T0191641

Lecture Notes in Computer Science 11747

More information about this series at http://www.springer.com/series/7409

David Lamas · Fernando Loizides ·
Lennart Nacke · Helen Petrie ·
Marco Winckler · Panayiotis Zaphiris (Eds.)

Human-Computer Interaction – INTERACT 2019

17th IFIP TC 13 International Conference
Paphos, Cyprus, September 2–6, 2019
Proceedings, Part II

Springer

Editors
David Lamas ⓘ
Tallinn University
Tartu, Estonia

Fernando Loizides ⓘ
Cardiff University
Cardiff, UK

Lennart Nacke ⓘ
University of Waterloo
Waterloo, ON, Canada

Helen Petrie ⓘ
University of York
York, UK

Marco Winckler ⓘ
Nice Sophia Antipolis University
Sophia Antipolis, France

Panayiotis Zaphiris ⓘ
Cyprus University of Technology
Limassol, Cyprus

ISSN 0302-9743   ISSN 1611-3349   (electronic)
Lecture Notes in Computer Science
ISBN 978-3-030-29383-3   ISBN 978-3-030-29384-0   (eBook)
https://doi.org/10.1007/978-3-030-29384-0

LNCS Sublibrary: SL3 – Information Systems and Applications, incl. Internet/Web, and HCI

This Springer imprint is published by the registered company Springer Nature Switzerland AG
The registered company address is: Gewerbestrasse 11, 6330 Cham, Switzerland

Foreword

The 17th IFIP TC13 International Conference on Human-Computer Interaction, INTERACT 2019, took place during September 2–6, 2019, in Paphos, Cyprus. This conference was held at the Coral Beach Hotel & Resort. The conference was co-sponsored by the Cyprus University of Technology and Tallinn University, in cooperation with ACM and ACM SIGCHI.

The International Federation for Information Processing (IFIP) was created in 1960 under the auspices of UNESCO. The Technical Committee 13 (TC13) of the IFIP aims at developing the science and technology of human-computer interaction (HCI). TC13 has representatives from 32 countries, 2 international organizations, apart from 14 expert members and observers. TC13 started the series of INTERACT conferences in 1984. These conferences have been an important showcase for researchers and practitioners in the field of HCI. Situated under the open, inclusive umbrella of the IFIP, INTERACT has been a truly international in its spirit and has attracted researchers from several countries and cultures. The venues of the INTERACT conferences over the years bear a testimony to this inclusiveness.

INTERACT 2019 continued the INTERACT conscious efforts to lower barriers that prevent people from developing countries to participate in conferences. Thinkers and optimists believe that all regions of the world can achieve human development goals. Information and communication technologies (ICTs) can support this process and empower people to achieve their full potential. Today ICT products have many new users and many new uses, but also present new challenges and provide new opportunities. It is no surprise that HCI researchers are showing great interest in these emergent users. INTERACT 2019 provided a platform to explore these challenges and opportunities, but also made it easier for people from developing countries to participate.

Furthermore, hosting INTERACT 2019 in a small country with a small HCI community presented an opportunity to expose the local industry and academia to the concepts of HCI and user-centered design. The rich history and culture of the island of Cyprus provided a strong networking atmosphere and collaboration opportunities.

Students represent the future of our community. They bring in new energy, enthusiasm, and fresh ideas. However, it is often hard for students to participate in international conferences. INTERACT 2019 made special efforts to bring students to the conference. The conference had low registration costs, and thanks to our sponsors, we could provide several travel grants.

Finally, great research is the heart of a good conference. Like its predecessors, INTERACT 2019 aimed to bring together high-quality research. As a multidisciplinary field, HCI requires interaction and discussion among diverse people with different interests and backgrounds. The beginners and the experienced, theoreticians and practitioners, and people from diverse disciplines and different countries gathered together in Paphos to learn from each other and to contribute to each other's growth.

We thank all the authors who chose INTERACT 2019 as the venue to publish their research.

We received a total of 669 submissions distributed in 2 peer reviewed tracks, 4 curated tracks, and 4 juried tracks. Of these, the following contributions were accepted:

- 111 Full Papers (peer reviewed)
- 55 Short Papers (peer reviewed)
- 7 Industry Case Studies (curated)
- 3 Courses (curated)
- 9 Demonstrations (curated)
- 18 Interactive Posters (juried)
- 2 Panels (curated)
- 9 Workshops (juried)
- 1 Field Trips (juried)
- 17 Doctoral Consortium (juried)

The acceptance rate for contributions received in the peer-reviewed tracks was 29% for full papers and 28% for short papers. In addition to full papers and short papers, the present proceedings feature contributions accepted in the form of industry case studies, courses, demonstrations, interactive posters, panels, and description of accepted workshops. The contributions submitted to workshops were published in adjunct proceedings.

INTERACT 2019 innovated the reviewing process with the introduction of sub-committees. Each subcommittee had a chair and set of associated chairs who were in charge of coordinating the reviewing process with the help of expert reviewers. Hereafter we list the ten subcommittees of INTERACT 2019:

- Accessibility and Assistive Technologies
- Design for Business and Safety/Critical Interactive Systems
- Design of Interactive Entertainment Systems
- HCI Education and Curriculum
- Information Visualization
- Interaction Design for Culture and Development
- Interactive Systems Technologies and Engineering
- Methodologies for User-Centred Design
- Social Interaction and Mobile HCI
- Understanding Human Aspects of HCI

The final decision on acceptance or rejection of full papers was taken in a Program Committee meeting held in London, United Kingdom in March 2019. The full papers chairs, the subcommittee chairs, and the associate chairs participated in this meeting. The meeting discussed a consistent set of criteria to deal with inevitable differences among the large number of reviewers. The final decisions on other tracks were made by the corresponding track chairs and reviewers, often after electronic meetings and discussions.

INTERACT 2019 was made possible by the persistent efforts across several months by 10 subcommittees chairs, 62 associated chairs, 28 track chairs, and 510 reviewers. We thank them all.

September 2019

Panayiotis Zaphiris
David Lamas

IFIP TC13 (http://ifip-tc13.org/)

Established in 1989, the International Federation for Information Processing Technical Committee on Human–Computer Interaction (IFIP TC 13) is an international committee of 32 member national societies and 10 Working Groups, representing specialists of the various disciplines contributing to the field of human-computer interaction. This includes (among others) human factors, ergonomics, cognitive science, computer science, and design. INTERACT is its flagship conference of IFIP TC 13, staged biennially in different countries around the world. The first INTERACT conference was held in 1984 running triennially and became a biennial event in 1993.

IFIP TC 13 aims to develop the science, technology, and societal aspects of HCI by encouraging empirical research; promoting the use of knowledge and methods from the human sciences in design and evaluation of computer systems; promoting a better understanding of the relation between formal design methods and system usability and acceptability; developing guidelines, models, and methods by which designers may provide better human-oriented computer systems; and, cooperating with other groups, inside and outside IFIP, to promote user-orientation and humanization in systems design. Thus, TC 13 seeks to improve interactions between people and computers, to encourage the growth of HCI research and its practice in industry and to disseminate these benefits worldwide.

The main orientation is to place the users at the center of the development process. Areas of study include: the problems people face when interacting with computers; the impact of technology deployment on people in individual and organizational contexts; the determinants of utility, usability, acceptability, learnability, and user experience; the appropriate allocation of tasks between computers and users especially in the case of automation; modeling the user, their tasks, and the interactive system to aid better system design; and harmonizing the computer to user characteristics and needs.

While the scope is thus set wide, with a tendency toward general principles rather than particular systems, it is recognized that progress will only be achieved through both general studies to advance theoretical understanding and specific studies on practical issues (e.g., interface design standards, software system resilience, documentation, training material, appropriateness of alternative interaction technologies, design guidelines, the problems of integrating interactive systems to match system needs, and organizational practices, etc.).

In 2015, TC13 approved the creation of a Steering Committee (SC) for the INTERACT conference. The SC is now in place, chaired by Anirudha Joshi and is responsible for:

- Promoting and maintaining the INTERACT conference as the premiere venue for researchers and practitioners interested in the topics of the conference (this requires a refinement of the topics above)
- Ensuring the highest quality for the contents of the event

- Setting up the bidding process to handle the future INTERACT conferences (decision is made up at TC 13 level)
- Providing advice to the current and future chairs and organizers of the INTERACT conference
- Providing data, tools, and documents about previous conferences to the future conference organizers
- Selecting the reviewing system to be used throughout the conference (as this impacts the entire set of reviewers)
- Resolving general issues involved with the INTERACT conference
- Capitalizing history (good and bad practices)

In 1999, TC 13 initiated a special IFIP Award, the Brian Shackel Award, for the most outstanding contribution in the form of a refereed paper submitted to and delivered at each INTERACT. The award draws attention to the need for a comprehensive human-centered approach in the design and use of information technology in which the human and social implications have been taken into account. In 2007, IFIP TC 13 launched an Accessibility Award to recognize an outstanding contribution in HCI with international impact dedicated to the field of accessibility for disabled users. In 2013, IFIP TC 13 launched the Interaction Design for International Development (IDID) Award that recognizes the most outstanding contribution to the application of interactive systems for social and economic development of people in developing countries. Since the process to decide the award takes place after papers are sent to the publisher for publication, the awards are not identified in the proceedings.

This year a special agreement has been made with the *International Journal of Behaviour and Information Technology* (published by Taylor and Francis) with Panos Markopoulos as editor in chief. In this agreement, authors of BIT whose papers are within the field of HCI are offered the opportunity to present their work at the INTERACT conference. Reciprocally, a selection of papers submitted and accepted for presentation at INTERACT are offered the opportunity to extend their contribution to be published in BIT.

IFIP TC 13 also recognizes pioneers in the area of HCI. An IFIP TC 13 pioneer is one who, through active participation in IFIP Technical Committees or related IFIP groups, has made outstanding contributions to the educational, theoretical, technical, commercial, or professional aspects of analysis, design, construction, evaluation, and use of interactive systems. IFIP TC 13 pioneers are appointed annually and awards are handed over at the INTERACT conference.

IFIP TC 13 stimulates working events and activities through its Working Groups (WGs). Working Groups consist of HCI experts from many countries, who seek to expand knowledge and find solutions to HCI issues and concerns within their domains. The list of Working Groups and their area of interest is given below.

WG13.1 (Education in HCI and HCI Curricula) aims to improve HCI education at all levels of higher education, coordinate and unite efforts to develop HCI curricula, and promote HCI teaching.

WG13.2 (Methodology for User-Centered System Design) aims to foster research, dissemination of information and good practice in the methodical application of HCI to software engineering.

WG13.3 (HCI and Disability) aims to make HCI designers aware of the needs of people with disabilities and encourage the development of information systems and tools permitting adaptation of interfaces to specific users.

WG13.4 (also WG2.7) (User Interface Engineering) investigates the nature, concepts, and construction of user interfaces for software systems, using a framework for reasoning about interactive systems and an engineering model for developing user interfaces.

WG 13.5 (Human Error, Resilience, Reliability, Safety and System Development) seeks a framework for studying human factors relating to systems failure, develops leading-edge techniques in hazard analysis and safety engineering of computer-based systems, and guides international accreditation activities for safety-critical systems.

WG13.6 (Human-Work Interaction Design) aims at establishing relationships between extensive empirical work-domain studies and HCI design. It will promote the use of knowledge, concepts, methods, and techniques that enable user studies to procure a better apprehension of the complex interplay between individual, social, and organizational contexts and thereby a better understanding of how and why people work in the ways that they do.

WG13.7 (Human–Computer Interaction and Visualization) aims to establish a study and research program that will combine both scientific work and practical applications in the fields of HCI and Visualization. It integrates several additional aspects of further research areas, such as scientific visualization, data mining, information design, computer graphics, cognition sciences, perception theory, or psychology, into this approach.

WG13.8 (Interaction Design and International Development) is currently working to reformulate its aims and scope.

WG13.9 (Interaction Design and Children) aims to support practitioners, regulators, and researchers to develop the study of interaction design and children across international contexts.

WG13.10 (Human-Centered Technology for Sustainability) aims to promote research, design, development, evaluation, and deployment of human-centered technology to encourage sustainable use of resources in various domains.

New Working Groups are formed as areas of significance in HCI arise. Further information is available on the IFIP TC13 website: http://ifip-tc13.org/.

IFIP TC13 Members

Officers

Chair

Philippe Palanque, France

Vice-chair for Awards

Paula Kotze, South Africa

Vice-chair for Communications

Helen Petrie, UK

Vice-chair for Growth and Reach Out INTERACT Steering Committee Chair

Jan Gulliksen, Sweden

Vice-chair for Working Groups

Simone D. J. Barbosa, Brazil

Treasurer

Virpi Roto, Finland

Secretary

Marco Winckler, France

INTERACT Steering Committee Chair

Anirudha Joshi

Country Representatives

Australia
Henry B. L. Duh
Australian Computer Society

Austria
Geraldine Fitzpatrick
Austrian Computer Society

Belgium
Bruno Dumas
Interuniversity Micro-Electronics Center
(IMEC)

Brazil
Milene Selbach Silveira
Brazilian Computer Society (SBC)

Bulgaria
Stoyan Georgiev Dentchev
Bulgarian Academy of Sciences

Canada
Lu Xiao
Canadian Information Processing Society

Croatia
Andrina Granic
Croatian Information Technology
  Association (CITA)

Cyprus
Panayiotis Zaphiris
Cyprus Computer Society

Czech Republic
Zdeněk Míkovec
Czech Society for Cybernetics
  and Informatics

Finland
Virpi Roto
Finnish Information Processing
  Association

France
Philippe Palanque
Société informatique de France (SIF)

Germany
Tom Gross
Gesellschaft fur Informatik e.V.

Hungary
Cecilia Sik Lanyi
John V. Neumann Computer Society

India
Anirudha Joshi
Computer Society of India (CSI)

Ireland
Liam J. Bannon
Irish Computer Society

Italy
Fabio Paternò
Italian Computer Society

Japan
Yoshifumi Kitamura
Information Processing Society of Japan

The Netherlands
Regina Bernhaupt
Nederlands Genootschap voor
  Informatica

New Zealand
Mark Apperley
New Zealand Computer Society

Norway
Frode Eika Sandnes
Norwegian Computer Society

Poland
Marcin Sikorski
Poland Academy of Sciences

Portugal
Pedro Campos
Associacão Portuguesa para o
  Desenvolvimento da Sociedade da
  Informação (APDSI)

Serbia
Aleksandar Jevremovic
Informatics Association of Serbia

Singapore
Shengdong Zhao
Singapore Computer Society

Slovakia
Wanda Benešová
The Slovak Society for Computer
  Science

Slovenia
Matjaž Debevc
The Slovenian Computer Society
  Informatika

South Africa
Janet L. Wesson and Paula Kotze
The Computer Society of South Africa

Sweden
Jan Gulliksen
Swedish Interdisciplinary Society for
  Human-Computer Interaction
Swedish Computer Society

Switzerland
Denis Lalanne
Swiss Federation for Information
  Processing

Tunisia
Mona Laroussi
Ecole Supérieure des Communications
  De Tunis (SUP'COM)

UK
José Abdelnour Nocera
British Computer Society (BCS)

UAE
Ghassan Al-Qaimari
UAE Computer Society

International Association Members

ACM
Gerrit van der Veer
Association for Computing Machinery
  (ACM)

CLEI
Jaime Sánchez
Centro Latinoamericano de Estudios en
  Informatica

Expert Members

Carmelo Ardito, Italy
Orwa, Kenya
David Lamas, Estonia
Dorian Gorgan, Romania
Eunice Sari, Australia/Indonesia
Fernando Loizides, UK/Cyprus
Ivan Burmistrov, Russia

Julio Abascal, Spain
Kaveh Bazargan, Iran
Marta Kristin Larusdottir, Iceland
Nikolaos Avouris, Greece
Peter Forbrig, Germany
Torkil Clemmensen, Denmark
Zhengjie Liu, China

Working Group Chairpersons

WG 13.1 (Education in HCI and HCI Curricula)

Konrad Baumann, Austria

WG 13.2 (Methodologies for User-Centered System Design)

Regina Bernhaupt, The Netherlands

WG 13.3 (HCI and Disability)

Helen Petrie, UK

WG 13.4/2.7 (User Interface Engineering)

José Creissac Campos, Portugal

WG 13.5 (Human Error, Resilience, Reliability, Safety and System Development)

Chris Johnson, UK

WG13.6 (Human-Work Interaction Design)

Barbara Rita Barricelli, Italy

WG13.7 (HCI and Visualization)

Peter Dannenmann, Germany

WG 13.8 (Interaction Design and International Development)

José Adbelnour Nocera, UK

WG 13.9 (Interaction Design and Children)

Janet Read, UK

WG 13.10 (Human-Centred Technology for Sustainability)

Masood Masoodian, Finland

Conference Organizing Committee

General Conference Chairs

David Lamas, Estonia
Panayiotis Zaphiris, Cyprus

Technical Program Chairs

Fernando Loizides, UK
Marco Winckler, France

Full Papers Co-chairs

Helen Petrie, UK
Lennart Nacke, Canada

Short Papers Co-chairs

Evangelos Karapanos, Cyprus
Jim CS Ang, UK

Interactive Posters Co-chairs

Carmelo Ardito, Italy
Zhengjie Liu, China

Panels Co-chairs

Darelle van Greunen, South Africa
Jahna Otterbacher, Cyprus

Demonstrations and Installations Co-chairs

Giuseppe Desolda, Italy
Vaso Constantinou, Cyprus

Courses Co-chairs

Parisa Eslambolchilar, UK
Regina Bernhaupt, The Netherlands

Workshops Co-chairs

Antigoni Parmaxi, Cyprus
Jose Abdelnour Nocera, UK

Doctoral Consortium Co-chairs

Andri Ioannou, Cyprus
Nikolaos Avouris, Greece

Student Design Consortium Co-chairs

Andreas Papallas, Cyprus
Eva Korae, Cyprus

Field Trips Chairs

Andreas Papallas, Cyprus
Anirudha Joshi, India
Panayiotis Zaphiris, Cyprus

Industry Case Studies Co-chairs

Aimilia Tzanavari, USA
Panagiotis Germanakos, Germany

Proceedings Chairs

Fernando Loizides, UK
Marco Winckler, France

Sponsorship Chair

Andreas Papallas, Cyprus

Student Volunteers Chair

Vaso Constantinou, Cyprus

Web and Social Media Chair

Aekaterini Mavri, Cyprus

Program Committee

Sub-committee Chairs

Elisa Mekler, Switzerland
Fabio Paterno, Italy
Gerhard Weber, Germany
Jan Gulliksen, Sweden
Jo Lumsden, UK

Laurence Nigay, France
Nikolaos Avouris, Greece
Philippe Palanque, France
Regina Bernhaupt, The Netherlands
Torkil Clemmensen, Denmark

Associated Chairs

Adrian Bussone, UK
Anirudha Joshi, India
Antonio Piccinno, Italy
Bridget Kane, Sweden
Bruno Dumas, Belgium
Carla Maria Dal Sasso Freitas, Brazil
Célia Martinie, France
Chi Vi, UK
Christine Bauer, Austria
Daniel Buzzo, UK
Daniela Trevisan, Brazil
Davide Spano, Italy
Denis Lalanne, Switzerland
Dhaval Vyas, Australia
Dorian Gorgan, Romania
Effie Law, UK
Elisa Mekler, Switzerland
Fabio Paterno, Italy
Frank Steinicke, Germany
Frode Eika Sandnes, Norway
Gavin Sim, UK
Gerhard Weber, Germany
Giuseppe Desolda, Italy
Jan Gulliksen, Sweden
Jan Stage, Denmark
Jan Van den Bergh, Belgium
Janet Wesson, South Africa
Jenny Darzentas, Greece
Jo Lumsden, UK
Jolanta Mizera-Pietraszko, Poland
Jose Abdelnour Nocera, UK

José Creissac Campos, Portugal
Katrina Attwood, UK
Kaveh Bazargan, Iran
Kibum Kim, South Korea
Laurence Nigay, France
Luis Teixeira, Portugal
Lynne Coventry, UK
Marcin Sikorski, Poland
Margarita Anastassova, France
Marta Laursdottir, Iceland
Matistella Matera, Italy
Nervo Verdezoto, UK
Nikolaos Avouris, Greece
Özge Subasi, Austria
Patrick Langdon, UK
Paula Kotze, South Africa
Pedro Campos, Portugal
Peter Forbrig, Germany
Peter Johnson, UK
Philippe Palanque, France
Regina Bernhaupt, The Netherlands
Sayan Sarcar, Japan
Simone Barbosa, Brazil
Simone Stumpf, UK
Stefania Castellani, France
Tom Gross, Germany
Torkil Clemmensen, Denmark
Valentin Schwind, Germany
Virpi Roto, Finland
Yoshifumi Kitamura, Japan
Zdenek Mikovec, Czech Republic

Reviewers

Adalberto Simeone, Belgium
Aditya Nittala, Germany
Adriana Vivacqua, Brazil
Aekaterini Mavri, Cyprus
Agneta Eriksson, Finland
Aidan Slingsby, UK
Aku Visuri, Finland
Alaa Alkhafaji, UK
Alasdair King, UK
Alberto Boem, Japan
Alberto Raposo, Brazil
Albrecht Schmidt, Germany
Aleksander Bai, Norway
Alessio Malizia, UK
Alexander Wachtel, Germany
Alexandra Covaci, UK
Alexandra Mendes, Portugal
Alexandre Canny, France
Ali Rizvi, Canada
Ali Soyoof, Iran
Alisa Burova, Finland
Alistair Edwards, UK
Alla Vovk, UK
Amina Bouraoui, Tunisia
Ana Cristina Garcia, Brazil
Ana Paula Afonso, Portugal
Ana Serrano, Spain
Anders Lundström, Sweden
Anderson Maciel, Brazil
Andre Suslik Spritzer, Brazil
André Zenner, Germany
Andrea Marrella, Italy
Andreas Sonderegger, Switzerland
Andrew Jian-lan Cen, Canada
Andrew MacQuarrie, UK
Andrew McNeill, UK
Andrey Krekhov, Germany
Andrii Matviienko, Germany
Andy Dearden, UK
Angus Forbes, USA
Anind Dey, USA
Anja Exler, Germany
Anke Dittmar, Germany

Anna Bramwell-Dicks, UK
Anna Feit, Switzerland
Anna-Lena Mueller, Germany
Annette Lamb, USA
Anthony Giannoumis, Norway
Antigoni Parmaxi, Cyprus
Antonio Gonzalez-Torres, Costa Rica
Antonio Piccinno, Italy
Arash Mahnan, USA
Arindam Dey, Australia
Aristides Mairena, Canada
Arjun Srinivasan, USA
Arminda Lopes, Portugal
Asam Almohamed, Australia
Ashkan Pourkand, USA
Asim Evren Yantac, Turkey
Aurélien Tabard, France
Aykut Coşkun, Turkey
Barbara Barricelli, Italy
Bastian Dewitz, Germany
Beiyu Lin, USA
Ben Morrison, UK
Benedict Gaster, UK
Benedikt Loepp, Germany
Benjamin Gorman, UK
Benjamin Weyers, Germany
Bernd Ploderer, Australia
Bineeth Kuriakose, Norway
Bosetti Bosetti, France
Brady Redfearn, USA
Brendan Cassidy, UK
Brendan Spillane, Ireland
Brian Freiter, Canada
Brianna Tomlinson, USA
Bruno Dumas, Belgium
Burak Merdenyan, UK
Cagatay Goncu, Australia
Cagri Tanriover, USA
Carlos Silva, Portugal
Carmen Santoro, Italy
Cecile Boulard, France
Célia Martinie, France
Chaolun Xia, USA

Liliane Machado, Brazil
Lilit Hakobyan, UK
Lisandro Granville, Brazil
Lonni Besançon, Sweden
Loredana Verardi, Italy
Lorisa Dubuc, UK
Lorna McKnight, UK
Loukas Konstantinou, Cyprus
Luciana Cardoso de Castro Salgado,
    Brazil
Luciana Nedel, Brazil
Lucio Davide Spano, Italy
Ludmila Musalova, UK
Ludvig Eblaus, Sweden
Luigi De Russis, Italy
Luis Leiva, Finland
Lynette Gerido, USA
Mads Andersen, Denmark
Mads Bødker, Denmark
Maher Abujelala, USA
Maliheh Ghajargar, Sweden
Malin Wik, Sweden
Malte Ressin, UK
Mandy Korzetz, Germany
Manjiri Joshi, India
Manuel J. Fonseca, Portugal
Marc Kurz, Austria
Marcelo Penha, Brazil
Marcelo Pimenta, Brazil
Márcio Pinho, Brazil
Marco Gillies, UK
Marco Manca, Italy
Marcos Baez, Italy
Marcos Serrano, France
Margarita Anastassova, France
María Laura Ramírez Galleguillos,
    Turkey
Maria Rosa Lorini, South Africa
Marian Cristian Mihaescu, Romania
Marianela Ciolfi Felice, France
Marion Koelle, Germany
Marios Constantinides, UK
Maristella Matera, Italy
Marius Koller, Germany
Mark Billinghurst, Australia
Mark Carman, Italy

Marko Tkalcic, Italy
Martin Feick, Germany
Martin Tomitsch, Australia
Mary Barreto, Portugal
Massimo Zancanaro, Italy
Matthew Horton, UK
Matthias Heintz, UK
Mauricio Pamplona Segundo, Brazil
Max Bernhagen, Germany
Max Birk, The Netherlands
Mehdi Ammi, France
Mehdi Boukallel, France
Meinald Thielsch, Germany
Melissa Densmore, South Africa
Meraj Ahmed Khan, USA
Michael Burch, The Netherlands
Michael Craven, UK
Michael McGuffin, Canada
Michael Nees, USA
Michael Rohs, Germany
Michela Assale, Italy
Michelle Annett, Canada
Mike Just, UK
Mikko Rajanen, Finland
Milene Silveira, Brazil
Miriam Begnum, Norway
Mirjam Augstein, Austria
Mirko Gelsomini, Italy
Muhammad Haziq Lim Abdullah,
    Malaysia
Muhammad Shoaib, Pakistan
Nadine Vigouroux, France
Natasa Rebernik, Spain
Naveed Ahmed, UAE
Netta Iivari, Finland
Nick Chozos, UK
Nico Herbig, Germany
Niels Henze, Germany
Niels van Berkel, UK
Nikola Banovic, USA
Nikolaos Avouris, Greece
Nimesha Ranasinghe, USA
Nis Bornoe, Denmark
Nitish Devadiga, USA
Obed Brew, UK
Ofir Sadka, Canada

Oscar Mayora, Italy
Panayiotis Koutsabasis, Greece
Panos Markopoulos, The Netherlands
Panote Siriaraya, Japan
Paola Risso, Italy
Paolo Buono, Italy
Parinya Punpongsanon, Japan
Pascal Knierim, Germany
Pascal Lessel, Germany
Patrick Langdon, UK
Paul Curzon, UK
PD Lamb, UK
Pedro Campos, Portugal
Peter Forbrig, Germany
Peter Ryan, Luxembourg
Philip Schaefer, Germany
Philipp Wacker, Germany
Philippe Palanque, France
Philippe Renevier Gonin, France
Pierre Dragicevic, France
Pierre-Henri Orefice, France
Pietro Murano, Norway
Piyush Madan, USA
Pradeep Yammiyavar, India
Praminda Caleb-Solly, UK
Priyanka Srivastava, India
Pui Voon Lim, Malaysia
Qiqi Jiang, Denmark
Radhika Garg, USA
Radu Jianu, UK
Rafael Henkin, UK
Rafał Michalski, Poland
Raian Ali, UK
Rajkumar Darbar, France
Raquel Hervas, Spain
Raquel Robinson, Canada
Rashmi Singla, Denmark
Raymundo Cornejo, Mexico
Reem Talhouk, UK
Renaud Blanch, France
Rina Wehbe, Canada
Roberto Montano-Murillo, UK
Rocio von Jungenfeld, UK
Romina Kühn, Germany
Romina Poguntke, Germany
Ronnie Taib, Australia

Rosa Lanzilotti, Italy
Rüdiger Heimgärtner, Germany
Rufat Rzayev, Germany
Rui José, Portugal
Rui Madeira, Portugal
Samir Aknine, France
Sana Maqsood, Canada
Sanjit Samaddar, UK
Santosh Vijaykumar, UK
Sarah Völkel, Germany
Sari Kujala, Finland
Sayan Sarcar, Japan
Scott Trent, Japan
Sean Butler, UK
Sebastian Günther, Germany
Selina Schepers, Belgium
Seokwoo Song, South Korea
Sergio Firmenich, Argentina
Shah Rukh Humayoun, USA
Shaimaa Lazem, Egypt
Sharon Lynn Chu, USA
Shichao Zhao, UK
Shiroq Al-Megren, USA
Silvia Gabrielli, Italy
Simone Kriglstein, Austria
Sirpa Riihiaho, Finland
Snigdha Petluru, India
Songchun Fan, USA
Sónia Rafael, Portugal
Sonja Schimmler, Germany
Sophie Lepreux, France
Srishti Gupta, USA
SRM Dilrukshi Gamage, Sri Lanka
SRM_Daniela Girardi, Italy
Stefan Carmien, UK
Stefano Valtolina, Italy
Stéphane Conversy, France
Stephanie Wilson, UK
Stephen Snow, UK
Stephen Uzor, UK
Steve Reeves, New Zealand
Steven Jeuris, Denmark
Steven Vos, The Netherlands
Subrata Tikadar, India
Sven Mayer, Germany
Taehyun Rhee, New Zealand

Sponsors and Partners

Sponsors

Research Centre on **Interactive** Media
Smart Systems and **Emerging** Technologies

 Springer

Partners

 ifip

International Federation for Information Processing

 Cyprus
University of
Technology

 TALLINN UNIVERSITY

 *In-Cooperation*

In-cooperation with ACM

SIGCHI

In-cooperation with SIGCHI

Contents – Part II

Education and HCI Curriculum II

Eye-Gaze Interaction

Games and Gamification

Human-Robot Interaction and 3D Interaction

Information Visualization

Information Visualization and Augmented Reality

Interaction Design for Culture and Development I

E-commerce

Discovering the Unfindable: The Tension Between Findability and Discoverability in a Bookshop Designed for Serendipity

Stephann Makri[1(✉)], Yi-Chun Chen[1,2,3], Dana McKay[2],
George Buchanan[2], and Melissa Ocepek[3]

[1] Centre for HCI Design, City, University of London, Northampton Square,
London EC1V 0HB, UK
Stephann@city.ac.uk
[2] iSchool, University of Melbourne, Parkville, VIC 3010, Australia
[3] iSchool, University of Illinois at Urbana-Champaign,
501 E. Daniel Street, Champaign, IL, USA

Abstract. Serendipity is a key aspect of user experience, particularly in the context of information acquisition - where it is known as *information encountering*. Unexpectedly encountering interesting or useful information can spark new insights while surprising and delighting. However, digital environments have been designed primarily for goal-directed seeking over loosely-directed exploration, searching over discovering. In this paper we examine a novel physical environment - a bookshop designed primarily for serendipity - for cues as to how information encountering might be helped or hindered by digital design. Naturalistic observations and interviews revealed it was almost impossible for participants to find specific books or topics other than by accident. But all unexpectedly encountered interesting books, highlighting a tension between findability and discoverability. While some of the bookshop's design features enabled information encountering, others inhibited it. However, encountering was resilient, as it occurred despite participants finding it hard to understand the purpose of even those features that did enable it. Findings suggest the need to consider how transparent or opaque the purpose of design features should be and to balance structure and lack of it when designing digital environments for findability and discoverability.

Keywords: Information encountering · Serendipity · Findability · Discoverability

1 Introduction

We can learn about designing digital information environments, such as search engines, digital libraries and e-commerce sites, by examining information behavior in *physical* places. Major models of information seeking, on which many digital information interfaces are founded, were all based in examining user behavior (see, for example, [1–3]). There are also several more direct examples of using physical behavior in information environments to generate design guidelines; these include music

© IFIP International Federation for Information Processing 2019
Published by Springer Nature Switzerland AG 2019
D. Lamas et al. (Eds.): INTERACT 2019, LNCS 11747, pp. 3–23, 2019.
https://doi.org/10.1007/978-3-030-29384-0_1

information seeking [4, 5], browsing physical libraries [6–8], and reading [9]. We follow this tradition of examining physical environments to inform digital design by investigating a novel type of information environment: a bookshop specifically designed to facilitate serendipity with features that include 'continuous' shelving, ambiguous section names, author-curated sections, recommendations, seating, and topically diverse display tables.

Digital and physical information environments are primarily optimized for findability over discoverability [10]. Even physical libraries, long heralded as discovery environments [11, 12], are predominantly designed for finding items; discovery via browsing is a secondary consideration [10]. This focus dramatically limits opportunities for (serendipitous) information encountering [13]. Information encountering is an important information experience; it can spark insight [11, 14], enhance knowledge [15] and propel users in new and exciting directions [11, 16], surprising and delighting [17].

Given the importance of information encountering as a form of Human Information Interaction, understanding how to support it online is highly topical in an age where information is increasingly digital; previous work in this area is limited. The work presented in this paper takes advantage of the rarity of an environment designed to facilitate information encountering to understand how it affects both serendipity and directed seeking. Our study is exploratory in nature, using observations and interviews to understand the information seeking and encountering experiences of 9 people, during both goal-directed seeking and loosely-directed exploring tasks.

Firstly, we introduce the concepts of serendipity and information encountering and review prior research. Next, we describe the physical bookshop's serendipity-related design features and how each might facilitate information encountering and explain our data collection and analysis approaches and limitations. Then, we present and discuss our findings first on the features of the bookshop, then on the overall design. Finally, we describe design implications for digital information environments.

2   Related Work

In this section, we first introduce the concepts of serendipity and information encountering, then discuss the influence of the design of physical space on information encountering. Next, we discuss how physical space affects how users find information, turning finally to discuss the literature on information encountering in bookshops.

2.1   Serendipity and Information Encountering

Serendipity is where unexpected circumstances and insight result in a valuable, unanticipated outcome [14]. In the past decade or so, it has become of increasing interest to HCI researchers (e.g. [13, 14, 46]), who are beginning to address the important, but difficult challenge of how best to design for it. HCI researchers have, however, noted a 'serendipity design paradox' - that 'hard-wiring' serendipity into algorithm design may lose some of its inherent 'unexpectedness,' potentially 'destroying' the experience [21]. This suggests the need to preserve user agency in making insightful connections. It is less contentious, however, that designing to facilitate serendipity, whether through AI, human insight, or a blend of the two, is worthwhile [13, 17, 20, 25, 46, 47].

Serendipity in the context of information acquisition is known as *information encountering* [18, 22]. It usually occurs as an embedded activity during information seeking [18]. It involves unexpectedly finding information considered useful or interesting [19]. This can be when looking for something specific (goal-directed seeking) or when not looking for anything in particular (loosely-directed exploration) [20]. While information-seeking is active, encountering is passive; it is characterized by the encounterer's low expectation of and involvement in finding the information [18, 19]. The process involves noticing a stimulus in the environment, stopping any active seeking task underway, examining the encountered information, then capturing or sharing it, before returning to the active task (if applicable).

Information encountering is an important form of Human-Information Interaction. It enhances user experience by 'surprising and delighting' [14] and facilitates processes such as creativity and ideation [21]. It is important in both physical and digital information environments; consider the examples of unexpectedly finding an interesting or useful: book in the library when browsing nearby shelves, or Webpage when searching for information on another (partly or seemingly unrelated) topic. However, no prior research has investigated information encountering in a physical environment specifically designed to facilitate it. This can inform digital information environment design.

2.2 Impact of Physical Environments on Information Encountering

Some research has found environmental factors can influence information encountering [19, 22]. However, very little research has examined how information environments might be designed to facilitate it.

Starting with a set of 'serendipity dimensions' identified from physical libraries [23], McCay-Peet et al. developed a measure of the propensity of digital information environments to facilitate serendipity [24, 25], comprising four factors (which may also apply to physical environments). These include the degree to which the environment is *trigger-rich* (contains a variety of information, ideas and resources that are interesting or useful), *highlights triggers* (brings interesting or useful information, ideas or resources to attention), *enables connections* (makes relationships between information, ideas or resources apparent) and *leads to the unexpected* (provides opportunities for unexpected interactions with information/ideas/resources) [25]. A theoretical framework [26], partly based on this earlier work, proposes ten 'sub-affordances' for serendipity in physical and digital information environments: *diversity* (heterogeneity of content); *cross-contacts* (collision of dissimilar resources); *incompleteness* (inconsistent features that offer users the potential to make their own meaning); *accessibility* (physical topology of the space and its impact on access); *multi-reachability* (ability to access the same place from many routes); *explorability* (how much of an invitation the environment offers for browsing and exploration); *slowability* (how well the environment invites users to slow down and look closer); *exposure* (how content is displayed trigger interest); *contrasts* (allowing items to stand out from the crowd) and *pointers* (ways the environment highlights content in specific ways, such as curation/recommendation).

Looking to research on physical environments, one observational study was partly conducted in a specialist bookshop, where most books (e.g. History and Fiction) were organized unconventionally by country [27], It did not, however, examine the impact of the bookshop's organization on reader behavior. Similarly, interviews with staff in a large bookshop [28] identified a design feature (table displays with books on diverse topics and with their covers showing) as potentially facilitating encountering. However, observations did not focus on use of the tables. This echoes the literature on libraries; regular visitors scout display tables and return trollies for interesting books [29, 30]. Libraries, with their rich classification schemes and information-dense environments, are generally seen as being supportive of encountering [7, 31]. Librarians are aware of this and have attempted to improve discovery by rearranging the shelves. One study rearranged fiction from alphabetical to by genre and found that while the change did not increase borrowing, it did increase browsing-based exploration [32].

Physical environments do not always support encountering, though; in libraries, an abundance of books can overwhelm [33] and top and bottom shelves are used less than those in the middle [31, 34]. Exploration can be hampered in very quiet environments as people feel self-conscious about moving items around [33]. Other environmental factors affect willingness to pause (i.e. slowability [26]); exploration is limited anywhere there is possibility of 'butt-brush' (people will even move away from items of interest to avoid being brushed from behind) [35]. Finally, particularly when there are heavy space constraints, physical books often only appear in a single location and this can inhibit discoveries that might otherwise be made through multi-reachability [21]. Findings from physical environments often cannot be directly transferred to digital ones [7]. But understanding the relative importance of physical design features for supporting encountering can indirectly inform digital design. This is the focus of this work.

2.3 Impact of Physical Environments on Goal-Directed Information-*Seeking*

In contrast to passive information encountering, there is the issue of active information-*seeking*. While there is much literature on wayfinding, including in libraries, work on how physical environments help or hinder finding known or highly describable items is limited. There is evidence library users get lost in the shelves and that a range of physical design features, including organization scheme and book visibility, inhibit goal-directed seeking [25]. Equally, target books may not be in stock [27], or may be missing or out [8]. Digital environments support highly goal-directed information-seeking well, provided good search functionality is available. The question, then, is whether it is possible to adequately support both goal-directed information seeking and exploration-driven information encountering in a single digital environment and, if so, how?

2.4   Bookshops as Information Environments

Information encountering in libraries has been widely discussed [36, 37], and occasionally observed [7, 33]. However, no studies have focused on observing encountering in bookshops. The few prior studies of information behavior in bookshops demonstrate very little evidence of encountering (or exploration in general). But this is perhaps because of their focus - on enquiries made by customers [27], collaborative interactions with books [38], children's book selection process for recreational reading [39] and general reading practices [28]. Although one study had a think-aloud element [39], all were primarily based on anonymous observations, which limits capture of rationale for choosing books. This rationale can include perceptions of unexpectedness.

In the bookshop customer enquiry study, most adults were found to 'grab-and-go,' demonstrating highly goal-directed rather than exploratory behavior [27]. This does not, however, speak to the behavior of those who did not talk to staff (who may have explored and potentially discovered more). While older children also engaged in goal-directed seeking for a specific book, author or topic, younger (pre-school and elementary) children did not have clear information needs and relied on "serendipitous encounters with a book that matches a preference" [39]. No further detail was, however, provided on the nature of these encounters. Many readers who visited bookshops in groups also had unclear needs [38]. While no information encounters were reported, it was concluded that digital information environments should support "both task-oriented and 'serendipitous' information-searching behaviors" [28]. Limited existing evidence of encountering in bookshops highlights the need for dedicated examination.

3   Bookshop Design

Libreria is a small independent bookshop in a trendy part of London's East End. It was chosen, as its website (Libreria.io) notes, because books are curated to 'maximize serendipity' and "every aspect of Libreria is designed to help you discover new books and ideas."

Libreria has two types of design features aimed at supporting serendipity: *physical* features and *informational* features. We describe each of these in turn.

3.1   Physical Design Features

Libreria is situated in an area peppered with other 'explorable' environments (e.g. vintage clothing stores and specialist music shops). The shop itself is long and narrow, and the sales counter is near the entrance (see Fig. 1). All elements of the store are visible from the entrance, which may help promote *explorability* [26]. There are several elements specifically designed to invite exploration, though - we describe these now.

The Appearance of Continuous Shelving. Libreria uses the linear, narrow layout of the shop - emphasized by a large mirror strategically placed opposite the entrance - to make the shelves seem 'infinite'. This infinity shelving is a nod to the inspiration of the shop's design: the infinite shelves in the library of Babel. The shelves in Libreria are divided horizontally into sections, but the shelf dividers are shallow and transparent to

Fig. 1. Bookshop layout showing continuous shelving

avoid visual disruption of the space (see Fig. 2). This is deliberate, to reinforce the impression of continuous shelving and downplay the semantic structure of the store. This design may *enable connections* and lead to the *unexpected discovery* of books in adjacent, different sections [25]. It could promote cross-contacts, *explorability* and *slowability* [26], by forcing close examination.

Fig. 2. 'Ways of Seeing' section marked by shallow, transparent acrylic sign

The Presence of Seating. Taking time to reflect is a known element of serendipity [21]. This *slowability* [26] is encouraged in Libreria by the presence of seating, not just the conventional kind regularly seen in bookshops, but also seating physically built into the shelves. The bookshop curator noted that seating is 'part of the bookshop tradition'; it encourages readers to try before they buy.

Exposing the Covers of (Some) Books. Most books are displayed on shelves with only spines showing, but some have their covers exposed - particularly those that are visually striking (see Fig. 2). Covers are widely used by savvy readers to make book selections [28, 40], so this information is important. Libreria makes more extensive use of this design feature than most bookshops. This may *highlight triggers* [25] by making covers immediately visible It could promote exposure by displaying covers in a way ready to trigger readers' visual sense, in contrast to those with only spines displayed [26].

3.2   Informational Design Features

In addition to Libreria's physical design features, there are several informational design features specifically for supporting serendipity. These are introduced below.

Broad, Ambiguous Organization Scheme and Section Labelling. The books in Libreria are classified by broad, unconventional themes such as 'Bad Feminism', 'Home and Hearth' and 'Enchantment for the Disenchanted', rather than by traditional subjects or genres. Each theme includes books on multiple subjects, e.g. 'Utopia' includes books on history, architecture and philosophy. The curator explained the thematic layout was *"to enhance chance finding...on different subject matters. It's about spurring ideas."*

Adjacent books are linked semantically; 'Home and Hearth,' for example, displayed 'The Vegetarian' and 'Aliens and Anorexia' next to each other - a possible example of *cross linking* [26] and *enabling connections* [25]. However, there were *"no hard and fast rules"* for curating content or linking books: *"too many guidelines would be restrictive. Diversity and playfulness engender a more creative approach."* (Curator).

The variety of themes and topical variance of books classified within themes could promote *diversity* and facilitate *cross-contacts* [23], through proximal placement of books that are simultaneously conceptually similar *and* dissimilar. This could *lead to the unexpected* [25], by broadening readers' interests.

The scheme's ambiguity demonstrates *incompleteness*, with imperfect 'cracks' that could *enable connections* [25] and spur new ideas. It may promote *slowability*, by forcing readers to "slow down, look closer and examine" [26] the shelves. The quirky section labels may act to *highlight triggers* [25], bringing books to the reader's attention.

Topically Diverse Table Displays. All tables contained piles of books, of the same title. None were intended to be topically-related to each other, or to those on nearby shelves. Books on tables were also shelved elsewhere. Juxtaposition of adjacent books on different topics may *enable connections* and *lead to the unexpected*, promoting *diversity*, *cross-contacts* and *multi-reachability* (by enabling books to be found by multiple routes, on the shelf or table) [26]. Covers were easily scannable, as tabletops were at waist height (see Fig. 1). This may create *exposure* and *contrasts* with books on the shelves [23], highlighting the covers as *visual triggers* [25].

Author Curated Sections. There were two author-curated sections, denoted by signs including the curator's name and background. A small section was curated by South London gallery owner Hannah Barry, containing books related to her artistic influences. A larger section on African literature was curated by African poet Belinda Zhawi. Author curation might provide *accessibility* to specially-selected books [26]. Curated sections could act as *pointers* [26] by *highlighting* specific books as potential *triggers* [25].

Recommendation Cards. Some books had recommendation cards with the recommender's name, occupation and recommendation reasons clipped to their covers (see Fig. 3). A 'Second Home members recommend...' sign was placed nearby, explaining

Second Home is a 'creative accelerator, workspace and cultural venue' (Libreria was incubated by Second Home). These cards can *highlight triggers* and *enable connections* [25]. They might provide *exposure* by *contrasting* with books without clipped-on cards [23]. Recommendations can also be considered a specific type of *pointer* [3].

Fig. 3. Recommendation cards, clipped to the covers of books, obscuring them

4   Method

Here, we outline our data collection and analysis approach and discuss limitations.

4.1   Data Collection

We conducted naturalistic observations and interviews with 9 participants (6 female, 3 male), all aged 22–30 and recruited through personal contacts. All were regular bookshop visitors (>6 times per year). Naturalistic observations are a common approach in this type of formative study of Human Information Interaction (see for example [7, 31, 39]). Similarly, exploratory studies of this nature are suited to small participant numbers, and frequently seen in the Human Information Interaction literature (see for example [8], which observed 9 information seekers, [7], which observed 8, and [9], which - despite being seminal work - used video observations of only 3 readers).

Participants were met before the study in a location near the bookshop. They were not told ahead of time which bookshop they would be visiting, to avoid them researching Libreria. None had previously visited the bookshop. Observations took place inside Libreria, during regular opening hours. However, to ensure a quiet task environment (and avoid disrupting business), we conducted the study at less busy times (e.g. beginning of the day). Observations comprised two tasks: a *goal-directed* seeking task, and a *loosely-directed* exploration task. To avoid task effect influence, we alternated which task was first. After each session, interviews were conducted in a nearby coffee shop.

We adapted guidance from previous research to minimize bias with task structure and briefing procedure [20, 41]. Participants were told they would spend 30 min in Libreria divided between two tasks, and asked to think aloud during both tasks. The instructions for the goal-directed seeking task were: *"Find a specific book you might want to read, or books written by an author or on a topic of interest. It doesn't matter if you find what you're looking for or not. Just do what you'd normally do in a bookshop when you have a goal."* The loosely-directed task instructions were: *"Explore the bookshop freely, without looking for anything in particular."* Participants were reminded before both tasks to 'be as natural as possible.' The self-directed nature of the tasks further supports naturalistic behavior. Intervention was limited to probing questions, such as 'what are you doing and why?' Due to the anticipated likelihood of either rapid resolution or rapid frustration during the goal-directed task, this task was limited to 8 min, leaving 22 min for the exploration task. After the observation, we interviewed participants to elicit their opinions on how well the environment supported them in their two active seeking tasks and in passive information encountering during them, and to verify their encounters. To avoid biasing their behavior, the study's information encountering focus was only revealed in the post-task interview.

To understand motivations for the bookshop's design, we also interviewed a curator - who was involved in the initial 'serendipity-inspired' stock selection and organization. The observations and interviews were audio recorded (we deemed video recording too intrusive). Rather than taking notes, the researcher made a photographic record of interactions with individual books, capturing both the book and the interaction. These photos were taken with permission from bookshop management and participants.

4.2 Data Analysis

We used inductive and deductive Thematic Analysis [42] to analyze our data. The inductive part of the analysis identified themes in the data, e.g. 'difficulty understanding section labels.' The deductive part looked for evidence for encountering and the impact of specific design features on goal-directed seeking, loosely-directed exploration and information encountering.

As with all qualitative analysis, caution is needed when interpreting prevalence of observations; *"more instances do not necessarily mean a theme itself is more crucial"* [42]. This is particularly true for studies of serendipity - which is 'regular but rare' [12], thus relatively few examples can be expected during observation. As such, we avoid quantifying observations, instead using relative, qualitative descriptions of prevalence.

4.3 Limitations

The user tasks were naturalistic, but not completely natural. Both goal-directed seeking and loosely-directed exploration are commonplace in bookstores, and indeed it is likely that shoppers switch between tasks while shopping. Whether goal-directed seeking is a task that people would normally attempt in a bookshop designed for serendipity, though, is an open question. Similarly, whether our participants' persistence in the face of observed difficulty would hold in their everyday life, or whether they would simply ask bookshop staff for help remains unclear. Nonetheless, both the goal-directed task and the persistence in the face of difficulty actually serve the purpose of our study: to identify which design elements support goal-directed seeking, which support exploration, and which simply hinder users in either type of information acquisition task.

The time-constraints imposed may have influenced how participants undertook the tasks; if unconstrained, they may have spent less or more time (potentially impacting encountering frequency), or made more extensive use of certain design features.

Finally, the relative rarity of information encounters and the small number of participants mean this study is necessarily exploratory. We cannot guarantee, for example, that the features most frequently found useful are the most important in supporting serendipity. However, our findings provide concrete evidence that design elements can affect both goal-directed seeking and loosely-directed exploration, sometimes in ways that counteract each other.

5   Findings

Each feature of the bookshop affected goal-directed seeking and loosely-directed exploration in one way or another. In this section we address each design feature identified above, describing their impact on both these types of information task.

5.1   Physical Design Features

The physical elements of Libreria's design, while somewhat dependent on the actual features of the shop building, had various implications for goal-directed seeking, loosely-directed exploration and information encountering (which was found to occur both during goal-directed seeking and loosely-directed exploration).

The Appearance of Continuous Shelving. This was one of the most striking design features, yet ultimately facilitated neither goal-directed seeking nor exploration. There was potential to unexpectedly find interesting books, including where one section ends and another begins, based on juxtaposition or novel adjacencies. However, no participant experienced this. Instead, the uneven spacing of bays and low visibility of the shallow section dividers made browsing the 'never-ending' shelves daunting for many. For example, P8 stated *"it makes me feel overwhelmed because there's no clear separation between categories. I can't tell where a category starts and where it ends."* This overwhelm is not uncommon in information seeking; information overload demonstrably limits users' cognitive capacity for finding information [43]. It further inhibits exploration and serendipity, which requires mental capacity for reflection [21].

P8 did suggest that continuous shelving *could* potentially facilitate encountering, as it encourages horizontal browsing along the shelf, across sections. She stated *"my eye is moving along with the shelf, even if the category changes. It's natural to keep looking at the shelf to see what else is on there."* So the intention of this intervention was noted by at least one participant as plausible, despite the lack of observations to support it.

The shallow, unobtrusive section dividers that are a necessary component of the illusion of continuous shelving actively inhibited directed seeking. Not one participant noticed the dividers right away, confirming that this feature worked as intended. However, even after spotting section dividers, seeing others was hard. P8 provides a classic example, noticing the labels only partway through her task and exclaiming *"there are labels! There are labels! Wow! I swear though, I don't see labels on other shelves."* The initial failure to notice labels also meant participants failed to understand the horizontal sectioning of the shelves *"there were a couple of books where I thought 'it makes sense these books are together.' But above them would be books that had nothing to do with them. There's not much connection."* They had to attempt to build mental models of the bookshop from the ground up, often unsuccessfully. P1, for example stated incorrectly *"I guess for the classics they're organized by author and for the history section it's by theme".* These findings echo those in physical libraries, where users find it hard to understand even conventional organization schemes such as Dewey [7, 44].

Seating. It is perhaps clear seating will not help with goal-directed seeking, which often leads to grab-and-go experiences [27]. However, seating could reasonably be expected to lead to encounters. We observed a single encounter that could be attributed to seating, and in particular Libreria's specific seating style. P4 sat on a wooden chair near 'Home and Hearth', where he noticed and examined an abandoned book on a nearby table.

While we might have expected to see more than just one encounter related to seating, our study design may have worked against this particular design element. Time to sit was limited during our study, and sitting and reading while being observed may feel 'creepy' to participants [45]. Our participants' comments confirmed our sense seating was underrepresented as a feature of support for exploration. Participants noted that seating may facilitate encountering by inviting them to *"stay...longer"* (P4) and examine books *"with no pressure"* (P2).

Book Cover Exposure. Several encounters were triggered by book cover exposure, on the shelves (P1, P3, P7, P8, P9) and on the tables (P4, P6). Exposure attracted readers' attention. For example, referring to a children's book, P7 stated *"I noticed this book because it was placed here on the shelf. All the other books nearby were darker, deeper colors. This light blue cover really caught my eye."* P7 reflected on the reasons for cover exposure, commenting *"I guess the owner intentionally wanted to let shoppers see this book."*

Some participants ignored the display tables in the center of the shop (more on this in Sect. 5.2), but for some the face-up covers facilitated encountering. Most participants, however, noticed and examined at least one table and, as with the shelves, exposed covers attracted their attention. For example, P6 picked up a book with striking cover art ('The Book of Joan' by Yuknavitch) from the center table. She stated *"people say don't judge a book by its cover, but I quite like the design."* This supports findings that covers play a key role in deciding whether to examine a book in detail [18, 31].

There were no examples of book cover exposure supporting goal-directed seeking, despite previous intimations that this could be the case. Previous work in bookshops have noted that queries about books sometimes include cover details, for example [27].

5.2   Informational Design Features

The information elements of Libreria could potentially be replicated in any space, or even online. In this section we report how they helped and hindered goal-directed seeking, loosely-directed exploration and information encountering.

Broad, Ambiguous Organization Scheme. This feature impacted both goal-directed seeking and loosely-directed exploration, as noted by the vast majority of participants.

The categories in Libreria were described by participants as too ambiguous to support goal-directed seeking. When P8 noticed 'Home and Hearth', she said *"such a weird label name! I wouldn't consider finding a book here."* She also highlighted they could have multiple meanings and therefore have many possible books 'correctly' classified within them. She stated *"the labels were vague. For example, with 'Identity,' what type of identity is it about? Racial identity? Gender identity? Surely lots of books in a bookshop can be classified under 'Identity'."*

Most participants also considered the labels too difficult to relate to individual books, which negatively impacted their goal-directed seeking. For example, P4 noticed the 'Wanderlust' sign and took out books from that section, stating *"oh, I like travelling."* He then noticed a book on 'London Craft Beer' in the same section and asked himself *"does it belong to Wanderlust?"*

In contrast to goal-directed seeking, the ambiguity of the organization scheme and associated section labels greatly encouraged exploration, and often encountering as a result. For example, P8 encountered a non-fiction book 'Assata: An Autobiography' after stating she usually prefers fiction. She commented *"it almost forces me to discover books I would not have considered otherwise. Because you have to browse by broad theme rather than by category."* Books were often placed next to each other in ways participants did not expect, and which facilitated discovery. P8 described these novel adjacencies as *"placing familiar things next to unfamiliar things, so you can discover something new"* and P3 said the sections *"repackage[d] the books and give them different meanings."* Novel adjacencies feature in the Bohemian Bookshelf [46], whose interactive visualizations of a library collection were designed for serendipity.

Some participants explicitly stated the broad organization scheme could lead to encounters that expanded their interests and burst their filter bubbles [47]. P4 stated *"in a normal bookstore often you already know what you're looking for and just go straight for it. And you end up reading stuff like what you've already read. This one makes you browse more."* He commented *"you may have to look through the entire store to find a specific book. But while you're looking you might find other books you like. It's like you can't filter anyway, even if you wanted to."* Topic diversity was regarded positively, as a means of potential discovery; referring to the 'Africana' shelf, P8 stated *"I don't think I've seen a category with such a diverse set of books in other bookshops. I quite like that."* P6 highlighted the need to balance staying within and venturing outside one's interests to promote useful discovery. She stated *"if you've got an author you like, you'd want to read other books by them again. But you also want to venture out of your existing interests,"* echoing the seeking-encountering tension seen in [33].

The section labels and unusual mix of books also encouraged 'slowability' [26] or taking the time to reflect [21]. P8 said the organization scheme forced him to *"browse more slowly, look at things in more detail and consider what I was looking at,"* referring to it as *"a different way of browsing"* that *"forced you to look at each shelf carefully and make your own meaning."* P5 commented *"these labels make my head think. In a common bookshop, you see fiction, non-fiction, poetry. It's easy to understand. But this bookshop is not like that. For example, you see the label 'Dark Times' and try to see what it's about and not about."*

Participants did express some caution about the way the organization scheme affected encountering, though. P8 noted *"I don't think [the structure] really hindered me, because I still discovered new books. But I almost wonder if I could discover more if there was a proper structure."* In contrast to P4, P7 said the structure meant she was 'always filtering' because the it was *"so random and chaotic."*

Topically Diverse Table Displays. These displays had mixed results. Three participants (P6-8) incorrectly applied mental models of traditional bookshops to the center table, assuming books on it were bestsellers or new releases. For example, P7 stated *"I don't look at tables like this because they're all bestsellers possibly. I have a prejudice against bestsellers. I think if they sold well, the content must be lame."* This can be considered a breakdown of the information encountering process [18, 19], where books are *noticed* but not *examined.* This was not true of all participants, though: some participants did find books on these tables, predominantly we suspect because they facilitate exposed covers. The topical diversity did not seem to have any impact on goal-directed seeking or loosely-directed exploration one way or the other, but the design of the tables was poorly understood generally. This element of Libreria's design can be considered broadly unsuccessful.

Author Curated Sections. Although author curated sections were noticed by most participants, some consciously avoided examining any type of recommendation. P5 stated this was because they usually did not align to her interests. She commented *"it's their story, not my story. I want to choose my own thing and not follow someone else's path."*

Those who *did* examine author-curated sections soon dismissed them as they were unfamiliar with the curator, e.g. P2 noticed the 'Curated by Hannah Barry' sign and said *"oh, there's a curator. But I don't know who she is, so don't really care. But if it was an author I loved, I might. If Margaret Atwood curated the bookshelf, I'd expect the books to be quite awesome."*

Recommendation Cards. These cards were also noticed but quickly dismissed by most. Several participants cited the cards obscuring the book cover as a reason for not examining them in more detail; P7 thought they were *"no use for discovering books at all"* as *"when they obscure the book covers, my interest sharply declines."* She stated although the card might still catch her attention, *"when I skim the text on one card and decide it's just promotional, I'd skip any others."* This misgiving about the cards' purpose was echoed by P5, who stated *"it feels suspicious"* as she thought books with cards were those the shop was trying to promote.

6   Libreria's Tension Between Findability and Discoverability

The finding that echoed across Libreria's design features is that there is a tension between findability and discoverability at play. This tension between supporting goal-directed seeking and discovery (often through loosely-directed exploration) was noted by several participants. For example, P3 stated *"you can always find something unusual in bookshops like this. But don't expect to find anything you already wanted. Finding particular books is nearly impossible."* P2 expressed a preference for organization that was *"more logical,"* but noted *"I guess this is good for browsing though, as you're looking from one book to another quickly."* On reflection, she decided a more logical organization scheme *"might also be less endearing and take some of the fun away."*

Participants found it almost impossible to find specific known items or topics, other than (ironically) by accident. However, all unexpectedly encountered interesting books, mostly when 'freely exploring' but also during goal-directed seeking. Some aspects of the environment design were key in facilitating encountering, particularly the broad, ambiguous organization scheme and book cover exposure. Other design features, particularly the continuous shelving, author curated sections and recommendation cards did not facilitate encountering. However, the follow-up interviews provided evidence that they might, if implemented differently.

Findings related to Libreria's support for goal-directed seeking and loosely-directed exploration are presented in Sects. 6.1 and 6.2. Example information encounters during directed and loosely-directed seeking are presented in Sects. 6.3 and 6.4.

6.1 Seeking but Not Finding: Libreria's Design Poorly Supports Goal-Directed Information-Seeking

Only one participant (P4) found what he was looking for in the goal-directed task - 'an interesting biography'. This may be because his (self-chosen) task was broader than all others. For example, P1 was unable to find books on East Asian History, P3 books by famous novelist Margaret Atwood, and P9 a biography of US president Johnson. However, some participants who performed the goal-directed task first found books (or sections of the shop) related to their goals during the loosely-directed task. For example, P6 did not find a book written by Popular Science author Steven Pinker during the finding task but found one later, by accident, during exploration.

Most participants voiced frustration, mostly due to difficulty understanding the organization scheme. When looking for 'When I Hit You' by Kandasamy, P8 said *"I don't know where it would be. No idea! I know it could be on the random shelves around the bookstore, but I don't know where I should look."* She stated *"if I want to find a specific book, this bookshop hinders me, as I don't know what the categorization is."* Other participants were also confused by the organization; P8 stated *"it made me want to stop browsing, it was so chaotic. There needs to be a balance."* P4 was frustrated as the section label ambiguity meant he had to scan the shelves unaided: *"- When you had something in mind it could be hard. It was very frustrating. Because the labels don't help you with anything. So you kinda have to walk through the entire store and scan through every bookshelf to find the books you want"* (P4).

Equally, there was confusion about the categories themselves, with P8 discovering books by a single author in disparate locations and P3 noting fiction was mixed with non-fiction. She stated *"the labels with such obscure themes didn't work as guidance. I just relied on memory - thought 'I've seen books about feminism in an area, maybe I can also find Atwood's books there."*

P6 considered Libreria only suitable for loosely-directed exploration, stating *"a bookshop like this might be less useful when you have a purpose. It's only good for browsing."* Similarly, P2 wished for a 'CTRL+FIND' equivalent to find known items. P6 though, commented that Libreria was not supposed to be for goal-directed seeking: other bookstores like Waterstones or Amazon were, and that one visited a place like Libreria *"to discover new books."* P1 stated if he wanted to find a specific book, he would normally ask staff, highlighting there are other avenues for finding known items.

6.2   Finding While not Seeking: Libreria's Design Supports Loosely-Directed Exploration Well

While participants struggled with goal-directed seeking, they reveled in exploring the bookshop through loosely-directed browsing. This engendered a highly-enjoyable experience and facilitated several serendipitous information encounters (discussed in Sect. 6.4). As explained by P9, *"even if you walked around the shop repetitively you'll still find new things you didn't see before."*

Unlike several participants, who said they disliked the bookshop's organization scheme, P9 liked Liberia precisely because of it, stating *"I like Libreria precisely because it has no clear labels or organization. I didn't know what to do at first, but then began to feel joy when freely browsing the books"* (P9).

When reflecting on how well Libreria supported exploration, P3 noted independent bookshops may be better suited than traditional ones because they encourage encountering: *"If I go to a normal bookshop, I usually want to find a particular book or latest releases. In an indie bookshop, I would go for an afternoon to browse, to discover. It's like going to a flea market. You might get some nice surprises"* (P3).

6.3   Finding While Looking for Something Else: Information Encountering During Goal-Directed Information Seeking

Three episodes of unexpectedly finding an interesting book during goal-directed seeking (by P5, P7 and P9) were observed. This suggests our reassurance that 'it doesn't matter if you find what you're looking for' may have partly mitigated the 'halo-effect' risk. This may also reflect real-life behavior; P6 said *"often I go to a bookshop for a specific book but end up buying others. It happens all the time."*

All encountered books were unrelated to the goal, for example P5 was browsing the 'Ways of Seeing' section for books on 21st century poetry and trying to understand the organization scheme. She pointed at some photography books, stating *"it's smart to put them together under 'Ways of Seeing'."* She then pulled out and put back several books in 'The Last Interview' series in quick succession and returned to the photography books, browsing them methodically. She picked up 'Movie Journal: The Rise of the New American Cinema 1959–1971' by Mekas and Bogdanovich, a book on the history of American filmmaking. She stated *"oh, Mekas! He's Lithuanian. Oh wow, he's been my hero since I was young. Very important in cinematic history in the 20th century. I knew the author, but I didn't know he'd written a book like this. Only when I saw the cover, I said to myself 'wow, it's him!' I met the icon that affected my life the most in a tiny bookshop in London!"* She commented *"it was especially unexpected to find a book about a little country in a small bookshop in a big city."*

6.4   Finding While Not Seeking: Information Encountering During Loosely-Directed Exploration

All participants bar P5 experienced at least one information encounter during loosely-directed exploration. Twelve encounters were observed overall. As the task was time bound and serendipity is 'regular but rare' [12], this number of encounters can be taken to reflect Libreria's 'explorability'. An example follows: In the goal-directed task, P2 struggled to find a Psychology or Science book as a gift for her brother. In the loosely-directed task, she noticed some illustration books shelved together. She pulled out a comic-book adapted version of 'American Gods' by Neil Gaiman but said she would not want to read it in comic form. As she put it back, she noticed another comic book next to it: 'Baking with Kafka' by Tom Gauld. She flicked through, mentioning she had seen Gauld's illustrations in newspapers and on Instagram, but was unaware he had published a book. She thought this would make a great present for her brother as it *"could spark some good conversations and make him laugh."* She kept the book with her and purchased it afterwards. She considered it an unexpected find as it was not a Psychology or Science book, so was outside her brother's usual interests. She thought he would find it interesting as her brother had previously liked some of Gauld's illustrations shared on a family instant messaging group.

7   Discussion and Design Implications for Digital Environments

All participants unexpectedly found interesting books in Libreria, providing empirical evidence that this bookshop, which was deliberately designed for serendipity, *did* encourage information encountering. However, the bookshop poorly supported goal-directed seeking. This highlights a tension between supporting findability on the one hand and discoverability on the other. Optimizing findability over discoverability may enable goal-directed seeking but inhibit loosely or un-directed seeking (i.e. exploration) and encountering. Libreria was, conversely, designed to optimize discoverability over findability: the opposite of the established focus of information retrieval. Its design enabled exploration and encountering, but inhibited goal-directed seeking.

Digital information environments are designed primarily for goal-directed information seeking, rather than the novelty, diversity and serendipity we saw facilitated by Libreria (see [48] for a review of non-accuracy-based approaches). However, digital information environments are notoriously poor for supporting serendipity, browsing and other forms of loosely-directed or undirected information seeking. The connection between findability-first design and poor experiences of serendipity has long been considered (e.g. see [7, 11]), but ours is the first work that has examined the opposite problem: what does serendipity-first design mean for findability? Our study demonstrates a tension between findability and discoverability. Designing a physical environment for serendipity by encouraging users to explore (even get a little bit lost), slow down, and wander makes it difficult for them to rapidly locate known or describable items of interest. It is likely that this is also true of digital environments.

Some, but not all, of Libreria's design features were noted to directly facilitate information encountering. However, some participants found it difficult to understand even those features that *did* facilitate encountering, such as the organization scheme and display tables. This lack of understanding created tensions in the user experience, but were not strong enough to entirely disrupt experiences of encountering.

Our participants distrusted design features they did not understand, such as curated sections and recommendations. This discouraged them from *examining* potentially interesting books: an essential part of the information encountering process [18, 19]. This highlights that even seemingly innocuous design decisions (e.g. curation by little-known authors, placing recommendation cards on book covers) can inhibit encounters. Designing digital serendipity-related design features to be readily understood should be a priority. Furthermore, these features should be carefully tested to ensure they do not unduly inhibit goal-directed seeking (and vice versa for goal-focused features).

Our participants had different expectations of mainstream bookshops, which were considered useful for finding specific items, and specialist shops, that were considered useful for exploration and encountering. These expectations made interpreting Libreria's unorthodox and at times scant structure hard. Libreria was perceived as deviating too much from norms: its loose structure made even the most specific known-item searches hard and was at times *counterproductive* in facilitating information encountering, confusing and overwhelming rather than inspiring users. In digital information environments there are few established norms. This may either help or hinder online information encounters: on the one hand, a lack of idioms can encourage users to 'slow down' and pay attention to information they might not otherwise have examined. On the other, it can induce reticence and caution, reducing opportunities for encountering.

Some participants made incorrect assumptions about the purpose of certain design features (e.g. display tables). Again, they carried expectations from mainstream bookstores, voicing cynicism that items were grouped for commercial rather than reader benefit. Understanding how to achieve authenticity and transparency in this context should reduce barriers to encountering associated with alien or manipulative structures.

Some disorganization or 'chaos' can liberate, but too much can constrain. Structure can be imposed to 'control' the chaos, but not too much as designers should not 'take the fun away' from what can be a joyful, delightful experience; it must still be perceived as 'endearing.' Others have advocated a similar need for balance for designing recommender systems [34], and 'inspiration-oriented' search tools [49]. The 'right' balance is likely to differ based not only on the environment's design, but also on informational factors such as user needs and tasks [34] and other individual factors, such as mood [19]. We are hopeful that it is possible to design flexible, versatile environments that provide some features that are better at supporting goal-directed seeking, and others more helpful in loosely or undirected exploration and encountering, allowing users to shift the seek-discover emphasis at will. How best to do this, particularly given variations in needs and contexts, is an empirical question for future research.

Our findings do not provide direct design solutions; the empirical insight to form an ironclad set of design guidelines does not yet exist. This study contributes to the still-open research question of how best to design for digital serendipity. However, some of Libreria's serendipity-related design features provide opportunities for potential digital analogues, such as supporting multiple (and perhaps unconventional) information organization schemes; some aimed at supporting known-item finding, others at loosely-directed exploration; providing tractable ways of showcasing or recommending content (e.g. for fiction, not just new releases or genre, but also books set in a particular location or historical period); introducing ways of 'slowing' information interaction, such as by providing meaningful, perhaps unconventional related content (e.g. trailers of the movie adaptations of a book), integrating annotation, sharing and personal information management functionality within digital environments; or providing 'continuity' by leveraging ontology-based links to facilitate browsing between related digital content. Illustrative design suggestions for addressing the findability-discovery tension include: reducing search-primacy by stronger visual and interaction signaling for browsing; providing novel browsing support (e.g. through socially-contributed subjectively meaningful connections between content) and integrating search and browse functionality in complementary ways that allow for seamless transition from goal-directed seeking to loosely-directed exploration and vice versa.

8 Conclusion

While prior work has suggested some types of environments may facilitate serendipity while others might not, our paper is the first investigation of a physical environment designed primarily for serendipity - a bookshop called Libreria. We used a combined observation and interview approach to assess which, if any, of Libreria's features facilitated serendipity, and whether designing for serendipity had an impact on more goal-directed forms of information seeking (it did, inhibiting goal-directed seeking).

Libreria had several features - such as ambiguous category names, seating, and exposed book covers that were effective in facilitating serendipitous information encountering, even if (as was the case with the ambiguous organization scheme) users did not understand them. Not all of Libreria's features were effective, though. The recommendation cards, for example, were too alien to participants to be trusted; not knowing where the recommendations came from invalidated them in their eyes. They further obscured a feature - book covers - that had the potential to facilitate serendipity. Leveraging the known affordances of serendipity when designing digital information environments will almost certainly result in more experiences of online information encountering, as this study demonstrated in the physical realm, but at what cost?

Digital information environments have traditionally been designed to support information seeking that is at least partly goal-directed; this is what search boxes are for. Digital environments are notoriously poor for supporting serendipity, though - perhaps because of their focus on directed seeking. Our study shows that designing for serendipity dramatically inhibits goal-directed seeking, so the tension between find-ability and discoverability operates in both directions. This poses an important challenge for digital design (and indeed for design generally): how can we best support all types of information acquisition - from highly to loosely goal-directed and from active to passive within a single interface, or digital information environment? How to address this challenge - ensuring that users can search when they need to, explore when they want to and experience information encounters as a surprising and delightful by-product - remains an important question for future work.

References

1. Marchionini, G.: Information seeking in electronic environments. In: Long, J. (ed.) Cambridge Series on Human-Computer Interaction, vol. 9. Cambridge University Press, Cambridge (1997)
2. Kuhlthau, C.C.: Inside the search process: information seeking from the user's perspective. JASIST **42**(5), 361–371 (1991)
3. Ellis, D.: A behavioral approach to information retrieval system design. J. Doc. **45**(3), 171–212 (1989)
4. Cunningham, S.J., Reeves, N., Britland, M.: An ethnographic study of music information seeking: implications for the design of a music digital library. In: JCDL 2003, pp. 5–16. IEEE Computer Society (2003)
5. Cunningham, S.J., Nichols, D.M.: Exploring social music behavior: an investigation of music selection at parties. In: ISMIR 2009, pp. Ismir (2009)
6. McKay, D., Buchanan, G., Chang, S.: It ain't what you do it's the way that you do it: design guidelines to better support online browsing. In: ASIST 2018. ASIS&T (2018)
7. Makri, S., et al.: A library or just another information resource? A case study of users' mental models of traditional and digital libraries. JASIST **58**(3), 433–445 (2007)
8. Stelmaszewska, H., Blandford, A.: From physical to digital: a case study of computer scientists' behavior in physical libraries. IJDL **4**(2), 82–92 (2004)
9. Marshall, C.C., Bly, S.: Turning the page on navigation. In: JCDL 2005, pp. 225–234. ACM (2005)
10. Svenonius, E.: The Intellectual Foundation of Information Organization. MIT Press, Boston (2000)
11. Foster, A., Ford, N.: Serendipity and information seeking: an empirical study. J. Doc. **59**(3), 321–340 (2003)
12. McBirnie, A.: Seeking serendipity: the paradox of control. Aslib Proc. **60**(6), 600–618 (2008)
13. Andre, P., et al.: Discovery is never by chance: designing for (un)serendipity. In: C&C 2009, pp. 305–314. ACM (2009)
14. Makri, S., Blandford, A.: Coming across information serendipitously: Part 1 - a process model. J. Doc. **68**(5), 685–704 (2012)
15. Yadamsuren, B., Erdelez, S.: Incidental exposure to online news. In: ASIST, pp. 1–8. American Society for Information Science (2010)
16. McCay-Peet, L., Toms, E.G.: The process of serendipity in knowledge work. In: IIIX, pp. 377–382. ACM (2010)
17. Race, T.M., Makri, S.: Accidental Information Discovery: Cultivating Serendipity in the Digital Age. Elsevier, Amsterdam (2016)
18. Erdelez, S.: Information encountering: a conceptual framework for accidental information discovery. In: ISIC 1997, pp. 412–421. Taylor Graham Publishing (1997)
19. Liu, F., Jiang, T., Chi, Y.: Online information encountering: modeling the process and influencing factors. J. Doc. **71**(6), 1135–1157 (2015)

20. Makri, S., et al.: Observing serendipity in digital information environments. ASIST Proc. **52** (1), 1–10 (2015)
21. Makri, S., et al.: "Making my own luck": serendipity strategies and how to support them in digital information environments. JASIST **65**(11), 2179–2194 (2014)
22. Erdelez, S.: Information encountering: it's more than just bumping into information. Bull. Am. Soc. Inf. Sci. Technol. **25**(3), 26–29 (1999)
23. Björneborn, L.: Serendipity dimensions and users' information behavior in the physical library interface. Inf. Res. **13**(4) (2008)
24. McCay-Peet, L., Toms, E.G.: The serendipity quotient. ASIST Proc. **48**(1), 1–4 (2011)
25. McCay-Peet, L., Toms, E.G.: Investigating serendipity: how it unfolds and what may influence it. JASIST **66**(7), 1463–1476 (2015)
26. Björneborn, L.: Three key affordances for serendipity: toward a framework connecting environmental and personal factors in serendipitous encounters. J. Doc. **73**(5), 1053–1081 (2017)
27. Buchanan, G., McKay, D.: In the bookshop: examining popular search strategies. In: JCDL 2011, pp. 269–278. ACM (2011)
28. Trager, K.: Reading in the borderland: an ethnographic study of serious readers in a mega-bookstore café. Commun. Rev. **8**(2), 185–236 (2005)
29. Ooi, K.: How adult fiction readers select fiction books in public libraries: a study of information seeking in context. School of Information Management, Victoria University of Wellington, Wellington (2008)
30. Saarinen, K., Vakkari, P.: A sign of a good book: readers' methods of accessing fiction in the public library. J. Doc. **69**(5), 736–754 (2013)
31. Hinze, A., et al.: Book selection behavior in the physical library: implications for ebook collections. In: JCDL 2012, pp. 305–314. ACM (2012)
32. Saarti, J.: Feeding with the spoon, or the effects of shelf classification of fiction on the loaning of fiction. Inf. Serv. Use **17**(2/3), 159 (1997)
33. Waugh, S., McKay, D., Makri, S.: 'Too Much Serendipity': the tension between information seeking and encountering at the library shelves. In: CHIIR 2017, pp. 277–280. ACM (2017)
34. Reutzel, D.R., Gali, K.: The art of children's book selection: a labyrinth unexplored. Read. Psychol. **19**(1), 3–50 (1998)
35. Underhill, P.: Why We Buy: The Science of Shopping. Simon and Schuster, New York (1999)
36. Carr, P.L.: Serendipity in the stacks: libraries, information architecture, and the problems of accidental discovery. C&RL **76**(6), 831–842 (2015)
37. Rimmer, J., et al.: An examination of the physical and the digital qualities of humanities research. IP&M **44**(3), 1374–1392 (2008)
38. Cunningham, S.J., Vanderschantz, N., Timpany, C., Hinze, A., Buchanan, G.: Social information behaviour in bookshops: implications for digital libraries. In: Aalberg, T., Papatheodorou, C., Dobreva, M., Tsakonas, G., Farrugia, C.J. (eds.) TPDL 2013. LNCS, vol. 8092, pp. 84–95. Springer, Heidelberg (2013). https://doi.org/10.1007/978-3-642-40501-3_9
39. Cunningham, S.J.: Children in the physical collection: implications for the digital library. In: ASIST, pp. 1–10. Association for Information Science and Technology (2011)
40. McKay, D., Hinze, A., Heese, R., Vanderschantz, N., Timpany, C., Cunningham, S.J.: An exploration of ebook selection behavior in academic library collections. In: Zaphiris, P., Buchanan, G., Rasmussen, E., Loizides, F. (eds.) TPDL 2012. LNCS, vol. 7489, pp. 13–24. Springer, Heidelberg (2012). https://doi.org/10.1007/978-3-642-33290-6_2
41. Bogers, T., Rasmussen, R.R., Jensen, L.S.B.: Measuring serendipity in the lab: the effects of priming and monitoring. In: iConference, pp. 703–706 (2013)

42. Braun, V., Clarke, V.: Using thematic analysis in psychology. Qual. Res. Psychol. **3**(2), 77–101 (2006)

43. Gerwe, P., Viles, C.L.: User effort in query construction and interface selection. In: DL 2000. ACM (2000)

44. McKay, D., Conyers, B.: Where the streets have no name: how library users get lost in the stacks. In: CHINZ 2010, pp. 77–80. ACM (2010)

45. Marshall, C.C.: Reading and writing the electronic book. In: Marchionini, G. (ed.) Synthesis Lectures on Information Concepts, Retrieval and Services. Morgan & Claypool, Chapel Hill (2010)

46. Thudt, A., Hinrichs, U., Carpendale, S.: The Bohemian bookshelf: supporting serendipitous book discoveries through information visualization. In: CHI 2012, pp 1461–1470. ACM (2012)

47. Pariser, E.: The Filter Bubble: What the Internet is Hiding from You. Penguin, New York (2011)

48. Kaminskas, M., Bridge, D.: Diversity, serendipity, novelty, and coverage: a survey and empirical analysis of beyond-accuracy objectives in recommender systems. ToIS **7**(1), 1–42 (2016)

49. Hill, T., et al.: "Searching for inspiration": user needs and search architecture in Europeana collections. In: ASIST, pp. 1–7. American Society for Information Science (2016)

Does the Pop-Out Make an Effect in the Product Selection of Signage Vending Machine?

Mitsuki Hosoya[1(✉)], Hiroaki Yamaura[1], Satoshi Nakamura[1],
Makoto Nakamura[2], Eiji Takamatsu[2], and Yujiro Kitaide[2]

[1] Meiji University, Nakano 4-21-1, Nakano-ku, Tokyo, Japan
ev60523@meiji.ac.jp
[2] Fuji Electric Co., Ltd, Fuji-cho 1-27, Yokkaichi, Mie, Japan

Abstract. When people select a product, they often face problems that they spend too much time to make a choice or tend to pick only popular items. As a solution to this problem, we focused on visual characteristics called pop-out, assuming that presenting the pop-out can lead to shortening the selection time and a wider variety of choice. In this study, we implemented a signage vending machine which had a pop-out function and conducted a long-term experiment (half year) to investigate the effect of the pop-out method in a real environment. From 2826 sales, we revealed that the selection time was short when the purchased items were popped-out, and a popped-out product was more likely to be selected by 1.51 times than chance level during the cold-only period that sold cold products only. On the other hand, there was no effect of the pop-out during the hot/cold mixed period that sold both cold and hot products.

Keywords: Choice behavior · Pop-out · Visual stimuli · Vending machine

1 Introduction

In everyday life, people encounter a lot of situations that require them to select something such as purchasing a drink at a vending machine, pick a lunchbox from a showcase, placing an order from a menu at a restaurant, and so on.

At the time of product selection, people often take time to consider which product to buy. However, there are several demerits in this behavior. For example, if a customer spends too much time to select items in a fast food restaurant, there would be a waiting line, the restaurant might get crowded, or other customers would become in a bad mood. So, it would be good for the providers if customers select items as fast as possible. In addition, spending a long time for selection is often considered to be a waste of time, so it is desirable to shorten the selection time. To solve these problems, we considered necessary to shorten the selection time by promoting the selection of products.

Electronic supplementary material The online version of this chapter (https://doi.org/10.1007/978-3-030-29384-0_2) contains supplementary material, which is available to authorized users.

© IFIP International Federation for Information Processing 2019
Published by Springer Nature Switzerland AG 2019
D. Lamas et al. (Eds.): INTERACT 2019, LNCS 11747, pp. 24–32, 2019.
https://doi.org/10.1007/978-3-030-29384-0_2

We then assumed that making a particular item stand out would be a way to encourage the selection of items. However, it is not desirable that only a particular item is highly likely to be selected when customers should have a wider variety of choice. For example, if people selected a particular product only in the vending machine, the product will be sold out, and others who want the item are no longer able to buy it. In addition, it is disadvantageous to the providers since they hope to eliminate the hesitation over the selection as much as possible and encourage diverse selection.

Thus it is considered to be important to reduce the time required for selection and to promote selection with a wider variety. Here, there is a visual characteristic of human beings called pop-out. The pop-out is a visual characteristic to perceive the stimulus immediately when only one different visual stimuli is present in the same visual stimulation group (Fig. 1). Then, we considered using the pop-out during the selection action would lead to shortening the selection time and diverse selection. For example, when multiple products are sold in vending machines, by popping out a particular product, it becomes easier for the customers to perceive the item immediately. With this, it is possible to induce the customers to select the target item and reduce the time for selection.

In this study, we implemented a vending machine with touch display which users could buy a drink only by touching its image (Fig. 2) and carried out a long-term investigation (half year) on whether pop-out leads to shortening the selection time and whether the range of selection becomes wider by performing pop-out. In addition, we placed the vending machine at our university. Furthermore, we clarified the advantages and problems of pop-out based on the results of the experiment.

Fig. 1. Example of a pop-out

Fig. 2. The signage type vending machine for the experiment

2 Related Work

Many kinds of research have been carried out to study pop-out. Maljkovic et al. [1] revealed that whether a person anticipates what is popped-out does not affect the target of their attention, and that pop-out cannot be ignored consciously. In addition, there are many studies that analyzed the target stimulus of pop out, and they found that pop-out can be affected by factors such as word group relevance (Diliberto et al. [2]), difference in directions (Nothdurft [3]), and whether the target stimulus is a face (Hershler et al. [4]). Based on the findings of these studies, Baldassi et al. [5] suggested that pop-out is not peculiar to the luminance or color, but may occur due to subjective factors such as personal experience or knowledge. Our current study focuses on these characteristics of pop-out introduced above and researches whether pop-out can reduce hesitation and time of selection.

Nudging is a term in behavioral economics that means a way to induce human behavior without restricting options. Specific examples and problems of nudging are summarized in Marteau et al. [6]. It is a nudging to induce selection by presenting pop-out before the action of selection, which is carried out in this study.

Digital signage is an information medium for transmitting information that displays images and characters with a display or projector. One of the examples is the digital signage guide interface in buildings or tourist spots, and the vending machine used in this study can also be an example. Digital signage has been becoming more and more common, and many studies have conducted along with it. For example, Muller et al. [7] pointed out a problem that digital signage is likely to be ignored when it shows advertising for which the viewers have no interest and proposed solutions for it. Digital signage is considered to match the technique introduced in the current study, which pops out a particular item because it is possible to control the information to present dynamically.

3 Experiment

The purpose of this study is to verify the usefulness of pop-out in solving the problems in product selection. Then, we implemented a signage type vending machine and investigated whether or not the pop-out is effective for reducing the selection time and promoting more variety of product selection by conducting an experiment using the machine.

Through the experiment, we collected data of the flow from when the research participants selected the item that is displayed on the screen of the vending machine to when they purchased it. We installed a function to present the effects of pop-out to highlight only one of the items in the vending machine at random for every purchase, and we investigated whether the selection behavior can be affected by the presence or absence of the pop-out. In addition, the system changes a popped-out product randomly. Moreover, we fixed the position of the products during the experiment period except when we replaced the products with new ones.

Fig. 3. An example of the product selection screen in the pop-out condition (bottom center of the product have been popped-out)

Firstly, we investigated the selectivity of pop-out. Then, we compared the situations with the pop-out presentation (henceforth referred to as pop-out condition) and without the pop-out presentation (henceforth referred to as normal condition). Here, we investigated whether the presence of the pop-out by itself affects the reduction of selection time, regardless of whether the popped-out items were selected. In addition, we compared the selection times of when people selected the popped-out product and when they did not select it in the pop-out condition. Furthermore, to see if the pop-out influences the choice of the items, we compared the distributions of the purchased products with the pop-out presentation (pop-out condition) and without the pop-out presentation (normal condition).

In the experimental system, we used the same background color for all the products in the normal condition. Here, in the pop-out condition, we changed the background color of a product that was randomly selected and applied the pop-out to the product. An example of the product selection screen in the pop-out condition (see Fig. 3). In the experiment, the background color of the popped-out products was gray (RGB values that are specified in 0.0 and 1.0 are 0.9 respectively), and the background color of the products without the pop-out was white (RGB values are 1.0 respectively). By making only one background color stand out this way, it becomes easy for the target item to attract attention, which is expected to increase the product selectivity and shorten the selection time.

We placed the system on the sixth floor of Meiji University. The experimental contributors were an unspecified number of people who stopped by the vending machine and were notified about the experiment by a poster on the vending machine telling that the experiment was underway. The experimental implementation period was from August 29, 2018, to February 28, 2019, which resulted in collecting data of 2826 sales. In addition, from August 29, 2018, to 1:00 pm on October 31, 2018, the vending machine sold only cold products (henceforth referred to as cold-only period), and the number of sales of this period was 1090. Then, we replaced six cold products with hot products at 1:00 pm on October 31, 2018, and since then both the hot products and cold products were sold (henceforth referred to as hot/cold mixed period). The number of sales in this period was 1736.

4 Result

The total number of sales to be analyzed was 2826, in which the number of sales in the pop-out condition was 1384 (526 during the cold-only period, and 858 during the hot/cold mixed period) and the number of sales in the normal condition was 1442 items.

Table 1 shows the number of sales in the pop-out condition and the selectivity of the pop-out product in each period. Here, if people selected the products randomly at chance level, the number of the sold items with the pop-out will be 15.94 (526/33) during the cold-only period, and 26.00 (858/33) during the hot/cold mixed period. The selection ratio of the popped-out products becomes 1.51 in cold-only period and 1.04 during the hot/cold mixed period. These results suggest that the effect of pop-out was seen during cold-only period, but not during the hot/cold mixed period.

Table 1. The results of sales in the pop-out condition in each period

Period	The number of sales	The number of sales of the popped-out product	Expected value (Chance Level)	Ratio
Cold-only	526	24	15.94	1.51
Hot/cold mixed	858	27	26.00	1.04

Figure 4 shows a comparison between the average selection time of when the customers selected the popped-out product and that of when they did not select the popped-out product in each period. In this figure, the average selection time of the user who selected the popped-out product was shorter than that of those who did not select the popped-out products. However, there was little difference in selecting time whether the products popped-out or not during the hot/cold mixed period. The result suggests that by presenting the pop-out during the cold-only period, it was possible to shorten the selection time of the user when they selected the pop-out product.

Figure 5 shows a comparison of the average selection time in the pop-out condition and the normal condition. From this result, there is no difference in the average selection time between in the pop-out condition and the normal condition.

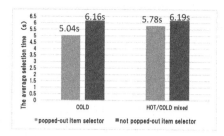 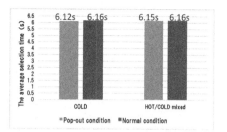

Fig. 4. Comparison of the average selection time between popped-out items and others

Fig. 5. Comparison of the average selection time between the pop-out condition and the normal condition

The products sold in the vending machine used in this experiment were placed in the 33 positions (see Fig. 6). The arrangement of the products during the hot/cold mixed period and the arrangement was the same during cold-only period. We made a comparison of the distribution of the sold products in the pop-out condition and in the normal condition to investigate whether the pop-out changed the distribution. In addition, we conducted two different investigations for the cold-only period and hot/cold mixed period respectively because of the difference in types of products sold in each period.

Figure 7 shows the distribution of sold products with the pop-out presentation and that with no pop-out presentation during the cold-only period, and Fig. 8 shows those distributions during the hot/cold mixed period. The horizontal axis of these figures represents the position number of the product shown in Fig. 6, and the vertical axis represents the number of sold products. The result shows that, regardless of whether or not there is a presentation of the pop-out, the distribution of products was mostly not changed. In addition, the most purchased products were products placed in No. 9 in both conditions with and without the presence of the pop-out. Based on these observations, we found that the distributions of sold products were similar in the pop-out condition, and the normal condition.

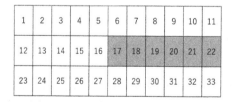

Fig. 6. Product placement during the HOT/COLD mixed period in signage vending machine.

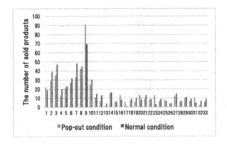 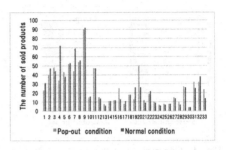

Fig. 7. Distribution of product sales in the pop-out condition and the normal condition during the cold-only period

Fig. 8. Distribution of product sales in the pop-out condition and the normal condition during the hot/cold mixed period

Figure 9 showed the distribution of the sold products in the pop-out condition in each period. The result shows that the products placed in No. 9, which was the most purchased products among all the products, had the biggest number of sales when they were with pop-out during the cold-only period. In addition, the products placed in No. 1 to 3 and No. 5 to 9 had a relatively large number of sales in each condition during the cold-only period, and they also tended to be sold well when they were popped-out. Moreover, the number of purchase of the products placed in No. 29 to 33 was extremely small, but it improved when they were popped-out. Therefore, we found that pop-out products were widely purchased during the cold-only period.

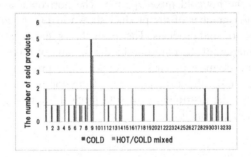

Fig. 9. Distribution of purchased popped-out products

5   Analysis

We found that the selectivity of popped-out products was high during the cold-only period. On the other hand, there is no difference in selectivity of the popped-out products during the hot/cold mixed period. The result would be because while cold products were displayed with blue text, hot products were displayed with red text (see Fig. 3), which resulted in popping out the hot products. In addition, the effect of the pop-out was not observed during the hot/cold mixed period because the customers were highly likely to know whether they would buy a cold drink or hot drink before starting the purchase.

As for shortening the selection time by pop-out, the average selection time of the users who selected the pop-out products was shorter than that of those who did not select the pop-out products. Thus, we could say that the pop-out contributed to shortening the selection time. On the other hand, there was no significant difference in the average selection times in the pop-out condition and the normal condition. This result would suggest that the presentation of the pop-out is less likely to cause negative effects, such as extending the selection time by increasing hesitation and confusion.

Here, the products placed in No. 1 to 3, and No. 5 through 9 had a large number of ales throughout the entire experiment, and they also held the high number of sales when they were popped-out during the cold-only period. From these results, we can say that a popped-out product that is originally popular would lead to increasing their sales. On the other hand, the products placed in No. 29-33 were observed to have a small number of sales throughout the entire experiment, but the number of their sales increased when they were popped-out during the cold-only period. The result would suggest a possibility that the pop-out can increase the sales of unpopular products as well.

During the hot/cold mixed period, there was a bias in the types of the purchased products when the user purchased the popped-out products. For example, the arrangement of the products in which hot items and cold items were mixed. To solve this problem, we will re-arrange the positions of cold products and hot products during the hot/cold mixed period.

The current study observed that the number of sales of the products placed on No. 1–9 was high while that of the products placed on No. 29–33 was small, and this result of the sales can be considered to be due to not only the users' preferences on the products but also the arrangement of the products (see Fig. 6). It is known that when people search for something, they generally start looking at the upper left, then move to the lower right. The result could account for the fact about the sales of the products that the products placed in No. 1 to 9, which were placed in the upper left of the vending machine and therefore are seen at first, recorded a large number of sales. On the other hand, the sales of products placed in No. 29 to 33, which were placed in the lower right of the vending machine and therefore are seen last, had only the small number of sales. However, it was also true that the products placed in No. 29 to 33 had been sold in the pop-out condition, so it can be said that the pop-out improved the negative effect of the position of the products to their sales.

Based on the observations above, we can say that the pop-out gives positive effect to the selection behavior. In addition, seriousness toward the selection was guaranteed in this experiment as it was conducted in the real environment in which the participants had actually to pay for the products. It is considered that we can apply the method to pop out to digital signage in general. Digital signage for selective actions has been widely used now and is suitable for this study, such as improving selection and selecting various products. In addition, we believe that the method used in the current study is applicable for any types of selective actions by touching the options on the display.

6 Conclusion

In this paper, we implemented a system which had a pop-out function and conducted a long-term experiment in the real environment. Then, we found that the products were more likely to be selected when they were popped-out than when they were not, and that the selection time was shorter when the users selected the popped-out products during the cold-only period. However, the result also suggested that the effect of the pop-out was not valid in the hot/cold mixed period. In addition, we found the possibilities that a wider range of selection would be available by popping out products randomly, and that the selection time can be shortened when users select the popped-out product.

In future work, we will analyze the behavior such as the number of human in front of the vending machine, and their gender, and age, and so on. In addition, since this research did not consider the possibility of the product package and popout competing, we believe that it is necessary to cluster and analyze the elements such as color, font, impression, and so on which related to package design. Additionally, since Gutwin et al. [8] shows that that popout effects away from a user's central vision are harder to notice, we will analyze the relationship between popped-out locations and purchased products. By doing this, it will be possible to make recommendations suitable for the situations, and the pop-out will be used more effectively.

Acknowledgments. This work was supported in part by JST ACCEL Grant Number JPMJAC1602, Japan.

References

1. Maljkovic, V., Nakayama, K.: Priming of pop-out-I. Role of features. Memory Cogn. **22**, 657–672 (1994)
2. Diliberto, K.A., Altarriba, J., Neill, W.T.: Novel popout without novelty. Memory Cogn. **26**, 429–434 (1998)
3. Nothdurft, H.C.: Texture segmentation and pop-out from orientation contrast. Vision. Res. **31** (6), 1073–1078 (1991)
4. Hershler, O., Hochstein, S.: At first sight: a high-level pop out effect for faces. Vision. Res. **45**, 1707–1724 (2005)
5. Baldassi, S., Burr, D.C.: "Pop-out" of targets modulated in luminance or colour: the effect of intrinsic and extrinsic uncertainty. Vision. Res. **44**, 1227–1233 (2004)
6. Marteau, T.M., Ogilvie, D., Roland, M., Suhrcke, M., Kelly, M.P.: Judging nudging: can nudging improve population health? Br. Med. J. **342**, d228 (2011)
7. Müller, J., et al.: Display blindness: the effect of expectations on attention towards digital signage. In: Tokuda, H., Beigl, M., Friday, A., Brush, A.J.B., Tobe, Y. (eds.) Pervasive 2009. LNCS, vol. 5538, pp. 1–8. Springer, Heidelberg (2009). https://doi.org/10.1007/978-3-642-01516-8_1
8. Gutwin, C., Cockburn, A., Coveney, A.: Peripheral popout: the influence of visual angle and stimulus intensity on popout effects. In: SIGHCI Conference on Human Factors in Computing Systems (CHI2017), New York (2017)

Exploring Spatial Menu Representation and Apartment-Based Categorization for Online Shopping

Marco Speicher[1(✉)], Nadja Rutsch[1(✉)], Antonio Krüger[1(✉)],
and Markus Löchtefeld[2(✉)]

[1] German Research Center for Artificial Intelligence (DFKI), Saarland Informatics
Campus (SIC), Saarbrücken, Germany
{marco.speicher,nadja.rutsch,antonio.krueger}@dfki.de
[2] Aalborg University, Aalborg, Denmark
mloc@create.aau.dk

Abstract. This work aims to explore, design and implement better
and intuitive categorization schemes and menu representations for online
shops that enrich and improve the shopping experience. We utilize the
Apartment metaphor, in which products are categorized into rooms and
furniture representing departments and shelves. Furthermore, we developed a realistic and interactive map-based spatial menu representation
based on prior research findings. In a comparative user study, we evaluated our new menu categorization and representation in comparison
with the current standard in online shops, based on real data from a
local retailer. The results show that our apartment-based categorization
in combination with a spatial representation outperforms all other conditions regarding all tested variables of performance (success rate, task
completion time) and preferences (user experience, usability, workload).

Keywords: Online shop · Product categorization ·
Menu representation · Usability · User experience

1 Introduction

Nowadays, online shops such as amazon.com or zalando.com are a well established and indispensable part of our everyday life. They often offer a better
product availability, time savings and higher comfort compared to physical stores
since purchases can be made from the comfort of ones home [35]. These factors
have lead to an enormous growth that is anticipated to continue [23,34]. While
in 2017, only 10.1% of worldwide purchases were made online this is expected
to grow to 15.5% by 2021[1].

---

[1] https://tinyurl.com/y8akourk.

Electronic supplementary material The online version of this chapter (https://
doi.org/10.1007/978-3-030-29384-0_3) contains supplementary material, which is available to authorized users.

© IFIP International Federation for Information Processing 2019
Published by Springer Nature Switzerland AG 2019
D. Lamas et al. (Eds.): INTERACT 2019, LNCS 11747, pp. 33–54, 2019.
https://doi.org/10.1007/978-3-030-29384-0_3

While the design and interaction techniques of online shops have changed and improved over the last years, due to a higher focus on user experience and usability [11,16,41], they are still mainly focused on product presentation and purchase transactions. Especially the search bar functionality, where powerful algorithms are used to improve efficiency of customer searches, has received most attention [26]. Compared to this, product search and explorations using a menu interface has been largely neglected. Even though contrary to common belief, product searches via a search bar have been proven to be not necessarily preferred by the user nor are they generally more effective [14]. Especially when an online shopper does not know the explicit name of the desired product or is simply "just looking", the search bars might not be a suitable solution. Customers that want to browse through the products using a specific category, e.g. if they are looking for a gift on menus for product exploration. Thus, it is important to further investigate possibilities of menu optimization.

Although the benefit of visualizations used in online shops is well known, menu representations are still mainly text-based. Furthermore, the underlying categorization depicted by the menu is often inconsistent throughout different online shops which makes it difficult for the customer to understand the underlying classification [27]. Therefore, in this paper we explore the usage of the Apartment metaphor [1] as a menu representation for online shops. It exploits the users familiarity with an apartment environment and categorizes products based on their association to rooms and furniture to make them easier to explore for the user. We present the development of the categorization of the different products as well as spatial visualization showing the floor plan of an apartment or a store to explore the different categories. Our comparative evaluation shows that an apartment-based online shop menu outperforms classic linear store-based menu structures in task performance, usability and user experience. Hence, this work contributes to the further development of online shop menus by:

- **A study of an online shop prototype** was conducted and evaluated four combinations of menu representation and categorization based on related work with respect to task performance and user preference.
- **User insights and actionable improvements** were provided for designing and developing future shopping environments.

2   Background

Prior works relevant to the here presented approach include those addressing (1) menu representations, as well as (2) menu categorization will be discussed here. Furthermore, we present an analysis of the menu structures of current popular online stores.

2.1   Menu Representation

Menu-guided interfaces have long been a prominent user interface component of software applications or websites and serve to structure the underlying amount of information hierarchically. Therefore a variety of different menu representations have been explored in the past. Miller et al. [21] examined the effects of menu width and depth on speed and accuracy. Their results were confirmed by Zaphiris et al. [42], which showed that flat hierarchies are easier and faster to use and lead to greater orientation and satisfaction, and shorten interaction times. This has been recently also confirmed by Zhang et al. [43] in their extensive study on web shop menus. But in their study they also investigated the difference of menu positioning. While early work showed no clear recommendation, and only a tendency towards menus at the top of the screen [24], Zhang et al. showed that top-positioned menus were faster for product search, while top and left-positioned menus were preferred. This confirms that linear menu variants are recommended for use in online shops. Based on these findings, we have developed a reference menu for our comparison study.

Cockburn et al. [5] investigated different approaches to improve the traditional linear menus in terms of performance and preference. They compared standard and shared menus [33], and showed that frequency split menus were the fastest. However, the use of frequency split menus in an online shop might be problematic as highlighting frequently selected but potentially unwanted objects would not lead to any improvement, and could lead to frustration and confusion [22]. Findlater et al. [6] used a prediction algorithm to determine menu items that the user probably needs and showed that they enable faster menu selection. As shopping is a changing process – i.e. the offer and the interests of customers are constantly varying – the use in online shops does not appear promising for the process of exploration and is therefore not considered in this work.

Ahlstrom et al. [2] compared different menu designs and their results show that a squared menu is faster and is preferred which indicates that a spatial and rasterized arrangement could lead to better usability. Similarly Scarr et al., structured items hierarchical in a grid in the *CommandMaps* menu [30]. Their comparison to a ribbon menu interface (known from Microsoft Word) demonstrated that *CommandMaps* are faster and require fewer pointing activities, since the user no longer needs to change menu levels and benefits from spatial memory. In the same line of exploiting spatial memory also Vrechopoulos et al. [39] examined how different "brick-and-mortar" layouts can be transferred into a virtual retail environment. They showed that a *grid* based on a tree structure is easier to handle, which is furthermore supported by Griffith [7].

In summary, an adjustment of the menu representation can lead to higher objective performance [6,21,30] and/or better subjective preference [2,5,42]. Deeper menus, i.e. menus with many layers, increase complexity and slow down interaction times, so that the width (number of menu items in the layer) is preferable to depth [13,14,21,25,40,42]. Moreover, it is advisable to minimize the menu depth without increasing the width extremely and on condition that the semantic data allow such a distribution [21]. The reference menu used in this paper is based on [43], representing the state-of-the-art of traditional linear menus in current online shops. Furthermore, we developed a spatial menu representation in the line of Vrechopoulos et al. and Griffith [7,39].

2.2 Menu Categorization

Besides the representation and arrangement, especially a meaningful and comprehensible categorization of the menu items is important for efficient menu interactions. Katz and Byrne's investigation of menu interfaces for e-commerce environments highlighted the importance of high quality categories [12]. This is also confirmed by the work of Tuch et al. [38], who showed that a good categorization with a high information content can lead to a higher feeling of user-friendliness. Larson and Czerwinski [14] recognized the importance of a semantically founded categorization and integrated this fact into their research on width and depth of menus. In addition, Miller and Remington [20] also emphasize the necessity of both aspects, menu representation and categorization, due to their direct interdependence, i.e. both aspects influence each other in terms of task performance and user preferences.

Usually one differentiates between hierarchical (or faceted) categories and automated clustering [10]. While fully automated clustering according to the similarity of words or phrases has the advantage here, a quick structuring of information collections often leads to logical inaccuracies in contrast to the manually created hierarchies, which are rather preferred by users [10]. Practical examples also show how the categorization of menu items influences user performance, more precisely that users work faster with optimized menu categorizations [32]. Resnick and Sanchez [28] confirm the influence and effect of high-quality menu labels against those with lower quality. The use of meaningful and comprehensive menu labels is therefore an essential.

Adam et al. [1] presented a new categorization and representation scheme to enable intuitive menu navigation. Their spatial "Apartment" metaphor maps the mental model of an apartment with different rooms (living room, kitchen, etc.) to a structure of a smart-home control interface. The top level of categorization corresponds to the room category, followed by a device level and finally a task level that contains the potentially possible system tasks of the selected device. A similar approach has been utilized by Speicher et al. [36] for a virtual reality store. They found that the apartment metaphor provided excellent customer satisfaction, as well as a high level of immersion and user experience. The positive effects of the Apartment metaphor on task performance and user preferences serves as a basis and motivation for the menu categorization of the online shop prototype developed in our work.

2.3 State-of-the-Art Analysis

Even though related work recommends to abandon linear store-based menu interfaces, most current online shops are still employing these. Table 1 lists a selection of popular online shops and their used categorization and representation. While we do not claim this to be the most representative selection it contains some of the most frequented stores. All of them use a linear representation in which the items are arranged horizontally or vertically. Some of them also integrate a multi-column menu display, e.g. the *IKEA* interface contains a two-column menu at the

Table 1. Overview of state-of-the-art online shops for groceries, electronics, furniture or fashion. For the representation the first number is the menu depth, the second is the width of the top-level. These online shops have been accessed on August 21st, 2018.

Online shop	Categorization	Representation
amazon.com	Product range, theme	$(4, 20)$
conrad.com	Product range, theme	$(4, 8)$
ikea.com	Product range, theme, room	$(3, 24)$
carrefour.fr	Product range, theme	$(3, 17)$
rewe.de	Product range, theme	$(3, 12)$
tesco.com/groceries	Product range, theme	$(4, 11)$
tesco.com/direct	Product range, theme	$(5, 12)$
zalando.com	Product range, theme, target group	$(4, 3)$

top level. There are significant differences in the menu width from 3 to 24 items, in contrast to the depths between 3 and 5 levels. This is in line with findings from previous work [14]. In current online shop menus, the individual menu items are predominantly text-based, while current research recommends more graphical methods. Only three of the eight online shops (*REWE, CARREFOUR, IKEA*) additionally integrate icons illustrating the associated text label, while three menus (*CONRAD, REWE, TESCO direct*) also show the number of sub-level items.

Besides the representation, the logical meaning of the underlying categorization is important. All considered menus in Table 1 use mixed categories, i.e. following different sorting strategies within a menu level. Mostly, however, the categories are based on a combination of assortments and themes known from physical shops. For example, the category "beverages" refers to an assortment, the category "baby" to a theme. Studies have shown that such a mixture of categories can be unclear to the users, since the labels do not clearly describe the underlying information space, which is essential to give the user an overall impression of the search space [10]. Especially occasional users or new customers who are not familiar with the specific occurrences of a new or existing shop interface could be particularly frustrated, resulting in a negative effect on performance and preference. In the worst case, it could lead to shopping attempts being cancelled and the shop not being visited again [18]. Our state-of-the-art analysis indicates that current online shops do not follow findings on menu optimization and tend to use classical methods that have already been established.

3   Approach

The purpose of this paper is to explore the usage of the Apartment metaphor for categorization in combination with a spatial representation as a new menu type for online shops. Therefore we re-categorized products from a set of previous categories (departments or themes and shelf names), which are more likely to be found in a physical market, to residential categories as part of a pilot study. Based on these categories we developed a spatial menu representation, as an alternative to the traditional linear menu. This results in the following summarized menu representations and categories to be compared in our conducted main experiment:

- Representations
  - Linear
  - Spatial
- Categorizations
  - Store
  - Apartment

To test and compare these four menu types and combinations of both representations and categorizations, they were integrated into an online shop prototype. As the basis for our menu we selected a set of 36 products, that represent the core areas of online trading. These products were selected from a local hypermarket with an associated online shop and is based on its frequently searched products. The 36 products included belong to various traditional product areas such as food, office supplies, clothing, electronics and others.

3.1 Representations

Representations of menus vary in the arrangement of the items on the screen. This can affect the search time to find a desired menu item visually, as well as the time to point and click [2,4,37]. We examine two different representations here: *linear* and *spatial*.

Linear. The linear menu is most common in today's web interfaces such as online shops [43]. Here the menu items are arranged so that they form either a horizontal or a vertical line, usually with text labels. Since horizontal linear menus are recommended at the top of the screen [43], this combination is used as a reference menu representation. The depth and width of a linear menu depends on the underlying categorization (see Fig. 1).

Spatial. Our spatial menu representation is influenced by earlier findings on the grid arrangement [2,30] and floor maps [19], which are often used in shopping malls, e.g. as printed maps. We use a spatial representation –a map–, based on real environments, where menu items are arranged according to the position they occupy in the real world either inside a store or an apartment depending on the used categorization (see Fig. 1). Thereby we hope to exploit the users spatial memory and improve the performance of the menus [8,29]. As with the linear menu representation, the depth and width of the spatial menu depends on the underlying categorization.

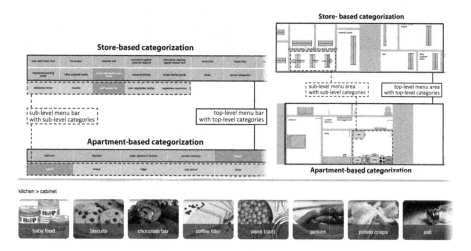

Fig. 1. Linear (left) and Spatial (right) representations, and product area relating to the sub-level "cabinet" under the top-level "kitchen".

3.2   Categorizations

The categorization determines the semantic structure of the menu and is usually structured hierarchically. In this paper, the categorizations are based on a three-level hierarchy (or menu depth) with top, sub and product levels. Overall, two different categories are investigated in this work: a traditional store- and an apartment-based categorization.

Store-Based. The traditional store-based categorization with different departments and themes, serves as the reference point for the evaluation as it represents the de-facto standard in current online shops [43]. The top-level categories of the hierarchy correspond to the product range that is typically separate departments, such as "milk & cheese" or "beverages". The subordinate categories describe shelves in these delimited market areas, e.g. "cream cheese" or "lemonades", followed by the product level as the lowest level (see Fig. 1).

Apartment-Based. The apartment metaphor used in our approach uses the fact that users are familiar with the structure of an apartment and the items (products) placed in it based on everyday habits and experiences [1]. As with the store-based categorization, this is also based on a three-level hierarchy: rooms (e.g. kitchen), furniture (e.g. refrigerator), and product (e.g. mustard). In order to develop these categories and define the corresponding product assignments a pilot study was carried out to find out where users assume that these products should be located inside an apartment.

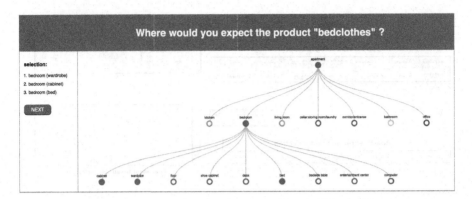

Fig. 2. The tree visualization representing the hierarchy of the apartment categories with room nodes on the first level and furniture nodes on the second level.

4   Pilot Study

To create the needed reclassification of the selected products from store- to apartment-based categorization, we conducted a pilot study. This study is divided into two phases. In the first phase, we focus on the categorization and product allocation inside the Apartment metaphor. In the second phase, we aim to create two groups of products with the same size and approximately the same average level of difficulty (product search error rate) from the pool of the 36 selected products. Each product is then classified according to its average search error rate in order to ensure comparability of product data. This will serve as the logical basis for the main study design.

4.1   Phase 1: Categorization and Product Allocation

In total, 42 participants (20 female) between 18 and 58 years ($M = 31.12, SD = 12.35$) volunteered in the pilot study, which consisted of two sessions. In the first qualitative session, we conducted a semi-structured on-site interview and asked the participants where, i.e. in which room on or in which furniture, they store or would store each of the selected products, followed by a demographic questionnaire. Most participants lived in a two-room apartment ($M = 2.17, SD = 0.85$) (which do not include bathroom, kitchen or hallway) with an average of two inhabitants ($M = 2.38, SD = 1.19$). One third lived in a partnership ($N = 14$), followed by singles ($N = 10$), with parents/family ($N = 9$) or in a shared flat ($N = 9$). All of them have already shopped online, most of them at least once a month ($N = 34$). Information about the housing situation of the participants was gathered. More precisely, the room types belonging to the apartment as well as the product storage habits, i.e. which furniture is used as storage space, such as milk in the refrigerator or newspapers on the table. This was done in a semi-structured interview to form a set of room and furniture categories (top and sub level).

The result of the first session was a preliminary set of apartment locations (rooms and associated furniture), which form an essential part of the apartment categorization, as they form the basis for the product allocation. A total of seven room categories were considered, as these were named by well over half of the participants: bathroom ($N = 41$), kitchen ($N = 41$), bedroom ($N = 41$), hallway ($N = 37$), living room ($N = 35$), pantry/cellar ($N = 32$) and office ($N = 30$). After these there was very little agreement between participants, the next room in this list would be the garden with only 5 mentions. Therefore these rooms create our top-level for the categorization.

After defining the rooms used for product allocation, the furniture or places within these rooms had to be specified. The data collected by the interview was qualitative. Characteristic keywords were chosen to organize the answers given. Furniture that is very similar in use has been combined. For the example "bed linen" in the bedroom, the "built-in cupboard" ($N = 1$), the "linen cupboard" ($N = 2$), the "chest of drawers" ($N = 2$) and the "cupboard" ($N = 11$) were combined under the most frequently used keyword "cupboard". Here is a complete overview of the rooms and associated furnitures (sub-level) in our categorization: **Bathroom**: cabinet, sink, sink cabinet, hook, toilet; **Bedroom**: bed, bedside table, cabinet, wardrobe; **Storage**: cabinet, washing machine; **Hallway**: cabinet, shoe cabinet; **Kitchen**: cabinet, drawer, fridge, sink, table, counter; **Living Room**: cabinet, computer, TV area, table; **Office**: cabinet, computer, desk.

In the second session, after we conducted and analyzed all 42 interviews, the same participants were asked to map the 36 selected products to one or multiple room-furniture pairs using an interactive web application. The web application consisted of three steps and was used to map the products to furniture and rooms (see Fig. 2). The current question *'Where do you expect product "X"?'* was displayed at the top of the screen. The current selection was listed left, as well as a next button to confirm the selection and to get to the next question. On the right, the apartment categories were visualized by an interactive hierarchical tree representation. The root represented the apartment itself, followed by the rooms as top-level and associated furniture as sub-level. This process supported multiple placement of products. In the main study, however, only one room-furniture pair was assigned to each product, namely the most frequently selected pair in this phase of the pilot study.

4.2   Phase 2: Product Groups

After selecting a suitable product set in the conceptual process, each product was assigned a level of difficulty to ensure better comparability. This was necessary to control learning effects within a categorization during the main study. The second phase took place in the local hypermarket, which provides us with the selected product data set, floor plan for the spatial store-based interface, and the departments and shelf names. Each participant ($N = 30$, 14 female) was provided with a worksheet, where the products had to be assigned to one of the store-based top categories. For each product, all incorrect answers were identified and statistical values were calculated for the error rates. Overall, the average error rate over all products was 21.67% ($SD = 27.20$). This finding also shows that there is considerable potential for improvement, at least for this particular retailer, since expectations often do not correspond to reality. The average statistical values resulting from the short classification led to two comparable product groups being formed in the following main study in order to eliminate learning effects in relation to the different categories. Therefore, the total package of 36 products was divided into two groups of 18 products each with comparable error rates (A: ~21.1%, B: ~22.2%).

5 Main Study

We conducted an experiment to compare the developed apartment metaphor for online shopping with more common menu representations in respect to task performance (success rate, task completion time), user preferences (user experience, usability and task workload), and unmet needs. We evaluated two menu representations (*Linear* vs. *Spatial*) and categorizations (*Store* vs. *Apartment*). Our main hypotheses were defined as:

- H_{1-1}: The task can be performed more efficiently using *Apartment* categorization with regard to task performance.
- H_{1-2}: *Apartment* is preferred over *Store* categorization with regard to user preferences.
- H_{2-1}: The task can be performed more efficiently using *Spatial* representation with regard to task performance.
- H_{2-2}: *Spatial* is preferred over *Linear* representation with regard to user preferences.

5.1 Participants

For the main experiment, 24 different unpaid participants (12 female) were recruited from the university's campus; they were aged between 20 and 33 years ($M = 25.3$, $SD = 3.6$). Most of the participants live in a two room apartment ($Median = 2, M = 2.04, SD = 0.86$), which do not include bathroom, kitchen or hallway, with two inhabitants ($Median = 2$). Seven participants live with their parents/family (29.17%), six in a partnership or shared apartment (25%) and five live alone (20.83%). On a 7-point scale from never to daily with regard to online shopping frequency, most participants regularly purchase online, i.e. 62.5% at least several times per month, and all participants shop online at least once per month with computer/laptop ($N = 24$), compared to less frequently with tablets ($N = 7$) or smart-phones ($N = 14$).

5.2 Apparatus

The experiment was conducted on a MacBook Pro running Mac OS (10.11.6) connected to a 24-in. monitor. A standard wireless mouse was used as input device with medium speed settings. The software was displayed in Google Chrome (v58.0.3029.110, 64-bit). HTML, CSS and JavaScript were used for the different menu interfaces in the prototype. Additionally, the JavaScript D3 library was used for data visualization purposes in the spatial menu condition. A database was set up using XAMPP (v7.0.5-0), data exchange was realized using PHP.

5.3 Evaluated Conditions

We evaluated two menu representations (linear, spatial) and two categorizations (store, apartment) to search products. In the linear menus, the menu items are arranged horizontally for all three vertical menu levels (top, sub and product level). In the spatial representations, items are arranged in a grid representing a virtual floor plan. Here, the participant clicks on the area with the corresponding text label to select a top-level category (see Fig. 1). As a result, the corresponding furniture or shelf icons are displayed within the selected area. After clicking on a shelf or furniture, the associated products are then displayed in the product area below the menu area (see Fig. 1). Although some products in the apartment concept should normally be placed in several positions per product, only one position was considered for each product in this main study in order to improve comparability of the conditions. This unique product placement refers to the most frequently mentioned placement from the pilot study.

5.4 Design

The experiment was a within-subjects design, with two independent variables with two levels each (representation: linear and spatial; categorization: store- and apartment-based) and five dependent variables related to the performance (task completion time, success rate) and preference of users (user experience, usability, workload). All representation and categorization conditions were counterbalanced using a Latin square. In order to eliminate learning effects concerning the different categorizations, the total set of 36 selected products was split into two comparable and equally difficult groups with 18 products respectively. Aside from training, this amounted to: 24 participants × 2 representations × 2 categorizations × 18 product searches = 1728 trials.

5.5 Task

During the main study, each participant performed a series of 18 search trials using a combination of the two representations (linear and spatial) and categorizations (store and apartment). The goal was to find and select a specific product and confirm the selection. The top-level categories were the departments of a local store for store-based and rooms for apartment-based categorization. The sub-level represented the shelves for store-based and furniture for apartment-based categorization (as developed in our pilot study). While the top- and sub-level visualizations differed depending on categorization and representation, the product level was displayed similar over all conditions by a product image and text label. A trial was successfully completed when the correct target product was selected and confirmed within a time limit of 30 s, or counted as failed otherwise.

5.6   Procedure

After welcoming the participant by the experimenter, she was introduced by an informed consent form. Each participant used all four menu types in Latin square order to search for products in the prototypical online shop. Before using a particular type of menu, the participant was introduced to the tested condition by watching a demonstration video that showed an example search task step by step. Then a set of 18 search trials was carried out in random order. Before each trial, the name and image of the target product appeared for five seconds. Then the product had to be found in the three-level menu and selected by clicking on it and confirming the selection. After each trial set per menu type, three post-task questionnaires (UEQ [15], SUS [3], NASA TLX [9]) were filled out by the participant to collect user preference ratings. The entire process was then repeated for the other three menu types. Afterwards, a final post-study questionnaire was answered, which included demographic questions. In total, the main study lasted about 50–60 min.

5.7   Evaluation Metrics

We measured task performance in the form of objective data (task completion time, success rate) and collected data describing users' preference to the methods, including subjective feedback (user experience, workload, motion sickness, immersion).

Task Performance. For each participant, we measured task completion time and success rate across the 18 product searches, in accordance with the common standards for product searches in online shops [17], as follows:

– **Task Completion Time (s)** was measured (in seconds) from when the countdown reaches zero to the product selection confirmation.
– **Success Rate (%)** was computed by calculating the number of correct product searches divided by all per set of trials for a tested menu interface.

User Preference. We collected a variety of subjective feedback to assess *user experience* and *workload*, but also *usability*, important in online shop applications. Therefore, we used the following questionnaires:

– **User Experience Questionnaire (UEQ):** rated on a 7-point scale [15]; The higher the score the better.

- **NASA Task Load Index (NASA TLX):** rated on a 21-point scale [9]; The lower the rating the better.
- **System Usability Scale (SUS):** rated on a 5-point scale [3]; The higher the score the better.

6 Results

Throughout this results section and in the following discussion we use abbreviations, fill patterns and color indications for the two menu representations and categorizations we tested: **Linear (striped)**, **Spatial (solid)**, **Store-based (orange)**, **Apartment-based (blue)**. The results of the experiment were analyzed using IBM SPSS Statistics 25. For the data analysis, we calculated repeated measures MANOVA and follow-up univariate ANOVAs. Using Wilks-Lambda statistic, there were significant differences for representations ($\Lambda = 0.13, F(6, 18) = 19.38, p < 0.01$) and categorizations ($\Lambda = 0.03, F(6, 18) = 92.70, p < 0.01$) for all tested dependent variables.

6.1 Task Performance

The task performance is measured quantitative through task completion time and success rate. These metrics indicate to what extent users are able to cope with the menu interfaces. They are computed per participant and condition as the average over the 18 trials.

Success Rate. The success rate describes the ratio between the number of successful and the total number of product searches. A product search is considered successful if the correct product has been selected and confirmed within the maximum execution time of 30 s. *Spatial/Apartment* achieved the highest average success rate ($M = 98.61, SD = 11.72$), and *Linear/Store* the lowest ($M = 69.44, SD = 46.12$). Univariate ANOVAs showed significant differences with regard to success rate between the representations ($F_{1,23} = 58.97, p < 0.01, \eta^2 = 0.72$) with *Spatial* ($M = 90.05, SD = 29.96$) better than *Linear* ($M = 80.44, SD = 39.69$), as well as between the categorizations ($F_{1,23} = 212.25, p < 0.01, \eta^2 = 0.90$) with *Apartment* ($M = 95.02, SD = 21.76$) better than *Store* categorization ($M = 75.46, SD = 43.06$). An interaction effect for success rate could be shown between the two tested conditions ($F_{1,23} = 4.38, p < 0.05, \eta^2 = 0.16$).

Task Completion Time. Task completion time was measured as the elapsed time in seconds to complete a single product search. The timer started when the countdown reaches zero and stopped automatically when the correct product has been selected and confirmed. In this analysis, we only included successful product searches. Furthermore, univariate ANOVAs showed significant differences for speed between representation ($F_{1,23} = 100.44, p < 0.01, \eta^2 = 0.81$) with

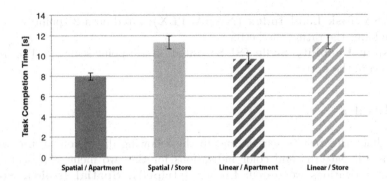

Fig. 3. Speed measurements (seconds) of successful trials. (Color figure online)

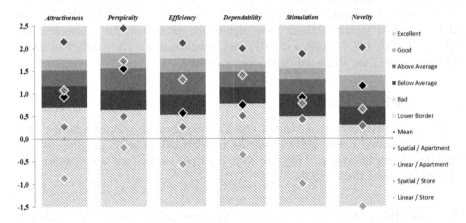

Fig. 4. User Experience Questionnaire (UEQ) results with respect to comparison benchmarks [31] (see shaded boxes). To make it easier to read, this figure shows a detail part between −1.5 and 2.5, while the original ranges between −3 and 3. (Color figure online)

Spatial ($M = 9.47, SD = 5.28$) faster than *Linear* ($M = 10.38, SD = 5.77$), and categorization ($F_{1,23} = 610.66, p < 0.01, \eta^2 = 0.97$) with *Apartment* ($M = 8.79, SD = 4.82$) faster than *Store* ($M = 11.31, SD = 6.04$).

6.2   User Preferences

User Experience. We chose the UEQ [15] as an end-user questionnaire to measure user experience (UX) in a quick and straightforward way. On a scale between −3 and 3 the overall UX, *Spatial/Apartment* achieved the highest score of 2.10 ($SD = 0.53$) on average, and *Linear/Store* the lowest ($M = -0.76, SD = 1.15$), with significant differences between representations ($F_{1,23} = 26.35, p < 0.01, \eta^2 = 0.53$) and categorizations ($F_{1,23} = 99.20, p < 0.01, \eta^2 = 0.81$) also differed significantly regarding the overall UX score. *Spatial* was rated higher with

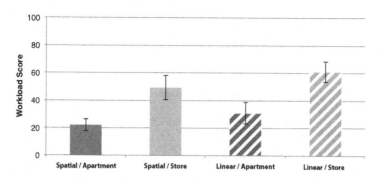

Fig. 5. The overall NASA TLX workload scores. (Color figure online)

an average of 1.24 ($SD = 1.30$) than *Linear* ($M = 0.20, SD = 1.50$) with respect to representation, whereas *Apartment* was rated higher ($M = 1.63, SD = 1.02$) than *Store* ($M = -0.19, SD = 1.33$) with respect to categorization. However, the data was also subjected to a factor analysis, including the six UEQ factors. *Spatial/Apartment* outperformed all other menu interfaces across the UEQ subscales, even 'excellent' in terms of all subscales, followed by the *Linear/Apartmentx*, *Spatial/Store*, and finally *Linear/Store* (see Fig. 4).

Usability. The SUS [3] is one of the most popular questionnaire for measuring attitudes toward system usability. It is a reliable and valid measure of perceived usability. *Spatial/Apartment* had the best score with 89.17 ($SD = 8.16$) on average, and *Linear/Store* ($M = 50.73, SD = 26.66$) the worst. Univariate ANOVAs pointed out a significance between the representations ($F_{1,23} = 8.32, p < 0.01, \eta^2 = 0.27$) and the categorizations ($F_{1,23} = 41.44, p < 0.01, \eta^2 = 0.64$). An interaction for usability between categorizations and representations could be found ($F_{1,23} = 8.32, p < 0.01, \eta^2 = 0.27$). Comparing the categorizations, *Apartment* had a higher average usability score ($M = 85.05, SD = 13.95$) than *Store* (M = 56.35, SD = 23.54). With regard to the representations, *Spatial* ($M = 75.57, SD = 19.89$) was higher than *Linear* ($M = 65.83, SD = 26.93$).

Task Workload. The task workload of the tested menu representations and categorizations was assessed with NASA TLX [9]. On average, *Spatial/Apartment* was rated the best ($M = 22.10, SD = 10.78$) and *Linear/Store* ($M = 61.04, SD = 18.69$) the worst (see Fig. 5). Univariate ANOVAs showed significant differences between the representations ($F_{1,23} = 18.00, p < 0.01, \eta^2 = 0.44$) and categorizations ($F_{1,23} = 134.24, p < 0.01, \eta^2 = 0.85$). *Spatial* was rated lower ($M = 35.68, SD = 22.06$) than *Linear* ($M = 45.96, SD = 24.27$), whereas *Apartment* achieved lower scores ($M = 26.49, SD = 16.19$) than *Store* ($M = 55.15, SD = 21.17$). We conducted a multivariate ANOVA with regard to these factors and found significant differences for all factors except

Table 2. NASA TLX contains six subscales (MD: Mental Demand, PD: Physical Demand, TD: Temporal Demand, PF: Performance, EF: Effort, FR: Frustration). The values refer to this format: $(F(x, 92) = .. , p < .. , \eta^2 = ..)$, with $x = 3$ for the menu types and $x = 1$ for representations and categorizations.

	Menu type	Representation	Categorization
Mental demand	(17.49, 0.01, 0.36)	-	(49.02, 0.01, 0.35)
Physical demand	-	-	(4.70, 0.05, 0.05)
Temporal demand	(17.34, 0.01, 0.36)	(4.41, 0.05, 0.05)	(47.51, 0.01, 0.34)
Performance	(11.01, 0.01, 0.26)	-	(29.01, 0.01, 0.24)
Effort	(15.13, 0.01, 0.33)	(4.73, 0.05, 0.05)	(40.65, 0.01, 0.31)
Frustration	(20.11, 0.01, 0.40)	(8.66, 0.01, 0.09)	(50.96, 0.01, 0.36)

physical demand between the four conditions, only for temporal demand, effort and frustration between the representations, and for all factors between the categorizations (Table 2):

7   Discussion

7.1   Task Performance

The average success rate of about 99% of the spatial apartment-based menu is significantly higher than all other tested conditions, and contrasts with the linear store-based menu with the lowest rate of 69%. The speed results are based on successful product searches only and show that the task was executed faster with spatial apartment-based menus than with all other menus. This suggests that its intuitive categorization and spatial representation help the user to better understand the underlying information space. In addition, the visual cues in the spatial menus actually seem to facilitate the visual search process.

The clear differences in task performance indicate that a spatial grid-based menu in conjunction with an apartment-based categorization was more efficient than all other tested combinations, which proves H_{1-1} and H_{2-1}. Since the menu with the worst average task performance is the commonly used menu type in today's online shops (see Sect. 2.3), our results show a remarkable potential for improvement.

7.2   User Preferences

The overall user experience results and highest ratings in all six UX subscales show that there is a clear advantage of the spatial apartment-based menu over all other tested menus. In particular, the significantly higher ratings of "Perspicuity", "Efficiency" and "Dependability" speak for more understanding, user-friendliness and reliability. Here, too, the visual hints of the spatial representation seem to facilitate the search process. High ratings in "Attractiveness", "Stimulation" and "Novelty" indicate that the more realistic and vivid presentation of the apartment categories seems to lead to a new and appealing experience.

Similar trends can be observed in the usability results. Here, too, the two apartment-based menus have achieved significantly better results. In addition, spatial menus achieved significantly higher usability values than linear menus within the respective categorization. Since values around 68 can already be interpreted as average to moderate[2], the two apartment-based interfaces with an average score of 85.05 can be described as 'excellent'. Whereas the spatial apartment-based menu even has a value of 89.17, which shows that comprehensibility is further supported by the illustrative character of the spatial representation. Overall, the results clearly show that spatial apartment-based menus were more usable than the other tested menus.

The task workload results show that store-based menus have scored more than twice as many points (55.15) as the apartment categorization (26.49). This indicates that the classification by rooms and furniture is cognitively less demanding than by product worlds and shelves. The spatial menus also achieved significantly lower utilization than the linear menus. For the individual subscales of the NASA TLX the spatial menu leads to significantly less effort, frustration and mental demand, which indicates that the visual cues facilitate and accelerate the orientation process. The apartment additionally minimizes the mental demand, since no complex and strenuous considerations were necessary. Overall, the new categorization and representation is less demanding and frustrating.

In summary, taking into account the results of user preference, it can be stated that there is a significantly higher preference with regard to user experience, workload and usability for the spatial apartment-based menu. Thus H_{1-2} and H_{2-2} can be accepted, since they are fulfilled in all aspects considered.

7.3   Observations and Comments

The participants' comments also confirm the overall impression of the previously discussed results. In the post-study questionnaire, the participants were explicitly asked for their opinion of the tested menus. Here, 23 out of 24 participants preferred the spatial apartment-based menu, only one the linear apartment-based menu. This choice was based on terms such as "intuitive", "easy", "entertaining", "clear" or "fast". The results of a pair comparison also showed that the combination of spatial apartment-based menus was preferred (98.61%), which faces the least preferred linear store-based one (15.28%). This was also confirmed by comments like "so hard" or "it will take a long time" for linear store-based and "this was cool", "great" or "very intuitive" for spatial apartment-based after the corresponding demonstration videos were shown. The majority of participants would like this combination to be integrated into current online shops.

---

[2] www.measuringu.com/sus.

7.4   Limitations

The major drawback of this study is the limited amount of 36 products tested. This applies in particular to the remarkably high ratings of preference questionnaires, which are often close to the optimal rating. Such 'excellent' results rarely occur in practice and are probably due to the limited test conditions. The scope and thus the number of products and categories of real online shops is usually much larger and therefore more complex. It might well be the case that the apartment metaphor does not scale with a large amount of products in its current form. A larger number of products would imply more level of categorizations, e.g. different parts of furniture. A fridge should therefore be partitioned into sublevels like door, vegetable drawer, and other layers. Each product can be categorized into different product variations and brands. Our 3-level approach has been chosen for a better overview and feasibility for our experiment. Our concept of an online shop using the apartment metaphor aims at products, which can be logically found in a standard apartment, e.g. no garage or garden products. Here, we would extend the apartment through e.g. a "home" metaphor. In addition, the exact categorization might be subject of cultural change.

Furthermore, online stores have a wider range of functions. The implemented prototype can therefore certainly not reflect the complexity of a real online shop, but forms the basis and new insights for a rethinking in the area of menus in online shops. In addition, the selected products are mainly based on a list of frequently sought-after products from a particular market. Thus it cannot be completely excluded that other products can be found more easily with the traditional categorization. Overall, expectations for preference evaluations and objective measurements in a fully functional online shop should be realistically lowered overall. However, the clear significant differences show that spatial apartment-based menus should still be preferred to the others.

8   Conclusion and Outlook

Especially when it comes to explorative setting in which a user tries to find something from a menu, current online shops can be significantly improved. Even though related work recommends to abandon linear and store-based menu interfaces [2,19,30], most current online shops are still employing these. Therefore, we investigated two representations (Linear, Spatial) and two categorizations (Store, Apartment) in an online shop prototype. The Apartment metaphor [1,36] turned out to be an effective way to support consumers to quickly and easily understand and use the offered information in terms of filtering out desired parts. Compared to the reference menu, the success rate was 42% higher and led to 42% faster search times than with our stored-based concept. Spatial grid-based menus performed significantly better than linear menus with a success rate about 12% higher on average. Excellent usability and user experience ratings indicate that spatial apartment-based interfaces increase understanding and reliability. The workload results also indicate that the intuitive apartment categories are less complex and could lead to less frustration. In addition, 23 out of 24 participants explicitly indicated that they preferred the apartment categories. Hence, our study confirmed previous approaches and demonstrated that our approach leads to significant performance increases. While we do not claim absolute generalizability for all online stores, this work highlights the potential for improvement.

In summary, this work opens up a large new field of research for the realization of menus in online shops. New methods for an enriched and facilitated shopping experience have been introduced. While the new menu types usually have the potential to improve menu interaction in online shops, further research is needed to ensure that this result is maintained in a complete and comprehensive shop system. We would extend the apartment through a Home metaphor including garage or garden. Furthermore, hybrid representations could also solve problems that might occur which a larger amount of products.

References

1. Adam, S., Mukasa, K.S., Breiner, K., Trapp, M.: An apartment-based metaphor for intuitive interaction with ambient assisted living applications. In: Proceedings of the 22nd British HCI Group Annual Conference on People and Computers: Culture, Creativity, Interaction, BCS-HCI 2008, vol. 1, pp. 67–75. British Computer Society, Swinton, UK (2008). http://dl.acm.org/citation.cfm?id=1531514.1531524
2. Ahlström, D., Cockburn, A., Gutwin, C., Irani, P.: Why it's quick to be square: modelling new and existing hierarchical menu designs. In: Proceedings of the SIGCHI Conference on Human Factors in Computing Systems, CHI 2010, pp. 1371–1380. ACM, New York, NY, USA (2010). https://doi.org/10.1145/1753326.1753534. http://doi.acm.org/10.1145/1753326.1753534
3. Brooke, J.: SUS: a retrospective. J. Usability Stud. 8(2), 29–40 (2013). http://dl.acm.org/citation.cfm?id=2817912.2817913
4. Cheng, H.I., Patterson, P.E.: Iconic hyperlinks on e-commerce websites. Appl. Ergon. 38(1), 65–69 (2007). https://doi.org/10.1016/j.apergo.2006.01.007. http://www.sciencedirect.com/science/article/pii/S0003687006000214
5. Cockburn, A., Gutwin, C., Greenberg, S.: A predictive model of menu performance. In: Proceedings of the SIGCHI Conference on Human Factors in Computing Systems, CHI 2007, pp. 627–636. ACM, New York, NY, USA (2007). https://doi.org/10.1145/1240624.1240723. http://doi.acm.org/10.1145/1240624.1240723
6. Findlater, L., Moffatt, K., McGrenere, J., Dawson, J.: Ephemeral adaptation: the use of gradual onset to improve menu selection performance. In: Proceedings of the SIGCHI Conference on Human Factors in Computing Systems, CHI 2009, pp. 1655–1664. ACM, New York, NY, USA (2009). https://doi.org/10.1145/1518701.1518956. http://doi.acm.org/10.1145/1518701.1518956
7. Griffith, D.A.: An examination of the influences of store layout in online retailing. J. Bus. Res. 58(10), 1391–1396 (2005). https://EconPapers.repec.org/RePEc:eee:jbrese:v:58:y:2005:i:10:p:1391-1396
8. Gutwin, C., Cockburn, A.: Improving list revisitation with listmaps. In: Proceedings of the Working Conference on Advanced Visual Interfaces, AVI 2006, pp. 396–403. ACM, New York, NY, USA (2006). https://doi.org/10.1145/1133265.1133347. http://doi.acm.org/10.1145/1133265.1133347

9. Hart, S.G., Stavenland, L.E.: Development of NASA-TLX (task load index): results of empirical and theoretical research. In: Hancock, P.A., Meshkati, N. (eds.) Human Mental Workload, pp. 139–183. Elsevier, Amsterdam (1988). http://ntrs.nasa.gov/archive/nasa/casi.ntrs.nasa.gov/20000004342_1999205624.pdf

10. Hearst, M.A.: Clustering versus faceted categories for information exploration. Commun. ACM **49**(4), 59–61 (2006). https://doi.org/10.1145/1121949.1121983. http://doi.acm.org/10.1145/1121949.1121983

11. Huang, Z., Benyoucef, M.: From e-commerce to social commerce: a close look at design features. Electron. Commer. Res. Appl. **12**(4), 246–259 (2013). https://doi.org/10.1016/j.elerap.2012.12.003. http://www.sciencedirect.com/science/article/pii/S156742231200124X. Social Commerce- Part 2

12. Katz, M.A., Byrne, M.D.: Effects of scent and breadth on use of site-specific search on e-commerce web sites. ACM Trans. Comput.-Hum. Interact. **10**(3), 198–220 (2003). https://doi.org/10.1145/937549.937551. http://doi.acm.org/10.1145/937549.937551

13. Kiger, J.I.: The depth/breadth trade-off in the design of menu-driven user interfaces. Int. J. Man-Mach. Stud. **20**(2), 201–213 (1984). https://doi.org/10.1016/S0020-7373(84)80018-8

14. Larson, K., Czerwinski, M.: Web page design: implications of memory, structure and scent for information retrieval. In: Proceedings of the SIGCHI Conference on Human Factors in Computing Systems, CHI 1998, pp. 25–32. ACM Press/Addison-Wesley Publishing Co., New York, NY, USA (1998). https://doi.org/10.1145/274644.274649

15. Laugwitz, B., Held, T., Schrepp, M.: Construction and evaluation of a user experience questionnaire. In: Holzinger, A. (ed.) USAB 2008. LNCS, vol. 5298, pp. 63–76. Springer, Heidelberg (2008). https://doi.org/10.1007/978-3-540-89350-9_6

16. Lazar, J.: User-Centered Web Development: Theory into Practice, 2nd edn. Jones and Bartlett Publishers Inc., Sudbury (2003)

17. MacKenzie, I.S.: Human-Computer Interaction: An Empirical Research Perspective, 1st edn. Morgan Kaufmann Publishers Inc., San Francisco (2013)

18. Madu, C.N., Madu, A.A.: Dimensions of e-quality. Int. J. Qual. Reliab. Manag. **19**(3), 246–258 (2002). https://doi.org/10.1108/02656710210415668

19. Meschtscherjakov, A., Reitberger, W., Lankes, M., Tscheligi, M.: Enhanced shopping: a dynamic map in a retail store. In: Proceedings of the 10th International Conference on Ubiquitous Computing, UbiComp 2008, pp. 336–339. ACM, New York, NY, USA (2008). https://doi.org/10.1145/1409635.1409680. http://doi.acm.org/10.1145/1409635.1409680

20. Miller, C.S., Remington, R.W.: Modeling information navigation: implications for information architecture. Hum.-Comput. Interact. **19**(3), 225–271 (2004)

21. Miller, D.P.: The depth/breadth tradeoff in hierarchical computer menus. Proc. Hum. Factors Soc. Annu. Meet. **25**(1), 296–300 (1981). https://doi.org/10.1177/107118138102500179

22. Mitchell, J., Shneiderman, B.: Dynamic versus static menus: an exploratory comparison. SIGCHI Bull. **20**(4), 33–37 (1989). https://doi.org/10.1145/67243.67247. http://doi.acm.org/10.1145/67243.67247

23. Moagăr-Poladian, S., Dumitrescu, G.C., Tănase, I.A.: Retail e-commerce (E-tail) – evolution, characteristics and perspectives in China, the USA and Europe. Glob. Econ. Observer **5**(1) (2017). https://ideas.repec.org/a/ntu/ntugeo/vol5-iss1-17-167.html

24. Murano, D.P., Sander, M.: User interface menu design performance and user preferences: a review and ways forward. Int. J. Adv. Comput. Sci. Appl. **7**(4), 355–361 (2016). https://doi.org/10.14569/IJACSA.2016.070447. http://dx.doi.org/10.14569/IJACSA.2016.070447

25. Norman, K.L.: Better design of menu selection systems through cognitive psychology and human factors. Hum. Factors **50**(3), 556–559 (2008). https://doi.org/10.1518/001872008X288411. pMID: 18689067

26. Petz, G., Greiner, A.: First in search – how to optimize search results in e-commerce web shops. In: Nah, F.F.-H. (ed.) HCIB 2014. LNCS, vol. 8527, pp. 566–574. Springer, Cham (2014). https://doi.org/10.1007/978-3-319-07293-7_55

27. Plechawska-Wojcik, M.: Heuristic evaluation and user experience assessment of online shopping portals using cognitive walkthrough and expert method. In: Human Capital without Borders: Knowledge and Learning for Quality of Life; Proceedings of the Management, Knowledge and Learning International Conference 2014, pp. 467–475. ToKnowPress (2014)

28. Resnick, M.L., Sanchez, J.: Effects of organizational scheme and labeling on task performance in product-centered and user-centered retail web sites. Hum. Factors **46**(1), 104–117 (2004). https://doi.org/10.1518/hfes.46.1.104.30390. pMID: 15151158

29. Robertson, G., Czerwinski, M., Larson, K., Robbins, D.C., Thiel, D., van Dantzich, M.: Data mountain: using spatial memory for document management. In: Proceedings of the 11th Annual ACM Symposium on User Interface Software and Technology, UIST 1998, pp. 153–162. ACM, New York, NY, USA (1998). https://doi.org/10.1145/288392.288596. http://doi.acm.org/10.1145/288392.288596

30. Scarr, J., Cockburn, A., Gutwin, C., Bunt, A.: Improving command selection with commandMaps. In: Proceedings of the SIGCHI Conference on Human Factors in Computing Systems, pp. 257–266 (2012). https://doi.org/10.1145/2207676.2207713

31. Schrepp, M., Hinderks, A., Thomaschewski, J.: Construction of a benchmark for the user experience questionnaire (UEQ). Int. J. Interact. Multimed. Artif. Intell. **4**(4), 40–44 (2017). https://doi.org/10.9781/ijimai.2017.445

32. Schwartz, J.P., Norman, K.L.: The importance of item distinctiveness on performance using a menu selection system. Behav. Inf. Technol. **5**(2), 173–182 (1986). https://doi.org/10.1080/01449298608914510

33. Sears, A., Shneiderman, B.: Split menus: effectively using selection frequency to organize menus. ACM Trans. Comput.-Hum. Interact. **1**(1), 27–51 (1994). https://doi.org/10.1145/174630.174632. http://doi.acm.org/10.1145/174630.174632

34. Shim, S., Eastlick, M.A., Lotz, S.L., Warrington, P.: An online prepurchase intentions model: the role of intention to search: best overall paper award-the sixth triennial AMS/ACRA retailing conference, 200011. J. Retail. **77**(3), 397–416 (2001). https://doi.org/10.1016/S0022-4359(01)00051-3. http://www.sciencedirect.com/science/article/pii/S0022435901000513. Decision made by a panel of journal of retailing editorial board members

35. Speicher, M., Cucerca, S., Krüger, A.: VRShop: a mobile interactive virtual reality shopping environment combining the benefits of on- and offline shopping. Proc. ACM Interact. Mob. Wearable Ubiquit. Technol. **1**(3), 102:1–102:31 (2017). https://doi.org/10.1145/3130967. http://doi.acm.org/10.1145/3130967

36. Speicher, M., Hell, P., Daiber, F., Simeone, A., Krüger, A.: A virtual reality shopping experience using the apartment metaphor. In: Proceedings of the 2018 International Conference on Advanced Visual Interfaces, AVI 2018, pp. 17:1–17:9. ACM, New York, NY, USA (2018). https://doi.org/10.1145/3206505.3206518. http://doi.acm.org/10.1145/3206505.3206518

37. Tsandilas, T., schraefel, m.c.: Bubbling menus: a selective mechanism for accessing hierarchical drop-down menus. In: Proceedings of the SIGCHI Conference on Human Factors in Computing Systems, CHI 2007, pp. 1195–1204. ACM, New York, NY, USA (2007). https://doi.org/10.1145/1240624.1240806. http://doi.acm.org/10.1145/1240624.1240806

38. Tuch, A.N., Roth, S.P., HornbæK, K., Opwis, K., Bargas-Avila, J.A.: Is beautiful really usable? toward understanding the relation between usability, aesthetics, and affect in HCI. Comput. Hum. Behav. **28**(5), 1596–1607 (2012). https://doi.org/10.1016/j.chb.2012.03.024

39. Vrechopoulos, A.P., O'Keefe, R.M., Doukidis, G.I., Siomkos, G.J.: Virtual store layout: an experimental comparison in the context of grocery retail. J. Retail. **80**(1), 13–22 (2004). https://doi.org/10.1016/j.jretai.2004.01.006. http://www.sciencedirect.com/science/article/pii/S002243590400003X

40. Wallace, D.F., Anderson, N.S., Shneiderman, B.: Time stress effects on two menu selection systems. Proc. Hum. Factors Soc. Annu. Meet. **31**(7), 727–731 (1987). https://doi.org/10.1177/154193128703100708

41. Wigand, R.T., Benjamin, R.I., Birkland, J.L.H.: Web 2.0 and beyond: implications for electronic commerce. In: Proceedings of the 10th International Conference on Electronic Commerce, ICEC 2008, pp. 7:1–7:5. ACM, New York, NY, USA (2008). https://doi.org/10.1145/1409540.1409550. http://doi.acm.org/10.1145/1409540.1409550

42. Zaphiris, P., Kurniawan, S.H., Darin Ellis, R.: Age related differences and the depth vs. breadth tradeoff in hierarchical online information systems. In: Carbonell, N., Stephanidis, C. (eds.) UI4ALL 2002. LNCS, vol. 2615, pp. 23–42. Springer, Heidelberg (2003). https://doi.org/10.1007/3-540-36572-9_2. http://dl.acm.org/citation.cfm?id=1765426.1765429

43. Zhang, F., Lin, S., Li, X., Shuai, Y., Jiang, H., Yao, C., Ying, F., Gao, F.: Navigation configuration and placement influences the visual search efficiency and preference. In: Proceedings of the 26th International Conference on World Wide Web Companion, WWW 2017, pp. 871–872. Companion, International World Wide Web Conferences Steering Committee, Republic and Canton of Geneva, Switzerland (2017). https://doi.org/10.1145/3041021.3054236

How to Improve the Interaction Design
of NFC Payment Terminals?

Poornigha Santhana Kumar[1(✉)], Michael Bechinie[1],
and Manfred Tscheligi[2]

[1] USECON, 1110 Vienna, Austria
{kumar,bechinie}@usecon.com
[2] University of Salzburg, 5020 Salzburg, Austria
manfred.tscheligi@sbg.ac.at

Abstract. Near field communication (NFC) payments also popularly known as contactless payments are increasingly used in retails shops like supermarkets and cafes nowadays. User studies on NFC payments show that NFC payments fail to provide users with the appropriate user experience. In this paper, we aimed to redesign the existing NFC payment experience design by altering 5 factors namely the audio feedback, the visual feedback, the haptic feedback, the screen design of the payment terminal and the NFC component. The results show that altering the aforementioned factors increase the usability of NFC payments and provides users with privacy and security-enhanced experience. We also framed 5 guidelines based on our evaluation results which will aid designers while designing or redesigning any system. We also believe that our research methods and guidelines contribute to the researches in the HCI community.

Keywords: NFC payments · Usability · User experience · Lived experience · Design guidelines

1 Introduction

User experience plays an important role in the systems/services/products we use in our everyday life. Each system we interact with leaves us with experience [1, 2]. This experience plays a vital role in the success of the system. For a system to be successful it should be designed considering 3 factors. The usability [4] of the system, the user experience [4] gained by the users from the system and the lived experience [1]. Figure 1 represents the relationship between usability, user experience and lived experience.

The different payment terminals used widely can be categorized into 4 main overlapping categories based on the feedback and hardware design. Namely,

Visual feedback on screen with audio feedback – The visual feedback on the state of the transaction and the visual feedback on the success of the transaction is displayed on the screen. The visual feedback is accompanied by sound feedback.

Visual feedback on hardware with audio feedback – The visual feedback on the state of the transaction and the visual feedback on the success of the transaction is

© IFIP International Federation for Information Processing 2019
Published by Springer Nature Switzerland AG 2019
D. Lamas et al. (Eds.): INTERACT 2019, LNCS 11747, pp. 55–68, 2019.
https://doi.org/10.1007/978-3-030-29384-0_4

displayed via lights in on the payment terminal hardware. The visual feedback is accompanied by sound feedback.

NFC scan pad on the screen – Payment terminals which lets users scan their NFC component on the side of the terminal. This terminal also delivers users with visual and audio feedback.

NFC scan pad on the side of the terminal – Payment terminals which lets users scan their NFC component on the screen of the terminal. This terminal also delivers users with visual and audio feedback.

All the above-mentioned terminal were initially designed for credit/debit card payments and were adapted to NFC payments. These terminals do not completely support NFC payments on scales of usability and user experience. NFC cards are in use for payments in the form of NFC cards since 2007 in the UK. This payment technology enables users to pay by simply tapping their NFC enabled component against any active payment terminal [5]. NFC technology is known for its fast interaction compared to existing interaction methods [6].

Researches have been carried out on NFC's security [7], acceptance [8, 9] and applications [5]. Only a few studies have been conducted on scales of usability on NFC. Research [10, 11] on NFC payments in supermarkets shows that there is a lack of usability and appropriate user experience in NFC payment in supermarkets. In this paper, we demonstrate how we addressed various factors of the payment terminal to support NFC payments and to improve its usability, user experience and lived experience of NFC payments.

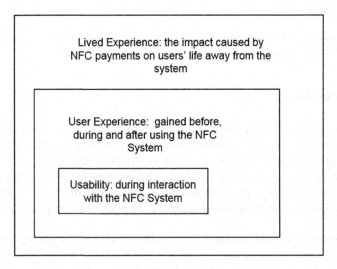

Fig. 1. The relationship between usability, user experience and lived experience of NFC payments

2 Method

We are following the well-established UCD [3] process throughout our project. As a first step, we conducted a user study to understand the existing practices and difficulties of NFC payments [10, 11]. During the user study, we also observed the design of payment terminals used in various supermarkets and cafes in Austria, Germany, Switzerland and the UK. We chose to work with supermarkets and cafes as a wide range of customers uses it on a daily basis. Our user study results portrayed that users feel less secured while paying with NFC compared to other payment methods. So to improve the usability and privacy & security related experience of the user, we redesigned the existing payment terminal.

2.1 Prototyping

We redesigned the payment terminal based on the user study data and the heuristics principles [12]. Five factors were considered for redesigning the prototype. We considered the possible feedbacks namely: visual feedback, audio feedback and haptic feedback. Additionally, the screen design of the payment terminal and the NFC component used to pay was also considered. To evaluate the effect of each factor on the usability and the user experience gained by the users, we designed prototypes corresponding to each factor. All the payment terminal prototypes were sized (19 × 9 cm) to the real world payment terminals.

Audio Feedback

Most existing payment terminals use sound feedback to notify the user. This sound feedback is not consistent in the pitch, length of the sound and the pattern across the supermarkets. In most supermarkets, the payment terminals provide audio feedback throughout the transaction as a long beep. In our prototypes, we used two different types of audio feedback.

Audio feedback only at the end of the transaction – short beep sound at the end of the transaction.
Audio feedback at each stage of the transaction – beep sound corresponding to the loading bar and at the end of the transaction.

Visual Feedback

One of the main disadvantages in adapting the credit/debit card terminals for NFC payment is the visual feedback provided on the screen is actively hidden by the users when scanning the NFC component against the payment terminal while paying. This makes the users lack feedback regarding the end of the transaction which leads to the users holding their NFC components against the payment terminal longer than it is required. NFC payments are known for being quicker than other payments. Since the lack of visual feedback obstructs this advantage, existing visual feedback needed to be improved. In our prototype (Fig. 2a), we placed the visual feedback on the hardware of the payment terminal. Payment terminals are used in environments which tend to be noisy like in cafes and supermarkets. As we cannot rely on audio feedbacks in such environments we also increased the size of the visual feedback. Green LED lights were placed around the payment terminal which acts as a loading bar during the transaction. The LED lights will be lit in a clockwise direction to show the state of the transaction to the users (Fig. 2b).

(a)   **(b)**

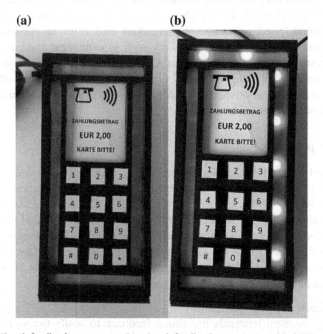

Fig. 2. (a) Visual feedback prototype (b) visual feedback prototype with LEDs lighting in a clockwise direction to indicate the state of the transaction (Color figure online)

Taking lived experience into account, the LED lights will act only as the feedback on the state of the transaction which in turn shows how long the users need to hold their card against the terminal. The success or failure of the transaction will be displayed only on the screen of the terminal. If the transaction fails the LED lights will not turn red. This is to prevent the negative lived experience gained by the users while using NFC payments in public places. Having a transaction declined in a public place might lead the user into never trying NFC payments again.

Haptic Feedback
We aimed to redesign the payment terminal such that it will support all the customers. We included haptic feedback to support any differently-abled peopled using the payment terminal. Differently abled customers may not be able to see the visual feedback or hear the audio feedback. So adding haptic feedback will help them feel the feedback and understand the state of the transaction. A vibrate feedback was added at the end of the transaction as feedback.

Screen Design
As explained in visual feedback, the feedback provided on the screen is hidden by the NFC component. To avoid this we redesigned the screen design of the payment

terminal (Fig. 3a). We split the screen into 2 parts. The top section is to scan the NFC component and the bottom section is to see the feedback provided by the payment terminal. The visual feedback is used to portray the state of the transaction and the bottom section is used to provide feedback on the end of the transaction. The bottom section of the screen shows the users if the transaction is successful or declined in a discreet manner without causing any social embarrassment thereby leaving them with positive lived experience.

(a)   **(b)**

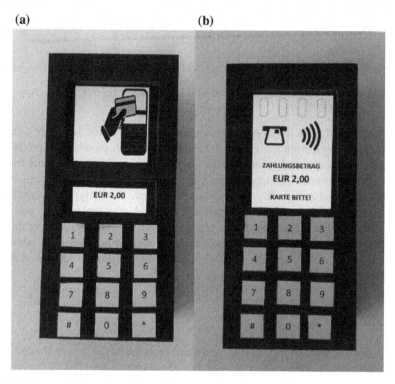

Fig. 3. (a) Screen design prototype with a modified screen design. (b) Base prototype – replication of the payment terminals used in supermarkets and cafes.

NFC Component

The type of NFC component used by the users influences the user experience gained by the users and these components also differ on scales of usability. We considered 3 NFC components in total (Fig. 4). First, the commonly used NFC component, the NFC debit cards and credit cards. The second NFC component considered was NFC mobile app. With apple pay and android pay mobile NFC is also spreading across many countries. We also considered the lesser-known NFC sticker as the third NFC component. The prototypes were made to match the real world dimension. The NFC card, NFC mobile app and NFC sticker measured 8.5 × 5.5 cm, 14 × 7 cm and 4 × 3 cm respectively.

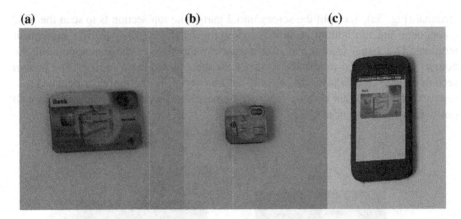

Fig. 4. NFC components (a) NFC card (b) NFC sticker (c) NFC mobile App

The prototypes were developed corresponding to each factor and other aspects of the payment terminal were not changed. In visual feedback prototype, a prototype of the payment terminals used in supermarkets was created and only the visual feedback in the payment terminal was replaced by our visual feedback. Other features like the audio feedback and screen designs were not modified. Similarly, for screen design prototype, the screen design of the payment terminal was replaced by our screen design. The visual feedback and audio feedback were not modified. Using the same procedure haptic and audio feedback prototypes were also developed. In addition to these prototypes, we also replaced the payment terminals used in supermarkets as a prototype to act as our base terminal (Fig. 3b).

3 Evaluation

The usability and user experienced gained from each prototype was evaluated during the evaluation phase. To measure the usability of the prototypes UMUX questionnaire [19] was used. The evaluation took place in Austria, a German-speaking country. To support our participants the standard UMUX questionnaire was translated to German by professional translators. The translation was back-translated to English by professional translators and was checked for equivalence to the original questionnaire.

To evaluate the privacy and security related user experience gained, a Likert scale was used. Any user paying with a payment terminal would prefer to feel secure. We aimed to improve the user experience gained by the users by delivering the users with a secured experience while paying with NFC. The users were questioned "How secured did they feel while paying with prototype a/b" and they were asked to rate their experience on a 1–5 (1 - low, 5 - high) Likert scale. We asked a simple question instead of using any standard privacy and security scales because we aimed to measure only the felt privacy and security user experience of the user.

Participants were recruited via USECON database (www.askus.at) for evaluation. Participants who have experience with NFC payments were recruited for evaluation and an incentive of 30€ was given to each participant. During the evaluation, the participants were asked to pay with an NFC debit card (prototype – Fig. 4a) with the base terminal and any one of the redesigned prototypes say the visual feedback prototype. Then they were asked to fill out the UMUX and Likert scale questionnaire for each prototype. After filling out the questionnaires the participants were asked an open question on their liking/disliking of the prototypes. Then the participants were again asked to pay with an NFC debit card (prototype – Fig. 4a) with the base terminal and any one of the redesigned prototypes say the audio feedback prototype followed by the questionnaires. This procedure was repeated for all the redesigned prototypes. The participants were asked to pay with only NFC card as it is the commonly used NFC payment component.

To evaluate the NFC component, the participants were asked pay with NFC card, NFC mobile app and NFC sticker on the base terminal. To provide participants with close to real-time feeling during evaluation they were asked to open the NFC application in the prototype prior to paying while paying with NFC mobile app. For NFC stickers, they were asked to choose anyone everyday object prototype (Fig. 5) and were asked to attach the NFC sticker to the object before paying with NFC sticker. The evaluation was then followed by questionnaires and open question.

During the evaluation, the order in which the prototypes were tested was changed for each participant to avoid order bias.

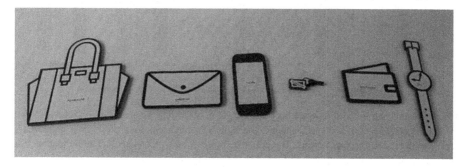

Fig. 5. Prototypes of everyday objects considered and used while evaluating NFC sticker

4   Results

Out of 33 participants, 14 were female and 19 were male with the mean age of 31. All the participants had prior experience with NFC payments. The UMUX scores represent the usability of the prototype and the Likert scale values represent the user experience gained from the prototype.

4.1 Usability Results

UMUX score for all the redesigned prototypes and base prototype was calculated. Figure 6 shows a comparison of mean UMUX scores of the prototypes and corresponding base terminals. The UMUX scores were compared by the Wilcoxon Signed-Rank test. The results show that there is a significant difference between the base prototype and redesigned prototypes. The visual feedback prototype and screen design prototype were significantly better than the base prototype with p < 0.05, z-value – 2.941 and –2.5495 respectively.

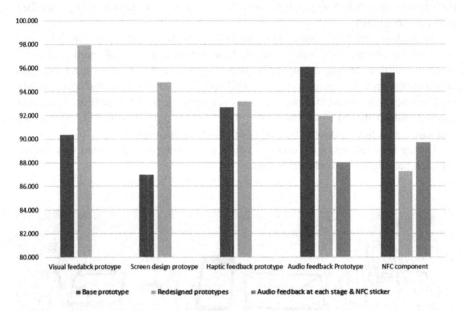

Fig. 6. Representing the difference between the mean of UMUX scores of base prototypes and the redesigned prototypes of each factor. The blue bars represent base prototype, orange bars represent the redesigned prototypes. The grey bars represent the prototype with audio feedback at each stage of the transaction and NFC sticker. (Color figure online)

The UMUX scores of the audio feedback show that the existing audio feedback (long beep throughout the transaction) is better than the redesigned audio feedbacks. The base terminal was significantly better than the audio feedback only at the end of the transaction and audio feedback at each stage of the transaction prototypes with p < 0.05, z-value –2.5205 and –3.0594 respectively.

NFC components' UMUX score portrays that NFC card is usable compared to NFC mobile app and NFC sticker. The NFC card is significantly better than NFC mobile app and NFC sticker with p < 0.05, z-value –3.1798 and –2.6656 respectively.

The haptic feedback prototype's UMUX scores (92.646) were similar to the base terminal's UMUX scores (93.137) with no significant difference. When questioned about their liking, 29 out of 33 participants felt the haptic feedback to be neutral. One participant mentioned that he/she thought it was his mobile phone as he always keeps his mobile on vibrate mode. Another participant said he/she did not like the vibrate feedback as it sounded like an error.

4.2   Results for Felt Security

The mean of Likert scale values was calculated for all the prototypes. These values were compared to know users' perceived security related experience from the prototypes. The user experience results were directly proportional to the usability results showing that usable prototypes deliver users with the appropriate user experience.

Participants felt secured while paying with the redesigned visual feedback and screen design prototype compared to the base terminal. Similar to UMUX score the base prototype was considered to be secured compared to other audio feedback prototypes. For haptic feedback, both the base terminal and the haptic feedback terminal had the same mean Likert score demonstrating that there is no difference in the experience gained. NFC cards provide users with secured user experience compared to NFC mobile app and NFC sticker. Figure 7 shows the mean Likert scale values of the prototypes and corresponding base terminals.

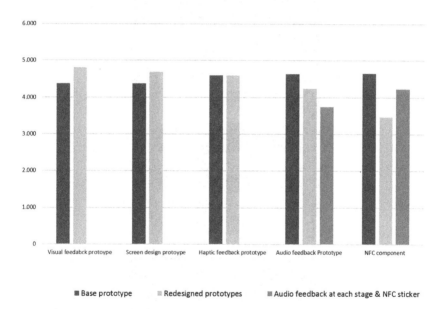

Fig. 7. Representing the difference between the mean of Likert scales values of base prototypes and the redesigned prototypes of each factor. The blue bars represent base prototype, orange bars represent the redesigned prototypes. The grey bars represent the prototype with audio feedback at each stage of the transaction and NFC sticker. (Color figure online)

5 Iteration

We designed a payment terminal comprising of all the factors which were usable and delivered users with security-enhanced experience. The redesigned prototype had the split screen design and visual feedback on the hardware of the payment terminal. Even though haptic feedback did not have an effect on usability and user experience, we added the haptic feedback to the redesigned payment terminal to support differently-abled customers. The audio feedback used in supermarkets was used without modification. Figure 8 shows the redesigned payment terminal. This payment terminal was then reevaluated against the base terminal on the scales of user experience provided.

Fig. 8. Final payment terminal design

The reevaluation was conducted in Austria and the participants were recruited directly from cafes and university campuses. In total, we had 113 participants out of which 71 (63%) were male and 42 (37%) were female with a mean age = 35. All the participants had prior experience with NFC payments. The participants were asked to pay with NFC card (prototype – Fig. 4a) on the redesigned payment terminal and the base payment terminal. They were then asked to rate their felt of security on a 1–5 Likert scale for each terminal. Finally, they were asked to share any comment regarding the payment terminals. Again the order in which the prototypes were tested was changed to avoid order biases.

The mean of the Likert scales values was compared using the Wilcoxon Signed-Rank test. The results demonstrated that the redesigned payment terminal provides significantly better user experience than the base payment terminal with $p < 0.01$, z – value -8.2164. Below are some answers from participants showing that the features in the redesigned payment terminal help them feel secured while paying with NFC.

"It vibrates, I need not even look into the screen I will know it"
"The lights are visible compared to the other one (base prototype)"
"I can see the amount while paying that make me feel secured"
"The vibration feature will help in supermarkets because it (the supermarkets) is usually noisy"

6 Discussion

The evaluation and reevaluation results clearly show that the redesigned payment terminals had a higher degree of usability and provide users with a secured experience. To generalize our findings and to contribute to the designing or redesigning process of any system/service/product, we framed 5 guidelines based on our evaluation results.

Redesigning is Crucial
Adapting an existing system for a different purpose may solve the need but it will not be successful as it is not developed for that particular purpose. The system should be redesigned based on the new needs to fully support the aroused need. Skipping the user analysis phase leads to usage problems. Adding a component to a system changes the context of use, so user analysis should be performed to ensure usability and appropriate user experience in the later design. In our case, the payment terminals designed for debit/credit card payments were adapted to support NFC payments in recent years. The adaptation allows users to pay with NFC components but this adaptation is not completely successful as it has usability and user experience flaws. A system should be redesigned for timely needs for successful functioning.

Visual Feedback is Key
Visual feedback plays an important role in any system. This is already stressed in the literature by many guideline sets [12, 13]. During the evaluation of our prototypes, we found that the visual feedback prototype was perceived to be the most usable and secured prototype. We should try to provide visual feedback on everything that happens in the system as human beings rely on visual feedback more than other feedback forms. Especially when designing or redesigning payment-related systems like payment terminals, online checkout pages and ticket machines, information like amount to be paid, the status of the transaction and the result of the transaction should be visually communicated to the users.

Black & White vs. Colour Interfaces

Colour has been studied in various directions in the literature. Psychological studies [14] and marketing studies [15] shows that certain colours trigger some emotions. [16] shows that colour also has an effect on human performance. In HCI, the law of simplicity states [17], when considering emotions we need to add components to achieve it. In our case, the considered emotion was triggered by coloured interfaces. One of our payment terminal interface was black & white. Users perceived the black & white interfaces to be outdated thereby considering it less secured. Adding some colour to the interfaces gave users more secured and updated feel. While designing any system, we should consider adding colour to the interfaces if applicable.

Failure of the System Does Not Imply the Failure of Feedback

A system might not be usable and deliver users with appropriate experience. This does not imply that the feedbacks used by the system is also not usable. In our case, the payment terminals used in the supermarkets were not usable for NFC payments and did not deliver them with the secured user experience. But the audio feedback used by these payment terminals did provide users with secured experience compared to other alternate audio feedbacks. Users might be used to certain feedbacks of the system which cannot be replaced. So while redesigning any system or designing any new system, each feedback from an old system or similar system should be considered.

Neutral Feedbacks for Efficient Designing

All feedback from a system need not be useful/informative for all users. Some types of feedback can be added in a way such that it is subtle for some users and dominant for other users. In our case, the haptic feedback did not add any value to users and was considered to be neutral. Haptic feedback will aid differently-abled people and will act as important feedback. Instead of designing a new system to support differently-abled users, we should try and incorporate neutral features into standard systems. This is not only economical but also helps to avoid the effect of exclusion and isolation [18] on differently abled users.

7   Limitations

The user studies were conducted in supermarkets in real-time whereas the evaluations were conducted in a lab setting. During the evaluation, we tried to recreate the real-time environment by giving them a supermarket scenario before testing the prototypes. Still the results acquired from lab setting might slightly vary when tested in real-time.

8   Next Steps and Conclusion

As a next step, we aim to achieve a universal design for the payment terminal. The redesigned payment terminal will be evaluated with differently abled participants and will be iterated according to needs. We will also update the guidelines list based on the evaluation results with the differently-abled people.

To conclude, the payment terminals used in supermarkets and cafés do not support NFC payments on scales of usability due to lack of lucid feedback. It also fails to provide users with an appropriate user experience which makes the users consider NFC payments to be less secured compared to other payments methods. We redesigned 3 factors namely visual feedback, haptic feedback and screen design of the payment terminal to support NFC payments. We also evaluated 2 other factors of NFC payments, the NFC component (NFC card, NFC mobile app and NFC sticker) and the audio feedback. Based on the evaluation results, we framed 5 guidelines for designing or redesigning a system to aid designers and other fellow researchers.

Acknowledgement. The project leading to these results has received funding from the European Union's Horizon 2020 research and innovation program under the Marie Sklodowska-Curie grant agreement No. 675730.

References

1. McCarthy, J., Peter, W.: Technology as experience. Interactions **11**(5), 42–43 (2004)
2. Garrett, J.J.: Elements of user experience, the: user-centered design for the web and beyond. Pearson Education, New York (2010)
3. International Organization for Standardization: Ergonomics of human system interaction - Part 210: human-centered design for interactive systems. ISO 9241-210:2010 (2010)
4. International Organization for Standardization: Ergonomics of human-system interaction – Part 11: usability: definitions and concepts. ISO 9241-11 (2010)
5. Ok, K., et al.: Current benefits and future directions of NFC services. In: International Conference on Education and Management Technology (ICEMT). IEEE (2010)
6. Massoth, M., Bingel, T.: Performance of different mobile payment service concepts compared with a NFC-based solution. In: Fourth International Conference on Internet and Web Applications and Services, ICIW 2009. IEEE (2009)
7. Madlmayr, G., et al.: NFC devices: security and privacy. In: Third International Conference on Availability, Reliability and Security. IEEE (2008)
8. Tan, G.W.-H., et al.: NFC mobile credit card: the next frontier of mobile payment? Telematics Inform. **31**(2), 292–307 (2014)
9. Schierz, P.G., Oliver, S., Wirtz, B.W.: Understanding consumer acceptance of mobile payment services: an empirical analysis. Electron. Commer. Res. Appl. **9**(3), 209–216 (2010)
10. Santhana Kumar, P., Bechinie, M., Tscheligi, M.: NFC payments – gaps between user perception and reality. In: Hansen, M., Kosta, E., Nai-Fovino, I., Fischer-Hübner, S. (eds.) Privacy and Identity 2017. IAICT, vol. 526, pp. 346–353. Springer, Cham (2018). https://doi.org/10.1007/978-3-319-92925-5_23
11. Santhana Kumar, P., Bechinie, M., Tscheligi, M.: Changed the cup, not the saucer – NFC payments in supermarkets. In: Stephanidis, C. (ed.) HCI 2018. CCIS, vol. 852, pp. 309–313. Springer, Cham (2018). https://doi.org/10.1007/978-3-319-92285-0_43
12. Nielsen, J.: Usability inspection methods. In: Conference Companion on Human Factors in Computing Systems. ACM (1994)
13. Norman, D.A.: The Psychology of Everyday Things, vol. 5. Basic Books, New York (1988)
14. Ou, L.-C., et al.: A study of colour emotion and colour preference. Part I: colour emotions for single colours. Color Res. Appl. **29**(3), 232–240 (2004)

15. Lichtlé, M.-C.: The effect of an advertisement's colour on emotions evoked by attitude towards the ad: the moderating role of the optimal stimulation level. Int. J. Advertising **26**(1), 37–62 (2007)
16. Hill, R.A., Barton, R.A.: Psychology: red enhances human performance in contests. Nature **435**(7040), 293 (2005)
17. Maeda, J.: The Laws of Simplicity. MIT Press, Cambridge (2006)
18. Kitchin, R.: 'Out of Place', knowing one's place': space, power and the exclusion of disabled people. Disabil. Soc. **13**(3), 343–356 (1998)
19. Bosley, J.J.: Creating a short usability metric for user experience (UMUX) scale. Interact. Comput. **25**(4), 317–319 (2013)

Places for News: A Situated Study of Context in News Consumption

Yuval Cohen[1], Marios Constantinides[2(✉)], and Paul Marshall[3]

[1] Interaction Centre, UCL, London, UK
yuval.cohen.14@ucl.ac.uk
[2] Department of Computer Science, UCL, London, UK
m.constantinides@cs.ucl.ac.uk
[3] Department of Computer Science, University of Bristol, Bristol, UK
p.marshall@bristol.ac.uk

Abstract. This paper presents a qualitative study of contextual factors that affect news consumption on mobile devices. Participants reported their daily news consumption activities over a period of two weeks through a snippet-based diary and experience sampling study, followed by semi-structured exit interviews. Wunderlist, a commercially available task management application and note-taking software, was appropriated for data collection. Findings highlighted a range of contextual factors that are not accounted for in current 'contextually-aware' news delivery technologies, and could be developed to better adapt such technologies in the future. These contextual factors were segmented to four areas: triggers, positive/conducive factors, negative/distracting factors and barriers to use.

Keywords: News consumption · Mobile · Snippet technique · Context awareness · Contextual factors

1 Introduction

News consumption is changing rapidly thanks to digital methods of consumption, reinforced by almost ubiquitous handheld mobile devices. Social networking platforms such as Facebook, Twitter and even direct messaging platforms such as WhatsApp and Snapchat are becoming de facto distribution channels for news stories. This wrests control over how news is presented to and consumed by users away from publishers [40]. Furthermore, news content is increasingly being presented in a 'contextually-aware' fashion, according to topics and locations.

While there has been a significant concern about and analysis of how emerging news consumption patterns can lead to the formation of 'filter bubbles' [41,45], and how fake news stories spread through social networks [33], there has been little focus on understanding exactly how social and personal context affect news consumption habits (cf. [22]). The study presented in this

© IFIP International Federation for Information Processing 2019
Published by Springer Nature Switzerland AG 2019
D. Lamas et al. (Eds.): INTERACT 2019, LNCS 11747, pp. 69–91, 2019.
https://doi.org/10.1007/978-3-030-29384-0_5

paper first aims to identify contextual factors relevant to news consumption, especially those of a more qualitative and experiential nature, which have typically been overlooked in previous research. Such research often defines context quite broadly [1] but tends to focus on objective quantifiable aspects of context, such as geographical location [19]. Our aim is to focus on what contextual factors are important prior to trying to use sensor data to identify them. Arguably, prior work has tended to focus on those contextual factors that are straightforward to measure rather than most salient from the users' perspective. Furthermore, the study aims to explore the effects of any identified contextual factors on user behaviour related to news consumption, and the influence it has on the news consumption experience.

Our findings highlight a range of social, cultural, affective and individual factors that drive the manner in which users consume news. We discuss these in relationship to opportunities for the development of new types of context-aware and adaptive news applications.

2   Background

2.1   Mobility and Context in HCI

The shift towards consumption on mobile devices is not an isolated phenomenon within news consumption, and can be categorised as part of a larger trend described by social scientists as a 'mobility turn' [56]. This perspective recognizes that human interaction with technologies is increasingly distributed over both time and space, and occurs in disparate social and physical contexts. Dourish and Bell [23] focus on mobility in the context of urbanism, and treat it as a spatial construct in which individuals render a space meaningful by acting in a certain way. Some approaches in social sciences describe a set of codes that govern interactions or non-interactions between individuals in public spaces [25]. Other perspectives, more relevant to the current study, have focused on the role of technologies in the isolation of individuals from their environment, creating "solitude and similitude" [3,26].

An additional area of mobility research is studies of mobile work. While news reading can generally be considered a non-work task, studies of mobile work have the potential for generalizable insights. For example, Perry et al. [46] note the existence of 'dead times' – periods of time which workers spend riding various forms of transportation or waiting for them to arrive, which creates opportunity for news reading on mobile devices [20]. Other studies have focused on issues such as battery life, connectivity and device limitations–all issues with relevance to everyday mobile information needs [10]. User experience of news applications has also been studied, particularly within the young generations, revealing factors such as quick understanding, consistency, fun, diversity, and interests [57].

A large body of research in relation has focused on context in the development of recommender systems. A comprehensive review of the state-of-the-art news recommendation systems can be retrieved from [30]. In addition to particular challenges of news recommendations (e.g., recency aspects), the advanced capabilities of today's smartphones open a new road to enhance and transform news consumption to a more personalized experience. The continuous connectivity and access to smartphones' sensors enable aspects of user's context to be incorporated into interaction with mobile apps. For example, Appazaar proposed by Bohmer et al. [38], generates app recommendations combining the actual app usage and user's current context. Similarly, Tavakolifard [54] leveraged users' location information to provide tailored news recommendation. Pessemier et al. [17] demonstrated the potential of a context-aware content-based recommendation engine which induces higher user satisfaction in the long run, and at the same time enables the recommender to overcome the cold-start problem and distinguish user preferences in various contextual situations.

Context in relation to news consumption has also been studied by analyzing social media behaviour. Social networking platforms such as Facebook and Twitter are becoming de facto distribution channels of news. Many apps leverage knowledge from users' social activities to recommend and deliver targeted news feed. Pulse, for example, developed by LinkedIn, is an example of one such app that delivers personalised news from a user's professional network. LumiNews [31], another example, leverages users' location, social feed, and their in-app actions to automatically infer their news interests. These, both implicit and explicit, signals were found to improve recommendations and improve user's satisfaction over time.

2.2   News Consumption and Adaptive News Interfaces

Data from Reuters [40] shows that the use of smartphones to view news media is rapidly growing, and is seen as the future for the news industry, especially with younger demographics [44] – a transformative change from times when mobile devices were thought of as "supplementary" to news-reading [58]. The Reuters report discusses 'gateways' through which news is discovered, such as search, social networks, and news-reading apps. It distinguishes between the different roles that Facebook and Twitter play in news consumption – initiated consumption vs. casual or play a central role in the discovery and presentation of content. However, while these platforms increasingly direct people to online news content and play a role in the spreading of 'fake news' (e.g., [33]), we still know little about the contextual factors that lead people to choose to consume that content in particular situations.

Previous work relating to contextually-aware news consumption technology has focused on appropriation of features and sensing technology within existing technological platforms. One of the uses for such appropriated data is the development of adaptive interfaces – systems that 'learn' user habits and use patterns, and adapt a user interface to better match those patterns [28]. Constantinides et al. [14,15] developed 'Habito News', an Android news app that presented participants with live news items while simultaneously logging frequency, time spent and location of reading, as well as speed and article completion rate using scroll-tracking. The goal of this research was to profile and classify reading habits into typical patterns of use, and to use those classifications as background to the development of adaptive, context-dependent news-reading interfaces to match them. Other notable work in this area [4,54] has focused on customization of content, rather than adaptation of the interface through which it is presented.

The current study aims to understand the contextual factors relating to news consumption in order to understand if they might be classifiable in a way that could drive the adaptation of content or the interface on which it is read.

3   Method

In recent years, HCI researchers have used a variety of in-situ methods that were previously limited to psychology and social sciences to better understand user behaviour in general and context of use in particular. Some methods, such as ethnography, typically require a researcher to be present among participants in order to collect data [55], while others such as diary studies and experience sampling rely on self-reporting by participants. Diaries have been used in studies of information needs, with computerized [2,9,11,32] and non-computerized [12,18,43] apparatus. The experience sampling method (ESM) has been used to obtain in-situ information that is more real-time [9,10,13], and can be supplemented by interviews aided by memory cues based on participant responses [7,8,36,39].

A particular focus of self-reporting studies has been to lower the data entry and overall participation burden inherent in such studies, especially when entries are done under mobile conditions. Brandt et al. [6] proposed a 'snippet' technique in which participants chose an input modality that they were most comfortable with, and captured small pieces ('snippets') of information about their experience in-situ. These later served as cues for a more detailed web-based diary. Sohn et al. [52] used an adaptation of the technique, as did Church et al. [10], where the snippet technique was used in combination with experience sampling and a diary study to explore daily information needs.

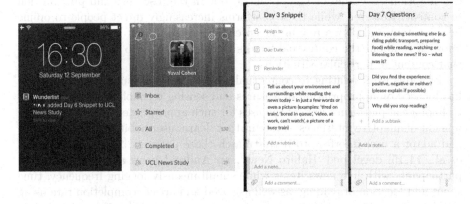

Fig. 1. Snippets and diary questions via the Wunderlist app

In the current study, snippets were used in combination with event-based ESM, triggered by participants' news reading. Participant responses to snippets were used as the basis for more detailed diary questions, and also served as memory cues during exit interviews. The user study consisted of three parts: (a) an instruction email; (b) snippet and diary questions; and (c) an exit interview.

A *Instruction email:* Participants received an email that included the study brief, installation and sign-up instructions for the Wunderlist app[1], and explanations on the types and timing of the questions that would be sent to them along with examples of how to answer the snippets, seeing as the snippets were designed to be more open and vague than the diary questions.

B *Snippets and Daily Questions:* Participants were sent two sets of questions every day through Wunderlist–snippets and diary questions, over a period of two weeks. Snippets were sent every morning, asking participants to add a short text or a picture of the context in which they consumed news that day. Sending times varied from one day to another, so as to minimize the potential cognitive bias associated with scheduled experience sampling alerts [13]. During the first 3–4 days of participation, instructions were given with examples (Fig. 1). In following days, the examples were removed. Four to five diary questions were sent every evening. Questions were limited in number so as not to impose too high a burden on participants, and were usually open ended so as to not limit the scope of responses. While questions varied in wording and order from one day to another, so they would not seem repetitive to participants, they were focused on four relatively distinct areas. Table 1 contains descriptions of these areas, as well as several examples for questions participants were asked about them. Initially, all participants received the same questions, which were modified from day to day in order to attain more detailed information about participant habits. However, as the goal of the study was exploratory and data analysis progressed throughout, the diary questions were customized for each participant on a daily basis.

C *Exit interviews:* Upon the 'snippets and diary questions' phase completion, participants were interviewed. Interviews were conducted either in person or via Skype, and were audio-recorded for later transcription and analysis. Each interview lasted between 20 to 30 min, and included three parts: (a) general and demographic data such as age and occupation; (b) targeted questions about the participant's responses during the situated study; and (c) questions about their experience regarding the data collection method.

3.1 Data Analysis

An iterative approach to data collection was taken, whereby collected snippets and diary responses were sampled on a daily basis and compared to concepts and insights that had begun to emerge. Interview audio was transcribed verbatim. Transcripts were then thematically analyzed [5]:

---

[1] https://www.wunderlist.com/.

Table 1. Diary question topics and examples

Question topic	Examples
Triggers for news-reading experiences	– What made you want to read (or listen to, or watch) the news today?
	– Why did you choose to read, watch or listen to the news at this specific time? (more than one answer is OK)
Environment and surroundings (e.g. concurrent activities, distractions, public or social settings)	– What did you like about your reading environment? What did you dislike?
	– Were you around others while reading? If yes – did this affect your reading in any way?
	– Did anything bother or distract you while reading? If so – what was it?
Feelings about news consumption experience as a whole	– Did you find the experience: positive, negative or neither? (please explain if possible)
	– Did reading the news affect your mood in any way? If yes – in what way?
Reasons for ending a news-reading experience	– Why did you stop reading?
	– What made you stop reading?

Open Coding: snippets, diaries and interviews were coded line-by-line using the NVivo qualitative data analysis software; pertinent statements were labelled.

Axial coding: relationships were identified between the concepts and categories that emerged during open coding. We sought to discern the phenomenon at hand (i.e. news consumption), with an additional emphasis on causal, contextual and intervening conditions, as these were the focus of the research, and would be the basis for later analysis. Analytic memos were used to note and highlight developing themes.

Themes were reviewed in a manner roughly corresponding to the six phases of thematic analysis set out by Braun and Clarke [5], though the process was recursive rather than linear, as noted by Braun and Clarke – we moved between phases as needed, repeating and re-evaluating themes and coded text as necessary.

3.2   Participants

Participants were recruited through personal contacts, social network posts, and notice-board adverts at three university campuses. The advert included information about remuneration, inclusion criteria and a link to an online sign-up form. The inclusion criteria required participants to live in the UK, be 18 years of age or above, use an iPhone or an Android based-smartphone (for purposes of compatibility with the data collection app), and read the news on a regular basis using a digital device, so that digital consumption habits could be gauged. The signup form asked respondents to enter contact and demographic information, and included several questions intended to confirm that participants meet the inclusion criteria. This information was also used to diversify the study sample in terms of age, gender and students vs. non-students. It was also used to gauge commute time. Each participant was remunerated with a small payment in cash or transfer upon completion of the study, and one larger value Amazon voucher was drawn between all participants.

Seventeen knowledge workers were recruited for the main user study (ten female). Participant ages ranged from 22 to 47 (M = 30, SD = 8). Fourteen participants lived in London, and three lived outside of it but commuted to the city on a daily basis. Eleven participants were students, and six were professionals.

3.3 Apparatus

The Wunderlist platform was used to implement the diary study and the 'snippet' technique/experience sampling components of the study. Wunderlist provides a basic tier of its platform and apps free of charge. Therefore, participants were not required to pay for downloading or using the app.

Participants installed the Wunderlist app on their mobile phone, where they would receive notifications of new snippets or diary questions, which they could tap in order to view and respond to each of these respective items. The app allows users to enter text in several fields: the 'task' fields adjacent to the task-completion checkboxes, a 'notes' area for freeform entry of text, and a comments thread. Users were not instructed where to answer, and were given the freedom to answer as they chose. On the researcher's side, participants were managed from Wunderlist's software for Mac, with each participant being added as a 'list' that was shared by the researcher with the participant. Both the researcher and the participant could freely add, edit and annotate items on the list.

4 Results

4.1 Triggers for Reading the News

Triggers were specific reasons described by participants for consuming news in a particular situation.

Break from Study or Work
A theme with nearly universal prevalence among participants was the use of news consumption as a break from a different activity that usually required a higher level of concentration. Reading, rather than listening or watching, was usually

cited as the way in which news was consumed. A very frequently discussed rationale for reading news during a break was that it is an activity that still requires engagement, but not at the level required by work or study.

"[...] it's sort of a quality break [...] switching to something that's relatively similar, the same kind of concentration is involved, but it's still different enough that it provides a rest from what I was working on." P2 - Interview

Many participants described reading the news as something that didn't need the same level of concentration as work, and therefore provided an opportunity to restore their ability to focus:

"If I'm really burnt out I won't absorb any of the news, but it gives me something to focus on that's not concentrated on writing or coding or any of the other things that I'm supposed to be doing... A few hours later I will be 'what did I read again?"' P3 – Interview

Furthermore, a number of participants mentioned the discrete nature of news content as being conducive to their subsequent resumption of work. For example, P2 (Interview) explained: *"[...] it also has a beginning and the end - when I finish reading an article I go back to work. I can obviously read another article, but that will extend it by only a little".*

Morning Habit

A majority of participants indicated that they consume news in bed or while preparing and eating breakfast. Participants described this behaviour as habitual, except in unforeseen circumstances such as lateness or being in a hurry. This morning habit is corroborated in a study conducted by Böhmer et al., which found news apps to be the most popular in the morning [37].

Two reasons were generally cited. The first is, to use the term given by several participants, 'wanting to know what's going on in the world':

"When I just wake up and I want to know what's going on in the world, so in the morning I always check it [...] it's a habit, because I wake up... I always wake up quite early, so I can take my time to start easily, have my breakfast, and while I have my breakfast I'll scroll down the news." P5 - Interview

The second reason for morning news consumption was procrastination. This was cited either together or apart from the need to be updated about the news.

"Maybe it's just that I don't want to start immediately with working, and I just need to ease myself into it" P2 - Interview

Notifications and Widgets

Notifications are small displays of text that appear on a computing device, usually a smartphone or a tablet, and alert the user to a certain occurrence or event. Widgets are slightly larger 'windows' of content, that usually show a string of informative text and an image or graphic; notifications are momentary and disappear within a few seconds while widgets permanently reside on the user's screen until they are removed. Both served as triggers for news consumption.

Participant responses indicated that they frequently decided whether to tap on a notification or widget to read a story in more depth. One indicated that this decision depends on the type of story, and whether she is otherwise busy. At times she will be content with consuming a news item exclusively via a notification.

"The push notifications from the Guardian app keep me informed without my having to read the story (or do anything)." P11 - Snippet

This participant later explained in detail: *"[...] 'England won the Ashes'.. I don't actually need more information than that, for example [...] It's completely dependent on how interested I am in the story and also what I'm doing at the time [...] they pop up at any time during the day, and I don't always have the liberty to check it immediately, because I'm doing something else, and sometimes I forget what it was before I've come back."* P11 - Interview

Social Feed Skimming

Participants described a logic for news consumption via social media that is similar to the one they described for notifications and widgets – i.e. a triage of whether to explore an item further or not.

"I pick up a lot of stuff that I read through the news feed of my Facebook page, [...] I find that more convenient way of accessing it, because it's sort of summarized in the posts that appear in my news feed" P14 - Interview

"[I] scroll down and see if there's anything interesting [...] If you're interested then you'll click on it [...] If not then just on to the next one. So it's just a quick scan of things to see if something really interesting has happened" P14 - Interview

Waiting for People or Technology

People were often triggered to look at news items when waiting either for people or for processes to complete. This can be viewed news consumption filling 'dead times' [46] or consumption of news in 'interstices' [20].

"[...] you're waiting for a friend for like an hour or something [...] it becomes a bit tedious, because I know that I'm using this just to fill time, as opposed to when I'm actually interested in something to read. [...] sometimes I really enjoy it when I'm actually saying 'OK, I actually want to see what's going on today', but other times it's just because I don't have anything to do... It's just to check whatever is going on there" P8 - Interview

Another participant discussed the effect of anticipation while waiting for people more poignantly, but pointed out that he sees news reading as a more productive 'time-killing' exercise than playing a game.

"[...] it's really just killing time until something happens or until someone will meet me; It can be a bit frustrating, because if it's something that you are waiting for and you know it starts at a certain time, you can kind of judge what you will read, but if you're waiting for someone, it's frustrating - they'll arrive and you are halfway through reading something... Because I tend not to go back to things as well, I think it's not as much of a relaxing experience. It's more killing time in a more productive way than playing a game, which I do sometimes." P14 - Interview

Situations of waiting for a certain process or machine to finish were also noted. The difference here, as opposed to waiting for a person, is that participants could better gauge the beginning and end time of the waiting experience.

Media Multitasking
Participants indicated that they sometimes read news on a digital device as a secondary activity while consuming content in another medium, such as television, but not being fully engaged (cf. [48,49]). One participant noted this happens when he is watching a television show together with his partner, and is not particularly interested in its content. In such a scenario of split attention between different forms of media, he will continuously evaluate the perceived benefit from each source and compare between them, terming this process as an 'interest/engrossment trade-off'.

"I will definitely scan a bit between the two [...] I guess it depends on how engrossed I am in either; I guess if the movie [...] has a slow part, then I'll move back to the news, and if the news is really interesting, then I'll get engrossed in that and focused on that, and then once I'm done I'll look back up and say 'this is going on' in the movie [...] I'll go back and forth. So it's about the interest/engrossment trade-off between the two, which will make me go back and forth." P3 - Interview

4.2   Conducive Contextual Factors

We define conducive contextual factors as those that have a positive effect on participants' news consumption experiences. Participants generally described these factors as being associated with a more pleasurable experience, and being more receptive to richer and longer content.

Alertness and Mood
Many participants highlighted how their emotional or cognitive capabilities in a given context are reflected in their likelihood of consuming 'hard news' - topics such as war or government corruption, or 'soft news' - topics such as celebrity news or 'man bites dog' stories [34]. This 'suitability spectrum' of hard news vs. soft news to the affective state of a user is outlined in Fig. 2.

One participant stated that a low level of alertness greatly reduces her attention and receptiveness to content, even to the point of stop reading.

"[...] that's a big factor [being tired]. I know that if I start reading an article and I'm tired I feel like I'm just LOSING IT, I feel like nothing is coming into my brain.. Nothing is going in. So at that point I stop" P2 - Interview

Another participant stated that while she will sometimes read news before she goes to sleep at night, she does not want to read upsetting stories .

"I won't try to read anything too harrowing [before going to sleep], you know, we're talking just interesting stuff... I try not to read about ISIS before I go to bed" P12 - Interview

Another participant described the positive end of this spectrum in reference to reading a newspaper on Sunday.

"Sunday is like the one day where I [...] just relax in the morning, because I just have such a busy life [...] that's my treat for Sunday, to just be able to lie in bed with a cup of tea and read the papers [...] I will read something much more in-depth, and longer, because I have the luxury of the time." P11 - Interview

Low alertness

Negative affective state

High alertness

Positive affective state

Soft News

Shorter Items

Hard news

Longer items

Fig. 2. User state - news consumption spectrum.

Background Activity

The issue of the suitability of different kinds of background activities for news consumption was one that split participants. Some stated that background sounds are conducive for working. Others expressed ambivalence towards background sounds while reading. Additionally, several participants were distracted by background activity, though the types of factors that would cause this varied between participants.

"I'm actually used to it for my studies [...] having music in the background. It doesn't divert my attention, it only makes me know there's something playing in the background; I can't concentrate without it. So when I want to listen to music and read the news, I stay concentrated, it doesn't split my attention. I mean, it does split my attention, but I'm focused on the news, not on the music." P6 - Interview

Another participant indicated that the background environment will affect the type of media she will choose for news consumption.

"[...] when I'm just walking on the street, I cannot read something and concentrate, so I prefer to listen to the podcast." P1 - Interview

Other participants noted visual and physical aspects of background activity as most affecting their news consumption experience. Some suggested that visual distractions were more detrimental to concentration than auditory ones.

"There was a lot of movement in the room, which I caught from the corner of my eye, so that kind of broke my attention [...] It can be less distracting [auditory stimulations], you can get into a sort of 'zone', where you tune it out." P2 - Interview

Other participants noted crowding as a detrimental factor to reading on public transport. One noted that he perceives as a personal safety issue.

"If I'm standing somewhere super-crowded, I'm not going to grab my phone and read the news, like on the bus [...] same with the overground [train] during rush-hour. It can get packed and I'm not going to break out my phone [...] it's just uncomfortable to do so, and also someone can just grab it and walk away" P3 - Interview

Another participant noted privacy aspects of standing within a dense crowd on the train.

"I tend to see other people looking. You get the feeling like someone else is also watching what you're reading, and that's not really nice and makes me a bit uncomfortable." P7 - Interview

It should be noted that even with the consensus among participants as to the distracting effects of crowding, some participants viewed them as tolerable and were not willing to forego news-reading unless the situation was extreme.

"Sometimes it's hard to [...] it's too crowded to even get your phone out and have a look at it [...] it's loud and it's bumpy [...] you can't really focus on what you're looking at, but equally it's something to do while you're spending those 12 min or however long on the tube." P11 - Interview

4.3 Negative Contextual Factors

We define *negative* contextual factors as those that hampered participants' news consumption experience, possibly causing them to alter it in some way, such as changing to another device, but not to end it.

Connectivity

Lack of Internet connectivity was cited by participants as a factor that hampers news consumption. They discussed various responses to this type of situation.

While dedicated article-saving apps such as Pocket[2] have been developed for offline reading scenarios, a prevalent solution among study participants was to open multiple tabs in their mobile Internet browser - an item 'hoarding' of sorts, though one user did note his frustration at the lack of serendipitous discovery.

"Usually on the public transport, I open news sites in different tabs and I activate it. So I find that not very comfortable, because in fact, I need to check the link, it doesn't go through because there is no signal." P6 - Interview

Another participant noted the use of the 'offline mode' in the news app she uses on her phone. *"[...] the Guardian app actually works offline, you just can't get the pictures and there's certain content that you can't get, but you can actually get the stories, even if you haven't got a signal, which is amazing, and really good."* P11 - Interview

For several participants, switching to a print newspaper was the preferable option in a situation of no connectivity.

"[...] if I'm on the tube as well, I tend to pick up the free papers... I read the news that way, so there's not much point in me looking at the BBC website when I'm on the tube. And also, I can't get reception [...]" P11 - Interview

As noted, some participants preferred to avoid the news consumption experience altogether when not connected.

"If I'm in the tube, I cannot access the Internet, so I don't think I will do anything if I was on the tube." P1 - Interview

---

[2] https://getpocket.com/.

Suboptimal Smartphone Experience

There was a consensus among participants that news-reading on a phone, while unavoidable on many occasions, did not provide what they perceived to be the optimal experience. A prevalent reason cited for this is that the phone is not conducive to serendipitous discovery of additional content. One participant, noting that the reading experience itself was satisfactory, suggested that following links was more difficult on the phone.

"The actual reading experience is fine when you're reading an article that you want to read and it's just text [...] but I feel like it doesn't facilitate easy links into other similar things [...] You can kind of scroll down through the article and there are related items on certain websites, at the bottom. I think it's something to do with the screen size, that it just feels very claustrophobic [...] If there was something in there that you wanted to read more about, it's not as simple as opening another tab in your browser on your laptop, for example." P14 - Interview

Another commonly cited issue was that certain websites were not customized for viewing on the small screen of the phone. One participant noted this in regard to serendipitous discovery while reading another piece of news.

"[...] it's also frustrating when people haven't [...] translated things properly for mobile, which happens quite a lot, where text doesn't resize properly. All of that sort of stuff makes it less, you know, comfortable." P14 - Interview

It should be noted that this perception of inconvenience was not universal among participants. Several, particularly younger, participants stated that a smartphone is their preferred device to consume news. One noted that when having the choice between her phone and a larger device such as a laptop, she will still choose her phone.

"[...] for reading at home, it's not on the computer; Basically, I will use my mobile phone [...] while I'm using the computer and doing some professional work like typing some important stuff, if I want to have some leisure time, I will take my mobile phone and send some message to my friends and also look for some news on my mobile phone." P1 - Interview

Multitasking

Participants indicated that in certain situations, they will consume news while performing another concurrent task. Concurrent tasks varied in both type and location, but generally had the effect of splitting attention, thereby decreasing engagement and making a breakaway from news consumption more likely.

One participant noted the effect of a concurrent task on the type of content she will choose to consume.

"[...] if I'm reading on my phone [...] in between things and in a situation where something else is going on, reading as a way to pass the time [...] If it's a story that requires me to think, to process what's going on, what the page is telling me, then I can't really get into it that much." P2 - Interview

Another participant noted productivity as a driver for multitasking while consuming news, and reiterated the effect it has on the type of content consumed.

"[...] if I'm at home I tend to feel more comfortable reading or watching the news when I'm doing something else [...] I tend to feel like I'm being unproductive if I spend an extended period of time reading or watching the news, so I tend to do it when I take a break from something else or am actually engaged in doing something else, so I sometimes have the news channel on while I'm sort of tidying up, or doing something that doesn't require [...] intellectual focus [...]. When I'm consuming news while I'm doing something else, it tends to be smaller articles or news." P14 - Interview

The tentativeness of user engagement in news consumption was also noted in the context of multitasking. One participant noted, in the context of reading on public transport, that news will always be secondary in terms of cognitive effort. This directly relates to the utilitarian role he assigned to news consumption.

"I don't think that there are many news items I would completely block everything out and not quite notice there's something else happening, it's like [...] just a distraction half the time. If I'm going to catch up with the news, it's really not important." P17 - Interview

Together, these statements indicate that there are instances in which participants will knowingly and willingly enter a situation in which they are not devoting their full attention to the news consumption experience, but it is nevertheless viewed by them as an appropriate activity.

4.4   Barriers to Use

Barriers are factors that lead to a situation where a user who would otherwise consume news chooses not to. This includes while already consuming news and choosing to end the experience, or alternatively choosing not to consume news in a certain situation at all.

'Me Time'
Several participants described some instances of their travel time on public transport as one in which they do not want to engage in any form of news consumption, or even any other activity. They described these occurrences as opportunities for introspection, reflection on their own thoughts, and even relaxation. In this scenario, participants would avoid consuming any sort of media.

"[...] sometimes when you're walking and you're on public transport, you just want your mind to be clear." P9 - Interview

Another participant described this experience not only as a way to 'clear the mind', but also as an environment in which she is secluded from unwanted individuals or pieces of information, despite being on a populated train.

"Sometimes I'll just be 'this is me time' [...] no one can get me, I'm not going to fill my head with more information, there's enough going on around me, my head's spinning with stuff, I just can't put any more stuff in it, even if it's a distraction, I need to relax my mind, and the train, for me, is the only place I can actually do that." P12 - Interview

While 'me time' describes a positive affective state, it was stated by participants as a reason for not consuming news, therefore is classified as a barrier.

News Overload

Some participants described negative emotions triggered by cumulative or successive instances of what they perceived as bad news, i.e. stories of a negative nature. While all participants who described this chose to stop consuming news as a result, the differences between them were in the intensity of emotions. One participant was relatively vivid:

"there are days when [...] especially if there's been a barrage of [...] Bad news, recently... Sometime you just want to put your head in the sand and go 'I don't want to know today'." P11 - Interview

Another participant described a state of disinterest:

"most of the news I don't find very interesting, like who killed who this weekend or a famous person that died, you know, doing something stupid, I don't find that interesting." P17 - Interview

Kinetosis

Several participants noted the issue of dizziness, nausea and an uncomfortable physical feeling while using a digital device to read in a moving vehicle.

One participant noted that she resolves the issues by only reading books, using a customized app that rectifies the motion-induced unpleasantness. This could possibly indicate a desire to carry on with the reading experience despite the physical obstacle, finding solutions to manage the issue.

"If I'm on public transportation I'll read a book, I don't usually read news. [...] I have a tendency to get motion sickness, and reading a book... I have a particular app on my phone that makes it very easy to read books, whereas reading pretty much anything else is very. It gives me motion sickness." P4 - Interview

Another participant indicated that she will avoid reading while she is standing on the train, as the simultaneous balancing and reading actions cause dizziness and nausea, however this does not occur when she is seated.

"[...] if it's too crowded then I wouldn't have a place to sit, I will have to hang on to something like hold the rails or just try to balance myself, and I don't want to read while I'm doing that, and usually I get this dizziness when I'm trying to read while I'm balancing... So, I switch to music and I won't read while I'm standing." P7 - Interview

For another participant, the way to prevent dizziness is to eliminate reading altogether and listen to a podcast instead:

"If I was on the bus, if I read news or if I read anything, I will feel dizzy, so I prefer to listen to podcasts. Also, this applies to when I'm just walking on the street, I cannot read something and concentrate, so I prefer to listen to the podcast." P1 - Interview

5   Discussion

5.1   Main Results

The current study discovered a variety of contextual factors that play an important role in news consumption, mostly of a phenomenological nature [21] - relating less to informational and computational aspects of a given context, and relating more to the social, cultural, affective and behavioural elements that comprise an individual's context of use.

The discovery of such contextual factors demonstrates the role of interpretation and sense-making processes on how users interact with technology, as well as the dynamic, momentary nature of user actions within a given context. This is especially noticeable in the fluid patterns of device use in relation to the space in which they are being used, such as participants' preference to read news on their phone at home or at work.

These findings, coupled with a news experience increasingly shaped by mobility, are important to the central finding of this paper–the creation of news consumption 'places' by users. Participants indicated that they appropriate different spaces and devices to create contexts and environments for news consumption that suit specific and dynamic momentary needs and affective states, often independently from physical location. These findings link to Harrison and Dourish's [27] discussion of the creation of place through situated meaning making.

5.2   Theoretical Implications

News Consumption Is Opportunistic: Situation Matters More Than Physical Location

To a considerable degree, the findings of our study demonstrate that users create their own meaningful contexts for news consumption, adapting and appropriating a wide range of situations. In many, participants saw elements such as background noise, lack of connectivity, waning alertness or an additional concurrent task not as barriers, but merely as detracting factors in an array of considerations that shaped their news consumption experience. In certain instances, factors such as suitability of news consumption to a specific situation took precedence over other detracting factors, suggesting an interplay between context, affective state, and consumption. In other cases, factors such as kinetosis (motion sickness) and the desire for 'me time' led to no news consumption or even technology use at all.

The findings show that the factors affecting participants' news consumption habits were not only numerous, but also changed within an experience as a perceived need to do so arose in ways that were situated [53]. In one example, participants indicated that they changed their actions in-situ as a result of both internal and external states. For example, participants indicated that when waiting for other people, they will continuously adapt the type of content they read in terms of topic and length, in order to suit the waiting time and level of concentration they predict they will have. Another example is in the case of media multitasking, where concurrent activities of watching television and reading the news encouraged a continuous in-situ reassessment of media consumption preferences, in what one participant described as an 'interest/engrossment trade-off'.

Consumption Characteristics Are Shaped by Momentary Needs and States – into Consumption 'niches'

Examined from a broad perspective, the results of this study indicate that momentary needs are a primary driver for news consumption. Participants generally viewed news consumption as a break or leisure activity, which they engaged in when they wanted to keep their mind busy, fill otherwise 'dead time' or in cases where news consumption is a daily or weekly ritual. Importantly, in some cases, such as daily or weekly rituals, the needs and context seemed to relate specifically to supporting the consumption of news content.

While contextual findings were segmented for presentation purposes, the interplay between the momentary needs that drove these factors was just as important. For example, a situation where news consumption was triggered by waiting for someone also included the distracting element of expectation. Participants indicated that this had an effect both on the type of news they consumed and on their level of concentration and immersion. It is this interplay that seemingly connects physical environment, affective state, and type of news being consumed.

A needs-based approach is an essential part of the assumption that users appropriate spaces for news consumption. In this appropriation process, users essentially match a momentary need with the availability of opportunity to realize that need, thereby creating their own unique news consumption 'places', or 'consumption niches'. Dimmick et al. [20] previously discussed the concept of 'niches' in terms of time and space interstices in which users 'fit' their news consumption, such as with their mobile devices while commuting, or on a desktop computer at work. By focusing on aspects of time and space, Dimmick perhaps addresses elements inherent in a view of context as something to be measured [20], rather than from the perspective of the individual experiencing it. Indeed, Dimmick concludes his paper by defining it as a call for further exploration into the intertwining of media consumption in mobile contexts and users daily lives. The results of the current study add to Dimmick's work by adding a phenomenological layer of context to the theory of niches in news consumption. The act of creating these 'consumption niches', and the needs that drive it, point to news consumption being an opportunistic activity.

5.3   Practical Implications

As this study was exploratory, its goal is to serve as a starting point for future exploration of the identified contextual factors. While today's sensing technology facilitates easy measurements of movement, lighting and latitude-longitude coordinates, elements such as user alertness, mood and distraction are not yet as easy to identify. However, significant advances are being made in classifying factors such as user mood [24,35,51] and boredom [47,49] from smartphone and wearable data, and it is likely that smartphones and wearable devices in the near future might be able to robustly detect users' affective state [29], which might have significant implications for the development of new kinds of context aware news applications. For example, the affective state of an individual could be used as a proxy to whether they are receptive to content that is 'hard news', or whether they will be more open to 'soft news'. In other words, a classifier could predict the 'user-alertness' based on user's emotional state, mobility patterns, or any other passive data.

Additionally, our work could expand the possibilities of previous adaptive content models such as the one proposed by Billsus and Pazzani [4] and Tavako-lifard et al. [54]. Just as importantly, it can expand upon the work started by Constantinides et al. [14–16] by adding to the range of factors by which adaptive interfaces match a user's habits, preferences and affective state. For example, factors such as the 'morning habit', the 'break from work or study', the 'media multitasking', the 'connectivity', and the 'suboptimal smartphone experience' could be easily identified from smartphones' sensors. In turn, the raw sensors signals could be translated into features to train models to detect these high-level factors. Having such models will be of particular use, for example, in the multitude of instances where contextual factors affected the length of text that users would read. For example, more concise descriptions of news content could be presented when users are more tired or distracted.

5.4   Limitations

The current study is subject to several limitations in the design and the results of the study. First, some of the methods used in the study carry the potential for certain biases. Diaries, being a reflective and self-reported method, have the potential for retrospective distortions [59]. Similarly, interviews are subject to recall errors, seeing as they are retrospective conducted even longer after participants' actions have taken place. However, the use of memory cues during interviews [42] and scheduling of the interviews as closely to the in-situ study as possible [50] were designed to alleviate this. An additional memory-related limitation pertains to the subset of users who, on several occasions, 'aggregated' snippets and diary questions and answered them all at once. While not rendering the collected data unusable by any means, this behaviour effectively negates the 'real-time' qualities of ESM and the value of snippets as memory cues, leaving the data as a traditional diary study. Similarly, there were also occurrences of participants responding to snippets, diary questions or both on the following day after they were sent. Seeing as uncued memory lasts for about one day [50], this behaviour might introduce some additional retrospective distortions, though supposedly not substantial ones. Finally, while the sample of 17 participants for this study is relatively standard for self-reporting studies such as diary studies and experience sampling, it would be ideal to further explore and gauge the effectiveness of the methodology presented in this paper, both for situated studies as a whole, and for news consumption and media studies in particular.

6   Conclusion

This study aimed to discover contextual factors that are of a qualitative nature, and that are currently not addressed by 'contextually-aware' research and software frameworks. The study produced findings that indicated a range of social, cultural and individual factors that drive the manner in which users consume news, and contextual factors. Most notably, the findings indicated that individuals often construct a context of use that is partially or wholly independent of the space in which their interaction with technology is taking place, reinforces earlier work by into the appropriation of spaces [27]. Participation rates and statements indicated a low participation burden, true to the original study design goal.

These results can be of use to the wider HCI community by serving as a starting point for further research into the phenomenological aspects of context, and enabling the development of news and media consumption technologies that will address these contextual factors, such as previous work into adaptive news interfaces [14]. Additionally, this research may herald further work into the design of in-situ methods that lower participant data-entry burden, as well as the appropriation of 'off the shelf' software applications for the purpose of in-situ research.

References

1. Abowd, G.D., Dey, A.K., Brown, P.J., Davies, N., Smith, M., Steggles, P.: Towards a better understanding of context and context-awareness. In: Gellersen, H.-W. (ed.) HUC 1999. LNCS, vol. 1707, pp. 304–307. Springer, Heidelberg (1999). https://doi.org/10.1007/3-540-48157-5_29
2. Amin, A., Townsend, S., van Ossenbruggen, J., Hardman, L.: Fancy a drink in canary wharf?: a user study on location-based mobile search. In: Gross, T., et al. (eds.) INTERACT 2009. LNCS, vol. 5726, pp. 736–749. Springer, Heidelberg (2009). https://doi.org/10.1007/978-3-642-03655-2_80
3. Augé, M.: Non-Places: Introduction to an Anthropology of Supermodernity. Verso, London (1995)
4. Billsus, D., Pazzani, M.J.: Adaptive news access. In: Brusilovsky, P., Kobsa, A., Nejdl, W. (eds.) The Adaptive Web. LNCS, vol. 4321, pp. 550–570. Springer, Heidelberg (2007). https://doi.org/10.1007/978-3-540-72079-9_18
5. Braun, V., Clarke, V.: Using thematic analysis in psychology. Qual. Res. Psychol. **3**(2), 77–101 (2006)
6. Brandt, J., Weiss, N., Klemmer, S.R.: Lowering the burden for diary studies under mobile conditions. In: Extended Abstracts on Human Factors in Computing Systems (CHI 2007), pp. 2303–2308 (2007)
7. Brown, B.A.T., Sellen, A.J., O'Hara, K.P.: A diary study of information capture in working life. In: Proceedings of the SIGCHI Conference on Human Factors in Computing Systems (CHI 2000), pp. 438–445 (2000). https://doi.org/10.1145/332040.332472
8. Carter, S., Mankoff, J.: When participants do the capturing: the role of media in diary studies. In: Proceedings of the SIGCHI Conference on Human Factors in Computing Systems (CHI 2005), pp. 899–908 (2005). https://doi.org/10.1145/1054972.1055098

9. Carter, S., Mankoff, J., Heer, J.: Momento: support for situated Ubicomp experimentation. In: Proceedings of the SIGCHI Conference on Human Factors in Computing Systems (CHI 2007), pp. 125–134 (2007). https://doi.org/10.1145/1240624. 1240644

10. Church, K., Cherubini, M., Oliver, N.: A large-scale study of daily information needs captured in situ. ACM Trans. Comput.-Hum. Interact. (TOCHI) **21**(2), 10 (2014)

11. Church, K., Oliver, N.: Understanding mobile web and mobile search use in today's dynamic mobile landscape. In: Proceedings of the 13th International Conference on Human Computer Interaction with Mobile Devices and Services, pp. 67–76 (2011)

12. Church, K., Smyth, B.: Understanding the intent behind mobile information needs. In: Proceedings of the 14th International Conference on Intelligent User Interfaces (IUI 2009), pp. 247–256 (2009). https://doi.org/10.1145/1502650.1502686

13. Consolvo, S., Walker, M.: Using the experience sampling method to evaluate ubicomp applications. IEEE Pervasive Comput. **2**(2), 24–31 (2003)

14. Constantinides, M., Dowell, J., Johnson, D., Malacria, S.: Exploring mobile news reading interactions for news app personalisation. In: Proceedings of the 17th International Conference on Human-Computer Interaction with Mobile Devices & Services (MobileHCI 2015), pp. 457–462 (2015). https://doi.org/10.1145/2785830. 2785860

15. Constantinides, M., Dowell, J.: A framework for interaction-driven user modeling of mobile news reading behaviour. In: Proceedings of the 26th Conference on User Modeling, Adaptation and Personalization, pp. 33–41. ACM (2018)

16. Constantinides, M.: Apps with habits: adaptive interfaces for news apps. In: Proceedings of the 33rd Annual ACM Conference Extended Abstracts on Human Factors in Computing Systems, pp. 191–194. ACM (2015)

17. De Pessemier, T., Courtois, C., Vanhecke, K., Van Damme, K., Martens, L., De Marez, L.: A user-centric evaluation of context-aware recommendations for a mobile news service. Multimed. Tools Appl. **75**(6), 3323–3351 (2016)

18. Dearman, D., Kellar, M., Truong, K.N.: An examination of daily information needs and sharing opportunities. In: Proceedings of the 2008 ACM Conference on Computer Supported Cooperative Work (CSCW 2008), pp. 679–688 (2008). https:// doi.org/10.1145/1460563.1460668

19. Dey, A.K.: Understanding and using context. Pers. Ubiquit. Comput. **5**(1), 4–7 (2001)

20. Dimmick, J., Feaster, J.C., Hoplamazian, G.J.: News in the interstices: the niches of mobile media in space and time. New Media Soc. **13**(1), 23–39 (2011)

21. Dourish, P.: Seeking a foundation for context-aware computing. Hum.-Comput. Interact. **16**(2), 229–241 (2001)

22. Dourish, P.: What we talk about when we talk about context. Pers. Ubiquit. Comput. **8**(1), 19–30 (2004)

23. Dourish, P., Bell, G.: Divining a Digital Future: Mess and Mythology in Ubiquitous Computing. MIT Press, Cambridge (2011)

24. Gloor, P.A., Colladon, A.F., Grippa, F., Budner, P., Eirich, J.: Aristotle said "Happiness is a State of Activity"—predicting mood through body sensing with smartwatches. J. Syst. Sci. Syst. Eng. **27**(5), 586–612 (2018)

25. Goffman, E.: Behavior in Public Places: Notes on the Social Organization of Gatherings. Free Press of Glencoe, New York (1963)

26. Gottschalk, S., Salvaggio, M.: Stuck inside of mobile: ethnography in non-places. J. Contemp. Ethnogr. **44**(1), 3–33 (2015)

27. Harrison, S., Dourish, P.: Re-place-ing space: the roles of place and space in collaborative systems. In: Proceedings of the 1996 ACM Conference on Computer Supported Cooperative Work (CSCW 1996), pp. 67–76 (1996). https://doi.org/10.1145/240080.240193

28. Jameson, A.: Adaptive interfaces and agents. In: Human-Computer Interaction: Design Issues, Solutions, and Applications (2009)

29. Kanjo, E., Al-Husain, L., Chamberlain, A.: Emotions in context: examining pervasive affective sensing systems, applications, and analyses. Pers. Ubiquit. Comput. **19**(7), 1197–1212 (2015)

30. Karimi, M., Jannach, D., Jugovac, M.: News recommender systems-survey and roads ahead. Inf. Process. Manag. **54**(6), 1203–1227 (2018)

31. Kazai, G., Yusof, I., Clarke, D.: Personalised news and blog recommendations based on user location, Facebook and Twitter user profiling. In: Proceedings of the 39th International ACM SIGIR conference on Research and Development in Information Retrieval, pp. 1129–1132. ACM (2016)

32. Kellar, M., Watters, C., Shepherd, M.: A field study characterizing Web-based information-seeking tasks. J. Am. Soc. Inf. Sci. Technol. **58**(7), 999–1018 (2007)

33. Kucharski, A.: Post-truth: study epidemiology of fake news. Nature **540**(7634), 525 (2016)

34. Lehman-Wilzig, S.N., Seletzky, M.: Hard news, soft news, "general" news: the necessity and utility of an intermediate classification. Journalism **11**(1), 37–56 (2010)

35. LiKamWa, R., Liu, Y., Lane, N.D., Zhong, L.: Moodscope: building a mood sensor from smartphone usage patterns. In: Proceedings of the 11 Annual International Conference on Mobile Systems, Applications, and Services (MobiSys 2013), pp. 389–402 (2013). https://doi.org/10.1145/2462456.2483967

36. Mancini, C., Thomas, K., Rogers, Y., Price, B.: From spaces to places: emerging contexts in mobile privacy. In: Proceedings of the 11th international conference on Ubiquitous computing (Ubicomp 2009), pp. 1–10 (2009). https://doi.org/10.1145/1620545.1620547

37. Böhmer M., Hecht, B., Schöning, J., Krüger, A., Bauer, G.: Falling asleep with angry birds, Facebook and Kindle: a large scale study on mobile application usage. In: Proceedings of the 13th international conference on Human computer interaction with mobile devices and services (MobileHCI 2011), pp. 47–56 (2001). https://doi.org/10.1145/2037373.2037383

38. Böhmer, M., Bauer, G., Krüger, A.: Exploring the design space of context-aware recommender systems that suggest mobile applications. In: 2nd Workshop on Context-Aware Recommender Systems (2010)

39. Nagel, K.S., Hudson, J.M., Abowd, G.D.: Predictors of availability in home life context-mediated communication. In Proceedings of the 2004 ACM Conference on Computer Supported Cooperative Work (CSCW 2004), pp. 497–506. ACM (2004). https://doi.org/10.1145/1031607.1031689

40. Newman, N., Levy, D.: The Reuters Institute Digital News Report 2015: Tracking the Future of News. University of Oxford, Reuters Institute for the Study of Journalism (2015)

41. Nguyen, T.T., Hui, P.-M., Harper, F.M., Terveen, L., Konstan, J.A.: Exploring the filter bubble: the effect of using recommender systems on content diversity. In: Proceedings of the 23rd International Conference on World Wide Web (WWW 2014), pp. 677–686 (2014). https://doi.org/10.1145/2566486.2568012

42. Novick, D.G., Santaella, B., Cervantes, A., Andrade, C.: Short-term methodology for long-term usability. In Proceedings of the 30th ACM International Conference on Design of Communication (SIGDOC 2012), pp. 205–212 (2012). https://doi.org/10.1145/2379057.2379097

43. Nylander, S., Lundquist, T., Brännström, A., Karlson, B.: "It's just easier with the phone" – a diary study of internet access from cell phones. In: Tokuda, H., Beigl, M., Friday, A., Brush, A.J.B., Tobe, Y. (eds.) Pervasive 2009. LNCS, vol. 5538, pp. 354–371. Springer, Heidelberg (2009). https://doi.org/10.1007/978-3-642-01516-8_24

44. Ofcom. News consumption in the UK: 2014 report. Ofcom (2014)

45. Pariser, E.: The Filter Bubble: What the Internet is Hiding From You. Penguin, New York (2011)

46. Perry, M., O'Hara, K., Sellen, A., Brown, B., Harper, R.: Dealing with mobility: understanding access anytime, anywhere. ACM Trans. Comput.-Hum. Interact. (TOCHI) 8(4), 323–347 (2001)

47. Pielot, M., Dingler, T., Pedro, J.S., Oliver, N.: When attention is not scarce-detecting boredom from mobile phone usage. In: Proceedings of the 2015 ACM International Joint Conference on Pervasive and Ubiquitous Computing (UbiComp 2015), pp. 825–836 (2015). https://doi.org/10.1145/2750858.2804252

48. Rigby, J.M., Brumby, D.P., Gould, S.J.J., Cox, A.L.: Media multitasking at home: a video observation study of concurrent TV and mobile device usage. In: Proceedings of the 2017 ACM International Conference on Interactive Experiences for TV and Online Video, pp. 3–10. ACM (2017)

49. Rooksby, J., Smith, T.E., Morrison, A., Rost, M., Chalmers, M.: Configuring attention in the multiscreen living room. In: Boulus-Rødje, N., Ellingsen, G., Bratteteig, T., Aanestad, M., Bjørn, P. (eds.) ECSCW 2015: Proceedings of the 14th European Conference on Computer Supported Cooperative Work, 19–23 September 2015, Oslo, Norway, pp. 243–261. Springer, Cham (2015). https://doi.org/10.1007/978-3-319-20499-4_13

50. Russell, D.M., Chi, E.H.: Looking back: retrospective study methods for HCI. In: Olson, J.S., Kellogg, W.A. (eds.) Ways of Knowing in HCI, pp. 373–393. Springer, New York (2014). https://doi.org/10.1007/978-1-4939-0378-8_15

51. Servia-Rodríguez, S., Rachuri, K.K., Mascolo, C., Rentfrow, P.J., Lathia, N., Sandstrom, G.M.: Mobile sensing at the service of mental well-being: a large-scale longitudinal study. In: Proceedings of the 26th International Conference on World Wide Web, pp. 103–112. International World Wide Web Conferences Steering Committee (2017)

52. Sohn, T., Li, K.A., Griswold, W.G., Hollan, J.D.: A diary study of mobile information needs. In: Proceedings of the SIGCHI Conference on Human Factors in Computing Systems (CHI 2008), pp. 433–442 (2008). https://doi.org/10.1145/1357054.1357125

53. Suchman, L.A.: Plans and Situated Actions: The Problem of Human-Machine Communication. Cambridge University Press, Cambridge (1987)

54. Tavakolifard, M., Gulla, J.A., Almeroth, K.C., Ingvaldesn, J.E., Nygreen, G., Berg, E.: Tailored news in the palm of your hand: a multi-perspective transparent approach to news recommendation. In: Proceedings of the 22nd International Conference on World Wide Web (WWW 2013 Companion), pp. 305–308 (2013). https://doi.org/10.1145/2487788.2487930

55. Taylor, A.S.: Ethnography in ubiquitous computing. In: Krumm, J. (ed.) Ubiquitous Computing Fundamentals, pp. 203–236. Chapman and Hall/CRC, Boca Raton (2009)

56. Urry, J.: Mobilities. Wiley, Oxford (2007)
57. Wang, W.-C.: Understanding user experience of news applications by Taxonomy of Experience (ToE). Behav. Inf. Technol. **36**(11), 1137–1147 (2017)
58. Westlund, O.: From mobile phone to mobile device: news consumption on the go. Can. J. Commun. **33**(3), 443 (2008)
59. Yarmey, D.A.: The Psychology of Eyewitness Testimony. FreePress, New York (1979)

Education and HCI Curriculum I

Education and HCI Curriculum I

Balance Talking and Doing! Using Google Design Sprint to Enhance an Intensive UCD Course

Marta Larusdottir[1]([⊠]), Virpi Roto[2], Jan Stage[3], Andrés Lucero[2], and Ilja Šmorgun[4]

[1] Reykjavik University, 101 Reykjavik, Iceland
marta@ru.is
[2] Aalto University, 00076 Aalto, Finland
[3] Aalborg University, 9100 Ålborg, Denmark
[4] Tallinn University, 10120 Tallinn, Estonia

Abstract. Design, evaluation and enhancement of teaching activities in user-centred design (UCD) is characterized by limited research. This is particularly paradoxical as effective high-quality teaching is a key prerequisite for professional work in UCD. This paper reports the development of a two-week intensive UCD course for university-level students in an international setting. The first edition of the course ran during the summer of 2017. Based on both qualitative and quantitative data collected from students, the course was enhanced and a new edition that introduced Google Design Sprint (GDS) was conducted during the summer of 2018. Similar student feedback data was collected during both years (i.e., 2017 and 2018). In both editions, the course included lectures and hands-on use of UCD and interaction design methods in a design assignment. In this paper, we focus on the 2018 edition of the course and the students' qualitative and quantitative feedback on that edition. The results illustrate that students liked the intensive teamwork, clear structure, and the international setting of the course. The main concerns from the students were on inefficient time management and the lack of user involvement in GDS. However, GDS was preferred to the traditional teaching methods, as the students saw the rapid development cycle to provide a good balance of talking and doing.

Keywords: User-Centred Design Education · Students feedback · Google Design Sprint

1 Introduction

While research in Human-Computer Interaction (HCI) and User-Centred Design (UCD) is characterized by extensive emphasis on concepts, methods and their use in practice, much less attention has been devoted to the teaching of these topics, although well-trained practitioners is a prerequisite for successful use in practice. It is a paradox that HCI and UCD research with its strong emphasis on concepts and methods for evaluation has very little concern for the teaching of these topics, not to mention the assessment of such teaching activities.

© IFIP International Federation for Information Processing 2019
Published by Springer Nature Switzerland AG 2019
D. Lamas et al. (Eds.): INTERACT 2019, LNCS 11747, pp. 95–113, 2019.
https://doi.org/10.1007/978-3-030-29384-0_6

Assessment has been a key topic for many years in general research on teaching. Cronbach was one of the early proponents of using assessment or evaluation as the basis for improving teaching activities. His aim was to use evidence gained through evaluation as the basis for developing and improving educational programs [4, 5]. A recent example of using quantitative data to improve teaching activities is provided by Aggarwal and Lynn [1] as they described how they improved a database management course through collection and interpretation of quantitative data. Quantitative data was also collected through questionnaires in a three week intensive course focusing on measuring the outcomes of learning outcomes [16].

Up to and during the 1990s, the field of teaching evaluation was re-shaped from this quantitative foundation by two parallel developments that were based on qualitative methods with a strong emphasis on context. First, the case study method was introduced to achieve a stronger focus on context of the teaching activities, and this was often combined with a participatory approach to teaching evaluation. Second, action research was introduced for "teachers [to] experiment in their own classrooms with how to improve teaching performance and enhance student learning" [17]. The effect of using practical exercises in a human-computer interaction course was studied recently and compared to using a more typical approach [19]. The results show that students involved in realistic projects are significantly more motivated and perceive that the HCI activities are more useful or important than students involved in a more general approach, with not as realistic projects to solve.

While there is significant research on the introduction of UCD in software organizations, few authors have discussed the design of courses on UCD. Seffah and Andreevskaia [15] describe how they developed a course in UCD for software practitioners. They developed the course over a period of eight years, and their approach embodies continuous improvement which is based on qualitative techniques such as class discussions combined with interviews and observation. In another study, students that had taken at least one master's level course in usability and user centered design (UCD) answered a survey to assess the value of a teaching philosophy that considered usability skills to be of value to future information professionals, even when they are not pursuing careers as usability engineers [2]. The survey results show that almost 95% of respondents regularly used the general principles of usability on the job, despite only 20% were hired to perform user centred design.

Over two years, we have developed a two-week course on UCD for university-level students. We gave the course for the first time in 2017 and evaluated it with 18 participants who had different nationalities. This has been reported with focus on the contents of the course, cf. [11]. Based on the evaluation, we redesigned the course, and in 2018 we gave it to a new group of 19 international students.

This paper reports from a case study of the evaluation of the second edition of the course that was given in 2018. The purpose of the paper is both to present the evaluation of the course and to provide a framework for evaluation of similar courses. In the following sections, we present the background for this paper by describing the overall rationale of the course, the first edition of the course briefly, the Google Design Sprint (GDS) process and the schedule of the course in 2018.

2   Background

In this section we describe the overall rationale for this UCD course and give an overview of the 2017 edition. We introduce the GDS process briefly, which was used in the 2018 edition of the course, and describe the structure of that edition of the course.

2.1   Overall Rationale for the Course

Over the past three decades we have witnessed shifts and re-framings in just about every area of interaction design: how it is done, who is doing it, for what goals, and what its results are. These changes show shift from designing things to designing interactions, first on micro-level and lately also on a macro level; and from designing for people to designing with people and very recently, to designing by people.

The university-level course targets higher education students in various fields and provides interaction design understanding and skills to new, but highly interested audiences. Additionally, we targeted non-ICT (Information and Communications Technologies) professionals. Upon completion of the course, higher education students and professionals should be able to conceptualize and prototype digital artefacts ranging from simple web-based services and small applications to wearable computing solutions and public space installations. The course was given in two weeks as a 4 ECTS intensive course, brought together, delivered, and hosted on rotation, by four partner universities: Aalto University, Ålborg University, Reykjavik University and Tallinn University.

2.2   Overview of the 2017 Edition of the Course

The first edition of the User-Centred Design Course was given at Tallinn University in 2017. It lasted for two weeks, Monday to Friday, between July 24 and August 4. The main learning objective of the course was that students would gain the ability to apply common user-centred design methods and interaction design tools in practice during a two-week intensive course. A total of 18 international students worked on designing and evaluating a software system, and used altogether 15 UCD methods along the way. The students worked in groups of three to four students, which were formed by the lecturers. Students brainstormed ideas for five different systems using similar methods for analyzing, designing and evaluating the system prototypes.

During the first three days the students were introduced to the following user-centred design methods: Visioning, Contextual interviews [7], Affinity diagram [12], walking the wall, personas and scenarios [7]. After an introduction of the method, the students used each of the methods with supervision from the lecturers. The next two days the students were introduced to user experience (UX) goals [9], they made low-fidelity paper prototypes of the user interface and evaluated those through heuristic evaluations [14]. They also used the System Usability Scale (SUS) questionnaire for evaluation [3] and additionally evaluated the interface according to their UX goals. During the second week the students were introduced to formal usability evaluations.

Students then prototyped the interface using the Just-in mind prototyping tool[1] and did an informal think aloud evaluation of that prototype. After redesigning the prototype, the students stated measurable usability and UX goals and made a summative user evaluation to check the measurable goals. At the end of the course all students gave a 15-min presentation to the class where they presented their work to each other. The methods introduced to the students were chosen partly based on results on what methods Information Technology (IT) professionals rate as good methods for UCD [8].

The feedback from the students was largely positive. Students liked being active during the class, since they used various methods during the class hours and could get guidance from the teachers. Students especially liked making the hi-fi prototypes and gave that method the highest rating. Students also liked working with international students with various backgrounds. Students disliked a mismatch between the description and the actual content during the course. The hi-fi prototyping started quite late, day seven, and it was difficult to get the prototype ready in time. The students also commented that they met real users quite late in the course, which was on the ninth day, and would have liked that to happen earlier in the course. They had used many UCD methods, but in those, they had "played" users for each other, so students from other groups participated in UCD activities.

With this feedback it was decided to structure the next edition of the course according to the Google Design Sprint (GDS) process. GDS offers a well-structured interaction design process, with one activity feeding into the next. Such a framework is especially important for the main target audience of the course - those encountering the interaction design process for the first time. As a result, the students would have a clearly defined process to follow that would allow them to reach tangible results fairly quickly, while also leaving the time for user evaluation.

2.3   Introduction to the Google Design Sprint

Created as a means to better balance his time on the job and with his family, Jake Knapp optimized the different activities of a design process by introducing a process called the Google Design Sprint (GDS) [10]. Knapp noticed that despite the large piles of sticky notes and the collective excitement generated during team brainstorming workshops, the best ideas were often generated by individuals who had a big challenge and not too much time to work on them. Another key ingredient was to have people involved in a project all working together in a room solving their own part of the problem and ready to answer questions. Combining a focus on individual work, time to prototype, and an inescapable deadline Knapp called these focused design efforts "sprints".

The GDS is a process to solve problems and test new ideas by building and testing a prototype in five days. The main premise for the process is seeing how customers react before committing to building a real product. It is a "smarter, more respectful, and more effective way of solving problems", one that brings the best contributions of everyone on the team by helping them spend their time on what really matters [10].

---

[1] Just-in Mind. https://www.justinmind.com/.

A series of support materials such as checklists, slide decks, and tools can be found on a dedicated website[2].

An important challenge is defined, small teams of about seven people with diverse skills are recruited, and then the right room and materials are found. These teams clear their schedules and move through a focused design process by spending one day at each of its five stages (i.e., map, sketch, decide, prototype, test). On Monday, a map of the problem is made by defining key questions, a long-term goal, and a target, thus building a foundation for the sprint week. On Tuesday, individuals follow a four-step process (i.e., notes, ideas, crazy 8s, and solution sketch) to sketch out their own detailed, opinionated, and competing solutions. On Wednesday, the strongest solutions are selected using a structured five-step "Sticky Decision" method (i.e., art museum, heat map, speed critique, straw poll, and supervote) and fleshed out into a storyboard. On Thursday, between one and three realistic-looking prototypes of the solutions proposed in the storyboard are built, using tools like Keynote to create the facade for apps and websites, a 3D printer to quickly prototype hardware, or just build marketing materials. Finally on Friday, the prototype is tested with five target customers in one on one interviews or think-aloud sessions. While only some of the resulting solutions will work, going through such sprints provides clarity on what to do next after spending only five days tackling that big important challenge.

While GDS is oriented towards quickly achieving tangible results and experimenting with a number of potential design solutions, it has some limitations that one needs to be aware of. The first one being that GDS assumes prior knowledge and familiarity with the context and user requirements. Thus, all background research should be done before GDS starts, as the process is more focused on putting together a team of experts, who can quickly propose workable solutions to the formulated problem. This also means that core UCD activities, such as the creation of personas and user scenarios, need to be carried out before hand, and later be used as input and guidance for the subsequent design activities. The second one being that although GDS includes basic user testing on the fifth day, more thorough evaluation might be necessary for achieving better results. Subsequent iterations could be planned to then incorporate the concerns the users voice during evaluation.

The GDS on our course differed a bit from the above in the initial preparations, as there were four to five students in one team. Each team was asked to create a small software application, designed either for a mobile device or a bigger screen. Each team formulated their own specific topic for the design exercise.

2.4   The Course Schedule in 2018

The User-Centred Design course given in 2018 at Reykjavik University, lasted for two weeks, Monday to Friday. Similar to the 2017 edition, the main learning objective of the course was the ability to apply common UCD methods and interaction design tools in practice during a two-week intensive interaction design sprint.

---

[2] Sprint book website. https://www.thesprintbook.com.

A total of 19 international students worked on designing and evaluating a software system in four groups of four to five students, which were formed by the lecturers before the beginning of the course. We applied a similar strategy while forming groups with varying backgrounds, gender, and nationalities in each group as in 2017. Five potential project ideas were suggested to the students but they were told that they could also brainstorm ideas themselves for the systems to be designed and evaluated during the course. Students worked on four different software systems ideas and used altogether 13 methods for analyzing, designing and evaluating the systems prototypes. The course schedule is illustrated in Fig. 1. The lectures are shown in bold text and the methods that the students practised are shown in italics. The results on the student evaluations of the methods are shown in Table 3, in the result section of this paper.

Week 1	Monday	Tuesday	Wednesday	Thursday	Friday
Morning	**Introduction lectures** *Discuss project ideas*	*Ask the experts* **Interaction design lecture**	*Voting on design* *Speed critique* **Storyboard lecture**	*Hi-fi prototyping*	*User evaluations*
Afternoon	*Making a map*	**Sketching lecture** *Lightning demos* *Sketching-crazy 8*	*Making a storyboard* **Prototyping lecture**	*Hi-fi prototyping* **User evaluation lecture**	*Interpret evaluation results* *Prepare students presentations*
Week 2	Monday	Tuesday	Wednesday	Thursday	Friday
Morning	*Student presentations* **Setting UX goal lecture**	*Prototyping for evaluation of UX goals*	**Evaluation lecture** *Choosing a target for the last evaluation*	**Agile UCD lecture** *Preparing summative UX evaluations*	*Preparing presentations*
Afternoon	*Setting UX goals*	*Evaluating against the UX goals*	*Prototyping for the last evaluation*	*Summative UX evaluations*	*Final presentations & Wrap up*

Fig. 1. The schedule of the UCD course in 2018. The text in italics explains hands-on activities.

The course schedule focused on running the GDS during the first week by conducting all the GDS methods in that process "by the book", following the checklists and descriptions in the process. Typically, there was a short lecture explaining how to use each method and right afterwards the students got one or two hours to practice that method under the supervision of the lecturers. During the second week user experience aspects were added to the design and the prototype was redesigned and evaluated with users to understand the user experience better of the prototype and the system idea. So in the second week, more emphasis was on lecturing and practicing user-centred design methods.

Upon completion of the course students should have acquired an understanding of what design is and should grasp the full cycle of the design process including the stages of discovering, defining, developing and delivering concepts targeting areas of their interest. There was a continuous assessment of the learning outcomes by observing the students while they practised the methods introduced in the course.

3   Method

In this section we describe the students taking part in the course in 2018 briefly, the course evaluation methods and the data analysis methods.

3.1   Students

Nineteen students participated in the course, 16 females and 3 males. Students living in Denmark, Estonia and Finland were selected and received grants to come to Iceland to participate in the course. Some of those students were originally from other countries, so we had participants from: Iceland (4), Estonia (4), Danmark (3), Poland (2) and one from each of the following countries: Belarus, Greece, Spain, Mexico, Russia and Vietnam. The participants were between 23 and 37 years old.

The participants had various backgrounds. Information is missing from three students, so the background information is based on 16 answers. Three students had a high school degree and were studying for BSc degree; eight had a Bachelor degree and were all studying on Master level, four had a Master degree, where three were studying further and one had a PhD degree. Several of the students had humanities and social sciences as their discipline, some had design sciences, and other computer science, technical science and engineering. Three students were not studying at the time of the course. Eleven students had some experience from working at a software company/organisation and the time varied from two to 36 months.

When the students registered to the course, they responded to question "What do you expect to learn on this course?". Out of 15 responses, six spontaneously mentioned Hands-on experience, and four specifically mentioned (Google Design) Sprint, four Prototyping and two Programming. Experiencing the full design process came up in six responses. The concepts mentioned were Interaction Design (5), UCD (3), User Interface (3), UX (2) and Usability (1). Evaluation was mentioned twice. In addition to learning these hard skills, collaborating with students from other cultures and disciplines was mentioned by five participants.

3.2   Course Evaluation Methods

Two data gathering methods were used to gather feedback from students on their opinions on the course. The Retrospective Hand technique was used as a weekly evaluation for collecting open-ended feedback from the students and a questionnaire form on the methods taught was used in the last session of the course. Both the questionnaire and the Retrospective Hand were distributed on paper. The data gathering methods will be described in more detail below.

The Retrospective Hand Technique. Students were asked to draw their right hand on an empty A4 sheet of paper as the last thing in the afternoon during both Fridays, so data was gathered twice with this technique during the course. In the space near the thumb, they were asked to write what they thought was good during the current week (i.e., thumb raised), in the space for the index finger, things they wanted to point out (i.e., indicate), in the third finger space what was not good (i.e., middle finger), in the space for the fourth finger what they will take home with them (i.e., ring finger), and the fifth finger what they wanted more of (i.e., pinky finger). The students wrote sentences in free text, so this was a qualitative technique. To keep anonymity, students handed in their feedback paper by putting it in a box that was placed at the back of the room, so that lecturers could not see who were returning the evaluation forms. When all the students had handed in their evaluations, we asked if there was something that they wanted to share with the group. There were open discussions for about 15 min of improvements that could be made to the course, but these discussions were not analysed for this publication.

The idea of this technique comes from industry and has been used by the first author on four different courses. The students like the method, since it has an open and somewhat creative format, so they can comment on various issues and it takes them around 10 min to complete. When used in the middle of the course, the instructors of the course have the possibility to respond to the comments of the students, and make enhancements accordingly, which the students appreciate.

The Method Questionnaire. The questionnaire was on paper and contained three pages. On the first page there were: four questions on the student's background, three questions on their currently highest achieved degree, one question on whether they were studying currently or not, and three on their current education field (if applicable). Also, on the first page they were asked if they had worked in a company/organisation developing software systems. If so, they were asked to fill in four more questions about the work role and company.

On the second page of the questionnaire the students were asked to rate their opinion of the 13 GDS/UCD methods used in the course. The first nine methods were all from the GDS process and four methods were more typical UCD methods. For each method they were asked to rate:

(a) If the method was thought provoking;
(b) If the method was useful for the course;
(c) If they thought that the method would be useful for their future job/education.

For each item we provided a 7-point scale from 1 = not at all to 7 = extremely so. The 13 GDS/UCD methods they evaluated were: *Making a map, Ask the experts, Lightning demos, Sketching (including crazy 8), Voting on design solutions, Speed critique of the designs, Storyboard making, Hi-fi prototyping, User testing (of the hi-fi prototypes), Setting UX goals, Evaluation of UX goals, Prototyping for the last evaluation, Summative UX evaluation.* Furthermore, students were asked to rate the whole GDS process (used during the first week) and the inclusion of the user aspects (the focus of the second week).

On the third page, there was just one open question for any other comments that they would like to share with us. They had a full A4 page to freely share their comments. Some student used the whole page to write detailed comments.

The questionnaire was filled in right after the retrospective hand evaluation during the last session of the class. The students typically used 20 min to fill in the questionnaire. When all the students had filled in this questionnaire, a group discussion was facilitated on the overall evaluation on the course and notes were taken by the lecturers on their comments.

3.3 Data Analysis Methods

The data from 2018 using the Retrospective Hand technique was analysed according to theme analysis [6]. The themes we used are shown in Table 1.

Table 1. The categorization themes from Steyn et al. used in this study.

#	Theme	Explanation according to Steyn et al.
1	Assessment	Assessment standards, structure, schedule, criteria and feedback
2	Staff quality	Tutor and lecturer availability, teaching skills, quality and frequency of communication with students and the number of lecturers on the module
3	Learning environment	Quality of lecture hall equipment, the size and comfort of lecture and tutorial venues and the quality of the learning environment created through group project work
4	Learning support	Adequate preparation for assessments and the provision of additional learning support, such as workshops and guest lecturers
5	Learning resources	The provision of additional resources and the quality, timeliness and affordability of resources provided
6	Teaching methods	*Steyn et al. definition:* Suggestions to make the lectures more interactive and application-based. *Our definition:* HOW the students learn, i.e., the format of activities on the course. The outcome of the design exercise
7	Course content	*Steyn et al. definition:* Relevance of the curriculum, and the workload. *Our definition:* WHAT the students learn
8	Course administration	*Steyn et al. definition:* Class scheduling. *Our definition:* Practical arrangements such as team formation and availability of practical course information

We based our themes on themes suggested by Steyn et al. [18] as shown in Table 1, but we adjusted some of the definitions to the characteristics of our course. Soon after starting to analyse the data, we noticed many data items did not fall to any of the themes in Table 1, and we needed more themes for the thematic analysis. The new themes are shown in Table 2.

Table 2. Additional themes added by the authors.

#	Theme	Explanation
9	Course structure	Structure and scheduling of the activities, days and the course. WHEN the learning activities take place
10	Soft skills	Critical thinking, problem solving, leadership and responsibility, communication, and collaboration (e.g., team work)
11	People	Personal relationships, selection of people on the course
12	Experience	Overall course experience, level of motivation, atmosphere, freetime activities, lunch and snacks, accommodation

We had to add the themes because our course was very different from Steyn et al. This intensive course ran for two weeks and many of the students comments were on the course schedule, so we decided to include a separate theme on Course structure. Our course included many problem-solving activities in teams, so we created a new theme for Soft skills. An intensive course with international students is a memorable experience, therefore themes for the comments regarding Experience and People were added.

The first two authors of the paper individually analysed the data according to the above themes. When both authors had analysed all the data, the inter-evaluator agreement was calculated to be 58%. Then each author re-evaluated their theme analysis in light of the other's category suggestion. After this, the evaluators discussed the disagreements until reaching consensus.

4 Results

In this section we first describe the results on the quantitative ratings from students and then the results on the qualitative feedback gathered.

4.1 Quantitative Ratings from Students

Rating of Methods: The average numbers on how students rated the methods and the focus of each week are summarized in Table 3 on a scale from 1 to 7, where 1 was "not at all" and 7 was "extremely so".

Table 3. The average quantitative rating of the methods from students in 2018.

GDS/UCD Methods and the focus each week	Thought provoking	Useful in the course	Useful in the future
Making a map	5,94	6,06	6,00
Ask the experts	4,81	4,44	5,63
Lightning demos	5,31	5,00	5,00
Sketching (incl. Crazy 8)	6,38	6,63	6,25
Voting on design solutions	5,00	6,13	5,56
Speed critique of the designs	5,63	6,00	5,44
Making a Storyboard	6,00	6,31	6,38
Hi-fi prototyping	5,50	6,25	6,50
User testing – 1st week	5,79	6,07	6,06
Setting UX goals	4,56	4,31	5,00
Evaluation against the UX goals	4,63	4,50	5,13
Prototyping for the last evaluation	4,81	5,50	5,31
Summative UX evaluation	5,19	5,06	5,25
Whole Google Design Sprint (1st week)	**6,69**	**6,75**	**6,63**
Including the user aspects 2nd week)	5,06	5,13	5,40

The students really liked the whole process of the GDS. It got the highest rating of all the course content in the questionnaire, for being thought provoking, useful in the course and useful in the future. Out of the GDS methods used during the first week, the students gave the highest ratings to the *Sketching* method, but they also rated the GDS methods, *Making a map* and *Making a storyboard* high.

The GDS/UCD method with the lowest numerical scores was *Setting UX goals* in the second week. Students were asked to do that during Monday morning in the second week, after being very productive during the first week. The structure of this session was maybe not as clear as for the sessions in the first week, so the students got all very tired. Many students commented that because of the looser structure they felt disconnected and not as motivated. There is clearly a challenge there, how to keep the motivation for the students from the first to the second week, and how user-centered design can best be included in the GDS process.

After the two weeks many students reflected that maybe it would have been good to have some team building activities and user research activities before beginning the GDS process. One student commented that because there were no user research activities before starting the GDS process, she felt like cheating. Actually the group the student was in, did describe one persona and one scenario, even though they were not instructed to do so. Some students also commented that the course could have been shorter, so the activities during the second week felt not as important as during the first week.

Comparing the Results from 2018 to the Results from 2017: In Table 4, the ratings from the students on GDS/UCD methods used both during the course in 2017 and 2018 are compared. In 2017 the UCD methods used during the first days of the course were the methods suggested by Holtzblatt et al. [7] in the Rapid Contextual Design process. In 2018, we followed the GDS process for the first week [10]. Some of the methods in these two processes are similar and can be compared. *Visioning* (in 2017) and *Making a map* (in 2018) have the same objective of giving an overview of the vision for the whole system. *Low-fi prototyping* on paper (in 2017) and *Sketching (including the Crazy 8)* according to GDS (in 2018) are also very similar. *Hi-fi prototyping* in 2018, was highly similar as in 2017, but in 2018 we followed predefined roles in the process according to the instructions in the GDS process. *User testing* of the prototypes was done in the same way in 2017 and 2018, by conducting think-aloud sessions with five users. *Setting UX goals* was also done in the same manner and taught by the same person both years, the *Evaluation of the UX goals* was also conducted in the same way. Additionally, the *Summative UX evaluation* at the end of the course was also conducted similarly.

In Table 4, it is interesting to see how the ratings of the methods differ between the two years. There is a significant difference between how the students rated how thought-provoking the two methods *Visioning* (used in 2017) and *Making a map* (used in 2018) are (t-test, $p = 0.01$) (shown in bold in the table). The reason for the higher rating could be that students received more precise instructions on the GDS method *Making the map*, than on *Visioning* the year before. But, there was not a statistical difference in the ratings of the other two aspects, how useful the methods were in the course and how useful the methods will be in the future.

Table 4. Average quantitative rating from students in 2017 and 2018 (standard deviation).

GDS/UCD method	Thought provoking		Useful in the course		Useful in the future	
	2017	2018	2017	2018	2017	2018
Visioning/Making a map	**4,6** **(1,68)**	**5,9** **(1,06)**	5,4 (1,69)	6,1 (1,12)	5,1 (1,86)	6,0 (0,89)
Low-fi prototyping/Sketching	**4,9** **(1,76)**	**6,4** **(1,02)**	5,9 (1,61)	6,6 (0,62)	5,5 (1,92)	6,3 (1,06)
Hi-fi prototyping	5,8 (1,42)	5,5 (1,15)	6,8 (0,53)	6,3 (1,13)	6,8 (0,71)	6,5 (0,97)
User testing (hi-fi prototypes)	5,6 (1,11)	5,8 (0,81)	6,2 (1,12)	6,1 (0,63)	6,2 (1,13)	6,2 (0,50)
Setting UX goals	**5,7** **(0,87)**	**4,6** **(1,21)**	**6,2** **(1,12)**	**4,3** **(1,01)**	**6,3** **(1,11)**	**5,0** **(1,21)**
Evaluation of the UX goals	5,0 (1,29)	4,6 (1,02)	5,4 (1,64)	4,5 (1,32)	5,1 (1,66)	5,1 (1,09)
Summative UX evaluation	5,7 (1,20)	5,1 (1,22)	**6,3** **(1,00)**	**5,1** **(1,24)**	**6,4** **(0,90)**	**5,4** **(1,48)**

Sketching was done more individually in 2018, as instructed by the GDS, than in 2017 when students did the *Low-fi prototyping* in groups. There is a significant difference between how the students rated how thought-provoking these two methods are (t-test, p = 0.01). There was not a statistical difference in the ratings of the two other aspects, how useful the methods were in the course and how useful the methods will be in the future.

The difference between ratings of the UCD method *Setting UX goals* in 2018 and 2017 was significant for the three aspects, if it was thought provoking, useful in the course and useful in the future (t-test, p = 0.01). The method was rated lower in 2018 than in 2017, when it was one of the most preferred methods. There was not a big difference in how the method was taught on the two coursers, so the reason for the difference may be in the scheduling and structure of this session. The students had been very active during the first week in 2018 and managed to make hi-fi prototypes of their brand new idea and evaluate it in one week. Then on Monday morning they were back to a traditional lecture + team exercise structure. Setting UX goals require in-depth consideration and discussion before they can be taken into use. That activity was not as straightforward and fast-paced as the methods in the GDS. It seemed to be hard for the students to switch from the pace of the GDS to a more open and less guided structure.

The method *Summative UX evaluation* got higher rating in 2017 than in 2018 and the difference was statistically different for the two aspects: the usefulness in the course and the usefulness in the future (t-test, p = 0.01). The reason could be that in 2018, the students felt it was a bit unnecessary to do the summative UX evaluation with users, because they had already done user testing with real users twice earlier in the course. So the last user testing sessions did not give that much additional information. On the contrary, in 2017, this was the first occasion where the students did evaluate with real users.

There was not a statistical difference in the ratings of the other methods and aspects that are compared in Table 4.

Based on this comparison it seems that the context of using a particular GDS/UCD method plays a very important role for how useful the methods are rated by students. Moreover, which GDS/UCD methods the students have used previously in the course and in which contexts seems to play an important role in how valuable the students think the methods are. In other words, evaluations are always relational to the students' previous experiences.

4.2   Qualitative Feedback During the Course

The data collected via the Retrospective Hand technique yielded 207 data items from 18 students (16 on the 2nd week). In total there were 52 comments on "What was good", 41 on "What was not so good", 39 on "I want to point out", 34 on "What I will take home" and 41 on "I want more of". This feedback method seemed engaging for the students, as only 4 (2.4%) of the comment points were left empty. Often, one student indicated several different data items in one finger feedback, e.g., a list of items considered good on the course. Each data item was assigned an ID in format 2018-w1 Good 16-1, i.e., starting with the year of the course, week number (w1), the finger where the comment was reported (Good), followed by a running number for the student (16) and a running number in case several data items were mentioned (1).

The items collected were categorised against the extended framework of Steyn et al. [18], see Sect. 3.3 for further explanation of the themes. The frequency of comments in each theme is shown in Table 5.

As can be seen from Table 5, more than half of the students' comments were about Course content (29%) and Course structure (27%).

Table 5. The frequency of data items collected analysed by themes.

Theme	Week 1	Week 2	Total
Course structure	25	30	55
Course content	31	30	61
Teaching methods	14	9	23
Learning support	10	7	17
Learning resources	4	0	4
People	6	4	10
Soft skills	3	4	7
Staff quality	2	9	11
Learning environment	2	0	2
Experience	9	3	12
Course administration	4	1	5
Total	110	97	207

We analysed these two themes further by calculating the percentage of comments in each category that the students were commenting in (on each finger). The results are shown in Table 6.

Table 6. Percentage of comments on each finger by week for the most frequently used themes.

Category/finger	Course structure			Course content		
	Week 1	Week 2	Total	Week 1	Week 2	Total
What was good	11%	7%	18%	13%	15%	28%
I'd like to point out	9%	20%	29%	5%	3%	8%
What was not so good	9%	15%	24%	10%	3%	13%
I will take this home	11%	0%	11%	7%	18%	25%
I would like more of	5%	13%	18%	16%	10%	26%
Total	45%	55%	100%	51%	49%	100%

Comments related to course structure were most prominent in the negative feedback responses of 'I'd like to point out' (29%) and 'What was not so good' (24%) fingers, which indicates that the course structure was still not optimal from the students' perspective. After the precisely structured first week of the GDS, the students missed a similar style for the second week, which was more focused on lectures and user evaluations, as these comments show: "was missing the structure from the first week" (2018-w2 NotGood 3) and "there was a bit of confusion on how to keep 1st week's pace" (2018-w2 NotGood 7).

The comments on course content were especially prominent in the 'What was good' (28%), 'I would like more of' (26%), and "I will take this home" (25%) fingers. Typical comments in 'I will take this home' were methodological, such as "Setting experience goals and testing according to them" (2018-w2 Take 10) or "Quick decision making. Short tasks - test, implementation!" (2018-w1 Take 9). Course content that students would have liked to hear more of related to user involvement, which GDS did not include: "I would like more of UCD" (2018-w1 More 10).

Teaching methods was the third most frequent category with 11% of all comments in this data set. Most of the comments were positive. The students clearly liked hands-on work in a team, like one student commented: "very good and efficient teamwork" (2018-w1 Good 5-3) and "not much theory:)" (2018-w1 Good 5-5). Another one commented that he/she would take home "the way a project like this should be organized and managed and how to find the right balance in talking and doing" (2018-w1 Take 13). The students also liked lectures that provided information to apply in the following teamwork, such as the UCD methods. "The things that I liked this week were lectures. I think it was nice to involve UX in the design process." (2018-w2 Good 5). The negative comments were mainly about the difficulty of doing high-fidelity prototyping as a team: "There was one person working no sharing" (2018-w1 NotGood 7-1).

On this intensive, international course, several students commented on the fellow students on the course. Comments in the 'What was good' finger report about the excitement to meet people from different countries, with different backgrounds, like:

"Variety of participants" (2018-w1 Good 4-4) and "The people - students and teachers were very interesting" (2018-w1 Good 12).

Looking at the shares of 'What was good' comments in the different categories we see the excitement of the fast-paced course structure during the GDS on the first week. Staff quality was praised after the second week. The students commented also about the general course experience, such as the location, free scholarship, and the food arrangements.

In 'What was not so good' section, many commented on the dramatic change in the course structure after the first week, and 31% of the comments after the 2nd week were about the Course structure. The negative comments on Course content were many but mild: "maybe also what would be alternatives to Google sprint" (2018-w1 NotGood 5-2), "Some of the lectures could be more advanced or go into more detail" (2018-w1 NotGood 10-1), and "I think there is a need in intro to UX research methods and tools" (2018-w2 NotGood 14).

5   Discussion

In this section we discuss the possible reasons behind the main results of student feedback presented in the previous section. We also discuss the challenges of integrating user-centred design into the GDS process.

5.1   Reflection on the Results

In this section, we discuss the main findings according to our observations and compare our experiences in 2018 with our experiences in 2017, which were reported in another paper [11].

The course content with GDS was preferred by the students. They all gave it a high numerical rating and commented that they liked the process and were highly motivated during the intensive week of the GDS. They liked detailed instructions, the timeboxing of activities and that the outcome of one activity was used while conducting the next method. They also felt that they had achieved much during the first week, having both done hi-fi prototypes and evaluated those with five real users just in one week. But they also got a bit tired after following the intense schedule, as one of the students explained: "The schedule was too intense, a day off to work on your own could be nice." (2018-w1 NotGood 8).

The change from the intense schedule of the first week to a more traditional and less structured UCD course schedule on the second week seemed too dramatic for most students. The nature of Iceland also attracted the international students, so some of them used the time until late Sunday evening to experience Iceland. We believe that communicating the pace and style of the course work right in the beginning of the course will help the students to prepare and stay motivated also outside the design sprint.

In the course description 2018, we promised to teach user-centred design and hands-on interaction design. Some comments from the students showed that during the first week when using the GDS process, students missed the user-centredness. Users were involved only on the last day of the sprint to get feedback on the hi-fi prototypes through user testing with real users. The next week, there were two more rounds of evaluations with users, which the students positively commented on. In 2017 the students did user testing sessions with real users once during the course, on the ninth day. But they did evaluations with fellow students and expert evaluation on previous days of the course. Some students commented that they would have wanted to meet real users earlier in the course. It was clear that the students were eager to meet real users and show the prototypes to them already in the first week, so it was very important for them to have the design process as realistic as possible.

Also during 2018, the students expressed interest in solving real-life problems. Students wanted to study people to find interesting problems before deciding the design focus. On the course the teachers provided six examples of suitable design topics, but only one group did choose a project idea from that pool. The other three groups came up with their own ideas to work on. Especially one of the groups seemed to have lost interest in the idea after evaluating with users on the fifth day, so the motivation to work further on the idea in the second week was not as high as during the first week. Choosing project ideas is a big issue for the students, not only to learn to use particular methods.

A clear limitation of this work is that the two courses were not run identically. They took place in different universities, with different students, and with different course structure. Three lecturers gave similar lectures during 2017 and 2018, but both years there were two lecturers who did not attend the other edition of the course. The courses in 2017 and 2018 used similar teaching methods with short lectures and hands-on training right after the lectures. Therefore, the comparison results between the two courses are indicative, and we can explain some differences in quantitative results by contextual changes only. However, the main contribution of this work is not based on the quantitative comparison but on the qualitative feedback on how the changed course structure with GDS was seen from the students' perspective.

5.2   Thoughts on Integrating UCD into Google Design Sprint

User-centred design requires that designers first envision how people are likely to use a product, and then to validate their user behaviour assumptions by conducting tests in the real world. With its main premise of seeing how customers react before committing to building a real product, GDS certainly shares the latter aspect of evaluation with UCD. However, people seem to be only indirectly involved in informing the envisioned designs.

Conducting user studies such as probes [13] or contextual inquiries [7] to gather rich information about people's needs, dreams, and aspirations can be time consuming. Due to GDS's focus on optimizing the different activities of a design process, people's input only comes through asking experts who know most about a given customer. Perhaps reacting to this lack of user input, it was earlier mentioned that one group felt they needed to create a persona and a scenario before starting with the GDS process. Based on what these students suggested, we feel there is an opportunity to extend people's involvement in the design sprint.

One simple way to involve users more in GDS is to invite one potential customer on the first day of GDS (i.e., Monday afternoon) to the activity called Ask the Experts. On top of having a person who knows most about technology, marketing, and business, the person who knows most about the customer could be further complemented by having one potential customer directly involved in these discussions. Involving a potential customer should, however, be carefully planned.

It may be the first time that some experts (e.g., technology) meet potential customers, and thus there could be a risk to turn the Ask the Experts activity into an ad hoc user study. Instead, the potential customer should act as 'one more expert', and the facilitator(s) should keep this in mind to keep the activity on track and within time. Such a setup would allow keeping GDS's focus on optimizing the design process and bringing the best contributions of everyone on the team, while increasing its user-centredness.

Additionally, the students could be asked to think more about the users while using the GDS process. Shortly after the mapping, students could be asked to describe better the user groups that are listed on the map, but either analysing the main characteristics of the user groups or making a persona for each user group. Furthermore, after making the paper prototypes and before making the storyboard, the students could be asked to set the user experience (UX) goals that they would like to enable with their prototype. This way, students would have the UX goals in mind when making the storyboard.

6   Conclusion

This paper has reported the development of a two-week intensive UCD course for university-level students in an international setting. The first edition of the course ran in the summer of 2017 and the second edition in the summer of 2018. We have presented and interpreted both qualitative and quantitative data collected from the students during the two editions of the course.

This paper contributes to the limited academic literature on teaching UCD methods, and this paper seems to be the first scientific publication discussing use of GDS in an academic interaction design class. There naturally remains much further work to do. Based on our experiences of the two-week intensive course, where the aim was to teach both user-centred design and hands-on interaction design methods, we propose the following improvements.

First, it seems important to spend a day for setting the scene for the teamwork and the design assignment before starting the GDS. Unlike in companies using GDS, the students on this class did not know each other and had varied educational and cultural backgrounds, therefore the need for team building was higher than normal. Second, UCD starts from understanding the users and the context, but this phase was missing in the 2018 class. In 2019, we are planning to go to the field to learn user research in a real context. Third, most students had just arrived to a foreign city without knowing anyone. Jumping to the intensive five-day GDS seemed to mostly go well, but may have influenced the tiredness of the students the second week. In 2019, the GDS could start the first Wednesday and continue after the weekend break. Fourth, students considered user evaluations highly useful for improving the design, so we need to find a way to integrate the evaluations to the design process. We also need to plan how to find external representatives of the target user group for each team.

Finally, this paper provides a methodological contribution for evaluating the students' course experience. We used the so-called 'Retrospective Hand' as a qualitative evaluation method for our course. In our case, it provided a significant amount of rich and relevant feedback on the design and content of the course. Since the results were promising, further validation of this student feedback collection method would be welcome. We utilized the framework by Steyn et al. [18] for the analysis of the Retrospective Hand data. Due to the different type of our course, the types of students' comments were differing from those in Steyn et al. [18] and we needed to create new categories to classify all comments. However, further work is required to test the categorization framework in other educational contexts. We expect both the categories and definitions of each category to become more comprehensive through future studies. While we find the open answers highly interesting on a smallish class like this, the emerged categories may help develop a quantitative questionnaire for collecting quick feedback on larger classes.

Acknowledgements. We would like to thank Nordplus for granting money to the project and to make it possible to invite students and lecturers to take part in the course. We would like to thank all the students that have participated in the two occasions of the course and given us access to the data which this paper is based on.

References

1. Aggarwal, A.K., Lynn, S.: Using continuous improvement to enhance an online course. Decis. Sci. J. Innovative Educ. **10**(1), 25–48 (2012)
2. Bias, R.G., Marty, P.F., Douglas, I.: Usability/User-centered design in the iSchools: justifying a teaching philosophy. J. Educ. Libr. Inf. Sci. **53**(4), 274–289 (2012)
3. Brooke, J.: SUS: A quick and dirty usability scale. In: Jordan, P.W., Thomas, B., Weerdmeester, B.A., McClelland, I.L. (eds.) Usability Evaluation in Industry, pp. 189–194. Taylor & Francis, London (1996)
4. Cronbach, L.J.: Course improvement through evaluation. Teachers Coll. Rec. **64**, 672–683 (1963)
5. Cronbach, L.J.: Evaluation for course improvement. In: Heath, R.W. (ed.) New Curricula. Harper & Row, New York (1963)
6. Ezzy, D.: Qualitative Analysis: Practice and Innovation. Psychology Press, London (2002)
7. Holtzblatt, K., Wendell, J.B., Wood, S.: Rapid Contextual Design: A How-to Guide to Key Techniques for User-Centered Design. Elsevier, San Francisco (2004)
8. Jia, Y., Larusdottir, M.K., Cajander, Å.: The usage of usability techniques in scrum projects. In: Winckler, M., Forbrig, P., Bernhaupt, R. (eds.) HCSE 2012. LNCS, vol. 7623, pp. 331–341. Springer, Heidelberg (2012). https://doi.org/10.1007/978-3-642-34347-6_25
9. Kaasinen, E., et al.: Defining user experience goals to guide the design of industrial systems. Behav. Inf. Technol. **34**(10), 976–991 (2015)
10. Knapp, J., Zeratsky, J., Kowitz, B.: Sprint: How to Solve Big Problems and Test New Ideas in Just Five Days. Simon and Schuster, New York (2016)

11. Larusdottir, M., Roto, V., Stage, J., Lucero, A.: Get realistic! - UCD course design and evaluation. In: Bogdan, C., Kuusinen, K., Lárusdóttir, M.K., Palanque, P., Winckler, M. (eds.) HCSE 2018. LNCS, vol. 11262, pp. 15–30. Springer, Cham (2019). https://doi.org/10.1007/978-3-030-05909-5_2

12. Lucero, A.: Using affinity diagrams to evaluate interactive prototypes. In: Abascal, J., Barbosa, S., Fetter, M., Gross, T., Palanque, P., Winckler, M. (eds.) INTERACT 2015. LNCS, vol. 9297, pp. 231–248. Springer, Cham (2015). https://doi.org/10.1007/978-3-319-22668-2_19

13. Mattelmäki, T., Lucero, A., Lee, J.-J.: Probing – two perspectives to participation. In: Markopoulos, P., Martens, J.-B., Malins, J., Coninx, K., Liapis, A. (eds.) Collaboration in Creative Design, pp. 33–51. Springer, Cham (2016). https://doi.org/10.1007/978-3-319-29155-0_3

14. Nielsen, J., Molich, R.: Heuristic evaluation of user interfaces. In: Proceedings of the SIGCHI Conference on Human Factors in Computing Systems, pp. 249–256. ACM (1990)

15. Seffah, A., Andreevskaia, A.: Empowering software engineers in human-centered design. In: Proceedings of the 25th International Conference on Software Engineering, pp. 653–658. IEEE Computer Society (2003)

16. Sigurgeirsson, D.B., Daniels, M., Larusdottir, M., Jonsson, B.Þ., Hamdaga, M.: Learning outcome outcomes: an evaluation of quality. In: Proceedings of the 48th Annual Frontiers in Education Conference (FIE). IEEE (2018)

17. Simons, H.: Utilizing evaluation evidence to enhance professional practice. Evaluation **10**(4), 410–429 (2004)

18. Steyn, C., Davies, C., Sambo, A.: Eliciting student feedback for course development: the application of a qualitative course evaluation tool among business research students. Assess. Eval. High. Educ. **44**(1), 11–24 (2019)

19. Urquiza-Fuentes, J., Maximiliano, P.-V.: Investigating the effect of realistic projects on students' motivation, the case of human-computer interaction course. Comput. Hum. Behav. **72**, 692–700 (2017)

Evaluating WELI: A Wrist-Worn Application to Assist Young Adults with Neurodevelopmental Disorders in Inclusive Classes

Hui Zheng[1], Vivian Genaro Motti[1(✉)], Kudirat Giwa-Lawal[2],
Anna Evmenova[2], and Heidi Graff[2]

[1] Volgenau School of Engineering, George Mason University, Fairfax, VA, USA
{hzheng5,vmotti}@gmu.edu
[2] College of Education and Human Development,
George Mason University, Fairfax, USA
{kgiwa,aevmenov,hgraff}@gmu.edu

Abstract. Numerous technologies have been explored to promote independence for neurodiverse individuals in their daily routines. Despite its importance, few applications though have focused on inclusive education for neurodiverse students following a postsecondary education program. Academic assistance for neurodiverse students still relies mainly on human intervention, leaving promising opportunities for wearable solutions to be explored. While some assistive wearable solutions exist, they have rarely been evaluated in field studies. It is unclear how neurodiverse students can benefit from the unobtrusiveness and consistency of wearable support in academic classes. To understand the effectiveness of assistive wearables for neurodiverse students in inclusive classes, we conducted a user study comprising 58 classes in a postsecondary inclusive setting. We developed and evaluated WELI (Wearable Life), an assistive wearable application that supports the communication between neurodiverse students and their assistants, providing interventions through smartwatches and smartphones. The results show that students are satisfied with WELI and that interventions should be primarily driven by context and events. Focus and Rewards stood out as the most helpful features implemented.

Keywords: Accessibility · Wearable · HCI · Smartwatch · Mobile · Neurodevelopmental disorder · IDDs · Autism · Inclusive education

1 Introduction

Neurodevelopmental disorders (including Autism Spectrum Disorders, Attention Deficit and Hyperactivity, Cerebral Palsy, and Down Syndrome) limit individuals' abilities to process and record information, manage time, regulate affective states, and interact with others. These limitations affect executive functioning and often result in difficulties for the individuals to integrate in society and live

© IFIP International Federation for Information Processing 2019
Published by Springer Nature Switzerland AG 2019
D. Lamas et al. (Eds.): INTERACT 2019, LNCS 11747, pp. 114–134, 2019.
https://doi.org/10.1007/978-3-030-29384-0_7

independently. Attending classes, finding and sustaining a job, and maintaining relationships are examples of daily activities that can be disproportionately challenging for people with neurodevelopmental disorders.

To successfully perform activities of daily living and better integrate themselves in society, individuals with neurodevelopmental disorders often require support from a personal assistant who continuously monitors them and intervenes when necessary. As these interventions are mostly and traditionally performed through human support, they tend to be costly, obtrusive, stigmatizing, and not scalable. There is a promising potential for technological solutions through wearable applications to support such interventions in a more scalable, unobtrusive, consistent, and less stigmatizing way.

A growing number of emerging technologies have been recently explored to assist individuals with neurodevelopmental disorders [1–3,30]. These solutions include interactive systems, games [4], mobile and wearable apps [5]. The application features include: teaching educational content, providing mood regulation, intervention tools, and exercises to sustain focus and attention [3]. The delivery formats for these assistive technologies range from tablets [6] and smartphones [7], to wearable computers [1] and physical installations [8].

Although the main target population for assistive technologies involves individuals with disabilities, some applications aim at supporting caregivers [9], assistants [26], parents, and teachers [10]. Prior work addressed the following neurodiverse conditions using assistive technologies: Down Syndrome, Autism Spectrum Disorders (ASD), Attention Deficit and Hyperactivity Disorders (ADHD), and Cerebral Palsy (CP) [30]. In the U.S., neurodevelopmental disorders affect 1 out of 6 children [11,12]. Their prevalence has increased 17% between 1997 and 2008 [11]. Neurodevelopmental disorders have lifelong consequences for individuals. In this context, technology can provide several benefits to them: (1) close contact with users; (2) remote and continuous monitoring; (3) record keeping of data for later analysis; (4) prompt interventions; and (5) reduced stigma.

Despite several opportunities and benefits associated to wearable technologies, they have been underexplored as assistive technologies for individuals with neurodevelopmental disorders. Also, the evaluation of assistive wearables have been carried out mostly in controlled settings during short periods [13]. To shed light on how smartwatch applications can assist postsecondary students with neurodevelopmental disorders in inclusive classrooms, we developed and evaluated WELI (Wearable Life) – a wearable application implemented to support neurodiverse students in mood regulation, interventions, reminders, and communication with their assistants. WELI was evaluated in a long-term IRB-approved study including two field studies in actual classes during two academic semesters.

The studies include data collected from users log (history of user interaction), focus groups, interviews, and questionnaires. The methods include two field studies, each carried out throughout one semester. The first study involved 11 participants – six neurodiverse students and their assistants. The second study involved 10 participants – six neurodiverse students and their assistants. The results show that the assistants find the application helpful to facilitate their job, and are willing to use it in inclusive classes. Additionally, most students find the application beneficial. Also, they feel proud wearing a smartwatch, and would like to continue using it in the future. Still, we noticed that there are situations in which the application may not fulfill specific needs of some users.

2   Related Work

A number of technologies to assist users with diverse abilities have been investigated by the scientific community in the past decades. Assistive wearables specifically, besides having a large potential for applications, also foster user acceptance, engagement and adoption due to their versatility, novelty, and conventional look [5,14]. Despite their promising potential and increasing popularity, the applications of wearables to assist neurodiverse users remain limited.

Assistive Wearables for the Users with Neurodevelopmental Disorders. Prior research on assistive wearables focuses on helping children with neurodevelopmental disorders for multiple purposes. To improve socialization for the children, TellMe uses interactive robot characters (incorporating microphone, sensors, and actuators) embedded in clothing to treat ASD symptoms of boys by encouraging them to speak out and express themselves while playing with the interactive robot characters on their clothing [2]. EnhancedTouch uses a bracelet with LED lights to provide visual feedback and augment human–human touch events (handshake) for children with ASD [15]. VRSocial uses virtual reality glasses to facilitate the proximity regulation in social communication for children with ASD, which augments the conversations between children with ASD and an avatar with the real-time visualizations of proximity, speaker volume, and duration of one's speech in VR [16].

Besides socialization, prior research on assistive wearables aimed at helping children in other aspects. For example, WatchMe is a prototype implemented to manage behavioral problems in children with neurodevelopmental disorders (Down Syndrome and ASD). The watch detects hand banging and delivers instructional interventions with visual-haptic cards [17]. CASTT (Child Activity Sensing and Training Tool) is a real-time assistive prototype that captures activities and assists the child in maintaining attention [3]. BlurtLine is an interactive belt aimed at supporting children with ADHD to control their impulsive speaking in classroom settings [18].

Several assistive wearables focus on helping not only children but also adults. For example, ProCom facilitates proximity awareness for individuals with ASD using chest-worn wearables with an infrared sensor module that connects to a mobile app to show the changes of distance and zones of proximity [19]. FOQUS is a smartwatch app that alleviates the anxiety and stress of adults with ADHD by providing tools for time management, guided meditation, and positive message priming [20,21]. Takt relies on touch and vision to enable individuals with ADHD to tell and read information of a clock using their senses (instead of relying on cognitive abilities) [1]. StretchBand is a wrist-band developed to analyze anxiety levels of adults with Autism by recording the user interaction with a digital stretch band [22].

Recent studies on assistive wearables focus mostly on children as the target population, rather than young adults. Furthermore, most studies support one unique feature at a time, e.g. communication or mood regulation. Most applications do not have a target scenario, and the evaluation is short and performed in controlled settings rather than in the field. Although the form factors of assistive wearable vary, including belts and chest-bands, wrist-worn wearables stand out among the solutions analyzed, possibly due to their conventional looks and versatility in terms of implementation, data collection, user interfaces, and interaction.

Design Considerations for Neurodiverse Users. The design approaches for technologies for special education must ensure a full understanding of the domain through user-centric design, seeking to facilitate the adoption of technology with solutions that are unobtrusive as well as easy to use and to adopt [9]. According to existing research guidelines for work with participants with disabilities [23]: (1) participants with disabilities should be directly involved with research; (2) they should be recruited with clear criteria; (3) collaboration with a group that focuses on the related disabilities should be established; (4) investigators should conduct primarily qualitative studies or a hybrid of quantitative and qualitative research, doing in-depth investigations to deal with small sample sizes; and (5) modifications to research methods for people with cognitive disabilities need to be made based on advice of those familiar with the specific cognitive disability. For Alper et al. (2012), four principles help to address the needs of end-users focusing on their perspectives rather than developers' mental models, namely: deep engagement, interdisciplinarity, individuality, and practicality [24]. We followed the design considerations and principles mentioned above to guide our field study, to ensure that the solution proposed meet actual users' needs, suit their individual abilities and preferences, and have a larger potential to be adopted in practical settings in a sustained way.

3 Evaluation Study

Unlike prior work on assistive wearables, evaluated briefly in controlled settings, WELI was assessed in a long-term evaluation in inclusive classrooms with young adults with neurodevelopmental disorders. More specifically, we conducted two field studies over two semesters. The studies were conducted in collaboration with a postsecondary academic program. Aiming at external validity, the studies took place in actual inclusive classes. The first study was carried out in the Fall 2017, and included 11 participants, being 6 neurodiverse students and 5 assistants. The second study took place in Spring 2018, including 10 participants – 6 students and 4 assistants. In the studies, the students and their assistants used WELI, a wearable and mobile application that facilitates assistance and communication in class. Assistants aided the students on demand as they traditionally do; however, instead of intervening verbally, they used WELI on smartphones and smartwatches to deliver the interventions in more unobtrusive and potentially less stigmatizing way.

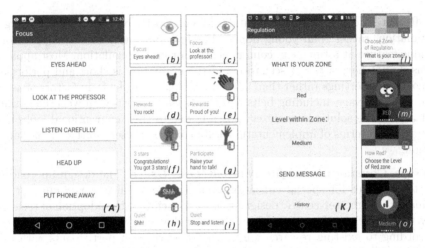

Fig. 1. WELI: examples of passive interactions are illustrated on the left (A), where assistants can choose in the mobile phone menu and send Focus–related interventions to the students' smartwatches (b to g); watch notifications are for Focus (b, c), Rewards (d, e, f), Participate prompt (g), and Quiet messages (h, i). Examples of active interaction are illustrated on the right, where the assistants can send assessment questions (K) via the phone, and the student can answer the questions using the smartwatch (l to o).

3.1 WELI (Wearable Life)

To attend a postsecondary program, students with neurodevelopmental disorders take inclusive classes accompanied by their assistants. The assistants help the students using verbal interventions and gestures. WELI was designed and developed through user-centered design following 8 user studies with 58 participants [26–28]. WELI supports coordination between young adults with neurodevelopmental disorders and their assistants in class. With a mobile and wearable solution [29], WELI (Fig. 1) fosters a more conducive environment for inclusive learning, enabling discreet communication without verbal interventions. WELI provides more unobtrusive assistance to neurodiverse students, minimizing disturbance to classmates and instructors and reducing the stigma of having an assistant visibly coaching students aloud in class. WELI delivers multimodal notifications of text messages and graphics on a smartwatch to students after a quick vibration. Interventions are timely, sent automatically or manually, triggered by the mobile app of WELI by an assistant. WELI has seven main features:

- **Focus:** helps students to concentrate in class;
- **Quiet:** moderates students' conversations and voice volume in class;
- **Participate:** helps students to be engaged in class;
- **Rewards:** gives students a positive reinforcement when they perform well;
- **Assessment:** enables students to self-assess their own mood (regulation);
- **Survey:** gathers feedback from students about their feelings after class;
- **Take a Break:** delivers a countdown reminder before a class break.

WELI includes two intervention styles: *passive*, without a reply, requiring the student to simply read the notification displayed on the smartwatch, sent by the assistant; and *active*, requiring the student to reply to the questions sent by the assistant and prompted on the smartwatch. The student answers are delivered to the assistant's phone. Among all features implemented, Focus, Quiet, Participation, and Rewards are passive, while Assessment, Survey, and Take a Break are active interventions that require a response. WELI has been developed on Android Wear OS, thus it can be conveniently used on different off-the-shelf commercial devices. For the evaluation studies, we employed a Sony Smartwatch 3 and a Moto G5 Plus smartphone.

4   Field Study: Assessing WELI

Field studies are suitable for technologies that are used in specific settings, such as inclusive classrooms. To evaluate WELI, two field studies were conducted in classes of an inclusive postsecondary education program during two semesters. The college-level inclusive classes met up to two times a week for 75 min at most. To avoid disturbing students taking classes and respect their privacy, video was not recorded but usage logs were recorded to collect app data in class. We applied a questionnaire and conducted a focus group after each semester for assessment.

The study participants, students with neurodevelopmental disorders and assistants, are young adults, English-speakers, of diverse ethnicities and genders. They were recruited by purposeful sampling [25] from Mason LIFE, a special education program. The students take college-level courses and special education classes. They understand and command expressive language and are technologically competent. They are able to willingly accept or decline participation in the study. The assistants are graduate or senior undergraduate students, majoring in Public Health, Education, and Psychology. Participation in the study was voluntary.

4.1   Study Protocol

Before the field study, each student and assistant received training to use WELI. In each class, the assistant observed the student and assisted them using WELI on a smartphone. The students wore a smartwatch to receive the haptic, text, and graphic notifications. Each student was paired with an assistant for the semester. The assistants followed traditional work practices to guide and assist students as needed. However, their communication was supported by WELI to assess its impacts in class interventions.

Features Evaluated. To avoid overwhelming the students and assistants in class, 6 features were selected for evaluation: Focus, Quiet, Participation, Rewards, Assessment, and Survey (Fig. 1). The usage of the features was on demand, i.e. based on student behaviors, except for the Survey, which was sent close to the end of each class to get the students' feedback.

Based on the feedback from the first study, we evaluated all WELI features in a follow-up study, including Take a Break and Customize which were added thanks to the feedback from the first study.

Logs of the User Interaction. To respect students' privacy, we did not record video in class. We strived to not overload the assistants, respecting their workload that includes observing the students, intervening when needed, and taking notes of the lecture. We recorded logs of app usage in class, including all interventions, messages sent from the mobile app and responses sent from the smartwatch. For each interaction, we logged the notification content and feature category with date and time. To allow data sharing with the investigators after class, we implemented a share function in WELI using gmail. The data was logged to monitor and analyze how the participants used WELI in classroom activities.

Follow-Up Study. We conducted follow-up surveys and focus groups after the field studies at the end of each semester. We employed questionnaires to gather student and assistant feedback on their experiences with WELI in class, and we conducted focus groups with the assistants to discuss WELI and assess its impacts on their workload and benefits to the students. Limitations and opportunities for improvement were also discussed. To evaluate WELI, we analyzed the data collected from all these studies.

5   Evaluation Results

5.1   First Field Study

The first field study occurred in the Fall 2017. Six neurodiverse students and five assistants volunteered to participate. One student withdrew during the first study. The five remaining students (3 male and 2 female, all white) were enrolled in four to six classes when using WELI. Their age ranged from 22 to 26 years old. They were in the 4th year of the postsecondary program. One student had both ID (Intellectual Disability) and ASD, one student had ASD, one had both ASD and ADHD, one had ID and CP, and one had ID. The five assistants were female, being three undergraduate and two graduate students majoring in Public Health and Special Education. We applied a questionnaire for the students and assistants at the end of the semester to evaluate WELI. To gather additional feedback about WELI, a 1-h focus group was conducted with the assistants.

5.2   Results of the Log Analysis

At the end of the study, we analyzed the log files of 24 classes, including 21 classes from the five students who participated in the entire study. The log analysis indicates the features that were used the most, how the intervention messages were used, and how usage varied in time, frequency and nature during classes.

Frequency of Usage per Feature. To assess the usage of different interventions in class, we counted the messages exchanged for each feature for all classes. To clarify, for the Assessment and Survey features requiring a student reply, we only accounted for the number of questions sent to treat it as one single action, without counting the answers repeatedly. In total, 431 messages were exchanged. The operations per feature used in class in order of frequency were:

- Focus: 162 (38%), Rewards: 133 (31%)
- Quiet: 57 (13%), Assessment: 37 (8.5%), Survey: 35 (8%)
- Participate: 7 (2%)

These results indicate that Focus and positive reinforcement (Rewards) are relevant for students, as they exceed 60% of all operations.

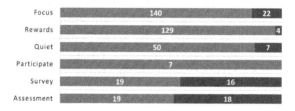

Fig. 2. The Notice Rate for each intervention in the first study. Per feature, there were messages successfully noticed (green bars) or ignored (blue bars). (Color figure online)

Notice Rate of the Features. Analyzing the logs, we found that the same message was sent consecutively sometimes in less than 1-min interval. In the focus group, the assistants mentioned situations where students did not notice, read, or react to the message on the smartwatch. In these cases, the assistant re-sent the notification until it was successfully delivered and perceived by the student. To identify how the students responded to the interventions, whether they noticed (read the message and reacted to it) or ignored it, we analyzed the 'notice rates' of the messages sent. We categorized repeated interaction patterns as follows: when the same message was sent consecutively within the 1-min interval for those passive notifications (not requiring a reply), and when the question did not receive responses for those active features requiring a reply. Otherwise, the interaction was considered successful.

Figure 2 shows notice rates of each feature. First, we analyzed four passive features: 129 out of 133 Rewards (97%) messages were noticed at once. Focus (142/162, 87.7%) and Quiet (50/57, 87.7%) messages had the same high success rate. Only seven Participate messages were delivered successfully, which left few possibilities for the student to disregard it. The reason why the Rewards had a higher notice rate might be because students are keen on receiving the positive reinforcement and barely miss them. For the features asking the reply, Survey got 54.3% (19/35) and Assessment had 51.4% (19/37) of messages replied by the students. The extra effort to provide input on the smartwatch might justify the lower success rate for Survey and Assessment. Survey had a higher success rate probably because it was sent after the class or near its end.

Temporal Analysis of Features. All the students who participated in the study were enrolled in 75-min courses. To analyze the temporal distribution of user interactions, we divided the classes into five intervals of 15 min each. The first interval corresponds to the time period during the first 15 min of each class, the second one ranges from 15 to 30 min, and so on.

To analyze the usage of WELI throughout the classes, for each student we calculated the average number of messages sent in each interval per class. Figure 3 shows the usage of WELI throughout the class intervals per student, and in each class interval it shows the average usage frequencies of two main features (Focus and Rewards) as well as the remaining features. Although we cannot identify any time patterns in WELI usage across all students, we note that student 2 required less interventions than the other four students. Also, we noticed more interventions during the second half of classes for 3 out of 5 students. Overall, Focus was the most common intervention for all students (P1, P3, and P5), except for student 4, who received more Rewards for positive reinforcement. The usage of Focus and Rewards varied across classes per student, but all students received both interventions in all class intervals (except student 2).

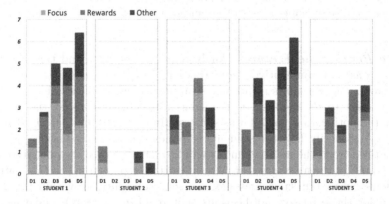

Fig. 3. Average usage of WELI features throughout the five 15-min class intervals (D1 to D5) per student in the first study, indicating the usage of Focus (orange), Rewards (green), and other (blue). (Color figure online)

Sequential Analysis of Features. To identify potential trends for intervention sequences, we discarded all the unnoticed messages and counted the sequences for each two successive operations. The results show that after a Focus intervention, the following interventions are mostly Focus (55%) again, showing that sustained interventions are needed when assisting neurodiverse students to concentrate. Additionally, 28% interventions after Focus are Rewards, showing the importance of positive reinforcement (after the students focus in class the assistant often encourages them). After a Rewards intervention, 44% are Rewards again, and 31% are Focus, which indicated that assistants try to sustain and encourage students' engagement.

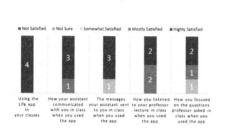

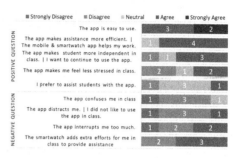

Fig. 4. The results of the questionnaire with 4 students who participated in the Study 1 concerning app usage, communication, messages, attention, and focus.

Fig. 5. The results of the questionnaire of 5 assistants in the first study. The top part includes 7 positive statements and the lower part shows 5 negative statements.

5.3 Results of the Questionnaires

Students' Responses. To assess the students' perceptions and experiences with WELI, at the end of the academic semester, we applied a 5-question questionnaire to the five students who participated in the entire study and received four qualified answers (one was discarded due to extreme answering bias [23]).

Overall, the students' responses were positive (Fig. 4). They were satisfied using WELI in their classes, and very satisfied with the communication between them and their assistants. They were also highly or mostly satisfied with how they listened to the class with WELI support. Concerning 'focus on the question the professor asked' and general 'messages sent to you by WELI' questions, one out of four students reported to be 'somewhat satisfied'. To triangulate the results and avoid acquiescence bias, we also asked the four assistants about their students' performance in class using WELI. All assistants reported to be very satisfied with WELI concerning how it motivates their students to be more engaged in class; three assistants were highly satisfied with WELI concerning how it helped their students with 'listening' skills, improved their ability to complete assignments and to follow the professor's instructions in class. One assistant reported to be 'somewhat satisfied' and 'not sure' about those aspects. The results suggest that WELI can improve the students' engagement and performance in class and that most students were satisfied with the communication and interventions they received via WELI. As expected, there were some variations on responses depending on the student though.

Assistants' Responses. In the first field study, we also applied a questionnaire to the five assistants. The experience of one assistant was limited to four classes since his/her student was not present in all classes. The questions focused on the assistants' opinions about using the application in what regards assistance, work impact, the students' reactions to WELI, as well as the benefits of the features used in class. We grouped questions that received similar responses to facilitate the presentation of the results. We presented 7 questions using positive statements and 5 using negative ones (Fig. 5).

All assistants (strongly) agreed that WELI is easy to use. Four assistants thought WELI made the assistance more efficient and helped their work in class without confusing or distracting them. Most assistants agreed on the aid and usability of WELI. Most assistants (3 out of 5) also wanted to continue using WELI in class and agreed that WELI made their students more independent (one was neutral and one disagreed). Most assistants were neutral about the preference to assist the student with WELI, which may due to the extra effort reported that the smartwatch added to them (3 agreed and 2 disagreed) when comparing it to the traditional assistance.

There were two multiple choice questions about the most and least useful features previously used in class. For the most useful features, Rewards and Focus received five votes, Quiet and Participate received two, Assessment received one. For the least useful features, Assessment and Survey received three votes. This result is nearly consistent with the frequency of feature usage from the log files, except for the Participate feature (2% in the log). Concerning the open questions, the assistants suggested WELI should enable customized messages to be more personalized to the student, including also a favorite page to access frequent messages faster and improve efficiency.

5.4   Results of the Focus Group

To complement, compare and contrast responses from the questionnaire, we conducted a one-hour focus group with five assistants. We discussed the pros and the cons of WELI, whether and how WELI facilitated their work, impacted the students, and asked for suggestions. A coordinator of the inclusive program and two designers facilitated and moderated the session. For documentation, the focus group was video recorded and notes were taken.

The **benefits** of WELI included making the assistance 'less obvious' by not requiring loud 'talk' to provide assistance as WELI provided 'discrete communication'. The 'buzz' along with the notification on smartwatch helped wake students up when they were sleepy. The **drawback** noted is that WELI was 'a bit distracting' to one student who was always 'paying attention to the watch'.

Concerning **usability**, four assistants judged WELI as 'user friendly' and 'easy to use and learn'. One assistant found initially challenging to 'find the right message in the menu'. Regarding how WELI facilitates the assistants' work, they reported that it could further 'encourage the student' by providing 'Rewards' 'consistently' and by providing 'feedback' from the student via WELI. For the workload, the assistants mentioned that sometimes the messages were not noticed by the student at first, so that they had to re-send it. For the **impact on students**, the students were 'excited' to use WELI in class, i.e. one student 'took off his Apple watch and wore WELI watch' in every class. Another student was proud and 'showed the watch to his classmates'. One assistant told that her student 'got better' with WELI, and she had to send *less interventions* because her student improved his behavior. Other assistant was able to *'sit farther away'* from her student thanks to WELI which allowed the student to become *'more independent'*. A student got 'a little frustrated' because he used to 'talk a lot' and still wanted to 'talk face-to-face' to get help in class. 'Focus', 'Rewards' and 'Quiet' were very useful **features** and the pictures showed in the notifications were appreciated. Sometimes the vibration of the watch was not long enough to notice. Also, the assistants suggested WELI to allow them add the student's name for each 'Rewards' message. Lastly, they wanted to be able to send 'customized' messages to the students in addition to the standard ones available in WELI.

5.5   Second Field Study

Customization Feature. Based on the feedback from the focus group in the first study, we extended the vibration, allowed assistants to add the student's name for Rewards, and added the Customize feature to WELI (Fig. 6). This feature made WELI more personalized, allowing assistants to add interventions that met specific needs of each student.

The second field study was conducted in the Spring 2018. Six neurodiverse students volunteered to participate, along with their four designated assistants. Among them, one student and two assistants had participated in the first field study. For field study 2, one student withdrew due to sleep issues. The remaining five students took five to eight classes with WELI. In total, we collected and analyzed log data from 34 classes. The five students who participated in the study included three male and two female participants, ranging from 21 to 26 years old. Two of them are Asian-American, two are White, and one is African-American. Two of them had ID, one had ID and ADHD, two had ASD and PDD (Pervasive Development Delay). The four assistants included one male and three female, being two senior students majoring in Psychology and Education, and two graduate students majoring in Public Health and Special Education. According to the feedback from the first study, we made the vibration for notifications on watch longer and evaluated two additional features in the second study: Customize and Take a Break.

Analogously to the first study, we applied a questionnaire to students and assistants in the end of the semester and conducted a one-hour focus group with the assistants.

5.6   Results of the Log Analysis

Frequency of Usage of WELI Features. In total 818 messages were exchanged, sorted by frequency, the number of operations per feature in class was:

Fig. 6. Customize feature enables assistant to add personalized messages for students (A). Each student has a list of customized messages (B), through which assistant can send notifications (c, d) to students.

Fig. 7. The Notice Rate for each intervention in Study 2. Per feature, the messages were either successfully noticed (green bar) or ignored (blue bar). (Color figure online)

– Focus: 588 (71%), Rewards: 124 (15%)
– Quiet, Participate, Customize: 17 (2%) each
– Survey: 32 (4%), Assessment: 20 (2.4%)
– Take a Break: 4 (0.5%)

As in the first study, Focus was the most popular intervention for students. Rewards was used oftentimes, and the other features were sparsely used.

Notice Rate of WELI Features. Figure 7 shows the notice rate of each feature. Focus (68.5%, 403/588), Customize (68.8%, 11/16), Assessment (70%, 14/20), Quiet (70.6%, 12/17), and Participate (70.6%, 12/17) had very similar notice rates (around 70%). For the four passive features, the notice rate of Rewards (96%, 119/124) is as high as in the first study, suggesting the students like to receive the Rewards messages. Comparing to Rewards, Focus, Quiet and Participate received lower notice rates. For other features requiring a reply, Survey (93.8%, 30/32), used near or after the end of class, was almost never disregarded. All four Take a Break messages were noticed successfully. Assessment and Survey had much higher notice rates than in the first study, most likely due to longer vibrations.

Temporal Analysis of Features. Figure 8 presents the average usage of WELI features throughout the five intervals for all classes per student. We notice no trends in the usage of WELI among all students along time. However, we notice two patterns in usage. Pattern 1 (students 2 and 3) received fewer interventions than the others. Being that student 2 and 3 received less than 1.5 interventions on average for the first 4 intervals and around 2 messages in the last interval when the survey was sent. Pattern 2 (students 4, 5 and 6) received more than 5 average interventions for all class duration. Compared to the pattern 2, Focus is not the main message received for pattern 1 (students 2 and 3), especially for student 2 who received few focus messages and more other messages including rewards. For pattern 2 (students 4, 5 and 6), focus stands out among all interventions, being more popular than rewards and any other messages. These two patterns might indicate that neurodiverse students who have focus issues need more interventions in class. Similarly to the first study, there is a relationship between the number of focus messages exchanged and overall usage of WELI for the students 4, 5 and 6. In other words, when students received more focus in one duration, they use more WELI in that duration. For Rewards, student 5 and 6 received rewards in all class duration, students 2 and 4 received them in 4 duration, and student 3 only received it in the first duration. Another interesting aspect is that the students 4 and 6 had the same assistant. Although their interventions show different patterns, we notice a similar behavior from their assistant in both cases, since she sent much more messages than other assistants (total of 17 messages for student 4 and total of 14 messages for student 6 for a single duration). While, the maximum number of messages exchanged by the other assistants was 8 in the second study. We note that the interventions varied among different students but there might be a potential similarity regarding the assistant work style.

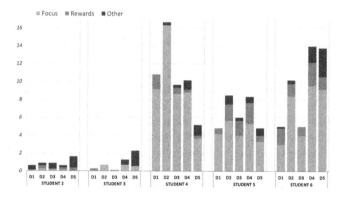

Fig. 8. WELI usage for the five 15-min class intervals per student in the second study. The average usage of Focus (orange), Rewards (green) and Others (blue) per class interval are shown, ranging from D1 (1st time interval) to D5 (5th time interval). (Color figure online)

Sequential Analysis of Features. As in the first study, the results of the second study show that after Focus, 73.7% interventions are again Focus. Also, the second most common intervention after Focus is Rewards (16.5%). After Rewards, 25.2% interventions are Rewards again. Focus (61.3%) is the most likely intervention to follow a Rewards. We note the need for sustained interventions when helping students to focus in class. There are less Rewards sent consecutively than in Study 1, and also a larger number of Focus.

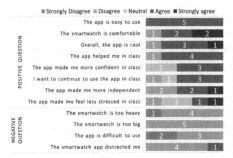

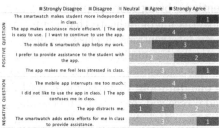

Fig. 9. The questionnaire results of 5 students in the second study. The top part includes 8 positive statements and the lower includes 4 negative statements.

Fig. 10. The questionnaire results of 4 assistants from the second study. 7 questions in positive statements (top), and 5 negative statements (bottom).

5.7   Results of the Questionnaire

As in the first study, we also applied a follow-up questionnaire to students and assistants who participated in Study 2.

Students' Responses. The questionnaire included 12 questions, responded by five students of the second study. Figure 9 shows the results. For the smartwatch, most students (4 of 5) agree it is 'comfortable' and no students judged it as too heavy or too big. All students believe WELI is 'easy to use' and 4 students agreed that WELI is 'cool' and helped them in class (only one disagreed). Most students were not 'distracted' by the smartwatch in class, except one. Most students (3) felt more confident in class with WELI and 2 were neutral. Most students (3) agreed WELI made them more independent and want to continue using WELI in class. There are mixed responses from students on whether WELI made them feel less stressed. Most students liked the smartwatch, and thought WELI helped them in multiple aspects in class, e.g. making them feel more comfortable. Some students have opposite feelings. This requires more in-depth studies to assess whether an *excessive* number of interventions causes more stress to students.

Assistants' Responses. In the second study, we applied the same questionnaire as in the first study to the 4 assistants (Fig. 10). All assistants agreed that WELI is 'easy to use', without confusing or interrupting their work, but making assistance more efficient by helping them. They also believe that it enabled the students to be more independent in class, and they wanted to continue using WELI. In comparison to the first study, there was overall a higher positive response about WELI on various aspects. However, there are neutral opinions about: the 'preference' to assist the student using WELI, WELI making their work 'less stressful' or more 'distracting' to them. Compared to the first study, only one assistant thought WELI added 'extra effort' to their workload. Overall, the assistants gave very positive feedback about using WELI in practice.

For multi-choice questions about the most useful features in class, three assistants chose 'Focus, Rewards, Quiet' and one assistant chose 'Focus, Rewards, Customize'. The Focus and Rewards were indeed the most used features according to the log analysis which validates such preference. Only one assistant chose 'Customize' rather than 'Quiet' as the third favorite feature. We noticed in logs that indeed one assistant sent more customized interventions than others. Concerning the open questions, three assistants suggested that WELI should allow the student to initiate the communication with them.

5.8   Results of the Focus Group

Analogously to the first study, in the second study we conducted a focus group with the four assistants. Among them, 3 assistants helped 3 students, and one helped 3 students in 3 different classes.

Among the **benefits** of WELI, most assistants found it supportive to the assistance and to the students, by 'consistently' helping the students with 'Focus' and with positive reinforcement through the 'Rewards' feature. Most students 'enjoyed' and 'loved' WELI and never felt 'bored' or 'tired' of it. One student had 'focus' issues, but with WELI he 'would look at the professor and try hard to focus and stay in class more' rather than 'gaze out the window or want to leave class' as before. The student was 'kind of attached to the smartwatch' and 'wanted to have it for his other classes as well' as a 'physical reminder' of behavior moderation even without receiving any intervention. One assistant sent his student customized messages like 'take your notebook out and leave the phone away' a few times and then her student *remembered* these customized messages as she would *perform the corresponding actions* each class even without receiving them. One assistant told her student became more independent with WELI, because in other classes without WELI the student kept asking her questions and 'relied more on her'.

Among the **limitations** pointed, one assistant mentioned that WELI worked well for her student in the first study but not in the second, as her student was neither interested nor responding, due to external factors. One assistant told that it was hard to help her student with discussions in class as the student would be often 'off-topic' and she used 'Take a Break' but her student did not want to come back, so she had to go out to call him back. While WELI may help assistants to locate their students, it may not help in engaging them in activities that they are not willing to participate in. Two assistants noticed that his/her student would be too excited when receiving 'Rewards' messages like 'you rock'. They suggested sending only 'thumbs up' or 'well done' as "milder" positive rewards. One assistant mentioned that she was about to use 'customized' feature in class, but she was afraid that editing and adding the message would take time necessary to observe and intervene with her student.

For **suggestions**, two assistants mentioned the students 'had trouble sliding on the watch' interface to answer questions for survey and assessment. They suggested to add brief instructions about the sliding direction with the question (an arrow prompt). Three assistants suggested to prepare 'customized' messages and add those as generic prompts, since most students will need them. Three assistants also wanted WELI to allow students to initiate the communication with them, so that they could know when the student wanted a 'restroom', 'water' or a 'longer break'. As WELI records the number of 'Rewards' to send stars, one assistant suggested to design a rule to transfer these stars to actual 'prizes' to further encourage students along the semester.

6   Discussion

Triangulation. From the analysis of the data collected from two user studies, triangulating methods was essential. Talking to assistants in the focus groups helped to validate (or to refute) findings based the initial log analysis. The questionnaires provided more comprehensive information, besides complementing the findings from focus groups.

Usage of WELI. Concerning the features, we learned the importance of Focus to help neurodiverse students in class and also of Rewards as positive reinforcement. There was no unified pattern in the interventions' frequency and time across students. However, there were some patterns depending on the intervention, e.g. Focus was more frequent than other interventions for some students. No unified usage patterns on time also proved that assistance is primarily driven by events and context (not time), and customized per student. It also indicated that the assistant interventions are indispensable, but can benefit from applications like WELI to improve their work efficiency, consistency and accountability, rather than replacing them.

Students. There is a fine trade-off in the assistance provided, leading to mixed results, in other words, the students who performed well and needed less intervention are not the key beneficiaries of some features (e.g. Focus, Quiet), as WELI would prove itself to be less useful for them. On the other hand, students who do not perform very well, e.g. having focus issues in class, get more help from WELI. What we learn is that we should provide two modes in WELI, one offering more functions to intervene and improve students' performance in class, and another dedicated to functions such as positive reinforcement or self regulation to encourage students to be more independent. The assistant could switch modes for the same student depending on his or her performance in class. As one assistant mentioned, her student "performed very well and focused with the help with app, except that he had bad days". We need further studies to verify the long term impacts of WELI, hypothesizing that the longer the students use the application, the less they need it, and also to identify the specific contexts in which WELI does not lend the expected results.

Assistant. Besides the diverse needs of each student, we noticed that the assistant style may impact the effectiveness of WELI. Although assistants send interventions on demand, based on the student's behaviors in class, we noticed certain tendencies of the assistant with the log analysis, Those include, one assistant always sent the student 'Smiley face' and 'Thumbs Up' at the beginning (the first minute) of the class like a greeting message. Another assistant helped two students for two different classes. Although the help the two students received was different, they received more interventions than all other participants of the study, and that assistant mentioned in focus group that her student 'took off the smartwatch once, which may due to the delivery of so many interventions to him'. We plan to add some restrictions on WELI and study protocol, and to improve the training, to prevent such situations in the future and to protect students from unnecessary stress.

External Factors. External factors had a strong influence in the evaluation of WELI in class. These factors are not always under the control of the evaluator but should be considered carefully, for instance by triangulating results from alternative methods, carefully selecting participants, and reaching out to a larger number of users. As two assistants informed us, there was one participant whose medication had recently been changed, therefore he/she was still in an adaptation process and was distracted in class. Hence, regardless of the format the intervention, it would not be effective.

7   Conclusion

Overall, the users had a positive response to use WELI. Also, certain students seemed to benefit the most from the wearable assistance than others. We believe that there is a threshold in the neurodiversity spectrum in which the solution not only help to assist the students but also to train them to become more independent in what regards self-regulation and attention. Focus and rewards interventions stood out as most used features for the assistance inclusive class in the wearable format. We did not find a universal temporal pattern of the interventions sent throughout the class intervals, indicating that the next-generation assistive technology for neurodiverse students following inclusive classes should rely neither on time nor on sequence of interventions, but be context as well as event-driven.

Individual profiles of students must be taken into account as well. Unsurprisingly, neurodiverse users have heterogeneous behaviors, therefore the assistance model should be flexible and distinct enough to accommodate for their individual characteristics. While this project helped to unveil the usefulness of wearable assistance to neurodiverse students, there are open questions we would like to explore further in the future. Those include, the implementation and assessment of functions to allow student to trigger the assistance through the watch, to intervene the 'off-topic' problem for discussion in class, to design enough messages to intervene in the students' behaviors not causing distraction or over-excitement, and to add a function to track student's location during class break by using the built-in GPS in the watch.

References

1. Eriksson, S., Gustafsson, F., Larsson, G., Hansen, P.: Takt: the wearable timepiece that enables sensory perception of time. In Proceedings of the 2017 ACM Conference Companion Publication on Designing Interactive Systems (DIS 2017 Companion), pp. 223–227. ACM, New York (2017). https://doi.org/10.1145/3064857.3079150
2. Helen, K.: 'TellMe': therapeutic clothing for children with autism spectrum disorder (ASD) in daily life. In: Proceedings of the 2014 ACM International Symposium on Wearable Computers: Adjunct Program (ISWC 2014 Adjunct), pp. 55–58. ACM, New York (2014). https://doi.org/10.1145/2641248.2641278
3. Sonne, T., Grønbæk, K.: Designing assistive technologies for the ADHD domain. In: Serino, S., Matic, A., Giakoumis, D., Lopez, G., Cipresso, P. (eds.) MindCare 2015. CCIS, vol. 604, pp. 259–268. Springer, Cham (2016). https://doi.org/10.1007/978-3-319-32270-4_26
4. Caro, K., Tentori, M., Martinez-Garcia, I., Zavala-Ibarra, I.: FroggyBobby: an exergame to support children with motor problems practicing motor coordination exercises during therapeutic interventions. Comput. Hum. Behav. **71**, 479–498 (2017). https://doi.org/10.1016/j.chb.2015.05.055
5. Benssassi, E.M., Gomez, J., Boyd, L.E., Hayes, G.R., Ye, J.: Wearable assistive technologies for autism: opportunities and challenges. IEEE Pervasive Comput. **17**(2), 11–21 (2018). https://doi.org/10.1109/MPRV.2018.022511239
6. Fage, C.: An emotion regulation app for school inclusion of children with ASD: design principles and preliminary results for its evaluation. SIGACCESS Access. Comput. **112**, 8–15 (2015). https://doi.org/10.1145/2809915.2809917
7. Escobedo, L., et al.: MOSOCO: a mobile assistive tool to support children with autism practicing social skills in real-life situations. In: Proceedings of the SIGCHI Conference on Human Factors in Computing Systems (CHI 2012), pp. 2589–2598. ACM, New York (2012). https://doi.org/10.1145/2207676.2208649
8. Cibrian, F., Peña, O., Ortega, D., Tentori, M.: BendableSound: an elastic multisensory surface using touch-based interactions to assist children with severe autism during music therapy. Int. J. Hum Comput Stud. **107**, 22–37 (2017). https://doi.org/10.1016/j.ijhcs.2017.05.003
9. Kientz, J.A., Hayes, G.R., Westeyn, T.L., Starner, T., Abowd, G.D.: Pervasive computing and autism: assisting caregivers of children with special needs. IEEE Pervasive Comput. **6**(1), 28–35 (2007). https://doi.org/10.1109/MPRV.2007.18
10. Zakaria, C., Davis, R., Walker, Z.: Seeking independent management of problem behavior: a proof-of-concept study with children and their teachers. In: Proceedings of the The 15th International Conference on Interaction Design and Children (IDC 2016), pp. 196–205. ACM, New York (2016). https://doi.org/10.1145/2930674.2930693
11. Boyle, C., et al.: Trends in the prevalence of developmental disabilities in US children, 1997–2008. Pediatrics **127**(6), 1034–1042 (2011)
12. Lipscomb, S., Haimson, J., Liu, A., Burghardt, J., Johnson, D., Thurlow, M.: Preparing for life after high school: the characteristics and experiences of youth in special education. Findings from the National Longitudinal Transition Study 2012, vol. 1: Comparisons with other youth: Full report (2017)

13. Sharmin, M., Hossain, M., Saha, A., Das, M., Maxwell, M., Ahmed, S.: From research to practice: informing the design of autism support smart technology. In: Proceedings of the 2018 CHI Conference on Human Factors in Computing Systems (CHI 2018), pp. 102–118. ACM, New York (2018) https://doi.org/10. 1145/3173574.3173676

14. Torrado, J.C., Gomez, J., Montoro, G.: Emotional self-regulation of individuals with autism spectrum disorders: smartwatches for monitoring and interaction. Sensors **17**, 1359 (2017). https://doi.org/10.3390/s17061359

15. Suzuki, K., Hachisu, T., Iida, K.: EnhancedTouch: a smart bracelet for enhancing human-human physical touch. In: Proceedings of the 2016 CHI Conference on Human Factors in Computing Systems (CHI 2016), pp. 1282–1293. ACM, New York (2016). https://doi.org/10.1145/2858036.2858439

16. Boyd, L.E., et al.: vrSocial: toward immersive therapeutic VR systems for children with autism. In: Proceedings of the 2018 CHI Conference on Human Factors in Computing Systems (CHI 2018), pp. 204–215. ACM, New York (2018). https:// doi.org/10.1145/3173574.3173778

17. Zakaria, C., Davis, R.: Demo: wearable application to manage problem behavior in children with neurodevelopmental disorders. In: Proceedings of the 14th Annual International Conference on Mobile Systems, Applications, and Services Companion (MobiSys 2016 Companion), p. 127. ACM, New York (2016) https://doi.org/ 10.1145/2938559.2938575

18. Smit, D., Bakker, S.: BlurtLine: a design exploration to support children with ADHD in classrooms. In: Abascal, J., Barbosa, S., Fetter, M., Gross, T., Palanque, P., Winckler, M. (eds.) INTERACT 2015. LNCS, vol. 9299, pp. 456–460. Springer, Cham (2015). https://doi.org/10.1007/978-3-319-22723-8_37

19. Boyd, L., Jiang, X., Hayes, G.: ProCom: designing and evaluating a mobile and wearable system to support proximity awareness for people with autism. In: Proceedings of the 2017 CHI Conference on Human Factors in Computing Systems (CHI 2017), pp. 2865–2877. ACM, New York (2017). https://doi.org/10.1145/ 3025453.3026014

20. Dibia, V.: FOQUS: a smartwatch application for individuals with ADHD and mental health challenges. In: Proceedings of the 18th International ACM SIGACCESS Conference on Computers and Accessibility (ASSETS 2016), pp. 311–312. ACM, New York (2016). https://doi.org/10.1145/2982142.2982207

21. Dibia, V., Trewin, S., Ashoori, M., Erickson, T.: Exploring the potential of wearables to support employment for people with mild cognitive impairment. In: Proceedings of the 17th International ACM SIGACCESS Conference on Computers and Accessibility (ASSETS 2015), pp. 401–402. ACM, New York (2015). https:// doi.org/10.1145/2700648.2811390

22. Simm, W., et al.: Anxiety and autism: towards personalized digital health. In: Proceedings of the 2016 CHI Conference on Human Factors in Computing Systems (CHI 2016), pp. 1270–1281. ACM, New York (2016). https://doi.org/10.1145/ 2858036.2858259

23. Lazar, J., Feng, J.H., Hochheiser, H.: Research Methods in Human-Computer Interaction. Wiley Publishing (2017). ISBN 0470723378, 9780470723371, 9780128093436

24. Alper, M., Hourcade, J., Gilutz, S.: Interactive technologies for children with special needs. In: Proceedings of the 11th International Conference on Interaction Design and Children (IDC 2012), pp. 363–366. ACM, New York (2012). https:// doi.org/10.1145/2307096.2307169

25. Reybold, L.E., Lammert, J.D., Stribling, S.M.: Participant selection as a conscious research method: thinking forward and the deliberation of 'Emergent' findings. Qual. Res. **13**(6), 699–716 (2013). https://doi.org/10.1177/1468794112465634

26. Zheng, H., Genaro Motti, V.: Assisting students with intellectual and developmental disabilities in inclusive education with smartwatches. In: Proceedings of the 2018 CHI Conference on Human Factors in Computing Systems, pp. 350–361. ACM, New York (2018). https://doi.org/10.1145/3173574.3173924

27. Zheng, H., Genaro Motti, V.: WeLi: a smartwatch application to assist students with intellectual and developmental disabilities. In: Proceedings of the 19th International ACM SIGACCESS Conference on Computers and Accessibility, pp. 355–356. ACM, New York (2017). https://doi.org/10.1145/3132525.3134770

28. Zheng, H., Genaro Motti, V.: Wearable life: a wrist-worn application to assist students in special education. In: Antona, M., Stephanidis, C. (eds.) UAHCI 2017. LNCS, vol. 10279, pp. 259–276. Springer, Cham (2017). https://doi.org/10.1007/978-3-319-58700-4_22

29. Evmenova, A.S., Graff, H.J., Motti, V.G., Giwa-Lawal, K., Zheng, H.: Designing a wearable technology intervention to support young adults with intellectual and developmental disabilities in inclusive postsecondary academic environments. J. Spec. Educ. Technol. (2018). https://doi.org/10.1177/0162643418795833

30. Motti, V.G., Evmenova, A.: Designing technologies for neurodiverse users: considerations from research practice. In: Ahram, T., Taiar, R., Colson, S., Choplin, A. (eds.) IHIET 2019. AISC, vol. 1018, pp. 268–274. Springer, Cham (2019). https://doi.org/10.1007/978-3-030-25629-6_42

How Do Typically Developing Children and Children with ASD Play a Tangible Game?

Amani Indunil Soysa[1]([✉]) [iD] and Abdullah Al Mahmud[2] [iD]

[1] Swinburne University of Technology, Melbourne, Australia
asoysa@swin.edu.au
[2] Centre for Design Innovation (CDI), Swinburne University of Technology,
Melbourne, Australia
aalmahmud@swin.edu.au

Abstract. A tangible user interface (TUI) brings a strong educational potential for both typically developing children and children with ASD, as it fosters tactile stimulation, development of cognitive skills and perceptual skills. However, no previous research has compared the commonalities and differences of using TUI for both groups in low-resource countries. This study examines the nature of using TUI in children with autism (ages 3–5; n = 14) compared to typically developing children (ages 3–5; n = 10) along with their performance in game-play. We used an iPad-based Picture to Object Mapping Activity (POMA) game that utilised tangible components using 30 interactive pretend play toys. We collected video recordings and logs of the POMA application to explore the commonalities and differences of using TUI among both groups of children. Results indicated that children with ASD performed lower than the typically developing children in group activities; however, both groups showed similar performance in individual activities. Furthermore, we observed children with ASD had difficulties in using TUI (e.g. placing the tangibles on the iPad) when compared to typically developing children. Based on our findings, we propose recommendations for developing low-cost TUI for children with ASD in Sri Lanka.

Keywords: Tangible user interface (TUI) · Autism · Technology · Developing countries · Game · Tangible interaction

1 Introduction

Tangible User Interfaces (TUI) have demonstrated its potential in supporting children for their learning activities in the past ten years. Numerous studies have shown that TUI-based tools can be used in educational activities such as geometry training [7], colour matching [30], science activities [41], computer programming [25] for typically developing (TD) children as physical objects interacting with virtual environments can cater playful learning environment [41]. According to Piaget developmental theory, manipulation of concrete physical objects can improve thinking and spatial skills for young children [52]. In addition to such skills, the work on TUI has suggested that

© IFIP International Federation for Information Processing 2019
Published by Springer Nature Switzerland AG 2019
D. Lamas et al. (Eds.): INTERACT 2019, LNCS 11747, pp. 135–155, 2019.
https://doi.org/10.1007/978-3-030-29384-0_8

TUIs might be suitable for engaging children and collaborative learning for children [32]. Therefore, a number of design-focused projects have researched on TUIs to improve social and cognitive skills for young TD children [40] as well as for children with social cognitive impairment such as Autism Spectrum Disorder (ASD) [2, 17, 51]. TUI is particularly beneficial for children with ASD as it supports tactile and sensory stimulation with digital feedback and effects, which are important factors for children with ASD as it can facilitate the sensory needs of children with ASD [29]. Although TUIs are beneficial for both TD children and children with ASD, we are not aware of any study, which has compared the ways of using TUIs among both groups. Therefore, in this paper, we evaluate a TUI-based collaborative educational game called POMA with TD children and children with ASD to explore the commonalities and differences when using TUI by both groups of children.

1.1   Use of TUI for Children With and Without ASD

ASD is a developmental disorder that can appear from a very early stage of childhood and it is associated with cognitive impairment in attention, social communication along with restrictive and repetitive interests and behaviours. Due to such impairments, children with ASD demonstrate problems in social engagement, impatience in turn-taking and waiting [10] that could potentially affect their day-to-day activities and their quality of life [24]. Therefore, it is imperative to diagnose children with ASD and direct them to proper intervention programs from a very early stage. These interventions often include tangible toys (i.e. cause and effect toys), visual support (flash cards) to represent both concrete and abstract real-world concepts [4]. For instance, occupational and special education teachers use cognitive therapies like object discrimination with pretend play toys (i.e. plastic toy fruits and vegetables) to empower very young (ages 4–6) children with ASD [54]. Similarly, some special education teachers and general education teachers used Montessori teaching methods and Montessori toys [34], to improve sensor-motor training and spatial abilities via physical objects (toys) that are relatable and natural for children. Further, such Montessori teaching methods highlight the importance of learning through exploration, physical play, repetition and simplicity, not only for TD children but also for children with ASD [5, 23]. For instance, in teaching children to understand the basic geometric shapes, teachers use flashcards containing the picture of the shape to match the correct physical object that represents the geometric shape in the flash card. The strengths of hands-on interaction with physical objects are that they can help understand the representations of relations within and between objects (e.g. shapes) [50]. Such skills are essential for early childhood development for both TD children as well as children with ASD. These significant factors such as learning through physical play, repetition and visual support can be considered when designing technologies and tools targeting young children.

With the advancement of technology, there have been many technological tools designed to support children [8, 27]. Most of these technological interventions support 2-dimensional learning with visual and auditory support such as touch-based technologies (iPad, tablets and tabletop applications) [35, 53], computer-based technologies (computer software) [20], virtual reality (computer software) [14] etc. Such technologies and tools can be beneficial for children especially children with ASD as these tools promote visual learning with immediate feedback. Though these tools and technologies provide interactive visual support for children, these tools lack the benefit of 3D learning and the use of real-world objects that support more effective or more natural learning [45]. TUI-based technologies can effectively be used to avoid such limitations, as it embeds digital technology into graspable forms blending the best of both digital and tangible worlds [30]. Prior research has shown that TUI-based technologies can be used to facilitate a wide array of learning topics from basic puzzles [55] to carpentry [12] for children. These studies focus on improving cognitive skills such as spatial cognition [6] of TD children; however, most research in TUI to support children with ASD mainly involves in skills like social interaction [18, 51] and cognitive skills [16, 44]. Most of these aforementioned TUI-based tools are designed using passive tangible objects such as toys with RFID-based tokens, magnet sensors and fiducial markers [22, 31]. These passive tangibles use digital displays such as tabletop devices, computer screens to provide visual and auditory feedback for the children, which enable children to engage in natural and direct interactions [31]. In addition to tabletop-based TUIs, researchers have built smart toys such as Polipo [49], which is an active TUI that offers various multisensory stimuli aimed at promoting fine-motor skills of children with ASD. Similarly, researchers have designed active tangible educational interfaces (i.e., "ReduCat") for therapists to engage with children with ASD in educational activities via social stories [2]. Furthermore, Francis et al. [21], has conducted a study with children with and without ASD in the UK to assess the promotion of social behaviour during free play with active TUI (i.e., Topobo) and passive toys (i.e., LEGO^{TM}). This study [21] found out that play with TUI leads to more social play compared to passive toys. Though Francis et al. [21] study provides useful insights on social behaviour during free-play for children with and without ASD, this study does not address the commonalities and differences of using TUI (i.e., how much help is required when using TUI, how TUIs are used among different groups). Further, this study focuses on TUI that is designed for developed countries, which may not be suitable for children in resource-challenged countries.

1.2   Use of Technology for Children in Low Resource Countries

Despite these cited works [16, 18, 44, 49, 51], the field of TUI for children with ASD is still relatively new. Furthermore, most of these studies mentioned earlier mainly focused on children in developing regions like the United States, the United Kingdom using expensive technologies such as tabletop devices. However, there have been a few studies that focused on assistive technology for children with ASD in low resource countries like India including the work conducted by Sharma et al. [42] and Sampath [39] to support decision making, mathematical and social skills of children with ASD. However, all these studies were limited to digital technology, which focused on 2-dimensional learning. For countries like Sri Lanka where autism prevalence is 1 in 93 children [37], and we are not aware of any study that focuses on assistive technology for the Sri Lankan children with ASD. Furthermore, there are several challenges of using technology for children with ASD in developing countries like Sri Lanka such as limited access to resources, equipment and knowledge may hinder parents and practitioners using technology at home and school setting [1]. For instances, prior studies have found that in Sri

Lanka, several vital factors inhibit families from seeking support for their child with ASD including, limited access to services, low-income, lack of knowledge, cultural and religious beliefs and limited services in their native languages [15]. However, Sharma et al. [43] have shown possible guidelines to avoid such challenges. For instance, designing with stakeholders (i.e., therapists and teachers) collaboratively may lead to more technology acceptance within autism communities. Furthermore, designing for diverse learners for collaborative use without individual use (i.e., classroom settings, therapy settings) to facilitate multiple users can also help low-economic autism communities. Educating parents and practitioners on how to use technology (i.e., limiting technology for 15–30 min) to reduce possible harmful effects of using technology for children with ASD (i.e., screen addiction) can also improve the awareness and the use of technology within lower resource regions. Additionally, Sharma et al. highlight that "Giving control to the educators" may also increase the technology acceptance in autism communities [43].

In the face of the challenges mentioned above and lack of research evidence on designing technologies for Sri Lankan children with ASD, we designed a TUI game called POMA (Picture to Object Mapping Activities) [48] to improve social and cognitive skills for Sri Lankan children with ASD. However, we assume that typically developing children in Sri Lanka would be able to use POMA without any difficulties. Therefore, we conducted an exploratory study comparing the use of POMA by TD children and children with ASD to verify our assumption. The primary focus of this study is to explore the commonalities and differences in POMA gameplay between both groups. The findings of the paper and its implications contribute to designing low-cost tangible games to support children in low resource countries.

2 POMA: Picture to Object Mapping Activity System

POMA (Picture to Object Mapping Activity) game is a TUI-based educational game running on an iPad that promotes picture to object mapping activities via placing tangible objects on top of the iPad surface. The target group for POMA is Sri Lankan children with ASD in the age of 3–6 years. However, educational and social components of POMA are based on the Sri Lankan standard preschool education system, which is applicable for both TD and children with ASD. Therefore, it is expected that POMA can be played equally by both TD children and children with ASD. The main objective of designing POMA is to get the children engaged in regular learning activities with social interaction in Sri Lankan autism therapy centres. POMA has been designed with consultation of parents and practitioners of Sri Lankan children with ASD. For the complete description of the POMA design process, please to refer our previous work [46–48].

2.1 Features of POMA

The architecture of POMA has two main parts namely software component, and tangible component (see Fig. 1). The software component is composed of four different activities with six levels. The four activities are related to (1) shapes, (2) fruits, (3) vegetables, and

(4) animal identification. During each activity, a tablet application displays a picture related to the activity, and children need to place the appropriate toy on top of the displayed picture. For instance, if the activity is shape identification, a shape related image (i.e., "starfish") will be displayed on the iPad screen. Once the children place the correct-toy (i.e., star-shaped toy) on the iPad screen, children will be reinforced by the iPad and directed to the next shape object. If children were not able to place the correct toy on the iPad screen, iPad would not provide any feedback to the children; however, the same picture will be displayed until children place the correct toy. The game will continue for the predefined duration (default 2 min), however, practitioners have the ability to change the game duration for each child. The levels of POMA start from beginner level to more advanced levels from single user modes to multi-user modes (see Figs. 1, 2). When children play the POMA application, practitioners get to select the child preferred background colour, child's level and the activity of their choice. Figure 1 lists the main activities and levels that are supported by POMA.

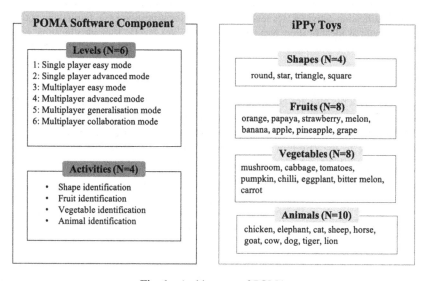

Fig. 1. Architecture of POMA

The tangible component of POMA consists of a set of interactive pretend play toys (iPPy toys) that can communicate with multi-touch surfaces. Tangible components of this prototype are designed using a set of pretend play toys that are commonly used by children with ASD in their therapy sessions. To make these pretend play toys interactive and recognisable by multi-touch surfaces (i.e., iPad) we embedded capacitive touch point patterns on the bottom layer of each interactive toy (see Fig. 2g, h). To improve the safety, robustness and durability of the tangible components as well as to reduce the cost of the tangibles, we have designed iPPy toys to be passive tangibles. Additionally, we also wanted the iPPy toys to be simple and relatable passive objects to avoid any fixation on toys for children with ASD. Passive tangibles are unpowered

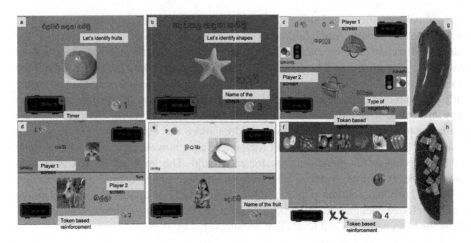

Fig. 2. Levels of POMA and iPPy toys, (a) level 1: vegetable identification activities, (b) level 2: shape identification activities, (c) level 3: vegetable identification basic turn-taking activities, (d) level 4: animal identification turn-taking activities, (e) level5: fruit identification generalization activities, (f) level5: fruits identification collaboration activities; (g, h) iPPy chilli-shaped toys.

physical components and are not tightly bound to the digital system [26]. Unlike active tangibles, iPPy toys do not have lights and audio embodied into the physical component. Therefore, the software component of POMA was used to provide audio and visual feedback to the children. To give a variety of iPPy toys for children, in consultation with the Sri Lankan therapists, we selected four different categories of toys that are commonly used by children with ASD in Sri Lanka (see Fig. 1).

3   Methodology

3.1   Participants

After obtaining approval from our university ethical review board, we recruited participants from Sri Lankan autism centres and preschools in Colombo. A total of 24 children participated in this study under two groups (group A and B). In group A, 14 children (nine males, five females) from 3–5.5 years ($M = 4.8$, $SD = 0.57$) were recruited from Sumaga autism centre, Kelaniya Sri Lanka. The eligibility requirements for the group A included (a) medical diagnosis of autism according to DSM V diagnosis criteria, (b) diagnosis of autism is mild, (c) verbal communication without the use of an augmentative alternative communication device as verified by the parents, (d) age group of 3–6 years, (e) hearing and vision within normal (6/6 vision, hearing ranging 0–20 dB) limits (aided or unaided) based on parents' report, (f) motor and physical abilities to manipulate a tablet device. In group B ten children (four males and six females) from 3–5 years ($M = 3.5$, $SD = 0.454$) were recruited from a Sumaga preschool in Kelaniya Sri Lanka. The eligibility requirement for the group B included

(a) no medical diagnosis of any psychological or physiological condition, (b) age group of 3–6 years, (c) hearing and vision within normal (6/6 vision, hearing ranging 0–20 dB) limits (aided or unaided) based on parents' report, and (d) motor and physical abilities to manipulate a tablet device.

In addition to the children, we recruited practitioners (five special education teachers and three primary school teachers) to conduct the study. The recruited practitioners have worked closely with the recruited children and have more than three years of experience working with children.

Fig. 3. Children with ASD and typically developing children playing with POMA; (a) child with ASD playing POMA-single-player mode, (b) child with ASD playing POMA with the practitioner, (c) A TD child playing POMA-single-player mode, and d) two TD children playing with POMA.

3.2 Procedure

The study was conducted in two different locations in Sri Lanka. For group A, we held the study in the autism centre classroom, in Sumaga autism centre Kelaniya Sri Lanka, and for group B, we held the sessions in the pre-school classroom in Sumaga preschool Kelaniya Sri Lanka. However, both groups of children were in the same age, therefore, both groups followed the similar steps (i.e., single-player to multiplayer modes) during the sessions. At the beginning of the session, the first author described the functionalities of the POMA application and iPPy toys to each practitioner and gave them time to explore POMA installed on an iPad.

Before conducting the sessions with children, practitioners locked the iPad to the POMA application using the guided access feature of the iPad, which disable the home button of the iPad. This was carried out to prevent children from accessing other apps such as YouTube application during the sessions. Then each practitioner introduced the iPPy toys to each child starting from iPPy shape-toys. Depending on the child's preference practitioners switched the iPPy shape-toys to the other toy categories namely iPPy animal-toys, iPPy vegetable-toys and iPPy fruit-toys. Furthermore, are two main modes of POMA namely single-player mode and multi-player modes. For the single-player mode levels (i.e., level 1 and 2), children played with the system by themselves (see Fig. 3a, c) and practitioners observed and helped the children when needed. For the multiplayer mode levels (level 3, 4, 5, and 6), practitioners selected another child from the same group of the participant to play in the group settings (see Fig. 3d). Furthermore, practitioners played with the children as their partner, whenever a specific child is not able to play with their peers (see Fig. 3b).

Practitioners started playing POMA with children from the single-player mode basic level (Level 1) to more advanced multiplayer modes. If a child performs well at a given level (if the child places the correct objects at least 60% of the time), he/she will be promoted to the next level by the practitioner. If the child does not perform well, the child will be asked to repeat the level until he/she performs well. Before repeating a level or going to another level, practitioners asked each child if they wanted to continue playing or if they wished to stop playing it. At the end of each activity, children were given 2–7 min' break (depending on the child's requirement), before moving to the next activity. After one hour of maximum duration, children were asked to stop playing with POMA by the practitioners to avoid any addictions.

3.3 Data Collection and Data Analysis

We collected objective data from the POMA application log and subjective data from the video recordings of all the sessions.

Log data: We collected objective data such as time-taken to complete levels and the total number of levels completed by a child from the POMA system log.

Video recordings: All sessions were video recorded with a total amount of footage of 9 h and 48 min. Table 1 describes the video coding scheme. We also coded common behaviour patterns of children (i.e., staring at toys, line-up toys) while playing POMA. These behaviour patterns were reported in relation to four main aspects, including; (1) time taken to play the POMA levels, (2) Playing POMA independently, (3) use of the tangible iPPY toys and (4) social engagements via turn-taking and vocal initiation.

We analysed the log data and video recordings against the two groups (TD children and children with ASD). For instance, we calculated the time taken to play POMA and vocal initiations by averaging the time taken to complete each level and averaging the number of vocal initiations for each level. Similarly, we calculated the help required from the practitioners by calculating the average percentage on the number of times practitioners helped children to play POMA from the total number of attempts. For object selection and placement, we calculated the average percentage of correct object

Table 1. Video coding scheme

Codes	Description
Help required from the practitioners	The occurrence of practitioner helping children to play POMA (i.e., hand holding, pointing)
Object selection and placement	How children place the iPPy toys on the iPad screen (i.e., upside down placement, correct placements and placing toys while touching the iPad screen)
Turn-taking	Child voluntarily giving the toys to their partner without being prompt
Vocal initiation	Vocal initiation due to gameplay (i.e., requesting toys, vocal compliments to the partner; "you can do this")
Behaviour patterns	Common behaviour patterns while playing POMA (i.e., staring at toys, line-up toys)

placement, the average percentage of correct object selection but incorrect object placement (i.e., upside down placement, finger touching placement), and the average percentage of incorrect object selection from the total number of attempts. Additionally, for turn-taking behaviour, we calculated average percentage on the number of times children turn-take the toys willingly with practitioners/peers from the total number of times POMA-game requested to turn-take the toys with the partner. Furthermore, we conducted an inferential statistical analysis using SPSS software where necessary.

4   Results

4.1   Time Taken to Play the POMA Levels

In general, both typically developing children and children with ASD showed similar capabilities when completing the POMA application. Results indicated that 50% of the TD children and 57% of children with ASD were able to complete up to level 5 of POMA application while the remaining children completed only up to level 4. None of the groups was able to complete level 6 of POMA application within their sessions. Additionally, we also found out that children with ASD spent more time (M = 32.85 min, SD = 7.19) while TD children spent lesser time (M = 24.5 min, SD = 4.42), even though both groups played similar number of levels (Minimum: 4, Maximum: 5). There was a significant difference on the overall time spent at the $p < 0.05$ level for two groups of children [F (1, 22) = 10.567, p = 0.004].

We also observed in video recordings that children with ASD spent more time looking and feeling the iPPy toys while playing the initial levels of POMA. For instance, to complete level 1 of POMA children with ASD took considerable time (M = 10 min; SD = 3.6) when compared to TD children (M = 3.6 min, SD = 1.6), see Fig. 4. The time taken to complete level 1, therefore, was significant, F (1, 22) =27.6, p = .000. However, both groups took the similar amount of time to complete level 2 and 3 and the time taken to complete levels was non-significant (Level 2, [F (1, 22) = 0.08, $p > 0.05$], Level 3, [F (1, 22) = 0.31, $p > 0.05$]). We also observed that both groups took a considerable amount of time (ASD: $M = 12.21$ min, $SD = 2$, TD: $M = 9.2$ min, $SD = 1.75$) to complete level 4, which includes turn-taking activities with multiple toys. The time taken to complete level 4 (see Fig. 4) was significant, $F (1, 22) = 12.99$, $p = 0.02$. However, we observed both groups took lesser time (ASD: $M = 4.28$ min, $SD = 2.44$; TD: $M = 5$ min, $SD = 1.4$) to complete level 5 with no significant difference $p > 0.05$.

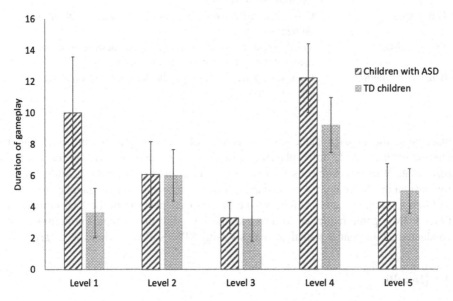

Fig. 4. Average time taken to complete each level of POMA.

4.2   Playing POMA Independently

To explore whether both groups of children can use POMA independently, we calculated the average percentage of help required from practitioners to complete a level. This was calculated by coding the number of times practitioners helped children for each level and a number of time children played without help from the video recordings. Then we calculated the percentage of help required from total attempts for each level.

In general, we found out that both group of children (ASD: $M = 17.95\%$, $SD = 11.5$ and TD children $M = 2.5\%$, $SD = 1.5$) required more help from the practitioners to complete the level 1 of POMA (see Fig. 5). However, there was a significant difference between the two groups of children to complete the level one, $F (1, 22) = 15.89$, $p = 0.01$. However, after level 1 TD children were much more confident to use POMA independently compared to children with ASD. For instance, to complete level 2, children with ASD required more help ($M = 12.1\%$, $SD = 10.6$) on average while TD children required lesser help ($M = 1\%$, $SD = 0.94$). An analysis of variance showed that the help required for children with ASD and TD children to complete level 1 was significant, $[F (1, 22) = 15.83, p = .001]$. Additionally, we also observed, even though

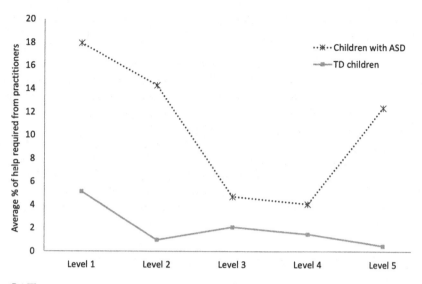

Fig. 5. The average percentage of help required from practitioners for children to play POMA

TD children required more help in the initial levels, they required lesser help in more advanced levels. For instance, to play level one TD children required more help ($M = 2.5$; $SD = 1.5$), compared to the help required in level two ($M = 2.5\%$; $SD = 0.9$), three ($M = 1\%$, $SD = 0.7$) and four ($M = 2.1\%$, $SD = 0.8$), [$F (4, 39) = 4.31, p = .006$].

Further, from our video analysis, we found out that children with ASD often (8 times on average per session) got distracted by aligning the toys and looking at the toys. Therefore, practitioners got more involved during play sessions to keep the children with ASD focused on the game.

4.3   Use of the Tangible iPPy Toys

We observed that both groups of children had similar cognitive skills in identifying correct tangible objects of the POMA application. On average 78.3% ($SD = 10.11$) of the time children ASD and 78.44% ($SD = 4.52$) of the time TD children were able to identify the correct tangible objects to place it on the iPad screen. Furthermore, we also observed that children with ASD scored less for levels that had multi-user modes (i.e., Level 3, Level 4, Level 5). For instance, on average TD children scored 24.2 points ($SD = 2.8$) for Level 3 while on average children with ASD scored 10.466 ($SD = 4.5$) for Level 3, [$F (1, 22) = 71.67, p = .000$].

Additionally, we further observed that 6.38% of the time children with ASD were able to identify the correct toy, but not able to place it correctly on the iPad screen. From the video data coding, we identified that children with ASD were unable to place the toys due to two main reasons. (1) FT- Fingers touch the iPad screen when placing the iPad; therefore, the touch point pattern gets distorted. (2) UD-putting the toys upside down; therefore, the iPad cannot recognise the touch point pattern. From the incorrect object placement, we found out that most of the FT-placements (M = 28.9%, SD = 10.4) were for vegetable type-iPPy toys and most (M = 16.7%, SD = 20.1) of the UD placements were for shape-type iPPy toys. When compared to children with ASD, TD children had very low (M = 0.105%, SD = 0.12) incorrect object placement [F (1, 22) = 14.04, p = .001]. Further, we observed from our video recordings that once typically developing children learn to place the tangible toys correctly in Level 1, and they avoided FT and UD placement completely.

In addition to FT and UD placements, we also observed that children with ASD spent some time (M = 87.64 s, SD = 62.4) aligning the toys properly, keeping the toys in a straight line after placing them on the iPad. Furthermore, we observed that some children with ASD (n = 7) got frustrated when they cannot place animal toys in the stand-up position throughout the levels. However, we did not find such behaviour in TD children.

4.4   Social Engagement via Turn Taking and Vocal Initiation

From the third level, POMA embeds social components using multiplayer functionalities along with turn-taking the tangible objects. From the practitioner observations, we found out that only two children with ASD were able to play multiplayer activities among each other (with peers) and the remaining children with ASD played the multiplayer activities with their respective practitioners. In contrast to children with ASD, all TD children were able to play multiplayer activities of POMA with their peers. To evaluate the social engagement throughout the sessions, we coded the two variables such as (1) the number of times children turn-take the toys willingly with practitioners/peers and cooperatively played with others and (2) the number of social interactions made via vocal initiation during the playtime.

The average percentage of turn-taking was determined by calculating the percentage of toys shared willingly by the children with their partner (i.e., peers or practitioner) with the total number of times POMA-game requested to turn-take the toys with the partner. In general, both children with ASD and TD children were able to share the physical toys among each other. We also observed (see Fig. 6) that TD children were more willingly turn-taking (M = 98.2%, SD = 1.92) compared to children with ASD (M = 81.5%, SD = 19.02). However, we did not observe any significant differences between both groups of children [F (1, 22) = 7.643, p = .006]. Additionally, we observed that over time both groups of children improved their willingness to take-turns among each other via sharing their toys. Furthermore, we noticed that all children who played level five (TD: n = 5; ASD: n = 5) took turns willingly without any hesitation.

Even though children with ASD were willingly sharing the toys among each other, we observed very few vocal initiations from children with ASD when compared to typically developing children (See Fig. 7). We observed significant differences in vocal initiation between the two groups. For instance, for the level 1, children with ASD spoke around 3–4 times on average (SD = 2.4) while TD children-initiated conversations around 8–9 times per session [F (1, 22) = 26.8, p = .000], indicating TD children are more verbal during POMA gameplay compared to children with ASD. Though

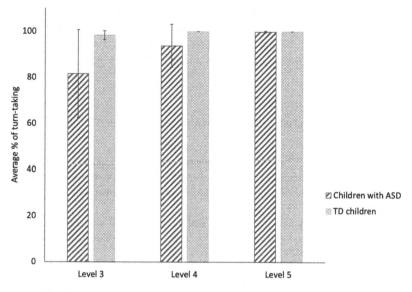

Fig. 6. Average percentage (%) of turn-taking during different levels

children with ASD had limited verbal communication between their partner, we also observed they kept on requesting for the toys using hand gestures. We also observed that both groups increased their verbal initiations throughout the levels (see Fig. 7). Additionally, we found that TD children helped each other by complimenting each other ("good job"), repeating the reinforcements generated by the iPad and also saying what objects needs to be picked verbally. In contrast to TD children, children with ASD

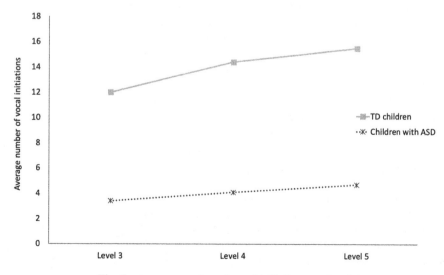

Fig. 7. Average number of vocal initiations per level

showed less interesting in helping each other verbally; however, we observed that they kept on repeating the audio feedback/reinforcements given by the iPad when his/her partner is doing well (i.e., "Well done", "You got it"). Table 2 summarizes the study findings by highlighting the commonalities and differences in gameplay between the two groups.

Table 2. Commonalities and differences in POMA-gameplay between TD children and children with ASD in Sri Lanka

Commonalities	
1	Both TD children and children with ASD were able to complete only unto level 5 (50% of the TD children and 57% of the children with ASD completed level 5 the others completed up to level 4)
2	Both TD children and children with ASD had the similar level of cognitive skills when identifying the iPPy toys correctly (78.545% of the time TD children and 79.23% of the time children with ASD identified the objects correctly)
3	Both TD children and children with ASD were able to share the objects among the other players and turn-take when playing multiplayer modes
Differences	
1	Children with ASD took a significant amount to complete level 1 and 4 when compared to TD children
2	Even though both groups had similar cognitive functionalities, children with ASD had difficulties placing the objects on the iPad screen (6.38% of the time)
3	Children with ASD required more help from the practitioners compared to TD children (children with ASD requested help 11.6% of the time throughout all the levels while TD children only needed help 1.2% of the time in the initial levels)
4	TD children had sufficient amount of social engagement via vocal initiation (8-10 times per session on average. However, children with ASD had a limited amount of social engagement via vocal initiation (4–5 times per session on average)
5	Only two children with ASD were able to play multiplayer modes with their peers. However, all TD children were able to play multiplayer modes with their peers

5 Discussion

In the following section, we reflect on the key findings and provide implications for designing TUI for children in Sri Lanka.

5.1 Reflection on the Key Findings

In this paper, we have presented how TD children and children with ASD in Sri Lanka play a TUI game, and we have illustrated the commonalities and differences in gameplay for both group of children. This study provides further evidence that well-designed TUI-based educational systems can leverage playful learning among children and promote social interaction in children. By comparing the progress reports of children with ASD and TD children, we were able to observe that cognitive skills (i.e., shape identification) overlapped between the two groups. Children in both groups were able to identify shapes, animals, veggies and fruits around 78–79% of the time. Hence, this study provides further support for the use of TUI in education for TD children [40] and children with ASD [44]. However, we observed qualitative differences between the two groups in the way they place the tangible toys on the iPad screen. For instances, 6.83% of the time children with ASD were not able to place the tangible toys even after correctly identifying them. We observed two reasons for such behaviour, (1) placing the objects while the fingertips were touching the iPad screen, and (2) putting the objects upside down. For both types of placements, iPad cannot identify the tangible toys as the touch point pattern gets distorted. In addition to incorrect toy placement on the iPad, we also observed children with ASD tend to line-up the tangibles during play time. The reason for behaviours like upside-down (UT) placement and line-up toys can be due to visual stimming that can be seen in many children with ASD due to sensory processing disorders [9]. Sensory processing issues occur in 92% of the individuals with ASD [33] leaving spectrum of strengths and deficits such as visual stimming, fine-motor movements [28, 38] and tactile profile. We believe that our recruited children with ASD had sensory processing issues that caused problems when placing slender surface toys such as fruits and vegetables on the iPad screen. In addition to object placement, we also observed that children with ASD required more time to complete the beginner levels of POMA when compared to TD children. The reasons for this may be due to their fine-motor skill limitations [28, 38], the unfamiliarity of the game and sensory integration deficits [28]. However, it is worth noticing that despite their sensory issues, children with ASD were able to complete the later levels (level 5) slightly faster than the TD children. The reason for this might be due to the predictability and the familiarity gained by playing the initial levels that led children with ASD to focus and concentrate more on the game [19].

Concerning independent playing, we observed both groups required help from practitioners when playing level 1 of POMA (children with ASD: 17.95% of the time and TD children 5.15% of the time). The main reasons for this might be because of the unfamiliarity of the POMA game since both groups of children were using TUI for the first time. Another reason for such behaviour might be because the majority of the Sri Lankan learning environments are teacher-centric and children in Sri Lanka rely on their teachers when learning new concepts [13]. We also found that over the time children required less help from the practitioners especially the TD children. TD children were found collaborating and turn-taking with each other without being forced by their partner to share their toys with their partner. However, we also observed even after level 1, children with ASD required additional help from the practitioners. For instance, we found children with ASD sometimes tend to get distracted by lining-up toys and staring at the toys, hence, practitioners were required to bring back the focus to the game. This may be one of the reasons why children with ASD took more help in level 5.

Similar to a prior study [17], we found that children with ASD show some degree of social interaction through turn-taking and co-operative play during multiplayer mode sessions of POMA. We also consider that enforcing co-operative play via multiplayer modes can leverage social interactions. For instance, our multiplayer mode play sequence findings suggest that level 3, 4 and 5 offer more opportunities for turn-taking and sharing in TD children as well as children with ASD. However, we also observed that limited vocal initiation in children with ASD when compared to TD children during multiplayer modes of POMA. Such behaviour is not surprising for children with ASD since children with ASD have limited verbal skills compared to TD children [3]. Despite having limited verbal abilities, children with ASD were able to socially engage among their partners using hand gestures while improving their verbal skills throughout the levels. Another important finding from this study is that only two children with ASD were able to play with their peers without adult directions, and remaining children with ASD (n = 12) required practitioners as their partners when playing the multiplayer modes. In contrast to our findings, prior studies have shown that adult directed play goal is not always necessary to promote socially-oriented free play when playing with construction-based TUI, especially when there are no specific goals [21]. However, in our study, we found out practitioner involvement was necessary to guide them while playing and keeping their focus on educational activities. The reasons for children with ASD required practitioner as their partner instead of their peers might be related to the characteristics of ASD such as the need for familiarity, predictability and consistency [11] that can be expected from their practitioners instead of their peers.

5.2   Design Implications for Developing TUI for Children with ASD

Based on our findings, we have listed a set of guidelines and lessons learned as implications for designing passive TUI for children. Some of these guidelines are specific to children with ASD, while others may apply to all children.

Socialisation: Percentage of social interactions via turn-taking and sharing was much higher than we envisioned during the design process of POMA. We observed both groups of children had above 80% turn-taking and sharing during the initial levels and improving this skill over-time up to 99%. The main reason for such success can be due to our digital interface, where we enforce parallel play with turn-taking through two-player functionalities. Additionally, we have also divided the POMA interface into two parts assigning collaborative roles to each player, which locks/unlocks the touch surface upon sharing and turn-taking. We also provided one set of toys at a given time to add the element of scarce resources. Hence, children had to collaborate to succeed in the game. Due to the limited resources (iPPy toys) and token-based reinforcement points, it is known to trigger competitive behaviour in children [36]. However, as seen in prior TUI-based autism studies [21, 49], our study provides further support that TUI-based systems promote collaborative elements in children instead of competition not only for children with ASD but also for TD children.

Structure of the Tangibles: The structure of the tangibles was an essential factor that significantly enhanced the progress of the child when using POMA. The central technology behind our passive tangible toys (iPPy toys) is touch point pattern matching. The objects on the digital screen are identified by matching the touch point pattern embedded under each toy. Further, we designed the iPPy toys rounded, graspable and tactile stimulating to both groups of children, since most children with ASD has sensory integration issues and limited fine-motor skills [28, 38]. However, we observed two issues when children with ASD were placing the iPPy toys on the digital display. The first issue we saw was, some of the times children with ASD placed the shape-related toys upside down on the digital screen. Hence, the touch point pattern could not be recognised by the system. To avoid such issues, we propose to provide more cues in the POMA applications in Graphics Interchange Format (GIF) demonstrating how to keep the toys properly on the iPad screen during the initial levels of POMA. The second issue we saw was, children with ASD tend to place their fingertips on the digital surface when placing the slender surface toys (fruits and vegetables) on the iPad that in turn, would modify the touch point pattern for identification. To avoid such issues, we propose to add an additional layer using non-conductive materials (i.e., plastic) around slender surface toys. This layer would prevent fingertips from being touched when placing the toys on the iPad screen.

Sustaining Attention: Even though the iPPy toys are passive tangibles (without lights and audio), children were distracted by the iPPy toys and paid more attention to the structure of the iPPy toys and keeping the iPPy toys line-up or stand-up position regardless of placing the toys on the digital surface. One reason for this could be that digital interface of POMA keep on waiting for children to keep the toys on the screen without trying to get the child's attention when in idle. It might be more appropriate to provide audio-visual feedback to the children when the iPad is idle to get the attention back to the game.

5.3   Strengths and Limitations

One limitation of this study is the unequal sample size with fewer TD children and more children with ASD. Although replication with the same number of children in both groups is required, this study offers preliminary evidence that both groups of children can play POMA effectively and POMA can facilitate social interaction and cognitive skills of children with ASD and TD children. In our study, for the ASD group, we had more boys (n = 9) compared to girls (n = 5). This may have an impact on the generalizability of our results. During the study period due to the unavailability of female participants at the therapy centres, we were not able to recruit more female participants. Furthermore, we also observed that 85.7% of the children played multi-player activities with their teachers while all TD children played multi-player activities with their peers, which may have some effect on their social engagement. However, due to the social impairments of children with ASD and the limited time given to play with POMA, most children with ASD were unable to play POMA (multi-player modes) with their peers. Therefore, practitioners took the role of being the partners of children with ASD who could not play with each other.

6   Conclusion and Future Work

In this paper, we have presented how children with ASD and TD children play a low-cost TUI-based game called POMA. Our results show that both groups of children were able to complete up to level 5 of POMA successfully and had similar success in object identification. However, children with ASD took a significant amount in completing levels compared to TD children. Furthermore, children with ASD showed difficulties in keeping the tangible toys on the iPad screen compared to TD children. Additionally, we found that children with ASD needed more help from the practitioners to complete the POMA levels and had lesser social interactions compared to TD children. However, we also observed children with ASD needed less help, less time to complete POMA levels and improve social interactions throughout the levels. Based on our findings, we have provided a set of guidelines for designing TUIs for children with ASD in low-resource countries. In our future work, we hope to improve POMA according to the findings of the current study and evaluate POMA in therapeutic settings for a more extended period to understand the effects of POMA in daily autism therapy practices.

Acknowledgement. We would like to acknowledge the support extended by the founder Mrs. Swarna Jayawardene and her staff of Sumaga Autism Centre and Sumaga pre-school, Kelaniya, Sri Lanka for this study. We are also grateful to the practitioners, parents and their children who took part in this study.

References

1. Ahmad, F.K.: Use of assistive technology in inclusive education: making room for diverse learning needs. Transcience **6**(2), 62–77 (2015)
2. Alessandrini, A., et al.: Designing ReduCat: audio-augmented paper drawings tangible interface in educational intervention for high-functioning autistic children. In: Proceedings of the 15th International Conference on Interaction Design and Children. ACM (2016)
3. Anderson, D.K., et al.: Patterns of growth in verbal abilities among children with autism spectrum disorder. J. Consult. Clin. Psychol. **75**(4), 594 (2007)
4. Asher, A.: Book review: visual supports for people with autism: a guide for parents and professionals. Can. J. Occup. Ther. **84**(3), 148 (2017)
5. Bartak, L., Rutter, M.: Special educational treatment of autistic children: a comparative study–1. Design of study and characteristics of units. J. Child Psychol. Psychiatry **14**(3), 161–179 (1973)
6. Baykal, G.E., et al.: A review on complementary natures of tangible user interfaces (TUIs) and early spatial learning. Int. J. Child-Comput. Interact. **16**, 104–113 (2018)
7. Bonnard, Q., et al.: Tangible paper interfaces: interpreting pupils' manipulations. In: Proceedings of the 2012 ACM International Conference on Interactive Tabletops and Surfaces. ACM (2012)
8. Boucenna, S., et al.: Interactive technologies for autistic children: a review. Cognit. Comput. **6**(4), 722–740 (2014)
9. Cardinaux, A., Gandhi, T.: Reduced anticipatory responses during dynamic object interactions in autism (2015)
10. CDC. Autism Spectrum Disorders: Data and Statistics, 11 July 2016 (2016). http://www.cdc.gov/ncbddd/autism/data.html
11. Church, C., Alisanski, S., Amanullah, S.: The social, behavioral, and academic experiences of children with Asperger syndrome. Focus Autism Other Dev. Disabil. **15**(1), 12–20 (2000)
12. Cuendet, S., et al.: An integrated way of using a tangible user interface in a classroom. Int. J. Comput.-Supp. Collaborative Learn. **10**(2), 183–208 (2015)
13. Dahanayake, S.: Implementation of the philosophical concept of student centred education at senior secondary level (2006)

14. Didehbani, N., et al.: Virtual reality social cognition training for children with high functioning autism. Comput. Hum. Behav. **62**, 703–711 (2016)
15. Eng, B., Foster, K.E.: Assessing the accessibility and integration of community resources for autism in Sri Lanka (2018)
16. Escobedo, L., et al.: Smart objects to support the discrimination training of children with autism. Pers. Ubiquit. Comput. **18**(6), 1485–1497 (2014)
17. Farr, W., Yuill, N., Raffle, H.: Social benefits of a tangible user interface for children with autistic spectrum conditions. Autism **14**(3), 237–252 (2010)
18. Farr, W.J.: Tangible user interfaces and social interaction in children with autism. University of Sussex (2011)
19. Ferrara, C., Hill, S.D.: The responsiveness of autistic children to the predictability of social and nonsocial toys. J. Autism Dev. Disord. **10**(1), 51–57 (1980)
20. Fletcher-Watson, A.: targeted review of computer-assisted learning for people with autism spectrum disorder: towards a consistent methodology. Rev. J. Autism Dev. Disord. **1**(2), 87–100 (2014)
21. Francis, G.A., et al.: Do tangible user interfaces promote social behaviour during free play? A comparison of autistic and typically-developing children playing with passive and digital construction toys. Res. Autism Spectr. Disord. **58**, 68–82 (2018)
22. Gelsomini, M.: Reflex: learning beyond the screen in a simple, fun, and affordable way. In: Extended Abstracts of the 2018 CHI Conference on Human Factors in Computing Systems. ACM (2018)
23. Gustafsson, C.: Montessori education. In: Fleer, M., van Oers, B. (eds.) International Handbook of Early Childhood Education. SIHE, pp. 1439–1456. Springer, Dordrecht (2018). https://doi.org/10.1007/978-94-024-0927-7_74
24. Heyvaert, M., et al.: Efficacy of behavioral interventions for reducing problem behavior in persons with autism: an updated quantitative synthesis of single-subject research. Res. Dev. Disabil. **35**(10), 2463–2476 (2014)
25. Horn, M.S., Crouser, R.J., Bers, M.U.: Tangible interaction and learning: the case for a hybrid approach. Pers. Ubiquit. Comput. **16**(4), 379–389 (2012)
26. Horn, M.S., Solovey, E.T., Jacob, R.J.: Tangible programming and informal science learning: making TUIs work for museums. In: Proceedings of the 7th International Conference on Interaction Design and Children. ACM (2008)
27. Hutchby, I., Moran-Ellis, J.: Children, Technology and Culture: The Impacts of Technologies in Children's Everyday Lives. Routledge, London (2013)
28. Jasmin, E., et al.: Sensori-motor and daily living skills of preschool children with autism spectrum disorders. J. Autism Dev. Disord. **39**(2), 231–241 (2009)
29. Joosten, A.V., Bundy, A.C.: Sensory processing and stereotypical and repetitive behaviour in children with autism and intellectual disability. Aust. Occup. Ther. J. **57**(6), 366–372 (2010)
30. Kubicki, S., et al.: RFID interactive tabletop application with tangible objects: exploratory study to observe young children' behaviors. Pers. Ubiquit. Comput. **19**(8), 1259–1274 (2015)
31. Marco, J., Cerezo, E., Baldassarri, S.: Bringing tabletop technology to all: evaluating a tangible farm game with kindergarten and special needs children. Pers. Ubiquit. Comput. **17**(8), 1577–1591 (2013)
32. Marshall, P.: Do tangible interfaces enhance learning? In: Proceedings of the 1st International Conference on Tangible and Embedded Interaction. ACM (2007)
33. Mayes, S.D.: Brief report: checklist for autism spectrum disorder: most discriminating items for diagnosing autism. J. Autism Dev. Disord. **48**(3), 935–939 (2018)
34. Montessori, M.: The Montessori Method. Transaction Publishers, New Brunswick (2013)

35. Muharib, R., et al.: Effects of functional communication training using GoTalk NowTM iPad® application on challenging behavior of children with autism spectrum disorder. J. Special Educ. Technol. 34, 71–79 (2018)
36. Pappert, A.T., Williams, A., Moore, C.: The influence of competition on resource allocation in preschool children. Soc. Dev. 26(2), 367–381 (2017)
37. Perera, H., Wijewardena, K., Aluthwelage, R.: Screening of 18–24-month-old children for autism in a semi-urban community in Sri Lanka. J. Trop. Pediatr. 55, 402 (2009)
38. Provost, B., Lopez, B.R., Heimerl, S.: A comparison of motor delays in young children: autism spectrum disorder, developmental delay, and developmental concerns. J. Autism Dev. Disord. 37(2), 321–328 (2007)
39. Sampath, H., Sivaswamy, J., Indurkhya, B.: Assistive systems for children with dyslexia and autism. ACM Sigaccess Accessibility Comput. 96, 32–36 (2010)
40. Schneider, B., et al.: Benefits of a tangible interface for collaborative learning and interaction. IEEE Trans. Learn. Technol. 4(3), 222–232 (2011)
41. Shaer, O., et al.: Designing reality-based interfaces for experiential bio-design. Pers. Ubiquit. Comput. 18(6), 1515–1532 (2014)
42. Sharma, S., et al.: Gesture-based interaction for individuals with developmental disabilities in India. In: Proceedings of the 18th International ACM SIGACCESS Conference on Computers and Accessibility. ACM (2016)
43. Sharma, S., et al.: Designing gesture-based applications for individuals with developmental disabilities: guidelines from user studies in India. ACM Trans. Accessible Comput. (TACCESS) 11(1), 3 (2018)
44. Sitdhisanguan, K., et al.: Using tangible user interfaces in computer-based training systems for low-functioning autistic children. Pers. Ubiquit. Comput. 16(2), 143–155 (2012)
45. Sluis, R., et al.: Read-it: five-to-seven-year-old children learn to read in a tabletop environment. In: Proceedings of the 2004 Conference on Interaction Design and Children: Building a Community. ACM (2004)
46. Soysa, A.I., Al Mahmud, A.: Beyond digital displays: design considerations for tablet applications targeting children with ASD in Sri Lanka. In: Extended Abstracts of the 2018 CHI Conference on Human Factors in Computing Systems. ACM (2018)
47. Soysa, A.I., Mahmud, A.A.: Assessing tablet applications focused on social interactions: what functionalities do Sri Lankan practitioners want for children with ASD? In: Proceedings of the 30th Australian Conference on Computer-Human Interaction. ACM (2018)
48. Soysa, A.I., Mahmud, A.A., Kuys, B.: Co-designing tablet computer applications with Sri Lankan practitioners to support children with ASD. In: Proceedings of the 17th ACM Conference on Interaction Design and Children. ACM (2018)
49. Tam, V., Gelsomini, M., Garzotto, F.: Polipo: a tangible toy for children with neurodevelopmental disorders. In: Proceedings of the Tenth International Conference on Tangible, Embedded, and Embodied Interaction. ACM (2017)
50. Verdine, B.N., et al.: Finding the missing piece: blocks, puzzles, and shapes fuel school readiness. Trends Neurosci. Educ. 3(1), 7–13 (2014)
51. Villafuerte, L., Markova, M., Jorda, S.: Acquisition of social abilities through musical tangible user interface: children with autism spectrum condition and the reactable. In: CHI'12 Extended Abstracts on Human Factors in Computing Systems. ACM (2012)
52. Wadsworth, B.J.: Piaget's Theory of Cognitive and Affective Development: Foundations of Constructivism. Longman Publishing, New York (1996)
53. Whitehouse, A.J., et al.: A randomised controlled trial of an iPad-based application to complement early behavioural intervention in autism spectrum disorder. J. Child Psychol. Psychiatry 58, 1042–1052 (2017)

54. Wimpory, D.C., Hobson, R.P., Nash, S.: What facilitates social engagement in preschool children with autism? J. Autism Dev. Disord. **37**(3), 564–573 (2007)
55. Xie, L., Antle, A.N., Motamedi, N.: Are tangibles more fun? Comparing children's enjoyment and engagement using physical, graphical and tangible user interfaces. In: Proceedings of the 2nd International Conference on Tangible and Embedded Interaction. ACM (2008)

StatPlayground: A Sandbox for Learning Practical Statistics

Krishna Subramanian[(⊠)], Jeanine Bonot, Radu A. Coanda, and Jan Borchers

RWTH Aachen University, 52056 Aachen, Germany
{krishna,borchers}@cs.rwth-aachen.de,
{jeanine.bonot,radu.coanda}@rwth-aachen.de

Abstract. Inferential statistics is a frequent task in several fields such as HCI, Psychology, and Medicine. Research shows that inferential statistics is often used incorrectly because the underlying statistical concepts are misunderstood. From interviews with students in an HCI lab, we find that, in addition to theoretical knowledge of statistics, novice analysts require statistical know-how, i.e., practical knowledge of how various data characteristics are inter-related and how they influence significance test selection and statistics, to analyze data. However, current learning resources such as books and online searches are not adequate to help learn statistical know-how. As a possible solution, we present StatPlayground, an interactive web app that supports exploratory learning of statistical know-how. StatPlayground does this by allowing users to modify data via direct-manipulation of visualizations, to see how those changes affect other data characteristics such as the shape of the distribution and variance of the data, as well as the resulting significance test and statistics such as effect size and p-value. StatPlayground can be combined with traditional teaching methods and can help prepare students for real-world analysis. Our evaluation of StatPlayground with graduate students shows the potential of StatPlayground to help learn statistical know-how and design implications for simulation tools for learning statistics.

Keywords: Statistical analysis · Exploratory learning · Data visualization

1 Introduction

Inferential statistics is used to validate experimental findings in several scientific fields such as HCI [6], Medicine [2], and Psychology [1]. Over the past two decades, however, research has shown that inferential statistics is often used incorrectly [6,16,19]. A potential reason is the lack of adequate understanding of statistical concepts [6,14,28].

Electronic supplementary material The online version of this chapter (https://doi.org/10.1007/978-3-030-29384-0_9) contains supplementary material, which is available to authorized users.

D. Lamas et al. (Eds.): INTERACT 2019, LNCS 11747, pp. 156–165, 2019.
https://doi.org/10.1007/978-3-030-29384-0_9

To understand how students prepare to do statistical analysis, we interviewed twelve students (undergraduate, graduate, and doctoral) from the HCI research lab at our university who analyze real-world data. We found that, while students had formal training in statistics, they had to learn practical statistics and statistical tool usage in order to perform analysis. We refer to this practical knowledge of statistics as *statistical know-how*. Examples include understanding the influence of outliers on the shape of a distribution, knowledge of which test to perform when data has a uniform distribution, and understanding how data transformations could affect test selection and statistics. Resources that students use in order to prepare to do analysis either do not help gather statistical know-how or are often inaccurate and untrustworthy. Furthermore, with these resources, applying the knowledge to the context of their own analysis was reported to be difficult.

As a potential solution to help students learn statistical know-how, we introduce StatPlayground. StatPlayground is a web app that visualizes *hypothetical* data, computes the inferential statistics automatically by checking the assumptions of the data, and visualizes the results. Users manipulate the data to see how this affects other data characteristics and the resulting statistics in real time. E.g., adding an outlier to a distribution that is normally distributed, might result in the distribution being no longer normal, and the selection of a non-parametric test. StatPlayground facilitates exploratory learning to help users construct their own statistical know-how at their own pace. Unlike current statistical simulations that focus on few concepts, StatPlayground can help users understand how several statistical concepts are interrelated. Although statistical significance testing is still the most common analysis method in HCI, it does suffer from methodological issues [10,19]. For this reason, StatPlayground supports frequently used significance tests, but encourages the use of methods considered more meaningful such as *effect-size* and *95% confidence intervals* [9].

This paper contributes the following: (1) Results of a formative study that informs us about current statistical practice in HCI, (2) StatPlayground, a web application for exploratory learning of statistical know-how, and (3) findings from a preliminary user study to validate StatPlayground and the resulting design implications for teaching statistics using simulations.

2   Motivation and Related Work

We first describe the formative study that motivated StatPlayground and then discuss prior research in statistical education, simulations, and direct manipulation techniques.

2.1   Motivational Study: Statistical Practice in HCI Research

While previous research has investigated how students learn statistics in schools, not much is known about how students in universities prepare for a real-world analysis task. To investigate this, we interviewed 12 students (3 female) from the local HCI lab. Our participants include two undergraduate, eight graduate, and two doctoral students. All participants but one had performed at least one analysis in the past two months (median = 10 days). Three participants had ongoing analysis during the time period of our study, which we observed. On average, interviews lasted 45 min and observations lasted 1 hour. We analyzed the transcripts and observation videos by applying the *contextual design* methodology [4]. While our sampling accounts for variations in participants' educational background and experience, it is limited to HCI domain. The major findings from our study are:

Formal Education is Not Adequate for Real-World Analysis: We found that although students had taken a statistical course earlier, most (11/12) had to learn statistics again before working on a real-world analysis task. This might be because statistical courses tend to teach predominantly theoretical concepts. To perform real-world analysis, students gather two types of knowledge: statistical know-how and statistical tool usage. Statistical know-how, as we discussed earlier, involves an understanding of how various statistical concepts are interrelated. *"Which test should I apply here?"*, *"How do outliers affect my distribution?"*, and *"What happens if my data is left skewed?"* are some examples of statistical know-how students reported having to learn before conducting analysis.

Current Resources Do Not Help Learn Statistical Know-How: Students reported resorting to *just-in-time learning* of statistics to gather statistical know-how. As a result, traditional learning methods like books, lecture slides, and online courses, while considered useful, were reported to be infeasible to help prepare to do statistics. Students reported that, while using these resources, they had to spend too much time to identify information that is *relevant* for their analysis. Tutorials like ps4hci[1] and hcistats[2] helped learn tool usage, but not statistical know-how. On the other hand, online searches and web articles helped students answer specific questions about statistical know-how, but often had inaccurate or unreliable information. Even when students found reliable sources, they had to apply the knowledge in those sources to the context of their analysis, which is not straightforward.

2.2   Statistical Literacy and Principles in Statistical Education

Prior research in statistical education has shown that *active learning* tools can benefit students. E.g., Garfield suggests that instructors should allow students to construct knowledge of statistical concepts on their own based on prior knowledge [14]. Learning tools that facilitate this should allow students' guesses and predictions to be confronted with actual results through real-time feedback. In a similar vein, Biehler also recommends the use of a *'sandbox'* tool that allows students to explore statistical concepts by themselves [5]. Furthermore, Stat-Playground has the potential to help students gain the ability to make sense of

---

[1] https://depts.washington.edu/madlab/proj/ps4hci/.
[2] http://yatani.jp/teaching/doku.php?id=hcistats:start.

statistical information [11], the ability to identify the relationships between statistical concepts [14], have better data awareness [23], and understand statistical procedures better [13], all of which are considered to be key skills a statistician should have.

2.3   Simulations

The use of simulations for learning is not novel. E.g., simulations have been used to teach electrical circuits [7] and mathematics [22]. In statistical education, Rice Virtual Lab in Statistics[3], Seeing Theory[4], and Wise Interface for Statistical Education[5] are some prominent simulations. While research on the effectiveness of simulations on statistical education is sparse, there are some promising results. Simulations lead to better learning outcomes in comparison to traditional teaching methods [27]. But there is a caveat—not all simulations are effective; their *design* and how they are used play a critical role. E.g., students learn better from simulations when they are given appropriate questions to answer [17].

StatPlayground extends current statistical simulation tools in two ways. First, while current simulations focus on teaching a few statistical concepts, StatPlayground can help users understand how several statistical concepts are inter-related. This helps users gain a more *holistic* understanding of statistical concepts. Second, current simulations are *rigid*—they depict one example under certain fixed conditions. As a result, the knowledge transfer from simulations to the context of user's own analysis could be tedious and lead to further complications. StatPlayground allows for more flexibility by allowing the user to shape the data in several ways: Change the distribution type, change measures of central tendency and spread, add or remove individual data points, etc.

2.4   Direct Manipulation of Visualizations

In StatPlayground, users directly manipulate visualizations to modify data characteristics. Direct manipulation [25] is an established interaction technique that offers several benefits like real-time feedback and more user engagement [20]. We used prior research works that utilized direct manipulation successfully to manipulate data [18,20,24] to design StatPlayground. E.g., *foreshadowing*, a technique we use in StatPlayground to provide *feedforward* to the user to preview resulting statistics (see Fig. 3), is inspired by *OctoPocus* [3] and *Design by Dragging* [8].

3   System Design

We used an iterative design process to develop StatPlayground[6]. Initially, a proof-of-concept prototype was evaluated with five experts, all of whom have at

---

[3] http://onlinestatbook.com/rvls.html.
[4] http://seeingtheory.io.
[5] http://wise.cgu.edu.
[6] See supplements.

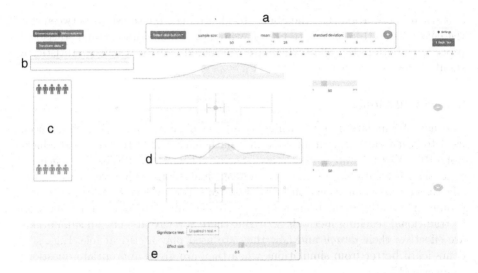

Fig. 1. StatPlayground contains three main panels: distribution generator (a), which can be used to generate the common data distributions by specifying parameters; results (e), which display the results of the current data configuration; plot, which uses box plot to visualize data distributions. Additionally, StatPlayground visualizes other data characteristics: shape of the distribution (d), homogeneity of the variances (b), and experimental design (c).

least two years of experience performing analysis; two experts teach statistics to undergraduate students. As a result of this evaluation, we identified features to be added to and removed from StatPlayground as well as some usability improvements.

Layout: StatPlayground has three panels: *data generation* (Fig. 1a), *plot*, and *results* (Fig. 1e). To begin with, the user generates common distributions like normal, uniform, and binomial distributions by setting the relevant parameters in the data generation panel. The generated data is then visualized as a box plot that shows the mean, median, inter-quartile range, and outliers of the distribution, as well as the confidence interval of the mean. Other data characteristics that influence inferential statistics are also visualized: shape of the distribution as a histogram curve (Fig. 1d), variance of each distribution as an animated bar chart at the top-left corner (Fig. 1b), and experimental design of the factor (Fig. 1c).

Interaction Design: Users interact with the plots in StatPlayground through *direct manipulation*. Click-and-dragging interface elements *modifies* the underlying data e.g., click-dragging a mean modifies the underlying mean of a distribution by modifying individual data points. Users can also create or delete data by clicking on either side of the whiskers and by clicking on an existing data point respectively. E.g., Fig. 3 (left) shows the interface after an outlier has been added; the histogram curve now indicates that the *test for normality* has failed.

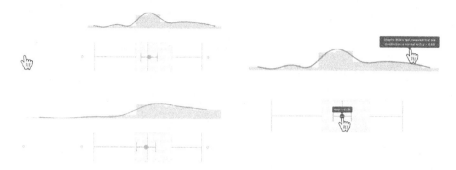

Fig. 2. Left: Users can create, edit, or delete data by directly interacting with the boxplot. Here, the user clicks to create an outlier. StatPlayground visualizes the change in data characteristics: the measures of central tendency shifts and the distribution is no longer normal! **Right:** StatPlayground uses progressive disclosure to reveal detailed information. User hovers over interface elements to view tooltips.

To avoid cluttering the interface, StatPlayground uses *progressive disclosure* to provide information on demand. E.g., hovering over any data point shows the characteristic and value (Fig. 3 bottom-right) and hovering over the histogram curve reveals statistics (Fig. 3 top-right).

Hovering over interface elements for 2 s shows *fine-level controls* that can be used to lock/unlock and set the range of values for data characteristics. This can be used to ask more fine-grained, what-if questions like *"Would the effect size of this comparison of two distributions increase even if the means of both distributions remain the same i.e., locked?"* Additionally, during direct manipulation, StatPlayground visualizes possible results the user can expect to reach along the path of her manipulation via *foreshadowing*. E.g., in Fig. 3, the user is click-dragging the mean of a distribution further away from the other distribution and foreshadowing helps see that moving them closer results in *smaller* effect sizes.

Statistical Computations in StatPlayground: Computing descriptive and inferential statistics from data is done mostly natively via JavaScript libraries[7]. However, inverse-computation of potential datasets from given inferential statistics (p-value, effect size), used in *foreshadowing*, is an interesting non-deterministic problem that has not been solved earlier. Prior research [21] is limited to inverse computation of datasets from *descriptive statistics*, not inferential statistics. Therefore, we built a Python package, *Cheno*[8] to perform inverse-computations of data from inferential statistics.

---

[7] https://github.com/pieterprovoost/jerzy, https://jstat.github.io.
[8] Cheno is an anagram of Cohen, a famous statistician who pioneered statistical power and effect size. See supplements.

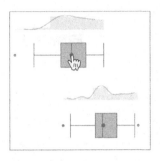 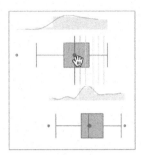 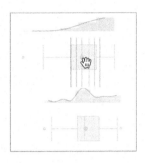

Fig. 3. StatPlayground uses *feedforward* to help users preemptively view statistical results. **Left:** Two distributions are being compared; user changes the mean of the distribution above by click-dragging it towards the mean of the distribution below. **Middle and right:** Feedforward elements indicate various effect sizes that would result upon further dragging.

4   Evaluation

We evaluated StatPlayground holistically to gauge its potential to help learn practical statistics.

Participants: 13 participants (4 female) volunteered to take part in the study. All participants are university students and have taken an introductory statistics course and/or performed an analysis earlier.

Procedure: Participants were presented with a hypothetical dataset and a set of questions to answer using StatPlayground. Questions were *story-driven* e.g., *"assume that of all participants in a text-entry experiment, one participant has practiced touch-typing; how does she (i.e., the outlier) affect your analysis?"* Follow-up questions were used to test if the participant was able to understand a concept that had come up earlier. We used a question-driven approach instead of open-ended exploration to motivate our participants. Participants were encouraged to think-aloud and we captured the audio and screen of the session.

Findings and Discussion: By analysing the collected data, we identified instances where StatPlayground helped participants gather statistical know-how e.g., how the measures of central tendency (mean, median) and spread (variance) influence the shape of the distribution, how effect sizes work in comparison to *p*-values, and how confidence intervals work. Participants found StatPlayground to be *easy to use* and *fun*. P3 compared StatPlayground to traditional learning methods, commenting *"this is a more intuitive way of grasping the concepts and understanding how they relate to each other."* P13 mentioned that if she were to continue using this tool, she could even *predict* the statistics from box plots. Nevertheless, some participants required more help than what was provided in the tutorial to understand certain concepts. Some participants also had difficulty using and interpreting fine-level control and homogeneity of variances graph respectively. We have since modified the app based on their feedback.

5   Implications and Future Work

Interaction Modes: Participants had varied motivation levels. Some participants were quite adventurous and explored StatPlayground without many prompts, while others were cautious (*"I could trial and error, but I am not sure whether what I observe will be interesting."* -P7). StatPlayground could cater to both of these target user groups. Cautious novices could use StatPlayground in a *guided mode*, where the interaction is driven by our prompts e.g., as in-place embellishments in visualizations [26]. More adventurous users and experts, e.g., course instructors, could use StatPlayground in an *unguided mode* to learn and teach statistical concepts. Before using StatPlayground in a classroom, however, instructors should use prior research on statistical education [12, 28] to design the prompts.

Help Compare Statistical Analysis Paradigms: During our study, we observed that participants compared the benefit of effect size and p-values, particularly noting how effect size tends to be less binary than p-values. StatPlayground could thus be used as a platform to compare paradigms of statistical methods e.g., Bayesian vs. frequentist inference.

Possible Misuse: Although StatPlayground is intended to be used as a learning tool, few participants wondered whether StatPlayground could be used for analyzing their own data e.g., as a quick-and-dirty way to *pilot test* analysis. However, since StatPlayground allows users to modify their data characteristics, using it for real-world analysis could lead the user to wander down the *"garden of forking paths"* [15]; the user would not be able to differentiate between exploratory and confirmatory analyses. To avoid this, StatPlayground currently does not allow users to work with their data.

6   Conclusion

We presented StatPlayground, an exploratory learning interface that allows students to construct their own understanding of statistical know-how by directly interacting with the visualization interface. While the user study indicates benefits of such an approach, future work can evaluate its effect on learning outcomes and statistical practice. Such exploratory learning interfaces provide an immersive, self-paced medium to bridge the gap between knowing the concepts in theory and applying them to a real-world problem. We are working on making StatPlayground available online at hci.rwth-aachen.de/statplayground.

Acknowledgements. We would like to thank Nur Hamdan and Chat Wacharaman-otham for their valuable feedback during the course of this project.

References

1. Aron, A., Coups, E., Aron, E.: Statistics for Psychology. Always Learning, 6th edn. Pearson, Upper Saddle River (2013). https://books.google.de/books?id=JtQPywAACAAJ

2. Banerjee, A., Jadhav, S., Bhawalkar, J.: Probability, clinical decision making and hypothesis testing. Ind. Psychiatry J. **18**(1), 64–69 (2009). https://doi.org/10. 4103/0972-6748.57864
3. Bau, O., Mackay, W.E.: OctoPocus: a dynamic guide for learning gesture-based command sets. In: Proceedings of the 21st Annual ACM Symposium on User Interface Software and Technology, UIST 2008, pp. 37–46. ACM, New York (2008). https://doi.org/10.1145/1449715.1449724
4. Beyer, H., Holtzblatt, K.: Contextual Design: Defining Customer-Centered Systems. Interactive Technologies. Elsevier Science (1998). https://books.google.de/books?id=sVKuMvaFzjQC
5. Biehler, R.: Software for learning and for doing statistics. Int. Stat. Rev. **65**(2), 167–189 (1997). https://doi.org/10.1111/j.1751-5823.1997.tb00399.x
6. Cairns, P.: HCI... not as it should be: inferential statistics in HCI research. In: Proceedings of the 21st British HCI Group Annual Conference on People and Computers: HCI...But Not As We Know It - Volume 1, BCS-HCI 2007, pp. 195–201. British Computer Society, Swinton (2007). http://dl.acm.org/citation.cfm?id=1531294.1531321
7. Carlsen, D.D., Andre, T.: Use of a microcomputer simulation and conceptual change text to overcome student preconceptions about electric circuits. J. Comput. Based Instruction **19**(4), 105–109 (1992). https://eric.ed.gov/?id=EJ457935
8. Coffey, D., Lin, C., Erdman, A.G., Keefe, D.F.: Design by dragging: an interface for creative forward and inverse design with simulation ensembles. IEEE Trans. Visual Comput. Graphics **19**(12), 2783–2791 (2013). https://doi.org/10. 1109/TVCG.2013.147
9. Cumming, G.: The new statistics: why and how. Psychol. Sci. **25**(1), 7–29 (2014). https://doi.org/10.1177/0956797613504966. pMID: 24220629
10. Dragicevic, P.: Fair statistical communication in HCI. In: Robertson, J., Kaptein, M. (eds.) Modern Statistical Methods for HCI. HIS, pp. 291–330. Springer, Cham (2016). https://doi.org/10.1007/978-3-319-26633-6_13
11. Gal, I.: Adults' statistical literacy: meanings, components, responsibilities. Int. Stat. Rev. **70**(1), 1–25. https://doi.org/10.1111/j.1751-5823.2002.tb00336.x
12. Garfield, J.: How students learn statistics. International Statistical Review/Revue Internationale de Statistique **63**(1), 25–34 (1995). http://www.jstor.org/stable/1403775
13. Garfield, J.: The challenge of developing statistical reasoning. J. Stat. Educ. **10**(3), null (2002). https://doi.org/10.1080/10691898.2002.11910676
14. Garfield, J., Ben-Zvi, D.: How students learn statistics revisited: a current review of research on teaching and learning statistics. Int. Stat. Rev. **75**(3), 372–396. https://doi.org/10.1111/j.1751-5823.2007.00029.x
15. Gelman, A., Loken, E.: The garden of forking paths: why multiple comparisons can be a problem, even when there is no "Fishing Expedition" or "p-Hacking" and the research hypothesis was posited ahead of time. Department of Statistics, Columbia University (2013)
16. Gray, W.D., Salzman, M.C.: Damaged merchandise? A review of experiments that compare usability evaluation methods. Hum. Comput. Inter. **13**(3), 203–261 (1998). https://doi.org/10.1207/s15327051hci13032
17. de Jong, T., Härtel, H., Swaak, J., van Joolingen, W.: Support for simulation-based learning: the effect of assignments in learning about transmission lines. In: Díaz de Ilarraza Sánchez, A., Fernández de Castro, I. (eds.) CALISCE 1996. LNCS, vol. 1108, pp. 9–26. Springer, Heidelberg (1996). https://doi.org/10.1007/BFb0022586

18. Kandel, S., Paepcke, A., Hellerstein, J., Heer, J.: Wrangler: interactive visual spec-
    ification of data transformation scripts. In: Proceedings of the SIGCHI Conference
    on Human Factors in Computing Systems, CHI 2011, pp. 3363–3372. ACM, New
    York (2011). https://doi.org/10.1145/1978942.1979444
19. Kaptein, M., Robertson, J.: Rethinking statistical analysis methods for CHI. In:
    Proceedings of the SIGCHI Conference on Human Factors in Computing Sys-
    tems, CHI 2012, pp. 1105–1114. ACM, New York (2012). https://doi.org/10.1145/
    2207676.2208557
20. Kondo, B., Collins, C.: DimpVis: exploring time-varying information visualizations
    by direct manipulation. IEEE Trans. Visual Comput. Graphics 20(12), 2003–2012
    (2014). https://doi.org/10.1109/TVCG.2014.2346250
21. Matejka, J., Fitzmaurice, G.: Same stats, different graphs: generating datasets
    with varied appearance and identical statistics through simulated annealing. In:
    Proceedings of the 2017 CHI Conference on Human Factors in Computing Sys-
    tems, CHI 2017, pp. 1290–1294. ACM, New York (2017). https://doi.org/10.1145/
    3025453.3025912
22. Reed, S.K.: Effect of computer graphics on improving estimates to algebra word
    problems. J. Educ. Psychol. 77(3), 285 (1985). https://doi.org/10.1037/0022-0663.
    77.3.285
23. Rumsey, D.J.: Statistical literacy as a goal for introductory statistics courses. J.
    Stat. Educ. 10(3), null (2002). https://doi.org/10.1080/10691898.2002.11910678
24. Rzeszotarski, J.M., Kittur, A.: Kinetica: naturalistic multi-touch data visualiza-
    tion. In: Proceedings of the SIGCHI Conference on Human Factors in Computing
    Systems, CHI 2014, pp. 897–906. ACM, New York (2014). https://doi.org/10.1145/
    2556288.2557231
25. Shneiderman, B.: Direct manipulation for comprehensible, predictable and con-
    trollable user interfaces. In: Proceedings of the 2nd International Conference on
    Intelligent User Interfaces, IUI 1997, pp. 33–39. ACM, New York (1997). https://
    doi.org/10.1145/238218.238281
26. Srinivasan, A., Drucker, S.M., Endert, A., Stasko, J.: Augmenting visualizations
    with interactive data facts to facilitate interpretation and communication. IEEE
    Trans. Visual Comput. Graphics 25(1), 672–681 (2019). https://doi.org/10.1109/
    TVCG.2018.2865145
27. Wackerly, D., Lang, J.: ExplorStat–active demonstration of statistical concepts.
    In: Joint Statistics Meeting, Chicago (1996)
28. Zieffler, A., Garfield, J., Alt, S., Dupuis, D., Holleque, K., Chang, B.: What does
    research suggest about the teaching and learning of introductory statistics at the
    college level? A review of the literature. J. Stat. Educ. 16(2) (2008). https://doi.
    org/10.1080/10691898.2008.11889566

Training Non-designers in Co-design Methods Through an Active Assisted Living Interactive Workshop

Paula Alexandra Silva[1(✉)] and Ana Dias Daniel[2]

[1] DigiMedia Research Centre, Universidade de Aveiro, Aveiro, Portugal
palexa@gmail.com
[2] GovCopp, Universidade de Aveiro, Aveiro, Portugal
anadaniel@ua.pt

Abstract. In the era of participation, design and development teams are called to utilize co-design methods in their work and thus required to master the use and appropriate application of those types of methods. However, not all teams, and certainly not all team members, are learned or trained in co-design. This raises challenges not only to the use of co-design methods, but also to its skilful application. This paper reports on an interactive co-design workshop with seventeen EU-funded project coordinators, to investigate their perception on the extent to which the workshop activities impacted their level of empathy towards others, ease of communication, and openness to employ co-design methods. Considering the hands-on and playful nature of the methods, we also investigate participants' perceptions on the methods' ease of application in a real-world context as well as their effectiveness in increasing participants' knowledge of co-design methods. Results indicate that the proposed activities positively contribute to all the dimensions investigated, with the highest effect being achieved in increasing participants' openness to employ co-design methods and the playful nature of the activities being perceived as contributing more to the learning effectiveness than the hands-on approach of the activities.

Keywords: Co-design methods · Training · Active and assisted living

1 Introduction

Product design has been around from the moment that the first artefact was created, received its functional shape, was adapted to satisfy its purpose, and personalised so that its user or owner could be identified. Since then, and as technology became more pervasive, much has changed and the more traditional-oriented approaches have gradually been replaced by more user-oriented ones. Among the latter, we find participatory design, or cooperative design (co-design), as it was originally referred to by the Scandinavian approach [1, 2]. Regardless of its maturity and the general endearment co-design receives from the design community, only recently has this approach been gaining momentum, with studies demonstrating its value [3, 4] and reporting on its use, for example in active and assisted living contexts [5–8]. However, employing a co-design approach can be complicated, demanding, costly, and time-consuming [9], so R&D teams might be sceptic or even resistant to the notion that user involvement

D. Lamas et al. (Eds.): INTERACT 2019, LNCS 11747, pp. 166–175, 2019.
https://doi.org/10.1007/978-3-030-29384-0_10

can bring value to the design process and outcomes [10]. One way to address this misbelief is to create opportunities for project coordinators to experience co-design activities and consequently develop their perception and openness to the approach. In this context, this paper reports on an interactive workshop organized with the purpose of introducing and training project coordinators on co-design and the type of activities that can be carried out while practicing it.

In the following sections, we provide a concise background on co-design and present the main design activities conducted during the workshop. Next, we present the research approach taken to identify the workshop impact on participants' skills acquisition, intention of use, perception towards applicability, and perceived learning effectiveness. In the later part of the paper, we present and discuss descriptive results and findings of the workshop impact on the participants' perception, through a post-workshop questionnaire, and outline the contribution of this case study – a set of suitable design activities and exercises – in the field of co-design.

2 Background

2.1 What Is Co-design?

The terms co-design and participatory design refer to a class of design-approaches that stresses the importance of the active, creative participation and collaboration of potential end-users and other stakeholders in the design process [1, 2]. Users are experts of their own experience [10] and as such, when implementing a co-design approach, potential end-users participate actively in the design process as domain experts, working in cooperation, as equal partners, with the design team [11]. As a result of this process, implicit knowledge surfaces, that can be used to inform product design. By working collaboratively with end-users, otherwise missed key design insights can be gathered, thus increasing the chances of creating design solutions and products which are both, relevant and accurate in meeting end-user needs [9, 10]. This generally involves engaging in a number of collaborative activities, the so-called 'generative tools' [11] or 'tools for conversation' [12], that allow users and stakeholders to dialogue and contribute their views, insights, and feedback, throughout the design process, at all stages. Examples of this kind of methods are scarce and the literature also fails to provide effective training approaches on how to develop/apply them.

2.2 Why Is Co-design Important and What Challenges Does It Pose?

Research suggests that including and engaging end-users in the design process allows for effective requirements gathering and increases both user satisfaction and level of acceptance of the final design [9]. To employ co-design practices is also key if aiming at novel [3], differentiated and inclusive solutions [10]. Therefore, if one strives that technology, devices or services are successfully adopted when market-ready [3, 4, 13], to practice a co-design approach is the recommended method. Still, although co-design enables everyone to have a 'voice', be an 'active agent of change', and to contribute their problem-solving capacity, employing a co-design approach can be a challenging endeavour, as it requires the involvement of a large number of stakeholders from diverse backgrounds, each with different personal characteristics [10]. The management of such a collaborative process can indeed be difficult, as the process involves negotiation among stakeholders (for e.g. older adults, formal/informal caregivers, municipalities) [14]. As a result, members of a co-design team need be enabled in order to successfully build familiarity and create trust [3]. Furthermore, for collective creativity to take place, a safe and inclusive environment, where space is made for open dialogues to happen naturally and respectfully, is essential. This requires that members develop skills not only of group communication, to allow for the successful conveying and sharing of ideas, but also of empathy towards others. Another challenge in co-design pertains to resource scarcity [9, 10] both in terms of time and/or money and access to qualified facilitators. If properly addressed, co-design challenges turn out to be unique advantages, especially in contrast to traditional design methods. Co-design is pivotal in building partnerships where feedback is celebrated and exchanged, and it is thus our role, as researchers and practitioners, to find efficient ways of practicing it and effectively training people in such approaches. A successful implementation of co-design may then be able to bypass the, too-often observed, dichotomy of 'us versus them' and create value for all stakeholders.

3   Interactive Co-design Workshop

3.1   Workshop Line-Up

The interactive co-design workshop, on which this exploratory study is based, took place on March 12th, 2019 in Brussels, Belgium, as part of a larger event, aimed at training EU-funded projects coordinators on topics, such as end-users' involvement, business approaches, and administrative reporting. The workshop aimed to introduce and train participants on co-design methods, under the motto "Designing for communities, with communities!" The associated design brief was: "Getting places when I can no longer drive".

The workshop was meant to mimic, as much possible, an actual workshop with real end-users and was organized in four parts: (i) workshop introduction; (ii) user understanding; (iii) prototyping and ideation; and (iv) workshop conclusion. Parts (ii) and (iii), respectively allocated to user understanding and prototyping and ideation, took the lion's share of workshop time. Part (ii), understanding user goals, resorted to two activities: a role-play and a sailboat exercise. Part (iii), dedicated to the early prototyping and ideation, was based on the 6-8-5, or the crazy eights, exercise. Given the absence of adequate training methods, the approach used in the workshop was developed from scratch, to specifically cater for the learning objectives defined for the workshop.

3.2   Role-Play and Sailboat Exercise

The opening session was followed by the role-play and sailboat exercises. Role-play was a workshop necessity, as no real end-users participated in the workshop. At the same time, role-playing a user can support participants' awareness and empathy for end-user needs, hence presenting a learning opportunity. For these purposes, a set of profile roles was created for groups to role-play when working together. Each set of profiles included four roles, each represented by a photo and a descriptive text (Fig. 1). The roles included a design researcher, a primary user (older adult), an informal care-giver (e.g. a neighbor, daughter/son), and a role representing a given domain expertise (e.g. company director, municipality representative, health insurance manager).

The sailboat exercise is inspired by agile team retrospectives [15] and has been adapted to be used as a co-design generative tool for user understanding and requirements gathering [16]. In this workshop, the sailboat exercise served as the basis for participants to engage in a shared activity that aimed at the elicitation of user goals and desires, in the context of the design brief "Getting places when I can no longer drive". To assist in this task, a drawing of a sailboat and its surrounding factors, i.e. trade winds, anchor, sun/land, ocean rocks (Fig. 2) and a set of prompt questions (Fig. 3) were made available, which were meant to facilitate communication and reasoning and to assist in the elicitation of beneficial and/or detrimental experiential aspects.

Fig. 1. Set of profiles

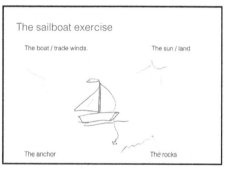

Fig. 2. Sailboat exercise support sheet.

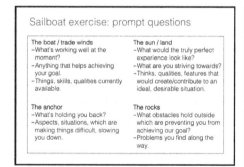

Fig. 3. Sailboat exercise prompt questions

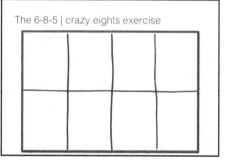

Fig. 4. 6-8-5 exercise support sheet.

3.3   6-8-5 Exercise

Having developed an understanding of users needs, it was possible to proceed to ideation and prototyping. To support this task, the workshop used the 6-8-5 exercise [17], a rapid ideation and early prototyping method that invites individuals, participating in a design activity, to draw six to eight sketches for a user interface concept in five minutes (allowing ∼40 s to be spent on each panel). In order to document and discuss the participants' design solution, a blank page with eight panels (Fig. 4) was made available to each participant for her/him to envision and draft design solutions.

3.4   Facilitator

The workshop facilitator was an experienced Human-Computer Interaction (HCI) lecturer and researcher with a vast experience in both methods for creativity and innovation as well as in designing solutions for the ageing population and its related ecosystems. A skilled and experienced facilitator is essential [10], as previous research has linked the skills of a facilitator with an overall higher workshop efficiency and increased participant motivation and enjoyment [18].

4   Research Approach

4.1   Participants

The workshop involved 17 participants (five female, 12 male), all of them coordinators of projects funded under the Active and Assisted Living Joint Programme [19]. Participant age varied, with two participants aged between 21–29, six between 30–39, four between 40–49, three between 50–59, and two participants, who were 60 or older. Participants indicated to reside in a variety of European countries, including Austria, Belgium, Denmark, Poland, Portugal, Romania, Spain, Switzerland, and the Netherlands. With regards to the level of education and specialization of the 17 participants, two reported holding a high school diploma, two a college degree, two a bachelor's degree, six a master's degree, one a professional degree, and four a doctorate degree. Participants were from diverse backgrounds, seven from an engineering-related background and four from a finance-related background. The remaining participants were from areas such as communication, psychology, gerontechnology, pharmacy, and marketing. In terms of their work context, most participants described themselves as working in and SME/Business, while another seven were from Research/Academia, and one from an End-user organisation.

4.2   Procedures and Data Gathering

The start of the workshop consisted of a facilitator introduction, an overview of the aim and goals of the workshop and the request to gather anonymous, non-identifying data of the participants through informed consent. Data was gathered through the research materials in the workshop and a questionnaire at the end of the workshop. All participants agreed to take part in the study. Next, participants introduced themselves and the facilitator made a short presentation on the value of co-design. From this point onwards, participants were introduced and given time to perform each of the planned activities, as introduced in Sect. 3.1. First, the participants were grouped into five teams (three groups of three and two of four). Then, after participants were introduced to the design brief and the rules for ideation[1] and discussion[2], the activities started. The profile roles for the role-play exercise were randomly picked from the available set of profiles. The sailboat exercise, which outcome was a set of user requirements, elicited with the support of the prompt questions, and the 6-8-5 exercise, which outcome was a conceptual low-fidelity paper prototype, were first performed individually and then collaboratively developed by the team as a group. As the group completed the activities and came up with a concept for their product or service, each group shared the final results with the whole group, in the debriefing session.

As the workshop activities came to an end, participants were invited to fill out a questionnaire about the session. This questionnaire (available on request) was the main tool used for data collection and was organized as follows: (i) Demographics: age, gender, level of education, background, country of living, work context, professional role/occupation; (ii) Experience and use of co-design methods: level of experience, frequency of use in work context, design cycle phase; (iii) Impacts on skills acquisition: empathy, communication; (iv) Intention of use and applicability: openness to future use, application to real-world context; and (v) Features of activities and learning effectiveness: hands-on approach, playful nature.

The answer format of the questionnaire sections (i) Demographic and (ii) Experience and use of co-design methods questions was a selection ranged items or an alternative, open-ended response. The remaining questionnaire sections (iii)–(v) were answered through a seven-point Likert-type scale, ranging from 'No experience' (1) to 'Very experienced' (7) for experience, from 'Never' (1) to 'At all times' (7) for frequency of use, and from 'Totally disagree' (1) to 'Totally agree' (7) for all other questions. From the questionnaire, a coding protocol was developed, after which data was entered and descriptively analyzed in IBM's Statistical Package for the Social Sciences (SPSS).

5   Results and Findings

5.1   Impacts on Skills Acquisition and Intention of Use

Table 1 shows, with regards to the impacts on skills acquisition and future intention of use, that the three exercises together was the best teaching approach to develop skills related to empathy towards the perspectives of others as well as to communication.

---

[1] Rules for ideation were: Do embrace creativity; Do encourage the craziness; Do get ideas on paper – write, scribble, draw, get them there; Do keep mindful of time – the clock is ticking; Do build on the ideas of others.

[2] Rules for discussion: Do treat each other with respect; Do let others speak; Do remember the design is not meant to suit your own preferences – don't judge based on them; Do discuss with harmony – don't be a negative critic; Do listen – the input from others is not going to be there forever.

This was also the approach that most increased participants' openness to employing co-design methods in future projects. Scrutinizing each particular exercise, participants considered that the role-play exercise was the least relevant for developing skills of empathy and communication, as opposed to the 6-8-5 exercise which was the most relevant across dimensions.

Table 1. Descriptive statistics on the impacts on skills acquisition and intention of use.

Variable		N	M	SD	Min	Max
Greater level of empathy	Role play	15	5.00	1.37	2	7
	Boat Exercise	15	5.07	1.44	3	7
	6-8-5 Exercise	14	5.21	1.01	3	6
	All exercise together	14	5.50	1.18	3	7
Facilitated communication	Role play	16	5.00	1.32	2	7
	Boat Exercise	16	5.25	1.09	3	7
	6-8-5 Exercise	14	5.57	0.90	4	7
	All exercise together	16	5.81	0.88	4	7
Openness to employing co-design	Role play	16	5.56	1.58	2	7
	Boat Exercise	16	5.56	1.46	2	7
	6-8-5 Exercise	15	5.73	1.39	2	7
	All exercise together	15	5.87	1.31	2	7

Legend: N = number of participants who answered; M = mean; SD = Standard deviation; Min = minimum; Max = maximum

5.2   Applicability and Learning Effectiveness

Table 2 shows, regarding the applicability of the different exercises in a real-world context, participants have a positive perception towards their usefulness. Into what concerns the effectiveness of the hands-on and playful nature of the exercises in increasing participant's knowledge on co-design methods, both features seem to be recognized as positive, with its playful nature showing slightly better ratings overall.

Table 2. Descriptive statistics on applicability and effectiveness in learning about co-design.

Variable	N	M	SD	Min	Max
Exercises are easy to apply to real contexts	17	5.20	1.52	3	7
Hands-on approach is effective in increasing knowledge of co-design methods	17	5.41	1.33	3	7
Playful nature is effective in increasing knowledge of co-design methods	17	5.82	1.10	3	7

Legend: N = number of participants who answered; M = mean; SD = Standard deviation; Min = minimum; Max = maximum

6 Discussion

The skills related to empathy and communication are crucial when employing co-design approaches, not only because they facilitate the interaction with others, but also because they are key in allowing design teams to identify and interpret peoples' needs and expectations. Prior research [20, 21] has stressed the importance of understanding how such social and emotional skills could be taught, thus becoming an emerging research area within HCI. The approach proposed in this workshop allows for the development of these skills, through stimulating empathy and communication skills as well as the openness to experimentation in the field. To recognize the value of employing such design approaches is particularly relevant when referring to project coordinators, who are often the one key decision makers in determining what activities to prioritize and which resources to spend in design projects.

In the case of the workshop described in this paper, it seems that the different exercises were complementary in the sense that they enabled for the development of skills crucial for the deeper understanding of the self and the others, addressing the needs highlighted in [14]. In doing so, the awareness of the importance of these types of methods was also developed. Still, the workshop participants did point out that, when carrying out the exercises with older adults, more time was likely to be needed in order to accommodate for any vision, auditory, or memory limitations. Contrasting the three different exercises used during the workshop, the role-play activity is the least valued activity in terms of improving empathy and communication. Arguably, this might be explained due to participants' awareness that, when in a real-world setting, outside a training room, they will indeed be working with actual end-users.

The positive impressions left by the workshop in terms of skills acquisition and intention of use were also observed when participants were inquired about the ease of application of the exercises in a real-world context. On the one hand, participants felt that the workshop was useful to understand the benefits of employing co-design methods, as well as its main characteristics, promoting the openness to its future use. On the other hand, through the hands-on approach followed, it was possible for participants to experience their playful nature. Playfulness is important in fostering motivation, involvement and fun, and thus central in the process of knowledge acquisition [22]. This again supports the idea that it is beneficial to run these types of workshops with multidisciplinary teams.

7 Conclusions and Future Work

In the form of an exploratory case study, this paper contributes a set of activities, here presented in the form of a workshop, to train multidisciplinary teams in co-design methods. Each of the exercises is described as well as the remaining procedures to allow for its future replication. Seventeen project coordinators were consulted to assess the value of the approach followed in terms of skill acquisition, intention of use, applicability, and learning effectiveness. Results show an overall positive opinion towards the approach, with participants recognizing it improved empathy and communication and increased their openness to employ co-design methods. The opinions also indicate the playfulness is valued when it comes the learning effectiveness.

As an exploratory study, with a relatively small sample, the study allows for limited extrapolation and can be seen as a first-step to conduct more detailed inquiries into co-design awareness and usage in the future. Regardless of the limitations, results are encouraging and indicate that workshops like this may indeed raise the required awareness on the necessity of engaging end-users through participatory approaches, if we are to design products and services that suit user needs and lifestyles. The contributions of this paper have implications for both researchers and practitioners working in the field. Not only does the paper provide the community with a replicable training tool, as the results have also indicated that the approach followed allowed for the development of the, much needed in design, social and emotional skills.

Acknowledgements. This research was developed with the support of the Research Program "CeNTER - Community-led Territorial Innovation" (CENTRO-01-0145-FEDER-000002), funded by Programa Operacional Regional do Centro (CENTRO 2020), PT2020. We would also like to express our gratitude to the workshop participants and to Phil Jordan, University of Hawai'i Manoa, for the suggestions on the manuscript.

References

1. Kyng, M.: Scandinavian design: users in product development. In: Proceedings of the SIGCHI Conference on Human Factors in Computing Systems, pp. 3–9. ACM, New York (1994)
2. Kyng, M.: Designing for cooperation: cooperating in design. Commun. ACM **34**, 65–73 (1991). https://doi.org/10.1145/125319.125323
3. Trischler, J., Pervan, S.J., Kelly, S.J., Scott, D.R.: The value of codesign: the effect of customer involvement in service design teams. J. Serv. Res. **21**, 75–100 (2018). https://doi.org/10.1177/1094670517714060
4. Wherton, J., Sugarhood, P., Procter, R., Hinder, S., Greenhalgh, T.: Co-production in practice: how people with assisted living needs can help design and evolve technologies and services. Implementation Sci. **10**, 75 (2015). https://doi.org/10.1186/s13012-015-0271-8
5. Doyle, J., Bailey, C., Ni Scanaill, C., van den Berg, F.: Lessons learned in deploying independent living technologies to older adults' homes. Univ. Access Inf. Soc. **13**, 191–204 (2014). https://doi.org/10.1007/s10209-013-0308-1
6. Lee, H.R., et al.: Steps toward participatory design of social robots: mutual learning with older adults with depression. In: 2017 12th ACM/IEEE International Conference on Human-Robot Interaction (HRI), pp. 244–253 (2017)
7. Branco, R.M., Quental, J., Ribeiro, Ó.: Personalised participation: an approach to involve people with dementia and their families in a participatory design project. CoDesign **13**, 127–143 (2017). https://doi.org/10.1080/15710882.2017.1310903
8. Vilarinho, T., Floch, J., Stav, E.: Co-designing a mHealth application for self-management of cystic fibrosis. In: Bernhaupt, R., Dalvi, G., Joshi, A., Balkrishan, D.K., O'Neill, J., Winckler, M. (eds.) INTERACT 2017. LNCS, vol. 10515, pp. 3–22. Springer, Cham (2017). https://doi.org/10.1007/978-3-319-67687-6_1
9. Kujala, S.: User involvement: a review of the benefits and challenges. Behav. Inf. Technol. **22**, 1–16 (2003). https://doi.org/10.1080/01449290301782

10. Co-Create Project: Co-Create Essentials (2019)
11. Sanders, E.B.-N., Stappers, P.J.: Co-creation and the new landscapes of design. CoDesign **4**, 5–18 (2008). https://doi.org/10.1080/15710880701875068
12. Sanders, E.B.-N.: Generative tools for co-designing. In: Scrivener, S.A.R., Ball, L.J., Woodcock, A. (eds.) Collaborative Design, pp. 3–12. Springer, London, London (2000). https://doi.org/10.1007/978-1-4471-0779-8_1
13. Hardisty, A.R., et al.: Bridging two translation gaps: a new informatics research agenda for telemonitoring of chronic disease. Int. J. Med. Inform. **80**, 734–744 (2011). https://doi.org/10.1016/j.ijmedinf.2011.07.002
14. Fitzpatrick, G., Malmborg, L.: Quadruple helix model organisation and tensions in participatory design teams. In: Proceedings of the 10th Nordic Conference on Human-Computer Interaction, pp. 376–384. ACM, New York (2018)
15. Krause, R.: UX Retrospectives 101. https://www.nngroup.com/articles/ux-retrospectives/
16. Silva, P.A.: The sailboat exercise as a method for user understanding and requirements gathering. In: Adjunct Proceedings INTERACT 2019 (2019)
17. Gray, D.: 6-8-5 (2011). https://gamestorming.com/6-8-5s/
18. Silva, P.A., Read, J.C.: A methodology to evaluate creative design methods: a study with the BadIdeas method. In: Proceedings of the 22nd Conference of the Computer-Human Interaction Special Interest Group of Australia on Computer-Human Interaction, pp. 264–271. ACM, New York (2010)
19. AAL Programme - Active Assisted Living Programme - Ageing Well. http://www.aal-europe.eu/
20. Slovák, P., Fitzpatrick, G.: Teaching and developing social and emotional skills with technology. ACM Trans. Comput.-Hum. Interact. **22**, 19:1–19:34 (2015). https://doi.org/10.1145/2744195
21. Slovák, P., Thieme, A., Murphy, D., Tennent, P., Olivier, P., Fitzpatrick, G.: On becoming a counsellor: challenges and opportunities to support interpersonal skills training. In: Proceedings of the 18th ACM Conference on Computer Supported Cooperative Work & Social Computing, pp. 1336–1347. ACM, New York (2015)
22. Llorens-Largo, F., Gallego-Durán, F.J., Villagrá-Arnedo, C.J., Compañ-Rosique, P., Satorre-Cuerda, R., Molina-Carmona, R.: Gamification of the learning process: lessons learned. IEEE Revista Iberoamericana de Tecnologias del Aprendizaje **11**, 227–234 (2016). https://doi.org/10.1109/RITA.2016.2619138

Education and HCI Curriculum II

Education and HCI Curriculum II

Embodied Interaction in Language Learning: Enhancing Students' Collaboration and Emotional Engagement

Panagiotis Kosmas[(⊠)][iD] and Panayiotis Zaphiris

Cyprus Interaction Lab,
Cyprus University of Technology, 3075 Limassol, Cyprus
panayiotis.kosmas@cut.ac.cy

Abstract. Embodied interaction enriches conventional educational practice and provides ways of integrating the physical body and movement into the learning process. The Embodied theoretical framework via the use of emerging technologies has significantly changed the direction of teaching allowing learners to be more active and engage in collaborative learning activities. This study investigates students' performance in a collaborative embodied learning environment using motion-based games within a real classroom language learning context. Participants were 52 elementary students (second and third graders) and five teachers. The analysis is based on a students' questionnaire, direct classroom observations and semi-structured interviews with participating teachers. Findings indicate that embodied learning interactions enabled students to work more collaboratively engaging them in the learning activities, physically and emotionally. The paper contributes to the HCI community by providing a better and evidence-based understanding of the potential of using embodied technology in collaborative settings within a real classroom environment.

Keywords: Embodied Interaction · Embodied learning ·
Collaborative learning · CSCL · Language learning · Emotional performance ·
Classroom · School

1 Introduction

With the significant growth of technology, massive efforts are underway to enrich traditional teaching and learning practices with the use of technology. Embodied learning is based on the idea that mind and body are closely interlinked emphasizing the inseparable link of brain, body, and environment [1]. Obviously, this approach offers new teaching and learning methods bringing the physical body and movement into the classroom. Previous literature reveals that movement and physical engagement has potential on students' cognitive and academic performance [2, 3]. Also, researchers in the field, argue that educational interventions based on the idea of embodied interaction make learning more accessible to all students giving them opportunities for active participation and engagement [4].

In Human Computer Interaction (HCI) field, Embodied Interaction, as proposed by Dourish [5], emphasised on the development of interactive experiences in the service of learning in different educational environments. Embodied interaction also attempts to

© IFIP International Federation for Information Processing 2019
Published by Springer Nature Switzerland AG 2019
D. Lamas et al. (Eds.): INTERACT 2019, LNCS 11747, pp. 179–196, 2019.
https://doi.org/10.1007/978-3-030-29384-0_11

explore the impact of embodiment and technology in creating new forms of meaningful interactive learning experiences. Embodied technologies include among other motion-based technologies, tangible tools, multi-sensor technologies and gesture technologies.

Over the last decades, the design and orchestration of computer-supported learning environments have been importantly influenced by the evolution of embodied learning approach. Recent explorations in educational settings indicate the positive impact of embodied learning technologies not only in students' learning outcomes [6] but also in students' emotional engagement and performance during the learning process [3].

Embodied interaction practices can enhance collaboration between students and facilitate the collaborative aim of educators through the use of technology. One example is the use of motion sensing technologies for educational purposes, which can engage students physically in the learning process. There are many motion-based technologies; most of them use the Microsoft Kinect camera.

Within the collaborative learning environment, students can work, produce and construct together with the new knowledge as the guidance from the teacher is limited. The role of technology in such learning environments is to support students' learning in order to create their own knowledge through group interaction [7]. Indeed, there is an ongoing interest in socially oriented theories of learning which propose a new perspective on learning based on Computer-supported collaborative learning [8].

Considering all of this, it is not surprising that the exploration of collaborative learning environments that integrate bodily movements into the classroom is gaining traction in the research community. International studies highlight the positive impact of movement on students' learning outcomes, on their engagement and on their attention. According to researchers [1, 3] learning takes place through the body and all its senses, whilst movement plays a significant role in how we control our body in space and in relation to others.

To that end, this study examines if the embodied interaction delivered through the use of motion-based games (i.e., Kinect educational games) can facilitate the collaboration between students. In particular, the study implements embodied learning as part of the learning activities in a real elementary classroom environment using motion-based technology to address:

- (a) the students' perceptions and feelings and
- (b) the teachers' perceived experiences regarding the collaboration and behavior of students during the educational intervention.

The contribution of this study is to provide empirical evidence of how embodied interaction can enhance the delivery of learning offering opportunities for effective collaboration between students.

The sections that follow review first the theoretical approach of embodied learning and interaction, specifically embodied cognition and its relationship with education emphasizing on the applications of this kind of learning in collaborative environments. Second, the methodology of the research is explained, and major findings are presented. The manuscript concludes with the discussion part highlighting the potential of embodied interaction in the computer-supported collaborative learning context.

2   The Embodied Perspective of Cognition

During the last century, embodied cognition emerged as a new theoretical model, promoting the integration of the body into the general system of cognition and introducing movement into learning and teaching practice. The general viewpoint of embodied cognition theory is founded on the idea that the mind must be understood only through its relationship to the bodily interactions in the world. Theorists argue that mind and body are closely interlinked [1] and emphasizes the role of bodily experience in education in relation to childhood and adolescence [9].

Collectively, the literature agrees that embodied cognition refers to the idea that the body influences the mind. Is the belief that humans' ability to gain knowledge, comprehend, remember, judge, and problem-solving are not confined to the brain. In this view, cognition then is influenced, if not determined, by humans' experiences with the world [10–13]. In the same line, embodied learning approach provides alternative learning strategies, especially those that take advantage of emerging embodied technologies.

In terms of embodied cognition's theoretical applications for education, several researchers have proposed frameworks or integration strategies/methodologies to explain how embodiment could work in educational and learning contexts. One of the first attempts in this direction was Barsalou's [14] framework of perceptual symbol systems. According to Barsalou [14], humans or learners develop multisensory representations of their environment using their sensory neural abilities.

Similarly, Gallagher and Lindgren [15] proposed the term "enactment". Enactment happens when bodily movements are used for specific learning tasks during the learning process. These bodily movements, or enactments, have a significant connection to their concomitant tasks/targets [15]. Regarding the integration of embodiment into digital learning media, Melcer and Isbister [16] created a framework that includes seven different categories which facilitate the implementation of embodied learning. Particularly, Melcer and Isbister [16] talked about the following categories: physicality, transforms, mapping, correspondence, mode of play, coordination, and the environment.

2.1   Embodied Interaction

Over the last few decades, HCI research has been increasingly influenced by embodied cognition theory with a great deal of theoretical and empirical implications. Indeed, the embodied perspective of learning and cognition has informed interaction and user-experience design. As Dourish [5] points out, "Embodiment is the property of our engagement with the world that allows us to make it meaningful", and thus, "Embodied Interaction is the creation, manipulation, and changing of meaning through engaged interaction with artifacts" (32, p. 3). In his work, Dourish [5] states the need for creating new ways of interacting with digital reality, techniques that can better satisfy the people's needs and abilities. For this purpose, the context seems to be one of the main issues for HCI design and interactive systems more broadly.

The ubiquitous computing era is bringing to the people the possibility to interact always and everywhere with digital information. However, the interaction means used to access this information exploit only a few of the human sensorimotor abilities. Most of these interactions happen through a traditional desktop or mobile interface, which often involve just vision and hearing senses and require the movement of only one or few fingers.

Theories of cognition have changed radically over the years upon recent trends in interaction and embodiment is the basis for a new foundational approach to HCI. Researchers in the area of HCI try to find a way to design forms for a wider range of engagements and interactions. Tangible computing and in general Tangible User Interfaces (TUIs) have this concern, to create a new more interactive and innovative context to facilitate the user's experiences [17, 18]. Thus, new forms of interaction such as the use of multi-sensory artifacts, gesture technologies, and whole-body interaction have created for Embodied interaction purposes [19].

With the emergence of ubiquitous technologies for learning in concepts of embodiment [20], many researchers have started to rethink about the design of these new technologies in order to create more embodied learning experiences [21]. Designers, researchers and educators confirm the need to move from abstract - theoretical teaching and learning to embodied teaching and learning, and this indeed is the challenge in education [22].

In conclusion, HCI has an important role in the implementation of these new kinds of interactivity based on the embodied framework. Given that, with the careful attention to existing practices and procedures, HCI has the key to push the boundaries of new technology, design, and evaluation, for the development of the field [23]. These new promising theories of embodiment, when they can apply to the HCI area, can make cognitive science productive and exciting again [24].

2.2   Embodied Cognition and Collaboration: Empirical Evidence

Empirical studies on embodied cognition and learning show that the bodily engagement and movement into the learning process has a positive impact on students' development of cognitive and academic performance [2, 3]. In particular, previous research in the area implementing embodied learning via technology has revealed that this kind of interventions and interactions has potential for cognitive functioning and academic performance for students [25]. Recent studies have also shown that the engagement of students in embodied learning contexts was also beneficial for students' emotional state [2, 26].

In collaborative learning contexts, some studies have indicated that collaborative methods led to high achievements comparing with other learning environments. Especially, a great deal of research studies has pointed out the value of computers and technologies in promoting collaboration between students in the classroom. However, some studies have revealed that students had difficulties to adjust their learning in these computer-based learning environments [27]. As Klemmer et al. [28] noted, the role of tangibility and in general the role of artifacts in collaboration is to facilitate all the collaborative aspects between learners. These technologies can also offer teachers opportunities to "orchestrate" or prepare the collaboration settings inside and between groups [29].

The study of Johnson-Glenberg, Birchfield, Tolentino, and Koziupa, [30] examining the students' learning outcomes in science, have revealed that the Embodied Mixed Reality Learning Environment (EMRELE) enhanced students' learning. Their conclusions indicate that the engagement of students in a collaborative embodied learning environment led to greater learning gains compared to other environments. In a recent study [31] the students' learning experiences enhanced by different ways of scaffolding. Results of this study indicated that the multi-touch device facilitated students' collaboration while experiencing bodily interactions with mathematical properties. As some researchers have noted that the collaboration in game-based worlds is at the same time complex, multi-causal and dynamic. For example, the study of Wendel, Gutjahr, Goebel, and Steinmetz [32] showed that group learning can be significantly affected by whether the group ends up with a leader or not.

Studies making use of different multi-touch devices highlighted that the interaction with these technologies led to effective collaborative learning and direct manipulation of a learning environment [33]. Alvarez, Brown, and Nussbaum, [34] agree that the use of a multi-touch interface can support the interaction between students enhancing the whole-group discussions and equal participation. In the same lines, Schneps et al., [35] claimed that the interaction with technology enables embodied learning experiences allowing learners to construct and produce new knowledge.

In general, taking into account the recent empirical work in this area, the collaborative learning in the classroom within the embodied learning context can significantly lead to higher learning outcomes, in terms of a higher level of reasoning, motivation, and social skills [36, 37] than conventional teaching practices. On the other hand, embodied learning activities in classrooms as Danish, Enyedy, Saleh, Lee, and Andrade, [38] said, may provoke off-task behavior and distract from the actual learning goals.

Additionally, some empirical studies have revealed the positive impact of embodied interaction in language learning, particularly in language development and comprehension [39, 40]. Findings of Cassar and Jang [41] demonstrated that the embodied learning activities improved the literacy skills of elementary students, while the study of Chang, Chien, Chiang, Lin, and Lai [42] showed that the embodied interaction enhanced the verbal information of students. Other studies in the context of language learning, revealed significant improvements in students' understanding and recall of information [43], and in second language acquisition [44].

Overall, despite the potential use of embodied learning technologies in various educational settings, little work has explicitly examined the integration of such technologies in collaborative environments in real classrooms. The present study examines if the delivery of embodied learning through technology can support the collaboration between students in the classroom within the language learning.

3   Methodology

The study implements embodied learning as part of the learning activities in a real elementary classroom environment using motion-based technology (Kinect-based educational games) to investigate:

- (a) the students' perceptions and feelings about the embodied interaction and,
- (b) the teachers' perceived experiences regarding the collaboration and behavior of students during the educational intervention.

The study adopts a mixed methods approach, in order to utilize the strengths of both quantitative and qualitative data. Specifically, we used a Likert scale questionnaire to access the students' perceptions in conjunction with direct classroom observations and semi-structured interviews with the participating teachers.

3.1   Participants

In the investigation participated 52 students (mean age: M = 8.2 years, 25 boys, 27 girls) from four different elementary classrooms in two primary schools. All elementary students (second and third graders) involved in embodied interaction activities using motion-based games in the classroom and completed 13 game sessions of 45 min during a four-month period. Five teachers were responsible for the delivery of embodied learning in their classrooms. Before the beginning of the study, teachers participated in a training workshop regarding the implementation of motion-based games in the classroom. Selection of children was by them being in the school class that was invited to participate. All participants (students and teachers) provided a consent form and all the approvals by the Ministry of Education were obtained.

3.2   The Use of Movement-Based Interactive Games for Embodied Learning

For the delivery of embodied learning in the classroom, a commercial suite of movement-based interactive educational games, known as Kinems [45] was used. We chose a well-tested tool, with no technical issues as we didn't want such issues to influence our results. This platform is specifically designed for elementary students and we found it to be adequate and applicable in our setting, thus allowing us to examine aspects of embodied interaction and collaboration in the classroom. Also, Kinems was the appropriate tool for this research because it engages students in learning through natural interaction, using only the hands and body, via the Microsoft Kinect camera (see Fig. 1). This suite of games includes several games which combine motor, academic, and cognitive goals with high adaptability for a different curriculum and can be used in early elementary classrooms [46]. These games are suitable for early elementary or pre-school/ kindergarten-aged children of typical development or for students with special educational needs [46]. Previous studies have shown the positive impact of Kinems games in students' overall performance and can be used to develop a variety of cognitive, academic and motor skills [25].

Kinems games have very easy implementation and the teachers can very easily adjust the games in their lesson. Specifically, teachers can change the games' settings based on their students' level and needs. They can configure the settings choosing the level of difficulty, the total number of questions, the time for each question, the duration of the session, number of words, categories of words, etc. For all these individual features above, we choose to use the Kinems professional tool.

Fig. 1. Kinems motion-based interactive games used in the study

In this study, we used three games from the Kinems game suite in order to examine if such embodied learning games can facilitate the collaboration between students (see Fig. 1). We choose the "Unboxit", "Lexis" and "Melody Tree", games which can be integrated into first language (L1) lessons enhancing the acquiring and retention of new words.

In particular, the Unboxit game (Fig. 2) designed to enhance the visual-spatial working memory and attention of young learners, based on the idea of previous traditional memory games with cards. In this game students must find the pairs of objects that are hidden in boxes, using his/her hand to select the appropriate objects.

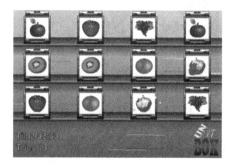

Fig. 2. Unboxit game

The second game was the "Lexis" (Fig. 3). The "Lexis" game takes place at an egg-packing plant. It is actually a missing letter game designed specifically to facilitate the students' spelling skills and acquisition of new words. Again, students should use their hands to fill in the words choosing the correct missing letter from a set of given letters. There are many categories or words based on classroom curriculum.

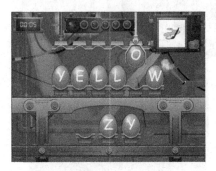

Fig. 3. Lexis game

Last, the "Melody tree" game (Fig. 4) aims to improve the audio-visual memory, attention, and concentration of students using sounds. Students should find the correct pairs of sounds that are hidden and select an object using their hands. In all the games ("Unboxit", "Lexis", "Melody Tree") the teacher can set the category of words/objects/sounds in his/her learning goals and adjust the game in the classroom curriculum.

Fig. 4. The Melody tree game

3.3   Interacting with Motion-Based Games in the Classroom

The research was conducted in four different classrooms during a fourth-month period. All students completed 13 embodied learning activities with motion-based games in their own classroom with their teacher once per week. The learning activities were implemented as a part of the language course. Teachers prepared and organized class-wide game sessions and all participated students were working in groups, based on the idea of computer-supported collaborative learning. The three games form Kinems platform ("Unboxit", "Lexis", "Melody Tree") were used to match the learning goals of the lesson. For that reason, teachers configured the settings of the games increasing the level of difficulty and changing the categories of words over time.

The teacher organized the lesson in such a way that all children have the opportunity to engage in the activities and to cooperate with each other. The lesson plan requires the participation of all students in all the collaborative activities, including the use of embodied games. The division of students into groups was made by the teacher of the class in order to facilitate the smooth running of all the activities. All members of the team had specific responsibilities within the group and the contribution of each member was essential in order to successfully complete their overall work as a group (see Fig. 5). The learning material given to the pupils was tailored to the games played every time in the classroom. Each group had to work together to solve the learning exercises at a predetermined time so that they can complete the activities before the course ends. The main activity was the interaction with motion-based games. All members of the team had to answer specific questions using the motion-based games in order to successfully complete their overall work as a group.

Fig. 5. Students working in groups

In practice, each member of the team played the games, one by one, while other members did relate learning activities to complete all the stages of the exercises, based on the lesson plan. Each group/team followed the same procedure following the instructions given by the teacher. The motion-based games were the most important activity of the group. The effective interaction with motion-based games allowed students to complete effectively all the group tasks and achieved learning gains. It is important to note that the teaching material was designed in such a way that it serves the delivery of specific learning subject, in this case, language acquisition. The learning material was linked to the games played by the children according to the curriculum.

Therefore, the game was fully integrated into the lesson in such a way that all children could benefit from it. In each session, teachers chose the appropriate category of words in three games "unboxit", "lexis" and "melody tree" in order to give children the opportunity to practice their existing knowledge and to enrich their knowledge on these particular units/chapters. In the following Fig. 6, we present some episodes of the implementation of embodied learning in the classroom using motion-based games as part of learning activities.

Fig. 6. Embodied interaction, learning and collaboration in the classroom

3.4   Data Collection

Following a mixed methods research approach, we collected data using quantitative and qualitative data.

Firstly, a short attitudinal Likert scale was administered to students participating in the study (N = 52) to assess their overall experience and perceptions of the learning approach. The questionnaire focused on the students' perceptions and feelings during the sessions. The questionnaire completed by students at the end of the fourth-month intervention.

Second, we used data from teachers' direct observations in the classroom. All the teachers (N = 5) made comments during each intervention session using observation protocols. The comments focused on monitoring how the students perceived the activities in the classroom and how they collaborated with other students. Teachers wrote their comments upon each intervention session in observation protocols in the form of a reflective diary concentrated particularly on:

1. Collaboration in the groups,
2. Students' emotional performance during the intervention

Third, semi-structured interviews were then conducted with all teachers (N = 5) who participated in the research to assess their overall experiences and perceptions of how embodied learning activities enhanced or not the collaboration between students. The qualitative data from semi-structured interviews were transcribed and coded as described in Saldana [47] and following the analysis procedure of Chi [48]. Table 1 presents some indicative questions from the interview.

Table 1. Some questions asked in interview sessions with teachers

Question	
1	Did the children have active participation in the learning process?
2	Did the students increase their participation in the class-activities with the use of motion-based games?
3	How was the motivation of the children during the sessions?
4	Could you describe the general performance of children across sessions?
5	What about the use of the body in the learning process?
6	How do you see embodied games helping children to improve their overall performance?
7	Regarding the collaboration, did you see any particular difficulties?
8	In what ways did the motion-based games enhance students' collaboration with other members of the group?

4 Findings

Our findings based on the quantitative analysis from students' questionnaire and qualitative analysis from classroom observations and semi-structured interviews are presented in this section.

4.1 Students' Perceptions and Feelings

At the end of intervention sessions and after completing 13 game sessions in the classroom, a short questionnaire was administrated to all students. The quantitative analysis derived from students' responses to the questionnaire demonstrated that the students enjoyed the lessons and experienced positive feelings during the sessions. The vast majority of students (90%) said that the lesson using motion-based games was more enjoyable and that they liked a lot to use their body movements in the classroom (67%). Moreover, most students (82%) claimed that enjoyed the collaboration with their classmates during the lesson while only 25% of students said that encountered difficulties. The following Fig. 7 illustrates the responses of students in the questionnaire.

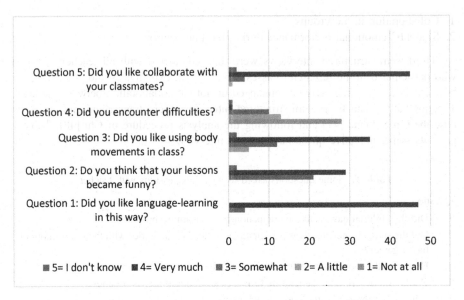

Fig. 7. Students perceptions and experiences (N = 52)

4.2 Teachers' Perceived Experiences Regarding the Collaboration

The qualitative data from semi-structured interviews were transcribed and coded as described in Saldana [47] in conjunction with the teachers' comments from direct classroom observations. Flowing the analysis procedure of Chi [48] we started with open coding and grouping of codes under higher-order categories. The next step was the review of the emerged categories and subcategories and then the interpretation for finalizing the categorization. Coding was done by two researchers. One was an independent researcher who participated in the data analysis process to allow a check for inter-rater agreement.

Qualitative analysis revealed many important insights into how embodied learning activities can facilitate students' collaboration within a real classroom environment. As derived from interviews and observations data, the essential point is that this movement-based intervention enabled all students to participate actively in learning and to collaborate with other students. As illustrated in Fig. 8, according to the teachers, the collaboration between students affected positively from: (a) the use of technology (b) the adjustment of learning material, (c) the funny way of leaning, (d) the establishment of group goals and (e) the clear and organized instructions given by the teacher.

All teachers claimed that the use of technology (in this case the motion-based games) was a very important incentive for students to progress and complete their activities successfully. As one teacher said (t1):

- *"The games were very funny for students. Each team was waiting for its turn to play. This has made them more effective in collaboration with others."*

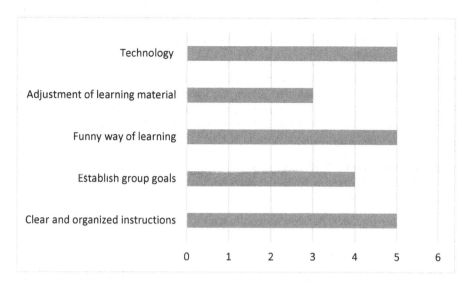

Fig. 8. Teachers discussing the collaboration between students (N = 5)

One other teacher agrees (t2):

– *"I think technology has helped children to follow the process more quickly and become actively involved in learning. I saw some guys encouraging other kids to participate in group activities to have the opportunity to play all the games".*

In line with others one teacher said (t4):

– *"I would think these embodied learning activities with the use of technology strengthened students' collaboration skills and increased their overall motivation to participate in the learning procedure. This kind of technology can complement traditional teaching and learning".*

Additionally, the adjustment of learning activities to the level of students allow all children to participate actively in the classroom and to work together harmoniously to achieve the best possible result.

As one of the teachers explained (t5):

– *"I strongly believe that this learning experience, organized and designed based on students' level and needs, helped all the children, even the difficult ones, to cooperate with others and improve their collaboration and communication skills. This is very important for children who have difficulties to collaborate with other students".*

Of course, according to the teachers, the clear establishment of the group's goals contributed significantly to the effective collaboration between students. As stated by a teacher (t2):

– *"Each group has very clear instructions and the activities were well organized and prepared. All the members of the group had something to do and all together had a common goal to achieve. This organization allowed students to work in a collaborative way without problems and misunderstandings".*

It is also important, as teachers claimed, to cultivate an atmosphere of cooperation in the classroom because such interventions require a high level of teamwork. Teachers discussed that it was often observed during the intervention that some children were encouraged to continue by their classmates. At other times, when students didn't understand instructions, they followed their classmates in order to advance to the next step, as one teacher highlighted (t3):

- *"During the intervention, I saw some students to encourage other students to continue the activity and finish the exercise. This was very essential for students with low self-confidence".*

Overall, the teachers' perceptions confirm positive results from the questionnaire and agree that this intervention enabled students to experience positive feelings and emotions. In a teacher's own words (t1):

- *"Through the sessions, students were very happy, careful and pay attention to the task following the instructions of the group. This activity motivated students a lot and increased their participation. The technology and the activities with body and hands helped students to improve their emotional state".*

5 Discussion

Given the documented positive effects of embodied interaction approach on students' performance, this study was undertaken to examine if this kind of intervention can facilitate the collaboration of students in the context of language learning. In particular, the research addresses the students' perceptions and feelings regarding these embodied learning activities with the use of technology (i.e., motion-based games). It also addresses the teachers' perceived experiences in relation to the collaboration of students in a real classroom. The contribution of this study is to provide evidence of how embodied interaction can enhance the delivery of learning offering opportunities for effective collaboration between students.

Findings based on students' questionnaire and qualitative data (from teachers' interviews and observations) support that embodied learning with the use of motion-based technology, can enhance significantly the students' collaboration engaging them actively in the learning process. These promising findings are in line with previous studies that demonstrated the potential of these interactive activities in students' learning outcomes and performance [2, 25, 34, 35, 39, 40].

Focusing on the qualitative analysis, we found that collaboration in the classroom associated with some important causal factors. Based on the teachers' perceptions the successful collaboration between students is linked with the use of technology, the adjustment of learning material on students' level and needs, the funny delivery of teaching, the establishment of group goals and finally with the clear and well-organized instructions given by the teacher.

In addition, one interesting finding of the study is that the educational intervention based on the idea of embodied learning with technology improved students' overall emotional performance. All participating teachers claimed that all the students were very motivated to participate in learning experienced positive emotions such as happiness and enjoyment during the sessions. Indeed, teachers argued that motion-based games not only improved the collaboration skills of children but also improved their emotional performance.

Overall the study contributes to the HCI community by providing an example of the embodied interaction via motion-based games in the real classroom. The empirical findings also provide a clearer understanding of the use of embodied learning activities in collaborative settings in elementary classrooms. Results from this study confirms the value of the integration of embodied idea in the collaborative environment resulting in increased collaboration between students and improved feelings and emotions. We believe that this manuscript could inform and encourage the implementation of embodied learning activities for educational purposes and collaboration in formal settings.

One limitation of the work is the lack of a control group. The documenting of differences between groups is beyond the purpose of this research. This work aimed to explore if embodied interaction could promote students' collaboration in an authentic classroom with the use of motion-based technologies. One other limitation of the study is that the use of motion-based games in this study was personalized. The Microsoft Kinect camera allows one person to interact with the game. Future studies could design and implement new interactions in order to allow students to play in a collaborative way. To that end, the future design should find ways for students to more deeply engage in technology-based embodied learning activities, creating more possibilities for collaboration.

5.1 Future Directions

The research on embodied interaction via the motion-based technologies in real classroom environments is still limited. There is still a lack of work on how we can implement embodied learning activities with the use of technology. More work is needed to get a deeper understanding of the body's engagement in the learning process. More investigation is needed to examine what aspects of the motion-based games specifically could lead to academic gains. Future studies could investigate the use of different embodied technologies in educational settings and work on the design of other technologies based on the idea of embodied cognition.

More research is also needed for developing and designing technologies for implementing embodied learning activities in different educational contexts. As mentioned earlier, in this study, students used the motion-based games one by one. In the future, it would be useful to design motion-based technologies for engaging the body in classrooms in collaborative ways and for a wider range of participants/students. To this end, the future design should find ways for students to more deeply engage in technology-based embodied learning activities, taking into consideration children's unexpected gestures and postures, their ages and the possibilities for more collaboration.

Finally, future researchers in the area of educational technology are particularly encouraged to implement embodied learning in real learning environments to explore whether movement and embodied learning principles can help meet specific collaboration skills. Further embodied learning implementations could use the findings of this study to create the appropriate atmosphere and the right type of activities to foster the collaboration of students.

Acknowledgements. We would like to thank all teachers and students, who voluntarily participated in this study, for their collaboration, hard work and engagement. We also thank Kinems educational games (https://www.kinems.com/) for providing the learning games free of charge.

References

1. Wilson, M.: Six views of embodied cognition. Psychon. Bull. Rev. **9**(4), 625–636 (2002)
2. Kosmas, P., Ioannou, A., Retalis, S.: Using embodied learning technology to advance motor performance of children with special educational needs and motor impairments. In: Lavoué, É., Drachsler, H., Verbert, K., Broisin, J., Pérez-Sanagustín, M. (eds.) EC-TEL 2017. LNCS, vol. 10474, pp. 111–124. Springer, Cham (2017). https://doi.org/10.1007/978-3-319-66610-5_9
3. Kosmas, P., Ioannou, A., Retalis, S.: Moving bodies to moving minds: a study of the use of motion-based games in special education. Tech Trends **62**(6), 594–601 (2018). https://doi.org/10.1007/s11528-018-0294-5
4. Foglia, L., Wilson, R.A.: Embodied cognition. Wiley Interdisc. Rev. Cogn. Sci. **4**(3), 319–325 (2013)
5. Dourish, P.: Where the Action Is: The Foundations of Embodied Interaction, vol. 36. The MIT Press, London (2001)
6. Marshall, P., Price, S., Rogers, Y.: Conceptualizing tangibles to support learning. In: Proceedings Conference on Interaction Design and Children, England, pp. 101–109. ACM (2003)
7. Zhu, C.: Student satisfaction, performance, and knowledge construction in online collaborative learning. J. Educ. Technol. Soc. **15**(1), 127 (2012)
8. McConnell, D.: Implementing Computing Supported Cooperative Learning. Routledge, Abingdon (2014)
9. Paloma, G.F. (ed.): Embodied Cognition. Theories and Applications in Education Science. Nova Science Publishers, New York (2017)
10. Atkinson, D.: Extended, embodied cognition and second language acquisition. Appl. Linguist. **31**(5), 599–622 (2010)
11. Anderson, M.L.: Embodied cognition: a field guide. Artif. Intell. **149**(1), 91–130 (2003)
12. Barsalou, L.W.: Grounded cognition: past, present, and future. Top. Cogn. Science **2**(4), 716–724 (2010)
13. Glenberg, A., Witt, J., Metcalfe, J.: From the revolution to embodiment 25 years of cognitive psychology. Perspect. Psychol. Sci. **8**(5), 573–585 (2013)
14. Barsalou, L.W.: Perceptions of perceptual symbols. Behav. Brain Sci. **22**, 637–660 (1999)
15. Gallagher, S., Lindgren, R.: Enactive metaphors: learning through full-body engagement. Educ. Psychol. Rev. **27**, 391–404 (2015)

16. Melcer, E.F., Isbister, K.: Bridging the physical divide: a design framework for embodied learning games and simulations. In: Proceedings of the 2016 CHI Conference Extended Abstracts on Human Factors in Computing Systems, pp. 2225–2233. ACM, New York (2016)

17. Cuendent, S., Jermann, P., Dillenbourg, P.: Tangible interfaces: when physical-virtual coupling may be detrimental to learning. In: Proceedings of British HCI, pp. 1–10 (2012). http://infoscience.epfl.ch/record/180395/files/

18. Shaer, O., Hornecker, E.: Tangible user interfaces: past, present, and future directions. Found. Trends® Hum.-Comput. Interact. 3(1–2), 1–137 (2009). https://doi.org/10.1561/1100000026

19. Farr, W., Price, S., Jewitt, C.: An Introduction to Embodiment and Digital Technology Research: interdisciplinary themes and perspectives. National Centre for Research Methods Working Paper, 1–18 (2012)

20. Price, S., Roussos, G., Falcão, T.P., Sheridan, J.G.: Technology and embodiment: relationships and implications for knowledge, creativity and communication. Beyond Curr. Horiz. 29, 1–22 (2009)

21. Riconscente, M.M.: Results from a controlled study of the iPad fractions game motion math. Games Cult. 8(4), 186–214 (2013). https://doi.org/10.1177/1555412013496894

22. Ionescu, T., Vasc, D.: Embodied cognition: challenges for psychology and education. Procedia Soc. Behav. Sci. 128, 275–280 (2014). https://doi.org/10.1016/j.sbspro.2014.03.156

23. O'Hara, K., Sellen, A., Wachs, J.: Introduction to special issue on body tracking and healthcare. Hum.-Comput. Interact. 31(3–4), 173–190 (2016)

24. Hurtienne, J.: Cognition in HCI: an ongoing story. Hum. Technol. 5, 12–28 (2009). https://jyx.jyu.fi/dspace/handle/123456789/20231

25. Kourakli, M., Altanis, I., Retalis, S., Boloudakis, M., Zbainos, D., Antonopoulou, K.: Towards the improvement of the cognitive, motoric and academic skills of students with special educational needs using Kinect learning games. Int. J. Child-Comput. Interact. 11, 28–39 (2016)

26. Lieberman, D.A., Chamberlin, B., Medina Jr., E., Franklin, B.A., Sanner, B.M., Vafiadis, D. K.: The power of play: innovations in Getting Active Summit 2011: a science panel proceedings report from the American Heart Association. Circulation 123(21), 2507–2516 (2011)

27. Bonk, C.J., Olson, T.M., Wisher, R.A., Orvis, K.L.: Learning form focus groups: an examination of blended learning. J. Distance Educ. 17, 97–118 (2002)

28. Klemmer, S.R., Hartmann, B., Takayama, L.: How bodies matter: five themes for interaction design. In: DIS 2006: Proceedings of the 6th Conference on Designing Interactive Systems, pp. 140–149 (2006). https://doi.org/10.1145/1142405.1142429

29. Evans, M.A., Rick, J.: Supporting learning with interactive surfaces and spaces. In: Spector, J.M., Merrill, M.D., Elen, J., Bishop, M.J. (eds.) Handbook of Research on Educational Communications and Technology, 4th edn, pp. 689–701. Springer, New York (2014). https://doi.org/10.1007/978-1-4614-3185-5_55

30. Johnson-Glenberg, M.C., Birchfield, D.A., Tolentino, L., Koziupa, T.: Collaborative embodied learning in mixed reality motion-capture environments: two science studies. J. Educ. Psychol. 106(1), 86 (2014)

31. Schmitt, L.J., Weinberger, A.: Collaborative learning on multi-touch interfaces: scaffolding elementary school students. In: Smith, B.K., Borge, M., Mercier, E., Lim, K.Y. (eds.) Making a Difference: Prioritizing Equity and Access in CSCL, 12th International Conference on Computer Supported Collaborative Learning (CSCL) 2017, vol. 1. International Society of the Learning Sciences, Philadelphia (2017)

32. Wendel, V., Gutjahr, M., Goebel, S., Steinmetz, R.: Designing collaborative multiplayer serious games. Educ. Inf. Technol. **18**, 287–308 (2013)
33. Roschelle, J., et al.: Scaffolding group explanation and feedback with handheld technology: impact on students' mathematics learning. Education Tech. Research Dev. **58**(4), 399–419 (2010)
34. Alvarez, C., Brown, C., Nussbaum, M.: Comparative study of netbooks and tablet PCs for fostering face-to-face collaborative learning. Comput. Hum. Behav. **27**(2), 834–844 (2011)
35. Schneps, M.H., Ruel, J., Sonnert, G., Dussault, M., Griffin, M., Sadler, P.M.: Conceptualizing astronomical scale: virtual simulations on handheld tablet computers reverse misconceptions. Comput. Educ. **70**, 269–280 (2014)
36. Johnson, D.W., Johnson, H.: Learning Together and Alone: Cooperation, Competition, and Individualization. Prentice Hall, Englewood Cliffs (1991)
37. Johnson, D.W., Johnson, R.T.: Cooperative Learning. Interaction Book Company, New Brighton (1984)
38. Danish, J.A., Enyedy, N., Saleh, A., Lee, C., Andrade, A.: Science through technology enhanced play: designing to support reflection through play and embodiment. In: Lindwall, O., Häkkinen, P., Koschman, T., Tchounikine, P., Ludvigsen, S. (eds.) Exploring the Material Conditions of Learning: The Computer Supported Collaborative Learning (CSCL) Conference 2015, vol. 1, pp. 332–339. The International Society of the Learning Sciences, Gothenburg (2015)
39. Kosmas, P., Ioannou, A., Zaphiris, P.: Implementing embodied learning in the classroom: effects on children's memory and language skills. Educ. Media Int. **56**(1), 59–74 (2018). https://doi.org/10.1080/09523987.2018.1547948
40. Kosmas, P., Zaphiris, P.: Words in action: investigating students' language acquisition and emotional performance through embodied learning. Innov. Lang. Learn. Teach. 1–16 (2019). https://doi.org/10.1080/17501229.2019.1607355
41. Cassar, A., Jang, E.: Investigating the effects of a game-based approach in teaching word recognition and spelling to students with reading disabilities and attention deficits. Aust. J. Learn. Difficulties **15**(2), 193–211 (2010)
42. Chang, C.Y., Chien, Y.T., Chiang, C.Y., Lin, M.C., Lai, H.C.: Embodying gesture-based multimedia to improve learning. Br. J. Educ. Technol. **44**(1) (2013). https://doi.org/10.1111/j.1467-8535.2012.01311.x
43. Donnelly, J.E., Lambourne, K.: Classroom-based physical activity, cognition, and academic achievement. Prev. Med. **52**, 36–42 (2011)
44. Lee, W., Huang, C., Wu, C., Huang, S., Chen, G.: The effects of using embodied interactions to improve learning performance. In: 2012 IEEE 12th International Conference on Advanced Learning Technologies (ICALT), 4–6 July 2012, pp. 557–559 (2012)
45. Kinems Learning Games Homepage. http://www.kinems.com/. Accessed 03 Feb 2019
46. Retalis, S., et al.: Empowering children with ADHD 21 learning disabilities with the Kinems kinect learning games. In: 8th European Conference on Games Based Learning, vol. 1, pp. 469–477 (2014)
47. Saldaña, J.: The Coding Manual for Qualitative Researchers. Sage, London (2009)
48. Chi, M.T.H.: Quantifying qualitative analyses of verbal data: a practical guide. J. Learn. Sci. **6**(3), 271–315 (1997)

Evaluation of a Massive Online Course Forum: Design Issues and Their Impact on Learners' Support

Anastasios Ntourmas[1](✉), Nikolaos Avouris[1], Sophia Daskalaki[1], and Yannis Dimitriadis[2]

[1] University of Patras, Patras, Greece
a.ntourmas@upnet.gr, {avouris,sdask}@upatras.gr
[2] Universidad de Valladolid, Valladolid, Spain
yannis@tel.uva.es

Abstract. Massive Open Online Courses (MOOCs) are delivered through dedicated platforms that provide educational opportunities to a large number of learners around the globe. The discussion forum is a key part of a MOOC platform. Structured communication between learners or between learners and instructors can take place through the forum. This communication has been shown that can have strong learning impact. Teaching Assistants (TAs) have a crucial role coordinating and supporting learners within a MOOC forum. In this paper, we investigate the impact a forum design can have on the TA's effectiveness while supporting the learners of a MOOC. Towards this objective, a mixed-methods study was performed on two MOOCs delivered through the OpenEdX platform. The goal was to reveal any design issues initially through a participatory ethnographic study and complementarily through a formal usability evaluation. Moreover, through interviews with the TAs, problems they faced while supporting learners were confirmed. The results of this study indicate that the OpenEdX forum design faces a variety of issues that need to be considered by course designers. Such issues cause various problems to teaching assistants, hindering effective support to learners and therefore affecting the learners' experience. It is further expected that the findings of this study may contribute to effective re-design of MOOC platform forums, more effective and efficient TA interventions and ultimately to improved learning.

Keywords: MOOC · Discussion forum · Learners support · Usability evaluation

1 Introduction

Massive Open Online Courses (MOOCs) open up learning opportunities to large numbers of people [1]. Most MOOCs are offered through dedicated online platforms, like Coursera, OpenEdX or Udemy, and most often attract thousands of learners. However, the effectiveness of learning in many MOOCs is questionable, as shown by the low student retention ratio [2]. It was found that in most cases completion rates of MOOCs do not exceed 20% and usually are between 7–11% [3]. There are several

© IFIP International Federation for Information Processing 2019
Published by Springer Nature Switzerland AG 2019
D. Lamas et al. (Eds.): INTERACT 2019, LNCS 11747, pp. 197–206, 2019.
https://doi.org/10.1007/978-3-030-29384-0_12

reasons for this low performance, among which, an important one has been recognized to be the lack of support and interactivity in MOOCs [4, 5]. Individual learners can receive support through the discussion forum, in the form of asynchronous communication and instructional interaction [6, 7]. It is therefore very important to study the way MOOC discussion forums are designed and used.

A significant user of a MOOC forum is the instructor and his/her assistants [8, 9]. Their role is to guide learners, pose interesting questions and provide insightful answers to learners' inquiries. Gamage et al. [10] suggest that the *usability dimension* of a MOOC platform and the help that is provided for any platform problems, are key factors for effective learning.

In this paper, a mixed-methods study is presented that aims to capture and explore encountered problems on the use of two MOOCs, delivered through OpenEdX technology, one of the major MOOC platforms [11]. The goal is to unveil and investigate the main problems that prevented TAs from supporting learners effectively within the discussion forum of this particular platform, and associate these problems with possible usability issues of the MOOC platform and to the ways the courses had been delivered. Moreover, this study aims to provide insights for a future alternative design of the MOOC forum platform that would improve the quality of the support it provides. It will also contribute to future design and development of tools that could assist TAs in providing more efficiently support to learners.

2   Literature Overview

Several past studies have shown that usability affects the participants' overall learning experience, while the design quality of a learning platform and the ease of using a learning management system contribute to the participants' satisfaction and performance [12]. In their survey on quality of MOOC designs, Yousef et al. [13] stated that usability, content, collaboration and instructional design play a major role in delivering successful MOOCs, while Soloway et al. [14] earlier had stated that learners should be placed at the center of their design process. Other studies have reported that usability problems are related to the poor design of e-learning courses, resulting in non-motivated and frustrated learners [15, 16]. Tsironis et al. [17] investigated the usability of three popular MOOC platforms, OpenEdX, Coursera and Udacity. The study revealed that all three platforms had usability problems in terms of navigation, finding resources and performing regular tasks.

On the other hand, the support that is provided by the course staff within a MOOC forum is an important part of the learning process [18]; it is a significant factor that affects learners' attrition within a MOOC [19]. In our case scenario, the main actors that provide support within the forum are the *teaching assistants*. Their role in online discussions is essential for maintaining the interest and motivation of learners [20]. They keep track of the discussions and intervene whenever there is a need for support. Their presence in the forum is crucial to keep learners engaged and may have positive impact to their performance [21]. In their research, Baxter and Haycock [22] stated that forums fail to handle high volumes of posts due to the fact that topics are fragmented over many threads and there is lack of search facilities. The difficulties of effective interaction and support in very large MOOC forums have been highlighted in many other studies, e.g. [23, 24]. Such studies indicate that a major increase in the forum participation may have negative effect to the support provided by TAs. This issue could be related to usability issues of the forum platform itself that scale up as forum participation increases. It is therefore understood that in order to support learners more efficiently there is need for new tools that could provide TAs a "bird's eye" view of the forum discussions [25].

Being motivated by such studies, we formulate the main research question of our work, that is to identify the key usability issues of the OpenEdX discussion forum and find out whether these affect the support that is provided to learners by the TAs. To answer this question, we followed a mixed-methods approach in order to capture the different aspects of problems TAs faced during their experience in the forum.

3 Methodology

The study was performed on two MOOCs offered in the mathesis.cup.gr, a major Greek MOOC platform based on OpenEdX technology. The first course, '*Differential Equations 1*' (DE course), aimed to introduce learners to the mathematical theory of differential equations and their practical use. The second one, '*Introduction to Python*' (PY course), aimed to introduce learners to computer programming through Python. The duration of both courses was 6 weeks and the enrolled learners were 2,153 for DE and 5,569 for PY. Within each course discussion forum, the support was provided by *Teaching Assistants* (TAs). The TAs were mostly learners that had attended former MOOCs of the same instructor and demonstrated high engagement and performance. They were subsequently contacted by the instructor, they were assigned the role of TA and were asked to contribute to subsequent editions of the course. For those particular courses, there were two active TAs for the DE and 5 for the PY.

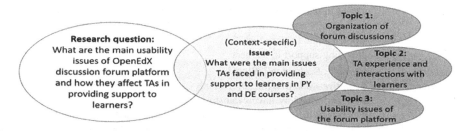

Fig. 1. Overview of research question, main issue and exploration topics of the study

To organize the study, we used an '*anticipatory data reduction method*' [26], where our research goals are addressed through three exploratory topics (see Fig. 1):

1. **Organization of the forum discussions**. The way discussions were organized and affected learners and TAs during their experience.

2. **TAs' experience and interactions within the forum**. Such experience and interactions provide us with insights about the TAs decisions over time.
3. **Usability issues of the forum platform.** We capture the main usability issues of the
platform and how they affected the TAs support to learners.

Triangulating different methods, data collection techniques (Table 1) and different
informants, allowed us to improve the quality, reliability, and rigor of the research and
its results [27]. In Table 1, we present the data collection methods employed: participatory ethnography, interviews, usability evaluation through cognitive walkthrough
and heuristics, forum log analysis. It should be observed that during the participatory
ethnography, we took a 'lurker' perspective, without intervening, so as to not affect
forum interactions. For the *cognitive walkthrough* method evaluators were asked to
perform typical user tasks in the forum, such as navigation in the forum, posting new
questions and modifying existing ones. Further down we present extracts from our data
collection methods using the format: [method/course/#TA].

Table 1. Data collection methods.

Method	Description	Purpose
Participatory Ethnography (PE method)	Recorded observations during our participation as regular users in the forum. Observations were guided by the exploration topics and were related to our individual experience as users of the forum and to the TAs interactions with learners	Gain a phenomenological account of participant's experience during the evolution of the forum over time. Record TA activities and interactions with learners. Capture main usability issues from a user's perspective
Interviews with TAs (INT method)	Qualitative, semi-structured, face-to-face interviews with the TAs of both courses. The interviews lasted 45 min. Two TAs of each course agreed to participate. The interviews were mainly concentrated on problems that occurred while providing support to learners	Provide an opportunity to view and understand the topic at hand [28]. Capture the TAs' opinions and experiences as broadly as possible following the analysis of observations made during the participatory ethnography
Usability evaluation	*Heuristic Evaluation* [29] and *Cognitive walkthrough* [30] methods were performed by three evaluators, which they had an advanced level of expertise. They consolidated common issues and discussed their differences, until a consensus could be achieved	Provide effective identification of problems arising from interaction with the forum interface and help to define users' assumptions
Discussion forum log analysis	Discussion forum log data of each course were retrieved and analyzed. The results of the analysis were related to the activities observed within the forum discussions	Provide quantitative data to validate our observations from the participatory ethnographic approach and the interviews with the TAs

4 Results

4.1 Exploratory Topic 1: Organization of the Forum Discussions

The discussion forum offered by the OpenEdX platform is organized according to a three-level hierarchy, shown in Fig. 2. The terminology used is that of 'discussions-responses-comments'. In most MOOC forums, a similar architecture is used, albeit with different terminology, e.g. in Coursera the three levels are called 'threads-posts-comments'. No further levels are allowed, as is the case with other discussion forums, beyond MOOCs, in which a comment can receive further comments, ad infinitum.

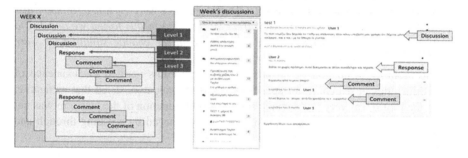

Fig. 2. Architecture of the OpenEdX discussion forum

During our participatory ethnographic study, it was observed that the organization of each week's discussions was *time-oriented*. Each new discussion that was created was added to the top of the left side-bar (see Fig. 2), that contained the week's discussions. It was observed that there were two kinds of discussions each week: *learner discussions*, i.e. discussions created by learners, and *course discussions*, i.e. discussions created by TAs or the course instructor.

Table 2. Activities related to learner and course discussions.

Course	Differential equations	Introduction to Python
Average number of discussions created per week (learner/course)	20.11/3.70	54.28/6.17
Average number of replies[a] per type of discussion each week (learner/course)	5.22/50.94	8.71/99.66
Percentage of *learner discussions* with TA participation	79.91%	67.52%

[a]responses and comments

As shown in Table 2, the average number of discussions created by learners was much higher than those created by the instructors. It is evident, that learners preferred to create their own discussions instead of participating in the *course discussions* set by TAs. This behavior increased complexity in the forum information space. During the interviews, TAs stated that the reason they created the topic specific *course discussions* was to discourage large numbers of *learner discussions*. They stated that they had problems in following new discussions and in providing prompt support to learners, as the number of *learner discussions* kept increasing. They also stated that such discussions usually related to a single question posed by the discussion creator and received just a few replies. On the other hand, *course discussions* were more popular; they received much higher number of replies as compared to *learner discussions*, as seen in Table 2. In general, we observed that there was no strict organization in the forum. TAs reported that in former MOOCs they participated, there were only *learner discussions* in the discussion forum. This resulted in a large number of *learner discussions* and a lot of questions remained unanswered. To resolve the issue, the TAs followed the approach of creating *course discussions* at the start of every week.

"In former MOOCs of Mr.[INSTRUCTOR], learners were creating so many discussions that it was impossible to keep track of them, so in this forum we decided to create specific discussions every week so as to avoid the chaotic situation we were facing previously." [INT/PY/TA1]

The usability evaluation performed in the two forums verified the existence of many difficulties in searching for specific items. The evaluators stated that navigation within the forum was very problematic and the search function of the platform was not helpful, so the search for questions of interest was achieved by scrolling through and reading every discussion's theme.

4.2   Exploratory Topic 2: TA Interactions with Learners

To collect information on this exploratory topic, we went through all the corresponding transcripts of the discussions that TA participated in. We focused on TA interactions that relate to issues they faced with learners. In some replies, the TAs were prompting learners to use the *course discussions* for posting their content-related questions and avoid creating their own. There were occasions where TAs did not even answer to learners' questions. An extract from PY forum (TA reply):

"There is a discussion that was created for questions on this material. Please use that to help your peers with their questions and us to provide you more effective support." [PE/DE/TA1]

During the interviews, TAs reported that such learner behavior did not comply with the forum policies, which stated: *"... learners should use course discussions to post their content-related questions ... questions posted in other discussions should not be answered by TAs"*. TAs however were not consistent in following this guide. We witnessed occasions where they were strict towards some learners that did not follow the rules, but in other occasions they kept answering questions within *learner discussions*. This somehow implied a change in their attitude, as if accepting eventually the situation and surrendering to policy violations. In fact, the TAs verified this behavior during the interviews. A related problem had to do with duplicate questions posted within *learner discussions* and inevitably appeared due to the large number of *learner discussions*. The TAs' frustration was conspicuous about it.

"Your question has already been answered in this discussion: [URL]. Please avoid posting questions that have already been answered elsewhere." [PE/PY/TA2]

Moreover, the TAs reported that many learners that follow such approach avoid engaging into a conversation, they just seek a solution to their problem. For example:

"There was a group of learners that were posting duplicate questions very frequently. It was obvious that they were unaware of other related discussions. They were using the forum just to get a direct answer." [INT/PY/TA2]

4.3   Exploratory Topic 3: Usability Issues of the Forum Platform

The *usability evaluation* unveiled a number of usability violations within the forum platform. Specifically, the evaluators reported that *navigation* was the main problem. The task of searching for discussions of interest to post new questions was difficult to perform. They also stated that during the evaluation of the PY course (attended by a much higher number of participants) this issue seemed to scale up. So navigation within a discussion of the PY course was much more time-consuming than the DE, due to the large number of replies in the former case. Another issue of the platform related to its search function. The evaluators reported that the search results were vague and didn't improve the navigation process. During the interviews it was stated:

"I usually used the browser's search function (cntrl-F) and searched with keywords like 'minutes' or question marks which I hoped to lead me to recent questions." [INT/PY/TA1]

This validated the evaluator's conclusions and implied that TAs often had to improvise for navigation. They also reported that the '*Create new response*' action was less prominent than the '*Create new discussion*'. The buttons for such actions were positioned in a way that users by mistake created a new discussion when they wanted to post a new question in an existing discussion. They also stated that '*Help and documentation*' (e.g. the forum's policies) was not included in the forum platform, but rather it was part of the course material. This may partially explain the limited compliance of learners to the forum policies.

5   Discussion

The results of our study revealed some significant limitations of the OpenEdX forum platform. The main issue refers to the difficulty in navigation within the forum discussions. Firstly, the organization of the discussions was not strict. This resulted in TAs not easily finding new interesting questions asking for their intervention. As the forum evolved over time, the number of new discussions increased and TAs had to contrive new ways of navigating. The forum itself provided email notifications for new messages but such method was treated as spam and was abandoned. The navigation issue was also verified during our participatory ethnography. Towards the end of each week, when the number of discussions had increased, it was very difficult to find conversations of interest. In the case of duplicate questions, we tried many times to find where the original one was answered, but we could hardly locate it. This may explain why learners were often unaware of their duplicate questions. It seems that the navigation problems had negative impact on them too. Usability evaluators also verified that navigation is problematic and specific tasks highlighted their violation.

During the participatory ethnography, we attempted to interpret the fact that learners often created their own discussions instead of using the *course discussions*. This could be attributed to the unawareness of the forum policies. *"Users that attend many MOOCs, take the MOOC policies for granted"* [INT/DE/TA1], stated one of the TAs. Usability evaluation also revealed that the policies should had been more visible as the evaluators struggled to find them. There is a need for new ways to inform learners about specific policies before they enter the discussion forum and the study showed that the forum platform lacks such feature. Clearly stated and implemented policies are very important to retain a 'healthy' forum as the course evolves over time.

It has been quite clear from the interviews, that such issues had negative effect on the support provided to learners by the TAs of both courses. TAs of PY course stated:

"I spent more time in searching than answering to new questions." [INT/PY/TA1,2]

Despite these issues, the TAs stated that they were pleased with their contribution. This is due to the fact that they are highly motivated, they participate in a voluntary basis and yet they choose to spend a lot of time in the forum. From the TA interviews, we concluded that the situation in the PY course was worse. They stated that navigation within the *course discussions* was difficult due to the large number of replies they received and had less time to answer questions due to the course size.

6 Conclusions

Our study highlighted several important usability issues of the OpenEdX platform and their negative impact on the TAs role. The negative impact was exacerbated in the PY course since it had more participants, which shows that the identified issues scale up with participation. We discovered that as participation in the forum increased, the TAs adapted more complex strategies in order to navigate and provide effective support to learners. This increases the required load of effort and detaches them from their main goal. Our study identified limitations of the platform in providing effective tools to assist the TAs on this issue. As a consequence, MOOC organizers resort to increasing the number of TAs as learner participation increases. However, in MOOCs with thousands of learners this cannot be a viable solution.

Due to the importance of the TAs role for supporting activities in a MOOC environment, it is now well understood that there is need for new policies and tools to ease and guide their interventions. Such tools could help TAs keep track of the discussions and provide support to learners efficiently and uninterruptedly while the forum evolves over time. The development of tools that assist TAs and automate their interventions [31] is a promising field of research. Classification algorithms that identify content-related discussions [32] may assist their development, while advanced visualization techniques may produce topic-related overview of the forum state, highlighting recurring topics. Development of such tools may be an interesting direction. Taking into consideration these recommendations, in our ongoing research we plan to follow a more design-based approach by experimentally implementing and validating such new approaches in future MOOCs delivered through the OpenEdX platform.

Acknowledgements. This research is performed in the frame of collaboration of the University of Patras with online platform mathesis.cup.gr. Supply of MOOCs data, by Mathesis is gratefully acknowledged. Doctoral scholarship "Strengthening Human Resources Research Potential via Doctorate Research – 2nd Cycle" (MIS-5000432), implemented by the State Scholarships Foundation (ΙΚΥ) is also gratefully acknowledged. This research has also been partially funded by the Spanish State Research Agency (AEI) under project grants TIN2014-53199-C3-2-R and TIN2017-85179-C3-2-R, the Regional Government of Castilla y León grant VA082U16, the EC grant 588438-EPP-1-2017-1-EL-EPPKA2-KA.

References

1. Hill, P.: Online educational delivery models: a descriptive view. EDUCAUSE Rev. **47**, 84–86 (2012)
2. Yuan, L., Powell, S.: MOOCs and open education: implications for higher education. Cetis White Paper (2013)
3. Liyanagunawardena, T.R., Parslow, P., Williams, S.A.: Dropout: MOOC participants' perspective. In: European MOOC Stakeholder Summit, pp. 95–100 (2014)
4. Daniel, J.: Making sense of MOOCs: musings in a maze of myth, paradox and possibility. J. Interact. Media Educ. **2012**(3), Art. 18 (2012). https://doi.org/10.5334/2012-18
5. Kizilcec, R.F., Halawa, S.: Attrition and achievement gaps in online learning. In: Learning@ Scale, pp. 57–66 (2015)
6. Mak, S., Williams, R., Mackness, J.: Blogs and forums as communication and learning tools in a MOOC. In: International Conference on Networked Learning, pp. 275–285 (2010)
7. Kumar, M., Kan, M.-Y., Tan, B.C., Ragupathi, K.: Learning instructor intervention from MOOC forums: early results and issues. In: International Educational Data Mining Society, pp. 218–225 (2015)
8. Berge, Z.L.: The role of the online instructor/facilitator. Educ. Technol. **35**, 22–30 (1995)
9. Brouns, F., Mota, J., Morgado, L.: A networked learning framework for effective MOOC design: the ECO project approach. In: Challenges for Research into Open & Distance Learning: Doing Things Better: Doing Better Things, pp. 161–171 (2014)
10. Gamage, D., Fernando, S., Perera, I.: Factors leading to an effective MOOC from participiants perspective. In: International Conference on Ubi-Media Computing, pp. 230–235 (2015)
11. Sandeen, C.: Integrating MOOCs into traditional higher education: the emerging "MOOC 3.0" era. Change Mag. High. Learn. **45**, 34–39 (2013)
12. Chang, S., Tung, F.: An empirical investigation of students' behavioural intentions to use the online learning course websites. Br. J. Edu. Technol. **39**, 71–83 (2008)
13. Yousef, A.M.F., Chatti, M.A., Schroeder, U., Wosnitza, M.: What drives a successful MOOC? An empirical examination of criteria to assure design quality of MOOCs. In: International Conference on Advanced Learning Technologies, pp. 44–48 (2014)
14. Soloway, E., Guzdial, M., Hay, K.E.: Learner-centered design: the challenge for HCI in the 21st century. Interactions **1**, 36–47 (1994)
15. Clark, R.C., Mayer, R.E.: E-learning and the Science of Instruction: Proven Guidelines for Consumers and Designers of Multimedia Learning. Wiley, Hoboken (2016)
16. O'regan, K.: Emotion and e-learning. J. Asynchronous Learn. Netw. **7**, 78–92 (2003)
17. Tsironis, A., Katsanos, C., Xenos, M.: Comparative usability evaluation of three popular MOOC platforms. In: Global Engineering Education Conference (EDUCON), pp. 608–612 (2016)

18. Onah, D.F., Sinclair, J.E., Boyatt, R.: Exploring the use of MOOC discussion forums. In: London International Conference on Education, pp. 1–4 (2014)
19. Yang, D., Wen, M., Kumar, A., Xing, E.P., Rose, C.P.: Towards an integration of text and graph clustering methods as a lens for studying social interaction in MOOCs. Int. Rev. Res. Open Distrib. Learn. **15**, 215–234 (2014)
20. Yang, D., Adamson, D., Rosé, C.P.: Question recommendation with constraints for massive open online courses. In: ACM Conference on Recommender Systems, pp. 49–56 (2014)
21. Mazzolini, M., Maddison, S.: Sage, guide or ghost? The effect of instructor intervention on student participation in online discussion forums. Comput. Educ. **40**, 237–253 (2003)
22. Baxter, J.A., Haycock, J.: Roles and student identities in online large course forums: implications for practice. Int. Rev. Res. Open Distrib. Learn. **15**(1), 20–40 (2014)
23. Onah, D.F., Sinclair, J., Boyatt, R.: Dropout rates of massive open online courses: behavioural patterns. In: EDULEARN14 Proceedings, pp. 5825–5834 (2014)
24. Kizilcec, R.F., Piech, C., Schneider, E.: Deconstructing disengagement: analyzing learner subpopulations in massive open online courses. In: International Conference on Learning Analytics and Knowledge, pp. 170–179 (2013)
25. Sharif, A., Magrill, B.: Discussion forums in MOOCs. Int. J. Learn. Teach. Educ. Res. **12**(1), 119–132 (2015)
26. Miles, M.B., Huberman, A.M., Huberman, M.A., Huberman, M.: Qualitative Data Analysis: An Expanded Sourcebook. Sage Publications, Thousand Oaks (1994)
27. Greene, J.C., Caracelli, V.J., Graham, W.F.: Toward a conceptual framework for mixed-method evaluation designs. Educ. Eval. Policy Anal. **11**, 255–274 (1989)
28. Stuckey, H.L.: Three types of interviews: qualitative research methods in social health. J. Soc. Health Diab. **1**, 56–59 (2013)
29. Nielsen, J.: Finding usability problems through heuristic evaluation. In: SIGCHI Conference on Human Factors in Computing Systems, pp. 373–380 (1992)
30. Lewis, C., Polson, P.G., Wharton, C., Rieman, J.: Testing a walkthrough methodology for theory-based design of walk-up-and-use interfaces. In: SIGCHI Conference on Human Factors in Computing Systems, pp. 397–404 (1990)
31. Chandrasekaran, M., Ragupathi, K., Kan, M.-Y., Tan, B.: Towards feasible instructor intervention in MOOC discussion forums. In: International Conference on Information Systems, pp. 2483–2491 (2015)
32. Wise, A.F., Cui, Y., Jin, W., Vytasek, J.: Mining for gold: identifying content-related MOOC discussion threads across domains through linguistic modeling. Internet High. Educ. **32**, 11–28 (2017)

Kahaniyan - Designing for Acquisition of Urdu as a Second Language

Saad Hassan[⊠], Aiza Hasib, Suleman Shahid, Sana Asif, and Arsalan Khan

Lahore University of Management Sciences, Lahore, Pakistan
{19100093,19100255,suleman.shahid,19100046,19100150}@lums.edu.pk

Abstract. This paper describes the design of Mobile Assisted Second Language Learning Application (MASLL) - Kahaniyan - created to assist non-native primary school children in learning Urdu. We explore the use of gamification to assist language learning within the context of interactive storytelling. The final design presented in this paper demonstrates how psychological and linguistic aspects coupled with contextual task analysis can be used to create a second language learning tool. The study also reports the results of the user study and the evaluation of the application which was conducted with 32 primary school students. Our results show a positive influence on learning outcomes, with findings that hold great significance for future work on designing MASLL for languages written in Arabic or Persian script.

Keywords: Second language learning · Book app · Mobile learning · Mobile technologies · MASLL · MALL · Urdu · Psycholinguistics

1 Introduction

Second language learners often face problems in the acquisition of writing skills in the concerned language. The problems are particularly relevant in languages written in Arabic or Persian scripts due to convoluted spellings and complex writing rules. Urdu writing system is one of the systems that borrow from these scripts. Students who learn Urdu as a second language often face multiple difficulties due to its writing style. In Pakistan, Urdu is the most common medium of instruction at primary schools despite the fact that only 8% of the total population speaks it as their first language [1]. Another common cause of difficulties particularly in the Pakistani context, therefore, is language transfer which arises due to the prevalence of a plethora of other first languages similar to Urdu. Linguistic interference of these first languages often results in negative transfer: the tendency of non-native speakers to transfer linguistic structures that are not the same in both languages [19]. Efforts to devise classroom-based solutions to remedy this situation have largely been unsuccessful. Moreover, students in traditional classroom settings often become self-conscious and refrain from participation in activities that promote their skills in the second language due to

ⓒ IFIP International Federation for Information Processing 2019
Published by Springer Nature Switzerland AG 2019
D. Lamas et al. (Eds.): INTERACT 2019, LNCS 11747, pp. 207–216, 2019.
https://doi.org/10.1007/978-3-030-29384-0_13

fear of making mistakes in front of their teachers and peers [5,6,12]. This raises the question, how to make the acquisition of Urdu as a second language easier for primary school students by developing a learner-centred framework [2].

In recent years, MASLL has become a popular mean for teaching a second language. It provides advantages over traditional methods such as mobility of learning, the ability to function in both classroom and informal settings, improvement of both individual and networked learning, and transformation from teacher-centred instruction into learner-centre learning [11]. Furthermore, these tools can help in creating personalized pedagogical approaches towards language learning which allow teachers to act as a facilitator and enhance the student's participation in learning activities beyond school timings [14]. However, to the best of our knowledge, no games or interactive storybooks to date have been designed to facilitate Urdu language learning specifically for non-native speakers and although 65% of research studies on designing MASLL have been conducted in Asia, none pertain to Pakistan [11]. These studies also have several limitations. They (a) have mostly been conducted on Chinese or English language, (b) prioritize higher or secondary school education over primary education and (c) rarely strive to make a comparison of their learning outcomes with classroom-based learning. Furthermore, while MASLL tools documented in these studies have been extensively used for learning within formal education where they are incorporated in language course curricula or class activities, their scope for independent learning has not been widely explored [11].

In this work, we discuss an approach that combines storytelling and gamification to address the problems in the acquisition of Urdu as a second language. The major learning outcome of most MASLL tools has been vocabulary building and rarely have efforts been made to address linguistic concerns specific to a language. Through a user study among 32 primary school children, we identified specific linguistic problems that primary school children face in identifying glyphs and creating meaningful Urdu sentences. We document how these problems in these two areas, along with psycho-social aspects of second language acquisition informed the design of our application Kahaniyaan. Our two research questions are (1) what effect does the usage of a MASLL based on learning through storytelling with incorporated elements of gamification have on the acquisition of Urdu as a second language? (2) how do psycho-social aspects such as language transfer and nonverbal communication inform the design of MASLL?

2   Literature Review

Psycho-Social Aspects of Second Language Learning. The nature of exposure to the second language impacts the learning process. Inadequate auditory perception and visual exposure to a language in informal settings at an early age slows the learning process which necessitates early language learning [20]. The linguistic and communicative competencies in the second language are partially a function of competencies in the first language before a child gets exposed to a second language [21]. The transfer of knowledge is dependant on the phonological contrast and correspondence of glyphs (smallest possible contrastive sub-unit of a writing system) between the two languages and may be positive (promotes learning ability) or negative (impedes the learning process) [18]. While creating a MASLL tool for Urdu, one has to account the language transfer from common first languages of non-native Urdu learners. A linguistic method that can be used to facilitate designers in this is contrastive analysis: the identification of structural differences and similarities between a pair of languages [3].

Initially, language learning is not about learning the writing system and grammar and the learner has to rely more on their social skills to master the language. According to social theorists such as Vygotsky, language originates from social activity and then becomes constructed as a cognitive and individual phenomenon [16]. A communicative act is only effective if the people involved, understand the intentional state of a partner [15]. The intentional state can be understood from contextual cues as well as the emotional display of the agent. While current MASLL tools are useful in improving verbal communication, they often fail to account for non-verbal components.

Tools for Language Learning. MASLLs in the form of Language learning games (LLG) have emerged as a popular tool for fostering language skills in young learners. LLG have the potential to engage students deeply with a particular topic because they allow children to actively participate in the learning process rather than just being passive observers [17]. Similarly, interactive storybooks have become another popular MASLL tool for language acquisition. Learning to read has a crucial impact on student's overall achievement and using computers to teach reading has been a goal of many educators since the technology was first introduced into schools [10]. Research shows that eBook features such as the pronunciation of words, narration, sound effects, and animations, that support the written text, allow children to focus on meaning, thus opening the way for high-level reading comprehension [4].

Based on the literature review, we incorporated contrastive analysis between Urdu words and words from native languages of migrant students into our study to account for linguistic transfer. While designing our contextual inquiry, we situated our tasks in a variety of familiar social contexts for children to best account for aspects of non-verbal communication. Lastly, based on the suitability of story-telling and gamification for MASLLs that we gauged from literature, we chose it as our design framework.

3   Research Method

The study was conducted in two primary community schools, "Qadam Community School" and "Punjab Public School," with total of 32 students from 2nd and 3rd, aged 7–9 years. These schools were selected because of the diversity of students enrolled, i.e. both native and non-native students. Both schools are located in the outskirts of Lahore, Pakistan. The medium of instruction in these schools is Urdu which is similarly also used by students for interpersonal communication. By 2nd and 3rd grade, students are assumed to have a basic understanding of written Urdu, the ability to comprehend instructions given in the language as well as the ability to communicate in it efficiently. Our four team members were proficient in writing and reading Urdu and had studied Urdu as their first or second language till 11th grade.

We employed a mixed-method approach and; (i) performed contextual inquiry through classroom observations and semi structured interviews with teachers of 2nd and 3rd grades from both the schools, (ii) conducted a survey to inquire students' background and (iii) administered a test accompanied by an activity to assess the students' language skills. Four teachers were interviewed about the teaching methods, the most common mistakes made by students in written assignments, and hindrances faced in speaking Urdu. We also inquired how these mistakes and hindrances varied across local and migrant students and whether there were any pronounced differences in their abilities and ease of acquisition. One person from our team sat through both classes in both the schools for a day each and noted the nature of mistakes made by the students while responding to the questions asked by the teacher and in communication with their peers.

A survey was administered to the students that asked about their demographic background and availability of and engagement with technological devices such as mobile phones/laptops in their home. A brief test, based on common mistakes in Urdu writing, was designed and administered to the students to gather quantitative data which was complemented by an activity. Four tables were set up, each with a different category of item (books, sweets, toys and stationary) and each student was given a paper with instructions (in Urdu or English) that required them to retrieve a specific item from a particular table. This activity was designed to assess the student's ability to understand instructions given in the language and their ability to employ the language in a social

Fig. 1. To avoid cognitive overload that can impact the self-efficacy of a learner, user exposed to a storyline through disintegration into scenes.

Fig. 2. Tracing feature in early storylines of the game whereby user has to identify alphabets and different shapes they take across a variety of words.

Fig. 3. Identify the correct action or emotion word being exhibited by the character and its correct form that renders the sentence meaningful.

Fig. 4. Everyday scenarios employed to enhance social communication skills, developed using familiar characters from earlier storylines.

context. Before the activity, students were encouraged to ask the two present members from our team if they faced any difficulties in reading the prompts. For each student, we noted the number of times they asked for help, the nature of help acquired (e.g pronouncing a particular word, comprehending the instruction etc.), and the time taken to both read the instruction and complete the task (Figs. 1, 2, 3 and 4).

4   Design and Implementation

All the students except one were allowed to use a smartphone for thirty minutes or less at home. The restricted usage of smartphones among primary school students necessitated using a framework to sustain the interest of the children over multiple sessions such as stories. This was complemented by the use of certain elements of gamification such as scores and unlocking of game features to allow learners to self-explain and self-evaluate their learning. Through contextual task analysis of the current method of teaching the Urdu language to primary school children, we identified common causes of error in Urdu writing. In Urdu language, alphabets take different shapes in different words depending on where they are occurring in a sentence - beginning, middle or end and with an increase in the length of a word, errors became more pronounced.

In Urdu script, digraphic combinations of characters represent vowels and non-native speakers lack the intuition of using the appropriate combination of characters to render vowel sounds in different words [13]. We observed that they often resorted to rules learnt in first languages to inform their choice of alphabets in the second language. This language transfer is often negative and results in mistakes in spellings. To further explore this, we performed a contrastive analysis of words that are commonly misspelt in Urdu, with their counterparts in the most prevalent first languages among non-native Urdu speakers and obtained a list of such words. This informed one of the in-game activity identify where students had to select the correct word form from common erroneous versions.

The proposed game design consists of three main components. The first part consists of adaptations of popular children's stories in Urdu Literature. The children periodically look at different scenes that constitute a story. After they view a scene and read the corresponding sentence, they are prompted to complete two-three tasks before progressing to the next scene. Based on the level the user is on, the task may consist of one of these: tracing alphabets on to word silhouettes, selecting correct word forms, identifying character's action and identifying the right emotion the character is exhibiting. In the second part of the application, the users have to make decisions based on information provided in the scene and the corresponding sentence. These scenes are not adaptations from stories but are rather stories crafted to embody routine interactions that require communication in Urdu. However, the characters and their actions and emotions are similar to those encountered by the children in the first part of the application. These characters are unlocked after completion of different storylines from the first part of the game. The third part of the application allows the users to create their own stories by incorporating the collections of characters. Paper-based low fidelity prototype of different plots and their subsequent scenes were created to test understanding and assign difficulty levels to the different stories. The final application was implemented using Unity for the Android as well as iOS platforms. Three stories for part one and two stories for part two were used for testing.

5   Evaluation

32 students were divided into four equal groups for evaluation: non-native and no application group, non-native and application group, native and non-application group, native and application group. Pre-tests, consisting of 5 questions each, based on the major learning outcomes of the application was administered. The testing spanned across five days, where children from the application groups, sat with one of the members from our team for 15–20 min each day as they navigated through the application and completed a storyline. Students from the non-application group were engaged in a 15–20-min session where the children were given a short story similar to the one in the application, accompanied by questions which they had to complete under the supervision of one of the members of our group. The members of our team rotated to eliminate any biases due to member's influence. Students were encouraged to ask questions and think out loud. Performance measures and lower level interaction issues were recorded for all the sessions conducted with each student. After each day's session, students from the application groups were asked among other things, to rate their levels of enjoyability, ease of navigation, motivation to engage with the application and identify the tasks they liked and disliked the most.

Following the five sessions, a sixth visit was performed to administer a post-test with all the students, similar to the pre-test. We also conducted an activity to test another aspect of learning that we aspired to achieve through the element of interactive storytelling in our design. It was hypothesized that interacting with the application would enhance the children's ability to extract meaning from a scene using non-verbal cues. We presented all four groups with the illustration of a scene from a new story and asked the children to describe it in their own words. We then counted the instances of correct usage of action and emotion terms in the students' description of the scene. We also showed the teachers from both the schools our final application and asked for their feedback.

6   Results

All our four groups showed an improvement in the post-test. An average of scores on pre-test and post-test out of 5, consisting of questions testing the major learning outcomes, was calculated. The post-test scores of children from the non-native and no application group, non-native and application group, native and non-application group, native and application group were on average +1.30, +0.70, +0.70 and +0.40 more than the pre-test scores. The most useful feature of the application was observed to be tracing the elements where 12 out of the 16 children who used the application, showed improvement in glyph identification compared to 5 out of the 16 children from the non-application group. The four students from the application group who showed no improvement were native Urdu speakers. Responses to questions on the post-test revealed that around 69% of the children using the application were able to entirely understand the plots as opposed to 37.5% from the non-application group. Moreover, the application group demonstrated a higher ability to extend the acquired skills of glyph identification to a wider range of structurally dissimilar words. Analysis of the students' description of the scenes from the activity showed that those who had used the application were more than twice as likely to include the description of the characters actions and emotions in their account. The number of times children in the application group asked for help decreased over the sessions with session 1 having the highest average of 4.2 times and session 5 having the lowest average of 1.1 times. Furthermore, although difficulty increased from plot 1 to plot 3, the game scores for each plot remained similar or showed a minor decrease. On average children rated the ease of use, feedback, enjoyability, the likelihood of recommending to others and learning to be 4.00, 3.42, 4.28, 4.00, 4.90 out of 5. These scores were calculated using the response to a 5-point Likert-type scale ranging from "Strongly Disagree" on one end (0) to "Strongly Agree" on the other (5). On average, students made 6 errors out of 42 clicks per plot. Observations made during the testing sessions showed that children were mostly able to read the storyline sentences independently. Non-native speakers enjoyed reading smaller sentences more while native speakers showed little or no preference for a particular type. While reading out a loud, the non-native speakers often pronounced words with vowels incorrectly but after completing several tasks to identify the correct version of similar words, these errors were reduced. Native Urdu speakers found some of the features such as tracing of the word to be uninteresting and showed a higher preference for features like identifying emotion and action words. However, both native and non-native students often faced difficulty in selecting between similar sounding alphabets such as "Hay". Many children suggested they should be allowed to start more than one plot at one time. The unlocking feature was almost always able to incentivize the children to complete the plot. We observed several children comparing scores among themselves and rejoicing at having unlocked a particular character. Based on their experience from non-educational games, some students reported that they expected to be able to move at least one character around the screen. A teacher from one of the schools, who viewed our final application recommended that we add a feature into our design which should allow teachers to create plots and incorporate them into the game. Another teacher remarked, "Students don't always do their homework but were very excited to play the game when your team would come."

7 Discussion and Conclusion

All MASLL projects previously studied show that mobile devices are beneficial in enhancing the second language (L2) learning process by either enhancing the proficiency in the concerned language, improving the learning motivation of the user, or both of them [11]. Many of these employ gamification and interactive elements to engage young learners. EBooks have also gained popularity to support the learning process as complements to their paper-based counterparts. In this study, we explored the use of stories with certain game elements for language learning. We applied this approach to teaching the Urdu language which has several unique properties in comparison to languages like English and presents its own design challenges.

Prior research has also shown that through developing a model that converges mobile technology, human learning capacity, and social interaction aspects, we can implement a solution that can be effectively used for formal and informal learning [7]. However, conscious learning that stresses on learning lexicon, formal rules, and grammar is often unsuccessful and there is a strong influence of the first language (L1) on second language learning (L2) that manifests through linguistic interference [8]. Therefore, while designing any learning pedagogy, psychological aspects of the human processing information system should be focused on [9]. While designing for non-native speakers, we accounted for psychological factors such as language transfer and social aspects by exploring their particular relevance in Urdu language acquisition. Our research explored whether a story-based game design, after accounting for aforementioned aspects, can inculcate an intuition in second language learners of Urdu similar to one in native learner. Nevertheless, the same design process can be replicated to create other second language learning tools for children for languages that follow writing systems similar to Arabic or Persian. Our evaluation showed that the game has a high potential to support second language acquisition of Urdu, particularly for non-native speakers. Findings also confirmed that without acquiring basic skills such as identifying different glyphs in a word, a child cannot understand whole words or create meaningful sentences using them. Results also affirmed that negative language transfer is a major challenge in Urdu language learning among non-native children but it can be overcome by repeated exposure. Learning is enhanced when broken down across several sessions as is done through the use of multiple storylines as it allows students to critically examine the structure of each sentence and hence develop a better intuition for what constitutes a proper sentence. Tasks following each scene ensured that they place focus on the more important components of the sentence such as action words. Progressing through a single storyline, keeps the child engaged with the learning process and sustains interest as opposed to games where a single skill is repetitively taught across a single level. Furthermore, the engagement is twofold; the student is kept engaged by the storyline and the gamified features such as scores and unlocking story characters. In future work, this design can be extended to allow teachers to design storylines and accompanying tasks based on stories that are part of the curriculum. In this way, teachers can facilitate the language learning process of non-native children and reduce the gap of proficiency between the native and non-native speakers in class. We hope that, with this paper, we have taken the first step towards exploring a framework for teaching Urdu to the non-native speaker in areas where it is used as the primary medium of instruction in primary schools. In this way, we want to motivate discussions in the INTERACT community on novel assistive applications for solving language acquisition problems in children.

References

1. Pakistan Demographic Profile 2018. In: IndexMundi. https://www.indexmundi. com/pakistan. Accessed 2 Feb 2019
2. Jaafar, W.A., Yahya, W., Leow, C.K., Samsudin, Z.: Mobile assisted second language learning: developing a learner-centered framework (2014)
3. Connor UM Contrastive rhetoric and text linguistics. Contrastive Rhetoric, pp. 80–99. https://doi.org/10.1017/cbo9781139524599.007
4. Longa, N.D., Mich, O.: Do animations in enhanced ebooks for children favour the reading comprehension process? In: Proceedings of the 12th International Conference on Interaction Design and Children - IDC 2013 (2013). https://doi.org/10. 1145/2485760.2485885
5. Gee, J.P.: Situated language and learning (2012). https://doi.org/10.4324/ 9780203594216
6. Hudson, J.M., Bruckman, A.S.: IRC Français: the creation of an internet-based SLA community. Comput. Assist. Lang. Learn. **15**, 109–134 (2002). https://doi. org/10.1076/call.15.2.109.8197
7. Koole, M.L.: A Model for Framing Mobile Learning (2009)
8. Walz, /j: Second language acquisition and second language learning. Stephen D. Krashen Oxford: Pergamon Press, 1981, Pp. 151. Stud. Second Lang. Acquisition **5**, 134 (1982). https://doi.org/10.1017/s0272263100004733
9. Mayer, R.E.: Cognitive theory of multimedia learning. In: The Cambridge Handbook of Multimedia Learning, pp. 43–71. https://doi.org/10.1017/ cbo9781139547369.005
10. Miller, L., Blackstock, J., Miller, R.: An exploratory study into the use of CD-ROM storybooks. Comput. Educ. **22**, 87–204 (1994). https://doi.org/10.1016/ 0360-1315(94)90087-6
11. Persson, V., Nouri, J.: A systematic review of second language learning with mobile technologies. Int. J. Emerg. Technol. Learn. (iJET) **13**, 188 (2018). https://doi. org/10.3991/ijet.v13i02.8094
12. Schmidt, R.W.: The role of consciousness in second language learning1. Appl. Linguist. **11**, 129–158 (1990). https://doi.org/10.1093/applin/11.2.129
13. Shah, A.: Teaching of Urdu: Problems and Prospects (2016)
14. Sung, Y.-T., Chang, K.-E., Yang, J.-M.: How effective are mobile devices for language learning? a meta-analysis. Educ. Res. Rev. **16**, 68–84 (2015). https://doi. org/10.1016/j.edurev.2015.09.001
15. Verga, L., Kotz, S.A.: How relevant is social interaction in second language learning? Front. Hum. Neurosci. (2013). https://doi.org/10.3389/fnhum.2013.00550
16. Vygotsky, L.: Thought and Language. MIT Press, Cambridge (1962). https://doi. org/10.1037/11193-000
17. Wallner, G., Kriglstein, S.: Design and evaluation of the educational game DOGeometry. InL Proceedings of the 8th International Conference on Advances in Computer Entertainment Technology - ACE 2011 (2011). https://doi.org/10.1145/ 2071423.2071441

18. Lee, M.-K.: The effects of learner variables on language competence among secondary ESL students in Hong Kong. https://doi.org/10.5353/thb3194464
19. Pulgram, E., Weinreich, U.: Languages in contact. findings and problems. Modern Lang. J. **37**, 429 (1953). https://doi.org/10.2307/320055
20. Wible, B.: Correlation between brainstem and cortical auditory processes in normal and language-impaired children. Brain **128**, 417–423 (2004). https://doi.org/10.1093/brain/awh367
21. Zorman, A.: Problems in reading acquisition in a second or a foreign language. Metodički obzori/Methodol. Horiz. **6**, 119–134 (2011). https://doi.org/10.32728/mo.06.1.2011.10

On Making, Tinkering, Coding and Play for Learning: A Review of Current Research

Stella Timotheou[1] and Andri Ioannou[1,2](✉) iD

[1] Cyprus Interaction Lab, Cyprus University of Technology, Limassol, Cyprus
{stella,andri}@cyprusinteractionlab.com
[2] Research Center on Interactive Media, Smart Systems and Emerging Technologies (RISE), Nicosia, Cyprus

Abstract. Although a few researchers have recently focused on the value of making, tinkering, coding, and play in learning, a synthesis of this work is currently missing, creating an unclear path for future research in this area. Computational-making-enhanced activities, framed as activities promoting making, tinkering, coding and play in the learning process, have gained a lot of attention during the last decade. This study provides a review of the existing research in this area, published in academic journals, from 2009 to 2018. We examine learning gains linked to learners' participation in computational making-enhanced activities in formal and non-formal education settings. We further overview the research methods, the educational level, and the context of the published studies. The review of selected studies has shown that most of the research has been conducted in non-formal and informal education settings, however a shift to formal education has appeared since 2016. Most studies have focused on programming and computer science with middle-school learners. Immediate action is needed to inform the design of computational-making-enhanced activities directly linked to curriculum goals. Given the lack of synthesis of work on computational-making, the review can have considerable value for researchers and practitioners in the field.

Keywords: Making · Tinkering · Coding · Play · Computational making · Technology-enhanced learning

1 Introduction

Current research findings support that making and tinkering activities can help with the development of skills, such as creativity, innovation, problem-solving, programming, computational thinking skills, which constitute the 21st century skill-set (Bevan et al. 2015; Moriwaki et al. 2012; Harnett et al. 2014; Kafai et al. 2013). Unlike, teaching methods which emphasize the existence of a single answer to a problem, or a determined process to the solution, methods that support making, tinkering, coding and play emphasize on the significance of the process, rather than the result. Also, such way of thinking can promote interdisciplinarity amongst the STEAM domains (Science, Technology, Engineering, Arts, and Mathematics), the importance of which has been underlined by many scholars (e.g., Jin et al. 2012).

© IFIP International Federation for Information Processing 2019
Published by Springer Nature Switzerland AG 2019
D. Lamas et al. (Eds.): INTERACT 2019, LNCS 11747, pp. 217–232, 2019.
https://doi.org/10.1007/978-3-030-29384-0_14

The movement of making, called "the maker movement" has gained enormous momentum during the last few years, as an active process of building, designing, and innovating with tools and materials for the production of shareable artifacts. Making is a learner-driven educative practice which supports learning, participation, and understanding (Vossoughi and Bevan 2014). Making is a process of creating something (Hsu et al. 2017), or "the act of creating tangible artifacts" (Rode et al. 2015, p. 8). Others describe making as a strategy in which individuals or groups of individuals are encouraged to create artifacts using software and/or physical objects (Papavlasopoulou et al. 2017).

Tinkering, as a part of making (Vossoughi and Bevan 2014) is a problem-solving technique and learning strategy, which promotes a practice of improvement and it is associated with experimentation and "trial and error" methods (Krieger et al. 2015). As Martinez and Stager (2013) argued, making and tinkering have evolved as a playful approach to solving problems through direct experience, experimentation and discovery. Programming, coding and physical computing are considered as making activities (Hsu et al. 2017) as they allow students to build and rebuild their artifacts (namely their robot), make the program design, code and debug.

Computational-making has been coined by Rode et al. (2015) to describe a combined set of skills that should be taught in STEAM education, namely computational thinking, aesthetics and creativity, visualizing multiple representations, understanding materials, and constructing (Rode et al. 2015). In other words, computational-making can describe making activities which require computation thinking skills and combine crafts with technology.

Play, as a dynamic, active and constructive behavior is naturally infused in all programming, making and tinkering activities. The playful nature of such activities promotes learner's interest (Ioannou 2018; Vossoughi and Bevan 2014). According to Martin (2015), learning environments organized based on making and tinkering settings are motivating and can support engagement and persistence and identity development.

Making, tinkering, coding and play activities might be seen as a relatively new practice in education, yet its theoretical roots are set in Papert's constructionism (Jones et al. 2017), which builds upon Piaget's constructivism. Piaget defined knowledge as an experience that can be built through the interaction of the learner with the world, people and things (Ackermann 2001) which is the experience that *making* offers to the learner. Similarly, Papert's theory of constructionism asserts that people construct internal knowledge when they design and build their own meaningful artifacts (Papert 1980). Making is also linked to Vygotsky's social constructivism in that it can support learning and cognitive development through children's interaction with others whilst sharing knowledge (Nussbaum et al. 2009).

Although a few researchers have recently focused on the value of making, tinkering, coding, and play in learning (Krieger et al. 2015; Hsu et al. 2017; Martinez and Stager 2013), a synthesis of this work is currently missing, creating an unclear path for future research in this area. A recent review of research in the making field was presented by Papavlasopoulou et al. (2017) but authors focused on making studies in extracurricular contexts only. The present review aims to summarize research findings, published from 2009 to 2018, on learning outcomes promoted through making, tinkering, coding and play in formal and non-formal education. The following research questions (RQs) are addressed:

RQ1: What types of learning outcomes can be derived from computational-making-enhanced activities?
RQ2: What research methods and research design are being used?
RQ3: What types of learning contexts for computational making are being used?

2   Methodology

2.1   Selection of Studies

The subject's range was wide enough, as we searched for studies published in academic journals concerned with making, tinkering, coding and play in education. First, we conducted a search in the following electronic databases: ERIC, JSTOR, ScienceDirect, Taylor and Francis Online, Scopus in additional to Google Scholar using the keywords "making", "tinkering", "coding" and "play" (and/in) "education", whilst restring the dates range to 2009–2018. The search initially resulted in a total of n = 3116 manuscripts.

By reading all the abstracts, we filtered the manuscripts using three criteria: (1) the study should be empirical. All studies that gathered empirical evidence through quantitative (e.g. surveys) or/and qualitative methods (e.g. interviews, focus groups, experiments) were included. Studies with no empirical findings, including reviews and theoretical perspectives were excluded (e.g., excluded review paper by Papavla-sopoulou et al. 2017), (2) the study should involve computational-making-enhanced activities, as defined in the introduction of this work (i.e., evidence of "computation"). Studies referred to making activities without any computational elements were excluded (e.g., a study conducted by Alekh et al. 2018), (3) the study should present learning outcomes, including outcomes on conceptual knowledge, attitudes and skills. Studies with no explicit reference to learning outcomes were excluded (e.g., Cohen et al. 2018). After applying the above-mentioned criteria, we concluded with 57 manuscripts.

2.2   Categorizing the Studies

We thoroughly read the 57 manuscripts and coded (i.e., open coding) the basic information derived from each work. A first round of open coding for learning outcomes was conducted, aiming to examine the types of learning outcomes derived from the computational-making-enhanced activities (RQ1). Based on evidence from 15% of studies, we identified three major categories of learning outcomes namely, content knowledge outcomes, attitudes, and 21st-century skills; these categories were then used for coding the rest of the studies. In a second round of coding, we coded for the types of research methods used (RQ2); in this case, we categorized the studies as qualitative, quantitative or mixed research methods whilst we recorded the sample size and age of the participants. Last, in a third round of coding we coded for formal and non-formal/informal learning context in which the computational-making-enhanced activities took place (RQ3). The coding was done by two researchers (authors) working closely together.

3 Findings

3.1 Learning Outcomes

The empirical findings on learning outcomes were organized in terms of content knowledge, attitudes, and 21st-century skills. Some of the studies reported outcomes in more than one category.

Content Knowledge. As P21 Framework (Partnership for 21st Century Learning, 2015) states, content knowledge refers to key subjects, such as science, mathematics, economics, arts, geography, world languages etc. Learning of programming or other computer science knowledge is also coded in this category. The results demonstrated that computational-making-enhanced activities were mostly linked to knowledge gains in programming and computer science. Fewer studies were concerned with science and engineering or arts and literacy. Major findings about knowledge gains are summarized in Table 1 and briefly discussed below.

To provide an example, in the study of Blikstein (2013) middle- and high- school students experienced digital design fabrication in FabLabs in schools. The authors found that through making, students had the opportunity to come across several concepts in engineering and science in highly engaging and meaningful ways. Furthermore, Kafai et al. (2014b), conducted a study in an e-textile computer science class with high school students; based on the analysis of project artifacts and interviews, the authors found that the experience promoted learning through making concerning circuitry and debugging. Students' engagement with simple computational circuits using e-textiles materials was also examined by Peppler (2013). This mixed-method research (pre and post-tests, surveys, interviews, journals, artifacts, and videotaped observations) took place in a summer workshop with children aged 7–12 years old and documented that students' understanding of key circuitry concepts was significantly increased through making. Another study with high school participants conducted by Searle et al. (2014), indicated that learning with e-textiles helped the students create a link between coding and making that contributed to their learning in computer science. Last but not least, Burke and Kafai (2012) found that middle school students learned the fundamentals of both programming and storytelling through making and tinkering and emphasized the potential of the connection between coding and writing.

Attitudes. Students' attitudes towards learning can be measured through assessment of the perceived levels of interest, challenge, choice, and enjoyment, which are dimensions linked to motivation and engagement. Self-efficacy is also an attitude concerned with perceived beliefs in the individual capacity for specific achievements. In line with findings by Vossoughi and Bevan (2014) and Martin (2015) about making and tinkering activities promoting learners' interest, most of the studies reported positive effects on students' attitudes (see Table 2).

Table 1. Major findings about knowledge gains.

	Authors	Findings on knowledge gains
1	Denner et al. (2012)	Underrepresented students learned concepts of programming and understanding software, that would prepare them for computer science courses
2	Khalili et al. (2011)	Students designed accurate visual representations of the constructs and verbally describe the concepts (biology and neurological concepts)
3	Kafai et al. (2014b)	Students learned about circuitry
4	Fields et al. (2015)	Students learning to work with programming tasks
5	Kafai et al. (2014a) Lee et al. (2014)	Students learned programming
6	Kafai and Vasudevan (2015)	Students learned about circuitry
7	Searle et al. (2014)	Students learned to design and program the electronic artifacts
8	Kafai et al. (2013)	Students learned computing concepts and practices
9	Burke and Kafai (2012)	Students gained fundamentals of programming and storytelling
10	Telhan et al. (2014) Basawapatna et al. (2013) Burge et al. (2013)	Students learned about programming
11	Schneider et al. (2015)	Learning gains were improved when students built the human hearing (biology) system without guidance
12	Qiu et al. (2013)	Learned programming via making activities using the combination of Modkit and LilyPad
13	Perner-Wilson et al. (2011)	Students learned to create technology (electronics) and programming
14	Franklin et al. (2013)	Students gained competence with several computer science concepts
15	Esper et al. (2014b)	Students learned about computer science, math and programming
16	Esper et al. (2014a)	Students understood basic programming.
17	Garneli et al. (2013)	Students who managed to change the game code did not improve their performance in math post-test. (negative results)
18	Posch and Fitzpatrick (2012)	Children learned about emerging technologies (electronics)
19	Peppler and Glosson (2013)	Students had significant gains in understanding of functional circuits
20	Litts et al. (2017)	Gains in students' understanding of circuitry
21	Worsley and Blikstein (2014)	Principle-based reasoning was associated with better quality designs and better engineering mechanism's understanding
22	Blikstein (2013)	Via digital fabrication the students experienced learning gains in computation and mathematics
23	Hartry et al. (2018)	Gains on STEM knowledge
24	Elkin et al. (2018)	Knowledge gains about programming and engineering, literacy and science

(*continued*)

Table 1. (*continued*)

	Authors	Findings on knowledge gains
25	Bull et al. (2017)	Students learned concepts about computer science, engineering and literacy
26	Patton and Knochel (2017)	Gains in art education
27	Bers et al. (2014)	Students learned concepts about robotics, programming
28	Chu et al. (2017a)	Students gained electronics and science knowledge

Table 2. Major findings about attitudes.

	Authors	Findings on attitudes
1	Denner et al. (2012)	Underrepresented students were engaged in the concepts of programming (engagement)
2	Harnett et al. (2014)	The experience of making helped students improve their attitudes towards engineering
3	Lane et al. (2013)	The acceptance of challenges was increased
4	Moriwaki et al. (2012)	Participants reported personal interest about science
5	Kafai et al. (2014b)	More realistic and positive attitudes were noted
6	Chu et al. (2015)	Increased interest and engagement incidents occurred
7	Searle et al. (2014)	Positive attitudes and perceptions towards computing
8	Kafai et al. (2013)	The making activities broadened students' perceptions of computing
9	Qiu et al. (2013)	Increased comfort, enjoyment and interest in working with electronics and programming
10	Mellis et al. (2013)	Participants felt comfortable and confident when working with crafts
11	Mellis and Buechley (2012)	Positive attitudes about electronics and laser cutting
12	Jacobs and Buechley (2013)	Engagement and positive attitudes towards programming
13	Qi and Buechley (2014)	Enjoyment, freedom and fluency to use the technology
14	Wagner et al. (2013)	Mobile computing gave opportunities to provide powerful new context about motivation in computational thinking
15	Burke and Kafai (2012)	Significant improvement in attitudes about computer science, computing, and mathematics
16	Giannakos and Jaccheri (2014)	Enjoyment was reported during children's programming experiences, lot of incidence of.
17	Giannakos and Jaccheri (2013)	The activity's easiness and usefulness significantly affected students' intention to participate
18	Garneli et al. (2013)	Participants' intention to learn programming was increased, positive attitudes towards programming were noted, as well as engagement and fun with the activity

(*continued*)

Table 2. (*continued*)

	Authors	Findings on attitudes
19	Giannakos et al. (2014)	Results showed positive effects of happiness and the negative effect of anxiety
20	Hartry et al. (2018)	Students reported that the program had strong impact on learners' interest on STEM
21	Wagh et al. (2017)	Tinkering with program code facilitated engagement with science
22	Elkin et al. (2018)	The children were all engaged in the making activities
23	Zajdel and Maharbiz (2016)	Significant increase of students' self-efficacy
24	Bers et al. (2014)	Kindergartners were engaged and interested in robotics, programming and computational thinking
25	Lane et al. (2013)	Significant increase in self-efficacy
26	Kolko et al. (2012)	Self-efficacy and identity were reported
27	Qiu et al. (2013)	Making activities increased students' technological self-efficacy

An indicative study comes from Chu et al. (2015), conducted with elementary school students in 3rd, 4th and 5th grades. Students used arts and craft materials, and electronics components to build a theatre kit. The results indicated that *making* lead to more robust learning for children as they sought to acquire STEM-knowledge to make the technological things of their interest. Similarly, results from a study conducted by Posch and Fitzpatrick (2012) in four workshops in Vienna, suggested that making in a FabLab can increase students' interest about learning emerging technologies. Another study with children (between 4–11 years old) working in an informal science learning environment with their parents indicated that the STEAM learning through making and tinkering nurtured learning both in personal interest and in concepts learned, enhanced engagement, and reinforced previous knowledge and basic motor skills (Moriwaki et al. 2012).

21st-century skills. For coding for 21st century skills, we adopted the Partnership for 21st Century Learning Framework (2015) which suggests three theme categories of skill: learning and innovation skills, information, media & technology skills, and life & career skills. This framework was previously followed by Harris et al. (2016) to collocate opportunities that tinkering experiences provide for developing 21st-century skills). Several types of 21st-century skills were reported in the 57 reviewed studies (see Table 3). Most of the studies reported skills from the first category (i.e., learning & innovation skills). In some cases, *making* appeared as a 21st-century skill itself.

To provide some examples, in Harnett et al. (2014), undergraduate students engaged in making activities demonstrating increased competence in problem-solving and project-planning activities. Also, a study with adults (Perner-Wilson et al. 2011), demonstrated that the participants were able to construct personally meaningful

Table 3. Findings on 21st-century skills

Learning & Innovation skills	
Problem-solving (and Project-planning)	Harnett et al. (2014)
	Kafai et al. (2014b)
	Schwartz et al. (2015)
	Searle and Kafai (2015)
	Esper et al. (2014a, b)
	Sheridan et al. (2014)
	Hartry et al. (2018)
	Bers et al. (2014)
Critical thinking	Kafai et al. (2014b)
	Hartry et al. (2018)
	Posch and Fitzpatrick (2012)
Collaboration – Co-operation Communication	Moriwaki et al. (2012)
	Mellis and Buechley (2012)
	Giannakos and Jaccheri (2013)
	Blikstein et al. (2017)
	Blikstein (2013)
	Hartry et al. (2018)
	Elkin et al. (2018)
	Bull et al. (2017)
	Fields et al. (2015)
Creativity	Kafai and Vasudevan (2015)
	Wagner et al. (2013)
	Rode et al. (2015)
	Hartry et al. (2018)
Information, Media & Technology skills	
Technology-technical skills	Jacobs and Buechley (2013)
	Kolko et al. (2012)
	Wagner et al. (2013)
	Litts et al. (2017)
Making skills	Chu et al. (2017)
	Okundaye et al. (2018)
	(Chu et al. 2017a, b, c)
Computational thinking	Rode et al. (2015)
	Kafai and Vasudevan (2015)
	Bers et al. (2014)
	Esper et al. (2014a, b)
	Peppler and Glosson (2013)
	(Basawapatna et al. 2013)
Information literacy skills	Bull et al. (2017)
Life & Career skills	
Decision making	Elkin et al. (2018)
Leadership	Okundaye et al. (2018)
Time management	
Presentation skills	

artifacts and that the approach made the technology more understandable allowing them to leverage existing skills to learn something new. The study also revealed that handcrafting technology fostered the realization of personal artifacts and afforded novel designs through the process of making. In a research conducted with children, in five out-of-school workshops (Posch and Fitzpatrick 2012), the researchers reported that 10–14 years old children were able to transfer learned skills and experiences in other projects.

3.2 Type of Research Methodology

In terms of methodology, 30 studies were qualitative, 20 were mixed-method studies and seven were quantitative (see Fig. 1). In terms of sample size, 23 studies involved fewer than 20 participants, 17 studies involved more than 21 but less than 50, six studied involved more than 50 people but fewer than 100, and another six studies involved more than 101 participants (Table 4). Most work has been done with middle school students; less work deals with younger or older learners (Table 5).

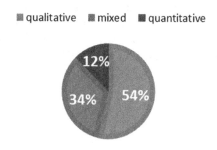

Fig. 1. Type of research method used in empirical studies

Table 4. Number of studies according to the sample size.

Sample size	Number of studies
<20	23
21–50	17
51–100	6
101<	6
Do not mention	5
Total	57

Table 5. Number of empirical studies per to educational level.

Age	Number of empirical studies
Kindergarden	1
Primary schools	10
Secondary schools	26
Primary & secondary	3
College/university	4
Primary & secondary & university	5
Adults	3
Children & adults	4
Doesn't mention	1
Total	57

Educational Context

Directly linked to the "maker movement", computational-making-enhanced activities have mostly taken place in informal and non-formal settings (e.g., libraries, science festivals, and museums). The general aim was to encourage students to design, experiment, create, explore and play with technological tools. Yet, since approximately 2016 (2018 only partially covered due to the time of conducting this review), there seems to be a growing interest in formal education (see Fig. 2), especially driven by K-12 educators (e.g., Bers et al. 2014; Chu et al. 2015; Fields et al. 2015; Wagh et al. 2017).

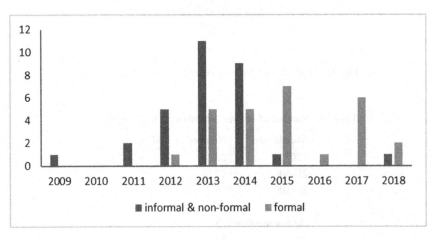

Fig. 2. Number of empirical studies throughout the last decade in formal and informal/non-formal education.

4   Discussion

The present review focused on making, tinkering, coding and play activities (i.e., computational-making-enhanced activities) for teaching and learning in formal and non-formal/informal learning settings. Below, we discuss the results of our review in relation to the initial research questions.

In terms of types of learning outcomes derived from computational-making-enhanced activities (RQ1), most of the studies in the review reported positive learning outcomes, namely outcomes on content knowledge, attitudes and skills. This is consistent with previous work arguing that making and tinkering are "potentially powerful contexts for learning" (Bevan et al. 2015, p. 21). As Vossoughi and Bevan (2014) also noted, such activities open space for learners to pursue personal interests and can broaden participation for many students.

In terms of research methods (RQ2) the review revealed that most of the studies in this area (computational-making) tend to use qualitative or mixed methodology. As the investigation of learners' attitudes or skills is a quite complex issue, the use of qualitative measures was deemed more suitable in most studies (Kafai et al. 2014a, b; Harnett et al. 2014) helping to understand issues of depth with computational-making. Yet, we now have enough evidence of the value of computation making, allowing for scaling-up the impact and measurement via quantitative studies. Quantitative methodology has only recently been used in computational making research, to document improvements in students' grades in formal education studies (e.g., Litts et al. 2017).

Non-formal and informal contexts were most common for computational-making-enhanced activities (RQ3), especially in year 2013. That could be justified by the Maker Movement's appearance (2009–2013) as a new trend in museums, makerspaces, hackerspaces, fablabs, after-school clubs, etc. Yet, since 2016 only two studies were found to have been conducted in non-formal/informal contexts, in contrast to the 16 studies conducted in formal education. This indicates that educators might be interested in computational-making-enhanced activities, yet empirical evidence in curricular areas is lacking.

The review revealed some open issues that are worth exploiting in the future. First, while a growing number of efforts in computational-making-enhanced activities in formal education is being recorded in the last three years, the design of learning activities and overall classroom implementation are not explicitly addressed in these studies. There is an immediate need for educative content and teaching/learning procedures linked to curriculum goals. Second, computational-making-enhanced activities have been mostly linked to content knowledge's gains in programming and computer science. Less attention has been given to science and engineering or arts and literacy. Possibilities and gains in these other domain areas are worth exploring and assessing. Third, most studies have been done with students in secondary education. There seems to be a need for more studies covering the spectrum of leaners in K-12 and up to higher education. Finally, most of the studies appear to aim at testing of making, tinkering, coding and play as a method for teaching and learning, yet the learning goals and design of computational-making tasks are not explicitly discussed in the research manuscripts. Studies which inform the design of computational-making-enhanced activities in relation to curriculum goals and expected learning outcomes are in need.

5   Conclusion

The present review demonstrates that the contribution of computational-making-enhanced activities in education is significant. Almost all the studies in the review, have indicated positive learning outcomes, often in more than one category (knowledge, attitudes and 21st-century skills). The focus has been on programming and computer science whilst the field should be exploited in engineering, arts and literacy. During the last three years empirical work has shifted from informal/non-formal education to formal education. This indicates the growing interest of researchers and educators to integrate computational-making-enhanced in the school classroom. Yet, immediate action is needed to inform learning design and the design of computational-making-enhanced activities directly linked to curriculum goals. Most of the empirical research studies were conducted in secondary-school education, while more work is needed with younger or older leaders. Although a few researchers have recently focused on the value of making, tinkering, coding, and play in learning, a synthesis of this work is currently missing, creating an unclear path for future research in this area. Therefore, the review can have considerable value in guiding future researchers and practice in the field.

Acknowledgement. This work has been partly supported by the project that has received funding from the European Union's Horizon 2020 research and innovation programme under grant agreement No 739578 (RISE – Call: H2020-WIDESPREAD-01-2016-2017-TeamingPhase2) and the Government of the Republic of Cyprus through the Directorate General for European Programmes, Coordination and Development.

References

* Articles in the review corpus

Ackermann, E.: Piaget's constructivism, Papert's constructionism: what's the difference. Future Learn. Group Publ. 5(3), 438 (2001)

Alekh, V., et al.: Aim for the sky: fostering a constructionist learning environment for teaching maker skills to children in india. In: Proceedings of the Conference on Creativity and Making in Education, pp. 87–94. ACM June 2018

* Basawapatna, A.R., Repenning, A., Lewis, C.H.: The simulation creation toolkit: an initial exploration into making programming accessible while preserving computational thinking. In: Proceeding of the 44th ACM Technical Symposium on Computer Science Education, pp. 501–506, March 2013

* Bers, M.U., Flannery, L., Kazakoff, E.R., Sullivan, A.: Computational thinking and tinkering: exploration of an early childhood robotics curriculum. Comput. Educ. 72, 145–157 (2014). https://doi.org/10.1016/j.compedu.2013.10.020

Bevan, B., Gutwill, J.P., Petrich, M., Wilkinson, K.: Learning through STEM-Rich tinkering: findings from a jointly negotiated research project taken up in practice. Sci. Educ. 99(1), 98–120 (2015). https://doi.org/10.1002/sce.21151

* Blikstein, P.: Digital Fabrication and 'Making' in Education: The Democratization of Invention. FabLabs: of Machines, Makers and Inventors, pp. 1–21 (2013). http://doi.org/10.1080/10749039.2014.939762

* Blikstein, P., Kabayadondo, Z., Martin, A., Fields, D.: An assessment instrument of technological literacies in makerspaces and FabLabs. J. Eng. Educ. **106**(1), 149–175 (2017)
* Bull, G., Schmidt-Crawford, D.A., McKenna, M.C., Cohoon, J.: Storymaking: combining making and storytelling in a school makerspace. Theory Pract. **56**(4), 271–281 (2017)
* Burge, J.E., Gannod, G.C., Doyle, M., Davis, K.C.: Girls on the go: a CS summer camp to attract and inspire female high school students. In: Proceeding of the 44th ACM Technical Symposium on Computer Science Education, pp. 615–620, March 2013
* Burke, Q., Kafai, Y.B.: The writers' workshop for youth programmers. In: Proceedings of the 43rd ACM Technical Symposium on Computer Science Education – SIGCSE 2012, pp. 433–438 (2012). http://doi.org/10.1145/2157136.2157264
* Chu, S.L., Angello, G., Saenz, M., Quek, F.: Fun in making: understanding the experience of fun and learning through curriculum-based Making in the elementary school classroom. Entertain. Comput. **18**, 31–40 (2017a). https://doi.org/10.1016/j.entcom.2016.08.007
* Chu, S.L., et al.: Becoming makers: examining making literacy in the elementary school science classroom. In: Proceedings of the 2017 Conference on Interaction Design and Children, June 2017, pp. 316–321 (2017b)
* Chu, S.L., Quek, F., Bhangaonkar, S., Ging, A.B., Sridharamurthy, K.: Making the maker: a means-to-an-ends approach to nurturing the maker mindset in elementary-aged children. Int. J. Child Comput. Interact. **5**, 11–19 (2015). https://doi.org/10.1016/j.ijcci.2015.08.002
* Chu, S.L., Quek, F., Deuermeyer, E., Martin, R.: From classroom-making to functional-making: a study in the development of making literacy. In: Proceedings of the 7th Annual Conference on Creativity and Fabrication in Education, October 2017, p. 3. ACM, (2017c)
Cohen, J.D., Jones, W.M., Smith, S.: Preservice and early career teachers' preconceptions and misconceptions about making in education. J. Digit. Learn. Teacher Educ. **34**(1), 31–42 (2018)
* Denner, J., Werner, L., Ortiz, E.: Computer games created by middle school girls: Can they be used to measure understanding of computer science concepts? Comput. Educ. **58**(1), 240–249 (2012)
* Elkin, M., Sullivan, A., Bers, M.U.: Books, Butterflies, and 'Bots: integrating engineering and robotics into early childhood curricula. In: English, L., Moore, T. (eds.) Early Engineering Learning. EMLD, pp. 225–248. Springer, Singapore (2018). https://doi.org/10.1007/978-981-10-8621-2_11
* Esper, S., Wood, S.R., Foster, S.R., Lerner, S., Griswold, W.G.: Codespells: how to design quests to teach java concepts. J. Comput. Sci. Coll. **29**(4), 114–122 (2014a)
* Esper, S., Foster, S.R., Griswold, W.G., Herrera, C., Snyder, W.: CodeSpells: bridging educational language features with industry-standard languages. In: Proceedings of the 14th Koli Calling International Conference on Computing Education Research, November 2014, pp. 5–14. ACM (2014b)
* Fields, D., Vasudevan, V., Kafai, Y.B.: The programmers' collective: fostering participatory culture by making music videos in a high school Scratch coding workshop. Interact. Learn. Environ. **23**(5), 613–633 (2015). https://doi.org/10.1080/10494820.2015.1065892
* Franklin, D., et al.: Assessment of computer science learning in a scratch-based outreach program. In: Proceeding of the 44th ACM Technical Symposium on Computer Science Education, pp. 371–376. ACM, March 2013
* Garneli, B., Giannakos, M.N., Chorianopoulos, K., Jaccheri, L.: Learning by playing and learning by making. In: Ma, M., Oliveira, M.F., Petersen, S., Hauge, J.B. (eds.) SGDA 2013. LNCS, vol. 8101, pp. 76–85. Springer, Heidelberg (2013). https://doi.org/10.1007/978-3-642-40790-1_8

* Giannakos, M.N., Jaccheri, L.: What motivates children to become creators of digital enriched artifacts? In: Proceedings of the 9th ACM Conference on Creativity & Cognition, pp. 104–113. ACM, June 2013

* Giannakos, M.N., Jaccheri, L.: Code your own game: the case of children with hearing impairments. In: Pisan, Y., Sgouros, N.M., Marsh, T. (eds.) ICEC 2014. LNCS, vol. 8770, pp. 108–116. Springer, Heidelberg (2014). https://doi.org/10.1007/978-3-662-45212-7_14

* Giannakos, M.N., Jaccheri, L., Leftheriotis, I.: Happy girls engaging with technology: assessing emotions and engagement related to programming activities. In: Zaphiris, P., Ioannou, A. (eds.) LCT 2014, Part I. LNCS, vol. 8523, pp. 398–409. Springer, Cham (2014). https://doi.org/10.1007/978-3-319-07482-5_38

* Harnett, C.K., Tretter, T.R., Philipp, S.B.: Hackerspaces and engineering education. In: 2014 IEEE Frontiers in Education Conference (FIE) Proceedings, pp. 1–8. IEEE, October 2014

Harris, E., Winterbottom, M., Xanthoudaki, M., Calcagnini, S., De Puer, I.: Tinkering: a practitioner guide for developing and implementing tinkering activities (2016). https://epale.ec.europa.eu/es/node/40449

* Hartry, A., Werner-Avidon, M., Hsi, S., Ortiz, A.: TechHive: a STEM learning lab for teens. In: 2018 CoNECD Conference, Crystal City, Virginia, pp. 1–13, April 2018

Hsu, Y.C., Baldwin, S., Ching, Y.H.: Learning through making and maker education. TechTrends 61(6), 589–594 (2017)

Ioannou, A.: A model of gameful design for learning using interactive tabletops: enactment and evaluation in the socio-emotional education classroom. Educ. Tech. Res. Dev. 67(2), 277–302 (2018)

* Jacobs, J., Buechley, L.: Codeable objects: computational design and digital fabrication for novice programmers. In: Proceedings of the SIGCHI Conference on Human Factors in Computing Systems, pp. 1589–1598. ACM, New York (2013)

Jin, Y.G., Chong, L.M., Cho, H.K.: Designing a robotics-enhanced learning content for STEAM education. In: 2012 9th International Conference on Ubiquitous Robots and Ambient Intelligence (URAI), pp. 433–436. IEEE, November 2012

Jones, W.M., Smith, S., Cohen, J.: Preservice teachers' beliefs about using maker activities in formal K-12 educational settings: a multi-institutional study. J. Res. Technol. Educ. 49(3–4), 134–148 (2017)

* Kafai, Y., Fields, D., Searle, K.: Electronic textiles as disruptive designs: Supporting and challenging maker activities in schools. Harv. Educ. Rev. 84(4), 532–556 (2014a)

* Kafai, Y.B., Searle, K., Kaplan, E., Fields, D., Lee, E., Lui, D.: Cupcake cushions, scooby doo shirts, and soft boomboxes: e-textiles in high school to promote computational concepts, practices, and perceptions. In: Proceeding of the 44th ACM Technical Symposium on Computer Science Education, pp. 311–316. ACM, March 2013

* Kafai, Y.B., Lee, E., Searle, K., Fields, D., Kaplan, E., Lui, D.: A crafts-oriented approach to computing in high school. ACM Trans. Comput. Educ. 14(1), 1–20 (2014b). https://doi.org/10.1145/2576874

* Kafai, Y., Vasudevan, V.: Hi-Lo tech games: crafting, coding and collaboration of augmented board games by high school youth. In: Proceedings of the 14th International Conference on Interaction Design and Children, pp. 130–139. ACM, June 2015

* Kafai, Y.B., Vasudevan, V.: Constructionist gaming beyond the screen: middle school students' crafting and computing of touchpads, board games, and controllers. In: Proceedings of the Workshop in Primary and Secondary Computing Education, pp. 49–54. ACM, November 2015

* Khalili, N., Sheridan, K., Williams, A., Clark, K., Stegman, M.: Students designing video games about immunology: insights for science learning. Comput. Sch. 28(3), 228–240 (2011)

* Kolko, B., Hope, A., Sattler, B., MacCorkle, K., Sirjani, B.: Hackademia: building functional rather than accredited engineers. In: Proceedings of the 12th Participatory Design Conference, vol. 1, pp. 129–138. ACM, August 2012

Krieger, S., Allen, M., Rawn, C.: Are females disinclined to tinker in computer science? In: Proceedings of the 46th ACM Technical Symposium on Computer Science Education - SIGCSE 2015, pp. 102–107 (2015). http://doi.org/10.1145/2676723.2677296

* Lane, H.C., et al.: The effects of a pedagogical agent for informal science education on learner behaviors and self-efficacy. In: Lane, H.C., Yacef, K., Mostow, J., Pavlik, P. (eds.) AIED 2013. LNCS, vol. 7926, pp. 309–318. Springer, Heidelberg (2013). https://doi.org/10.1007/978-3-642-39112-5_32

* Lee, E., Kafai, Y.B., Vasudevan, V., Davis, R.L.: Playing in the arcade: designing tangible interfaces with MaKey MaKey for scratch games. In: Nijholt, A. (ed.) Playful User Interfaces. GMSE, pp. 277–292. Springer, Singapore (2014). https://doi.org/10.1007/978-981-4560-96-2_13

* Litts, B.K., Kafai, Y.B., Lui, D.A., Walker, J.T., Widman, S.A.: Stitching codeable circuits: high school students' learning about circuitry and coding with electronic textiles. J. Sci. Educ. Technol. 26(5), 494–507 (2017). https://doi.org/10.1007/s10956-017-9694-0

Martin, L.: The promise of the maker movement for education. J. Pre-College Eng. Educ. Res. 5 (1) (2015). http://doi.org/10.7771/2157-9288.1099

Martinez, S.L., Stager, G.S.: Invent to learn: making, tinkering, and engineering in the classroom, p. 237, December 2013. http://doi.org/10.1093/intimm/dxu021

* Mellis, D.A., Buechley, L.: Case studies in the personal fabrication of electronic products. In: Proceedings of the Designing Interactive Systems Conference, pp. 268–277. ACM, June 2012

* Mellis, D.A., Jacoby, S., Buechley, L., Perner-Wilson, H., Qi, J.: Microcontrollers as material: crafting circuits with paper, conductive ink, electronic components, and an untoolkit. In: Proceedings of the 7th International Conference on Tangible, Embedded and Embodied Interaction, pp. 83–90. ACM, February 2013

* Moriwaki, K., et al.: Scrapyard challenge Jr., Adapting an art and design workshop to support STEM to STEAM learning experiences. In: IEEE 2nd Integrated STEM Education Conference, ISEC 2012 (2012). https://doi.org/10.1109/ISECon.2012.6204175

Nussbaum, M., Alvarez, C., McFarlane, A., Gomez, F., Claro, S., Radovic, D.: Technology as small group face-to-face collaborative scaffolding. Comput. Educ. 52(1), 147–153 (2009). https://doi.org/10.1016/j.compedu.2008.07.005

* Okundaye, O., Chu, S., Quek, F., Berman, A., Natarajarathinam, M., Kuttolamadom, M.: From making to micro-manufacture: catalyzing STEM participation in rural high schools. In: Proceedings of the Conference on Creativity and Making in Education, pp. 21–29. ACM, June 2018

Papavlasopoulou, S., Giannakos, M.N., Jaccheri, L.: Empirical studies on the maker movement, a promising approach to learning: a literature review. Entertain. Comput. 18, 57–78 (2017)

Papert, S.: Mindstorms: Children, Computers, and Powerful Ideas. Basic Books, Inc., New York (1980)

* Patton, R.M., Knochel, A.D.: Meaningful makers: stuff, sharing, and connection in STEAM curriculum. Art Educ. 70(1), 36–43 (2017). https://doi.org/10.1080/00043125.2017.1247571

* Perner-Wilson, H., Buechley, L., Satomi, M.: Handcrafting textile interfaces from a kit-of-no-parts. In: Proceedings of the Fifth International Conference on Tangible, Embedded, and Embodied Interaction - TEI 2011, p. 61 (2011). http://doi.org/10.1145/1935701.1935715

* Peppler, K., Glosson, D.: Stitching circuits: learning about circuitry through e-textile materials. J. Sci. Educ. Technol. 22(5), 751–763 (2013)

* Peppler, K.: STEAM-powered computing education: using e-textiles to integrate the arts and STEM. Computer 46(9), 38–43 (2013)

* Posch, I., Fitzpatrick, G.: First steps in the FabLab. In: Proceedings of the 24th Australian Computer-Human Interaction Conference on - OzCHI 2012, pp. 497–500 (2012). http://doi.org/10.1145/2414536.2414612

* Qi, J., Buechley, L.: Sketching in circuits: designing and building electronics on paper. In: Proceedings of the SIGCHI Conference on Human Factors in Computing Systems, pp. 1713–1722. ACM, April 2014

* Qiu, K., Buechley, L., Baafi, E., Dubow, W.: A curriculum for teaching computer science through computational textiles. In: Proceedings of the 12th International Conference on Interaction Design and Children, pp. 20–27. ACM, June 2013

Rode, J.A., et al.: From computational thinking to computational making. In: Proceedings of the 2015 ACM International Joint Conference on Pervasive and Ubiquitous Computing and Proceedings of the 2015 ACM International Symposium on Wearable Computers - UbiComp 2015, pp. 401–402 (2015). http://doi.org/10.1145/2800835.2800926

* Schneider, B., Bumbacher, E., Blikstein, P.: Discovery versus direct instruction: learning outcomes of two pedagogical models using tangible interfaces, pp. 364–371. International Society of the Learning Sciences, Inc. (2015)

* Schwartz, L.H., DiGiacomo, D., Gutiérrez, K.D.: Designing "contexts for tinkerability" with undergraduates and children within the El Pueblo Magico social design experiment. Int. J. Res. Ext. Educ. 3(1), 94–113 (2015)

* Searle, K.A., Fields, D.A., Lui, D.A., Kafai, Y.B.: Diversifying high school students' views about computing with electronic textiles. In: Proceedings of the Tenth Annual Conference on International Computing Education Research - ICER 2014, pp. 75–82 (2014). http://doi.org/10.1145/2632320.2632352

* Searle, K.A., Kafai, Y.B.: Boys' needlework: understanding gendered and indigenous perspectives on computing and crafting with electronic textiles. In: ICER, pp. 31–39, July 2015

* Sheridan, K., Halverson, E.R., Litts, B., Brahms, L., Jacobs-Priebe, L., Owens, T.: Learning in the making: a comparative case study of three makerspaces. Harv. Educ. Rev. 84(4), 505–531 (2014)

* Telhan, O., Kafai, Y.B., Davis, R.L., Steele, K., Adleberg, B.M.: Connected messages: a maker approach to interactive community murals with youth. In: Proceedings of the 2014 Conference on Interaction Design and Children, pp. 193–196. ACM, June 2014

Vossoughi, S., Bevan, B.: Making and tinkering: A review of the literature. National Research Council Committee on Out of School Time STEM, pp. 1–55 (2014)

Wagh, A., Cook-Whitt, K., Wilensky, U.: Bridging inquiry-based science and constructionism: exploring the alignment between students tinkering with code of computational models and goals of inquiry. J. Res. Sci. Teach. 54(5), 615–641 (2017). https://doi.org/10.1002/tea.21379

* Wagner, A., Gray, J., Corley, J., Wolber, D.: Using app inventor in a K-12 summer camp. In: Proceeding of the 44th ACM Technical Symposium on Computer Science Education, pp. 621–626. ACM, March 2013

* Worsley, M., Blikstein, P.: Assessing the "Makers": the impact of principle-based reasoning on hands-on, project-based learning. In: Proceedings of the 2014 Conference of the Learning Sciences, pp. 1147–1151 (2014)

* Zajdel, T.J., Maharbiz, M.M.: Teaching design with a tinkering-driven robot hack. In: 2016 IEEE Frontiers in Education Conference (FIE), pp. 1–6. IEEE, October 2016

Rexy, A Configurable Application for Building Virtual Teaching Assistants

Luca Benedetto[(⊠)] and Paolo Cremonesi

Politecnico di Milano, Milan, Italy
{luca.benedetto,paolo.cremonesi}@polimi.it

Abstract. In recent years, virtual assistants gained a pervasive role in many domains and education was not different from others. However, although some implementation of conversational agents for supporting students have already been presented, they were *ad hoc* systems, built for specific courses and impossible to generalize. Also, there is a lack of research about the effects that the development of systems capable of interacting with both the students and the professors would have. In this paper, we introduce *Rexy*, a configurable application that can be used to build virtual teaching assistants for diverse courses, and present the results of a user study carried out using it as a virtual teaching assistant for an on-site course held at Politecnico di Milano. The qualitative analysis of the usage that was made of the assistant and the results of a post study questionnaire the students were asked to fill showed that they see conversational agents as useful tools for helping them in their studies.

Keywords: Artificial intelligence · Conversational agents · Human-computer interaction · Virtual teaching assistants · NLP

1 Introduction

For several years research has been exploring the usage of conversational agents - also referred to as chatbots - in education, due to their capability of bringing advantages both to students and to teachers. Recent works, such as [3], suggested the use of chatbots as Virtual Teaching Assistants (VTA) to enable scalable teaching and reduce instructors' workload. Thanks to VTAs, students can have most of their requests answered immediately without having to wait for the teacher to write back; at the same time, instructors can focus on other aspects of the teaching activity that necessarily require a direct human interaction.

Regardless of these promising characteristics of conversational agents, there is a lack of studies to show the efficacy of VTAs. Previous works proposed chatbots as virtual teaching assistants, but they were either concepts without a working implementation or systems with limitations: in particular, even though VTAs are unavoidably able to understand only part of the requests they receive, the existing implementations can interact only with students and are not capable of asking human teaching assistants for help.

© IFIP International Federation for Information Processing 2019
Published by Springer Nature Switzerland AG 2019
D. Lamas et al. (Eds.): INTERACT 2019, LNCS 11747, pp. 233–241, 2019.
https://doi.org/10.1007/978-3-030-29384-0_15

In this paper, we introduce *Rexy* - a configurable application that can be used to build VTAs about any types of courses - and present a user study in which *Rexy* was deployed as a virtual assistant for an on-site course held at Politecnico di Milano in order to understand how the students perceived the assistant, whether it was useful and how it could be improved.

The main contributions of this work consist in:

- the introduction of *Rexy*, a novel application to implement VTAs that can interact with both students and professors;
- the implementation and deployment of an assistant based on *Rexy*;
- a qualitative user study, which shows that students are willing to leverage VTAs and see conversational agents as useful supporting tools.

The rest of the paper is organized as follows. Section 2 presents the state of the art; Sect. 3 introduces *Rexy*; Sect. 4 provides the details of the user study, whose results are presented in Sect. 5. Lastly, Sect. 6 presents the final discussion and the directions for future works.

2   Related Work

The effectiveness and usefulness of instant messaging applications and forums to support online and on-site students has been proved by several works [12–14]. Unfortunately, there are many constraints that limit the supplying of continuous human support, such as the cost and availability of Teaching Assistants (TA); a possible solution consists in automating student's support via the usage of conversational agents.

Conversational agents and their possible applications in diverse domains have been studied for years [10], and researchers already tried to use them in education several years ago [9,11], creating the first implementations of what we call "virtual teaching assistants" (VTA). However, although some of these results are still relevant today, the technology available at the time did not allow the implementation of chat-based VTAs that were really effective in improving the students' learning experience. More precisely, conversational agents rely on natural language processing (NLP) [4] techniques to understand the users' requests and provide meaningful responses, and the algorithms available at the time were not accurate enough for the tasks that had to be solved in VTAs.

In recent years, thanks to the improvements in NLP, researchers returned to explore the usage of conversational systems in education, but there is still a lack of studies to show the efficacy of VTAs. In particular, no previous works explored the possibility of building a VTA capable of interacting with both students and human TAs, and most works did not focus on the perception that the students have of a VTA, even though this is an important aspect to consider and might affect the effectiveness of such systems [8].

Goel et al. in [7] introduced Jill Watson (JW), a VTA for online education similar to the ones that can be implemented with *Rexy*; the authors showed the possible applications of JW in a MOOC, but they did not present the details of the implementation and always considered it as a black-box. Also, *Rexy* leads to the development of VTA that have a different role: JW aimed at completely replacing human TAs, therefore it encountered some issues that still have to be dealt with [5]; on the other hand, our application is meant to work together with the professors (as suggested in [11]) and therefore does not have to deal with conversations that are out of the scope of the specific course for which it is deployed. This is an important difference between the two approaches: VTAs built upon *Rexy* are meant to cooperate with human TAs in order to answer the requests they cannot deal with on their own, and can do so by proactively starting a conversation with a TA and asking for help.

Ventura ct al. [15] and Akcora et. al [1] proposed conversational agents as virtual teaching assistants, but their objective was different from ours: indeed, the systems presented in both the works can be defined as tutors whose role is guiding a student while he's consuming the content of an online course, not being assistants that can answer general requests. Also, while Ventura et al. already presented preliminary results of the use of their assistant, the system proposed in [1] is only a concept which will require further work.

3   The Application: *Rexy*

We propose a configurable application that can be used to implement different VTAs, extending the work done in [2]. The only step required to build from *Rexy* an assistant for a specific course consists in creating the appropriate knowledge base and feeding the application with it. As shown in Fig. 1 this application is composed of three components: (i) messaging application, (ii) application server, (iii) natural language processing component.

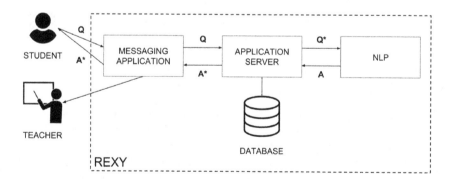

Fig. 1. Architecture of *Rexy*

3.1 Messaging Application

The front-end of the system consists of a Slack application that enables students to interact with the VTA. Although several messaging applications feature the possibility of implementing conversational agents, we decided to use Slack since it allows both one-to-one and one-to-many interactions: indeed, a Slack workspace can be used in the educational domain as a hub where students can interact not only with the VTA, but also with each other and with the professors. Additionally, Slack has two interesting features: it allows conversational agents (i) to send interactive messages and dialogs, thus enriching the way in which students can communicate with the VTA (e.g. with multi-choice questions), and (ii) to begin the conversation with a student, therefore enabling proactive assistants that can send messages to students that are struggling.

3.2 Application Server

The role of the application server consists in processing the requests Q coming from the students and managing how the NLP component interacts with the database in order to create the response message $A*$. In particular, its tasks can be grouped into three categories.

- **Preprocessing:** this is necessary when the creation of the response requires some information which is not available in the NLP component. More precisely, the application server has to keep track of the context of the conversation, since the memory of the NLP component is limited to the current interaction with the student and, if he references something previously said, the server must take care of this and modify the input request before sending it to the NLP component. In Fig. 1, Q is the original question while $Q*$ is the question after it has been preprocessed. Let's consider this example:

  Student(Q) : How many inhabitants does London have?
  Rexy : As of 2019, it has 9,126,366 inhabitants.
  Student(Q) : How many inhabitants did **it** have in 1750?
  Student(Q^*) : How many inhabitants did **London** have in 1750?
  Rexy : In 1750, 740,000 persons were living in London.

  In the second request, the student refers to "London" with the pronoun "it"; therefore, the application server has to modify the message in order to make the NLP component understand the request.

- **Post-processing:** analogously to preprocessing, if the response requires some information that is out of the reach of the NLP component, the application server has to modify the message before forwarding the answer to the messaging application. In Fig. 1, A is the original answer while $A*$ is the question after it has been post-processed. An example is shown here:

  Student : How many inhabitants does London have?
  Rexy(A) : As of 2019, it has <*num_london_inhabitants*> inhabitants.

Rexy(A*) : As of 2019, it has 9,126,366 inhabitants.

The NLP component creates the template answer A and the application server fills the gap with the information gathered from the database.

- **Interaction with a human teaching assistant:** every time the NLP component receives a request forwarded by the application server, it generates a response and sends it, together with an estimated confidence level c, back to the server; a low value of c means that the NLP component is not confident in the generated response. A threshold t_L is defined in the application server; if $c < t_L$ the assistant forwards via Slack the question to the human TA and sends to the student a notification stating that the request will be answered as soon as possible by a human. When the TA writes the response, this is sent to the student and the correct request-response pair is sent to the NLP component as well, in order to update the dataset used for future retraining.

The application server contains the information about the course, the information about the students and the history of all the conversations.

3.3   NLP Component

The NLP component leverages IBM's Watson Assistant [6], an AI engine offering services for natural language understanding and natural language processing; in order to make it work in the educational domain, we can train it with data consisting of a set of request-response pairs. Each request is labelled with an *intent* and/or an *entity*: *intents* represent the objectives of the users, while *entities* give a context to the interaction between the user and the assistant, thus affecting the way in which it reacts to each *intent*.

Intents are specific of the educational domain but do not depend on the particular course. Therefore, once we have defined the ones related to education, they can be used without modifications for every course; in particular, we defined 71 *intents*. Examples of intents we defined are *exam_date*, which indicates that the student is interested in knowing the date of the exam; *content_references*, when the student wants to know where to find a specific course topic in the material; and *course_program*, meaning that the student wants to know the program of the course.

Differently from *intents*, *entities* are, in general, course dependent. Each *entity* does not represent a unique concept, but instead a set of concepts (named *values* in Watson).

Let's consider the same example as above:

STUDENT : How many inhabitants does London have?

Here, "London" is a value of the entity *course_topic*, "inhabitants" is a value of the entity *attribute* and the intent is *retrieve_topic_information*.

When implementing an assistant using this application, it is sufficient to enlarge the set of *entities* by inserting the ones that are specific to the course for which the VTA is being built. In our case, we configured and deployed *Rexy* as a VTA to support the students enrolled in an introductory course about recommender systems held on-site at Politecnico di Milano. In order to adapt *Rexy* to this scenario, we only had to store in the database server the knowledge base containing the information specific to this course, and to define the course-specific entities. In total, we defined 231 values grouped in 4 entities.

A very interesting feature of Watson Assistant consists in the possibility of continuously retraining the model, thus enabling active learning. Our architecture leverages this in order to keep improving the accuracy of the model: every time a request is correctly answered (by the assistant or a human TA), the request-response pair is inserted in the training set so that it will be used for retraining. Thanks to this approach, the number of required interactions with the human TA is likely to continuously decrease as more training samples are being collected.

4   User Study

The course was attended by 107 students and they were informed about the possibility of using the VTA to answer their questions; however, they were not forced to use it and could still interact with human TAs for help. Moreover, in order to stimulate the use of the VTA, we let the students join the Slack workspace with arbitrary nicknames, therefore they could not be identified and associated with the final score of the exam.

Our qualitative study has two goals: (i) understanding the effectiveness of the assistant by analyzing the interaction logs, (ii) collecting feedback from the students in order to understand how they perceive conversational agents as VTAs.

At the end of the semester, the students were given a post-study questionnaire to capture their opinion about the assistant: the questionnaire comprised both closed-ended and open-ended questions. In particular, the following questions were asked:

- How would you evaluate the support provided by *Rexy*?
- Do you think virtual teaching assistants could help you, as a student?
- Which was the best feature of *Rexy*?
- Which was the biggest limitation of *Rexy*?
- How could *Rexy* be improved, in your opinion?

5   Evaluation

At the time of writing, 22 students have interacted with the assistant in 263 conversation turns, thus having an average of 11.95 messages per student.

5.1   System Usage

Not all the messages required both the identification of an *intent* and an *entity*: more precisely, 182 questions required *intent* classification and the remaining

81 both *intent* and *entity* classification. Manual inspection of the activity log showed that the VTA was always capable of correctly detecting the *entity*, while the accuracy on *intent* classification was about 70%: 127 out of 182 *intents* were correctly classified. Diving a bit more into the details, we noticed that out of the 55 requests that were not handled only 26 were questions that should have been answered, the remaining 29 were random messages or messages mocking the assistant. Therefore, the actual *intent* classification accuracy was 83%.

Most of the students' requests were related to two aspects of the course: (i) definitions and examples about the topics presented during the lectures and (ii) lecture and exam schedule. This suggests that VTAs can be particularly useful as helping tools for reviewing the course and quickly retrieve information about it; indeed, students can obtain the information they are looking for without having to search the course material or the course website for it.

The students' requests involved only 43 *intents* out of the 71 we had defined (60.56%). This is reasonable, since *intents* were arbitrarily chosen while designing *Rexy*, future work should focus on this aspect to understand whether a reorganization of them would bring some improvements to the effectiveness of *Rexy*.

5.2 Post-study Questionnaire

The questionnaire was answered by 40 students, 11 of them interacted with *Rexy* at least once.

When asked whether they see VTAs as useful supporting tools for students, only 4 students claimed that they did not see any advantages coming from them. Interestingly, these 4 students had not tried *Rexy*, suggesting that the ones who tried to interact with the assistant foresaw the advantages that such system could bring to their learning experience.

When asked why they did not use the assistant, most of the students replied that the support received from the human TAs and the other students was usually sufficient. However, one answer to this question was particularly interesting: a student said that he did not use *Rexy* because he did not feel comfortable talking to a bot. This aspect should definitely be taken into consideration in future research in order to understand whether similar problems could be overcome, especially because in MOOCs the interaction with human TAs necessarily introduces long delays in the communication.

Only 3 students rated in a negative way the assistant; the others appreciated the possibility of receiving immediate answers, specifically for quickly finding online video lectures and information about the schedule and the topics presented in each lecture, which is in agreement with the usage we observed in the interaction log.

Although only few students rated in a negative way the assistant, we received some comments about the limitations of this first implementation of *Rexy*. In particular, some students criticized the fact that sometimes the assistant has to forward the requests to a human TA. At the same time, however, they appreciated the fact that they were not asked to resend the question because *Rexy* was able to manage everything on its own and they only had to wait a bit longer before receiving the answer.

6   Conclusions and Future Work

In this paper we have introduced *Rexy*, a novel configurable architecture that can be used to build virtual teaching assistants. We have shown the implementation of a VTA built upon *Rexy* for an on-site course held at Politecnico di Milano and reported the results of a qualitative user study in which we analyzed the effectiveness of this application. *Rexy* received positive feedback from the students and proved capable of answering most of their requests. In doing so, it reduced both the workload on the Professor and the average time elapsed between sending a question and receiving the answer.

The proposed application leverages IBM's Watson Assistant for the majority of the tasks related to NLP and thus offers a fairly easy solution for implementing virtual teaching assistants. Indeed, the only effort required consists in the curation of the knowledge base related to the target course to feed the database with.

Feedback from students suggests that some improvement could be made: in particular, enlarging the training set would make *Rexy* more accurate in detecting the correct *intent* and therefore reduce the need of interventions from human TAs. Indeed, even though the students appreciated the fact that they were not requested to perform any additional request when *Rexy* could not understand a question, the delay introduced by waiting for a human teaching assistant to answer was the one element that was criticized by the students.

Future work should focus more on the choice of *intents* made while developing *Rexy*. Indeed, they were arbitrarily chosen while designing the application and, although they proved very effective once *Rexy* was deployed, it is possible that some slightly different configurations could work even better in recognizing the students' requests.

Another aspect to consider in future work is the value that is used as threshold in the application server to decide whether *Rexy* is confident in the generated answer. Indeed, it has a direct impact on the system's performance since it determines whether the assistant should contact a human teaching assistant for help and some improvements could be obtained by performing performance tuning to find the optimal value for the threshold.

The current architecture only deals with one-to-one interactions, communicating with students in private conversations; however, one of the reasons of choosing Slack as the front-end application consisted in the possibility of enabling one-to-many interactions and we are currently working on implementing such feature.

References

1. Akcora, D.E., et al.: Conversational support for education. In: Penstein Rosé, C., et al. (eds.) AIED 2018. LNCS (LNAI), vol. 10948, pp. 14–19. Springer, Cham (2018). https://doi.org/10.1007/978-3-319-93846-2_3
2. Benedetto, L., Cremonesi, P., Parenti, M.: A virtual teaching assistant for personalized learning. arXiv preprint arXiv:1902.09289 (2019)
3. du Boulay, B.: Artificial intelligence as an effective classroom assistant. IEEE Intell. Syst. **31**(6), 76–81 (2016)
4. Collobert, R., Weston, J., Bottou, L., Karlen, M., Kavukcuoglu, K., Kuksa, P.: Natural language processing (almost) from scratch. J. Mach. Learn. Res. **12**, 2493–2537 (2011)
5. Eicher, B., Polepeddi, L., Goel, A.: Jill Watson doesn't care if you're pregnant: grounding AI ethics in empirical studies. In: AAAI/ACM Conference on Artificial Intelligence, Ethics, and Society, New Orleans, LA, vol. 7 (2017)
6. Ferrucci, D., et al.: Building Watson: an overview of the deepQA project. AI Magaz. **31**(3), 59–79 (2010)
7. Goel, A.K., Polepeddi, L.: Jill Watson: a virtual teaching assistant for online education. Technical report, Georgia Institute of Technology (2016)
8. Hill, J., Ford, W.R., Farreras, I.G.: Real conversations with artificial intelligence: a comparison between human-human online conversations and human-chatbot conversations. Comput. Hum. Behav. **49**, 245–250 (2015)
9. Kerlyl, A., Hall, P., Bull, S.: Bringing chatbots into education: towards natural language negotiation of open learner models. In: Ellis, R., Allen, T., Tuson, A. (eds.) Applications and Innovations in Intelligent Systems XIV. SGAI 2006, pp. 179–192. Springer, London (2007). https://doi.org/10.1007/978-1-84628-666-7_14
10. Ramesh, K., Ravishankaran, S., Joshi, A., Chandrasekaran, K.: A survey of design techniques for conversational agents. In: Kaushik, S., Gupta, D., Kharb, L., Chahal, D. (eds.) ICICCT 2017. CCIS, vol. 750, pp. 336–350. Springer, Singapore (2017). https://doi.org/10.1007/978-981-10-6544-6_31
11. Shawar, B.A., Atwell, E.: Chatbots: are they really useful? Ldv forum, vol. 22, pp. 29–49 (2007)
12. So, S.: Mobile instant messaging support for teaching and learning in higher education. Internet High. Educ. **31**, 32–42 (2016)
13. Sun, Z., Lin, C.H., Wu, M., Zhou, J., Luo, L.: A tale of two communication tools: discussion-forum and mobile instant-messaging apps in collaborative learning. Br. J. Educ. Technol. **49**(2), 248–261 (2018)
14. Timmis, S.: Constant companions: instant messaging conversations as sustainable supportive study structures amongst undergraduate peers. Comput. Educ. **59**(1), 3–18 (2012)
15. Ventura, M., et al.: Preliminary evaluations of a dialogue-based digital tutor. In: Penstein Rosé, C., et al. (eds.) AIED 2018. LNCS (LNAI), vol. 10948, pp. 480–483. Springer, Cham (2018). https://doi.org/10.1007/978-3-319-93846-2_90

Two-Way Gaze Sharing in Remote Teaching

Oleg Špakov[1], Diederick Niehorster[2], Howell Istance[1](✉), Kari-Jouko Räihä[1], and Harri Siirtola[1]

[1] Tampere University, Kalavantie 4, Tampere, Finland
`howell.istance@tuni.fi, howell.istance@staff.uta.fi`
[2] Lund University, Paradisgatan 2, Lund, Sweden

Abstract. On-line teaching situations where a tutor and their students are remote from each other mean that contact between them is reduced compared with teaching in a classroom. We report an initial study of two-way gaze sharing between a tutor and a group of students, who were in different locations. A 45-min class consisted of an introductory lecture followed by an exercise in using two software tools, one for building an experiment and the other for analysis of the data collected. The tutor went through an exercise step by step and the students followed. This was run twice with four students on each run. The tutor had a view of the students' desktops with their gaze markers overlaid and each student had a view of the tutor's desktop and gaze marker. Students found seeing the tutor's gaze marker helpful during the exercise but distracting when reading the text on the lecture slides. The tutor found the view of the students' gaze point helpful as an indicator of their current object of attention when giving assistance to individuals.

Keywords: Gaze sharing · Remote teaching · Two-way

1 Introduction

A feature of classroom teaching is the ability of the tutor to gauge problems students have and progress made by them while listening to something being explained or when completing exercises. Observing cues from students who have difficulties can enable the tutor to help those students. Some students will ask for help if they need it, but others will not.

The possibility for tutors to observe students will be much reduced in remote internet-mediated teaching situations. This reduction in non-verbal contact can be offset by sharing an indication of a student's current object of visual attention with the tutor. There are also benefits in sharing where the tutor is currently looking with the students, as has been demonstrated in a classroom teaching situation [15]. It is very possible that the value of these benefits would be enhanced in a remote teaching situation.

© IFIP International Federation for Information Processing 2019
Published by Springer Nature Switzerland AG 2019
D. Lamas et al. (Eds.): INTERACT 2019, LNCS 11747, pp. 242–251, 2019.
https://doi.org/10.1007/978-3-030-29384-0_16

If a remote eye tracker is to be used to measure where the student is looking, then the area of measurement is typically restricted to a screen in front of them. This screen can display a copy of the tutor's screen as well as the desktop of the student's own computer. Real-time remote teaching is facilitated by bi-directional voice communication between the tutor and students. We can characterize the teaching situations using the CSCW classification [9] as 'same time - same place' (classroom) and 'same time - different place' (internet mediated teaching). We are not considering here 'different place - different time' (as would be the case with MOOCs for example).

The research question is twofold. First, to what extent does the tutor having access to information about where the student is looking help him or her to be aware of problems the student may have in understanding what is currently being taught? Second, to what extent does the student knowing where the tutor is looking in relation to the teaching material help the student?

This paper presents the outcomes from two remote teaching sessions. In each, four students sat separated from each other in a digital classroom where all computers were equipped with eye trackers. The tutor sat in a separate room with two screens, one was their teaching screen and the other contained views of each student's screen with the student's gaze point overlaid. Each student had a window on their desktop containing a view of the tutor's teaching screen with his gaze point overlaid. The contribution of this paper is that it is the first to the knowledge of the authors to investigate the value of simultaneous two-way gaze sharing in a remote teaching situation.

2   Background and Previous Work

The value of *gaze sharing* has been studied in several different contexts in addition to education. This means showing someone in real-time where someone else is looking. These contexts include remote expert assistance in problem solving [1,6], collaborative visual search [2,11,13], remote pair programming [3] and games [10].

Educational applications of gaze sharing have used different numbers of sharers of gaze.

One-to-One. Sharing the gaze of an expert (tutor) with a novice (student) has been found to be useful in teaching software debugging [14]. The gaze was shared continuously and not intentionally or deliberately (like a mouse pointer). It was found that the expert's gaze functioned as a useful cue and assisted the student in problem solving.

One-to-Many. Replacing the tutor's pointer with an marker of the tutor's current gaze point has been compared to more traditional pointing methods [15]. The *GazeLaser* system was compared with the PowerPoint pointer and with a conventional laser pointer for manual pointing. GazeLaser performed on a par with the PowerPoint pointer, surpassing manual pointing. The PowerPoint pointer was rated highest by the participants, but GazeLaser was most easily noticed.

In a study of gaze sharing in a MOOC [12], it was found that displaying the gaze point of the tutor on video teaching material made understanding what the tutor was referring to in complex situations easier for the student. Also, students stopped and replayed parts of the video less frequently compared with situations where the gaze overlay was absent. Similarly, eye-movement modelling examples demonstrated the value of using an expert's gaze point to guide the attention of students looking at case videos in medical educational situations [5, 7, 8].

Many-to-One. A system for sharing the gaze information from students to a tutor's display during a computer science studio session was studied in [16]. On the teacher's display, each student's gaze was visualized with a colored circle having a 70 pixel radius. In addition, each student's location in the code editor was indicated with a color-coded line in the scroll bar. It was found out that the system was useful for getting confirmation that the students are following along, and monitoring the students while they were working independently. In addition, the teachers did not find the real time gaze visualization distracting as some of the earlier studies have suggested [4].

The study reported in this paper is effectively a combination of the one-to-many and many-to one situations. The tutor's gaze point is presented to all participating students and each of the student's displays containing their gaze points is presented to the tutor.

3   Setting Up a Teaching Situation with Two-Way Gaze Sharing

3.1   Digital Classroom

The experiment took place in the Lund University Humanities Lab's Digital Classroom. In this facility, 25 computer stations are available that were each equipped with an SMI RED-m remote eye tracker and that are connected together through a gigabit Ethernet network. The stations in this setup were arranged in a large O, with all sitting on the outside of the O facing inward.

3.2   The Gaze Sharing Solution

The screen image and gaze marker position were shared separately from the students' machines to the tutor's machine, and from the tutor's machine to each of the student machines. The gaze marker was overlaid on the image of the remote screen at the receiver's end.

GazeNet. The tool was built to share gaze data between multiple PCs. It consists of server and client components. The GazeNet Server[1] runs as a NodeJS application on a local university server that interconnects GazeNet Client instances. All data streams are grouped into named channels, and all clients connected to a same channel exchange gaze data with each other.

---

[1] Available at https://github.com/uta-gasp/gazenet-server.

The GazeNet Client[2] is a local .NET application that connects to an eye tracker installed on the local PC (using ETU-Driver[3] and UDPMultiCast[4] as middle-ware) and streams gaze data to the GazeNet Server using a named channel defined in its settings. The tool can be configured to display the local and/or remote gaze points on screen as semitransparent colored circles. GazeNet Client is supplied with several plugins, one of which starts UltraVNC Server and Ultra-VNC Viewer instances and scales remote gaze points to fit them into corresponding UltraVNC Viewer windows.

UltraVNC. UltraVNC was chosen as a highly configurable and robust VNC solution to share the images of the desktops. The UltraVNC Server tool captures a PC desktop into a video-stream and delivers it to UltraVNC clients connected to it. At the endpoints of these streams, the UltraVNC Viewer tool was used as the VNC client, which was controlled by the GazeNet Client software.

Skype. All students and the tutor were connected to the group chat created in Skype. Only speech was transmitted over Skype, as the pilot tests revealed that video streams over Skype tend to delay or even halt regularly. The chat was the main communication channel between the participants in the session.

Tutor's Workstation. This had two monitors, one showed the tutor's own desktop and the eye tracker tracked the gaze position on this monitor. The other monitor showed the desktops of the 4 students with their respective gaze positions overlaid. In each of these desktops the student's view of the tutor's desktop is shown in the top right corner. The tutor's gaze point on his or her own desktop is shown to the student in this view. It was not visible when the tutor was looking at the monitor with the students' desktops. The layouts are shown in Fig. 1.

3.3   Class Teaching Exercise

The digital classroom was being used for a course on eye tracking. A lecture and class exercise, lasting 45 min and dealing with collecting and analyzing eye tracking data was devised and delivered twice to four course students on each occasion. The lecture lasted about seven minutes and used PowerPoint slides. Students were asked to maximize the window with the view of the tutor's screen during this. Following this, students were asked to return the window to its normal size. There then followed a demonstration of BeGaze (the data analysis tool) to visualize previously collected eye tracking data from a reading experiment. Then the use of Experiment Builder was demonstrated to set up a simple procedure for collecting reading data. Finally, the students collected their own reading data, and then used BeGaze to visualize and analyze this. In the practical exercise the tutor demonstrated and explained each step, and the students followed on their own computer. This was supported by a paper handout that the students could refer to during the exercise.

---

[2] Available at https://github.com/uta-gasp/gazenet-client.

[3] Available at https://www.sis.uta.fi/~csolsp/downloads.php.

[4] Available at https://github.com/dcnieho/UDPMulticast.

4   Outcomes and Evaluation

4.1   Student Evaluation of Shared Gaze

Eight students participated in total, five female and three male. There were two teaching sessions with four students in each. In the second session, two of the students had used the BeGaze analysis tool previously. Seven of the eight students answered an evaluation questionnaire after their session was over, which was followed by a discussion with all students in the session. One student left shortly before the end of their session by prior agreement and did not complete the questionnaire.

Some questions dealt with the usefulness of seeing the tutor's gaze marker. Other questions dealt with how students felt about having their own eyes tracked and the tutor seeing their gaze position. The replies are summarized in Table 1.

4.2   Tutor Evaluation of Shared Gaze

One tutor gave both lectures. They reported not looking at the students' desktops at all during the lecture part of the session. During the practical exercise, they reported using the screen containing the desktops in two ways. First looking at the desktops showed whether a student was keeping up with the exercise or whether they had encountered a problem and was falling behind. Second, when

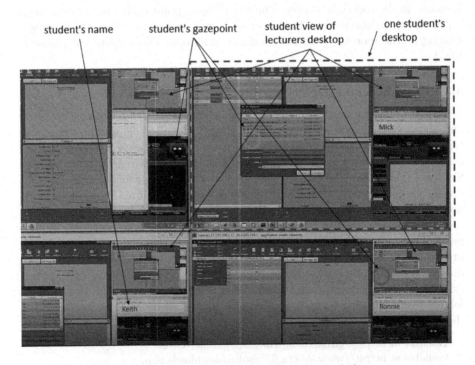

Fig. 1. Part of tutor's view of the 4 student's desktops

Table 1. Summary of responses from student questionnaires and interviews

how much attention was paid to the tutor's gaze point

– 6 reported following the tutor's gaze indicator 50% to 70% of the time of the session

situations where the tutor's gaze marker was helpful

– 3 said using the gaze marker to find where to find specific elements in the interface that the tutor referred to, especially when the instruction was not heard properly or was unclear

– 2 used it to confirm they were looking at the same general area as the tutor

– 2 said it was helpful

situations where the tutor's gaze marker was distracting

– 4 reported this was most of the time during the lecture slides: it was hard to listen, read slides and also see the gaze marker

– It was distracting as the gaze marker did not align with the tutor's mouse marker that was also displayed on the slide

– When the tutor's desktop window was restored to its normal size and location in the top right corner after the initial lecture, the marker was not distracting

whether the visual form of the gaze marker was appropriate

– 4 thought it was good, although 1 thought it obscured the text on the slides

whether the tutor's gaze marker was sufficiently stable

– 3 thought it was, 2 thought it unstable part of the time, but 2 thought it was unstable and disturbing

how to make better use of the tutor's gaze marker

– 1 suggested having the option to replay the path of the marker

– 2 suggested showing it only when the students were supposed to be doing something and not displaying it during the lecture part of the session

– 1 said that there were times when they wanted more information but the normal size of the tutor's desktop window was too small

whether having their eyes tracked was disturbing

– 4 said no, 2 said only initially, and 1 said yes

whether having their eyes tracked caused fatigue

– 2 said no, but 5 reported some fatigue by the end of the session

whether having their eyes tracked caused them to behave differently

– 3 said no, other than trying to sit in the same position in front of the screen

– 4 said yes in some way they were more conscious of where they were looking. "I sometimes tried to make my gaze be where the teacher wanted at the moment, even if I already knew what to do."

the tutor was helping a particular student, their gaze point provided a valuable indicator of the location of the student's attention. Each student's name appeared in a text box on the right hand side of their desktop, so the tutor could easily identify the student, and could address them directly.

It was seen quickly whether the student was looking at the object referred to by the tutor, or whether they had difficulties locating this. There was no need to describe the absolute location if a student had problems, or to indicate the location by moving a mouse pointer to the object. The object could be referred to in relation to the gaze point, for example, 'No.. no.. up from where you're looking .. and right .. yes, there'.

4.3 Observations from the Teaching Sessions

An advantage of a setup where the content of the desktop can be manipulated by the students is that it allows them to work in their preferred fashion. Most students simply made use of the small view of the tutor's window, switching their gaze back and forth between their own work area and the tutor's window when following instructions. One student had problems setting up the experiment and fell a little behind. The tutor was able to get them back on track by individual tutoring a couple of times, but before that they had missed some of the verbal instructions. Therefore they decided to get a more detailed view of the tutor's desktop, maximizing and minimizing it ten times and spending nearly three minutes watching the large view without acting themselves. Their mode of operation was to make a plan and execute it after minimizing the tutor's view, even if it was not in synchrony with the verbal instructions.

5 Discussion

This paper has reported an initial study into two-way gaze sharing in a realistic remote teaching situation. A lecture and accompanying exercises to illustrate the collection and visualization of eye tracking data during a course were produced, and the class was repeated twice. One limitation was that only four students took part in each class. This was intentional to enable the views of all students' desktops to be displayed simultaneously to the tutor. The study was not repeated subsequently with larger numbers of students. Another limitation was that no analysis was made of objective measures indicating learning or teaching behaviour on the part of the students or the tutor, and there was no comparison of these indicators with and without shared gaze.

During the initial lecture part of the session, the view of the lecturer's desktop was shown maximized on the students' screens. The slides were shown full screen with the lecturer's gaze marker overlaid. Many students felt that seeing the lecturer's gaze marker was distracting, partly because it was new to them, but mostly because it interfered with their own reading of the text on the slides. Quoting one student, "Very distracting in the beginning! I could not attend to what [the tutor] was saying the first minutes, because I was too focused on following his eye movements and thinking about my own." However as most slides contained both text and illustrations, the gaze marker did work as an indicator for the students when to look at the pictures instead of the text. For this purpose it seemed to work well.

The two-way connection between the teacher and the students allowed the teacher to instruct individual students if they got stuck. For instance, one student was unable to follow the instructions concerning gaze replay, and asked a question using the audio channel. The tutor walked them through step by step and helped them catch up with the others. During this time the other students had to wait, but this is no different from what would happen in a traditional in-class tutoring session.

There are several issues to consider for a larger study of two-way gaze sharing. First, should students be given control of when they see the tutor's gaze marker? This would be in order to switch the marker off to prevent it being a distraction, such as when the tutor is looking at text on slides. It would be possible to detect automatically when the tutor is reading text on slides and suppress display of the tutor's gaze point on the student's view. Second, is the added value of gaze sharing worth the overhead of eye tracking in comparison with using deliberate movements of the mouse pointer to communicate the objects being attended to when the need arises? Third, what are the means of increasing the number of students being taught remotely from four to a more realistic number?

5.1 Increasing the Number of Participating Students

The problem with presenting each student's desktop all the time is the amount of screen space required and the bandwidth to stream all desktops to the tutor's workstation. The display in this study (Fig. 1) provides more information than the tutor has in a real classroom. One way to increase the number of students that a tutor can monitor concurrently could be to use another tutor. Their role would be to check several pages of tiled screens for students who appear to have difficulties. Another way is to enable students to request help, and then display only one student desktop and gaze marker to the tutor at a time. This is the equivalent of a student putting their hand up in class and the tutor coming to look over their shoulder. During this 1-to-1 help, voice communication could be restricted to the tutor and the individual student. A third way would be to detect automatically the distance between the tutor's marker and the student's marker and alert the tutor if the distance is consistently large.

In a classroom, the tutor may also look at students' faces to judge who might be having problems and ask if they need help. If the number of students is not large, Skype could be used in conference call mode to provide a view of the faces of all students. The tutor could select a student, and talk to them directly with only their desktop and marker being presented.

6   Conclusions

This initial study into two-way gaze sharing, in addition to voice, during remote teaching has shown that enabling the tutor to see where a student is looking on their desktop can facilitate helping that student. Little or no negotiation is needed to identify which objects are being referred to. Students reported finding that following the tutor's gaze point was very useful in completing the exercise but distracting when students were reading the text on slides. This work suggests that two-way gaze sharing can be a valuable asset for both tutor and student in a situation where students undertake exercises under tutor supervision. Further research in this area should focus on how these finding can be scaled onto a larger classroom.

Acknowledgments. This research was funded by the Academy of Finland, project Private and Shared Gaze: Enablers, Applications, Experiences (GaSP, grant number 2501287895).

References

1. Akkil, D., James, J.M., Isokoski, P., Kangas, J.: GazeTorch: enabling gaze awareness in collaborative physical tasks. In: Proceedings of the 2016 CHI Conference Extended Abstracts on Human Factors in Computing Systems, pp. 1151–1158. ACM (2016)
2. Brennan, S.E., Chen, X., Dickinson, C.A., Neider, M.B., Zelinsky, G.J.: Coordinating cognition: the costs and benefits of shared gaze during collaborative search. Cognition **106**(3), 1465–1477 (2008). http://www.sciencedirect.com/science/article/pii/S0010027707001448
3. D'Angelo, S., Begel, A.: Improving communication between pair programmers using shared gaze awareness. In: Proceedings of the 2017 CHI Conference on Human Factors in Computing Systems, pp. 6245–6290. ACM (2017)
4. D'Angelo, S., Gergle, D.: Gazed and confused: understanding and designing shared gaze for remote collaboration. In: Proceedings of the 2016 CHI Conference on Human Factors in Computing Systems, pp. 2492–2496. ACM (2016)
5. van Gog, T., Jarodzka, H., Scheiter, K., Gerjets, P., Paas, F.: Attention guidance during example study via the model's eye movements. Comput. Hum. Behav. **25**(3), 785–791 (2009). https://doi.org/10.1016/j.chb.2009.02.007
6. Gupta, K., Lee, G.A., Billinghurst, M.: Do you see what I see? The effect of gaze tracking on task space remote collaboration. IEEE Trans. Vis. Comput. Graph. **22**(11), 2413–2422 (2016)
7. Jarodzka, H., et al.: Conveying clinical reasoning based on visual observation via eye-movement modelling examples. Instr. Sci. **40**(5), 813–827 (2012). https://doi.org/10.1007/s11251-012-9218-5
8. Jarodzka, H., van Gog, T., Dorr, M., Scheiter, K., Gerjets, P.: Learning to see: guiding students' attention via a model's eye movements fosters learning. Learn. Instr. **25**, 62–70 (2013). https://doi.org/10.1016/j.learninstruc.2012.11.004
9. Johansen, R.: Groupware: Computer Support for Business Teams. The Free Press, New York (1988)
10. Lankes, M., Maurer, B., Stiglbauer, B.: An eye for an eye: gaze input in competitive online games and its effects on social presence. In: Proceedings of the 13th International Conference on Advances in Computer Entertainment Technology, ACE 2016, pp. 17:1–17:9. ACM, New York (2016). https://doi.org/10.1145/3001773.3001774. http://doi.acm.org/10.1145/3001773.3001774
11. Niehorster, D.C., Cornelissen, T., Holmqvist, K., Hooge, I.: Searching with and against each other: spatiotemporal coordination of visual search behavior in collaborative and competitive settings. Atten. Percept. Psychophys. **81**(3), 666–683 (2019). https://doi.org/10.3758/s13414-018-01640-0

12. Sharma, K., Jermann, P., Dillenbourg, P.: Displaying teacher's gaze in a MOOC: effects on students' video navigation patterns. In: Conole, G., Klobučar, T., Rensing, C., Konert, J., Lavoué, É. (eds.) EC-TEL 2015. LNCS, vol. 9307, pp. 325–338. Springer, Cham (2015). https://doi.org/10.1007/978-3-319-24258-3_24

13. Siirtola, H., Špakov, O., Istance, H., Räihä, K.J.: Shared gaze in collaborative visual search. Int. J. Hum. Comput. Interact. (2019). https://www.tandfonline.com/doi/abs/10.1080/10447318.2019.1565746

14. Stein, R., Brennan, S.E.: Another person's eye gaze as a cue in solving programming problems. In: Proceedings of the 6th International Conference on Multimodal Interfaces, ICMI 2004, pp. 9–15. ACM, New York (2004). http://doi.acm.org/10.1145/1027933.1027936

15. Špakov, O., Siirtola, H., Istance, H., Räihä, K.J.: GazeLaser: A hands-free highlighting technique for presentations. In: Proceedings of the 2016 CHI Conference Extended Abstracts on Human Factors in Computing Systems, CHI EA 2016, pp. 2648–2654. ACM, New York (2016). https://doi.org/10.1145/2851581.2892504. http://doi.acm.org/10.1145/2851581.2892504

16. Yao, N., Brewer, J., D'Angelo, S., Horn, M., Gergle, D.: Visualizing gaze information from multiple students to support remote instruction. In: Extended Abstracts of the 2018 CHI Conference on Human Factors in Computing Systems, CHI EA 2018, pp. LBW051:1–LBW051:6. ACM, New York (2018). https://doi.org/10.1145/3170427.3188453

Eye-Gaze Interaction

Designing Interactions with Intention-Aware Gaze-Enabled Artificial Agents

Joshua Newn[(✉)] [iD], Ronal Singh [iD], Fraser Allison [iD], Prashan Madumal [iD], Eduardo Velloso [iD], and Frank Vetere [iD]

School of Computing and Information Systems, The University of Melbourne, Melbourne, Australia
{newnj,rr.singh,f.allison,madumalp,evelloso,f.vetere}@unimelb.edu.au

Abstract. As it becomes more common for humans to work alongside artificial agents on everyday tasks, it is increasingly important to design artificial agents that can understand and interact with their human counterparts naturally. We posit that an effective way to do this is to harness nonverbal cues used in human-human interaction. We, therefore, leverage knowledge from existing work on gaze-based intention recognition, where the awareness of gaze can provide insights into the future actions of an observed human subject. In this paper, we design and evaluate the use of a proactive intention-aware gaze-enabled artificial agent that assists a human player engaged in an online strategy game. The agent assists by recognising and communicating the intentions of a human opponent in real-time, potentially improving situation awareness. Our first study identifies the language requirements for the artificial agent to communicate the opponent's intentions to the assisted player, using an inverted Wizard of Oz method approach. Our second study compares the experience of playing an online strategy game with and without the assistance of the agent. Specifically, we conducted a within-subjects study with 30 participants to compare their experience of playing with (1) detailed AI predictions, (2) abstract AI predictions, and (3) no AI predictions but with a live visualisation of their opponent's gaze. Our results show that the agent can facilitate awareness of another user's intentions without adding visual distraction to the interface; however, the cognitive workload was similar across all three conditions, suggesting that the manner in which the agent communicates its predictions requires further exploration. Overall, our work contributes to the understanding of how to support human-agent teams in a dynamic collaboration scenario. We provide a positive account of humans interacting with an intention-aware artificial agent afforded by gaze input, which presents immediate opportunities for improving interactions between the counterparts.

Keywords: Human-AI interaction · Intention recognition ·
Explainable interface · Human-AI teaming · Intention awareness ·
Eye tracking · Gaze awareness

© IFIP International Federation for Information Processing 2019
Published by Springer Nature Switzerland AG 2019
D. Lamas et al. (Eds.): INTERACT 2019, LNCS 11747, pp. 255–281, 2019.
https://doi.org/10.1007/978-3-030-29384-0_17

1   Introduction

Gaze is an important nonverbal communication signal in everyday human-human interaction [4], and has become a popular research topic for technology-mediated interaction [17,43,60]. The ability to tell what someone is looking at—'gaze awareness'—is a useful way to gauge the attention of others [1,2,14,63]. Gaze observed over time is an effective predictor of human intention [26,27,50,56]. A common approach for gaze awareness is to visually overlay a user's gaze over a shared interface, which provides others rich insights into the mind of the tracked user. This complementary layer of communication has numerous benefits such as improved coordination [2,12,14] and situation awareness [50]. Despite these benefits, overlaying gaze on the interface can add a highly distracting element to the task at hand [50], confuse users when there is a mismatch with other modes of communication such as speech [14], and scales poorly with multiple users.

In this paper, we explore how an artificial agent that interprets eye movements can alleviate issues commonly associated with visual gaze awareness, and how humans respond to agent-derived intentions from gaze and observable actions. A socially interactive agent that can understand human gaze can potentially improve the interaction with its human counterparts [27,56], such as by adapting its behaviour to their anticipated intentions, or even support the user by communicating the intentions of others. However, much investigation is still needed from an interaction design perspective before humans can work alongside such agents effectively, with each counterpart playing to its strengths.

Our work presents a step towards artificial agents that can interpret and communicate human intentions based on nonverbal behavioural signals. We designed and evaluated the communication protocols of a proactive gaze-enabled artificial agent for communicating intentions to a human player in the context of an online strategy game. The agent assists by making inferences about the opponent's intentions based on their gaze and actions, allowing the user to focus on formulating better strategies with improved awareness of the situation. By abstracting the gaze data into a written prediction of what the opponent intends to do, we avoid the distracting nature of gaze visualisation as found in past research [14,50,51,63]. As nonverbal cues are challenging to articulate, our first step was to build a linguistic model of intention recognition derived from human observers. This process resulted in a general model of intention communication, which we incorporated into the artificial agent.

Our following step evaluates the model while comparing the existing approach of using gaze visualisation to infer intentions in strategic gameplay to our proposed approach of abstracting the intentions from gaze input into written predictions through an artificial agent. We designed a within-subjects user study with three conditions, in which we provide varying levels of information to an assisted player. In the first condition, we provide players with a live visualisation of their opponent's gaze, allowing them to interpret the information as they see fit. In the second condition, the agent sends the player inferences about the opponent's plans, followed by an explanation of the observed behaviours that it used to form the prediction in an attempt to be transparent about its reasoning process. In the third condition, the agent sends the is predictions about their opponent's plans without an explanation of its reasoning process, to allow the player to have their own beliefs about the agent's logic, and without any direct knowledge of the data that led to that inference.

We conducted the within-subjects study with 30 player pairs, in which the evaluated players reported a positive experience when engaging with the agent in terms of preference and usefulness for situation awareness, and a perceived reduction in cognitive workload and distraction. Though our results show that the agent can facilitate awareness of another user's intentions without adding visual distraction to the interface, there was no significant difference in the players' cognitive workload for the written prediction conditions, as compared to the live gaze visualisation condition. These findings suggest that the manner in which the agent communicates requires further exploration.

All in all, our work presents two primary contributions to the design of artificial agents that collaborate with humans, from both sides of the interaction. From the agent end, we show that it is possible to develop agents that can not only predict intentions through gaze but communicate and reason about them as well. On the other end, we show that the human counterpart can be supported by a proactive agent that communicates intentions through verbal means (e.g. written language), which maintains situation awareness while reducing visual distraction when compared to using a live gaze visualisation approach.

2   Related Work

2.1   Shared Gaze Awareness

Gaze visualisation is by far the most common approach for utilising gaze input in technology-mediated human-human interaction. This approach provides a complementary layer of nonverbal communication, especially beneficial in remote settings where users cannot see where other the users they are interacting with are looking. Observers can derive rich information from gaze behaviours displayed over an interface (e.g. scanning, focus on an object, and repeated comparisons of different objects [57]). These gaze behaviours provide clues about the other person's cognitive processes, i.e. the ability to discern their intentions [51]. The benefits are well demonstrated in multi-user scenarios, improving communication and coordination in collaborative settings (e.g. [2,12,24,63]). Gaze visualisation has also been explored in competitive gameplay [46,59], highlighting its potential for increasing social presence between remote players [36,45], and for enabling players to recognise the intentions of others in real-time [50,51].

Despite its numerous benefits, researchers have commonly found that using live gaze visualisation can be 'distracting' and 'confusing' for an observer to interpret [14,51,63]. We believe this is because humans are not accustomed to interpreting visual representations of gaze, as the focal point of gaze is 'invisible' in normal everyday interpersonal interaction [50], and that an added layer of continuous information draws the user's attention away from the task at hand when displayed. As gaze visualisation is highly dependent on context and individual preference [15,50], software for visualising gaze in real-time often allows users to control its parameters such as by adjusting the colour, opacity and smoothness [7,13]. The recent release of Tobii Ghost[1]—a free commercial software designed to allow eSports audiences to view customised gaze visualisations of players in real-time—further exemplifies the growing popularity of this feature in gaze visualisation applications.

2.2 Gaze-Based Intention Recognition

Though human attention can be easily inferred by the direction of a person's gaze, discerning their intention through their gaze is a far more complicated process. The observer must distinguish between intentional and unintentional behaviours, and gaze direction alone provides very few clues to do so. In our previous study, we demonstrated that using an aggregated visualisation of gaze can enable human-human intention recognition in competitive gameplay, with benefits such as early inference of intentions [50]. Despite such benefits, the study found that players who could see the gaze of their opponent had no gain in performance, due to its cost in time and attention—by attempting to infer their opponents' strategies, they ended up neglecting their own. Players who did manage to reach a balance stated that the broad clues provided by gaze awareness were beneficial to formulating and adjusting their strategy. For instance, they could ignore certain areas of the game-board if they noticed that their opponent had not looked there. Overall, these findings suggest that effectively managing the cognitive demands of inferring the opponent's strategy and devising one's own is the key to successfully making use of the opponent's gaze information.

However, it is unlikely that humans can fully operationalise gaze while performing complex tasks without assistance, due to the limits of human working memory. As visual behaviour is intrinsically linked to how humans plan and execute actions [34], researchers have explored the use of computational techniques to perform intention recognition from gaze, typically employing a machine learning approach (e.g. [5,26]). In a previous paper, we proposed an alternative approach that incorporates visual behaviour into model-based intention recognition using automated planning [56]. We leveraged the fact that humans plan ahead in strategic scenarios and that the incorporation of gaze as priors in a planning-based model resulted in the computation of predictions with high accuracy, earlier and with no additional computational cost when compared with a base planning model that did not use gaze input. Overall, such works, exemplify the use of computational techniques to harness the rich information available from the observation of gaze behaviour.

---

[1] https://tobiigaming.com/software/ghost/.

2.3 Human-Agent Teaming

In 1960, Licklider proposed the vision of *man-computer symbiosis*, where computers would be able to work with humans to solve problems that are not easily addressed if attempted by either counterpart individually [38]. For instance, while computers can perform complex calculations and repetitive tasks far better than humans, humans are better at visual-spatial reasoning and at exercising judgement. However, enabling this symbiosis through mixed teams comes with significant challenges with regards to effectiveness [33]. One such challenge is a lack of agent transparency, which hinders the human partner's ability to understand the decisions of the artificial agent [30,48]. The lack of transparency can lead to adverse effects for the human partner, such as a reduction in trust when working together, and therefore, a potential for disuse [6,10,35,62].

Researchers in AI argue that providing explanations supports transparency and may improve trust in the system [23,41,47,52,62]. Moreover, when using an agent as a decision aid, users would often seek an explanation of its output to improve their own decision making [61]. However, for an explanation to be effective, it must be at the right level of detail [31]. An explanation of how something works will fail if it presupposes too much and skips over essential information, or if it provides a level of detail that leads to an increase in cognitive workload, hence decreasing its effectiveness [52]. Further, we need to consider the application domain, the audience of the explanation [21], as well as the *presentation format* (how to explain) and the *content* (what to explain) [19,31].

From a different perspective, dissimilarities between human language and computer language pose another consideration for real-time cooperation, which Licklider states *"may be the most serious obstacle for true symbiosis"* [38]. Licklider explains that humans think more naturally and easily in terms of goals than specific itineraries, implying the existence of human goals during communication. Computers, however, communicate better in terms of procedural instruction, which may be redundant or not meaningful to a human collaborator.

In summary, there are numerous benefits for implementing gaze input for computer-mediated interaction afforded by advances and availability of eye-tracking technology. However, information overload, interpretation difficulty and scalability using the conventional approach of gaze visualisation hinder its full potential for multi-user settings. Recent work in AI has shown that intelligent agents have the potential to perform intention recognition from gaze input, which is often a complex task in human-human interaction, especially when the user is already preoccupied. Our work intersects these areas by using an intelligent collaborative agent to support a human counterpart by recognising the intentions of others based on their gaze for them. To do this effectively, we must first consider how an ideal agent would communicate intentions once recognised, addressing Licklider's language mismatch prerequisite. Second, we must consider an agent's explanation capabilities to support transparency, where the agent can provide insights into its reasoning process to gain the trust of the user. Lastly, we need to consider the optimum level of support as different levels of artificial agent support can result in changes in cognitive workload, positively or negatively [9].

3   Research Design

From our review of the literature, an ideal intention-aware agent for human-agent interaction in the context of teaming should possess the following capabilities:

1. Infer a users' intentions accurately based on gaze observation and other available sources of information (e.g. observable explicit actions) in a timely manner.
2. Communicate inferred users' intentions to an assisted user in a way that the user finds easy to understand, such as through natural language.
3. Increase the users' situation awareness while reducing the users' cognitive workload (in comparison with current approaches, e.g. gaze visualisation).

We conducted two studies to evaluate the prospects of an agent possessing these capabilities. Our first study identified the language that humans use to describe the intentions of third parties over short text-based messages. The findings from the study provided the language requirements for our artificial agent. In the subsequent study, we evaluated our enhanced artificial agent with participants using an online strategy game. We obtained ethics approval from our University's ethics committee, as both studies involved mild deception of the participants. Both studies required a scenario in which participants were required to deduce another person's intentions through a computer system. For our purposes, we used the digital version of an online competitive turn-based strategy board game called *Ticket to Ride*. In this game, players compete to build connections between cities based on drawn 'ticket' cards (e.g. Dallas to New York). The core of the game is to keep their intentions hidden as an opposing player can gain a significant advantage by correctly guessing their hidden plans. Therefore, players must plan their routes carefully to minimise the risk that an opponent will guess their intentions and block them by claiming the routes that they need first. More detailed information on the rules of *Ticket to Ride* can be found on the game's website[2].

4   Study 1: Language Identification

In this study, we developed an effective language model for a gaze-aware artificial agent to communicate an opponent's intentions to a user through text, and conducted a study to generate specific language data for our broader scenario. We used a variation of the Wizard of Oz prototyping method in which participants played the role of the 'artificial agent' to produce language according to what they think is appropriate to the task, instead of the language being determined by the researchers or system designers.

---

[2] http://www.daysofwonder.com/tickettoride/en/usa/.

The goal of our artificial agent is to promote the user's *situation awareness*, defined by Endsley [20] as: *"perception of elements in the environment within a volume of time and space, the comprehension of their meaning, and the projection of their status in the future"*. Gaze awareness has been shown to be especially beneficial for situation awareness, particularly when a player is in a strategic game can make correct inferences about their opponent's strategy early in the game [50]. However, prior literature on agent transparency in general tasks indicates two important aspects of agent communication: *presentation format* and *content* [19,31]. We used the Situation Awareness-Based Transparency Model (or SAT Model) [11] as a model of agent transparency to support a user's situation awareness. In this model, the agent communicates different types of information at three levels to support the user. At the lowest level, the agent communicates its own state, which includes the agent's intentions. At the middle level, the agent communicates information regarding its reasoning process, and at the top level, the agent communicates information regarding potential future states.

For this study, we recruited 20 participants (11M/9F) from The University of Melbourne, aged between 20 and 32 years (M = 25, SD = 3.7), to take on the role of a 'predictor-explainer'. We selected participants based on their self-rated English proficiency in our recruitment questionnaire, as we required participants to produce a rich vocabulary around gaze behaviours, observable actions and the communication of intentions. We provided participants with the rules of the game at the time of recruitment, and we compensated them with a $15 (AUD) gift card upon completion of the study.

4.1 Experimental Setup and Procedure

Upon arrival, we sat the participant in front of a computer and obtained the participant's written consent to participate in the study. The participant and experimenter sat at opposite ends of the table so that the experimenter's display was not visible to the participant. Figure 1-Right shows the technical setup consisting of a laptop connected to two 23-inch monitors on a rectangular table, located in a study room. The experimenter then introduced the task by explaining that there were two other players in separate rooms preparing to play *Ticket to Ride* against each other. The experimenter told the participant that they had been randomly selected to take on the role of a 'predictor-explainer' (or appraiser), who would watch the game between the two other players via the computer and send assistive messages to one of them, their 'teammate'.

In reality, there was only one participant in each session (i.e. themselves). The game of *Ticket to Ride* shown to the participant was pre-recorded, and we used each recording only once. To clarify, we showed 20 different games played by 20 different player pairs from our previous study data set [50]. The recorded player was naive to the fact their gaze was being observed, meaning that the participant observes natural gaze behaviours. We did this for two reasons, (1) in order to elicit a wide range of textual representations from different game scenarios and (2) there was no need for anyone to receive the participant's messages, as the lexical content of those messages was the focus of the study.

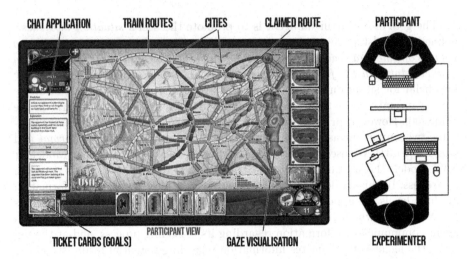

CHAT APPLICATION   TRAIN ROUTES   CITIES   CLAIMED ROUTE   PARTICIPANT

PARTICIPANT VIEW

TICKET CARDS (GOALS)   GAZE VISUALISATION   EXPERIMENTER

Fig. 1. Left: Participant view. **Right**: Experimental setup.

The recording of the game included a 'live' dynamic heatmap visualisation of the gaze of the 'opponent' player (as shown in Fig. 1-Left). We designed and employed a protocol to continually reinforce the participants' belief that they were engaged in a live online game with two other players throughout the study. For example, as each session was designed to last a maximum of an hour, we informed the participant in advance that the game would begin at a fixed time, partway through the session, as all "three" participants needed time to be introduced to the study and familiarise themselves with *Ticket to Ride* through the game's tutorial. The researcher was only allowed to clarify the rules about the game when prompted during the study to avoid any influence on the data.

We describe this approach as an 'inverted' Wizard of Oz protocol. In a typical Wizard of Oz study, a researcher secretly plays the role of the computer system while a participant interacts with it [32,54]. In our study, the participant is asked to play the role of the computer system, and the secret is that there is no end-user. The benefit of this is that it allows us to directly collect a large number of different messages that reflect how the participants think the computer 'should' communicate in an assistive fashion. A similar approach has been used in the context of machine learning to 'bootstrap' a Reinforcement-Learning-based dialogue system on human-generated activity [55].

Before it was 'time to join the game', the experimenter showed the participant four short clips (introduced as pre-recordings rather than a live game), representing four scenarios with the live dynamic gaze visualisation. This was to start the participant thinking about how they could form *predictions* from the information available, particularly the gaze visualisation, and then from *explanations* in text about their reasoning process. This step allowed them to develop confidence in their ability to observe and communicate simultaneously during the live game. We reminded participants to provide messages that their 'teammate' would find helpful, and to build the teammate's trust by being transparent in how they derived their predictions through their explanations.

Next, we demonstrated a simple chat application that served as the means of communication with their teammate (see Fig. 1-Left). The application contained two text fields to input their *prediction* and *explanation* respectively, a send button and a window showing the conversation. The application logged all messages sent and included a validation to ensure both text fields are not empty. We augmented the application to select a response from a range of automated natural language responses in reply to every message sent by the participant to keep up the deception. The responses mimicked a 'busy player': one that replied with a short delay, sometimes did not reply at all, and often with a brief response. The majority of responses consisted of acknowledgements, while the remaining introduced expressions of uncertainty about the participant's messages to convey human-like qualities (e.g. "I don't think so", "Hmmm ok").

At the prescribed start time, the experimenter streamed the recorded game as if it was a live game feed and informed the participant that the game had started. We posed no restrictions on the syntax or semantics participants could use for their messages, which allows them to freely formulate them as they saw fit, as long as each contained a prediction of their opponent's intentions followed by an explanation for their prediction. At the end of the study, the researchers conducted a short interview with the participant to find their experience embodying the role. Lastly, we debriefed participants about the deception and provided participants with the opportunity to inquire about our objectives.

4.2 Findings

We elicited a total of 249 raw messages ($mean = 12.4$ messages per participant), with a high deviation between participants ($min = 4$, $max = 23$). The ability to successfully formulate messages depended on several factors, including individual ability, experience with the game, the communication strategy adopted, and the recorded game shown. We discarded messages where participants attempted to communicate with their teammate casually or provided recommendations instead. However, we included recommendations that resemble a prediction that included a clear explanation (e.g. *"You should block Helena to Duluth, our opponent is likely to claim this the route next as he has repeatedly been looking at it."*). We also split messages that contain two mutually exclusive predictions (e.g. *"The opponent is interested in the west coast. Opponent may build routes around New York."*), which typically occurs when participants formed another prediction while forming an initial unrelated prediction but have the same reasoning process for both. Finally, we obtained a total of 246 messages after our filtering process for analysis.

Prediction Format. For the prediction part of each message, we stripped them into its essential and meaningful components to obtain a minimal format for predictions (e.g. From [City] to [City] through [City]), which gave us a total of 45 initial formats. We merged formats that were similar in nature into key prediction formats (examples shown in Fig. 2), each demonstrating unique characteristics in terms of abstraction. We also noted that participants conveyed their level of confidence when providing their predictions, using words that express uncertainty (e.g. i think/maybe/will try). As studies on explanations argue for showing system uncertainty [3,39], we will introduce uncertainty when communicating predictions, including stating alternate routes when the likelihood of the plan is similar (e.g. To [City] or [City] through [City] from [City] or [City]).

Explanation Content. Participants provided a wide range of explanations for their predictions. We found that complex explanations contain *spatial, temporal* and *quantitative* properties, in line with findings using expert explainers [16]. Simplistic explanations, on the other hand, typically described observed behaviours and often only with one property (e.g. *"The opponent was looking at those routes."*). In order to build a general model, we turn to Malle and Knobe [44]'s explanation model for labelling the properties for more complex explanations elicited with the assumption that the model can be generalised to explain human nonverbal or combined inputs. Following the model, explanations can include information about past and potential future actions, i.e. *Causal History of Reasons*, defined as O_A, and *Intentional Action*, defined as I_A. As our logs showed that participants had a strong reliance on gaze to explain the predictions, we include gaze (O_g) as part of every explanation generated using our piece-wise function below. We believe that gaze being 'always on' [28], becomes a valuable source of information for participants throughout the game, especially when the opponent has performed only a few observable actions.

$$Explanation = \begin{cases} O_g, O_A & \text{if ontic actions observed} \\ O_g, I_A & \text{if intentional action likely} \\ O_g, I_A, O_A & \text{otherwise} \end{cases} \quad (1)$$

Therefore, combination of all three sources of information forms an explanation that is *detailed*, for example:

"The opponent is building a route from Washington to New Orleans through Nashville in the South East [Prediction (i)]. The opponent has claimed part of this route [O_A], has been looking at the routes between Raleigh and Little Rock repeatedly [O_g] and is likely to claim Nashville to Raleigh next [I_A]."

Reasoning and Communication Strategies. Participants adopted two general strategies for reasoning about and communicating the intentions of their opponent, which they maintained either strategy throughout, or interchanged between the two depending on the situation. We found that the strategies were reflective of the two systems of Kahneman's Dual Process Theory [29]—*System 1* (heuristic, intuitive) and *System 2* (systematic, analytical). The first strategy was to send as many messages as possible, in fear of missing out on communicating predictions that may be important to their perceived teammate. Due to this time pressure, we believe participants adopted System 1, where they made use of their intuition, and that their rate of communication was limited to their typing speed. In contrast, the second strategy was closer towards System 2, where participants took a conscious effort to reason about the opponent's intentions and overall strategy, as they wanted to provide the best possible prediction accompanied by a detailed explanation of their reasoning process. This strategy resulted in fewer predictions, especially if the current prediction or reasoning did not change.

Participants on average generated more predictions at the beginning of the game and followed by fewer predictions towards the end of the game, representing its relevance. Unless the opponent's plan changes, more recent predictions will be less relevant, especially if the new predictions were part of the plan that has already been predicted. In our interviews, participants noted the most difficult aspects of explaining is to come up with the best possible explanation, and also what to communicate when unsure how they have come about the prediction. This is when System 1 (or simply: intuition) often comes into play, which makes it hard to quantify certain aspects such as how much the opponent has looked at one part as compared with another. Participants also noted that timely predictions would be most helpful, but this is difficult to tell how far in advance the opponent will perform the predicted action (e.g. in how many turns).

5   Study 2: Evaluation

By combining the language model derived from Study 1 with an instance of an intention-aware artificial agent from our previous work, we can now evaluate the experience of playing an online strategy with and without agent assistance. Figure 2 summarises our experimental setup of two observation rooms and a control room. Each session involved three researchers, two to facilitate the players and the third, an unseen human to assemble the predictions from the artificial agent into natural language following a set of rules. Both setups were identical for both players, except for the eye trackers attached to the bottom of their screens; the evaluated player (P_A) was equipped with Tobii Pro X2-30 (for pupillary data), and 'naive' opponent (P_B) was equipped with a Tobii 4C eye tracker.

We recruited 60 players (34M/26F) for the study and allocated them randomly into two equal groups according to gender (17M/13F in each). At the time of recruitment, we informed players that the purpose of the study was to collect physiological data while they played a strategic game. The first group (Group A) consisted of 'aware' assisted players, aged between 18 and 50 years (M = 26.9, SD = 6.9), while the second group (Group B) consisted of 'naive' players, aged between 18 and 33 (M = 25.6, SD = 3.8) to be the opponents. 17 assisted players and 10 naive opponents have played the game before. All players were compensated with a \$20 (AUD) gift card for their participation.

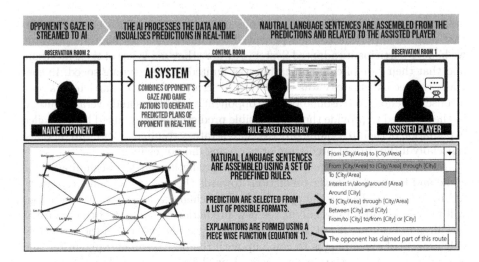

Fig. 2. Top: Experimental Setup and Communication Flow. **Bottom**: AI System Visualisation and Assembly Process. Opponent's intentions are displayed by increasing the line thickness of routes. The thicker the line, the more likely the route will be claimed. Coloured lines represent the claimed routes (player: green, opponent: red). The size of the city indicates where the opponent has fixated upon (the larger the city, the more the opponent has looked upon). (Color figure online)

5.1   Intention-Aware Gaze-Enabled Artificial Agent

We instantiated an artificial agent that performs intention recognition using the combination of ontic actions and gaze using a planning-based model from our previous work [56]. The approach uses a 'white-box' approach that allows us to understand the underlying algorithms and data structures, which makes it simpler to interrogate the model and its predictions, and therefore generate explanations when compared to other approaches. Further, research has shown that humans prefer working with an agent through planning; reporting the perceived reduction of cognitive workload, and the ability to maintain situation awareness for short-term tasks [49]. The objective of the agent assistance in this work is not to solve the *Ticket to Ride* game by providing step-by-step recommendations to the assisted player but to explore how an agent can assist a human player by maintaining and communicating its beliefs of an opponent's intentions.

Our decision to adopt an artificial agent instead of a Wizard of Oz approach as used in Study 1 was for three reasons. First, using the data set from our previous study [50], the agent scored positively higher compared to a human interpreter using gaze visualisation (F_1-*Score*: 0.57 versus 0.37 respectively) in terms of plan recognition. This means that an assisted player playing alongside the agent would receive more accurate predictions than with a human assistant (or wizard), which gave us confidence in its adoption. Second, the more accurate agent provides better ground truths overall, meaning that even if we provide the goals of the opponent (destination cities) to the wizard, the system remains far better at discriminating and predicting the most likely plans and can provide this information earlier as well. This capability ensures relative consistency of predictions and provides a realistic impression of what such systems can do across participants. Third, as found in our previous study [50], human interpreters can be subject to biases, especially when the human interpreter fixates on incorrect predictions and overlooks other predictions.

As part of this work, we developed a graph visualisation to display the predictions made by the agent to assist in the rule-based assembly stage (shown in Fig. 2-Bottom). The graph displays the combination of the top 10 most likely plans of the opponent. The thickness of the edges (representing routes) increases according to the number of times it appears in the top 10 plans; indicating the likelihood of the player choosing that particular plan. Further, the graph not only shows the opponent's plans at a macro-level but also the possible combinations that the opponent may use to achieve their intentions, i.e. alternate plans.

5.2 Study Conditions

We designed three conditions representing three levels of information abstraction. At the lowest level (GAZE VIZ), we show the assisted player (P_A) the gaze of the naive opponent (P_B) throughout the game using a live heatmap visualisation (as shown in Fig. 1-Left). This condition allowed players to make their inferences on their opponent's plans at the cost of their attention and serves as a baseline condition as we displayed the visualisation throughout the game.

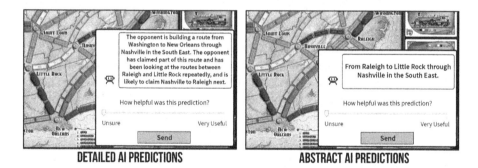

DETAILED AI PREDICTIONS   ABSTRACT AI PREDICTIONS

Fig. 3. AI prediction examples.

At the mid-level (DETAILED AI PREDS), we assemble the intentions and observed behaviours into our text-based language model informed by Study 1. Here, we presented the prediction as an *Intentional Action* [44]—what the opponent intends to do next, while being transparent about its reasoning process. As part of natural language, we conveyed uncertainty when communicating the predictions and provided temporal, spatial and quantitative elements where possible. At the highest level (ABSTRACT AI PREDS), the agent provided an abstract about the predicted plan through one of the formats from our language model. As both AI prediction levels are reflective of the Dual Process Theory [29] systems and the strategies described in Sect. 4.2, we simulate the communication frequency accordingly. For DETAILED AI PREDS, we require the formation of detailed messages and therefore set the frequency to every 2 minutes so that the system can make a sufficient observation to form the best possible prediction and explanation. For ABSTRACT AI PREDS, the frequency was set to a minute (60 seconds), as we only need to send the best possible prediction at that point in time. We counterbalanced the study conditions using a Latin square to minimise any learning effects. As this is a within-subject study, we only subjected the conditions to the assisted player (P_A), in which we presented as a 'mode of assistance'. For both AI conditions, the researcher made it explicit to the assisted player that the AI uses their opponent's gaze behaviour and observable game actions to generate the predictions.

5.3 Measures and Analysis

To evaluate the player experience in each condition, we designed a repeated-measures questionnaire. As there was no specifically designed questionnaire to measure the experience of intention awareness, we formed our questions based on our previous work on gaze-based intention recognition [50], which measures the subjective experience of players when performing intention recognition with and without gaze visualisation. For each measure, we employed a 7-point Likert scale (1 being full disagreement, 7 being full agreement), and included questions to measure the participant's perceived ability to discern intentions and formulate strategy, the effects of information presented during gameplay (such as whether it has influenced the outcome or have caused them to play differently), and whether the condition presented were distracting and were informative.

For the AI conditions, we included two additional measures, which asked the players how well they *understood* the AI predictions and how *reliable* the AI performed in predicting the opponent's intentions, and only in the DETAILED AI PREDS condition, we asked players about the *clarity* of the explanations to validate messages formed using our model. At the end of the study, we measured the overall experience of using all three conditions, we asked players to rate the conditions with regards to *preference*, *demand* and *usefulness* from most to least. We then prompted the players on the ratings for each measure as part of our subsequent post-study semi-structured interview.

To measure cognitive workload unobtrusively, we used the recently proposed Index of Pupillary Activity (IPA) metric [18], which measures the frequency of pupil diameter oscillation. The metric shows a direct correlation with working memory, making it a plausible way to measure cognitive workload. Further, we employed traditional measures of the cognitive workload from eye movement behaviour from prior work (e.g. [9]), such as *long fixations* (i.e. fixations >500 ms), which indicate deeper cognitive processing. We also used NASA-TLX questionnaire [22] to capture perceived workload based on six subscales—mental demand, physical demand, temporal demand, performance, effort and frustration.

5.4 Participants and Procedures

To manage the complexities of the study, all three researchers involved in the experiment followed a strict rehearsed protocol. Both players were given an initial briefing together upon arrival that explains that we will track their physiological signals throughout the study for post-study analysis. We then provide players with the written overview of the study, consent form and basic demographic questionnaire to fill out before separating randomly into one of the two observation rooms with the allocated facilitator. We instructed the players to play the game's interactive tutorial for up to 10 minutes to get familiar with the game and its controls, regardless of experience. Players then played three rounds of *Ticket to Ride* against each other, with each testing a different study condition.

At the start of each round, we requested each player to pick all three randomly assigned 'ticket' cards for them to attempt to complete (each representing a pair of 'goal cities', potentially having up to six initial goal cities). Players were asked to 'think aloud' during the game about their strategy; their opponent's strategy; what they were thinking and what their opponent might be thinking. Each player was given a 12-minute cumulative time allowance for their total turns in each round to ensure timely completion. If either player ran out of time, we manually calculated the scores for that round. We video-recorded the screen and rooms for both players for the entire duration of the session. Each session lasted approximately 120 minutes in total. For the remainder of the section, we describe the procedure for each player separately for clarity.

Player A (Assisted Player) Procedure. Once the players entered their respective rooms, the facilitator (F_A) informed the player that they had been randomly selected to be the 'aware' player while making it clear at no point during the study that their information will be exposed to their opponent (P_B). The facilitator then calibrated the player's eyes with the eye tracker using the default calibration before starting the tutorial. We then informed the player that they would play three rounds of the game against player P_B and will receive 'additional information' about their opponent's intentions without their knowledge, which will vary according to the condition.

In all conditions, the player received prompts with a slider (see Fig. 3). The primary purpose of the rating scale is for players to reflect on the information that is being presented to them. The players were instructed to verbalise why they had given a particular rating. At the end of each condition, we administered the NASA-TLX immediately before asking them to fill up a questionnaire on their experience about the round they just played. This ordering was intentional as their subjective workload may change after filling up the questionnaire. Once completed, the facilitator conducted a short interview on the game they just played and prompted the player on any extremities in their subjective ratings.

Player B (Naive Opponent) Procedure. The procedure for the naive opponent (P_B) was straightforward, where the player was required to play three regular games against player P_A while being eye tracked, therefore acted as the control group. Once the players entered their respective rooms, the facilitator (F_B) calibrated the player to the eye tracker before the tutorial. At the end of each condition, we administered the NASA-TLX questionnaire and a Games Experience Questionnaire (GEQ) [8]. The primary purpose of both questionnaires was for the player to fill up the time while player P_A went through a longer post-study questionnaire and interview. Any gaps in time were filled up by facilitator F_B, who will engage in a conversation about the game they just played.

5.5   Results

The first part of this section presents the overall results from our various subjective and objective measures, as previously outlined in Sect. 5.3 (Measures and Analysis). In the second part, we present and discuss the experience of the players with and without the agent from the insights provided by the post-study semistructured interviews in relation to our various measures. Figure 4 summarises the median scores for the responses in our repeated-measures questionnaire.

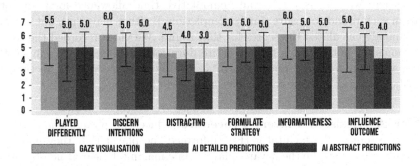

Fig. 4. Questionnaire results.

A Kruskal-Wallis test revealed no significant differences between the conditions for each of the measures. The figure shows that the conditions were found to be comparable except for the decreasing trend in distraction as we reduced the information. In addition to these measures, players in both AI conditions rated an agreeable median score for reliability (5.0) and when asked if they understood the AI predictions (6.0). The results suggest that although the communication was clear, the AI was unable to meet the expectation of the player, such as by not providing correct predictions, predictions that the player already guessed or that the predictions were not timely enough for them to act on it.

Table 1 below shows the rating given for each condition in relation to *preference*, *demand* and *usefulness*. A Friedman test showed no significant differences between the conditions for all three ratings. These ratings, however, served as prompts for discussion during the post-study semi-structured interview as players were asked to reflect on their reasoning behind their given ratings.

Table 1. Post-study ratings for each condition.

	Preferred			Demanding			Useful		
	Most	Middle	Least	Most	Middle	Least	Most	Middle	Least
GAZE VIZ	**15**	13	2	**15**	9	6	**13**	12	5
AI DETAILED	7	8	**15**	6	12	12	9	6	**15**
AI ABSTRACT	8	9	13	8	10	12	8	12	10

Table 2. Results of cognitive workload measures.

	IPA (Hz)	Average long fixations (>500 ms)	Average saccade velocity (m/sec)	NASA-TLX
GAZE VIZ	0.0127	0.02 (0.02)	47.80 (27.9)	49.1
AI DETAILED	0.0138	0.22 (0.10)	54.71 (29.2)	45.4
AI ABSTRACT	0.0148	0.02 (0.02)	49.49 (31.3)	45.9

Table 2 summarises the results of our cognitive workload measures. We ran a Mann-Whitney U test for all the objective measures and only found significant differences for the average long fixations measure. A post hoc analysis showed differences between the GAZE VIZ and DETAILED AI PREDS conditions ($W = 0$, $Z = 4.78$, $p < 0.05$, $r = 0.87$) and between both AI conditions ($W = 0$, $Z = 4.78$, $p < 0.05$, $r = 0.87$). The results show that players on average had longer fixations in the DETAILED AI PREDS condition, which could simply be because participants needed time to process the predictions. We found no significant differences between GAZE VIZ and ABSTRACT AI PREDS conditions, which suggests that players did not require a longer time to parse the predictions in ABSTRACT AI PREDS condition, indicating that the ABSTRACT AI PREDS case did not introduce any significant burden while achieving similar awareness as the GAZE VIZ condition. Though the AI did not decrease the cognitive workload as compared with the current approach of gaze visualisation, the NASA-TLX questionnaire scores indicated that players perceived the GAZE VIZ condition to be more demanding overall than when being assisted by the agent. However, although the overall mean score for the measure suggests the perceived workload for the GAZE VIZ condition was higher when compared to the AI conditions, a Kruskal-Wallis test showed no significant differences among the three conditions.

AI Predictions. Players who spoke positively about the predictions often referred to the specific properties in the predictions, including temporal and spatial properties as found in prior work (e.g. *"I like the temporal information ('since the beginning of the game...'), and precise information about where the opponent was looking."* – [P17$_A$]). The uncertainty provided in the explanations was also well received by players, noting that they only needed to know the areas than the specific cities (e.g. P8$_A$), or that the agent communicated alternate paths the opponent may take (e.g. P30$_A$). Player P12$_A$ explicitly noted that the predictions were useful when the agent predicted longer (distal) routes instead of shorter (proximal) routes, especially for strategy formulation.

There is some evidence to suggest that the AI predictions drew their attention to areas of the board they overlooked. For example, P5$_A$ mentioned *"It made me take notice of what my opponent was doing."* A third of players (10/30) noted that they had to invest time in deciphering the AI predictions, mostly attributed to their unfamiliarity with the map, despite each prediction having an overall indication of the area in the predictions where applicable (e.g. From [City] to [City] in the South East). This finding also brings forward an issue with the textual representation of intentions (*"I like the predictions that were short; I did not like the visuals. It was easier to take the AI info but not as pop-up prompts."* – [P29$_A$]; *"It took me out of the game a little to have the prompt pop up and then look at the map to interpret."* – [P10$_A$]). Player P1$_A$ mentions that *"...it would be better if the route was highlighted"*, as a suggestion to complement the predictions with a concise visual component.

Players who least preferred the AI conditions found the prediction prompts distracting because it interrupted their thought process. As they were required to reflect on the prediction sent each time, it took them further away from their current task. Between the AI conditions, players preferred the abstract AI predictions over the detailed AI predictions in general as the messages were more concise and therefore needed less time investment in deciphering them and subsequently utilising the information:

– **P8$_A$**: *"I liked the simplicity of the information it [the artificial agent] gave me, it was very easy to filter."*
– **P10$_A$**: *"I liked the short form prompts, they were actually quicker to read, and I was still able to formulate a plan around my interpretation of the prompt."*
– **P23$_A$**: *"Shorter and brief hints were easy to understand and helpful."*

There were overarching reports that predictions became less useful as the game progressed, as expected, especially towards the end of the game, as P12$_A$ mentions *"I liked the initial predictions, but it was less helpful towards the end of the game"*. A possible explanation is because there was enough evidence in the form of routes claimed and players could make their own inferences through the observable opponent actions. As the agent lacked awareness of the context, players also noted several limitations in the AI conditions, such as not being able to predict whether the opponent was going to block them (e.g. P17$_A$).

Further, the agent was expected to communicate when prior predictions are no longer relevant or when the plans of the opponent have changed, as P15$_A$

states *"I'm not sure how helpful the AI was. It could be that the opponent did not have enough cards to carry out his original plan, or I blocked him successful at the beginning"*. Moreover, players also mentioned that they did not pay attention to their opponent's plans throughout the game, as their plans were not affected by their own. This finding suggests that the AI made them aware of their opponent's plans, but in some ways annoyed them as the AI kept informing them about the opponent's plans when it did not affect their plans throughout the game.

Gaze Visualisation. A third of players (10/30) explicitly mentioned that the gaze visualisation was 'distracting', mentioning it *"moved too much"* [P1$_A$], occupied their time and attention [P15$_A$], which then caused them to play longer turns [P10$_A$]. When prompted further, three players (P12$_A$, P25$_A$, P29$_A$) mentioned it was mentally demanding to focus on their own and their opponent's strategies (or plans) at the same time, causing a distraction.

Half the players (16/30) found the gaze visualisation to be informative and therefore useful, with a general consensus that it was good to know the general areas the opponent was looking at. Player P17$_A$ enjoyed the challenging aspect of inferring the opponent's intentions on their own, while P12$_A$ found it interesting to reaffirm their assumptions. Though these players found the visualisation informative, players also were not able to utilise the information that was available to them, especially if they were not experienced in the game (e.g. *"It was good to know the general areas the opponent was going for, but don't think I'm experienced enough to act well on the information."* – P23$_A$). These findings are also reflected in our questionnaire results, as shown in Fig. 4.

Table 1 shows that although gaze was found to be most demanding, it was rated most preferred and useful. There are two possible explanations for this. First, experienced players were able to utilise the additional information better through gaze. Second, players noted that the fact that the gaze was overlaid over the game made it easy to determine the areas of interest spatially, which was sufficient to gauge their opponents' intentions at a glance.

A few players drew comparisons with the AI predictions, for example, *"I prefer it [gaze visualisation] to the AI because I didn't have to bother with reading the pop-ups."* as mentioned by P23$_A$. Players also mention that it was possible to ignore gaze when they want to, attributing it to visual background noise on the interface. However, players did note the ability to access the additional information at all times in the GAZE VIZ condition. In comparison with the AI conditions, new information was only available when the predictions appeared, leaving the players on occasion to wait longer for new information to be sent.

6   Discussion

In this paper, we evaluated the prospects of an ideal intention-aware artificial agent, which we designed in line with the existing literature. We present the first step towards artificial agents that can interpret and communicate intentions afforded by gaze input to assist a user by improving the user's situation awareness. Further, we evaluated whether the agent can alleviate the distracting nature of live gaze visualisation used to recognise intentions in prior work. To that end, we conducted two studies: first to derive a language model used by our agent to communicate the predicted intentions using natural language, and second to evaluate the effectiveness and experience of interacting with our agent.

The predictions and explanations provided by the agent early in the game allowed the participants to formulate better strategies, but overall, the agent neither impacted the players' performance nor decreased the cognitive workload as initially hypothesised. It was possible that the game itself introduced cognitive workload, which is difficult to isolate as players had different abilities and set of goals. However, the overall perceived cognitive workload was lower in the agent-assisted conditions, with reduced distraction as compared to the gaze visualisation approach. We further acknowledge that irrespective of the mode of communication, the processing of information generates cognitive workload.

Our subjective assessments indicate that the agent was successful in deriving intentions from gaze and communicating them to the players in a way that matched the informativeness of the gaze visualisation. These results suggest that there is vast potential in using artificial agents to take on such roles when provided with complementary inputs such as gaze. We also note that an agent-assisted approach can potentially scale well for multiple users, where the agent can determine what is the most relevant information to communicate, compared to visualising multiple user's gaze on the same interface which could potentially clutter the interface and cause confusion. Due to the limitations of our approach concerning representation and context, we have only partially achieved our goals for a collaborative intention-aware artificial agent. Following, we discuss the considerations when designing such agents derived from our findings.

Information Presentation. A significant limitation of our approach is the full use of textual representations to convey human intentions. While this serves as a good starting point, it caused participants in our study who were unfamiliar with the game to underutilise the predictions from the agent, as they needed to be spatially aware of the layout of the interface, i.e. the location of cities or map areas, to understand the predictions. Our findings suggest that an overlay of precise intentions over the interface using visual augmentation by the agent coupled with natural language annotations, can potentially be a more understandable way to communicate predictions and explanations.

Context-Awareness. In our user study, we evaluated two sides of the interaction simultaneously. On one side, whether the agent can process and communicate intentions in real-time by observing a human player (the opponent), hence the *sender*. On other, the experience of the *receiver* of intentions, in our case, the agent-assisted player. Ideally, the agent should consider what the agent-assisted player already knows by deriving their intentions as well, either implicitly or explicitly. With context-awareness, the agent would only communicate relevant predictions, such as predictions that directly affect the user and therefore, better relevance to the user regardless of the mode of communication. The DETAILED AI PREDS condition was an extreme case where we gave the most complete explanation possible without considering what the player already knew, leading to the communication of redundant information. The subjective assessment of this condition shows that it is necessary to keep a model of what the player already knows, or what has already been communicated, to reduce distracting information and increase the effectiveness of each communication.

Moreover, context-awareness would allow the agent to adjust the *level of detail* when communicating intentions. The combination of more concise information and more timely predictions would improve the human's ability to respond to the agent. Furthermore, if the agent understood the intentions of all observable users, it would be possible for the agent to negotiate the broader goals of each of the users derived from their intentions. Our work closely resembles *iTourist*, in which an agent could recognise gaze patterns of a 'tourist' and provide recommendations on transport or accommodation alternatives [53], but only for a single user at a time. We extend this work by demonstrating the ability of an automated system to understand long-term human intentions, and by providing insights on how these intentions can be communicated effectively, in a way that can be scaled easily to multiple users.

Nonverbal Communication. This work provides an empirical assessment in a real-time setting of the intention prediction model that we developed in a previous paper [56], and shows that nonverbal inputs such as gaze can be used as a basis for natural language explanations. Further, this work demonstrates the usefulness of multimodal human inputs in the context of human-agent teaming. Our broader aim in this work is to provide a generalisable approach for designing such agents (we do not claim ecological validity for our study setting).

Our work aims to improve on current approaches for human-awareness by not only detecting human presence or actions, but also predicting their intentional actions. As an example, we use the work of Unhelkar et al. [58]'s human-robot collaborative assembly task. In their task, the work area was divided into cells, some shared by humans and robots, which were required to cease operating entirely whenever a human enters a shared cell. They developed and tested a model that incorporated predictions of human motion to improve the efficiency and safety of the assembly task. However, if the robot's motion planner could 'see' that as the human was moving towards their cell, and could 'see' that the human is consistently looking at a bench in a cell that was not their own. The robot then could easily fuse the gaze and motion information to determine the cell that the human was going to and continue its work rather than stop, improving its task efficiency and the interaction with the human. Hence, agents with the ability to process intentions can not only improve their interactions with their human counterparts but improve their proactiveness as well.

Explainable Agency. Our first study formed the basis of a general model of intention communication, which can support the cognitive process of generating explanations involving observable actions and gaze behaviours. As explanations in an explainable agency [35,40] involves both a cognitive process to derive an explanation and a social process of communicating the explanation to a human [42,47], there is a clear scope of expanding our approach to generalise our findings to other settings, evaluate our existing approach [25], and to explore two-way communication between the human and the agent (e.g. dialogue).

In essence, our agent possesses the ability to maintain the mental model of users with regards to short and long-term intentions that we can interrogate at any point in time using our 'white-box' approach. Lastly, our work focused on intention recognition aspect of explanation, which goes beyond question-answering, and differs from existing approaches where the presence of features is used to explain instead of the long-term observation of human behaviours.

7   Conclusions

In this paper, we have demonstrated a viable approach for designing the communication and interaction means for socially interactive agents, addressing various prerequisites for effective human-agent collaboration [37,38]. Our approach uses a proactive agent to assist a human player engaged in an online strategy game by improving the player's situation awareness through the communication of an opponent's intentions. We developed a language model based on human communication that allows our intention-aware agent to communicate inferred intentions through the observation of gaze behaviours and actions. In a user study, we evaluated the experience with and without the agent and found that players were receptive to the agent due to its ability to provide situation awareness of future intentions without the distractions of gaze visualisation. The agent's ability to digest gaze information into contextual and useful representations has broad implications for future systems. We provide several considerations on the design of such agents, including the presentation of information, the need for context-awareness, and opportunities in harnessing nonverbal communication.

Overall, the paper highlights the use of nonverbal behavioural inputs in Human-Agent Interaction and further provides an approach that can be applied in scenarios where it is important to know the intentions of others (e.g. air traffic control, wargaming). In future work, we plan to extend the agent with the ability to consider additional input from the user and to generate alternative predictions about another user based on 'what-if' queries (such as querying about an action that another user is most likely to take). These extended capabilities will be particularly useful in collaborative scenarios, where an agent can assist, mediate or negotiate with knowledge of multiple users' intentions.

Acknowledgements. We acknowledge the Australian Commonwealth Government, Microsoft Research Centre for Social Natural User Interfaces and Interaction Design Lab for their support on this project. We extend our gratitude to our colleagues, particularly Vassilis Kostakos, Tilman Dingler and Ryan Kelly for their input on the paper.

Dr. Eduardo Velloso is the recipient of an Australian Research Council Discovery Early Career Award (Project Number: DE180100315) funded by the Australian Commonwealth Government.

References

1. Akkil, D., Dey, P., Salian, D., Rajput, N.: Gaze awareness in agent-based early-childhood learning application. In: Bernhaupt, R., Dalvi, G., Joshi, A., Balkrishan, D.K., O'Neill, J., Winckler, M. (eds.) INTERACT 2017. LNCS, vol. 10514, pp. 447–466. Springer, Cham (2017). https://doi.org/10.1007/978-3-319-67684-5_28
2. Akkil, D., Thankachan, B., Isokoski, P.: I see what you see: gaze awareness in mobile video collaboration. In: Proceedings of the 2018 ACM Symposium on Eye Tracking Research & Applications, ETRA 2018, pp. 32:1–32:9. ACM, New York (2018). https://doi.org/10.1145/3204493.3204542
3. Antifakos, S., Schwaninger, A., Schiele, B.: Evaluating the effects of displaying uncertainty in context-aware applications. In: Davies, N., Mynatt, E.D., Siio, I. (eds.) UbiComp 2004. LNCS, vol. 3205, pp. 54–69. Springer, Heidelberg (2004). https://doi.org/10.1007/978-3-540-30119-6_4
4. Argyle, M., Cook, M.: Gaze and Mutual Gaze. Cambridge University Press, Cambridge (1976)
5. Bednarik, R., Eivazi, S., Vrzakova, H.: Eye gaze in intelligent user interfaces. In: Nakano, Y., Conati, C., Bader, T. (eds.) A Computational Approach for Prediction of Problem-Solving Behavior Using Support Vector Machines and Eye-Tracking Data, pp. 111–134. Springer, London (2013). https://doi.org/10.1007/978-1-4471-4784-8_7
6. Biran, O., Cotton, C.: Explanation and justification in machine learning: a survey. In: IJCAI 2017 Workshop on Explainable AI (XAI), p. 8 (2017)
7. Brewer, J., D'Angelo, S., Gergle, D.: Iris: gaze visualization design made easy. In: Extended Abstracts of the 2018 CHI Conference on Human Factors in Computing Systems, CHI EA 2018, pp. D504:1–D504:4. ACM, New York (2018). https://doi.org/10.1145/3170427.3186502
8. Brockmyer, J.H., Fox, C.M., Curtiss, K.A., McBroom, E., Burkhart, K.M., Pidruzny, J.N.: The development of the game engagement questionnaire: a measure of engagement in video game-playing. J. Exp. Soc. Psychol. 45(4), 624–634 (2009). https://doi.org/10.1016/j.jesp.2009.02.016
9. Buettner, R.: Cognitive workload of humans using artificial intelligence systems: towards objective measurement applying eye-tracking technology. In: Timm, I.J., Thimm, M. (eds.) KI 2013. LNCS (LNAI), vol. 8077, pp. 37–48. Springer, Heidelberg (2013). https://doi.org/10.1007/978-3-642-40942-4_4
10. Chen, J., Barnes, M.: Human-agent teaming for multirobot control: a review of human factors issues. IEEE Trans. Hum. Mach. Syst. 44(1), 13–29 (2014). https://doi.org/10.1109/THMS.2013.2293535
11. Chen, J.Y.C., Lakhmani, S.G., Stowers, K., Selkowitz, A.R., Wright, J.L., Barnes, M.: Situation awareness-based agent transparency and human-autonomy teaming effectiveness. Theor. Issues Ergon. Sci. 19(3), 259–282 (2018). https://doi.org/10.1080/1463922X.2017.1315750
12. D'Angelo, S., Begel, A.: Improving communication between pair programmers using shared gaze awareness. In: Proceedings of the 2017 CHI Conference on Human Factors in Computing Systems, CHI 2017, pp. 6245–6290. ACM, New York (2017). https://doi.org/10.1145/3025453.3025573

13. D'Angelo, S., Brewer, J., Gergle, D.: Iris: a tool for designing contextually relevant gaze visualizations. In: Proceedings of the 11th ACM Symposium on Eye Tracking Research & Applications, ETRA 2019, pp. 79:1–79:5. ACM, New York (2019). https://doi.org/10.1145/3317958.3318228

14. D'Angelo, S., Gergle, D.: Gazed and confused: understanding and designing shared gaze for remote collaboration. In: Proceedings of the 2016 CHI Conference on Human Factors in Computing Systems, CHI 2016, pp. 2492–2496. ACM, New York (2016). https://doi.org/10.1145/2858036.2858499

15. D'Angelo, S., Gergle, D.: An eye for design: gaze visualizations for remote collaborative work. In: Proceedings of the 2018 CHI Conference on Human Factors in Computing Systems, CHI 2018, pp. 349:1–349:12. ACM, New York (2018). https://doi.org/10.1145/3173574.3173923

16. Dodge, J., Penney, S., Hilderbrand, C., Anderson, A., Burnett, M.: How the experts do it: assessing and explaining agent behaviors in real-time strategy games. In: Proceedings of the 2018 CHI Conference on Human Factors in Computing Systems, CHI 2018, pp. 562:1–562:12. ACM, New York (2018). https://doi.org/10.1145/3173574.3174136

17. Duchowski, A.T.: Gaze-based interaction: a 30 year retrospective. Comput. Graph. **73**, 59–69 (2018). https://doi.org/10.1016/j.cag.2018.04.002

18. Duchowski, A.T., et al.: The index of pupillary activity: measuring cognitive load vis-à-vis task difficulty with pupil oscillation. In: Proceedings of the 2018 CHI Conference on Human Factors in Computing Systems, CHI 2018, pp. 282:1–282:13. ACM, New York (2018). https://doi.org/10.1145/3173574.3173856

19. Eiband, M., Schneider, H., Bilandzic, M., Fazekas-Con, J., Haug, M., Hussmann, H.: Bringing transparency design into practice. In: 23rd International Conference on Intelligent User Interfaces, IUI 2018, pp. 211–223. ACM, New York (2018). https://doi.org/10.1145/3172944.3172961

20. Endsley, M.R.: Toward a theory of situation awareness in dynamic systems. Hum. Factors J. Hum. Factors Ergon. Soc. **37**(1), 32–64 (1995). https://doi.org/10.1518/001872095779049543

21. Harbers, M., van den Bosch, K., Meyer, J.-J.C.: A study into preferred explanations of virtual agent behavior. In: Ruttkay, Z., Kipp, M., Nijholt, A., Vilhjálmsson, H.H. (eds.) IVA 2009. LNCS (LNAI), vol. 5773, pp. 132–145. Springer, Heidelberg (2009). https://doi.org/10.1007/978-3-642-04380-2_17

22. Hart, S.G., Staveland, L.E.: Development of NASA-TLX (task load index): results of empirical and theoretical research. In: Hancock, P.A., Meshkati, N. (eds.) Human Mental Workload, Advances in Psychology, vol. 52, pp. 139–183. North-Holland (1988). https://doi.org/10.1016/S0166-4115(08)62386-9

23. Hayes, B., Shah, J.A.: Improving robot controller transparency through autonomous policy explanation. In: Proceedings of the 2017 ACM/IEEE International Conference on Human-Robot Interaction, HRI 2017, pp. 303–312. ACM, New York (2017). https://doi.org/10.1145/2909824.3020233

24. Higuch, K., Yonetani, R., Sato, Y.: Can eye help you? Effects of visualizing eye fixations on remote collaboration scenarios for physical tasks. In: Proceedings of the 2016 CHI Conference on Human Factors in Computing Systems, CHI 2016, pp. 5180–5190. ACM, New York (2016). https://doi.org/10.1145/2858036.2858438

25. Hoffman, R.R., Mueller, S.T., Klein, G., Litman, J.: Metrics for explainable AI: challenges and prospects. arXiv preprint arXiv:1812.04608 (2018)

26. Huang, C.M., Andrist, S., Sauppé, A., Mutlu, B.: Using gaze patterns to predict task intent in collaboration. Front. Psychol. **6**, 1049 (2015). https://doi.org/10.3389/fpsyg.2015.01049

27. Huang, C.M., Mutlu, B.: Anticipatory robot control for efficient human-robot collaboration. In: The Eleventh ACM/IEEE International Conference on Human Robot Interaction, HRI 2016, pp. 83–90. IEEE Press, Piscataway (2016). http://dl.acm.org/citation.cfm?id=2906831.2906846

28. Jacob, R.J.K.: What you look at is what you get: eye movement-based interaction techniques. In: Proceedings of the SIGCHI Conference on Human Factors in Computing Systems, CHI 1990, pp. 11–18. ACM, New York (1990). https://doi.org/10.1145/97243.97246

29. Kahneman, D., Egan, P.: Thinking, Fast and Slow, vol. 1. Farrar Straus and Giroux, New York (2011)

30. Kass, R., Finin, T.: The need for user models in generating expert system explanation. Int. J. Expert Syst. 1(4), 345–375 (1988). http://dl.acm.org/citation.cfm?id=58447.58452

31. Keil, F.C.: Explanation and understanding. Annu. Rev. Psychol. 57(1), 227–254 (2006). https://doi.org/10.1146/annurev.psych.57.102904.190100

32. Kelley, J.F.: An iterative design methodology for user-friendly natural language office information applications. ACM Trans. Inf. Syst. 2(1), 26–41 (1984)

33. Klien, G., Woods, D.D., Bradshaw, J.M., Hoffman, R.R., Feltovich, P.J.: Ten challenges for making automation a "team player" in joint human-agent activity. IEEE Intell. Syst. 19(6), 91–95 (2004). https://doi.org/10.1109/MIS.2004.74

34. Land, M.F.: Vision, eye movements, and natural behavior. Vis. Neurosci. 26(1), 51–62 (2009). https://doi.org/10.1017/S0952523808080899

35. Langley, P., Meadows, B., Sridharan, M., Choi, D.: Explainable agency for intelligent autonomous systems. In: Twenty-Ninth IAAI Conference (2017)

36. Lankes, M., Maurer, B., Stiglbauer, B.: An eye for an eye: gaze input in competitive online games and its effects on social presence. In: Proceedings of the 13th International Conference on Advances in Computer Entertainment Technology, ACE 2016, pp. 17:1–17:9. ACM, New York (2016). https://doi.org/10.1145/3001773.3001774

37. Lesh, N., Marks, J., Rich, C., Sidner, C.L.: Man-computer symbiosis revisited: achieving natural communication and collaboration with computers. IEICE Trans. 87(6), 1290–1298 (2004)

38. Licklider, J.C.R.: Man-computer symbiosis. IRE Trans. Hum. Factors Electron. HFE-1 1, 4–11 (1960). https://doi.org/10.1109/THFE2.1960.4503259

39. Lim, B.Y., Dey, A.K.: Investigating intelligibility for uncertain context-aware applications. In: Proceedings of the 13th International Conference on Ubiquitous Computing, UbiComp 2011, pp. 415–424. ACM, New York (2011). https://doi.org/10.1145/2030112.2030168

40. Madumal, P.: Explainable agency in intelligent agents: doctoral consortium. In: Proceedings of the 18th International Conference on Autonomous Agents and MultiAgent Systems, AAMAS 2019, pp. 2432–2434. International Foundation for Autonomous Agents and Multiagent Systems, Richland (2019). http://dl.acm.org/citation.cfm?id=3306127.3332137

41. Madumal, P., Miller, T., Sonenberg, L., Vetere, F.: Explainable reinforcement learning through a causal lens. arXiv preprint arXiv:1905.10958 (2019)

42. Madumal, P., Miller, T., Sonenberg, L., Vetere, F.: A grounded interaction protocol for explainable artificial intelligence. In: Proceedings of the 18th International Conference on Autonomous Agents and MultiAgent Systems, AAMAS 2019, pp. 1033–1041. International Foundation for Autonomous Agents and Multiagent Systems, Richland (2019). http://dl.acm.org/citation.cfm?id=3306127.3331801

43. Majaranta, P., Bulling, A.: Eye Tracking and eye-based human-computer interaction. In: Fairclough, S.H., Gilleade, K. (eds.) Advances in Physiological Computing. HIS, pp. 39–65. Springer, London (2014). https://doi.org/10.1007/978-1-4471-6392-3_3

44. Malle, B.F., Knobe, J.: Which behaviors do people explain? A basic actor-observer asymmetry. J. Pers. Soc. Psychol. **72**(2), 288 (1997)

45. Maurer, B., Lankes, M., Stiglbauer, B., Tscheligi, M.: EyeCo: effects of shared gaze on social presence in an online cooperative game. In: Wallner, G., Kriglstein, S., Hlavacs, H., Malaka, R., Lugmayr, A., Yang, H.-S. (eds.) ICEC 2016. LNCS, vol. 9926, pp. 102–114. Springer, Cham (2016). https://doi.org/10.1007/978-3-319-46100-7_9

46. Maurer, B., Lankes, M., Tscheligi, M.: Where the eyes meet: lessons learned from shared gaze-based interactions in cooperative and competitive online games. Entertainment Comput. **27**, 47–59 (2018). https://doi.org/10.1016/j.entcom.2018.02.009, http://www.sciencedirect.com/science/article/pii/S1875952117300629

47. Miller, T.: Explanation in artificial intelligence: insights from the social sciences. Artif. Intell. **267**, 1–38 (2019). https://doi.org/10.1016/j.artint.2018.07.007

48. Moore, J.D., Paris, C.L.: Requirements for an expert system explanation facility. Comput. Intell. **7**(4), 367–370 (1991)

49. Narayanan, V., Zhang, Y., Mendoza, N., Kambhampati, S.: Automated planning for peer-to-peer teaming and its evaluation in remote human-robot interaction. In: Proceedings of the Tenth Annual ACM/IEEE International Conference on Human-Robot Interaction Extended Abstracts, HRI 2015 Extended Abstracts, pp. 161–162. ACM, New York (2015). https://doi.org/10.1145/2701973.2702042

50. Newn, J., Allison, F., Velloso, E., Vetere, F.: Looks can be deceiving: Using gaze visualisation to predict and mislead opponents in strategic gameplay. In: Proceedings of the 2018 CHI Conference on Human Factors in Computing Systems, CHI 2018, pp. 261:1–261:12. ACM, New York (2018). https://doi.org/10.1145/3173574.3173835

51. Newn, J., Velloso, E., Allison, F., Abdelrahman, Y., Vetere, F.: Evaluating real-time gaze representations to infer intentions in competitive turn-based strategy games. In: Proceedings of the Annual Symposium on Computer-Human Interaction in Play, CHI PLAY 2017, pp. 541–552. ACM, New York (2017). https://doi.org/10.1145/3116595.3116624

52. Nunes, I., Jannach, D.: A systematic review and taxonomy of explanations in decision support and recommender systems. User Model. User-Adap. Inter. **27**(3–5), 393–444 (2017). https://doi.org/10.1007/s11257-017-9195-0

53. Qvarfordt, P., Zhai, S.: Conversing with the user based on eye-gaze patterns. In: Proceedings of the SIGCHI Conference on Human Factors in Computing Systems, CHI 2005, pp. 221–230. ACM, New York (2005). https://doi.org/10.1145/1054972.1055004

54. Riek, L.D.: Wizard of Oz studies in HRI: a systematic review and new reporting guidelines. J. Hum.-Robot Interact. **1**(1), 119–136 (2012). https://doi.org/10.5898/JHRI.1.1.Riek

55. Rieser, V.: Bootstrapping reinforcement learning-based dialogue strategies from wizard-of-Oz data. DFKI (2008)

56. Singh, R., Miller, T., Newn, J., Sonenberg, L., Velloso, E., Vetere, F.: Combining planning with gaze for online human intention recognition. In: Proceedings of the 17th International Conference on Autonomous Agents and Multiagent System, AAMAS 2018. International Foundation for Autonomous Agents and Multiagent Systems, Richland (2018). http://dl.acm.org/citation.cfm?id=3237383.3237457

57. Stein, R., Brennan, S.E.: Another person's eye gaze as a cue in solving programming problems. In: Proceedings of the 6th International Conference on Multimodal Interfaces, ICMI 2004, pp. 9–15. ACM, New York (2004). https://doi.org/10.1145/1027933.1027936

58. Unhelkar, V.V., et al.: Human-aware robotic assistant for collaborative assembly: integrating human motion prediction with planning in time. IEEE Robot. Autom. Lett. **3**(3), 2394–2401 (2018). https://doi.org/10.1109/LRA.2018.2812906

59. Velloso, E., Carter, M.: The emergence of eyeplay: a survey of eye interaction in games. In: Proceedings of the 2016 Annual Symposium on Computer-Human Interaction in Play, CHI PLAY 2016, pp. 171–185. ACM, New York (2016). https://doi.org/10.1145/2967934.2968084

60. Vertegaal, R.: The gaze groupware system: mediating joint attention in multiparty communication and collaboration. In: Proceedings of the SIGCHI Conference on Human Factors in Computing Systems, CHI 1999, pp. 294–301. ACM, New York (1999). https://doi.org/10.1145/302979.303065

61. Wang, D., Yang, Q., Abdul, A., Lim, B.Y.: Designing theory-driven user-centric explainable AI. In: Proceedings of the 2019 CHI Conference on Human Factors in Computing Systems, CHI 2019, pp. 601:1–601:15. ACM, New York (2019)

62. Wang, N., Pynadath, D.V., Hill, S.G.: Trust calibration within a human-robot team: comparing automatically generated explanations. In: The Eleventh ACM/IEEE International Conference on Human Robot Interaction, pp. 109–116. IEEE Press (2016)

63. Zhang, Y., Pfeuffer, K., Chong, M.K., Alexander, J., Bulling, A., Gellersen, H.: Look together: using gaze for assisting co-located collaborative search. Pers. Ubiquit. Comput. **21**(1), 173–186 (2017). https://doi.org/10.1007/s00779-016-0969-x

GazeLens: Guiding Attention to Improve Gaze Interpretation in Hub-Satellite Collaboration

Khanh-Duy Le[1]([⊠]), Ignacio Avellino[2], Cédric Fleury[3], Morten Fjeld[1], and Andreas Kunz[4]

[1] Chalmers University of Technology, Gothenburg, Sweden
{khanh-duy.le,fjeld}@chalmers.se
[2] ISIR, CNRS, Sorbonne Université, Paris, France
ignacio.avellino@sorbonne-universite.fr
[3] LRI, Univ. Paris-Sud, CNRS, Inria, Université Paris-Saclay, Paris, France
cedric.fleury@lri.fr
[4] ETH Zurich, Zurich, Switzerland
kunz@iwf.mavt.ethz.ch

Abstract. In hub-satellite collaboration using video, interpreting gaze direction is critical for communication between hub coworkers sitting around a table and their remote satellite colleague. However, 2D video distorts images and makes this interpretation inaccurate. We present *GazeLens*, a video conferencing system that improves hub coworkers' ability to interpret the satellite worker's gaze. A 360° camera captures the hub coworkers and a ceiling camera captures artifacts on the hub table. The system combines these two video feeds in an interface. Lens widgets strategically guide the satellite worker's attention toward specific areas of her/his screen allow hub coworkers to clearly interpret her/his gaze direction. Our evaluation shows that *GazeLens* (1) increases hub coworkers' overall gaze interpretation accuracy by 25.8% in comparison to a conventional video conferencing system, (2) especially for physical artifacts on the hub table, and (3) improves hub coworkers' ability to distinguish between gazes toward people and artifacts. We discuss how screen space can be leveraged to improve gaze interpretation.

Keywords: Remote collaboration · Telepresence · Gaze · Lens widgets

1 Introduction

In hub-satellite communication, a remote team member (satellite) collaborates at a distance with colleagues at the main office (hub). Typically, hub coworkers sit around a table with artifacts such as paper printouts, with a screen placed at one

Electronic supplementary material The online version of this chapter (https://doi.org/10.1007/978-3-030-29384-0_18) contains supplementary material, which is available to authorized users.

edge of the table showing a video feed of the satellite worker. The satellite worker sees the hub office in a deep perspective as it is captured by a camera placed at the edge of the table. Hub coworkers see a closer view of their colleagues, with a much more shallow perspective. Simply put, due to these differences in perspective, it is difficult to interpret the satellite's gaze (where s/he's looking at). While video conferencing systems can support non-verbal cues as people can see each others' faces and gestures, it is not always coherent: non-verbal cues such as gaze and deictic gestures are disparate between hub coworkers and the satellite, making communication asymmetric as co-located hub coworkers easily understand each others' non-verbal cues but not those of the satellite worker.

Gaze is important in collaboration - it is a reliable predictor of conversational attention [1,4], offering effortless reference to spatial objects [29], supporting remote instruction [5,30], and improving users' confidence in distributed problem solving on shared artifacts [2]. Kendon [27] argues that gaze is a signal through which a person relates their basic orientation and even intention toward another. Falling short on conveying gaze in remote collaboration can lead to confused communication [3], reduce social intimacy [3], decrease effectiveness [32] and increase effort for collaborative tasks [2,5].

Previous work has tried to improve gaze perception in remote collaboration, but has mainly focused on conveying either gaze awareness between distant coworkers [7,8,25] or gaze on shared digital content [11,14], leaving the problem of conveying gaze on physical artifacts rather under attended. Achieving this often requires specialized and complex hardware setups on the satellite side [9,13,16], which might be unrealistic for traveling workers. We focus on designing a mobile solution to improve hub coworkers' interpretation of the satellite worker's gaze both toward themselves and hub physical artifacts using minimal equipment.

We present *GazeLens*, a hub-satellite video conferencing system that improves hub coworker's accuracy when interpreting the direction of a satellite worker's gaze. At the hub side, *GazeLens* captures two videos: a view of the coworkers, using an off-the-shelf 360° camera, and a view of the artifacts on the table, using a ceiling-mounted camera. The system presents these videos simultaneously on the satellite worker's laptop screen, eliminating the need for stationary or specialized hardware on the remote end. *GazeLens* displays lenses on the satellite's screen, which the satellite worker can move to focus on different parts of the two videos, such as a hub coworker on the 360° view and an artifact on the table view. These lenses are strategically positioned to explicitly guide the direction of the satellite worker's gaze. As with conventional video conferencing, hub coworkers simply see a video stream of their remote colleague's face shown on the screen placed on the edge of their table. Our aim is to provide a more coherent picture for hub coworkers of where exactly their satellite colleague is directing his/her attention, thus improving clarity of communication.

We evaluate the performance of *GazeLens* in two studies, where we compare it to conventional video conferencing (*ConvVC*) using a wide-angle camera on the hub side. The first study shows that *GazeLens* helps hub coworkers distinguish whether a satellite worker is looking at a person or at an artifact on the hub side. The second study shows that *GazeLens* helps hub coworkers interpret which artifact on the hub table the satellite worker is looking at. Early feedback on usability show the benefits for satellite workers, by improving visibility of hub artifacts and hub coworkers' activities while maintaining their spatial relations. We show that screen space can be better leveraged through strategic placement of interface elements to support non-verbal communication in video conferencing and thus convey a satellite worker's gaze direction.

(a)   **(b)**   **(c)**

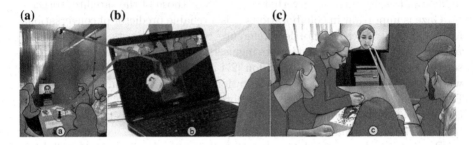

Fig. 1. *GazeLens* system. (a) On the hub side, a 360° camera on the table captures coworkers and a webcam mounted on the ceiling captures artifacts on the table. (b) Video feeds from the two cameras are displayed on the screen of the remote satellite worker; a virtual lens strategically guides her/his attention towards a specific screen area according to the observed artifact. (c) The satellite's gaze, guided by the virtual lens, is aligned towards the observed artifact on the hub space.

2   Related Work

2.1   Gaze Awareness Among Remote Coworkers

One-to-one Remote Collaboration: Gemmel et al. [24] and Giger et al. [25] proposed using computer vision to manipulate eye gaze in the remote worker's video. They focused on achieving direct eye contact by correcting the disparity between the location of the video conferencing window and the camera.

Multi-party Remote Collaboration: In the Hydra system [7], each remote party was represented by a hardware device containing a display, a camera, and a microphone. These were spatially arranged in front of the local worker, helping convey the worker's gaze.

Group-to-Group Remote Collaboration: For each participant, Multi-View [8] used one camera and one projector to capture and display each person on one side from the perspective of each person on the other. Similarly, MMSpace [13] placed multiple displays around the table of a local group, each representing a worker on the remote side, replicating the sitting positions of the remote workers. Both systems maintained correct gaze awareness between remote coworkers.

Hub-Satellite Remote Collaboration: Jones et al. [15] installed a large screen on the satellite's side to display the hub's video stream and employed multiple cameras to construct a 3D model of the satellite worker's face to help hub coworkers perceive their gaze. Pan and Steed [9] and Gotsch et al. [16] also used an array of cameras to capture the satellite worker's face from different angles, selectively displaying the images to hub coworkers on a cylindrical display.

While most previous work focused on direct eye contact and gaze awareness between remote coworkers, only a few have attempted to provide correct interpretation of gaze toward shared artifacts - either virtual artifacts shared through a synchronized system or physical artifacts at either location - mandatory in hub-satellite collaboration that involves shared objects on the hub table. In addition, the above systems often require specialized hardware, which is not suitable for a traveling satellite worker who needs a lightweight and mobile device.

2.2   Gaze Support for Shared Virtual Artifacts

ClearBoard [11] creates a write-on-glass metaphor by overlaying a shared digital canvas on the remote coworker's video feed, inherently conveying gaze between two remote people working on the canvas. Similarly, Holoport [14] captures images of the hub's workers using a camera behind a scree, which helps convey coworkers' gaze among each other as well as towards on-screen artifacts. GAZE and GAZE-2 [1,18] introduce a 3D virtual environment where the video stream of each worker is displayed on a 3D cube that could change direction to convey the worker's gaze toward others. Hauber et al. [12] evaluated a setup where workers were equipped with a tabletop showing a shared display, coupled with a screen showing the video feeds of the remote workers. A camera was mounted on top of the screen to capture remote workers' faces. They also compared this technique with the a 3D virtual environment of GAZE [1]. Finally, Avellino et al. [31] showed that video can be used to convey gaze and deictic gestures toward shared digital content in large wall-sized displays.

All these systems convey gaze direction to shared virtual artifacts by keeping the spatial relation of the video feed to the digital content. While they demonstrate that people can interpret gaze direction from a video feed, these techniques are not applicable in the context of hub-satellite collaborations involving physical artifacts on the hub table. These systems are designed for symmetric and specific settings such as large interactive whiteboards or wall-sized displays, which are not appropriate for mobile workers or small organisations.

2.3   Gaze Support for Physical Artifacts

Visualizations that indicate remote gaze direction have been explored for supporting physical collaborative tasks [2,5,29]. Otsuki et al. [17] developed ThirdEye, an add-on display that conveys the remote worker's gaze into the 3D physical space. It projects a 2D graphic element, controlled by eye tracking data of the remote worker, onto a hemispherical surface that looks like an eye. However, such mediated representations might introduce spatial disparities when compared to unmediated gaze, potentially leading to confusion and reducing the value of the satellite's video feed. These solutions add complexity to the satellite worker's setup, by adding specialized hardware such as an eye tracker.

Xu et al. [6] introduce an approach for conveying the satellite worker's attention in hub-satellite collaboration. The satellite worker can view a panoramic video stream of the hub on their screen, captured by a 360° camera, and manually select the area of interest in the video. A tablet on the hub's side, horizontally placed under the 360° camera, showed an arrow pointing at the area selected by the satellite worker. This solution cannot convey the satellite's attention toward physical artifacts as it lacks the vertical dimension of their gaze, and using an arrow to represent gaze might also be distracting and unnatural for the hub coworkers as compared to an unmediated gaze.

Finally, CamBlend [19] used video effects to blur the 180° video of the remote side, encouraging the user to focus on an area of interest in order to view it in high resolution. This mimics a human's visual system, where foveal (central) vision has much higher acuity than peripheral vision [20]. CamBlend did not however aim to convey the satellite's gaze. *GazeLens* leverages this technique to provide the satellite worker with an overview of the hub's space, while guiding the satellite worker's attention to strategic locations in order to explicitly convey their gaze to the hub workers.

3   GazeLens Design

GazeLens is designed to improve the hub coworkers' perception of the satellite worker's gaze. It is motivated by the limitations of current video conferencing systems in conveying gaze.

3.1   Gaze Perception in Video Conferencing

Stokes [22] and Chen [10] showed that when the angle between the gaze direction and the camera is less than 5° in video conferencing between two people, the remote person perceives direct eye contact. Moreover, when one person looks towards the right of the camera, the remote person feels they are looking at their right shoulder, and so on. While this effect can be leveraged to establish eye contact between pairs of video conferencing endpoints [10], it may also be used for gaze interpretation in groups, such as hub-satellite settings.

3.2   Limitations of Hub-Satellite Communication Systems

The screen on the hub side showing the satellite's video often uses a wide-angle camera that captures an overview of the hub environment, so the satellite worker

Fig. 2. Hub table captured by a camera placed (a) below and (b) above the hub screen (image courtesy requested).

can view the hub (Fig. 2). Two typical placements for this camera are just above the screen, such as in the Cisco MX Series [34] and Polycom RealPresence Group Series [35] or below the screen, as in the Cisco SX80 [36] or AVS solutions [37]. Neither of these setups effectively conveys the satellite worker's gaze back to hub coworkers nor at the artifacts on the table. When the camera is placed below the screen, artifacts on the table are largely occluded or difficult to see, but the satellite sees hub worker's faces straight on (Fig. 2a). With a placement above the screen, the hub's artifacts are less occluded, but the hub's environment as a whole seems distant, with a distortion of deep perspective where coworkers appear small (Fig. 2b, note the distant table edge). This "mapping" of the hub's environment onto the satellite's computer screen leads to hub coworkers being unable to distinguish the satellite's gaze toward different people and artifacts. Additionally, hub coworkers near the camera appear lower on the satellite's computer screen, making it harder for them to discern whether the satellite worker is looking at a coworker or at an object on the table.

3.3 Design Requirements

With these limitations in mind, we derived the following design requirements for a video conferencing system that can convey the satellite worker's gaze toward their hub coworkers and physical artifacts:

DR1: the system needs to display a view of the hub to the satellite worker in which they can see both the hub coworkers' faces and the artifacts on the table without occlusions.

DR2: the system should allow hub coworkers to clearly distinguish if the satellite worker is gazing toward individual coworkers or hub table artifacts.

DR3: the system should allow hub coworkers to accurately interpret the satellite worker's gaze toward physical artifacts.

DR4: the system should only rely on video to convey the satellite worker's gaze, and avoid mediated gaze representations such as arrows, pointers or virtual arms, which introduce spatial and representational disparities.

DR5: the system for the satellite worker should consist of a lightweight and mobile device which does not require any calibration, suitable for traveling.

3.4   *GazeLens* Implementation

Hub side: to ensure *DR1*, *GazeLens* captures the panoramic video of the cowork-ers sitting around the hub's table using a 360° camera placed at the center of it, and it captures the scene using a camera mounted on the ceiling to avoid occluding artifacts on the hub table (see Fig. 1a).

Fig. 3. *GazeLens* interface with (a) a lens showing a close-up of an artifact on the table and (b) a lens highlighting a hub worker's position around the table. Lenses are triggered when users click on the video feeds, the lens on artifacts is rotated either by dragging the handle or simply clicking on the border at the desired direction.

Satellite Side: GazeLens presents the two video feeds to the satellite worker on a standard laptop with a camera, satisfying *DR5* (see Fig. 1b). Their presenta-tion is designed so that it improves the interpretation of the satellite's gaze. To fulfill *DR2*, the video feed displaying hub coworkers should be placed near the satellite's laptop camera, located above the screen. This panoramic video is then segmented on the satellite's display to maintain spatial fidelity: the hub cowork-ers sitting in front of their screen are shown in the center of the satellite's video, while those on the sides of the hub table are displayed on their corresponding sides. The overview video of the hub table is displayed below the panoramic video of the hub coworkers (Fig. 3).

To address *DR3*, the video of the hub table view is scaled to fit the satel-lite's screen and to maximize the size of any objects on it, although this leads to different gaze patterns depending on table shape. Stretching this video to main-tain a specific size would solve this problem, but would also distort the objects. Instead, we chose a focus-based approach mimicking foveal and peripheral vision to maximize variation of the satellite worker's gaze, while preventing the hub table representation from becoming distorted.

The focus-based interaction is implemented as a widget in the form of a virtual lens that focuses on content. The hub's table video is displayed in the table's actual aspect ratio and "out of focus," using a video effect to mimic the indistinct quality of peripheral vision. The satellite worker thus sees an arrangement of artifacts but not their details. To see an object's details, the satellite selects it and a round virtual lens appears on the side showing a high-resolution detail of the selected area. This lens is strategically placed on the satellite's screen so that when the satellite worker gazes at it, the hub coworkers are able to correctly interpret which object is being looked at based solely from the direction of the satellite's gaze (see Fig. 1c). This supports *DR4*. The lens position is interpolated by mapping the hub table's video onto as much screen space as possible below the hub coworker's panoramic video. As artifacts can be placed on the table from different directions, we implemented a rotation control on the lens, which the satellite worker can use to rotate its content if needed (Fig. 3a).

To keep the satellite worker aware of the hub coworkers' spatial arrangement around the table, we segmented the hub's panoramic video based on the table's aspect ratio, and placed the segments around the table at their corresponding sides. These segments are then also displayed out of focus. When the satellite worker wants to look at one of their hub coworkers, they select it within the panoramic view at the top of the screen a square lens widget appears to guide their gaze toward a specific person (see Fig. 3b).

GazeLens is implemented using C# and .NET 4.5 framework[1]. In its current implementation, the panoramic video height is equal to 20% of the entire screen height. When displayed on a 14-in. 16:9 conventional laptop screen, this creates a distance of around 4 cm from the built-in camera to the top edge of the screen showing the panoramic video of the hub. Assuming that the satellite worker is 45 cm from their screen, and the hub screen is placed at the center of the table edge, this 4 cm distance creates the desired visual angle of 5° between the satellite's camera and the panoramic video showing their hub coworkers, establishing direct gaze [10]. This size is also sufficient to avoid distortions in the panoramic video. The lenses are activated by a left-button mouse click event on non-touch screen computers, and by a touch down event on touch devices.

4   Study 1: Accuracy in Interpreting Satellite's Gaze

We evaluate whether *GazeLens* can improve hub coworkers' ability to interpret a satellite's gaze by comparing it to a conventional video conference system (*ConvVC*). *ConvVC* displays the hub side in full screen on the satellite's screen, still guiding their gaze towards right direction. To our knowledge, no off-the-shelf video conferencing interfaces for laptop/tablet offer better unmediated gaze towards people and artifacts than a *ConvVC*. We test the following hypotheses:

– H1: *GazeLens* improves accuracy of gaze interpretation compared to *ConvVC*;
– H2: *GazeLens* outperforms *ConvVC* for gaze interpretation accuracy both when the hub coworker sits in front of and to the side of screen; and,
– H3: *GazeLens* incurs a lower perceived workload than *ConvVC*.

4.1   Method

The study has a within-subjects design with the following factors:

- INTERFACE used by the satellite worker with levels: *GazeLens* and *ConvVC*;
- POSITION of the hub participants around the hub table with levels: *Front* and *Side* of the screen.

We controlled two secondary factors ACTOR and TARGET. We recorded 3 video sets of different ACTORs to mitigate possible effects tied to one of them in particular. Each ACTOR gazed at 14 TARGETs located on and around the table (Fig. 4) as if he/she was the satellite worker.

Conditions were grouped by POSITION, then by INTERFACE and then by ACTOR. The presentation order of these three conditions was counterbalanced using Latin squares. Each Latin square row was repeated when necessary. For each POSITION × INTERFACE × ACTOR condition, the order of the 14 TARGETs was randomized so that successive videos never showed the same target as the previous one (and with a different ACTORs). Participants performed in total 168 trials (2 POSITIONs × 2 INTERFACEs × 3 ACTORs × 14 TARGETs).

4.2   Participants

Twelve participants (7 male), aged 22 to 33 (median = 25), with backgrounds from computer science, interaction design, and social science participated in the study. This sample size is the average one reported in CHI studies [38] and also used in related work [17,31]. Pilot studies determined that effects are strong enough to be observed with this sample size. All participants had normal or corrected-to-normal vision. Three never used video conferencing applications, two used them on a monthly basis, five on a weekly basis, one on a daily basis and one multiple times a day. Each received a movie ticket for their participation.

4.3   Hardware and Software

For video recording the stimuli, we used a conventional laptop, a typical commercial foldable laptop with a screen size of 11–17 in. (here, 14 in.) with a built-in front facing camera, for the satellite worker, as it is still one of the most common device used by travelers. Due to the low resolution of our laptop's built-in camera, we used a Plexgear 720p webcam[2] mounted at the same position as the laptop's built-in camera to record ACTORs. Using a high-res camera does not reduce the validity of the study as we are not investigating the effect of image quality. Also, many current conventional laptop models have high resolutions.

On the hub side, we used a 80 cm × 140 cm rectangular table with a height of 60 cm to accommodate 6 people. The 14 TARGETs (12 cm × 12 cm) were divided into two groups: 9 (labeled from 1 to 9) arranged in a 3 × 3 grid on the hub table represented artifacts, and 5 (labeled from A to E) around the table representing coworker targets. This left one edge occupied by the screen, two targets on each 140 cm vertical edge and one on the 80 cm horizontal edge (Fig. 4). We used 5

---

[2] https://www.kjell.com/se/sortiment/dator-natverk/datortillbehor/webbkameror/plexgear-720p-webbkamera-p61271.

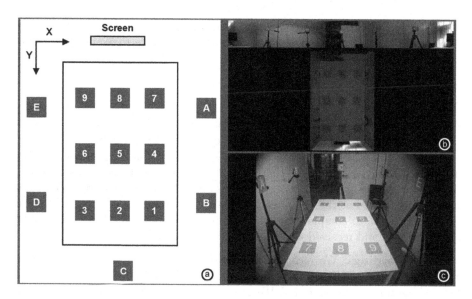

Fig. 4. (a) Hub space with target arrangement as used in Study 1. (b) *GazeLens* interface and (c) conventional interface *ConvVC* with the experimental setup.

hub coworkers in the study as it is a typical small team size and offers sufficient challenge for interpreting gaze. Hub coworkers were 65 cm higher than the table, approximated to the average eye-level height of a person sitting on a 45 cm-high chair, the average for office chairs [23]. The distance from a coworker to its nearest neighbor (proxy or hub screen) was 80 cm, and to the nearest edge of the table was 35 cm. We used a 25-in. monitor to display the satellite's video stream, placed on a stand with the same height as the table.

To capture all the hub's targets in the *ConvVC* condition, due to our laboratory's hardware constraints, we simulated a wide-angle camera by coupling the 12-megapixel back camera of a LG Nexus 5X phone with a 0.67X wide-angled lens. The phone was mounted above the screen and adjusted so that the proxies were captured near the top edge of the video to convey the satellite worker's direct eye contact when looking at these targets (Fig. 4-right/bottom). For the *GazeLens* condition, we used a Ricoh R 360° camera to capture panoramic video and a Logitech HD Pro Webcam C910 to capture the overview video of the table (Fig. 4-right/top).

Participants sat at two positions around the hub's table: in *Front*, opposite the screen and at the of the screen (positions A and C respectively on Fig. 4a). The distance from the participant's body to the nearest edge was around 35 cm. As the table was symmetric, the evaluation result from one side could be applied to the other. We chose position A as it was closer to the screen than B or D, causing the so-called Mona Lisa effect (where the image of a subject looking into the camera is seen by remote participants as looking at them, irrespective of their position) that could affect the gaze interpretation. The recorded videos were displayed at full screen. The videos' aspect ratio (4:3) mismatched the hub's screen (16:9). However, we did not modify the videos' size to avoid a partial or distorted view of the hub.

4.4 Procedure

After greeting participants, they signed a consent form and read printed instructions. Participants answered a pre-study questionnaire providing their background and self-assessing their technological expertise. They completed a training session before starting the experiment. We encouraged them to take a 5-min break between the two POSITION conditions and a 2-min break between each 21 videos (middle and at the end of each INTERFACE condition). It took 1 h 15 min for a participant to complete the study. Finally, they answered the post-study questionnaires and received a movie ticket.

Video Recordings. We recorded 6-s videos of 3 different ACTORS gazing at 14 targets in the satellite worker interface displayed on a 14-in. laptop screen, for both *GazeLens* and *ConvVC*. We observed in pilots that 6 s are long enough to make ACTOR's gaze movements perceivable while avoiding fatigue. *ActorA* was a 29-year-old man with brown medium-length hair and hazel eyes, *ActorB* a 34-year-old man with short blonde hair and brown eyes, and *ActorC* a 44-year-old woman with brown pulled back hair and hazel eyes.

ACTORS sat on a 45 cm-high office chair 45 cm away from the laptop screen, which was placed on a 70 cm-high office desk. In order to recreate a more realistic gaze, actors first looked at a starting point and then at the target. This causes relative movements in the satellite worker's gaze, which provides a context with easier interpretation for the viewer. A target's starting point was decided by choosing its nearest neighboring label at an arbitrary point of 50 cm, with the exception of labels on the same grid row and column as the target. As humans are less sensitive to vertical changes of gaze [10] and the distance between two targets on the same row in conventional videos is smaller, satellite workers eye movements become be noticeable. For each target, we recorded actors gazing at them from three different starting points. We did not use a chin-rest for the actors to make the recording realistic, however they were instructed to keep their head straight. They were also instructed to look at the targets in natural ways (i.e. they could turn their head if needed).

Task. Participants were advised to sit upright at POSITIONS, and could lean back if they got tired. However, if seated at the *Side*, they were not allowed to lean toward the screen. Participants watched each video playing in an infinite loop to avoid missing gaze movements due to distractions. There was thus no time pressure for the participants as we focused on accuracy. When they were ready to answer which target the ACTOR was looking at, they tapped a large "Stop" button on an Asus Nexus 9 tablet. The tablet then showed a replica of the table with the targets and hub coworkers laid out in the same fashion as on the participant's screen to make selection easier.

4.5   Data Collection and Analysis

We collected participants' responses for each trial, i.e. which target they thought was being gazed at, and their confidence in their answer (on 5-point Likert scale: 1 = not confident, 5 = very confident). We also recorded response time. When two INTERFACE conditions for each POSITION were completed, participants answered a post-questionnaire indicating their perceived workload (based on NASA TLX [33]), perceived ease to differentiate gazes at targets on and around the table, perceived ease to interpret the satellite's gaze and their interpretation strategies in both conditions.

We define *Gaze Interpretation Accuracy* as the proportion of correct trials. We define *Differentiation Accuracy*, i.e. the participant's ability to differentiate gaze at targets *around* or *on* the table, as the proportion of trials with gaze at the correct set of targets on or around table.

4.6   Results

To analyze *Gaze Interpretation Accuracy* we perform a two-way factorial ANOVA (INTERFACE × POSITION). The result (Fig. 5) shows an effect of INTER-FACE ($F_{1,44} = 7.33$, $p < 0.001$), POSITION ($F_{1,44} = 6.88$, $p < 0.01$) and no interaction effect INTERFACE × POSITION ($p > 0.1$). *GazeLens* significantly improves interpretation of the satellite gaze in comparison to *ConvVC* (31.45% ± 4.67% vs 25% ± 3.51%, an increase of 25.8%, 6.45% effect size), supporting H1. As expected, participants interpreted the satellite's gaze significantly more precisely at the *Front* than *Side* POSITION (31.35% ± 4.96% vs 25% ± 3.13%). As there is no interaction effect, we cannot reject H2. Data in Fig. 5 suggests that participants performed better with *GazeLens* at both sitting positions.

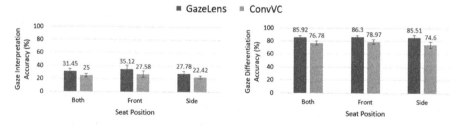

Fig. 5. *Gaze Interpretation Accuracy* (in %) (left) and *Gaze Differentiation Accuracy* (in %) (right) for INTERFACE ×POSITION. Error bars show 95% confidence interval (CI).

To analyze *Differentiation Accuracy* we perform a two-way factorial ANOVA (INTERFACE × POSITION). The result (Fig. 5) shows an effect of INTERFACE ($F_{1,44} = 20.77$, $p < 0.001$), no effect of POSITION nor an interaction effect of INTERFACE × POSITION ($p > 0.1$). Participants using *GazeLens* could better differentiate gaze at targets around or on the table compared to *ConvVC* (85.92% ± 2.38% vs. 76.78% ± 3.14%, $p < 0.001$).

A two-way factorial ANOVA analysis (INTERFACE × POSITION) did not yield any effect of INTERFACE × POSITION on perceived workload (not supporting H3), neither for answer time nor confidence (all p's > 0.1). Finally, we did not find any effect of ACTOR on *Gaze Interpretation Accuracy* nor *Differentiation Accuracy* at targets on or around table, neither learning effects.

5   Study 2: Accuracy in Interpreting Gaze at Hub Artifacts

Study 1 showed that *GazeLens* improves gaze interpretation accuracy in general. We wanted to further investigate how accurately hub coworkers can interpret the satellite worker's gaze towards physical artifacts on the hub table. In reality, arrangements of physical artifacts on the table can vary from sparse (e.g. meetings with some paper documents) to dense (e.g. brainstorming with sticky notes, phones, physical prototypes). This prompts the need to explore how the granularity of artifact arrangement impacts a hub coworker's gaze interpretation. We also investigate if *GazeLens* can increase hub coworkers' accuracy at interpreting the satellite's gaze compared to *ConvVC*, especially regarding error distance along the two table dimensions: horizontal (X) and vertical (Y). We used a similar experiment design to Study 1, where participants have to determine the satellite's gaze in prerecorded videos displayed on the screen at the hub table.

We operationalize artifacts arrangements through the granularity of layouts:

- 3 × 3 (9 objects in a 3 × 3 grid): low-granularity arrangements to investigate gaze interpretation accuracy in meeting scenarios involving paper documents,
- 5 × 5 (25 objects in a 5 × 5 grid): high-granularity arrangements to investigate gaze interpretation accuracy in scenarios such as brainstorming.

We formulate the following hypotheses:

- H1: *GazeLens* improves the hub coworkers' interpretation accuracy for gaze toward objects on the hub table compared to *ConvVC*;
- H2: *GazeLens* outperforms *ConvVC* for gaze interpretation accuracy at both levels of granularity;
- H3: *GazeLens* reduces X and Y error distance compared to *ConvVC*.

5.1   Method

The within-subject study design has the following factors:

- INTERFACE used by the satellite to view the targets, with two conditions: *GazeLens* and *ConvVC*; and,

– LAYOUT of the artifacts on the table with two conditions: 3×3 and 5×5 grid.

For each participant, the conditions were grouped by LAYOUT, then by INTERFACE and then by ACTOR. ACTORs were the same as in Study 1.

The order of presentation was counterbalanced across conditions using Latin squares for the first three conditions and randomized order for TARGET. Each Latin square was repeated when necessary. For each LAYOUT × INTERFACE × ACTOR condition, the order of the targets (9 for 3×3 and 25 for 5×5) was randomized so a different succession of videos was shown for each target. Participants took a 5-min break between the two layout conditions, and performed a training session before starting the experiment, where we ensured they covered all TARGETs, INTERFACEs and LAYOUTs.

5.2   Participants

Twelve participants—different from those in Study 1—8 males, aged 22 to 38 (median = 29), with backgrounds from computer science, interaction design, and social science participated in the study. All had normal or corrected-to-normal vision. Three used their computer on daily basis, eight multiple times a day and one on a weekly basis. One had never used video conferencing applications, eight used them on a monthly basis, one on a weekly basis, one on a daily basis, and one multiple times a day. Each received a movie ticket for their participation.

5.3   Hardware and Software

We used the same cameras, hub table, hub screen, and screen placement as in Study 1. To investigate gaze interpretation accuracy for different artifact sizes, we used two different layouts on the table (Fig. 4). We removed targets representing hub coworkers in Study 1 to avoid distracting actors and participants.

5.4   Procedure

We employed a similar procedure as in Study 1. However, participants took a 2-min break after every 18 videos in the 3×3 layout, and after every 15 videos in the 5×5 layout (the dense layout was more tiring).

Video Recordings. We recorded 306 6-s videos for the hub's targets of the same three ACTORs as in study 1:81 videos for the 3×3 layout and 225 for the 5×5 layout. We used the same laptop, camera, placements of the devices and ACTORs as in Study 1. Each video was also recorded in a similar procedure as in Study 1: each ACTOR first looked at a starting point and then at the target. We used the same criteria for choosing starting points for targets.

Task. We used a similar task as in Study 1, although participants only sat at position A (*Front*) to watch the videos. The positions of the screen and those of participants in relation to it remained the same.

5.5   Data Collection and Analysis

We collected data as in Study 1. We measure *Gaze Interpretation Accuracy* as in Study 1 and two error measures: *X-Axis Error* and *Y-Axis Error*, denoting the error between the correct and selected target along the table's horizontal and vertical orientation (X and Y axis in Fig. 4a) respectively.

5.6   Results

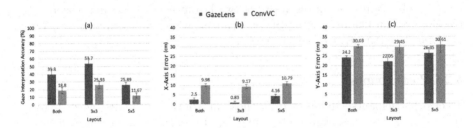

Fig. 6. (a) Gaze interpretation accuracy (in %) for each INTERFACE × LAYOUT condition. (b) X-axis error (in cm) and (c) Y-axis error (in cm) for each INTERFACE × LAYOUT condition. Bars indicate 95% CI.

We analyze *Gaze Interpretation Accuracy* as in Study 1 by performing a two-way factorial ANOVA (INTERFACE and LAYOUT). The result shows an effect of INTERFACE ($F_{1,44} = 69.26$, $p < 0.001$), supporting H1, LAYOUT ($F_{1,44} = 69.50$, $p < 0.001$) and INTERFACE × LAYOUT ($F_{1,44} = 7.214$, $p < 0.05$). A post-hoc Tukey HSD test showed that *GazeLens* significantly improves *Gaze Interpretation Accuracy* in both 3×3 layout (53.7% ± 7.06% vs 25.93% ± 4.81%, $p < 0.001$) and 5 × 5 layout (25.89% ± 3.55% vs 11.67% ± 3.5%, $p < 0.001$) supporting H2. Post-hoc Tukey HSD tests showed significant differences between *GazeLens* with 3 × 3 and *GazeLens* with 5 × 5 ($p < 0.001$), between *GazeLens* with 3 × 3 and *ConvVC* with 5×5 ($p < 0.001$), between *ConvVC* with 3 × 3 and *ConvVC* with 5 × 5 ($p < 0.01$). Figure 6a shows gaze interpretation accuracy in each INTERFACE × LAYOUT condition.

To examine *X-Axis Error*, we perform a two-way factorial ANOVA analysis with INTERFACE and LAYOUT as factors. The analysis shows an effect of INTERFACE ($F_{1,44} = 251.59$, $p < 0.001$), partially supporting H3, LAYOUT ($F_{1,44} = 27.54$, $p < 0.001$) and no effect of INTERFACE × LAYOUT ($F_{1,44} = 3.255$, $p > 0.05$). For *Y-Axis Error* we perform a two-way factorial ANOVA analysis with INTERFACE and LAYOUT as factors. The analysis shows an effect of INTERFACE ($F_{1,44} = 11.29$, $p < 0.005$), partially supporting H3, but no effect of LAYOUT and INTERFACE × LAYOUT (all $p > 0.1$).

We did not find any effect of INTERFACE on answer time, self-confidence, perceived workload and perceived ease of gaze interpretation (all $p > 0.1$). No learning effect was found in term of gaze interpretation accuracy, X and

Y-axis error. Figure 7 visualizes the X and Y error distances at each target by
INTERFACE and LAYOUT. Figure 6(b, c) shows X and Y error distance in each
INTERFACE × LAYOUT condition.

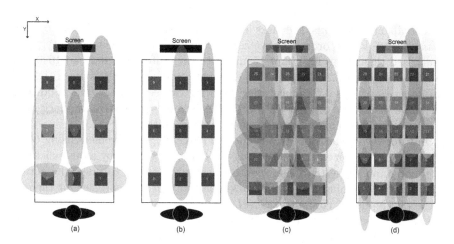

Fig. 7. X and Y-axis error visualization at each target in Study 2, in (a) 3 × 3 layout using *ConvVC*, (b) 3 × 3 layout using *GazeLens*, (c) 5 × 5 layout using *ConvVC*, (d) 5 × 5 layout using *GazeLens*. Zero error is shown by an ellipse-axis equal to the target size.

6   Early User Feedback of GazeLens

The two previous experiments evaluated *GazeLens* on the hub side. We gather in
a last study early user feedback on its usability from the satellite worker's perspective. We recruited five pairs of participants (8 male, 2 female, aged from 23
to 50, median 31) to solve a remote collaborative task. Participants had various
backgrounds from computer science, software engineering, and social sciences.
Participants in each pair knew each other well. Designing an experimental collaborative task for hub-satellite collaboration involving physical artifacts is complicated by the complex communication required between coworkers and artifacts.
To our knowledge, there is still no standardized experimental task for this. As we
focus on gathering feedback on the satellite's side, for simplicity, we chose a standard task commonly used when investigating remote collaboration on physical
tasks: solving a puzzle by arranging a set of pieces into a predefined picture.

Each pair of participants consisted of a *worker* on the hub side and an *instructor* on the satellite side. The *worker* had all the puzzle pieces on the hub table,
but did not know the solution. The *instructor* knew the solution and communicated with the worker via audio and video to guide them selecting and arranging
the pieces. This task can trigger movements of the hub worker, their hands, and

the artifacts on and around the table, which could be perceived differently by the satellite worker on different video conferencing interfaces. Each puzzle consists of 16 rectangular pieces, chosen so that they were hard to be verbally described by color and visual patterns. We used the same laboratory setup as in Study 1 and 2.

Participants performed the tasks in both interfaces on the satellite side, *Gaze-Lens* and *ConvVC*, in order to have comparative views on their usability. They familiarized themselves for about 15 min with each interface, and had 10 min to solve the task in each condition. Two different 50 cm × 80 cm puzzles with comparable levels of visual difficulty were used for two conditions. The conditions and puzzle tasks were counter-balanced. We gathered qualitative feedback in an interview after participants went through both conditions.

Only one *instructors* our of four reported perceiving inconvenient using *Gaze-Lens* lenses. He reported that activating the lens on the table by mouse click was quite tiring and suggested using mouse wheel scroll events to make the activation similar to zooming. All *instructors* reported that it was easier for them to see the puzzle pieces' content in *GazeLens*, as those at the far edge of the table were hard to see in *ConvVC*, where they sometimes had to ask the performer to hold and show it to the camera. One *instructor*, who often uses Skype for hub-satellite meetings, really liked the concept of people around the table in a panoramic video connected via a virtual lens. He could imagine that it could help him clearly see everyone while knowing where they are sitting around the table and what they are doing on the table during a meeting. Besides that, two *instructors* reported that when the virtual lens was on the top of *GazeLens'* table area it might obscure *workers'* hand gestures.

7   Discussion

7.1   GazeLens Improves Differentiating Gaze Towards People vs. Artifacts

Study 1 showed that *GazeLens* improves the satellite worker's gaze interpretation accuracy toward hub coworkers and, in particular, they are able to distinguish with more than 85% accuracy if the satellite worker is gazing towards them or towards the physical artifacts on the table. This is due to the position of the panoramic video of hub coworkers' at the top of the satellite interface, close to the camera, and the position of the artifact overview at the bottom of the interface. To further improve this, we could explore increasing the gap between these two views to obtain a larger, more distinguishable, difference in gaze direction.

7.2   GazeLens Improves Gaze Interpretation Accuracy

Study 2 showed that *GazeLens* improved gaze interpretation accuracy for table artifacts not only in sparse (3 × 3) but also dense (5 × 5) arrangements. This can be explained by how the entire laptop screen is used to make the satellite's worker's gaze better aligned with the hub artifacts as compared to the *ConvVC* condition, as stated by P10: *"To determine where the satellite worker was gazing, I could imagine a line of sight from his eyes to the table/person"*. We argue that in *ConvVC*, due to the perspective projection of the hub table, distances between objects at the far edge of the table appear too small, making gaze toward them indistinguishable. This was confirmed by participant comments about the satellite's gaze in *ConvVC*: *"It was hard compared to the other condition [*GazeLens*] because they just stared at the table and I had no clue which number was the exact one"* (P6); *"the differences between different gazes felt very small"* (P5) and *"They were looking more at the center"* (P9). In contrast to *ConvVC*, partic ipants perceived the satellite worker's gaze in the *GazeLens* condition as *"more obvious"*, *"clearer"* and *"easier to determine where they are looking"*.

Small between-object distances in *ConvVC* also caused negligible eye movements in the videos where the satellite worker gazes from the starting point to the target: *"They moved less and thus gave me fewer references to be able to get a picture of what they were looking at"*; *"Eye movements were very small and the angles were hard to calculate in my head"* and *"The eyes did not move and I got confused"*. In contrast, participants perceived eye movement in *Gaze-Lens* condition as *"clearer"*, *"easy to distinguish from side to side"*, *"enough to follow"*, *"sometimes added with head movements, easier to determine"*.

When investigating X-Axis and Y-Axis Error, it was not surprising that horizontal gaze changes were perceived more accurately than vertical ones, as people are more sensitive to horizontal gaze changes, especially when the gaze is below the satellite's camera [10]. Furthermore, laptops have landscape screens, leaving less vertical space to position the lens than in the horizontal direction-making gaze differences more distinguishable in the horizontal orientation. In future work, we want to explore how to improve gaze perception in the vertical dimension.

7.3   Limitations and Future Work

Although most of the participants reported that the satellite worker's gaze was clear and easy to interpret with *GazeLens*, two participants in Study 1 reported that they did not feel the satellite worker was looking at any markers in particular, and their answers were just an approximation based on gaze. This can be explained by the fact that at that moment *GazeLens* did not precisely calculate the screen mapping based on the actual size of the table and the distance from the coworkers to the hub table. Achieving geometrically corrected gaze in video communication is almost impossible, as it depends on several parameters that cannot all be easily acquired in real-life hub-satellite scenarios, such as camera focal length, camera position, video size, camera-scene, and screen-viewer distance. *GazeLens'* mapping strategy is effective at improving gaze interpretation and yet simple enough to be deployed in realistic scenarios. In future, we will consider replacing the ceiling-mounted camera with a depth-sensing camera, which can acquire the table size and coworkers's distance from the table in order to improve mapping. We are also interested to further study *GazeLens* with different hub table shapes, sizes and layouts, using the current screen mapping strategy and others. Likewise, due to the emerging use of tablets for work purposes, it would be valuable to study *GazeLens* on tablet devices both in portrait and landscape display mode.

In our last study, participants perceived *GazeLens* positively, without usability issues. Still, we plan to improve the system by making the virtual lens over the table less occlusive in the future setup using a depth-sensing camera, by detecting the presence of hub workers' hand gestures and dynamically adjusting the opacity of the lens. Besides that, we plan to study how expertise might influence time needed to learn *GazeLens*, as we think that probably this is not enough to make an impact on the hub side, which is unaware of what is shown on the satellite's interface. Lastly, we plan to extended *GazeLens* to support multiple satellites, for instance by representing each one by a screen placed around the hub table and the corresponding video feeds adjusted accordingly (e.g. re-segment panoramic video, change orientation of the table's video).

8 Conclusion

While conventional hub-satellite collaboration typically employs video conferencing, it is difficult for hub coworkers to interpret the satellite worker's gaze. Previous work supporting gaze between remote workers has not addressed shared physical artifacts used in collaboration, and support for conveying gaze in remote collaboration with asymmetric setups is still limited. We designed *GazeLens*, a novel interaction technique supporting gaze interpretation that guides the attention of the satellite worker by means of virtual lenses focusing on either hub coworkers or artifacts. In our first study, we showed that *GazeLens* significantly improves gaze interpretation over a conventional video conferencing system; and also that it improves hub coworkers' ability to differentiate the satellite's gaze toward themselves or artifacts on the table. In our second study, we found that *GazeLens* improves hub coworkers' interpretation accuracy for gaze toward objects on the table, for both sparse and dense arrangements of artifacts. Early user feedback informed us about the advantages and potential drawbacks of *GazeLens*' usability. *GazeLens* shows that the satellite worker's laptop screen can be fully leveraged to guide their attention and help hub coworkers more accurately interpret their gaze.

References

1. Vertegaal, R.: The GAZE groupware system: mediating joint attention in multi-party communication and collaboration. In: Proceedings of the SIGCHI Conference on Human Factors in Computing Systems, CHI 1999, pp. 294–301. ACM, New York (1999)
2. Akkil, D., James, J.M., Isokoski, P., Kangas, J.: GazeTorch: enabling gaze awareness in collaborative physical tasks. In: Proceedings of the 2016 CHI Conference Extended Abstracts on Human Factors in Computing Systems, CHI EA 2016, pp. 1151–1158. ACM, New York (2016)

3. Vertegaal, R., van der Veer, G., Vons, H.: Effects of gaze on multiparty mediated communication. In: Proceedings of Graphics Interface 2000, pp. 95–102. ACM, New York (2010)

4. Vertegaal, R., Slagter, R., Van der Veer, G., Nijholt, A.: Eye gaze patterns in conversations: there is more to conversational agents than meets the eyes. In: Proceedings of the SIGCHI Conference on Human Factors in Computing Systems, CHI 2001, pp. 301–308. ACM, New York (2001)

5. Higuch, K., Yonetani, R., Sato, Y.: Can eye help you? Effects of visualizing eye fixations on remote collaboration scenarios for physical tasks. In: Proceedings of the 2016 CHI Conference on Human Factors in Computing Systems, CHI 2016, pp. 5180–5190. ACM, New York (2016)

6. Xu, B., Ellis, J., Erickson, T.: Attention from afar: simulating the gazes of remote participants in hybrid meetings. In: Proceedings of the 2017 Conference on Designing Interactive Systems, DIS 2017, pp. 101–113. ACM, New York (2017)

7. Sellen, A., Buxton, B., Arnott, J.: Using spatial cues to improve videoconferencing. In: Proceedings of the SIGCHI Conference on Human Factors in Computing Systems, CHI 1992, pp. 651–652. ACM, New York (1992)

8. Nguyen, D., Canny, J.: MultiView: spatially faithful group video conferencing. In: Proceedings of the SIGCHI Conference on Human Factors in Computing Systems, CHI 2005, pp. 799–808. ACM, New York (2005)

9. Pan, Y., Steed, A.: A gaze-preserving situated multiview telepresence system. In: Proceedings of the SIGCHI Conference on Human Factors in Computing Systems, CHI 2014, pp. 2173–2176. ACM, New York (2014)

10. Chen, M.: Leveraging the asymmetric sensitivity of eye contact for videoconferencing. In: Proceedings of the SIGCHI Conference on Human Factors in Computing Systems, CHI 2002, pp. 49–56. ACM, New York (2002)

11. Ishii, H., Kobayashi, M.: ClearBoard: a seamless medium for shared drawing and conversation with eye contact. In: Proceedings of the SIGCHI Conference on Human Factors in Computing Systems, CHI 1992, pp. 525–532. ACM, New York (1992)

12. Hauber, J., Regenbrecht, H., Billinghurst, M., Cockburn, A.: Spatiality in video-conferencing: trade-offs between efficiency and social presence. In: Proceedings of the 2006 20th Anniversary Conference on Computer Supported Cooperative Work, CSCW 2006, pp. 413–422. ACM, New York (2006)

13. Otsuka, K.: MMSpace: kinetically-augmented telepresence for small group-to-group conversations. In: Proceedings of 2016 IEEE Virtual Reality (VR). IEEE (2016)

14. Küchler, M., Kunz, A.: Holoport-a device for simultaneous video and data conferencing featuring gaze awareness. In: Proceedings of Virtual Reality Conference 2006, pp. 81–88. IEEE (2006)

15. Jones, A., et al.: Achieving eye contact in a one-to-many 3D video teleconferencing system. ACM Trans. Graph. (TOG) 28(3) (2009)

16. Gotsch, D., Zhang, X., Meeritt, T., Vertegaal, R.: TeleHuman2: a cylindrical light field teleconferencing system for life-size 3D human telepresence. In: Proceedings of the 2018 CHI Conference on Human Factors in Computing Systems, CHI 2018, p. 552. ACM, New York (2018)

17. Otsuki, M., Kawano, T., Maruyama, K., Kuzuoka, H., Suzuki, Y.: ThirdEye: simple add-on display to represent remote participant's gaze direction in video communication. In: Proceedings of the 2017 CHI Conference on Human Factors in Computing Systems, CHI 2017, pp. 5307–5312. ACM, New York (2017)

18. Vertegaal, R., Weevers, I., Sohn, C., Cheung, C.: GAZE-2: conveying eye contact in group video conferencing using eye-controlled camera direction. In: Proceedings of the SIGCHI Conference on Human Factors in Computing Systems, CHI 2003, pp. 521–528. ACM, New York (2003)

19. Norris, J., Schnädelbach, H., Qiu, G.: CamBlend: an object focused collaboration tool. In: Proceedings of the SIGCHI Conference on Human Factors in Computing Systems, CHI 2012, pp. 627–636. ACM, New York (2012)

20. Bailey, R., McNamara, A., Sudarsanam, N., Grimm, C.: Subtle gaze direction. ACM Trans. Graph. (TOG) 28(4) (2009)

21. Hata, H., Koike, H., Sato, Y.: Visual guidance with unnoticed blur effect. In: Proceedings of the International Working Conference on Advanced Visual Interfaces, AVI 2016, pp. 28–35. ACM, New York (2016)

22. Stokes, R.: Human factors and appearance design considerations of the Mod II PICTUREPHONE station set. ACM Trans. Graph. (TOG) 17(2), 318 (1969)

23. Average human sitting posture dimensions required in interior design. https://gharpedia.com/average-human-sitting-posture-dimensions-required-in-interior-design/

24. Gemmell, J., Toyama, K., Zitnick, C.L., Kang, T., Seitz, S.: Gaze awareness for video-conferencing: a software approach. IEEE MultiMedia 7(4), 26–35 (2000)

25. Giger, D., Bazin, J.-C., Kuster, C., Popa, T., Gross, M.: Gaze correction with a single webcam. In: 2014 IEEE International Conference on Multimedia and Expo (ICME). IEEE (2014)

26. Venolia, G., et al.: Embodied social proxy: mediating interpersonal connection in hub-and-satellite teams. In: Proceedings of the SIGCHI Conference on Human Factors in Computing Systems, CHI 2010, pp. 1049–1058. ACM, New York (2010)

27. Kendon, A.: Some functions of gaze-direction in social interaction. Acta Psychologica 26, 22–63 (1967)

28. Brennan, S.E., Chen, X., Dickinson, C.A., Neider, M.B., Zelinsky, G.J.: Coordinating cognition: the costs and benefits of shared gaze during collaborative search. Cognition 106(3), 1465–1477 (2008)

29. Akkil, D., Isokoski, P.: I see what you see: gaze awareness in mobile video collaboration. In: Proceedings of the 2018 ACM Symposium on Eye Tracking Research & Applications, ETRA 2018, p. 32. ACM, New York (2018)

30. Yao, N., Brewer, J., D'Angelo, S., Horn, M., Gergle, D.: Visualizing gaze information from multiple students to support remote instruction. In: Extended Abstracts of the 2018 CHI Conference on Human Factors in Computing Systems, CHI 2018, p. LBW051. ACM, New York (2018)

31. Avellino, I., Fleury, C., Beaudouin-Lafon, M.: Accuracy of deictic gestures to support telepresence on wall-sized displays. In: Proceedings of the 33rd Annual ACM Conference on Human Factors in Computing Systems, pp. 2393–2396. ACM, New York (2015)

32. Monk, A.F., Gale, C.: A look is worth a thousand words: full gaze awareness in video-mediated conversation. Discourse Process. 33(4), 257–278 (2002)

33. Hart, S.G., Staveland, L.E: Development of NASA-TLX (task load index): results of empirical and theoretical research. Adv. Psychol. 52, 139–183 (1998)

34. Cisco TelePresence MX Series. https://www.cisco.com/c/en/us/products/collaboration-endpoints/telepresence-mx-series/index.html. Accessed 26 Jan 2019

35. RealPresence Group Series. http://www.polycom.com/products-services/hd-telepresence-video-conferencing/realpresence-room/realpresence-group-series.html. Accessed 26 Jan 2019

36. Cisco CTS-SX80-IPST60-K9 TelePresence (CTS-SX80-IPST60-K9). https://www.bechtle.com/ch-en/shop/cisco-cts-sx80-ipst60-k9-telepresence-896450-40-p. Accessed 26 Jan 2019

37. Enterprise Video Conference. http://www.avsolutions.com/enterprise-video-conference. Accessed 26 Jan 2019

38. Caine, K.: Local standards for sample size at CHI. In: Proceedings of the 2016 CHI Conference on Human Factors in Computing Systems, pp. 981–992. ACM, New York (2016)

Influences of Mixed Reality and Human Cognition on Picture Passwords: An Eye Tracking Study

Christos Fidas[1], Marios Belk[2,3]([✉]), George Hadjidemetriou[3], and Andreas Pitsillides[3]

[1] Department of Cultural Heritage Management and New Technologies, University of Patras, Patras, Greece
fidas@upatras.gr
[2] School of Sciences, University of Central Lancashire, Cyprus Campus, Larnaca, Cyprus
mbelk1@uclan.ac.uk
[3] Department of Computer Science, University of Cyprus, Nicosia, Cyprus
{ghadjil2, andreas.pitsillides}@cs.ucy.ac.cy

Abstract. Recent research revealed that individual cognitive differences affect visual behavior and task performance of picture passwords within conventional interaction realms such as desktops and tablets. Bearing in mind that mixed reality environments necessitate from end-users to perceive, process and comprehend visually-enriched content, this paper further investigates whether this new interaction realm amplifies existing observed effects of individual cognitive differences towards user interactions in picture passwords. For this purpose, we conducted a comparative eye tracking study ($N = 50$) in which users performed a picture password composition task within a conventional interaction context *vs.* a mixed reality context. For interpreting the derived results, we adopted an accredited human cognition theory that highlights cognitive differences in visual perception and search. Analysis of results revealed that new technology realms like mixed reality extend and, in some cases, amplify the effect of human cognitive differences towards users' visual and interaction behavior in picture passwords. Findings can be of value for improving future implementations of picture passwords by considering human cognitive differences as a personalization factor for the design of user-adaptive graphical passwords in mixed reality.

Keywords: Picture passwords · Human cognition · Mixed reality · Eye tracking · Visual behavior · Usability · Security

1 Introduction

Mixed reality technologies are being continuously embraced by researchers and practitioners for developing immersive applications and services which favor multimodal human computer interaction techniques like touch-, hand gesture- or gaze-based. Such technology advancements open unprecedented opportunities for designing new

© IFIP International Federation for Information Processing 2019
Published by Springer Nature Switzerland AG 2019
D. Lamas et al. (Eds.): INTERACT 2019, LNCS 11747, pp. 304–313, 2019.
https://doi.org/10.1007/978-3-030-29384-0_19

visually enriched interaction experiences for end-users in a variety of application domains that include healthcare, military training, aviation, interactive product management, remote working, games, etc. [29–31].

A cornerstone user activity in mixed reality environments is related to *user authentication*. User authentication is an act which aims at verifying that a user is who she claims to be and therefore has eligible rights to access sensitive information and services. Since mixed reality contexts introduce new challenges and opportunities for designing visually enriched user experiences, researchers have explored existing and alternative user authentication schemes (*e.g.*, pin, passwords, patterns, graphical) in mixed and virtual reality contexts, aiming to gain new knowledge on the interplay between human behavior, usability, and security in such schemes [1–5].

In this context, picture passwords, which require users to draw secret gestures on a background image to unlock a device or application, have been introduced as viable mixed reality user authentication schemes since they leverage on hand gesture interaction modalities. Figure 1 depicts Microsoft's Picture Gesture Authentication (PGA), a widely deployed picture password scheme that has been introduced in Windows 8™ (and further deployed in Windows 10™) as a promising alternative login experience to text-based passwords. Picture passwords necessitate from humans to perform visual search and visual memory processing tasks, aiming to view, recognize and recall graphical information. Given that individuals differ in the way they perceive and process visual information [6–8], researchers have investigated the effects of human cognitive differences towards human behavior, experience and security of graphical passwords within conventional environments, such as desktop and mobile [9–12].

Fig. 1. Example of Microsoft Windows 10 PGA on a traditional desktop computer [18]. Users are required to draw three gestures on a background image to create their graphical password.

Research Motivation. Given the increased adoption of mixed reality technologies in a variety of application domains [13], we are motivated in investigating effects of human cognitive differences and mixed reality technology towards user's interaction and visual behavior within graphical password composition tasks. Such new knowledge would allow application designers to draw conclusions on the interplay between human cognitive and design factors of graphical passwords within mixed reality, and apply this knowledge for the provision of human cognitive-centered password experiences that are best-fit to each user's cognitive characteristics, and consequently assist visual information search and processing.

For doing so, we adopted an accredited human cognition theory and conducted a between-subjects eye tracking study ($N = 50$) in which users performed a picture password composition task that was seamlessly deployed in mixed reality and traditional desktop contexts. To the best of our knowledge, this is amongst the first works which investigate the effects of human cognition and mixed reality picture password composition towards users' interaction and visual behavior.

2 Human Cognition Theory

We adopted Witkin's field dependence-independence theory (FD-I) [9, 14, 15] which suggests that humans have different habitual approaches, according to contextual and environmental conditions, in retrieving, recalling, processing and storing graphical information [8]. Accordingly, the theory distinguishes individuals as being field dependent and field independent. *Field dependent (FD)* individuals view the perceptual field as a whole, they are not attentive to detail, and not efficient and effective in situations where they are required to extract relevant information from a complex whole. *Field independent (FI)* individuals view the information presented by their visual field as a collection of parts and tend to experience items as discrete from their backgrounds. With regards to visual search abilities, studies have shown that FIs are more efficient in visual search tasks than FDs since they are more successful in dis-embedding and isolating important information from a complex whole [14, 15].

3 Method of Study

3.1 Null Hypotheses

H_{01}. There is no interaction effect between FD-I differences and the technological context (desktop *vs.* mixed reality) towards time needed to create a picture password; *by investigating this research question we examine the effects of mixed reality's multimodal interaction capabilities towards task efficiency of FD-I users.*

H_{02}. There is no interaction effect between FD-I differences and the technological context (desktop *vs.* mixed reality) towards users' visual behavior; *by investigating this research question we examine the effects of mixed reality's enriched visual content presentation capabilities towards gaze behavior of FD-I users.*

H_{03}. There is no correlation between the time to create a picture password and visual behavior; *by investigating this research question we examine the interdependencies between FD-I users' interaction and visual behavior in mixed reality's environments.*

3.2   Research Instruments

Cognitive Factor Elicitation. Users' FD-I was measured through the Group Embedded Figures Test (GEFT) [16] which is a widely accredited and validated paper-and-pencil test [14, 15]. The test measures the user's ability to find common geometric shapes in a larger design. The GEFT consists of 25 items; 7 are used for practice, 18 are used for assessment. In each item, a simple geometric figure is hidden within a complex pattern, and participants are required to identify the simple figure by drawing it with a pencil over the complex figure. Based on a widely-applied cut-off score [14, 15], participants that solve 11 items and less are FD, while 12 items and above are FI.

Graphical Password Scheme. We developed a picture password mechanism, coined HoloPass, following guidelines of Microsoft Windows 10™ Picture Gesture Authentication (PGA) [17] in which users draw passwords on a background image that acts as a cue (Fig. 2-left). Implementation details and suitability of HoloPass is reported in [18]. Three gestures were implemented, *i.e.*, *dot, line, circle* which can be achieved through *hand-based gestures* or *clicker-based gestures* (Fig. 2-right). For each gesture, the following data are stored: for dots, the coordinates of the point, for lines the coordinates of the starting and ending point, and for circles the coordinates of the point's center, radius and direction.

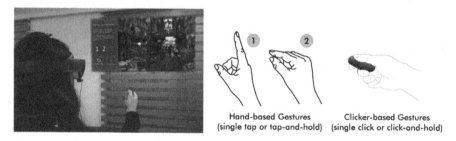

Fig. 2. A user interacting with HoloPass that resembles PGA in mixed reality (left); and types of user input through hand gestures or using the HoloLens clicker (right) [18].

Interaction Devices. The picture password scheme was deployed on a conventional desktop computer and a mixed reality device. The desktop computer was a typical PC, with Intel core i7, 8 GB RAM, 21-in. monitor, standard keyboard/mouse. For mixed reality we used Microsoft HoloLens which is a popular and widely adopted head mounted display for mixed reality, and features see-through holographic lenses. To measure the users' visual behavior and fixations, we have used and integrated Pupil Labs' eye tracker [19] in HoloLens using Pupil Labs' Binocular Add-on.

3.3   Sampling and Procedure

A total of 50 individuals (10 females) participated in the study, ranging in age from 18 to 40 ($m = 24.46$; $sd = 3.58$). Based on their scores on the GEFT; 24 participants

(48%) were FD; 26 participants (52%) were FI. No participant was familiar with picture passwords and all had no or limited prior experience with mixed reality devices. The study involved the following steps: *(i)* participants were informed that the collected data would be stored anonymously for research purposes, and they signed a consent form; *(ii)* they were familiarized with the picture password and equipment, following an eye-calibration process; *(iii)* participants then created a picture password to unlock a real service in order to increase ecological validity; and finally *(iv)* they were asked to log in to ensure that the passwords were not created at random.

3.4   Data Metrics

For interaction behavior we measured time required to create the picture password which started as soon the user was shown with the task until the user successfully completed the password creation. For visual behavior we used the following measures: *(i)* fixation count and duration; and *(ii)* transition entropy [25] between Areas of Interests (AOIs) which measures the lack of order aiming to capture eye movement variability.

4   Analysis of Results

In the analysis that follows, data are mean ± standard error. Residual analysis was performed, outliers were assessed by inspection of a boxplot, normality was assessed using Shapiro-Wilk's normality test for each cell of the design and homogeneity of variances was assessed by Levene's test. There were no outliers, residuals were normally distributed and there was homogeneity of variances.

4.1   Password Creation Time Differences

To investigate H_{01}, we ran a two-way ANOVA to examine the effects of FD-I and interaction context on graphical password creation time (Fig. 3-left). There was a significant effect of FD-I on the time to create the picture password in both interaction context, $F(1, 50) = 4.846$, $p = .033$, *partial* $\eta^2 = .095$. FD users spent significantly more time to create a picture password than FI users, in both interaction contexts (FD-Desktop: 37.25 ± 19.34; FD-HoloLens: 29.16 ± 14.29; FI-Desktop: 26.28 ± 13.78; FI-HoloLens: 17.87 ± 12.22). An analysis across groups (FD and FI) revealed that mixed reality interactions were completed faster in both groups compared to desktop contexts.

4.2   Visual Behavior Differences

To investigate H_{02}, a two-way MANOVA was run with two independent variables (FD-I and interaction context) and two dependent variables (fixation count and mean fixation duration). The combined fixation metrics were used to measure visual behavior. The interaction effect between FD-I and interaction context on the combined dependent variables was not statistically significant, $F(2, 45) = .745$, $p = .48$,

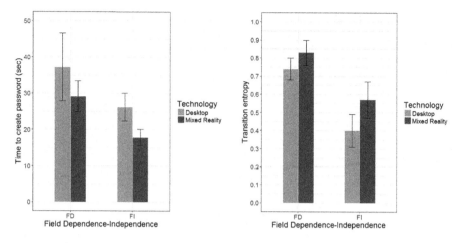

Fig. 3. Time to create (left) and transition entropy (right) per user group.

Wilks' Λ = .968, *partial η^2* = .032. There was a statistically significant main effect of interaction context on the combined dependent variables, $F(2, 45)$ = 13.302, $p <$ .001, *Wilks' Λ* = .628, *partial η^2* = .372. Follow up univariate two-way ANOVAs were run, and the main effect of intervention considered. There was a statistically significant main effect of interaction context for fixation duration, $F(1, 50)$ = 24.640, $p <$ .001, *partial η^2* = .349, but not for fixation count, $F(1, 50)$ = .722, $p =$ .4, *partial η^2* = .015. As such, Tukey pairwise comparisons were run for the differences in mean fixation duration between interaction contexts. The marginal means for fixation duration were 981.38 $\pm$ 35.42 for desktop interactions, and 732.7 $\pm$ 35.42 for mixed reality inter-actions. For FD users, there was a statistically significant mean difference between the desktop-based fixation duration and the mixed reality fixation duration of −230.73 (95% CI, −376.16 to 85.3), $p =$ .003, while for FI users the difference was −266.61 (95% CI, 406.34 to 126.89), $p <$ .001.

We further ran a two-way ANOVA to examine the effects of FD-I and interaction context on transition entropy (Fig. 3-right). There was a significant effect of FD-I on transition entropy, $F(1, 50)$ = 27.089, $p <$ .001, *partial η^2* = .371. FD users had sig-nificantly higher transition entropy than FI users since they had higher randomness and variability in their visual behavior. There was also a significant effect of interaction context on transition entropy, $F(1, 50)$ = 5.259, $p =$ .027, *partial η^2* = .102 with mixed reality interaction triggering higher transition entropies than conventional interaction contexts.

4.3 Correlation Between Time to Create a Picture Password and Visual Behavior

To investigate H_{03}, we performed a Pearson's Product Moment correlation test, between time to create the password and transition entropy (Fig. 4). The analysis revealed a strong positive correlation between creation time and transition entropy for desktop interactions ($r =$ .505, $p =$ .01) as well as for mixed reality interactions

($r = .438$, $p = .028$). The higher the transition entropy, the more disordered the visual behavior is. These results explain the previous analyses, since FD users spent significantly more time and had higher transition entropies than FI users.

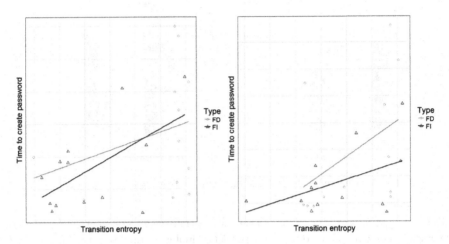

Fig. 4. Scatter-plots depicting creation time of passwords and transition entropy for desktop interactions (left) and mixed reality interactions (right).

5   Interpretation of Results

Interpretation with Regards to H_{01}. Mixed reality scaffolded more efficient graphical password task execution for both user groups (FD and FI) compared with the desktop context. A between cognitive factor analysis revealed that within mixed reality, FI users were significantly faster than FD users. This can be explained due to FI users' positive adaptation and independence in regards with contextual and field changes (desktop *vs.* mixed reality). This finding suggests that the device, and eventually the field change, towards mixed reality interactions (context-wise and interaction-wise) was adopted more efficiently and effectively by FI users compared to FD users. This further supports previous findings which state that FD users depend on their surrounding field whereas FI users are not significantly influenced by their surrounding field and context of use [24, 26, 27]. Furthermore, this finding can also be explained by the fact that FD users follow a more holistic and exploratory approach during visual search compared to FI users that primarily focus on specific focal points of an image during interaction. Based on qualitative feedback, the increased amount of time for FDs did not negatively affect their interaction experience.

"*I was excited to draw a password on an image. At first, I spent some time to view the whole content and then I made my selections*" ~ *P20 - FD individual*

"*It is much easier to draw my password than using the virtual keyboard. I created my password in no time by selecting the people in the image*" ~ *P24 - FI individual*

Interpretation with Regards to H_{02}. The interaction context has a main effect on the fixation duration during picture password composition. Users in the mixed reality interaction context fixated longer on areas of the image than users during desktop-based interactions. With regards to transition entropy, results revealed significant differences among FD and FI users. Specifically, FD users had significantly higher transition entropies (higher randomness in eye movements) compared to FI users. Hence, these observable differences in eye gaze behavior among FD and FI users allows to better explain the previous finding related to task completion efficiency.

"The most difficult part was finding where to draw the gestures, but I believe that adds up to the security of the password" ∼ *P15 - FD individual*

"It is a more creative way to create a password and escapes the dullness of the keyboard" ∼ *P30 - FI individual*

Interpretation with Regards to H_{03}. A strong positive correlation between password creation time and transition entropy was revealed which further supports Finding 2 and Finding 3. The higher the transition entropy, the more disordered the visual behavior is. These results explain the previous analyses, since FD users spent significantly more time and hence triggered higher transition entropies compared to FI users.

"I checked out the whole image to see all the items. I tried to avoid objects that were obvious for someone to guess my password so I tried to find less obvious objects to select" ∼ *P33 - FD individual*

"I focused on specific objects and made my selections" ∼ *P42 - FI individual*

6   Conclusions

This paper revealed underlying effects between individual cognitive differences and mixed reality interaction realms towards users' eye gaze behavior and task execution during picture password composition tasks. Analysis of eye-tracking data further validated that user's individual differences of visual information perception and processing are reflected by their eye gaze behavior in both conventional and mixed reality interaction realms, but with a stronger effect within mixed reality interaction contexts. As such, the enriched visual content presentation of mixed reality environments has a rather catalyst effect, in terms of visual content exploration and task execution, for FD users than FI users. A comparative analysis between the conventional and mixed reality interaction contexts revealed that the technology shift towards a visually enriched content presentation triggered FD users to explore longer and comprehensively the content. Hence, FD users spent more time and produced longer fixation durations and transition entropies within mixed reality environments when compared to FI users.

Bearing in mind that transition entropies of users have been correlated with security strength of graphical passwords [9, 28] such findings can be of value for mixed reality researchers and experience designers for considering: *(a)* users eye gaze patterns as early predictors of password security strength [28]; and *(b)* human cognitive characteristics as important design factors in picture password schemes [9, 24, 34]. We anticipate that this work will inspire similar research endeavors (*e.g.*, see the approaches discussed in [9, 10, 23, 24, 32, 33] on how human factors can be incorporated in personalized user authentication schemes) aiming to incorporate novel authentication schemes based on eye tracking methods and users' eye gaze patterns.

Acknowledgements. This research has been partially supported by EU Horizon 2020 Grant 826278 "Securing Medical Data in Smart Patient-Centric Healthcare Systems" (Serums). We thank all participants for their time and valuable comments provided during the studies.

References

1. Yu, Z., Liang, H.N., Fleming, C., Man, K.L.: An exploration of usable authentication mechanisms for virtual reality systems. In: IEEE APCCAS 2016, pp. 458–460. IEEE (2016)
2. Roesner, F., Kohno, T., Molnar, D.: Security and privacy for augmented reality systems. Commun. ACM **57**(4), 88–96 (2014)
3. George, C., et al.: Seamless and secure VR: adapting and evaluating established authentication systems for virtual reality. In: USEC 2017 (2017)
4. Yadav, D.K., Ionascu, B., Krishna Ongole, S.V., Roy, A., Memon, N.: Design and analysis of shoulder surfing resistant PIN based authentication mechanisms on Google glass. In: Brenner, M., Christin, N., Johnson, B., Rohloff, K. (eds.) FC 2015. LNCS, vol. 8976, pp. 281–297. Springer, Heidelberg (2015). https://doi.org/10.1007/978-3-662-48051-9_21
5. Schneegaß, S., Oualil, Y., Bulling, A.: SkullConduct: biometric user identification on eyewear computers using bone conduction through the skull. In: CHI 2016, pp. 1379–1384. ACM (2016)
6. Mayer, R.E., Massa, L.J.: Three facets of visual and verbal learners: cognitive ability, cognitive style, and learning preference. J. Educ. Psychol. **95**(4), 833–846 (2003)
7. Riding, R., Cheema, I.: Cognitive styles – an overview and integration. Educ. Psychol. **11**(3–4), 193–215 (1991)
8. Witkin, H.A., Moore, C.A., Goodenough, D.R., Cox, P.W.: Field-dependent and field-independent cognitive styles and their educational implications. Res. Bull. Ser. **1975**(2), 1–64 (1975)
9. Katsini, C., Fidas, C., Raptis, G., Belk, M., Samaras, G., Avouris, N.: Influences of human cognition and visual behavior on password security during picture password composition. In: ACM SIGCHI Human Factors in Computing Systems (CHI 2018), paper 87. ACM (2018)
10. Belk, M., Fidas, C., Katsini, C., Avouris, N., Samaras, G.: Effects of human cognitive differences on interaction and visual behavior in graphical user authentication. In: Bernhaupt, R., Dalvi, G., Joshi, A., K. Balkrishan, D., O'Neill, J., Winckler, M. (eds.) INTERACT 2017, Part III. LNCS, vol. 10515, pp. 287–296. Springer, Cham (2017). https://doi.org/10.1007/978-3-319-67687-6_19
11. Belk, M., Germanakos, P., Fidas, C., Samaras, G.: A personalization method based on human factors for improving usability of user authentication tasks. In: Dimitrova, V., Kuflik, T., Chin, D., Ricci, F., Dolog, P., Houben, G.-J. (eds.) UMAP 2014. LNCS, vol. 8538, pp. 13–24. Springer, Cham (2014). https://doi.org/10.1007/978-3-319-08786-3_2
12. Raptis, G., Fidas, C.A., Avouris, N.: Effects of mixed-reality on players' behaviour and immersion in a cultural tourism game: a cognitive processing perspective. Int. J. Hum. Comput. Stud. **114**, 69–79 (2018)
13. Bellini, H., Chen, W., Sugiyama, M., Shin, M., Alam, S., Takayama, D.: Virtual & augmented reality: understanding the race for the next computing platform. Technical report. The Goldman Sachs Group (2016)

14. Angeli, C., Valanides, N., Kirschner, P.: Field dependence-independence and instructional-design effects on learners' performance with a computer-modeling tool. Comput. Hum. Behav. **25**(6), 1355–1366 (2009)
15. Hong, J., Hwang, M., Tam, K., Lai, Y., Liu, L.: Effects of cognitive style on digital jigsaw puzzle performance: a GridWare analysis. Comput. Hum. Behav. **28**(3), 920–928 (2012)
16. Oltman, P.K., Raskin, E., Witkin, H.A.: GEFT. Consulting Psychologists Press, Palo Alto (1971)
17. Johnson, J.J., et al.: Picture gesture authentication (2014). https://www.google.com/patents/US8910253
18. Hadjidemetriou, G., Belk, M., Fidas, C., Pitsillides, A.: Picture passwords in mixed reality: implementation and evaluation. In: ACM CHI 2019 Extended Abstracts. ACM Press (2019)
19. Kassner, M., Patera, W., Bulling, A.: Pupil: an open source platform for pervasive eye tracking and mobile gaze-based interaction. In: ACM UbiComp 2014, pp. 1151–1160 (2014)
20. Zhao, Z., Ahn, G., Seo, J., Hu, H.: On the security of picture gesture authentication. In: USENIX Security 2013, pp. 383–398. USENIX Association (2013)
21. Zhao, Z., Ahn, G., Hu, H.: Picture gesture authentication: empirical analysis, automated attacks, and scheme evaluation. ACM Trans. Inf. Syst. Secur. **17**(4), 37 (2015)
22. Biddle, R., Chiasson, S., van Oorschot, P.: Graphical passwords: learning from the first twelve years. ACM Comput. Surv. **44**(4), 41 (2012)
23. Liu, D., Dong, B., Gao, X., Wang, H.: Exploiting eye tracking for smartphone authentication. In: Malkin, T., Kolesnikov, V., Lewko, A.B., Polychronakis, M. (eds.) ACNS 2015. LNCS, vol. 9092, pp. 457–477. Springer, Cham (2015). https://doi.org/10.1007/978-3-319-28166-7_22
24. Belk, M., Fidas, C., Germanakos, P., Samaras, G.: The interplay between humans, technology and user authentication: a cognitive processing perspective. Comput. Hum. Behav. **76**, 184–200 (2017)
25. Krejtz, K., et al.: Gaze transition entropy. ACM Trans. Appl. Percept. **13**(1), 1–20 (2015)
26. Davis, J.K.: Educational implications of field dependence–independence, pp. 149–175 (1991)
27. Messick, S.: The Matter of Style: Manifestations of Personality in Cognition, Learning, and Teaching. Educational Testing Service, Princeton (1993)
28. Katsini, C., Raptis, G.E., Fidas, C., Avouris, N.: Towards gaze-based quantification of the security of graphical authentication schemes. In: ACM ETRA 2018. ACM Press (2018)
29. Bogle, A.: ebay launches a world-first virtual reality department store (2016). https://mashable.com/2016/05/18/ebay-virtual-reality-shopping
30. Medenica, Z, Kun, L., Paek, T., Palinko, O.: Augmented reality vs. street views: a driving simulator study comparing two emerging navigation aids. In: MobileHCI 2011, pp. 265–274 (2011)
31. Kim, S., Dey, A.K.: Simulated augmented reality windshield display as a cognitive mapping aid for elder driver navigation. In: ACM CHI 2009, pp. 133–142 (2009)
32. Constantinides, A., Belk, M., Fidas, C., Samaras, G.: On cultural-centered graphical passwords: Leveraging on users' cultural experiences for improving password memorability. In: ACM UMAP 2018, pp. 245–249. ACM Press (2018)
33. Belk, M., Pamboris, A., Fidas, C., Katsini, C., Avouris, N., Samaras, G.: Sweet-spotting security and usability for intelligent graphical authentication mechanisms. In: ACM WI 2017, pp. 252–259. ACM Press (2017)
34. Katsini, C., Fidas, C., Raptis, G., Belk, M., Samaras, G., Avouris, N.: Eye gaze-driven prediction of cognitive differences during graphical password composition. In: ACM IUI 2017, pp. 147–152. ACM Press (2018)

ScaffoMapping: Assisting Concept Mapping for Video Learners

Shan Zhang[1]([⊠])[iD], Xiaojun Meng[2], Can Liu[1,3], Shengdong Zhao[1],
Vibhor Sehgal[1], and Morten Fjeld[4]

[1] NUS-HCI Lab, National University of Singapore, Singapore 117418, Singapore
shan_zhang@u.nus.edu, zhaosd@comp.nus.edu.sg, sehgalvibhor@gmail.com
[2] Noah's Ark Lab, Huawei Technologies, Shenzhen, China
mengxiaojun2@huawei.com
[3] School of Creative Media, City University of Hong Kong, Kowloon, Hong Kong
canliu@cityu.edu.hk
[4] t2i Lab, Chalmers University of Technology, Gothenburg, Sweden
fjeld@chalmers.se

Abstract. Previous research has shown that having learners construct concept maps can bring better learning outcome. However, in video learning scenario, there is not sufficient support for learners to create concept maps from educational videos. Through a preliminary study, we identified two main difficulties video learners face in creating concept maps: navigation difficulty and learning difficulty. To help users to overcome such difficulties, we design scaffolds to assist learners in concept mapping. We present ScaffoMapping, a system aiming for scaffolded concept map creation on educational videos through automatic concept extraction and timestamp generation. Our study, which compares ScaffoMapping with the baseline approach, shows that (1) Learners can create higher quality concept maps with ScaffoMapping. (2) ScaffoMapping enables better learning outcomes in video learning scenario.

Keywords: Concept map · Scaffolding · Video learning

1 Introduction

Concept map is a well-established model of organizing and representing knowledge [27]. It has a graph structure where labeled nodes represent concepts and labeled links represent relationships among concepts. The process of constructing a concept map, which calls "concept mapping", has showed many benefits in facilitating meaningful learning [26]. Compared with rote learning, meaningful learning occurs when students relate new knowledge to their existing knowledge model [7]. Previous research has introduced concept mapping as an effective

Electronic supplementary material The online version of this chapter (https:// doi.org/10.1007/978-3-030-29384-0_20) contains supplementary material, which is available to authorized users.

© IFIP International Federation for Information Processing 2019
Published by Springer Nature Switzerland AG 2019
D. Lamas et al. (Eds.): INTERACT 2019, LNCS 11747, pp. 314–328, 2019.
https://doi.org/10.1007/978-3-030-29384-0_20

learning tool in classroom learning environment for decades [35]. Concept maps finished by students can also inform teachers to what extent the learning material is understood by the students, so that they can make adjustments on teaching plans. As such, the exercise of concept mapping can be used as instructional materials and guides and testing vehicles.

As plenty of video-based learning platforms emerge, video has become a popular medium of online education. However, video-based learning has a number of challenges in promoting meaningful learning. For example, novice learners may feel difficult to process new concepts scattered in the video and incorporate them without close guidance from teachers [5]. Moreover, while some videos are well-organized and enjoyable to watch, relying solely on the video content may leave the learners disengaged and lose the chance to reflect on what they have learned [6]. For instructors, gauging learners' experience and comprehension level is also difficult and currently mainly through course reviews, forum posts and quizzes [34].

Previous research has shown that the use of concept map can complement videos in facilitating meaningful learning. Liu et al. [22] showed that editing an existing expert-crafted concept map help learners understand the video content. In their work, the same effects on learning driven by using concept map is observed in video learning context as well, such as reinforcing video learners' understanding by promoting recall, reflection on the video content, and helping learners identify the knowledge gaps between new information and their existing mental model. Finished concept maps also provide a concept-oriented overview of video content, which can further be used as the feedback to video instructors, and future reference to students when preparing for tests.

However, it is not always easy for students to build concept maps from scratch. Novice learners who are unfamiliar with the video content tend to feel frustrated to identify key concepts and their relationships [40]. And the linear representation of video content may bring challenges for learners, which is shown in our preliminary study with 12 participants. We first observed learners building concept maps for video content with a conventional authoring interface (the baseline system in Fig. 1). We saw that they had difficulty in navigating concepts, gaining the overview and video flow, identifying key concepts and relationships.

To mitigate these challenges, we designed scaffolds that aims for easier concept map creation while preserving the learning benefits. We introduce ScaffoMapping, a system to assist the creation of concept maps for video content with automatic concept extraction and automatic timestamp generation. Individual concepts are automatically linked to video timestamps to facilitate content navigation. To evaluate the effectiveness of ScaffoMapping, we conducted a controlled study, comparing ScaffoMapping with the baseline system. Results showed that ScaffoMapping provides better learning outcomes and improves the quality of user-created concept maps. Such system can make concept maps widely accessible and used for online videos.

Overall, the contributions of this paper are:

1. We identified and categorized video learners' difficulties in concept mapping.

2. We designed ScaffoMapping, a system which provides scaffolding help in concept mapping.
3. We empirically evaluated ScaffoMapping by comparing it with the baseline system, and our results showed that ScaffoMapping enables better learning outcomes and higher-quality concept map creation.

2   Related Work

As our work introduces scaffolding concept mapping to facilitate video learning, we review related work on improving the video learning experience, applying concept map in video learning and scaffolding concept mapping.

2.1   Research in Improving Video Learning Experience

Many factors impede video learning platforms in supporting deep and meaningful learning [16] like the lack of personalized instructions and usability problems. Linear representation is one of the biggest problems that prevents learners from exploring video content effectively. Current research provides new ways to improve video learning experience. First, a large body of work focus on the video preview or navigation technique. Some research focuses on creating summaries of segmented video content [29,32,39]. Some research uses visual representation, for example Fisheye [15], video trees [19] and customized word-clouds [38] as navigation aid to help users preview and select some portion of video. However, they either do not provide a concept-oriented view or help learners understand relationships of concepts. NoteVideo [25] identifies conceptual objects to create a summarized image, but is limited to the blackboard-style video. Other research focuses on providing a more engaging learning experience. For example, in-video prompting questions [34] are used to increase learning and help instructors get feedback.

2.2   Applying Concept Map in Video Learning

Previous research has shown the value of providing concept maps in video learning. Some research utilizes the non-linear property of concept map to organize learning materials across different media (e.g., using hierarchical concept maps to support dynamic non-linear learning plans [31]). For integrating concept map within the video content, the most relevant work is done by Liu et al. [22], which utilizes experts or crowd workers to generate interactive concept maps for lecture videos, and has shown the learning benefits on supporting learners' understanding and reflection.

However, previous works focus on the concept maps instead of concept mapping process. They provide complete concept maps generated by crowd workers, experts [22] or Natural Language Processing techniques [40] to learners. While providing complete concept maps saves time, it may put learners in a position where they only passively take in knowledge with little autonomous learning [10], and finally undermine learners' learning performance [17,24]. What's more, editing concept maps by learners are poorly supported in video learning scenario. Extending previous work, we focus on the concept mapping process to facilitate video learning.

2.3 Scaffolds in Concept Mapping

Showing a complete concept map done by crowd workers or experts may result in little autonomous learning. On the contrary, concept mapping by learners themselves can promote autonomous learning and foster deeper processing, but it is time-consuming. What's more, this process requires effort, which usually leads to cognitive overload and finally decreases the learning outcomes as well as learners' motivation [11,20]. Therefore, researchers have been exploring using scaffolds to strike the balance between automation and manual composition [11]. Scaffolds are supports designed to assist learners in mindfully participating in work that would otherwise be too difficult or complex for a novice [13]. Numerous works have explored additional tool-based scaffolds to reduce the cognitive workload in concept mapping [28].

Luchini et al. [23] recognized users' difficulties in concept mapping on handheld computers and designed Pocket PiCoMap to help learners create better concept maps on handheld computers. Cheung et al. [12] proposed a collaborative concept mapping tool, which helps participants co-construct concept maps and improves understanding of the subject matter. Although these tools were successful in some ways, none of them focused on video learning scenario, which probably brings an extra burden for concept mapping. In this research, we focus on the video learning scenario and conduct the following studies.

3   Preliminary Study

To understand how and where learners need to be supported when creating concept maps for videos, we implemented a baseline system (Fig. 1) consisting of a web-based video player for playing lecture video and a canvas for creating concept maps. Learners can watch, pause, replay and navigate the video content. They can use keyboard/mouse shortcuts to create a blank concept, link and label them on the canvas. They can also zoom in/out the canvas according to their needs.

3.1   Study Design

We recruited 12 participants [P1–P12] (5 female) ranging from 22–30 years old from a local university. They were instructed to watch a video (Consciousness-Psychology[1]) and author the concept map in the best quality as they can according to what they had learned. There were no constraints on completion time,

---

[1] https://www.youtube.com/watch?v=jReX7qKU2yc.

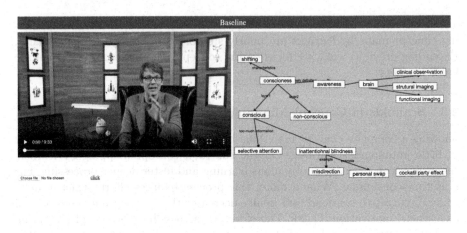

Fig. 1. An example concept map created by P5. The rectangle nodes represent concepts and the directed edges represent the relations. The baseline system interface consisting of a video player and a canvas. Users can create concepts, links and link labels on the canvas.

and they were free to navigate the video (fast-forward or rewind) and author the concept map as they want.

After they finished this task, they were asked to fill in a post-questionnaire. The questionnaire included questions to understand their prior knowledge about the video topic, their engagement level, and perceived difficulty of the video. We also carried out a semi-structured interview for each participant to know more about his/her experience in the experiment.

3.2   Results

Participants reported relatively low levels of prior knowledge on the video topic (10-scale Likert question: 1: never heard about it, 10: understand very well) with $M = 4.16$ ($SD = 2.22$). Their engagement while watching the video was high (10-scale Likert question: 1: not engaged at all, 10: Very engaged) with $M = 7.5$ ($SD = 1.76$). The perceived difficulty of video (10-scale Likert question: 1: very easy, 10: very difficult) was high with $M = 7$ ($SD = 2.97$).

Overall, participants reported that authoring concept maps facilitated their learning of the video content. They were able to remember more concepts compared with only watching the video [P2, P7], understand the relationships among concepts [P2, P9] and understand the video structure [P7]. Some reported that authoring concept maps was similar to taking notes during lectures [P6, P10]. In terms of authoring strategy, most participants noted down concepts during the first time watching as they had limited memory in remembering concepts [P2, P3, P5, P7, P9]. Some watched most of the video to get an overview of the video [P11, P12] and authored concept maps during the second time watching; they regarded authoring concept map as a distraction while watching the video [P8].

All participants reviewed the concept map to add more links and organize the structure. On average, they spent 24 min 46 s (SD = 5 min 16 s) on finishing the task (watching video plus authoring).

Participants reported several difficulties in concept mapping from video content. Based on their experiences, we identified two types of difficulties in concept mapping from video. The first type was the navigation difficulty caused by the linear representation of video content. Gaining an overview and identifying the main topic at the beginning was difficult [P3, P11, P12]. They also struggled to continuously pause the video to type and add concepts. As more concepts were created, they lost the order of the concepts' creation time [P5, P12]. Furthermore, a lot of time was spent on navigating back and forth in the video to find a specific concept or identify relationships between two concepts.

The second type was the learning difficulty in understanding the concepts and their relationships during the concept mapping process. Some learners reported less confidence in finding out important concepts and thus noted down everything they did not understand [P1, P4]. Most learners noted down some important concepts in their mind based on cues, like whether a concept appeared many times [P1, P2, P3, P5] or the video lecturer gave an explanation [P7, P9]. All participants remarked that finding the relationships between concepts was the most difficult part as they could not form the spatial structure and relationships during a single time viewing.

4   System Design

4.1   Designing Scaffolds

Based on the insights gained from the preliminary study, we designed scaffolding solutions to alleviate the navigation and learning difficulty. We searched for the previous literature on scaffolding concept mapping and improving video learning experience. Wang et al. [37] demonstrated the benefits of a hyperlink feature in concept mapping. When the students create concept nodes, the nodes in the concept map are hyperlinked to segments of text that the nodes represent. The hyperlink feature creates a consistent connection between the concept map and the content and enables easier concept map reviewing and editing. In the video learning scenario, previous research also established the effectiveness of linking video timestamps with conceptual objects to facilitate navigation [22,25]. For example, Notevideo [25] identified conceptual objects and linked them with timestamps, which serves as an effective navigation aid. Learners can directly jump to the video frame where that object first appeared. Thus, to mitigate the difficulty learners face in navigating concepts during concept mapping, we proposed the first scaffolding solution as linking concepts that learners created with video timestamps automatically.

Second, many research works demonstrated the benefits of providing students with incomplete concept map templates prepared by experts [10,11]. It creates a quick summary of the learning material and helps in students' understanding of content. In the video learning scenario, audio transcripts [2,4] or visual information [19,38] are used to provide a preview of video content. For example, Yadav et al. [38] provided customized word-clouds, which is an aggregated view of concepts in the video and helps learners understand video content. Thus, to mitigate the difficulty learners face in gaining an overview, we proposed the second scaffolding solution as to extract concepts in the video subtitle to provide a visual preview, which also serves as an incomplete template for concept mapping.

Our other design solutions are based on work done by Liu et al. [22] and Luchini et al. [23]. The concept node size can be bound with the importance of that concept. Relationship hints and time information are also added accordingly. To make them suitable for video scenario, we took an iterative design process by conducting informal pilot studies to get feedback from users. The final design solutions are listed in Tables 1 and 2.

Table 1. Navigation difficulties and scaffolding solutions

Navigation difficulties	Scaffolding solutions
Difficult to navigate concepts	Link concepts with video timestamps
Difficult to gain an overview	Extract concepts to provide a visual preview
Difficult to understand the video flow	Bind concepts' color with time information

Table 2. Learning difficulties and scaffolding solutions

Cognitive difficulties	Scaffolding solutions
Difficult to identify important concepts	Bind concepts' size with frequency
Difficult to find the relationship	Provide the relationship hints

4.2 System Implementation

To support scaffolds design, we utilized video and its subtitle file as input. The subtitle file is a text file in SRT or VTT format [18]. A single subtitle block, also called a cue, consists of three parts: the cue index, the timing information and the text (Fig. 2). The text feature of the subtitle has been widely used in identifying video topics to support video classification [8], and the timing information is usually combined with visual information to improve the interactivity of video [18,33].

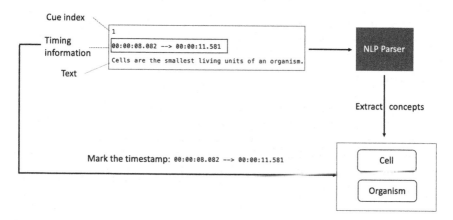

Fig. 2. An example of a subtitle block (the cue index, the timing information and the text) and ScaffoMapping work flow

Automatic Concept Extraction: We first used Google Natural Language API [1] to do text analysis and extract potential key concepts from subtitles. This API was used to analyze the structure of sentences and identify proper nouns in subjects or objects. These nouns are often regarded as key concepts. The Great Noun List [3] was used to identify the stems that are related to a given topic. Those extracted nouns (or stems) are more likely to contain the meaning that relates to the topic in a video. After generation of the concepts, we calculate the frequency that each concept appears in the subtitle. The more frequent concepts get larger font sizes and rectangle sizes.

Automatic Timestamp Generation: Each concept was coded with the time information of the subtitle cue. As a concept may appear more than once in the subtitle, after we marked all the timestamps of the concept, we marked the first one as the time of creation, which was the yellow dot in Fig. 3(a). Each concept was automatically assigned with a color from white to orange according to their creation time. Learners could click a concept to see all the moments it appeared in the video (Fig. 3(a)) and double click to navigate to the creation time. We also visualized in-video progress by highlighting mentioned concepts in every frame (blue colored concepts in Fig. 3(d)).

Concept relationships were made explicit by the hierarchical structure of the concept map as follows: We first sorted the concepts according to their frequency and creation time (Fig. 3(c)), then developed relationship hints, so that when a user linked two concepts in the same sentence, the text of that sentence would show below the video and the timestamp of the sentence would be marked in the timeline (Fig. 3(b)). The system would give the hint "No direct link" if none occurred, which means the two concepts users want to link don't appear in the same sentence. In this case, they need to build the relationship based on their own understanding. Keyboard shortcuts and zoom in/out were provided in the same way as in the baseline system. A release nodes function allowed users to remove all isolated nodes and keep linked ones.

5   Evaluation Study

ScaffoMapping is designed to facilitate video learning through scaffolding concept mapping for video learners, so we are interested in knowing: (1) Will the learners be able to create better concept maps with the help of ScaffoMapping interface? (2) How's the learning outcome in ScaffoMapping compared with the baseline interface? With these questions in mind, we conducted a user study to compare ScaffoMapping with the baseline system.

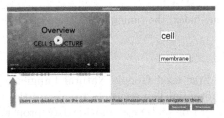

(a) Click a concept to see its timestamps in the video

(b) Relationship hint when users want to link "cell" and "membrane"

(c) Display all the concepts for reference

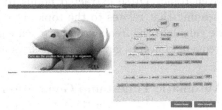

(d) Mentioned concepts are highlighted in blue as video plays

Fig. 3. The ScaffoMapping interface integrates interactive concept mapping into the video player. Each concept users created is automatically linked to its timestamps in the video. Relationship hints are given when users create links. All the concepts are displayed as the reference and lecture progress is visualized in blue. (Color figure online)

5.1   Study Design

Participants and Materials: We recruited 12 participants [P1–P12] (6 male and 6 female) ranging from 21–27 years old from a local university. We selected two videos on two different topics from the same YouTube education channel (V1: Immune System[2], V2: Consciousness[3]) with similar styles and similar lengths

---

[2] https://www.youtube.com/watch?v=GIJK3dwCWCw.

[3] https://www.youtube.com/watch?v=jReX7qKU2yc.

(V1: 9:12; V2: 9:32). Participants rated their prior knowledge level through a 10-point Likert Scale (1: Never heard about it, 10: understand very well) and perceived difficulty of video content (1: very easy, 10: very difficult) after watching them. As the participants were neither from psychology nor from biology major, there was little risk that they were familiar with the advanced content of the videos. This was consistent with their self-reported similar level of prior knowledge (V1: M = 3, SD = 2.37; V2: M = 3.25, SD = 1.54 (t(11) = 0.491, p = 0.633)). Videos were pilot tested with three users to ensure the similar difficulty level, which was consistent with participants' perceived difficulty level (V1: M = 6.08, SD = 2.06; V2: M = 5.08, SD = 2.31 (t(11) = 0.964, p = 0.356)).

Tasks and Procedure: We began by providing introductions of the two systems to each participant: baseline version and scaffolds version. Before starting the experiment, participants had time to practice and get familiar with the two systems. Then each participant experienced two experimental sessions where they watched the videos (V1, V2) and created concept maps using both systems (baseline, ScaffoMapping). The order of the systems was counter-balanced while the order of the video remained the same (e.g., P1 watched V1 using baseline system, then watched V2 using ScaffoMapping; P2 watched V1 using ScaffoMapping, then watched V2 using baseline system). They had the freedom to author concept maps during or after watching the videos, pause and resume, and watch multiple times, but the time for each session was limited to be the video duration plus 10 min. They could not take further notes such as with paper and pencil.

5.2 Analysis

Concept Map Quality Evaluation: To measure the quality of the concept maps, two domain experts were invited for each video to evaluate the concept maps generated from the baseline system and from ScaffoMapping. They watched the videos and evaluate the validity of concepts and relationships (links and link phrases). Adopted from [21], one valid concept or relationship was given 1 point. Invalid concepts and relationships were those containing typos or were incorrect, as determined by the experts. The interrater reliability correlations of the experts for V1 and V2 were 0.94 and 0.96, which indicates high reliability.

Learning Outcome Evaluation: To measure the learning gain, a 5-question test was administered to each participant after each session. The questions consisted of 3 True or False questions and 2 multiple choice questions from the video content. For example, for V1 on immune system, Q1: "The skin only supplies simple physical protection. T/F" Q4: "Which one of the following is not the internal defense? A. Phagocytes B. Mucous membranes C. Antimicrobial proteins D. Neutrophils". Participants did not have access to videos and concept maps during the test. After they had finished the two experiment sessions, we conducted a semi-structured interview asking their system preference and experiences.

Participants were told in advance that their performance indicator was the total of test scores (5 points) plus the concept map scores (convert concept map quality to a full-score of 5 points). They received \$10 for finishing the experiment and an extra \$10 for the best performance.

6   Results

Although the number of participants is relatively small, effects in the valid concept/link number, learning outcome and user preference are observed with statistical significance.

6.1   Concept Map Quality

We calculated the numbers of concepts and links participants generated. Two domain experts for each video rated the number of valid concepts and links as we described earlier. The summary of results are shown in Fig. 4(a) and (b).

There was no significant difference in the total numbers of concepts and links in the baseline system and ScaffoMapping. However, there was significant difference in the numbers of valid concepts $(t(11) = 8.072, p < 0.001)$ and valid links $(t(11) = 3.906, p < 0.01)$. This result shows that ScaffoMapping can facilitate learners to create concept maps with higher quality concepts and links with the scaffolding solutions provided.

6.2   Learning Outcome Test

Overall, participants using ScaffoMapping $(M = 3.92, SD = 1.38)$ outperformed baseline systems $(M = 3, SD = 1.21)$ in the tests. A paired t-test revealed significant improvement in the test score $(t(11) = 3.19, p < 0.01)$. Our results showed that ScaffoMapping assists effective video learning.

There are two reasons explaining the learning benefits of ScaffoMapping. First, ScaffoMapping supports efficient navigation through the automatic timestamp generation. Considerable time was saved and users could focus on construction work which involves more analytical thinking, e.g. identifying relationships. According to the interview result, all participants reported that they like the automatic timestamp generation, which provides the hyperlink from concepts to the video content. Second, with the extracted concepts, users reported a more positive learning experience when they found the gap between existing concepts and their mental model. With the template concepts provided, participants try to link between the template concepts and the knowledge they learned in the video, e.g. "I pay attention to the concepts and try to make sense of them" [P11], "I can identify the missing gaps and digest the information on the spot." This was consistent with the learning theories [9], which shows that meaningful learning is facilitated when learners integrate new concepts and propositions into their existing cognitive structure.

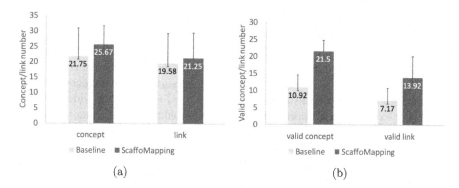

Fig. 4. (a) Mean of concept and link number of baseline system and ScaffoMapping. The result shows no significant difference. (b) Mean of valid concept and link number of baseline system and ScaffoMapping. The result shows learners use ScaffoMapping can create more valid concepts and links.

6.3   User Preference

We collected participants' feedback through the semi-structured interview. The majority of participants preferred ScaffoMapping (10/12) over the baseline system. Participants reported that ScaffoMapping made the authoring process easier and more efficient. The extracted concepts remove the burden of tedious typing and makes them focus on constructing links between concepts. The highlighting feature visualizes the in-video progress and can help them find connection easier [P3, P5, P7, P12]. And the automatic timestamp linking helps them navigate and review concept maps easily. They also indicated that they would like to save the concept maps as interactive notes for the video, and refer to them when they want to review or prepare for exams.

The remaining two participants [P4, P10] reported that they wanted a combination of baseline system plus automatic timestamp generation feature. In ScaffoMapping, they were confused by the extracted concepts appearing in the beginning, and after they identified key concepts, they needed to check their existence in the canvas, which created extra burden for them. While the baseline system gave them a sense of more "control", navigating back and forth to find the concept was tedious. Thus, they preferred to have a combination system.

7   Limitation and Future Work

We conducted an interview to gather feedback from learners about their video learning experience with ScaffoMapping. While the majority gave positive feedback to ScaffoMapping, two participants reported an expectation of baseline system combining automatic timestamp generation. It is still unclear whether expertise or domain knowledge has an influence on the choice of scaffolding systems. Due to the small size of participants, no correlation between system preference and prior knowledge with test performance was found. Furthermore, since our participants were recruited from the university community, more advanced scaffolding may be needed for less skilled learners. While some design solutions may solve this problem to some extent (e.g. triggering the automatic concept extraction by user control), it is worth investigating designing personalized scaffolding strategies according to learners' knowledge level to maximize video learning results. For example, combining with psychophysiological computing to measure the learners' frustration or attention to provide scaffolds at proper time [14].

We utilized video subtitle as the text source to provide relationship hints, which is supported by previous research that speech is the main carrier of information in nearly all lectures [39]. Inspired by the TF-IDF indices [30], if two concepts appeared in the same sentence(s), the sentence(s) would be displayed as the hint to help learners identify relationships. However, this feature can be interfered by pronouns like "it", or "them". For example, if the learner want to link concept A and B whose relationship is shown in sentence C, but A is referred as "it", the system will fail to identify sentence C as the relationship hint. To provide high-quality relationship hints, external sources or databases like Wikipedia [36] can be added to help with the relationship analysis.

While learner-generated concept maps can provide valuable feedback for video lecturers, analyzing concept maps can bring an extra burden for lecturers especially when a video has a large number of learners. To make ScaffoMapping more useful for lecturers and educational video developers, automatic concept map evaluation could be explored as an extension work. Finally, our evaluation study focused on video learners. In the future, we will extend this work to larger group of people. We expect to see how teachers, practitioners, educational video developers make use of this system to support learners.

8   Conclusion

In this paper, we proposed scaffolding solutions to assist concept mapping for video learners. We implemented these solutions in the ScaffoMapping system. Our evaluation study indicated that learners can create concept maps with better quality, as well as obtaining higher learning outcomes using ScaffoMapping. Our investigation on scaffolding solution shows promising benefits of semi-automation in learning systems. We encourage future research on similar solutions and believe this will have a wide impact on digital learning communities.

Acknowledgements. This research was funded by National University of Singapore Academic Research Fund T1 251RES1617. We thank Philippa Beckman and Barrie James Sutcliffe for proofreading, and Samangi Wadinambi Arachchi for her generous help with designing Fig. 4.

References

1. Cloud natural language API. https://cloud.google.com/natural-language/docs
2. Edx. https://www.edx.org
3. The great noun list. http://www.desiquintans.com/nounlist
4. Khan academy. https://www.khanacademy.org
5. Ally, M.: Foundations of educational theory for online learning. Theory Pract. Online Learn. **2**, 15–44 (2004)
6. Anderson, T., Kanuka, H.: Online social interchange, discord, and knowledge construction. J. Distance Educ. **13**, 57–74 (1998)
7. Ausubel, D.P.: The psychology of meaningful verbal learning (1963)
8. Brezeale, D., Cook, D.J.: Automatic video classification: a survey of the literature. IEEE Trans. Syst. Man Cybern. Part C (Appl. Rev.) **38**(3), 416–430 (2008)
9. Cañas, A.J., Novak, J.D.: Concept mapping using Cmaptools to enhance meaningful learning. In: Okada, A., Shum, S.B., Sherborne, T. (eds.) Knowledge Cartography. AIKP, pp. 25–46. Springer, London (2008). https://doi.org/10.1007/978-1-84800-149-7_2
10. Chang, K.E., Sung, Y.T., Chen, I.D.: The effect of concept mapping to enhance text comprehension and summarization. J. Exp. Educ. **71**(1), 5–23 (2002)
11. Chang, K.E., Sung, Y.T., Chen, S.F.: Learning through computer-based concept mapping with scaffolding aid. J. Comput. Assist. Learn. **17**(1), 21–33 (2001)
12. Cheung, L.S.: A constructivist approach to designing computer supported concept-mapping environment. Int. J. Instr. Media **33**(2), 153–165 (2006)
13. Collins, A., Brown, J.S., Newman, S.E.: Cognitive apprenticeship: teaching the crafts of reading, writing, and mathematics. In: Knowing, Learning, and Instruction: Essays in Honor of Robert Glaser, vol. 18, pp. 32–42 (1989)
14. Dirican, A.C., Göktürk, M.: Psychophysiological measures of human cognitive states applied in human computer interaction. Procedia Comput. Sci. **3**, 1361–1367 (2011)
15. Divakaran, A., Forlines, C., Lanning, T., Shipman, S., Wittenburg, K.: Augmenting fast-forward and rewind for personal digital video recorders. In: Consumer Electronics, pp. 43–44 (2005)
16. Garrison, D.R., Cleveland-Innes, M.: Facilitating cognitive presence in online learning: interaction is not enough. Am. J. Distance Educ. **19**(3), 133–148 (2005)
17. Griffin, C.C., Malone, L.D., Kameenui, E.J.: Effects of graphic organizer instruction on fifth-grade students. J. Educ. Res. **89**(2), 98–107 (1995)
18. Hu, Y., Kautz, J., Yu, Y., Wang, W.: Speaker-following video subtitles. ACM Trans. Multimedia Comput. Commun. Appl. (TOMM) **11**(2), 32 (2015)
19. Jansen, M., Heeren, W., van Dijk, B.: Videotrees: improving video surrogate presentation using hierarchy. In: International Workshop on Content-Based Multimedia Indexing, CBMI 2008, pp. 560–567. IEEE (2008)
20. Katayama, A.D., Robinson, D.H.: Getting students partially involved in note-taking using graphic organizers. J. Exp. Educ. **68**(2), 119–133 (2000)
21. Kwon, S.Y., Cifuentes, L.: The comparative effect of individually-constructed vs. collaboratively-constructed computer-based concept maps. Comput. Educ. **52**(2), 365–375 (2009)
22. Liu, C., Kim, J., Wang, H.C.: ConceptScape: collaborative concept mapping for video learning. In: Proceedings of the 2018 CHI Conference on Human Factors in Computing Systems, p. 387. ACM (2018)

23. Luchini, K., et al.: Scaffolding in the small: designing educational supports for concept mapping on handheld computers. In: CHI 2002 Extended Abstracts on Human Factors in Computing Systems, pp. 792–793. ACM (2002)

24. McCagg, E.C., Dansereau, D.F.: A convergent paradigm for examining knowledge mapping as a learning strategy. J. Educ. Res. **84**(6), 317–324 (1991)

25. Monserrat, T.J.K.P., Zhao, S., McGee, K., Pandey, A.V.: NoteVideo: facilitating navigation of blackboard-style lecture videos. In: Proceedings of the SIGCHI Conference on Human Factors in Computing Systems, pp. 1139–1148. ACM (2013)

26. Novak, J.D.: Concept maps and Vee diagrams: two metacognitive tools to facilitate meaningful learning. Instr. Sci. **19**(1), 29–52 (1990)

27. Novak, J.D., Cañas, A.J.: The theory underlying concept maps and how to construct and use them (2008)

28. Oliver, K.: An investigation of concept mapping to improve the reading comprehension of science texts. J. Sci. Educ. Technol. **18**(5), 402–414 (2009)

29. Pavel, A., Hartmann, B., Agrawala, M.: Video digests: a browsable, skimmable format for informational lecture videos. In: Proceedings of the 27th Annual ACM Symposium on User Interface Software and Technology, pp. 573–582. ACM (2014)

30. Ramos, J., et al.: Using TF-IDF to determine word relevance in document queries. In: Proceedings of the First Instructional Conference on Machine Learning, vol. 242, pp. 133–142 (2003)

31. Schwab, M., et al.: Booc.io: an education system with hierarchical concept maps. IEEE Trans. Vis. Comput. Graph. **23**(1), 571–580 (2017)

32. Seidel, N.: Making web video accessible: interaction design patterns for assistive video learning environments. In: Proceedings of the 20th European Conference on Pattern Languages of Programs, p. 17. ACM (2015)

33. Shin, H.V., Berthouzoz, F., Li, W., Durand, F.: Visual transcripts: lecture notes from blackboard-style lecture videos. ACM Trans. Graph. (TOG) **34**(6), 240 (2015)

34. Shin, H., Ko, E.Y., Williams, J.J., Kim, J.: Understanding the effect of in-video prompting on learners and instructors. In: Proceedings of the 2018 CHI Conference on Human Factors in Computing Systems, p. 319. ACM (2018)

35. Taylor, B.M., Beach, R.W.: The effects of text structure instruction on middle-grade students' comprehension and production of expository text. Reading Res. Q. **19**, 134–146 (1984)

36. Wang, F., Li, X., Lei, W., Huang, C., Yin, M., Pong, T.-C.: Constructing learning maps for lecture videos by exploring Wikipedia knowledge. In: Ho, Y.-S., Sang, J., Ro, Y.M., Kim, J., Wu, F. (eds.) PCM 2015. LNCS, vol. 9314, pp. 559–569. Springer, Cham (2015). https://doi.org/10.1007/978-3-319-24075-6_54

37. Wang, S., Walker, E., Wylie, R.: What matters in concept mapping? Maps learners create or how they create them. In: André, E., Baker, R., Hu, X., Rodrigo, M.M.T., du Boulay, B. (eds.) AIED 2017. LNCS (LNAI), vol. 10331, pp. 406–417. Springer, Cham (2017). https://doi.org/10.1007/978-3-319-61425-0_34

38. Yadav, K., et al.: Content-driven multi-modal techniques for non-linear video navigation. In: Proceedings of the 20th International Conference on Intelligent User Interfaces, pp. 333–344. ACM (2015)

39. Yang, H., Siebert, M., Luhne, P., Sack, H., Meinel, C.: Automatic lecture video indexing using video OCR technology. In: 2011 IEEE International Symposium on Multimedia (ISM), pp. 111–116. IEEE (2011)

40. Zubrinic, K., Kalpic, D., Milicevic, M.: The automatic creation of concept maps from documents written using morphologically rich languages. Expert Syst. Appl. **39**(16), 12709–12718 (2012)

Shared Gaze While Driving: How Drivers Can Be Supported by an LED-Visualization of the Front-Seat Passenger's Gaze

Sandra Trösterer[✉], Benedikt Streitwieser, Alexander Meschtscherjakov, and Manfred Tscheligi

Center for Human-Computer Interaction, University of Salzburg, 5020 Salzburg, Austria
{sandra.troesterer,benedikt.streitwieser, alexander.meschtscherjakov,manfred.tscheligi}@sbg.ac.at
http://hci.sbg.ac.at

Abstract. The front-seat passenger in a vehicle may assist a driver in providing hints towards points of interest in a driving situation. In order to communicate spatial information efficiently, the so-called shared gaze approach has been introduced in previous research. Thereby, the gaze of the front-seat passenger is visualized for the driver. So far, this approach has been solely investigated in driving simulator environments. In this paper, we present a study on how well shared gaze works in a real driving situation ($n = 8$). We examine identification rates of different object types in the driving environment based on the visualization of the front-seat passenger's gaze via glowing LEDs on an LED-strip. Our results show that this rate is dependent on object relevance for the driving task and movement of the object. We found that perceived visual distraction was low and that the usefulness of shared gaze for navigational tasks was considered high.

Keywords: Shared gaze · Driving · Front-seat passenger · LEDs · Ambient light systems

1 Introduction

Driving can be demanding since the driver constantly needs to observe the environment in order to drive safe. The driver needs to identify, interpret, and react to traffic signs and signals, road markings, and the behavior of other drivers and road users. Previous research has shown that front-seat passengers might support the driver by additionally monitoring the environment and providing according hints (e.g., [3,6]). Since gestures and verbal cues provided by the front-seat passenger might be ambiguous and not properly perceived by the driver, the *shared gaze* approach has been suggested to support front-seat passenger and driver communication [17,30,31].

© IFIP International Federation for Information Processing 2019
Published by Springer Nature Switzerland AG 2019
D. Lamas et al. (Eds.): INTERACT 2019, LNCS 11747, pp. 329–350, 2019.
https://doi.org/10.1007/978-3-030-29384-0_21

Fig. 1. Setup in the car. The gaze of the front-seat passenger is captured with an eye-tracking system and is visualized for the driver with blue glowing LEDs on an LED-strip mounted at the bottom of the windshield. The front-seat passenger is currently looking at the speed sign ahead on the right side of the street.

The basic idea of this approach is that the gaze of the front-seat passenger is visualized for the driver in the vehicle, allowing the driver to see where the front-seat passenger is looking at. This is achieved by using an eye-tracking system to capture the front-seat passenger's gaze, which is visualized in real-time for the driver. The visualization could be done in various ways by using, e.g., full windshield visualizations (via an head-up display) or ambient light information (e.g., LEDs). Previous research indicates that using ambient light information is more beneficial in terms of less visual distraction for the driver (e.g., [15,31]). In our case, we used an LED-strip mounted at the bottom of the windshield in order to provide horizontal spatial information. For example, a front-seat passenger wants to point to a speed limit sign ahead. While looking at the sign, an LED segment is lit at the bottom of the windshield at the corresponding position in line of sight between the driver and the traffic sign, i.e., the gaze visualization is mapped to the driver's perspective (see Fig. 1).

The usefulness of shared gaze has been successfully shown in previous research [17,30,31]. However, a drawback of these studies is that they were conducted solely in a driving simulator environment, lacking ecological validity. Our aim was to leave the driving simulator and investigate the approach in a real driving situation with the vehicle moving in a realistic three-dimensional environment with a dynamically changing scenery, vibrations in the vehicle and forces affecting the driver and passenger. Transferring the approach from the simulator to the real world required changes of the gaze calibration and mapping procedure and the influences of the real driving environment were not yet clear. Therefore, the present study focused primarily on how well and accurately drivers could perceive the gaze visualization under these new circumstances since an accurate perception is crucial in order for the shared gaze approach to be beneficial.

We conducted an in-situ study with eight participants with the above mentioned LED visualization of the front-seat passenger's gaze. The main aim of the study was to investigate drivers' perception of the gaze visualization and the usefulness of the approach for drivers in a real driving situation. Therefore and for safety reasons, the front-seat passenger's role was taken over by a researcher. In particular, we had the following research questions:

1. How well do drivers perceive the LED-visualization of the front-seat passenger's gaze during actual driving?
2. How well can drivers identify objects in the driving environment based on the visualization and how do specific object properties influence the object identification rate?
3. How distracting do drivers perceive the LED-visualization?
4. How useful do drivers experience the shared gaze approach?

Our study provides insights on different levels: First, it introduces a methodological approach how to map three-dimensional eye tracking data to a one-dimensional representation for the driver's perspective in a car. Second, we provide results on how well the gaze visualization is perceived by drivers in the real driving context. Third, the study provides insights on how natural gazing behavior affects the usability and usefulness of the approach. Our study extends existing research on the use of shared gaze by adding a new domain. Implications for the shared gaze while driving are discussed and recommendations for improvement are provided.

2 Related Work

2.1 The Front-Seat Passenger as Supporter of the Driver

The role of passengers in a car has been highlighted in previous research. The presence of passengers can influence experiences (e.g., [9,10]) or collaboration happening in the car (e.g., [3,6,11]). It was also shown that passengers may assist drivers in different situations. Specifically in navigation scenarios, the front-seat passenger can become a supporter by guiding the driver, or helping in interpreting misleading information provided by a navigation system [3,6]. However, so far, the ways how the front-seat passenger can communicate with the driver are limited. The sitting position side-by-side and the need of the driver to pay attention to the driving task can hinder efficient communication. It was found that drivers and passenger indeed experience problems due to ambiguity in the communication [5]. Hence, it has been outlined that there is a need for interfaces to support driver and passenger collaboration [4,6,20,23,24]. One approach was introduced by Perterer et al. [24], who provide the front-seat passenger with more detailed information about a route on a tablet in order to enable better support. In contrast to this, the shared gaze approach aims at enhancing driver and front-seat passenger communication directly.

2.2 Ambient Light Systems

The main reason for choosing glowing LEDs for visualizing the front-seat passenger's gaze, is that ambient light can draw driver's attention while keeping visual distraction low. In the automotive domain, LED-visualizations are used in various ways, e.g., for take over requests in automated driving scenarios [1,2], as support of anticipatory driving [12], as aid in lane change scenarios [13,14], or for gaze and attention guidance of the driver [25,26,28]. LEDs also have been used in steering wheels to provide warnings or information [8,15,21], in the a-pillars to alter drivers' perception of speed [7,19], and mounted in glasses to keep up situation awareness [32]. Particularly, Matviienko et al. [15] have shown that an ambient light system could significantly reduce distraction of the driver compared to a GUI-based navigation system. In their design guidelines for the usage of ambient light systems [16], they further state that the position of an LED visualization is one of the essential parameters. An approach to increase the accuracy of LED visualizations was introduced by Trösterer et al. [29], who showed that accuracy could be increased by conducting an individual calibration procedure for the driver.

2.3 Shared Gaze in the Car

So far, the shared gaze approach has solely been investigated in driving simulator studies. While Maurer et al. [17] presented findings from a first exploratory study, Trösterer et al. [30] investigated the approach in an elaborate driving simulator study with driver/front-seat passenger pairs as participants. Thereby, the gaze of the front-seat passenger was visualized as dot in the simulation. In the study, a combination of verbal hints and shared gaze was compared to a condition, where the front-seat passenger only provided verbal hints during a navigational task. The benefit of the shared gaze approach could be successfully shown. A further driving simulator study focused on the kind of gaze visualization, i.e., the dot visualization was compared with an LED visualization shown on a LED-strip mounted at the bottom of the windshield [31]. The LED visualization was perceived as less accurate, but reduced driver's search time and was less distracting for the driver. As outlined, the main aim of the study presented here, was to investigate the approach in a real driving situation, taking into account these previous findings.

3 Method

The study was conducted in a car, which was equipped with an eye-tracking system for capturing the gaze of the front-seat passenger and an LED-strip mounted at the bottom of the windshield for visualizing the gaze.

During a study trial, three people were in the car: the driver (i.e., the study participant), the front-seat passenger, and the experimenter, who was sitting on the right rear seat. The front-seat passenger was a briefed research fellow involved in the project, who was the same individual across all study trials. His task was to aid the driver with the LED calibration, to guide the driver along a predefined route, and to provide hints about objects in the environment with his gaze. The front-seat passenger knew the route by heart. Note that we as researchers had the agreement to refrain from showing the gaze visualization in complex traffic situations, as well as to refrain from showing the gaze visualization at all, if we felt safety was comprised. Additionally, participants could interrupt the study anytime.

Task of the participant was to drive along the predefined route guided by the front-seat passenger. The front-seat passenger told the driver where to go, and at times additionally used the LED visualization to show the way (e.g., the front-seat passenger would say *"We have to turn right there."* and simultaneously showed his gaze to point out what *"there"* means). The use of the LEDs during navigation was intended to give subjects a first impression how the gaze visualization could aid navigation and allowing for a more differentiated feedback with regard to the usefulness and usability of the approach.

In order to find out how well and accurately drivers could perceive the gaze visualization in the real setting, participants had to perform an object identification task during the drive. Thereby, the front-seat passenger visualized his gaze without saying anything while looking at a certain object in the environment (e.g., traffic lights, traffic signs, other traffic participants). In order to share his gaze, the front-seat passenger used a knob to switch the LED visualization on and off. When turned on, the front-seat passenger's gaze was visualized with glowing LEDs on the LED-strip in real time. The driver then needed to tell, which object the front-seat passenger was referring to (e.g., *"The 50 km/h speed sign"*) solely based on the visualization. When a driver had given his/her answer, the front-seat passenger replied verbally whether the given answer was correct or not. In case the driver did not say anything when the front-seat passenger showed his gaze, it was a miss (no reaction), i.e., in such case the driver had not perceived the LED visualization. Note that the participants were instructed accordingly to avoid confusion of the object identification task and navigation, i.e., they knew in advance that navigational guidance will include an according verbal hint by the front-seat passenger.

The object identification task allowed us to objectively and distinctly verify how well drivers perceived the gaze visualization, since it was based on visual information only. Note that combining shared gaze with verbal hints from the outset would have provided less clear evidence, since verbal cues in a realistic scenario usually reduce the search space and may compensate for inaccuracies of the visualization (cf. [30,31]).

3.1   Technical Setup

The car used in the study was a Ford Galaxy with automatic transition. For the LED-visualization, a 1.5 m LED-strip with 216 LEDs was mounted at the bottom of the windshield of the car. The LED-strip was controlled by an Arduino controller. For the LED-visualization, three blue glowing LEDs were used.

We chose this number and the color based on pretests. The light intensity was chosen considering proper visibility without being visually distractive. Since the weather was sunny during the whole study, the intensity was set at the highest value.

For capturing the gaze of the front-seat passenger, we used a SmartEye Pro eye-tracking system with 60 Hz. Three cameras were mounted in front of the front-seat passenger's seat. Since the SmartEye system allows to define a 3D world model of the environment, we measured and defined the windshield of the car as a plane in the model. That is, if the front-seat passenger looks at an object outside, his gaze intersects with the windshield and the eye-tracking system provides the x- and y-coordinates of the intersection. In turn, the x-coordinate can be easily transferred in the according LED-pixel position, since the LED-strip covers the windshield width.

A Java application was developed for controlling the setup. The application provides a graphical user interface for conducting a calibration procedure for the driver and the front-seat passenger, and for managing settings (e.g., LED visualization width and intensity). It further executes the transformation and mapping of the gaze data to the LED-strip. The application was running on a laptop. In addition, two hardware devices (a rotary knob to manually change the position of the glowing LEDs for the calibration and a knob to switch on and off the LEDs) were used.

In order for the setup to work, an LED calibration (cf. [29]) and gaze mapping procedure needed to be performed. This was done in four steps: (1) Driver and front-seat passenger agreed on two distinct points in the environment, which could be perceived by both and could be mapped to the LED-strip (preferably in-plane in about 5–10 m distance to the car). (2) Using the rotary knob, the driver manually adjusted the position of one glowing LED shown on the LED-strip until it reflected the position of the outside point most accurately from his/her point of view. S/he then pressed the knob and the LED-position was saved in LED-pixel. (3) The front-seat passenger looked at the point outside and when he pressed the knob, the gaze position was captured, transferred in LED-pixel (see above) and saved. In this way, position data was provided in LED-pixel for each point and each perspective (driver's and front-seat passenger's). (4) Based on the values and by using linear interpolation, the final mapping of the gaze visualization for the driver's perspective was done mathematically.

For analysis purposes, two GoPro Hero 7 cameras were mounted in the car. One was fixated at the top center of the windshield filming the scenery in front of the car including the windshield and the LED-strip. The other one was mounted at the left side window, filming the driver.

3.2 Participants

All participants were recruited at our research institution. This was deliberately done due to safety and ethical reasons. Participants were selected based on their self-assessment of driving experience, driving safety, and regularity of driving. Our sample included daily commuters, as well as drivers, who had particular experience in driving unfamiliar (rental) cars. None of the participants was familiar with the study setup. In total, eight subjects (five male, three female) participated in the study. The youngest participant was 24, the oldest participant 36 years old (M = 30 years, SD = 4.12). On average, participants had their driver's license for 12 years (SD = 3.45). Half of the subjects possessed an own car. On average, subjects reported an annual mileage of 8,300 km (min = 300; max = 25,000 km).

Three subjects indicated that they usually drive alone, while five subjects reported to often have one passenger or more. Two subjects reported that they rarely drive on routes they are unfamiliar with, five subjects did this sometimes, while one subject reported that this happens often. All subjects were familiar with using a navigation system during driving. Seven subjects reported to have been supported by a passenger in finding a route before. Thereby, the support by the passenger was perceived as helpful by six subjects.

3.3   Procedure

The participant was welcomed and accompanied to the car, which was parked in the underground garage of our institution. The participant was asked to sit down in the driver's seat and was introduced to the front-seat passenger, who already sat in the car. The experimenter sat down in the right rear seat of the car.

Introduction. First, the participant was given a short introduction into the shared gaze approach and the purpose of the study. They had to read a sheet containing general information about the study including safety instructions. The participant was told to drive carefully and to follow traffic rules at all time. Whenever a participant felt uncomfortable or unsafe s/he could interrupt the study. S/he then had to sign an informed consent. After checking the participant's driver's license, the experimenter asked the subject to adjust the seat and mirrors, and to buckle up. Furthermore, the subject was given a short introduction into the car. After that, the subject was asked to drive to a nearby parking lot outside in order to get familiar with the car.

LED Calibration and Gaze Mapping. At the parking lot, the front-seat passenger asked the participant to park at a specific position. For the LED calibration and gaze mapping, front-seat passenger and driver verbally agreed on two distinct points in the environment (like, e.g., a back-light of a specific parked car). The LED calibration and gaze mapping procedure was conducted following the steps described in the technical setup section. After that, the accuracy of the LED visualization was controlled. Therefore, the front-seat passenger looked at some points in the environment and pressed the knob to show his gaze, which was visualized for the driver with three glowing LEDs on the LED-strip. It was task of the driver to tell, which points were meant. In case of inaccuracies, the calibration procedure was repeated.

Drive and Object Identification Task. The participant was then told that his/her task was to drive to a village nearby and that the front-seat passenger would tell him/her where to go. It was explained that the front-seat passenger may simultaneously use the LED visualization to show the way. Furthermore, the participant was instructed for the object identification task. It was explained that during the drive the front-seat passenger would point at certain objects in the environment (e.g., traffic signs, other vehicles, buildings) with his gaze and without saying anything. It was pointed out that it was the participant's task to tell, which objects were meant solely based on the LED-visualization of the gaze. In case the driver had no further questions, the video camera recordings were started and the drive began.

During the drive, the front-seat passenger could visualize his gaze by pressing the knob. Foremost, the front-seat passenger chose objects depending on the traffic situation. The front-seat passenger also indicated verbally, whether the answer of the driver was correct or not, or whether the driver had missed a visualization (i.e., did not respond verbally to a visualization). The experimenter in the rear seat noted these comments. When arriving at the village, the subject was directed to a parking lot and parked the car. In case any problems (e.g., an apparent offset of the LED-visualization, eye-tracking problems) had been observed up to this point, the LED and/or eye-tracking calibration was repeated. Otherwise, the subject could immediately begin with the drive back. Again, the front-seat passenger told the driver where to go and pointed to objects with his gaze. At the end of the drive, the subject was asked to park the car in the underground garage of our institution.

Questionnaires and Final Interview. The subject was then asked to fill in a questionnaire with several self-generated items and the Driving Activity Load Index (DALI) [22]. This questionnaire allows to evaluate mental workload and is specifically designed for the driving context. Finally, a semi-structured interview was conducted. Interview questions focused on the usefulness of the gaze visualization, perceived distraction, possible problems, suggestions for improvement, and the use of shared gaze as a driver or front-seat passenger. The subject was then thanked for participation and left the car. The duration of one study trial was about one hour.

3.4   Route

The driving route we used in the study was predefined. Our requirements were that it should allow fluent driving, while comprising different driving scenarios. Starting point was our research institution near the city boundary of Salzburg. The route led along a national highway (with driving speeds up to 100 km/h) and through some smaller villages. It contained several roundabouts and traffic lights. Turning point was a village about 7.5 km away from the starting point. When entering the city on the way back, a detour was made through the city, before arriving at our research institution. The total length of the route was about 17 km. The driving side was right. During the study, traffic along the route was dense but fluent (i.e., no traffic jams). Driving time varied between 22 and 25 min (24 min on average). Half of the subjects were familiar with parts of the route, i.e., they knew about the village and had a basic idea how to get there. Note that in the village and the last part of the route, they also needed to rely on the navigational guidance by the front-seat passenger.

4   Data Analysis

For the analysis of data, we coded the video recordings showing the forward scenery and the LED-strip. For the coding, we used the following parameters: Each time, the LED-visualization was used by the front-seat passenger, we noted

- to which object the front-seat passenger was referring to with his gaze (*object type*),
- where the object was placed in the scenery (right side of the road, left side of the road, central in front of the car) (*object position*),
- whether the object itself was moving (e.g., another driving car) or not (e.g., a traffic sign) (*object movement*),
- whether the object itself was relevant for the driving task (e.g., traffic sign) or not (e.g., bus station) (*object relevance*),
- whether the subject correctly identified the object or not (*object identification*),
- whether the subject corrected a previously given answer immediately (*object correction*), or
- whether s/he had perceived the visualization at all (*object perception*).

Furthermore, we noted all verbal navigational hints, and whether the gaze visualization was used for support or not. All data was entered in Microsoft Excel for further analysis. We also transcribed comments of the participants during the drive. Questionnaire data was analyzed with IBM SPSS Statistics 24. The final interviews were transcribed as well, categorized, and analyzed following the basics of a qualitative content analysis [18].

5   Results

In the following, we provide a detailed description of the results including object identification rates, general functionality, perceived distraction, and usefulness of the approach.

5.1   Object Identification Rates

For the object identification task, the front-seat passenger visualized his gaze without saying anything while looking at a certain object. The driver needed to tell, which object the front-seat passenger is referring to solely based on the visualization. In total, the front-seat passenger notified the participants about objects in the environment 483 times. The amount of notifications varied between 49 and 77 times per drive (M = 60, SD = 10.48), depending on the traffic situation. On average, a notification was provided every 24 s within a drive (the average duration of a drive was 24 min).

Overall Rates. With regard to our first research question (RQ1), whether drivers do perceive the LED-visualization of the front-seat passenger's gaze, we found that in only 2% of the cases, the driver did not react to the visualization, i.e., they said nothing when the visualization was shown. In all other cases (98%), the drivers commented verbally what they thought the front-seat passenger was referring to.

Table 1. Object identification rates per object categories and overall.

Object category	N	Identified	Corrected	Not identified	No reaction
Traffic signs, lights, markings	**233**	**78%**	**7%**	**13%**	**2%**
information sign	25	84%	0%	12%	4%
place-name sign	17	82%	0%	18%	0%
road mirror	16	63%	6%	25%	6%
road sign	100	73%	11%	16%	0%
speed limit sign	52	88%	4%	6%	2%
traffic light	21	76%	10%	10%	5%
zebra crossing	2	100%	0%	0%	0%
Other vehicles	**109**	**76%**	**6%**	**17%**	**1%**
incoming vehicle	5	80%	0%	20%	0%
oncoming vehicle	75	80%	5%	15%	0%
parked vehicle	27	63%	7%	26%	4%
vehicle ahead	2	100%	0%	0%	0%
Vulnerable road users	**60**	**85%**	**3%**	**10%**	**2%**
cyclist	22	77%	5%	18%	0%
motor cyclist	8	100%	0%	0%	0%
pedestrian	30	87%	3%	7%	3%
Points of interest	**81**	**67%**	**15%**	**16%**	**2%**
billboard	41	83%	7%	10%	0%
building	8	100%	0%	0%	0%
bus stop	19	32%	26%	32%	11%
miscellaneous	13	46%	31%	23%	0%
Overall	**483**	**77%**	**7%**	**14%**	**2%**

Table 2. Object identification rates based on object relevance for the driving task and per object categories.

Object relevance for driving task	N	Identified	Corrected	Not identified	No reaction
Relevant	**223**	81%	6%	12%	1%
traffic signs, lights, markings	208	80%	6%	12%	1%
other vehicles	7	86%	0%	14%	0%
vulnerable road users	8	100%	0%	0%	0%
Irrelevant	**260**	73%	9%	17%	2%
traffic signs, lights, markings	25	60%	12%	24%	4%
other vehicles	102	75%	6%	18%	1%
vulnerable road users	52	83%	4%	12%	2%
points of interest	81	67%	15%	16%	2%
Overall	**483**	77%	7%	14%	2%

The overall correct object identification rate was 77% (min = 65%, max = 85%; SD = 7.64). This result is significantly above chance level ($\chi^2 = 29.16$, p < .001). In 7% of the cases, the drivers said something different first, but corrected their answer immediately, thus, the object was correctly identified in the end. In 14% of the cases, the object was not correctly identified. Table 1 provides an overview of the object identification rates overall and per object categories. Most objects fell in the category *traffic signs, lights, and markings*, followed by *other vehicles*, *points of interest*, and *vulnerable road users*. Correct object identification was highest when the front-seat passenger was referring to vulnerable road users (85%; $\chi^2 = 49.00$, p < .001), and lowest when referring to other points-of-interest (67%; $\chi^2 = 11.56$, p < .05 when comparing it to an equal distribution of correct and incorrect answers).

Object Properties. Regarding object properties (RQ2), we took a look at object relevance, movement, and position. As a first step, we analyzed to which degree the relevance of the object for the driving task impacts object identification rates. As depicted in Table 2, we could find that the object identification rate tended to be higher when the object was relevant for the driving task (81% for relevant vs. 73% for irrelevant objects). Both rates are significantly above chance level ($\chi^2 = 38.44$, p < .001 for relevant and $\chi^2 = 21.16$, p < .001 for irrelevant objects). Among the relevant objects, *vulnerable road users* were identified correctly in all cases.

As indicated in Table 3, most of the referred objects were static (n = 353), while *other vehicles* and *vulnerable road users* could also be in movement (n = 130). We could find that the object identification rate tended to be higher when the objects were in movement (83% for moving vs. 74% for static objects). Identification rates were highest, when the objects were also relevant for the driving task (93% for moving and 80% for static objects). The rates were lower when the objects were irrelevant for the actual driving task (82% for moving and 66% for static). Again, all rates were significantly above chance level.

Table 3. Object identification rates based on object movement and per object categories.

Object movement	N	Identified	Corrected	Not identified	No reaction
Moving	**130**	**83%**	**5%**	**12%**	**0%**
other vehicles	79	80%	5%	15%	0%
vulnerable road users	51	88%	4%	8%	0%
Static	**353**	**74%**	**8%**	**15%**	**2%**
traffic signs, lights, markings	233	78%	7%	13%	2%
other vehicles	30	67%	7%	23%	3%
vulnerable road users	9	67%	0%	22%	11%
points of interest	81	67%	15%	16%	2%
Overall	**483**	**77%**	**7%**	**14%**	**2%**

Finally, we analyzed the object identification rates for the different object positions. Since the driving side was right, a large portion of objects were also located on the right side (n = 297). We found, that objects in front of the car (n = 12, central position), were correctly identified in 92% of the cases ($\chi^2 = 70.56$, p < .001). Those objects were also all relevant for the driving task, since they could impact driving behavior. For objects at the side of the road, the object identification rate was comparable (74% for left and 77% for right objects).

5.2 Use of the LED-Visualization for Navigation

As outlined, the front-seat passenger navigated the driver along the route by telling him/her where to go, and at times he complemented verbal hints with the visualization of his gaze. The average number of navigational hints was 21 per drive (min = 18, max = 27). About 21% of the navigational hints were given solely verbally, 76% verbally with simultaneous LED-visualization of the gaze, and in 3% of the cases, the LED-visualization was used alone for guidance (i.e., subsequently to a verbal hint). Most navigational hints were advice, where to turn right (49%) or left (21%), or to drive straight on (3%). Furthermore, the front-seat passenger communicated, where to exit the roundabouts on the route (27%).

Seven of the eight drivers followed the navigational hints properly and drove along the route without any problems. One driver missed a roundabout exit (and drove an additional round in the roundabout) and missed a further road exit later on (the driver needed to stop and turn around to follow the route again). The roundabout exit was solely communicated via LED-visualization. In the latter case, the driver overlooked the exit, which was located shortly behind a bend, despite verbal and LED notification.

5.3 General Functionality of the Eye-Tracking and LED-Calibration

For two subjects, it was necessary to recalibrate the LED-visualization when arriving at the turning point since an offset became apparent during the drive. In all other cases, we could continue with the initial calibration. In general, the eye-tracking system worked stable during the study and it was never necessary to repeat the eye-tracker calibration for the front-seat passenger within a study trial. However, during the drives, it sometimes happened that eye-tracking errors occurred, causing the LED-visualization to jump or freeze. Nonetheless, this happened very seldom - in total, we noted 11 cases, where such problems occurred.

5.4 Perceived Distraction and Usefulness of the Shared Gaze Approach

In order to capture participants' perceived distraction (RQ3) and impressions regarding the usefulness of the approach (RQ4), we used different questionnaire items and conducted a semi-structured final interview.

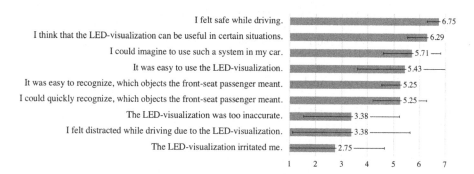

Fig. 2. Means and standard deviations of drivers' ratings of statements (1 = does not apply at all, 7 = does fully apply).

Figure 2 provides an overview of drivers' ratings of statements, which had to be rated on a 7-point Likert scale (1 = does not apply at all, 7 = does fully apply). It is apparent that the ratings regarding the usefulness of the visualization (M = 6.29, SD = 0.76), or whether one could imagine to use it in their own car (M = 5.71, SD = 1.11) are rather high. Participants also tended to agree that it was easy to use the LED-visualization (M = 5.43, SD = 1.81), and that they could easily (M = 5.25, SD = 0.71) and quickly (M = 5.25, SD = 1.04) recognize, which objects the front-seat passenger meant. Mean ratings regarding LED-visualization inaccuracy (M = 3.38, SD = 1.85), perceived distraction (M = 3.38, SD = 2.26), and irritation by the LED-visualization (M = 2.75, SD = 1.91) were below average. In general, participants felt safe while driving (M = 6.75, SD = 0.46).

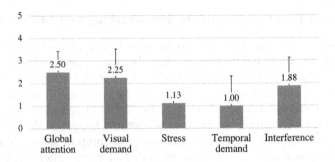

Fig. 3. Means and standard deviations for selected factors of the DALI questionnaire (0 = low, 5 = high).

In order to capture constraints with regard to the driving task, we used the DALI questionnaire (note that we left out the auditory demand factor, since the notification of the driver during the object identification task was purely visual). Figure 3 provides an overview of the mean ratings for each factor. It is apparent that the ratings for temporal demand (M = 1.00, SD = 1.31) and stress (M = 1.13, SD = 0.35) are particularly low. Also, drivers rated interference (M = 1.88, SD = 1.25) and visual demand (M = 2.25, SD = 1.28) below average. The mean rating of global attention was average (M = 2.5, SD = 0.93).

5.5   Findings from the Interviews

At the end of a study trial, participants were interviewed. Interview questions targeted their general impression about the shared gaze approach, its usefulness, perceived distraction, and suggestions for improvement.

All participants found the gaze visualization to be useful. *"I think it's useful. It's often the case that other people see things, which you don't perceive - like for example a speed limit sign."* (P3). Seven participants outlined that they found the approach worked well and was practical, specifically for navigation. *"I think it worked surprisingly well, particularly for navigation. I could also imagine it for a navigation system - when the computer gives directions."* (P4). *"I think it's cool for navigation. I hope this will break into the market."* (P2). Two subjects meant that the accuracy of the LED-visualization could have been generally better for object identification, while four subjects outlined that it was sometimes difficult to tell which object was meant when objects were overlapping from their point of view. For example, P8 stated *"Sometimes it was not possible to identify the object, because there were several objects in one line."* *"When there was a sign in front of a bus stop, it was difficult."* (P1).

Participants generally considered the shared gaze approach to be helpful for navigation and providing directions. However, it was also outlined by four participants that the LED-visualization rather served as additional source of information, when they already knew where to go (because they knew parts of the route, read the information provided on the information signs, or the verbal hint by the front-seat passenger was enough). Participants stated that the approach could be particularly feasible when navigating in unfamiliar regions or more complex driving scenarios. *"I think, if the driving situation is more complex, like in cities, it could help"* (P8). Two participants had doubts that the LED-visualization would provide the adequate accuracy for navigation scenarios. *"I would not be sure, whether I could really tell which street I should take when there are three in a row."* (P6). Three participants also outlined that the timing (i.e., at which point the front-seat passenger shows his/her gaze) may be a crucial factor. Specifically, with regard using the LED-visualization to indicate a roundabout exit, three subjects expressed concerns. *"Sometimes I had the feeling that I should continue to drive in the roundabout, because the light started to move to the right quite late."* (P5).

As regards distraction, seven participants stated that they didn't feel visually distracted by LED-visualization. Only P8 meant *"I think I looked at the visualization directly, because the LEDs were not so bright."* However, almost all participants (n = 7) outlined that they rather felt a bit distracted by the task they had to do, i.e., that they were rather cognitively distracted. *"I was distracted by the task. The anticipating - what does he* [the front-seat passenger] *mean."* (P7). *"When I was unsure, whether it was the bus stop or the sign - then it was a bit distracting, because I had to think about it. But when it was unambiguous, it was not distracting at all"* (P1). *"Usually, the front-seat passenger would look at something that is important for the driver. So it does not distract, but rather guide the driver."* (P2).

As regards the LED-visualization itself, seven participants stated that they found the visualization with three LEDs to be adequate. *"I think it's fine with three LEDs. Using just one LED might be difficult to perceive, using more LEDs would decrease accuracy."* (P7). Participants were also fine with blue as color. Suggestions for improvement were, e.g., to implement an additional audio or vibration signal so that the driver can additionally perceive when the front-seat passenger starts showing his/her gaze. It was suggested that head tracking of the driver could increase accuracy, or that gaze tracking of the driver could be used for gaze guidance, i.e., that it is also considered where the driver is currently looking. Color and brightness of the LED visualization should be adapted depending on the weather conditions. All participants stated that they had no problems with the LED-calibration, which had to be done at the beginning. *"That was super easy."* (P5).

We also asked study participants, whether they could imagine to use the shared gaze approach as a front-seat passenger. Seven participants stated that they could imagine it, particularly for navigation. *"It really makes sense to use it, when I know where to go and the driver doesn't."* (P7). *"Yes, I can imagine to use it. For example, when searching for a parking space, there are often agile discussions in the car. Here it would be really helpful."* (P5). P6 had doubts he would use it, but he noted that the approach could be probably very beneficial for rally co-pilots, who guide the rally driver. *"The rally co-pilot is a real expert*

and knows where to go. That's mostly not the case for normal passengers." P4
also thought that rally drivers could benefit from the approach.

Finally, we asked participants whether they could imagine to use the system
in their own car. Seven participants said that they could imagine to use it. They
found the system to be *"unagitated"*, *"simple"*, *"funny"*, *"supportive in typical
scenarios"*, and *"nice to have"*.

6   Discussion

6.1   Drivers' Perception of the LED-Visualization

With regard to our first research question, we found that drivers did perceive
the LED-visualization in almost all cases (98%). As regards the question, how
well the drivers could identify objects in the environment based on the visualization (RQ2), we found an overall object identification rate of 77%. We consider this as a good rate, taking into account that inaccuracies could happen
on three different levels. That is, the eye-tracking accuracy in general plays a
role, as well as the accuracy of the mapping of the gaze to the LED-strip and
the mapping of the LED-visualization to the driver's perspective. Furthermore,
the three-dimensional spatial information is reduced to a simple one-dimensional
representation, i.e., depth or height information was not provided. It also needs
to be outlined that the found rate basically reflects the worst case, since solely
visual information was available for the driver during the object identification
task. We expect the rate to be even higher, when according verbal hints are provided by the front-seat passenger. As outlined in the method section, the object
identification task was chosen to ensure that an objective and distinct verification, how well drivers perceive the gaze visualization in a real driving situation,
is possible.

Our results also suggest that certain object properties play a role when it
comes to correct identification. We found that the object identification rate
tended to be higher, when the object was relevant for driving task and was
especially high when the object was a vulnerable road user. Also, objects were
identified more easily when they were in movement or central in front of the car.
Several factors need to be considered when interpreting these tendencies.

First, *anticipation* is certainly an important factor, i.e., drivers had a certain
expectation, what the front-seat passenger could mean most likely. This was
also mentioned in the final interviews. As pointed out, a front-seat passenger
would usually refer to something that's relevant for the driver. Therefore, it also
seems likely that the driver would rather identify a relevant object based on the
visualization. That is, anticipation might influence how the LED-visualization is
perceived.

Another factor, which plays a role here, is the *saliency* of the object in the
respective scenery. Driving is dynamic and involves constant changes of the environment. Hence, when the front-seat passenger showed his gaze, the scenery
could be more or less cluttered, thus, making it more or less difficult to identify

the object. Furthermore, the different viewing perspectives of driver and front-seat passenger can have an impact. An object, which can be clearly perceived by the front-seat passenger, may appear to be overlapping with other objects from the driver's perspective. This was also mentioned as a problem in the final interviews.

As outlined, the LED-visualization of the gaze is a one-dimensional representation of spatial information. However, we found that the LED-visualization provided another quality, i.e., the *movement* of the glowing LEDs depending on the gazing behavior. That is, if the front-seat passenger fixates a static object while the car is moving, the visualization will move accordingly depending on the object position and distance. If the front-seat passenger looks at a moving object and follows it with his gaze, this results in much quicker movements. We believe that this superordinate information made it easier for drivers to identify moving objects.

On the other hand, we also found that the natural gazing behavior of the front-seat passenger could be misleading. This became most apparent when using the gaze to point at a roundabout exit, since the front-seat passenger looked in the roundabout first and then at the exit (i.e., the LED-visualization was moving from the left to right, which was experienced as too late by some drivers).

6.2 Perceived Distraction and Usefulness of the Shared Gaze Approach

Participants generally indicated that they were not visually distracted by the LED-visualization. This is in line with previous findings [15,30,31] and is also supported by the ratings in the questionnaires. Mean ratings for distraction and irritation caused by the LED-visualization were low. Also, visual demand and interference were rated below average in the DALI questionnaire.

However, it turned out that the participants felt rather cognitively distracted by the object identification task, especially when the LED-visualization was not distinct. This finding can be seen twofold. On the one hand, it is a consequence of our chosen methodological approach. Our aim was to gain sufficient data about object identification accuracy without the need to make an extensive drive. On the other hand, our results underline that it needs to be considered in the future that an ambiguous visualization of the front-seat passenger's gaze may cause cognitive distraction of driver. It should be noted, though, that (opposed to the object identification task in the study) the gaze visualization would usually be accompanied by some verbal comment of the front-seat passenger, thus, reducing the cognitive effort for the driver.

Drivers could also experience this during the study, since the shared gaze approach was used for navigation as well. Thereby, the front-seat passenger used the gaze visualization in addition to his verbal hints where to go. Almost all participants agreed that the shared gaze approach could be useful and helpful for navigation. This is in line with what was found in the driving simulator studies [30,31]. Especially for unknown areas and more complex driving scenarios, shared gaze might be valuable. However, our results also show that there still might be some problems that need to be solved. For example, the timing (i.e., when gaze is visualized) may play a crucial role in such scenarios. Also, natural gazing behavior needs to be considered, which might be misleading (like, e.g., in the roundabout scenario).

6.3 The Role of the Front-Seat Passenger and Further Application Scenarios for Shared Gaze

In our study, the role of the front-seat passenger was taken over by a researcher, who was used to the approach and controlled his gaze to a certain degree, e.g., he knew that he had to fixate an object for some time to be recognizable for the driver. It is questionable if similar results in detection rates can be achieved when the front-seat passenger is not used to the approach, or whether a certain training would be necessary. Indeed, Trösterer et al. [30] found in their first simulator study, that a proper instruction of the front-seat passenger may be crucial. Nonetheless, the important role of a front-seat passenger to support the driver was expressed by almost all participants. This also includes the willingness to use shared gaze as front-seat passenger. Also, shared gaze could be a valuable approach in professional areas (for, e.g., rally co-pilots, driving instructors).

With respect to design considerations, the in-situ study showed that the number of glowing LEDs (three) and their color (blue) was perceived positively by the participants. Also, the merely horizontal spatial information was perceived positively. In contrast to what was expressed by participants in the driving simulator study [31], provision of additional depth or height information turned out to be less relevant in real driving situations.

Potential improvements of shared gaze with LEDs could be a *gaze lock* (i.e., the possibility for the front-seat passenger to "lock" the gaze after having looked at an specific object, so that s/he needs not to stare at the object all the time), gaze guidance (i.e., also taking into account where the driver looks at; cf. [26,27]), or a different way to activate or deactivate the gaze visualization (e.g., by means of gestures instead of using a knob).

6.4 Limitations

There are some limitations with respect to the study presented here. First, we only investigated the perspective of the driver and not the role of the front-seat passenger. It is unclear, whether detection rates would be similarly high with an inexperienced front-seat passenger. Second, the number of participants was rather low in order to be able to generalize the results for a broad range of different drivers. However, the large number of identified objects and the high identification rates suggest that the shared-gaze approach and the LED visualization is effective. Third, the object identification task was rather artificially with respect to frequency and mental effort. However, as pointed out, the task was necessary in order to get a clear verification of drivers' perception of the gaze visualization in the real driving context. Fourth, the chosen route was rather short and in parts familiar to the drivers. Future work should focus on unknown areas and more complex driving environments. Finally, we only assessed perceived visual distraction of the driver. Future studies should use eye-tracking of the driver to investigate visual distraction also objectively.

7 Conclusion

Based on our results, we conclude that the shared-gaze approach and its implementation with glowing LEDs on an LED-strip worked well in the real driving scenario. The adapted gaze calibration and mapping procedures showed to be successful. The LED-visualization was recognized in almost all of the cases and the correct object identification rate was with 77% significantly above chance level. We found that this rate was influenced by different object properties and assume that drivers' anticipation, object saliency, and the natural gazing behavior of the front-seat passenger determined the differences in perception. The study participants experienced the shared gaze approach as particularly useful for navigation, however, the role of the front-seat passenger needs to be further examined. In future work, we plan on a comparative study in a more complex driving environment to further investigate the approach for navigation and with front-seat passengers as study participants as well.

References

1. Bazilinskyy, P., Petermeijer, S.M., Petrovych, V., Dodou, D., de Winter, J.C.: Take-over requests in highly automated driving: a crowdsourcing survey on auditory, vibrotactile, and visual displays. Transp. Res. Part F Traffic Psychol. Behav. **56**, 82–98 (2018)
2. Borojeni, S.S., Chuang, L., Heuten, W., Boll, S.: Assisting drivers with ambient take-over requests in highly automated driving. In: Proceedings of the 8th International Conference on Automotive User Interfaces and Interactive Vehicular Applications, AutomotiveUI 2016, pp. 237–244. ACM, New York (2016). https://doi.org/10.1145/3003715.3005409. http://doi.acm.org/10.1145/3003715.3005409
3. Bryden, K.J., Charlton, J., Oxley, J., Lowndes, G.: Older driver and passenger collaboration for wayfinding in unfamiliar areas. Int. J. Behav. Dev. **38**(4), 378–385 (2014)
4. Forlizzi, J., Barley, W.C., Seder, T.: Where should I turn: moving from individual to collaborative navigation strategies to inform the interaction design of future navigation systems. In: Proceedings of the SIGCHI Conference on Human Factors in Computing Systems, pp. 1261–1270. ACM (2010)
5. Gärtner, M., Meschtscherjakov, A., Maurer, B., Wilfinger, D., Tscheligi, M.: "Dad, stop crashing my car!": making use of probing to inspire the design of future in-car interfaces. In: Proceedings of the 6th International Conference on Automotive User Interfaces and Interactive Vehicular Applications, AutomotiveUI 2014, pp. 27:1–27:8. ACM, New York (2014). https://doi.org/10.1145/2667317.2667348. http://doi.acm.org/10.1145/2667317.2667348

6. Gridling, N., Meschtscherjakov, A., Tscheligi, M.: I need help!: exploring collaboration in the car. In: Proceedings of the ACM 2012 Conference on Computer Supported Cooperative Work Companion, CSCW 2012, pp. 87–90. ACM, New York (2012). https://doi.org/10.1145/2141512.2141549. http://doi.acm.org/10.1145/2141512.2141549

7. van Huysduynen, H.H., Terken, J., Meschtscherjakov, A., Eggen, B., Tscheligi, M.: Ambient light and its influence on driving experience. In: Proceedings of the 9th International Conference on Automotive User Interfaces and Interactive Vehicular Applications, AutomotiveUI 2017, pp. 293–301. ACM, New York (2017). https://doi.org/10.1145/3122986.3122992. http://doi.acm.org/10.1145/3122986.3122992

8. Johns, M., Mok, B., Talamonti, W., Sibi, S., Ju, W.: Looking ahead: anticipatory interfaces for driver-automation collaboration. In: 2017 IEEE Intelligent Transportation Systems (ITSC), pp. 1–7. IEEE (2017)

9. Juhlin, O.: Social media on the road: mobile technologies and future traffic research. IEEE Multimed. **18**(1), 8–10 (2011)

10. Knobel, M., et al.: Clique trip: feeling related in different cars. In: Proceedings of the Designing Interactive Systems Conference, DIS 2012, pp. 29–37. ACM, New York (2012). https://doi.org/10.1145/2317956.2317963. http://doi.acm.org/10.1145/2317956.2317963

11. Krischkowsky, A., et al.: The impact of spatial properties on collaboration: an exploratory study in the automotive domain. In: Proceedings of the 19th International Conference on Supporting Group Work, GROUP 2016, pp. 245–255. ACM, New York (2016). https://doi.org/10.1145/2957276.2957304. http://doi.acm.org/10.1145/2957276.2957304

12. Laquai, F., Chowanetz, F., Rigoll, G.: A large-scale led array to support anticipatory driving. In: Proceedings of the IEEE Systems Men and Cybernetics (SMC 2011), Anchorage, AK, USA (2011)

13. Löcken, A., Heuten, W., Boll, S.: Supporting lane change decisions with ambient light. In: Proceedings of the 7th International Conference on Automotive User Interfaces and Interactive Vehicular Applications, AutomotiveUI 2015, pp. 204–211. ACM, New York (2015). https://doi.org/10.1145/2799250.2799259. http://doi.acm.org/10.1145/2799250.2799259

14. Löcken, A., Müller, H., Heuten, W., Boll, S.: An experiment on ambient light patterns to support lane change decisions. In: 2015 IEEE Intelligent Vehicles Symposium (IV), pp. 505–510. IEEE (2015)

15. Matviienko, A., Löcken, A., El Ali, A., Heuten, W., Boll, S.: NaviLight: investigating ambient light displays for turn-by-turn navigation in cars. In: Proceedings of the 18th International Conference on Human-Computer Interaction with Mobile Devices and Services, pp. 283–294. ACM (2016)

16. Matviienko, A., et al.: Deriving design guidelines for ambient light systems. In: Proceedings of the 14th International Conference on Mobile and Ubiquitous Multimedia, MUM 2015, pp. 267–277. ACM, New York (2015).https://doi.org/10.1145/2836041.2836069. http://doi.acm.org/10.1145/2836041.2836069

17. Maurer, B., et al.: Shared gaze in the car: towards a better driver-passenger collaboration. In: Adjunct Proceedings of the 6th International Conference on Automotive User Interfaces and Interactive Vehicular Applications, AutomotiveUI 2014, pp. 1–6. ACM, New York (2014). https://doi.org/10.1145/2667239.2667274. http://doi.acm.org/10.1145/2667239.2667274

18. Mayring, P.: Qualitative content analysis: theoretical foundation, basic procedures and software solution (2014)

19. Meschtscherjakov, A., Döttlinger, C., Rödel, C., Tscheligi, M.: ChaseLight: ambient led stripes to control driving speed. In: Proceedings of the 7th International Conference on Automotive User Interfaces and Interactive Vehicular Applications, AutomotiveUI 2015, pp. 212–219. ACM, New York (2015). https://doi.org/10.1145/2799250.2799279. http://doi.acm.org/10.1145/2799250.2799279

20. Meschtscherjakov, A., Perterer, N., Trösterer, S., Krischkowsky, A., Tscheligi, M.: The neglected passenger—how collaboration in the car fosters driving experience and safety. In: Meixner, G., Müller, C. (eds.) Automotive User Interfaces: Creating Interactive Experiences in the Car. HIS, pp. 187–213. Springer, Cham (2017). https://doi.org/10.1007/978-3-319-49448-7_7

21. Mok, B., Johns, M., Yang, S., Ju, W.: Reinventing the wheel: transforming steering wheel systems for autonomous vehicles. In: Proceedings of the 30th Annual ACM Symposium on User Interface Software and Technology, pp. 229–241. ACM (2017)

22. Pauzié, A.: A method to assess the driver mental workload: the driving activity load index (DALI). IET Intell. Transp. Syst. **2**(4), 315–322 (2008)

23. Perterer, N.: Safety through collaboration: a new challenge for automotive design. In: Proceedings of the 19th ACM Conference on Computer Supported Cooperative Work and Social Computing Companion, CSCW 2016 Companion, pp. 167–170. ACM, New York (2016). https://doi.org/10.1145/2818052.2874344. http://doi.acm.org/10.1145/2818052.2874344

24. Perterer, N., Meschtscherjakov, A., Tscheligi, M.: Co-navigator: an advanced navigation system for front-seat passengers. In: Proceedings of the 7th International Conference on Automotive User Interfaces and Interactive Vehicular Applications, AutomotiveUI 2015, pp. 187–194. ACM, New York (2015). https://doi.org/10.1145/2799250.2799265. http://doi.acm.org/10.1145/2799250.2799265

25. Pfromm, M., Cieler, S., Bruder, R.: Driver assistance via optical information with spatial reference. In: 2013 16th International IEEE Conference on Intelligent Transportation Systems (ITSC), pp. 2006–2011. IEEE (2013)

26. Pomarjanschi, L., Dorr, M., Barth, E.: Gaze guidance reduces the number of collisions with pedestrians in a driving simulator. ACM Trans. Interact. Intell. Syst. (TIIS) **1**(2), 8 (2012)

27. Pomarjanschi, L., Dorr, M., Bex, P.J., Barth, E.: Simple gaze-contingent cues guide eye movements in a realistic driving simulator. In: Human Vision and Electronic Imaging XVIII, vol. 8651, p. 865110. International Society for Optics and Photonics (2013)

28. Schmidt, G.J., Rittger, L.: Guiding driver visual attention with leds. In: Proceedings of the 9th International Conference on Automotive User Interfaces and Interactive Vehicular Applications, AutomotiveUI 2017, pp. 279–286. ACM, New York (2017). https://doi.org/10.1145/3122986.3122994. http://doi.acm.org/10.1145/3122986.3122994

29. Trösterer, S., Döttlinger, C., Gärtner, M., Meschtscherjakov, A., Tscheligi, M.: Individual led visualization calibration to increase spatial accuracy: findings from a static driving simulator setup. In: Proceedings of the 9th International Conference on Automotive User Interfaces and Interactive Vehicular Applications, AutomotiveUI 2017, pp. 270–278. ACM, New York (2017). https://doi.org/10.1145/3122986.3123012. http://doi.acm.org/10.1145/3122986.3123012

30. Trösterer, S., et al.: Four eyes see more than two: shared gaze in the car. In: Abascal, J., Barbosa, S., Fetter, M., Gross, T., Palanque, P., Winckler, M. (eds.) INTERACT 2015, Part II. LNCS, vol. 9297, pp. 331–348. Springer, Cham (2015). https://doi.org/10.1007/978-3-319-22668-2_26

31. Trösterer, S., Wuchse, M., Döttlinger, C., Meschtscherjakov, A., Tscheligi, M.: Light my way: visualizing shared gaze in the car. In: Proceedings of the 7th International Conference on Automotive User Interfaces and Interactive Vehicular Applications, AutomotiveUI 2015, pp. 196–203. ACM, New York (2015). https://doi.org/10.1145/2799250.2799258. http://doi.acm.org/10.1145/2799250.2799258

32. van Veen, T., Karjanto, J., Terken, J.: Situation awareness in automated vehicles through proximal peripheral light signals. In: Proceedings of the 9th International Conference on Automotive User Interfaces and Interactive Vehicular Applications, AutomotiveUI 2017, pp. 287–292. ACM, New York (2017). https://doi.org/10.1145/3122986.3122993. http://doi.acm.org/10.1145/3122986.3122993

TEXTile: Eyes-Free Text Input on Smart Glasses Using Touch Enabled Textile on the Forearm

Ilyasse Belkacem[1], Isabelle Pecci[1(✉)], Benoît Martin[1], and Anthony Faiola[2]

[1] Laboratoire de Conception, Optimisation et Modélisation des Systèmes, LCOMS EA 7306, Université de Lorraine, Metz, France
{ilyasse.belkacem,isabelle.pecci,
benoit.martin}@univ-lorraine.fr
[2] Department of Biomedical and Health Information Sciences, University of Illinois, Chicago, IL, USA
faiola@uic.edu

Abstract. Smart glasses are autonomous and efficient computers that can perform complex tasks through mobile applications. This paper focuses on text input for mobile context. We present a new connected fabric to smart glasses as a device for text entry. This device, integrated into clothing, provides a new interaction technique called TEXTile. It allows typing without requiring users to hold a device. Users can put fingers anywhere on the fabric surface and release them, without needing to look at the fabric or using markers on the fabric. The text entry technique is based on eight combinations of fingers in contact or released, identified as pleasant among 15 in a survey involving 74 participants. A first user's study with 20 participants establishes that the eight combinations for TEXTile were significantly reliable (98.95% recognition rate). A second study with nine participants evaluates the learning curve of TEXTile. Users achieved a mean typing of 8.11 WPM at the end of ten 12-min sessions, which can be slow, but sufficient with short text compared to other advantages of the technique. Results show low error rates for tasks completed and good usability (76% in SUS questionnaire). The NASA-TLX questionnaire establishes there is no important mental or physical workload to accomplish the task.

Keywords: Wearable · Smart glasses · Textile · Forearm interaction · Text entry

1 Introduction

Today, the smartphone is the most widespread device in the world offering access to a broad range of apps, tools, and services. However, the mobile device has some practical limitations: it is often in the pocket or bags [1], and it does not allow quick access. In addition, during use, the user's hands are occupied, even if they are not interacting with the device, which makes its use frustrating in some context.

© IFIP International Federation for Information Processing 2019
Published by Springer Nature Switzerland AG 2019
D. Lamas et al. (Eds.): INTERACT 2019, LNCS 11747, pp. 351–371, 2019.
https://doi.org/10.1007/978-3-030-29384-0_22

Smart glasses can overcome these limitations. This device looks like conventional eyeglasses including electronic components: a processor, sensors (Wifi, Bluetooth, GPS, accelerometer, gyroscope, etc.) and a transparent display screen that allows a simultaneous vision of physical and digital worlds. Current smart glasses are autonomous and efficient computers that can perform more complex tasks for mobile applications. When using smart glasses, users may need to enter text: to search for information, to reply to a message or to write a note. Common text entry used with smartphones or computers may be complex to use with smart glasses.

The first commercial smart glasses, the Google Glass [2], provided speech recognition to enter text. However, this technique is inappropriate in noisy environments [3], and users didn't like it in public places [4]. There is a need to design a new text entry system for use in conjunction with smart glasses beyond what is currently available [5].

In this paper, we propose a new text entry technique called "TEXTile". This technique uses a new one-dimensional tactile fabric device that is placed on the forearm while being connected to the smart glasses. We did an online survey to identify the most comfortable combinations of fingers in contact with the fabric device. With these combinations, we built a grammar for our new text entry technique. Two user studies were conducted: one demonstrated the performance and reliability of the device, and one experimented the performance of the new text entry technique. The contribution of our work includes:

1. A smart textile for input with smart glasses based on a literature review and conceptual modeling.
2. A low cost and reliable prototype integrated into the fabric of one's clothing, e.g., on the forearm.
3. A new text entry technique using a grammar based on a user study that matches with the conceptual framework of our prototype.

2   Motivating Goal and Design Rational

In a mobile environment, the text entry task can be done standing, walking or sitting. The user cannot hold additional devices because his hands can be busy, and he cannot always use audio input due to respect privacy. Such a context would include for example a pedestrian that sends a message while walking in the street, a worker attending a meeting and taking short notes, or a clinician accessing patient records while interacting with the patient. To meet the needs of this context, we have set the following requirements for our design:

- (Req 1) The location of the interaction: interaction with the device should not hamper the user work. He should not carry an extra device in his hand or wear a glove. Wrist and forearm interactions are the most socially acceptable [6].
- (Req 2) The discretion of the device: the device must be invisible and comfortable during a mobility situation. It should not be cumbersome to affect the user work (e.g., a smartphone placed on the forearm).

- (Req 3) Eyes-free interaction: since the smart glasses screen is in front of the eyes, the user must be able to interact while remaining engaged to both real and digital worlds.

3 Related Works

With the emergence of mobile and wearable technologies, many research has been interested in text entry because this task requires effective hardware or software solutions to compensate for the absence of classic keyboards. With smart glasses, the great advantage is to be able to interact while remaining attentive to the real world, since the smart glasses screen is in front of the eyes. This advantage becomes a challenge for tasks like text entry. Usually, the user looks at the keyboard to enter text and looks at the screen to check for text accuracy. With smart glasses, the user can look at the real-world, while walking and interacting with the virtual environment. In this context, it is ineffective and cumbersome to look at a text entry device.

Many classifications exist for text entry techniques. In this paper, we divide text entry techniques into two groups: those that require a single action and those that require multiple actions to select a character. We define an action as a gesture, a flick, a selection by pointing one or more touch simultaneously, etc.

3.1 Text Entry Techniques Using a Single Action to Select a Character

The best known single action technique is the standard keyboard: one character maps to one physical key. It can be physical or virtual. Small versions of Qwerty keyboard for wearable exist, but they failed to gain acceptance due to their lower text performance and their fatigue level [7]. To overcome space limitation, chorded keyboards were introduced to decrease the number of keys. A chord is a combination of keys pressed simultaneously. One of the most common is the one-handed Twiddler keyboard [8]. Other research has proposed several chording techniques based on Braille encodings: BrailleTouch [9] and Perkinput [10]. These techniques are implemented on smartphones. Although designed primarily for visually impaired people, they can be used for text entry on smart glasses. The disadvantage of chorded keyboards is the effort needed to learn chords.

Single-action techniques involve also gestures based input. Gestures can be performed with a two-dimensional device. To ease learning, Graffiti [11] and EdgeWrite [12] use gestures that are more or less related to the shape of the Latin letters. Graffiti [11] supports quick learning and aid retention through the similarity of most characters to the Romain alphabet, but it requires accuracy. EdgeWrite [12] needs less accuracy but requires edges to perform the gestures and gestures are less related to the shapes of the letters. With QuikWriting [13] and 8pen [14], users trace gestures around a central region of the layout to one or more zones around the center to enter a character. Since the layout of the characters determines the gestures, it is challenging to support text entry in a mobile situation: the gestures require users to find locations of the character. Gestures can be performed as well in the air. A sensor captures the gesture, and the user can perform a gesture in the air associated with a character as in Airwriting [15] or Airstroke [16]. These techniques have some human factors limitations because it causes fatigue in the arms [17]. This technology requires the user to make gestures publicly in front of the face, but users do not appreciate [18]. PalmType [26] is a technique that uses the palm of the hand as a keyboard to enter text. A virtual keyboard is displayed on the smart glasses, and the user touches his palm. Infrared sensors located on the forearm detect each touch. This technique requires the user to locate the specific region on the palm to enter the characters. As some smart glasses have a tactile surface, Yu et al. [27] proposed a system of gestures on this surface: each character is a set of one-dimensional lines that mimic the representation of the character with handwriting. This system does not support numbers and special characters.

3.2   Text Entry Techniques Using Multiple Actions to Select a Character

Multiple actions to select a character allow reducing the space to interact and simplify the learning. Actions are sequential and they allow navigating in the space of characters. Users first select a group of characters and a character among this group. MessageEase [19] was primarily designed for 12-button keypad of mobile phones. It uses a tap for the first action followed by a tap or a slide-lift for the second action. With FlickKey [20] and ThumbText [21], the keyboard layout is divided into six large keys. The user selects a group of characters by pointing a position on the surface and make a flick for the second action to select the character. All of these three techniques may imply accuracy issues because they require to locate where to tap for the first action. More than two actions can be performed in H4-writer [22], H4-TEG [23], MDITIM [24] to select a character depending on the frequency of the character. The Huffman coding using four keys represent the characters, but it requires learning.

Swipezone [28] was adapted from SwipeBoard technique [29] to smart glasses. By using this technique, each character is encoded with two actions: a first swipe that selects the region on the keyboard, and a second swipe that selects the character. This technique is very efficient and does not require a lot of learning because it uses the Qwerty layout. Holdboard [30] uses the same interaction technique, but unlike in Swipezone, it merges the selection of the region and the selection of the character in one gesture. The location of the thumb touching the edge of the smartwatch selects a group of characters (starting point of the gesture), and then, a swipe selects the desired character. That's why we consider it in the multiple actions category. This technique has also a problem with localization.

3.3   Devices Used for Text Entry

Many devices can be associated with a text entry technique on smart glasses.

Handheld Devices. In this category, we can find small versions of the Qwerty keyboard or Twiddler chorded keyboard with different buttons [8]. Another technology is a gyroscope-based handheld device [31], and it consists in entering the text by using a handheld controller to select the character on a keyboard with hand movement. The user must hold the controller in the hand and tilt it to different angles to select targets (characters) on the screen. Holding an extra device does not satisfy our requirement.

Hand Wearables. DigitTap [32] is a wrist-worn device with an accelerometer to detect tap time and a camera to detect tap location. The acquisition of tap location cannot be accurately recognized in the occlusion environment or with wrist movement. Another work, DigitSpace [33], includes a pair of magnetic-sensing nail-ring chains mounted in the hand of the user. The prototype is very cumbersome in some mobile contexts. Other works use thumb-to-fingers interaction, but by wearing a glove [23, 34–36]. The more recent and advanced work is DigiTouch [36], which senses a continuous touch position and detects the thumb position along the length of a finger by using conductive fabric strips and a conductive patch on the thumb pad. This technique uses one action by using the two hands. Though the technique is promising and can achieve high text entry speed, wearing a glove during the interaction may hamper the user in a mobile situation and may make his tasks difficult to master. Other wearable devices use eyes-free text entry, such as a ring [37], miniature touch surface [21] or even a nail-mounted device [38]. For example, asking the user to tap the finger that carries the ring [37] on a surface in different directions to select a character, has a variable performance that depends on the surface quality. Also, users of [21, 38] may have difficulty because the interaction surface is limited to a small portion and can suffer from precision.

Eye or Head Tracking. With significant advances in eye-tracking performance, we can use eye movement for text entry [39] with smart glasses. In eye-tracking systems, people are usually asked to fix long enough on a character to select it. In a mobile context, the user could not keep visual attention to his environment. Moreover, interacting with the head using a gyroscope [40] requires learning and can be a source of fatigue if the text is long. It requires considerable visual attention while typing, along with constant head movement, which seems to be difficult in situations of needed mobility, making this technology also socially troublesome.

Microphone. Text entry using voice seems to be the most natural technique with a good performance outcome [25]. However, it raises issues of reliability and confidentiality in mobile situations.

Interactive Textile. Many new inexpensive interactive textile materials are marketed. They can be made for invisible and ubiquitous interactions [41]. Several studies are interested in interactive textiles. One of the earliest is PocketTouch [42], that inserts a capacitive device grid in the pocket, but not integrated on the fabric of the pocket. Other works such as [43] and [44] have designed a resistive surface in the form of a matrix of pressure sensors, on the textile surface. Resistive technology does not detect multiple points in an efficient way. zPatch [45] combines resistive and capacitive technology, making a patch to detect hover, touch, and pressure on its interface. It does not yet allow multi-finger interactions.

4 The Text Entry Technique TEXTile

4.1 Description of the Prototype

To meet the needs defined above (Sect. 2), we chose to use an interactive textile that can be placed on clothing. We have designed a textile surface with a capacitive grid, which allows us the recognition of several simultaneous contact points, as outlined in detail below.

Hardware Device. Our prototype is a tactile fabric with a size of 11.9 cm × 10 cm. The prototype consists of 36 parallel conductive threads (thin, stainless, and washable), sewn in a linear array onto the fabric with a spacing of 3.5 mm. Three "12-cap-touch breakout MPR121" [46] cards are used to connect the threads. These cards allow us the capacitive sensing of touch on the tactile fabric. The cards manage the sensitivity. In addition, cards connect the 12 threads. All three cards are connected to a FLORA microcontroller (see Fig. 1).

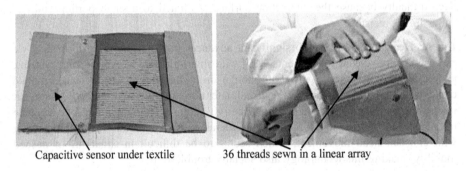

Capacitive sensor under textile   36 threads sewn in a linear array

Fig. 1. The prototype has 36 parallel conductive threads sewn in a linear array connected to capacitive sensors. (Color figure online)

The microcontroller receives the touch events (contact or release) of each entry among the 36 entries. The device is connected to smart glasses with an OTG cable. A Bluetooth module can be integrated for a wireless solution if desired. The touch surface is framed by a red plastic rectangle so that the user can feel if their fingers are moving away from the touch surface.

To meet the first requirement (Req 1), we explored the idea of attaching the device to the sleeve of a white lab coat, with snap buttons. Thus, when the user wears the coat, he can interact with the surface on the forearm.

Processing Software. The data transmitted by the MPR121 cards are processed at two levels. The first level, on the Arduino platform based on C/C++. This platform can detect touch events (contact or release) on the thread, and knows on which thread the event has been performed. After detection, the information is sent using the I2C serial bus communication protocol at the second level.

The second level is programmed in JAVA using the Android SDK because the smart glasses run under the Android system. This level interprets the state of the threads, in terms of fingers in contact or released. The combination of fingers is validated after a time without changing of states on the threads. The prototype can identify the numbers of fingers in contact with the textile surface by extracting the touch groups on the surface. Then, if the user releases fingers, the algorithm identifies which fingers are released by eliminating the touch groups from the start position. Once the operations are interpreted by the algorithm, in terms of interaction, specific actions on the system can be triggered.

Prototype Limitation. Our prototype was simplified to perform 1D interactions anywhere on the surface in order to have reliability in fingers in contact and released detection. However, it has some limitations in the type of gestures that we can perform on the surface. The prototype does not identify which fingers are on the surface, that is why we need a start position to detect released fingers. Another limitation to the detriment of the simplicity of the prototype is that we cannot perform two-dimensional gestures as in many common techniques.

4.2 Preliminary Study

Our goal was to find a language of interaction based on simple contacts-and-releases of the four fingers (forefinger, middle finger, ring finger and little finger). The thumb was ignored because of its shifted position from the other fingers. We define a combination of 4 values $d_1 d_2 d_3 d_4$ where the state of each finger d_i is defined by:

$$d_i = \begin{cases} 0, \text{ if finger } i \text{ is released} \\ 1, \text{ if finger } i \text{ is in contact with the device} \end{cases}$$

$$forefinger = 1 \leq i \leq 4 = little\,finger$$

We started by conducting an online survey to identify comfortable combinations by using our prototype. The online survey was an effective tool for obtaining quick feedback on acceptability, as well as related to comfort with a gestural interface [47].

Participants. An email was sent requesting volunteers for the study. The email was dispatched on a university mailing list. Participants were encouraged to send it to others to participate in the study. We sent it to our families and friends too. 74 participants (37 females, 64 right-handed) answered to the online survey, 62% aged between 15–24, 18% between 25–34, 5% between 35–44, 4% between 45–54, 3% between 55–64 and 7% more than 65 years old. 69% were students, 19% workers, 5% retired persons, 3% unemployed, 3% housewife and 1% at college student.

Task and Procedure. The online survey examined the possible types of interaction while using our prototype: the RELEASE, i.e. release fingers "simultaneously" from a start combination. We have chosen as the start combination the one where the four fingers (index, middle, ring and little) are in contact with the surface. The thumb was ignored because of its position being too offset from the others. We have 15 possible combinations of finger released. We have explored this "RELEASES" because they can (1) be performed in our 1D interaction surface, (2) be detected in an accurate way on our device, and (3) meet the eyes-free interaction without needing to look at the fabric or using markers on the fabric.

Before starting the survey, we inform the participants that the purpose of the study was to evaluate the comfort of these combinations to be used as part of an interface.

The survey illustrated the 15 combinations, with animated demonstrations in the form of a hand that performs the combination on the surface and with a brief description. In this way, the participants of the study could reproduce the combination. The videoed action took about two seconds, played in a loop. Participants were asked to reproduce and rate each combination, according to the comfort level they felt by using a five-point Likert scale—from "Not at all comfortable" to "Very comfortable". All combinations are displayed in the same order on a single page with scrolling. The user can go back and correct a rate he gave.

Each combination was coded as follows: the finger in contact with the surface is represented by a 1 (or 0 if it is released). We presented the four fingers by a sequence of 4 digits where the high weight is associated with the index and the low weight with the little finger. For example, "RELEASE_0110" maps to "release the forefinger and the little finger from the start combination".

Results. Figure 2 shows the average scores for the 15 combinations.

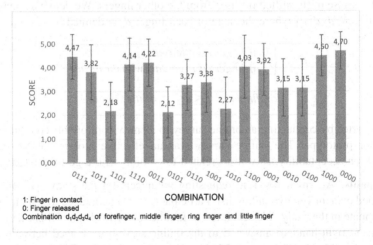

Fig. 2. Mean score of each combination for the RELEASE operation.

We only retained the comfortable combinations that had a score of more than 3.5 to eliminate the combinations with negative or neutral score—giving us 8 combinations:

- 3 combinations with a one released finger: 0111, 1011, 1110.
- 2 combinations with two released fingers: 0011 et 1100.
- 2 combinations with three released fingers: 0001, 1000.
- 1 combination with four released fingers: 0000.

From our analysis, we learned that comfortable combinations do not require the user to release non-adjacent fingers.

4.3 Evaluation of Device Reliability

The purpose of the experiment is to evaluate the reliability of the device.

Participants. Twenty unpaid volunteer participants (average age 21.6 years, all right-handed) were recruited from the University's Computer Science PhD program. Participants never used smart glasses neither connected textile surfaces in the past.

Task. The goal is to evaluate the performance of the detection of the start combination (four fingers in contact with the textile surface) and the number of fingers released detected from the start combination. Participants had to interact with the textile surface in response to a visual stimulus displayed on the smart glasses. The stimulus (see Fig. 3) asked the user to put the four fingers in contact. Once the fingers are in contact with the surface, arrows indicates the fingers to release.

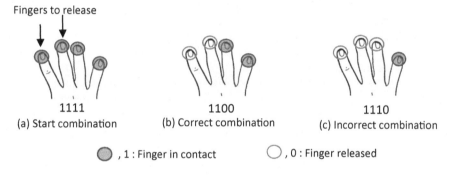

Fig. 3. Screenshot of the task

Procedure. Our study follows a single-variable plan: the operation (start combination, RELEASE) with an intra-subject configuration. The RELEASE operation had 8 possibilities (the selected combinations). Each combination was tested 10 times. Each participant performed 80 tests as follows: 0000 → 1111 → RELEASE. We collected data for 0000 → 1111 (8 × 10) and 1111 → RELEASE (8 × 10). The task order was randomized with only one constraint: a RELEASE task always comes after a starting position task.

Before starting the tests, participants were asked to read a document that specifies the purpose of the experiment, the task to be performed, and the devices to use. They also fill out a pre-questionnaire for demographic information (age, gender, laterality). Participants began the test with a visual feedback on the smart glasses that gives them instructions.

Apparatus. The experiment was performed using Epson binocular transparent smart glasses. This model offers very good image quality with its OLED display at a 1280 × 720 pixels resolution. The screen of smart glasses maps to a screen of 80 in by 5 m. The smart glasses can be worn over eyeglasses. They embed various sensors (GPS, compass, gyroscope, accelerometer, etc.). They are connected to a controller through a cable. This controller contains buttons and a tactile surface used as a trackpad. The smart glasses run under an Android 5.1 operating system.

Our textile surface is connected to the glasses and placed on the left sleeve of a lab coat worn by the participant. The participant is standing, wearing the glasses and interacting with the textile surface with his right hand. The experiment took place in the same room with the same lighting conditions (closed window shutters and interior lights under the ceiling).

Collected Data. During the study, we recorded each interaction task with the textile surface (the expected interaction and the interaction detected), i.e.1600 (20 participants × 80 operations) of start combinations and 1600 operations release.

Results. Overall, our prototype successfully identified 99.19% of starting positions and 98.69% of RELEASE operations performed. Table 1 summarizes the detailed recognition rates.

The detailed error analysis revealed two causes of error. In some situations, the user's finger was not sufficiently in contact with the surface. In addition, the user sometimes hesitated and did not release the requested fingers simultaneously, which was interpreted as more than one action. For example, if it requested to release the middle finger, the ring finger and the little finger (RELEASE_1000), the user releases the middle finger and the ring finger and after a time longer than he/she releases the little finger, which considered as (RELEASE_1001). We distinguish device errors and participants errors by observation.

In addition, the reliability test showed that our textile surface can be used to put in contact four fingers (forefinger, middle, ring and little fingers) on the surface and release them. Hence, it could be used to test our text input technique.

Table 1. Recognition operations' rate by observation.

	Device errors	Participant errors	Reliability of the device
Starting position	13/1600	0/1600	99.19%
	0.81%	0%	
Release	21/1600	94/1600	98.69%
	1.31%	5.87%	

4.4 Definition of TEXTile

TEXTile is a text entry technique that encodes each character into a sequence of two actions (see Fig. 4). For each action, the user needs to put in contact the four fingers on the textile surface (called start combination) and to release between one and three fingers. If the user releases the four fingers, the text entry interaction is cancelled.

The advantage of this technique is that it does not require the visual attention of the user to look at the tactile surface which is being typed on. As the user has the glasses screen in front of their eyes, a view of the keyboard is displayed to help him to perform the right actions.

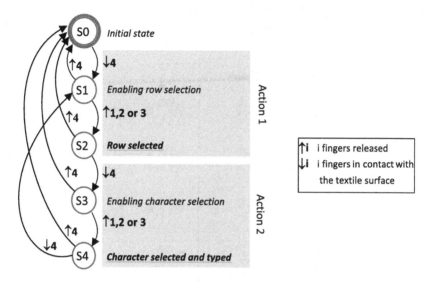

Fig. 4. Two actions to perform the typing of a character.

As the goal is to support novice users to enter a short text, we opted for a Qwerty layout as in Swipezone [28]. The keyboard is divided into two regions of three rows, which gives a distribution of characters on six rows. Each row is divided into two regions of three characters. This division allows us to reach all the characters in two actions as mentioned in Fig. 4. To facilitate learning, we chose an intuitive method to select a row or a character:

- The number of the row to be selected maps to the number of fingers to release. If the row is located on the left region, the user needs to release its fingers by starting from forefinger. If the row is located on the right region, the user needs to release its fingers from little finger to forefinger.
- To choose the character in the row selected, it's the same technique as row selection. The user just needs to release the number of fingers matching to the position of the character on the region of the row. If the character is located on the left region of the row, the user needs to release its fingers by starting from forefinger. If the character is located on the right region, the user needs to release its fingers from little finger to forefinger.
- To select another character, the user just needs to do the start combination (put the four fingers in contact with the textile surface).

A visual help is displayed on the keyboard that user can see on smartglasses to help him which fingers to release (see Fig. 5): the numbers indicate how many fingers to release and the arrows under the numbers indicate from which finger to start. For example, to select the second row of the right region, the user must release two fingers starting from the right: little and ring fingers (RELEASE_1100). Table 2 summarizes how to select each region from the start combination. Figure 5 shows how to write the word "CAP" with visual feedback on the smart glasses.

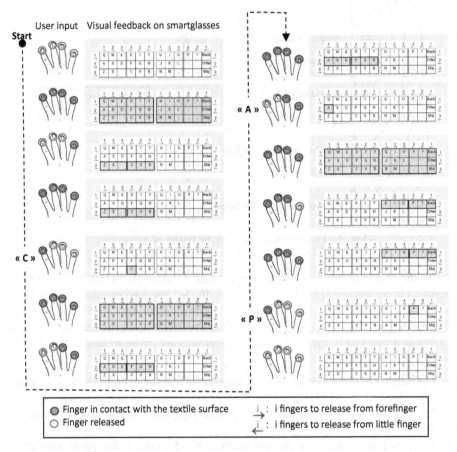

Fig. 5. Example of text entry: the word "CAP".

Among the eight combinations selected during the preliminary study, RELEASE_1011 (release middle finger) combination remains available. This combination was used to switch to the numeric and special characters view of the keyboard. Initially, the QWERTY view was displayed.

Table 2. The combinations to select a row or a column (character) on the keyboard.

Number of fingers to release	Combination	Result of action 1	Result of action 2
0 finger	RELEASE_0000	No row selected	No column selected
1 finger	RELEASE_0111	Left row #1	Left column #1
1 finger	RELEASE_1110	Right row #1	Right column #1
2 fingers	RELEASE_0011	Left row 2 left	Left column #2
2 fingers	RELEASE_1100	Right row 2 right	Right column #2
3 fingers	RELEASE_0001	Left row 3 left	Left column #3
3 fingers	RELEASE_1000	Right row 3 right	Right column #3

5 Experiment of TEXTile: Evaluation of the Learning Curve

The purpose of this experiment was to evaluate novice performance and the learning curve of the TEXTile technique on smart glasses.

5.1 Participants

Nine unpaid volunteers (two female) participated in the experiment (average age 24 years, all right-handed) were recruited from the University's Computer Science program for a five-days study. Participants never used smart glasses neither connected textile surfaces in the past. In addition, they did not participate in any of the previous studies we conducted.

5.2 Task

Participants completed a text entry task with the TEXTile technique. The experiment was structured into 10 sessions that were split into five days, two sessions each day, to observe the learning curve and fatigue levels. Each session lasted 12 min. During this time the participants entered short text phrases as quickly and accurately as possible randomly selected from the MacKenzie and Soukoreff corpus [48].

5.3 Procedure

The experiment was a within-subjects design, with one independent variable, the session. The sessions (1–10) were used to check the learning effect and the novice performances. On the first session and before starting the tests, participants are asked to read a document specifying the purpose of the experiment, the tasks to be performed, and the devices to be used. The document explains also the text entry technique and how to perform typing and releasing to write letters based on visual aid on smart glasses. After that, they completed a training session where they had to enter the sentence "hello world" to get familiar with the smart glasses, the fabric and the technique. No prior training was performed because the goal of our evaluation is to observe how the performance varied over time. During this pre-test, if a participant had a problem, then they could ask the experimenter for help. Data from this session were discarded and this was done only one time, at the beginning of the first session.

Following the training session and after a short break, the test application started. Each participant typed sentences for 12 min. The timing started after the participants typed the first letter. A sentence was validated once typing the "enter" key. Error correction was allowed using the "back" key. It is up to the user to make as few mistakes as possible while keeping a good speed of data entry. The test procedure for other sessions was the same as the first session, not including the training session. During the experiment, the experimenter took notes from the observations of the behavior of the participants.

At the end of the experiment (i.e., after session 10), the participants shared their comments on the experiment and the tested device. They also filled out the NASA-TLX evaluation, a subjective feedback form to assess perceived workload. They also complete a SUS questionnaire to measure the usability of the tested technique.

5.4 Apparatus

We conducted this experiment under the same conditions as the previous experiment, with the same equipment.

5.5 Collected Data

During this study, we recorded the expected sentence, each operation on the surface (Start position, RELEASE) with the time of the event. In addition, to the data collected during the interaction, we collected all questionnaire answers (SUS, NASA-TLX), the informal comments from the participants and the observations we noted during the experiment.

5.6 Results

Text Entry Speed - The Learning Curve. Figure 6 shows the text entry speed overage over each session. The one-way repeated measures ANOVA showed a significant effect of the sessions ($F_{8,72} = 19,53, p < .001$). Tukey's HSD post hoc tests on sessions were carried out for text entry speed. Comparisons using the Tukey HSD test indicated that sessions six and nine, seven and ten were significantly different.

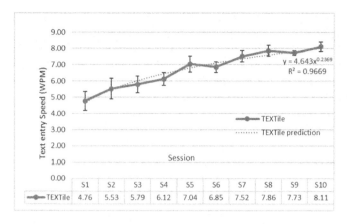

Fig. 6. Text entry speed by session.

We derive the regression model in the form of the power law of learning. The equation and the squared correlation coefficients are shown in Fig. 6.

Errors. We distinguish two levels of errors:

- Corrected error: error that caused an entry of a wrong character with correction.
- Uncorrected error: error that caused an entry of a wrong character without correction.

Figure 7 shows the average rate of the corrected errors over each session and Fig. 8 shows the average rate of the uncorrected errors by session.

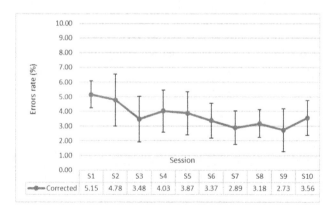

Fig. 7. Corrected text entry errors by session.

The one-way repeated measures ANOVA showed that the difference between the session is significant for corrected errors and for uncorrected errors.

Another type of error that was reported is soft error when the users make a row selection error (i.e., an error during the first action and the user cancels without causing an entry of a character, the passage S2 → S0 and S3 → S0 in Fig. 4). The soft error rate was 5.65% (SD 0.74) in the first session to 4.17% (SD 0.51) in the last session.

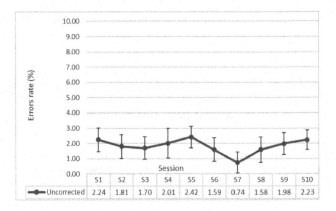

Fig. 8. Uncorrected text entry errors by session.

Participant Feedback. The results of the SUS questionnaires demonstrated an average of 76.5 (SD 6.89) for the TEXTile technique. The NASA-TLX questionnaires administered after the last session produced subjective ratings. Responses to these questions are summarized in Fig. 9.

When interviewing the participants about the TEXTile technique, they stated that: "at the beginning we look for how to reach a character, and it becomes a reflex action", "it requires a little concentration at first, but we take over quickly", "As we go along, the position of the letters are retained and automatically actions are made without looking at the keyboard" and "it takes a little time to get used with."

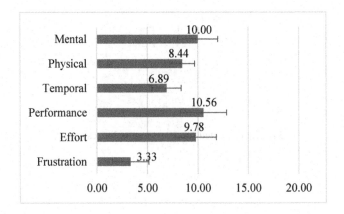

Fig. 9. Average NASA-TLX score of TEXTile technique.

Our primary findings from study 2 is related to the position of the arm carrying the textile. The participants who started the test with the arm in front of the eyes to write finished with their arm along the body.

6 Discussion

The results of our study show that although the TEXTile technique started with a relatively low speed (4.76 WPM; SD 0.58), the participants were still able to learn the technique as the study progressed. That is, they eventually achieved an entry speed of 8.11 WPM (SD 0.29) in the last session, after 2 h of practice. These results are not surprising, because participants never practiced text input with the TEXTile technique. They were also not in a comfortable position because they were standing to simulate a standing mobility context.

Although our longitudinal study lasted 10 sessions, it did not last long, so the participants never became experts. It is hard to judge the performance of TEXTile technique after 2 h of use but the results of our study show that users were able to type using TEXTile and meet the requirement of mobility context.

The error rate is relatively low (see Fig. 7). Increasing speed through sessions is not done at the expense of error. We also noticed a soft error rate from 5.65% (SD 0.74) in the first session to 4.10% (SD 0.51) in the last session. These errors can be explained by the fact that the participants choose a combination and then cancelled. Part of the errors was due to a combination that was not done correctly. For example, if it requested to release the middle finger, the ring finger and the little finger (RELEASE_1000), then the user releases the middle finger and the ring finger and after a time longer than the validation time he/she releases the little finger, and thus, the combinations were perceived as sequentially, which caused a misinterpretation of the combination and considered as (RELEASE_1001).

The results of the SUS questionnaire indicated a score of 76% for the TEXTile technique. This value can be considered as reaching a good level of satisfaction [49]. The results of the NASA-TLX questionnaire were also very encouraging in the absence of negative scores, while highlighting the mental and physical requirements necessary to accomplish the task.

Although the TEXTile technique was new to the participants, they found it very instructive. Participants also noted that their learning of the TEXTile technique text entry became quite eventually automatic, without the need to look at the keyboard. As our goal was to provide eyes-free interaction with the device and not with the visual help displayed on the smartglasses, another study will be necessary to measure when this visual help is no more useful.

7 Conclusion and Future Work

We designed a new text entry technique referred to as TEXTile, in conjunction with the use of smart glasses. This technique uses a new connected fabric as a device that can be integrated into one's clothing. It provides typing without requiring users to hold a device. The user performs multi-touch of fingers anywhere on the fabric surface with no anchored targets for typing. The results of our user study demonstrated that the TEXTile technique had a good performance by reaching 8.11 WPM showing the feasibility of using TEXTile for text entry. After 2 h of practice, the participants speed of input continued to grow throughout the study.

There are several limitations to the study that should be noted. First, the participants of the study were limited with high degrees of experience with technology and computing. However, the research findings presented here were only intended to be exploratory; and as such, we used a convenience sample of users, i.e., students. Next steps will include testing using a more general population, to assess the value of the technology in other real-world settings. We hope to test TEXTile on a broader participant population to assess usability and learning, in a fairer context. Another perspective is to conduct a blind experiment setting for experts where users do not have visual feedback to limit the visual attention the user devotes to smart glasses visual feedback.

For our future work, we plan to make improvements to TEXTile, in order to address several issues. The first would be to improve our prototype and to keep up with new advances in digital fabrics technology. One possibility will be to have a two-dimensional textile surface to compare our text entry technique to other techniques like Graffiti [11] or EdgeWrite [12]. This improvement will allow us to use the textile surface for other type of interaction, other than the text entry like pointing and manipulating interfaces in smart glasses.

We plan to permit users to edit their text (selection, copy, paste, etc.) and control the interface. We still have several possibilities with combinations of fingers that have not been explored, e.g., combinations with three fingers as starting position. Now, our technique uses two actions to enter a character. As such, we will increase the input speed by evaluating our technique using the first action to select the region and a prediction model to replace the second action to select the character. Lastly, we will also focus our revised version of TEXTile on providing an auto-completion and auto-correction function.

References

1. Wiese, J., Saponas, T.S., Brush, A.J.: Phoneprioception: enabling mobile phones to infer where they are kept. In: Proceedings of the SIGCHI Conference on Human Factors in Computing Systems, pp. 2157–2166. ACM, April 2013
2. Google Glass Project (2017). https://en.wikipedia.org/wiki/GoogleGlass/. Accessed 5 Nov 2018

3. Yi, S., Qin, Z., Novak, E., Yin, Y., Li, Q.: GlassGesture: exploring head gesture interface of smart glasses. In: IEEE INFOCOM 2016-The 35th Annual IEEE International Conference on Computer Communications, pp. 1–9. IEEE, April 2016
4. Kollee, B., Kratz, S., Dunnigan, A.: Exploring gestural interaction in smart spaces using head mounted devices with ego-centric sensing. In: Proceedings of the 2nd ACM Symposium on Spatial User Interaction, pp. 40–49. ACM, October 2014
5. McCall, R., Martin, B., Popleteev, A., Louveton, N., Engel, T.: Text entry on smart glasses. In: 2015 8th International Conference on Human System Interactions (HSI), pp. 195–200. IEEE, June 2015
6. Profita, H.P., et al.: Don't mind me touching my wrist: a case study of interacting with on-body technology in public. In: Proceedings of the 2013 International Symposium on Wearable Computers, pp. 89–96. ACM, September 2013
7. Kim, H., Sohn, M., Kim, S., Pak, J., Lee, W.: Button keyboard: a very small keyboard with universal usability for wearable computing. In: Baranauskas, C., Palanque, P., Abascal, J., Barbosa, S.D.J. (eds.) INTERACT 2007. LNCS, vol. 4662, pp. 343–346. Springer, Heidelberg (2007). https://doi.org/10.1007/978-3-540-74796-3_32
8. Lyons, K., et al.: Twiddler typing: one-handed chording text entry for mobile phones. In: Proceedings of the SIGCHI Conference on Human Factors in Computing Systems, pp. 671–678. ACM, April 2004
9. Frey, B., Southern, C., Romero, M.: BrailleTouch: mobile texting for the visually impaired. In: Stephanidis, C. (ed.) UAHCI 2011. LNCS, vol. 6767, pp. 19–25. Springer, Heidelberg (2011). https://doi.org/10.1007/978-3-642-21666-4_3
10. Azenkot, S., Wobbrock, J.O., Prasain, S., Ladner, R.E.: Input finger detection for nonvisual touch screen text entry in Perkinput. In: Proceedings of Graphics Interface 2012, pp. 121–129. Canadian Information Processing Society, May 2012
11. Tinwala, H., MacKenzie, I.S.: Eyes-free text entry on a touchscreen phone. In: 2009 IEEE Toronto International Conference on Science and Technology for Humanity (TIC-STH), pp. 83–88. IEEE, September 2009
12. Wobbrock, J.O., Myers, B.A., Kembel, J.A.: EdgeWrite: a stylus-based text entry method designed for high accuracy and stability of motion. In: Proceedings of the 16th Annual ACM Symposium on User Interface Software and Technology, pp. 61–70. ACM, 2003 November
13. Perlin, K.: Quikwriting: continuous stylus-based text entry. In: ACM Symposium on User Interface Software and Technology, pp. 215–216, November 1998
14. 8pen Project (2019). http://www.8pen.com/. Accessed 14 Apr 2019
15. Amma, C., Georgi, M., Schultz, T.: Airwriting: hands-free mobile text input by spotting and continuous recognition of 3D-space handwriting with inertial sensors. In: 2012 16th International Symposium on Wearable Computers (ISWC), pp. 52–59. IEEE, June 2012
16. Ni, T., Bowman, D., North, C.: AirStroke: bringing unistroke text entry to freehand gesture interfaces. In: Proceedings of the SIGCHI Conference on Human Factors in Computing Systems, pp. 2473–2476. ACM, May 2011
17. Hincapié-Ramos, J.D., Guo, X., Moghadasian, P., Irani, P.: Consumed endurance: a metric to quantify arm fatigue of mid-air interactions. In: Proceedings of the 32nd Annual ACM Conference on Human Factors in Computing Systems, pp. 1063–1072. ACM, April 2014
18. Hsieh, Y.T., Jylhä, A., Orso, V., Gamberini, L., Jacucci, G.: Designing a willing-to-use-in-public hand gestural interaction technique for smart glasses. In: Proceedings of the 2016 CHI Conference on Human Factors in Computing Systems, pp. 4203–4215. ACM, May 2016
19. Nesbat, S.B.: A system for fast, full-text entry for small electronic devices. In: Proceedings of the 5th International Conference on Multimodal Interfaces, pp. 4–11. ACM, November 2003
20. FlickKey keyboard (2017). http://www.flickkey.com/. Accessed 14 Apr 2019

21. Kim, J., Delamare, W., Irani, P.: ThumbText: text entry for wearable devices using a miniature ring. In: Proceedings of Graphics interface Conference (2018)
22. MacKenzie, I.S., Soukoreff, R.W., Helga, J.: 1 thumb, 4 buttons, 20 words per minute: design and evaluation of H4-Writer. In: Proceedings of the 24th Annual ACM Symposium on User Interface Software and Technology, pp. 471–480. ACM, October 2011
23. Bajer, B.R., MacKenzie, I.S., Baljko, M.: Huffman base-4 text entry glove (H4 TEG). In: 2012 16th International Symposium on Wearable Computers (ISWC), pp. 41–47. IEEE, June 2012
24. Isokoski, P., Raisamo, R.: Device independent text input: a rationale and an example. In: Proceedings of the Working Conference on Advanced Visual Interfaces, pp. 76–83. ACM, May 2000
25. Hoste, L., Dumas, B., Signer, B.: SpeeG: a multimodal speech-and gesture-based text input solution. In: Proceedings of the International Working Conference on Advanced Visual Interfaces, pp. 156–163. ACM, May 2012
26. Wang, C.Y., Chu, W.C., Chiu, P.T., Hsiu, M.C., Chiang, Y.H., Chen, M.Y.: PalmType: using palms as keyboards for smart glasses. In: Proceedings of the 17th International Conference on Human-Computer Interaction with Mobile Devices and Services, pp. 153–160. ACM, August 2015
27. Yu, C., Sun, K., Zhong, M., Li, X., Zhao, P., Shi, Y.: One-dimensional handwriting: inputting letters and words on smart glasses. In: Proceedings of the 2016 CHI Conference on Human Factors in Computing Systems, pp. 71–82. ACM, May 2016
28. Grossman, T., Chen, X.A., Fitzmaurice, G.: Typing on glasses: adapting text entry to smart eyewear. In: Proceedings of the 17th International Conference on Human-Computer Interaction with Mobile Devices and Services, pp. 144–152. ACM, August 2015
29. Chen, X.A., Grossman, T., Fitzmaurice, G.: Swipeboard: a text entry technique for ultra-small interfaces that supports novice to expert transitions. In: Proceedings of the 27th Annual ACM Symposium on User Interface Software and Technology, pp. 615–620. ACM, October 2014
30. Ahn, S., Heo, S., Lee, G.: Typing on a smartwatch for smart glasses. In: Proceedings of the 2017 ACM International Conference on Interactive Surfaces and Spaces, pp. 201–209. ACM, October 2017
31. Jones, E., Alexander, J., Andreou, A., Irani, P., Subramanian, S.: GesText: accelerometer-based gestural text-entry systems. In: Proceedings of the SIGCHI Conference on Human Factors in Computing Systems, pp. 2173–2182. ACM, April 2010
32. Prätorius, M., Valkov, D., Burgbacher, U., Hinrichs, K.: DigiTap: an eyes-free VR/AR symbolic input device. In: Proceedings of the 20th ACM Symposium on Virtual Reality Software and Technology, pp. 9–18. ACM, November 2014
33. Huang, D.Y., et al.: DigitSpace: designing thumb-to-fingers touch interfaces for one-handed and eyes-free interactions. In: Proceedings of the 2016 CHI Conference on Human Factors in Computing Systems, pp. 1526–1537. ACM, May 2016
34. Kuester, F., Chen, M., Phair, M.E., Mehring, C.: Towards keyboard independent touch typing in VR. In: Proceedings of the ACM Symposium on Virtual Reality Software and Technology, pp. 86–95. ACM, November 2005
35. Lee, S., Hong, S.H., Jeon, J.W.: Designing a universal keyboard using chording gloves. In: Proceedings of the 2003 Conference on Universal Usability (CUU 2003), pp. 142–147. ACM, New York (2003)
36. Whitmire, E., Jain, M., Jain, D., Nelson, G., Karkar, R., Patel, S., Goel, M.: DigiTouch: reconfigurable thumb-to-finger input and text entry on head-mounted displays. Proc. ACM Interact. Mob. Wearable Ubiquitous Technol. 1(3), 113 (2017)

37. Nirjon, S., Gummeson, J., Gelb, D., Kim, K.H.: TypingRing: a wearable ring platform for text input. In: Proceedings of the 13th Annual International Conference on Mobile Systems, Applications, and Services, pp. 227–239. ACM, May 2015

38. Chan, L.R., et al.: FingerPad: private and subtle interaction using fingertips. In: Proceedings of the 26th Annual ACM Symposium on User Interface Software and Technology, pp. 255–260. ACM, October 2013

39. Majaranta, P., Aula, A., Räihä, K.J.: Effects of feedback on eye typing with a short dwell time. In: Proceedings of the 2004 Symposium on Eye Tracking Research & Applications, pp. 139–146. ACM, March 2004

40. Yu, C., Gu, Y., Yang, Z., Yi, X., Luo, H., Shi, Y.: Tap, dwell or gesture?: Exploring head-based text entry techniques for HMDs. In: Proceedings of the 2017 CHI Conference on Human Factors in Computing Systems, pp. 4479–4488. ACM, May 2017

41. Poupyrev, I., Gong, N.W., Fukuhara, S., Karagozler, M.E., Schwesig, C., Robinson, K.E.: Project Jacquard: interactive digital textiles at scale. In: Proceedings of the 2016 CHI Conference on Human Factors in Computing Systems, pp. 4216–4227. ACM, May 2016

42. Saponas, T.S., Harrison, C., Benko, H.: PocketTouch: through-fabric capacitive touch input. In: Proceedings of the 24th Annual ACM Symposium on User Interface Software and Technology, pp. 303–308. ACM, October 2011

43. Zhou, B., Cheng, J., Sundholm, M., Lukowicz, P.: From smart clothing to smart table cloth: design and implementation of a large scale, textile pressure matrix sensor. In: Maehle, E., Römer, K., Karl, W., Tovar, E. (eds.) ARCS 2014. LNCS, vol. 8350, pp. 159–170. Springer, Cham (2014). https://doi.org/10.1007/978-3-319-04891-8_14

44. Schneegass, S., Voit, A.: GestureSleeve: using touch sensitive fabrics for gestural input on the forearm for controlling smartwatches. In: Proceedings of the 2016 ACM International Symposium on Wearable Computers, pp. 108–115. ACM, September 2016

45. Strohmeier, P., Knibbe, J., Boring, S., Hornbæk, K.: zPatch: hybrid resistive/capacitive eTextile input. In: Proceedings of the Twelfth International Conference on Tangible, Embedded, and Embodied Interaction, pp. 188–198. ACM, March 2018

46. Ian Adafruit MPR121 12-Key Capacitive Touch Sensor Breakout (2019). https://learn.adafruit.com/adafruit-mpr121-12-key-capacitive-touch-sensor-breakout-tutorial/overview. Accessed 14 Apr 2019

47. Rico, J., Brewster, S.: Usable gestures for mobile interfaces: evaluating social acceptability. In: Proceedings of the SIGCHI Conference on Human Factors in Computing Systems, pp. 887–896. ACM, April 2010

48. MacKenzie, I.S., Soukoreff, R.W.: Phrase sets for evaluating text entry techniques. In: CHI 2003 Extended Abstracts on Human Factors in Computing Systems, pp. 754–755. ACM, April 2003

49. Bangor, A., Kortum, P.T., Miller, J.T.: An empirical evaluation of the system usability scale. Int. J. Hum.-Comput. Interact. **24**(6), 574–594 (2008)

Games and Gamification

"I Don't Fit into a Single Type":
A Trait Model and Scale of Game Playing
Preferences

Gustavo F. Tondello$^{(\boxtimes)}$ (iD), Karina Arrambide (iD), Giovanni Ribeiro,
Andrew Jian-lan Cen, and Lennart E. Nacke (iD)

University of Waterloo, Waterloo, ON, Canada
gustavo@tondello.com, karina.arrambide@gmail.com,
ggsribei@uwaterloo.ca, jin.lan.cen@gmail.com,
lennart.nacke@acm.org

Abstract. Player typology models classify different player motivations and behaviours. These models are necessary to design personalized games or to target specific audiences. However, many models lack validation and standard measurement instruments. Additionally, they rely on type theories, which split players into separate categories. Yet, personality research has lately favoured trait theories, which recognize that people's preferences are composed of a sum of different characteristics. Given these shortcomings of existing models, we developed a player traits model built on a detailed review and synthesis of the extant literature, which introduces five player traits: aesthetic orientation, narrative orientation, goal orientation, social orientation, and challenge orientation. Furthermore, we created and validated a 25-item measurement scale for the five player traits. This scale outputs a player profile, which describes participants' preferences for different game elements and game playing styles. Finally, we demonstrate that this is the first validated player preferences model and how it serves as an actionable tool for personalized game design.

Keywords: Player traits · Player types · Player experience ·
Video games · Games user research

1 Introduction

The Games User Research (GUR) community has been collectively studying and classifying player preferences to understand what playing styles and game elements are enjoyed by what people. This knowledge can help designers create games better targeted to their audience, so they can offer their players the content they want [26, 36]; marketers segment their player base [15], so their campaigns can be more effective; and researchers explain the variables that influence the player's experience and enjoyment. This can also lead to the design of more effective games with a purpose, such as educational or health-related games.

© IFIP International Federation for Information Processing 2019
Published by Springer Nature Switzerland AG 2019
D. Lamas et al. (Eds.): INTERACT 2019, LNCS 11747, pp. 375–395, 2019.
https://doi.org/10.1007/978-3-030-29384-0_23

But despite the efforts of the community and the recent advances, we still lack a player preferences model that is backed by empirical evidence and a validated measurement instrument [15].

Given these shortcomings of the existing literature, we present and validate a player traits model with an accompanying measurement scale. More specifically, we build upon the research of Tondello et al. [35], which suggested the investigation of five player traits: action orientation, goal orientation, social orientation, aesthetic orientation, and immersion orientation. Their suggestion was based on the study of prior attempts to classify player preferences in types (e.g., [1,26]). However, type theories have been criticized as inadequate in personality research, giving ground to trait theories [13,23]. Trait theories interpret an individual as a sum of different characteristics, whereas type theories try to classify people in separate categories. But player type models rarely work in practice because people actually have several overlapping motivations, some weaker and some stronger. Rarely is someone motivated by a single factor. Therefore, trait theories have been suggested to also be a better approach to classify player motivations and behaviours in games [4,15,35]. In this context, the BrainHex [4,26] was developed; a top-down player types model tentatively created to help understand player preferences and develop a definitive player traits model. Thus, Tondello and colleagues continued this line of investigation by analyzing the BrainHex data [26] and devising the five-trait player preferences model.

In the present work, we created a survey based on Tondello et al.'s [35] suggested five-trait model and validated its factor structure and content. We devised a survey with ten items per trait and collected data from 332 participants to validate it. Then, we conducted a factor analysis and a reliability analysis to retain the five items that contributed most to each subscale. Next, we conducted a confirmatory factor analysis with structural equation modelling to validate the final 25-item (five per trait) survey. Finally, we compared participants' player trait scores with their preferences for different game elements and game playing styles [36]. We found several significant correlations, demonstrating that the five player traits correspond to different playing preferences.

It is important to understand the relationship between personality, playing preferences, and enjoyment of game elements because this knowledge has uses in the design of targeted and adaptive games, as well as targeted multimedia advertising campaigns. Our research contributes to the HCI gaming community by shedding light on what playing styles are enjoyed with what specific game elements by what people. Our work introduces and validates a novel player traits model, with a standard 25-item survey to score people on the five traits. We also demonstrate that participants' scores in these five player traits help explain their preferences for different game elements and playing styles.

2   Related Work

Player motivations can be studied from three distinct perspectives: the general reasons why people play games, how people play different games, or how different game dynamics or mechanics motivate distinct player experiences. The present work and the extant literature reviewed in this section focus on the later topic. Thus, we are not concerned with why people play games, but rather with how they interact with and are more or less motivated by the diverse game dynamics that they experience. The objective of this research field so far has been to represent these preferences in player typologies. However, this paper aims to build a testable model of player traits instead of player types because traits can better represent the diverse range of playing motivations.

Caillois [9] was the first to present a typology of playful behaviour with four categories: *Agôn* (games of challenge), *Alea* (games of chance), *Mimicry* (playing as someone or something else), and *Ilinx* (visceral impact). Later, Malone's theory of motivating instruction [21] identified three categories of fun: challenge, fantasy, and curiosity. Based on these categories, a set of design heuristics was presented, where curiosity is used as an incentive to keep players engaged.

Bartle [1] presented the first modern player typology, which was based on two axes that represent players' interaction with the virtual world or with other players. In this typology, Achievers are constantly seeking to earn points or other virtual rewards in the game; Socialisers are focused in social interactions within the game and in forming relationships with other players; Explorers are interested in discovering and learning the game world; and Killers are focused in competitive game play and defeating other players. Bartle later expanded the model with a third dimension: whether the players actions are implicit or explicit [2]. However, Bartle never presented a validated measurement scale. Although many informal scales exist and are used online, they are more recreational rather than a scientific scoring system. Thus, it is not possible to confidently screen players using Bartle's typology or make assumptions about their gaming preferences.

Following a more systematic approach, the BrainHex [26] was developed, based on a series of demographic game design studies [3,4] and neurobiological research [5]. It presents seven player types: Seeker (motivated by curiosity), Survivor (motivated by fear), Daredevil (motivated by excitement), Mastermind (motivated by strategy), Conqueror (motivated by challenge), Socialiser (motivated by social interaction), and Achiever (motivated by goal completion). A survey was conducted among more than 50,000 players establishing a relationship between them and the Myers-Briggs Type Indicator (MBTI) [25]. The BrainHex has been used in several studies to investigate players' motivation in games (e.g., [6,28]). However, two independent studies [8,35] found several issues related to its psychometric properties (factor validity, stability, and consistency). Additionally, the development of BrainHex was based on type theories, and particularly on the MBTI, which itself has several reliability and validation issues and is being replaced by trait theories in the psychology literature [23]. Therefore, the BrainHex scale cannot be reliably used to classify player preferences.

Yee et al. also employed a systematic approach throughout several studies [41,44], ultimately leading to an analysis with over 140,000 participants of all game genres and the development of the gamer motivation profile [42]. In this model, 12 dimensions are grouped into six clusters: Action (destruction and excitement), Social (competition and community), Mastery (challenge and strategy), Achievement (competition and power), Immersion (fantasy and story), and Creativity (design and discovery). They also established correlations between these dimensions and personality traits [43]. This gamer motivation profile could be used to aid in the design of personalized games; however, its survey is a proprietary instrument, which makes it difficult to apply in every situation, especially for smaller game studios. On the other hand, we are making our measurement scale publicly available in this work; thus, it can be widely used by anyone.

Vahlo and Hamari [38] recently presented a five-factor inventory of intrinsic motivations to gameplay: Relatedness, Autonomy, Competence, Immersion, and Fun. Although their model is somewhat similar to ours because both introduce five different factors that motivate gameplay, their work is explicitly aimed at understanding the general motivations why people play games, without differentiating which gameplay activities they find more enjoyable. On the other hand, our work has the opposite goal of classifying the different gameplay styles preferred for each player, instead of the general reasons why they play games.

Hamari and Tuunanen [15] presented a literature review and a meta-synthesis of the existing player typologies. They identified five common constructs, which appear in some form in many of the available typologies: Achievement, Exploration, Sociability, Domination, and Immersion. Nonetheless, they also noted that not all models have been properly validated, that there are numerous methodological differences between them, and claimed for more research towards a definitive player preferences model. We answer this call in the present work.

2.1 The Proposed Model of Five Player Traits

As we mentioned before, the BrainHex was created as an interim model, aimed at providing the grounds for the development of a definitive player traits model. Building upon that work, Tondello et al. [35] conducted a series of analyses over the original BrainHex dataset [26]. The results showed that the BrainHex scale was only able to discriminate three types instead of the proposed seven: (1) *action orientation* (represented by the conqueror and daredevil archetypes); (2) *aesthetic orientation* (represented by the socializer and seeker archetypes); and (3) *goal orientation* (represented by the mastermind, achiever, and survivor archetypes). Furthermore, by inspecting the results and considering the existing literature on player typologies, Tondello and colleagues suggested that two additional traits should be considered, even though they were not originally captured by the BrainHex: *social orientation* and *immersion orientation*. The first, because social motivations are present in all existing player motivation theories, and the second because immersion is also a motivation listed in many existing theories [15] and evidence has been found that participants' attitudes towards story are related to their gaming preferences [35].

The present study builds upon Tondello et al.'s [35] work by introducing a new scale and providing evidence of the structural and construct validity of the player traits model, while also investigating player preferences for different elements of play and analyzing new player preferences data to provide a wider scope. This scale and its validation provide a more robust model for future applications. In summary, we base our work off the following player traits. Below, we also discuss some of the theoretical grounds for each proposed player trait, based on personality [10,13] and motivation [11,32] theories. However, it is important to note that these theories only partly explain the player traits, which were derived from data analyses from the aforementioned works, rather than from theory. Thus, it is not clear what other psychological factors influence them.

Social orientation: the player's preference for playing together with others online or in the same space. The motivation fostered by this kind of player experiences is explained by the psychological need for relatedness (the need to have meaningful interactions with others) discussed by self-determination theory (SDT) [11,32,33]. Moreover, people with more extraverted and agreeable personalities are usually more open to social experiences.

Aesthetic orientation: the player's preference for aesthetic experiences, such as exploring the game world and appreciating the game's graphics, sound, and art style. People are mainly motivated towards this type of gameplay by their openness to experience and the psychological need for autonomy [33], which is satisfied when the player can explore new paths and tailor their own journey.

Action orientation: the player's preference for challenging and fast-paced gameplay. As explained by SDT [33], this kind of experiences satisfies the psychological need for competence when the player can overcome the challenges.

Goal orientation: the player's preference for gameplay that involves completing quests or tasks, collecting digital objects, or similar experiences. This preference is also motivated by the psychological need for competence [33], but it is more focused on the amount or percentage of tasks completed, whereas action orientation is more focused on overcoming a few highly difficult challenges.

Immersion orientation: the player's preference for complex stories or narratives within games. This preference is also fostered by the player's openness to experience, but recent research has also showed that some people might simply be naturally more inclined to enjoy narratives [27].

2.2   Game Elements and Game Playing Styles

Tondello et al. [36] noted that past approaches to studying player types and preferences have ignored the relationship between those types and the activity elements of games. Those works focused only on high-level factors such as achievement or immersion. The issue with this is that it makes the application of those frameworks to the design of games difficult. Hence, Tondello et al. mapped constructs on an intermediate granularity level, commonly referred to as game dynamics or elements. In addition, they also investigated the different modes or styles of play such as a preference for single or multiplayer gameplay. These game playing styles can be combined with various game elements to create a variety of experiences. The game elements bore out by their work include strategic resource management, puzzle, artistic movement (such as music or painting), sports and cards, role-playing, virtual goods (dynamics of acquisition and collection), simulation, action (fast-paced play), and progression. The game playing styles found to be reliable were multiplayer (including cooperative and competitive), abstract interaction (such as from an isometric point of view), solo play, competitive community (such as streaming and e-sports), and casual gaming.

Similarly, Vahlo et al. [39] also provide a categorization of common game dynamics, structured in five factors: assault (dynamics of killing and murdering), manage (acquisition and development of resources), journey (exploration of the gameworld), care (showing affection and taking care of pets), and coordinate (matching tiles or music). In addition, they propose a clustering of player preferences based on their scored interest for each one of these groups of dynamics, identifying seven player types: mercenary, adventurer, commander, daredevil, companion, patterner, and explorer.

The five-trait model we propose and validate in this work is meant to address the building blocks of actionable game design. Therefore, we need to investigate if these player traits will correspond to participants' preferences for different elements of gaming. Thus, we compare participants' player traits scores with their preferences for game elements and playing styles from Tondello et al. [36], which we chose because their study considered a larger pool of game dynamics and identified a more diverse number of categories in comparison to Vahlo et al. The goal of this comparison is to validate the content of our player traits model and its usefulness for predicting player preferences.

3   Methods

We conducted an online survey between February and August 2018 using the Qualtrics platform provided by the University of Waterloo.

3.1   Survey Development

The player traits survey items were collaboratively developed by four researchers in two phases. In the first phase, we used a brainstorming approach to generate tentative items. First, each researcher studied the description of each of the five player traits from [35]. Next, each researcher wrote several suggested items that could be used to score someone on that trait. In the second phase, we put together all the suggested items from all researchers and collectively selected those that seemed the best. For the selection, each researcher read all the items available for each trait and voted for the items they thought would best represent the trait. Each researcher could vote on an unlimited number of items. In the end, the ten items per trait that received the highest amount of votes were included in the player traits survey. The complete list of items is presented in Table 1.

The online survey included the following sections. We used a 7-point Likert scale for all sections, except the demographic information, due to its prevalence in prior studies and its ability to detect subtle participant preferences.

Table 1. All the player traits survey items.

#	Items
T1	I like to build or create new things or objects or characters in games
T2	I like games with unique art styles
T3	I often feel in awe with the landscapes or other game imagery
T4	I like to customize how my character looks in a game
T5	I like it when games have an element of exploration
T6	I care more about gameplay than about graphics and sound. (R)
T7	The quality of the graphics and sound are really important for my appreciation of a game
T8	I like to spend some time exploring the game world
T9	I like it when games look unique or vibrant
T10	I usually choose gear, weapons, or other game items based on what they look like
I1	I like games which make me feel like I am actually in a different place
I2	I enjoy complex narratives in a game
I3	I like games that allow me to make decisions over the story
I4	I like games with detailed worlds or universes to explore
I5	I like it when I can be someone else in the game
I6	I like games that pull me in with their story
I7	I usually skip the story portions or the cutscenes when I am playing. (R)
I8	I feel like storytelling often gets in the way of actually playing the game. (R)
I9	Story is not important to me when I play games. (R)
I10	I like it when playing a game makes me lose track of time
G1	I usually do not care if I do not complete all optional parts of a game. (R)
G2	I enjoy games that provide many optional goals for me to complete
G3	I like games with lots of collectibles to find
G4	I often start quests in games that I don't finish. (R)
G5	I am not concerned with whether or not I finish a game. (R)
G6	I feel stressed if I do not complete all the tasks in a game
G7	I like to complete all the tasks and objectives in a game
G8	I like completing games 100%
G9	I like finishing quests
G10	I ignore most side quests when I play games. (R)
S1	I like to interact with other people in a game
S2	I often prefer to play games alone. (R)
S3	I like it when I have to collaborate with other players to solve a challenge
S4	I don't like playing with other people. (R)
S5	I feel I can become friends with the people I play online with
S6	I like to play online with other players
S7	I like it when games require co-operation between players
S8	I like games that let me play in guilds or teams
S9	I don't enjoy multiplayer games. (R)
S10	I like it when games allow me to communicate to other players online
A1	I enjoy highly difficult challenges in games
A2	I usually play games at the highest difficulty setting
A3	I like it when games challenge me
A4	I like it when games get my heart beating fast
A5	I like it when keeping my character alive is difficult
A6	I usually avoid playing games at the highest difficulty setting. (R)
A7	I like it when progression in a game demands skill
A8	I like easy games. (R)
A9	I like it when goals are hard to achieve in games
A10	I like games that let me move at high speed

Notes. Items marked with (R) were reversed for scoring.
The codes beside each item correspond to their position in the survey and the original intended trait for the item: T = Aesthetic, I = Immersion, G = Goal, S = Social, A = Action.

1. Demographic information
2. Personality inventory (BFI-10 [29])
3. Player traits items (see Table 1)
4. Game elements preferences (the top three elements by group from [36])
5. Game playing style preferences (the top three styles by group from [36])

Regarding sections 4 (game elements preferences) and 5 (game playing style preferences) of the survey, Tondello et al. [36] classified player preferences in nine groups of three to 13 game design elements each, and five groups of one to six game playing styles each. But to score participants on these groups, we just asked them about their preferences for the three highest-loading game elements and playing styles for each group, as three items are usually enough to obtain a score for a latent variable.

3.2   Participants

We recruited participants through social media (Twitter, Facebook, and Reddit) and mailing lists. Participants were only required to be 15 years or older and have a working understanding of English. As an incentive, they were offered the possibility to enter a draw for one of two $50 international gift cards. In total, 350 participants completed the survey. However, we had to discard one participant who took less than five minutes to complete the survey (which we considered the minimum time to respond carefully according to our tests) and 17 responses that did not include answers to all the player trait items. Therefore, the final dataset contained 332 responses (212 men, 100 women, 11 transgender, 6 nonbinary, and 3 identified as other). Participants were between 15 and 57 years old ($M = 25.7$, $SD = 7.1$).

Participants were from all continents, with the following distribution: North America (53.3%), Europe (27.1%), Asia (11.4%), Oceania (4.8%), South and Central Americas (3.0%), and Africa (0.3%). However, 318 participants (95.8%) reported a high English proficiency and 14 (4.2%) reported a medium proficiency. Therefore, we assume that language understanding was adequate.

Regarding game playing habits, 305 (91.9%) participants reported playing regularly on desktop or laptop computers, 240 (72.3%) play regularly on consoles, and 230 (69.3%) play regularly on smartphones or tablets. Moreover, 156 (47.0%) participants reported playing 1–10 h per week, 101 (30.4%) play 11–20 h per week, 72 (21.7%) play more than 20 h per week, and only three (0.9%) participants reported playing less than one hour per week.

We also asked participants if they would be willing to complete a follow-up survey, which included only the player traits items, so we could calculate the test-retest reliability of the scale. 157 participants agreed to participate and were invited for the follow-up, but only 70 actually completed it. The follow-up surveys were completed between one and four weeks after the original responses.

4 Results

We present the study results with the following organization. First, we present the results of the initial factor analysis used to validate the traits structure and select the best five survey items per trait. Next, we present the results of the confirmatory factor analysis (CFA) used to evaluate the goodness of fit of the measurement model represented by the 25-item survey (five per trait), as well as the test-retest reliability analysis. Then, we discuss the player traits nomenclature and evaluate the correlations between them and with the Big-5 personality traits [13]. These analyses help to better understand the player traits and their meaning. Finally, we present the correlations of the player traits with participants' preferences for different game elements and game playing styles, which allows us to establish the model's usefulness for predicting gaming preferences.

For the factor analyses, we randomly split the dataset in two, so we could carry out the initial analysis and the CFA with different datasets. Therefore, the dataset for the initial factor analysis contained 175 responses (115 men, 49 women, 5 transgender, and 6 non-binary; $M_{age} = 25.6$, $SD = 7.1$). The dataset for the CFA contained 157 responses (97 men, 51 women, 6 transgender, and 3 other genders; $M_{age} = 25.8$, $SD = 6.9$). The number of responses in each group was not identical because of the random assignment to groups.

4.1 Initial Factor Analysis

We conducted an initial factor analysis with 175 responses to validate the trait structure and reduce the number of items in the survey. Our goal was to keep only the needed amount of items to enable scoring participants in the player traits with sufficient reliability, without making the survey too long. Prior to carrying out the analysis, we verified the sample adequacy. Regarding sample size, we considered literature that specifically investigated the conditions that influence the stability of the results, instead of the generic suggestions from textbooks, which usually do not consider the characteristics of each sample and each instrument. Three studies [14,20,40] independently concluded that good factor analysis results can be achieved with even 100–150 participants if the number of items per factor and the loading saturation (how much each item loads into their respective factor) are good. Our study included 10 items per factor (considered a good variable sampling) and the five items retained per factor had most loadings above 0.60 (considered good) or above 0.80 (very good). Thus, our sample of $N = 175$ was more than enough to produce stable results. Furthermore, the Kaiser-Meyer-Olkin (KMO) measure of sampling adequacy was .808, meaning that the sample was large enough to perform the analysis, and Bartlett's Test of Sphericity was significant ($\chi^2_{1275} = 5043.0, p < .001$), indicating that the correlations between items were sufficiently large.

The responses to the Likert items are non-parametric, with several variables showing absolute values of skewness and/or kurtosis above 1.0. Therefore, we used a polychoric correlation matrix, as recommended by Muthén and Kaplan [24]. Moreover, we employed an Oblimin rotation because we expected that the

Table 2. Factor analysis (structure matrix) of the player traits.

Items	Components				
	1 (T)	2 (I)	3 (G)	4 (S)	5 (A)
I1	**.724**				
I4	**.721**				
T8	**.694**				
T4	**.684**				
T5	.681				
T3	**.631**				
I5	.556				
G2	.537				
T2	.520				
T9	.508				
I3	.468				
T1	.426				
T10	.415				
I10					
T7					
I7 (R)		**−.840**			
I9 (R)		**−.686**			
I2	.480	**−.650**			
I6	.535	**−.622**			
I8 (R)		**−.613**			
G7			**.812**		
G1 (R)			**.804**		
G8			**.771**		
G6			**.566**		
G9	.437		**.563**		
G10 (R)		.507	.513		
G4 (R)		.366	.496		
G5 (R)			.438		
G3	.401		.422		
S6				**.874**	
S1				**.837**	
S4 (R)				**.819**	
S8				**.804**	
S2 (R)				**.793**	
S10				.791	
S7				.755	
S3				.747	
S9 (R)				.741	
S5				.681	
A9					**.846**
A1					**.842**
A3					**.821**
A2					**.795**
A7					**.785**
A6 (R)					.766
A5					.724
A4					.504
A8 (R)					.487
A10					.433
T6 (R)					
Eigenvalues	9.906	6.815	5.021	3.177	2.600
% of variance	19.424	13.363	9.845	6.230	5.098
Internal reliability (α) with five items by factor	.753	.843	.819	.914	.854

Notes. Extraction method: Unweighted Least Squares (ULS). Rotation method: Normalized Direct Oblimin. For improved visualization, the loadings <.36 (absolute values) are suppressed. The items marked in bold were the five items kept per factor. Items marked with (R) were reversed for scoring.
T = Aesthetic, I = Immersion, G = Goal, S = Social, A = Action.

components could partially overlap. In addition, we considered factor loadings greater than .36 as significant, following Field's [12] (p. 644) recommendation for a sample size of ~200 and $\alpha = .01$. An inspection of the screen plot showed a large drop of the eigenvalues after the fifth factor, suggesting that five factors should be retained, which was expected because the survey structure and the items were based on the five-trait model already described. The analysis was carried out using **FACTOR 10.8.02** [18]. The results are presented in Table 2.

After inspecting the results, we decided to keep five items per trait. Therefore, our final player traits survey contains 25 items. This number results in a survey with a good length, which can be quickly completed, while still keeping a good reliability: Cronbach's α for all traits with five items was $\geq .753$ (see Table 2). The retained items are marked in bold in Table 2. The five items selected per factor were those with the highest loadings, except the last item for factor 1 (aesthetic orientation): since the fifth highest loading item (T5) was semantically similar to the second and third, we decided to keep the sixth (T3) instead.

4.2 Confirmatory Factor Analysis and Test-Retest Reliability

After selecting the final five items per trait to keep, we conducted a confirmatory factor analysis (CFA) with the second half of the dataset (157 responses) using structural equation modelling (SEM) to verify the goodness of fit of the measurement model for the player traits. We carried out the analysis using the maximum likelihood method on **lavaan** [30], an open-source **R** package for SEM. The five player traits were modelled as latent variables, with the five items per trait as the observed measures. Figure 1 shows the SEM path model and the calculated coefficients.

The calculated fit statistics show that the model is adequate: Comparative Fit Index $(CFI) = .927$ (a $CFI \geq .90$ represents a good fit [17]); Root Mean Square Error of Approximation $(RMSEA) = .058$ (90% CI $= .051, .064$; $p < .05$) (a $RMSEA < .08$ represents a good fit [17]); and Standardized Root Mean Square Residual $(SRMR) = .067$ (a $SRMR < .08$ represents a good fit [17]). We did not

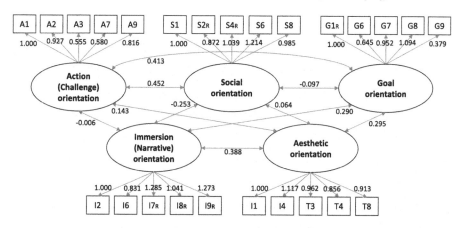

Fig. 1. Structural equation path model with calculated coefficients.

use the chi square test because it is a poor measure of model fit for large sample sizes and models with strong correlations [22,31]. Similarly, we did not use the Goodness of Fit Index (GFI) because its value is influenced by the sample size and degrees of freedom, thus rendering the interpretation very difficult [19,34].

Furthermore, we evaluated the discriminant validity of the factors using the Heterotrait-Monotrait ratio of correlations (HTMT) [16], calculated by the **semTools** package for **R**. Values below .90 indicate good discriminant validity [16]. Therefore, the results (see Table 3) showed no problems of discriminant validity, meaning that our traits are sufficiently different from each other.

Table 3. Heterotrait-Monotrait ratio of correlations (HTMT) between the player traits.

Player traits	1 (T)	2 (I)	3 (G)	4 (S)	5 (A)
1- Aesthetic orient	–				
2- Immersion orient	0.499	–			
3- Goal orient	0.300	0.271	–		
4- Social orient	0.128	0.200	0.090	–	
5- Action orient	0.142	0.109	0.225	0.264	–

We also calculated the test-retest reliability of the 25-item scale to ensure that it leads to similar scores each time someone completes it. We calculated the player trait scores using the retained five items per trait for the 70 participants who completed the follow-up survey, then compared their follow-up with their original scores. The correlations between test and retest scores are all significant with $p < .01$ (Pearson's r, one-tailed) and the following coefficients: social orientation: $r = .906$; aesthetic orientation: $r = .763$; action orientation: $r = .813$; goal orientation: $r = .844$; and immersion orientation: $r = .768$. This demonstrates that the scale is stable, meaning that a person is likely to obtain similar scores each time they take it, provided that they still have similar preferences.

4.3 Player Traits Nomenclature

Upon completion of the analyses and inspection of the five items retained per trait, we better understood what gaming preferences are associated with each trait. Therefore, we were able to reevaluate the nomenclature originally suggested by Tondello et al. [35] and we propose two modifications (see Table 4).

While factor 2 had been tentatively named as *immersion orientation*, the retained items for this factor are all related to narrative and story, whereas other aspects of immersion did not strongly contribute to this trait. Thus, we contend that *narrative orientation* is a better name for this trait. Additionally, a closer inspection of the five retained items for factor 5 (*action orientation*) shows that they are all related to challenge and difficulty. Hence, we contend that *challenge orientation* is a better name for this trait. From this point on, we only refer to the player traits using this newly proposed nomenclature.

Table 4. Tentative and definitive trait names.

Factor	Originally suggested name		Newly proposed name
1	Aesthetic orientation	→	Aesthetic orientation
2	Immersion orientation	→	Narrative orientation
3	Goal orientation	→	Goal orientation
4	Social orientation	→	Social orientation
5	Action orientation	→	Challenge orientation

4.4 Correlation Between Traits and with Personality

Table 5 presents the mean scores for each player trait, as well as the bivariate correlations (Pearson's r) between them. We calculated the trait scores for each participant as a mean percentage of the values of the 7-point Likert scale. This was also how the scores were presented to participants because a percentage is generally easier to understand than a 1–7 scale. The results suggest that aesthetic orientation and narrative orientation are the strongest player traits overall. In addition, weak or strong aesthetic and narrative playing orientations seem to generally occur together, with a correlation of $r = .377$ between them. Other significant correlations were not further examined because they are weaker.

Table 5. Descriptive statistics (mean and standard deviation) for the player traits and bivariate correlations (Pearson's r) of the traits between themselves. ($N = 332$)

Player traits	M	SD	1 (A)	2 (N)	3 (G)	4 (S)	5 (C)
1- Aesthetic orientation	80.1%	14.8	–				
2- Narrative orientation	77.7%	18.6	.377**	–			
3- Goal orientation	58.2%	19.9	.174**	.182**	–		
4- Social orientation	51.4%	24.7	.069	−.184**	−.049	–	
5- Challenge orientation	64.8%	18.6	.093	−.033	.180**	.236**	–

** $p < .01$.
A = Aesthetic, N = Narrative, G = Goal, S = Social, C = Challenge

Table 6 presents the bivariate correlations between the player traits and the Big-5 personality traits [13]. Since many studies in games user research try to understand playing preferences through personality traits, it is important to determine if the player traits proposed here are sufficiently different from, and a better alternative to understanding player preferences than personality traits.

Upon inspection of Table 6, aesthetic and narrative orientations are correlated with openness to experience. It is to be expected that more open people would be more interested in aesthetic experiences, which explains these correlations. In addition, a negative correlation exists between narrative orientation and extraversion, showing that more introverted tend to enjoy games with strong

Table 6. Bivariate correlations (Pearson's r) between players traits and Big-5 personality traits, game elements, and game playing styles. ($N = 332$)

Personality traits	1 (A)	2 (N)	3 (G)	4 (S)	5 (C)
1- Extraversion	−.106	−.169**	−.033	.254**	.060
2- Agreeableness	−.024	−.035	.086	.149**	.067
3- Conscientiousness	−.054	−.022	.141*	.077	.052
4- Neuroticism	.104	.004	.118*	−.129*	−.175**
5- Openness	.248**	.127*	.055	−.082	−.062
Game elements	1 (A)	2 (N)	3 (G)	4 (S)	5 (C)
1- Strategic resource mgmt	.039	.063	.131*	.205**	.202**
2- Puzzle	.163**	.100	.180**	−.005	.234**
3- Artistic movement	.006	−.113*	.037	.154**	−.027
4- Sports and Cards	−.130*	−.224**	−.010	.199**	.130*
5- Role-playing	.479**	.492**	.210**	.015	.111*
6- Virtual Goods	.305**	−.020	.248**	.229**	.086
7- Simulation	.521**	.396**	.133*	.071	.033
8- Action	.311**	.035	.040	.241**	.403**
Game playing styles	1 (A)	2 (N)	3 (G)	4 (S)	5 (C)
1- Multiplayer	.088	−.166**	.041	.818**	.263**
2- Abstract interaction	−.045	.028	.039	.103	.145**
3- Solo playing	.363**	.256**	.088	−.115**	.238**
4- Competitive community	.097	−.133*	−.021	.460**	.271**
5- Casual play	.098	−.036	−.055	.115*	−.173**

* $p < .05$. ** $p < .01$.
A = Aesthetic, N = Narrative, G = Goal, S = Social, C = Challenge

narratives and stories. Next, we can see correlations of goal orientation with conscientiousness and neuroticism. This is to be expected because more conscientious people tend to be more organized and industrious; thus, they would feel more satisfaction from completing goals. On the other hand, social orientation is correlated with extraversion and agreeableness, and also negatively correlated with neuroticism. It is to be expected that more extraverted and agreeable people would be more inclined to play together with others. Finally, there is a negative correlation between challenge orientation and neuroticism. The reason for this correlation could be that difficult challenges would make more neurotic people anxious; therefore, they would probably prefer less challenging games. However, it is important to note that all these correlations are weak. Therefore, we can conclude that the player traits and personality traits are related, but they cannot be considered the same. Likely, a person's personality has some sort of influence in the way that they play games, but personality alone does not explain all the different playing preferences between people.

4.5 Correlations with Game Elements and Game Playing Styles

In this section, we show evidence that the player traits are actually related to different preferences when people play games, thus supporting the model's construct validity. We do this by analyzing the bivariate correlations of participants' player traits scores with their self-reported preferences for different game elements and game playing styles.

Regarding participants' preferences for different game elements (see Table 6), the significant correlations between aesthetic and narrative orientation with role-playing and simulation game elements are expected because these kind of games are generally focused on narrative and other aesthetic experiences. Aesthetic orientation is also correlated with virtual goods and action, showing that players likely perceive some sort of aesthetic experience when interacting with these game elements. Narrative orientation is also negatively correlated with sports and cards, which makes sense if we consider that these kinds of games usually have no story at all. Next, the correlation of goal orientation with puzzle, role-playing, and virtual goods can be explained because these kinds of elements are strongly based on setting goals for players to complete (e.g., to solve a puzzle, to enhance a character, or to acquire a specific in-game good). On the other hand, the correlations of social orientation with sports and cards, virtual goods, and action are explained because these three kinds of games have some element of player interaction, such as multiplayer modes or a virtual economy where players can exchange virtual goods. Finally, the correlation of challenge orientation with strategic resource management, puzzle, and action makes sense because these game elements pose difficult challenges for players to overcome. We did not consider the correlations with $r < .2$ relevant due to their very weak effect size. Because of a data collection error, we did not have the data to analyze the correlations with progression game elements. We suppose that participants with high goal orientation will enjoy progression game elements, but unfortunately we were not able to confirm this assumption due to the lack of data.

Considering participants' preferences for different game playing styles (see Table 6), the strong correlation between social orientation and multiplayer gaming is to be expected because several items of the social orientation trait refer to playing together. For a similar reason, a moderate correlation exists between social orientation and competitive community. Additionally, the significant correlations of aesthetic and narrative orientations with solo playing are understandable because playing alone usually gives the player more space to immerse themselves in the game's narrative and the aesthetic experience than when playing with others. Finally, challenge orientation is negatively correlated with casual playing and positively correlated with all other playing styles. This can be explained by casual games generally offering shorter and less challenging gameplay, thus they will be less appreciated by players who seek challenging experiences. Goal orientation did not show any significant correlation, meaning that it does not influence people's preferences for different playing styles.

5 Discussion

In the present work, we contribute a new, validated, 25-item survey to score people regarding their playing traits. Moreover, we present evidence that our player traits model is consistent and reliable. Furthermore, the player traits are helpful in understanding player preferences for different game elements and game playing styles, and are sufficiently different from the Big-5 personality traits.

Summarizing the results detailed in the previous section, these are the main characteristics of each player trait:

Aesthetic orientation: players who score high on this trait enjoy aesthetic experiences in games, such as exploring the world, enjoying the scenery, or appreciating the quality of the graphics, sound, and art style. On the other hand, players who score low might focus more on gameplay than the aesthetics of the game. Players who score higher on this trait are usually more open to experience, enjoy role-playing and simulations games, and enjoy playing alone.

Narrative orientation (formerly Immersion orientation): players who score high on this trait enjoy complex narratives and stories within games, whereas players who score low usually prefer games with less story elements and might skip the story or cutscenes when they feel that those get in the way of gameplay. Players who score high on this trait tend to be more open to experience and introverted, enjoy role-playing and simulation games, and enjoy playing alone.

Goal orientation: players who score high on this trait enjoy completing game goals and like to complete games 100%, explore all the options, and complete all the collections. On the other hand, players who score low might leave optional quests or achievements unfinished. Players who score higher in this trait tend to be slightly more conscientious and neurotic.

Social orientation: players who score high on this trait generally prefer to play together with others. They enjoy multiplayer games and competitive gaming communities, whereas players who score low would prefer to play alone. Players who score higher in this trait tend to be slightly more extraverted, more agreeable, and less neurotic.

Challenge orientation (formerly Action orientation): players who score high on this trait generally prefer difficult games and hard challenges. On the other hand, players who score low prefer easier or casual games. Players who are more neurotic tend to score lower in this trait. Players who score high on this trait tend to enjoy all game playing styles, except casual games.

There is a partial correlation between aesthetic and immersion orientations (see Table 5). This is why items I2 and I6 load significantly in both factors in Table 2. Therefore, it is important to understand the differences between them. Players with high aesthetic orientation might enjoy narratives as a type of aesthetic experience, but they will still enjoy a game with a simpler story if there are other aesthetic elements to appreciate. On the other hand, players with high immersion orientation will not enjoy games without elaborate stories or narratives. Additionally, players with low aesthetic orientation are not likely to feel that the story prevents their enjoyment of the gameplay, whereas players with low immersion orientation will probably feel that complex stories get in the way of gameplay and are more likely to skip narratives and cutscenes.

5.1 Applications of the Model

There are many ways to use the player traits model in game design, marketing, and research. Game designers can use it by adding our 25-items to their intake survey for potential playtesters, which allows more focused playtesting. For example, when testing Destiny [7], a multiplayer first-person science-fiction shooter, it is important to test players with high scores in social, aesthetic, and challenge orientations, as they are most likely to be satisfied by the gameplay.

Our survey can also be used earlier in production by giving designers more information on the preferences of their audience. For example, a game studio might want to explore options for a new game. By asking players to fill out the player traits survey, they can learn what are their most prominent traits. Then, they can look at the list of game elements and game playing styles correlated to these traits to seek ideas that will satisfy their players. Or, if the trait scores for a player are available during gameplay, some mechanics may be dynamically activated or deactivated, thus providing a personalized gaming experience.

Those in marketing departments can also use our model by applying our items to their existing surveys, allowing them to target players whose orientations will be best served by the elements of their game. For example, it would be important to target those with narrative, goal, and challenge orientations when marketing Far Cry 5 [37] because it contains game elements that would be appealing to players with those traits, such as branching storyline and side quests.

These potential applications would not be possible with any of the existing models described in the Related Work, either because a measurement instrument is not available for them, or because the existing instrument is not reliable.

5.2 Comparison with Existing Models

Our work presents the first publicly available model of player preferences based on traits instead of categorical types, and with a validated measurement scale. Nevertheless, we provide a specific comparison with some of the existing works.

Since the development of the player traits was inspired by the BrainHex [26], there is a correspondence between them: social orientation with BrainHex's socialiser archetype; aesthetic orientation with seeker; challenge orientation with conqueror and daredevil; goal orientation with mastermind, achiever, and survivor; but narrative orientation is a new trait. However, our player traits model uses a well accepted approach inspired by trait theories instead of types and differently from the BrainHex, our measurement survey has demonstrated validity.

Regarding Bartle's typology [1,2], social orientation would correspond to Bartle's socialiser; goal orientation would correspond to achiever; and aesthetic orientation would correspond to explorer; but there is no player trait which corresponds directly to killer. However, these are only theoretical assumptions because we did not conduct any empirical comparison of these models.

Comparing our player traits model with Yee's gamer motivation profile [42], social orientation is present in both models; aesthetic orientation corresponds to creativity; challenge orientation to mastery; goal orientation to achievement; and narrative orientation to immersion. But there is no player trait corresponding to action motivations. Although Tondello et al. [35] had initially suggested an action orientation trait, in our study the challenge-oriented motivations were more pronounced than action-oriented ones. Future studies could explore if action orientation should be a sixth player trait, which our work did not discern.

Moreover, social orientation is similar to the sociability concept from Hamari and Tuunanen's [15] meta-synthesis of player types; aesthetic orientation to exploration; goal orientation to achievement; and narrative orientation to immersion. Challenge orientation may lead some players to the domination behaviours from their meta-review, but these concepts are not exactly the same. Future work could investigate the similarities and differences between these two constructs to better understand what drives players in each case.

Finally, although we employed SDT to help explain the theoretical background of the player traits, SDT alone cannot be used to understand player preferences. SDT-based scales such as the Player Experience of Need Satisfaction [33] and the inventory of intrinsic motivations to gameplay [38] can only explain the general motivations that lead people to play and enjoy games, but they say nothing about different player preferences.

5.3   Limitations and Future Work

Although we present considerable evidence of the validity of the five-factor player traits model and the 25-item measurement scale, our study has a few limitations. First, all data came from self-reported answers. Therefore, future studies should confirm if players' self-reported preferences correspond to their actual behaviour when playing games. In addition, although our dataset was large enough to carry out all the statistical analyses, further validation of the model with more participants would contribute to increasing confidence in it. Moreover, the personality traits scale that we used (BFI-10) is short and less accurate than longer ones. This can be a reason for low correlations detected with player traits. Future studies could employ longer personality scales for a new analysis of these correlations. Finally, our study validated the existence of the five player traits. However, these traits only partially explained participants' gaming preferences. Thus, we cannot determine if these are the only traits that affect gaming preferences, or if more traits should be added to the model in the future.

6   Conclusion

This research introduces a new player preferences model that solves the issues identified in previous work. The player traits model had been initially proposed by Tondello et al. [35] based on previous player typologies, in particular the BrainHex scale. Now, our work introduces a validated measurement scale and provides empirical evidence of the model's construct and discriminant validity. It is the first model based on player traits instead of types, which better captures the full range of individual preferences. Its use to the game design, marketing, and research communities is abundantly evident as it can inform and analyze the design of games, marketing campaigns, and user research studies.

Acknowledgments. This work was supported by the CNPq, Brazil; SSHRC [895-2011-1014, IMMERSe]; NSERC Discovery [RGPIN-2018-06576]; NSERC CREATE SWaGUR; and CFI [35819, JELF].

References

1. Bartle, R.: Hearts, Clubs, Diamonds, Spades: players who suit MUDs. J. MUD Res. **1**(1), 19 (1996)
2. Bartle, R.: Virtual worlds: why people play. Massively Mult. Game Dev. **2**(1), 3–18 (2005)
3. Bateman, C., Boon, R.: 21st Century Game Design. Game Development Series. Charles River Media, Hingham (2006)
4. Bateman, C., Lowenhaupt, R., Nacke, L.E.: Player typology in theory and practice. In: Proceedings of DiGRA 2011 (2011)
5. Bateman, C., Nacke, L.E.: The neurobiology of play. In: Proceedings of Futureplay 2010, Vancouver, BC, Canada, pp. 1–8. ACM (2010). https://doi.org/10.1145/1920778.1920780
6. Birk, M.V., Toker, D., Mandryk, R.L., Conati, C.: Modeling motivation in a social network game using player-centric traits and personality traits. In: Ricci, F., Bontcheva, K., Conlan, O., Lawless, S. (eds.) UMAP 2015. LNCS, vol. 9146, pp. 18–30. Springer, Cham (2015). https://doi.org/10.1007/978-3-319-20267-9_2
7. Bungie: Destiny. Game [XBOX 360]: Activision, Santa Monica, CA, September 2014
8. Busch, M., Mattheiss, E., Orji, R., Fröhlich, P., Lankes, M., Tscheligi, M.: Player type models – towards empirical validation. In: Proceedings of the 2016 CHI Conference Extended Abstracts on Human Factors in Computing Systems. ACM (2016). https://doi.org/10.1145/2851581.2892399
9. Caillois, R.: Man, Play, and Games. University of Illinois Press, Champaign (1961)
10. Costa Jr., P.T., Mccrae, R.R.: Trait theories of personality. In: Barone, D.F., Hersen, M., Van Hasselt, V.B. (eds.) Advanced Personality. The Plenum Series in Social/Clinical Psychology, pp. 103–121. Springer, Boston (1998). https://doi.org/10.1007/978-1-4419-8580-4_5
11. Deci, E.L., Ryan, R.M.: Intrinsic Motivation and Self-Determination in Human Behavior. Plenum, New York and London (1985)
12. Field, A.: Discovering Statistics Using SPSS, 3rd edn. Sage Publications, London (2009)
13. Goldberg, L.R.: The structure of phenotypic personality traits. Am. Psychol. **48**(1), 26–34 (1993). https://doi.org/10.1037/0003-066X.48.1.26
14. Guadagnoli, E., Velicer, W.F.: Relation of sample size to the stability of component patterns. Psychol. Bull. **103**(2), 265–275 (1988). https://doi.org/10.1037/0033-2909.103.2.265

15. Hamari, J., Tuunanen, J.: Player types: a meta-synthesis. Trans. Digit. Games Res. **1**(2) (2014). http://todigra.org/index.php/todigra/article/view/13

16. Henseler, J., Ringle, C.M., Sarstedt, M.: A new criterion for assessing discriminant validity in variance-based structural equation modeling. J. Acad. Mark. Sci. **43**(1), 115–135 (2015). https://doi.org/10.1007/s11747-014-0403-8

17. Kline, R.B.: Principles and Practice of Structural Equation Modeling, 3rd edn. The Guilford Press, New York (2010)

18. Lorenzo-Seva, U., Ferrando, P.: FACTOR 9.2: a comprehensive program for fitting exploratory and semiconfirmatory factor analysis and IRT models. Appl. Psychol. Meas. **37**(6), 497–498 (2013)

19. MacCallum, R.C., Hong, S.: Power analysis in covariance structure modeling using GFI and AGFI. Multivar. Behav. Res. **32**(2), 193–210 (1997). https://doi.org/10.1207/s15327906mbr3202_5

20. MacCallum, R.C., Widaman, K.F., Zhang, S., Hong, S.: Sample size in factor analysis. Psychol. Methods **4**(1), 84–99 (1999)

21. Malone, T.W.: Toward a theory of intrinsically motivating instruction. Cogn. Sci. **4**, 333–369 (1981)

22. Matsunaga, M.: How to factor-analyze your data right: do's, don'ts, and how-to's. Int. J. Psychol. Res. **3**(1), 97–110 (2010). https://doi.org/10.21500/20112084.854

23. McCrae, R.R., Costa, P.T.: Reinterpreting the Myers-Briggs type indicator from the perspective of the five-factor model of personality. J. Pers. **57**(1), 17–40 (1989). https://doi.org/10.1111/j.1467-6494.1989.tb00759.x

24. Muthén, B., Kaplan, D.: A comparison of some methodologies for the factor analysis of non-normal Likert variables. Br. J. Math. Stat. Psychol. **38**, 171–189 (1985)

25. Myers, I.B.: The Myers-Briggs Type Indicator. Consulting Psychologists Press, Palo Alto (1962)

26. Nacke, L.E., Bateman, C., Mandryk, R.L.: BrainHex: a neurobiological gamer typology survey. Entertain. Comput. **5**(1), 55–62 (2014). https://doi.org/10.1016/j.entcom.2013.06.002

27. Newman, K.: The case for the narrative brain. In: Proceedings of the Second Australasian Conference on Interactive Entertainment, pp. 145–149. Creativity & Cognition Studios Press (2005)

28. Orji, R., Mandryk, R.L., Vassileva, J., Gerling, K.M.: Tailoring persuasive health games to gamer type. In: Proceedings of the SIGCHI Conference on Human Factors in Computing Systems - CHI 2013, pp. 2467–2476 (2013). https://doi.org/10.1145/2470654.2481341

29. Rammstedt, B., John, O.P.: Measuring personality in one minute or less: a 10-item short version of the big five inventory in English and German. J. Res. Pers. **41**(1), 203–212 (2007). https://doi.org/10.1016/j.jrp.2006.02.001

30. Rosseel, Y.: lavaan: an R package for structural equation modeling. J. Stat. Softw. **48**(2), 1–36 (2012). https://doi.org/10.18637/jss.v048.i02

31. Russell, D.W.: In search of underlying dimensions: the use (and abuse) of factor analysis in personality and social psychology bulletin. Pers. Soc. Psychol. Bull. **28**(12), 1629–1646 (2002). https://doi.org/10.1177/014616702237645

32. Ryan, R.M., Deci, E.L.: Self-determination theory and the facilitation of intrinsic motivation, social development, and well-being. Am. Psychol. **55**(1), 68–78 (2000). https://doi.org/10.1037/0003-066X.55.1.68

33. Ryan, R.M., Rigby, C.S., Przybylski, A.: The motivational pull of video games: a self-determination theory approach. Motiv. Emot. **30**(4), 347–363 (2006). https://doi.org/10.1007/s11031-006-9051-8

34. Sharma, S., Mukherjee, S., Kumar, A., Dillon, W.R.: A simulation study to investigate the use of cutoff values for assessing model fit in covariance structure models. J. Bus. Res. **58**(7), 935–943 (2005). https://doi.org/10.1016/j.jbusres.2003.10.007

35. Tondello, G.F., Valtchanov, D., Reetz, A., Wehbe, R.R., Orji, R., Nacke, L.E.: Towards a trait model of video game preferences. Int. J. Hum. Comput. Interact. **34**, 732–748 (2018). https://doi.org/10.1080/10447318.2018.1461765

36. Tondello, G.F., Wehbe, R.R., Orji, R., Ribeiro, G., Nacke, L.E.: A framework and taxonomy of videogame playing preferences. In: Proceedings of the 2017 Annual Symposium on Computer-Human Interaction in Play - CHI PLAY 2017, Amsterdam, Netherlands, pp. 329–340. ACM (2017). https://doi.org/10.1145/3116595.3116629

37. Ubisoft Montreal, Ubisoft Toronto: Far Cry 5. Game [Microsoft Windows], Ubisoft, Montreuil, France, March 2018

38. Vahlo, J., Hamari, J.: Five-factor inventory of intrinsic motivations to gameplay (IMG). In: Proceedings of the 52nd Hawaii International Conference on System Sciences (HICSS), pp. 2476–2485. University of Hawai'i at Manoa (2019). http://hdl.handle.net/10125/59686

39. Vahlo, J., Kaakinen, J.K., Holm, S.K., Koponen, A.: Digital game dynamics preferences and player types. J. Comput. Mediat. Commun. **22**(2), 88–103 (2017). https://doi.org/10.1111/jcc4.12181

40. Velicer, W.F., Fava, J.L.: Affects of variable and subject sampling on factor pattern recovery. Psychol. Methods **3**(2), 231–251 (1998). https://doi.org/10.1037/1082-989X.3.2.231

41. Yee, N.: Motivations for play in online games. CyberPsychology Behav. **9**(6), 772–775 (2006). https://doi.org/10.1089/cpb.2006.9.772

42. Yee, N.: Gamer motivation model overview and descriptions. Quantic Foundry, December 2015. http://quanticfoundry.com/2015/12/15/handy-reference/

43. Yee, N.: Gaming Motivations Align with Personality Traits. Quantic Foundry, January 2016. http://quanticfoundry.com/2016/01/05/personality-correlates/

44. Yee, N., Ducheneaut, N., Nelson, L.: Online gaming motivations scale: development and validation. In: Proceedings of the SIGCHI Conference on Human Factors in Computing Systems - CHI 2012, pp. 2803–2806. ACM (2012). https://doi.org/10.1145/2207676.2208681

Comparing the Applicability of Pressure as a Game Metric to Self-assessment and Physiological Metrics

Ea Ehrnberg Ustrup, Mads Mathiesen, Joakim Have Poulsen,
Jesper Vang Christensen, and Markus Löchtefeld[✉]

Aalborg University, Aalborg, Denmark
{eustru14,mmat13,jpou14,jchr14}@student.aau.dk, mloc@create.aau.dk

Abstract. Recently, the amount of pressure that is exerted on an input device during a gaming session has been shown to correlate with several aspects of the game experience. While studies have used this metric in a game analysis perspective with promising results, there is still a lack of comparison between the performance of this metric compared to physiological metrics or self-assessment method. Therefore, we conduct an experiment in which we compare exerted pressure against the electrodermal activity (EDA), heart rate (HR) and self-assessment of a subject during a gaming session. Our results indicate that pressure can be used to assess the perceived game difficulty, possibly even better than EDA and HR.

Keywords: Game metrics · Pressure · Self-assessment · Physiological metrics

1 Introduction

In recent years, a variety of approaches have explored how to measure and analyze game experiences, especially in relation to different methods and types of data to use, which has given rise to a plethora of options. Recently, pressure exerted on an input device - which can be categorized as behavioural data - has been shown to be a promising measurement of arousal [13,27], as well as possibly indicating levels of immersion, types of frustration and different player actions [19,30,31]. However, there's a lack of research on how well this metric performs against other metrics such as physiological and self-assessment methods. This is important to understand, as it can help to make an informed choice on which metrics to use in a game analysis context. Furthermore, pressure is an attractive metric to use, as some devices such as newer smartphones (e.g. Apple iPhone 6s) are already able to measure different levels of applied pressure. This would mean that a game analysis based on pressure would not necessarily require additional equipment, allowing for data collection on a larger scale without having to spend additional time or effort. In comparison, physiological metrics require external sensors to be attached to the player, which is both obtrusive to the player and limits how much data can

D. Lamas et al. (Eds.): INTERACT 2019, LNCS 11747, pp. 396–405, 2019.
https://doi.org/10.1007/978-3-030-29384-0_24

be collected within a time frame based on how many sensors and test facilitators are available. In the case of self-assessment metrics, the collection and analysis of qualitative data is a very time-consuming process compared to the alternatives. This paper aims to compare the performance of exerted pressure against electro-dermal activity (EDA), heart rate (HR) and self-assessment as metrics for measuring game experiences. To this end, we conduct an experiment in which all four metrics are used, and follow up with a discussion of the possibilities and limitations of pressure as a game metric.

2   Related Work

In order to properly compare pressure against other metrics, it is important to first understand the different methods that exist for analyzing game experiences. One such validated method is through self-assessment. To this end, various questionnaires have been developed. The Game Experience Questionnaire (GEQ) [14] and its associated modules, used in several previous studies [1,7,13,20,28]. The Self-Assessment Manikin (SAM) [2] was developed to measure a person's affective reactions to stimuli. Previous studies have used SAM in conjunction with other methods to form a coherent understanding of the game experience [9,21,25,30]. Another self-assessment method is think-aloud protocols [5,6,12]. However, these self-assessment methods have previously been criticized as being too disruptive or inhibiting the experience [11,18]. Players may have to pause mid-game to answer questions, or they have to focus on the task of thinking aloud while simultaneously playing the game. Post-game questionnaires or retrospective video-cued think-aloud sessions also present the issue of being reflective rather than reactive, and players may not remember all details after the game has ended [29]. The issues with self-assessment methods caused researchers to look into the use of physiological metrics as a possible supplement or alternative to self-assessment data [7,16,18]. While several different physiological metrics have been explored, the most popular metrics appear to be electrodermal activity (EDA) and facial electromyography (fEMG), followed by heart rate (HR) [29]. These metrics relate well to the emotional dimensions defined by Russell [24], as EDA and HR has previously been linked to arousal, while fEMG has been linked to valence [15,23,26]. However, while physiological data is objective and has a high temporal precision, it lacks the contexts that self-assessment data may provide [29]. This shortcoming can be made up for through triangulation, i.e. combining the physiological metrics with other metrics (such as self-assessment [22], logging player behaviour [10] or analyzing video recordings [28]).

In recent years, there has also been an increasing interest in using exerted pressure as a possible game metric. Sykes and Brown [27] found that there was a significant difference in the mean pressure exerted on a gamepad when subjects played *Space Invaders* at varying difficulties, which suggests a connection between pressure and arousal. This finding was supported by van den Hoogen et al. [13], who found a connection between the game difficulty and the max pressure exerted on a mouse button when subjects played three levels of varying difficulty in *Half-Life 2*. In another study by van den Hoogen et al. [30], aside from finding a connection between pressure and arousal, it was also suggested that there is a connection between the pressure and the level of presence and dominance felt by the player. It was found that when playing levels of varying difficulty in the racing game *Need for Speed: Pro Street*, the pressure was higher in the cases where self-report measures also indicated a higher feeling of arousal, presence and dominance. Furthermore, using an adapted version of a basic infinite runner game, Miller and Mandryk [19] found a connection between the pressure exerted on a touch surface and the type of frustration the player was feeling (in-game frustration versus at-game frustration). Finally, van den Hoogen et al. [31] did a study that suggests that there is a connection between the exerted pressure and the type of player action (avoidance versus approach) in racing car games (*Colin McRae, Trackmania*) and shooter games (*Battlefield 1942, Hitman Contracts*).

As evident from the research, the applicability of pressure as a game metric has been studied and validated in several contexts. However, there are still aspects to explore. Current research has considered pressure in relation to behavioural metrics or self-assessment data, but have failed to include physiological metrics. Comparing pressure in relation to multiple metrics at a time may provide insight on previously unknown correlations, or could aid in giving a better overview of pros and cons of pressure as a game metric.

3   Evaluation

The purpose of the experiment was to collect data to be used to explore the eventual connections and correlations between the different types of metrics.

3.1   Materials and Setup

The game used in the main experiment was an adapted version of the arcade game *Breakout*. The game follows the design and rules of the original *Breakout* from 1976 by Atari Inc. However, the game was adapted to easily switch between two different difficulties. This could be done at the start of a level, and it changed the amount of speed the ball have. It was decided to use *Breakout* for the experiment as the arcade game genre has been used in previous studies on pressure as a game metric [27]. Furthermore, the game has simple controls and the difficulty could easily be changed.

Figure 1 shows the custom reader that was built to measure EDA and the exerted pressure using an Arduino. The pressure was measured through two Force Sensitive Resistors (FSR) attached to the left and right arrow keys, and the EDA was measured through two copper bands made of copper tape with velcro on the back (seen to the right of the keyboard), which were to be worn around two fingers on the hand. Both signals are sampled at 20 Hz. The Empatica E4 wristband was used to obtain the blood volume pulse (BVP) sampled at 64 Hz. While the E4

Fig. 1. Left: The custom reader that was used to obtain pressure and EDA signals during the test. Right: The subject can be seen wearing the E4 wristband and the copper bands for the EDA reader. FSRs were attached to the left and right arrow key. The screen shows *Breakout*.

is technically also able to measure EDA, in preliminary test it proved to be less reliable than our custom-built reader due to a faulty sensor in the wristband. Self-assessment data was collected by distributing the iGEQ and SAM questionnaires to the subjects. The statements for the immersion aspects ('I was interested in the game's story' and 'I found it impressive') were excluded from the iGEQ as the statements did not seem relevant in this particular game. Furthermore, video recordings of the game and the subject's face while playing were also collected. To assess the difficulty of the levels that the subjects played, a difficulty questionnaire by van den Hoogen et al. [13] was also distributed. It consists of the single item 'How difficult did you find it to play the level?', which is rated on a scale from −2 ('too easy') to 2 ('too hard'), with 0 being 'optimal'. Furthermore, a camera was angled to record the subject's left hand (which wore the E4 wristband and the copper bands). These recordings could be used during data analysis to assess whether noise or artifacts in the physiological signals were generated by hand movement. Figure 1 shows a photo of the setup of the experiment.

3.2   Subjects and Procedure

The results of the experiment consist of data from 25 tests. The subjects were University students aged 20–25 years old (18 males and 7 females). At the beginning of each test, the subject was briefed about the test procedure and asked to sign a consent form. They were then asked to rate how often they play games on a scale from 0 ('never') to 5 ('daily'). One participant reported 'never' (4%), one reported 'less than once a year' (4%), one reported 'monthly' (4%), seven reported 'weekly' (28%) and 15 reported 'daily' (60%). The E4 wristband and the copper bands for the EDA readings were attached to their left hand, and they were asked to place their hand within a hand-shaped outline on the table and keep it still for the remainder of the test. Before playing, they watched a calming video with nature sounds for 3 min to allow for their physiological signals to fall to an acceptable base level. The subject was then asked to play two levels of *Breakout*, one of an easy difficulty and one of a hard difficulty. The order of the given difficulty was counterbalanced. After each level, they were asked to fill out the iGEQ, SAM and difficulty questionnaire. Furthermore, after filling out the questionnaires between the two levels, they watched 1 min of the calming video to reduce carry-over effects for the second playthrough.

4   Results

It should be noted that while pressure sensors were attached to both the left and right arrow keys on the keyboard, only the data from the FSR on the left arrow key is used during the following data analysis due to some issues with the readings of the right FSR. In regards to calculating the mean pressure, datapoints that were not connected to a keypress were excluded from the calculations. This ensures that readings that did not contain user input would not influence the calculated mean pressure, even when slight noise in the FSRs was recorded. Prior to data analysis, the EDA signal (measured at 20 Hz) was denoised by calculating the centered moving average with a window of 21 (i.e. calculating the centered moving average over 1 s). The HR was calculated from the interbeat interval (IBI) signal provided by the E4 wristband, which calculates the IBI signal from the BVP. Wrong peaks, i.e. noise in the BVP, are automatically removed by algorithms in the E4 wristband software. As a final pre-processing step, the EDA, HR and pressure signals were normalized (min-max) per subject. This meant that rather than finding a minimum and maximum value per playthrough for a given signal, a minimum and maximum value was found per subject (i.e. in each subject's easy and hard playthroughs combined). This ensured that the individual differences between subjects were removed, while each subject's difference between the easy and hard playthrough was preserved. To determine which statistical tests to use, a series of Lilliefors tests were performed to assess whether the obtained data come from a normal distribution. Table 1 shows the resulting p-values of performing Lilliefors tests on the mean (and max) values of the different signals in each difficulty, as well as the difficulty ratings (n = 25 for each test). The data that were found to come from a normal distribution (i.e. when the p-value was above a significance level of 0.05) have been emboldened in the table.

Table 1. Lilliefors p-values

	Easy	Hard
Max pressure	0.024	<0.001
Mean pressure	**0.272**	**>0.5**
Mean EDA	0.034	0.003
Mean HR	**0.356**	**>0.5**
Difficulty ratings	0.001	0.001

Table 2. T-test and Wilcoxon

Variable	Test	p-value	Effect size r
Max pressure	Wilcoxon	<0.001	−0.546
Mean pressure	t-test	<0.001	0.852
Mean EDA	Wilcoxon	0.367	0.127
Mean HR	t-test	0.557	0.121
Difficulty rating	Wilcoxon	<0.001	−0.470

Two-tailed Student's t-tests or Wilcoxon signed-rank tests were then performed with the different variables (n = 25 for each test). In the case of normally distributed interval data, a Student's t-test was used, while in the case of ordinal data or data that was not normally distributed a Wilcoxon signed-rank test was used. Table 2 shows the resulting p-values of the student's t-tests and Wilcoxon signed-rank tests, with the independent variable being the difficulty (easy/hard), and the dependent variable being specified in each row.

With a significance level of 0.05, we can interpret these results as that the difficulty ratings, max pressure and mean pressure are significantly different between the easy and the hard difficulty. By inspecting the max and mean pressure values in the easy and hard difficulty, it can specifically be determined that the harder difficulty resulted in a higher max and mean pressure. As for the effect size, following the general guidelines by Cohen [3], an r of 0.1 is considered small, 0.3 is considered medium and 0.5 is considered large. Thus, the r of the differences in max and mean pressures can be considered large, while the r for the difference in difficulty ratings can be considered medium, but on the verge of being large. Thus, the magnitude of the difference in the mentioned variables can for the most part be interpreted as being large.

To explore any eventual linear relationships between variables, it was furthermore decided to calculate a set of Spearman's and Pearson's correlation coefficients (depending on whether ordinal data, i.e. answers to the iGEQ, were included in the calculations). The variables consist of the difference between the easy and hard difficulty. Calculating correlation coefficients using the differences between the difficulties rather than the raw values ensures that the correlation coefficients are based on the *change* that was experienced between the difficulties. As an example, a subject rating tension as '2' and '3' in the easy and hard difficulty respectively will have a tension difference of '1', which would also be the case if they had instead rated it '4' and '5'. The correlations that were found to be significant are listed in Table 3. Following general guidelines [8], it can be said that all relationships listed in the table are moderate, with the exception of the relationship

Table 3. Significant correlation coefficients between variables

Variable 1	Variable 2	Correlation coefficient	P-value
Max pressure	Mean pressure	0.469*	0.017
Max pressure	Flow	−0.465	0.018
EDA	Negative affection	−0.447	0.018
EDA	Flow	0.370**	0.068
HR	Competence	0.423	0.034
HR	Positive affection	0.559	0.003
Difficulty	Tension	0.467	0.018
Difficulty	Challenge	0.529	0.006

Pearson's correlation coefficient
**p-value above 0.05*

marked with a double-asterisk which is mild or weak. As expected, the difficulty correlates positively with the tension and challenge. Furthermore, the EDA can be said to correlate with whether the player was in their optimal flow. The reason for this is it correlates positively with flow (consisting of the statement 'I forgot everything around me' and 'I felt completely absorbed'), while correlating negatively with the negative affection (consisting of the statements 'I felt bored' and 'I found it tiresome'). Following the definition of flow by Csikszentmihalyi [4], the negative affection seems to describe 'boredom' which is outside of the flow channel. Finally, looking at Table 3, it also seems that HR correlates with how good the player felt. The reason for this is that HR correlates positively with both the positive affection (consisting of the statements 'I felt good' and 'I felt content') and the competence (consisting of the statements 'I felt successful' and 'I felt skillful').

5 Discussion

The performed Student's t-tests and Wilcoxon signed-rank tests indicate that the pressure exerted while gaming was affected by how difficult the game was, and more specifically, that a harder difficulty resulted in a higher mean and max pressure. Furthermore, looking at the calculated correlation coefficients, it has been found that difficulty relates with tension and challenge, i.e. the arousal of the subject. This finding - that pressure relates to difficulty and arousal - is also backed by previous research [13, 27, 30] in which different games and lengths of play sessions were used. Notably, as opposed to max and mean pressure, no significant difference could be found in the mean EDA and HR between the difficulties. This may indicate that pressure can be a better metric for measuring game difficulty than EDA and HR, at least in the case of short play sessions.

In contrast to findings by van den Hoogen et al. [13], we have not been able to find any significant correlations between pressure and the different player experience aspects covered in the iGEQ. This may be explained by the fact that the experiment designs were not similar and different games were used in the tests. In their experiment the subject played Half-Life 2 in three 10-min sessions, and the pressure on the left mouse button was measured. In our experiment the subject played Breakout in two 5-min sessions, and the pressure on the left and right arrow keys was measured. This dissimilarity in findings suggests that pressure is not necessarily indicative of player experience aspects. For a more conclusive discussion on this, further research would be required.

The calculated correlation coefficients indicate that the mean HR correlates positively with competence and positive affection, which can be summarized as emotional valence. This correlation is not backed by previous research, and while there is most likely an underlying cause of the correlation, it is currently not possible to pinpoint the exact explanation. Therefore, this result of the data analysis will be disregarded.

The correlation coefficients related to the mean EDA can be interpreted as that the mean EDA rose the more excited the subject felt, which has also been found in previous research [7, 17]. Firstly, the mean EDA correlated negatively with negative affection (which describes how bored or disinterested the subject felt) and, secondly, it correlated positively with flow.

5.1 Impact for Practitioners

Our results indicate that pressure relates to the arousal of the player and the perceived difficulty of the game. This in turn suggests that pressure can be used to create adaptive games that alter the difficulty to better fit the player's skill level based on the amount of pressure they apply to the input device. This application has multiple benefits compared to using self-assessment or physiological metrics:

- Pressure is a non-obtrusive metric as opposed to physiological metrics that require sensors to be attached to the body.
- Pressure data is real-time compared to self-assessment data that is typically obtained during or after a game session through interviews or questionnaires.
- Some devices (e.g. styluses, trackpads, phones and tablets) have in-built technology that is able to detect different levels of pressure. This means that using it as a game metric does not necessarily acquire additional equipment for these platforms.

5.2 Limitations

It should be noted that the obtained results are based on subjects within a narrow age range that can be considered to be at least fairly experienced with games (88% reported 'weekly' or 'daily' gaming). This may have had an effect on the results. The strength of the calculated correlation coefficients can be interpreted as 'moderate', or in one case 'weak'. It is possible that play sessions longer than 5 min could increase the strength of the correlation coefficients, but this is a matter for further research. Finally, the game used for the experiment was specifically chosen due to being action-focused which is in line with prior work [13,19,30,31]. Performing a similar experiment with other games may not produce the same results.

6   Conclusion

With this paper, we set out to explore the possibilities and limitations of pressure as a game metric in relation to other widely used game metrics. The results of the experiment firstly indicate that pressure relates to arousal, which means it can be used as an indication of the perceived difficulty of a game. As pressure is unobtrusive compared to physiological metrics and real-time compared to subjective metrics it enables developers to use it easily. Secondly, pressure has been better at indicating arousal in our experiment setup compared to the physiological metrics. Thirdly, we have not found any significant correlations between pressure and player experience aspects like others before us. We would advise that further research on this subject is conducted before anything conclusive can be said on the matter.

References

1. Plass-Oude Bos, D., et al.: Brain-computer interfacing and games. In: Tan, D., Nijholt, A. (eds.) Brain-Computer Interfaces. HCIS, pp. 149–178. Springer, London (2010). https://doi.org/10.1007/978-1-84996-272-8_10
2. Bradley, M.M., Lang, P.J.: Measuring emotion: the self-assessment manikin and the semantic differential. J. Behav. Ther. Exp. Psychiatry 25(1), 49–59 (1994)
3. Cohen, J.: Statistical Power Analysis for the Behavioral Sciences, 2nd edn, p. 82. Routledge, New York (1988)
4. Csikszentmihalyi, M.: Flow: The Psychology of Optimal Experience. Harper Perennial, New York (1991)
5. Desurvire, H., Caplan, M., Toth, J.A.: Using heuristics to evaluate the playability of games. In: CHI 2004 Extended Abstracts on Human Factors in Computing Systems, pp. 1509–1512. ACM (2004)
6. Desurvire, H., El-Nasr, M.S.: Methods for game user research: studying player behavior to enhance game design. IEEE Comput. Graphics Appl. 33(4), 82–87 (2013). https://doi.org/10.1109/mcg.2013.61
7. Drachen, A., Nacke, L.E., Yannakakis, G., Pedersen, A.L.: Correlation between heart rate, electrodermal activity and player experience in first-person shooter games. In: Proceedings of the 5th ACM SIGGRAPH Symposium on Video Games, pp. 49–54. ACM (2010)
8. Evans, J.D.: Straightforward Statistics for the Behavioral Sciences. Brooks/Cole Publishing Company, Pacific Grove (1996)
9. Gabana, D., Tokarchuk, L., Hannon, E., Gunes, H.: Effects of valence and arousal on working memory performance in virtual reality gaming. In: 2017 Seventh International Conference on Affective Computing and Intelligent Interaction (ACII). IEEE, October 2017. https://doi.org/10.1109/acii.2017.8273576
10. Gagné, A.R., El-Nasr, M.S., Shaw, C.D.: A deeper look at the use of telemetry for analysis of player behavior in RTS games. In: Anacleto, J.C., Fels, S., Graham, N., Kapralos, B., Saif El-Nasr, M., Stanley, K. (eds.) ICEC 2011. LNCS, vol. 6972, pp. 247–257. Springer, Heidelberg (2011). https://doi.org/10.1007/978-3-642-24500-8_26
11. Hazlett, R.L.: Measuring emotional valence during interactive experiences: boys at video game play. In: Proceedings of the SIGCHI Conference on Human Factors in Computing Systems, pp. 1023–1026. ACM (2006)
12. Hong, J.C., Liu, M.C.: A study on thinking strategy between experts and novices of computer games. Comput. Hum. Behav. 19(2), 245–258 (2003). https://doi.org/10.1016/s0747-5632(02)00013-4
13. van den Hoogen, W.M., Ijsselsteijn, W., De Kort, Y.: Exploring behavioral expressions of player experience in digital games. In: Proceedings of the Workshop on Facial and Bodily Expression for Control and Adaptation of Games ECAG 2008, pp. 11–19 (2008). https://pure.tue.nl/ws/files/2937671/Metis223106.pdf
14. IJsselsteijn, W., De Kort, Y., Poels, K.: The game experience questionnaire (2013)
15. Kivikangas, J.M., et al.: A review of the use of psychophysiological methods in game research. J. Gaming Virtual Worlds 3(3), 181–199 (2011)
16. Klarkowski, M., Johnson, D., Wyeth, P., Phillips, C., Smith, S.: Psychophysiology of challenge in play: EDA and self-reported arousal. In: Proceedings of the 2016 CHI Conference Extended Abstracts on Human Factors in Computing Systems, pp. 1930–1936. ACM (2016)

17. Mandryk, R.L., Atkins, M.S.: A fuzzy physiological approach for continuously modeling emotion during interaction with play technologies. Int. J. Hum. Comput. Stud. **65**(4), 329–347 (2007). https://doi.org/10.1016/j.ijhcs.2006.11.011

18. Mandryk, R.L., Atkins, M.S., Inkpen, K.M.: A continuous and objective evaluation of emotional experience with interactive play environments. In: Proceedings of the SIGCHI Conference on Human Factors in Computing Systems, pp. 1027–1036. ACM (2006)

19. Miller, M.K., Mandryk, R.L.: Differentiating in-game frustration from at-game frustration using touch pressure. In: Proceedings of the 2016 ACM International Conference on Interactive Surfaces and Spaces, pp. 225–234. ACM (2016)

20. Nacke, L., Lindley, C.A.: Flow and immersion in first-person shooters: measuring the player's gameplay experience. In: Proceedings of the 2008 Conference on Future Play: Research, Play, Share, pp. 81–88. ACM (2008)

21. Nacke, L.E., Nacke, A., Lindley, C.A.: Brain training for silver gamers: effects of age and game form on effectiveness, efficiency, self-assessment, and gameplay experience. CyberPsychology Behav. **12**(5), 493–499 (2009). https://doi.org/10.1089/cpb.2009.0013

22. O'Brien, H., McLean, K.: Measuring the user engagement process. In: Engagement by Design Pre-Conference Workshop, CHI, April 2009

23. Ravaja, N.: Contributions of psychophysiology to media research: review and recommendations. Media Psychol. **6**(2), 193–235 (2004)

24. Russell, J.A.: A circumplex model of affect. J. Pers. Soc. Psychol. **39**(6), 1161–1178 (1980). https://doi.org/10.1037/h0077714

25. Schneider, E.F.: Death with a story. Hum. Commun. Res. **30**(3), 361–375 (2004). https://doi.org/10.1111/j.1468-2958.2004.tb00736.x

26. Shi, Y., Ruiz, N., Taib, R., Choi, E., Chen, F.: Galvanic skin response (GSR) as an index of cognitive load. In: CHI 2007 Extended Abstracts on Human Factors in Computing Systems, pp. 2651–2656. ACM (2007)

27. Sykes, J., Brown, S.: Affective gaming: measuring emotion through the gamepad. In: CHI 2003 Extended Abstracts on Human Factors in Computing Systems, pp. 732–733. ACM (2003)

28. Tan, C.T., Bakkes, S., Pisan, Y.: Inferring player experiences using facial expressions analysis. In: Proceedings of the 2014 Conference on Interactive Entertainment - IE 2014. ACM Press (2014). https://doi.org/10.1145/2677758.2677765

29. Tan, C.T., Leong, T.W., Shen, S.: Combining think-aloud and physiological data to understand video game experiences. In: Proceedings of the SIGCHI Conference on Human Factors in Computing Systems, pp. 381–390. ACM (2014)

30. Van den Hoogen, W., IJsselsteijn, W.A., de Kort, Y.A.: Effects of sensory immersion on behavioural indicators of player experience: movement synchrony and controller pressure. In: DiGRA 2009 - Proceedings of the 2009 DiGRA International Conference: Breaking New Ground: Innovation in Games, Play, Practice and Theory. Brunel University, September 2009. http://www.digra.org/wp-content/uploads/digital-library/09287.18127.pdf

31. Van Den Hoogen, W., Braad, E., Ijsselsteijn, W.: Pressure at play: measuring player approach and avoidance behaviour through the keyboard. In: DiGRA - Proceedings of the 2014 DiGRA International Conference, August 2014

Fall-Prevention Exergames Using Balance Board Systems

Miguel Brito[1,2], Rui Nóbrega[1,2(✉)], João Jacob[1], Rui Rodrigues[1,2], and António Coelho[1,2]

[1] Faculdade de Engenharia da Universidade do Porto, Porto, Portugal
migueldiasbrito@gmail.com,
{ruinobrega,joao.jacob,rui.rodrigues,acoelho}@fe.up.pt
[2] INESC TEC, Instituto de Engenharia de Sistemas e Computadores Tecnologia e Ciência, Porto, Portugal

Abstract. The prevention of falls in older adults is an issue that can only be solved with regular exercises, sometimes with the supervision of therapists. This paper presents a game framework that uses devices such as the Wii Balance Board (WBB) to replicate fall-prevention programs, such as the Otago Exercise Programme. The objective is to increase the adherence of senior users to these exercises, while increasing their autonomy by enabling them to conduct unsupervised games. Two interactive games were developed and tested using the WBB and other available devices such as smartphones. The main contribution of this paper is the proposal of several metrics for exergames for the elderly and the combination of digital games with fall-prevention exercises and automatic balance measures based on Centre of Pressure (COP) tracking.

Keywords: Exergames · Fall prevention · Balance metrics · Human Computer Interaction

1 Introduction

The increase in quality of healthcare over the past century led to the growth of life expectancy. With this change, age-related problems are more common. One of these problems is related to falls and their potentially serious consequences. As age degrades biological elements that control body balance, falls become more frequent and more severe. Fall prevention programs usually integrate several complementary methods. One of them is doing exercises that improve balance [3] in older adults [1], decreasing fall risk, but also strengthening the body, mitigating fall consequences [8]. However, motivating seniors to do healthy exercises is difficult. Affordable motion sensing devices have been shown to bring motivation as they turn physiotherapy sessions into entertaining and engaging interactive environments. One of those devices, the Nintendo Wii Balance Board System (WBB), uses four pressure sensors that measure the user's center of pressure

© IFIP International Federation for Information Processing 2019
Published by Springer Nature Switzerland AG 2019
D. Lamas et al. (Eds.): INTERACT 2019, LNCS 11747, pp. 406–426, 2019.
https://doi.org/10.1007/978-3-030-29384-0_25

(COP) which has been proved to be useful in helping the therapists evaluate their patients' balance [1,9,28].

The main objective of this paper is to propose a methodology for creating and evaluating interactive exergames that provide a solution for motivating older adults towards regular exercise practice [26], as well as automating data collection for healthcare professionals. The usage of multiple sensors and devices can provide the system with input both for exergames and for balance metrics. A combination of game development techniques and fall-prevention exercises may not only motivate older adults as it combines the pleasure of playing video games with the need to promote balance [27], but also provide physiotherapists with data from remote game play sessions.

To test the proposed methodology and metrics, two interactive exergames were developed. These games require the user to perform exercises that are part of the main fall-prevention programs [8], such as the Otago Exercise Programme or the Fitness and Mobility Exercise (FAME), and balance assessment scales as well, such as the Berg Balance Scale [22]. While the senior plays the game, the system uses the COP and compute balance assessment metrics used by physiotherapists, namely the COP's mean velocity and total oscillation. This data can be further processed and COP's path, amplitude-over-time and frequency maps can be generated.

2   Related Work

The scope of this work involves exergames in health [17,31]. Digital games can provide enjoyment to people, defined here as an individual's positive response towards technology and its context. Experiencing enjoyment is the main reason why people play games [23]. A difficult game for a novice player can create anxiety making him quit, while a very easy game can cause boredom [18,19]. Increasing challenges' difficulty as the player progresses and gains skill is then important [24]. This way, fun can be achieved throughout the whole game [7]. Game style factors can be determinant when providing enjoyment to players. Fantasy inclusion, narrative, avatar resemblance and player's identification with it, other playable characters, sound and music effects, high quality realistic graphics, use of humor, character development over time and game medium duration (few days or weeks) affects the way players feel about the game [23,24]. Psycho-social characteristics, which are player-dependent, also affect the way a person enjoys a game. The most important player's traits are sensation seeking, self-forgetfulness, desire of being in control, self-efficacy and need of satisfaction (mood repair or recovery of an experience) [23]. Games that cause guilt, e.g. violent games for some players, are not effective to provide enjoyment [23]. Several authors studied enjoyment in games such as Mellecker et al. [24], Zaczynski et al. [38] and Nawaz et al. [27].

2.1 Therapy-Oriented Exergames

Deutsch et al. [11] made a first approach to the use of Nintendo Wii console in physical rehabilitation. An adolescent student with spastic diplegia cerebral palsy was subjected to eleven sessions during four weeks where he would play games from a set of four Wii games and given the liberty to play each game for as long as he wanted. The therapist observed that while playing the digital games, the patient did not feel he was in therapy and did more effort in the exercises.

Exergames to improve balance in older adults is a topic that was explored in Agmon et al. [1]. In this work it was asserted that limited supervised balance training at home was safe and feasible. Furthermore, several other games studied the use of exergames in older adults [3] and in unsupervised scenarios [28].

Lange et al. [21] developed an exergame for neurological injury rehabilitation using the WBB. More recent works indicate important factors to be considered to develop motivational rehabilitation exergames. Geurts et al. in [14] concluded that it was important to be possible to calibrate the exergames according to the patients' needs and capabilities. Uzor and Baillie [36] developed five exergames for seniors, as well as wireless inertial sensors to interact with them. These sensors detect nine movements, four of those are used in each game, which are: sit-to-stand, side steps, marching, knee bends.

Vines et al. [37] elaborated a critical analysis of over 30 years of HCI research for the elderly with the goal of finding its main concerns and give advices for future studies. Elderly adults enjoy interacting with Nintendo Wii controllers and find them useful for therapy despite technology and physical limitations [6]. Nielsen and Störring [29] also proposed a method to create an interface with hand gestures.

Recently, Clark et al. shown that the WBB can be used in clinics to compute quantitative balance measures, namely center of pressure, path length and velocity, with high correlation with precise commercial force plates that are the gold standard in quantitative balance measurement [9]. González et al. developed a Center of Mass estimation system which uses the Kinect and the WBB using the statically equivalent serial chain method [15]. The solution is a portable and affordable alternative to other systems despite its limitations. Improper light, loose fitting clothes and large objects surrounding the user interferes Kinect's readings while WBB area limits the number of poses the user can make [15]. Other balance therapy projects include Kennedy et al. [20] and Ayoade and Baillie [2].

2.2 Balance Rehabilitation Overview

Balance maintenance requires coordination from sensory, neurological and musculoskeletal systems [22]. Commercial force plates are used to compute a person's COP while standing. These devices can be used to identify older adults with higher fall risk even when there is no evidence of a balance impairment [30]. With the COP values over some time, one to two minutes, several variables can be determined for balance assessment [12]. COP can be measured in two axis: backward and forward or anterior-posterior direction (AP), and side-to-side or medial-lateral direction (ML). The most useful metrics are the stabilogram's bandwidth and the COP path, medium velocity, oscillation area and total displacement [12]. Higher COP bandwidth, alongside inability to tandem standing (stand with a foot in front of the other with the front foot's heel touching other's toe) and higher body mass index, indicates higher probability of a fall occurrence due to intrinsic factors [30]. The COP test should be done two to four times as too many repetitions may cause fatigue and learning, which can result in a wrong analysis [12].

Laboratory testing of balance using treadmills or sway platforms is impractical in most clinics [32]. Therapists nowadays use subjective scales thoughtfully tested based on functional balance tests. Functional balance tests are exercises based on basic movements such as getting up from a chair, standing or picking up objects. One of those tests is the Time Up and Go test (TUG). The TUG consists in getting up from an arm chair, walk three meters, turn, come back and sit in the chair [32]. Evaluation is given relative to the time the patient takes to complete the task. Patients who take less than twenty seconds were shown to be independent for basic mobility activities whereas those who took more than thirty had difficulties getting up of bed, sitting and getting up of a toilet and getting in and off a tub [32]. TUG is a reliable test to assess patient's balance, gait manoeuvre and functional abilities and track physical mobility deterioration [32]. However, TUG does not give enough information to detail the source of balance impairments [22].

Other tests include the Berg Balance Scale (BBS) [1,22], the Fullerton Advanced Balance Scale (FAB) [33], the Brunel Balance Assessment (BBA) [35] and the Functional Independence Measure (FIM) [20]. Different exercise programs have been created and successfully tested regarding fall-prevention. In New Zealand, Campbell and Robertson's Otago Exercise Programme has decreased fall frequency by one third in four trial tests and improved senior's self-confidence for daily activities [8].

3   Proposed Solution

The main contribution of this work is that it provides a methodology for integrating known physiotherapists' exercises in exergames that can be played with relative autonomy while providing feedback to the therapists. This methodology focuses on the definition of a set of metrics to ascertain balance as well as sensors and devices to collect data.

To validate this methodology, two exergames, fit to be played by elderly people and with specific exercise movements to prevent falls, are described and tested. The goal is to implement balance assessment with automatic metrics used by physiotherapists to provide a mean to monitor the player's evolution while keeping subjects motivated.

The designed exergames are digital games where the player must perform one or multiple exercises to control a character and solve problems. Problem-solving levels and game rewards are important as they were shown to be effective to motivate patients for therapy sessions [5]. The exercises were chosen from main used fall-prevention exercise programs to hopefully improve older adults balance and decrease fall risk [8].

The methodology consists of the following steps: (1) choose exercises, (2) choose devices, (3) choose metrics, (4) create exergame and (5) evaluate with therapists.

4   Balance Metrics

The main input device chosen was the Nintendo Wii Balance Board (WBB). The WBB was developed and commercialized by Nintendo initially as a controller for some WiiFit mini-games. In these games, the WBB tracks the player's Centre of Pressure (COP) whose position has to be controlled in order to progress.

Data from the WBB is sent via bluetooth connections and includes the pressure measured by each sensor and total. This way, COP value can be computed using Eq. 1. Let $i = 1..4$ be an identifier for each sensor (front left, front right, rear left, rear right), P_i the position of sensor i and W_i the weight read by sensor i. Then:

$$COP(ML, AP) = \sum_{i=1}^{4} \frac{W_i * P_i(ML, AP)}{\sum_{i=1}^{4} W_i} \tag{1}$$

Manipulating the position of each sensor in the equation according to a rotation from the WBB original position will give a correct COP in Medial-lateral (ML) and Anterior-Posterior (AP) directions. Tracking the user's COP, several movements or exercises can be detected or measured.

One goal for this project was to provide physiotherapists or care-takers a mean to monitor a senior's balance evolution. Equation 1 allows COP computation with data from the WBB. However COP alone is not useful for balance assessment [12]. Duarte and Freitas [12] indicated that the best COP related metrics for balance assessment were COP's mean velocity, total oscillation, path chart and displacement (amplitude) over time.

5   Game Design and Implementation

Following the methodology, after identifying certain exercises and considering the balance metrics to be collected, two exergames were designed.

For both games we describe the design and implementation steps. Both games have a small calibration stage and a tutorial as seen in Fig. 1, followed by the game logic. They are based on a city environment, divided in several streets. The city has several objects, such as cars and boxes that the player has to avoid. This provides a setting that is familiar to all players.

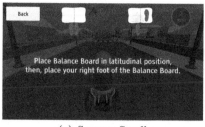 

(a) Segway Stroll   (b) Scooter Chase

Fig. 1. Tutorial messages for Segway Stroll and Scooter Chase.

The games display information to the player in order to help him. As previously mentioned, tutorial messages appear to the player in the beginning of the game, either to instruct the player to calibrate the devices or to explain the game's logic and mechanics, as seen in Fig. 1.

The next sections briefly describe the features of each game.

5.1 Segway Stroll - Description

In this game, the player has to drive a virtual Segway (http://www.Segway.com). To interact, the user has to stand in the WBB and perform forward reaching movements or weight shifts. These movements can be read by the WBB alone. However, other sensors can be added in order to force the user to do them correctly. Other movements can be included by introducing obstacles in the levels. Figure 2 is a sketch of the idea for this game.

In the game the player is leaving home to try out the newly bought Segway and takes a stroll in the town with the objective of reaching the end of a path. The user has to forward reach in order to move, stand to stop and perform weight shift to turn.

Exercise: To perform a forward reach, the player must stand with feet shoulder-width apart. Then, raise one arm to the shoulder height and lean forward as far as possible. To finish the forward reach the player must return to the initial position. In this exercise the player should alternate the raising of their arms. The initial position for forward reaching and weight shifts are the same. To perform a weight shift, the player should bend one of the legs placing more weight over that leg. Weight shifts should be done for each leg, alternately. First levels have shorter paths and require fewer movements and have shorter game play sessions. Higher levels have more complex paths with more demanding exercises.

Benefits: These game's movements help seniors train balance control when their centre of gravity changes [25]. Forward reaching improves the limits of forward stability [25]. Weight shifts are present in FAME [13] and BBA [35], forward reaching is present in FAME, Melo's program [25], BBA and BBS [4] and standing is part of BBS and BBA and provides quantitative data for balance assessment [9].

Fig. 2. Segway Stroll sketch. The player has to perform a forward reaching to accelerate and weight shifts to turn.

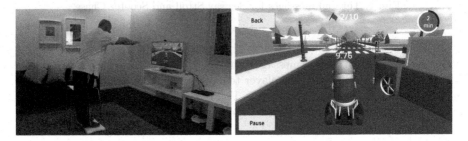

Fig. 3. Senior performing a forward reach movement while playing Segway Stroll.

Evaluation: Sensors used to read the player's movements provide useful data for analysis. The WBB can track changes to the player's centre of pressure in all movements. An external camera and body tracking software can be used to force the player to do the movements correctly, in terms of body pose. Smartphones or smartwatches can also be used when forward reaching in the player's hand or wrist.

Evaluation measures taken from this exercise are: the number of repetitions and duration of each movement, the amplitude of forward reaching and weight shifts and the COP while the player is standing which can be used to compute other metrics useful for balance assessment, e.g. COP path and COP velocity [9].

This game presents an interactive way to assess balance, as the movements tracked are part of several measures. While useful for assessment, these exercises aim to promote balance when done regularly and consequently, decrease fall risk.

5.2   Segway Stroll - Implementation

In this game the main goal is to follow a path given by the system. The player uses the WBB with two different exercises to fully control the character as seen in Fig. 2. A senior playing this game can be seen in Fig. 3.

A level is comprised of ten checkpoints, each represented as a pair of flags placed on the road. The player has to pass between the two flags to complete the checkpoint and earn points. If the player surpasses a checkpoint without passing between the flags, it will disappear and the player does not get a second chance to earn points in it. A time limit of 150-s exists for the game to be completed.

Game Interface. The game is placed in a city with several static elements, except for the cars that come from different directions. This game's main goal is to pass between the flags of each checkpoint. The player has a time limit to reach the next checkpoint and the remaining number of seconds appears in the screen. The number of checkpoints successfully surpassed and the total of checkpoints are displayed on the top of the screen. Lastly, traffic lights are present as well as other obstacles to the player. The game interface can be seen in Fig. 3.

Calibration and instruction messages are shown to the player in the beginning of the game. A message display can be seen in Fig. 1. The same method is also used to warn the player that he was not supposed to advance when the traffic light is red or a car is crossing the street.

The score screen presents the number of surpassed checkpoints, the number of obstacle hits, the number of times the player mistakenly advanced through the street (i.e., crossed the street with red light on or when a car was crossing in front) and the total COP's amplitude in the AP direction as an evaluation metric.

Basic Gameplay and Controls. To accelerate, the user performs a forward reaching exercise. Forward reaching is detected by the system using the readings from the WBB. The Segway will accelerate more if the COP further moves forward in the AP axis, motivating the player to increase the amplitude of this exercise. A chair is recommended to be used as support to avoid injuries from the player falling forward. The senior playing this game on Fig. 3 is performing this exercise to accelerate the Segway.

The second interaction is turning the Segway. This can be made by weight shifting to the desired side while forward reaching. This mechanic was implemented to add another degree of interaction to the game. The WBB sensitivity to turn is very high in order to make this interaction effortless.

Lastly, to brake the Segway, the player must perform a toe raise. This exercise was added as it is used in fall-prevention exercise programs. The Segway will lose velocity gradually when not accelerating, but braking was added to provide the ability to perform sudden stops which are important to avoid traps. Once again, a support should be present in order to avoid the player falling backward as the WBB front may rise when the player performs a toe raise. This exercise can be seen on Fig. 4.

Exercise Analysis. In order to evaluate the forward reaching exercise, therapists usually measure the maximum distance the patients can reach with their arm. This analysis is hard to assess using the WBB, and further sensors should be added for better exercise tracking, as previously suggested. Nevertheless, the system collects the maximum distance the COP reaches in the AP direction and presents it to the user in the score screen.

Fig. 4. Senior performing a toe raise movement on the WBB required to play Segway Stroll.

The purpose of traps in this game is to force the player to stand still for a few seconds. This way, quantitative metrics can be taken for further analysis as indicated by Duarte and Freitas [12]. However, the traps are activated for 10 s, at most, instead of the minimum of 30 s required for a correct assessment according to Duarte and Freitas [12]. This decision was made because seniors could get bored with the game if they had to stand for an extended period of time, thus failing to motivate them to play. Figure 5 presents a COP's path chart, a COP's frequency map and an amplitude-over-time chart. All the examples were taken from a participant gameplay during test phase, which will be described in the Evaluation section. These metrics could provide data to physiotherapists so they can perform a balance assessment on their patients.

5.3   Scooter Chase - Description

In this game, the player has to do a tandem stand, i.e., stand with a foot in front of the other, in order to balance while riding a scooter. The movement performance is read by the WBB and transmitted to the game. A smartphone is used as a steering wheel.

The player notices something is missing: the cat ran away. The player follows the cat, but it is too fast. The player sees the grandson's scooter, gets on it and accelerates to catch the cat. Tandem standing is needed to keep balance and avoid falling from the scooter. The main goal of this game is to catch the cat and return without falling.

Exercise: In order to perform a tandem standing, the player must place a foot directly in front of the other and hold for some seconds. For the movement to be read by the WBB, the player should turn it 90° from its usual position and place one foot on the rear side and the other in the front side of the board, as seen in Fig. 1(b). In higher levels, the scooter's sensitivity to COP changes and the time needed for the player to stand in a tandem position increases.

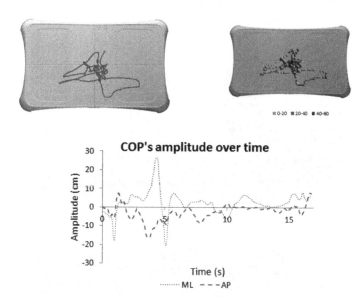

Fig. 5. COP's path chart on the left, COP's frequency map on the center and COP's amplitude-over-time chart on the right while standing, taken from Segway Stroll.

Benefits: Heel-to-toe standing is indicated in Otago [8] and FAME [13] programs as a means to promote older adults' balance. In addition, tandem standing is also used as a balance measure in the BBS [4].

Evaluation: The WBB provides information about the tandem standing. These readings can be used to determine the number of repetitions and the duration of each standing. COP path and sway in this exercise may be useful to assess balance as well.

Tandem standing promotes balance and consequently, decreases fall risk. At the same time, it can also be used to assess balance.

5.4 Scooter Chase - Implementation

To simulate a scooter's base, the system relies on a WBB, rotated 90° from its normal position, and a smartphone to simulate the handlebar. This game can be used to promote balance improvements and to assess it as well. A senior playing this game can be seen in Fig. 6. The main goal is to catch the cat. However, it is not enough to catch it one time, as it runs away again several times. The player has a 150 s time limit for reaching the cat on ten occasions.

To achieve a better result, the player should avoid obstacles in the scenario such as cars and streetlights. Balance performance is also considered when computing the final result to motivate the player to sustain the tandem standing longer and tremble less.

Fig. 6. A senior playing Scooter Chase.

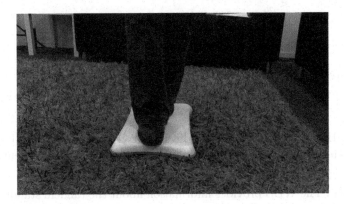

Fig. 7. Heel-toe standing on top of the WBB required to play Scooter Chase.

Basic Gameplay and Controls. There are two interactions possible in Scooter Chase: move and turn.

The main development goal was to use a tandem standing exercise as an interaction to move the player. An algorithm was written to detect when the player is doing the exercise and when it does, the game character moves at constant speed, stopping when the player leaves the position. Stopping can also be used to figure what to do next. A player performing the tandem stance in order to play this game can be seen in Fig. 7.

The possibility of turning was added to make the game more dynamic and attractive, enabling the cat to make curvilinear trajectories and adding obstacles in the path which the cat can jump, as well as requiring the player to coordinate the movement of the handlebar with the stance. The first approach to this interaction was to use COP's sway in the medial-lateral direction using arms wide open rotations to cause it. However, this decision did not affect the COP coordinates: that arm rotation barely affected COP because the human body tends to compensate these movements with the feet, causing the COP's to actually move

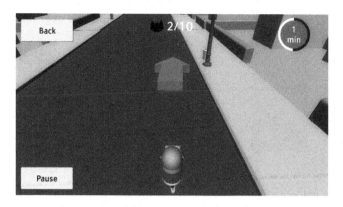

Fig. 8. Scooter Chase screenshot.

in the unintended direction in most cases. Ultimately, smartphone interaction was added, as an handlebar, to surpass those difficulties, using changes in its three-dimensional orientation to rotate the character. Adding a second device was more effective than using the WBB to turn while tandem standing.

This game has four difficulty levels where the path the cat runs is different and has more obstacles for the player. The cat and scooter's speed and handlebar's sensibility increase in higher levels. The first level has a small tutorial to explain to the players the mechanics and the logic.

When the player catches the cat for the tenth time or the time limit is surpassed, the game ends and a score is given and displayed to the player. This score takes into account the number of times the cat was caught. The score screen also shows the number of times the player hit an obstacle, the total time standing in the tandem stance and the balance performance according to the Tandem Stance Test [16] described in the exercise analysis.

Game Interface. Scooter Chase displays several information to the player in order to assist. During gameplay, the player can see in the top of the screen the total number of stops the cat does during the level, as well as the number of times it was already caught. A clock is also present to indicate the remaining time the player has to finish the game at the top right corner. An arrow will appear above the character if the cat is far way to help the player locate it. A game's screenshot can be seen in Fig. 8.

As stated above, tutorial messages will appear to the player in the beginning of the game, either to instruct the player to calibrate the devices or to explain the game's logic and mechanics as seen in Fig. 1. The score screen, seen at the end of the game, presents scores to the user, which are the number of times the cat was caught, the number of times the player hit an obstacle, the total time standing in the tandem stance and Tandem Stance Test (TST) result.

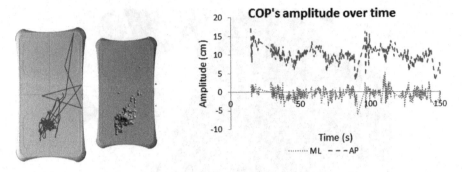

Fig. 9. COP's path chart on the left, COP's frequency map on the center and COP's amplitude-over-time, all taken while performing a tandem stance in Scooter Chase.

Exercise Analysis. The first balance assessment metric present in this game is the Tandem Stance Test (TST) [16]. This test is clearly appropriate to use in this game as it takes into consideration the maximum time a patient can maintain a heel-toe standing pose. The result from this test can be low, if the maximum time is between 0 and 9 s, medium if between 10 s and 29 s, or high otherwise. The terminology was changed to weak, fair and good to inform the players better about the assessment. A classification of excellent was added if the player can maintain the pose through all the game.

In addition, the COP's mean velocity and total oscillation are computed and recorded in a file. This file also contains the COP tracking needed to generate the COP's path, amplitude-over-time and frequency map. On Fig. 9 it is presented, on the left, an example of a COP's path chart, on the center a COP's frequency map and on the right is a COP's amplitude-over-time chart, all taken from one participant's tryout. These metrics could be useful for a balance assessment from a physiotherapist. This approach may be a feasible way to regularly evaluate patients remotely through the use of exergames.

6   Evaluation

The test focused on the system's usability and satisfaction, and in field-testing a set of proposed metrics. The volunteers experimented the final versions of Scooter Chase and Segway Stroll. This test phase counted with eleven participants. These volunteers were seniors who lived independently with ages between sixty-four and eighty years old ($\bar{x} = 72.09 \pm 5.75$). Six participants were of the female gender.

6.1   Methods

Before interacting with the developed exergames, the volunteers were asked to perform the Time Up and Go (TUG) test. Then, the participants would experiment the system following the instructions of a mediator. The mediator instructed the volunteers as follows:

1. Perform the TUG test. (a) Begin seated. (b) When the mediator says "go", the volunteer should get up, walk three meters, return and sit again where the participant was. (c) The three meters distance is pointed out by the mediator. (d) The mediator must start a stopwatch when saying "go", stop when the participant sits and write the time.
2. Play the Scooter Chase game. (a) Read the calibration instructions and interact accordingly. (b) Read the game instructions and play the game. (c) If the player does the calibration wrong or does not understand something, the game should be restarted. (d) If the player has not understood, the mediator should explain or demonstrate the instructions.
3. Play the Segway Stroll game. (a) Read the calibration instructions and interact accordingly. (b) Read the game instructions and play the game. (c) If the player does the calibration wrong or does not understand something, the game should be restarted. (d) If the player has not understood, the mediator should explain or demonstrate the instructions.
4. Answer the questions on the questionnaire.

This protocol provides a balance test result for comparison with the automatic system analysis to evaluate if the system assessment was consistent. The questionnaire has questions about physical exercise habits and motivation to play these games. All the measured metrics are described in detail in the next section.

6.2 Measured Metrics

As stated, with this work we aim for solutions that can motivate older adults. Knowing that technological barriers and complex mechanics can hamper the perception of the games, and hence their acceptance, we chose a set of metrics to assess these issues in the case of our proposed games. Metrics M1, M2 and M3 cover the technological expertise level, needs for explanation, and the game's difficulty perception (Table 1).

The second set of metrics (M4, M5 and M6) focuses on the automation of data collection for healthcare professionals (another of the goals of this work). Therefore they cover data obtained automatically by the system regarding COP (described in Sect. 4), TST and TUG (supported by the literature).

For the Segway Stroll, the system tracks the COP when the player is standing still for more than 10 s. It records all COP readings and respective time during the tracking in order to draw the COP's path, COP amplitude over time in AP and ML directions and a frequency map. In addition, it records the COP's total mean velocity, total oscillation, standard deviation and variance. A summary of all metrics used in the tests is described on Table 1.

For the Scooter Chase analysis this data was taken from the system: total time in tandem stance, maximum time in tandem stance (which is used by the system to evaluate the player's balance using the TST [16]), COP's mean velocity and total oscillation through the game, the number of repetitions, for each of them, the standard deviation and the variance in AP and ML direction and

Table 1. Metrics summary.

ID	Metric	Source	Description
M1	Technological expertise level	Questionnaire	Number of devices regularly used (phone, PC, tablet) [0, 3]
M2	Explanation level required	Annotation	Explanation required from the mediator [1, 5] based on annotations (see Table 2)
M3	Games' difficulty perception	Questionnaire	Median of Likert scores [1, 5] of questions (see Table 3)
M4	COP's mean velocity	System	COP's mean velocity while performing a tandem or standing stance measured by the system
M5	TST	System	Maximum time maintaining a tandem stance
M6	TUG	System	Results from TUG test

lastly, COP read while in the stance and the time it was taken, used to draw the COP's path, COP frequency map and COP's amplitude over time.

6.3   Results and Analysis

This section presents the main results of the tests. The technological expertise (M1) for this population was characterised in terms of regular use of smartphones, tablets and computers or laptops. Three participants said they do not use any of the devices regularly, two stated that they used the smartphone and two other said they used smartphones and computers. From the remaining participants, one said he uses only computers, another uses only the tablet, the third uses the smartphone and the tablet and the last said he uses all the devices regularly. As such, this group had disparate technological habits.

The explanation level required (M2) to play the exergames is detailed in Table 2 while median values of the answers to the games' difficulty questionnaire (M3) can be seen in Table 3. The average of the TUG result and automatic retrieved answers (Metrics M4 to M6) are presented in Table 4.

The annotations (M2) seen in Table 2 use a 5 point Likert-scale. With these annotations we could see that most users could understand well the WBB interface, namely in Scooter Chase users did understand how to move with the heel-toe standing ($M = 5$) and how to move using a forward reach in Segway Stroll ($M = 5$). Most users were able to understand the calibration system in both games without much explanation. The usage of the smartphone to steer the Scooter was not very successful ($M = 3$). Some interface elements such as the arrow to track the cat were not obvious ($M = 1$).

The data was retrieved from the system to compare with the results of the TUG test. Few participants had their standing stance assessed by the system, as seen in the last columns of Table 4. First, almost all participants thought they

Table 2. Explanation level required - Mediator Annotations, Metric M2 (Medians and Interquartile Range), some annotations were only made for one application

#	Question	Scooter Chase			Segway Stroll		
		M	Q3	Q1	M	Q3	Q1
1	How to move	5	0	0	5	0	0
2	WBB calibration	5	0	0	5	0	0
3	Smartphone calibration	5	0	−2			
4	How to steer	3	2	−1	5	0	−4
5	Must catch the cat	2	2.5	−1			
6	How to brake				3	0	0
7	Must avoid obstacles	4	1	−3	5	0	−4

Table 3. Questionnaire Metric M3 (Medians and Interquartile Range)

#	Question	M	Q3	Q1
1	I practice physical exercise regularly	5	0	−1
2	I enjoyed playing Scooter Chase	4	1	−0.5
3	I enjoyed playing Scooter Stroll	4	1	0
4	I would like to play these games regularly	5	0	−0.5
5	I felt I was doing physical exercise/effort	4	1	0
6	These games motivate physical exercise practice	5	0	−0.5
7	Device calibration was simple	3	0.5	0
8	Controlling the vehicles was simple	3	0	−1
9	Objective fulfilment was simple	3	0	−1

had to raise their calves. One participant after corrected stated "in fact, in the image the figure is also raising the toes". The second reason was that they had difficulties in doing an acceleration-brake movement and were not being able to surpass the first trap before the time ran out. In the future a more thorough exemplification of the exercise and additional time to complete the exercise can help prevent these issues.

All participants scored less than $20s$ in the TUG test as expected for older adults who live independently [32]. With the exception of one participant, all seniors scored more than $30s$ in the TST which indicates the same lack of balance impairments [16]. As an exception one participant stopped the stance many times to stop the scooter and figure what to do and not because he could not maintain the position. This means that some results may be directly influenced by game design and the learning capacity of the players and not due to physical or motor impairments. This should be further explored in the future.

In the questionnaire (M3) (seen in Table 3), all volunteers, except one, said in the first question that they practice exercise regularly. Some even commented

Table 4. Automatic measures for each participant (Metrics M4, M5 and M6).

Gender	Age	Tech. Expertise	TUG (s)	Tandem stance			Standing stance	
				TST Time (s)	Mean velocity (cm/s)	Total oscillation (cm)	Mean velocity (cm/s)	Total oscillation (cm)
F	80	0	15.0	33.9	10.7	837.6		
F	66	2	8.3	35.3	25.2	1778.6		
M	64	3	5.6	54.2	27.7	1757.6	6.2	92.1
F	67	2	5.0	61.7	81.6	932.9		
M	77	2	9.7	118.0	34.3	1482.5	14.3	181.8
F	69	0	5.0	149.9	7.6	1236.6	16.3	308.7
M	78	1	6.2	96.9	18.2	1319.7		
M	68	0	4.6	14.3	10.3	571.4	9.6	237.4
F	76	1	12.7	103.5	24.1	1731.7		
F	78	1	8.5	41.1	9.7	1367.4	8.9	72.9
M	70	1	10.4	41.9	12.6	825.9		
Average		1.8	8.3	68.4	23.9	1258.3	11.1	178.6
STD Dev		1.0	3.4	42.5	21.1	418.6	4.1	98.8

what exercises they usually do, such as gymnastics or tai-chi. The results of TUG and TST may be explained by these practices. Despite the obvious difficulties in playing these games, most seniors claimed they liked Scooter Chase, and also enjoyed Segway Stroll. All the seniors said they would like to play these games regularly and by doing so, it would motivate them to do exercise. Most seniors also expressed they felt they were doing physical exercise or effort. The last three questions were focused on the usability and received less favourable answers, which was expected given the level of explanation required for playing.

6.4 Discussion

The tests showcased the importance of using a set of metrics to systematically collect and measure performance of older adults in an exergame scenario. The participants claimed they enjoyed playing the games (Metric M3) and they would like to do it regularly, showing motivation towards regular exercise practice.

In this small sample, age analysis suggests users with age below 70 years old understand better the games, but balance is similar across all ages. As almost all the participants exercise regularly, this result is not surprising. Quantitative balance comparison between metrics did not find any relevant relations, as the metrics used are more related to finding balance impairments than quantifying balance in healthier individuals. Further testing these measures with physiotherapists may help reach additional conclusions, which can culminate in the revision of these proposed metrics. Still, qualitative measures between TUG and TST did obtain similar results, which indicates that this metric could be used to supervise the players.

TST, COP's mean velocity, total oscillation, path, amplitude-over-time and frequency maps (Metrics M4 to M6) can give a mean for physiotherapists and care-takers to supervise the elderly adults who play the games, thus it can be practicable. Frequent exercise has benefits, so it is expected that regular exergaming sessions would have too. The proposed exergames have to be further studied to reveal their practicability to monitor patients' balance and benefits related to fall prevention. In Segway Stroll the game instructions were considered good, with the exception of the toe raise problem. The forward reaching detection algorithm had some problems as some players had difficulty to move the character. This happened in the preliminary tests during implementation phase. Another difficulty was to avoid traps. As this was the first interaction with the system, players were not expecting the traps and did not stop in time. Then, the participants had problems doing a quick acceleration and braking immediately.

7 Conclusion

Digital games for rehabilitation are an important topic of research nowadays and multiple works have presented positive results in using motion sensing devices in therapy despite being originally created for entertainment [1,7,28]. Exergaming has been shown to have potential to improve traditional therapy exercises and fall-prevention exercise programs in the works of Deutsch et al. [11], Geurts et al. [14], Uzor and Baillie [36], Davies et al. [10], Santos et al. [34] and others. Our methodology combines this research with a proposed set of balance metrics and therapeutical exercises, such as those proposed by Clark et al. [9] and Kennedy et al. [20] to allow for supervised domestic exergames.

We have proposed a set of balance metrics to be computed while the user plays the games. These proposed metrics for evaluating balance exergames seem to be relevant but further studies are required in the future to refine them.

All participants in the user studies stated they enjoyed playing the games, would like to do it regularly and that the games motivate physical exercise practice. This indicates that home exercise through the use of exergames can be motivating although further studies are needed. Nevertheless there is still room for improvements taking into account the suggestions and difficulties observed in the user studies.

Acknowledgments. We would like to thank Fraunhofer Portugal for their support. This work is financed by the ERDF – European Regional Development Fund through the Operational Programme for Competitiveness and Internationalisation – COMPETE 2020 Programme and by National Funds through the Portuguese funding agency, FCT – Fundação para a Ciência e a Tecnologia within project POCI-01-0145-FEDER-030740 – PTDC/CCI-COM/30740/2017.

References

1. Agmon, M., Perry, C.K., Phelan, E., Demiris, G., Nguyen, H.Q.: A pilot study of Wii Fit exergames to improve balance in older adults. J. Geriatr. Phys. Ther. **34**(4), 161–167 (2011). https://doi.org/10.1519/JPT.0b013e3182191d98
2. Ayoade, M., Baillie, L.: A novel knee rehabilitation system for the home. In: Proceedings of the 32nd Annual ACM Conference on Human Factors in Computing Systems - CHI 2014, pp. 2521–2530 (2014). https://doi.org/10.1145/2556288.2557353
3. Bateni, H.: Changes in balance in older adults based on use of physical therapy vs the Wii Fit gaming system: a preliminary study. Physiotherapy (United Kingdom) **98**(3), 211–216 (2012). https://doi.org/10.1016/j.physio.2011.02.004
4. Berg, K., Wood-Dauphinée, S., Williams, J.I., Gayton, D.: Measuring balance in the elderly: preliminary development of an instrument. Physiother. Can. **41**(6), 304–311 (1989)
5. Betker, A.L., Szturm, T., Moussavi, Z.K., Nett, C.: Video game-based exercises for balance rehabilitation: a single-subject design. Arch. Phys. Med. Rehabil. **87**(8), 1141–1149 (2006). https://doi.org/10.1016/j.apmr.2006.04.010
6. Bhuiyan, M., Picking, R.: Gesture-controlled user interfaces, what have we done and what's next. In: Proceedings of the 5th Collaborative Research Symposium on Security, E-Learning, Internet and Networking, pp. 59–69 (2009)
7. Brito, C.M., Jacob, J., Nóbrega, R., Santos, A.M.: Balance assessment in fall-prevention exergames. In: Proceedings of the 17th International ACM SIGACCESS Conference on Computers' Accessibility, pp. 439–440 (2015). https://doi.org/10.1145/2700648.2811342
8. Campbell, A.J., Robertson, M.C.: Otago exercise programme to prevent falls in older adults (2003)
9. Clark, R.A., Bryant, A.L., Pua, Y., McCrory, P., Bennell, K., Hunt, M.: Validity and reliability of the Nintendo Wii Balance Board for assessment of standing balance. Gait Posture **31**, 307–310 (2010). https://doi.org/10.1016/j.gaitpost.2009.11.012
10. Davies, T.C., et al.: Developing Wii balance games to increase balance: a multidisciplinary approach. Int. J. Virtual Worlds Hum. Comput. Interact. **1** (2013). https://doi.org/10.11159/vwhci.2013.002
11. Deutsch, J.E., Borbely, M., Filler, J., Huhn, K., Guarrera-Bowlby, P.: Use of a low-cost, commercially available gaming console (Wii) for rehabilitation of an adolescent with cerebral palsy. Phys. Ther. **88**(10), 1196–1207 (2008). https://doi.org/10.2522/ptj.20080062
12. Duarte, M., Freitas, S.M.S.F.: Revisão sobre Posturografia Baseada em Plataforma de Força para Avaliação do Equilíbrio. Revista Brasileira de Fisioterapia **14**(3), 183–192 (2010)
13. Eng, J., Dawson, A., Pang, M.: Fitness and mobility exercise program: a community-based group exercise program for people living with stroke (2006)
14. Geurts, L., et al.: Digital games for physical therapy: fulfilling the need for calibration and adaptation. In: Design, pp. 117–124 (2011)
15. González, A., Hayashibe, M., Fraisse, P.: Estimation of the center of mass with Kinect and Wii balance board. In: International Conference on Intelligent Robots and Systems, pp. 1023–1028 (2012)

16. Hile, E.S., Brach, J.S., Perera, S., Wert, D.M., VanSwearingen, J.M., Studenski, S.A.: Interpreting the need for initial support to perform tandem stance tests of balance. Phys. Ther. **92**(10), 1316–1328 (2012). https://doi.org/10.2522/ptj. 20110283
17. Jacob, J., Nóbrega, R., Coelho, A., Rodrigues, R.: Adaptivity and safety in location-based games. In: 2017 9th International Conference on Virtual Worlds and Games for Serious Applications (VS-Games), pp. 173–174, September 2017. https://doi.org/10.1109/VS-GAMES.2017.8056592
18. Jacob, J., Lopes, A., Nóbrega, R., Rodrigues, R., Coelho, A.: Player adaptivity and safety in location-based games. In: Cheok, A.D., Inami, M., Romão, T. (eds.) ACE 2017. LNCS, vol. 10714, pp. 219–238. Springer, Cham (2018). https://doi. org/10.1007/978-3-319-76270-8_16
19. Jacob, J., Lopes, A., Nóbrega, R., Rodrigues, R., Coelho, A.: Towards player adaptivity in mobile exergames. In: Cheok, A.D., Inami, M., Romão, T. (eds.) ACE 2017. LNCS, vol. 10714, pp. 278–292. Springer, Cham (2018). https://doi.org/10. 1007/978-3-319-76270-8_20
20. Kennedy, M.W., Schmiedeler, J.P., Crowell, C.R., Villano, M., Striegel, A.D., Kuitse, J.: Enhanced feedback in balance rehabilitation using the Nintendo Wii balance board. In: 2011 IEEE 13th International Conference on e-Health Networking, Applications and Services, HEALTHCOM 2011, pp. 162–168 (2011)
21. Lange, B.S., et al.: Development of an interactive rehabilitation game using the Nintendo WiiFitTM Balance Board for people with neurological injury. In: International Conference on Disability, Virtual Reality & Associated Technologies, pp. 249–254 (2010)
22. Langley, F.A., Mackintosh, S.F.H., Applsc, B.: Functional balance assessment of older community dwelling adults: a systematic review of the literature. Internet J. Allied Health Sci. Pract. **5**(4), 1–11 (2007)
23. Mekler, E.D., Bopp, J.A., Tuch, A.N., Opwis, K.: A systematic review of quantitative studies on the enjoyment of digital entertainment games. In: Proceedings of the 32nd Annual ACM Conference on Human Factors in Computing Systems - CHI 2014, pp. 927–936 (2014). https://doi.org/10.1145/2556288.2557078
24. Mellecker, R., Lyons, E.J., Baranowski, T.: Disentangling fun and enjoyment in exergames using an expanded design, play, experience framework: a narrative review. Games Health J. **2**(3), 142–149 (2013). https://doi.org/10.1089/g4h.2013. 0022
25. Melo, M.C.P.A.: The impact of a specific home based exercise programme on fal risk factors in older Portuguese people. Ph.D. thesis, University of Brighton (2008)
26. Mitty, E., Flores, S.: Fall prevention in assisted living: assesment and strategies. Geriatr. Nurs. **28**(6), 349–357 (2007)
27. Nawaz, A., Skjæret, N., Ystmark, K., Helbostad, J.L., Vereijken, B., Svanæs, D.: Assessing seniors' user experience (UX) of exergames for balance training. In: Proceedings of the 8th Nordic Conference on Human-Computer Interaction Fun, Fast, Foundational - NordiCHI 2014, New York, NY, USA, pp. 578–587 (2014). https:// doi.org/10.1145/2639189.2639235
28. Nicholson, V.P., McKean, M., Lowe, J., Fawcett, C., Burkett, B.: Six weeks of unsupervised Nintendo Wii Fit gaming is effective at improving balance in independent older adults. J. Aging Phys. Act. **23**(1), 153–158 (2015). https://doi.org/ 10.1123/JAPA.2013-0148
29. Nielsen, M., Störring, M.: A procedure for developing intuitive and ergonomic gesture interfaces for HCI. In: The 5th International Workshop on Gesture and Sign Language Based Human Computer Interaction, pp. 1–12 (2003)

30. Pajala, S., Era, P., Koskenvuo, M., Kaprio, J., Törmäkangas, T., Rantanen, T.: Force platform balance measures as predictors of indoor and outdoor falls in community-dwelling women aged 63–76 years. J. Gerontol. Ser. Biol. Sci. Med. Sci. **63**(2), 171–178 (2008). https://doi.org/10.1093/gerona/63.2.171

31. Pinto, D., Costa, J., Nóbrega, R., da Silva, H., Coelho, A.: Graphical simulation of clinical scenarios for medical training. In: 2018 International Conference on Graphics and Interaction (ICGI), pp. 1–8, November 2018. https://doi.org/10.1109/ITCGI.2018.8602866

32. Podsiadlo, D., Richardson, S.: The timed "Up & Go": a test of basic functional mobility for frail elderly persons. J. Am. Geriatr. Soc. **39**, 142–148 (1991)

33. Rose, D.J., Lucchese, N., Wiersma, L.D.: Development of a multidimensional balance scale for use with functionally independent older adults. Arch. Phys. Med. Rehabil. **87**(11), 1478–1485 (2006). https://doi.org/10.1016/j.apmr.2006.07.263

34. Santos, A., Guimarães, V., Matos, N., Cevada, J., Ferreira, C., Sousa, I.: Multisensor exercise-based interactive games for fall prevention and rehabilitation. In: 2015 9th International Conference on Pervasive Computing Technologies for Healthcare (PervasiveHealth), pp. 65–71, May 2015. https://doi.org/10.4108/icst.pervasivehealth.2015.259115

35. Tyson, S.: Brunel Balance Assessment (BBA). University of Salford (2004)

36. Uzor, S., Baillie, L.: Investigating the long-term use of exergames in the home with elderly fallers. In: Proceedings of the 32nd Annual ACM Conference on Human Factors in Computing Systems - CHI 2014, pp. 2813–2822 (2014). https://doi.org/10.1145/2556288.2557160

37. Vines, J., Pritchard, G., Wright, P., Olivier, P.: An age-old problem: examining the discourses of ageing in HCI and strategies for future research. TOCHI **22**(1), 1–27 (2015). https://doi.org/10.1017/S0269888900008122

38. Zaczynski, M., Whitehead, A.D.: Establishing design guidelines in interactive exercise gaming. In: Proceedings of the 32nd Annual ACM Conference on Human Factors in Computing Systems - CHI 2014, pp. 1875–1884 (2014). https://doi.org/10.1145/2556288.2557329

Mobile Mapmaking: A Field Study of Gamification and Cartographic Editing

Manousos Kamilakis$^{(\boxtimes)}$ and Konstantinos Chorianopoulos

Ionian University, Corfu 49100, Greece
cl6kami@ionio.gr

Abstract. Digital mapmaking has traditionally been a desktop computing activity with dedicated graphical (native or web) applications that strongly depend on the precision of mouse input. In addition, digital mapmaking also has a strong pillar on field observations, which have remained a separate task to the final mapmaking. In this work, we present to users a mobile application that combines the strengths of graphical mapmaking user interfaces with the actual geographical context into an integrated and collaborative user interface. In particular, the application implements three representative mobile mapmaking tasks (path recording, path editing and path reviewing) and includes gamification elements. A field experiment was conducted with thirty-six participants for two twenty-day periods during which they were asked to provide information about the pedestrian network of an urban region using the app. The results from questionnaire responses and contribution data showed that most users prefer recording their path, which is also the work with the lowest interaction. Moreover, gamification did not bring the expected results and the more difficult tasks were undertaken by few devoted users. Further research is needed to examine how interface design could better engage committed users in the aforementioned mapmaking task types.

Keywords: Mobile interaction · Mapmaking · VGI

1 Introduction

The emergence of digital maps and modern geographic tools (sensors, devices, software) that automate and abstract complex processes has made it possible for untrained people to participate in cartographic projects despite lacking the specialized knowledge and education of professional cartographers. It has come to a point where users perceive such systems differently than before. This tendency has unfolded a research space which deals with cartographic interaction mediated by computing devices [1]. Moreover, commercial smartphone devices have become capable of collecting location data and therefore offer valuable geographic information. This led to the logical consequence of mobile apps becoming a powerful tool for obtaining Volunteered Geographic Information (VGI) [2].

Human interaction with geographic applications has been studied in various contexts and largely in map use. On the other hand, mapmaking interaction research is limited as it has not been a long time since mapmaking has been widely introduced to

© IFIP International Federation for Information Processing 2019
Published by Springer Nature Switzerland AG 2019
D. Lamas et al. (Eds.): INTERACT 2019, LNCS 11747, pp. 427–435, 2019.
https://doi.org/10.1007/978-3-030-29384-0_26

non-geographers. User data analysis in VGI applications has shown the heterogeneity of the contributors in terms of usage patterns which could be exploited in HCI related decisions of resembling applications [3, 4]. Concerning pedestrian mapmaking, Kapenekakis et al. [5] confirmed the feasibility of making an abstract map by pedestrians employing common smartphone devices and an Android app. Although the app's functionality is similar with the one presented here, we additionally introduce and examine the function of map editing in the urban environment. This is considered important because many crowdsourcing map editing or VGI applications use distant editing techniques like satellite images, aerial photographs, street level images [6, 7]. In contrast, in our approach the user experiences the path network on site, as he walks. Hence, we suppose he can make more qualitative edits than in desktop applications. If this holds true, it is worth concentrating the interest on mobile variants of such systems.

Although some mapmaking mobile apps have already emerged, it is yet unclear how users operate them and generate content. There is a wide variety of functionalities from the simplistic recording of courses, to more sophisticated like applying corrections to geographic data. Since they target large numbers of users, it is expected that users will have different task preferences, cartographic skills and knowledge, and motivation in contributing. In this paper we give emphasis to selected types of functionalities typically found in such applications, which we consider to represent discrete types of map interaction tasks. We present an Android app which is utilized to explore how users interact with these tasks. The mapmaking app's main goal is to collect data and information by the users in an attempt to create a map for pedestrians based on their walking experience.

Contribution. This paper discusses lessons learnt from an experiment with a mobile mapmaking map interface. In particular, we discuss user interaction, task preference and the design considerations which arise.

2   Application Design

An Android app was developed which is based on the previous work of Kapenekakis et al. [5]. It is a crowdsourcing gamified application which generally aims at collecting location information from pedestrians. The system is complemented by a database for data storage and a server for serving requests from user devices. Its main purpose is to collect pedestrian routes resulting in an aggregated path network/map for pedestrian use.

Path Recording: The core function of the application is to collect user's location data while walking through an urban environment with minimal interaction (see Fig. 1 left). The location information collected can be considered as the basis of a new pedestrian network of paths or map, which is not identical to the vehicle roads. The task of recording paths, from a user's perspective, is analyzed as such: Tap button to start path recording → Walk - passive recording of path (during walk, user can optionally select a type of path from a list) → Tap button to stop path recording → Confirm to save recorded path and data (includes getting informed for points gained).

Path correction: A feature that is commonly found in desktop cartographic applications is correcting street network or other geographic shapes of interest. We included an analogous functionality in the app, which allows the user to "draw" a suggestion of path correction (see Fig. 1 middle). We consider this an important addition as, inevitably, recorded paths are inaccurately recorded due to sensory limitations and environmental obstructions. The actions the user has to undergo to correct a path are: Walk checking the screen until find a recorded path that needs correcting (only near recorded paths appear) ➔ Tap to select path for correction ➔ Draw correction in straight line (Long tap to start correction ➔ Long tap to stop correction) ➔ Confirm correction (includes getting informed for points gained).

Path reviewing: Besides correcting paths, users can also review other users' paths on walkability (see Fig. 1 right). Peer reviewing of paths has a double aim. Firstly, it is necessary to objectify paths' walkability values and secondly to discourage and limit the effects of malicious behavior. Evaluating a path, the user must follow these actions: Walk checking the screen until find a path to evaluate (only near recorded paths appear) ➔ Tap to select path for reviewing ➔ Review path by selecting predefined choices from lists (walkability reviewing, tags reviewing, new path) ➔ Confirm upload of review (includes getting informed for points gained).

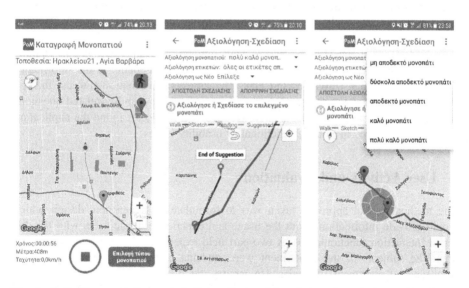

Fig. 1. Left: User recording a path (green line), while other paths are shown (red lines). **Middle:** User making a suggestion for correction (blue line) of a path (red line). **Right:** User reviewing a path (red line). (Color figure online)

It is noted that the above functionalities include locality as a necessary attribute for data input. For path recording this is self-explanatory. For the other two functionalities, the situated path reviewing and correcting is ensured by restricting them for paths only in the vicinity of the user.

To motivate users to provide as much information as possible, a gamification system was applied. The gamification system involved a scoring and an achievement system on Google Play for each of the actions that have already been explained. Also, a leaderboard was created to enhance competition. To explain briefly, the scoring and achievements system favor (a) recording long paths; (b) recording new paths; (c) reviewing paths; (d) reviewing unreviewed paths; (e) suggesting a path correction; (f) providing a new suggestion for path correction. It also discourages users from providing low quality, inaccurate or mischievous information. Depending on the reviews of other users, a path or a suggestion of a player may gain extra points or receive a point penalty.

The app's three core functionalities can be seen as three different interactivity functionalities usually found on VGI mobile applications. The path recording represents a minimal interaction, with fragmented engagement functionality. The user mostly interacts at the start and the end of the task, with the option of turning his attention elsewhere in the meantime. The path reviewing is a more classic interaction functionality and requires constant attention until the task is finished and a moderate interaction load. For this task to be completed the user has to find a path (both physically and on screen), to select it, to review it (from predefined choices) and to confirm the transaction. The most demanding interaction process is the path suggestion/correction. In this case the user has to find a path needing correction, to select it, to carefully apply the correction by "drawing" it on the smartphone screen and confirm the transaction.

In order to test whether the app is well implemented and free of considerable usability problems, a pilot study was conducted with six students of the Informatics Department of Ionian University in Corfu. The subjects were requested to use the app in the field for ten days, answer a short questionnaire with usability-related questions and to report any problems encountered. Generally, the subjects found the application easy to use and free of notable functional or usability issues.

3   User Activity and Evaluation

The methodological approach taken was to formulate an experiment design which would provide information about the usage and experience of the users with the different interaction functionalities. A two-part field experiment was conducted with the app. The subjects of the experiment were students of the Information Science & Informatics Department of Ionian University and were offered a bonus grade on specific courses for completing a minimum of tasks using the app. The field trial took place in the city of Corfu, a city of approximately thirty thousand inhabitants. The street layout of Corfu is variformed and hardly linearized, as it comprises of a new and an old region. The participants were invited to complete tasks, which covered all the main functionalities. More specifically, they had to record paths, review other users' paths and design corrections to recorded paths. They were also provided with an online manual (which included the details of the point system) and a link to a video demo showing the full capabilities and functions of the app.

In the first trial, the subjects were encouraged to perform all the above function-alities in the form of a game and finish with filling an online questionnaire. Short time usage was expected as the experiment was an unsupervised field experiment [8]. In order to address potential low contribution levels, we introduced both internal and external incentives. They involved bonus grades in a course of their degree and the gamification of the app with scores for each contribution and a leaderboard. Moreover, it was stated to potential participants that the ultimate goal of the game, besides player rankings, was to collect enough data to produce a new, more appropriate map for pedestrians. As in the first trial there were no pre-recorded paths, it was easier for the subjects to focus on recording paths. In the end of the first trial there were indeed a large number of recorded paths. Thus, the second trial focused only on the reviewing and designing of paths in order to draw more solid conclusions regarding these functionalities. In both of the trials of the experiment the subjects were given a twenty-day period of app usage to fulfill the tasks given.

Totally, thirty six (36) participants installed the app and twenty (20) of them made at least one valid contribution (uploading) to the database (Table 1). As valid contri-bution we consider a recording, or an action on a path, inside the boundaries that roughly contain the city. Also, the recorded paths had to be at least twenty (20) m long. We chose a short minimum path distance because of the short alleys that make up blocks of buildings in the old region, assuming that even a path that short could contain noteworthy information.

Table 1. User participation in each stage

Action	Participants
App installation	36
Valid contribution	20
First experiment	
Path recording	19
Path reviewing	8
Path correction	4
Questionnaire response	14
Review experiment	
Path reviewing	3
Path correction	3

3.1   Questionnaire Results

The aim of the questionnaire was to assess how the app's functionalities appeal to the user and which are the factors that motivate users to use them. The replies from the relevant questions showed that most of the respondents have never edited a map (71.4%) but where very interested in the idea of contributing in the creation of a pedestrian map. About half of the participants were motivated from the contribution in the creation of the pedestrian map, approximately the other half were motivated from the gamification features of the app and only one was participating for the extra grade.

It is impressive that while many of the participants were motivated by the score system and achievements, all of them claimed that they did not use any strategy to gain more points. Concerning the preference type of contribution among recording new paths, reviewing other users' paths, and editing existing paths, the answers dominated the recording new paths choice (92.9%).

3.2   Contribution Data Results

The participants seemed to enjoy more to record paths as nineteen (19) of them recorded 415 paths. About half of them recorded less than ten paths (52.6%), four recorded twenty to thirty paths (21%), and another four recorded more than thirty paths (21%). Although the paths are many, they considerably differ in size. In cartography, one of the most important features of contributions is coverage. From this aspect, the subjects displayed different levels of zeal as it is shown from the total path distance presented in Fig. 2. The total distance of the paths reached 254002 m. The mean path distance was 612 m, which is a reasonable walking distance according to Yang et al. [9] as trips longer than 400 m are common and the median distance of waking trips among walkers is 800 m. This may indicate that users did not put more effort than usual walks to record paths. Consequently, this could explain why users preferred this type of functionality. It is minimal, does not explicitly require the attention of the user and it can be undertaken while the user is occupied with other activities like taking a regular walk or going somewhere where he is already supposed to go. The responses from the questionnaires also support this, based on the result that not one user tried to gain more points using a strategic behavior.

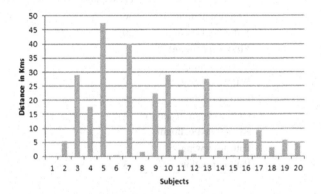

Fig. 2. Total path distance per subject

The functionalities of reviewing and correcting paths were barely used during the first experiment. At the early stage of the experiment there were only few paths to be found for reviewing and corrections. To exclude the possibility of users not fully understanding the concept of these functionalities at the early stage, we conducted a review experiment with the recorded paths from the first experiment already loaded and the recording of paths deactivated. In this way, the subjects could focus in these specific actions.

The combined results showed again little interest of the participants for these functionalities. The fact is that eight (8) subjects reviewed at least one path and five (5) suggested at least one path correction. It is interesting that of them, only three (3) contributed the vast majority of these edits (Fig. 3). Comparing path reviewing and path correcting, the total number of reviews was 152 (45.8%), little less than the total number of suggestions for path corrections which was 180 (54.2%).

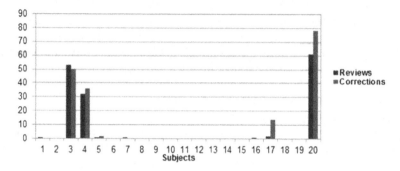

Fig. 3. Path reviews and corrections per subject

4 Discussion

The experiments revealed some behavioral aspects of users while interacting with our app, which could be generalized to relevant smartphone apps. Knowing and interpreting user behavior is important in designing interactivity.

Firstly, the majority of our subjects stated that they prefer recording paths which was also evident from the uploaded data. Thus, we assume that casual users prefer minimalistic, with lighter cognitive load interactivity for this kind of cartographic apps. In agreement with the conclusion of Poplin et al. that users find difficulties or neglect some operations due to lack of training in mapping platforms [4], our results from contribution data indicate that users' task acceptance differs highly among users. Most participants engaged more with the lightweight tasks and functionality which required less interaction, while only few users were receptive to the harder and more complex interactions. This is also in line with the research on map editing applications such as the Cyclopath geowiki and OpenStreetMap which show that a small portion of users contribute the most in mapping content [3, 10]. It is indicative that most participants did not bother at all with the more demanding tasks. This should not be understood simplistically and isolatedly, because there are also other factors involved, such as motivation, which impact avocation. However, it can be assumed that path recording may be preferred by users in similar mobile apps for interaction load or other reasons. In case of the first, similar apps should be carefully designed in order to minimize user interaction. Another solution could be to focus work on specific tasks which are less appealing. For example, in the context of a cycling geowiki, Priedhorsky et al. try to elicit volunteered work acknowledging that preference in "work types" can be correlated with personal characteristics, specifically familiarity with the region [11].

Our app serves a specific purpose. Therefore, it is understandable that not all people will be willing to participate in its goal. In anticipation of this lack of willingness to participate in the cause, we employed a gamification system. More than half of the subjects refused that the scoring system and the achievements motivated them for using the app. This is consistent with the absence of strategy for most players for gaining many points. It is also consistent with the observation that few participants offered much geographic information regardless of the scoring system. Taking the above into account, we propose that specific-purpose contributing applications such as the one studied, are better to be designed considering not the casual user, but users devoted to the goal of the app who are more likely to considerably use it. Moreover, it seems that gamification is not a panacea for increasing user engagement in every case. In contrast, Salomoni et al. reported positive results from the gamification of a mobile app which collected urban data about accessibility [12]. However, we argue that the game mechanics of our app were considerably different.

Regarding the comparison between path reviewing and path correction, we expected that users would significantly use more the path reviewing function because it is easier from an interactivity perspective and can be applied in every recorded path the user finds in his way. On the other hand, the path correction is more demanding as a task, especially when performed in a small smartphone screen, and has to be performed only on paths which can be corrected. Nevertheless, as the users who contributed more to these tasks were the few 'devoted' ones, we can assume that this kind of users are more receptive to undergo more complex and effortful interactions to fulfill tasks.

Cartographic activities play a significant role when designing user-centered carto-graphic interactions and interfaces should be adjusted to the corresponding users' tasks [13]. This paper analyzed the behavior of users with a serious-purpose app which included different interaction functionalities. It is evident that users contribute differently in mapmaking tasks. We believe that in some degree this is due to cognitive and interaction workload. We don't claim that there are interface shortcomings as this was not a finding from the pilot experiment, but there is a need to improve interaction in such mobile apps in order to benefit from on-site provision of geographic information. Moreover, simple forms of gamification like point gathering, leaderboard and achievement systems may not yield better results in terms of contribution in every case. When designing interactivity for similar applications, it is important to first clarify the target users for each of the functionality offered. Cartographic apps include complex tasks, which in some occasions are difficult to be performed without training. Thus, we find it logical to use different interaction functionalities and complexity per type of user, as Brock et al. also suggest in the case of bespoke map customization [14]. Further experiments and data analysis of our app might provide additional insights into building community GIS systems as mobile systems.

Acknowledgments. We would like to thank Mr. Antonios Papapolizos for his valuable work in developing the app.

References

1. Roth, R.E.: Interactive maps: what we know and what we need to know. J. Spat. Inf. Sci. **2013**(6), 59–115 (2013)
2. Goodchild, M.F.: Citizens as sensors: the world of volunteered geography. GeoJournal **69** (4), 211–221 (2007)
3. Panciera, K., Priedhorsky, R., Erickson, T., Terveen, L.: Lurking? Cyclopaths? A quantitative lifecycle analysis of user behavior in a geowiki. In: Proceedings of the SIGCHI Conference on Human Factors in Computing Systems, pp. 1917–1926. ACM, April 2010
4. Poplin, A., Guan, W., Lewis, B.: Online survey of heterogeneous users and their usage of the interactive mapping platform worldmap. Cartographic J. **54**(3), 214–232 (2017)
5. Kapenekakis, I., Chorianopoulos, K.: Citizen science for pedestrian cartography: collection and moderation of walkable routes in cities through mobile gamification. Hum.-centric Comput. Inf. Sci. **7**(1), 10 (2017)
6. Hara, K., Le, V., Froehlich, J.: Combining crowdsourcing and google street view to identify street-level accessibility problems. In: Proceedings of the SIGCHI Conference on Human Factors in Computing Systems, pp. 631–640. ACM, April 2013
7. Hara, K., Sun, J., Moore, R., Jacobs, D., Froehlich, J.: Tohme: detecting curb ramps in google street view using crowdsourcing, computer vision, and machine learning. In: Proceedings of the 27th Annual ACM Symposium on User Interface Software and Technology, pp. 189–204. ACM, October 2014
8. Henze, N., Pielot, M., Poppinga, B., Schinke, T., Boll, S.: My app is an experiment: experience from user studies in mobile app stores. Int. J. Mobile Hum. Comput. Interact. (IJMHCI) **3**(4), 71–91 (2011)
9. Yang, Y., Diez-Roux, A.V.: Walking distance by trip purpose and population subgroups. Am. J. Prev. Med. **43**(1), 11–19 (2012)
10. Haklay, M., Weber, P.: Openstreetmap: User-generated street maps. IEEE Pervasive Comput. **7**(4), 12–18 (2008)
11. Priedhorsky, R., Masli, M., Terveen, L.: Eliciting and focusing geographic volunteer work. In: Proceedings of the 2010 ACM Conference on Computer Supported Cooperative Work, pp. 61–70. ACM, February 2010
12. Salomoni, P., Prandi, C., Roccetti, M., Nisi, V., Nunes, N.J.: Crowdsourcing urban accessibility: some preliminary experiences with results. In: Proceedings of the 11th Biannual Conference on Italian SIGCHI Chapter, pp. 130–133. ACM, September 2015
13. Dransch, D.: User-centred human-computer interaction in cartographic information processing. In: International Cartographic Conference-ICC, pp. 1767–1774, August 2001
14. Brock, A.M., Hecht, B., Signer, B., Schöning, J.: Bespoke map customization behavior and its implications for the design of multimedia cartographic tools. In: Proceedings of the 16th International Conference on Mobile and Ubiquitous Multimedia, pp. 1–11. ACM, November 2017

Play and Learn with an Intelligent Robot: Enhancing the Therapy of Hearing-Impaired Children

Andri Ioannou[1,2(✉)] [iD] and Anna Andreva[3]

[1] Cyprus Interaction Lab, Cyprus University of Technology, Limassol, Cyprus
andri@cyprusinteractionlab.com
[2] Research Center on Interactive Media, Smart Systems and Emerging
Technologies (RISE), Nicosia, Cyprus
[3] Department of Logopedics, Faculty of Public Health, Health Care and Sport,
South-West University "Neofit Rilski", Blagoevgrad, Bulgaria

Abstract. This study suggests an innovative way of using an intelligent robot to support speech therapy for hearing impaired children through play. Although medical technology (e.g., hearing aid, cochlear implant) for children with hearing impairment has advanced significantly, the amplification itself does not provide optimal development of hearing and speaking; it must be combined with specialized therapy. The present study focuses on the use of the humanoid robot NAO in auditory-verbal therapy, an approach to the development of auditory and verbal skills, which does not allow lipreading or other non-verbal cues to facilitate communication. NAO does not have a human mouth and therefore children with hearing impairment cannot do lipreading; this unique characteristic of the technology has been successfully used in the study to create playful and engaging auditory-verbal therapy sessions for six kindergarten hearing impaired children, allowing them to improve their ability to follow instructions using the hearing aid/cochlear implant rather than visual clues in the environment. Our results, although preliminary, seem to encourage further research in supporting hearing-impaired children via play with intelligent robots.

Keywords: NAO · Intelligent robot · Humanoid robot · Hearing impairment · Deaf · Speech therapy · Auditory-Verbal therapy · Special education · Playful learning · Technology-enhanced learning

1 Introduction

Children with hearing impairment are at high risk for language, academic and social difficulties [1]. Fortunately, the advancement of medical technology (e.g., hearing aid, cochlear implant) has significantly changed the prospects of children with hearing impairment. As Levy (2012) explained, with reference to the invention of the cochlear implant, there is now a device that allows a large proportion of deaf people to hear; this has dramatically changed the deaf community and deaf education [2]. Because of the advancement of medical technology, the education of children with hearing impairment

© IFIP International Federation for Information Processing 2019
Published by Springer Nature Switzerland AG 2019
D. Lamas et al. (Eds.): INTERACT 2019, LNCS 11747, pp. 436–452, 2019.
https://doi.org/10.1007/978-3-030-29384-0_27

has evolved into a change in speech therapy, educational audiology, and special education [3]. Educational programs that serve hearing impaired children have changed and keep changing, especially since most of these children are now placed in mainstream schools rather than schools for the deaf in the developed countries [4]. Regional school administration and councils have stopped training programs for children with hearing impairment, on the idea that these students, supported by medical technology, should not be educated separately; instead, they are included to general/mainstream classroom whilst they receive additional therapy and support from speech therapists and educational audiologists [3]. Despite the medical technology advancement, amplification itself does not provide optimal development of hearing and speaking; it must be combined with a specialized program for early intervention [5].

The focus of this study is on the integration of an intelligent robot, NAO, as a supportive tool for learning through play in this early intervention, particularly in auditory-verbal therapy for hearing impaired children, an approach to the development of auditory and verbal skills that does not allow lipreading or other non-verbal cues to facilitate communication. In general, play is crucial for the communication, cognitive, physical, social, and emotional development of young children [6]. While initiating and taking part in playful activities children are motivated to communicate and practice their language [7]. For this reason, play is extensively used in therapy and education. There are many studies exploring play and language learning in groups of children with hearing disorders. Some studies are related to play and deaf children in special schools [8]; other studies compare the ability of children with hearing impairment to play with their hearing peers [9–13]. NAO is well documented as a tool that can be used successfully in learning and therapy through play (e.g., [14–18], although not with hearing impaired children.

Furthermore, NAO has a unique characteristic and a great affordance in the context of the present study. The robot does not have a human mouth and therefore children with hearing impairment cannot do lipreading. The unique feature of the technology has been identified by the authors of this work (an educational technologist and a speech therapist - researcher and practitioner) and has been used in this study to create a unique environment for auditory-verbal therapy sessions for children with hearing impairment. This study was inspired by a true need for engaging hearing-impaired children in auditory-verbal therapy sessions, as identified during previous work of the authors [19] as well as practical experience of the therapists involved. The present manuscript focuses on:

1. What are the children's gains in auditory skills, name the ability of the hearing-impaired child to detect sounds and follow instructions?
2. What is the perceived value of the robot-enhanced environment for auditory-verbal therapy?

The rest of this manuscript begins with an overview of deaf studies and technology. Then, we elaborate on the methods and procedures of the study, including details on the robot-enhanced activities. We finally present our findings followed by a discussion of implications for future research and practice.

2   State of the Art

2.1   Therapy of Children with Hearing Disorder

Humans use speech to share information, to predict and explain behavior such as desires, beliefs, and feelings [20]. Young children learn to participate in communication situations through listening to the speech of their parents and caregivers. The first years of life are crucial for language development, while about 85% of neural development happens till the third year of life. Early access to the auditory brain is of importance for developing spoken language adequate to the norm for certain age [21]. If mild or partial hearing loss occur in this sensitive period, it could result in delay of language development.

Today, there are about 34 million children with hearing loss worldwide [22]. Various factors affect the communication skills of hearing impaired children, ranging from the degree of hearing loss, age of onset of hearing loss, age of identifying the child's hearing disorder, etiology of the disorder, adequacy of intervention, the presence of other disabilities, age of receiving intervention, type of intervention program, family and environmental influences, consistency of use of medical technology (e.g., hearing aid, cochlear implant), and the attitudes of the child or parents [7, 9–13].

One of the main issues the family of a deaf child has is whether to use manual or verbal communication with their child [23]. Initially the parents of children with hearing impairment and later the children themselves can choose a communication approach to learn speech and language. Parents seek information from the professionals (medical doctors, audiologist, speech and language pathologist, and teacher) about the communication method. Those who choose the oral communication method expect from their child an ability to fit in with typically developing children [24]. According to Gallaudet Research Institute report (2008), around 96% of hearing impaired children have hearing parents [25]. Consequently, hearing parents want to give the opportunity to their child with hearing impairment to communicate verbally. Unfortunately, there is no data that clearly illustrates the best communication approach [20, 24].

According to Harris (2014), the degree of a child's hearing loss has been a primary factor used by parents to decide which communication modality is applicable for their child. Usually the parents of children with mild or moderate hearing loss choose oral mode (i.e., listening and spoken language) whereas with more severe losses, parents opt for a manual form of communication such as Sign Language and finger spelling. Socialization, academic achievement and self-esteem may also influence the decision of the parents regarding the communication modality [11]. Researchers in Australia [26] have investigated the way of decision making about the communication mode in families of deaf children. They found out that most of the children with hearing impairment use oral communication; only one third have experience using a type of non-verbal communication mode. The caregivers choose the communication mode depending on source of information – professionals, family and friends, own research by parents; child individual needs and preferences; accessibility of communication – languages and communication modality used in family and community; access to intervention; audiological characteristics; child's future life [26, 27]. The aim of all communication approaches is to give the opportunity to the child with hearing impairment to develop sufficient skills to be able to communicate.

2.2 Medical Technology and Therapy of Hearing Impaired

The advancement of medical technology has significantly improved the prospects of children with hearing impairment. Amplification via electronic devices such as hearing aids or cochlear implants can provide a sense of sound to hearing impaired people, although they do not restore hearing loss. In any case, speech therapy and early intervention upon use of an appropriate aid (hearing aid or cochlear implant) is a major factor for development of the child's communication skills.

Hearing aid amplifies sounds and makes them louder. The microphones of the device pick up the sounds and after the amplification, they are sent into the ear canal, through the middle ear to the cochlear where the hair cells are activated and provide sound signals to the brain. Hearing aid is suitable for people with mild to severe hearing loss. Cochlear implant is surgically implanted electronic medical device. Cochlear implants are suitable for people with severe-to-profound sensorineural hearing loss, who cannot benefit from hearing aid. It has two main parts – internal (receiver/simulator) and external (speech processor). The internal part is implanted by surgery under the skin behind the ear. Electrodes are placed by medical professionals into the cochlear to stimulate the auditory nerve. Cochlear implant substitutes the function of the damaged hair cells in the inner ear and directly stimulates the auditory nerve that provides the signals to the brain. The external part is behind the ear. It is attached via transmitter cord to the transmitter coil, which magnetically attaches itself to the internal receiver [20, 28]. Children with successful surgery could hear the whole range of speech sounds and they have the possibility to learn and use the verbal speech; however, it is difficult to predict whether the cochlear implant(s) surgery will be successful or not [29]. Then, there are situations when the surgery is successful but the child is not using the implant due to other communication preferences, lack of family support, psychological weakness to accept the implant, the school that the child is attending, the difficulty to get used to the signal of the implant [11]. Resent research has shown that cochlear implant children trained without the use of sign language have shown significant advantage in their narratives, range of vocabulary and use of expressions, and in the complexity of the syntax used in their language [30].

Assuming an appropriate aid (hearing aid, cochlear implants) is used, support from speech therapists and educational audiologists in the early years of age is critical. This puts strong emphasis on the options of auditory-oral and auditory-verbal therapy approaches to development of verbal communication skills for the child who uses amplification [31]. In the auditory-oral approach, the child listens to others while s/he pays attention to lipreading (i.e. receiving visual information from the lips) and body language. Instead, the auditory-verbal method is a very strict approach that does not allow the use of lipreading or other non-verbal cues (e.g. gestures) to facilitate communication [20]. Auditory-verbal approach is child-directed, based on the child's interests and using play. It includes strategies that encourage joint attention, turn-taking, thus facilitates the development of listening skills, speech and language [32]. In this case, during therapy sessions, speech therapists stay in position which does not allow lipreading to force the child use his/her amplification device (hearing aid or cochlear implant) to hear the speech sounds. This enables children to make auditory images of what they hear in their brains and to create neural pathways for speech and language development [30, 33].

Overall, research of Cole and Flexer (2015) has shown that learning through listening is the most effective way of developing spoken language and cognition [30]. Thus, the auditory-verbal method is a very attractive in early intervention and therapy of children with all kind of amplification (e.g., hearing aid, cochlear implant). A technique that has been associated with auditory-verbal therapy is covering the therapist's mouth with his/her hand to eliminate lipreading. In their recent work, Estabrooks et al. (2016) encourage therapists to act more naturally during auditory-verbal therapy. They argue that covering the mouth might disrupt sensorimotor input during infancy and may have negative implications for the development of speech motor control; it can also provoke stress in young children which, in turn, negatively affects speech perception. The listening skill should be stimulated, but therapists should find ways to eliminate lipreading without having to cover their mouth, a rather atypical act in social interaction [32]. The humanoid robot NAO has a unique characteristic in this case - it does not have a human mouth and therefore children with hearing impairment cannot do lipreading. This unique feature of the technology has been identified by the researchers and has been used in this work to create a unique environment for auditory-verbal therapy sessions that can be playful and effective.

2.3 Play and Learning with Robots

Play has an adaptive function when children explore new situation, new environment, like games with a humanoid robot. It could support the development of sensorimotor skills and cognitive development – in our case stimulating the listening skills and the language [44].

The published studies about use of intelligent robots in interaction with children with and without disabilities are rapidly increasing during the past decade. Some of them explore the human-robot interaction in play scenarios with typically developing children (e.g., [16, 34]). Others investigate play and learning with intelligent robots in the therapy of children with disabilities, e.g., diagnosed with cerebral palsy [35] or Autism Spectrum Disorder (ASD) [14, 17, 18, 36–38]. One example is the program known as ASKNAO (Autism Solution for Kids) by Aldebaran Robotics, which uses NAO as a tool to help ASD children; the program has supported ASD children in learning about the social and communicative skills they lacked [39]. Intelligent humanoid robots show effectiveness with ASD children because they are simple and predictable with basic conversational function; they can be used as mediators to interact with the professional in therapy sessions, with the parents at home or with their peers at school [18]. Overall, research on the use of robots for play and learning shows that children (with disabilities or not) tend to interact with the intelligent robot smoothly, accept it as a peer in play, and are willing to initiate communication with the robot.

Studies on using intelligent robots with deaf children are scarce. Sawada et al. (2008) used a robotic voice simulator for speech therapy with hearing impaired children; the invented robot consisted of motor-controlled vocal organs (vocal cords), a vocal tract and a nasal cavity to generate a natural voice imitating a human vocalization. The robot reproduced the vocalization of the deaf children and taught them how to generate clearer speech through repeating the correct vocalization [40]. Moreover, NAO has been used in play activities for the assessment of listening and speaking skills of seven hearing-impaired students who use cochlear implant(s) deaf children [19]. A couple of other studies used intelligent robots with deaf children for manual communication. One such study involved NAO to assist a story telling by showing signs from the Turkish sign language, therefore facilitating non-verbal communication [41]. Then, unlike NAO that has only three fingers and thus, limited ability to present all signs used in manual communication, [42] used a robotic platform with five fingers (Robovie R3) for teaching sign language to deaf participants. There are virtually no studies focused on the use of intelligent robots in therapy of children with hearing impairment aiming specifically at the development of auditory and verbal communication skills.

3 Methodology

This was a mixed-method study which made use of quantitative and qualitative data to realize gains in the ability of the hearing-impaired child to detect sounds and follow instructions as well as the value of the robot-enhanced experience based on the observations of the participating speech therapist and special teacher.

3.1 Participants and Setting

The study took place in a mainstream public kindergarten-preschool in an Eastern Mediterranean country. This kindergarten-preschool (2–5 years old children) has the largest percentage of children with hearing impairment of the country. It is located next to and shares facilities and staff with the single school for the deaf in the country. Upon completion of the kindergarten, the parents of hearing impaired children have to decide to mainstream their children (i.e., put them in a general school) or keep them at the school for the deaf, with only 3% choosing the latter, as of today's data (personal communication with school principal). Children with hearing impairment in the kindergarten are supported by special teachers and speech therapy experts who focus on the child's development of auditory and communication skills.

Six kindergarten children, 3–4 years old, participated in the study. Detailed characteristics of the children (e.g., current speech and language skills, degree of hearing loss, age at identification of hearing loss, age at intervention for hearing loss) were unknown to the researchers, as requested by the school principal for confidentiality purposes. Despite the unfortunate fact, the researchers decided that the study was still worth pursuing in order to detect and document, even preliminary, the added value of an intelligent robot in the particular context. All children were supported by either a cochlear implant or a hearing aid or both, as seen in Table 1. These children attended regular kindergarten lessons together with eight hearing children in the same class. They also attended personal speech therapy sessions at the school's special unit.

Table 1. Participants profile

Child (Gender)	Cochlear implant	Hearing aid
P1 (Girl)	X	
P2 (Girl)	X	
P3 (Boy)	X	
P4 (Boy)	X	X
P5 (Girl)		X
P6 (Girl)		X

Participants were also the school therapist (audiology and speech therapy expert) and the special teacher of the school (also speech therapy expert). The school therapist worked with the researchers in the co-design of the activities for the study; she was also active during the implementation of the study and data collection as described below. The special teacher of the school was an observer in most (80%) of the therapy sessions. During the implementation and data collection the researchers (educational technologist and a speech therapist) were observers of the experience.

3.2   Activities and Co-design

The activities were co-designed by the researchers (an educational technologist and a speech therapist - researcher and practitioner) and the school therapist, based on previous experiences in research and practice, although such activities are considered general practice in speech therapy. Based on the school therapist, she had used similar activities with her students in the past, but there was no structured way of doing these activities (how often, what duration, what kinds of animals, what kinds of sounds). Also, in applying the auditory-verbal therapy method she was concerned about covering her mouth and acting unnaturally in any way that could disturb the child.

A total of four activities were designed and deployed on NAO. In accordance to the auditory-verbal method, all activities involved listening, followed by spoken instructions by NAO in order to assess children's ability to correctly respond to the spoken sounds using their cochlear implant and/or hearing aid, rather than other cues in the environment. For every correct answer, NAO praised the child and NAO's eyes turned green; for every mistake, NAO said "try again" and his eyes turned red. The visual clue of "green" and "red" eyes was the only visual clue in the environment. These four activities are briefly described below (see also Fig. 1).

1. *Ling Sounds Story.* An object for each of the six Ling Sounds is placed on the desk (i.e., /m/: ice cream, /i:/: mouse, h/a/: Plane, sh/ʃ/: baby who sleeps, /s/: Snake, /u/: ghost). These six sounds represent speech in different frequencies (low, mid and high). They are used to check how well children are hearing with their cochlear implant and /or hearing aid. This check is used in order to detect changes in child's quality of hearing. NAO tells a story and when the above sounds are spoken, the child picks the appropriate object to give to NAO e.g., "Maria spent a wonderful weekend riding with her family in the mountain. As they walked she heard a sound / iii /, what can it be? [child picks up the mouse]. However, her dad saw something

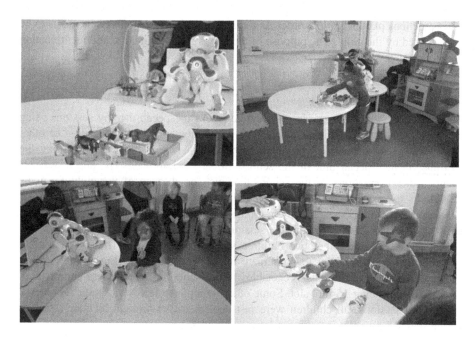

Fig. 1. Implementations of farm animals (top), Ling sounds story (bottom)

terrible /sss /[child picks up the snake]. "Dad, this snake is very big !!"…". The story changes from session to session so that the Ling Sounds are spoken in different order.

2. Music Density. The child holds a musical toy-instrument of his/her selection e.g., a drum (child selects from a box of a few toy-instruments). As NAO signs a rhyme in gentle intensity, the child beats the drum gently. When the intensity goes stronger at unexpended time, the child needs to immediately respond by beating the drum louder, and vice versa. In a round of play, after a medium starting density of the song, there are three unexpended changes in sound intensity (louder or lower). The game is used in order to develop child's ability of discrimination and identification of sound intensity.

3. Farm animals. Various animals (farm and jungle animals) and a farm built of blocks are placed on the desk. NAO asks the child to place in and out of the farm one animal at a time, based on the animal's sound e.g., "Take [cow audio sound] and place it in the farm", "Take [dog audio sound] and place it out of the farm". The seven farm animals are cow, sheep, dog, cat, rooster, pig, horse and duck; instructions play in random order for animals in and out of the farm. In a round of play, there are six statements to be executed by the child. With this game children develop their ability to discriminate and identify animal sounds which are with different frequency (e.g. low frequency – cow sound, high frequency – cat sound).

4. Vegetables. Vegetable-toys and a basket are placed on the desk. The child listens to NAO's simple statements, such as "Put x in the basket", "Take x and y from the basket". The five vegetables are: potato, tomato, lettuce, cucumber and carrot;

instructions play in random order. In a round of play, there are five statements to be executed by the child. The purpose of the game is discrimination and identification of vegetables.

3.3 Procedures

The study took place during six consecutive weeks of speech therapy sessions using strictly the auditory-verbal therapy method, which does not allow lipreading or other non-verbal cues to facilitate communication. Therapies were done daily, during the morning, in the special unit of the school. Some sessions were lost due to schools events, other obligations of the school therapist, or absence of the child from the school. In six weeks, children completed between 16 and 22 sessions with NAO. Children arrived at the special unity in groups of three (i.e., 2 groups of 3 children) and the session lasted 45-min. Within the session, the children performed in the activities one by one, while the other two children waited for their turn. That is, each child typically had a 15-min slot to participate in the four activities (Ling sounds story, Music density, Farm Animals, Vegetables). Some children managed to complete all four activities in their 15-min slot. Some others completed fewer activities. By week 3 (around 10 sessions) all children were fast enough to get through all four activities within their 15 min slot in each session.

The week before the investigation begun, all spoken sounds in the activities were pilot-tested with all participating children. For each child, NAO's pitch tone and speed of spoken words was adjusted and noted for subsequent session, based on the school therapist's input from observing the child's respond to the sounds. NAO's speak volume was set nearly to maximum for all children, which according to the therapist approximated how loud a teacher spoke in a typical lesson in the classroom. NAO's language was set to the national language of the country. We used NAO's robotic voice only for the instructions e.g., "take [audio sound for cow] and place it in the farm." However for the sounds in the activities, such as the "cow "sound in the farm game or "/i:/" for mouse or "h/a/" for the plane in the Ling sounds game, the sounds were downloaded as audio files in high quality and per screening of the school therapist for quality and appropriateness for the activity.

During the study, NAO was sitting without nay interaction with the child other than verbal. We used strictly the auditory-verbal therapy method, which does not allow lipreading or other non-verbal cues to facilitate communication. Any cues from NAO or in the environments could have jeopardize the philosophy of the auditory-verbal therapy method. Moreover, NAO was semi-autonomous. NAO could play the activities and randomize the order of sounds within each activity. The therapist could touch NAO's head (head-sensor on NAO) for NAO to act a positive response whilst a touch on his foot (foot-sensor on NAO) triggered a negative response (e.g., switching between activities, activating positive feedback or "try again" via touching as relevant). Although the experience could be manageable by the school therapist only, due to the exploratory nature of the present study, a student programmer was also in close proximity to the robot to ensure everything would work as planned. The special teacher of the school as well as the two researchers (authors of this work) observed the study from a seated position and without interfering.

In terms of data collection, the school therapist recorded each child's performance in every activity completed (Ling sounds story, Music density, Farm Animals, Vegetables) in every session. Although NAO gave a "try again" option for the sake of play and learn, for data collection purposes the therapist marked a correct answer only on child's first trial and only for correctly detected sounds. Table 2 presents an example of data recording for the "Ling Sounds Story." Similar tables were used for data recording of other activities in every session and for each participating child. At the end of the activity the therapist together with the special teacher who observed the study participated in a group-interview with the researchers (authors of this work). The interview aimed to elicit details about the overall experience and perceived added value of the technology.

Table 2. Sample data recording and interpretation table.

Week X - Child name - Ling Sounds Story						
	/m/: ice cream	/i/: mouse	/a/: plane	Sh/ʃ/: baby who sleeps	/s/: snake	/u/: ghost
Monday	√	√	√	√	–	√
Tuesday	√	√	√	–	–	–
Wednesday	√	√	√	–	–	√
Thursday	√	√	√	–	–	–
Friday	√	√	√	√	–	–

Note: Interpreting the above results:
- /ah/, /m/, and /i/were all detected consistently and correctly
- /sh/and /u/are not being detected consistently
- /s/is not being detected at all.

4 Findings

4.1 Gains in Detecting Sounds and Following Instructions

Using the detailed data recording as of Table 2, a percent success score was computed for each child per activity per week; see Table 3 for the average percent success scores across children. Plotting of participates' success scores across weeks allowed us to realize the progress of each participating child's gains in the ability to understand tasks presented through NAO over time. Some children mastered the detection of sounds earlier than others (e.g., by week 3; around 10 daily sessions), while all of them presented a consistent record of detecting sounds correctly by the last week of the study (i.e., week 6; 16–22 daily sessions). Figure 2 illustrates the progress charts of two of a participating child, as example. All participating children had steadily progress on all activities until a consistent correct pattern of detecting sounds occurred towards the last two weeks of the study.

Table 3. Average percent (%) success score across participants, on weekly activities

Weeks (up to 5 sessions per week)	Vegetables (child follows instruction correctly)	Farm animals (child follows instruction correctly)	Music density (child beats the drum louder or lower immediately after the density changes)	Ling sounds story (child picks the correct object)
Week 1	19%	20%	14%	12%
Week2	28%	30%	14%	12%
Week3	28%	50%	24%	22%
Week4	55%	70%	70%	42%
Week5	90%	88%	100%	82%
Week6	100%	90%	100%	95%

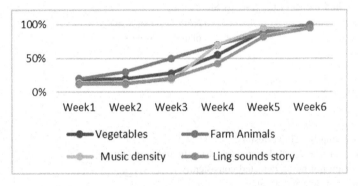

Fig. 2. An example of child's progress chart in terms of % correct answers across weeks (percent of correct answers on y-axes)

With respect to observed gains in detecting sounds and following instructions, the perspectives of the school therapist and special teacher were consistent with the quantitative outcomes. Both argued that the auditory-verbal therapy with NAO seemed to improve the children's auditory skills, including their ability to pay attention to NAO and to use their amplifier technology rather than relying on external cues. They also noted their observation of increased self-confidence for the participating children, as they performed better and better from session to session and as NAO positively reinforced their responses ("good job" and green eyes). As the therapist explained:

"NAO kept children's attention, which is very important in developing verbal communication skills. NAO is interesting and cute enough to keep the child playing and completing the tasks while s/he is forced to listen. In early sessions, I noticed that all of them looked at me again and again seeking for clues. Because I directed their attention to NAO, they learnt to rely less on other cues, and use their amplifiers more, to play with NAO. I think the use of the robot in this sense is brilliant! [...]. I also noticed gains in self-confidence from session to session and as children started learning to listen and to recognize the sounds that NAO spoke, for example [child's name] was very shy at the beginning, but gradually she became confident and enthusiastic in playing with NAO."

4.2   Playful and Engaging Therapy Sessions

The therapist elaborated on how the children responded positively and enthusiastically to the activities during the auditory-verbal therapy. As she explained,

> *"...the auditory-verbal therapy is not always pleasant for the child with hearing impairment. The child seeks for cues and s/he is confused and annoyed when I cover my mouth. I often hold a picture in front of my mouth, to distract him/her from the fact that I am covering my mouth on purpose."*

Yet, both therapist and special teacher thought that NAO robot made auditory-verbal therapy fun for the child with hearing impairment, engaging them in a playful learning experience. In the teacher's own words:

> *"Children were happy playing with NAO and I saw their enthusiasm, in completing the tasks and working with NAO. Their joy lasted for the duration of the activity, and even after therapy, for the duration of the school day."*

In addition to NAO's great prospects for speech therapy, a rather unforeseen idea in teachers' feedback was the potential of play and learn with NAO in inclusive education settings. In their view, the experience could be beneficial for both hearing impaired students and their hearing peers (i.e., the activities could serve all students in class). For example, as the special teacher explained, the Music Density game could involve more density variations, from sharp & steep to smooth & gradual changes; this could make it challenging for hearing children of this age, in a fun, class-wide, music activity. Also, the special teacher thought that 3–4-year old hearing children do not necessarily know the sounds of farm animals and with some more customization (e.g., to include less familiar animal sounds) the activity could easily challenge the hearing child. This way all children could enjoy sessions of play and learn with NAO. Furthermore, in the special teachers' view, the use of NAO in typical lessons both learning and children with hearing impairment could expand the auditory-verbal therapy time for these children who unavoidably do much lipreading and use other non-verbal cues as the teachers interacts with the whole class. As stated by the special teacher:

> *"I think it is a given that NAO can be used successfully in auditory-verbal therapy sessions. But he could work equally well in the inclusive classroom. Some of our hearing 3-year old children do not necessarily know the farm animals yet, neither the vegetables, so there could be value for them in playing with NAO [...]. I just think the possibilities of this technology are beyond individual speech therapy sessions. Also, consider that in class, my students with hearing impairment continue to do lipreading, which is unavoidable. NAO could help me expand the auditory-verbal therapy time for them without taking anything away from my hearing children [...]."*

5   Discussion

This study aimed to examine an innovative way of using an intelligent robot to support speech therapy for hearing impaired children through play. The study presented a unique environment for auditory-verbal therapy for hearing impaired children. NAO does not have a human mouth and therefore it is not supporting lipreading during auditory-verbal therapy; this unique characteristic of the technology was successfully used in this study to create playful therapy sessions for six kindergarten children with hearing impairment over the course of six weeks. The co-designed activities and implementation procedures were detailed in this work. The authors believe that the innovative idea can be successfully transferred and replicated with success in similar circumstances and learning/therapy contexts.

Are there gains in the ability of the hearing-impaired child to detect sounds and follow instructions? The study demonstrated quantitative gains in hearing impaired children's ability to respond correctly to sounds and to follow directions. All participating children had steadily progress on all activities until a consistent correct pattern of detecting sounds occurred towards the last two weeks of the study. We need to acknowledge however, that because no baseline measurements were provided as to how well the children could complete the tasks in non-NAO contexts, or data about their level of development in speech, language, or listening (please see discussion of confidentiality earlier), the results presented can only describe children's gains in the ability to understand tasks presented through NAO over time, which may or may not, reflect a change in their level of skill in listening and language. Future work should aim to address these important limitations of the present work.

What is the perceived value of the robot-enhanced environment for auditory-verbal therapy? The added value of the intelligent robot during the auditory-verbal therapy was documented by the speech therapist and special teacher-observer in a couple of ways. The views of the researchers are also consistent with these reported observations. First, they noted observed gains in children's ability to pay attention to NAO and to use their amplifier technology rather than relying on external cues. In other words, the hypothesized affordance of the intelligent robot was well materialized in the implementation. Second, they noted the playfulness of the learning experience and the children's overall positive attitude towards the lack of non-verbal cues. This finding replicates previous work on children learning through play with intelligent robots, especially involving ASD children (e.g., [14, 18, 36]). Overall, the study might be suggesting that NAO can make auditory-verbal therapy fun and engaging for children with hearing impairment, compared to an experience in which the therapist must hide all non-verbal cues (i.e., covering mouth). Of course, we need to acknowledge that the input for the therapist may be biased because of her involvement in the design of the activities and implementation with NAO. We were bounded by this limitation in the context of this study; despite the speech therapy (research and practice) and educational technology expertise of the researchers, the direct involvement of the school therapist was instrumental for the investigation in an authentic school-therapy setting and practice. Overall however, the findings suggest an innovative way of using an intelligent robot in this context and justify further investigation.

Furthermore, the technology and experience were perceived as a promising pathway to inclusive education, an unforeseen finding, which however, the authors, consider a significant reflection. A complete suite of NAO applications with customizable content and difficulty levels can support the inclusive (kindergarten) classroom and benefit both hearing and students with hearing impairment. How intelligent robots can support the educator in adopting an inclusive education approach is a very promising direction for future research, considering the rise of children with hearing impairment in mainstream schools vis-à-vis the underutilization of novel technologies [43]. Yet, while the above-mentioned idea presents an exciting opportunity for future research in inclusive education settings, the present study does not yet provide evidence that NAO would be appropriate for or beneficial for use with children without hearing loss. Also, in a mainstream classroom (i.e., an inclusive setting) background noise in the class-room could make the task impossible for the children with hearing loss. These ideas coupled with plausible difficulties merit investigation in future research.

All in all, this study aimed to explore the humanoid robot's potential for assisting therapists auditory-verbal exercises. Our conclusions are provisional and at this stage, we can only claim that NAO has potential in this context. A potential is only a pos-sibility; we cannot offer any certainties, based on this initial work, but we do share our positive initial impression. The study remains a subject of future work and replication. We have offered our lessons learned as well as initial evidence that NAO could be an important means of assisting therapy of children with hearing impairment. We further demonstrated that NAO is an attractive tool in this therapy context because of the lack of visual clues (has no mouth) while at the same time it is fun and friendly [16]. We believe that a laptop or tablet could not have had the same effect, although future work could address this hypothesis via an experiment design with a control/comparison group.

6   Conclusion

The presented study focused on the use of the humanoid NAO robot in auditory-verbal therapy, an approach to the development of auditory and verbal skills, which does not allow lipreading or other non-verbal cues to facilitate communication. This is, in our view, innovative and is worthy of further exploration while aiming to address the limitations of the present study.

Play with intelligent robots is now a reality. The question of interest is how to best utilize such technology-mediated experiences for the sake of learning, including therapy. The study contributes to the technology-enhanced learning, speech therapy and special education communities by presenting a case of practical utility of humanoid robots with real world impact. The findings of this study are encouraging and warrant further investigation to fully exploit the possibilities of intelligent robots in the context of education and therapy for children with hearing impairment.

Acknowledgements. This work has been partly supported by the project that has received funding from the European Union's Horizon 2020 research and innovation programme under grant agree-ment No 739578 (RISE – Call: H2020-WIDESPREAD-01-2016-2017-TeamingPhase2) and the Government of the Republic of Cyprus through the Directorate General for European Programmes, Coordination and Development.

References

1. Spencer, P.E., Marschark, M.: Evidence-Based Practice in Educating Deaf and Hard-of-Hearing Students. Oxford University Press, Oxford (2010)
2. Lee, C.: Deafness and cochlear implants: a deaf scholar's perspective. Child Neurol. J. 27(6), 821–823 (2012). https://doi.org/10.1177/0883073812441248
3. Beal-Alvarez, J., Cannon, J.E.: Technology intervention research with deaf and hard of hearing learners: levels of evidence. Am. Ann. Deaf 158(5), 486–505 (2014)
4. Kelman, C.A., Branco, A.U.: (Meta) Communication strategies in inclusive classes for deaf students. Am. Ann. Deaf 154(4), 371–381 (2009)
5. Wilkins, M., Ertmer, D.J.: Introducing young children who are deaf or hard of hearing to spoken LanguageChild'sVoice, an oral school. Lang. Speech Hear. Serv. Schools 33(3), 196–204 (2002)
6. Ginsburg, K.R.: The importance of play in promoting healthy child development and maintaining strong parent-child bonds. Pediatrics 119(1), 182–191 (2007)
7. Mills, P.E., Beecher, C.C., Dale, P.S., Cole, K.N., Jenkins, J.R.: Language of children with disabilities to peers at play: impact of ecology. J. Early Interv. 36(2), 111–130 (2014)
8. Qayyum, A., Khan, A.Z., Rais, R.A.: Exploring play of children with sensory impairments in special schools at Karachi, Pakistan. Qual. Rep. 20(2), 1–17 (2015)
9. Bobzien, J., Richels, C., Raver, S.A., Hester, P., Browning, E., Morin, L.: An observational study of social communication skills in eight preschoolers with and without hearing loss during cooperative play. Early Child. Educ. J. 41(5), 339–346 (2013)
10. Cejas, I., Barker, D.H., Quittner, A.L., Niparko, J.K.: Development of joint engagement in young deaf and hearing children: effects of chronological age and language skills. J. Speech Lang. Hear. Res. 57(5), 1831–1841 (2014)
11. Harris, L.G.: Social-emotional development in children with hearing loss. Theses and Dissertations - Communication Sciences and Disorders, vol. 4 (2014). http://uknowledge.uky.edu/commdisorders_etds/4/. Accessed 01 Aug 2017
12. Sininger, Y.S., Grimes, A., Christensen, E.: Auditory development in early amplified children: factors influencing auditory-based communication outcomes in children with hearing loss. Ear Hear. 31(2), 166–185 (2010)
13. Yuhan, X.: Peer interaction of children with hearing impairment. Int. J. Psychol. Stud. 5(4), 17–25 (2013)
14. Arendsen, J., Janssen, J.B., Begeer, S., Stekelenburg, F.C.: The use of robots in social behavior tutoring for children with ASD. In: 28th Proceedings on Annual European Conference on Cognitive Ergonomics, pp. 371–372. ACM (2010)
15. Fridin, M.: Storytelling by a kindergarten social assistive robot: a tool for constructive learning in preschool education. Comput. Educ. 70, 53–64 (2014)
16. Ioannou, A., Andreou, E., Christofi, M.: Preschoolers' interest and caring behaviour around a humanoid robot. TechTrends 59(2), 23–26 (2015)
17. Kartapanis, I., Ioannou, A., Zaphiris, P.: NAO as an assistant in ASD therapy sessions: the case of Joe. In: INTED2015 Proceedings (2015)
18. Lee, H., Hyun, E.: The intelligent robot contents for children with speech-language disorder. J. Educ. Technol. Soc. 18(3), 100–113 (2015)
19. Polycarpou, P., Andreeva, A., Ioannou, A., Zaphiris, P.: Don't read my lips: assessing listening and speaking skills through play with a humanoid robot. In: Stephanidis, C. (ed.) HCI 2016. CCIS, vol. 618, pp. 255–260. Springer, Cham (2016). https://doi.org/10.1007/978-3-319-40542-1_41

20. Welling, D.R., Ukstins, C.A.: Fundamentals of Audiology for the Speech-language Pathologist. Jones & Bartlett Learning (2017)
21. Shonkoff, J.P., Phillips, D.A. (ed.): From Neurons to Neighborhoods: The Science of Early Childhood Development. National Academies Press, Washington (DC) (2000). https://www.ncbi.nlm.nih.gov/books/NBK225557/ https://doi.org/10.17226/9824
22. World Health Organization. https://www.who.int/news-room/fact-sheets/detail/deafness-and-hearing-loss. Accessed 28 Aug 2018
23. Marshark, M., Hauser, P.C.: How Deaf Children Learn: What Parents and Teachers Need to Know. Oxford University Press, New York (2012)
24. Decker, K.B.: Influences on Parental Decisions Regarding Communications Options for Children Identified with Hearing Loss. Human Development and Family Studies, p. 1409. Michigan State University, Michigan (2010)
25. Gallaudet Research Institute: Regional and national summary report of data from the 2007–08 annual survey of deaf and hard of hearing children and youth (2008)
26. Crowe, K., McLeod, S., McKinnon, D.H., Ching, T.Y.C.: Speech, sign, or multilingualism for children with hearing loss: Quantitative insights into caregivers' decision-making. Lang. Speech Hear. Serv. Schools **45**, 234–247 (2014)
27. Crowe, K., Fordham, L.A., McLeod, S., Ching, T.Y.C.: Part of our world: Influences on caregiver decisions about communication choices for children with hearing loss. Deafness Educ. Int. **16**(2), 61–85 (2014)
28. Paul, P.V., Whitelaw, G.M.: Hearing and Deafness an Introduction for Health and Education Professionals. Jones & Bartlett Publishers, Sudbury (2011)
29. Cooper, H., Craddock, L.: Cochlear Implants: A Practical Guide, 2nd edn. Whurr Publishers, London and Philadelphia (2006)
30. Cole, E.B., Flexer, C.: Children with Hearing Loss: Developing Listening and Talking Birth to Six. Plural Publishing, San Diego (2015)
31. Ling, D.: Speech and the Hearing Impaired Child: Theory and Practice, 2nd edn. Alexander Graham Bell Association for the Deaf, Washington, DC (2002)
32. Estabrooks, W., MacIver-Lux, K., Rhoades, E.A.: Auditory-Verbal Therapy: For Young Children with Hearing Loss and their Families, and the Practitioners who Guide Them, p. 286. Plural Publishing, San Diego (2016)
33. MuSiEk, F.E.: Neurobiology, Cognitive Science, and Intervention. Handbook of Central Auditory Processing Disorder, Volume II: Comprehensive Intervention, vol. 2, p. 1. Plural Publishing (2013)
34. Keren, G., Ben-David, A., Fridin, M.: Kindergarten assistive robotics (KAR) as a tool for spatial cognition development in pre-school education. In: International Conference on Intelligent Robots and Systems 7–12 October 2012, Vilamoura, Algarve, Portugal (2012)
35. Malik, N.A., Yussof, H., Hanapiah, F.A.: Development of imitation learning through physical therapy using a humanoid robot. In: International Conference on Robot PRIDE 2013–2014 - Medical and Rehabilitation Robotics and Instrumentation, ConfPRIDE 2013–2014, Procedia Computer Science, vol. 42, pp. 191–197. Elsevier (2014)
36. Hamzah, M.S.J., Shamsuddin, S., Miskam, M.A., Yussof, H., Hashim, K.S.: Development of interaction scenarios based on pre-school curriculum in robotic intervention for children with autism. In: International Conference on Robot PRIDE 2013–2014-Medical and Rehabilitation Robotics and Instrumentation, ConfPRIDE 2013–2014, Procedia Computer Science, vol. 42, pp. 214–221. Elsevier (2014)
37. Robins, B., Dautenhahn, K., Boekhorst, R., Billard, A.: Robotic assistants in therapy and education of children with autism: can a small humanoid robot help encourage social interaction skills? Univ. Access Inf. Soc. **4**, 105–120 (2005)

38. Srinivasan, S.M., Park, I.K., Neelly, L.B., Bhat, A.N.: A comparison of the effects of rhythm and robotic interventions on repetitive behaviors and affective states of children with autism spectrum disorder (ASD). In: Research in Autism Spectrum Disorders, vol. 18, pp. 51–63. Elsevier (2015)

39. Salleh, M.H.K., et al.: Experimental framework for the categorization of special education programs of ASKNAO. Procedia Comput. Sci. **76**, 480 (2015)

40. Sawada, H., Kitani, M., Hayashi, Y.: A robotic voice simulator and the interactive training for hearing-impaired people. In: BioMed Research International 2008 (2008)

41. Kose-Bagci, H., Yorganci, R.: Tale of a robot: humanoid robot assisted sign language tutoring. In: 11th IEEE-RAS International Conference on Humanoid Robots, pp. 105–111. IEEE, Bled Slovenia (2011)

42. Uluer, P., Akalin, N., Kose, H.: A new robotic platform for sign language tutoring humanoid robots as assistive game companions for teaching sign language. Int. J. Soc. Robot. **7**, 571–585 (2015)

43. Constantinou, V., Ioannou, A., Klironomos, I., Antona, M., Stephanidis, C.: Technology support for the inclusion of deaf students in mainstream schools: a summary of research from 2007 to 2017. Univ. Access Inf. Soc. 1–6 (2018)

44. Besio, S.: The need for play for the sake of play. In: Besio, S., Bulgarelli, D., Stancheva-Popkostadinova, V. (eds.) Play Development in Children With Disabilities (2017)

Understanding the Digital and Non-digital Participation by the Gaming Youth

Iikka Pietilä[⊠], Jari Varsaluoma, and Kaisa Väänänen

Computing Sciences, Human-Centered Technology, Tampere University,
Tampere, Finland
iikka.pietila@tuni.fi

Abstract. It is important for the inclusiveness of society that the youth actively participate in its development. Even though the means of digital participation have advanced in the past decade, there is still lack of understanding of digital participation of the youth. In this paper, we present a study on how youth aged 16–25 years perceive social and societal participation and more specifically, how youth currently participate in non-digitally and digitally. We conducted a mixed method study in a large gaming event in Finland using a questionnaire (N = 277) and face-to-face interviews (N = 25). The findings reveal that the gaming youth consider digital participation to include discussions in different social media services or web discussion forums. Creating digital content (e.g. videos) and answering surveys were also emphasized. Perceived advantages to participate digitally include the freedom regarding location and time, ease and efficiency in sharing information, and inexpensiveness. Central disadvantages include lack of commitment, anonymity, misinformation and cheating. We also found that frequently playing gamers are more likely to participate online in social activities than those who play occasionally. Youth who reported that they play strategy games were more active in civic participation than those who do not play strategy games. We discuss the implications of our findings to the design of tools for digital participation.

Keywords: Youth · Gaming · Games · Digital participation ·
Societal participation

1 Introduction

The participation of Finnish citizens has decreased significantly during the last three decades (Pessala 2009; Myrskylä 2012; Sutela et al. 2018). By lack of participation, we refer to people who do not participate in the processes of society, and people that are not employed or in education (Myrskylä 2011). The Finnish National Institute for Health and Welfare (THL) (Isola et al. 2017) define participation ("osallisuus" in Finnish) to be (1) The ability to decide about one's own life and the possibility to regulate one's own doings, (2) engaging in processes that have effects in groups, services, living environments, and in the society, (3) local, when one is able to participate and contribute to the common good, and (4) to engage in creating meaningfulness and experience social relationships. Participation is also described to include

© IFIP International Federation for Information Processing 2019
Published by Springer Nature Switzerland AG 2019
D. Lamas et al. (Eds.): INTERACT 2019, LNCS 11747, pp. 453–471, 2019.
https://doi.org/10.1007/978-3-030-29384-0_28

the processes that the youth is able to be involved with, for instance education, environment, and housing. Participation can make the young people able to engage with issues of their choice, and to engage actively without the preset adult agencies. Checkoway (2011.) According to Michels and De Graaf (2010), it is crucial to enable citizens to participate in various societal processes and decision making to improve democracy. Stolle and Hooghe (2011: 120) summarize the changes in participation affiliated with the past decades "...citizens today, especially younger generations, seem to prefer participating in the extra-parliamentary realm, in non-hierarchical and informal networks, and in a variety of sporadic campaigns that are not institutionalized."

Although youth participation and gaming have been studied extensively, it seems that the number of studies on the relationship of different kinds of digital gaming habits and participation is very limited. The public discourse related to gaming is controversial, and gaming is sometimes affiliated with social hardship (e.g. Przybylski 2014). In this study, our goal was to understand youth's perceptions and motivations for digital and non-digital participation. We also elucidate how participation and societal satisfaction could differ between frequent and less frequent young gamers, and young people who play different genres of digital games. As a practical contribution, we also propose design implications for digital services that aim at motivating youth to participate in societal discussion.

2   Background and Related Work

2.1   Youth's Digital and Non-digital Societal Participation

According to Meriläinen et al. (2018), digital participation can be for instance reading blogs and answering digital surveys. Sæbø et al. (2008) assert that eParticipation activities can include but is not necessarily limited to voting, taking part in political discourse, and decision-making. In this paper, we use the concept of digital participation to denote a wide spectre of participational activities, similar to what Meriläinen et al. (2018) define digital participation to be. In Fig. 1, we have described how participation, digital participation and eParticipation relate to each other in the context of this paper. Pessala (2009) arguments that the otherwise politically passive young people are primarily interested in political activities that happen online, which might play a key factor to succeed in enhancing active participation and citizenship.

eParticipation or electronic participation denotes a form of participation in which information and communication technology is applied. eParticipation can be used to address the participation of individual persons, groups or governmental policy-making parties (Albrecht et al. 2008). Panopoulou et al. (2014: 195) refer to electronic participation as "...the use of information and communication technologies to enhance political participation and citizen engagement." Sæbø et al. (2008) state that eParticipation has an intrinsic goal in enhancing active citizenship by enabling wider accessibility and availability of ways of engagement allowing society and government to grow fairer and more efficient. It is further discussed that "e" in eParticipation refers to the use of information and communication technologies, especially the Internet. However, meaning of "participation" might vary and it can be used to refer to "taking

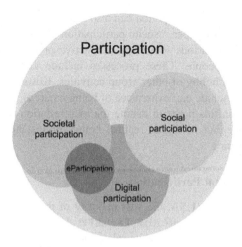

Fig. 1. Relationships of participation, digital participation and eParticipation in the context of this paper.

part in communal discussion or activity, or in the sense of taking some role in decision making". On more general level, eParticipation can be associated ambiguously with political deliberation and decision-making, and can occur in formal or informal settings (Sæbø et al. 2008).

According to Meriläinen et al. (2018), obstacles among youth for participating in digital settings include absence of interest, belief of lack of impact, inadequate communication between youths and officials, and having no knowledge of the channels to utilize. In a literature review, Ianniello et al. (2018) capsulize the key dimensions obstructing participation to be information inaccessibility, officials' attitudes, community representations, process designs, group dynamics, and collaboration quality. Ianniello et al. (2018) also summarize that to overcome these obstacles, long-term interaction, involving participants in research, diversity, participation institutionalization, allowing multiple participation methods, and clarifying rules and mechanics must among other solutions be addressed.

Digital participation can also be approached through addressing the relationship of the Internet and political participation. Polat (2005) dissects the Internet enabling participation in three different dimensions: The Internet providing information, the Internet functioning as a communication medium, and the Internet functioning as a virtual public sphere. Polat (2005) also criticizes the existing tendency to think that the Internet is a technology first and information sharing and communication enabling platform second, which might accentuate technological determinism in the affiliated discourse. Pessala (2009) states that digital participation can be seen as a wider way of engagement than just participation through political parties, and it can also be used when referring to electronic societal participation.

In this paper, we use "Societal participation" to denote the participation of an individual or a group of individuals in the processes of the society, such as voting or participating in decision making, or engaging in political discussions. According to

Harris et al. (2010), societal participation can also mean for instance joining a political party. In the context of this paper, "Social participation" means the participation of an individual or a group in various social and interactive processes that can take place between two or more people. These processes include constructions such as for instance friendships and hobby or other group activities. Kowert et al. (2014) describe social participation to include e.g. experience of being a part of a group. "Social digital participation" is used in this paper to denote the manifestation of these social participation activities happening in digital realms, being for instance online friendships, chatting, or social gaming.

2.2 Gaming and Digital Participation

Similarly, as for instance in USA, the vast majority of the young people play digital games in Finland (Pelaajabarometri 2018; Lenhart et al. 2008). As the nature of gaming is ubiquitous, studying the varying habits related to it might offer valuable insight on how to model successfully possible elements in systems that aim to enhance youth participation. Lenhart et al. (2008) state that gaming is a comprehensive phenomenon that is relevant to the lives of majority of the youth despite of for instance socioeconomic status. It is also articulated that online gaming poses a key role in young people's social interactions.

The study conducted by Lenhart et al. did not exhibit a connection between the amount of gaming and the participation in civic or political activity of youth. Furthermore, it is said that there might be differences in engagement in political activity between those who play with others in physically same space and those who play with others only online. These activities include getting information on politics, participating in charity, being committed to civic participation, and persuading others to vote in election. In addition, the meta activities related to gaming, that can be for instance participating in game related discussions online and engaging in activities in gaming communities, are linked to higher civic and political engagement. (Lenhart et al. 2008). Ferguson and Garza (2011), state that online social activity could be higher among those who play action games, but gaming is not linked to civic engagement in either way. However, their finding suggest that among action game players the parent's involvement can have a positive effect in the gaming youth's civic participation, whereas similar effects were not present in the non-gaming youth. It is further discussed that the multiplayer dimension with shared goals may contribute to the positive outcomes of gaming (Ferguson and Garza 2011). Lenhart et al. (2008) established no link between civic activities or attitudes and gaming. Still, the teens that had played games that offer social experiences like helping other players, learning about societal problems, and facing moral or ethical dilemmas reflected significantly higher civic engagement than those, who did not have such experiences. These activities included raising money for charity, getting information on politics online, and participating in protests.

3 Studying the Gaming Youth's Digital and Non-digital Participation

This study is part of a multidisciplinary research project exploring the capacities of young people (aged between 16 and 25) and the obstacles that hamper their engagement with society. This study is one of the several studies aiming to understand the perceptions and motivations of youth in relation to digital participation. One of the focus areas of the research project is in supporting the design of digital services that can motivate youth taking part in societal activities on different levels, from local to national level participation. The gaming youth are an interesting group to study since they are active in digital surroundings and may have specific motivations for societal participation.

The following research questions were formed:

RQ1:   What kind of perceptions (e.g. definitions, and positive and negative aspects) do the gaming youth have about digital participation?

RQ2:   What kind of obstacles and motivations do the gaming youth have for societal participation?

RQ3:   How do types of digital and non-digital participation vary among different kinds of gamers?

    3A: Are there differences in societal participation or digital or non-digital social participation between frequent and less frequent gamers?

    3B: Are there differences in societal participation or digital or non-digital social participation between game genres played?

    3C: Are there differences in personal life and societal satisfaction between frequent and less frequent gamers?

3.1 Participants

Data was gathered with a questionnaire and interviews (see Sect. 3.2). Altogether 277 people answered the questionnaire. Participant age varied between 16 and 25 years, mean and median age being 20 years. Roughly, a third of the participants were under eighteen years of age. Three quarters of participants reported their gender to be male (n = 206), one fifth identified as female (n = 58) and 12 participants identified as other or did not want to disclose their gender.

According to the Finnish gamer barometer (Pelaajabarometri 2018), almost all of the Finnish people aged between 10 and 75 years play games generally. Digital games are played by more than two thirds. It is also asserted that 97% of 10–19-year-olds and 91% of 20–29-year-olds play digital games more frequently than weekly. Barometer states that, 1/3 play daily and 2/3 play weekly, but in this study, 2/3 of the respondents play daily and 2/3 play weekly. In this study, the respondent's gaming is more frequent than in national barometer on average (Fig. 2).

In total 25 people participated the interviews. Age of the participants ranged between 16–25 years (average 20.4 years, with standard deviation 3.5 years). Sixteen were male, 8 female and one identified as other. From the participants, 16 were studying full-time, 6 were working part-time or full-time and 3 were unemployed.

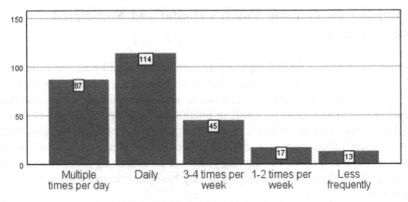

How often do you play digital games

Fig. 2. Respondents' gaming frequency.

The level of education ranged from 9 primary school students to 7 vocational school students, 7 high school graduates and one with a university degree. All participants were familiar with gaming culture and games in general. Only one person (ID19) was not actively playing games as a hobby at the time of the study.

3.2   Procedure

Data was acquired at the Assembly 2018. Assembly is an event about digital culture and arts, electronic gaming, and meeting old and new friends. Assembly is organized at the Expo and Convention Centre of Helsinki, located in Helsinki, the capital city of Finland. Over 5000 friends of digital arts and culture, demoscene, and gaming attend assembly every year. Most of Assembly visitors are of suitable age (From 16 to 25 years), and presumably active users of various digital services thus offering a plausible venue for conducting the study. Assembly 2018 was organized during 2.–5.8.2018.

Participants were able to answer the questionnaire both online and offline. The online version was executed on Webropol survey tool and could be taken at any suitable time during the event on participants' own device. The participation link was distributed to the event visitors through event website and on the event Facebook page. The questionnaire link and a small commercial of the research project was visible on info screen in the main hall. Mobile devices were supported by the online questionnaire. Researchers administered offline version during daytime on paper. Paper questionnaires were answered on-site next to the project's stand. All the participants were able to take part in lottery to win gift cards, regardless of the medium. In addition, participants were offered sweets at the stand after answering the questionnaire.

In addition to the questionnaire, interviews were conducted with the youth participating the Assembly event. People walking past or stopping by the stand were actively invited to take part to the interviews. At the beginning of the interview, participant answered a short background questionnaire on a paper. The interview sessions were audio recorded and varied from 17 to 69 min, with most interviews taking half an hour. After the session, participant was awarded with a movie ticket.

3.3 Instruments

A questionnaire and interview aimed for youth (age 16–25) were prepared in order to study the research questions. Questionnaire consisted of 11 main questions and had seven additional open-ended questions. Paper version of the questionnaire was laid on 11 pages. Five of the main questions were Likert scale questions consisting of 5–10 claims that were to be assessed on a scale of 1–7, 1 being "Fully disagree" and 7 being "Fully agree". Eighth option on the scale represented answer "I do not know or do not want to say/Does not apply to me". Lastly, also the background variables were inquired with optional participation to lottery. Participants were additionally able to give feedback on the questionnaire by assessing suitability of questionnaire length and how interesting the questions were. Background questions consisted of age, gender, nature of living area, postal number, province, marital status, employment status, and educational level. Main questions concerned the amount and frequency of playing digital games, gaming platforms and genres, ICT skills, societal participation, society and personal life satisfaction, social relationships, digital social participation, social gaming, and online relationships. Open-ended questions inquired news consumption habits, obstacles for participation, desires to legislative changes, and future dreams and aspirations. Formed sum variables and questions are described more specifically in Table 1.

A semi-structured interview was prepared to study youths' perceptions regarding different topics. Interview themes included societal and digital participation, gaming culture, future plans and dreams, future technology trends, and legislation. In this paper, the focus is in the results related to the themes of societal and digital participation. In the questions related to the societal participation, participants were asked how they have previously participated in political discussions, societies/clubs/associations, voluntary work, or other activities related to their living environment or society. These questions were followed by asking about the reasons for not participating and factors that motivate or could motivate participation in these activities. Next were the questions related to digital participation. Participants were asked to define "digital participation" and if they had utilized digital services to participate in the previously discussed societal activities. Finally, the positive and negative aspects of digital participation were discussed.

In summary, data used in this study consists of 277 respondents in questionnaire that consists of 18 questions and background questions and interviews of 25 participants with two interview themes included in the study.

3.4 Analysis

Overall sampling size is 277 after removing inappropriate subjects. For analysis of quantitative data, threshold for statistical significance alpha value of .05 was selected. A Python script was written to execute the two-tailed Mann-Whitney-U test on a set of multiple dichotomous variables.

Table 1. All the sub variables and formed sum variables presented with their Cronbach's alphas. * Ylilauta is a Finnish image and conversation board (http://www.ylilauta.fi)

Sum variable	Social participation	Digital social participation	Personal life satisfaction	Societal participation
Variable 1	I constantly feel myself lonely (REVERSED)	Online gaming has a significant role in my friend relationships	I am satisfied with my life as it is	I discuss timely domestic or foreign events with my friends or family often
Variable 2	I enjoy other people's company	A significant part of my social interactions happen online (for instance in games, social media or chats)	I am satisfied with my work/studies/other professional status	Under 18: I would vote in the next election if i could/Over 18: I will vote in the next election
Variable 3	I feel like I am a relative part of some group or team	I produce content in image boards or message boards (Like for instance Ylilauta* or 4chan, for instance text or images)	I have good daily routines	I feel like I would succeed well if I were to rationalize and discuss my views on some controversial political or societal question
Variable 4	I believe that others enjoy my company	I read/watch content on image boards or message boards (Like for instance Ylilauta or 4chan)	I am satisfied with my free time	It is easy for me to find a suitable political party
Variable 5	I like doing things with others			I am interested in politics
Variable 6	I have good friends			I read/watch the news to get information on timely events
Variable 7	I get new friends easily			
Number of items	7	4	4	6

(continued)

Sum variable	Social participation	Digital social participation	Personal life satisfaction	Societal participation
Cronbach's Alpha	.88	.70	.82	.81
Distribution is normal	No	Yes	No	No

Running a factor analysis for test variables was considered appropriate as KMO test value was .787 and Bartlett's test of sphericity produced a significant value ($p < .001$, $df = 210$). After addressing the Scree plot, maximum quantity of components was set to four. Principal component analysis was chosen as extraction method and rotation was done with Varimax. Factor loadings for each observed variable are represented in Table 2. Values under .300 were excluded from the table for clarity. Factor analysis results suggest a rather clear positioning of the observed variables in the four distinct components. However, some of the variables under the construct "Social participation" seem to contribute also to construct "Personal life satisfaction".

Questions related sum variables were created and can be seen in Table 1. All sum variables except one received more than $\alpha = .70$ as their Cronbach's alpha value reflecting an acceptable or good inner consistency. Additionally, the sub variables were inspected in a cross-correlation matrix. Sum variables were tested for their distribution normality with Kolmogorov-Smirnov and Shapiro-Wilk tests and the distributions were also visually assessed. The used tests are explained in more detail along with the results.

Interviews were transcribed and qualitatively analyzed by categorizing similar responses to categories that were derived from the data. Similar categorization process was followed with the open questions of the questionnaire.

Table 2. Loading and cross-loading values for each observed variable in four factors

Observed variable	Loading in each factor			
	1	2	3	4
I enjoy other people's company	0.783			
I like doing things with others	0.761			
I believe that others enjoy my company	0.725		0.340	
I have good friends	0.724			
I get new friends easily	0.719			
I feel like I am a relative part of some group or team	0.636		0.378	
I constantly feel myself lonely REVERSED	0.467		0.399	
I am interested in politics		0.823		
I feel like I would succeed well if I were to rationalize and discuss my views on some controversial political or societal question		0.792		
I often discuss with my friends and family the current events abroad or in Finland		0.790		

(*continued*)

Table 2. (*continued*)

Observed variable	Loading in each factor			
	1	2	3	4
I read/watch the news to get information on current events		0.630		
Under 18-yo: I would vote in the next election if I was eligible/Over 18-yo: I will vote in the next election		0.609		
It is easy for me to find a suitable political party		0.506		
I am satisfied with my life as it is			0.845	
I am satisfied with my work/study/other professional status			0.830	
I am satisfied with my free time			0.807	
I have good daily routines			0.590	
A significant part of my social interactions happen online (for instance in games, social media or chats				0.835
Online gaming has a significant role in my friend relationships				0.764
I read/watch content on image boards or message boards (Like for instance Ylilauta or 4chan				0.692
I produce content in image boards or message boards (Like for instance Ylilauta or 4chan, for instance text of images				0.617

4 Results

4.1 RQ1: What Kind of Perceptions Do the Gaming Youth Have About Digital Participation?

How did the interview participants define "digital participation"? The most often mentioned aspect (11/25 respondents, 44%) when defining digital participation related to utilizing social media services, such as Facebook, Twitter or WhatsApp. Six respondents (24%) considered that digital participation includes active participation in discussions (e.g. Slack) or discussion forums in the Internet (e.g. Reddit, 4chan). For instance, one respondent (ID9) commented that digital participation is "something more clever than evening paper's comment section. I don't consider that yet as digital participation, but taking part in discussion forums. I am mainly in Slack and some hobby-specific subreddit. Maybe 4chan is counted [as digital participation], maybe not". Four participants (16%) emphasized the creation of digital content in the Internet, such as videos, graphics and texts as a way of participation. Three mentions (12%) related to answering or creating own digital surveys and two people mentioned commenting or liking existing content as a way of participation. Rest of the individual comments related to citizen's initiatives in the Internet, voting (in web), web courses for teaching, taking part in software development, and "doing something together in different locations" e.g. charity.

When asked about the positive aspects of digital participation, the following topics were brought up: (1) low threshold for participation because you can do it on your own time, from any location (e.g. from a bus in countryside) and it suits for anyone (e.g. introvert personality, people with disabilities), (2) sharing information and reaching people is easy and fast, (3) organizing e.g. events via digital channels is cheap and easy, and (4) the freedom of expression. Negative aspects in relation to digital participation included the following: (1) lack of commitment as it is easy to ignore or change one's mind about participation e.g. in event, (2) anonymity leads more easily to aggression, harassment and unfriendly behavior, (3) misinformation and provocation ("trolling"), (4) misuse, cheating and hijacking (e.g. Twitter hashtag), and (5) technical issues (e.g. poor Internet connection or web-cam).

4.2   RQ2: What Kind of Obstacles and Motivations Do the Gaming Youth Have for Societal Participation?

The questionnaire results (N = 217) regarding the sum variable Societal participation (scale 1–7, 6 items, see Table 1) suggest that the gaming youth perceive themselves as slightly more towards active in societal participation (Mean = 4.64, SD = 1.29).

In the interviews (N = 25), participants were asked how they have previously participated in political discussions, societies/clubs/associations (e.g. non-governmental organizations), voluntary work, or other activities related to their living environment or society. First, regarding politics, 12 out of 25 participants tend to discuss politics, some rarely and others more actively, with their family or friends, but 10 of them not in any public channel. News from politics are followed with varying interest, mainly from digital newspapers and social media sites (7 respondents), such as Facebook and Reddit. Few examples of different political activities were brought up: one respondent had participated in protest marches and one had signed a petition. In school context, two people had participated in student council and one in a "parliament club". From digital participation perspective, examples from individual respondents included (1) answering digital surveys about political parties (ID12) or life in the city (ID19), (2) sharing references to information sources in social media discussions (ID8), (3) discussing political topics during live video stream (ID8) or creating political videos (ID6) in YouTube, and (4) participating in Slack discussions for preparing a feedback for a legislative proposal from European Aviation Safety Agency (ID9).

Next, the results concerning obstacles for gaming youths' participation in societal/political discussions are presented. This topic was included in both the questionnaire and interviews. Figure 3 presents the questionnaire results, illustrating the main reasons that gaming youth propose for not taking part in societal discussions.

The interview results are in line with the questionnaire results, suggesting that the main reasons for youth not being more active in political discussions are (1) lack of interest (7 out of 25 responses), (2) conflicts, aggressive discourse (5), (3) lack of information (3), (4) not a suitable life situation due the young age (3), and one of each of the following: it would not have any effect, no opportunities to have an impact, lack of political discourse in family or with people around you, badly moderated discussion forums, things happen too slowly, and "all that you put in the Internet stays there".

What would motivate youth to take part in political discussions? This was asked in the interviews. The motivational factors included the following: (1) topics relevant for oneself or one's own life (e.g. student life, sexual minorities, the environment, morally meaningful choices) (4 responses out of 25), (2) topics that are interesting (e.g. political

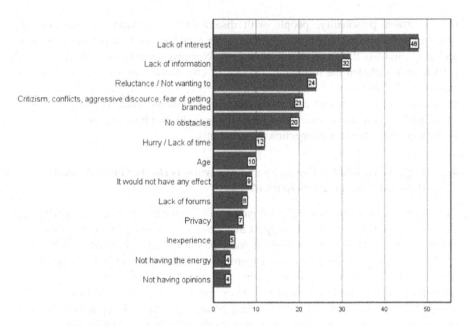

Fig. 3. Categorization of the questionnaire responses to the open question "Reasons that prevent me from taking part in societal discussions are…" The following single responses were also received: unspecific fear, religion, poverty, language barriers, and ethnic background. (N = 277).

science, technology, games) (3), (3) desire to share your opinion (e.g. in contrast to your friend's opinion, because of your own persona, or in order to provide facts to the discussion) (3), (4) visible results from your activity in the community or in relation to your goal (2), and one of each of the following motivational aspects: friends' activity and opinions, clearly presented information aimed for young people, meeting politically active youth such as youth parliament representatives, supporting candidates with similar interests, opinions that strongly differ from yours, restricting your rights, acknowledging individuals when evaluating impacts of decisions, and safe environment for youth to present their opinions.

4.3   RQ3: How Do Types of Digital and Non-digital Participation Vary Among Different Kinds of Gamers?

3A: Are there differences in societal participation or digital or non-digital social participation between frequent and less frequent gamers?
Results shown in Table 3 and Fig. 4 suggest that people who play more often might be more active also in other social digital activities. Running a Kruskal-Wallis test on variables "Social participation" (χ^2 (4) = .78, p = .94) and "Societal participation" (χ^2 (4) = 4.74, p = .32) in classes of gaming frequency did not exhibit a statistically significant difference. However, a statistically significant difference was found in variable "Digital social participation" in categories of gaming frequency when testing with one-way ANOVA [F(4, 258) = 7.05, p < .01]. Post-hoc comparison using the Tukey HSD

test revealed multiple differences between groups indicating increased values in variable "Digital social participation" among categories of more frequent gamers than categories of less frequent gamers. In Table 3, the statistically significant differences are described in more detail, each category mean is displayed and significance values (*p*) of differences between categories are presented.

Table 3. Statistically significant differences in variable "Digital social participation" between categories of gaming frequencies. In addition, category means and significance *p*-value of each difference are displayed.

Category	Mean	Category	Mean	p
Multiple times per day	4.46	3–4 times per week	3.69	.02
Multiple times per day	4.46	1–2 times per week	3.35	.03
Multiple times per day	4.46	Less frequently	2.60	<.01
Daily	3.96	Less frequently	2.60	.01

3B: Are there differences in societal participation or digital or non-digital social participation between game genres played?

Multiple statistically significant differences between whether a certain genre is played or not were found in various sum variables. For instance, the results assert that respondents that reportedly play strategy games would be more likely to participate in societal activities (U = 4178, $p < .01$). This difference is presented in Fig. 5.

In the light of effect sizes, especially the difference between those who play shooter games and those who do not in the variable "Digital Social Participation" is exceptionally noticeable ($d = .81$), and the difference between those who play strategy games and those who do not in variable "Societal participation" ($d = .45$) as these effect sizes can be considered large and medium respectively.

In Table 4, all the statistically significant differences in corresponding dependent variables between playing or not playing a specific genre are displayed with both categories medians, Mann-Whitney-U values and *p*-values. Also, effect sizes are displayed in the table. Rest of the effect sizes remain small, however none of the effects of statistically significant differences between categories of playing or not playing distinct genres should be considered trivial or non-existent. Genre "Shooters" should be approached with care, because the number of those who did not reportedly play this genre, is only 28. For instance, strategy gaming genre on the other hand represents a good balance between those who play or do not play games that belong to this genre (Yes: 133, No: 84). Number of observational units in each genre under each category are also displayed in the table under column "Played Y/N".

3C: Are there differences in personal life and societal satisfaction between frequent and less frequent gamers?

The study results suggests that the people who play multiple times per day are less satisfied with the Finnish society than those who play only daily. Executing the Kruskal-Wallis test on variable "Personal Life Satisfaction" in categories of gaming frequency variable did not show a statistically significant difference (χ^2 (4, N = 267) = 1.99, $p = .74$). However, a statistically significant difference was detected

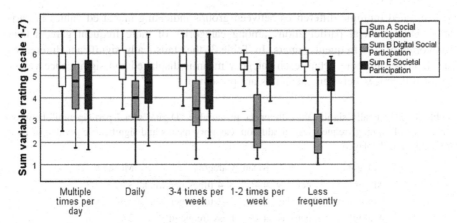

Fig. 4. People who play more often, might be more active in other digital social settings also – a statistically significant difference was found for instance between categories "Multiple times per day" and "3–4 times per week" in variable "Digital Social Participation"

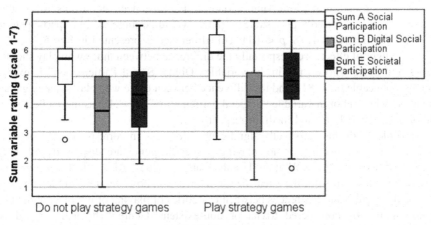

Fig. 5. A statistically significant difference between those who play strategy games and do not play strategy games was found in sum variables "Digital Social Participation" and "Societal Participation", indicating that strategy game players might be more prone to societal activities.

in the sum variable "Finnish Society Satisfaction" when comparing categories of gaming frequency (χ^2 (4, N = 206) = 13.66, $p < .01$). Running a Dunn's post-hoc test reveals a statistically significant difference between categories of gaming frequency "Multiple times per day" and "Daily" (χ^2 (4, 206) = 13.66, $p = .02$). No other statistically significant differences were found between categories.

Table 4. Statistically significant differences in sum variables between categories of playing or not playing a certain gaming genre

Gaming genre	Sum variable a difference was found in	Median Yes	Median No	Played Y/N	U	p	Effect size (d)
Puzzles and Card games	Societal Participation	5.00	4.50	63/154	3900	.02	0.34
Shooters	Social Participation	5.71	6.14	235/27	4135	.01	0.41
Shooters	Digital Social Participation	4.00	3.25	236/28	1939	<.01	0.81
Strategy	Societal Participation	4.83	4.33	133/84	4178	<.01	0.45
Action	Digital Social Participation	4.00	3.75	152/112	7144	.03	0.29
Simulation	Societal Participation	5.00	4.50	76/141	4221	.01	0.40
Multiplayer Online	Digital Social Participation	4.00	3.75	157/107	7004	.02	0.32
Multiplayer Online	Societal Participation	4.67	4.33	124/93	4800	.03	0.31
Roleplaying	Digital Social Participation	4.25	3.75	101/163	6489	<.01	0.36
Roleplaying	Societal Participation	5.00	4.33	84/133	4404	.01	0.37
Online roleplaying	Digital social participation	4.25	3.75	57/207	4836	.04	0.33

5   Discussion

The activities that the interviewed youth affiliate with digital participation were mainly related to social media use, activity in discussion forums, creating digital content and answering digital surveys. Similar activities were suggested in Meriläinen et al. (2018). Only a few described activities related to digital participation were related to eParticipation activities as described by Sæbø et al. (2008). These included voting and starting citizen's initiatives in the Internet, as a way of taking part in political discussions or decision making that are some of the key aspects of eParticipation. Furthermore, the array of obstacles for youth participation in digital setting found in this study is analogous to the proposed obstacles by Meriläinen et al. (2018). However, this study suggests some additional obstacles, in specific fear of conflicts and young age, although the latter can relate to the belief of lack of impact.

Also, the results related to gaming and its relationship to participation are mostly coincident with the research executed by Lenhart et al. (2008), as for instance the digital social activities show higher rating among those who play action games compared to those who do not play action games. Similarly, no statistically significant difference was found in societal participation between more or less frequent players. The difference between people who play or do not play a game of certain genre in the variables "Social Participation" and "Societal Participation" could be affiliated with the contents and mechanics of the games. Lenhart et al. (2008) assert that playing games that include social experiences, helping others, and facing moral dilemmas, can be linked to heightened civic engagement. The game genres that exhibit in this study these kinds of positive phenomena, do in some instances include the described activities: In strategy games, resource division problematics are addressed and multiplayer online games include social activities and helping others, and these indeed were, among others, the genres that showed positive effect in societal participation.

5.1   Implications to the Design of Digital Services that Activate Youth to Societal Participation

Based on the results of our study we propose the following initial design implications for digital services that aim at motivating youth to participate in societal discussion and other activities.

Providing Safe Environment for Youth Participation. The environment should be user-friendly and supportive towards newcomers, those interested but not yet familiar in political debate. Many young people are afraid of conflicts and discussions about sensitive topics such as immigrants. Therefore, discussion area should include clear rules and be well moderated in order to prevent inappropriate behavior, such as personal insults and harassment. In addition, it could be emphasized that the they are not too young to participate.

Offering Information that Entices Participation. Lack of grounding information was one of the main obstacles for participation. There should be sufficient depth of background information about the topics to enable insightful discussion. The service should offer easy access and means for finding areas of own interest (e.g. tags, favorites, recommendations). Furthermore, the subject matters should be presented in an interesting way, targeted at the youth - for example, in a visual way, instead of long textual descriptions. Possibilities of applying information representation conventions from games should be considered in for instance showing societal objectives, progress, and resources.

Matching Digital Participation to Personal Needs. Youth's interest to participate in societal discussions varies greatly. Participation should be enabled on different "requirements levels", for example for users who can spare little time and effort, and for people who have more motivation to dig deeper into the topics. The digital service could offer match making between youth of similar "spirit" - and at the same time avoiding users staying solely in the circles ("bubbles") of like-minded people.

Rewarding Participation. The users should be able to see the results of their own activities easily and concretely, e.g. through visual indicators. The system could provide the users with some kind of digital or even physical reward. Digital rewards, such as badges, could be posted within the same service but also in users' other social media services - naturally only with the user's permission.

5.2   Study Limitations

Although the study has been conducted with great regard to data acquisition, handling, analysis, and reporting, some limitations need to be mentioned. The questionnaire question sets have not been validated in a large-scale study and thus the indicators can be limited in their reliability, however they were applied and combined from several credible studies, and reviewed by three researchers. In addition, the results of the conducted factor analysis further reflect sum variable validity. In addition, the inner consistency was considered high in all the sum variables that exhibited statistically significant discrepancies, which can reflect instrument reliability. The sum variable "Digital Social Participation" had a 1/4 of its value from online gaming and thus might be biased, as respondents were mostly active gamers. It also must be mentioned that the results are generalizable only in a certain section of Finnish youth, as for instance gaming amount related variables differ from the national equivalent. Considering the abovementioned limitations in instruments and analysis, the effect sizes are additionally addressed in relation to the results and sincerely described. Also, the Bonferroni (in which, the significance value is multiplied by each pairwise test in set) correction method is used in subsequent testing scenarios where applicable. Finally, the qualitative interview data were analyzed and categorized by a single researcher, while with multiple analyzers there could have been some differences in the final categorization.

5.3   Future Work

In our future work we are conducting field studies of the youth's participation behavior. Furthermore, we will do design research on how, using participatory design methods, various youth groups could be motivated to digital societal participation. One of the approaches used in the human-centered design of novel digital services is gamification, which is a promising approach for digital service design (e.g. Deterding et al. 2011; Da Rocha Seixas et al. 2016; Gabarron et al. 2013). This approach is expected to be valuable for both gaming and non-gaming youth, and it may give rise to novel forms of participation. In the coming two years, we will design and implement digital service prototypes and utilize them in actual youth participation tasks such as city planning, work mentoring and commenting of legislative proposals.

6 Conclusions

This study produced relevant information on the societal and social activities and tendencies exhibited by the gaming youth. In specific, the findings point out that there are several obstacles for societal participation but also a multitude of motivators that can be used to understand requirements for design for societal inclusion. The findings shed light to the phenomenon of youth participation as part of the development of inclusive society. The proposed design implications can be applied when designing digital services for the youth. The findings contribute to the field of HCI by providing insights of youth's needs and motivations to use digital services for societal participation. The suggested design implications can give guidance for developers of digital services for youth participation. Designers should aim to remove the identified obstacles and support user motivation by providing safe environment for youth participation, offering information that entices participation, matching digital participation to personal needs, and by rewarding active participation.

Acknowledgements. We are grateful to the reviewers for their time and effort. We thank Niina Meriläinen, Eero Saukkonen, and Marika Hölttä for their support in data acquisition.

The research was funded by the Strategic Research Council at the Academy of Finland, project ALL-YOUTH with decision no. 312689.

References

Albrecht, S., et al.: eParticipation – Electronic Participation of Citizens and the Business Community in eGovernment. Institut für Informationsmanagement Bremen GmbH (ifib) (2008)

Checkoway, B.: What is youth participation? Child. Youth Serv. Rev. **33**(2), 340–345 (2011). https://doi.org/10.1016/j.childyouth.2010.09.017

Da Rocha Seixas, L., Gomes, A.S., De Melo Filho, I.J.: Effectiveness of gamification in the engagement of students. Comput. Hum. Behav. **58**, 48–63 (2016). https://doi.org/10.1016/j.chb.2015.11.021

Deterding, S., Sicart, M., Nacke, L., O'Hara, K., Dixon, D.: Gamification: using game-design elements in non-gaming contexts. In: CHI 2011 Extended Abstracts. On Human Factors in Computing Systems, pp. 2425–2428. ACM (2011)

Stolle, D., Hooghe, M.: Shifting inequalities. Eur. Soc. **13**(1), 119–142 (2011)

Ferguson, C.J., Garza, A.: Call of (civic) duty: action games and civic behavior in a large sample of youth. Comput. Hum. Behav. **27**(2), 770–775 (2011). https://doi.org/10.1016/j.chb.2010.10.026

Gabarron, E., Schopf, T., Serrano, J.A., Fernandez-Luque, L., Dorronzoro, E.: Gamification strategy on prevention of STDs for youth (2013). https://doi.org/10.3233/978-1-61499-289-9-1066

Harris, A., Wyn, J., Younes, S.: Beyond apathetic or activist youth: 'ordinary' young people and contemporary forms of participation. Young **18**(1), 9–32 (2010)

Ianniello, M., Iacuzzi, S., Fedele, P., Brusati, L.: Obstacles and solutions on the ladder of citizen participation: a systematic review. Public Manag. Rev. **21**(1) (2018)

Isola, A-M., et al.: Mitä osallisuus on? Osallisuuden viitekehystä rakentamassa. Terveyden ja hyvinvoinnin laitos. Juvenes Print – Suomen Yliopistopaino Oy (2017)

Kowert, R., Domahidi, E., Festl, R., Quandt, T.: Social gaming, lonely life? The impact of digital game play on adolescents' social circles. Comput. Hum. Behav. **36**, 385–390 (2014)

Lenhart, A., Kahne, J., Middaugh, E., Macgill, A.R., Evans, C., Vitak, J.: Teens, Video Games, and Civics. Pew Internet & American Life Project. 202-415-4500 (2008)

Meriläinen, N., Pietilä, I., Varsaluoma, J.: Digital services and youth participation in processes of social change: World Café workshops in Finland. Presented at 2018 ECPR General Conference Universität Hamburg (2018)

Michels, A., De Graaf, L.: Examining citizen participation: local participatory policy making and democracy. Local Gov. Stud. **36**(4), 477–491 (2010). https://doi.org/10.1080/03003930.2010. 494101

Myrskylä, P.: Hukassa - Keitä ovat syrjäytyneet nuoret? EVA Analyysi, vol. 12, 1.2.2012 (2012)

Myrskylä, P.: Young people outside the labour market and studies. Työ ja yrittäjyys 12/2011. Ministry of Employment and Economy (2011)

Mäyrä, F., Karvinen, J., Ermi, L.: Pelaajabarometri 2018: Monimuotoistuva Mobiilipelaaminen. TRIM Research Reports 28. Tampere: Tampereen yliopisto (2018). http://urn.fi/URN:ISBN: 978-952-03-0153-8

Panopoulou, E., Tambouris, E., Tarabanis, K.: Success factors in designing eParticipation initiatives. Inf. Organ. **24**(4), 195–213 (2014). https://doi.org/10.1016/j.infoandorg.2014.08. 001

Pessala, H.: Suomalaisten yhteiskunnallinen osallistuminen internetissä. Viestinnän tutkimus-keskus, CRC, Helsingin yliopisto, viestinnän laitos. Oikeusministeriön demokratiayksikkö (2009)

Polat, R.K.: The internet and political participation: exploring the explanatory links. Eur. J. Commun. **2005**(20), 435 (2005)

Przybylski, A.K.: Electronic gaming psychosocial adjustment. Pediatrics **134**(3), e716–e722 (2014)

Sutela, E., Haapakorva, P., Marttila, M., Ristikari, T.: Haavissa? Aktivointitoimissa olleiden nuorten taustat ja tilanteet toimien jälkeen. Vertailu Suomen kuuden suurimman kaupungin välillä Kansallinen syntymäkohortti 1987 -aineiston valossa. Terveyden ja hyvinvoinnin laitos (THL). Työpaperi 5/2018 (2018)

Sæbø, Ø., Rose, J., Skiftenes Flak, L.: The shape of eParticipation: characterizing an emerging research area. Gov. Inf. Q. **25**(3), 400–428 (2008). https://doi.org/10.1016/j.giq.2007.04.007

Human-Robot Interaction and 3D Interaction

DupRobo: Interactive Robotic Autocompletion of Physical Block-Based Repetitive Structure

Taizhou Chen[1], Yi-Shiun Wu[2], and Kening Zhu[1(✉)]

[1] School of Creative Media, City University of Hong Kong, Kowloon, Hong Kong
taizhou.chen@my.cityu.edu.hk, keninzhu@cityu.edu.hk
[2] Department of Micro Engineering, EPFL, Lausanne, Switzerland
alan830908@gmail.com

Abstract. In this paper, we present DupRobo, an interactive robotic platform for tangible block-based design and construction. DupRobo supported user-customizable exemplar, repetition control, and tangible autocompletion, through the computer-vision and the robotic techniques. With DupRobo, we aim to reduce users' workload in repetitive block-based construction, yet preserve the direct manipulatability and the intuitiveness in tangible model design, such as product design and architecture design. Through a user study with 12 participants, we found that DupRobo significantly reduced participants' perceived physical demand, overall efforts, and frustration in the process of block-based structure design and construction, compared to the situation without DupRobo. In addition, the participants rated DupRobo as easy to learn and use.

Keywords: Block assembly · Robotics · Autocompletion · Tangible user interface · Programming by demonstration · Tangible programming

1 Introduction

Assembly blocks (e.g. LEGO) have been widely applied in various creative areas, such as product design [19] and architecture design [29]. Different from sketching which is thought of as 2D visual design thinking [7], physical block building, with its emphasis on assembly and manipulation, ought to be considered 3D physical design thinking, a more tangible, interactive way of exploring design [29].

However, it is still confusing and tedious for non-experienced user to construct large physical models through the piece-by-piece block-building process [30]. It is even more difficult to create new models from scratch. Several researches have been done to tackle this problem, via the automatic generation of block-building

Electronic supplementary material The online version of this chapter (https://doi.org/10.1007/978-3-030-29384-0_29) contains supplementary material, which is available to authorized users.

instruction [20,23,35] and automatic construction of digital design with robots [10,11,21,28]. However, automatic instruction generation still requires users to build the structure by themselves. Although robotic automatic construction could reduce users' workload on physical building, most of them required the software-based modelling process, in which the complex modelling procedure disconnected users from the material investigation of the actual artefact being designed [16], leading to the lack of creative artistry or craftsmanship [6]. In addition, designing 3D models with CAD software requires additional expertise to organize and structure operations [18]. Research further indicated that interacting with a 3D model virtually can be far less intuitive than actually making the physical model [13,37], and tangible interfaces supported better problem-solving process than the software interfaces did [26,41]. In addition, tangible artefacts and interfaces have demonstrated their benefits to design iteration [5], digital fabrication [39], digital entertainment [38,40], and medical service [31].

Many large complicated structures often involve many repetitive parts. For example, the Parthenon model contains multiple similar pillar structure, and the Great Wall model consist of many embattlements. Meanwhile, it is observable that highly creative patterns can be generated through controlling the repetition of a primitive exemplar. The exemplar repetition, also knowns as autocompletion, has been widely supported in many 2D/3D design software [14,25,33,34]. Considering the physical block-building process, there is a need to reduce the manual workload in repetitive physical block-based construction through physical autocompletion yet preserve the direct manipulability and the intuitiveness in tangible modelling.

In this paper, we present DupRobo (Fig. 1), an interactive robotic platform for tangible block-based design and construction. Inspired by the drawing autocompletion, DupRobo supported physical exemplar creation, repetition control, and physical autocompletion. The setup of DupRobo consists of a KinectV2 sensor above the workbench platform to track the user input (i.e. the exemplar building and the marker-based commands), a robotic arm for automatic construction, and a block inventory management mechanism. Our user study with 12 participants showed that DupRobo significantly reduced participants' perceived physical demand, overall efforts, and frustration in the process of block-based structure design and construction, compared to the situation without DupRobo. In addition, the participants rated DupRobo as easy to learn and use, and they commented that DupRobo could assist them to achieve their desired structures.

2   Related Work

DupRobo was inspired by the existing works on the 2D drawing autocompletion, the block-assembly tracking and generation, and the robot assistant system.

2.1   Software-Based Autocompletion: 2D and 3D

The research on automatic repetitions of visual patterns has been greatly advanced in recent data-driven methods [14,33]. These works impose a list of

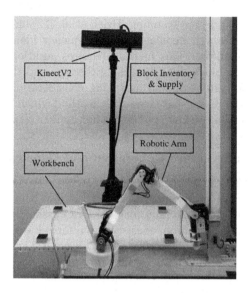

Fig. 1. System setup of DupRobo.

sequential orders with the user-defined exemplar to be cloned to the desired output region through various gestural commands, such as brushes. Similar autocompletion techniques were recently applied on 3D surface sculpting [25], which support brushing and stippling for modeling repeated part such as tentacles, hairs, and repeated texture on meshes. Although the autocompleted 3D virtual surface can be physicalized through 3D printing, it still requires users to edit the 3D model in graphical user interfaces which could be less direct or intuitive than the tangible user interface. Moreover, the autocompletion concept was also used on animation autocompletion, Xing et al. [34] introduced a method that simplify the process of creating frame-by-frame animation through manual sketches. It allows users to define character animation such as motion and trajectory easily by adding some command-based strokes. Taking one step further, we implement the concept of autocompletion into a fully tangible interface, with DupRobo supporting the physical block-based modeling autocompletion with tangible commands.

2.2 Block-Assembly Tracking

There have been several researches on tracking the procedure of block assembly. Miller et al. [22] and Van de Leemput et al. [17] both developed Kinect-based systems to track the construction of LEGO models. Their methods assumed that the physical model always stays with the base on the table, to reduce the complexity of tracking. Gupta et al. [8] presented Duplotrack, a real-time system to track the assembly process of Duplo blocks in 6 degrees of freedom. They used one Kinect sensor, thus requiring the physical model to be continually rotated to conduct 360-degree scanning. Hsieh et al. [12] introduced RFIBricks, a system that use ultrahigh frequency radio-frequency identification for block-based structure recognition. This method requires addition components, such as RFID tags on each block, thus increasing the cost and the size of the block. To make a low-cost system as well as taking consideration of the block size, DupRobo adopted the Kinect-based tracking method which is similar to [17, 22], for both block-structure tracking and command-marker recognition.

2.3 Block-Based Structure Generation and Construction

Besides block-assembly tracking, several researches were conducted on block-based structure generation and automatic construction. Kim et al. [15] presented a thorough literature review on automated LEGO assembly construction. Luo et al. [20] introduced Legolization, consisting of a force-based analytic algorithm and a layout refinement algorithm that allows automatic generation of a LEGO brick layout from a given 3D model. Mueller et al. [23] developed faBrickation, a rapid-prototyping method that combined hand-made LEGO structures and 3D-printed parts for functional objects. More recently, Yun et al. [35] developed a Legorization framework that produces a LEGO model through voxelization from user-specified 3D mesh model.

To automatically build block-based structures, Sekijima et al. [28] developed a reconfigurable 3D prototyping system that can automatically assemble the octahedron-shape blocks with embedded magnetic joints. Hiller and Lipson [10] introduced a method that 3D-printed a model in voxel with advantages of perfect repeatability and supporting multiple materials. Hiller developed a "VoxJet" printer using spherical voxels [11]. Maeda et al. [21] have developed a 3D-block printing system that allows reconstructing 3D CAD models into physical block-based structures. Their system can automatically convert a 3D model to a block structure that consisting of primitive LEGO blocks, then trigger the robot for automatic assembly. Although these systems support automatic block building with robotic technology, they still requires users' software-based model design, which require extensive learning and practice. Research have proved that tangible modelling interfaces helped users achieve better learning and task performance than pure software interfaces did [26]. DupRobo leverages these advantages of tangible interfaces, offering an intuitive physical prototyping environment.

2.4 Robotic Assistant

DupRobo is also strongly inspired by the recent development in interacting with robotic assistants for industrial and in-home purpose. Zhao et al. [36] utilized AR markers to control house-keeping robots. Orendt et al. [24] validated the intuitiveness and robustness of a One-Shot programming-by-demonstration robotic system. More recently, Sefidgar et al. [27] developed a set of physical blocks with visual markers for robot programming in a pick-and-place task context. Their studies proved the high intuitiveness and learnability of situated tangible programming for robotic assistants. Thus, the similar interaction techniques were adopted in DupRobo. Wang et al. [32] proposed a framework for describing human-robot collaboration. Van den Bergh et al. [2] developed a low-cost robot setup for collaborative personal fabrication activities in Fab Labs and Makerspaces. Smithwick et al. [29] envisioned an intelligent robotic platform that assists architects in tangible prototype design. DupRobo was directly motivated by this vision and stepped further with tangible control interface for the robot. More importantly, DupRobo distinguished itself by offering tangible modelling and control interfaces which could be more intuitive than the graphical user interfaces.

3   DupRobo

DupRobo is an interactive robotic platform aiming to support tangible block-based repetitive structure design and construction. It allows users to design and construct complicated repeated assembly block architecture in a few simple steps from scratch. There are three key features in DupRobo:

Firstly, DupRobo supports tangible design with physical blocks and command markers, motivated by the proven benefit of tangible interfaces on problem solving and creative design processes [26]. Many repeated block-based structures can be represented by: a single element repeats according to certain rule. Thus, we decoded repetitive block structures into two parts: the exemplar and the repeat rules. We designed a set of tangible marker blocks that define specific rules for repetition in an intuitive way, allowing users to easily explore and create their own repetitive block structures by arranging and combining the placement of different markers.

Secondly, DupRobo provides an integrated workbench-type environment by connecting the virtual and physical world with our preview system. To reduce the gap between the virtual and physical world during the design process, every user input (i.e. exemplar construction and marker placement) will be captured, calculated, and showed on the screen in real time. Our preview system also supports navigation operation, allowing users to preview and understand the current state of the generated structure from different perspectives in 3D space.

Lastly, DupRobo emphasizes on human-robot collaboration. We aim to use robotic arms to assist human for constructing complicated and tedious block structure. Human-robot collaboration is defined as: a sequence of interdependent actions in a Human-Robot interaction setting towards a shared goal [4]. DupRobo builds physical blocks based on the user's exemplar and physical commands. Therefore, users and DupRobo collaborate and contribute to the complete design and construction pipeline.

3.1   Hardware

Workbench. The workbench consists of a wood platform and a block inventory. The wood platform (60 cm × 30 cm) was drilled by the laser cutter with 18 rows by 37 columns, in total 666 holes with the diameter of 3 mm and the depth of

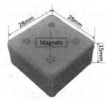

Fig. 2. DupRobo building block.

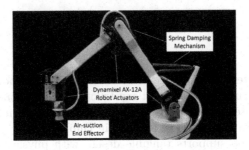

Fig. 3. DupRobo robotic arm.

2 mm to embed the neodymium magnets. The distance between two neighboring magnets was 15 mm. The platform was attached on a sliding mechanism with a 200-step stepping motor for the vertical movement. Every 200 steps movement of the stepping motor moves the platform 5 mm vertically.

The block inventory/supply mechanism was consisted with a 3D printed gear structure with an embedded servo motor (Model No.: MG-996R). A switch was attached on the storing compartment to detect the level of blocks. Once the number of the blocks is low, the LED will light up as an indication to notify the user. When there is no block left, a loud buzz will warn the user and pause the process until the user refill the blocks.

Building Blocks. As shown in Fig. 2, the 3D-printed block sizes 28 mm by 28 mm and 15 mm in height. We designed the size of the block slightly smaller than the gap between two adjacent magnets on the platform, a smooth placement

Fig. 4. (left) Anchor marker; (middle) Up marker; (right) Go marker.

by robotic arm. There were 4 neodymium magnets square-distribute embedded in both the top and bottom side of the block.

Robotic Arm. The robotic arm (Fig. 3) consists of six Dynamixel AX-12A Robot Actuators, an air-suction cap as the end effector, and the 3D printed frames with springs as the damping system to reduce the load of and ensure the stable movement of the actuators. To grip a block, the system turns on the air pump and the valve by the relay-controlled switch circuit. To build a block, the microcontroller receives the 3D coordinate of the to-build block, and calculate the real-time movement of each actuator based on the inverse kinematics and a real-time PID control algorithm. The air pump creates a vacuum state of the suction cap and enable it to hold the block. The valve will release air into the suction to release the block once reaching the targeted coordinate.

Command Makers. We designed three marker-base commands: *Anchor* marker, *Up* marker, and *Go* marker, as shown in Fig. 4.

The *Anchor* marker is the main command in DuoRobo. With the *Anchor* marker, DupRobo will generate the structure that lines up between the last exemplar-building position and the marker position using the exemplar (Fig. 5(b)). If one or more *Anchor* markers already exist on the platform, the newly placed *Anchor* marker will start lining at the end point of the last *Anchor* marker's operation and end the line at the current *Anchor* marker (Fig. 5(d)).

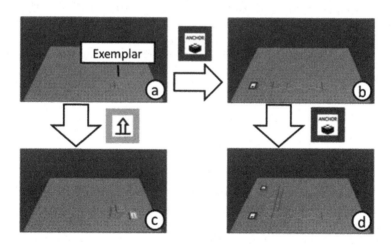

Fig. 5. (a) Workbench without any marker, (b) Workbench with the first *Anchor* marker, (c) Workbench with the first *Up* marker, (d) Workbench with more *Anchor* markers.

The *Up* marker will repeat the exemplar toward the up direction twice (Fig. 5(c)). It is also possible to set the repeat time as a controllable parameter, which means that we can have an additional marker associate with the *Up*

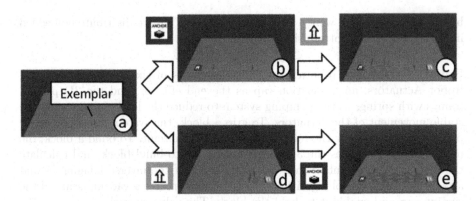

Fig. 6. (a) Workbench without any marker, (b) Workbench with the first *Anchor* marker, (c) Workbench with the *Up* marker after the *Anchor* marker, (d) Workbench with the first *Up* marker, (e) Workbench with the *Anchor* marker after the *Up* marker.

marker that control the repeat time. In the current prototype as the proof of concept, we set the repeat time with a constant value of two, due to the limited building space.

Combination of the *Anchor* marker and the *Up* marker provides diversified outputs. If an *Up* marker was set after one or more *Anchor* marker (Fig. 6(b)), the exemplar will be extended linearly upward from the start position to the last *Anchor* marker (Fig. 6(c)), instead of building upward perpendicularly. On the other hand, if the anchor marker was set after the *Up* marker (Fig. 6(d)), then the up operation will be conducted first and the result structure will be set as repeated element before the *Anchor* marker's operation using the new exemplar (Fig. 6(e)).

3.2 Software

The software of DupRobo consists of two main parts: block/marker-placement recognition, and repetition generation/preview.

Block/Marker-Placement Recognition. The recognition part was developed using C++ with the Kinect library and the OpenCV library. We used the depth frame for the block-placement tracking, and the RGB frame from the KinectV2 for the marker detection. Since the relative position between Kinect and the workbench platform are stationary (40 cm vertically), and the possible positions for the block placement are fixed with the embedded magnets' positions on the platform, we mapped each possible position to the 3D coordinate in the depth frame. Therefore, we can track each block's position on the platform according to the 2D coordinate in the depth frame. We can also get the height of that particular position from the depth information. To increase the tracking accuracy, we utilize four sets of 2D coordinates to track one block. Once detecting

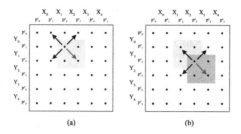

(a)   (b)

Fig. 7. (a) If depth change was detected at point (p_2^x, p_1^y), then scan through (p_1^x, p_0^y), (p_3^x, p_0^y), (p_1^x, p_2^y), (p_3^x, p_2^y), as indicated by the black arrows. Another detection of depth change was found at (p_3^x, p_2^y), as indicated by the red arrow, thus it is selected as a block placement at layer 1. (b) If there is another depth change at (p_3^x, p_2^y), we conduct the same diagonal-point-scanning process to detect the block at (X_3, Y_2) at layer 2. (Color figure online)

the simultaneous depth changes (i.e. the change of grayscale color in the depth frame) at two diagonal points, the system triggered the event of block-placement detection. Figure 7 illustrates an example of block-placement detection for two blocks at different height levels ((X_i, Y_j) denotes the coordinate of the block, and (p_i^x, p_j^y) denotes the coordinate of the to-scan pixel).

For marker detection, the system obtained the marker mask by calculating the L2 distance between the pre-defined RGB value of a particular marker and each pixel in the current RGB frame. The system then performed the rectangle-detection process on the marker mask to retrieve the center of the detected rectangle as the marker's position respectively.

Repetition Generation and Preview. Given the structure and the position of the exemplar, and the type and the position of the marker, the preview program calculated the positions of to-build blocks, which is done by a vector-base algorithm. For the *Anchor* marker, we adopted a recursive process, *anchorRepetition*, as described in Fig. 8. For the *Up* marker, the preview part naively calculated the positions of the to-built blocks towards the up direction.

4   Walkthrough

4.1   Step 1: Ideation and Exemplar Building

Users firstly decide what they want to build with DupRobo before considering the shape of the exemplar and the repetitive structure. For better recognition performance as well as for distinguishing users' input blocks, we use wooden blocks for creating the exemplar.

Use Case: A master student on architecture design, Alan, would like to build a close area with blocks that look like the wall of an ancient castle. He decided to use 3 blocks to create a reversed T-shape structure as the exemplar. As he built

```
Algorithm: anchorRepetition
anchorRepetition (E, M)
Input: A list E of blocks of the exemplar, marker M
Output: A list R of repeated blocks

get Distance D from E.position() to M.position()
get Direction d from E.position() to M.position()

loop through the position p for each potential
placement of the repeated exemplar E', given the
E'.boundingBox() is adjacent to E.boundingBox();
and select position p' whose direction to E has the
smallest angle to d.

get Distance d' from p' to M.position()

if (d' < D)
          instantiate R_next at position p'
          anchorRepetition (R_next, M)
else
          return R
```

Fig. 8. Psuedocode of repetition generation for the *Anchor* marker.

Fig. 9. Physical exemplar construction.

the exemplar by placing blocks on the workbench, DupRobo software executed the recognition process after each block placement, and rendered the blocks in the preview (Fig. 9).

4.2 Step 2: Marker Placement

After creating the exemplar, users need to place markers on the workbench for generating the to-build repetitive structure. For every camera frame, DupRobo software will detect whether there are markers on the platform or not. Once detected a particular marker, the system will generate and render the repetitive structure in the virtual environment for preview.

Use Case: Alan then started to place marker on the workbench. Since he would like to add some height for the wall structure, he first put an *Up* marker on the platform. From the preview system he saw the exemplar was repeated perpendicularly twice (Fig. 10(a)). He then put an *Anchor* marker on the right of the exemplar, as he wanted the expand the exemplar to the right. From the preview

Fig. 10. (a) Place an *Up* marker, (b)–(d) Place the first, second, and third *Anchor* marker. (Color figure online)

system, he saw what he expected (Fig. 10(b)). He then put the second *Anchor* marker in front of the first one (Fig. 10(c)), and lastly put the third *Anchor* marker on the left of the second (Fig. 10(d)). He saw the structure repeating the exemplar to the second and the third *Anchor* marker correctly on the preview screen.

4.3   Step 3: Correction and Fine-Tuning

DupRobo contains a buildability checking process for each marker detection, to ensure that the physical autocompletion process could be accomplished. In the current prototype, we prepared in total 64 3D-printed blocks with neodymium magnets. DupRobo software will calculate the number of blocks needed to build the repetitive structure. While there needs more than the current total number of blocks (i.e. 64) for building, the exceeding part will be rendered in a semi-transparent manner in the preview window. If there is a collision detected between the newly generated block and the previous block, the newly generated block would be rendered in red for warning.

Use Case: After placing the third anchor marker, Alan noticed that some blocks in the preview system are semi-transparent (highlighted in the red box in

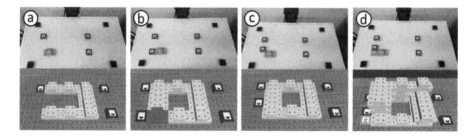

Fig. 11. (a) Correction by removing the *Up* marker, (b) Place the fourth *Anchor* marker and collision was detected, (c) Adjust the placement of the fourth *Anchor* marker, (d) Lastly, place the *Up* marker. (Color figure online)

Fig. 10(d)), meaning that the current set of blocks is not enough for DupRobo to finish the physical autocompletion. He did not want this happen so he decided to reset the marker. He then removed the *Up* marker from the workbench (Fig. 11(a)), and placed the fourth *Anchor* marker to close the shape (Fig. 11(b)). However, he noticed that subsequently there are some blocks become red on the preview window, indicating collision. This was caused by the wrong position of the fourth marker. Therefore, he adjusted the position of the fourth marker to form a perfect close area (Fig. 11(c)). Lastly, he placed a up marker to generate a stair-like wall structure (Fig. 11(d)).

4.4   Step 4: Physical Autocompletion

Users can trigger the autocompletion process by placing the *Go* marker. DupRobo software will check the buildability again before triggering the robotic arm. In order to prevent from physical collision during the physical construction process, the architecture will be constructed from left to right meanwhile from nearby to faraway.

Use Case: Alan was satisfied with the generated structure. He put the go marker to trigger the physical autocompletion process. Finally he got a will-built structure as what he saw in the preview system (Fig. 12).

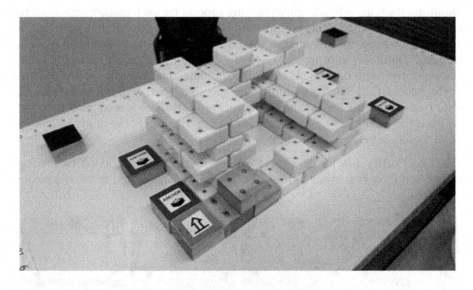

Fig. 12. Final product constructed by DupRobo.

5   Workshop Study

To evaluate the usefulness and usability of DupRobo, we conducted 10 individual workshops with an emphasis on the following questions:

- How do users evaluate the intuitiveness and learnability of DupRobo?
- Do users find DupRobo useful and engaging?
- How does DupRobo reduce the workload of repetitive block building?

We have adopted the evaluation strategy and procedure followed by other creative systems [3, 39, 42] for our evaluation.

5.1   Participants

Our workshops had a total 12 participants (one per workshop) consisting of five males and five females with ages ranging from 22 to 33 years (M = 27.3, SD = 4.63). The workshops were held in a research laboratory with a dimension of $10\,m \times 7\,m$. Prior to conducting the workshops, we recorded the information on each participant's professional background (five on computer graphics & rendering, three on interface design, and two on product design).

5.2   Apparatus

Each participant worked with a DupRobo system, which consisted of hardware (the workbench, the robotic arm, the 3D-printed blocks with embedded magnets, and the marker-based command blocks) and a software interface for result preview installed in a Dell Optiplex 990DT desktop PC.

5.3   Procedure

The workshop was conducted in four sessions:

1. Introduction. (10 min) The workshop facilitator gave a brief introduction of DupRobo, and showed a few examples that can be made using DupRobo, through powerpoint slides.
2. Guided Task. (15–20 min) After the briefing, the participant was given a printed tutorial on how to make a repetitive structure that can be auto-completed by DupRobo. The participant were asked to recreate this example to familiarize themselves with DupRobo. The activity involved creating the exemplar from scratch, placing the command markers, and triggering the robotic arm for auto-completion.
3. Free Task. (30–40 min) The participant was asked to explore their creativity and imagination by creating a new repetitive structure. This session aimed to provide us insights on how DupRobo allows users to explore their creativity. In addition, once satisfied with his/her design, the participant needed to construct one physical model of the design by him/herself, besides triggering the robotic arm. The participant constructed his/her design manually while DupRobo was building. This was to compare users' workload on repetitive structure building with and without DupRobo.
4. Demo. (10 min) After make his/her own structure, the participants was asked to present their design to the facilitator and explain the design rationale.

Table 1. Participants' ratings of the user-experience questionnaire. P#: Participant ID.

	P1	P2	P3	P4	P5	P6	P7	P8	P9	P10	P11	P12	Mean	SD
It is easy to learn to use this toolkit	5	4	5	5	5	5	4	5	4	5	4	5	4.67	0.49
It is easy to use this toolkit to create the physical structure that I want	4	5	4	4	4	4	5	5	4	4	4	4	4.25	0.45
It is easy to use the software to design and plan the physical structure	4	4	4	5	5	4	4	5	4	4	3	5	4.25	0.62
This toolkit is useful in creating physical block structures	5	4	4	5	4	4	3	5	4	4	4	5	4.25	0.62
Making physical block structures with this toolkit is fun	5	4	4	5	4	5	4	4	2	5	4	5	4.25	0.87
I enjoy creating physical block structures using this toolkit	5	4	4	5	4	4	4	5	2	5	4	5	4.25	0.87
I became creative in creating physical block structures with this toolkit	4	3	5	4	4	4	3	5	4	4	4	4	4.00	0.60
I became productive in creating physical block structure with this toolkit	5	4	4	5	5	5	4	4	5	4	5	4	4.5	0.52
I would recommend it to my friends	5	3	4	5	5	3	3	5	4	4	4	5	4.17	0.83

Fig. 13. The repetitive structures created by the workshop participants.

The workshop process was video recorded with the participants' consent. After the workshop, the participant answered a user-experience questionnaire on their impressions of the system (1 - strongly disagree, 5 - strongly agree). In addition, the participant was asked to two copies of a modified version (1 - very low, 7 - very high) of NASA TLX questionnaire [9] on their perceived workload with and without DupRobo.

5.4   Results

User Evaluation of DupRobo's Intuitiveness and Learnability. Table 1 shows the detailed ratings of the user-experience questionnaire from all the participants. Participants found DupRobo's marker-based command interface intuitive and easy to learn. One participant reported that it was *"easy to get used to the system after the guided task"*. Other participants commented: *"It was interesting to see the robot following my commands"*, that DupRobo can be easily and quickly understood, and that *"it was like having a robot as a building assistant"*. The results of the questionnaire showed that intuitiveness earned a score of 4.25/5 while the learnability scored 4.67/5.

All the participants were able to finish the guided task within the allotted time of 20 min. In the 40-min free task, the participants were able to come up with different structures and implement them through the autocompletion by DupRobo. They were allowed to ask questions when they faced difficulties, but very few did. There were, at most, two questions asked during each of the 12 workshops, which suggested that the toolkit was self-explanatory.

Nonetheless, the questions posed did help us to identify minor usability problems of the interface. Examples were *"Can I use the structure created by the robot as a new exemplar?"*, *"Can I change my design while the robot is building?"*, *"Can the system give any suggestion on resolving the collision?"*, and *"Can I have blocks in different shapes, such as circle and triangle? It seems I only have cube-shape."*, indicating that the reuse function, the recommendation function, and the variety of blocks can be improved in our current system.

User Opinions on DupRobo's Usefulness and Capacity to Be Engaging. Workshop participants unanimously agreed that the toolkit is useful (4.25/5) and that it can be employed in the following: architecture design; product design; furniture design; and pure entertainment. In terms of the creative process, we observed that one user made a few drafts outside of the board before he put the exemplar and the marker on the platform. Two users commented that they can mentally visualize the end results based on the markers. The rest of the users mentioned that they didn't have a clear idea on what they could build at the beginning, and the markers and the preview function assisted them to explore different ideas through "try and error". They tended to refer to the visualization on the screen, to decide the next step of design. The statement of "I became creative in creating physical block structures with this toolkit." was averagely rated 4/5.

Overall enjoyment scored 4.25/5. It was observed that enjoyment increased when the participants were allowed to be creative in the free task. They were excited by the opportunity to create repetitive structures with DupRobo. Figure 13 shows the examples of the products created by the participants during the free tasks. Participants generally liked the toolkit, and most of them agreed (4.17/5) that they wanted to recommend it to their friends.

Workload Reduction and Productivity Support. The average total NASA-TLX score with DupRobo is 17.67/42 (SD = 4.94), and the average total score without DupRobo is 26.25/42 (SD = 8.24). Table 2 shows the detailed ratings of the NASA-TLX questionnaire from all the participants. Wilcoxon Signed Ranks Test showed that the participants rated significantly less workload (Z = 2.675, p < 0.01) with DupRobo than without DupRobo. For the individual items of NASA TLX questionnaire, Wilcoxon Signed Ranks Test showed that the participants rated significantly less physical demand (Z = 2.715, p < 0.05), overall effort (Z = 2.537, p < 0.05), and frustration (Z = 2.132, p < 0.05) with DupRobo than the process of building by themselves without DupRobo. One participants explicitly commented that *"It reduces tedious work"*. Furthermore, the participants rated 4.5/5 on the statement "I became productive with DupRobo", although the building speed of the robotic arm was generally slower than the speed of the participants themselves.

Table 2. Participants' ratings of the NASA-TLX questionnaire. P#: Participant ID.

		P1	P2	P3	P4	P5	P6	P7	P8	P9	P10	P11	P12	Mean	SD
Mental demand	With DupRobo	5	4	2	3	2	2	4	2	3	6	5	2	3.33	1.43
	Without DupRobo	6	3	1	5	6	5	3	7	5	4	3	6	4.50	1.73
Physical demand	With DupRobo	2	1	2	3	2	1	2	2	1	2	2	1	1.75	0.62
	Without DupRobo	5	1	1	5	5	5	6	7	7	5	6	5	4.83	1.95
Temporal demand	With DupRobo	6	1	1	3	5	1	2	2	1	6	4	2	2.83	1.95
	Without DupRobo	5	1	1	5	3	1	3	7	6	5	4	2	3.58	2.07
Effort	With DupRobo	4	1	2	3	3	2	2	2	3	3	3	1	2.42	0.90
	Without DupRobo	6	3	1	5	4	5	3	7	5	5	4	4	4.33	1.56
Performance	With DupRobo	6	3	6	4	3	6	3	7	6	4	5	5	4.83	1.40
	Without DupRobo	6	3	6	4	5	5	5	4	4	4	5	6	4.75	0.97
Frustration level	With DupRobo	5	1	2	3	2	2	4	2	2	3	3	1	2.50	1.17
	Without DupRobo	7	1	1	5	3	2	6	7	6	5	3	5	4.25	2.18
Total score	With DupRobo	28	11	15	19	17	14	17	17	16	24	22	12	17.67	4.94
	Without DupRobo	35	12	11	29	26	23	26	39	33	28	25	28	26.25	8.24

6   Limitation and Future Work

Despite the capabilities we have shown, the current prototype of DupRobo could be improved in several aspects.

6.1   Variety of Command Markers

While the three markers in our current prototype could cover most basics repetitive block-based structures, there is a need for more variation of marker-based commands to support more complicated structures. For example, we currently defined the *Up* operation with a default parameter of two as the proof of concept, due to the limited space for construction. We could have another marker associate with the Up marker to control the time of vertical repetition.

In our current prototype, the orientation of the exemplar repetition was fixed according to the user input. It is possible to design another command marker, in the future work, that control the direction of the autocompleted part, to support more diversities for the final product. In addition, we would include the grouping operation for the future version, which allow users to group the current repeated structure as an exemplar for the new repetition.

Furthermore, in our current setting, the possible paths were mostly straight lines. To this end, we will include more marker for constructing curved paths in our future work. Curves can be easily represented using quadratic function or Bessel function. Therefore, we could include more markers (e.g. quadratic marker, Bessel marker) for generating curved structures.

As a systematic step of the future work, we will conduct a series of participatory design sessions with users to co-design new marker-based commands for DupRobo.

6.2 Speed of Autocompletion

Some workshop participants commented on the slow building speed of the robotic autocompletion process. It currently took approximately 25 s for the robotic arm to grip and build one block on the workbench. The speed of the robotic arm was fine-tuned to ensure the stability of griping and building. Another reason is that the servo motor we used is not powerful enough to stably support the robotic arm, especially the base joint in which even a small fluctuation caused a large shake on the end effector. Furthermore, the 3D-printed robotic arm limited the range of movements and the capability of building large structures. While the DIY mechanical implementation was used in the current prototype as a proof of concept, we will incorporate high-quality industrial robotic arms in the future.

6.3 Recognition Distortion

In the current prototype, wed use a top-down-facing KinectV2 sensor for both exemplar tracking and marker recognition. Our current algorithm would suffer from the problem of image distortion, especially when the exemplar was set on the edge of the platform. Thus, we limited the area of the workbench for a better recognition result. Therefore, we will tackle this problem by improving the current algorithm with the method of lens distortion rectification [1], to restore the Kinect images.

6.4 Multi-robot Collaboration

While DupRobo is inspired by Smithwick et al.'s vision of robotic design assistant [29], we further envision that the robotic assistant in tangible creative process could duplicate the designer's initial design, and perform iterations of the initial design, enabling rapid prototyping of different design configuration. In addition, the robotic assistant can experiment and construct complex possibilities that are difficult for manual efforts, and further provide new design suggestions to the designer. As the future work, we will investigate coordinating multiple robots with different shapes and functionalities to construct more complex shapes.

7 Conclusion

In this paper, we present DupRobo, an interactive robotic platform for tangible block-based design and construction. DupRobo supported user-customisable exemplar, repetition control with command markers, and physical autocompletion by the robotic arm. A user study with 12 participants showed that the participants rated DupRobo as easy to learn and use. More importantly, DupRobo significantly reduced participants' perceived physical demand, overall effort, and frustration in the process of block-based repetitive structure design and construction, while being compared to the situation without DupRobo. While this system is currently limited by the variety of the command marker and the speed of the autocompletion process, it can be considered as the first attempt to explore building repeated assembly blocks structure using physical marker-based command. The current system can be easily expanded with more functionalities. With DupRobo, we envision that the robotic assistant could provide tangible creative design support by duplicating, iterating, and experimenting complicated structure design with minimum input from the human designers, yet preserving the craftsmanship, the materiality, and the intuitiveness of physical artefact design.

Acknowledgments. This research was partially supported by grant from the Centre for Applied Computing and Interactive Media (ACIM) of School of Creative Media, the Strategic Research Grants (Project No. 7005021 & 7005172), the Teaching Development Grant (Project No. 6000623 & 6000639), the Applied Research Fund (Project No. 9667189), City University of Hong Kong, and grants from the Research Grants Council (Project No. CityU 21200216) and the Environment and Conservation Fund (Project No. EECA1956) of the Hong Kong Special Administrative Region, China.

References

1. Benligiray, B., Topal, C.: Lens distortion rectification using triangulation based interpolation. In: Bebis, G., et al. (eds.) ISVC 2015. LNCS, vol. 9475, pp. 35–44. Springer, Cham (2015). https://doi.org/10.1007/978-3-319-27863-6_4
2. Van den Bergh, J., van Deurzen, B., Veuskens, T., Ramakers, R., Luyten, K.: Towards tool-support for robot-assisted product creation in Fab Labs. In: Bogdan, C., Kuusinen, K., Lárusdóttir, M.K., Palanque, P., Winckler, M. (eds.) HCSE 2018. LNCS, vol. 11262, pp. 219–230. Springer, Cham (2019). https://doi.org/10.1007/978-3-030-05909-5_13

3. Buechley, L., Eisenberg, M., Catchen, J., Crockett, A.: The LilyPad Arduino: using computational textiles to investigate engagement, aesthetics, and diversity in computer science education. In: Proceedings of the SIGCHI Conference on Human Factors in Computing Systems, pp. 423–432. ACM (2008)

4. Bütepage, J., Kragic, D.: Human-robot collaboration: from psychology to social robotics. arXiv preprint arXiv:1705.10146 (2017)

5. Dancu, A., et al.: Emergent interfaces: constructive assembly of identical units. In: Proceedings of the 33rd Annual ACM Conference Extended Abstracts on Human Factors in Computing Systems, pp. 451–460. ACM (2015)

6. Evernden, C.B.: Digital imperfections: analog processes in 21st century cinema. Ph.D. thesis, Lethbridge, Alta.: University of Lethbridge, Dept. of New Media (2014)

7. Goldschmidt, G.: On visual design thinking: the vis kids of architecture. Des. Stud. **15**(2), 158–174 (1994)

8. Gupta, A., Fox, D., Curless, B., Cohen, M.: DuploTrack: a real-time system for authoring and guiding Duplo block assembly. In: Proceedings of the 25th Annual ACM Symposium on User Interface Software and Technology, pp. 389–402. ACM (2012)

9. Hart, S.G., Staveland, L.E.: Development of NASA-TLX (Task Load Index): results of empirical and theoretical research. Adv. Psychol. **52**, 139–183 (1988)

10. Hiller, J., Lipson, H.: Design and analysis of digital materials for physical 3D voxel printing. Rapid Prototyping J. **15**(2), 137–149 (2009)

11. Hiller, J.D., Lipson, H.: Fully recyclable multi-material printing. In: Solid Freeform Fabrication Proceedings, pp. 98–106. Citeseer (2009)

12. Hsieh, M.J., Liang, R.H., Huang, D.Y., Ke, J.Y., Chen, B.Y.: RFIBricks: interactive building blocks based on RFID. In: Proceedings of the 2018 CHI Conference on Human Factors in Computing Systems, p. 189. ACM (2018)

13. Ishii, H., Ullmer, B.: Tangible bits: towards seamless interfaces between people, bits and atoms. In: Proceedings of the ACM SIGCHI Conference on Human Factors in Computing Systems, pp. 234–241. ACM (1997)

14. Kazi, R.H., Igarashi, T., Zhao, S., Davis, R.: Vignette: interactive texture design and manipulation with freeform gestures for pen-and-ink illustration. In: Proceedings of the SIGCHI Conference on Human Factors in Computing Systems, pp. 1727–1736. ACM (2012)

15. Kim, J.W., Kang, K.K., Lee, J.H.: Survey on automated LEGO assembly construction (2014)

16. Kourteva, E., Mc Meel, D.: Entropy: unpacking the form through post digital making. Des. J. **20**(sup1), S172–S183 (2017)

17. Van de Leemput, S., Van Otterlo, M.: DUPLOG: probabilistic logical interpretation of Duplo assemblies from 3D vision (2013)

18. Leen, D., Ramakers, R., Luyten, K.: StrutModeling: a low-fidelity construction kit to iteratively model, test, and adapt 3D objects. In: Proceedings of the 30th Annual ACM Symposium on User Interface Software and Technology, pp. 471–479. ACM (2017)

19. Lofaro, D.M., Le, T.T.G., Oh, P.: Mechatronics education: from paper design to product prototype using LEGO NXT parts. In: Kim, J.-H., et al. (eds.) FIRA 2009. CCIS, vol. 44, pp. 232–239. Springer, Heidelberg (2009). https://doi.org/10.1007/978-3-642-03986-7_27

20. Luo, S.J., et al.: Legolization: optimizing LEGO designs. ACM Trans. Graph. (TOG) **34**(6), 222 (2015)

21. Maeda, Y., Nakano, O., Maekawa, T., Maruo, S.: From CAD models to toy brick sculptures: a 3D block printer. In: 2016 IEEE/RSJ International Conference on Intelligent Robots and Systems (IROS), pp. 2167–2172. IEEE (2016)

22. Miller, A., White, B., Charbonneau, E., Kanzler, Z., LaViola Jr., J.J.: Interactive 3D model acquisition and tracking of building block structures. IEEE Trans. Visual Comput. Graphics 18(4), 651–659 (2012)

23. Mueller, S., Mohr, T., Guenther, K., Frohnhofen, J., Baudisch, P.: faBrickation: fast 3D printing of functional objects by integrating construction kit building blocks. In: Proceedings of the SIGCHI Conference on Human Factors in Computing Systems, pp. 3827–3834. ACM (2014)

24. Orendt, E.M., Fichtner, M., Henrich, D.: Robot programming by non-experts: intuitiveness and robustness of one-shot robot programming. In: 2016 25th IEEE International Symposium on Robot and Human Interactive Communication (RO-MAN), pp. 192–199. IEEE (2016)

25. Peng, M., Xing, J., Wei, L.Y.: Autocomplete 3D sculpting. arXiv preprint arXiv:1703.10405 (2017)

26. Schneider, B., Jermann, P., Zufferey, G., Dillenbourg, P.: Benefits of a tangible interface for collaborative learning and interaction. IEEE Trans. Learn. Technol. 4(3), 222–232 (2011)

27. Sefidgar, Y.S., Agarwal, P., Cakmak, M.: Situated tangible robot programming. In: Proceedings of the 2017 ACM/IEEE International Conference on Human-Robot Interaction, pp. 473–482. ACM (2017)

28. Sekijima, K., Tanaka, H.: Reconfigurable three-dimensional prototype system using digital materials. In: ACM SIGGRAPH 2015 Posters, p. 89. ACM (2015)

29. Smithwick, D., Kirsh, D., Sass, L.: Designerly pick and place: coding physical model making to inform material-based robotic interaction. In: Gero, J.S. (ed.) Design Computing and Cognition 2016, pp. 419–436. Springer, Cham (2017). https://doi.org/10.1007/978-3-319-44989-0_23

30. Strobel, J.: All the better to see you with: a comparison of approaches to delivering instructions for LEGO construction tasks. Ph.D. thesis, Bowling Green State University (2010)

31. Tsai, S.C., Samani, H., Kao, Y.W., Zhu, K., Jalaian, B.: Design and development of interactive intelligent medical agent. In: 2018 IEEE International Conference on Artificial Intelligence and Virtual Reality (AIVR), pp. 210–215. IEEE (2018)

32. Wang, X.V., Kemény, Z., Váncza, J., Wang, L.: Human-robot collaborative assembly in cyber-physical production: classification framework and implementation. CIRP Ann. 66(1), 5–8 (2017)

33. Xing, J., Chen, H.T., Wei, L.Y.: Autocomplete painting repetitions. ACM Trans. Graph. (TOG) 33(6), 172 (2014)

34. Xing, J., Wei, L.Y., Shiratori, T., Yatani, K.: Autocomplete hand-drawn animations. ACM Trans. Graph. (TOG) 34(6), 169 (2015)

35. Yun, G., Park, C., Yang, H., Min, K.: Legorization with multi-height bricks from silhouette-fitted voxelization. In: Proceedings of the Computer Graphics International Conference, p. 40. ACM (2017)

36. Zhao, S., Nakamura, K., Ishii, K., Igarashi, T.: Magic cards: a paper tag interface for implicit robot control. In: Proceedings of the SIGCHI Conference on Human Factors in Computing Systems, pp. 173–182. ACM (2009)

37. Zhu, K.: A framework for interactive paper-craft system. In: CHI 2012 Extended Abstracts on Human Factors in Computing Systems, pp. 1411–1416. ACM (2012)

38. Zhu, K., Chen, T., Han, F., Wu, Y.S.: HapTwist: creating interactive haptic proxies in virtual reality using low-cost twistable artefacts. In: Proceedings of the 2019 CHI Conference on Human Factors in Computing Systems, p. 693. ACM (2019)

39. Zhu, K., Dancu, A., Zhao, S.S.: FusePrint: a DIY 2.5D printing technique embracing everyday artifacts. In: Proceedings of the 2016 ACM Conference on Designing Interactive Systems, pp. 146–157. ACM (2016)

40. Zhu, K., Fernando, O.N.N., Cheok, A.D., Fiala, M., Yang, T.W.: Origami recognition system using natural feature tracking. In: 2010 IEEE International Symposium on Mixed and Augmented Reality, pp. 289–290. IEEE (2010)

41. Zhu, K., Ma, X., Wong, G.K.W., Huen, J.M.H.: How different input and output modalities support coding as a problem-solving process for children. In: Proceedings of the The 15th International Conference on Interaction Design and Children, pp. 238–245. ACM (2016)

42. Zhu, K., Zhao, S.: AutoGami: a low-cost rapid prototyping toolkit for automated movable paper craft. In: Proceedings of the SIGCHI Conference on Human Factors in Computing Systems, pp. 661–670. ACM (2013)

Esquisse: Using 3D Models Staging to Facilitate the Creation of Vector-Based Trace Figures

Axel Antoine[1]([⊠]), Sylvain Malacria[2], Nicolai Marquardt[3], and Géry Casiez[1]

[1] Univ. Lille, CNRS, Centrale Lille, Inria, UMR 9189 - CRIStAL -
Centre de Recherche en Informatique Signal et Automatique de Lille,
59000 Lille, France
{axel.antoine,gery.casiez}@univ-lille.fr
[2] Inria Lille - Nord Europe, Lille, France
sylvain.malacria@inria.fr
[3] University College London, London, UK
n.marquardt@ucl.ac.uk

Abstract. Trace figures are contour drawings of people and objects that capture the essence of scenes without the visual noise of photos or other visual representations. Their focus and clarity make them ideal representations to illustrate designs or interaction techniques. In practice, creating those figures is a tedious task requiring advanced skills, even when creating the figures by tracing outlines based on photos. To mediate the process of creating trace figures, we introduce the open-source tool *Esquisse*. Informed by our taxonomy of 124 trace figures, *Esquisse* provides an innovative 3D model staging workflow, with specific interaction techniques that facilitate 3D staging through kinematic manipulation, anchor points and posture tracking. Our rendering algorithm (including stroboscopic rendering effects) creates vector-based trace figures of 3D scenes. We validated *Esquisse* with an experiment where participants created trace figures illustrating interaction techniques, and results show that participants quickly managed to use and appropriate the tool.

Keywords: Trace figures · 3D models staging · Vector graphics · Blender

1 Introduction

Trace figures are static illustrative figures created to capture the essence of a situation, removing unnecessary details by limiting the graphical representation to the most important contours/outlines of the shown objects and people (for

---

Electronic supplementary material The online version of this chapter (https://doi.org/10.1007/978-3-030-29384-0_30) contains supplementary material, which is available to authorized users.

D. Lamas et al. (Eds.): INTERACT 2019, LNCS 11747, pp. 496–516, 2019.
https://doi.org/10.1007/978-3-030-29384-0_30

example, the visual abstract of our Fig. 1 includes several trace figures). Trace figures, even when augmented with graphical annotation overlays (such as text, arrows or circles), minimize visual clutter and are effective at describing the essence of an interactive scenario.

Likely because of their clarity and focus, trace figures are gaining popularity in the HCI community, especially for illustrating a novel interaction technique or interactive systems. As a result, they can be found in many papers, presentations or posters: over three years of UIST proceedings [1–3] for instance, more than 25% of the published papers used trace figures, often used to demonstrate gestures, provide an overview of a system setup or illustrate a design space.

Producing trace figures from scratch without a model requires very good drawing skills. Therefore, many users have to rely on manual photo tracing in order to produce the outlines of devices and people shown in the illustrations [9]. This manual tracing is a time-consuming and tedious task and eventually results in a limited workflow where even small changes of the drawn people, postures or devices might require starting again the manual tracing process from scratch. This is even more of a problem in cases where several hand postures must be produced or when users are required to change the point of view of the illustration. So far, research on the production of illustrations has been mostly focused on facilitating the production of new types of illustrations such as animated or interactive illustrations [18,19], whether they illustrate interactive scenarios or not. However, despite the frequent use of trace figure to illustrate interactive scenarios, and the challenges of the process to produce them, we are lacking software tools that are targeted at facilitating their production.

In this paper, we support the hypothesis that 3D staging is a good alternative to mediate the production of static trace figures to illustrate interactive scenarios. More precisely, we present *Esquisse*, an open-source tool implementing an innovative 3D staging workflow for producing trace figures (Fig. 1). In particular, the underlying idea behind *Esquisse* is to capitalize on the flexibility of a 3D modeling software for staging 3D scenes that are subsequently rendered as a trace-figure vector file that can still be post-edited in a vector-graphics software afterwards. We provide 3D models, tools and techniques to make this workflow accessible to every people even if they do not have previous experience with 3D modeling software.

The workflow implemented by *Esquisse* works as follows. Users open a 3D scene using one of the provided templates. If needed, they can directly modify the position and pose of the objects using interaction techniques provided by *Esquisse* that simplify the manipulation of these 3D objects. For instance, users can easily specify a hand posture using a Leapmotion hand tracking camera[1], or by adding a *contact point anchor* which will snap a desired finger to this contact point and modify the hand pose according if the point is moved on the display. They can also add other avatars and objects to the scene if required. Users then position the camera in the 3D space according to their needs. They can also integrate interface screenshots in various displays. Optionally they can add a

---

[1] LeapMotion – https://www.leapmotion.com/.

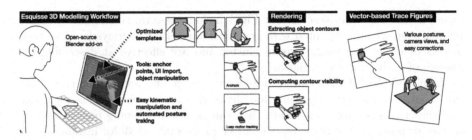

Fig. 1. Workflow of *Esquisse*: (left) facilitating staging of 3D scenes with templates, anchor points, direct UI import, kinematic manipulation and automated posture tracking, (center) *Esquisse*'s algorithm rendering the tracing images, and (right) final vector-based trace figures.

stroboscopic effect to illustrate the motion of a finger or object. A simple click to a *Render* button then calls *Esquisse*'s rendering algorithm which generates a trace figure of the scene, integrating all added interface images, and outputs a vector-based file (examples of trace figures produced with *Esquisse* can be seen in Fig. 1 and other figures throughout the paper; further renderings can be found in the Supplementary Material).

In summary, *Esquisse*'s workflow facilitates the rapid production of trace figures, as well as the adaptation of existing figures. Our work makes the following contributions:

 (i) introducing a novel workflow for quickly creating vector based trace figures;
 (ii) presenting the design of interaction techniques to facilitate this workflow;
(iii) developing an innovative rendering pipeline, adapted from existing techniques;
(iv) implementing this workflow into a Blender add-on.

To allow members of the HCI community to create trace figures with *Esquisse*, it is released as a free open-source[2] add-on for the 3D modelling software Blender [14].

The remainder of the paper is structured as follows. After presenting a taxonomy of illustrative figures for HCI scientific contribution, we discuss the existing workflows for creating trace figures. We then describe details of *Esquisse*'s interaction techniques and its implementation, before discussing the evaluation and figures created by participants.

2 Taxonomy of Trace Figures

We define trace figures as graphical representations of the most essential features of a scene by using contours/outlines of objects, people and the environment. In this section, we will introduce a classification of different kinds of trace figures and discuss typical characteristics. To better understand the use of trace

---

[2] Github Esquisse – http://ns.inria.fr/loki/esquisse/.

figures within the HCI community, we analysed the use of trace figures in the papers published over three years (2015–2017) of UIST proceedings [1–3]. Many publications at UIST include details on gestural interaction techniques, use of interaction techniques and technical details on device use, and are a subset of the spectrum of publications published in the HCI community. Our initial sampling of proceedings indicated a common use of photo tracing in UIST papers, but our analysis below similarly translates to other HCI publications (e.g., Interact or ACM CHI), though the overall counts and percentages would probably differ.

Overall, we found 124 trace figures (often multiple per paper) in the 222 accepted UIST papers of these three years (trace figures in 29% of the papers). We constrained our search so that all trace figures included in our sample set need to include at least one part of a person's body (e.g., a person's fingers, hand or full body), and therefore we did not include pure technical line drawing of components or devices. By following a systematic coding (by two researchers) and iterative thematic analysis of the figure sample set we identified the following five categories:

1. **Demonstration of gestures (64):** this most common type of trace figure illustrates a hand or body gesture (e.g., swiping, pressing, turning). Trace figures work well to clearly illustrate the accurate postures of hands or a person's body ([13, Fig. 13], [29, Fig. 1]).
2. **Overview of system setup or assembly (26):** these illustrations show, for example, the setup of tracking cameras, the setup of hardware (e.g., [9, Fig. 1d]) or the technical assembly of a wearable device.
3. **Interaction sequences (14):** these sequences show multiple frames of an interaction with a system (e.g., key steps of the interaction with a screen interface).
4. **Design space illustrations (13):** this can be a technical design space (e.g., variations of a tangible form factor) or a design space of gestures (e.g., a collection of 8 different hand postures).
5. **Other (7):** this includes any other uses of trace figures, for examples as part of tables, flow diagrams, etc.

By continuing our analysis and coding, we further identified the following characteristics of trace figure illustrations:

– **C1 — Person's body, hands or fingers:** the most common drawn element across all figures was a person's hand (total of 218 drawings of a person's hand, often multiple per figure, in 43 papers). This corresponds to the high number of figures in HCI papers demonstrating gestures ([9, Fig. 1d]). A person's body (or most of the body, like the upper torso) was drawn as part of Figs. 158 times across 22 papers. Individual fingers were drawn 51 times in 7 papers ([13, Fig. 13]) and a person's head (without rest of the body) 16 times (in 5 papers).
– **C2 — Devices and objects:** phones/tablets (32) and wearable devices such as smartwatches (20) were the most commonly drawn devices in our sample.

37 of the trace figures included some kind of tangible devices or other physical objects (e.g. active tokens, door handles). Other less frequently drawn objects and devices included: white boards and interactive tabletops (12), VR/AR headsets (7), tracking cameras (4), and car interiors (2) for automotive UI interaction.

– **C3 — Screen user interfaces:** 31 of the trace figures included screenshots of graphical user interfaces. For example, screenshots show the interface elements on mobile phones or smartwatch screens (see screenshots embedded in [13, Fig. 13] and [16, Fig. 3]).

– **C4 — Environment:** most photo traces (116) do not include any drawn details of the physical environment (e.g., background, furniture). Only 8 figures (e.g., [22, Fig. 1]) include traces lines delimiting the size of a room, or showing furniture and other objects in the environment. Since an important goal of photo traces is to reduce visual clutter, it seems that most figures strictly limit the traced details.

– **C5 — Use of colour:** photo traces can be pure black-and-white line drawings (34) but many include colour: 45 drawings used coloured areas within the drawing (e.g., solid fill of a person's hand in a skin-coloured tone), and 58 drawings used colour for making annotations and labels that stand out against the black and white trace figure (e.g., coloured arrows on top of the drawing, or coloured text labels).

– **C6 — Annotations:** most of the trace figures (121) include meta annotations such as labels, text descriptions, arrows or motion path lines. Most common annotations (besides text labels) are arrows (63) and touch contact point visualisations (37), for example by showing a coloured circle at the position where a person's fingers are touching the screen ([13, Fig. 13] and [16, Fig. 3]).

– **C7 — Static vs dynamic:** most figures depict a static scene (e.g., a single moment in time, a static setup), but a small number of figures (6) were designed for illustrating motion or movement (e.g., moving arms for a body gesture). Those usually used stroboscopic effect, where previous states/positions are drawn in different colours or line styles. McAweeney *et al.* made the same observation in their taxonomy focused on how gestures can be represented [26].

– **C8 — Use of perspective:** 55 trace figures in 43 papers use some sort of perspective (e.g., [25, Fig. 2] and [22, Fig. 1]), which can be required to illustrate specific interactive scenarios (*e.g.* users around a table top, device tilting).

Our categorization and identified characteristics are of course depending on our sample and the kind of publications at UIST, and it is likely that further categories and properties can be identified when widening the sample. However, our categories and characterizations are a first-order approximation of the kind of interaction technique trace figures created for publications within the HCI community.

We used this characterisation of trace figures to directly inform the design of *Esquisse*. We decided to support various hand gestures and full-body models in the application to capture much of the use cases for trace figures we found in the literature. Commonly used device types (such as phones, tablets and smart-watches) became part of our template library (explained shortly). We also decided to directly integrate different colouring and tracing mechanisms (e.g., see through lines, coloured areas), and to simplify the use of human body representations in the visualisations (through templates and automated hand tracking).

3   Practices for Creating Trace Figures

3.1   Model-Based Methods

While producing trace figure is a common practice, especially for HCI researchers, surprisingly little work has been devoted to ease the production of such materials. The most commonly used method remains manual photo-tracing [9,33] which can be described as follows. First, users stage the situation they want to illustrate using physical devices and other people standing in as actors, and take a photo of it. Then, they transfer this photo to a computer or a tablet, and open it as a background layer in an image editing software. Third, they sketch traces on top of the photo using their favourite input device and graphics editing software (usually Inkscape or Adobe Illustrator). Once the sketch is complete, they may add visuals such as overlaying an interface over a display or adding arrows, texts or contact points. Finally, they export the trace figure, most of the time as a vector graphic file so it can be resized at will.

This manual photo-tracing workflow still suffers from several limitations. First, it is time consuming and relatively tedious. It also requires users to have devices as well as friends or colleagues available that can be used as models. It may also require users to build physical props, for instance to illustrate inter-action with devices they do not actually own or that exist only as 3D models. Another limitation is that some "minor" modifications (for instance a change in hand posture) might require users to start the whole process from the begin-ning. Similarly, changing the angle of the illustration requires users to repeat the process with a new photo.

Some of the vector graphics editing software provide tools to convert a photo into a drawing-like vector figure. However, these methods rely on juxtapositions of colour fills and result in a different visual quality than trace figures. Typically for a hand, the skin will result in several colour fills to recreate the gradient resulting of the lightning condition. Moreover, such an approach will vectorize the entire image, including background or elements that will ultimately be removed from the trace figure. A method letting the user perform local adjustment has thus been proposed [34].

Edge detection algorithms, based on the seminal work by John Canny [6], seem an alternative solution for tracing the contours of a model photography, but these algorithms usually fill pixels rather than producing a vector path, and may result in low-quality results depending on lighting conditions and quality of the source image. Mixed initiative [28,30] lets the human *lead* the edge detection, but still suffers from lighting conditions and blurry objects.

Specifying the contours of an object is also typical from rotoscoping technique[3] used in animation, which consists in drawing on top of consecutive images (typically a video). The traditional workflow for rotoscoping however differs from the manual photo-tracing as it still consists in creating several closed shapes for each object in order to ease subsequent manipulation [24]. As a result, tools specifically designed for easing rotoscoping, such as Roto++ [24], are less suitable for producing trace figures.

The comic book drawing tool ClipStudio Paint[4] could facilitate the production of trace figure when a photo model cannot be provided, since it provides 3D avatars that can be used as support to manually photo trace on top of them. However, this tool is mostly targeted at drawing characters and is not adapted to the illustration of HCI scenarios. Finally, DemoDraw [9] captures whole body movements from a user through a Microsoft Kinect and produces a minimalist illustration that can be overlaid with arrow annotations or using stroboscopic effects. *Esquisse* extends beyond this earlier related work by supporting the easy creation of vector-based photo tracings of both body movements, gestures and input devices.

3.2   Staging-Based Methods

2D staging can be used to produce illustrations similar to trace figures, typically by using cliparts found online or suggested by Google AutoDraw[5] (a tool based on machine learning that retrieves clipart images based on approximate sketches drawn by the user) to rapidly produce trace figures without relying on a photo model. Those approaches require the appropriate cliparts (which are not necessarily available in vector format), and the 2D nature of clipart does not allow changes to correct the perspective of the figure which can be essential for illustrating interactive scenarios involving multiple users in a smart living room, or interaction techniques on a smartphone based on device tilting (for example, see Fig. 1 in [22] and [31]).

SketchStudio is a 2.5D staging tool for prototyping animated design scenarios, based on body avatars and graph nodes that depict the journey of that avatar in space and time [21], scenes that can be played back through a dedicated viewing interface. There are, however, limitations when using this tool for the creation of photo traces. First, it is focused on *large scale* interactive scenarios involving a user that moves around devices, making it more difficult to use for fine interactions such as touch-based interaction on a smartphone. Furthermore, all interactive devices and interfaces must still be sketched, thus requiring drawing skills from the user, and the tool does not produce a vector-graphics rendering of the scene. Finally, several participants in an experiment conducted with SketchStudio mentioned that it becomes limited for ideas that need to be illustrated in 3D form, which is why Kim et al. suggest to improve their system to support the use of 3D models.

---

[3] Rotoscoping – https://en.wikipedia.org/wiki/Rotoscoping.

[4] ClipStudio Paint – https://www.clipstudio.net/en/.

[5] AutoDraw – https://www.autodraw.com/.

Finally, ComiPo![6] is a design tool that relies on 3D models to make it possible to design manga-like comic books. 3D staging to produce 2D renderings here solves many problems associated with perspective. However besides the type of rendering, this tools could not be used for the production of trace figures for HCI because of the lack of support for aspects like the inclusion of interfaces or the production of vector format. Moreover, it does not use a camera system, which means that changing the perspective of a scene requires users to independently rotate all the objects of that scene.

4   Esquisse Workflow and Interaction

To use *Esquisse* the user starts Blender with the *Esquisse* add-on[7] previously installed. We chose Blender as it is a free and cross-platform software widely used to model, animate and render 3D scenes. However, as a complete 3D modelling environment, Blender provides controls with many degrees of freedom that are not needed for illustration production, which is why we overrode most default controls with simpler interaction techniques specifically implemented for *Esquisse*. These techniques are located in a dedicated panel located on the left side of the Blender interface (see Fig. 2, left). To create a vector graphics illustration with *Esquisse*, users stage a 3D scene using one of the pre-existing templates as starting point or manually adding 3D objects to the scene. For objects featuring a screen (e.g. a smartphone) they can optionally load an external file with a screenshot image of the interface, which gets automatically rendered as part of the screen of the selected device. They then position and align the objects using the specific interaction techniques of *Esquisse* built to ease the manipulation of articulated objects (and in particular simplifying the modification of hand postures), but they can still use default Blender controls if they prefer. Next they orient the viewport to the desired point of view. If wanted, they can add a stroboscopic effect to illustrate the motion of a finger, for example. Last they render the scene to create the trace figure as a vector-based SVG file. Optionally, they can tweak or add graphical elements using any vector graphics editing software like Inkscape or Illustrator. Note that these steps do not necessarily have to be performed in that specific order. In the following we detail each step of this workflow.

4.1   Choosing a Template and Objects

We identified in our taxonomy (C1 and C2) that many trace figures only vary in details, which is why *Esquisse* provides TEMPLATES with pre-arranged sets of people and objects used in these typical scenarios. Each TEMPLATE defines a 3D scene in Blender whose objects are loaded in the scene currently opened, for example two hands holding a phone, a person interacting with a smartwatch, or

---

[6] ComiPo! – https://www.comipo.com/.
[7] Esquisse on GitHub – http://ns.inria.fr/loki/esquisse/.

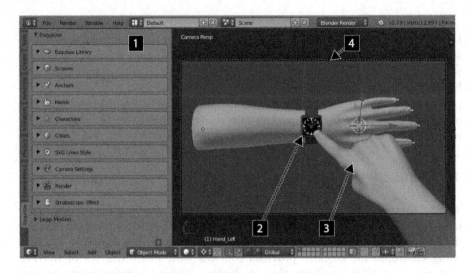

Fig. 2. Blender with the *Esquisse* add-on. All controls specific to *Esquisse* are located in a dedicated panel located on the left side of the interface (1). The right side shows the 3D view of the scene with several objects from the *Esquisse* library such as a SmartWatch with its GUI (2) and hand models (3)), and the frame of the current camera view (4).

two people around an interactive tabletop. TEMPLATES can be easily selected from the gallery of thumbnail images of all currently available templates (Fig. 2, (1) *Esquisse Library* tab). We created TEMPLATES based on the most commonly used postures and devices from our taxonomy, but new templates can be easily added by saving a scene and adding it to the *Esquisse* library.

In a similar way, users can complete a 3D scene by adding new objects (e.g., phones, avatars) from the object library of *Esquisse*. Custom 3D objects can obviously also be added to the scene using the import feature from Blender.

4.2   Adding GUIs in the Scene

Esquisse allows users to insert UIs (which was the case of 31 figures from our taxonomy, see C3) on 3D objects featuring a screen. A *screen* is a 3D plane object with a specific tag on which a user interface (defined in an external file) can be imported and displayed on.

Common objects with displays (smartphones, tablets, TVs, smartwatches and tabletops) are already provided in *Esquisse* with a defined *screen* area. It is also possible to add a *screen* to any other 3D object directly in *Esquisse*, by adding a *screen* object to the scene and setting the corresponding 3D object as its parent.

4.3   Facilitating Object Positioning

Simple objects like smartphones or tabletops can be positioned in the 3D scene easily using the 3-axis manipulator already available in Blender for translating, rotating and scaling the objects. However, when it comes to complex objects like a person's hand or body, manipulating the global position, rotation and scale of the combined object is not enough as these models are more complex and the position and orientation of each of their sub-objects (e.g., bones for a hand model) need to be modified. *Esquisse* provides *rigged* models that take into account child-parent relationships between bones. That being said, modifying a body or hand posture while keeping a coherent visual appearance can be a difficult and a time-consuming process for novice users [4,32]. In the following, we introduce techniques to simplify this task.

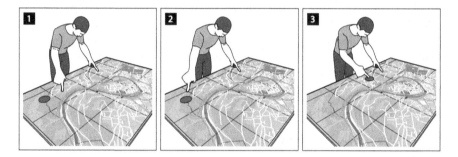

Fig. 3. (1) A red anchor is added to the SCREEN of the tabletop. (2) The index of the right hand is LINKED to the anchor. (3) The anchor is moved and the arm follows. (Color figure online)

Anchors. We define an ANCHOR as a point on an object that can be used to constrain the posture of another 3D object (*e.g.* a hand model). For example, ANCHORS allow users to specify a contact point on a display, attach a specific finger of a hand model to it, and then to modify the location of this contact while preserving the kinematic constraints of the hand (i.e., *Esquisse* makes sure that the fingers are touching the ANCHOR points with a realistic hand posture when reachable).

Once in ANCHOR mode, anchors can be added on any object (*e.g.* a screen) by clicking on the desired locations on the object. The user then links anchors to parts of another another object (*e.g.* fingertips of a hand). The anchors define constrains between the two objects that are then used by the Blender inverse kinematic solver to compute the position and orientation of the armature when the anchors are moved in 3D. *Esquisse* also provides a mode to move a linked object with the anchors, to avoid changing the current pose of the armature.

Fingers Flexion and Extension. The manipulation of non-anchored fingers may remain difficult [4, 32], therefore *Esquisse* provides two specific controls for modifying hand poses. Inspired by Achibet *et al.* who control the pose of a virtual hand using sliders on a tablet [4], we added slider controls to manipulate the flexion of every finger of our hand model. Changing the value of a slider updates the flexion of the corresponding finger in the 3D scene in real time by adjusting the orientation of each bone of the finger. This method allows users to rapidly modify hand poses, for instance to describe a mid-air gestural vocabulary.

We also implemented a LeapMotion integration so the hand posture can be demonstrated. Similarly, body postures could be demonstrated using a Kinect like in DemoDraw [9].

4.4 Snap to Camera Point of View

In Blender cameras can be moved and rotated like any other object. As rotations can be difficult to perform, we implemented a feature to snap the camera object to the current viewport position. In this way the user can simply move the viewport to the desired point of view and then 'teleport' the camera so it matches its location and orientation.

4.5 Stroboscopic Effect

Esquisse allows users to generate stroboscopic figures, used to convey the movement of objects over time [27], by rendering each step with an increasing amount of transparency (C7 in our taxonomy). Once the scene is set up (Fig. 4, top left), the user can enter in stroboscopic mode by clicking on the appropriate button in the interface. This allows users to define different *keyframes*, each saving the positions of all the current objects in the scene. *Esquisse* uses keyframes to detect the objects that moved and create a version of the corresponding objects (i.e. a copy of the objects displayed in wireframe) as illustrated Fig. 4, top right (a keyframe version of the anchor and the linked hand are created when the anchor is moved). Keyframe objects can also be manipulated in the scene if necessary. Additional frames can be defined between keyframes in *Esquisse* using linear interpolation (see Fig. 4, bottom left, where two steps are defined using interpolation).

All of the presented techniques in this section are designed to allow users inexperienced with 3D modelling softwares to rapidly stage a scene with 3D models. Most importantly, the techniques allow rapid iteration and experimentation (e.g., quickly changing the posture of a hand or camera view of the scene), something that is not possible to do when manually creating trace figures.

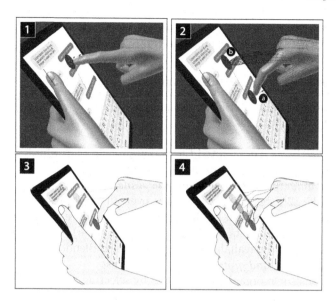

Fig. 4. (1) The index of the right hand is linked to a red anchor. (2) As soon as the hand moves in stroboscopic mode (a), a wireframe version of the object is created (b). (3) *Esquisse* rendering of the scene. (4) *Esquisse* rendering of the scene when 2 additional frames are defined by interpolation between the two keyframes.

5   Esquisse Rendering Process

From the 3D scene, *Esquisse* is rendering vector images focusing on the contours of the objects. One important requirement of our rendering approach is to create closed contours only, so users can modify if they want the rendered objects in a vector graphics editing software afterwards (*e.g.* moving objects or modifying the colour or opacity of an object).

A first possible approach consists in propagating virtual points along the edges of an object mesh, by considering their visibility, to form the contours of the 3D object [17]. Unfortunately, this technique requires a high mesh density to accurately compute meshes' visibility, which yields to time consuming renderings. A second approach [12] consists in building a view map assigning properties to edges and then extracting contours by selecting specific edges based on their nature and visibility in order to chain them to form strokes. Unfortunately, extracted contours are split in several strokes which can be problematic to produce accurate polygons filling in a vector-based format. A third approach consists in creating layers containing full objects with the most effective cuts [10]. This facilitates the edition of SVGs in a graphics editing software but at a cost of longer rendering times to compute the depth order of the different layers.

As a result we chose to adapt the approach proposed by Eisemann *et al.* [11] which provides fill regions support by using the 2D arrangement package of the

CGAL[8] library to extract 2D regions formed by 2D strokes. In that way, it is possible to extract at the same time line contours and fill polygons.

5.1   Esquisse 3D to SVG Rendering

This section explains how paths are calculated and how the final SVG rendering is performed.

From 3D to 2D Paths We adapted the two approaches introduced in [11,12] to our needs and implemented them in Blender as follows.

Step 1: *Computing a view map for the scene*
Similarly to [11,12], the first step iterates over all the edges of the objects to build a view map of the scene, by characterizing the *nature* of each edge (crease, silhouette, etc.) as well as its *visiblity* (visible or hidden). We use the Freestyle implementation already available as an extension in Blender.

Step 2: *Selecting and grouping edges of interest*
Second step consists in organizing the edges by selecting all the edges that correspond to a SILHOUETTE, CONTOUR or a CREASE, and to group them depending on their visibility. Note that keeping hidden edges is crucial as it can be required to illustrate some interactive scenarios (typically instances of back-of-device interaction).

Step 3: *Computing and associating filling regions*
Once all the edges of interest of the different objects have been grouped, we compute the regions formed by the 2D projection of the visible ones. As [11], we use the *2D arrangement* package provided by CGAL, which provides the regions formed by the 2D projection of the edges.

Step 4: *Associating 2D regions to their corresponding 3D objects*
We associate a region to its corresponding object in the scene by picking for a random point inside the region (using the GPC library[9]) and raycasting this point to the 3D scene to identify the corresponding 3D object. This step is used to group regions of a same object, as well as select a default filling colour for each region.

From Paths to SVG Rendering. The SVG file produced by *Esquisse* comprises two main layers, one for fillings and visible strokes, and a second for hidden strokes (which must be drawn on top of fills to be visible). The first layer contains one sublayer per object grouping all its fillings and visible strokes, which eases the postediting using other softwares. The line style used for each type of contour, as well as the colour of each object can also be specified by the user in the *Esquisse* interface. Filled contour layers are produced to avoid stroke layers from overlapping.

Generating Filled Contours Containing Holes. To appear as a hole, the points of the inside contour have to be oriented counter-clockwise while the points of the outer contour should be clockwise[10] for a *non-zero* fill rule. As CGAL

---

[8] https://www.cgal.org.
[9] http://www.cs.man.ac.uk/~toby/gpc/.
[10] https://www.w3.org/TR/SVG/painting.html.

2D arrangement package returns regions under a hierarchy, regions inside other regions can be considered as holes and thus, be drawn in a counter-clockwise way.

Projecting UIs on Screens. Our algorithm also needs to project possible images of graphical user interfaces on their corresponding screens in the 3D scene. For that, we use numpy linear algebra solver to compute the planar homography from the four corners of the user interface to the four corners of the screen object in the scene. However, considering SVG does not currently support perspective matrix transformations, we apply the homography to all the geometric objects of the user interface by computing the new coordinates. Some elements like ellipses, arcs or text first need to be discretized into segments or Bezier curves in order to be projected. All the projected elements are then grouped and a clipping path is applied to this group using the visible contours of the screen object, in order to avoid overlapping artefacts (*e.g.* a finger in front of the smartphone's display).

Rendering a Stroboscopic Figure. To render a stroboscopic figure, we adapt the rendering pipeline as follows. First, it computes the four rendering steps for each keyframe. Then it iterates over these keyframes and computes the SVG rendering for an object only if it has moved since the previous keyframe.

Doing multiple renderings implies having multiple contours for some of the objects (keyframes and final), and thus, requires to carefully choose the z-index of each object in the SVG file.

First, all objects that did not move in the scene are positioned with a low z-index. Then, we iterate over each keyframe and draw its objects with increased transparency and z-index.

Note that these modifications marginally deter rendering time, which remains below 5 s for the Figs. 3 and 4, when running on the i7 4 GHz computer described in the study section.

6   Study: Illustrating Interactions

We evaluated *Esquisse* by asking HCI students and researchers to produce visual illustrations of interaction techniques from the literature using our tool.

6.1   Method

Participants and Apparatus. We recruited 8 participants ($\bar{x}=33$, $\sigma=10$), all researchers in HCI. Three were academic researchers, three PhD students and two Post-graduate students. None of these participants had previous experience with the Blender software. The experiment was conducted with Blender v2.79 with the *Esquisse* add-on installed, running on an iMac 27' 5K display with i7 4Ghz. Three input devices were available: a Logitech G9 Laser computer mouse, an Apple Magic Trackpad 2 and a LeapMotion. Adobe Illustrator and Inkscape were also installed and available to use at anytime if the participants wanted to complete the vector graphics file produced with *Esquisse*.

Procedure. Participants were invited to sit in front of the computer and were instructed that the experiment consisted in producing trace figures. We first showed them a set of trace figures extracted from the taxomony to clearly explain what trace figures are. After this introduction, we introduced the main task which consisted in illustrating one interaction technique from a set of four published in the HCI community (AuraSense [37], Put-that-there [5], TiltReduction [7] and Stitching [15]) that were described using the original accompanying videos. We chose these interaction techniques because they rely on a variety of devices (*e.g.* smartphone, smartwatch, large display) and input modalities (device motion, touch, skin and speech input).

Participants were first presented with a 10 min long video explaining Blender basic controls and Esquisse features, and were then given 30 min to illustrate one interaction using Esquisse. They were also told that they could edit the produced SVG file afterwards with a graphics editing software.

Since the experiment's main focus was not the production of 2D interfaces, we provided a set of 2D interfaces associated to the 4 interaction techniques, to be used as screen interfaces. We measured the time it took participants to create the tracing figure (up to 30 min) and made observer notes about the strategy used by each participant. This experiment employed a *think aloud* protocol [23] encouraging participants to comment on *Esquisse* while producing the illustration. Figures produced by the participants can be found as additional material to this paper.

6.2   Interaction and Strategy in *Esquisse*

Templates. All participants but two started their illustration using one of the predefined templates. Interestingly, the two participants who did not [P3, P8] were producing illustrations for *Stitching* which consists of a pen gesture spanning over two interactive tablets, a situation for which *Esquisse* does not provide a template for. Both P3 and P8 manually added two mobile devices and one right hand with a stylus and placed them in the scene. In the other cases, *Esquisse* provides predefined templates close enough to the interactions to illustrate.

Anchors. As for templates, all participants used anchors except the two participants who had to illustrate *Stitching* [P3, P8]. In this case, all participants adopted a similar workflow: they simply moved the right hand with the stylus over the two devices on an axis without using anchors. Interestingly, one of these participants wanted to anchor the stylus [P8], which is not available in *Esquisse* but could be quickly implemented. His idea was to put an anchor on the tablet screen, then link the anchor to the stylus tip, and so, moving the stylus and the hand at the same time when moving the anchor. Overall, all participants understood and adopted the use of anchors very quickly.

Stroboscopic Effect. All participants but one used the stroboscopic feature of *Esquisse* in order to illustrate motion. Two of them [P1,P2] who had to illustrate *AuraSense* used the interpolation feature in order to generate additional frames between the two defined keyframes. Once again, these participants exhibited a similar workflow, positioning the right hand with an anchor, adding a keyframe, moving the right hand to a different position and then set the interpolations. The participant who did not use the stroboscopic effect [P5], considered himself as figure expert, and did it intentionally to build instead a storyboard-like figure for *TiltReduction* using 3 distinct illustrations.

3D Manipulations. All participants but two used the anchoring system and the 3-axis translation manipulator to make all the displacements they wanted, without expressing difficulties. The only two participants [P5, P6] who rotated objects during staging had to illustrate *TiltReduction*, which involves a rotation from the wrist to tilt a smartphone. One of them [P6] was the only participant who had difficulties with Esquisse and failed to create what he wanted, commenting that *"3D manipulations are too difficult for me"*. That being said, he ignored easier alternative strategies that could be used to rotate objects, such as anchoring all the fingers to force the hand pose, only move the camera to a different point of view, or to use the Leap Motion. The latter was adopted by [P5] to more easily change the hand orientation. Overall, only two participants used the Leap Motion for changing the hand posture, the other one [P2] was illustrating *AuraSense* and used it to define an index pointing posture for the right hand. Finally, all the participants used the camera snapping functionality and no one moved using the 3-axis manipulator.

SVG Post-editing. While all participants were invited to do so, only three participants [P4, P5, P7] post-edited the figure produced with *Esquisse* in a vector-grahics editing software. While two performed only minor adjustments, [P5] built a 3 images storyboard and overlaid an arrow depicting motion over one figure.

6.3   Participants Subjective Feedback

Learning and Use. Overall, participants appreciated *Esquisse*, reporting that it was *"easy to use and fun"* [P4, P5, P8] and *"fast"* [P5, P7, P8], even if *Esquisse* requires a learning phase for objects manipulation and Blender interface [P1, P3, P8]. Participants quickly understood all the functionalities by just watching the 10 min tutorial video [P1, P3, P4, P5]. Even better, [P1] was *"impressed"* and said it was *"fast to learn and master the different functionalities"*, making *Esquisse* *"interesting considering [his] poor artistic skills"*.

Post Editing. Globally, participants were satisfied with the *Esquisse* rendering results, but some still prefer to refine the figure afterwards in a graphics editing software [P4, P5, P7]. More importantly, participants saw *Esquisse* as a rapid prototyping tool *"for making quick illustrations using complex objects to be modified afterwards"* [P5, P7].

Improvements. Participants were enthusiastic with *Esquisse* and commented on several additional features that could enrich its functionalities. [P2] commented that the capacity to control any object of the scene using motion sensing (as Yoon *et al.* did with a smartphone [35]) could be useful to make 3D staging even easier. [P4] would have liked to identify the keyframes objects in the scene, for example by using a different colour or a number associated to the keyframe index. [P8] commented that the ability to modify a User Interface file within *Esquisse* directly in the scene would optimize the workflow. Finally, two participants [P5, P8] commented that the capacity to overlay arrows *"between here and there"* directly within *Esquisse*, either using the anchors or optionally displaying arrows between the keyframes, would remove the need to open the produced SVG file in a graphics-editing software afterwards. These suggested improvements are not challenging and will be implemented in the future versions of *Esquisse*.

7   Discussion and Conclusion

Trace figures are powerful and frequently used materials for illustrating HCI research papers. Based on a characterization of trace figures used in the HCI community, we designed *Esquisse*, a tool that implements a novel workflow based on 3D objects manipulation to stage a 3D scene and export it as a vector trace figure. We contributed interaction techniques to facilitate this workflow (including the use of anchor points to help the manipulation of complex articulated objects such as hands and the integration of stroboscopic effects) and a rendering pipeline to extract the different contours, fill them and finally generate a vector-based SVG file. We implemented *Esquisse* as an add-on for the open source 3D modelling software Blender and evaluated its usability in a qualitative experiment with 8 participants. The results of this experiment suggest that users, even when not familiar with Blender nor used to produce trace figures, managed to quickly produce trace figures illustrating interaction techniques from the literature with little to no experience in the production of trace figures or use of a 3D modelling software.

Esquisse thus provides an alternative workflow to produce trace figures, that can be used by users who believe they do not have the skills required to perform manual photo-tracing. *Esquisse* can also benefit users who usually rely on manual photo-tracing, for instance, as a rapid-prototyping tool as reported by participants in our experiment. A 3D scene staged with *Esquisse* can also be exported *as is* as a model for manual photo-tracing, which could be useful in situations where one has to illustrate a "complex and heavy" interactive scenario (for instance involving tabletops, large displays, several users, etc.) without having to prepare the physical setup required to take a photo of the scene.

There are limitations when using *Esquisse*. Typically, while adding models to *Esquisse* is as easy as adding a scene to its template sub-folder, designing these templates still need basic 3D modeling and staging skills. We anticipate that in the future, progress in computer vision and computer graphics research will allow to extract 3D objects from a photography to automatically create templates [8, 20, 36].

An aspect of *Esquisse* that can be seen as both an advantage or a drawback is that it has been implemented as a Blender add-on. We made this decision because Blender provides a solid environment for 3D modelling and object manipulation that *Esquisse* benefits from, as well as because it simplifies its distribution and maintenance. Because of this, however, the interaction with *Esquisse* is constrained by what the Blender environment allows add-ons to do (e.g., the design of the user interface for add-ons is limited). In that respect, we designed *Esquisse* by trying to provide the best user experience and interaction that Blender allowed us to design. For example, we added dedicated slider controls to ease the definition of hand and body poses and implemented a direct Leap-Motion integration to help users to manipulate hand poses. Similarly, inspired by DemoDraw [9], we plan to implement a Microsoft Kinect integration to ease the manipulation of body poses.

Most trace figures overlay meta annotations (such as texts or arrows). Besides contact points, *Esquisse* does not currently support a way to add these annotations and the user still has to open the produced SVG file in a graphic editing software to add them afterwards. However, meta annotation are usually simple geometric shapes or text layers that should be straightforward to integrate in the add-on. Adding meta-annotation support to *Esquisse* could be added by mimicking how anchors are currently added: the meta-annotation would be a shape or text that would be positioned over an invisible plan that would not be rendered when the SVG file is produced.

We hope our open-source release of *Esquisse* will help the production of trace figures that are gaining popularity in the HCI community as they are effective in capturing the essence of interactive scenarios.

References

1. UIST 2015: Proceedings of the 28th Annual ACM Symposium on User Interface Software and Technology. ACM, New York (2015)
2. UIST 2016: Proceedings of the 29th Annual Symposium on User Interface Software and Technology. ACM, New York (2016)
3. UIST 2017: Proceedings of the 30th Annual ACM Symposium on User Interface Software and Technology. ACM, New York (2017)
4. Achibet, M., Casiez, G., Lécuyer, A., Marchal, M.: Thing: introducing a tablet-based interaction technique for controlling 3D hand models. In: Proceedings of the 33rd Annual ACM Conference on Human Factors in Computing Systems, CHI 2015, pp. 317–326. ACM, New York (2015). https://doi.org/10.1145/2702123.2702158
5. Bolt, R.A.: Put-that-there: voice and gesture at the graphics interface. In: Proceedings of the 7th Annual Conference on Computer Graphics and Interactive Techniques, SIGGRAPH 1980, pp. 262–270. ACM, New York (1980). https://doi.org/10.1145/800250.807503
6. Canny, J.: A computational approach to edge detection. In: Readings in Computer Vision, pp. 184–203. Elsevier (1987)

7. Chang, Y., L'Yi, S., Koh, K., Seo, J.: Understanding users' touch behavior on large mobile touch-screens and assisted targeting by tilting gesture. In: Proceedings of the 33rd Annual ACM Conference on Human Factors in Computing Systems, CHI 2015, pp. 1499–1508. ACM, New York (2015). https://doi.org/10.1145/2702123. 2702425

8. Chen, T., Zhu, Z., Shamir, A., Hu, S.M., Cohen-Or, D.: 3-sweep: extracting editable objects from a single photo. ACM Trans. Graph. (TOG) **32**(6), 195 (2013)

9. Chi, P.Y.P., Vogel, D., Dontcheva, M., Li, W., Hartmann, B.: Authoring illustrations of human movements by iterative physical demonstration. In: Proceedings of the 29th Annual Symposium on User Interface Software and Technology, UIST 2016, pp. 809–820. ACM, New York (2016). https://doi.org/10.1145/2984511.2984559

10. Eisemann, E., Paris, S., Durand, F.: A visibility algorithm for converting 3D meshes into editable 2D vector graphics. In: ACM SIGGRAPH 2009 Papers, SIGGRAPH 2009. pp. 83:1–83:8. ACM, New York (2009). https://doi.org/10.1145/1576246. 1531389

11. Eisemann, E., Winnemöller, H., Hart, J.C., Salesin, D.: Stylized vector art from 3D models with region support. In: Computer Graphics Forum, vol. 27, pp. 1199–1207. Wiley Online Library (2008)

12. Grabli, S., Turquin, E., Durand, F., Sillion, F.X.: Programmable style for NPR line drawing. In: Proceedings of the Fifteenth Eurographics Conference on Rendering Techniques, EGSR 2004, Aire-la-Ville, Switzerland, pp. 33–44. Eurographics Association, Switzerland (2004). https://doi.org/10.2312/EGWR/EGSR04/033-044

13. Han, J., Lee, G.: Push-push: a drag-like operation overlapped with a page transition operation on touch interfaces. In: Proceedings of the 28th Annual ACM Symposium on User Interface Software & Technology, UIST 2015, pp. 313–322. ACM, New York (2015). https://doi.org/10.1145/2807442.2807457

14. Hess, R.: The Essential Blender: Guide to 3D Creation with the Open Source Suite Blender. No Starch Press, San Francisco (2007)

15. Hinckley, K., Ramos, G., Guimbretiere, F., Baudisch, P., Smith, M.: Stitching: pen gestures that span multiple displays. In: Proceedings of the Working Conference on Advanced Visual Interfaces, AVI 2004, pp. 23–31. ACM, New York (2004). https:// doi.org/10.1145/989863.989866

16. Huang, D., Zhang, X., Saponas, T.S., Fogarty, J., Gollakota, S.: Leveraging dual-observable input for fine-grained thumb interaction using forearm EMG. In: Proceedings of the 28th Annual ACM Symposium on User Interface Software & Technology, UIST 2015, pp. 523–528. ACM, New York (2015). https://doi.org/10.1145/2807442.2807506

17. Karsch, K., Hart, J.C.: Snaxels on a plane. In: Proceedings of the ACM SIGGRAPH/Eurographics Symposium on Non-Photorealistic Animation and Rendering, NPAR 2011, pp. 35–42. ACM, New York (2011). https://doi.org/10.1145/2024676.2024683

18. Kazi, R.H., Chevalier, F., Grossman, T., Fitzmaurice, G.: Kitty: sketching dynamic and interactive illustrations. In: Proceedings of the 27th Annual ACM Symposium on User Interface Software and Technology, UIST 2014, pp. 395–405. ACM, New York (2014). https://doi.org/10.1145/2642918.2647375

19. Kazi, R.H., Chevalier, F., Grossman, T., Zhao, S., Fitzmaurice, G.: Draco: sketching animated drawings with kinetic textures. In: ACM SIGGRAPH 2014 Posters, SIGGRAPH 2014, pp. 5:1–5:1. ACM, New York (2014). https://doi.org/10.1145/2614217.2614221

20. Kholgade, N., Simon, T., Efros, A., Sheikh, Y.: 3D object manipulation in a single photograph using stock 3D models. ACM Trans. Graph. (TOG) **33**(4), 127 (2014)

21. Kim, H.J., Kim, C.M., Nam, T.J.: SketchStudio: experience prototyping with 2.5-dimensional animated design scenarios. In: Proceedings of the 2018 Designing Interactive Systems Conference, DIS 2018, pp. 831–843. ACM, New York (2018). https://doi.org/10.1145/3196709.3196736

22. Lander, C., Gehring, S., Krüger, A., Boring, S., Bulling, A.: GazeProjector: accurate gaze estimation and seamless gaze interaction across multiple displays. In: Proceedings of the 28th Annual ACM Symposium on User Interface Software & Technology, UIST 2015, pp. 395–404. ACM, New York (2015). https://doi.org/10.1145/2807442.2807479

23. Lewis, C., Rieman, J.: Task-Centered User Interface Design. A Practical Introduction (1993)

24. Li, W., Viola, F., Starck, J., Brostow, G.J., Campbell, N.D.F.: Roto++: accelerating professional rotoscoping using shape manifolds. ACM Trans. Graph. **35**(4), 62:1–62:15 (2016). https://doi.org/10.1145/2897824.2925973

25. Lo, J., et al.: Aesthetic electronics: designing, sketching, and fabricating circuits through digital exploration. In: Proceedings of the 29th Annual Symposium on User Interface Software and Technology, UIST 2016, pp. 665–676. ACM, New York (2016). https://doi.org/10.1145/2984511.2984579

26. McAweeney, E., Zhang, H., Nebeling, M.: User-driven design principles for gesture representations. In: Proceedings of the 2018 CHI Conference on Human Factors in Computing Systems, CHI 2018, pp. 547:1–547:13, ACM, New York (2018). https://doi.org/10.1145/3173574.3174121

27. McCloud, S.: Understanding Comics: The Invisible Art (1993)

28. Mortensen, E.N., Barrett, W.A.: Intelligent scissors for image composition. In: Proceedings of the 22Nd Annual Conference on Computer Graphics and Interactive Techniques, SIGGRAPH 1995, pp. 191–198. ACM, New York (1995). https://doi.org/10.1145/218380.218442

29. Nancel, M., Vogel, D., De Araujo, B., Jota, R., Casiez, G.: Next-point prediction metrics for perceived spatial errors. In: Proceedings of the 29th Annual Symposium on User Interface Software and Technology, UIST 2016, pp. 271–285. ACM, New York (2016). https://doi.org/10.1145/2984511.2984590

30. Neufeld, E., Popoola, H., Callele, D., Mould, D.: Mixed initiative interactive edge detection. In: Graphics Interface, pp. 177–184 (2003)

31. Ruiz, J., Li, Y.: DoubleFlip: a motion gesture delimiter for mobile interaction. In: Proceedings of the SIGCHI Conference on Human Factors in Computing Systems, CHI 2011, pp. 2717–2720. ACM, New York (2011). https://doi.org/10.1145/1978942.1979341

32. Wu, Y., Huang, T.S.: Hand modeling, analysis and recognition. IEEE Signal Process. Mag. **18**(3), 51–60 (2001)

33. Xie, J., Hertzmann, A., Li, W., Winnemöller, H.: PortraitSketch: face sketching assistance for novices. In: Proceedings of the 27th Annual ACM Symposium on User Interface Software and Technology, UIST 2014, pp. 407–417. ACM, New York (2014). https://doi.org/10.1145/2642918.2647399

34. Xie, J., Winnemöller, H., Li, W., Schiller, S.: Interactive vectorization. In: Proceedings of the 2017 CHI Conference on Human Factors in Computing Systems, CHI 2017, pp. 6695–6705. ACM, New York (2017). https://doi.org/10.1145/3025453.3025872

35. Yoon, D., Lee, J.H., Yeom, K., Park, J.: Mobiature: 3D model manipulation technique for large displays using mobile devices. In: 2011 IEEE International Conference on Consumer Electronics (ICCE), pp. 495–496, January 2011. https://doi.org/10.1109/ICCE.2011.5722702

36. Zheng, Y., Chen, X., Cheng, M.M., Zhou, K., Hu, S.M., Mitra, N.J.: Interactive images: cuboid proxies for smart image manipulation. ACM Trans. Graph. 31(4), 99–1 (2012)

37. Zhou, J., Zhang, Y., Laput, G., Harrison, C.: AuraSense: enabling expressive around-smartwatch interactions with electric field sensing. In: Proceedings of the 29th Annual Symposium on User Interface Software and Technology, UIST 2016, pp. 81–86. ACM, New York (2016). https://doi.org/10.1145/2984511.2984568

Examining the Effects of Height, Velocity and Emotional Representation of a Social Transport Robot and Human Factors in Human-Robot Collaboration

Jana Jost[1], Thomas Kirks[1(✉)], Stuart Chapman[1], and Gerhard Rinkenauer[2]

[1] Fraunhofer Institute for Material Flow and Logistics,
Joseph-von-Fraunhofer-Str. 2-4, 44227 Dortmund, Germany
{jana.jost,thomas.kirks,stuart.chapman}@iml.fraunhofer.de
[2] Leibniz Research Centre for Working Environment and Human Factors,
Ardeystraße 67, 44139 Dortmund, Germany
rinkenauer@ifado.de

Abstract. In nowadays industrial facilities robots play a major part in assisting the human worker. To ensure an effective process not only safety aspects have to be considered. For increasing the acceptance of humans towards robots, social aspects are important as well. In this paper we examine how the behaviour of humans towards other humans can be adapted to the robots behaviour. Especially, the usage of social rules regarding the distance between people are studied with different robot characteristics for height, velocity and emotional expressions as well as human factors.

Keywords: Empirical studies in HCI · User experience design · Social robots

1 Introduction

Human-robot collaboration (HRC), a field of human-robot interaction (HRI), was established in various work fields. Most robots installed in warehouses are doing monotonous work and are surrounded by fences to ensure the safety of workers. Further, these robots do not mirror human behaviour and therefore cannot correctly be interpreted by the human which leads to discomfort [7]. However, to foster HRC in this field of application, the robot has to move autonomously and react according to its environment including the human. An essential factor for an effective collaboration is that the human feels safe, comfortable and interprets the actions of the robot correctly. A straightforward assumption is that people will approach social robots the same way as they would do with other people, thereby extending the computers are social actors theory [9,19] to HRI. In approaching its user, the social theory of proxemics [9] has to be maintained to this goal. Here, two classifications of "safety" will be scrutinized. The

© IFIP International Federation for Information Processing 2019
Published by Springer Nature Switzerland AG 2019
D. Lamas et al. (Eds.): INTERACT 2019, LNCS 11747, pp. 517–526, 2019.
https://doi.org/10.1007/978-3-030-29384-0_31

physical safety focuses on avoiding collisions and is a decisive requirement for autonomous robots in HRC. The mental safety means ensuring that the robot does not cause fear for people. Mental safety is as important as physical safety [16]. If the presence or actions of the robot cause fear, the human will feel uncomfortable and use avoidance techniques to compensate the behaviour of the robot, although the physical safety is secured. For a pleasant and effective interaction, it is crucial that the robots meet the needs and expectations of the user. In particular, the robot needs to match social norms. In this case the proxemics is examined which can help to ensure mental safety. The examined social robot has the ability to show different faces via a display according to it's state, which plays a major role in human communication [5]. The impact of facial expressions in human and robot interaction has to be analysed. Emotional representations in robotics may add a new element in HRC and can strengthen the acceptance of robots [6]. By giving information about the robot's emotional state, the user will be able to predict the robots behaviour and therefore feel comfortable. The findings may contribute to a change in implementation of social robots in order to realise a better individualisation of robots when interacting with humans in a more personal manner.

2   Background

2.1   Human-Robot-Interaction

Today, robots can be found in various fields of application. Their tasks and capabilities have changed in the last decades from heavy industrial robots to more flexible and cognitive robots [22]. These offer direct interaction with the human without safety equipment and therefore are used also in other applications e.g. surgery [18]. Although the usage of robots in industrial applications is increasing, the human worker will always play a key role [13]. Therefore, the development of new interaction modalities for humans and robots is important.

According to ISO 8373 [12] HRC is defined as the exchange of information or actions between humans and robots to fulfil a given task. It is one interaction form besides cooperation and co-existence in HRI. In HRC humans and robots have the same goal or subgoals, for what coordination methods are needed [18]. For designing robots for HRC one has to consider various guidelines e.g. DIN EN ISO 10218 [8]. Those guidelines focus on safety aspects. Robots available on the market for HRC like ABB Dual-Arm [15] already fulfil the safety criteria but for HRC further issues e.g. psychological ergonomics have to be regarded to maximize the acceptance of humans towards robots.

2.2   Proxemics

As autonomous robots are collaborating with its human colleague, it is important to ensure safety and acceptance of the user. Hall [9] introduced the theory of proxemics and stated that people have distinct spaces surrounding them in elliptic circles. These four spaces are called intimate (0.15 m–0.45 m), personal (0.45 m–1.2 m), social (1.2 m–3.6 m) and public (>3.6 m). Each is defined by the kind of people entering the area. For example, partners and good friends are in the intimate or personal zone, whereas in the social zone acquaintances are positioned. A problem occurs as one enters a space he is not allowed to. The person feels anxious and might use avoidance techniques e.g. distancing himself from the other person. This avoidance behaviour is stated in the intimacy equilibrium model by Argyle [2]. Therefore, the robot needs to detect these zones and react in a manner that the human feels safe and comfortable.

An experiment examining the effects of three robot sizes on anxiety, conducted by Hirori and Ito [10], showed that participants felt more anxious and kept the greatest distance with the tallest robot (1.8 m). Concerning the robot velocity, Sakai et al. [20] revealed that the subjective distance kept to the robot correlated proportionally with the moving speed of the robot. They analysed five velocities ranging from 0.2 m/s to 1.0 m/s. Velocities equal and greater than 0.8 m/s caused anxiety. Ikeura et al. [11] confirmed this by analysing galvanic skin response and evaluating subjective ratings. The main aim of proxemics in HRI focuses on maximizing the user experience and enhancing the productivity of the collaboration. Human factors that determine how people react to approaching robots are their general attitudes towards robots [21], their experience in robotics, gender and age [7]. Other factors that have an impact on the distance between the two agents are the height, the velocity and mutual gaze of the robot.

2.3   Analysis Methods

In the following section the questionnaires will be outlined and general information will be given about these. The User Experience Questionnaire (UEQ), developed by Laugwitz et al. [14], was designed to enable a rapid assessment by the user, based on a comprehensive impression of the user experience. It should enable users to express feelings that arise during the experience with the product in a simple way. The UEQ is a valid method to evaluate how a robot is being perceived by the participants.

Normura and Kanda [17] proposed a concept to measure anxiety towards robots, resulting in the negative attitude towards robots scale (NARS). This scale was successfully used to explain differences in the behaviour of the participants in HRI studies. The Godspeed questionnaire was developed by Bartneck [3] as an HRI-specific measure of participants' perception across multiple dimensions, each one being applied with a set of semantic differential scales. We used the Godspeed questionnaire to measure the participants' perception of the robot.

3   Research Hypotheses

The intention of the socio-technical system, consisting of a social, autonomous transport vehicle (ATV) and the human worker is to provide an agreeable working environment, where the worker can fulfil his tasks and is supported by the

ATV. According to the proxemic concept of Hall [9], we expect that the distance control of humans to a robot is influenced by factors of the robot, which are characterized either by the threat of the own safety or by social aspects. Aspects of safety, for example, refer to the size and speed of the robot, whereas social aspects are influenced by emotional expression. For this reason, we hypothesize the following points:

1. The speed of the robot affects the personal space. Faster robots lead to a greater distance between user and robot than slower ones.
2. The height of the robot affects the personal space. Smaller robots can enter further into the personal space than higher robots.
3. The facial expression of the robot influences the distance kept. A "happy" robot can enter further into the personal space than a sad one (Fig. 1).
4. The last point investigates the difference between human-robot and robot-human approach. The distance kept is smaller if the participant approaches than if the robot does.

4   Methodology

A laboratory experiment was conducted to explore what effects the height, the velocity and the two emotions happiness and sadness have on the distance between a social ATV and the participant.

4.1   Experimental Setup

In this study, the interaction with the social ATV is in the scope of research. It has the size of a small load carrier and is able to drive autonomously. The social ATV is designed for collaborating with human workers. With the integrated scissor lift, the carried load can be extended up to an ergonomic height.

Through webservices, the user can acquire its state or control it via wearables. The ATV has an e-paper display at its front. It displays emoji like faces, pictograms and textual hints to express the state of the robot in a comprehensible way. We are interested if humans notice the change of the emotional expression on its display and further if a significant difference is measurable between the two states, "happy" and "sad" (see Fig. 1(a) and (b)). While the robot expresses emotions in a human-like manner, we are interested if a human-like relationship is being created and social human-human norms are being transferred onto the robot. Further, we investigate the dichotomy between utility and pleasure in the ATV's height. According to ergonomic reasons, the robot can heighten its lift from 220 mm to 820 mm, also while driving. Now the question arises, if the user is pleased or feels uncomfortable and distances himself from the robot or approaches the robot from the side, which may cause longer working operations and decreases usability.

We prepared an area of four by four meters and installed the OptiTrack [1] motion tracking system with multiple cameras to track the ATV and the head

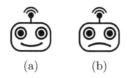

(a)   (b)

Fig. 1. Social ATV's face is either (a) happy or (b) sad

of the participant. Therefore, we attached markers on the ATV's front and the participant is wearing a marker beanie. Hence, with the recorded data from the tracking system the distances between ATV and human can be calculated. Inside the tracking area we installed an optical guidance track on the ground which the ATV uses to follow a straight track to approach the human at different velocities.

4.2 Experimental Procedure

Each participant received an introduction to the anonymised experiment. They could stop the experiment at any time. Before the experiment started, the participants provided their demographic variables. Afterwards, the participants were asked to stand on a specific position in the laboratory setting, which provided a distance of three meters to the ATV. The factors height, velocity and emotion are varied to mitigate an order bias. For example, the ATV is driving with a velocity of 0.4 m/s, an extended lift and represents a happy emotional state. The tasks involve approaching the ATV or being approached in the altered conditions. With a push button, the participant can stop the ATV from approaching in case of discomfort. Figure 2 illustrates the testing environment. During the experiment, the movement of the social ATV as well as of the participant were recorded by using OptiTrack. Since, the ATV is using a new approach of interaction, participants could have a negative tendency towards the technology itself and therefore negative emotions could emerge towards the ATV. Hence, after the experiment, the participant filled in the UEQ "Attractiveness" Scale, NARS and the Godspeed questionnaire.

(a)   (b)

Fig. 2. ATV (left) and test subject (right). (a) retracted lift (b) extended lift

5   Results

Sixteen participants took part in the experiment (3 females, 6 with experience in robotics) and the mean age was 31 (SD = 9.04) years. We analyzed the two conditions separately (robot approaches participant vs. participant approaches robot).

Robot approaches Participant

An ANOVA with the within subject factors velocity (0.4 m/s vs. 0.6 m/s), height (low vs. high) and emotion (happy vs. sad) and the between subject factor robot experience (no, yes) was conducted. In agreement with our hypothesis, the distance was closer when the robot was low (449 mm) than when the robot was high (504 mm), $F(1,14) = 6.13$, $p = .03$. A significant interaction between robot experience and emotion, $F(1,14) = 8.3$, $p = 0.01$, suggests that the influence of the robot's emotional expression is opposite for the two robot experience groups (cf. Fig. 3(a)). Separate ANOVAs for each factor levels of robot experience, however, reveal that the emotion expression of the robot influenced the distance for the participants with no prior robot experience, $F(1,9) = 5.9$, $p = .04$, but showed only a trend for the participants with robot experience, $F(1,5) = 4.6$, $p = .08$. In line with our hypotheses the inexperienced group tolerates a shorter distance of the robot with a happy face. Interestingly, in the experienced group the influence of emotional expression seems to be damped or even inverted. Such a result can also mean, however, that for experienced participants the expressiveness of the facial features was not strong enough. With regard to the speed of the robot, our first hypothesis could not be confirmed, since the speed manipulation is not reflected in the behaviour of the test persons.

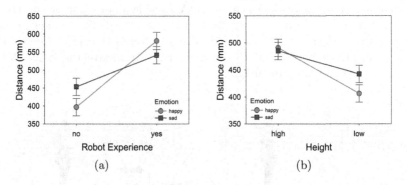

(a)   (b)

Fig. 3. Distance as a function of (a) robot experience and emotion and (b) height and emotion. The error bars represent Fisher's least significant difference (LSD)

Participant Approaches Robot

ANOVAs for the within subject factors height and emotion and the between subject factor robot experience were conducted. Because the approaching velocity of the participants was not manipulated, the factor velocity is not relevant. To compare the situations in which either the participants move towards the robot or the robot moves towards the participants, the within factor movement condition (human vs. robot) was defined. Since the participants approached the robot only slowly, the slow robot movement condition (0.4 m/s) was chosen as comparison. Again a significant main effect of factor height is revealed in the expected direction, $F(1,14) = 9.7$, $p < .01$ (cf. Fig. 3(b)). The interaction between emotion and height just failed to be significant, $F(1,4) = 4.7$, $p = .057$. Figure 3(b) depicts this interaction, whereby the mean values suggest that the emotional expression of the robot only affects the distance of the low robot, viz. the distance to the happy robot was shorter.

Finally, the analysis of variance revealed a three-way interaction, $F(1,14) = 4.7$, $p = .049$, which is depicted in Fig. 4. This results suggest different patterns for the two robot experience groups. Separate ANOVAs for the two groups revealed no significant effects of factor height and movement condition for the experienced group, p's $> .1$, which may also be due to the low statistical power because of the small group size. For the inexperienced group there is a main effect for the factor height, $F(1,9) = 7.8$, $p = .02$, viz. for the low robot a closer distance is tolerated. Furthermore, there was a trend for the interaction of movement condition and height, $F(1,9) = 3.4$, $p = .097$, which may suggest that the distance control for the low and high robot size differs when the participants move towards the robot in comparison when the robot approaches the participants. In sum, the analyses of the moving participants in comparison to the moving robot provide additional insights into the HRI. The results suggest that the influence of the emotional expression of the robot on the proximity behaviour of the participants depends on the height of the robot. Furthermore, people who have no prior experience with robots seem to be more sensitive in regulating their distance as a function of robot height when moving towards the robot than people who have already prior experience.

The results of the "Attractiveness Scale" of the UEQ revealed a positive rating of the robot (Mean = 0.83, SD = 0.64, CI = [0.48, 1,18]). Overall, the robot was rated as sympathetic and friendly. Analysis of NARS "Negative Attitudes toward Situations and Interactions with Robots" suggests rather positive attitudes in our experimental situation towards the robot, Mean = 3.7, SD = 0.8, CI = [3.3, 4.1]. The analysis of "Negative Attitude toward Social Influence of Robots" revealed a rather neutral attitude of the participants with regard to the social influence, Mean = 3.0, SD = 0.7, CI = [2.7, 3.4]. The reversed "Negative Attitudes toward Emotions in Interaction with Robots" suggests also a rather neutral attitude towards the robot used in this study, M = 3.0, SD = 0.7, CI = [2.6, 3.4]. The Godspeed survey is divided into four factors: perceived safety (Mean = 3.5, SD = 0.5, CI = [3.3, 3.8]), likeability (Mean = 4.0, SD = 0.6, CI = [3.7, 4.3]), anthropomorphism (Mean = 2.5, SD = 0.8, CI = [2.0, 2.9]) and animacy (Mean = 2.8, SD = 0.5, CI = [2.5, 3.1]). In sum, the subjective ratings

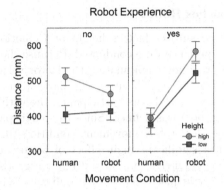

Fig. 4. Distance as a function of movement condition, height and robot experience. The error bars represent Fisher's LSD.

suggest that the robot rated rather sympathetic and pleasant. The perceived safety was slightly positive and the likeability scale supports the findings from the UEQ that the robot was perceived as a rather convenient interaction partner but, however, not as a human counterpart.

6 Discussion

The factors are discussed in an order according to the importance of the findings. As stated in other studies, several factors of the robot and the personal background of the human have impact on the distance kept. The main factor in our study influencing the distance has been the height of the robot. Participants kept smaller distances to the robot with retracted lift (448 mm) than with extended lift (503 mm). Therefore, the second hypothesis can be confirmed whereas the first hypothesis cannot be verified. One reason could be that the given velocities were not fast enough (see findings [20]). Our fourth assumption refers to the approaches, robot approaching human vs. human approaching robot. As a result, people kept smaller distances, when they approached the ATV. According to prior robotic experience, the analysis revealed that participants kept greater distance to the robot. Without robotic experience, the facial representation of the social ATV played a role. They were excited to collaborate with a robot whereas people with robotic experience tended to show less excitement and might payed no attention to the display. This is only valid as the ATV does not extend its lift. When extended, the facial expressions had no influence, because people focused on the highest point of the ATV and ignored the display. Therefore, the third hypothesis can just partially be validated. According to the social theory of proxemics, the robot entered the personal space, in some cases even the intimate space. The intimate zone is supposed for familiar people. This may be caused by the appearance of the ATV. The factor "Attractiveness" of the UEQ was rated pleasant and likeable and as we know people tend to decrease the distance to agents they like. These findings are supported by the results of the Godspeed Questionnaire. Participants felt secure and found the robot likeable.

7 Conclusion and Outlook

In conclusion, we gained insights in how the social ATV is being perceived and could adjust the design and behaviour of it to optimize the collaboration with the human worker. The height influences the distance kept to the robot whereas the chosen velocities do not affect it. Small effects have been found between the two emotional representations. This is caused by the position of the display and the experience of the participant with robots. To communicate with its surrounding the display should always be at the highest position. Further, the facial features need to be stronger for experienced people.

The next steps in evaluating the interaction between the social robot and its user is to abstract design guidelines concerning the appearance of social robots in HRC. For this reason, further theoretical concepts regarding emotion regulation, such as emotional reactivity, should also be considered [4]. Furthermore, we consider to evaluate the multiple interaction modalities, like speech recognition and gesture control with mobile devices such as tablets or smartphones, and test them in usability tests. Concerning proxemics, the minimum distance in which the user is willing or feels comfortable to communicate with the ATV or the user notices the display of it in the first place, has to be identified. We will conduct this experiment in a real-world industrial case study. Since the robot's appearance may be compared to pets, we also think about including questions of preliminary experience about and ownership of pets in the questionnaire.

References

1. Optitrack motion capture system. http://optitrack.com/
2. Argyle, M., Dean, J.: Eye-contact, distance and affiliation. Sociometry **28**(3), 289–304 (1965). http://www.jstor.org/stable/2786027
3. Bartneck, C., Croft, E., Kulic, D.: Measurement instruments for the anthropomorphism, animacy, likeability, perceived intelligence, and perceived safety of robots. Int. J. Soc. Robot. **1**(1), 71–81 (2009). https://doi.org/10.1007/s12369-008-0001-3
4. Becerra, R., Campitelli, G.: Emotional reactivity: critical analysis and proposal of a new scale. Int/ J. Appl. Psychol. **3**(6), 161–168 (2013). https://doi.org/10.5923/j.ijap.20130306.03
5. Boyle, E., Anderson, A., Newlands, A.: The effects of visibility on dialog and performance in a cooperative problem-solving task. Lang. Speech **37**, 1–20 (1994)
6. Breazeal, C.: Affective interaction between humans and robots. In: Kelemen, J., Sosík, P. (eds.) ECAL 2001. LNCS (LNAI), vol. 2159, pp. 582–591. Springer, Heidelberg (2001). https://doi.org/10.1007/3-540-44811-X_66
7. Butler, J.T., Agah, A.: Psychological effects of behavior patterns of a mobile personal robot. Auton. Robots **10**(2), 185–202 (2001). https://doi.org/10.1023/A:1008986004181
8. Deutsches Institut für Normung: DIN EN ISO 10218:2012 Industrieroboter - Sicherheitsanforderungen (2012)

9. Hall, E.: The hidden dimension. Doubleday Anchor Books, Doubleday (1966). https://books.google.de/books?id=u-wyAAAAMAAJ

10. Hiroi, Y., Ito, A.: Are bigger robots scary? The relationship between robot size and psychological threat. In: 2008 IEEE/ASME International Conference on Advanced Intelligent Mechatronics, pp. 546–551 (2008). https://doi.org/10.1109/AIM.2008.4601719

11. Ikeura, R., Otsuka, H., Inooka, H.: Study on emotional evaluation of robot motions based on galvanic skin reflex. Jpn. J. Ergon. **31**(5), 355–358 (1995). https://doi.org/10.5100/jje.31.355

12. International Organization for Standardization: ISO 8373:2012–03 Robots and robotic devices - Vocabulary (2012)

13. Jost, J., Kirks, T., Mättig, B., Sinsel, A., Trapp, T.U.: Der Mensch in der Industrie – Innovative Unterstützung durch augmented reality. In: Vogel-Heuser, B., Bauernhansl, T., ten Hompel, M. (eds.) Handbuch Industrie 4.0 Bd.1. SRT, pp. 153–174. Springer, Heidelberg (2017). https://doi.org/10.1007/978-3-662-45279-0_86

14. Laugwitz, B., Held, T., Schrepp, M.: Construction and evaluation of a user experience questionnaire. In: Holzinger, A. (ed.) USAB 2008. LNCS, vol. 5298, pp. 63–76. Springer, Heidelberg (2008). https://doi.org/10.1007/978-3-540-89350-9_6

15. Matthias, B., Ding, H., Miegel, V.: Die Zukunft der Mensch-Roboter Kollaboration in der industriellen Montage (2013)

16. Mutlu, B., Forlizzi, J., Hodgins, J.: A storytelling robot: modeling and evaluation of human-like gaze behavior. In: 2006 6th IEEE-RAS International Conference on Humanoid Robots, pp. 518–523, December 2006. https://doi.org/10.1109/ICHR.2006.321322

17. Nomura, T., Kanda, T., Suzuki, T., Kato, K.: Psychology in human-robot communication: an attempt through investigation of negative attitudes and anxiety toward robots. In: 2004 IEEE International Workshop on Robot and Human Interactive Interactive Communication, Kurashiki, Okayama, Japan, pp. 35–40, September 2004

18. Onnasch, L., Maier, X., Jürgensohn, T.: Mensch-Roboter-Interaktion - Eine Taxonomie für alle Anwendungsfälle., baua:Fokus, vol. 1 (2016)

19. Reeves, B., Nass, C.: The media equation: how people treat computers, television, and new media like real people and places (1996)

20. Sakai, T., Nakajima, H., Nishimura, D., Uematsu, H., Kitano, Y.: Autonomous mobile robot system for delivery in hospital. Technical report of Matsushita Electric Works, vol. 53, no. 2, pp. 62–67 (2005)

21. Syrdal, D.S., Dautenhahn, K., Koay, K.L., Walters, M.L.: The negative attitudes towards robots scale and reactions to robot behaviour in a live human-robot interaction study (2009)

22. Weber, M.: Mensch-Roboter-Kollaboration (2001). https://www.arbeitswissenschaft.net/fileadmin/Downloads/Angebote_und_Produkte/Zahlen_Daten_Fakten/ifaa_Zahlen_Daten_Fakten_MRK.pdf

Towards Participatory Design of Social Robots

Aduén Darriba Frederiks[1]([✉]), Johanna Renny Octavia[1], Cesar Vandevelde[2], and Jelle Saldien[1,2]

[1] imec-mict, Ghent University, Miriam Makebaplein 1, Ghent, Belgium
info@mict.be, aduen.darribafrederiks@ugent.be
[2] Department of Industrial Systems Engineering and Product Design, Ghent University, Graaf Karel de Goedelaan 5, 8500 Kortrijk, Belgium
http://mict.be

Abstract. With an increase in research and development of social robotics and commercial robots entering the market, there is a need for design tools that enable non-experts to design, build and use customized social robots. Human Computer Interaction researchers have a rich evolving tool-set when it comes to user-centered design. To encourage the use of user-centered design techniques in early design iterations of social robots, we propose the use of Opsoro. We present a case study which exhibits participatory design sessions using a Do-It-Yourself platform to enable the creation of social robots with non-experts.

Keywords: Social robots · Do-It-Yourself · Participatory design · Toolkit · Open source

1 Introduction

Recent years have been characterized by an increased interest in robotics, and analysts have steadily pointed at robotics as one of the next big trends in technology. Gradually, robotics research has shifted its attention from robots that function within their own predefined space to robots that coexist with humans in the human's natural habitats. In conjunction, the research domain shifted from technological to a multidisciplinary form including social sciences. This new paradigm in robotics is focused on creating meaningful interactions with their contextual surrounding. This resulted in the study of social robotics, a field that is concerned with natural interaction between robots and humans. Social robots are robots that can communicate using social affordances [4] that we find intuitive, for example through body posture, facial expressions, speech, and gaze.

A coincidental trend shaping and disrupting our modern society is the revival of the Do-It-Yourself (DIY) paradigm. Contemporary DIY trends, such as the maker movement and the open source hardware movement, draw attention to

© IFIP International Federation for Information Processing 2019
Published by Springer Nature Switzerland AG 2019
D. Lamas et al. (Eds.): INTERACT 2019, LNCS 11747, pp. 527–535, 2019.
https://doi.org/10.1007/978-3-030-29384-0_32

the empowering feeling of making things. We should not restrict ourselves to being just consumers of technology, but that we should also become creators of technology in order to shape the world around us. These trends have been responsible for democratizing previously complex technology, including social robotics technology, in a creative, hands-on setting. Many engineering challenges that were considered extremely difficult in the past can now be accomplished with the help of open designs and off-the-shelf parts. However, it is not obvious to rapidly design DIY custom social robots. It generally requires a great amount of time, effort and relevant prior knowledge of the designer.

The work described in this paper is situated at the intersection of three trends: robotics, DIY and Participatory Design (PD). Our work foresees the possibility of providing a DIY platform to support the PD process when designing and creating custom social robots. This paper discusses how Opsoro, is used to facilitate the PD sessions conducted to design customs social robots, which we demonstrated in a case study. Through Opsoro as an (online) platform approach, it is expected to make social robotics technology accessible for a wider audience.

2   Opsoro: Open Platform for Social Robots

We have recognized an opportunity for an open DIY platform that facilitates the design, construction, and production of new social robot characters. To address the current difficulties of designing custom social robots, an open source, DIY-friendly toolkit approach called Opsoro [12] has been developed. This platform is based on an existing social robot, named Ono (Fig. 1). Ono is designed in the context of robot-assisted therapy for children with Autism Spectrum Disorder (ASD). It is a low cost, open source social robot that can be made using DIY tools and techniques [14].

Opsoro contains an open-source programming, hardware, and embodiment framework. We focus on non-experts to go from a character concept to a functional social robot. Emphasizing low-cost and DIY aspects and aiming primarily at characters with animated facial expressions and limited body/limb motion. Opsoro has showed the feasibility of supporting the design and creation of social robots by using only DIY techniques and materials [13].

2.1   Hardware

The various components are grouped into subunits of related actuators and mechanisms, called modules (Fig. 2). This has a number of important advantages. It simplifies assembly; modules can be put together outside of the body of the robot, where there is more room to manipulate components and perform assembly steps. Secondly, in case of damage, modules can be removed and replaced or repaired quickly. Thirdly, the modular architecture makes the system ideally suited for accelerating the design of new robots, as complex functionality is packaged in easy-to-use building blocks. Finally, the modules allow for upgrades and customization, enhancing the lifespan and potential usefulness of

Fig. 1. Ono, the open source social robot

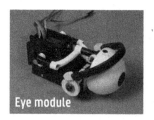  

Fig. 2. Assembled Open source modules including the off-the-shelf servo motor

robots built using the system. Each module encapsulates the functionality of one specific facial/body feature, such as an eye or a mouth. As of yet, the modules focus on actuation only, though it is also possible to incorporate sensors.

2.2 Software

The robots made with Opsoro can be controlled via a web interface running on the Raspberry Pi. The platform contains an application called Social Script to provide a very user-friendly app (Fig. 3) to control facial expressions with text-to-speech. Custom programming is facilitated with the Opsoro Blockly API (Fig. 4), which is a visual programming language based on Blockly[1] to allow participants to program behaviors. Simple interactive scenarios can be created using this language by dragging and connecting puzzle-shaped blocks.

2.3 Embodiment

This design approach shares similarities with the concept of "untoolkits" [5] in the sense that the toolkit is not just a collection of modules, but that the step of creating a custom embodiment is an intrinsic part of the kit. Thus, digital manufacturing techniques such as laser-cutting can be seen as intangible components

---

[1] Blockly – https://developers.google.com/blockly/.

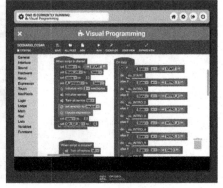

Fig. 3. Social Script App   **Fig. 4.** Opsoro Blockly programming

of the Opsoro toolkit. A large degree of design freedom is afforded through this approach, as the design of the modules does not have a large influence on the aesthetics and design of the robotic character. In the first approach the toolkit consisted of modules that are attached to a custom made frame [12]. This will serve as the skeleton of the robot where the embodiment will be fitted onto. This version allows for full freedom in customization but comes at a higher workload. For short design sessions there is a simplified version called Opsoro Grid. This will be the version used in the case study. In this toolkit the modules can be connected to a grid plate using a single screw. The holes of the grid plates are spaced 8 mm apart, making the system compatible with LEGO Technic bricks. The modules contain two locating pins in addition to a single threaded hole. The locating pins are used to position the module on the grid, preventing rotation. A screw is then used to fasten the module to the grid, locking the connection. Robots created using this principle are easier to produce and can be regarded as $2^{1}/2$ dimensional robots due to their flat appearance.

3   Participatory Design in Social Robotics

The combination of cheap off-the-shelf components and open-source software made prototyping interactive products easier and faster. What used to be high-fidelity prototyping is now considered low-fidelity. Adding interactivity to a paper prototype is now cost-efficient and easy [15]. Before the rise of the DIY maker culture, designing the hardware and software was too labor intensive to be considered part of a low-fidelity prototyping stage. The introduction of paper and technology prototyping enables new paradigms in the hybrid area of PD. Beaudouin-Lafon and Mackay describe *offline* prototyping as a means to eliminate the constrains of modern day development tools. "Prototypes are less likely to constrain the designer's thinking ... even if the developer ends up using a standard set of interface widgets, usually results in a more creative design." [2]. The new field of paper and technology prototyping should never restrict the offline and unlimited creativity of having just pens, paper, glue, and scissors.

Participatory Design in literature, also often referred to as co-creation or co-design, refers to the act of collective creativity of designers and people not trained in design working together in the design development process [10]. By applying co-creation or PD in the field of social robotics, designers and non-experts are encouraged to creatively work together in the design and creation of social robots. In the field of human-computer interaction, PD has been widely considered to be used as a design approach or design methodology in the creation of interactive systems and applications [6].

In robotics research, there is little work within human-robot interaction that apply PD approach in the design process of creating social robots [6]. PD method has been used to elicit design recommendations, from a group of designers and target users who had a range of visual abilities, in the design process of building service robots that interact with and guide a blind person through a building in an effective and socially acceptable way [1]. A series of participatory design sessions with teenagers has also been conducted in the design of a social robot envisioned to measure their stress [8]. The use of the participatory design approach for developing social robots has also been explored in a case study with older adults diagnosed with depression [3]. Another case of co-designing social robots is with cognitively-impaired citizens, who are adults with acquired brain damages across the wide spectrum of cognitive impairments [7]. Based on these previous works, we observed two main concerns: there is a need of personalized social robots designed according to each individual's needs, and the process of co-creating such social robots can be very time consuming. The latter concern is due to a lack of practical tools that bridge the knowledge gap from both sides. Allowing both parties, research-designers and robot users, to share their knowledge through the creation of an interactive artifact. In participatory design, tacit knowledge is not only explored, it is in many cases made material [11]. In the following case study we aim to evaluate the participants confidence in their tacit knowledge for building a robot with the Opsoro system.

4   Case Study

As a way towards the implementation of the Opsoro platform in the participatory design of custom social robots, we carried out one design workshop as a case study to learn and observe how non-experts can build their custom DIY social robots from scratch. This workshop served as part of the iterative design process that ultimately led to the current state of Opsoro platform. To evaluate how non-experts design and build social robots from scratch using Opsoro, a design workshop was conducted during the "Classroom of the Future" event at the Frankfurt Book Fair. The purpose of the workshop was to evaluate the Opsoro system with secondary school students. Over the course of a two-hour workshop, the students created and programmed custom robots using cardboard, craft materials, and Opsoro modules, as depicted in Fig. 5.

Fig. 5. Participants building custom robots using the Opsoro modules and craft materials

Fig. 6. Cardboard embodiments designed by the participants

4.1 Procedure

During the workshop, participants worked together in small groups (2–5 persons per team) to design and program their robots. Four groups worked in parallel. The experiment ran over the course of a day, each team took approximately two hours to complete a robot. The kit consists electronics, five actuator modules, and a large grid plate. Keeping in line with the efforts to simplify and reduce costs of the Opsoro system, we chose to use smaller, simplified modules, as informed by the results of the previous workshop. The modules used during this workshop were smaller, had less DOF, and were built using micro-sized servos (as opposed to standard-sized servos). To design robots, participants first positioned and affixed the modules on the grid plate. Then, they created cardboard "skins" (Fig. 6) to go over the modules and backplate. The grid system afforded participants the ability to position modules wherever they wanted. The less prescriptive design of the modules in combination with the low weight of the materials enabled functionality such as moving arms and ears.

As part of the evaluation, participants were asked to fill in a questionnaire. The large number of participants, the limited amount of time, as well as the language barrier meant that a paper questionnaire was the best evaluation tool for the workshop. The questionnaire, translated in German, consisted of the following questions:

- General personal details: name, age, and gender.
- 7-point Likert scale statements, with a value of one indicating complete disagreement, and seven indicating complete agreement:
  - "I could build what I wanted to build."
  - "The connection system is easy to use."
  - "The modules are adaptable."
  - "I like the aesthetics of the Opsoro system."
  - "I like the functionality of the Opsoro system."
  - "I like the novelty of the Opsoro system."

- The AttrakDiff-Short questionnaire. This variant of the AttrakDiff questionnaire consists of only ten antonym-pairs, as opposed to 28 antonym-pairs in the full AttrakDiff questionnaire.
- Open questions:
  - "Which workshop aspects did you like?"
  - "What was the most annoying aspect, or where did you experience the most problems?"
  - "What did you learn from the workshop?"

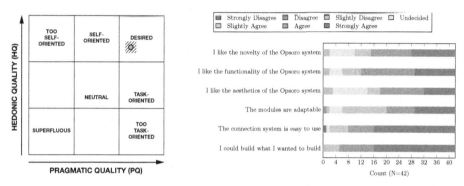

Fig. 7. Results of the AttrakDiff-Short questionnaire. The hatched area represents the confidence rectangle ($n = 46$, PQ $= 1.52 \pm 0.26$, HQ $= 1.64 \pm 0.24$)

Fig. 8. Results from the Likert scale questions ($n = 42$)

4.2 Results

In total, 48 workshop participants filled in the questionnaire. The average age of respondents was 17.35 years old, with a spread of $\sigma = 1.86$. The youngest respondent was 14 years old and the oldest was 23 years old. Respondents were predominantly female (66%), with 32 girls versus 16 boys. Figure 7 shows the result of the AttrakDiff-Short questionnaire and position the Opsoro Grid system firmly within the quadrant of desirable products. Two incomplete questionnaires were discarded for the AttrakDiff, resulting in a sample size of $n = 46$, and six for the Likert scale questions resulting in $n = 42$. The latest iteration of the Opsoro system is situated firmly in the category of desirable products, a notable improvement compared to the previous workshop. With a value of 1.84, the overall attractiveness of the system (ATT) was also rated fairly high. The large number of participants resulted in a narrower, more precise confidence interval, as indicated by the hatched area. Figure 8 shows the results of the six Likert scale questions.

In the feedback from the open questions, we noticed that "creativity" is frequently mentioned as a positive aspect of the Opsoro system. From the 41 participants that filled in the open questions, 20 mentioned "creativity" in their responses (48.8%), 10 mentioned fun (24.4%), and 7 mentioned technology (17.1%). Multiple participants also said that building robots is not as hard as it appears, and that it is fun to combine technology with creativity. As expected, negative feedback was mostly related to technical problems, such as defective servos and problems with the audio quality and the volume of the speaker. Comments from the open questions also hint at the potential of Opsoro for the Science, Technology, Engineering and Mathematics (STEM) education, as indicated by remarks such as *"Technology does not have to be boring"* and *"You can do many cool things with technology"*.

5   Conclusions

This paper presented a case study describing the participatory design process of creating custom social robots by using Opsoro, an open platform for DIY social robots. The platform enables designers and non-experts to design, build, and use custom social robots for face-to-face communication. Opsoro provides social robotic technology to a wide audience of users. It builds upon contemporary DIY principles and practices e.g. the open source hardware movement and the maker movement. Designing a platform is different than designing a single system, not only from a technical standpoint, but in the way they are used. For this reason, traditional engineering paradigms were eschewed in favor of an iterative, user-centered design process that emphasizes user experience aspects. Each iteration has led to a better understanding of different DIY approaches in the *design*, *build*, and *use* phases of the platform. The result is an inexpensive, open source, DIY-friendly platform for the design, development and use of custom emotionally expressive robotic characters. The platform lends itself for participatory design sessions early in the development process of a social robot and it can serve as a toolkit for educational purposes.

Using a participatory design approach early in the development of a social robot can be advantageous for embodiment- and interaction design. The design iterations for Opsoro have led to the simpler form named *Opsoro Grid* that shows great potential as a design tool. The ability of taking the concept out of the lab environment and evaluate it with stakeholders through participatory design methods has already been proved valuable in the HCI community [3,7–9]. Having the right tools with these methods will open up new possibilities for robot design research and development. Opsoro adds physical robot modules to the design toolbox for the future researchers.

References

1. Azenkot, S., Feng, C., Cakmak, M.: Enabling building service robots to guide blind people: a participatory design approach. In: The Eleventh ACM/IEEE International Conference on Human Robot Interaction, HRI 2016, pp. 3–10. IEEE Press, Piscataway (2016)
2. Beaudouin-Lafon, M., Mackay, W.E.: Prototyping tools and techniques. In: Jacko, J.A. (ed.) The Human Computer Interaction Handbook, 3 edn., Chap. 47, pp. 1081–1104. CRC Press, Boca Raton (2012)
3. Lee, H.R., et al.: Steps toward participatory design of social robots: mutual learning with older adults with depression. In: Proceedings of the 2017 ACM/IEEE International Conference on Human-Robot Interaction, HRI 2017, pp. 244–253. ACM, New York (2017)
4. McArthur, L.Z., Baron, R.M.: Toward an ecological theory of social perception. Psychol. Rev. **90**(3), 215–238 (1983)
5. Mellis, D.A., Jacoby, S., Buechley, L., Perner-wilson, H., Qi, J.: Microcontrollers as material: crafting circuits with paper, conductive ink, electronic components, and an untoolkit. In: Proceedings of the 7th International Conference on Tangible, Embedded and Embodied Interaction, pp. 83–90 (2013)
6. Muller, M.J.: Participatory design: the third space in HCI. In: The Human-Computer Interaction Handbook, pp. 1051–1068. L. Erlbaum Associates Inc., Hillsdale
7. Rodil, K., Rehm, M., Krummheuer, A.L.: Co-designing social robots with cognitively impaired citizens. In: Proceedings of the 10th Nordic Conference on Human-Computer Interaction, NordiCHI 2018, pp. 686–690. ACM, New York (2018)
8. Rose, E.J., Björling, E.A.: Designing for engagement: using participatory design to develop a social robot to measure teen stress. In: Proceedings of the 35th ACM International Conference on the Design of Communication, SIGDOC 2017, pp. 7:1–7:10. ACM, New York (2017)
9. Šabanović, S., Chang, W.-L., Bennett, C.C., Piatt, J.A., Hakken, D.: A robot of my own: participatory design of socially assistive robots for independently living older adults diagnosed with depression. In: Zhou, J., Salvendy, G. (eds.) ITAP 2015. LNCS, vol. 9193, pp. 104–114. Springer, Cham (2015). https://doi.org/10.1007/978-3-319-20892-3_11
10. Sanders, E.B.N., Stappers, P.J.: Co-creation and the new landscapes of design. CoDesign **4**(1), 5–18 (2008)
11. Spinuzzi, C.: The methodology of participatory design. Tech. Commun. **52**(2), 163–174 (2005)
12. Vandevelde, C., Saldien, J.: An open platform for the design of social robot embodiments for face-to-face communication. In: Proceedings of the 11th International Conference on Human-Robot Interaction, Christchurch, New Zealand, pp. 287–294
13. Vandevelde, C., Saldien, J.: Demonstration of OPSORO - an open platform for social robots. In: 2016 11th ACM/IEEE International Conference on Human-Robot Interaction (HRI), pp. 555–556, No. 1, IEEE, March 2016
14. Vandevelde, C., Saldien, J., Ciocci, C., Vanderborght, B.: Ono, a DIY open source platform for social robotics. In: Butz, A., Greenberg, S., Bakker, S., Loke, L., De Luca, A. (eds.) Proceedings of the 8th International Conference on Tangible, Embedded and Embodied Interaction
15. Zhu, K., Zhao, S.: AutoGami: a low-cost rapid prototyping toolkit for automated movable paper craft. In: Proceedings of the SIGCHI Conference on Human Factors in Computing Systems, pp. 661–670. ACM

User Needs in Smart Homes: Changing Needs According to Life Cycles and the Impact on Designing Smart Home Solutions

Olivia De Ruyck[1,2,3(✉)] , Peter Conradie[1,2] ,
Lieven De Marez[1,3] , and Jelle Saldien[1,2]

[1] imec-mict-UGent, Ghent, Belgium
{olivia.deruyck, peter.conradie, lieven.demarez,
jelle.saldien}@ugent.be
[2] Department of Industrial Systems Engineering and Product Design,
Ghent University, Kortrijk, Belgium
[3] Department of Communication Sciences, Ghent University, Ghent, Belgium

Abstract. Smart home solutions are gaining popularity but hold a large untapped potential. This paper presents smart home needs from a user point of view. Based on co-creation workshops with residents of different life cycles in Belgium, it draws conclusions about key issues related to user needs. Starting from these insights we can describe characteristics of inhabitants according to their life cycle. We conclude that their needs for smart solutions and the way they want to equip their homes differ. The younger generation looks for modular systems with possibilities to expand or move them. They are moment oriented and buy Internet of Things (IoT) appliances according to their current needs and budget. The older generation, by contrast, searches for quality and all-in-one solutions. They want a complete solution that does not require any updates or extras and is proof for their future needs. The results of this study in the form of eight guidelines can be considered when designing smart home solutions.

Keywords: Smart homes · Life cycle · User study · Design guidelines

1 Introduction

In the last decade, popular and scientific attention for smart homes has augmented with consultancy firms like Gartner [16] and Deloitte [10] reporting growing consumer interest. Contrary to the traditional home were appliances respond to commands via fixed buttons and switches, smart homes and smart appliances are controlled from anywhere in the house or over the internet, often through smartphone apps.

Market research in the United States, confirms the increasing interest. Eighty-one percent of US internet users are aware of the concept of smart devices and the connected home after being given a description [38]. Moreover, global consumer research carried out in seven countries worldwide, including the United States and Germany, suggests a high level of market support. Half of all respondents believe that smart home solutions will have an impact in their lives in the next few years [17].

D. Lamas et al. (Eds.): INTERACT 2019, LNCS 11747, pp. 536–551, 2019.
https://doi.org/10.1007/978-3-030-29384-0_33

However, while consumer interest is increasing, data from Flanders (Belgium) shows that adoption remains limited, as only 8.8% of respondents report owning either a smart thermostat, lighting or lock. More surprisingly, 27,4% reported ever hearing of any of these applications [47].

These findings highlight the existing discrepancy between people's needs and the currently available market offerings. Hargreaves and Wilson [21] emphasize this problem by noting that to date, the majority of visions on smart home technologies have not been based on a clear understanding of user–centric benefits. Furthermore, users have not been engaged in a clear, systematic way. The slow adoption rate of smart products, together with the technology push [18, 43] instead of a market pull in the market, nurtures the urge to better understand current user needs [35, 53].

Most user studies regarding smart home technology focus on elements that can stimulate adoption of smart home technology. For instance, in the context of the benefits [52] and barriers [1] of existing smart products. Venkatesh [5] developed a model to predict the adoption of a technology in the home. In his MATH model, he states that life cycles are an important predictor. Limited research, however, is to be found on understanding characteristics and needs of home owners and tenants and comparing them over different life cycles.

Current smart home products are not designed with a focus on the user or the life cycle, therefore the goal of this study is to understand different needs per life cycle for smart home products. This leads to the following research objectives:

- to determine characteristics of inhabitants' life cycles
- to determine specific needs and interactions for smart home solutions per life cycle
- to determine possible barriers for adoption according to inhabitants' life cycle

Information gathered from this study should provide managers and designers with a greater understanding of the user needs in the context of the smart home and give them the ability to create new meaningful smart products and interactions.

The remainder of this paper is structured as follows. First, we review prevalent research within the domain of smart home needs. Secondly, we discuss the methods used in this study followed by our results. Finally, we present guidelines for developing smart home solutions taking life cycle into account.

2 Literature Review and Background

Through a review of existing literature, this section will give a short overview of what we mean by the term of smart home, the detected barriers and benefits and who the users of smart homes are. We will briefly describe the existing literature and models on household lifecycles.

2.1 What Is a Smart Home

Terms such as 'smart home' [8], 'smart living', 'smart product', 'IoT product' are often conflated. In this paper, we discuss the needs of users in residential homes and thus exclude related smart living environments [44] like smart cities [22] and smart factories [56], which expand the concept beyond the home environment.

Most homes today have appliances and devices like dishwasher, music installation, garage door, heating and lighting. These are operated manually, mostly by pushing a button. Products are not connected, and users need to be present to start interactions. In smart homes, in contrast, it is possible to access them with remote electronic control. In this paper, the term 'smart home' is used as a generic describer for a residence where sensors and appliances can be (remotely) controlled over a network [27]. User interaction happens through buttons, interfaces, gestures, voice or through automatic commands between appliances.

The provided services by smart homes are not restricted to energy management [8] but include all services that correspond to the needs of its inhabitants [1, 7].

Smart homes are predicted to remain a hot topic for many years, with an impressive estimated compound annual growth rate (CAGR) of around 24% between 2016 and 2020 [45]. Nevertheless, not everything that is technologically possible, matches a need on the user side or is economically feasible. It is from this perspective that we believe that by studying the user needs we add a valid contribution to this domain.

2.2 Barriers and Benefits

To tap into this large potential of smart homes, several papers have studied the barriers for market adoption of smart homes [1, 28, 52]. Cost, privacy, security, reliability, and the interoperability of different technologies are described as current most important obstacles for adoption. A set of sociotechnical concerns with smart home technologies include an increased dependence on technology, electricity networks or outside experts, and the spread of non-essential luxuries inducing laziness in domestic life [1].

Benefits of existing smart home technologies are described by Wilson, Hargreaves and Hauxwell [52]. Following their study, the smart home is dominantly seen through an energy management lens. Over 86% of UK respondents agreed or strongly agreed that the main purpose of smart home technologies is to control energy, heating and appliances. The study provides a thorough overview of user' perception on smart home technologies through, among others, a national survey and an analysis of marketing material. Other benefits of smart homes are improved security, enhanced leisure, entertainment and extended personal independence for assisted living [7, 39].

2.3 Research and Users of Smart Homes

Solaimani et al. [44] noted that research on smart homes is dominated by research on technological developments. Most studies focus on the acceptance of a technology and the user experience by installing smart products, sensors and actuators in the homes of the users [19, 30, 54, 55]. Other types of studies in this domain are participatory design studies [42] in which people intended to use the system, help to design. Research typically start from a specific idea or target group, the main goal is to develop or improve a product [25]. With our study, on the contrary, we want to take a step back from technology and want first to understand the needs in the homes to, in a later stage, develop products based on these user needs.

Hargreaves and Wilson [20], list types of prospective smart home users: elderly or vulnerable house-holders, rational energy users, technophiles, home improvers and differentiated families. From these groups, elderly or vulnerable house-holders, such as people with disability, visual- and hearing impairments or people with dementia, have most been studied. They have very specific and differentiating characteristics. Smart homes improve their independence, self-determination and freedom of choice [14]. As note by Hargreaves and Wilson [20] elderly in smart homes benefit from safety measurements such as easy access to emergency contacts, fall prevention, or visual and hearing assistance [2, 6, 23, 29, 32].

In the domain of energy policy, benefits and risks of smart home technologies [52] have been looked at from different stakeholders' point of view including early adopters versus non-users and industry. In the same domain, Balta-Ozkan [1] found that social barriers such as control, security and cost to smart home diffusion vary by expertise, life-stage and location.

As mentioned in the introduction, in our study we look at the specific context of Belgium where there has traditionally been an emphasis of home ownership [9]. Seventy percent own and build or renovate a house which is slightly above the European average [12]. Belgians tend to buy at their thirties [3].

2.4 Household Life Cycle

To conclude our literature study, we looked into studies around household life cycles. Hill and Rodgers (1964), as cited in Wilkes [51], describe different events impact a life cycle and the relation between different family members like age, having a first child, departure of the last child out of the home, divorce, dissolution of marriage, decease of a spouse and the age of the main earner.

Wells and Gubar [50] describe a traditional model of family life ignoring for example all singles other than young, never married and older. Later studies from Gillis and Enis [34] modernize the life cycle model and base category membership more on age of the woman rather on the age of the man, as her age will be a better predictor for the age of children. They capture the complexity of households by creating a model with 12 stages. Although the model is created in 1982 it already describes newer familial forms as single parents and same sex couples. Previous studies prove the important effect of age and life cycle on the expenditure [4, 13, 31]. We have chosen to use age as the main criterion for categorization of inhabitants' characteristics, but we emphasize that this is not a strict categorization, since persons in the same age groups might have different lifestyles.

3 Methodology

To gather information about the user needs and interactions, the qualitative technique of co-design is used [42]. We give preference to this technique, because as noted by Visser et al. [49], generative techniques give access to latent and tacit knowledge, while techniques like observations and interviews are more likely to reveal explicit and observable knowledge. The use of card-based tools during similar workshops are found effective, and characteristics are summarized by Mora [36]. Research projects have found the cards effective in supporting idea generation [46], presenting theoretical constructs and transferring knowledge between theory and practice [11], keeping people at the center of the design process [26, 33] and facilitating a shared under-standing or steering a discussing when it becomes unproductive [24]. Our intent to use the cards lays more in the ability to encourage conversation than to stimulate idea generation.

A few card tools have specially targeted IoT ideation [15, 36]. These cards are intended to support IoT design space and to provide triggers for creative reflective ideation of augmented objects. A description of the card deck used follows in the workshop description.

3.1 Sampling

Different recruitment strategies were explored in order to attract participants with a high diversity in age and social background. There was a message displayed on a digital wall in the public library, messages were sent through different online channels like Facebook groups and University contact lists, and the project was presented during computer literacy lectures for seniors.

Participants were divided over five focus groups of two hours. The ages of par-ticipants ranged between 21 and 71 years because we wanted to focus on people that have purchasing power and possible changing needs. This way we exclude minors with no buying power and dependent elderly who's changing needs are mainly related to health problems as previously mentioned.

The sample consisted of 24 participants, the main criterion to divide our groups was age (age = 21–71y; M = 41,6; SD = 16,9). Next to this we tried to attain a male-female balance (m = 11; f = 13) and a balance in the type of homes. Eleven participants live in a home which has not been renovated in the last ten years, 13 participants live in (totally) renovated or recently new build home. Prior to the workshops, participants were asked to fill in a questionnaire with socio demographic questions, experience with renovation or building a house. Additionally, we used a limited 10 item version of the Technology Readiness Index (TRI) [37, 48]. The TRI measures the readiness of a respondent to adopt a new technology. This was important for our research as we wanted to focus on the "somewhat resistant" (TRI −10 to −1) and "somewhat technology ready" (TRI 0 to 10) respondents. "Very technology resistant" (TRI −20 to −11) participants were excluded. We measured TRI to prevent our workshop being skewed towards too many highly technology ready or resistant persons.

Finally, participants were compensated with a movie ticket for their time (Fig. 1).

Fig. 1. Picture taken during a workshop. Cards encourage workshop participants to discuss their needs and indicate their preferences.

3.2   Workshop Description

The workshops were conducted in a creative co-creation space in the Main Library of Ghent at different moments within a four-week period. Consistency between the different groups was ensured by following the same schedule for each session. All sessions were led by 2 researchers, who which facilitated the translation of first ideas around needs in idea sheets. The workshop consisted of short exercises, a discussion moment, a brainstorm to express solutions for their needs and a short presentation of generated ideas by the participants.

To reveal user needs three consecutive exercises were used: first we used a 'day in the life' exercise in which users could describe a week or weekend day. This allowed them to reflect on their activities at home. This was followed by a second exercise in which they had to come up with needs based on these previous mentioned activities. Participants were encouraged to share their needs and frustrations at home out loud.

To help people pronouncing their needs a third exercise consisted of 30 "need cards" with different categories like safety, comfort, energy use entertainment and health. The cards were custom made for the exercise since no existing card decks could be found which described specific user needs in smart homes.

Fig. 2. Picture of need cards used during the workshop. Participants can indicate their most important needs with adhesive dots. This enables the researchers to link needs to different life cycles.

The need cards are paper cards with a theme, a need and a picture (Fig. 2). Examples are protection against burglary; pleasant temperature in the home; control slumber consumption; create a TV moment; good air quality. We iteratively updated the card set during the workshop whenever need sets seemed to be too limited, outdated or duplicated. We encouraged participants to discuss the needs and finally we used the dot selection method to prioritize the needs. Each participant received five stickers with their initials to indicate their top five. The initials allowed the researchers to connect the needs to the socio-demographics of the participants during the analysis of the workshop.

The final part of the workshop consisted of an idea generation based on the most important needs which came out of the dot selection exercise or differently said: the cards with the most votes. Needs could thus vary between the different workshops. The group was now divided in two and both groups needed to come up with a solution for the need they had. If possible, they also needed to describe the way of interaction with the new solution and points of attention like "the door should only close automatically when none else is inside the home". As a short intermezzo, barriers towards IoT products in the home were discussed.

As an additional experiment, one of the groups received interaction cards. This is a card kit that describes different ways of interaction. Like the need cards, they are paper cards with a theme, a picture and a description of an interaction like press a button, clap in your hand, talk to something… The kit holds 20 cards which are selected out of existing card sets [33, 36] and other existing interactions. The evaluation of the use of these interaction cards is beyond the scope of this paper, but first findings indicate a low influence of the cards on the richness of the generated ideas.

To close the workshop, teams presented on average three ideas to each other. These small presentations push the participants to better prepare and think about solutions and helps researchers to better capture the idea.

4 Findings

The five workshops -with insights of 24 people aged between 21 and 71 years- resulted in a rich dataset. Over ten hours of video was captured, more than 100 needs were discussed, 31 idea sheets filled in and different discussion themes were cited. The data gathered was consistent across all the sessions. Next, we will present our findings concerning 1. Characteristics of living over life cycles, 2. User needs and interactions according to life cycles and 3. Barriers towards IoT in the home.

Measured TRI levels ranged between 14 and -8, with an average of 3 (standard deviation of 4.67). Our sample was thus not skewed in favor of too many highly or lowly technologically ready.

4.1 Characteristics of Living Over Life Cycles

Insights are based on the 'day in the life exercise' in which participants describe their activities, and a discussion during the co-creation workshops.

Results show that people of the same life cycle show similarities in the characteristics of living, needs, and solutions for the home. The presence of children, the size of the home and the ownership impacts the time someone expects to live in a home. This impacts in turn the willingness and the type of investments done in a home.

Life cycles are more easily identified by age. However, this should not be viewed as a rigid categorization. For example, a divorced man in his forties, who moved out of his home to a flat, have more resemblance of living with someone of age group 25–35 year than with other men of his age living with a partner and children in a bigger house. A parallel finding was described by Wilkes in his study on household life cycles [51].

The four following names -mentioned from young to old- describe our groups best: Dependent Youngsters, Independent Youngsters, Family Life, Independent Elder. Following we give a description of the common characteristics of these groups, gained from the first workshop exercise.

Dependent Youngsters. Mainly between 18–25 years old. Are characterized for being active and adaptive. This group of people moved -only partially- out of the home. During the week they live in students houses, small apartments or studios. During the weekend, they spend their time at the family home. This new living situation means a reduction of their comfort with smaller and less comfortable rooms. They have little to no impact on the choice of light, heating or energy in their home. They often share spaces with other tenants. While they own few smart home appliances, products like an internet connected sound system are mentioned. *"The lights in the corridor of my student house are always on (it is installed this way), I find this so annoying and a wastage." (woman, 22y.)*

Independent Youngsters. Mainly between 25–35 years old. This group of people moved out from their family home and live alone or with a partner, possibly with small children. They often plan to buy or just bought a property and make purchases to make their home smarter and more efficient (e.g. roof insulation, ventilation, thermostat, smart lamps...). The majority wishes to do this in different phases, often from a cost perspective. They have a preference for appliances which are not built-in and don't come with installation costs, so they can take them along in case they move again to a house which is better adapted to their growing household. *"I bought these IKEA lamps which can be controlled by an app. Inexpensive and easy to install in the fittings. If I have more money, I'll buy that smart lock." (man, 30y.)* They own a variety of smart home appliances both for augmented control as for entertainment. Products like a smart lock, smart alarm, smart thermostat, air quality sensor, smart lights or internet connected sound system are mentioned.

Family Life. Mainly between 35–55 years old. This group lives with their children in a home they bought and refurbished a while ago. They have made large investments in the house in the past. New purchases for the house primarily happen when a product is out of function (e.g.; cooker hood, boiler) or when they hear very positive feedback about a product. *"We had mold/fungus on the walls in our house and they needed to install a whole new ventilation system. An expensive case, but now the problem is solved, and we are happy for that." (woman, 50y.)*

They have a low level of information about smart home products and other novel solutions for the house. They own fewer smart home appliances compared to the independent youngsters. Mentioned appliances are functional, like a smart thermostat and a connected fire alarm.

Independent Elder. Mainly between 55–75 years old. They used to live with their children in the home but when they move out, their home often becomes too big. This group of people is searching for new living situations (e.g. co-housing, assistant living, apartment). Construction works to adapt their homes to their new needs (everything on one floor, large doors, smaller home and garden) are often so radical that they opt to move or build again. This makes that they either live in old houses (>20y.) or in properties with the newest technologies. Contrary to what many would think about this target group, a part of them recently rebuilt and are well informed about new building solutions and technology. *"I live in a big gentleman's house, since the children moved out, I'm thinking about new ways of living like co-housing or B&B" (woman, 65y.)*

"We bought a land last year and are making the plans with an architect at the moment. In the home everything will be on one floor with large doors in case one of use will need a wheelchair one day. It must be built following latest energy norms with light sensors for convenient living." (man, 67y.)

Participants from this group living in old houses own little to no smart home appliances but own complete wired sound systems, home automation, automated rolling shutters, sensor lights on the driveway. Inhabitants of new houses are more likely to own a smart fire alarm or light sensors in the hallway.

Based on these insights we can propose that Independent Youngsters and Independent Elder are most interesting groups to target; they have high needs in combination with the willingness to invest in new IoT solutions for their homes. However, they want to equip their homes in different ways. The Independent Youngsters search for modular systems with possibilities to expand or move them. They are moment oriented and buy IoT appliances according to their current needs and budget.

The Independent Elder on the other hand, search for quality and all-in-one solutions. They are future oriented and want a complete solution that won't need any updates or extras.

4.2 User Needs and Interaction According to Life Cycles

During the co-creation workshops a selection exercise with a set of 30 need cards was used. Participants were asked to write their initials on the dots and stick them on their five highest needs. Priority needs per life stage of our participants are listed in the table below (Table 1).

Table 1. List with priority needs per life stage based on needs card exercise.

Dependent youngster (18–25y)	Independent youngster (25–35y)	Family life (35–55y)	Independent elder (55–75y)
Reminders for chores in the home	Air quality in the home	Air quality in the home	Fire prevention
Give others access to your home	Reminders for chores in the home	Reminders for chores in the home	Theft prevention
Air quality in the home	Give others access to your home	Theft prevention	Temperature control
Control lights	Control lights	Temperature control	Air quality in the home
Manage groceries	Reduce slumber consumption	Natural light	Set nice atmosphere

By linking the top five needs to the respondents we found differences in needs according to the life cycle. Based on our respondent sample, Youngsters and Elder have most opposite needs.

For young people, products that help them to remind chores in the home and enable remote access to third parties like family members or cleaning personnel score very high. *"I would love a fridge with camera and screen that can help you to know what to buy or reminds you to place the garbage outside." (female, 26y.) "I have a smart lock at home. It is great, I can open the door for workmen or the cleaning lady without needing to be there." (man, 31y.)*

Older people, in contrast, place security and safety like theft prevention, fire alarms… highest in their ranked needs. Unlike youngsters, they are not fond of the reminders and remote access. *"Safety like fire alarms and lights in my garden that switch on to prevent burglary are a priority."* (woman, 65y.) *"I write paper notes and leave them on the table and my neighbor has my keys. I don't need any product to do this for me"* (man, 67y.)

Needs of the Family Life group are less pronounced. A better knowledge of the air quality in and around the home is of common interest between all groups. *"Air quality is important for me. I think that my house is healthy, but it is just a guess. I wonder whether it is better or not to open the windows to ventilate the room in the morning when there are traffic jams in my street."* (man, 36y.)

Interactions According to Life Stages. In addition to the difference in functions, also the type of interactions varies between life stages. The Independent Elder understand the advantage of new interactions and are open for them. However, they are more careful. Many would like an additional physical button or switch in case of failure.

"My father-in-law has automatic rolling shutters because he couldn't lift the old manual ones anymore. To open them, you still have to push a button so he would keep the feeling of control, and we would know that something is wrong when the shutters are not open in the morning." (woman 54y.)

Dependent and Independent Youngsters are more exposed to new types of interactions (contactless payment, check in through bio data, speech control on the phone) and thus have more confidence. They do not ask for buttons to fall back on. Full automation when interacting with products is accepted. They expect products to be customizable and that settings can be changed.

"I don't mind that products are personalized and automated, it is so easy that my agenda knows me; but the way we interact with products should not disturb others. A smart mat which switches on the lights in the morning when stepping on it, or products with speech control are perfect to me now. They would not be appropriate for families with sleeping children." (man, 29y.) *"To enter the gym, I unlock the door with a finger scan (bio data). Great! Fast and easy!"* (woman, 22y.)

4.3   Barriers Towards Acceptance of Smart Home Solutions

Previous research [53] indicates acceptability of smart homes is closely linked to issues of security, privacy and trust as well as practical and ergonomic concerns with user friendliness. During a discussion moment, participants were questioned about barriers towards IoT products. Here again we find some similarities and differences among the life cycles.

Over generations, there is a fear for the effects of Wi-Fi on health. However, rarely this a reason not to accept smart products in the home. This fear was clearly present in all sessions and was not found in previous research on barriers of IoT products [1]. *"All this radiance, like while charging an object from a distance and all the smartphones, this can't be healthy, but yes we just buy what is on the market if it is easy."* (woman, 65y.) *"I don't want Wi-Fi in my home. It can't be healthy to constantly live in that."* (woman, 26y.)

Other fears are more outspoken by the Independent Elder. IoT solutions are feared by them for the loss of control and apathy. They think that letting products make their own decisions, will lead to frustration and breakage of the product. *"Sensors make me nervous. We had that at work. Sun is there, the screens roll out, sun is gone, screens go up, sun is there again... Terrible!... until it breaks."* (man, 71y.)

Another close related fear is the cost and availability of a technician. The fear is that the major cost is not the product itself but the technician in case of problems with the hard- or software.

The last age-related fear is laziness. The Independent Elder fear that all sensors and automation will make them and others lazy and decrease their mobility. Here again this fear is more outspoken with older than younger people. They perceive closing curtains, switching off lights... as physical activities which they want to conduct themselves. However, when they think of themselves or others in case of reduced mobility, they find such kind of solution very useful. Younger respondents don't think these solutions will reduce their physical activity.

"I am here to tell these kids that you need to stand up to switch a light, if not you'll become lazy. But my wife had a hip surgery, I need to do everything for her. In her case, automatic solution are useful." (man, 63y.)

4.4 Recommendations for Designers and Managers Developing Smart Home Solutions

From the findings we can draw some conclusions for different types of designers or managers when developing new smart home solutions. They are shortly summarized below.

1. Prior to the development of smart home solutions, the organization of workshops with designated tools help to understand most important needs.
2. User needs for smart home solutions change according to the life cycle. To create a market-pull, a designer should be aware for who he is designing.
3. Needs of Independent and Dependent Youngsters and Independent Elder differ the most. Needs of the Family Life group are less outspoken and have similarities with both other groups.
4. The Independent and Dependent Youngster equip their homes with modular solutions with possibilities to expand the system in the future. Older generations are more future oriented and need built-in solutions without any updates required.
5. The Independent Elder can't be neglected when designing smart home solutions since a part of them rebuilds and equips the home with the newest technology.
6. When designing new types of interaction in the home, all groups are open for new interfaces, however, Independent Elder lack confidence and wish for buttons as back up in case of defect.
7. Next to the described barriers for the acceptance of smart home products in previous literature as security, cost, privacy, reliability, interoperability of technologies, dependence on technology, electricity networks or outside experts and laziness. Inhabitants fear the effect of Wi-Fi on health. These barriers should be taken into account in the design or the marketing of the product.

8. Highest ranked needs for smart home solutions of younger people are related to reminding chores in the home and enable remote access to the home to third parties. In contrary, these above-mentioned needs are unwanted by the older target group. Improved safety (fire-, burglary detection) is a priority for them. A better knowledge of the air quality in and around the home is of common interest between all groups.

5   Discussion and Conclusion

This study investigated through workshops the needs of the tenants and home owners in different lifecycles. More specific the research objectives are to determine characteristics of inhabitants' life cycles, specific needs for smart home solutions per life cycle and possible barriers for adoption according to life cycle.

This study is new to our knowledge since it starts from a technology pull: discovering user needs. Were the majority of studies in the smart home have a technology push attitude. Secondly it compares needs for smart home solutions between younger and older inhabitants in the area of Belgium. It can help designers, product managers or software developers of smart products to bring products on the market which take the different life cycle and specific needs into account.

Previous research on barriers to smart home solutions as cost, trust, privacy and loss of control [1] are found in common. An additional unexpected fear for smart home solutions is the effect of Wi-Fi on health. A possible explanation could be that it is described as a fear, rarely as a real barrier not to accept any internet in the home. Another possible reason could be that Belgians are more sensitive about health concerns.

Recommendations should be read bearing in mind the limited number of respondents (24). Sample bias is a possible concern because of the partial recruitment through the library and University website. This may lead to a more educated and socially engaged group. Another potential shortcoming of the study is the fact that participants were questioned out of their home context. The chosen research method of groups discussions did not allow for home interviews. This means that the interaction with other products and other inhabitants could not been taken into account and that the focus of the research lays on understanding explicit needs, not implicit needs.

The aim for future research is to translate some of these needs into meaningful interactions. We will amongst others study the design for different rhythms of use (multiple times a day versus some time a year) and how people of different life cycles living together interact with a same product. In this upcoming stage, different mock-ups will be first tested in a smart home lab setting and later implemented in the homes of the participants.

Acknowledgments. We thank all participants for cooperating in this study. We would also like to thank the reviewers for their feedback on early drafts of this article.

References

1. Balta-Ozkan, N., et al.: Social barriers to the adoption of smart homes. Energy Policy **63**, 363–374 (2013)
2. Beringer, R., Sixsmith, A., Campo, M., Brown, J., McCloskey, R.: The "Acceptance" of ambient assisted living: developing an alternate methodology to this limited research lens. In: Abdulrazak, B., Giroux, S., Bouchard, B., Pigot, H., Mokhtari, M. (eds.) ICOST 2011. LNCS, vol. 6719, pp. 161–167. Springer, Heidelberg (2011). https://doi.org/10.1007/978-3-642-21535-3_21
3. Bouyon, S.: Recent trends in EU home ownership. ECRI Comment 15, vol. 15, pp. 1–8 (2015)
4. Brown, S., et al.: Household technology use: integrating household life cycle and the model of adoption of technology in households. Inf. Soc. **22**(4), 205–218 (2006)
5. Brown, S.A., Venkatesh, V.: Model of adoption of technology in households: a baseline model test and extension incorporating household life cycle. MIS Q. **29**(3), 399–426 (2005)
6. Cesta, A., et al.: Monitoring elderly people with the ROBOCARE domestic environment: interaction synthesis and user evaluation. Comput. Intell. **27**(1), 60–82 (2011)
7. Chan, M., et al.: Smart homes - current features and future perspectives. Maturitas **64**(2), 90–97 (2009)
8. Cook, D.J.: How smart is your home? Science **335**(6076), 1579–1581 (2012)
9. De Decker, P., Dewilde, C.: Home-ownership and asset-based welfare: the case of Belgium. J. Hous. Built Environ. **25**(2), 243–262 (2010)
10. Deloitte: Switch on to the connected home - The Deloitte Consumer Review (2017)
11. Deng, Y., et al.: Tango cards: a card-based design tool for informing the design of tangible learning games. In: Proceedings of 2014 Conference on Designing Interactive System, pp. 695–704 (2014)
12. Eurostat: People in the EU: who are we and how do we live? 2015 (2015)
13. Fernández-Villaverde, J., Krueger, D.: Consumption over the life cycle: facts from consumer expenditure survey data. Rev. Econ. Stat. **89**(3), 552–565 (2007)
14. Friedewald, M., et al.: Perspectives of ambient intelligence in the home environment. Telematics Inform. **22**, 221–238 (2005)
15. Futurice: IoT Service Kit. http://iotservicekit.com
16. Gartner: Leading the IoT: Gartner Insights on How to Lead in a Connected World (2017)
17. GfK: The truth behind the hype - insights on consumer attitudes to the smart home (2016)
18. Haines, V., et al.: Probing user values in the home environment within a technology driven smart home project. Pers. Ubiquit. Comput. **11**(5), 349–359 (2007)
19. Hargreaves, T., et al.: Keeping energy visible? exploring how householders interact with feedback from smart energy monitors in the longer term. Energy Policy **52**(November), 126–134 (2013)
20. Hargreaves, T., Wilson, C.: Smart Homes and Their Users. Springer, Cham (2017). https://doi.org/10.1007/978-3-319-68018-7
21. Hargreaves, T., Wilson, C.: Who uses smart home technologies? Representations of users by the smart home industry. In: ECEEE Summer Study, pp. 1–14 (2013)
22. Harrison, C., et al.: Foundations for smarter cities. IBM J. Res. Dev. **54**(4), 1–16 (2010)
23. van Hoof, J., et al.: Ageing-in-place with the use of ambient intelligence technology: perspectives of older users. Int. J. Med. Inform. **80**(5), 310–331 (2011)
24. Hornecker, E.: Creative idea exploration within the structure of a guiding framework: the card brainstorming game. In: Proceedings of Fourth International Conference on Tangible Embedded Embodied Interaction, vol. 10, pp. 101–108 (2010)

25. Hwang, A., et al.: Using participatory design to determine the needs of informal caregivers for smart home user interfaces. In: Proceedings of 6th International Conference on Pervasive Computing Technologies for Healthcare, pp. 41–48 (2012)
26. IDEO: IDEO Method Cards: 51 Ways to Inspire Design., Palo Alto (2003)
27. International Telecommunication Union: Measuring the Information Society, Geneva (2010)
28. Jakobi, T., et al.: The Catch(es) with smart home – experiences of a living lab field study. In: Proceedings of CHI, pp. 1620–1633 (2017)
29. Kim, M.J., et al.: A critical review of user studies on healthy smart homes. Indoor Built Environ. 22(1), 260–270 (2013)
30. Kim, S., Paulos, E.: InAir: sharing indoor air quality measurements and visualizations. In: Proceedings of the Conference on Human Factors in Computing System, pp. 1861–1870 (2010)
31. Lawson, R.: Patterns of tourist expenditure and types of vacation across the family life cycle. J. Travel Res. 29(4), 12–18 (1991)
32. Lorenzen-Huber, L., et al.: Privacy, technology, and aging: a proposed framework. Ageing Int. 36(2), 232–252 (2011)
33. Lucero, A., Arrasvuori, J.: The PLEX cards and its techniques as sources of inspiration when designing for playfulness. Int. J. Arts Technol. 6(1), 22 (2013)
34. Mary, C., Gilly, B.M.E.: Recycling the family life cycle: a proposal for redefinition (1982). http://www.acrwebsite.org/volumes/display.asp?id=6007
35. Mennicken, S., et al.: From today's augmented houses to tomorrow's smart homes : new directions for home automation research, pp. 105–115 (2014)
36. Mora, S., et al.: Tiles: a card-based ideation toolkit for the internet of things. In: Proceedings of 2017 Conference on Designing Interactive System - DIS 2017, pp. 587–598 (2017)
37. Parasuraman, A., Colby, C.L.: Techno-Ready Marketing: How and Why your Customers Adopt Technology. The Free Press, New York (2007)
38. PWC: Smart home, seamless life - Unlocking a culture of convenience. PWC Consum. Intell. Ser., January 2017
39. Røpke, I., Nyborg, S.: Energy impacts of the smart home – conflicting visions. In: ECEEE 2011 Summer Study, pp. 1849–1860 (2011)
40. Sanders, E.B.-N., Stappers, P.J.: Co-creation and the new landscapes of design. CoDesign 4(1), 5–18 (2008)
41. Sanders, E.B.-N., Stappers, P.J.: Probes, toolkits and prototypes: three approaches to making in codesigning (2014). http://dx.doi.org/10.1080/15710882.2014.888183
42. Simonsen, J., Robertson, T.: Routledge International Handbook of Participatory Design. Routledge, London (2013)
43. Solaimani, S., Bouwman, H., Baken, N.: The smart home landscape: a qualitative meta-analysis. In: Abdulrazak, B., Giroux, S., Bouchard, B., Pigot, H., Mokhtari, M. (eds.) ICOST 2011. LNCS, vol. 6719, pp. 192–199. Springer, Heidelberg (2011). https://doi.org/10.1007/978-3-642-21535-3_25
44. Solaimani, S., et al.: What we do- and don't- know about the smart home: an analysis of the smart home literature. Indoor Built Environ. 24(3), 370–383 (2015)
45. Technavio: Global Smart Appliances Market 2016-2020 (2016)
46. Vaajakallio, K., Mattelmäki, T.: Design games in codesign: As a tool, a mindset and a structure (2014). http://dx.doi.org/10.1080/15710882.2014.881886
47. Vanhaelewyn, B., De Marez, L.: imec.Digimeter 2017: measuring digital media trends in flanders (2017)
48. Victorino, L., et al.: Exploring the use of the abbreviated technology readiness index for hotel customer segmentation. Cornell Hosp. Q. 50, 342–359 (2009)

49. Visser, F.S., et al.: Contextmapping: experiences from practice. CoDesign **1**(2), 119–149 (2005)
50. Wells, W.D., Gubar, G.: Life concept in marketing research. J. Mark. Res. **3**(4), 355–363 (1966)
51. Wilkes, R.E.: Household life-cycle stages, transitions, and product expenditures. J. Consum. Res. **22**(1), 27 (1995)
52. Wilson, C., et al.: Benefits and risks of smart home technologies. Energy Policy. **103**, 72–83 (2017)
53. Wilson, C., et al.: Smart homes and their users: a systematic analysis and key challenges. Pers. Ubiquit. Comput. **19**(2), 463–476 (2015)
54. Woo, J., Lim, Y.: User experience in do-it-yourself-style smart homes. In: Proceedings of 2015 ACM International Joint Conference on Pervasive Ubiquitous Computing – UbiComp 2015, pp. 779–790 (2015)
55. Yang, R., Newman, M.W.: Learning from a learning thermostat: lessons for intelligent systems for the home, pp. 93–102 (2013)
56. Zuehlke, D.: SmartFactory-towards a factory-of-things. Annu. Rev. Control **34**(1), 129–138 (2010)

Information Visualization

A Formative Study of Interactive Bias Metrics in Visual Analytics Using Anchoring Bias

Emily Wall[1]([✉]), Leslie Blaha[2], Celeste Paul[3], and Alex Endert[1]

[1] Georgia Tech, Atlanta, GA, USA
{emilywall,endert}@gatech.edu
[2] Air Force Research Laboratory, Pittsburgh, PA, USA
leslie.blaha@us.af.mil
[3] U.S. Department of Defense, Washington, D.C., USA
clpaul@tycho.ncsc.mil

Abstract. Interaction is the cornerstone of how people perform tasks and gain insight in visual analytics. However, people's inherent cognitive biases impact their behavior and decision making *during* their interactive visual analytic process. Understanding how bias impacts the visual analytic process, how it can be measured, and how its negative effects can be mitigated is a complex problem space. Nonetheless, recent work has begun to approach this problem by proposing theoretical computational metrics that are applied to user interaction sequences to measure bias in real-time. In this paper, we implement and apply these computational metrics in the context of anchoring bias. We present the results of a formative study examining how the metrics can capture anchoring bias in real-time during a visual analytic task. We present lessons learned in the form of considerations for applying the metrics in a visual analytic tool. Our findings suggest that these computational metrics are a promising approach for characterizing bias in users' interactive behaviors.

Keywords: Cognitive bias · Anchoring bias · Visual analytics

1 Introduction

Human-in-the-loop approaches to data analysis combine complementary strengths of humans and computers. In visual data analysis, people leverage cognitive and perceptual systems to think about data by analyzing the views created. However, cognitive science tells us that people are inherently biased [31]. At times, biases act as mental shortcuts and help people analyze data quickly [15]. Yet there are situations where biases may lead to suboptimal analysis processes

Electronic supplementary material The online version of this chapter (https://doi.org/10.1007/978-3-030-29384-0_34) contains supplementary material, which is available to authorized users.

© IFIP International Federation for Information Processing 2019
Published by Springer Nature Switzerland AG 2019
D. Lamas et al. (Eds.): INTERACT 2019, LNCS 11747, pp. 555–575, 2019.
https://doi.org/10.1007/978-3-030-29384-0_34

or decisions. **Anchoring bias**, for example, describes the tendency for people to rely too heavily on initial information when making a decision [12]. In the analytic process, this tendency leads people to preferentially weight some information and neglect other information, often leading to poorly informed decisions.

The impact of bias on decision making can be further compounded in mixed-initiative visual analytic approaches. Mixed-initiative visual analytics systems leverage adaptive computational models that learn from and adjust to user feedback [19]. These models incorporate latent knowledge about the data or the domain from users through interactions. However, what if mixed-initiative systems learn from biased behaviors or even amplify the users' biases [13]?

In cognitive science, bias is typically measured by analyzing decisions people make during controlled laboratory experiments (e.g., [12,24,32]). It is understood that bias can influence perceptual judgments, memory recall, and deliberative choice making, each of which are involved in visual analytics [25]. In the context of data visualization and visual analytics, researchers have begun to characterize bias from analysis of perceptual judgments [6,7,35] or interaction data [3], where a user's behavior with an interactive tool is treated as a proxy for their cognitive state. All of these works, however, rely on post-hoc analysis of user data. While informative to the ways visualization design can influence the severity of bias, waiting until a task is completed does not allow for online intervention by systems prior to a potentially erroneous decision.

Enabling mixed-initiative systems to adapt to or mitigate cognitive biases requires an understanding of bias in real-time, during the analysis process [16]. Recently, we introduced theoretical metrics to quantify bias from user interactions in real-time during the visual data analysis process [36]. The metrics focus on characterizing *human* bias rather than other forms of bias that may be present in the analysis process (i.e., bias in analytic models, data sampling, etc.). The metrics track user interactions with the visualization, data, and analytic models in the system to create a quantitative representation of analytic provenance. The theoretical formulation in [36], however, relies on assumptions untested on actual user data, leaving many open questions regarding how to implement and apply the theory in a visual analytic tool.

In this paper, we explore how to bring the theoretical metrics into practice; specifically: **how to incorporate the interactive bias metrics into a visual analytic tool**. To do so, we implemented the metrics in a tool and conducted a formative study to examine how bias can be observed in users' interactions through the lens of the bias metrics. Our goal is to leverage a well-known and highly studied form of bias (anchoring [12,14]) to influence participants' analysis processes in a controlled way, to study the metrics under predictably biased behavior patterns. Our analysis suggests anchoring bias can be observed in users' interactive behavior through the lens of the bias metrics. The primary contributions of this paper include (1) guidelines for applying the bias metrics in visual analytic systems (Sect. 6), and (2) results of a formative study showing how the metrics can be used to capture anchoring bias (Sect. 5).

2   Related Work

Bias in Cognitive Sciences. Bias is a concept that has been widely studied in cognitive science. Cognitive bias refers to subconscious errors or inefficiencies resulting from the use of heuristics for decision making [20,21,31]. There are dozens of these types of errors that commonly impact decision making, and specifically data analysis and sensemaking [18]. A prominent example is confirmation bias, the tendency to search for and rely on evidence that confirms an existing belief [24,38]. In this paper, we focus on anchoring bias, defined earlier.

Framing describes the manner in which a choice is presented to people, including the language used, the context provided, and the nature of the information displayed [32,33]. For example, a positive framing of a medical treatment risk would present probability of lives saved; a negative framing presents the same information in terms of lives lost. Framing has been found to strongly shape decision making [30]. The way that information or task goals are introduced to people has a strong impact on how they will conduct their analyses. Thus in our formative study, described later, we leverage task framing to induce anchoring bias in participants. Doing so allows us to evaluate how anchoring bias manifests in user interaction patterns for a visual data exploration and classification task.

Bias in Visual Analytics. The topic of bias in visual analytics has recently garnered increasing attention. Gotz et al. [16] addressed the issue of selection bias in examining healthcare data. They proposed a way to quantify how subsets of data may be unintentionally biased due to correlated attributes in a filtered dataset. Dimara et al. [7] examined the attraction effect in information visualization, the phenomenon where a person's decision between two alternatives is altered by an irrelevant third option. They observed that this bias is present in the use of data visualizations [7] and can be mitigated by altering the framing of the task [6]. Other recent work has begun to organize and formalize the types of bias relevant in the visualization and visual analytic domains [5,8,34,37].

Perhaps most similar to our work is Cho et al. [3] who replicated effects of anchoring bias in a visual analytic tool. In their study, participants were tasked with predicting protest events by analyzing Twitter data. They elicited anchoring bias in participants through priming, then measured reliance on particular views in a multi-view system through post-experiment metrics like total proportion of time in each view. We similarly aim to show over-reliance on some visual information sources, but we will instead quantify the behavioral effects of anchoring bias through the bias metrics [36].

3   Bias Metrics

In this section, we review our prior work defining the theoretical bias metrics, which is the emphasis of the analysis for the present study. The bias metrics utilize user interactions in a visual analytic tool as input. User interaction is the means by which users express their intent to the system [26,28]. User interaction has been shown to have the power to support steering analytic models [1,10,11,22], inferring a user's personality traits [2], reasoning about their analytic methods and strategies [9], and understanding the generation of insights [17]. Thus, interaction can be thought of as a proxy, although lossy and approximate, for capturing a user's cognitive state. While the design of interactive behaviors in visual analytic tools may not precisely capture a user's state of mind, it can nonetheless provide coarse information about a user's sensemaking process.

Table 1. Metrics used in this study. Each metric computes a specific behavior which can be analyzed to detect bias.

Metric	Description	Example behavior
Data Point Coverage (DPC)	measures *how much* of the dataset the user has interacted with	user interacted with only 3 of 100 players
Data Point Distribution (DPD)	measures *how evenly* the user is focusing their interactions across the dataset	user interacted with some data points dozens of times while ignoring others
Attribute Coverage (AC)	measures the *range of an attribute's values* explored by the user's interactions	user interacted with only players over 84 in. tall, when height ranges from 67 to 88 in.
Attribute Distribution (AD)	measures the *difference in the distribution* of the user's interactions to the distribution of a particular attribute in the dataset	user interacted with a uniform sample of data while the attribute follows a normal curve
Attribute Weight Coverage (AWC)	measures the *range of weights* for a particular attribute explored by the user's interactions	user sets weight values between 0–0.2, ignoring weight values less than 0 and greater than 0.2
Attribute Weight Distribution (AWD)	measures the *difference in the distribution* of the user-defined weights for an attribute to a baseline of unbiased information weighting	user weights follow an exponential distribution, with higher probability for low weight values than high attribute weights

We operationally define bias as patterns of interaction that reflect a systematic deviation from unbiased behavior consistent with a cognitive bias. The metrics are computed on logged interactions with a visualization to determine levels of bias with respect to different facets of the data. Each metric computation results in a value between 0 and 1, where 0 represents low bias and 1 represents high bias. Over time, we obtain a sequence of [0, 1] metric values for each facet representing the user's level of bias throughout their analytic process. Rather than analyzing the accuracy or appropriateness of a decision *after* the decision is made, the metrics provide an interaction-by-interaction bias measurement.

The metrics compute bias with respect to *data points*, *attributes*, and *attribute weights* within the dataset and visual analytic model. For example, if a user is examining a dataset of basketball players, the bias metrics are designed to quantify a user's focus on specific players (data points), stats about players like height or free-throw percentage (attributes), and the way that the user places relative importance of those stats in analytic models (attribute weights). For our purposes, attribute weights fall in the range $[-1, 1]$ and are used to quantify the relative importance of each data attribute [22]. The attribute and attribute weight metrics are computed separately for each attribute in the dataset.

For each concept of data points, attributes, and attribute weights, there are metrics representing *coverage* and *distribution*. Coverage quantifies the proportion of elements that have been interacted with. Distribution, on the other hand, compares the user's (potentially repeated) interactions to the underlying distribution of the data. For example, if the user performs many interactions with only a handful of basketball players, the data point coverage bias value will be closer to 1. This indicates an incomplete sampling of the data points. Similarly, if the user focuses primarily on Point Guards, for example, the distribution of interactions may significantly differ from the distribution of the player positions in the full dataset; the computed attribute distribution bias will be higher, indicating a sampling of the set dissimilar to the underlying data.

Table 1 summarizes the bias metrics. Each metric compares the user's sequence of interactions to a baseline of "unbiased" behavior. Our current baseline for unbiased behavior makes a simple assumption that all data points, attributes, or attribute weights will be interacted with in a uniform pattern. Hence, in the current formulation, we utilize a uniform distribution as the baseline for the data point and attribute weight metrics. We utilize the true underlying distribution of the attributes of the data in the attribute distribution metrics, assuming unbiased interactions will closely match the underlying distributions.

Our initial formulation of the metrics [36] was theoretical and relied on untested assumptions (e.g., about which interactions to compute on). In this work, we conduct a formative study to inform the implementation of the metrics in real visual analytic systems and to demonstrate how the metrics can be used to quantify instances of anchoring bias.

4 Methodology

We conducted a formative study to explore the implementation of the bias metrics and the ways they capture anchoring bias in real-time through users' interactive behavior. The purpose of this study is two-fold: (1) serve as a formative approach to implementing and applying the bias metrics, and (2) understand if the bias metrics can characterize participants who are exhibiting anchoring bias toward different data attributes. To test the hypothesis that the metrics can capture bias in real-time, we manipulated task framing to elicit predictably biased behaviors from participants and examined the ability of the metrics to detect patterns consistent with anchoring bias. Participants in the study were tasked with categorizing a dataset of basketball players. Using the visual analytics tool InterAxis [22] (Fig. 1), users were instructed to examine all of the available data to label 100 anonymized basketball players according to one of five positions. We deliberately encouraged participants to anchor on different data attributes (see Table 2) by randomly assigning them to a framing condition; each condition described the five positions using different attributes.

InterAxis. Participants used a scatterplot-based visual analytics tool to categorize basketball players by their position (Fig. 1). Pilot studies led us to modify the InterAxis interface from its presentation in [22] and [36] for the present study. Changes include: the y-axis custom axis options were removed; data point colors were changed to reflect participants' labels; options for saving the plot settings were removed; and experiment control options (e.g., position labels, Continue button) were added. The data from the pilot was only for testing and feedback on our protocol and are not included in the results.

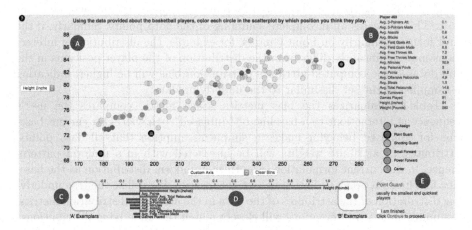

Fig. 1. A modified version of the system InterAxis [22], the interface used by participants to complete the task of categorizing basketball players.

The primary view in InterAxis is a scatterplot, where each of 100 basketball players is represented by a circle (Fig. 1A). Hovering on a circle reveals details about that player (Fig. 1B). Data points can be dragged from the scatterplot into the Exemplar bins on either side of the x-axis (Fig. 1C). The system, in response, will compute a custom axis using a linear dimension reduction technique. The result is a set of attribute weights that represents the differences between the A and B Exemplar bins. The attribute weights are visualized as bars along the axis (Fig. 1D). The bars can also be interacted with by click-and-drag to directly manipulate the weights that make up the custom axis. Participants can read a description of each position by clicking on the colored circles on the right side (Fig. 1E). If they select a position on the right, the user can then label players as the selected position by clicking on the points in the scatterplot.

We selected InterAxis due to the system's highly interactive nature—to encourage users to explore and interact with the data, because the bias metrics ultimately rely on user interactions. InterAxis allows users to browse data points and attributes, and leverage an analytic model consisting of weighted attributes to project the data. This allows us to use the full set of bias metrics.

Table 2. Position descriptions used in the two framing conditions. We expected *Size* condition participants to rely more heavily on size-related attributes (i.e., Height and Weight). We expected *Role* condition participants to rely more heavily on the role-related attributes called out in the descriptions.

Position	Size condition	Role condition
Center (C)	Typically the *largest* players on the team	Responsible for protecting the basket, resulting in lots of *blocks*
Power Forward (PF)	Typically of *medium-large* size and stature	Typically spends most time near the basket, resulting in lots of *rebounds*
Small Forward (SF)	Typically of *medium* size and stature	Typically a strong defender with lots of *steals*
Shooting Guard (SG)	Typically of *small-medium* size and stature	Typically attempts many shots, especially long-ranged shots (i.e., *3-pointers*)
Point Guard (PG)	Usually the *smallest* and quickest players	Skilled at passing and dribbling; primarily responsible for distributing the ball to other players resulting in many *assists*

Analytic Task and Framing Conditions. Studies of anchoring bias within the cognitive science community rely on highly controlled experiments to isolate a cognitive phenomenon. However, in visual data analysis, cognitive processes are often much more complex than can be captured from such experiments. Pirolli and Card describe the sensemaking process as a series of iterative tasks involving searching for information, schematizing, presentation, and so on [27]. Hence we sought a task with enough complexity to simulate decision making within a realistic analysis scenario while maintaining tractable experimental conditions.

There are many tasks associated with performing data analysis in a visual analytic tool, such as ranking, clustering, or categorizing data [11,29]. What bias looks like can be quite different across these tasks; for this study we narrowed our scope to focus on categorization-based analysis. We found through pilot studies that categorizing basketball players was a sufficiently challenging task that led users to interact with the visual analytics tool for approximately 30 min. This provided a balance of task complexity and study tractability.

Participants were instructed to categorize a set of 100 basketball players by their positions by analyzing all of their stats using the InterAxis visual analytic tool [22] in Fig. 1. We used a dataset of professional (NBA) basketball player[1] statistics with names and team affiliations removed. After filtering out less active players (whose statistical attributes were too small to be informative), we randomly selected 20 players for each of five positions: Center (C), Power Forward (PF), Small Forward (SF), Shooting Guard (SG), and Point Guard (PG). Each player had data for the following stats: 3-Pointers Attempted, 3-Pointers Made, Assists, Blocks, Field Goals Attempted, Field Goals Made, Free Throws Attempted, Free Throws Made, Minutes, Personal Fouls, Points, Offensive Rebounds, Steals, Total Rebounds, Turnovers, Games Played, Height, and Weight.

Participants were assigned to one of two conditions. The two conditions differed in the descriptions provided for the five positions. In the *Size* condition, the descriptions are based on physical attributes (Height and Weight). In the *Role* condition, positions were described with respect to their typical role on the court and performance statistics. These descriptions were based on analysis of the distributions of attributes for each position as well as position descriptions recognized by the NBA[2]. Table 2 shows the text used to describe the positions in each condition, which was available throughout the task (Fig. 1E). Similar to other experiments utilizing task framing, we described the positions from two different perspectives (sets of attributes) between the two conditions. Participants in each condition should then anchor on the attributes used in the framing to which they were assigned. We emphasize that, while the player position descriptions were framed differently, participants in both conditions were instructed to utilize all of the data to make their decisions.

Generally, anchoring bias describes an over-reliance on some information, often to the neglect of other relevant information about a decision. We operationally define interaction-based biases as increased interaction with limited subsets of data, attributes, or attribute weights over a more evenly or uniformly distributed pattern of interactions. Anchoring specifically, then, will be observed if there is biased interactions with information to which the participant has been cued and is relying on more than other information to make analytic decisions.

Verifying the Task Framing Effects. To see how the bias metrics quantify anchoring bias, we first analyzed how framing impacted user behaviors. We compared the frequencies of attributes selected for the scatterplot axes between the two framing conditions. We predicted that participants in the Size framing condition would select the Height or Weight attributes on the axes more than participants in the Role framing condition. Likewise, we predicted that participants in the Role framing condition would select the other attributes used in the position descriptions (Blocks, Rebounds, Steals, 3-Pointers, or Assists; see Table 2) on the axes more than participants in the Size framing condition.

---

[1] http://stats.nba.com/.

[2] http://www.nba.com/canada/Basketball_U_Players_and_Posi-Canada_Generic_Article-18037.html.

Figure 2 shows the results of this analysis. Each boxplot shows the number of times the given attribute was selected on the axis for participants in the Role condition (left) and the Size condition (right). Larger separation of mean and quartile values suggests that the framing condition impacted the frequency of interaction with a given attribute, while highly overlapping boxplots suggest little or no difference for that attribute between the framing conditions. The boxplots reveal that some attribute axis selections show clear differences supporting our predictions (outlined in blue), while others exhibit little difference between conditions (e.g., Weight, Total Rebounds, 3-Pointers Made, and Assists). Participants in the Size condition interacted more frequently with Height than the Role condition participants. And participants in the Role condition interacted more frequently with performance-related attributes (Blocks, Offensive Rebounds, Steals, 3-Pointers Attempted) than participants in the Size condition. These results suggest that the participants from the two conditions anchored on the attributes described in the respective framing conditions, as predicted. These results confirm that the Role and Size conditions influenced the overall categorization behaviors in ways consistent with our intended manipulations.

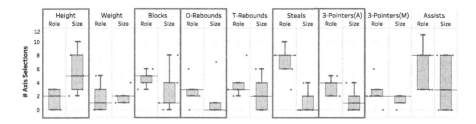

Fig. 2. Boxplots for number of attribute interaction via InterAxis axis manipulation. The thick middle line indicates the median; the box delineates the inner quartiles, and the whisker bars give the outer quartiles. Green dots indicate the sum of observations for each participant (not outliers). The blue boxes indicate attributes for which a substantial difference is seen between the two conditions. (Color figure online)

Participants. Ten participants (4 female, mean age 25.5 ± 2.7 years) were recruited from a large university. Nine participants had experience playing basketball, and six participants watched at least a few (NCAA, NBA, WNBA) games per season (self-reported). The one participant who never played basketball watches it regularly. All participants were moderately familiar with information visualization, based on Likert ratings provided in a background survey. Participants were randomly assigned to either the Size or Role condition.

Procedure. Participants began with informed consent, completed a demographic questionnaire, and were shown a 5-min video describing the task and demonstrating use of the InterAxis tool to complete the task. The demonstration used different position descriptions than the study. Participants then completed the main task, using InterAxis to categorize 100 basketball players into one of five positions. There were no time limits for completing the task. After completing the task, participants completed a post-study questionnaire about their experience and were compensated with a $10 Starbucks gift card.

A moderator observed participants' interactions during the task. Participants were encouraged to ask questions as needed regarding the interface, the underlying algorithmic transformations, or the meaning of an attribute. The moderator did not reveal information about the underlying distribution of positions in the dataset or additional attributes that might be used to help categorize players.

Timestamped logs of the users' interactions were automatically recorded, including interactions with data points (labeling, hovering to reveal details, and dragging to axis bins), interactions with axes (selecting a new attribute for an axis, dragging to adjust attribute weights, and recomputing attribute weights based on interactions with the bins), and interactions with position descriptions (clicking to reveal a description and double clicking to de-select a position description). The interaction logs serve as the input data for the bias metrics.

5   Analysis and Results

We analyzed the user study data with the high-level goal of understanding how to use the bias metrics to quantify and characterize *anchoring bias*. The bias metrics provide us with the ability to characterize a user's analytic process in real-time by quantifying aspects of their interaction patterns in which they may be exhibiting bias. In particular, we analyzed the bias metrics from the granularity of (1) the sequences of $[0, 1]$ metric values over time, and (2) where in the distribution of the data user interactions deviated from expected behavior. From the perspective of the bias metrics, participants subject to anchoring bias could be observed to have (1) higher $[0, 1]$ bias metric values for the anchored attributes, and/or (2) instances during the analytic process where they interact more heavily with part of the distribution of the anchored attribute.

To analyze if the metrics can capture bias, we used the collected interaction logs to simulate the real-time computation of the bias metrics after each user's session to avoid influencing the analysis process[3]. We note that the bias metrics created 74 unique time series per participant (Data Point Coverage + Data Point Distribution + 18 attributes × {Attribute Coverage, Attribute Distribution, Attribute Weight Coverage, Attribute Weight Distribution}). In the scope of this work, we narrow the focus of our discussion to only attributes that were referenced in the framing of position descriptions (Table 2). We discuss a few selected examples of findings from the computed bias metrics. Visualizations of all metrics can be found in the supplemental materials.[4]

---

[3] Note that while the ultimate goal of the metrics is online interpretation and mixed-initiative adaptation, the present work collected full interaction sequences of metrics for post-hoc analysis, to ensure the metrics can capture bias and to elucidate how to effectively put the metrics into practice.

[4] https://github.com/gtvalab/bias-framing.

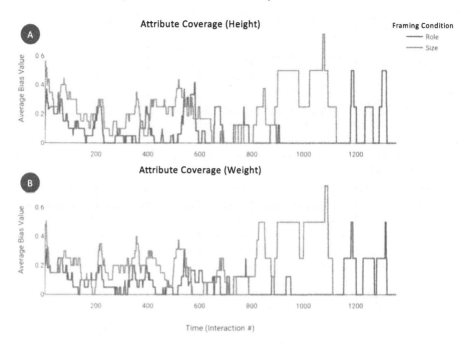

Fig. 3. A visualization of the average Attribute Coverage (AC) metric for the attributes (A) Height and (B) Weight. Size condition participants (orange) tended to have higher AC bias for both Height and Weight than Role condition participants (blue), consistent with our predictions. (Color figure online)

Participants' accuracy for categorizing players averaged 53% $(SD = 18\%)$ over the mean duration 33.6 min $(SD = 14$ min$)$. Some interactions were filtered out to reduce noise in the bias metric computations. According to Newell's time scale of human action [23], deliberate cognitive actions are on the order of 100 ms+. Because hovering in the interface shows a data point's details, particularly short hovers were likely not intentional interactions. Thus, hovers with duration less than 100 ms were removed as likely "incidental" interactions performed unintentionally while navigating the cursor to a different part of the interface. Participants performed an average of 1647 interactions $(SD = 710)$, which filtered down to an average of 791 non-incidental interactions $(SD = 300)$. For additional discussion on which interactions are included in the bias metric computations, see Sect. 6.

Metrics over Interaction Sequences. Computed over time, the bias metrics produce a sequence of $[0, 1]$ values quantifying the level of bias throughout the analysis process, which can be visualized as a time series. We hypothesized that the attributes explicitly described in each condition (Height and Weight for the *Size* condition; Blocks, Rebounds, Steals, 3-Pointers, and Assists for the *Role* condition) will have higher metric values in the associated condition than in the other. For example, we expected the time series of Attribute Distribution values for Assists to be higher for Role condition participants than for Size condition participants. To evaluate this hypothesis, we visualized all 74 metrics' time series.

Figure 3 shows the Attribute Coverage (AC) metric for (A) the Height attribute and for (B) the Weight attribute. The blue line represents the AC metric time series averaged over all Role condition participants. The orange line represents the AC metric time series averaged over all Size condition participants. Figure 3 shows that Size condition participants tended to have higher peaks (metric values closer to 1) and longer peaks (over greater spans of time) in the AC bias metric for the Height and Weight attributes than Role condition participants, consistent with the framing condition predictions.

We confirm this trend by comparing bias values averaged over the full interaction sequence for participants in each condition. Size condition participants had an average value of $M_{\text{Size}} = 0.2211$ ($SD = 0.066$) for the *Height* AC metric compared to $M_{\text{Role}} = 0.0952$ ($SD = 0.016$). Similarly, for the Weight AC metric, the Size condition participants had an average value of $M_{\text{Size}} = 0.2120$ ($SD = 0.098$) compared to the Role condition participants $M_{\text{Role}} = 0.0849$ ($SD = 0.042$).

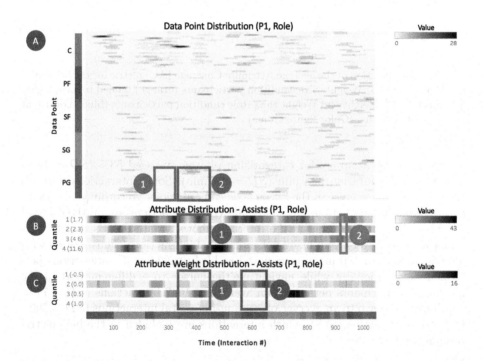

Fig. 4. Visualizations of three of the bias metrics for a Role condition participant: (A) the DPD metric, (B) the AD metric for Assists, and (C) the AWD metric for Assists. While labeling PGs (blue boxes), (A) the participant showed more bias toward PGs than while labeling other positions (SF; green). (B) The participant also showed greater bias toward the high end of the distribution for Assists while labeling PGs than other positions (C; purple), and (C) weighted Assists more heavily while labeling PGs than while labeling other positions (PF; red). (Color figure online)

This evidence supports our hypothesis; however, not all metrics show a discernible difference in $[0, 1]$ values between the two conditions. One potential explanation for inconsistent effects is the level of granularity in the analysis. The bias metric values indicate the degree of bias; however, they do not indicate the source of the bias. For example, a user focusing on particularly tall players might have the same metric value as a user focusing mostly on short players. That is, simply knowing the metric value informs us of a bias; however, the number itself does not differentiate the source within the data distributions. Next, we address this by examining the underlying coverage or distribution.

Coverage and Distribution of Bias Metric Values. To compute the metric values, an intermediate step is to break down the user's interactions with data points, attributes, and attribute weights into quantiles and distributions to see how they deviate from unbiased interactive behavior. One way to show the framing effects on user interaction patterns is to compare the metrics broken down into components of coverage and distribution rather than just summative $[0, 1]$ values. In this analysis we visualized the breakdown of coverage and distribution metrics using a heatmap. Note that because the bias metrics are computed independently for each participant, the color scale used to shade the cells is likewise normalized for each participant. The scales are defined in each plot.

Figure 4 illustrates the metrics Data Point Distribution (DPD), Attribute Distribution (AD) for Assists, and Attribute Weight Distribution (AWD) for Assists for one Role condition participant. All of the metrics share a common x-axis of time, captured as the interaction number. The colored bars beneath the time represent the type of position being labeled during that time period (blue = Point Guard, orange = Shooting Guard, green = Small Forward, red = Power Forward, and purple = Center). The shading in a particular (x, y) position represents the count of interactions that fall within the given bin at the given point in time; darker shades represent a greater number of interactions.

In Fig. 4(A), the y-axis shows a row for each data point to illustrate DPD. This type of plot can visually indicate the user's bias toward (interaction with) particular players based on their interactive behavior during different time periods. For example, the DPD metric shows more bias toward players who are Point Guards (PGs) while attempting to label PGs (Fig. 4(A,2)) than while attempting to label Small Forwards (Fig. 4(A,1)), consistent with correct categorizations.

In Fig. 4(B), the y-axis illustrates the distribution of attribute values (AD) broken down into four quantiles. The AD metric for Average Assists shows a stronger bias toward players with a high number of Average Assists while labeling PGs (Fig. 4(B,1)) than while labeling Centers (Fig. 4(B,2)), consistent with Role framing. In Fig. 4(C), the y-axis illustrates the breakdown of attribute weight ranges (AWD) into four quantiles. The AWD metric for Average Assists indicates a bias toward higher weighting of the attribute while labeling PGs (Fig. 4(C,1)) than while labeling Power Forwards (Fig. 4(C,2)). The Role condition PG description is intended to influence participants to anchor on the Average Assists attribute. Hence, Figs. 4(B) and (C) visually capture a user's anchoring bias toward an attribute.

Figure 5(A) visually compares Attribute Weight Coverage (AWC) for Height between two users from different conditions. The position descriptions used in the Size condition were designed to anchor participants on Height and Weight attributes. The Size condition participant (top) showed greater coverage of the range of attribute weights (as shown by the black bars in all four quartiles) and spent more time with a high, positive weight applied to the Height attribute. Comparatively, the Role condition participant (bottom) covered less of the range of possible attribute weights and spent the vast majority of their analysis with a low weight applied to the Height attribute. We can quantify this difference using the L metric from recurrence quantification analysis [4]. L gives the average length of diagonal segments in a recurrence analysis. Applied to the metric state, larger L values reflect staying in a state longer while smaller L values reflect switching more frequently between quartiles. For the Size participant (top), $L = 14.9$ indicating more switching, and $L = 229.8$ for the Role participant (bottom), reflecting a very long time in a single quartile which is seen in Fig. 5(A). Heatmaps for all metrics and all participants are in the supplemental material.

Similarly, Fig. 5(B) shows how Attribute Distribution (AD) for Average Total Rebounds compares for one Size condition participant (top) and one Role condition participant (bottom). Role condition participants were told that Power

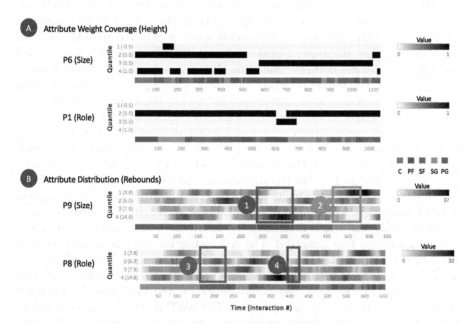

Fig. 5. (A) Visualization of the AWC metric for Height. The Size condition participant (top) showed greater *coverage* of the range of Height attribute weights than the Role condition participant (bottom). (B) Visualization of the AD metric for Total Rebounds. Participants focused more on upper parts of the Rebounds distribution while labeling PFs (red boxes) than other positions. (Color figure online)

Forwards (PF) typically have a high number of Rebounds. While labeling PFs, both the Role condition participant (4) and the Size condition participant (1) showed interactions with greater focus toward the upper parts of the distribution (Q3 and Q4). Similarly, both the Role condition participant (3) and the Size condition participant (2) interacted with lower parts of the distribution (Q1 and Q2) while labeling other positions. While the Size condition participants were not explicitly told about the importance of Rebounds for PFs, there is a correlation between the Weight of PFs and Rebounds ($r = 0.414$, $p = 0.069$), which could explain the similar patterns across the two conditions. Looking at the distribution patterns, we see both participants spent some time in all quartiles for the AD metrics. For the participant in the Size condition (top), $L = 21.2$, and for the Role condition participant (bottom), $L = 16.8$. The participants had similar L magnitudes, but the relatively larger value for Size condition participant indicates less switching between quartiles.

In summary, the task framing impacted which attributes people rely on in their interactive analysis process. These visualizations collectively demonstrate the promise that the real-time interaction-based bias metrics can detect anchoring bias toward particular attributes of the data.

6   Applying the Bias Metrics

This study constitutes the first application of the real-time bias metrics in [36], and explores how to analyze them to capture a specific type of cognitive bias. Consequently, we identified a number of challenges to consider and extracted several lessons learned in moving from theory to implementation in measuring bias through interactions. Additional sources of variability in user activities arise in the real-world analysis process that challenge theoretical assumptions. Implementation choices made early in the design process may need to adjust or adapt on the fly to accommodate unforeseen activities by the experimental participants. In this section, we present guidelines and considerations for integrating and applying the bias metrics, including a discussion on interaction design for the bias metrics, which interactions should be included in the bias metric computations, and how to interpret the metrics.

Designing for Measurement vs. Usability. Designing a visualization system often involves understanding potential user needs, including things like ease-of-use, learnability, or analytic capabilities. These goals each necessitate particular design decisions. Incorporating interaction-based bias metrics in an interface likewise entails its own design requirements which may conflict with other goals. While incorporating bias computation in a visualization has the potential to promote better analysis behaviors, it ultimately relies on interpreting user interactions as a meaningful capture of the analytic process. Hence, the design must facilitate sufficient, meaningful, recordable interactions. In other words, the analysis process must be explicit in the interaction design of the interface.

For example, in the modification of the InterAxis [22] system for the evaluation discussed in the user study methodology section, we debated the interaction design for labeling basketball players' positions. A lasso tool could be an efficient way to label players in bulk; however, providing such a tool would make the interpretation of the aggregate interaction difficult from the perspective of the bias metrics. Further, participants would be less likely to interact with specific data points, read their individual attributes, and make a decision.

Given that the bias metrics rely on abundant interaction data, we instead decided to use single click to label data points and hover to reveal details about individual data points. This decision came at the expense of a potentially less frustrating user experience, as echoed by participants after the study. Such trade-offs must be considered when integrating bias metrics into practical tool design. When the risk of biased analysis is low or the potential consequences are low, designers and developers may opt to focus on designing for usability. An important question to consider for future research is *if the interaction design of an interface does not organically produce sufficient interaction data to measure, to what extent is it acceptable to violate user experience to achieve it?*

Which Interactions to Compute On. *Incidental Interactions:* The bias metrics rely on recording and computing on sequences of user interactions. Just as we must ensure that a system's interactions are designed to explicitly capture as much of the decision making process as possible, we also need a way of knowing if some of the interactions were unintentional. For example, a user may want to hover on a particular data point in the scatterplot to get details; however, due to the particular axis configuration or zoom level, the scatterplot may be overplotted. Thus, in attempting to perform a single deliberate interaction, the user might accidentally hover on several other data points along the way. These "incidental" interactions do not reflect the user's intent in any way and should thus ideally be discarded from the bias computations to remove noise. As an initial proxy for filtering out noisy incidental interactions, we ignored all hovers less than 100 ms. Some amount of noise is to be expected when leveraging user interaction as a proxy for cognitive state. However, the fidelity of models can be improved by taking care to ensure, even with rough approximations, that the interactions computed on reflect a meaningful capture of user intent.

Interaction Windowing: Wall et al.'s [36] prior work presents a formulation of metrics for characterizing bias based on user interaction histories; however, it does not inform us *when* to compute the metrics or *how many past interactions* should be computed on. In this study, we experimented with three different techniques for scoping the metric computations. Our first approach was to compute the bias metrics after every interaction and use the *full interaction history* for every computation. Next, we tried a *rolling window* of the previous n interactions around each current interaction. The window size n then introduced another variable whose value can lead to potentially very different results. We experimented with window sizes ranging from 25 to 100 previous interactions. Lastly, we tried using key *decision points*, where the bias metrics could be computed using all of the interactions that occurred since the last decision point. We computed two variations of this: (1) using each data point label as a decision point, and (2) using the activation of a position (Fig. 1E) as a decision point.

Generalizing this windowing technique, however, requires that decision points be known, which may not be the case depending on the task and interface.

Each of these windowing techniques gives a slightly different perspective on the user's bias. For example, using the *full interaction history* can shed light on long-standing biases throughout the user's analytic process, while using a *rolling window* can capture more short-lived biases. Alternatively, using only the interactions between key *decision points* can be used to characterize bias in a user's interactions associated with individual decisions. As we did not know what strategies people might use, we captured short-lived biases using a *rolling window*, size $n = 50$, computed after each interaction.

Interpreting the Bias Metrics. The bias metrics are formulated such that a value $b \in [0, 1]$ is produced, where 0 indicates no bias and 1 indicates high bias (e.g., as shown in Fig. 3). While an objective characterization of bias, the value b itself is not actionable from a user's perspective. That is, the bias value alone does not provide sufficient detail to a user to facilitate effective reflection and correction of their behavior. For example, a user might have a high bias value for the Height AD metric. This could be due to the user focusing unevenly on short players, on tall players, or on *any* part of the distribution.

To draw actionable conclusions from the bias metric values, it is important to provide additional information to the user, specifically about where in the data or the distribution the user's interactions depart from the objective expectation. In the evaluation results, we showed one potential solution, which visualizes the *coverage* and *distribution* of interactions across data points, attributes, and attribute weights as heatmaps (Figs. 4 and 5). Combining both the [0, 1] bias values along with the *coverage* and *distribution* that comprises the bias value computation might be ideal in some situations. For example, the [0, 1] bias values could be used by automated techniques to select the most concerning dimension(s) in the user's behavior. Then, using the *coverage* and *distribution* information, systems can visualize the source of bias as the imbalance between the unbiased baseline behavior and the user's interactions to encourage user reflection.

7   Limitations and Future Work

Study Limitations. One limitation of the current study was the lack of consideration for visual salience as a confounding explanation for some interactive behavior. Because users could change axis configurations, zoom, and pan on the scatterplot, different emerging clusters of points or outliers might draw the user's attention. In future work, we would like to explore redefining the unbiased baselines for the metrics that account for visual salience. Other factors can also impact users' interactive behaviors, including incidental interactions, task-switching, environmental distractions, and so on. It is of general interest to improve unbiased baseline models to account for such factors.

We have focused our analysis on an exploration of within-subjects patterns in the data, toward our goal of within-user, online use of the metrics. The present data includes, on average, 74 metrics × 791 interactions per participant, in addition to overall metrics like task accuracy. While ten participants is large enough for our present formative analysis, it is too few for strong between-subjects statistical power. Because these metrics are new, we are simultaneously developing the analyses for the metrics while testing their validity and applicability. Ultimately, our goal is to determine an effective analysis pipeline to facilitate larger data collection efforts for both within and between subjects analyses.

Generalizing Tasks and Interfaces. In this study, participants were tasked with categorizing basketball players by position in a visual analytic tool. Our goal was to study the metrics' ability to quantify a psychological concept (bias) in the context of a real-world problem (using a visual analytic system for categorization). However, the study focused on a single constrained subtask of data analysis. In reality, data analysis can be much messier with analysts examining alternative hypotheses and switching between potentially very different subtasks in diverse analytic interfaces. In future work, we would like to examine how bias materializes in other types of interfaces and analytic subtasks (e.g., ranking, clustering, etc.) as well as how these subtasks combine into more complete sensemaking. We would also like to enable handling multiple data sources, which will challenge the current definitions of the metrics. For example, handling text documents may be challenging because clicking to open the document constitutes one interaction but the time spent reading the document without any explicit interface interactions could be significant. It is important to identify meaningful ways to incorporate time on task into the metric computations.

Temporal Interaction Weighting. We discussed above how different windowing techniques impact bias metric computations. A potential improvement on these variations would be to develop a temporal weighting scheme, where all interactions are used to compute the bias metrics, and the interactions are weighted by recency. The most recent interactions would be weighted more highly than those performed early in the user's analysis process. A rigorous evaluation of windowing and interaction weighting schemes could inform the way that we account for how current analytic processes are informed by previous ones.

8   Conclusion

The visualization and visual analytics communities are becoming increasingly aware that biases, from the way data is collected, modeled, or analyzed, may negatively impact the process of visual data analysis. Specifically for interactive data exploration, a user's cognitive biases play a role in shaping the analysis process and ultimately the analytic outcome. In this paper, we focused on implementing and applying real-time bias metrics by studying how anchoring bias materializes in user interactions. We presented the results of a formative study where participants were assigned to one of two conditions for a categorization task using a visual analytic system. We captured interaction logs from their analyses and used real-time bias metrics [36] to characterize the interactions. Comparing the two conditions, we found that user interactions interpreted through bias metrics captured strategies and behaviors reflecting the manipulated anchoring bias. These encouraging results open the potential for discovering biased behavior in real-time during the analytic process, which can have broad-reaching impact on the design and implementation of visual analytic systems.

Acknowledgements. This research is sponsored in part by the U.S. the Department of Defense through the Pacific Northwest National Laboratory, the Siemens Future-Maker Fellowship, and NSF IIS-1813281. The views and conclusions contained in this document are those of the authors and should not be interpreted as representing the official policies, either expressed or implied, of the U.S. Government.

References

1. Brown, E.T., Liu, J., Brodley, C.E., Chang, R.: Dis-function: learning distance functions interactively. In: IEEE Conference on Visual Analytics Science and Technology (VAST), pp. 83–92 (2012)
2. Brown, E.T., et al.: Finding Waldo: learning about users from their interactions. IEEE Trans. Visual Comput. Graphics **20**(12), 1663–1672 (2014)
3. Cho, I., Wesslen, R., Karduni, A., Santhanam, S., Shaikh, S., Dou, W.: The anchoring effect in decision-making with visual analytics. In: IEEE Conference on Visual Analytics Science and Technology (VAST) (2017)
4. Coco, M.I., Dale, R.: Cross-recurrence quantification analysis of categorical and continuous time series: an R package. Front. Psychol. **5**, 510 (2014)
5. Cottam, J.A., Blaha, L.M.: Bias by default? A means for a priori interface measurement. In: DECISIVe: Workshop on Dealing with Cognitive Biases in Visualizations (2017)
6. Dimara, E., Bailly, G., Bezerianos, A., Franconeri, S.: Mitigating the attraction effect with visualizations. IEEE Trans. Visual Comput. Graphics **25**, 850–860 (2018)
7. Dimara, E., Bezerianos, A., Dragicevic, P.: The attraction effect in information visualization. IEEE Trans. Visual Comput. Graphics **23**(1), 471–480 (2017)
8. Dimara, E., Franconeri, S., Plaisant, C., Bezerianos, A., Dragicevic, P.: A task-based taxonomy of cognitive biases for information visualization. IEEE Trans. Visual Comput. Graphics (2018)
9. Dou, W., Jeong, D.H., Stukes, F., Ribarsky, W., Lipford, H.R., Chang, R.: Recovering reasoning process from user interactions. IEEE Comput. Graphics Appl. **29**, 52–61 (2009)
10. Endert, A., Han, C., Maiti, D., House, L., Leman, S.C., North, C.: Observation-level interaction with statistical models for visual analytics. In: IEEE VAST, pp. 121–130 (2011)
11. Endert, A., et al.: The state of the art in integrating machine learning into visual analytics. In: Computer Graphics Forum. Wiley Online Library (2017)
12. Englich, M., Mussweiler, T.: Anchoring effect. Cognitive Illusions: Intriguing Phenomena in Judgement, Thinking, and Memory, p. 223 (2016)
13. Friedman, B., Nissenbaum, H.: Bias in computer systems. ACM Trans. Inf. Syst. (TOIS) **14**(3), 330–347 (1996)
14. Furnham, A., Boo, H.C.: A literature review of the anchoring effect. J. Socio-economics **40**(1), 35–42 (2011)

15. Gigerenzer, G., Goldstein, D.G.: Reasoning the fast and frugal way: models of bounded rationality. Psychol. Rev. **103**(4), 650 (1996)

16. Gotz, D., Sun, S., Cao, N.: Adaptive contextualization: combating bias during high-dimensional visualization and data selection. In: Proceedings of the 21st International Conference on Intelligent User Interfaces, pp. 85–95. ACM (2016)

17. Gotz, D., Zhou, M.X.: Characterizing users' visual analytic activity for insight provenance. Inf. Vis. **8**(1), 42–55 (2009)

18. Heuer Jr., R.J.: Psychology of Intelligence Analysis, Washington, DC (1999)

19. Horvitz, E.: Principles of mixed-initiative user interfaces. In: Proceedings of the SIGCHI Conference on Human Factors in Computing Systems, pp. 159–166, May 1999

20. Kahneman, D.: Thinking, Fast and Slow. Macmillan (2011)

21. Kahneman, D., Frederick, S.: A model of heuristic judgment. In: The Cambridge Handbook of Thinking and Reasoning, pp. 267–294 (2005)

22. Kim, H., Choo, J., Park, H., Endert, A.: InterAxis: steering scatterplot axes via observation-level interaction. IEEE Trans. Visual Comput. Graphics **22**(1), 131–140 (2016)

23. Newell, A.: Unified Theories of Cognition. Harvard University Press (1994)

24. Nickerson, R.S.: Confirmation bias: a ubiquitous phenomenon in many guises. Rev. Gen. Psychol. **2**(2), 175–220 (1998)

25. Patterson, R.E., et al.: A human cognition framework for information visualization. Comput. Graphics **42**, 42–58 (2014)

26. Pike, W.A., Stasko, J., Chang, R., O'Connell, T.A.: The science of interaction. Inf. Vis. **8**(4), 263–274 (2009)

27. Pirolli, P., Card, S.: Sensemaking processes of intelligence analysts and possible leverage points as identified though cognitive task analysis. In: Proceedings of the 2005 International Conference on Intelligence Analysis, McLean, p. 6 (2005)

28. Pohl, M., Smuc, M., Mayr, E.: The user puzzle - explaining the interaction with visual analytics systems. IEEE Trans. Visual Comput. Graphics **18**(12), 2908–2916 (2012)

29. Shneiderman, B.: The eyes have it: a task by data type taxonomy for information visualizations. In: The Craft of Information Visualization, pp. 364–371. Elsevier (2003)

30. Thomas, A.K., Millar, P.R.: Reducing the framing effect in older and younger adults by encouraging analytic processing. J. Gerontol. B Psychol. Sci. Soc. Sci. **2**, 139 (2011)

31. Tversky, A., Kahneman, D.: Judgment under uncertainty: heuristics and biases. Science **185**, 1124–1131 (1974)

32. Tversky, A., Kahneman, D.: The framing of decisions and the psychology of choice. Science **211**, 453–458 (1981)

33. Tversky, A., Kahneman, D.: Rational choice and the framing of decisions. J. Bus. **59**, S251–S278 (1986)

34. Valdez, A.C., Ziefle, M., Sedlmair, M.: A framework for studying biases in visualization research. In: DECISIVe 2017: Dealing with Cognitive Biases in Visualisations (2017)

35. Valdez, A.C., Ziefle, M., Sedlmair, M.: Priming and anchoring effects in visualization. IEEE Trans. Visual Comput. Graphics **1**, 584–594 (2018)

36. Wall, E., Blaha, L.M., Franklin, L., Endert, A.: Warning, bias may occur: a proposed approach to detecting cognitive bias in interactive visual analytics. In: IEEE Conference on Visual Analytics Science and Technology (VAST) (2017)

37. Wall, E., Blaha, L.M., Paul, C.L., Cook, K., Endert, A.: Four perspectives on human bias in visual analytics. In: DECISIVe: Workshop on Dealing with Cognitive Biases in Visualizations (2017)
38. Wason, P.C.: On the failure to eliminate hypotheses in a conceptual task. Q. J. Exp. Psychol. **12**(3), 129–140 (1960)

Benefits and Trade-Offs of Different Model Representations in Decision Support Systems for Non-expert Users

Francisco Gutiérrez[1], Xavier Ochoa[2], Karsten Seipp[1], Tom Broos[1], and Katrien Verbert[1(✉)]

[1] Department of Computer Science, KU Leuven,
Celestijnenlaan 200A, 3001 Leuven, Belgium
{francisco.gutierrez,Katrien.verbert,tom.broos}@kuleuven.be,
karsten.seipp@gmail.com
[2] NYU Steinhardt, New York, NY, USA
xavier.ochoa@nyu.edu

Abstract. Researchers have reported a lack of experience and low graph literacy as significant problems when making visual analytics applications available to a general audience. Therefore, it is fundamental to understand the strengths and weaknesses of different visualizations in the decision-making process. This paper explores the benefits and challenges of an intuitive, a compact, and a detailed visualization for supporting non-expert users. Using objective and subjective means proposed by earlier work, we determine the benefits and trade-offs of these visualizations for different task complexity levels. We found that while an intuitive visualization can be a good choice for easy level and medium level tasks, hard level tasks are best supported with a richer, yet visually more demanding visualization.

Keywords: Visual analytics · Laymen · Graph literacy · Decision-making

1 Introduction

In our daily lives, we may consider multiple risks when planning a financial investment, a project strategy, or when finding a clean and safe place to live. Visual analytics offers a promising approach to facilitate such decision-making tasks. Thomas and Cook [60] define visual analytics (VA) as the science of analytical reasoning facilitated by interactive visual interfaces. In its core, VA supports this analytic reasoning with automated visual data analysis [32]. VA tools can provide control over a variety of settings, interactive discovery, exploration, and understanding of real-world complex systems [5]. Moreover, VA gradually supports users in their sense-making process, allowing them to gauge the effects of different parameters and to gain more insight with each step of the human-computer dialogue [66].

© IFIP International Federation for Information Processing 2019
Published by Springer Nature Switzerland AG 2019
D. Lamas et al. (Eds.): INTERACT 2019, LNCS 11747, pp. 576–597, 2019.
https://doi.org/10.1007/978-3-030-29384-0_35

While the interactive steering of algorithms allows insight into massive data sets, such as social data streams [18] and geospatial data [4], there is a need for research concerning an adequate presentation of such analysis with regards to users inexperienced with visual analysis [14] or unfamiliar with the given visual representation [37]. In the remainder of this paper, we refer to this group of users as *non-expert users*.

Despite the growing needs of non-expert users to control complex analytic processes, little work has been done to support them. Examples include researchers in the humanities who want to apply analysis techniques to large text corpora [26] and non-expert users making decisions about storm forecasts [45]. Different visual representations might have different levels of "visual literacy" that impact the cognitive activities of users [9,38]. For instance, simple and intuitive visualizations may be easier to understand, but general ones might offer more detail and insight into the underlying data and processes at the cost of "representational compatibility" [55]. Although much effort has been geared towards finding the most suitable representation of different types of data [64], researchers report challenges that non-expert users face when using these interactively in VA [23]. To address this issue, we investigate the strengths and weaknesses of different representations to support non-expert users in decision-making. Our research questions are as follows:

1. Regarding objective factors such as accuracy and efficiency, *how do the intuitive, detailed, and compact visualizations relate to the task difficulty?*
2. Regarding subjective factors such as usability and uncertainty, *what are the benefits and challenges of intuitive, detailed, and compact visualizations in an interactive decision-making process?*

To answer these questions, we designed and evaluated an intuitive, a detailed and a compact visualization to support non-expert users with their decision-making under uncertainty. Using subjective and objective means, we provided a set of tasks to the participants and evaluated the three visualizations. The study focuses on stock prices investment, using market indicators to support non-expert users.

2 Background

2.1 Decision Support and Visualization

Decision support systems literature has modelled decision-making as an iterative process of problem recognition, perspective development, perspective synthesis, actions, and results [42]. Visualization plays a crucial role to support the development of these multiple perspectives.

More specifically, visualization facilitates human decision-making by providing structured views about information pertaining to the decision-making problem space [51]. Visualization is a well-established method to support decision-making in a wide variety of domains. Verbert et al. [62] showed that accuracy of recommender systems that suggest relevant items to a user increases with a set-based cluster map representation compared to a traditional ranked list of recommendations. Speier and Morris [57] showed that particularly when the solution set is large, visual query interfaces help users with greater effectiveness than text-based interfaces. Recent studies show how visualization affects and supports user decision-making in the context of financial services [6].

Decision-making usually relies on perception-based information [3]. However, adequate interpretations for perceptions may not always be easy to find under uncertain situations, and thus defining models of this outstanding capability is a difficult, yet a highly promising research area [3]. More specifically, visualization facilitates human decision-making by providing structured views about models related to the decision-making problem space [51]. When making decisions in the real world, information visualization not only helps decision-making, but also offers a means of knowledge creation, as well as an appropriate communication channel [2]. Several application areas have been using visual techniques, including health-care [1], supply chain management [43] and financial services [6].

However, there is a lack of knowledge about which visualization and interaction techniques work best for particular settings and particular users [20]. Also, research has shown that the choice of representation of data influences decision-making outcomes [56]. For instance, Gettinger et al. [13] found that different visual representations have an impact on the decision-making process when giving simple and complex tasks to the participants. We are interested in researching further the factors that influence decision-making, such as the effects of the visualization context, uncertainty representation and trust [27].

2.2   Visual Analytics

In recent years, the importance of Visual Analytics to support decision-making has grown [32]. Visual analytics extends interaction of traditional information visualization techniques with facilities for updating, steering and improving the analytic processes. The key objective is to incorporate feedback from end-users to improve an automatic analysis process.

Examples of VA tools in decision making include the work of Senaratne et al. [49] that explores the use of a VA approach to tackle the inherent uncertainty in urban mobility patterns. Data collected from citizens' mobile communication is used to help to determine the urban dynamics of a city. Afterwards, city planners can use these tools to improve decision-making processes. Moreover, Höferlin et al. [22] introduced a VA approach to analyze video content supported by the communication of uncertainty generated from computer vision feature extraction to end-users. Goda and Song [15] presented a framework for visualizing Tsunami risks using VA techniques to support decision-making in emergency response capability. Their work emphasizes the importance of uncertainty modeling and visualization. The framework was developed through a case study for the 2011 Tohoku tsunami. Other examples include non-expert interpretations of hurracaine prediction [45], climate change data [19], and uncertainty in climate prediction [59]. Visual analytics is also a useful tool to improve understanding of data in predictions [34]. For instance, Ming et al. [41] introduced an interactive visualization technique to support non-expert users in machine-learning to explore and understand predictive models.

Several researchers have compared different visualizations of analysis outcomes and uncertainty associated to these outcomes to support decision-making for non-experts. Ibrekk and Morgan [25] compared nine different visualizations, including error bars, pie chart and density functions, to communicate uncertainty to users with no experience in statistical analysis. The authors suggest to use a combination of cumulative and probability distribution functions (PDF) to avoid misinterpretation. More recently, Greis et al. [16] compared different representations of uncertainty for non-expert users. Results indicate that even though a PDF plot is the best way to communicate uncertainty information, qualitative factors are also important to consider in representations for decision-making. Dynamic visualizations have been researched as well. Hullman et al. [24] compared the effects of an animated visualization against two static visualizations, and measured levels of difficulty by considering one and two variables in the model. Even though accuracy was similar in all representations for single-variable distributions, participants tended to be more accurate with their judgments when using the animated visualization with two variables. Tak et al. [58] compared seven visual representations of uncertainty for non-expert users, including solid and dashed borders, colour-band, gradient, thinning and random lines, and error bars. Results indicate that the visual representation of uncertainty affects the perceived certainty of participants. However, further exploration is required towards the use of other visual variables such as the use of colour and uncertainty range.

In this paper, we build on this earlier research and focus specifically on the design and evaluation of different types of visualizations (*intuitive, compact, detailed*) for non-expert users. We extend the work of [58] by including the uncertainty range in different representations. As in work of [13], we consider different levels of problem complexity. We evaluate different aspects of the utility and effectiveness of different designs, including ease of use and visual appeal as identified by [16]. We discuss these evaluation metrics in the next section.

2.3 Evaluation Metrics

Metrics to evaluate VA applications comprise a variety of criteria. However, definitive, generalizable guidelines do not appear to exist. Therefore, we analyzed previous work to define a set of objective and subjective metrics that may be considered useful in measuring an application's adequacy for supporting the decision-making process. Yang et al. [65] evaluated information graphics based on user preference and their capability to provide different levels of insight. While they could establish a link between information type and presentation, similar to Wongsuphasawat et al. [64], they did not investigate how well the representations would perform as part of an interactive analysis in a VA application. Mckenzie et al. [40] considered objective measures such as *time spent* and

Table 1. List of objective and subjective measures considered.

Metric	Question	Ref.
Objective measures		
Accuracy	How does precision compare across the visualizations?	[40]
Time spent	Is the use of the visualization resulting in longer or shorter decision times?	[40]
Actions	How many interactions are required to solve the tasks?	[47]
Subjective measures, usability-related		
Visual appeal	The visualization was visually appealing	[16]
Ease of use	The visualization was easy to use	[16]
Suitability	The visualization was suitable for solving the tasks	[50]
Likability	The preference towards the uncertainty visualization method	[50]
Task difficulty	Solving the tasks using the visualization was easy	[65]
Subjective measures, uncertainty-related		
Trust	The visualization was trustworthy	[30]
Confidence	I felt confident using the visualization	[11]
Credibility	The visualization was credible	[39]
Understanding	The visualization was easy to understand	[16]
Accuracy	I find the accuracy of this visualization acceptable	[16]

accuracy, whereas Bertini et al. [47] measured the *actions* in an uncertainty-aware interactive interface.

When comparing visual representations, Senaratne et al. [50] ranked visual representations towards their *suitability* according to the user domain. They explored metrics such as *performance* and *likability*, defined as the preference towards the uncertainty visualization method. Using a set of tasks, Lee et al. [36] used objective measures such as *time spent* and, as the work of Greis et al. [16], they used subjective measures such as *ease of use*, *visual appeal* and *easiness to understand*. To evaluate uncertainty factors, Kay et al. [31] proposed a questionnaire to evaluate *acceptance of accuracy* in visual analysis, considering *ease of use* and *intent to use*. [46] defined guidelines towards uncertainty propagation in VA systems, indicating that *trustworthiness* is a critical factor towards uncertainty awareness. Deitrick et al. [11] evaluated different uncertainty representations and their influence on the *confidence* of participants decisions. To conceptualize a framework for uncertainty, MacEachren et al. [39] defined *credibility* as an important subjective measure that has an impact on the user's decision-making and analysis. We compiled a list of objective and subjective measures in Table 1.

3   Study Design

In this study, we collected financial data and implemented intuitive, compact and detailed model representations to support financial decisions for non-expert users[1].

3.1   Design Motivation

As indicated above, there is a lack of knowledge about which visualization and interaction techniques work best for particular settings and particular users [20]. Research has also shown that the choice of representation of data influences decision-making outcomes [56]. We are interested in researching further the factors that influence decision-making, such as the effect of the complexity of the visualization, uncertainty representation and trust. Overall, our decision motivations follow Shneiderman's visual information-seeking mantra [52]:

- With a **detailed representation**, we aim to provide a general context for understanding the predicted data. A detailed visualization addresses the representation of uncertainty considering the data used in the model.
- A **compact representation** provides a close-up, allowing to examine the distribution of data in limited screen spaces and high data complexity situations, as viewing every detail might be impractical. This visualization provides focused insight into a particular risk, clearly showing its spread and uncertainty. Yet, providing detail for a single factor comes at the price of depicting relationships between multiple factors.
- An **intuitive representation** is a visualization that is commonly used and familiar by the end-user to resolve tasks. These representations might include a minimal depiction of uncertainty and might not explain a model in detail.

A typical scenario for decision-making is the investment in stocks. Such a task is subject to uncertainty due to many variables that are involved. We used data related to stock prices to compare different model representations that support users in their decision-making while investing in stocks.

What and When: Intuitive Representation *(Time Series)*. Investing capital in stocks requires to see the behavior of the company stock price in the past. Typically, stock prices fluctuate a lot over time, partly depending on different external factors, such as worldwide news, oil price, and world economy. For the intuitive representation, we asked a financial expert about typical time series visualization. Based on this expert feedback, we designed a time series visualization showing the last year historic fluctuation of the stock value and a next year forecast. The time-series visualization is suited for answering simple questions concerning aspects of what and when.

Why: Detailed Representation *(Scatter Plot)*. A detailed visualization of the prediction model allows users to investigate why and how a prediction

---

[1] https://github.com/FranciscoGutierrez/stockprices.

is made. By inspecting the variables in the model, users can identify possible sources of uncertainty. Differences between the distributions of observations can be depicted and users can see with high precision how data is being correlated [28]. As the approach requires a certain degree in graph literacy, it is important to investigate when and how such a representation is appropriate to support decision-making for non-expert users.

How: Compact Representation *(Dot Plots).* The compact representation used probability distribution functions (PDF), as also used by [25] and [29]. The visualization focuses on showing a clear representation of future events to happen showing discrete outcomes. The dot plot is less detailed than the scatter plot representation, as it does not represent the observations and model. However, it does show a clear representation of probability outcomes. The most likely predicted value was shown above the mean of the distribution, while the predicted value was displayed below the visualization.

The visualization of uncertainty is important to correctly interpret an algorithm's prediction [53]. In our earlier work [48], we investigated quantitative and qualitative performance of different visual variables, such as opacity, blur, contour lines, grid size, and texture, for representing uncertainty. We found that overall opacity performed best, followed by texture. Therefore, we chose a change in opacity in the three visualizations for depicting uncertainty.

3.2   Application Design

We created a set of visualizations to represent the predicted stock price for different companies. A different visualization was used for each of the three study applications resulting in three identical applications, one with a set of six intuitive visualizations, a second with a set of six detailed visualizations and a third with a set of six compact visualizations.

3.3   Data

A typical scenario for decision-making is the investment in stocks. Such a task is subject to uncertainty due to many of the variables that are involved, (e.g., consumer trust, worldwide news, economic growth, Dow Jones index). We used stock prices data to compare different model representations that support non-expert users in their decision-making process while investing in stocks.

To simulate a real scenario we asked for advice from the financial expert. Based on experience, the financial expert selected six companies from the Dow Jones share that had a similar behaviour in their stock prices: Disney (NYSE: DIS), Home Depot (NYSE: HD), Apple (NASDAQ: AAPL), Chevron (NYSE: CVX), IBM (NYSE: IBM), and McDonalds (NYSE: MCD). We used the Quandl API [44] to get the current and one-year historical records of stocks from the selected companies. With the advice of the financial expert, we collected tweets mentioning the selected companies for topics such as worldwide news, and consumer trust that might serve as an indicator of the stock market [7]. We aimed for tweets containing the following hashtags and keywords: "news", "#news", "trust", "confident", "confidence". Then, we used the sentiment analysis API [54], to assign a score from negative (0) to positive (1).

3.4 Model

To estimate the stock price, we built a simple regression model:

$$StockPrice = CI_i\beta_0 + \beta_1 \tag{1}$$

where CI is a compound indicator, β_0 is the slope of the line and β_1 is the *Stock Price* intercept. CI is based on the average normalized values of the market indicators: consumer trust, worldwide news, economic growth, and the Dow Jones index. This allowed users to adjust the market indicators using sliders in the user interface, updating the predictions in the visualization section. Note that we present this simplified forecasting model solely for the purpose of demonstration.

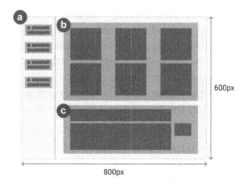

Fig. 1. Layout used in the applications. (a) The settings section shows sliders for adjusting the variables. (b) Visualization section where predictions are shown. (c) Questions section that users have to answer together with the visuals.

3.5 Interaction

We divided the application into three main sections: settings, visuals and questions, see Fig. 1. The settings section used the following market indicators: consumer trust, worldwide news, economic growth, and Dow Jones index. The application presented the market indicators as checkboxes with sliders, see Fig. 2 (left). Selecting a checkbox determines whether the model considers the market indicator as a variable in the prediction. Each slider enables the users to set the level of importance of the variable in the model, according to their beliefs.

When the user selected variables or changed their importance with sliders, the visualization outcome was updated instantly, see Fig. 1b. Next, the questions section, see Fig. 1c, shows a set of easy-to-hard questions reviewed by the financial expert. The users had to interact with a combination of variable settings to respond to all the questions.

3.6   Visualization

The intuitive, compact and detailed visualizations were separated in three different applications, see Fig. 2. Each of the visualizations represented stock price predictions of the same six companies.

Figure 2a: Intuitive Visualization *(Time-Series).* In this visualization, the stock prices predictions were shown using time-series. We implemented a line chart to show the variation of the stock price divided in two sections: historical and forecast. The historical section depicted the stock prices from the past 12 months as historical data. The forecast section showed the expected predicted value for the next 12 months. We also showed the value of the last stock price for the historical data, the value of the fore-casted stock price and the percentage difference between these two values, coloured by red (negative) or green (positive). In addition, we showed the prediction interval for such prediction. We used an opacity scale that indicated the likelihood for the predicted value from unlikely (light grey) to likely (dark grey). In other words, the opacity scale highlighted the quantiles of the predicted probability distribution and showed the range of accuracy for the value. The visualization was updated immediately after when the user adjusted the importance of different variables in the settings section.

Figure 2b: Detailed Visualization *(Scatterplots).* The visualization consisted of the plot of the regression model together with the observations of trust, worldwide news, economic growth and the Dow Jones index. The spread of stock prices of a variable was mapped to the X-axis, the corresponding distribution of the variables describing the economic factors to the Y-axis and then plotted into the coordinate system. Different colours were used to distinguish between the variables. The predicted value for the stock price was written next to the visualization at the Y-axis coordinate of the corresponding point of the regression line.

Figure 2c: Compact Visualization *(Dot Plots).* We used opacity in the dots to represent the accuracy in the forecast. The most likely predicted stock value was shown above the graph. The percent differences were displayed below. Colour was used to depict increase (green) or decrease (red) of the stock price in all visualizations.

3.7   Study Formulation

The financial expert analyzed the data, the model and the visualizations to create a set of 20 candidate questions for the main study. We conducted a

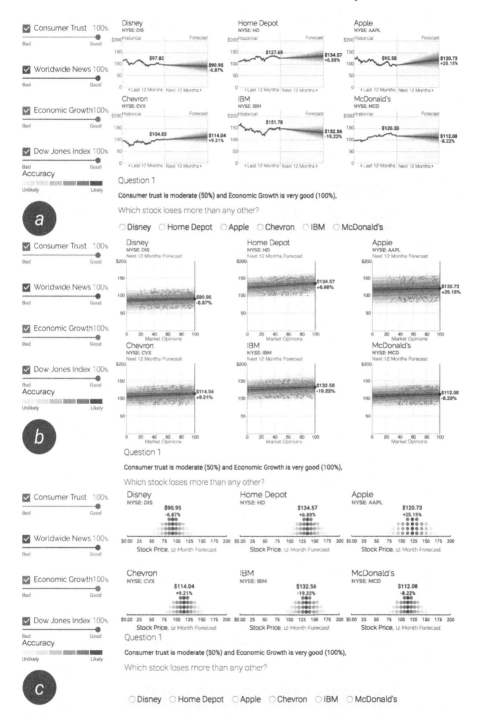

Fig. 2. The three different applications used in the financial decisions study: (a) intuitive, (b) detailed, and (c) compact. (Color figure online)

Table 2. Final groups of participants from the user study

Group	# participants	Gender	Mean age	SD
Intuitive	98	36F, 61M, 1 did not say	32.3	8.9
Detailed	84	29F, 55M	34.8	10.5
Compact	83	28F, 54M, 1 did not say	32.5	9.47

preliminary study in Amazon Mechanical Turk (AMT), where we evaluated the 20 questions with ten participants (10 males) with no expertise with data analysis or visualization. Based on the number of actions required by the participants to answer the questions, we ranked them and selected the top 12 questions. After, we organized the questions into three different categories (easy, medium and hard).

3.8 Main Study

We recruited 360 participants on AMT, 120 per application. To qualify for the study, users had to indicate that they had no professional experience in data analysis and that they were reasonably proficient in the English language. Also, participants were required to have a minimum approval rate of 95%. To catch "gaming" users that simply clicked through the questions, we included five "gold standard" questions randomly into our task list [63]. These were simple questions, such as "What is $1 + 2$?", which used similar controls as the "normal" tasks. In addition to these, we added three training questions to familiarize users with the application. We deemed this necessary as a pilot study showed low performance at the beginning with a learning effect. Each user could only participate once and received a minimum payment of $0.50. To motivate users to try harder, we offered bonuses. For answering at least 66% of questions correctly, users received $2.50, for more than 80%, they received $3.50.

After a short tutorial, the application presented the training and study questions. The average time of the study for each participant was 21 min. At the start of each task, the visualization and controls were hidden, with only the question and a "start" button being visible in the middle of the screen. Upon clicking "start", the visualization, controls, and questions became visible. Recording started when users clicked "start" and ended when they clicked "submit". The following properties were recorded: time spent, number of actions, and the answer given. After users had completed all tasks, they were invited to answer questions regarding usability: *visual appeal, ease of use, suitability, likability, ease of tasks* and questions related to uncertainty: *trust, confidence, credibility, understanding, accuracy representation*, presented in Table 1. Answers were given on a five-point Likert scale, from strongly disagree (1) to strongly agree (5). Users who had failed more than one of the gold questions, had less than three correct answers or did not finish the evaluation were removed, leaving the groups presented in Table 2.

Table 3. Questions by level of difficulty. We show the mean accuracy from all participants.

Diff.	Question	Acc.
Easy	If you consider all four factors to be moderate (50%), which company has the least certain stock price value?	1.00
	If you consider all four factors to be good (75%), which stocks are expected to grow more than 5%?	0.88
	Consumer trust is moderate (50%) and *economic growth* is very good (100%): which stock loses more than any other?	0.87
	If you consider all four factor to be very bad (0%), which is the most profitable stock to invest?	0.83
Medium	You expect a very good *consumer trust* (100%) and a very bad *Dow Jones index* (0%). McDonald's loses more than (...)	0.80
	You expect IBM's stock to be exactly $127.91 and you only consider one factor. Which factor needs to be very good (100%) to confirm your expectation?	0.79
	Economic growth and *consumer trust* are moderate (both 50%). What is the value for the *Dow Jones index* when the chevron stock is $110.11?	0.78
	You have very precise expectations, *consumer trust* at 39%, *worldwide news* at 68%, *economic growth* at 38% and the *Dow Jones index* at 62%. The (...) stock is expected to gain more than (...) but less than (...)	0.74
Hard	You expect the *economic growth* to be moderate (50%). How does the Dow Jones index have to be, so that the growth of apple is exactly the opposite of the growth of IBM?	0.68
	Consumer trust is moderately bad (25%), *economic growth* and the *Dow Jones index* are good (75%). What is the value for the *worldwide news* when the home depot's stock is $129.99?	0.58
	Worldwide news are very good (100%). Which two companies have the highest predicted stock value?	0.46
	If you discard all other indicators, the difference between very bad (0%) and very good (100%) *worldwide news* has the strongest effect on (...)	0.37

4   Results

We ranked the answers of the participants by their accuracy and grouped them in three levels of difficulty, see Table 3. Based on this ranking, we assigned easy, medium and hard levels of difficulty to each question. Also, to further understand the usage of the interface and answer our research questions, we calculated the participants efficiency. Frøkjær et al. [12] defined efficiency as the relation between the accuracy with which users achieve certain goals and the resources expended in achieving them.

The evaluation of VA applications is a big challenge in the visual analytics field [61]. So far, evaluation guidelines are not well established. However, accuracy and efficiency are amongst the most accepted criteria [46]. Moreover, VA studies have used efficiency in the past to measure human-computer interaction techniques in the decision-making process. As such, efficiency is a relevant measurement in our study, as it can tell us how the visual representation is used to efficiently communicate the outcome to the end-user [33].

We define efficiency as follows:

$$efficiency = \sum_{j=1}^{R} \sum_{i=1}^{N} a_{i,j} / \sum_{j=1}^{R} \sum_{i=1}^{N} r_{i,j} \qquad (2)$$

where N is the total number of tasks; R is the number of users; $a_{i,j}$ is the accuracy of task i by user j; $r_{i,j}$ is the amount of resources expended by the user j to solve task i. Resource is defined as the actions per minute performed by the user.

Figure 3 shows the mean values for accuracy and efficiency, using 95% CI, and sorted by level of difficulty. Factorial ANOVA tests were conducted to compare the accuracy of participants, and their efficiency with the visualizations and levels of difficulty. As a follow up to the findings, a post-hoc Tukey HSD test was used. Also, we report the results in Table 4.

Accuracy: participant's accuracy was significantly different for all levels of difficulty ($p < 0.001, \eta_p^2 = 0.23$). In general, participants tended to be significantly ($p < .01, \eta_p^2 = 0.018$) less accurate while using the *compact* visualization. No other significant differences were found.

- *Easy tasks*: no significant differences were found. Participants tended to be more accurate with the intuitive (*mean* = 92%) and the detailed (*mean* = 91%) visualizations, followed by the compact (*mean* = 85%) visualization.
- *Medium tasks*: participants were significantly more accurate ($p < .05, \eta_p^2 = 0.005$) when using the intuitive visualization (*mean* = 82%). They were less accurate with the detailed (*mean* = 78%) and compact (*mean* = 69%) visualizations.
- *Hard tasks*: participants were significantly more accurate ($p < .05, \eta_p^2 = 0.005$) while using the detailed visualization (*mean* = 60%). They were less accurate with the intuitive (*mean* = 52%) and compact (*mean* = 47%) visualizations.

Efficiency: efficiency was significantly different for all levels of difficulty ($p < 0.01, \eta_p^2 = 0.035$) and visualizations, ($p < 0.001, \eta_p^2 = 0.24$). In general, participants were significantly more efficient ($p < 0.001, \eta_p^2 = 0.031$) while using the *detailed* and *intuitive* representations. No other significant differences were found.

Table 4. Results of the study. Objective measures are presented with the mean, subjective measures are presented with their mean and median. Best-scoring values are highlighted in **bold**.

Metric	Difficulty	Intuitive		Detailed		Compact	
Accuracy	Easy	**92%**		91%		85%	
	Medium	**82%***		78%		69%	
	Hard	52%		**60%***		47%	
Efficiency	Easy	**34%**		29%		11%	
	Medium	**34%*****		18%		8%	
	Hard	20%		**23%*****		5%	
Usability		*Mdn*	*M*	*Mdn*	*M*	*Mdn*	*M*
Visual appeal		**5**	4.46	4	**4.47**	4	4.46
Ease of use		**5***	**4.43**	5	4.38	4	4.37
Suitability		**5*****	4.55	**5****	**4.58**	4	4.35
Likability		**5**	**4.5**	4	4.46	**5**	4.46
Tasks were easy		**5*****	**4.28**	**4****	4.16	3	4.18
Uncertainty		*Mdn*	*M*	*Mdn*	*M*	*Mdn*	*M*
Trust		**4*****	4.15	4	4.1	3	**4.21**
Confidence		**5*****	4.41	**4.5*****	**4.42**	3	4.35
Credibility		4	4.23	4	4.15	4	**4.31**
Understanding		**5*****	**4.41**	**5**	4.26	4	4.3
Accuracy		**5*****	**4.49**	4	4.23	4	4.3

* significant at $p < .05$; ** significant at $p < .01$;
*** significant at $p < .001$.

- *Easy tasks*: no significant differences were found. Participants tended to be more efficient with the intuitive visualization ($mean = 34\%$), followed by the detailed ($mean = 29\%$) and the compact ($mean = 11\%$) visualizations.
- *Medium tasks*: participants were significantly more efficient ($p < .001, \eta_p^2 = 0.005$) using the intuitive visualization ($mean = 34\%$). They were less efficient with the detailed ($mean = 18\%$) and compact ($mean = 8\%$) visualizations.
- *Hard tasks*: participants were significantly more efficient ($p < .001, \eta_p^2 = 0.005$) using the detailed visualization ($mean = 60\%$). They were less efficient with the intuitive ($mean = 20\%$) and compact ($mean = 5\%$) visualizations.

A Kruskal Wallis U non-parametric test was used to find a difference in the responses related to usability and uncertainty. Mann-Whitney tests were used as a follow-up in the findings.

- **Visual appeal**: no significant differences were found. Participants preferred the intuitive ($Mdn = 5$) visualization, followed by the compact ($Mdn = 4$) and the detailed ($Mdn = 4$) visualizations.

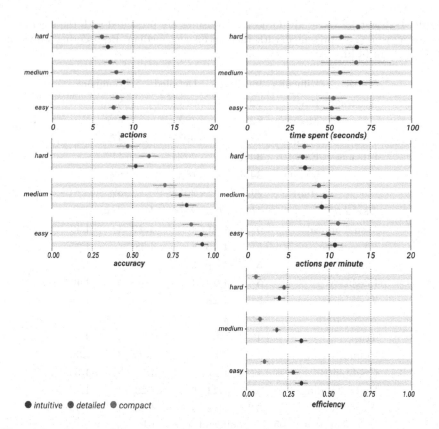

Fig. 3. Results regarding *actions*, *time spent*, *actions per minute*, *accuracy* and *efficiency*, grouped by *easy*, *medium*, and *hard* levels of difficulty.

- **Ease of use**: participants had a significant preference ($p < .05$) towards the intuitive ($Mdn = 5$) visualization, followed by the detailed ($Mdn = 5$) and compact ($Mdn = 4$) visualizations.
- **Suitability**: participants had a significant preference ($p < .001$) towards the intuitive ($Mdn = 5$) and detailed ($Mdn = 5$) visualizations ($p < .01$), followed by the compact ($Mdn = 4$) visualization.
- **Likability**: no significant differences were found. Participants preferred the intuitive ($Mdn = 5$) and compact ($Mdn = 5$) visualizations, followed by the detailed ($Mdn = 4$) visualization.
- **Tasks were easy**: participants had a significant preference ($p < .001$) towards the intuitive ($Mdn = 5$) and the detailed ($Mdn = 4$) visualizations ($p < .01$), followed by the compact ($Mdn = 3$) visualization.
- **Trust**: participants had a significant preference ($p < .001$) towards the intuitive ($Mdn = 4$) visualization, followed by the compact ($Mdn = 4$) and the detailed ($Mdn = 3$) visualizations.

- **Confidence**: participants had a significant preference $(p < .001)$ towards the intuitive $(Mdn = 5)$ and the detailed $(Mdn = 4.5)$ visualizations $(p < .001)$, followed by the compact $(Mdn = 3)$ visualization.
- **Credibility**: no significant differences were found. Participants showed a similar preference towards the intuitive, detailed and compact $(Mdn = 4)$ visualizations.
- **Understanding**: participants had a significant preference $(p < .001)$ towards the intuitive $(Mdn = 5)$ visualization, followed by the compact $(Mdn = 4)$ and the detailed $(Mdn = 4)$ visualizations.
- **Uncertainty**: participants had a significant preference $(p < .001)$ towards the intuitive $(Mdn = 5)$, followed by the detailed $(Mdn = 4)$ and compact $(Mdn = 4)$ representations.

5   Answering the Research Questions

RQ1: Regarding objective factors such as accuracy and efficiency, how do the intuitive, detailed, and compact visualizations relate to the task difficulty?

The selection of a suitable visualization for the task at hand has a significant impact on evaluation results. Results indicate that an *intuitive* visualization works well for easy and medium-level tasks where the participants were the most accurate and efficient. In both studies, participants that used the *detailed visualization* tended to be more accurate as the level of difficulty increased, particularly for hard tasks. Participants tended to be more accurate and more efficient while using this representation, particularly for hard tasks. The *compact* visualization was in general the least accurate and efficient.

RQ2: Regarding subjective factors such as usability and uncertainty, what are the benefits and challenges of intuitive, detailed, and compact visualizations in an interactive decision-making process?

The *intuitive visualization* scored best on most usability and uncertainty factors. These results indicate that the careful selection of an *easy to use* and *suitable* visualization has a strong impact towards uncertainty factors such as *trust*, *understanding* and *confidence*. Participants also indicated that the tasks seemed easy to solve and the accuracy representation was good. Participants that used the *detailed visualization* indicated the visualization was suitable for solving the tasks and tended to show a positive attitude towards the uncertainty representation. Although the *compact visualization* was rated good for factors such as understanding, accuracy representation and likability, further exploration is required on factors such as trust, confidence, and task difficulty.

6   Recommendations for Implementation

Visualization for non-expert users requires careful measurement of qualitative and quantitative analysis of behaviour to solve a problem. Modern approaches such as immerse analytics demand that the choice of the visualization should be progressively adapted to the complexity of the task [8]. Communication of uncertainty is essential in the decision-making and should be an integral part of visualization. Based on our findings, we give the following recommendations.

- **Detailed visualization**: we recommend the use of this visualization as the level of difficulty increases, mainly when looking for efficiency and accuracy on hard level tasks. However, one of the potential drawbacks is the responsiveness of the visualization on small screens. A detailed visualization would shine in larger spaces, where users can manipulate the variables and inspect the details as the information is updated.
- **Intuitive visualization**: the visualization scored best on most usability and uncertainty aspects and was highly accurate for easy and medium level tasks. Participants tended to be more accurate and efficient with the intuitive representation of easy and medium level tasks.
- **Compact visualization**: we recommend being cautious using a compact visualization when accuracy is a critical factor for medium and hard tasks. A compact visualization has potential because it can show a deep insight towards explaining uncertainty. According to participant's feedback, the visualization was credible and understandable, but they were not sure when asked about their trust or confidence. Further research is required about the effects of a compact visualization in the decision-making for VA applications.

7 Conclusion

Exploring the challenges of VA for non-experts is a growing research field [35]. While advice on mapping types of data to an ideal representation does exist [64], information about different visualizations' qualitative and quantitative performance in an interactive decision-making process for non-experts does not. To address this research gap, we have examined the suitability of intuitive, compact, and detailed visualizations in the risk-based decision-making process for non-experts in an application facilitating the exploration of variables involved in a prediction model. By allowing the users to interactively change the importance of different variables, users could steer an algorithm predicting these aspects from a dataset.

Using objective and subjective means proposed by earlier work, we determined the benefits and trade-offs of different uncertainty representations using tasks with different difficulty levels. We found that intuitive visualizations can be a good choice for easy and medium level tasks and that a more demanding visualization may be required for hard level tasks, potentially at the cost of usability aspects. Our research extends previous work on the challenges of supporting non-experts with VA: Kwon et al. [35] reported a set of "roadblocks" inhibiting non-experts from successfully using popular VA applications. As these are commonly built for experts, their utility can be "unreachable" to non-experts due to their limited domain experience, low graph literacy, and inaccurate mental model.

Some applications of our work include the education domain where visualization of prediction outcomes plays a critical role to support the decision-making process of academic advisers [17]. Moreover, in the employment domain, interactive VA tools can be useful to visualize prediction and recommendation output and support a dialogue between job mediator and job seeker [10]. Here VA tools increase *explainability*, providing mediators with control over the information that is presented to job seekers.

Therefore, if we want to extend the user-base of VA to non-experts, we may have to take a step back from these specialized and robust applications. Instead, this endeavour may call for a new generation of closely tied applications to a user's abilities, preferences, and the difficulty of the problem to be solved. Huang et al. [23] explored the challenges of PVA and suggested that an application that is to be successful in this field needs to consider the user's context and provide "appropriate baselines to support reasoning about data". Our work presents a step towards providing such a baseline: defining user context as the difficulty of the problem to be solved or level of insight to be gained, we have evaluated the adequacy of a certain visualization for supporting the VA process of non-experts. Following Shneiderman's visual information seeking mantra [52] of increasing information density as required, we suggest increasing the complexity and capability of a model's representation as the task difficulty and the required level of insight increases.

Regarding the relationship between accuracy and uncertainty, we observed an increment of accuracy with the intuitive visualization for medium and easy tasks where participants also indicated an increase of trust and confidence. This was followed by the detailed representation where participants where significantly more accurate for hard tasks and they reported to have confidence with the visualization. However, with the compact representation, participants where less accurate and gave the lowest scores regarding uncertainty factors.

Our results and those of Kwon et al. [35] have indicated that confronting non-experts with a powerful, but unnecessary complex visualization is detrimental to solving simple problems. Instead, our results indicate that by adapting the visualization to the difficulty of the task, a favourable balance may be struck between various objective and subjective aspects and the decision-making process optimally supported. By defining strengths and weaknesses of three visualization types for problems of varying difficulty, we provided a step towards the definition of a set of visualizations that may be chosen to support non-expert users.

8 Limitations

We used a crowd-sourcing platform to gather data. Previous work has shown the suitability of AMT for conducting studies in the visualization domain [21,65]. Even though our interface was simple, guiding the users with questions to facilitate evaluation, and only four control variables were used to simplify interaction, results should be interpreted with caution, as studies were unsupervised. Moreover, we have detailed the accuracy results per difficulty level, however, the subjective data related to perceived uncertainty is not captured individually for the different difficulty levels. Also, while we were able to identify the benefits and challenges of the visualizations, the effect sizes are relatively small. Future work will investigate further the perceived uncertainty and examine performance in a purely exploratory environment. We will also investigate whether the findings can be extended to other domains.

Acknowledgements. Part of this research has been supported by the KU Leuven Research Council (grant agreement no. C24/16/017 and RUN/16/003), the Research Foundation Flanders (FWO, grant agreement no. G0C9515N), and the European Union (Horizon 2020 research and innovation programme, grant agreement no. 780751).

References

1. Abidi, S.S.R.: Knowledge management in healthcare: towards knowledge-driven decision-support services. Int. J. Med. Inform. **63**(1), 5–18 (2001)
2. Al-Kassab, J., Ouertani, Z.M., Schiuma, G., Neely, A.: Information visualization to support management decisions. Int. J. Inf. Technol. Decis. Mak. **13**(02), 407–428 (2014)
3. Aliev, R.A., Huseynov, O.H.: Fuzzy geometry-based decision making with unprecisiated visual information. Int. J. Inf. Technol. Decis. Mak. **13**(5), 1051–1073 (2014)
4. Andrienko, G., et al.: Geovisual analytics for spatial decision support: setting the research agenda. Int. J. Geogr. Inf. Sci. **21**(8), 839–857 (2007)
5. Basole, R.C., Qamar, A., Park, H., Paredis, C.J., McGinnis, L.F.: Visual analytics for early-phase complex engineered system design support. IEEE Comput. Graph. Appl. **35**(2), 41–51 (2015)
6. Ben-Assuli, O.: Assessing the perception of information components in financial decision support systems. Decis. Support Syst. **54**(1), 795–802 (2012)
7. Bollen, J., Mao, H., Zeng, X.: Twitter mood predicts the stock market. J. Comput. Sci. **2**(1), 1–8 (2011)
8. Bonada, S., Veras, R., Collins, C.: Personalized views for immersive analytics. In: Proceedings of the 2016 ACM Companion on Interactive Surfaces and Spaces, ISS Companion 2016, pp. 83–89. ACM, New York (2016)
9. Boy, J., Rensink, R.A., Bertini, E., Fekete, J.D.: A principled way of assessing visualization literacy. IEEE Trans. Visual Comput. Graph. **20**(12), 1963–1972 (2014)
10. Charleer, S., Gutiérrez Hernández, F., Verbert, K.: Supporting job mediator and job seeker through an actionable dashboard. In: Proceedings of the 24th IUI Conference on Intelligent User Interfaces. ACM (2018)
11. Deitrick, S., Edsall, R.: The influence of uncertainty visualization on decision making: an empirical evaluation. In: Riedl, A., Kainz, W., Elmes, G.A. (eds.) Progress in Spatial Data Handling, pp. 719–738. Springer, Heidelberg (2006). https://doi.org/10.1007/3-540-35589-8_45
12. Frøkjær, E., Hertzum, M., Hornbæk, K.: Measuring usability: are effectiveness, efficiency, and satisfaction really correlated? In: Proceedings of the SIGCHI Conference on Human Factors in Computing Systems, pp. 345–352. ACM (2000)
13. Gettinger, J., Kiesling, E., Stummer, C., Vetschera, R.: A comparison of representations for discrete multi-criteria decision problems. Decis. Support Syst. **54**(2), 976–985 (2013)

14. Gettinger, J., Koeszegi, S.T., Schoop, M.: Shall we dance? - The effect of information presentations on negotiation processes and outcomes. Decis. Support Syst. **53**(1), 161–174 (2012)
15. Goda, K., Song, J.: Uncertainty modeling and visualization for tsunami hazard and risk mapping: a case study for the 2011 tohoku earthquake. Stoch. Env. Res. Risk Assess. **30**(8), 2271–2285 (2016)
16. Greis, M., Ohler, T., Henze, N., Schmidt, A.: Investigating representation alternatives for communicating uncertainty to non-experts. In: Abascal, J., Barbosa, S., Fetter, M., Gross, T., Palanque, P., Winckler, M. (eds.) INTERACT 2015. LNCS, vol. 9299, pp. 256–263. Springer, Cham (2015). https://doi.org/10.1007/978-3-319-22723-8_21
17. Gutiérrez, F., Seipp, K., Ochoa, X., Chiluiza, K., De Laet, T., Verbert, K.: LADA: a learning analytics dashboard for academic advising. Comput. Hum. Behav. (2018). https://www.sciencedirect.com/science/article/pii/S0747563218305909
18. Hao, M., et al.: Visual sentiment analysis on Twitter data streams. In: 2011 IEEE Conference on Visual Analytics Science and Technology (VAST), pp. 277–278. IEEE (2011)
19. Harold, J., Lorenzoni, I., Shipley, T.F., Coventry, K.R.: Cognitive and psychological science insights to improve climate change data visualization. Nat. Clim. Chang. **6**(12), 1080 (2016)
20. He, C., Parra, D., Verbert, K.: Interactive recommender systems: a survey of the state of the art and future research challenges and opportunities. Expert Syst. Appl. **56**, 9–27 (2016)
21. Heer, J., Bostock, M.: Crowdsourcing graphical perception: using mechanical turk to assess visualization design. In: Proceedings of the SIGCHI Conference on Human Factors in Computing Systems, pp. 203–212. ACM (2010)
22. Höferlin, M., Höferlin, B., Weiskopf, D., Heidemann, G.: Uncertainty-aware video visual analytics of tracked moving objects. J. Spat. Inf. Sci. **2011**(2), 87–117 (2011)
23. Huang, D., et al.: Personal visualization and personal visual analytics. IEEE Trans. Vis. Comput. Graph. **21**(3), 420–433 (2015)
24. Hullman, J., Resnick, P., Adar, E.: Hypothetical outcome plots outperform error bars and violin plots for inferences about reliability of variable ordering. PLoS ONE **10**(11), e0142444 (2015)
25. Ibrekk, H., Morgan, M.G.: Graphical communication of uncertain quantities to nontechnical people. Risk Anal. **7**(4), 519–529 (1987)
26. John, M., Koch, S., Heimerl, F., Müller, A., Ertl, T., Kuhn, J.: Interactive visual analysis of German poetics. In: Digital Humanities 2015 Book of Abstracts (2015)
27. Johnson, C.R., Sanderson, A.R.: A next step: visualizing errors and uncertainty. IEEE Comput. Graph. Appl. **23**(5), 6–10 (2003)
28. Kay, M., Heer, J.: Beyond Weber's Law: a second look at ranking visualizations of correlation. IEEE Trans. Vis. Comput. Graph. **22**(1), 469–478 (2016)
29. Kay, M., Kola, T., Hullman, J.R., Munson, S.A.: When (ish) is My Bus? User-centered visualizations of uncertainty in everyday, mobile predictive systems. In: Proceedings of the 2016 CHI Conference on Human Factors in Computing Systems - CHI 2016, pp. 5092–5103 (2016)
30. Kay, M., Morris, D., Kientz, J.A., et al.: There's no such thing as gaining a pound: reconsidering the bathroom scale user interface. In: Proceedings of the 2013 ACM International Joint Conference on Pervasive and Ubiquitous Computing, pp. 401–410. ACM (2013)

31. Kay, M., Patel, S.N., Kientz, J.A.: How good is 85%?: A survey tool to connect classifier evaluation to acceptability of accuracy. In: Proceedings of the 33rd Annual ACM Conference on Human Factors in Computing Systems, pp. 347–356. ACM (2015)
32. Keim, D.A., Mansmann, F., Schneidewind, J., Thomas, J., Ziegler, H.: Visual analytics: scope and challenges. In: Simoff, S.J., Böhlen, M.H., Mazeika, A. (eds.) Visual Data Mining. LNCS, vol. 4404, pp. 76–90. Springer, Heidelberg (2008). https://doi.org/10.1007/978-3-540-71080-6_6
33. Keim, D.A., Mansmann, F., Thomas, J.: Visual analytics: how much visualization and how much analytics? SIGKDD Explor. Newsl. **11**(2), 5–8 (2010)
34. Kim, Y.S., Reinecke, K., Hullman, J.: Explaining the gap: visualizing one's predictions improves recall and comprehension of data. In: Proceedings of the 2017 CHI Conference on Human Factors in Computing Systems, CHI 2017, pp. 1375–1386. ACM, New York (2017). https://doi.org/10.1145/3025453.3025592
35. Kwon, B.C., Fisher, B., Yi, J.S.: Visual analytic roadblocks for novice investigators. In: VAST 2011 - IEEE Conference on Visual Analytics Science and Technology 2011, Proceedings, pp. 3–11. IEEE (2011)
36. Lee, B., Robertson, G.G., Czerwinski, M., Parr, C.S.: CandidTree: visualizing structural uncertainty in similar hierarchies. Inf. Vis. **6**(3), 233–246 (2007)
37. Lee, S., Kim, S.H., Hung, Y.H., Lam, H., Kang, Y.A., Yi, J.S.: How do people make sense of unfamiliar visualizations?: A grounded model of novice's information visualization sense making. IEEE Trans. Vis. Comput. Graph. **22**(1), 499–508 (2016)
38. Lee, S., Kim, S.H., Kwon, B.C.: VLAT: development of a visualization literacy assessment test. IEEE Trans. Vis. Comput. Graphics **23**(1), 551–560 (2017)
39. MacEachren, A.M.A., et al.: Visualizing geospatial information uncertainty: what we know and what we need to know. Cartogr. Geogr. Inf. Sci. **32**(3), 139–160 (2005)
40. McKenzie, G., Hegarty, M., Barrett, T., Goodchild, M.: Assessing the effectiveness of different visualizations for judgments of positional uncertainty. Int. J. Geogr. Inf. Sci. **30**(2), 221–239 (2016)
41. Ming, Y., Qu, H., Bertini, E.: RuleMatrix: visualizing and understanding classifiers with rules. IEEE Trans. Vis. Comput. Graph. **25**(1), 342–352 (2019)
42. Park, H., Basole, R.C.: Bicentric diagrams: design and applications of a graph-based relational set visualization technique. Decis. Support Syst. **84**, 64–77 (2016)
43. Park, H., Bellamy, M.A., Basole, R.C.: Visual analytics for supply network management: system design and evaluation. Decis. Support Syst. **91**, 89–102 (2016)
44. Quandl: Quandl api (2017). https://www.quandl.com/docs/api
45. Ruginski, I.T., et al.: Non-expert interpretations of hurricane forecast uncertainty visualizations. Spat. Cogn. Comput. **16**(2), 154–172 (2016)
46. Sacha, D., Senaratne, H., Kwon, B.C., Ellis, G., Keim, D.A.: The role of uncertainty, awareness, and trust in visual analytics. IEEE Trans. Vis. Comput. Graph. **22**(1), 240–249 (2016)
47. Sarkar, A., Blackwell, A.F., Jamnik, M., Spott, M.: Interaction with uncertainty in visualisations. In: Bertini, E., Kennedy, J., Puppo, E. (eds.) Eurographics Conference on Visualization (EuroVis) - Short Papers. The Eurographics Association (2015)
48. Seipp, K., Gutiérrez, F., Ochoa, X., Verbert, K.: Towards a visual guide for communicating uncertainty in visual analytics. J. Vis. Lang. Comput. **50**, 1–18 (2019)
49. Senaratne, H., et al.: Urban mobility analysis with mobile network data: a visual analytics approach. IEEE Trans. Intell. Transp. Syst. **19**(5), 1537–1546 (2018)

50. Senaratne, H., Reusser, D., Schreck, T.: Usability of uncertainty visualisation methods: a comparison between different user groups (2013)
51. Shim, J.P., Warkentin, M., Courtney, J.F., Power, D.J., Sharda, R., Carlsson, C.: Past, present, and future of decision support technology. Decis. Support Syst. **33**(2), 111–126 (2002)
52. Shneiderman, B.: The eyes have it: a task by data type taxonomy for information visualizations. In: Proceedings 1996 IEEE Symposium on Visual Languages, VL 1996, pp. 336–343. IEEE Computer Society (1996)
53. Skeels, M., Lee, B., Smith, G., Robertson, G.G.: Revealing uncertainty for information visualization. Inf. Vis. **9**(1), 70–81 (2010)
54. Smedt, T.D., Daelemans, W.: Pattern for Python. J. Mach. Learn. Res. **13**(Jun), 2063–2067 (2012)
55. Sparrow, J.A.: Graphical displays in information systems: some data properties influencing the effectiveness of alternative forms. Behav. Inf. Technol. **8**(1), 43–56 (1989)
56. Speier, C.: The influence of information presentation formats on complex task decision-making performance. Hum.-Comput. Stud. **64**(11), 115–1131 (2006)
57. Speier, C., Morris, M.G.: The influence of query interface design on decision-making performance. MIS Q. **27**(3), 397–423 (2003)
58. Tak, S., Toet, A., van Erp, J.: The perception of visual uncertainty representation by non-experts. IEEE Trans. Vis. Comput. Graph. **20**(6), 935–943 (2014)
59. Taylor, A.L., Dessai, S., de Bruin, W.B.: Communicating uncertainty in seasonal and interannual climate forecasts in Europe. Philos. Trans. R. Soc. A: Math. Phys. Eng. Sci. **373**(2055), 20140454 (2015)
60. Thomas, J.J., Cook, K.A.: Illuminating the path: the R&D agenda for visual analytics national visualization and analytics center. In: National Visualization and Analytics Center-US. Department of Homeland Security (2005)
61. Thomas, J., Kielman, J.: Challenges for visual analytics. Inf. Vis. **8**(4), 309–314 (2009)
62. Verbert, K., Parra, D., Brusilovsky, P.: Agents vs. users: visual recommendation of research talks with multiple dimension of relevance. ACM Trans. Interact. Intell. Syst. **6**, 1–46 (2016)
63. Wang, J., Ipeirotis, P.G., Provost, F.: A framework for quality assurance in crowdsourcing, p. 38 (2013)
64. Wongsuphasawat, K., Moritz, D., Anand, A., Mackinlay, J., Howe, B., Heer, J.: Voyager: exploratory analysis via faceted browsing of visualization recommendations. IEEE Trans. Vis. Comput. Graph. **22**(1), 649–658 (2016)
65. Yang, H., Li, Y., Zhou, M.X.: Understand users' comprehension and preferences for composing information visualizations. ACM Trans. Comput.-Hum. Interact. **21**(1), 1–30 (2014)
66. Yi, J.S., ah Kang, Y., Stasko, J.T., Jacko, J.A.: Toward a deeper understanding of the role of interaction in information visualization. IEEE Trans. Vis. Comput. Graph. **13**(6), 1224–1231 (2007)

Customizing Websites Through Automatic Web Search

Iñigo Aldalur(✉), Alain Perez(✉), and Felix Larrinaga(✉)

Mondragon University, Loramendi 4, Arrasate, Spain
{ialdalur,aperez,flarrinaga}@mondragon.edu

Abstract. The WorldWide Web has endured an incredible growth in the last decades. Nowadays, we can visit an unimaginable number of websites from different devices (laptops, mobiles, tablets...) in order to obtain immediate information. However, this information is separated in different resources and Web information search is unpleasant. The feeling of the users is frustrating when collecting information from different resources. Techniques such as Web personalization and Web customization have been an important research area during the last years. Web customization techniques have been widely used to develop website adaptation along the WorldWide Web. This customization is frequently performed by end-users that use the numerous tools available to carry out this assignment.

This article presents Excore, a Web customization tool that permits end-users to customize their websites with automatic Web searches. The article presents the benefits introduced by Excore as a response to the drawbacks end-users experience while they perform their Web activities. Evaluation of the Web customization tool is also addressed in the paper. Evaluation is performed with stakeholders by means of tests and surveys. Results show that testers overcome the detected drawbacks with the use of Excore.

Keywords: Human-Computer Interaction · End-User Development · Customization · Automation · Web search

1 Introduction

Customization is the mechanism that enables users to adapt content, design and functionality to their necessities. Customization might include redefining colors, relocating components, removing features, adding new elements... even adapting web content to people with dyslexia [37]. In order to achieve this goal, the web application is accommodated to the end-user requirements. The increasing volume of website content and actions available on the Web, triggers an

Electronic supplementary material The online version of this chapter (https:// doi.org/10.1007/978-3-030-29384-0_36) contains supplementary material, which is available to authorized users.

© IFIP International Federation for Information Processing 2019
Published by Springer Nature Switzerland AG 2019
D. Lamas et al. (Eds.): INTERACT 2019, LNCS 11747, pp. 598–618, 2019.
https://doi.org/10.1007/978-3-030-29384-0_36

increasing yearning for controlling the Web experience. Often, with a view to carry out actions conducted through the Web, various websites are needed [18]. Generally those websites are completely independent from one another. As a result, end-users are forsaken on their own to obtain the information required by accomplishing their inter-site explorations. The problem is that users feel frustration when repetitive tasks are involved in extracting content from different websites. [2] studied that multiple windows and tabs have significant flaws that hinder users' performance. Here, the approach is to empower end-users to develop extracting content functionality by themselves avoiding this problem.

Lieberman et al. [24] define End-User Development as "a set of methods, techniques and tools that allow users of software systems, who are acting as nonprofessional software developers, at some point to create, modify or extend a software artifact". End-users are capable of commencing with basic adaptation mechanisms and step by step advance to more powerful adaptation mechanisms without facing insuperable barriers [39]. There is an ongoing shift to end-user centered technology, and even users with humble or no skill in Web-based programming languages might perceive the necessity of customizing Web applications according to their preferences [26]. End-user customization is a desired feature in products and in Information Technology there is no difference. Allowing end-users to accommodate content to their requirements enhances usability and might support the removal of accessibility barriers as well [37]. This work looks into Web Customization as a mechanism to adapt Web pages by end-users through a Chrome browser extension for automatic web search.

The remainder of the paper is organized as follows. Section 2 analyses the problem we want to solve, its causes and its consequences. Section 3 discusses related work in order to give the reader an idea of what has been done in this area. Sections 4 and 5 describe Excore (External Content Retriever), a browser extension that customizes web pages for repetitive web search tasks. Section 6 presents the evaluation and its results, Sect. 7 shows features we would like to enhance about Excore and Sect. 8 concludes the paper.

2 Problem Analysis

The Problem

Websites have evolved in the last decade but they still present shortcoming features in the form of repetitive assignments (opening new tabs, scrolling, dozens of clicks to finish with a task...). [20] has accomplished a study on user's feelings when performing web interactions and they have detected a feeling of frustration on users with repetitive tasks, such as gathering information from different resources. Furthermore, the study detected cognitive disorientation in user's daily web activities when looking for information in diverse sources.

Causes

Nowadays users open different tabs to search for information on the Web (multitasking) and they are continuously altering the view from one another (branching). For example, preparing a trip might require three web sessions: finding a flight, booking a hotel and checking the weather. Multi-tasking is a common phenomenon at present time. [30] found that web users' multi-tasking takes up to 76% of the time of their common web activities (about 20% of the sessions had 5 or more tasks). Only 24% of the users use the web for an unique task. A multi-task session occurs when the Web navigation requires more than one web session to be completed and it has a definable point as to when the task is finalized or it is abandoned [27]. In the web literature, branching is defined as the act of initiating a new tab (or window), allowing people to pleasantly navigate multiple websites concurrently [16].

Consequences

When users are obliged to carry out cross-site activities in their daily routine, even when they have to do it occasionally, they lost the focus with their constant tab switching [9]. As a consequence, their tasks will prolong in time and can be inadequately completed.

Constant tab switching is one way of obtaining information from websites contained in different tabs. Nonetheless, users might switch through tabs to locate a previously opened tab or click on a tab by accident. In these cases, tab switching results in transient page views. Users do not actually aspire to gather information from these sites [43]. In fact, [17] found that users switch tabs at least 57.4% of the time, but user activity, measured in page views, is split among tabs rather than increasing overall activity. [32] claims that when multiple sessions are involved it becomes necessary to understand and represent the information contained in each session, which is essential to differentiate them.

Transferring data across applications is a common end-user task, and copying and pasting via the clipboard allows users to do so relatively easily. Using the clipboard, however, can also introduce inefficiencies and errors in user tasks [40]. Roberts et al. [34] researched on errors due to the copying and pasting data in the context of medical information. Should you add this drawback to tab-switching and loss of focus, end-users will have an unsatisfactory web experience.

[29] shows that interruptions can cause frustration, distract people, cause people to make mistakes, reduce their efficiency and increase the time that is needed for the primary task. And this is not all, [35] remarks that multitasking over different types of tasks can reduce productivity and [38] states that the ability of humans to accomplish simultaneous mental operations is limited by the ability of human brains. That is why users have desperate reasons to conclude a branching multi-task successfully. Our objective is to reduce these drawbacks and as a result, end-users will have a satisfactory web experience.

3   Related Work

An activity is defined as a coordinated set of actions by people towards a common objective, mediated by tools and subject to situational constraints [19]. It is exceedingly common to see how people are doing different activities at the same time or switching activities. In fact, people average about three minutes on a pursuit before switching activity [15]. This instance is called task fragmentation which has been studied frequently; showing that it is very common in the workplace [4,15,36]. These studies have shown that work fragmentation is noxious to the actual work: after such a context switch, time is necessary for people to regain their bearings [36]. It must be taken into considerations that nowadays most people work with computers and that [4] research has shown that computers are notoriously bad at supporting the management of parallel activities and interruptions. Interruptions are a particularly detrimental kind of activity fragmentation in which an external signal forces a person to switch activity at an unplanned period and for an unknown duration [36]. This means that computer workers are constantly losing track of their activities. Some other works have tried to avoid this drawback, for instance Cowpath [9], WildThumb [25] and AwToolkit [12].

Cowpath [9] focuses on "Web trails", i.e. recurring navigation paths across distinct Web sites. Rather than switching between tabs and typing once and again the same URLs (Uniform Resource Locator), Cowpath augments the affected websites with additional hyper-links that "pave the way" of these Web trails. [9] mentions that if there is no need to go through the welcome page of a site, it saves clicks and facilitates focus and hence avoids task fragmentation. [42] proposes an algorithm that extracts information from a web search and avoids end-users repeating a secondary search. WildThumb [25] suggests a change in the web interface to support efficient task management in Web browsing. It provides the user with a visual overview of all tabs and reduces the error by opening the correct one. Nonetheless, it does not avoid multi-tasking or losing track. If the user has dozens of tabs opened, the visual overview does not help to find the correct tab, the user must look for it and in this process, he would lose track of the active task. Another example is AwToolkit [12]. It consists of a set of user interface widgets that assist users in maintaining awareness of display changes. The main objective is to offer the ability to detect changes when users are not looking at a specific display, and then notifying users of these changes.

Wikipedia defines mashups as a web page or web application that uses content from more than one source to create a single new service displayed in a single graphical interface[1]. With Web users' search tasks becoming increasingly complex, a single information source cannot necessarily satisfy their information needs [23]. Joining content from different websites circumvents tab switching when locating information from diverse resources. FaceMashup [28] is an End-User Development environment that empowers social network users, supporting them in creating their own procedures for inspecting and controlling their data. MashupEditor [13] is a novel environment for End-User Development of Web mashups. MashupEditor adds content from different websites. The tool avoids tab switching during the composition process. End users exploit an intuitive copy and paste metaphor, which provides component composition for existing Web applications. This means that MashupEditor eludes using copy and paste in repetitive activities. MAMS [41] is the first existing Mashup development process for Modeling and Simulation. Following a new Box/Wiring/Mashup method, users

---

[1] https://en.wikipedia.org/wiki/Mashup.

Fig. 1. Filmaffinity website original website (top) and after customized with IMDB information (bottom)

can develop resources as mashup components, compose them as mashups and run these mashups in web browsers quickly.

Not only are mashups appropriate to join content from different websites in a single one but other methods are possible to be used. WebMakeup [1] is a Chrome browser extension that copies content from diverse web pages and end-users insert or paste this content in a single website. Moreover, it permits them to remove unnecessary web elements and move them if they wish through the website. With CrowdMock [11], users may define their own requirements (adding and removing content) and share them with the community, who can reproduce, edit and evolve them collaboratively. Bosetti [5] proposes a solution to reduce user interaction during web searches thanks to existing web engines. Chudnoskyy et al. [7] take a step forward to create mashups by assisting users with recommendations and automatic composition. [10] shows a tool that proposes a data acquisition system capable of capturing the user interaction in mashups interfaces. Subsequently, these interactions can be reproduced automatically without any human action, which can be a method to limit task fragmentation.

Web automation tools provide a system to increase human productivity by conducting repetitive tasks autonomously. We agree with [3] when they state that "any repetitious behavior should be a candidate for automation because automating things". TellMe [14] is an automation system that enables via natural language instructions to record Web based tasks and then replay them to automate those tasks in the future. SUGILITE [22] is a mobile system that enables the user to create an automation for different tasks across any or multiple smartphone apps and to execute automated tasks through a multi-modal interface.

Despite the existence of applications to automate and customize web interactions, these are insufficient to guarantee the accomplishment of user goals when changes in relevant context cannot be fully anticipated at design time [6]. The goal of this article is to provide end-users with a way to customize their own web searches in their favorite or most visited web pages, therefore reducing frustration in repetitive tasks to solve the problem analyzed in Sect. 2.

4   Automating Web Interactions

The following may be an example of someone's morning routine before going to work: Sit in front of the computer, open the browser, write an URL (e.g. New York Times), read the news headlines, click and open the most interesting ones in new tabs, copy the headlines and search on Google for more info about those news... How often do people do the same action on the net? Which actions do they repeat weekly or monthly? How many repetitive tasks do people do every day? Human beings are undoubtedly animals of habits and hence, we constantly repeat the same activities o a daily basis.

Why do not people develop a script to execute these routines automatically? Most of them are end-users and they do not have the skills to create these routines. What is more, even if they have the knowledge, they might not have the time to develop a script to automatize actions. Excore assists end-users to create automatic web searches with simple interactions (clicks and copy and paste) in very few minutes. With the intention of illustrating the situation we have developed an example to compare film rating in two film websites: IMDB[2] and Filmaffinity[3]. Let's imagine someone is keen on films and he watches a film every night at home. To know if the film deserves being watched he compares the opinion of people about films in both websites. Why cannot we have both opinions in a single search? Fig. 1 shows the original website of Filmaffinity (top) and the same website including IMDB valuation of the same film (bottom).

4.1   Creation

Excore is a Chrome browser extension for end-users. Chrome is the most used browser around the world[4]. That is why, Excore has been developed as a Chrome extension. Once it is installed, the Excore icon can be seen on the top right corner of the browser. Two options will be shown by clicking on it: "New" and "Delete". New is the option to create an automatic task, the definition of the process that provides enough information to the browser extension to repeat the task itself. At the first stage, the background will change its color to certify where the new content is going to be inserted. After that, the user inserts the URL of the website the system has to extract the new content from, in this example, the IMDB website. Figure 2 illustrates the next step that consist of copying the element that the user wants to look for, such as the title of the film.

Figure 3 shows the beginning of the next step of the creation process, the website previously inserted by the user. End-users must follow instructions that appear at the top of the website, i.e. paste and clicks. At the end of the process the users have to select the element the system will locate and copy it to be inserted in the initial website.

4.2   Execution

Now end-users are totally passive with regard to Excore because the system checks if Excore must be enacted based on the website address. The system inspects the URL allowing two possible scenarios.

1. **It is the same Web address.** The customization is always executed.
2. **Website in the same domain.** the customization is executed only when the system is able to locate the element to be searched. Otherwise, the system stops the execution until a new load event is triggered with the same domain.

Excore automation process repeats the interactions done by the user during the creation by locating the desired node, making a copy of it and inserting this node code and style into the customizable website. This process avoids completely the tab switching and copy and pasting actions on the part of the user. This action

---

[2] https://www.imdb.com/.
[3] https://www.filmaffinity.com.
[4] http://gs.statcounter.com.

Fig. 2. Copying yearning element in Filmaffinity

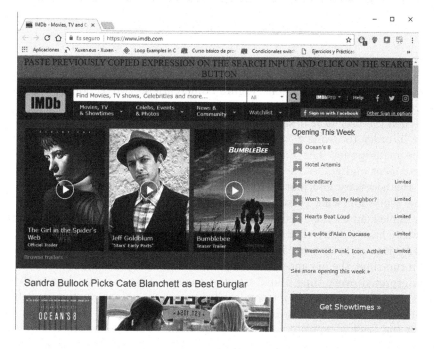

Fig. 3. Pasting process with Excore

saving should increase user focus in their task because he does not have to change the content on his screen. In order to confirm this idea, an evaluation has been accomplished and explained in Sect. 6 in depth.

Once the user is not interested in using the automated task further, the user is able to delete it by clicking on Excore extension icon and every single time he visits the website, the customization will not be enacted.

4.3   Architecture

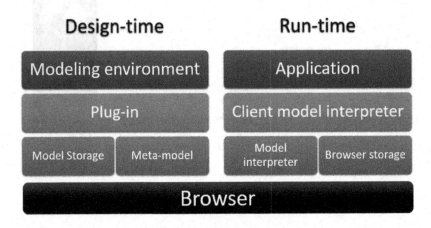

Fig. 4. Excore architecture by layers

In this subsection, we present the architecture of Excore and how it fulfills the goals in the previous subsections. Figure 4 differentiates two sections: design-time or creation and run-time or execution.

When the user is at design-time, Excore web extension provides an environment in order to define a web search step by step. This web search is defined in the meta-model. The Excore extension provides the user with a modeling environment and guides them on the meta-model definition. The user will only read the necessary information for the next step and they will interact with the mouse while following these instructions. Instances are developed visually, no code implementation is needed. At the end, an instance is stored in the browser. Browsers have a space that allow extensions to store some information which is used by Excore to save the instance of the meta-model.

In run-time, the instance of the meta-model stored in the browser is analyzed or interpreted every time a load event is enacted. Once Excore detects that it must come into action, it interprets all events and actions previously defined by the user. These actions are executed in the background, allowing the user watch the original website without changes. Once the application has finished all actions in the background and it detects the final node, the original website will show a copy of the content trough the application, i.e. Excore.

5   Excore Internal Definition

End-User Development tools can be divided into 5 categories: Visual Programming, Spreadsheets, Programming By Demonstration, Domain Specific Languages and Model-Based [1]. Visual Programming tools include visual symbols and graphical notations which are used by end-users as if they were small boxes in which users interact with those components to create their own executable programs. These executable programs must be interpreted by the system thanks to a simple and expressive domain-specific language. Domain-Specific Languages are considered as an approach to decrease complexity of software systems development. Accompanied by Domain Specific Language good practices [31] all requirements have been captured by our feature diagram (see Fig. 5). Next subsections will explain the feature diagram.

5.1   Hosting

Web customization is a set of changes performed by users in order to personalize their most visited or favorite websites. Customization is executed when the web page with a marked host is loaded and the load event is enacted (it has no sense to execute the customization before the event because some nodes might not be loaded and the customization would not take place). The host can be portrayed by a URL expression and when this expression matches the current address of the website, the customization is executed. The host and the current URL can be equal or they can have identical domain to enact web customization. Following the filmAffinity example illustrated by Fig. 1, the user is interested in comparing hundreds of films in the same domain. Otherwise Fig. 1 example would only work for "The dark knight rises" film and the user would have to repeat the automation task for every single film they want to compare. This would be nonsense.

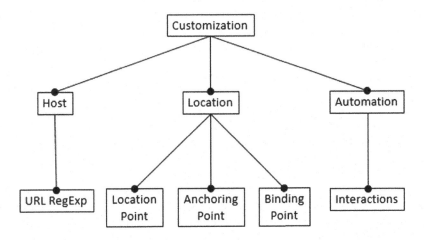

Fig. 5. Feature diagram for Web search customization

5.2   Location

As soon as the customization has started, three different elements must be located to perform the customization successfully. In order to obtain these elements three different locators must be defined. A Web locator can be defined as a mechanism for unique identification of an element in the Document Object Model (DOM) [33]. These locators are:

- **Location Point.** This locator points out from where the desired element is going to be extracted.
- **Anchoring Point.** This information indicates the position where the node extracted with the previous locator is going to be inserted in the target website. The element can be inserted before or after the node has been found with the anchoring locator.
- **Binding Point.** This designates the location of the parameter the system uses to do the automatic web search. In our example, the title of the film.

There are diverse types of locators: first generation, based on coordinates; second generation, based on the structure, (i.e. xpath) and node attributes and third generation, based on image [21]. The robustness of this type of locators is different. First generation locators are not being used nowadays due to their lack of robustness, they are extremely sensitive to modest changes in the DOM structure and web page layout. If the position of the nodes changes a pixel, first generation locator will probably not find the node. According to [21], locators based on node attributes are more robust than those based on structure and these are more robust in time than image based locator. Additionally, third generation locators are not appropriate to be used in Excore owing to the fact that this type of locator tries to find always exactly the same element (image). Each execution is different. If we had to use an image locator in the example of Fig. 1, it would only have worked for this film and not for the rest of films on the website. Hence, we have implemented a multiple locator algorithm. We use a Xpath to find the element and an attribute locator when possible. It is important to remark that it is impossible to use attribute locators all the time because some nodes do not have ID attributes or because their class or other attributes are not unique.

5.3   Automation

One of the aims of Excore is to do the search automatically. For that reason, the system must record all interactions users do to be able to repeat them automatically in execution time. First, the system saves the web page with which it will interact later. Once this website is ready (the load event has been enacted), Excore, that has saved the interaction type (i.e. click, copy, paste...) and the location of the element in which the system has to recreate that action, completes interactions one by one to the end. When the last interactions are completed, the location point acts by extracting the target element and the anchoring point to be inserted on the defined position of the customized website.

6   Evaluation

The main objective of Excore is to allow end-users to customize their favorite and most visited Web pages by including a mechanism to look for required content in diverse Web pages automatically. Allowing users to adapt content to their needs improves usability [37]. In order to validate if Excore accomplishes its purpose, we have evaluated Excore following the ISO 9241-11[5]. ISO definition of usability (ISO 9241-11, Guidance on Usability) comprises three quality characteristics: effectiveness (whether or not end-users are able to complete successfully the tasks), efficiency (if end-users conclude the assignment with Excore faster than manually) and satisfaction (the opinion of the end-user about Excore).

6.1   Research Method

Setting. The study was conducted in Mondragon University laboratory (Arrasate-Mondragon, Spain). All participants did not use computers with the same features but they had some minimum requirements(i.e., Intel Core i5, 4 GB RAM and Windows 10) and an installation of Chrome.

Procedure. Before participants started with the evaluation, they were informed of the purpose of the study and were given a brief description of it. Afterwards, an Excore instance was presented to exemplify the main functionality of the application. The example consisted of creating and automatic Web search to compare the opinion of people on some films in IMDB and Filmaffinity websites. Next, participants were given a leaf with the instructions to create a new automatic Web search. They had to do the evaluation with another example, a book price comparative. First they had to compare the price of ten different books manually from Powells[6] and Amazon[7]. They must find out which platform sells the book at a better price and after that, they had to compare another set of ten books by using Excore. Participants were asked to note down the time at which they started and finished both activities. In order to accurately measure evaluation time, there was a clock so that participants kept track of time. Finally, the participants were directed to a Google Forms on-line questionnaire.

Subjects. Twenty people participated in the study and 60% of the participants were female. As for their age, all of them were in the 20–39 age range. Participants were from Arrasate-Mondragon and the nearby towns. Most subjects were single and with a degree in Mondragon University and other universities but nobody had a technical degree, the aim of the evaluation was to test Excore with end-users. The day the evaluation was accomplished, all of them were working in different fields, such as financial, construction, teaching, agricultural or sports. 70% of participants have installed at least one plug-in in their browser with an average of 1.5. 70% of the participants spend more than 1 h on the Internet

---

[5] https://www.iso.org/standard/16883.html.

[6] http://www.powells.com/.

[7] https://www.amazon.com/.

Table 1. Satisfaction results from 1 (completely disagree) to 5 (completely agree)

Item	Mean	2-5 tabs	6-10 tabs	10+ tabs	St. Dev.
1-When I access the Web, I often have to change the tab ("tab switching")	3.5	2.75	3.5	4.5	1.24
2-Having to do "tab switching" is a nuisance/frustration	3.25	2.12	3.83	4.17	1.37
3-When I constantly change tabs I lose the focus/goal of what I am doing	2.65	1.75	2.67	3.83	1.35
4-I usually lose the focus/objective of what I am doing when I am on the Internet	2.55	1.87	2.33	3.66	1.28
5-I usually use the "copy and paste" options when I am browsing the Internet	4.05	4	3.83	4.33	0.99
6-Having to "copy and paste" is a nuisance/frustration	2.5	2.12	2.33	3.17	1.19
7-Using Excore helps me not to lose the focus/goal of the task I am doing	3.4	2.75	3.33	4.33	1.10
8-Diminish the possibility of losing focus on my task is useful	3.8	3.12	3.67	4.83	1.19
9-Reducing the need to navigate between different tabs is useful	3.85	3.62	3.83	4.17	1.09
10-Not having to "copy and paste" in web searches is useful	3.65	2.88	3.83	4.5	1.14
11-I think that being able to insert content from other web pages within a page is useful	4.05	4	3.83	4.33	0.94
12-I plan to use Excore in the future	3.2	3	3.17	3.5	0.77
13-I think Excore is interesting enough to recommend it to my friends	3.4	3	3.5	3.83	1.14
14-It has been easy to create a new Excore	3.4	3.12	3.5	3.67	1.05
15-It has been easy to remove an Excore	3.3	2.88	3	4.17	0.92
16-It has been easy to compare Powells and Amazon prices with Excore	4.1	3.38	4.17	5	1.12
17-During the use of Excore, I have known at all times how to do the things I had to do	3.65	3.12	4.17	3.83	1.09
18-In general, I am satisfied with what I have been able to do with Excore	3.6	3.62	3.17	4	0.82

everyday in their job and additionally, 55% of them connected for more than 1 h in their free time.

Instrument. A questionnaire was used to collect users' experience in the evaluation. The questionnaire was composed of four sections; background, effectiveness (true false to mark the completeness of the tasks), efficiency (time in minutes to complete tasks) and satisfaction. Satisfaction was measured using different questions with a 5-point Likert scale (1 = completely disagree, 5 = completely agree).

Data Analysis. Descriptive statistics have been used to characterize the sample and to evaluate the participants' experience using Excore.

6.2 Results

The results[8] show the conclusion we can draw from the answers to the questionnaire. Some subjects have added some comments about Excore to the questionnaire:

- *Despite the fact that the state of development of Excore is not optimized, I think it is a very useful tool.*
- *It is a useful extension, the next thing would be to implement the redirection towards the website in which is cheaper to buy the book.*
- *I find Excore useful and easy to use.*

These comments convey the idea that the subjects in the evaluation have had a positive opinion about Excore and they may use it in the future.

In this section, we are going to analyze usability results in ISO 9241-11 considering its three characteristics:

Effectiveness. Both tasks were successfully completed by all subjects. The first task consisted of installing the extension on their browser. The second one consisted of creating an automatic web search and compare the prices of ten books in Powells and Amazon first manually and later automatically. No problems occurred during either process.

Efficiency. Efficiency is measured regarding the time required to conclude the manual search and the automatic search. The time needed in the manual search by all subjects on average has been 9 min and 6 s whereas the time needed in the automatic search has been 6 min and 54 s. This means that automatic web search has been an 24,2% swifter than the manual one. Due to this result, we might infer that the more automatic web search in parallel we have, the more efficient will be. All subjects needed less time to compare book prices with Excore than manually. The time difference needed to complete both task varies from one subject to another. This may be because during the evaluation, some of them were doing the manual search in parallel and some others did not.

We have compared the manual and the automatic searches to know if there are statistically significant differences between both. We have calculated that there is a statistical significant difference of 99,9% in the time needed to carry out each activity which decidedly supports the efficiency of Excore compared to manual web searches.

Satisfaction. Davis [8] said that satisfaction is determined by three dimensions: perceived usefulness, perceived ease of use and willingness to use it in the future. Perceived usefulness by subjects is answered through the first questions in Table 1 (items 1–11). In the middle of the table, willingness to use in the future questions

---

[8] https://tinyurl.com/y9bhva6v.

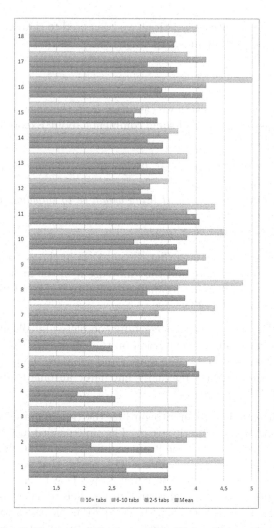

Fig. 6. Excore satisfaction results (Color figure online)

show subjects intention to do so (items 12–13). At the end of Table 1 it is shown what subjects answered whether Excore was easy to use for them (items 14–17). The last question reflects their general opinion about the tool and its utility.

Table 1 is divided in six columns. "Items" are the questions subjects answered after doing the evaluation, "Mean" is the average value from 1 (completely disagree) to 5 (completely agree) subjects gave to each item and "St. Dev." is the standard deviation in each question. The other three columns show the average value subjects gave to each question based on the average number of tabs they usually have opened in their browsers. At the beginning of the questionnaire subjects were asked about how many tabs they usually have opened during their web assignments. Eight subjects said that they have between 2 and 5 tabs opened all the time, six subjects have between 6 and 10 tabs and 6 subjects more than 10 tabs. There is a relation between the amount of tabs the users open and the rating they give to Excore.

Items from 1 to 6 (yellow) are questions referring to the consequences cited in Sect. 2 (tab switching, lost of focus and copy & paste) about their feeling while browsing. Item 1 remarks that the more tabs a person has, the more tab switches he performs (Mean 2–5tabs = 2.75, Mean 10+tabs = 4.5) and the more frustration he feels (Mean 2–5tabs = 2.12, Mean 10+tabs = 4.17)(item 3). These results are logical because users with 3 tabs opened will do less tab switching than users with 11 tabs and people with a big number of tabs opened make more mistakes and as a consequence they feel frustration. Item 3 evaluates whether tab switching is the main cause of focus lost for users with more than 10 tabs (Mean 10+tabs = 3.83). Users also lost their focus when they were on the Internet and they had a large number of tabs opened (Mean 2–5tabs = 1.87, Mean 6–10tabs = 2.33, Mean 10+tabs = 3.66)(item 4). Copy & paste is a frequent action users do (Mean = 4.05) independently of the number of tabs(item 5). However, user fell frustration when they have a large number of tabs (Mean 2–5tabs = 2.12, Mean 10+tabs = 3.17) (item 6).

We have calculated statistically significant differences between groups of users. The users in those groups have been divided according to the amount of tabs they usually have opened. Users with 2–5 tabs and users with 6–10 tabs opened have statistically significant differences in items 2 and 3. Differences in item 2 validates our premise because the more tabs a user has, the more frustration they will feel at tab switching. It also makes sense that users with few tabs do not lose their focus as much as users with several tabs opened. There are statistically significant differences in items 1, 3 and 4 between users with 6–10 tabs opened per session and users with 10+tabs opened tabs per session. For item 1, it seems that users have to do more tab switching when they have a large number of tabs in their browser session. Items 3 and 4 are related to focus during their activities. This result validates our hypothesis due to the fact that the more tabs opened a user has, the easier it is to lose focus on the current activity. Finally, we analyzed the differences between 1–5tabs and 10+tabs users and the results show significant differences in all items except for item 5. Item 5 is about copy and paste activities and all type of users copy and paste during their web activities. The significant difference in items 1 to 4 is of 99%, items related to tab switching and the lose of focus. The significant difference of item 6 is 95%, showing that the bigger the number of opened tabs are, the bigger the nuisance of copying and pasting it is. The results on items 1 to 4 strongly validates the analysis previously done in the problem analysis section.

Items from 7 to 11 (blue) are questions about their experience with Excore during evaluation. Regarding item 7, users consider that the higher number of tabs the more Excore helps to maintain their focus on their activities (Mean 2–5tabs = 2.75, Mean 6–10tabs = 3.33, Mean 10+tabs = 4.33). Furthermore, users claim that it is useful to minimise the chance of losing focus (Mean 2–5tabs = 3.12, Mean 10+tabs = 4.83) (item 8), reducing tab switching (Mean

2–5tabs = 3.62, Mean 10+tabs = 4.17) (item 9) and copying and paste (Mean 2–5tabs = 2.88, Mean 10+tabs = 4.5) (item 10). It is remarkable that in this occasion subjects with more tabs consider Excore more useful regarding the three drawbacks: copy and paste, tab switching and lost of focus. Finally, subjects claim that inserting content from different websites in a single one is useful (Mean = 4.05) (item 11).

Regarding the statistically significant differences, the greater differences are in 10+tabs users. Items 7, 8 and 10 are affected by those differences. Items 7 and 8 are about the focus and users claim that Excore helps them to maintain the focus depending on the number of tabs opened. These results validate the fact that Excore helps to mitigate the consequences explained in the problem analysis section.

As for willingness to use in the future (orange), subjects are interested in using Excore in the future and recommending it to their acquaintances. Similar to usefulness, in this case people with more tabs opened are more interested in using and in recommending Excore.

Concerning subject's perception on Excore's easiness to use, they found easy to create a new automatic search and to remove it. Thanks to Excore, they thought it was really easy to compare prices from Powells and Amazon (Mean = 4.1) in particular people that have more than 10 tabs, because all of them value this question with 5. Lastly, subject did not have problems during the evaluation because they knew what they had to do (Mean = 3.65) and it is relevant to remark that subjects were satisfied when they finished their first experience with Excore (Mean = 3.6).

Figure 6 helps to illustrate these results visually. Numbers on the left indicate the items or question numbers, and bottom values are results users gave to each one. Yellow columns (results of people that have on average more than 10 tabs opened) are always higher than the other results. With the exception of item 5 and 18, the more tabs a user usually has opened, the more frustrated they feel when they are surfing the net. Excore contributed to mitigate this frustration. Figure 6 shows how people with an average of 6–10 tabs opened (gray column) are close to the mean (blue column) in all items. This might indicate that in general most people have between 6 to 10 tabs opened every session and that their opinion is reliable in web matters.

Figure 6 also gives visual evidence of subjects opinions on most significant consequences on multi-tasking, their opinion about web actions and if in their opinion Excore mitigates those problems or not.

7 Future Work

On the future, the first goal is to be capable of doing more than one web search in parallel. We have calculated that using the current version of Excore, the time reduction in repetitive tasks will be more than the 24.2%. Additionally, our purpose is to be able to include iterative web searches based on one result, i.e. when Excore inserts the new content, conduct a new automatic web search based on the new content in another website. It is important to remark that some of this content could be dynamic and as a consequence, every time the dynamic content is updated, Excore should refresh all content based on the dynamic element.

In order to reduce user's frustration we must do more research in common user interactions like clicks, URL typing, scrolling, etcetera which can increase this feeling. Website customization is the precise technique to mitigate these problems.

Finally, we would like to enhance locator robustness in order to increase automatic search life expectancy. As mentioned in Sect. 5, we have implemented two different locator mechanisms owing to the fact that when one fails, the other could find the element. Excore requires several locators to successfully complete the web search and if one fails, the automation will come to nothing. This is why it is highly relevant to implement new locator mechanisms because if one fails another one might succeed. Furthermore, we are interested in improving our actual Xpath algorithm to adapt to web upgrades.

8   Conclusions

This article has presented Excore, a Chrome browser extension that enables end-users to customize their favorite websites with automatic web searches by using simple interactions such as clicks, copy and paste. The aim of this tool is to reduce the frustration users have when they carry out repetitive tasks by decreasing the consequences of this problem (tab switching, copy and paste actions and lost of focus in their daily activities). Evaluation results support the problem analysis. They reflect that people that on average have more opened tabs feel that tab switching, copy and paste are a problem and that they lose their focus more often than people who have few tabs opened. Results also show that Excore helps people who have a large number of tabs opened all the time to reduce these three shortcomings (copy and paste, tab switching and lost of focus). They also remark that it is easy to use. Moreover, Excore reduces the time needed to do frequent web searches around 25%.

References

1. Aldalur, I., Winckler, M., Díaz, O., Palanque, P.: Web augmentation as a promising technology for end user development. In: Paternò, F., Wulf, V. (eds.) New Perspectives in End-User Development, pp. 433–459. Springer, Cham (2017). https://doi.org/10.1007/978-3-319-60291-2_17
2. AlSada, M., Nakajima, T.: Parallel web browsing in tangible augmented reality environments. In: Proceedings of the 33rd Annual ACM Conference Extended Abstracts on Human Factors in Computing Systems, Seoul, CHI 2015 Extended Abstracts, Republic of Korea, 18–23 April 2015, pp. 953–958 (2015)

3. Amershi, S., Mahmud, J., Nichols, J., Lau, T., Ruiz, G.A.: LiveAction: automating web task model generation. TiiS **3**(3), 14:1–14:23 (2013)

4. Bardram, J.E., Bunde-Pedersen, J., Søgaard, M.: Support for activity-based computing in a personal computing operating system. In: Proceedings of the 2006 Conference on Human Factors in Computing Systems, CHI 2006, Montréal, 22–27 April 2006, pp. 211–220 (2006)

5. Bosetti, G., Firmenich, S., Fernandez, A., Winckler, M., Rossi, G.: From search engines to augmented search services: an end-user development approach. In: Cabot, J., De Virgilio, R., Torlone, R. (eds.) ICWE 2017. LNCS, vol. 10360, pp. 115–133. Springer, Cham (2017). https://doi.org/10.1007/978-3-319-60131-1_7

6. Castaneda, L., Villegas, N.M., Müller, H.A.: Self-adaptive applications: on the development of personalized web-tasking systems. In: Proceedings of the 9th International Symposium on Software Engineering for Adaptive and Self-managing Systems, SEAMS 2014, Hyderabad, 2–3 June 2014, pp. 49–54 (2014)

7. Chudnovskyy, O., et al.: End-user-oriented telco mashups: the OMELETTE approach. In: Proceedings of the 21st World Wide Web Conference, WWW 2012, Lyon, 16–20 April 2012 (Companion Volume), pp. 235–238 (2012)

8. Davis, F.D.: Perceived usefulness, perceived ease of use, and user acceptance of information technology. MIS Q. **13**(3), 319–340 (1989)

9. Díaz, O., Sosa, J.D., Trujillo, S.: Activity fragmentation in the web: empowering users to support their own webflows. In: 24th ACM Conference on Hypertext and Social Media (Part of ECRC), HT 2013, Paris, 02–04 May 2013, pp. 69–78 (2013)

10. Fernández-García, A.J., Iribarne, L., Corral, A., Criado, J., Wang, J.Z.: A flexible data acquisition system for storing the interactions on mashup user interfaces. Comput. Stand. Interfaces **59**, 10–34 (2018)

11. Firmenich, D., Firmenich, S., Rivero, J.M., Antonelli, L., Rossi, G.: Crowdmock: an approach for defining and evolving web augmentation requirements. Requir. Eng. **23**(1), 33–61 (2018)

12. Garrido, J.E., Penichet, V.M.R., Lozano, M.D., Quigley, A.J., Kristensson, P.O.: Awtoolkit: attention-aware user interface widgets. In: International Working Conference on Advanced Visual Interfaces, AVI 2014, Como, 27–29 May 2014, pp. 9–16 (2014)

13. Ghiani, G., Paternò, F., Spano, L.D., Pintori, G.: An environment for end-user development of web mashups. Int. J. Hum.-Comput. Stud. **87**, 38–64 (2016)

14. Gil, Y., Ratnakar, V., Fritz, C.: TellMe: learning procedures from tutorial instruction. In: Proceedings of the 16th International Conference on Intelligent User Interfaces, IUI 2011, Palo Alto, 13–16 February 2011, pp. 227–236 (2011)

15. González, V.M., Mark, G.: "Constant, constant, multi-tasking craziness": managing multiple working spheres. In: Proceedings of the 2004 Conference on Human Factors in Computing Systems, CHI 2004, Vienna, 24–29 April 2004, pp. 113–120 (2004)

16. Huang, J., Lin, T., White, R.W.: No search result left behind: branching behavior with browser tabs. In: Proceedings of the Fifth International Conference on Web Search and Web Data Mining, WSDM 2012, Seattle, 8–12 February 2012, pp. 203–212 (2012)

17. Huang, J., White, R.W.: Parallel browsing behavior on the web. In: Proceedings of the 21st ACM Conference on Hypertext and Hypermedia, HT 2010, Toronto, 13–16 June 2010, pp. 13–18 (2010)

18. Karsai, G., Lang, A., Neema, S.: Design patterns for open tool integration. Softw. Syst. Model. **4**(2), 157–170 (2005)

19. Kuutti, K.: The concept of activity as a basic unit of analysis for CSCW research. In: Bannon, L., Robinson, M., Schmidt, K. (eds.) Proceedings of the Second European Conference on Computer-Supported Cooperative Work ECSCW 1991. Springer, Dordrecht (1991). https://doi.org/10.1007/978-94-011-3506-1_19

20. Lee, T.Y., Bederson, B.B.: Give the people what they want: studying end-user needs for enhancing the web. PeerJ Comput. Sci. **2**, e91 (2016). https://doi.org/10.7717/peerj-cs.91, https://doi.org/10.7717/peerj-cs.91

21. Leotta, M., Clerissi, D., Ricca, F., Tonella, P.: Capture-replay vs. programmable web testing: an empirical assessment during test case evolution. In: 20th Working Conference on Reverse Engineering, WCRE 2013, Koblenz, 14–17 October 2013, pp. 272–281 (2013)

22. Li, T.J., Azaria, A., Myers, B.A.: SUGILITE: creating multimodal smartphone automation by demonstration. In: Proceedings of the 2017 CHI Conference on Human Factors in Computing Systems, Denver, 06–11 May 2017, pp. 6038–6049 (2017)

23. Li, X., Liu, Y., Cai, R., Ma, S.: Investigation of user search behavior while facing heterogeneous search services. In: Proceedings of the Tenth ACM International Conference on Web Search and Data Mining, WSDM 2017, Cambridge, 6–10 February 2017, pp. 161–170 (2017)

24. Lieberman, H., Paternò, F., Wulf, V. (eds.): End User Development. Human-Computer Interaction Series. Springer, Dordrecht (2006). https://doi.org/10.1007/1-4020-5386-X

25. Liu, S., Tajima, K.: Wildthumb: a web browser supporting efficient task management on wide displays. In: Proceedings of the 15th International Conference on Intelligent User Interfaces, IUI 2010, Hong Kong, 7–10 February 2010, pp. 159–168 (2010)

26. Macías, J.A., Paternò, F.: Customization of web applications through an intelligent environment exploiting logical interface descriptions. Interact. Comput. **20**(1), 29–47 (2008)

27. MacKay, B., Watters, C.R.: Exploring multi-session web tasks. In: Proceedings of the 2008 Conference on Human Factors in Computing Systems, CHI 2008, Florence, 5–10 April 2008, pp. 1187–1196 (2008)

28. Massa, D., Spano, L.D.: FaceMashup: an end-user development tool for social network data. Future Internet **8**(2), 10 (2016)

29. McFarlane, D.C., Latorella, K.A.: The scope and importance of human interruption in human-computer interaction design. Hum.-Comput. Interac. **17**(1), 1–61 (2002)

30. Mehrotra, R., Bhattacharya, P., Yilmaz, E.: Characterizing users' multi-tasking behavior in web search. In: Proceedings of the 2016 ACM Conference on Human Information Interaction and Retrieval, CHIIR 2016, Carrboro, 13–17 March 2016, pp. 297–300 (2016)

31. Mernik, M., Heering, J., Sloane, A.M.: When and how to develop domain-specific languages. ACM Comput. Surv. **37**(4), 316–344 (2005)

32. Raghavan, S., Parampalli, U., Raghavan, S.V.: Re-engineering simultaneous internet sessions process-separated browsers. In: Proceedings of the Australasian Computer Science Week Multiconference, ACSW 2017, Geelong, 31 January–3 February 2017, pp. 70:1–70:10 (2017)

33. Ricca, F., Leotta, M., Stocco, A., Clerissi, D., Tonella, P.: Web testware evolution. In: 15th IEEE International Symposium on Web Systems Evolution, WSE 2013, Eindhoven, 27 September 2013, pp. 39–44 (2013)

34. Roberts, K., Cahan, A., Demner-Fushman, D.: Error propagation in EHRs via copy/paste: an analysis of relative dates. In: American Medical Informatics Association Annual Symposium, AMIA 2014, Washington, DC, 15–19 November 2014

35. Rubinstein, J.S., Meyer, D.E., Evans, J.E.: Executive control of cognitive processes in task switching. Exp. Psychol. Hum. Percept. Perform. **27**(1), 763–797 (2001)

36. Sanchez, H., Robbes, R., González, V.M.: An empirical study of work fragmentation in software evolution tasks. In: 22nd IEEE International Conference on Software Analysis, Evolution, and Reengineering, SANER 2015, Montreal, 2–6 March 2015, pp. 251–260 (2015)

37. de Santana, V.F., de Oliveira, R., Almeida, L.D.A., Ito, M.: Firefixia: an accessibility web browser customization toolbar for people with dyslexia. In: International Cross-Disciplinary Conference on Web Accessibility, W4A 2013, Rio de Janeiro, 13–15 May 2013, pp. 16:1–16:4 (2013)

38. Schweickert, R., Boggs, G.J.: Models of central capacity and concurrency. Math. Psychol. **28**(3), 223–281 (1984)

39. Spahn, M., Dörner, C., Wulf, V.: End user development: approaches towards a flexible software design. In: 16th European Conference on Information Systems, ECIS 2008, pp. 303–314 (2008)

40. Stolee, K.T., Elbaum, S.G., Rothermel, G.: Revealing the copy and paste habits of end users. In: Proceedings of IEEE Symposium on Visual Languages and Human-Centric Computing, VL/HCC 2009, Corvallis, 20–24 September 2009, pp. 59–66 (2009)

41. Wainer, G.A., Wang, S.: MAMS: mashup architecture with modeling and simulation as a service. J. Comput. Sci. **21**, 113–131 (2017)

42. Winckler, M., Cava, R., Barboni, E., Palanque, P., Freitas, C.: Usability aspects of the inside-in approach for ancillary search tasks on the web. In: Abascal, J., Barbosa, S., Fetter, M., Gross, T., Palanque, P., Winckler, M. (eds.) INTERACT 2015, Part II. LNCS, vol. 9297, pp. 211–230. Springer, Cham (2015). https://doi.org/10.1007/978-3-319-22668-2_18

43. Zhang, H., Zhao, S.: Measuring web page revisitation in tabbed browsing. In: Proceedings of the International Conference on Human Factors in Computing Systems, CHI 2011, Vancouver, 7–12 May 2011, pp. 1831–1834 (2011)

Influence of Color and Size of Particles on Their Perceived Speed in Node-Link Diagrams

Hugo Romat[1,2]([✉]), Dylan Lebout[1]([✉]), Emmanuel Pietriga[1],
and Caroline Appert[1]

[1] Université Paris-Sud, CNRS, INRIA, Université Paris Saclay, Saint-Aubin, France
{hugo.romat,dylan.lebout,emmanuel.pietriga}@inria.fr,
caroline.appert@lri.fr
[2] TecKnowMetrix, Voiron, France

Abstract. Edges in networks often represent transfer relationships between vertices. When visualizing such networks as node-link diagrams, animated particles flowing along the links can effectively convey this notion of transfer. Variables that govern the motion of particles, their speed in particular, may be used to visually represent edge data attributes. Few guidelines exist to inform the design of these particle-based network visualizations, however. Empirical studies so far have only looked at the different motion variables in isolation, independently from other visual variables controlling the appearance of particles, such as their color or size. In this paper, we report on a study of the influence of several visual variables on users' perception of the *speed* of particles. Our results show that particles' *luminance*, *chromaticity* and *width* do not interfere with their perceived *speed*. But variations in their *length* make it more difficult for users to compare the relative *speed* of particles across edges.

Keywords: Graph Visualization · Animation · Perception

1 Introduction

Networks consist of vertices connected by edges, that can encode different sorts of relationships between those vertices depending on the particular application domain considered. Often, these edges represent transfer relationships, especially when the network is directed. Such transfer relationships are closely related to the concept of *flow*: vehicles moving through a transportation network, message dissemination on social networks, disease propagation, power distribution through an electrical grid, *etc.*

Electronic supplementary material The online version of this chapter (https://doi.org/10.1007/978-3-030-29384-0_37) contains supplementary material, which is available to authorized users.

© IFIP International Federation for Information Processing 2019
Published by Springer Nature Switzerland AG 2019
D. Lamas et al. (Eds.): INTERACT 2019, LNCS 11747, pp. 619–637, 2019.
https://doi.org/10.1007/978-3-030-29384-0_37

When visualizing networks as node-link diagrams, this concept of flow can be illustrated by animating the links that represent transfer relationships, typically by having small glyphs – often referred to as *particles* – traverse those links. Depending on the nature of the relationships, particles will encode individual entities traversing the network (*e.g.*, a specific plane going from one airport to another); or they will form repeating patterns that encode more abstract properties of the edges (*e.g.*, the daily average number of passengers on that route). In the latter case, the repeating patterns of particles can be modeled as *animated edge textures* [29]. These textures enable visualization designers to map data attributes to both the variables that define the visual appearance of particles and those that define their behavior. Variables that define the visual appearance of particles include color, shape and size. Variables that define their behavior are essentially related to motion. They include particle speed, and the frequency of the particle pattern.

Enabling visualization designers to map data attributes to motion properties provides them with a larger design space. They have the opportunity to visually represent additional data attributes, in an otherwise fairly limited set of visual variables that basically consists of edge color, stroke width, dash pattern, and to some extent link curvature [20]. But designers can also consider motion variables as alternatives, as they have different qualities and might be more effective at illustrating flow-related attributes.

Many examples from the visualization literature feature animated edge textures or animated particles at large (see, *e.g.*, [11,12,21,24]), sometimes serving specific purposes such as helping to relate groups of consecutive edges [7], guiding visual search [36], or illustrating dynamic propagation or contagion [1,25]. They can also be found in more art- or design-oriented projects (*e.g.*, [6,13,28]) as well as in some commercial dashboard applications.

These diverse uses of animated particles hint at their potential. However, they have often been used in a relatively *ad hoc* manner, without clear guidelines about how to create effective visual mappings. Romat *et al.* [29] recently introduced a framework to explore the design space of motion-based visual mappings in node-link diagrams and to study their effectiveness in terms of perception. The initial studies reported in that article evaluated different motion variables, but studied them in isolation as a necessary first step. As discussed in Sect. 2, the visual perception literature suggests that the interplay between encoding channels could be complex, calling for additional studies that cross different channels. Indeed, motion variables might interfere with one another; and they might also interfere with variables that control the visual appearance of particles.

In this paper, we report on a study that investigates the interplay between particle *speed*, two particle-color attributes (*luminance* and *chromaticity*), and two particle-size attributes (*length* and *width*). Results show that neither the *luminance*, nor the *chromaticity*, nor the *width* of particles interferes with their perceived *speed*. Only variations in their *length* interfere with the perception of their relative *speed* across edges. We discuss these findings and illustrate applications with simple examples of mappings that make effective use of combinations of encoding channels to represent multivariate edges.

2   Background and Motivation

Motion started to be investigated in HCI as an *"abstractly codable dimension in its own right"* [3] as early as 1997. Focusing more specifically on its use in data visualization, motion can be useful for presentations [16] and data storytelling [30], for filtering and brushing [4,14,36], for emphasizing spatial relationships, explaining functionality, illustrating causality [5,27]. Motion is also used extensively in flow visualizations [19,23,26] and representations of other scientific data such as cosmological particles [18].

Focusing even more specifically on network visualization, we find multiple examples of node-link diagrams that make use of some form of particles to visually encode data. Recent work on confluent graph drawing also hints at the potential of particles in combination with edge bundling [2]. Some visualizations map particles to individual entities that move through the network; others use more abstract encodings such as the previously-mentioned animated edge textures [22,29]. Figure 1-a shows an example of the former: a visualization of bike sharing data in New York City [28]. Figure 1-b shows an example of the latter: a visualization of the information flow between relays in the Tor network.

The above two examples share one commonality: they encode multiple data attributes on visual variables that define the appearance and motion of particles. In Fig. 1-a, particles move along trails that represent the bike routes. The shape of particles (brighter and taller at the front end) gives additional information: in what direction that bike is moving;[1] and how fast it is going, the particle's length representing how much distance has been covered in a range of two minutes. In Fig. 1-b, particles show how much data flow between pairs of nodes in the network. Particles can move at different speeds, and can have different colors depending on the type of service (general services *vs.* hidden services). But while such encodings do seem to make sense in these two particular cases, they remain, as most others, *ad hoc* design decisions.

Indeed, our understanding of the interplay between the different visual encoding variables that can be used with particles is limited. Romat *et al.* [29] studied different motion-related encoding variables (particle speed, particle pattern, pattern frequency). But as mentioned earlier, they only studied those variables in isolation, quantifying how many different levels participants could discriminate by comparing pairs of edges, only varying one motion variable at a time, and studying them in a single experimental configuration: white particles, all of the same width, traversing black links.

Yet, the perception literature suggests that there might be a complex interplay between different encoding variables. This might have a direct impact on which ones can be effectively combined, *i.e.*, without variations of one variable

---

[1] Which is redundant with the green *vs.* orange color and with the actual motion when animating the visualization, but becomes more useful when looking at a still image.

interfering with the perception of values of another variable involved in the mapping. For instance, vision research tells us that contrast has an effect on perceived speed, motion direction and on the speed discrimination threshold. More specifically, chromaticity contrast and luminance contrast [38] both have an effect. See, e.g., [8,17,33,34,37] for a complementary set of references.

Such psychophysiological-level findings can guide and inform the design of motion-based visualizations, but they are insufficient to assess the perceptual efficiency of visual encodings involving moving particles in node-link diagrams. Indeed, no matter how large the motion perception literature [31], the experimental setups involved in these studies mostly involve participants evaluating

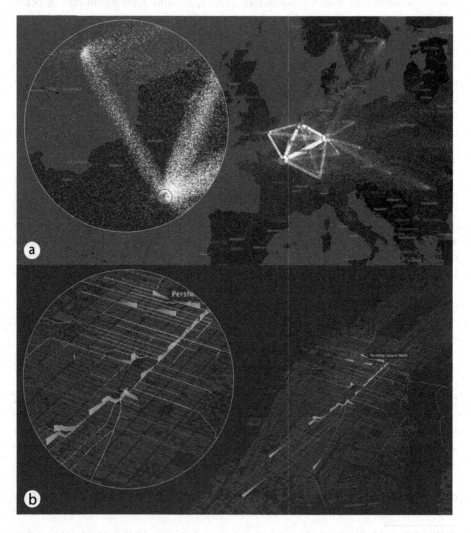

Fig. 1. (a) Information flow between Tor network relays [6]; (b) bike sharing data [28].

speed differences by looking at simple gratings or plaids. While these setups are appropriate in that context, they fail to capture the subtleties of visual perception in the context of complex visualizations that involve larger numbers of small graphical marks, that in our case might have more elaborate motion patterns. As recently stated by Szafir in her work about modeling color differences for visualization design: *"[these] models [...] isolate the capabilities of the human visual system from the complexities introduced by real-world viewing"* [35]. Her *isolation assumption*[2] and *geometric assumption*[3] also represent limits in our case, that call for studies about the perception of particle motion in node-link diagrams. Indeed, the use of motion on links is quite specific. Particles only move along predefined visual paths. The nature of the movement and the number of different directions, considering that edges have different orientations and that they can be curved, is very particular compared to the conditions evaluated in the above psychophysiological experiments. Beyond orientation, the distance between links to be compared might also have an effect, as spatial distance has been shown, for instance, to influence color difference perception [10].

Empirical studies that focus on observing potential interferences between different visual and motion variables (chromaticity, luminance, size, speed) are necessary to get a clear understanding of their interplay, and then identify effective visual mappings that combine some of them to represent multivariate data in node-link diagrams.

3   Experiment Design

We report on a series of experiments that assess users' ability to compare motion speed between two edges, when particles flowing along those edges also vary along a static visual variable. Each participant takes part in four experiments, presented in a random order, and performed in separate, non-consecutive sessions. Each experiment investigates the combination of speed and one of the following four visual variables (VV): *Length*, *Width*, *Luminance*, and *Chromaticity*. For example, for VV = *Width*, the experiment aims at answering the following practical question: do users perceive particles to be moving at the same speed when they are thin and when they are thicker?

3.1   Task

Figure 2 illustrates the experimental task. Participants are instructed to focus on two edges only (indicated by A and B). They have to adjust the speed of particles on *response* edge B so as to make it match that of particles on *reference* edge A. Moving the slider knob toward the left decreases the speed of particles flowing along edge B. Moving the knob toward the right increases it. At the beginning of a trial, the slider knob is always positioned in the middle of the slider. The slider

---

[2] Marks are presented in isolation or in pairs at best.

[3] Marks do not vary in their size and shape.

has 120 steps, each step corresponding to an increment (resp. decrement) in speed that is proportional to the speed of reference edge A ($slider\_unit = \frac{speed(A)}{40}$). This design ensures that the target speed (*i.e.*, that of reference edge A) is contained in the slider's range, but that it does not always correspond to the same position of the knob relative to the slider across trials.

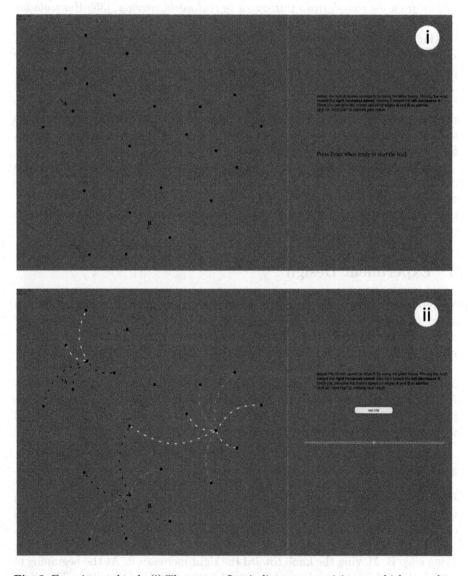

Fig. 2. Experimental task. (i) The system first indicates to participants which two edges they will have to compare. (ii) When participants press the **Enter** key, the visualization gets animated. Participants have to adjust the speed of particles on edge B so that it matches that of particles on edge A, using the slider on the right.

We generate eight planar graphs, which are drawn without edge crossings. The presentation of these graphs is counterbalanced across experimental conditions. Layouts consist of 20 to 28 links, and 21 to 29 nodes, and are generated using D3's force-directed algorithm [9]. Each layout meets the following requirements:

- nodes are distributed in a spatially uniform way;
- there is no pair of nodes that are too close to each other.

The resulting node-link diagrams have the following characteristics:

- average distance between connected nodes: 61 mm (min = 18, max = 165, median = 59);
- average distance of the two links to be compared: 147 mm (min = 105, max = 194, median = 148)[4];
- average length of these links: 66 mm (min = 42, max = 106, median = 64)[5];
- average relative difference in orientation between two links (modulo 180°): 56° (min = 1°, max = 172°, median = 36°).

All eight layouts are available on the companion website, as well as the data collected during the study.[6]

The study of phenomena related to motion perception requires that we are very careful about the visual design of the experimental setup. In particular, we have to ensure that differences in luminance will not impact participants' perception of particles' color (*i.e.*, avoid phenomena such as "dark particles on a light background appear darker than they actually are"). Szafir [35] showed that the minimal difference in luminance that is required in order not to impact the perception of color depends on the size of the visual mark considered. Based on her recommendations and on the minimal size that particles can have in our series of experiments, we computed a minimal difference of luminance of 11%.[7] A background color of $(50,0,0)_{CIELAB}$ and link color of $(49,0,0)_{CIELAB}$ ensure that particles always have a minimal 16% difference in luminance with both the background and the link itself, in all tested conditions.

Each of the four experiments follows a within-subject design considering four factors:

- SPEED_A: the speed of *reference* edge A, $\text{SPEED}_A \in \{Low, Medium, High\}$;
- $\text{SPEED}_{B/A}$: the initial speed of *response* edge B relative to that of *reference* edge A, $\text{SPEED}_{B/A} \in \{Low, Higher\}$;

---

[4] Distance between links is computed as the minimum distance among all four pairs of endpoints between the two links.

[5] Calculation of link length ignores the link's curvature.

[6] To keep the submission anonymous, the companion website is provided only as supplemental material for now.

[7] We use formula (8) in [35] considering that particles are small elongated marks that can have various orientations.

– Δ_{VV}: the difference in value between the *reference* and *response* edges for the considered visual variable (*Length*, *Width*, *Luminance* or *Chromaticity*). The difference can be small, medium, large or there can be no difference ($\Delta_{VV} \in \{Same, Small, Medium, Large\}$). Figure 3 details the exact values corresponding to these different levels, per visual variable. Factor Δ_{VV} is handled differently in the case of *Chromaticity* as it is two-dimensional, compared to *Length*, *Width* and *Luminance*, which are one-dimensional. For *Chromaticity*, we consider the four colors that correspond to the extrema of the two axes defining the chromaticity space in the CIELAB model (at a constant luminance level of 75), and test the following four difference cases: no difference (*Same*), and difference with one of the three other colors.

Perception studies with animated gratings have shown that visual variables can alter perceived velocity to a different extent depending on how fast the grating moves (*e.g.*, [17,38]). They have also shown that the relative speed of another 'modifier' grating can affect the perceived velocity of the grating of interest [32]. In our experiment, factors SPEED$_A$ and SPEED$_{B/A}$ are introduced to account for these potential effects in the context of animated edge textures. To limit the duration of the experiment, we chose a sample of three values ($\{Low, Medium$ and $High\}$) for the speed of *reference* edge A out of the six that were tested in [29]. Initial speed for *response* edge B was set relative to that of edge A in order to make the difference between edges sufficient to be perceivable without significant effort. Table 1 details the actual speeds we test in the different SPEED$_A$ × SPEED$_{B/A}$ conditions. According to recommendations from [29], the emission frequency of particles is adjusted depending on their speed, in order to preserve a constant spacing between them.

Table 1. Tested speeds in the experiment, in millimeters per second. The first column corresponds to the speed of *reference* edge A, which remains fixed throughout a trial. The second (resp. third) column corresponds to the initial speed of *response* edge B in condition SPEED$_{B/A}$ = *Lower* (resp. SPEED$_{B/A}$ = *Higher*).

Speed of edge A (SPEED$_A$)	Initial speed of edge B (SPEED$_{B/A}$ = *Lower*)	Initial speed of edge B (SPEED$_{B/A}$ = *Higher*)
(*Low*) 5.36 mm.s^{-1}	1.55 mm.s^{-1}	10.18 mm.s^{-1}
(*Medium*) 19.35 mm.s^{-1}	10.18 mm.s^{-1}	36.76 mm.s^{-1}
(*High*) 36.76 mm.s^{-1}	19.35 mm.s^{-1}	69.94 mm.s^{-1}

After a series of four practice trials (corresponding to a sample of possible conditions), each participant completes two blocks. Each block contains 48 trials, corresponding to the 24 (3 × 2 × 4) conditions, repeated twice. Conditions SPEED$_A$ × Δ_{VV} are presented in a random order. For each SPEED$_A$ × Δ_{VV} condition, the two conditions SPEED$_{B/A}$ = *Lower* and SPEED$_{B/A}$ = *Higher* are presented in series, but in a random order across conditions.

In each of the four experiments, motion variable *speed* is combined with a different visual variable vv: *Length, Width, Luminance, Chromaticity*. We have computed fifteen random orders of the four experiments to counterbalance their presentation across our fifteen participants.

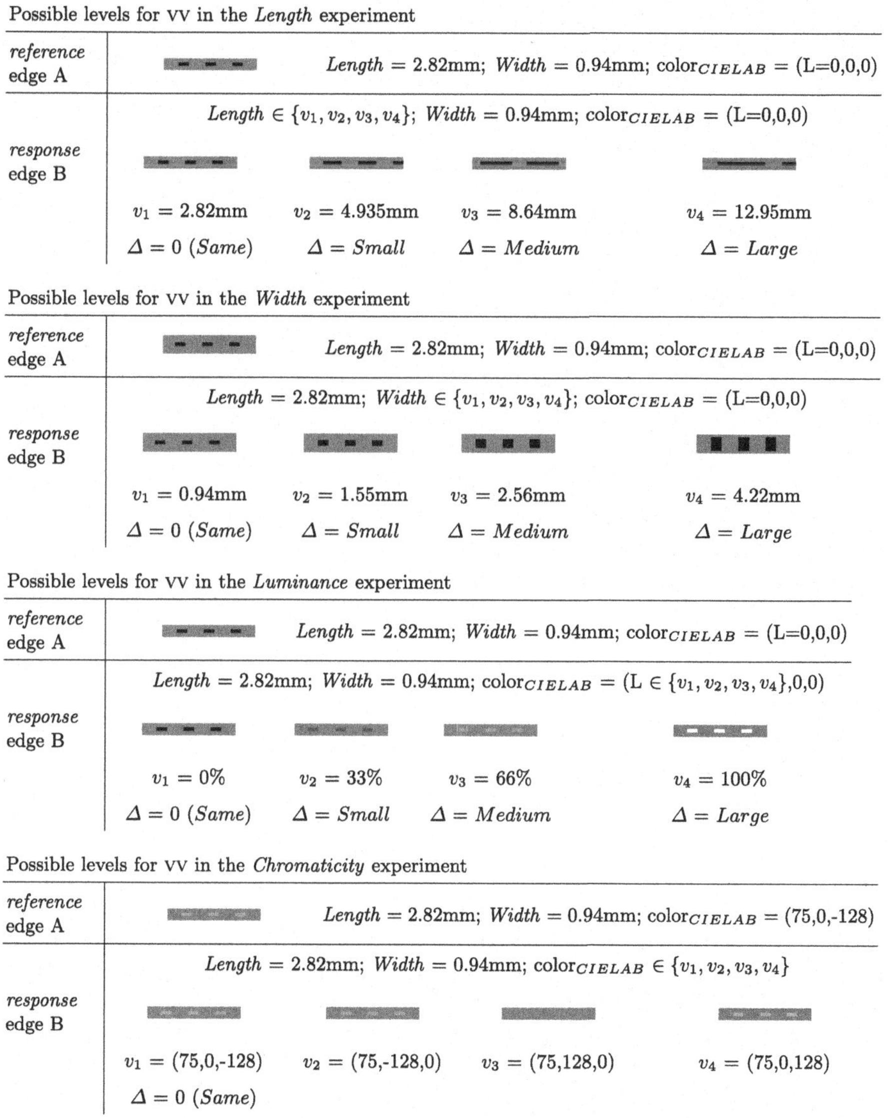

Possible levels for vv in the *Length* experiment

reference edge A	*Length* = 2.82mm; *Width* = 0.94mm; color$_{CIELAB}$ = (L=0,0,0)			
response edge B	*Length* ∈ {v_1, v_2, v_3, v_4}; *Width* = 0.94mm; color$_{CIELAB}$ = (L=0,0,0)			
	v_1 = 2.82mm	v_2 = 4.935mm	v_3 = 8.64mm	v_4 = 12.95mm
	Δ = 0 (*Same*)	Δ = *Small*	Δ = *Medium*	Δ = *Large*

Possible levels for vv in the *Width* experiment

reference edge A	*Length* = 2.82mm; *Width* = 0.94mm; color$_{CIELAB}$ = (L=0,0,0)			
response edge B	*Length* = 2.82mm; *Width* ∈ {v_1, v_2, v_3, v_4}; color$_{CIELAB}$ = (L=0,0,0)			
	v_1 = 0.94mm	v_2 = 1.55mm	v_3 = 2.56mm	v_4 = 4.22mm
	Δ = 0 (*Same*)	Δ = *Small*	Δ = *Medium*	Δ = *Large*

Possible levels for vv in the *Luminance* experiment

reference edge A	*Length* = 2.82mm; *Width* = 0.94mm; color$_{CIELAB}$ = (L=0,0,0)			
response edge B	*Length* = 2.82mm; *Width* = 0.94mm; color$_{CIELAB}$ = (L ∈ {v_1, v_2, v_3, v_4},0,0)			
	v_1 = 0%	v_2 = 33%	v_3 = 66%	v_4 = 100%
	Δ = 0 (*Same*)	Δ = *Small*	Δ = *Medium*	Δ = *Large*

Possible levels for vv in the *Chromaticity* experiment

reference edge A	*Length* = 2.82mm; *Width* = 0.94mm; color$_{CIELAB}$ = (75,0,-128)			
response edge B	*Length* = 2.82mm; *Width* = 0.94mm; color$_{CIELAB}$ ∈ {v_1, v_2, v_3, v_4}			
	v_1 = (75,0,-128)	v_2 = (75,-128,0)	v_3 = (75,128,0)	v_4 = (75,0,128)
	Δ = 0 (*Same*)			

Fig. 3. Possible values for all four visual variables (vv): *Length, Width, Luminance, Chromaticity*.

3.2 Participants and Apparatus

Fifteen volunteers (4 female), aged 21 to 42 year-old (average 26, median 24), all with normal or corrected to normal vision, no color blindness, participated in the experiments. There was no remuneration involved. We conducted the experiments on a PC Dell Precision 5520, equipped with an Intel core i7-7820HQ processor (3.9GHz), 16GB RAM, and an NVidia Quadro M1200 graphics card (4GB), driving an 27" DELL U2715H external monitor (2560 × 1440 QHD, 109 ppi). The monitor features a 16:9 ratio and a luminosity of 350 cd.m^2. Contrast ratio is 1000:1 (native), and 2000000:1 (dynamic). Participants are seated at a distance of 0.6 m from the screen.

4 Results

The main measure of the experiment is Δ_{speed}: the absolute difference in speed between *response* edge B and *reference* edge A at the end of the trial. The lower this difference, the better participants are at estimating speed regardless of variations along another visual variable. In other words, Δ_{speed} is a measure of how much a visual variable (*Length*, *Width*, *Luminance* or *Chromaticity*) interferes with the speed motion variable.

As all participants took part in each of the four conditions and experienced varying presentation orders, data collected across the four experiments can be handled as a single experiment with four factors (VV, SPEED$_A$, SPEED$_{B/A}$, Δ_{VV}), whose design can be summarized as follows:

        15 users
    ×   4 levels of VV
    ×   2 blocks
    ×   3 levels of SPEED$_A$
    ×   4 levels of Δ_{VV}
    ×   2 levels of SPEED$_{B/A}$
    = 2880 trials in total

A repeated measure ANOVA of the four factors on Δ_{speed} reveals a main effect for each of them.

We start our analysis with factor SPEED$_{B/A}$ as it has a main effect ($F_{1,14} = 10.9$, $p < 0.0001$, $\eta_G^2 = 0.03$), but no interaction effect with other factors ($p > 0.05$). Participants were slightly less precise when they had to decrease the speed of response edge B to reach that of edge A ($\Delta_{speed} = 4.1$ mm.s^{-1} when SPEED$_{B/A}$ = *Higher*) than when they had to increase it ($\Delta_{speed} = 3.1$ mm.s^{-1} when SPEED$_{B/A}$ = *Lower*). This difference might be due to the fact that our ability to perceive changes is not linear. Actually, according to the Weber-Fechner law [15], detecting a change from an initially-high level requires a higher-amplitude change than detecting a change from an initially-low level. However, the effect of SPEED$_{B/A}$ is rather small and, as it has no or negligible interaction with other factors, we ignore it for the rest of our analyses.

The remaining three factors all have a significant effect on Δ_{speed}, and they all interact with each other. First, factor SPEED$_A$ has a large effect on Δ_{speed}

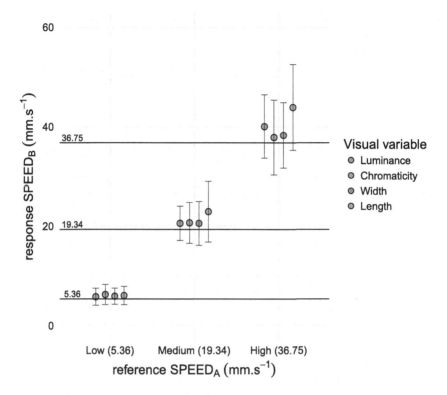

Fig. 4. Average final speed of response edge B per SPEED$_A$ × VV condition. Error bars represent the 95% confidence interval.

$(F_{2,28} = 51.8, p < 0.0001, \eta_G^2 = 0.31)$, which supports the Weber-Fechner law mentioned above: participants were worse at estimating difference at high speeds than they were at low speeds. We then look at factor VV, which is our primary factor of interest, in order to observe whether visual variables of different nature have different levels of interference with the speed motion variable. An ANOVA reveals a significant effect of VV on Δ_{speed} $(F_{3,42} = 18, p < 0.0001, \eta_G^2 = 0.11)$. As illustrated in Fig. 4, participants seem to have more trouble in estimating particle speed when the particles vary in their length. Pairwise comparisons between VV conditions using paired t-tests show that only the *Length* condition is significantly different from all other VV conditions $(p < 0.0001)$. The other three visual variables are not significantly different from each other. Figure 4 also illustrates the interaction effect between VV and SPEED$_A$ on Δ_{speed} $(F_{6,84} = 8, p < 0.0001, \eta_G^2 = 0.07)$. Differences in luminance and length of particles have a higher impact on their perceived speed when particles move at a high speed. However, even in the SPEED$_A$ = *High* condition, only the effect of the *Length* visual variable is significant.

The last factor, Δ_{VV}, is the magnitude of the difference between the values of the considered visual variable on the reference and response edges. Its value must be interpreted relative to that of VV. We thus break down the rest of our analyses by VV condition, in order to better understand what happens under the different visual variable conditions. Figures 5 and 6 illustrate our results for each visual variable. For *Chromaticity*, *Luminance* and *Width*, only the effect of SPEED$_A$, already mentioned above, is significant on Δ_{speed} ($F_{2,28} = 22$, $p < 0.0001$, $\eta_G^2 = 0.41$, $F_{2,28} = 39$, $p < 0.0001$, $\eta_G^2 = 0.54$ and $F_{2,28} = 31$, $p < 0.0001$, $\eta_G^2 = 0.44$ respectively). Neither Δ_{VV} nor SPEED$_A$ $\times$ Δ_{VV} have a significant effect ($p > 0.05$). The situation is a bit different for *Length*. We observe three significant effects on Δ_{speed}: the effect of SPEED$_A$ as for other visual variables ($F_{2,28} = 43$, $p < 0.0001$, $\eta_G^2 = 0.54$), but also the effect of Δ_{VV} ($F_{3,42} = 13$, $p < 0.0001$, $\eta_G^2 = 0.23$), and of the interaction SPEED$_A$$\times$$\Delta_{VV}$ ($F_{6,84} = 7$, $p < 0.0001$, $\eta_G^2 = 0.12$). The accuracy in estimating speed gets worse on average with larger differences in length, and this phenomenon gets amplified with the speed of particles. Pairwise comparisons between $\Delta_{VV}$$\times$SPEED$_A$ support this interpretation. For example, in the SPEED$_A$ = *Low* condition, only *Same* is different from *Medium* and *Large* ($p < 0.05$), while in SPEED$_A$ = *High* condition, almost all pairs of conditions significantly differ ($p < 0.05$). We tentatively attribute this to the size-speed illusion studied in experimental psychology (smaller objects appear to move faster than larger ones–see, *e.g.*, [39]), although this remains speculation at this stage.

5   Summary of Findings

In our experiment, the color of particles did not interfere with their perceived speed, suggesting that visualization designers can safely communicate two attributes on links using *Speed* and *Color* as the encoding channels. Regarding color, designers can make use of either chromaticity, which is typically useful to encode categorical attributes, or luminance, which is better suited to quantitative attributes. The perceived speed of particles was not affected by either of those variables in our empirical observations.

On the contrary, our study shows that variations in the length of particles' do have an impact on their perceived speed, and that interferences between speed and length get more important with large differences in length and at high speeds. This means that using *Speed* and *Size* in combination should be done with caution.

In particular, our results support that a *Speed+Width* encoding should be preferred over a *Speed+Length* one.

We illustrate these findings on two examples of possible combinations that do not cause interferences. The first combines *Speed* and *Color* to visually encode two edge attributes. The second combines *Speed* and *Size*. Animated versions of these node-link diagrams are available on the companion website.

Speed+Color. Figure 7 shows an example of a node-link diagram that encodes edge attributes using a combination of particle speed and color. This node-link diagram shows data about air traffic in the USA, where nodes represent airports and links aerial routes connecting airports. The graph data are multivariate, with multiple attributes for both airports and routes that call for the use

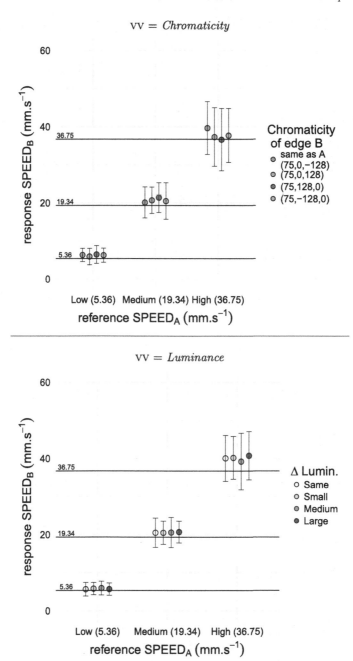

Fig. 5. Average final speed of response edge B for each SPEED$_A$ × Δ_{VV} condition corresponding to color visual variables. Error bars represent the 95% confidence interval.

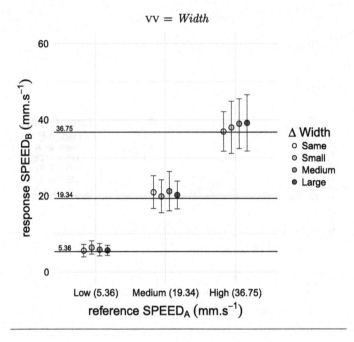

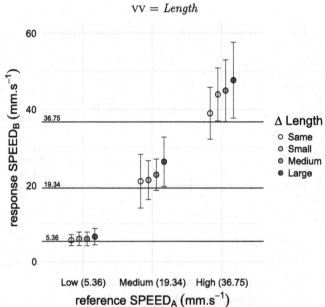

Fig. 6. Average final speed of response edge B for each SPEED$_A$ × Δ_{VV} condition corresponding to size visual variables. Error bars represent the 95% confidence interval.

Fig. 7. A node-link diagram representing air traffic from Salt Lake City to other airports in the USA. Particle chromaticity encodes the main category of payload: passengers in red, mail in blue and freight in yellow. Particle speed encodes the average number of planes on that route. (Color figure online)

of multiple encoding channels. A particle-based node-link diagram is especially well suited to represent air traffic, as it effectively conveys the notion of transit from one airport to the other. The color of particles encodes the main type of payload on a route (mail, freight or passengers). The speed of particles encodes the average number of planes traveling on that route.

The resulting visualization makes it possible to make comparisons per type of payload and across types of payloads. For example, the visualization shows that there are more planes with passengers traveling from Salt Lake City to Chicago than to Seattle, and that the number of planes carrying people to Chicago is higher than the number of planes carrying mail to San Francisco.

Speed+Size. Figure 8 illustrates another example of an animated node-link diagram that shows Twitter activity of some politicians about two key topics: immigration and global warming. While the air traffic example above was using flowing particles to encode two attributes of different type (a categorical one and a quantitative one), this example makes use of particles to encode two quantitative attributes. Particle speed encodes the number of tweets mentioning a hashtag (shown as destination node) over the last year; particle width encodes the number of such tweets over the last month. This design choice makes it possible to see actors' engagement on both a short- and a longer-term basis in the same node-link diagram. For example, if we consider hashtag "global warming", the speed of particles shows that Emmanuel Macron and Angela Merkel were more active over the entire year than Vladimir Putin and Donald Trump were, while the thick particles for Macron reveal that he was the most active over the last month.

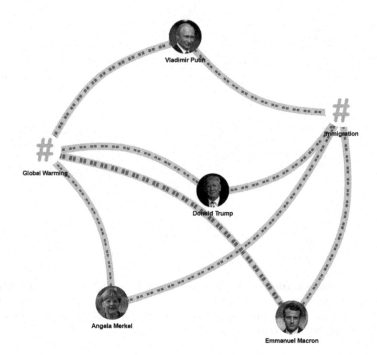

Fig. 8. A node-link diagram representing activity of some politicians about key topics on the Twitter social network (*the data are fictional, generated randomly for illustration purposes only*). The width of particles encodes the number of tweets mentioning the destination hashtag (*e.g.*, Global Warming) over the last month. The speed of particles encodes the number of such tweets over the last year.

6   Conclusion and Future Work

When designing node-link diagrams that feature animated particles, combining particle speed with other visual variables should be handled with caution. In this article, we observed that variations in chromaticity, luminance and width did not alter the perceived speed of particles, while variations in their length did. These empirical findings provide guidelines about which combinations between particle speed and these four visual variables can be effective. But these findings also suggest that the particle *pattern*, a motion variable proposed in [29], should probably not be combined with particle speed. Indeed, particle patterns are obtained by introducing variable-length interspaces to delimit series of particles that form a pattern. An interspace between particles is conceptually close to a transparent particle, which should thus not feature variations in length so as not to interfere with perceived speed.

The effectiveness of animated edge textures in node-link diagrams might also be challenged in the context of graphs that are larger than the ones tested in this study. Larger graphs will introduce a potentially larger distance between pairs of links that can make comparison based on motion difficult. Similarly, animated edge textures might be challenged with dense and non-planar graphs. A high density of links might introduce many motion 'distractors', while link crossings might impact users' ability to follow flows of particles. Such effects remain to be studied in order to assess how the use of animated particle flows, as encoding channels, scale with graph size and complexity. Finally, our results provide guidelines about combining speed with static visual variables when considered in isolation. Combinations of multiple static variables in the context of animated edge textures should be studied next. For example, luminance and chromaticity taken together might interfere with the perception of motion [38].

References

1. Archambault, D., Purchase, H.C.: On the effective visualisation of dynamic attribute cascades. Inf. Vis. **15**(1), 51–63 (2016). https://doi.org/10.1177/1473871615576758
2. Bach, B., Henry Riche, N., Hurter, C., Marriott, K., Dwyer, T.: Towards unambiguous edge bundling: investigating confluent drawings for network visualization. IEEE Trans. Visual. Comput. Graph. **23**(1), 541–550 (2017). https://doi.org/10.1109/TVCG.2016.2598958
3. Bartram, L.: Perceptual and interpretative properties of motion for information visualization. In: Proceedings of the Workshop on New Paradigms in Information Visualization and Manipulation, NPIV 1997, pp. 3–7. ACM (1997). https://doi.org/10.1145/275519.275520
4. Bartram, L., Ware, C.: Filtering and brushing with motion. Inf. Vis. **1**(1), 66–79 (2002). https://doi.org/10.1057/palgrave.ivs.9500005
5. Bartram, L., Yao, M.: Animating causal overlays. In: Computer Graphics Forum, vol. 27, pp. 751–758. Wiley Online Library (2008). https://doi.org/10.1111/j.1467-8659.2008.01204.x
6. Birk, K., Dickson, C., Schroh, D.: Data flow in the Tor network (2015). https://torflow.uncharted.software/
7. Blaas, J., Botha, C., Grundy, E., Jones, M., Laramee, R., Post, F.: Smooth graphs for visual exploration of higher-order state transitions. IEEE Trans. Visual. Comput. Graph. **15**(6), 969–976 (2009). https://doi.org/10.1109/TVCG.2009.181
8. Blakemore, M.R., Snowden, R.J.: The effect of contrast upon perceived speed: A general phenomenon? Perception **28**(1), 33–48 (1999). https://doi.org/10.1068/p2722
9. Bostock, M., Ogievetsky, V., Heer, J.: D3 data-driven documents. IEEE Trans. Visual. Comput. Graph. **17**(12), 2301–2309 (2011). https://doi.org/10.1109/TVCG.2011.185
10. Brychtová, A., Çöltekin, A.: The effect of spatial distance on the discriminability of colors in maps. Cartography Geogr. Inf. Sci. **44**(3), 229–245 (2017). https://doi.org/10.1080/15230406.2016.1140074
11. Buschmann, S., Trapp, M., Döllner, J.: Animated visualization of spatial-temporal trajectory data for air-trac analysis. Vis. Comput. **32**(3), 371–381 (2016). https://doi.org/10.1007/s00371-015-1185-9

12. Cornec, O., Vuillemot, R.: Visualizing the scale of world economies. In: VisWeek 2015 Electronic Conference Proceedings - Poster (2015)
13. Cruz, P.: Wrongfully right: applications of semantic figurative metaphors in information visualization. In: IEEE VIS Arts Program, pp. 14–21. VISAP (2015)
14. Etemadpour, R., Murray, P., Forbes, A.G.: Evaluating density-based motion for big data visual analytics. In: IEEE International Conference on Big Data, pp. 451–460, October 2014. https://doi.org/10.1109/BigData.2014.7004262
15. Fechner, G.: Elements of Psychophysics, vol. 1. American Psychological Association, Washington, DC (1966)
16. Fisher, D.: Animation for visualization: opportunities and drawbacks. In: Beautiful Visualization, chap. 19, pp. 329–352. O'Reilly Media (2010)
17. Gegenfurtner, K.R., Hawken, M.J.: Perceived velocity of luminance, chromatic and non-fourier stimuli: influence of contrast and temporal frequency. Vision Res. **36**(9), 1281–1290 (1996). https://doi.org/10.1016/0042-6989(95)00198-0
18. Haroz, S., Ma, K.L., Heitmann, K.: Multiple uncertainties in time-variant cosmological particle data. In: IEEE Pacific Visualization Symposium, pp. 207–214, March 2008. https://doi.org/10.1109/PACIFICVIS.2008.4475478
19. Haroz, S., Whitney, D.: Temporal thresholds for feature detection in flow visualization. In: Proceedings of the 7th Symposium on Applied Perception in Graphics and Visualization, APGV 2010, p. 163. ACM (2010). https://doi.org/10.1145/1836248.1836285
20. Henry Riche, N., Dwyer, T., Lee, B., Carpendale, S.: Exploring the design space of interactive link curvature in network diagrams. In: Proceedings of the International Working Conference on Advanced Visual Interfaces, AVI 2012, pp. 506–513. ACM (2012). https://doi.org/10.1145/2254556.2254652
21. Hinrichs, U., Butscher, S., Müller, J., Reiterer, H.: Diving in at the deep end: the value of alternative in-situ approaches for systematic library search. In: Proceedings of the CHI Conference on Human Factors in Computing Systems, pp. 4634–4646. ACM (2016). https://doi.org/10.1145/2858036.2858549
22. Holten, D., Isenberg, P., Van Wijk, J.J., Fekete, J.D.: An extended evaluation of the readability of tapered, animated, and textured directed-edge representations in node-link graphs. In: 2011 IEEE Pacific Visualization Symposium, pp. 195–202. IEEE (2011)
23. Huber, D.E., Healey, C.G.: Visualizing data with motion. In: Proceedings of IEEE Visualization, pp. 527–534 (2005). https://doi.org/10.1109/VISUAL.2005.1532838
24. Itoh, M., Yokoyama, D., Toyoda, M., Tomita, Y., Kawamura, S., Kitsuregawa, M.: Visual exploration of changes in passenger flows and tweets on mega-city metro network. IEEE Trans. Big Data **2**(1), 85–99 (2016). https://doi.org/10.1109/TBDATA.2016.2546301
25. von Landesberger, T., Diel, S., Bremm, S., Fellner, D.W.: Visual analysis of contagion in networks. Inf. Vis. **14**(2), 93–110 (2015). https://doi.org/10.1177/1473871613487087
26. McLoughlin, T., Laramee, R.S., Peikert, R., Post, F.H., Chen, M.: Over two decades of integration-based, geometric flow visualization. In: Computer Graphics Forum, vol. 29, pp. 1807–1829. Wiley Online Library (2010). https://doi.org/10.1111/j.1467-8659.2010.01650.x
27. Michotte, A.: The Perception of Causality. Methuen's Manuals of Modern Psychology. Basic Books, New York (1963)
28. Nagel, T., Pietsch, C., Dork, M.: Staged analysis: from evocative to comparative visualizations of urban mobility. In: VIS Arts Program (VISAP), pp. 1–8. IEEE (2017). https://doi.org/10.1109/VISAP.2017.8282374

29. Romat, H., Appert, C., Bach, B., Henry-Riche, N., Pietriga, E.: Animated edge textures in node-link diagrams: a design space and initial evaluation. In: Proceedings of the CHI Conference on Human Factors in Computing Systems, CHI 2018, pp. 187:1–187:13. ACM (2018). https://doi.org/10.1145/3173574.3173761

30. Segel, E., Heer, J.: Narrative visualization: telling stories with data. IEEE Trans. Visual. Comput. Graph. **16**(6), 1139–1148 (2010). https://doi.org/10.1109/TVCG. 2010.179

31. Sekuler, R., Watamaniuk, S., Blake, R.: Perception of visual motion. In: Stevens' Handbook of Experimental Psychology: Vol. 1 Sensation and Perception, 3rd edn. pp. 121–176. Wiley (2004)

32. Smith, D.R.R., Derrington, A.M.: What is the denominator for contrast normalisation? Vision Res. **36**(23), 3759–3766 (1996). https://doi.org/10.1016/0042-6989(96)00100-9

33. Sotiropoulos, G., Seitz, A.R., Seriès, P.: Contrast dependency and prior expectations in human speed perception. Vision Res. **97**, 16–23 (2014). https://doi.org/ 10.1016/j.visres.2014.01.012

34. Stone, L.S., Thompson, P.: Human speed perception is contrast dependent. Vision Res. **32**(8), 1535–1549 (1992). https://doi.org/10.1016/0042-6989(92)90209-2

35. Szafir, D.A.: Modeling color difference for visualization design. IEEE Trans. Visual. Comput. Graph. **24**(1), 392–401 (2018). https://doi.org/10.1109/TVCG. 2017.2744359

36. Ware, C., Bobrow, R.: Motion to support rapid interactive queries on node-link diagrams. ACM Trans. Appl. Percept. **1**(1), 3–18 (2004). https://doi.org/10.1145/ 1008722.1008724

37. Weiskopf, D.: On the role of color in the perception of motion in animated visualizations. In: IEEE Visualization. pp. 305–312, October 2004. https://doi.org/10. 1109/VISUAL.2004.73

38. Willis, A., Anderson, S.J.: Colour and luminance interactions in the visual perception of motion. Proc. Roy. Soc. London B Biol. Sci. **269**(1495), 1011–1016 (2002). https://doi.org/10.1098/rspb.2002.1985

39. Yong, Z., Hsieh, P.J.: Speed-size illusion correlates with retinal-level motion statistics. J. Vis. **17**(9), 1 (2017)

Information Visualization and Augmented Reality

Augmented Reality Technology for Displaying Close-Proximity Sub-Surface Positions

Kasper Hald$^{(\boxtimes)}$, Matthias Rehm, and Thomas B. Moeslund

Department of Architecture, Design and Media Technology, Aalborg University,
Aalborg, Denmark
`kh@create.aau.dk`

Abstract. When designing human-system collaboration to assist in strenuous manual tasks we need to develop methods of communication between the system and the human. In this paper we are evaluating augmented reality (AR) technologies for displaying task-relevant information when the target is on a work surface for a typically standing work operation. In this case we are testing AR interfaces for displaying sub-surface positions. To do this we compare four types of AR interfaces, a head-mounted see-through display, a mounted see-through display, top-down surface projection and graphical overlays on a static monitor. We performed the experiment with 48 participants. Data analyses show significant difference between the AR interfaces in terms of task completion times and user satisfaction with the projection-based display being the fastest and most satisfying to the participants.

Keywords: Augmented reality · Usability testing

1 Introduction

Repetitive strenuous movements involved in production work can lead to musculoskeletal diseases in the long term [9]. This issue can be addressed by introducing assistive and collaborative systems that can relieve some of the strain. This also has the potential to increase productivity. In order to do this we need to develop communication methods between the system and the human, from here referred to as the operator. The communication from the system to the operator in the production context will involve conveying the details pertaining to the current task, and for this study we seek to utilize augmented reality (AR) interfaces for this purpose.

The studies and development are done in the context of industrial meat production in which employees stand on the meat processing lines. In this case the term operator will refer to a single production employee collaborating with an instance of the system's assisting agents. The system will be assisting in tasks involved in sequential meat processing where each employee performs one task

© IFIP International Federation for Information Processing 2019
Published by Springer Nature Switzerland AG 2019
D. Lamas et al. (Eds.): INTERACT 2019, LNCS 11747, pp. 641–659, 2019.
https://doi.org/10.1007/978-3-030-29384-0_38

on each piece of meat for a period of time. These tasks include positioning the meat, cutting it down to size, trimming fat layers or picking out impurities. For this test we focus on the latter task and develop methods for the system to show the position of an impurity, whether it be on or under the surface of the meat, that it can be addressed and removed by operator.

Because the operators will be working in close proximity with potentially hazardous hardware it is critical that task-relevant information can be displayed non-obstructively to the operator in order to communicate the current objective of the system. This will allow the operator to anticipate the actions of the system, leading to safer collaboration and improve human trust in the system as the communication is developed further.

We focus on evaluating AR interfaces since these can be used hands-free. The goal is to evaluate and compare four different types of AR interfaces in terms of effectiveness, ergonomics and user acceptance when showing sub-surface positions in an opaque mass acting as the analog for the meat. The four types of AR interfaces are a head-mounted see-through display, a tablet-based see-through display mounted to an adjustable arm, top-down surface projection and graphical overlays on a static monitor.

2   Related Research

The communication from the system to the operator in the manufacturing context will involve conveying the details pertaining to the current task. Novak-Marcinin et al. [8] define augmented reality-aided manufacturing (ARAM) as the overlap of AR-aided robot control, AR-aided testing, AR-aided assembly and AR-aided transport and storage. The experiment in this paper is to evaluate interfaces for AR-aided assembly, because of the meat production context, where it will be used to aid production staff.

Regarding preliminary evaluation of AR devices, Elia et al. [3] proposed a 4-step model to be applied in specific manufacturing processes. The fist step is a multi-criteria analysis for ranking the most effective AR systems for the purpose, which is the current stage of this project. The ranking is performed by comparing the hardware options in terms of output modalities, reliability, responsiveness and agility. The ranking is done using pair-wise comparison followed by analysis and ranking of the AR devices. Elia et al. [3] categorize types of AR hardware as head-mounted displays (HMD), handheld devices, projectors and haptic force feedback systems. The second step is obtaining a judgment matrix using pair-wise comparison between criteria, followed by evaluation of local weights and consistency of comparison in step 3, with final ranking of devices as step 4.

Kruijff et al. [6] classified potential issues with AR caused by a combination of the environment of use, capturing the environment, the method of augmentation, the types of display device and user. They also point out whether these issues are predominant with particular display types which are categorized similarly to Elia et al. [3]: Head-mounted displays (video see-through or optical see-through), handheld mobile devices or projector-camera system (stationary or mobile). Relevant issues for this study include wearable see-though displays having limited field of view (FOV) and vergence-accommodation conflict for virtual objects and surface-based distortions for projector-based setups.

For this experiment we consider the environment of use be recreating the relevant working conditions pertaining to freedom of movement and posture allowed in a standing task. The four categories outlined by Elia et al. and Kruijff et al. have all been considered for the experiment. However, seeing as all of them are primarily visual aids as opposed to haptic force feedback systems, the latter is not included in this experiment. Since the context of the study allows for handheld devices to be implemented in combination with existing production tools, we would consider haptic feedback as a possible addition to visual augmented reality, so it may be evaluated as an addition at a later stage.

Human-system collaboration enabled by AR has been studied previously, often in the context of human-robot collaboration. However, often these tests have not been performed in the context of a close-proximity task with the user standing at a table. Green et al. [4] tested a human-system collaboration system utilizing an HMD where the operator was sitting at a table. However, the headset used in this case, rather than being a see-through AR display, was an eMagin Z800 headset using OLED displays with the augmented video fed from a mounted webcam. With the potential to have the webcam pointed downwards toward the table the operator would be relieved from bending their neck to look directly down at the tracking markers. The paper does not specify any angle adjustment in the implementation. This solution is not considered for this comparison due to the potential hazard or limiting the operators field of view as opposed to see-through HMDs which allow the user to still see outside of the display field. Even-though not pertaining to a task specifically, Vogel et al. [13] proposed using projection-based AR to show an outline of a safe working area in relation to the collaborative system.

Schwerdtfeger et al. [10] go into depth describing the projected AR, specifically using lasers. They points out the cons of HMD AR devices, those being narrow field of view, limited resolution, swimming effect, multiple focus planes as well as eye fatigue. While laser-projected AR can address some of these issues it is limited to displaying information on surfaces in the environment and the image must be distorted to compensate for environment geometry and viewing angle, whether the projector is head-mounted or stationary. In addition, it also introduces the challenge of occlusion by either the user or other objects. In order to avoid surface distortion for this test we use an even surface for this comparison.

Swan et al. [12] studied how depth perception is affected while using AR devices in that subjects tended to underestimate distance in AR when they are projected at less than 23 meters distance to the user, after which the bias switches to overestimation. Comparing this to short distance error, Singh et al. [11] estimated an error of $-5.5\,cm$ at most for distances less than $50\,cm$. From these finding we should expect our participants to underestimate the target distances in our test. However, we can not know if this is true when the user can judge distance in relation to a real surface as opposed to judging a target hanging in the air.

Similarly to showing sub-surface positions, augmented reality has previously been used to imitate x-ray vision. Avery et al. [1] emphasized that when showing the content beyond the surface using an graphical overlay it should include an edge overlay representing the surface as a depth cue, using occlusion as a depth cue so the object does not appear to float in front of the surface. We are implementing the same method in our test applications by projecting a graphical grid overlay on the surface of our meat analog.

The main contribution of this experiment to the fields of human-robot collaboration and ARAM is in the comparison between the AR devices, but the significance is in the environment and conditions it will be utilized, as comparing the systems in a low-distance setup while standing at a work surface has rarely been done.

3   Setup

The experiment is performed using a tray of sand as the analog for a cut section of meat, as it allows the test subject to poke into it with a tool to address the impurities that will be displayed in it using the AR devices. We use dry loose sand with low density so allow easy entry and to prevent visible entry points to stay throughout a test session. The sand also allows for the surface to be smoothed out by hand.

The participant's performance is measured using an HTC Vive controller with a nail mounted to the bottom as shown in Fig. 1. Using the six degrees of freedom tracking capabilities of the controller the participants are using the tip of the nail to poke into the body of sand as closely as they can while holding the controller in their dominant hand. A second Vive controller is held in the non-dominant hand and the participants will use a button on it to confirm when they have hit a target. Confirming with the non-dominant hand prevents shaking the tip of the nail during a button press.

The HTC Vive tracking space is running using a Windows 10 PC which also acts as the host for the test application, developed in Unity 3D. In order to show the target position on the HMD and the mounted tablet, both of which run Android, the PC acts as network host and sends target positions to the devices acting as clients over a wifi connection throughout the test sessions.

The surface position of the sand is calibrated in the tracking space using the tracked nails on the Vive controller along with a printed piece of calibration paper which also fits in-between the tracking markers used for the HMD and mounted tablet. The tracking markers are positioned at either side of the testing area with the goal of having at least one visible to the tracking camera regardless of where the user is looking and to prevent occlusion of the trackers. The full test setup is shown in Fig. 2.

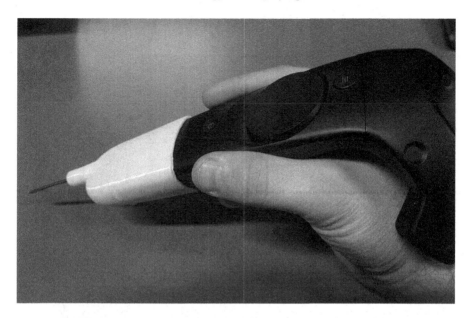

Fig. 1. The needle used for the experiment, made from a 3D printed mount and a nail attached with a bolt in the loop designed for the wrist strap.

4   AR Devices

We are testing four different types of AR devices. Three of them are based on three of the types outlined by both Elia et al. [3] and Kruijff et al. [6]; head-mounted see-through display from here referenced as HMD, see-though mobile display and projection-based AR. In addition, we are comparing a video feed on a monitor augmented with graphical overlays because this is currently a typical way of displaying information in meat production settings. The software for the four AR devices are developed using Unity 3D. Similar to all of the versions is that a green grid is projected aligned with the surface of the sand, similarly to what is described by Avery et al. [1].

The targets are shown as a red sphere or circles at 10 mm in diameter projected into the sand. Due the nature of the devices the display methods for the targets differ between the displays. Because the image for the top-down projector and the stationary screens are limited to 2D projections on the surface of the sand, the red dot is shown along with a number indicating the depth of the target in millimeters. We considered using similar labels for HMD and tablet devices, but because the user will see the target projected from different angles depending on their viewing angle as opposed to always seeing it from the top and directly down. Both the HMD and tablet show 3D-rendered images, allowing for occlusion and motion parallax as occlusions by the green grid as cues, which is not possible for the remaining displays without using head-coupled perspective.

Fig. 2. The full setup for the AR test [5].

Because of the varying nature and performances of the displays, accurate calibration between all devices proved very difficult. Because of this, this study focuses on the accuracy spread between each device. In practice this means that the accuracy for each device is measured by the offsets from the median offset from the targets for each participant. By doing this we assume that the median hit is an accurate hit as adjusted to the user.

4.1   Head-Mounted See-Through Display

The HMD using an Epson Moverio Bt-300 which is an Android-based device and is equipped with 0.43 in. wide panel 720p displays at a 30 Hz refresh rate. The software is implemented using Unity 3D with the Vuforia AR plugin. The HMD is shown in Fig. 3. The impurities are projected into the sand on the glasses while also utilizing the overlay grid.

Using Vuforia along with the build-in 5 megapixel camera on the right-hand side of the headset the system is tracking using the AR markers at either end of the surface of the sand. The goal is to avoid the participants occluding the trackers by only having to use one hand for the tasks, leaving the tracker on the opposite side exposed. The feed from the camera itself is not displayed on the HMD, only the grid targets are displayed. The overlay is manually offset and rotated to best fit the surface of the sand. This process includes adjusting the rendering FOV to fit the display area of the glasses. In this case the FOV is set to 21°, despite the manufacturer advertising 23° FOV for the device.

Since we are not able to perform eye tracking using the hardware to determine the convergence point, rendering the position in stereo would leave the user with difficulty focusing. Because of this the target is not rendered in stereo, but rather as a 2D overlay similarly to the see-through display, and when analyzing the data the participants' dominant eye must be taken into consideration.

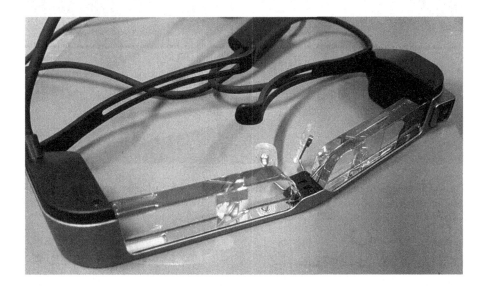

Fig. 3. The Epson Moverio Bt-300 glasses used for the experiment [5].

4.2 Mounted See-Through Display

Similarly to the HMD, the see-through tablet display is running Android and Unity with Vuforia. The display is shown in Fig. 4. The tablet is mounted to an adjustable stand, so it can be positioned according the user's height while oriented to show the entire surfaces area of the sand and all the targets in frame. For this test the tablet is manually adjusted to each subject and remains stationary where an AR tracking marker is visible.

We focus on the marker opposite the user's dominant hand to prevent occlusion. The participant also has to be able to reach underneath the tablet and their hands are visible throughout the test sessions and they can coordinate their movement with the targets in the camera feed. Since the tablet remains mostly stationary during each session, Vuforia is mainly used when the tablet is initially adjusted for the user, this device is less susceptible to errors and latency introduced by Vuforia.

Fig. 4. The arm-mounted see-through display setup with impurity projected into the sand as a red dot assisted by a grid overlay aligned with the surface [5]. (Color figure online)

4.3   Top-Down Projection

This device is set up using a projector mounted to a tripod with a 3D printed adapter and pointed down towards the sand. The projection is shown in Fig. 5, bottom left. The projection is adjusted using a piece of paper with a grid printed on it matching the green grid overlay. The projected overlay features the green grid and the targets are shown as red dots with depth in millimeters shown next to them.

4.4   Stationary Screen

The monitor setup utilizes a 25 in. PC monitor with an aspect ratio of 16 by 10. The monitor is shown in Fig. 6, bottom right. We use a Logitech C920 on an adjustable mount pointed straight down to the surface of the sand. Similarly to the top-down projection setup, the camera feed on the monitor features the green grid overlay and the targets are displayed along with label indicating their depth. Similarly to the tablet setup, the user will be seeing their hands in the video feed during the test sessions. The camera position is calibrated using the printed grid and by placing an HTC Vive controller in the video feed and matching its position with the representation on the monitor.

Fig. 5. The grid projected onto the sand with the targets shown as a red dot [5]. (Color figure online)

5   Experiment

Each participant is introduced to the topic at the beginning of the experiment and they are asked to sign a consent form, followed by a questionnaire pertaining to their age, sex, height, dominant hand and dominant eye. In cases where participants do not know their dominant eye, it is determined with the Miles Test [7].

5.1   Pointing Tasks

Each participant performs a set of pointing tasks with each AR device. The order of the devices is counterbalanced between participants in order to counter bias and initial confusion about the tasks with the first devices. With four systems we have 24 possible combinations. We do each combination twice to reach a total of 48 participants.

While wielding the HTC Vive controller the participant is asked to point the tip of the nail in the center of the target as they appear, as quickly and precisely as they can. To do this they will be asked to have the HTC Vive controller rest on the side of their dominant hand between the thumb and index finger as shown in Fig. 1. When the participant believes they have reached the target center, they must confirm by pressing the trackpad on the controller in the non-dominant hand. To prevent accidental double-presses there is a delay of one second from when a target is confirmed to when the next target is shown, during which the confirm button is disabled. This also allows the participants to return their hand to a natural position close to their body, but they are not instructed to do so.

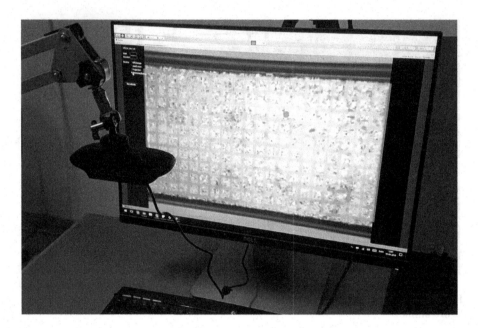

Fig. 6. The monitor and top-down camera [5].

The sand is held in a rectangular plastic tray and has a depth of 5 cm. The targets are shown at depths of 0, 5 and 10 mm, meaning that participants can not expect to drive the nail to the bottom of the tray and get a precise hit. At each of the three depths the targets are distributed on two rows and four columns with 10 cm of spacing in both dimensions, so the participants will get to both reach across and away from the center of their body. With a 24 targets per device per user, we get a total of 4608 samples. The rectangular shape for the tray and the sand is appropriate for the experiment considering that at the points of fine operation in meat production, such as picking out impurities, the meat has been cut down to these shapes.

For each target we measure the task completion time from when a new target appears until the participant confirms a hit. This includes time spend searching for the targets. The accuracy is measured as the offsets from the target center to the tip of the nail at confirmation for the three dimensions individually as well as the absolute distance from target to tip. After using each of the four devices the participants get to evaluate the device in terms of acceptance and ease of use with System Usability Scale (SUS) [2].

5.2 Hypotheses

With the experiment we aim to prove that there are significant differences in the effectiveness and user experience between the AR display types, specifically in terms of the following hypotheses:

- H1: Spotting and hitting sub-surface targets when using different AR devices will yield different task completion times.
- H2: Hitting sub-surface targets using the different AR devices will yield different hit accuracy.
- H3: The different AR devices have different usability based on the Standard Usability Score.

6   Results

As described in Sect. 4, the four devices can be split into two categories, the AR glasses and mounted tablet showing depth through perspective, occlusion and parallax while the remaining are limited to 2D overlays. In this section these categories are described as the 3D and the 2D enabled devices, respectively.

The experiment was performed with 48 participants, average age 24 years, ranging between 20 and 34. Nine participants were female, ten were left-handed. 21 reported having left-eye dominant, 25 reported right, one reported both eyes to be dominant and one could not be determined. Eight participants had positive eyeglass prescriptions, ten had negative prescriptions and two had unknown prescriptions.

6.1   Data Analyses

Performing analyses of variance with significance threshold at .05 shows significant difference among the AR devices in task completion times when comparing them individually ($F(2,3926) = 333.3$, $p < .001$) and when comparing the 3D and 2D enabled devices ($F(1,3926) = 124.7$, $p < .001$) with Tukey's HSD post-hoc analysis showing significant difference between all devices. The projection-based display yielded the lowest average time (2.3 s), followed by the stationary screen (3.55 s), the mounted see-through display (4.5 s) and the AR glassed (9.92 s) had the longest average task time. A summary of the task time data is shown in the box plot in Fig. 7. These results confirm the first hypothesis.

To analyze the accuracy between AR devices, in order to compensate for dominant eye and calibration inaccuracies between test participants, the samples are corrected according to their per-session median hit value. By doing this we make the assumption that the median offsets are for a precise hit, making the median values zero for the data sets used. Figure 8 shows the per-session median hit values for each condition and participants. The high median offsets for depth suggest a calibration error.

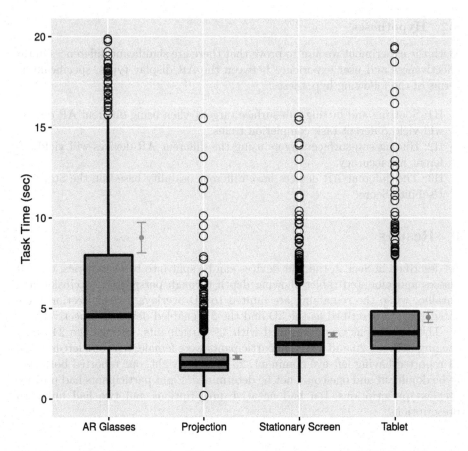

Fig. 7. Box plot of the task completion times between the four AR interfaces. Next to each box plot are their mean values and confidence intervals.

Performing a multiple analysis of variance, dependent values being the hit offsets on three separate dimension, there is significant difference between the four AR devices ($F(2,3926) = 6$, $p < .01$) as well as when comparing the 3D and 2D enabled devices ($F(1,3926) = 3$, $p < .002$), confirming the second hypothesis. The handedness of the user did not yield significant difference in hit offsets.

Looking at hit spread, the AR glasses have the largest average standard deviation at 51 mm in target hit offsets for all three dimensions. In comparison, the stationary screen, projection and tablet displays have averages of 10, 28 and 30 mm, respectively.

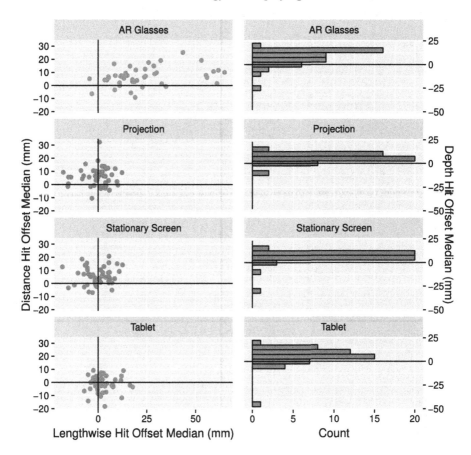

Fig. 8. Per-session surface median hit offset values for each participant (left) and histogram for depth offset medians in bins of 5 mm (right) for each condition.

Investigating the difference in sideways offsets in relation to the user for the four devices ($F(2,3926) = 3.36$, $p < .05$), a Tukey's HSD post-hoc analysis shows no significant difference between any pair of devices, suggesting the difference depends on whether the interfaces were 3D or 2D enabled ($F(1,3926) = 9.26$, $p < .003$). Similarly for offsets going towards or away from the body is only significantly difference between the two groups ($F(1,3928) = 8.27$, $p < .005$). The average offsets along with standard deviations along the surface are shown in Fig. 9.

For the depths offsets as well there is only significant difference between the two categories ($F(3,3926) = 3.4$, $p = .017$) and all of the average offsets are within one millimeter of each other. The depth offsets are shown in Fig. 10.

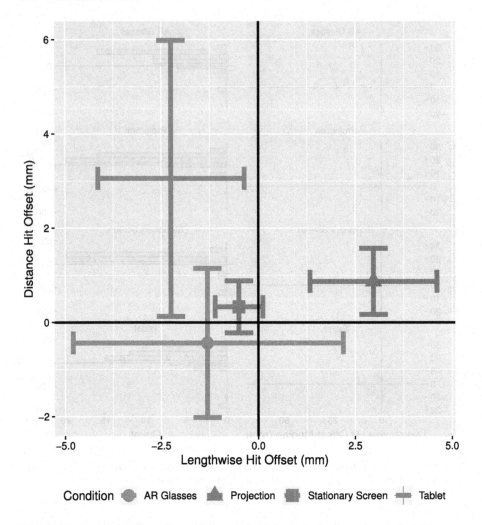

Fig. 9. The average offsets along with standard deviations along the surface between the four AR devices.

The SUS scores show significant difference between the four devices ($F(3,186)$ = 92.03, p < .001) with Tukey's HSD post-hoc analyses showing significance between all four devices. There is not significant difference in user acceptance when comparing 2D and 3D devices. However, two of the four devices do not have normally distributed scores according to the Shapiro-Wilk normality test, the AR glasses (p = .062) and the mounted see-through display (p = .16), making the third hypothesis harder to retain. The SUS scores are summarized in Fig. 11.

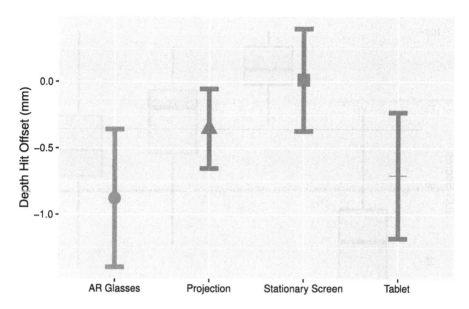

Fig. 10. Average depth offsets between the four AR devices along with confidence intervals.

6.2 Observations

The AR glasses had the longest overall task completion time. The long task times are likely due to the narrow FOV, for multiple reasons. Firstly, the FOV does not allow for the user to see the augmentation overlay on the entire surface at once, requiring additional search time to the task. Despite them being able to see all of the surface at once, the AR glasses only cover a small segment of their FOV, creating a letterbox effect. Despite the mounted tablet display tracking and showing targets in similar way, its position and FOV did allow for user to see the entire surface at once, eliminating the need for search time.

The limited FOV of both the display and the camera used for the tracking in combination with the short distance to the surface of the sand made it difficult for the participants to inspect the entire surface area while also keeping the tracking marker in view of the camera. This in combination with errors and latency introduced by Vuforia made a sub-par user experience.

In addition, the glasses' FOV does not allow the user to glance downwards, leading them to turn their head downwards to an uncomfortable degree as they leaned in over the tray, while also having to turn their head to look around and search for targets. A few test participants commented on this, stating that using the glasses was starting to give them neck pains. Many participants who tried other devices after the glasses would comment out loud on how much easier it was.

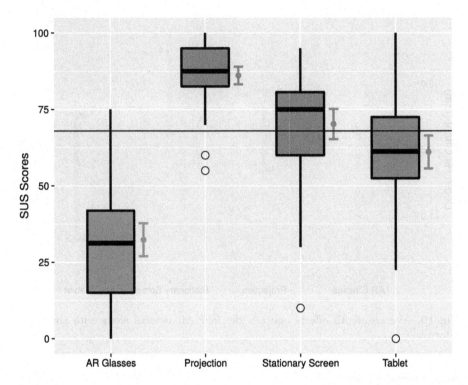

Fig. 11. Box plot of the SUS scores between the four AR interfaces and a line at the cut-off value of 68. Next to each box plot are their mean values and confidence intervals.

7 Discussion

Despite the accuracy of the AR devices proved significantly different, it is hard to define a concrete set of tendencies, seeing as significance differs between devices and axes and the average hit positions differ as seen in Fig. 9. Also, the average hit accuracy in depth, though significantly different, are within one millimeter of one another, making it less relevant in a real-world context. It does show, however, that the projection based AR and the monitor were the two devices with the lowest standard deviations along the surface.

The analyses show significant differences when comparing the 2D and 3D enabled interfaces, both for task completion time and accuracy. For the latter this grouping is more consistently significant, because the post-hoc analyses show no significant difference in pairwise comparison. This may be due to both of them being static and showing the positions from a top-down perspective as opposed to the see-through display which required interpretation of perspective and occlusion as depth clues and the glasses that required constant tracking as the user moves, introducing noise. The tracking noise would also be introduced for the mounted displays in a real-world setting as the display would be moved around. Nevertheless, the inaccuracy for the projection and the monitor can likely be fixed with hardware and software adjustment, where the remaining devices have the challenge of tracking and depths communication.

The SUS results show that the projection-based AR and the monitor-based AR were the only two devices with averages scores reaching above the standard cut-off point of 68. The analysis of variance was used despite not all of the groups being normally distributed because due to the nature of the SUS scale where groups will be tailed in different directions dependent on their average position on the scale, making them hard to fit in any statistical model.

The low task completion time combined with the high SUS score for the projection-based AR system is likely due to the direct connection between the display and the target, the interfaces being on the target itself. Eliminating the requirement of coordinating hands with a display offset from the target seems to make the interface more accessible. This is despite the problem with projection-based AR that the user will occlude the projection when interacting with it.

The issues with the AR glasses described in Sect. 6.2 make the Epson Moverio non-viable for near-distance tasks. An alternative would be the technique used by Green et al. [4] where the user's viewing direction would be shifted downwards, compensating for the FOV. However, whether this approach, occluding part of the user's FOV during a potentially hazardous task, would work is uncertain. It would be beneficial to repeat the experiment using a HMD specifically designed for the context of close-proximity tabletop operations. This would involve expanding the display FOV, allowing the user to search by scanning with their eyes rather than turning their head straight at the target. Another required feature is eye-tracking in order to properly implement stereo display.

It is worth considering after this experiment whether 2D and 3D enabled AR devices are comparable in terms of accuracy and user experience due to differences in affordances. Because the projection-based overlay and the screen are static displays, the only tracking involved in a real-life scenario is of the meat and the targets as the subject is moved around work surface. As such, these two displays potentially introduce less tracking noise, which is also likely to have affected the test results.

The results and conclusions to this experiment are mainly valid in the simulated context and would benefit from repeating in a setup with real meat. In that case, the results and observations illustrate the limitations of the AR glasses as implemented in this experiment, which should be addressed before they are assessed with real meat, either by different hardware or tracking solutions.

8   Conclusion

This paper presents a comparative study of the usability of four types of AR displays for showing sub-surface impurities in meat by having the participants point to targets inside an analog made of sand. The four display types are wearable AR glasses, a mounted see-through display, projection-based AR and a monitor displaying a top-down video feed with graphical overlay. The goal is to determine suitable interfaces for augmented meat production.

After performing the evaluation with 48 participants our three hypotheses were retained with significantly different task completion time, accuracy and user acceptance depending on the AR display type used. Data analysis indicates that projection-based AR yields the second-lowest variance in combination with the lowest task completion times and the highest SUS score, making it the most suited for the task with the mounted see-through display and stationary screen being viable alternatives, while the AR glasses showed to be non-viable for near-distance tasks as they were implemented for the experiment.

Even though the research is aimed at the meat production industry, the results are relevant to any industry that utilized manual processes while standing at a work surface. Whether the results would pertain to sitting tasks at a desktop might require further testing due to the difference in distance and postures.

As stated in Sect. 7, for further comparison between the devices, the limitations of some of the devices have to be addressed with more suitable hardware and tracking solutions before they are tested further in a real-world context. That is if the 2D and 3D-enabled devices can be considered comparable from an accuracy perspective due to the difference in affordances. Even so, at early stages of development it is relevant to compare them in terms of the usability and user acceptance that stems from the different affordances.

Acknowledgement. This research is sponsored by Innovation Fund Denmark and is part of the project, Augmented Cellular Meat Production.

References

1. Avery, B., Sandor, C., Thomas, B.H.: Improving spatial perception for augmented reality x-ray vision. In: 2009 IEEE Virtual Reality Conference, pp. 79–82. IEEE, March 2009. https://doi.org/10.1109/VR.2009.4811002, http://ieeexplore.ieee.org/document/4811002/
2. Brooke, J., et al.: Sus-a quick and dirty usability scale. Usability Eval. Ind. **189**(194), 4–7 (1996)
3. Elia, V., Gnoni, M.G., Lanzilotto, A.: Evaluating the application of augmented reality devices in manufacturing from a process point of view: an AHP based model. Expert Syst. Appl. **63**, 187–197 (2016). https://doi.org/10.1016/j.eswa.2016.07.006. http://linkinghub.elsevier.com/retrieve/pii/S0957417416303505
4. Green, S.A., Chase, J.G., Chen, X., Billinghurst, M.: Evaluating the augmented reality human-robot collaboration system. In: 2008 15th International Conference on Mechatronics and Machine Vision in Practice, pp. 521–526. IEEE, December 2008. https://doi.org/10.1109/MMVIP.2008.4749586, http://ieeexplore.ieee.org/document/4749586/
5. Hald, K., Rehm, M., Moeslund, T.B.: Testing augmented reality systems for spotting sub-surface impurities. In: Barricelli, B., et al. (eds.) HWID 2018. IAICT, vol. 544, pp. 103–112. Springer, Cham (2019). https://doi.org/10.1007/978-3-030-05297-3_7
6. Kruijff, E., Swan, J.E., Feiner, S.: Perceptual issues in augmented reality revisited. In: 2010 IEEE International Symposium on Mixed and Augmented Reality, pp. 3–12. IEEE, October 2010. https://doi.org/10.1109/ISMAR.2010.5643530, http://ieeexplore.ieee.org/document/5643530/

7. Miles, W.R.: Ocular dominance demonstrated by unconscious sighting. J. Exp. Psychol. **12**(2), 113 (1929)
8. Novak-Marcincin, J., Barna, J., Janak, M., Novakova-Marcincinova, L.: Augmented reality aided manufacturing. Procedia Comput. Sci. **25**, 23–31 (2013). https://doi.org/10.1016/J.PROCS.2013.11.00. https://www.sciencedirect.com/science/article/pii/S187705091301209X
9. Punnett, L., Wegman, D.H.: Work-related musculoskeletal disorders: the epidemiologic evidence and the debate. J. Electromyogr. Kinesiol. **14**(1), 13–23 (2004). https://doi.org/10.1016/J.JELEKIN.2003.09.015. https://www.sciencedirect.com/science/article/pii/S1050641103001251?via%3Dihub
10. Schwerdtfeger, B., Pustka, D., Hofhauser, A., Klinker, G.: Using laser projectors for augmented reality. In: Proceedings of the 2008 ACM Symposium on Virtual Reality Software and Technology - VRST 2008, p. 134. ACM Press, New York (2008). https://doi.org/10.1145/1450579.1450608, http://portal.acm.org/citation.cfm?doid=1450579.1450608
11. Singh, G., Swan, J.E., Jones, J.A., Ellis, S.R.: Depth judgment measures and occluding surfaces in near-field augmented reality. In: Proceedings of the 7th Symposium on Applied Perception in Graphics and Visualization - APGV 2010, p. 149. ACM Press, New York (2010). https://doi.org/10.1145/1836248.1836277, http://portal.acm.org/citation.cfm?doid=1836248.1836277
12. Swan, J., et al.: A perceptual matching technique for depth judgments in optical, see-through augmented reality. In: IEEE Virtual Reality Conference (VR 2006), pp. 19–26. IEEE. https://doi.org/10.1109/VR.2006.13, http://ieeexplore.ieee.org/document/1667622/
13. Vogel, C., Poggendorf, M., Walter, C., Elkmann, N.: Towards safe physical human-robot collaboration: a projection-based safety system. In: 2011 IEEE/RSJ International Conference on Intelligent Robots and Systems, pp. 3355–3360. IEEE, September 2011. https://doi.org/10.1109/IROS.2011.6094550, http://ieeexplore.ieee.org/document/6094550/

Bubble Margin: Motion Sickness Prevention While Reading on Smartphones in Vehicles

Alexander Meschtscherjakov[1][✉][iD], Sebastian Strumegger[2],
and Sandra Trösterer[1]

[1] Center for Human-Computer Interaction, University of Salzburg, Salzburg, Austria
{alexander.meschtscherjakov,sandra.troesterer}@sbg.ac.at
[2] University of Salzburg, Salzburg, Austria
s.strumegger@gmx.at
https://hci.sbg.ac.at/

Abstract. The shift towards autonomous driving will allow people to read and work while riding in such a vehicle. Some people suffer from motion sickness while being engaged in these activities in a moving vehicle since the signals of the visual and vestibular systems of the human body are mismatched. One approach to mitigate motion sickness is to provide visual cues for the affected person. We present Bubble Margin, a smartphone application to reduce motion sickness while reading in a moving vehicle. It is built as a stand-alone, semi-transparent overlay application that visualizes motion cues in form of bubbles at the margins of a smartphone while other applications may be used in the remaining area. Forces to move these bubbles are taken from smartphone sensors. An initial within-subject design study ($N = 10$) with participants performing a reading task in a real driving scenario showed mitigating effects on motion sickness symptoms.

Keywords: Motion sickness · Nausea · Smartphone application · Peripheral vision

1 Introduction

People have always had an urge to put their free time to good use while traveling and modern technology has introduced various ways for us to entertain and educate ourselves while being on the move. For example, one third of Canadian college students choose to use their smartphones when riding on buses [15]. However, several people suffer from motion sickness symptoms such as nausea, sweating, and dizziness when using their smartphones in moving vehicles. Susceptibility to motion sickness varies depending on multiple factors such as age, gender, vestibular diseases and the type of transportation and movement (e.g., [3,7,12,18,24]).

© IFIP International Federation for Information Processing 2019
Published by Springer Nature Switzerland AG 2019
D. Lamas et al. (Eds.): INTERACT 2019, LNCS 11747, pp. 660–677, 2019.
https://doi.org/10.1007/978-3-030-29384-0_39

The future of automated cars is likely to bring about an even greater amount of people being exposed to activities inducing motion sickness. Recent studies by Sivak and Schoettle [27] have shown, for example, that 37% of adult U.S. citizen passengers in fully self-driving vehicles are expected to be involved in activities that increase the frequency and severity of motion sickness, such as reading or watching movies. According to their estimations, about 6–12% of U.S. citizen passengers will experience moderate or severe motion sickness at some time.

The prevailing theory suggests that in many cases motion sickness is caused by a sensory conflict between the visual and vestibular systems of the human body, whenever there is a mismatch between the anticipated and the actual signal [25]. This is often the case when passengers are riding in a vehicle, especially when the roads are curvy. Thereby, motion sickness symptoms occur especially on low frequency motion (<1 Hz) and seem to peek around 0.2 Hz [14]. It was shown by Bos [5] that adding high frequency motion in form of non-sickening vibration can reduce the sickening effect of low frequency motions.

If a passenger sitting in a bus looks out the window and fixates a point, e.g., a road sign, the vestibular and visual systems cooperate in order to stabilize the eyes as the bus turns. However, this vestibulo-ocular reflex is repressed by the visual pursuit mechanism if the passenger is reading a newspaper [6]. As a result the passenger's eyes do not follow the bus' motion, creating a sensory conflict. If the passenger's eyes are not focused on the road ahead the linear acceleration and deceleration of the vehicle can cause motion sickness [4].

There are several fundamentally different approaches when it comes to preventing or mitigating motion sickness. *Pharmalogical* countermeasures have been proven to be effective, but the developed drugs can provoke unwanted side effects and oral administration must be planned well in advance for the body to absorb the necessary substances in time [12]. Those drawbacks may be acceptable for long ship cruises but they are not for everyday car or bus drives.

Habituation has proven to be very effective against motion sickness by the military, as jet pilots cannot be allowed to deal with undesirable side effects. Cowings and Toscano [8] have shown that habituation to the repeated stimulus is superior to pharmacological treatment. While being very effective, this method is also very time-consuming and the training can last several weeks [12].

Orientation is another element having an influence on motion sickness. Sailors, for example, have long used the method of fixating their vision oTurner1999n the horizon as a reference point in order to reduce the sensory conflict of the visual and vestibular systems [26]. In the automotive domain it is known looking through the windshield onto the road might mitigate motion sickness symptoms [28].

Another key factor in preventing motion sickness closely related to orientation is *anticipation*. Drivers, for example, tend to get less sick than passengers since in addition to them having a clear view on the road, they are in control and therefore can anticipate the incoming motion [9]. The common believe that backwards seating passengers are more likely to suffer from motion sickness symptoms lines up with the theory that an awareness of the road ahead mitigate the symptoms, as shown by Griffin and Turner [28].

Recently, there have been several approaches to use technology to mitigate motion sickness symptoms. Most of them use visual stimuli to help with orientation and anticipation, such as the MotionReader [16] the Motion Sickness Prevention System (MSPS) [23], or the Peripheral Visual Feedforward System (PVFS) [19]. Our approach is to utilize visual feedback on linear acceleration forces in real-time for people riding in a vehicle to fight motion sickness. Thereby visual stimuli are presented at the margin of a smartphone display. Passengers are perceiving the stimuli in their peripheral view while interacting or reading at the remaining area of the smartphone.

Motivated by these thoughts we are presenting Bubble Margin, an Android application designed to mitigate motion sickness symptoms by providing visual feedback on linear acceleration forces. Bubble Margin works as a stand-alone application. It visualises moving objects within a semitransparent frame on a smartphone screen. By choosing a border design, we believe to have created a non-disruptive smartphone experience while providing visual motion cues. The effect of our interface was tested in an initial within-subjects study (N=10), assessing motion sickness severity before and after test drives in a real driving scenario. Participants were further asked to make changes to the design (e.g., border size, number of bubbles, color) in order to gather information about user preferences.

The approach to use visual stimuli in that way to mitigate motion sickness is not knew, as we have outlined above. The novelty lies in that fact, that our approach does not need any additional hardware and can run as an overlay on any application running on a smartphone.

2   Related Work

Visual information about upcoming car movements raises situation awareness and as a result can mitigate the effects of motion sickness, as shown by the Peripheral Visual Feedforward System (PVFS) of Karjanto et al. [19]. The PVFS used LED lights next to two displays to inform video-watching study participants about the next turn. The undeniable benefit of this system is that the displayed visual cue does not affect the viewed content, since LED lights are placed outside of the screen. However, it requires additional hardware to be installed, as well as information about upcoming movements.

Apart from visual feedback cues, Yusof et al. [29] have created a haptic feedback device consisting of several vibrating mini motors. They have increased passenger's situation awareness about upcoming movements by emitting vibrations to the forearms. A preliminary study has shown promising results regarding the connection of motion sickness and situation awareness. Apart from navigation information, the challenge with providing anticipatory information is, that it requires accurate estimation of future vehicle movements. One approach is to use GPS data, which has been shown to be rather inaccurate in smartphone GPS sensors [2].

Thinking about a future of fully automated cars and the constantly improving technologies in the virtual reality sector, passengers are likely to be using VR Head Mounted Displays (HMDs) while driving. However, the limited visual information about motion is destined to create a sensory conflict while driving. McGill *et al.* [22] have explored this possibility by conducting a study with participants wearing VR HMDs, establishing a baseline for future work. It was shown that there is no universal presentation of motion on the display that eases motion sickness. Different participants had different preferences and the wrong presentation could actually even have a negative effect on motion sickness symptoms.

Hock et al. [17] have present CarVR an HMD that maps vehicular movements to the visual information presented within a virtual reality world. This allows users to feel the kinesthetic forces produced while riding during the VR experience. The cars acceleration was taken into consideration for rendering the virtual environment to mitigate simulator sickness. They have shown that simulator sickness is reduced compared to a stationary VR experiences.

In HCI research, only little work has been published picking up the context of smartphone or tablet displays in combination with motion sickness. Hanau and Popescu [16] studied bus passengers using e-readers by presenting their approach MotionReader. They have developed two interfaces. One showing a ball-spring gizmo which moves according to acceleration sensor data received from the device. The disadvantage of such an approach is that the visualization overlays content on the smartphone and thus, may be annoying for the user. The second interface moved the whole text displayed on the smartphone according to incoming acceleration forces. Study results for both interfaces did not suggest a significant improvement on the symptoms of motion sickness. Nonetheless, their study setup of filling a bus with participants and having them wear view-limiting hoods was innovative. It allowed them to evaluate a reasonable sample size (N = 26) at the same conditions.

Miksch *et al.* [23] took a different approach and provided a live video feed in their Motion Sickness Prevention System (MSPS). The video stream was visualized in form of a semi-transparent background for tablets behind a text. Most participants stated that they rated the implemented interface as very helpful and their results emerging from the conducted motion sickness survey [20] showed just as much. This system has the technical barrier that a front-facing camera would have to be mounted and the video data transmission delays need to be kept at a minimum.

In addition, there are several apps for mobile devices promising mitigating effects on motion sickness. However, most of them concentrate on instructing the driver on a driving style that induces less motion sickness. Two applications were found that took a related approach to Bubble Margin. The Anti Motion Sickness App[1] simulates radial waves across the screen. The KineStop - Car sickness aid[2]

---

[1] https://play.google.com/store/apps/details?id=com.scy.chaeyoung.tbsm2 - Accessed 26.01.2019.

[2] https://play.google.com/store/apps/details?id=com.urbandroid.kinestop - Accessed 26.01.2019.

provides a semi-transparent artificial horizon overlay. For both apps no empirical evidence of actual mitigating effects is available. Various other interfaces trying to prevent motion sickness for travelers circulate on social media platforms. For example, car manufacturer Citroën has recently launched a product called SEETROËN[3] in form of eyeglasses with a liquid-filled frame.

These approaches have shown that there is potential for mitigating motion sickness by providing visual cues. For our approach, we wanted to use a passenger's smartphone for visualizing such cues, since most people take their smartphones with them anyways and everywhere. In the next section, we describe design decisions and implementation information for the Bubble Margin approach.

3   Bubble Margin Prototype

For the Bubble Margin prototype we need to make sure to be able to visualize the motion cues without interfering with a primary task such as reading on the smartphone. Secondly, motion cues need to have access to linear acceleration data in real-time. To increase accessibility, we decided not to use additional hardware on top of built-in sensors in a modern smartphone.

Most modern Android phones provide linear acceleration data out of the box in form of a software-based motion sensor using the device's gyroscope. For older devices, as well as modern low-budget devices a low-pass filter can be implemented in order to filter gravitational force from the accelerometer's data and further obtain linear acceleration data. Prior to designing the interface we had to ensure the possibility of drawing overlays on the device's screen. Android provides the SYSTEM_ALERT_WINDOW[4] permission that needs to be granted once by the user and further allows an application or background service to draw above all other applications.

This also allowed us to implement Bubble Margin as a semitransparent graphical overlay with no touch functionalities. Touch gestures are handled by the layer below the Bubble Margin visualization and thus scrolling gestures are not affected.

3.1   Interface Design

To discuss various design ideas for the interface we have conducted an internal workshop with three HCI researchers and two interaction designers. Inspired by designs, as described in the related work section, various visualizations were discussed.

A design presenting visual cues in a single spot on the screen as in the ball-spring gizmo by Hanau and Popescu [16] was decided to be not suitable for smaller displays such as smartphones' as compared to those of tablets or e-readers.

---

[3] https://www.youtube.com/watch?v=aih3LgMoyvY - Accessed on 26.01.2019.

[4] See https://developer.android.com/reference/android/Manifest.permission for more information - Accessed on 26.01.2019.

The visual cue would take up too much screen space in order to be of reasonable size. Creating a fullscreen overlay design that simulates outgoing radial waves could cope with the above mentioned problem of size. However, we did not want the visual cue to lower usability of the smartphone itself by displaying information all over the screen. A fullscreen visualization might also distract from a primary task such as reading on the smartphone. Another idea was to show a banner at one side of the screen. While this idea was considered little intrusive, the movement space for objects would be rich for one planar axis but small for its perpendicular axis. Compensating inferior movement with additional metaphors, such as colors, did not seem intuitive enough for user's peripheral vision to comprehend.

In general, we ruled out all design ideas that were deemed as too disturbing or as too small to provide the necessary space for moving visual feedback cues. It is known that peripheral vision is good at detecting motion compared to detecting form [1], hence the interface should provide a rich movement space for visual feedback. That is why the final decision was made for a design based on a semi-transparent border, drawn at the margins of the screen. In addition to being mostly scrollable, text documents and websites tend to have unused space at the margins of the display. This enabled us to implement a little disruptive interface with enough room for indicators to move notable distances.

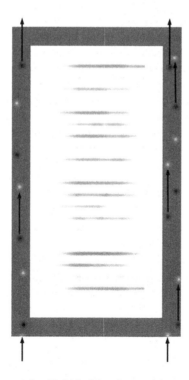

Fig. 1. Illustrated movement for Bubble Margin used in a car that is slowing down. Black bubbles show the position before braking. White bubbles show the position while slowing down. Arrows demonstrate bubble movement.

3.2   Visualization

Having decided to use the border of the smartphone as visualization area, we needed to decide how movement should be visualized. Again, we discussed several ideas. The two most promising were metaphors of raindrops and bubbles. Raindrops would have a fixed anchor point and display movement by morphing their form in the direction of the force. Since raindrops are familiar in the automotive context this metaphor was expected to be intuitive and natural. On the other hand, animating and visualizing raindrops in a natural way would require a lot of computational power. The effect of different amplitudes of forces might not be noticed by a user [1].

Thus, we decided to display movable objects indicating linear acceleration in form of circles, making them resemble floating bubbles (see Fig. 1). Bubbles would have no fixed anchor-points but move freely inside the border. They are easier to implement than raindrops and open-up the possibility to be adaptable to user preferences. All bubbles move according to the direction and amplitude of a registered linear acceleration force. Additionally, a small random variance in movement amplitude was introduced in order to get a more natural feeling, such that they do not seem to move as one unit. Whenever a bubble moves outside the device's display or out of the border, it appears on the opposite site respectively.

Figure 1 illustrates the conceptual design of Bubble Margin. Bubbles move forward as the car is slowing down. Black bubbles indicate the position before braking, whereas white bubbles show a snapshot of its position while slowing down. Arrows demonstrate the way a bubble has moved. They are solely used for demonstration and are not a part of the actual interface. We have further implemented the option for users to freely change Bubble Margin's settings. Color, transparency and width of the border can be freely adjusted. Border size can be set to a specific dp (density-independent pixel)[5] value. Bubbles can be adjusted in size and number. Additionally, transparency and color can be chosen. The user can set three colors independently forming a radial gradient.

3.3   Movement Design

As stated previously we used the smartphone's sensors to access linear acceleration data. To access gyroscope sensor data we used the android hardware package to implement a Sensor_Event_Listener registered with a Sensor_Manager. We then constantly saved the sensor values into an array updated every 20 ms. These values were then used to inform the movement of the bubbles.

We factored raw data form the gyroscope to represent a smooth and natural bubble movement in the following way. First we simply added sensor data in x and y direction to the bubbles current position. This resulted in a smooth but

---

[5] Density-independent pixels (dp) are an abstract unit based on the physical density of the screen. Units are relative to a 160 dpi (dots-per-inch) screen. One dp is one pixel on a 160 dpi screen. The ratio of dp-to-pixel will change with the screen density. $px = dp * (dpi/160)$ from https://developer.android.com - Accessed on 26.01.2019.

to little magnitude movement. Thus, we amplified the movement by a factor 3.5, which we determined by trail-and-error until we were satisfied in the visual appearance. Additionally, we altered this factor randomly in a range from 50% to 150% in order to make the movements of the individual bubble more *natural* i.e. all bubbles moving in the same direction, but not all behaving exactly in the same magnitude.

The initial placement of bubbles was randomly inside the Bubble Margins border by randomly generating x and y coordinates within the Bubble Margin border, which then were used as the center for bubbles.

In case the phone would not by equipped with a gyroscope, we used the acceleration sensor data from which we extracted earth gravitation by means of a low pass-filter and then removed this gravity by means of a high-pass filter. The basic idea behind that is to iteratively extract earth gravitation from the data by thresholding[6]. Feasibility testing with older devices where the low-pass filter was executed did not result in noticeable delays. For the study presented later we only used newer devices (all of the same kind to be able to compare results) and thus built-in gyroscope sensors were available.

In order to get the best results form sensor data the smartphone would need to be aligned in a horizontal position. Since sitting people hold their smartphone in an angle between zero and 20-degrees [21], acceleration data was interpolated in a vertical direction to cope with this. Additionally, it was made possible to set the current slope for continuous uphill or downhill rides, which allows for more accurate bubble movement.

4   Study Setup

In order to test the effect of Bubble Margin on mitigating motion sickness, a small-scale (N = 10), within-subjects study was conducted in a real-driving scenario. The experimental setup aimed to recreate the common situation of passengers reading a text on their smartphone while driving on curvy countryside roads.

A test condition (TC) and a control condition (CC) were introduced, in which participants had to read a text with (TC) or without (CC) Bubble Margin while sitting in a driving vehicle. The vehicle was driven by a researcher. All participants needed to take part in both conditions. To rule out cumulative effects of motion sickness a minimum pause of two days was required between the conditions. Condition order was alternated to reduce the risk of one-sided habituation-affected results.

The control condition and the test condition both consisted of a 20-min drive on a preselected road, known for little traffic and for allowing speeds up to 100 km/h. The route included serpentines and curvy roads. Distance was 15.3 km with an altitude difference of 211 m. The driven course on the pre-selected road is shown in Fig. 2.

---

[6] https://developer.android.com/guide/topics/sensors/sensors_motion - Accessed on 2.06.2019.

Fig. 2. Preselected route used for studying the mitigating effect of Bubble Margin on motion sickness.

In order to reduce study effort, we allowed up to three people participating in one ride. Thus, we needed to have three similar smartphones on which the Bubble Margin app was installed. All Android smartphones used for drives were *Sony Xperia Compact* models, providing a 4.6 in. display and a resolution of 720 × 1280 pixels at a 16:9 aspect ratio. The device has a built-in gyroscope sensor. In order to have comparable situations, screen brightness was set to the highest available level and not adjusting automatically.

Two different texts describing countries were prepared for participants to read, differing for both conditions. The font used for the texts was *Roboto* measuring a font size of 24pt visualized as pdfs in *WPS Office*[7]. The text was shown inside the Bubble Margin borders. We chose the reading task specifically as it is often attributed to induce motion sickness. It is a typical task on mobile devices and we could validate whether subjects were actually looking at the smartphone by asking comprehension questions. With respect to validity regarding the reading task, we counterbalanced the visualized text and used differently ordered conditions.

In the final version of Bubble Margin users will have the possibility to choose how many bubbles they want to have visualized, in customised color and size, etc. For the study we wanted to have comparable conditions. Thus, we tried out various settings on our own. We experimented with different margin sizes and number and sizes of bubbles. The margin should be small enough so that the

---

[7] *WPS Office - Word, Docs, PDF, Note, Slide & Sheet* by *Kingsoft Office Software Corporation LimitedEffizienz.*

Fig. 3. The Bubble Margin is a smartphone application to mitigate motion sickness while reading in a moving vehicle visualizing motion cues in form of bubbles at the margins of a smartphone.

text in the center is still visible, but broad enough to visualize enough bubbles. Our aim was to get enough bubbles that are equally distributed within the BubbleMargin border (all areas i.e. left, right, bottom, top). We then presented different variations to colleagues. They were given the chance to change settings keeping in mind that the bubbles shall be noticeable when reading a text but not too distractive.

This resulted in 200 bubbles, measuring a radius of 10 dp and filled by a white to transparent radial gradient color. They were randomly placed inside a 16 dp wide, semi-transparent gray border. For the study these values were kept the same for all participants. We do not claim that this is the most usable setting, but they seemed to be a fair balance between readability of the text in the center of the screen and enough visual information for the Bubble Margin approach to be perceivable by users. Figure 3 visualises the setup for subjects. For demonstration reasons the border width as well as text content and colours were changed.

As individual drives included up to three participants, seating positions were noted and it was assured that they did not differ for both conditions. For each ride, the driver was instructed to record the outside temperature, weather conditions, as well as traffic conditions. Temperature inside the car was to be constantly kept at 20.0 °C.

4.1   Demographics

Six females and four males of age between 21 and 60 volunteered to take part in the study. They were recruited among colleagues not familiar with the project. All of them stated to have experienced more or less severe effects of motion sickness as passengers before.

Prior to the first ride, participants were asked to fill in a short version of the Motion Sickness Susceptibility Questionnaire Short-form (MSSQ-Short) [11,13] to get a measurement of their general susceptibility to motion sickness. The MSSQ-Short was scored as proposed and percentiles were approximated using the polynomial described by Golding [13]. The resulting MSSQ percentiles ranged from 28.6 to 100 with a median of 77.85. A high MSSQ percentile suggests high susceptibility to motion sickness.

4.2   Subjective Well-Being

Prior to each of the two rides participants were asked to report their physical state. This included questions regarding alcohol or drug consumption within the last 24 h. We additionally assessed how long ago they had eaten food or drunken fluids. In order to establish a general baseline, all participants were asked to score their overall well-being from 1 to 9 before both conditions.

4.3   Study Procedure

The study procedure is shown in Fig. 4. Before the first ride participants were informed about the aims and risks of the study. We especially, informed participants about the risk of becoming motion sick during a ride. They were informed that they could stop the ride at any time, if they felt too uneasy to continue. After signing an informed consent participants filled in demographic data and the MSSQ.

Then for each of the two conditions participants had to answer the above mentioned subjective well-being questions. As proposed by Karjanto *et al.* [19], the change in participants' motion sickness level was determined by applying the Motion Sickness Assessment Questionnaire (MSAQ) [10] before and after each drive. The MSAQ is used to assess four dimensions of motion sickness, defined as *gastrointestinal*, *central*, *peripheral*, and *sopite-related*. An overall score can be derived by ignoring dimensions and calculating the percentage of total points scored. Bubble Margin's effect on easing motion sickness was determined by taking the difference in scores for the control condition and the test condition.

During the ride participants were asked to take note on a protocol whenever they had to move their vision away from the text. The protocol consisted of three images on a sheet of paper: look away from the phone, look outside the window, stop. Participants should indicate with a dash next to the image whenever they looked away from the screen or outside the window. The effort for participants was very low. We wanted to record this behavior in order to be informed about coping strategies of participants with respect to motion sickness. If a participant would require the vehicle to stop, we would have noted time and reason.

After they had finished riding and completed the second MSAQ, a post-study questionnaire was filled-in. Questions with respect to readability and understandability needed to be answered on a Likert-like scale from one to nine. To validate the participants' attention to the text, they had to answer ten dichotomous questions regarding its content.

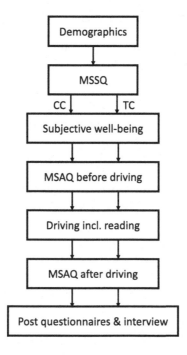

Fig. 4. Flow diagram showing the study procedure.

After the control condition, we further asked participants to state on a scale from 0 (never) to 3 (often) if they had intentionally or unintentionally looked at the moving bubbles. A Likert-like scale (1–9) was used to assess if participants felt disturbed by Bubble Margin and if they would consider using the application in the future. Participants were also asked to change Bubble Margin's settings according to their own preferences in order to give feedback on their preferences. That was done stationary and not in the moving vehicle. These settings were not used as an input to the study but as a feedback afterwards.

5   Results

A Wilcoxon signed rank test (WSRT) was applied to the overall well-being baseline score. The analysis showed that overall well-being was not significantly different at the beginning of both conditions ($z = -0.707$, n.s.).

WSRT results on MSAQ score differences showed that the total motion sickness level was significantly lower in the test condition, compared to the control condition ($z = -2.346$, $p = 0.0095$, one-tailed). Changes for specific motion sickness dimensions were significant for gastrointestinal, central, and sopite-related dimension, as well as for the total score (see Table 1 for detailed results). Only the motion sickness change for the peripheral dimension was found to be not significant. This result leads to the assumption that Bubble Margin does have a potential positive effect on motion sickness symptoms.

672   A. Meschtscherjakov et al.

Table 1. MSAQ results from Wilcoxon signed rank test as well as means and medians for the control condition (CC) and the test condition (TC). Scores for statistical analysis were derived by subtracting the pre-drive MSAQ scores from the post-drive MSAQ scores.

	Mean CC	Mean TC	Median CC	Median TC	z-value	p-value (two-tailed)	p-value (one-tailed)
Total	12.082	2.638	8.335	0.040	-2.346^a	0.019	0.0095*
Gastro	16.112	4.999	12.500	0.000	-2.549^a	0.011	0.0055*
Central	15.333	3.779	7.775	0.000	-1.859^a	0.063	0.0315*
Sopite	11.945	0.833	9.725	0.000	-2.176^a	0.030	0.015*
Peripheral	1.481	0.740	0.000	1.850	-0.142^b	0.887	0.5565

* The result is significant for $p < .05$, one-tailed.
[a] Based on positive ranks.
[b] Based on negative ranks.

We further conducted a Spearman-Rho rank correlation in order to check upon a correlation of susceptibility (MSSQ-score) and occurred motion sickness (MSAQ-score). We found a highly significant positive correlation (Spearman-Rho $= 0.796$, $p < .01$) for the control condition. The correlation was a bit lower for the condition with the Bubble Margin (Spearman-Rho $= 0.723$, $p < .05$). In general that means that participants, who were more susceptible to motion sickness, were also more likely to get motion sick during the study.

Outside temperatures varied from $15.0°$ to $27.0\,°C$ with medians of $19\,°C$ for the control condition and $25\,°C$ for the test condition. The weather ranged from sunny to cloudy and traffic was trivially low at most times. For the control condition, one test person (TP8) has stated to have drunk alcohol within 24 h prior to the study. The test condition consisted of three participants (TP3, TP7, TP8) drinking alcohol within 24 h prior to the study. After asking for details they all confirmed to have drunk a trivial amount the night before. TP7 and TP10 have taken medication 24 h prior to driving in both conditions, while TP8 only stated likewise for the test condition. General well-being was rated between 6 and 9 for both conditions for all participants but one, meaning that they felt well before the rides. TP7 rated general well-being only with 4 for the test condition, mentioning that he felt a little bit dizzy.

Regarding looking out of the window to mitigate motion sickness the following answers were given. During control condition, two participants (TP 2,3) looked away from the text and out of the window once and TP1 did so twice. For the test condition TP1 looked out twice and TP7 once. All others stated to have constantly had their vision fixed on the phone. Three people (TP 2,5,6) have stated that they had intentionally looked at the moving bubbles at times. More than half of the participants (TP 1,2,3,7,8,10) unintentionally moved their vision to the bubbles rarely or sometimes. Percentages scored in the text understanding test ranged from 60% to 100% with medians of 90% (CC) and 95% (TC).

For both conditions median values for font readability was 8.5 and for text understandability 9, rated on the Likert-like questionnaires scaled from 1 (not at all) to 9 (very much). The median for Bubble Margin being irritating was 1.5. For participants considering to use the application in private the median value was 9. With respect to individual configuration most participants were satisfied with the pre-settings. TP1 would have liked less bubbles on display (100 instead of 200), as well as slower movement. TP5 wished for the border to be wider (30 dp instead of 16 dp). Color configurations for bubbles and the border were individually different and based on personal preference.

6 Discussion

The study has shown that the overall assessment of the Bubble Margin approach was positive both with respect to its mitigating effect on motion sickness, as well as to usability related aspects.

We could show a significant improvement regarding motion sickness symptoms for the test condition. The only dimension that did not create a significant effect was the peripheral score. This score included questions with respect to subjective temperature feeling. Although, we tried to have a stable temperature inside the vehicle the outside temperature was not consistent for all drives. This could be a possible reason for these results.

In the study participant could sit on different seats in the front or at the back. We only made sure, that they sat at the same position for both rides (CC and TC). We did not find any effects on motion sickness based on the sitting position of participants. Although none of the participant felt really sick during rides, some indicated that they had to look outside the window because they felt uneasy. This was not only the case during the control condition, but also while using Bubble Margin. This leads us to the assumption, that there are limits to the mitigating effects of Bubble Margin.

We could also show, that applications like Bubble Margin have a stronger effect on people who are more susceptible to motion sickness. This result does not come as a surprise, since Bubble Margin seems to be unnecessary for people not being susceptible to motion sickness. One participant (TP5) complained about migraine prior to the test conditions drive. This was not the case for the control condition. It is worth mentioning that Bubble Margin had an opposite effect on her, amplifying motion sickness symptoms. Her migraine might have had an effect on this outcome, which has already been shown in [18]. This, also shows that there is no universal applicable visualization of motion that mitigates motion sickness, supporting [22].

With respect to the Bubble Margin design the visualization was not perceived as being peripheral at all times since participants either intentionally or unintentionally looked at the bubbles from time to time. Since the application was new to them this could be due to novelty effects. However, participants stated that this had a positive effect on subjective well-being. One could argue that looking at the Bubble Margin may be positive since mental distraction was shown to have a positive effect on motion sickness [5].

The overall functionality and stability of the Bubble Margin application proved to be faultless and stable. None of the participants reported any problems with regards to dysfunctioning visualizations or inconsistencies. These facts allow for Bubble Margin's source code to be used as a foundation for future projects to build on.

From a methodological point of view, the reading task was conducted well by all participants, which implies that the Bubble Margin visualization allows for doing such tasks while being visible at the smartphone margin, even with relatively small displays as we used in the study. With the current increase of size of new smartphones and phablets Bubble Margins might be even more effective.

6.1   Limitations

One limitation of the study is the low number of participants. The decision was ultimately one between breadth and depth. Since motion sickness is not yet fully understood with influencing factors sometimes differing from individual to individual, we opted for an in-depth assessment on a smaller sample. We chose a within-subject study design in order to find individual differences, which we did in the end. People are different in their susceptibility to motion sickness and this is also dependent within a subject (e.g., time of the day, general well-being, medication). While we tried to limit confounding factors as much as possible e.g., chose the same route for both rides, chose the same time of the day (to have similar light and traffic conditions), asked for influencing factors such as alcohol consumption, or eating behavior.

Another limitation is the recruiting among colleagues not familiar with the project. This had mainly procedural reasons. We wanted to conduct a within subject-study having participants to drive twice in a reasonable timely distance to each ride not to have sequence effects, at the same time wanting to have both rides as soon as possible after each other. Additionally, we wanted contextual factors to be as stable as possible (weather, outside temperature) since they also might have an influence on motion sickness. We argue that, the subjective feedback about the Bubble Margin approach in general might be biased, but whether it helps to fight motion sickness is probably not subject to such a bias.

The decision to inform participants in advance about potential risks could have priming effects on motion sickness. Due to ethical reasons we decided to inform participants about potential well-being related risks in advance. We cannot entirely exclude biases with respect to that.

Our study indicates that the Bubble Margin has a mitigating effect on an individual, subjective level. Participants were eager to use Bubble Margin for their private purposes in the future. That showed us the potentials of it. Results show the potentials of Bubble Margin, but cannot be generalized and need further verification. Data on acceleration forces could provide additional insight into the severity of induced motion sickness, as shown by Karjanto et al. [19].

7   Conclusions

In this paper, we have presented a novel approach to mitigate motion sickness while driving. Bubble Margin provides visual cues, shown at the border of a smartphone based on acceleration forces in real-time. Bubble Margin is designed to run on a mobile device regardless of the content displayed in the center of the screen. Its value lies in the fact that it does not need any addition al hardware and might be used as an overlay for any possible application. As such it is crucial that it is not perceived as being distractive from a primary task, such as reading, while still having a mitigating effect on motion sickness. An initial study showed, that Bubble Margin has mitigating effects on motion sickness during a reading task. With the raise of autonomous vehicles and the omnipresence of smartphones we believe, that approaches such as Bubble Margin have the potential to reach a large number of people.

Future work, needs to investigate what effect different designs have on mitigating motion sickness. For example, what is the minimum number of bubbles to evoke these effects? What effects have margin width and color?

References

1. Anstis, S.: Motion perception in the frontal plane: sensory aspects. In: Handbook of Perception and Human Performance, pp. 16.1–16.27. Wiley, Hoboken (1986)
2. Bauer, C.: On the (in-)accuracy of GPS measures of smartphones: a study of running tracking applications. In: 2013 Proceedings of International Conference on Advances in Mobile Computing & Multimedia, MoMM, pp. 335:335–335:341. ACM, New York (2013). https://doi.org/10.1145/2536853.2536893
3. Bertolini, G., Straumann, D.: Moving in a moving world: a review on vestibular motion sickness. Front. Neurol. **7**, 14 (2016). https://doi.org/10.3389/fneur.2016. 00014. https://www.frontiersin.org/article/10.3389/fneur.2016.00014
4. Bles, W., Bos, J., de Graaf, B., Groen, E., Wertheim, A.: Motion sickness: only one provocative conflict? Brain Res. Bull. **47**, 481–487 (1998)
5. Bos, J.E.: Less sickness with more motion and/or mental distraction. J. Vestib. Res. Equilibr. Orientation **25**(1), 23–33 (2015)
6. Bronstein, A., Lempert, T.: Dizziness: A Practical Approach to Diagnosis and Management. Dizziness with Downloadable Video, pp. 147–166. Cambridge University Press, Cambridge (2016)
7. Cohen, B., et al.: Motion sickness on tilting trains. FASEB J. **25**(11), 3765–3774 (2011). https://doi.org/10.1096/fj.11-184887
8. Cowings, P., Toscano, B.: Autogenic-feedback training exercise is superior to promethazine for control of motion sickness symptoms. J. Clin. Pharmacol. **40**, 1154–1165 (2000)
9. Diels, C., Bos, J.E.: Self-driving carsickness. Appl. Ergon. **53**, 374–382 (2016)
10. Gianaros, P.J., Muth, E.R., Mordkoff, J.T., Levine, M.E., Stern, R.M.: A questionnaire for the assessment of the multiple dimensions of motion sickness. Aviat. Space Environ. Med. **72**(2), 115–119 (2001)
11. Golding, J.F.: Motion sickness susceptibility questionnaire revised and its relationship to other forms of sickness. Brain Res. Bull. **47**(5), 507–516 (1998)

12. Golding, J.F.: Motion sickness susceptibility. Auton. Neurosci. Basic Clin. **129**, 67–76 (2006)

13. Golding, J.F.: Predicting individual differences in motion sickness susceptibility by questionnaire. Pers. Individ. Differ. **41**(2), 237–248 (2006)

14. Golding, J.F., Mueller, A., Gresty, M.A.: A motion sickness maximum around the 0.2 hz frequency range of horizontal translational oscillation. Aviat. Space Environ. Med. **72**(3), 188–192 (2001)

15. Guo, Z., Derian, A., Zhao, J.: Smart devices and travel time use by bus passengers in Vancouver, Canada. Int. J. Sustain. Transp. **9**(5), 335–347 (2015). https://doi. org/10.1080/15568318.2013.784933

16. Hanau, E., Popescu, V.: Motionreader: visual acceleration cues for alleviating passenger e-reader motion sickness. In: 2017 Proceedings of the 9th International Conference on Automotive User Interfaces and Interactive Vehicular Applications Adjunct AutomotiveUI, pp. 72–76. ACM, New York (2017). https://doi.org/10. 1145/3131726.3131741

17. Hock, P., Benedikter, S., Gugenheimer, J., Rukzio, E.: CarVR: enabling in-car virtual reality entertainment. In: Proceedings of the 2017 CHI Conference on Human Factors in Computing Systems, CHI 2017, pp. 4034–4044. ACM, New York (2017). https://doi.org/10.1145/3025453.3025665, http://doi.acm.org/ 10.1145/3025453.3025665

18. Jeong, S.H., Oh, S.Y., Kim, H.J., Koo, J.W., Kim, J.S.: Vestibular dysfunction in migraine: effects of associated vertigo and motion sickness. J. Neurol. **257**(6), 905–912 (2010). https://doi.org/10.1007/s00415-009-5435-5

19. Karjanto, J., Yusof, N.M., Wang, C., Terken, J., Delbressine, F., Rauterberg, M.: The effect of peripheral visual feedforward system in enhancing situation awareness and mitigating motion sickness in fully automated driving. Transp. Res. Part F Traffic Psychol. Behav. **58**, 678–692 (2018)

20. Kennedy, R.S., Lane, N.E., Berbaum, K., Lilienthal, M.G.: Simulator sickness questionnaire: an enhanced method for quantifying simulator sickness. Int. J. Aviat. Psychol. **3**, 203–220 (1993)

21. Kim, Y.L., et al.: The comparison of muscle activity according to various conditions during smartphone use in healthy adults. Phys. Ther. Rehabil. Sci. **5**, 15–21 (2016). https://doi.org/10.14474/ptrs.2016.5.1.15

22. McGill, M., Ng, A., Brewster, S.: I am the passenger: how visual motion cues can influence sickness for in-car VR. In: 2017 Proceedings of the 2017 CHI Conference on Human Factors in Computing Systems, CHI 2017, pp. 5655–5668. ACM, New York (2017). https://doi.org/10.1145/3025453.3026046

23. Miksch, M., Steiner, M., Miksch, M., Meschtscherjakov, A.: Motion sickness prevention system (MSPS): reading between the lines. In: Adjunct Proceedings of the 8th International Conference on Automotive User Interfaces and Interactive Vehicular Applications. AutomotiveUI 2016 Adjunct, pp. 147–152. ACM, New York (2016). https://doi.org/10.1145/3004323.3004340

24. Paillard, A., et al.: Motion sickness susceptibility in healthy subjects and vestibular patients: effects of gender, age and trait-anxiety. J. Vestib. Res.: Equilibr. Orientation **23**(4/5), 203–209 (2013)

25. Reason, J., Brand, J.J.: Motion Sickness. Academic Press, Cambridge (1975)

26. Shupak, A., Gordon, C.R.: Motion sickness advances in pathogenesis, prediction, prevention, and treatment. Aviat. Space Environ. Med. **77**, 1213–1223 (2007)

27. Sivak, M., Schoettle, B.: Motion sickness in self-driving vehicles. Technical report, University of Michigan, Ann Arbor, Transportation Research Institute (2015)

28. Turner, M., Griffin, M.J.: Motion sickness in public road transport: therelative importance of motion, vision and individual differences. Br. J. Psychol. **90**(4), 519–530 (1999)
29. Yusof, N.M., Karjanto, J., Kapoor, S., Terken, J.M.B., Delbressine, F., Rauterberg, M.: Experimental setup of motion sickness and situation awareness in automated vehicle riding experience. In: AutomotiveUI 2017: Proceedings of the 9th International Conference on Automotive User Interfaces and Interactive Vehicular Applications Adjunct, 24–27 September 2017, Oldenburg, Germany, pp. 104–109. Association for Computing Machinery Inc., United States (2017). https://doi.org/10.1145/3131726.3131761

CyclAir: A Bike Mounted Prototype for Real-Time Visualization of CO$_2$ Levels While Cycling

Eike Schneiders[✉] and Mikael B. Skov

Department of Computer Science, Human-Centered Computing Group,
Aalborg University, Selma Lagerløfsvej 300, 9220 Aalborg, Denmark
{eike,dubois}@cs.aau.dk

Abstract. With the increased global focus on the environment, pollution, greenhouse gases, as well as carbon footprint, a multitude of initiatives have emerged in order to reduce air pollution and also increase awareness of air quality. In this paper, we developed CyclAir, a system enabling cyclists to monitor the traffic-related air pollution, measured in carbon dioxide (CO_2) levels, both in real-time as well as retrospectively. Based on a first user study with seven test participants, we found that our participants were often confirmed about their preconceptions of the immediate CO_2 level and air quality, but interestingly they were also sometimes surprised. 6 out of the 7 participants expressed willingness to change route choosing behavior when presented with new evidence about the air quality, even when this increased the route length.

Keywords: Air quality measurement · CO_2 sensing ·
Real-time CO_2 visualization · Participatory Sensing in the Wild ·
Traffic based air pollution

1 Introduction

Global warming is a significant environmental concern and various initiatives e.g. by the European Union [5] or the United Nations [4] attempt to address and tackle this problem - including reduction of carbon dioxide (CO_2) emissions. One way to reduce CO_2 is to better utilize transportation means with no or limited CO_2 emissions, such as cycling. However, while cycling for transportation is favorable in terms of CO_2 emission, cyclists often expose themselves to air pollution and low air quality as they move around cities. Therefore, HCI research has studied effects on cyclists behavior and attitudes of air quality and pollution by collecting data for a retrospective analysis [2,11,14]. However, we have a limited understanding of the implications of real-time air quality feedback on cyclists behavior and awareness.

In this paper we developed CyclAir, which is a bike mounted prototype that visualizes real-time measurements of CO_2 levels when cycling through a simple LED-based, traffic light inspired, interface. The aim of our work is twofold.

© IFIP International Federation for Information Processing 2019
Published by Springer Nature Switzerland AG 2019
D. Lamas et al. (Eds.): INTERACT 2019, LNCS 11747, pp. 678–687, 2019.
https://doi.org/10.1007/978-3-030-29384-0_40

Firstly, we present a prototype developed in order to explore the possibility to increase awareness about air quality by giving cyclists real-time feedback of the air quality in their immediate surroundings. Thereby rendering something invisible visible, namely the local CO_2 level. Secondly, we want to identify if there exists a willingness for a behavioral change when it comes to the choosing of the cycling route when presented with previously unknown information about air quality.

2   Related Work

Several studies investigate mobile air quality tracking among others [1, 2, 7–9, 11, 14]. These studies usually employ a multitude of different sensors in order to collect data about air quality and often for various purposes. The studies have employed different means of transportation and data collection e.g. bikes [7, 8, 11], motorized vehicles [2, 11, 14] or mobile phones [9].

Aoki et al. [2] and Westerdahl et al. [14] both made use of motor vehicles equipped with different sensors in order to capture data about the air quality of San Francisco. Aoki et al. developed a system attached to street sweepers in San Francisco in order to collect three different air quality measurements as well as temperature, humidity, motion, and GPS data. Their primary focus was the development of a research vehicle for data collection for researchers, government agencies as well as public health NGOs. They identified shortcomings when using motorized vehicles which themselves have air pollution emissions, which resulted in the need of additional calibration of the system itself, in order to account for the street sweepers. Carvalho et al. [3] developed a system for measuring air quality, which can be attached to taxis and buses in Lisbon, in order to generate a real-time overlay for google maps on air quality which can be accessed through a web browser. Just like Aoki et al. they made use of emission causing vehicles for the collection of data which can involve some additional challenges. Westerdahl et al. [14] chose a zero-emission electric vehicle (Toyota Rav4 SUV) which did not contribute to emission. Their main contribution was the development of a sophisticated real-time mobile air quality measuring platform that got tested in Los Angeles. Furthermore, they identified strong differences in ultrafine particle density, depending on the road type and truck density at the given time.

An alternative to the mentioned motorized vehicles is the use of bicycles. Among others Anowar et al., Elen et al., Eisenman et al., and Hertel et al. [1, 7, 8, 11] conducted research in relation to bicycles and air pollution. Anowar et al. [1] tried to identify the willingness to chose alternative cycling routes to lower air pollution exposure, even if this resulted in longer routes. They investigated this using a survey, and concluded, that participants were willing to drive up to 4 min longer, given a reduction of NO_2 by 5ppb. For data collection Elen et al. [8] developed a research bike, the Aeroflex. They used the research bike to generate map representations for hot spot identification, air quality mapping as well as exposure monitoring. Although attached to a bike, the system still requires a certain degree of technical expertise, making the use hard for every-day cyclists. Furthermore, it required the transportation of a Laptop, batteries as well as a lot of other equipment which makes it less everyday friendly. Eisenman et al. [7] developed the BikeNet, which is a system for cyclist experience mapping in terms of fitness and environment tracking. They developed a bike and helmet mounted sensing system for the collection of several factors such as noise, roughness of the terrain or CO_2. Given their Health index definition, they calculated the healthiness of a given route which can be accessed through a web portal. Hertel et al. [11] compared a variety of air pollutants on three different routes, shortest bike route, less trafficked bike route and bus taking route. They performed a study with two groups of 25 people traveling from home to work and vice-versa. They could conclude, that the slower "greener" route reduced the intake of the measured pollutants on average by 10%–39%, although the increased travel time increased the exposure time to the pollutants.

Froehlich et al. [9] developed the UbiGreen mobile phone system in order to increase awareness about transportation habits. They conducted a field study using semi-automatic tracking while giving feedback to the users via the mobile phone in order to encourage green transportation. They concluded that test participants value the feedback about traveling behavior, which could lead to a lasting behavior change.

In this study, I aim at developing a system for real-time air quality monitoring in the wild, without the need for any technical expertise or complex to setup system. CyclAir has been developed with simplicity in mind, both in terms of compatibility with every bike, as well as in terms of non-intrusive feedback while cycling.

3   CyclAir

CyclAir is a system enabling cyclists to monitor the CO_2 levels both in realtime while cycling as well as retrospectively. CyclAir consists of a water-resistant encasing (IP44) in order to be durable enough for outdoor use on a bicycle. An Arduino Uno, running a custom C++ implementation, was used to control the system. The Adafruit SGP30 Air Quality Sensor Breakout Board (SGP30) was attached in order to measure CO_2-equivalent, which corresponds to the greenhouse gases measured, converted to the equivalent amount of CO_2 concentration. In order to increase air contact with the SGP30, the sensor was mounted on the handlebar of the bike. Air holes on the bottom of the SGP30 encasing increased air exchange within the encasing. Beside the SGP30 sensor, the NeoPixel 16 LED RGB lighting system (LED-ring) was mounted on the handlebar for visual feedback about CO_2 level to the cyclist. The LED-ring mounted on the bike's handlebar can be seen in Fig. 1B.

To ensure visibility while maintaining water resistant qualities, both the LED-ring as well as the SGP30 were mounted on the handlebar in a 3d printed enclosure. In order to enable the mapping of air quality measurements to a specific location, the Neo6M-V2 GPS module was used. The GPS module was used to acquire timestamps, date, longitude, as well as latitude. All measurements were collected and written to a micro SD-Card in 1-s intervals which were deemed sufficient. The average cycling speed in Copenhagen is 16.4 km/h which would correspond to a distance of 4.5 m/s using a 1-s interval [13].

Fig. 1. A: CyclAir system in context - here on a high traffic road in the center of Aalborg waiting at a red light. **B:** Close-up of visual feedback based on the 10 s average CO$_2$ level.

The design of CyclAir was developed in a preliminary design workshop. One button is installed in order to turn the system on/off. This starts the data collection in 1 Hz intervals. Visual feedback was provided in-situ via the handlebar mounted LED-ring. Through this the cyclist was receiving timely information about the CO$_2$ content of the air traversed during the last 10 s. Both shorter (down to 3 s) and longer (up to 30 s) intervals were experimented with, but this felt either too distracting when the interval was shorter, or not informative enough, for longer intervals. Each LED would light up in green, yellow or red (LowCO$_2$, MediumCO$_2$, HighCO$_2$), as illustrated in Fig. 1, dependent on the average CO$_2$ level in the last 10 s interval. The LED notification system was chosen in order to provide a subtle, non-intrusive notification approach using light [10,12] in an environment where distractions are not acceptable. The led-ring was chosen in order to give the possibility to identify tendencies while cycling, by providing current real-time information, which is comparable to the previous data points represented through earlier LEDs. After each cycling trip, the data was collected and visualized. This gave the cyclists the possibility to correlate the CO$_2$ levels on the traversed route, represented on a line graph, with the specific location, plotted using Google Maps, see example in Fig. 2.

4   Field Study

We conducted a field study of CyclAir using seven test participants (5 female; age: 25–55; mean age: 33.3, sd: 11.4) to evaluate our prototype and to gain a deeper understanding of cyclists experiences, motivation and use of CyclAir. The test participants were unpaid and were recruited through word-of-mouth.

All seven test participants ride bikes at least several times each week. Test participant T1 and T6 used the system on multiple days whereas the others used CyclAir once. Each test participant drove between ~3–16 km (mean: 6.7 km, sd: 4.1 km), resulting in a total of ~47 km. The system was in use for a total duration of ~3.5 h across all seven test participants with an average use time of 28.3 min per participant.

All cycle tours were performed in the two Danish cities Aalborg (~116000 citizens) and Haderslev (~22000 citizens), with four test participants in Aalborg and three in Haderslev. Both cities have a very good cycling infrastructure with predominantly dedicated bike lanes next to the road whereas cycling on the road is the exception.

In order to give in-situ air quality feedback to the cyclists, the test participants got visual notifications about the air quality using the LED-ring attached to the handlebar of the bike. This was an averaged value for the CO_2 over the last 10 s. Depending on the average, the next LED on the LED-ring would light up in green, yellow or red. In order to give the user insight into which LED was the next to light up, the two LED lights following the current one were turned off, leaving 14 lit LEDs and two turned off, see Fig. 1. The two threshold values, for the switch between the colors, were chosen to represent Danish air quality, meaning that even red was not necessarily representational for bad air quality when compared to the global air quality levels. After each bicycle tour, the data was collected and processed. Using a custom python script, the GPS data was plotted using Google Maps, and the CO_2 was smoothed using a 10-s moving average without overlap, and plotted into a line graph. With the map and the line graph as a basis, a semi-structured interview was conducted to gain some insight into the cyclist's experiences and thoughts of the CyclAir system.

5 Results

The cycling trips for the seven participants covered a total of ~47 km. When asked on what basis the test participants chose the cycling route, five of the seven test participants replied that the route choice was based on the expectation of seeing a red LED - meaning they chose roads which they hypothesized had high traffic density and therefore would lead to a reduction in air quality. Test participants T4 and T5 simply used the system for work-related commuting.

The CO_2 zone ratio overall tours for all test participants was of 73.7% LowCO2, 16.3% MediumCO2, and 10.0% HighCO2. Test participant T4, who was cycling in Aalborg, was the only test participant who did experience the HighCO2, and therefore did not see the red LED. The average CO_2 level, based on the 10-s moving window, was 442.1 parts-per-million (ppm) (max: 10163 ppm, sd: 265.7). The CO_2 value was LowCO2 for 73.7% of the time, meaning below 425 ppm, while it only exceeded 475 ppm, HighCO2, for 10.0% the measurements.

Based on the interviews and the collected data, we identified four themes on real-time visualization of CO_2-levels. ① **Increased awareness** about the air quality in the cyclist's immediate surroundings, which correlated with their

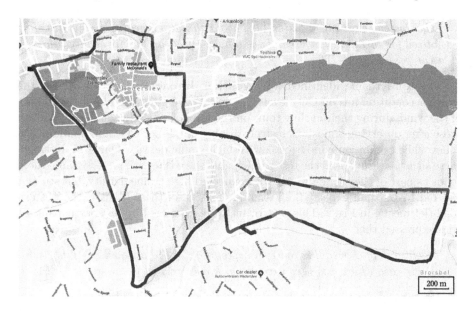

Fig. 2. First route driven by test participant T1, with color coded LowCO$_2$ (Green), MediumCO$_2$ (Yellow), and HighCO$_2$ (Red) peaks. (Color figure online)

sensual experiences. Cyclists became more aware of the differences in air quality in their immediate surroundings and could often identify, using their senses, why CyclAir would change color. Especially the HighCO$_2$ indications given by CyclAir matched with the cyclist's senses, which often could be identified using the sense of smell. Furthermore, T7 stated that at one point during the drive his eyes felt slightly irritated which, according to his own judgment, might have been related to low air quality. The second theme was the ② **High curiosity** in terms of linking the real-time information presented by CyclAir to a visible cause. Test participants expressed that when observing a red LED, or identifying bad air quality using their sense of, primarily, smell, they were trying to identify a visible cause. Test participants identified three typical causes for HighCO$_2$. (1) while crossing larger roads, (2) cycling parallel to high traffic roads with cars passing by, (3) or while standing at red intersection lights near cars, buses or other motorized vehicles, as illustrated in Fig. 1A. The first two themes are supported by, quotes made independently by several test participants. T7 for instances stated that:

> *"There was a good connection between the peaks [referring to HighCO$_2$ areas] and the impression I got through my senses when driving through these areas." - T7.*

This statement was independently supported by test participants T1 and T6. T2 expressed that he became increasingly aware of the local differences in air quality, especially when driving parallel to high-traffic roads, by stating:

"The system gave me a better idea about the difference in air quality, I noticed for instance that it can have a huge effect [on the air quality] when a car passes me." - T2

The third theme identified, ③ **Weather impact**, relates to impact the weather condition has on CO_2 levels. T1 and T3 were curious about the impact of the wind, during their cycling tour, on the level of air pollution. This curiosity arose after observing almost exclusively driving in the LowCO2 and MediumCO2 zones while cycling on windy roads with high traffic density. Quite interestingly these situations surprised the test participants since they deliberately chose these roads as part of the cycling route, with expected high traffic density, but still got less red LEDs than expected, an example for one of these roads is the western road (leftmost), in Fig. 2. This was for instance expressed by test participant T1 who expressed that:

"I deliberately choose this route in expectation of bad air quality - this was not the case which was very surprising. Maybe related to the wind?" - T1.

T4, who chose the route based on work-related commuting was the only one experiencing a rainy cycling tour. T4 was also the only test participant not experiencing HighCO2. To identify if there exists a correlation between rain and an effect on the CO_2 levels was not investigated and is left for future work.

The last theme, ④ **Confirmation of beliefs**, relates to the possibility the test subject had during the use of CyclAir, in order to confirm previously unconfirmed assumptions or beliefs about air quality. T6, who already chose an alternative route, compared to the fastest, for work-related commuting, stated that, after cycling the comparison, CyclAir confirmed her assumption that the air quality on the chosen route was better in comparison the fastest route. T1 partially made the same observation, on some roads where she expected low air quality, the use of CyclAir could confirm this.

Although the information CyclAir revealed did not feel entirely new to all test participants, it increased the awareness to local air quality changes and made test participants think about differences in air quality in their local environment. When asked about route choosing behavior, T6 stated that she already now chooses a route, for work-related commuting, that she expected to have less traffic-related air pollution compared to the alternative, sometimes more direct, routes. This expectation was confirmed during her cycling tours with CyclAir. T1, T5, T6, and T7 explicitly stated that they without a doubt would take alternative routes even when slightly longer, if they could reduce exposure to traffic-related air pollution. Test participants T2 and T3 stated that they might consider choosing a different route, and only T4 would not be willing to consider an alternative, longer, route to decrease air pollution exposure. Thereby we could confirm the willingness to drive detours to lower CO_2 exposure, even at the cost of increased distance, which confirms the findings in [1].

T1 asked if it would be possible to get route recommendations based on air quality, instead of the typical time or distance minimization's when planning a route pre-trip. This feature could be relevant both for a web interface, for the planning of the cycling trip, as well as in-situ based on current data. In relation to the, originating in the preliminary design workshop, CyclAir design all test participants agreed on the intuitiveness of the output given by the system. The traffic light inspired output was easy to understand and, with only one change every ten seconds, not too distracting. Several test participants indicated that the 140-s history, that was accessible at all times given the 14 simultaneously active LEDs each representing 10 s, was longer than necessary while cycling. The main focus was on the current and the last measurement which made it possible to identify if the air quality is improving or worsening.

All test participants agreed on, that by giving them real-time information about the local air quality, that the system either increased their awareness about air quality, which was the case for five of the seven test participants, or confirmed previously held, yet unconfirmed, assumptions the test participant had.

6   Discussion and Conclusion

In this paper we described the development and the field study, using 7 test participants, of the bike mounted prototype CyclAir. We ventured out to identify a possibility to give cyclists an increased awareness of air quality in their immediate surroundings. This was done by providing the 10 s average for the CO$_2$ value, using a traffic light inspired green, yellow and red system, representing LowCO$_2$, MediumCO$_2$ and HighCO$_2$, on the bike's handlebar, and thereby giving real-time in-situ information about something invisible made visible, namely the traffic-related air pollution in the current area. We extend on the current HCI research with findings based on real-time experiences while cycling, which were expressed during post cycling tour interviews. All test participants stated that they, after the use of CyclAir, had an **increased awareness** of the air quality differences, or at least a **confirmation** of previously unconfirmed assumptions about their local environment. An additional interesting finding is the impact of different **weather conditions** such as rain and wind on air pollution. Both seem to have an impact on air pollution, although confirmation of this is left for future work. The impact of the weather on air quality supports tendencies observed by Devarakonda et al. [6]. The impact of the weather, as well as the easy to understand visualization of traffic-related air pollution incited the test subjects **curiosity**. We confirmed that the CyclAir was able to increase air quality awareness, additionally, we could confirm [1]s identification of the cyclist's willingness to consider longer routes - if a reduced exposure to traffic-related air pollutants can be achieved.

This work opens up for several different areas of research for future work. One possibility would be how to optimize route planning, pre-cycling tour, based on information supplied by CyclAir. This could be supported with the development of a web-based platform, making the air quality data accessible for all cyclists. A different direction would be the exploration of in-situ directional information based on the current data for air quality in the given location. This can be followed by supplying deeper insights into the bike trip data for post-session analysis and tracking. The usefulness of user input, for instance when experiences particularly bad air, could be explored in a future study.

During this study a single pollutant, CO_2, was chosen to give the test participants a simplified representation of real-time air quality in their immediate surroundings. A topic for future work would be the system optimization with increased complexity by adding additional metrics such as Particulate Matter ($PM_{2.5/10}$), Ozone (O_3) or Carbon Monoxide (CO).

Given a large enough user base, the generation of heat maps based on air pollution is another area for future research. This can have several different application areas like for instance route planning for cyclists or air quality information for urban planners. Here a heat map could be useful in order to identify areas with, particularly high air pollution. This would gain additional potential with an extended set of sensors as described earlier.

Acknowledgement. We thank all participants of this user study for their time. Furthermore, we would like to thank the additional cyclists who helped us pilot test the system.

References

1. Anowar, S., Eluru, N., Hatzopoulou, M.: Quantifying the value of a clean ride: how far would you bicycle to avoid exposure to traffic-related air pollution? Transp. Res. Part A Policy Pract. **105**, 66–78 (2017). https://doi.org/10.1016/j.tra.2017.08.017
2. Aoki, P.M., et al.: A vehicle for research: using street sweepers to explore the landscape of environmental community action. In: Proceedings of the SIGCHI Conference on Human Factors in Computing Systems, CHI 2009, pp. 375–384. ACM, New York (2009). https://doi.org/10.1145/1518701.1518762
3. Carvalho, V., Lopes, J.G., Ramos, H.G., Alegria, F.C.: City-wide mobile air quality measurement system. In: SENSORS, 2009 IEEE, pp. 546–551, October 2009. https://doi.org/10.1109/ICSENS.2009.5398299
4. U.N.F.C. on Climate Change: Action on climate and SDGs (2015). https://unfccc. int/action-on-climate-and-sdgs
5. European Commission: European climate change programme. https://ec.europa. eu/clima/policies/eccp_en
6. Devarakonda, S., Sevusu, P., Liu, H., Liu, R., Iftode, L., Nath, B.: Real-time air quality monitoring through mobile sensing in metropolitan areas. In: Proceedings of the 2nd ACM SIGKDD International Workshop on Urban Computing, UrbComp 2013, pp. 15:1–15:8. ACM, New York (2013). https://doi.org/10.1145/2505821. 2505834
7. Eisenman, S.B., Miluzzo, E., Lane, N.D., Peterson, R.A., Ahn, G.S., Campbell, A.T.: The BikeNet mobile sensing system for cyclist experience mapping. In: Proceedings of the 5th International Conference on Embedded Networked Sensor Systems, SenSys 2007, pp. 87–101. ACM, New York (2007). https://doi.org/10.1145/ 1322263.1322273
8. Elen, B., Peters, J., Poppel, M.V., Bleux, N., Theunis, J., Reggente, M., Standaert, A.: The aeroflex: a bicycle for mobile air quality measurements. Sensors **13**(1), 221–240 (2013). https://doi.org/10.3390/s130100221

9. Froehlich, J., et al.: UbiGreen: investigating a mobile tool for tracking and supporting green transportation habits. In: Proceedings of the SIGCHI Conference on Human Factors in Computing Systems, CHI 2009, pp. 1043–1052. ACM, New York (2009). https://doi.org/10.1145/1518701.1518861

10. Hansson, R., Ljungstrand, P.: The reminder bracelet: subtle notification cues for mobile devices, pp. 323–324, January 2000. https://doi.org/10.1145/633292.633488

11. Hertel, O., Hvidberg, M., Ketzel, M., Storm, L., Stausgaard, L.: A proper choice of route significantly reduces air pollution exposure–a study on bicycle and bus trips in urban streets. Sci. Total Environ. **389**(1), 58–70 (2008). https://doi.org/10.1016/j.scitotenv.2007.08.058

12. Müller, H., Kazakova, A., Pielot, M., Heuten, W., Boll, S.: Ambient timer – unobtrusively reminding users of upcoming tasks with ambient light. In: Kotzé, P., Marsden, G., Lindgaard, G., Wesson, J., Winckler, M. (eds.) INTERACT 2013. LNCS, vol. 8117, pp. 211–228. Springer, Heidelberg (2013). https://doi.org/10.1007/978-3-642-40483-2_15

13. Technical and Environmental Administration City of Copenhagen: The Bicycle Account 2014 (2017). http://www.cycling-embassy.dk/wp-content/uploads/2015/05/Copenhagens-Biycle-Account-2014.pdf

14. Westerdahl, D., Fruin, S., Sax, T., Fine, P.M., Sioutas, C.: Mobile platform measurements of ultrafine particles and associated pollutant concentrations on freeways and residential streets in Los Angeles. Atmos. Environ. **39**(20), 3597–3610 (2005). https://doi.org/10.1016/j.atmosenv.2005.02.034

Dissecting Pie Charts

Harri Siirtola, Kari-Jouko Räihä[⊠], Howell Istance, and Oleg Špakov

Faculty of Information Technology and Communication, Tampere University,
Tampere, Finland
{harri.siirtola,kari-jouko.raiha,howell.istance,oleg.spakov}@tuni.fi

Abstract. Pie charts can be regularly found both in the popular media and research publications. There is evidence that other forms of visualizations make it easier to evaluate the relative order of the data items. Doughnut charts have been suggested as a variation that has advantages over pie charts. We investigated how pie charts and doughnut charts are affected by the number of sectors in the chart, the difference in sector sizes, and the size of the hole. We carried out an eye tracking study to find out how the charts are read. Our study reveals the distribution of visual attention for each type of chart. The results indicate that doughnut charts with a medium size hole have a slight edge over the other chart types we studied. We also show that contrary to common claims, for information extraction also the area and length of sector arc are used in addition to the angles of the sectors.

Keywords: Pie charts · Doughnut charts · Readability · Effectiveness

1 Introduction

Pie charts are omnipresent. Whenever there is an election to be reported, a budget to be explained, or a poll to be published we see them, and usually many of them. Pie charts are practically the *de-facto* standard to represent how some part relates to a whole, or to other parts of the (same) whole. Perhaps the greatest strength of pie charts is that they are self-explanatory – or at least supposed to be so.

The pie chart is also one of the most controversial data graphic representations ever. Many prominent experts advice to avoid them completely because human visual system is better in perceiving length than angle (*'The only thing worse than a pie chart is several of them'* (Tufte 1983), *'Save pies for the dessert'* (Few 2007), *'Pie charts are bad'* (Fenton 2009), *'Death to pie charts'* (Nussbaumer 2011)), but there are advocates as well (*'Why Tufte is flat-out wrong about pie charts'* (Gabrielle 2013), *'In defense of pie charts'* (Kosara 2011), and also Spence and Lewandowsky (1991); Peck et al.(2013)). We are not trying to solve this debate or take sides – our approach is pragmatic: since pie charts are used anyway, we need to understand them better.

© IFIP International Federation for Information Processing 2019
Published by Springer Nature Switzerland AG 2019
D. Lamas et al. (Eds.): INTERACT 2019, LNCS 11747, pp. 688–698, 2019.
https://doi.org/10.1007/978-3-030-29384-0_41

One possible explanation for the tumult over pie charts is that they are often misused. The most important guidelines with pie charts are that there should be no more than about 7 slices, slices should not be exploded (taken out from the pie), there should be no separate legend (requiring movement between slices and labels), and there should be no 3D effects (a generally bad idea in data graphics). Making a Google image search for "pie chart" shows that these rules are often recklessly violated.

We study in this paper how pie charts are read by reporting an experiment where participants were requested to list the sectors of pie charts in a decreasing order of size while their gaze was recorded with an eye tracker. We also include the most popular variation of pie chart, the doughnut chart, and investigate how the size of the hole in the middle of the doughnut affects the reading. The chosen experimental task is perhaps the most common operation with pie and doughnut charts as they are really geared towards relative comparisons. Sometimes the slices of these charts can be freely sorted by magnitude which would render the task trivial, but often the variables represented by slices have a natural order which precludes this (e.g. political parties, ratings about something).

2   Previous Work

Lima (2018) presents two explanations for the popularity of pie charts: historical and evolutionary ones. His examples suggest that the preference for round pie charts might be too deep-rooted to be removed with any kind of reasoning.

Eells (1926) did the first comparisons between pie charts and stacked bar charts. This was a justified experimental setup – both have parts as well as a whole. His experimental task was to estimate the percentage of the whole represented by an element, as a number. He concluded that pie charts could be read as rapidly as stacked bar charts, and that the accuracy of pie charts was better. As a response, von Huhn (1927) criticized Eells's experimental task, because neither of the visualizations is meant to be used for absolute judgements, but relative ones. In addition, von Huhn suspected that the missing scales and labels from the stimulus ruined the ecological validity and the results. Despite von Huhn's criticism, the same experimental setup was later repeated in a number of studies. A recent comparison of pie charts and bar charts (with relative judgments) is presented by Siirtola (2019).

According to a seminal paper by Cleveland and McGill (1984), the accuracy of judgements (from the most accurate to least accurate) in elementary perceptual tasks is length, angle, and area. However, this result is for extracting quantitative information from graphs (absolute judgement), and in our experiment only relative judgement is needed. In addition, the judgement based on the curved lengths in our experiment might be more difficult than on straight ones. The study was later replicated using Mechanical Turk by Heer and Bostock (2010) with similar results.

Spence and Lewandowsky (1991) give a comprehensive review of the earlier research on pie charts, and point out that the practitioners of display graphics keep using pie charts despite the harsh criticism from experts – and the practitioners probably have a good sense of what works and what doesn't work.

Skau and Kosara (2016) did a comparison of pie charts, doughnut charts, and 'angle only charts' (two line segments depicting an angle), and argued that angle is not the primary or only factor when pie charts are read. They did not use eye tracking, but deconstructed pie and doughnut charts into their constituent parts. Their experimental task was absolute judgement ("*What percentage of the whole is indicated?*") which we find unnatural in part-whole visualizations.

Although there thus is a wealth of research on pie charts and doughnut charts, it is targeted at their performance: how fast and how correctly can the information represented by the chart be extracted. There are no studies on how this extraction process takes place, i.e., where in the chart do viewers attend to. This can only be found out by tracking the gaze of the viewers. Ours is the first eye tracking study on this issue. Our goal is to shed light on *how* pie charts and doughnut charts are read.

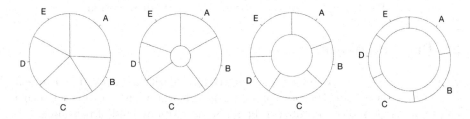

Fig. 1. Variations of stimulus, from left to right: Pie Chart (no hole), Doughnut-25 (a doughnut chart with hole having radius of 25% of the pie radius), and correspondingly, Doughnut-50 and Doughnut-75 variations.

3   Method

3.1   Participants

In our experiment participants were recruited from an introductory course in human-computer interaction, where they received course credit for participating. 29 students volunteered to take part in the test. Reliable gaze data could not be collected for two of them: for one the tracker could not be calibrated, and for the other there were big gaps in the gaze point stream produced by the eye tracker. Thus 27 participants (17 male, 10 female) calibrated well and produced data that is reported in this paper.

The age of the participants ranged from 19 to 56 years, with median age of 23 years. All had normal vision or corrected to normal vision (7 wore eye glasses and 2 had contact lenses). Only one participant had previously used an eye tracker. Pie charts were previously familiar to all participants, but doughnut charts were equally familiar to only five participants, and somewhat familiar to another five participants.

3.2 Apparatus

A Tobii T60 eye tracker with a 17-inch TFT color monitor with 1280 × 1024 resolution was used to track the gaze. A PC running Windows 10 was used for the experiment. The stimuli were presented using the Tobii Pro Lab software.

3.3 Task

The participants were shown a sequence of pie charts in random order. The charts varied based on the number of segments (4, 5, 6 or 7). They also were of varying difficulty, with the difference between the value of the segments being depicted at least 6%, 10%, 14% or 18%. Finally, the radius of the hole was varied from 0% of the doughnut radius (corresponding to a full pie), to 25%, 50%, and finally 75%, corresponding to the slimmest doughnut (Fig. 1). Altogether there were thus 4 (number of segments) × 4 (angle difference) × 4 (hole size) = 64 different charts.

The pies were centered on the screen and had a radius of 356 pixels. The sectors of the charts were labelled outside the perimeter of the pie with capital letters starting from A for the top right sector, and running clockwise from there on. The participants were asked to say aloud the order of the sectors from the biggest to the smallest by stating the labels of the sectors in that order.

3.4 Procedure

Upon entering the lab the participants first signed an informed consent form.

The experimenter then explained the task and showed on paper some sample images of pie charts and doughnut charts. The participant was told to speak clearly, and explained that they could revise their judgment of the order of the sectors during the presentation of a stimulus, as long as the order they eventually chose was clear.

They were asked to work quickly and accurately. As a motivation, the five best (using a combined measure of speed and correctness) were promised a monetary reward of 10 euros. The details of the metric used for ordering the performance were not revealed.

The participants were then seated in front of the eye tracker at a distance of about 60 cm from the screen. The eye tracker was calibrated using a 5-point calibration. The quality of the calibration was measured after the calibration. Both the accuracy and precision were less than 0.5°, on average, and always at most 1°.

After calibration the experimenter started an audio recording using a Samsung A3 mobile phone and moved to another computer for entering the orders of sectors that the participant uttered. After the experiment the audio recording was used to double check that the experimenter had transcribed the participant's answers correctly.

The data collection then began. The participant advanced to the next chart by pressing the space bar. A dot with a 10 pixel radius was first shown in the center of the screen for 2.5 s. The next chart then appeared automatically. After uttering the order of the sectors the participant pressed the space bar again to move to the next chart, and the process was repeated with the dot appearing in the center.

Since viewing 64 charts in a row is a monotonous task, the participant was given information on progress. After the first four charts, instead of the picture with a dot, a circle containing the number 60 was shown for five seconds in the center to indicate that 60 charts still remained. Similar information was then given after every 10 graphs.

After finishing the task the participant was interviewed. Finally they were shown live visualizations of their gaze path when viewing some of the charts.

4   Results

4.1   Time and Correctness

Two factors affect the performance of pie charts and doughnut charts inversely: number of sectors and difference of values depicted. The fewer sectors there are, the easier the task, and the smaller the difference, the more difficult it becomes.

For visualizing the distribution of the data points it is useful to define a metric that combines the effect of the two factors. We define an index of difficulty as

$$IOD = ln(5 \times (Number\ of\ Sectors)/(Difference\ as\ Percentage)).$$

This function distributes the stimuli to cover the whole stimulus space so that all cases have a positive IOD value. The easiest case is one with 4 sectors and value difference of 18%, producing an IOD of 0.105. The most difficult case has 7 segments with difference of 6%, producing an IOD of 1.764. In the first case the data values that are represented by the sectors in the chart are 70.9, 83.6, 96.4 and 109.1. In the latter case the data values range from 43.6 to 59.3 with a difference of 2.6 between consecutive values, which can be expected to be a very difficult ordering task.

Figure 2 (on the left) shows the IOD versus the mean of task time (from appearance of stimulus to its disappearance when the participant pressed the space bar) for each visualization type, aggregated per the levels of IOD. The overlaid curves are smoothed with loess local polynomial regression. The figure suggests that Doughnut-50 might be the fastest visualization to interpret in medium-to-difficult cases, but this difference is not statistically significant according to our mixed-effects modeling.

Figure 2 also shows the IOD versus the number of errors for each visualization type (on the right). There is practically no difference between curves: the number of errors increases with the same rate in each visualization as tasks become more difficult.

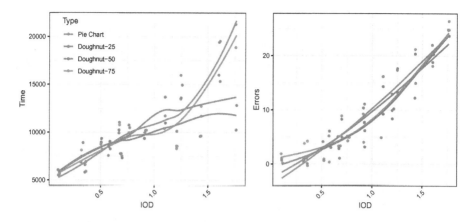

Fig. 2. IOD (Index of Difficulty) vs. mean task time (on the left) and number of errors (on the right).

Table 1 shows the mean and standard deviation for task execution time, and the error count per visualization type. Again, the numbers suggest that Doughnut-50 has a slight advantage in terms of time and errors, but there is no statistical significance.

Table 1. Summary of task times and standard deviations, in milliseconds, and error counts.

Type	Mean of task time	SD	Error count
Doughnut-75	10,309	5,982	137
Doughnut-50	9,791	5,169	130
Doughnut-25	10,450	6,380	137
Pie Chart	10,423	6,925	142

4.2   Distribution of Visual Attention

In comparing the relative sizes of sectors in a circular visualization there are four features which can be used for comparison, illustrated in Fig. 3. We can use the angle of sectors, either explicitly shown or imagined. In addition, we can use the length of sector arcs, either the outer one in case of pie chart, or inner and outer one in case of doughnut chart. We can also base our judgement on the area of sectors. In reality a combination of the features is likely to be used.

In this section we use the raw gaze points and their empirical distribution to estimate the focus of visual attention. We do not cluster the gaze data into saccades and fixations but use the lowest level raw data available.

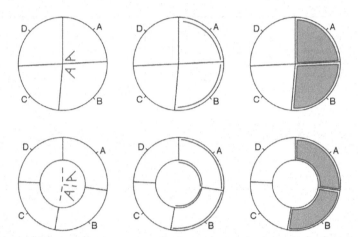

Fig. 3. What to look at when deciding the relative order of sectors, from the left: the angle, the length of inner or outer arc, and the area of sector.

4.2.1   Gaze Distance from the Origo

Figure 4 shows the overall distribution of the gaze point distance from the origo in our four conditions as percentage of visualization diameter. The density distributions are clearly different (Pie Chart: $Mean = 58.1\%, SD = 30.5\%$, Doughnut-25: $Mean = 60.6\%, SD = 28.1\%$, Doughnut-50: $Mean = 68.0\%, SD = 23.1\%$, and Doughnut-75: $Mean = 77.8\%, SD = 20.1\%$).

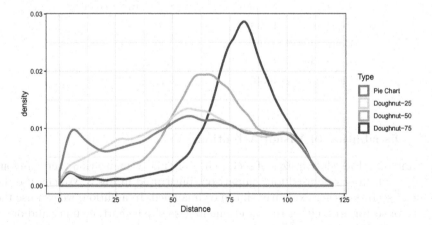

Fig. 4. Overall density of gaze distance from the origo per visualization type.

4.2.2   Proportion of Time in Areas of Visualization

With the empirical distribution function we can also estimate what proportion of time the participants spent in each area of the charts. The areas of interest in our study are the surroundings of the origo, area around the lower ring, area within the band (between rings), and the upper ring (Fig. 3). They correspond to estimating the magnitudes of sectors by using angles, lengths, and areas.

Figure 5 shows the overall distance of gaze points from the origo as a binned density graph (with 6 bins). The black dot denotes the median value, and the dashed lines show where the 'ring' of the chart resides. With all charts types the participants had to read the labels outside the ring (appr. 100–130% of diameter) which shows as a similar bar far right. Personal variation was high: participant P20's median attention is almost on the inner arc when participant P23's attention is clearly on the outer arc.

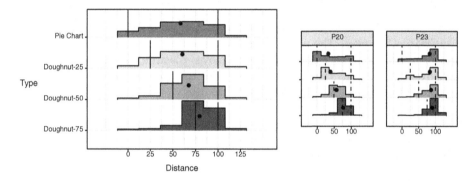

Fig. 5. Overall density of gaze distance as percentage of diameter from the origo per visualization type. The black point indicates the median of distance from the origo, and the dashed lines show the ring of the corresponding visualization. P20 and P23 were the two extreme cases.

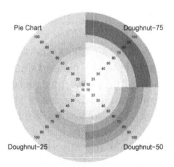

Fig. 6. Overall density of gaze distance from the origo per visualization type. The gaze distance has been divided into 10% bands, and each quadrant shows one visualization. The color scale is from white to red – deeper red indicates higher amount of gaze hits in that band (Color figure online).

Finally, Fig. 6 is a summary how the visual attention is allocated within the four chart types. This image summarises all gaze data from all participants in 10% steps.

5   Discussion

Figure 4 shows that the information-extracting of Pie Chart is not concentrated on the origo, i.e. comparison of angles, which has been a common assumption (e.g. by Simkin and Hastie (1987)). This was observed by Skau and Kosara (2016) as well. The figure suggests that participants use angle, area, and arc length almost evenly. Another interesting point is the comparison of Pie Chart and Doughnut-25 – the densities are similar except in the vicinity of the origo. The use of angle for comparisons is reduced because of the hole, and even more so in case of Doughnut-50 and Doughnut-75.

Figure 5 shows the overall differences in the allocation of visual attention more vividly. There are several trends in visual attention as the hole in the visualization increases: the use of the angle decreases, the use of inner and outer arcs increases, and the median attention moves towards the inner edge of the visualization. It seems that participants prefer the inner arc over the outer arc for comparisons.

Figure 6 shows the distribution of visual attention as co-centric 10% circles for all participants and conditions. It is easy to see how the hole in the middle changes the attention allocation – it is easier to use the area of a sector or length of the arc to estimate the size. For Pie Chart the area of a sector appears to be the dominant method to compare size, not the angle. Overall, Pie Chart is the most evenly-allocated visualization type, and participants used all three methods for size comparisons. For doughnuts the hole decreases the use of angle for estimation.

The participants were also interviewed about their preferences and observations. They provided comments, e.g. P10: *"If there's a hole, then the inner arcs are closer to each other than the outer arcs, so it is easier to compare them. ...And the angle then, it had to be like divided in four sectors and then one could really use the angles."*

Finally, it is important to be clear about the scope of this study. We have focused only on the graphical side of the pie and doughnut charts, and removed aspects that are essential parts of properly constructed charts. For the graphical side, we have followed the gold standard: no more than seven sectors and start the sectors from 12 o'clock, proceed clock-wise. We have named our sectors, but it is often useful to include the sector size in the label, especially if the values are close to each other. We did not use any color in the charts, as its benefits vary among participants. Thus this study is focused only on how the graphical aspects of pie and doughnut charts are read and perceived. Further research is needed for richer forms of pie charts.

6   Conclusions

Pie charts are one of the most common types of visualizations encountered in the media, so it is important to understand how readers extract information from them. We show that pie charts are not only used for comparing angles. Instead, the area and the outer arc are used as well in making judgments of the relative order of the sectors. This contradicts the claim made in the literature (e.g. Simkin and Hastie (1987)).

Including a hole in the center of the diagram, i.e. using a doughnut instead of a pie, might seem like a step in the wrong direction, as it makes the angles of the sectors less prominent. However, with a suitable size of the hole the advantages may overcome this disadvantage. Concerning the time used for the judgments and the correctness of the judgments (Fig. 2 and Table 1), there is a trend (but not statistically significant) that a hole that extends halfway through the radius of the diagram makes judgments slightly faster and less error prone than the other variations, including the standard pie chart.

Acknowledgements. This research was funded by the Academy of Finland, project *Private and Shared Gaze: Enablers, Applications, Experiences* (GaSP, grant number 2501287895). We acknowledge the use of the *Statistical System R* (R Core Team 2019) and *tidyverse* packages (Wickham 2017; Wickham and Grolemund 2016), especially *ggplot2* (Wickham 2010).

References

Cleveland, W.S., McGill, R.: Graphical perception: theory, experimentation, and application to the development of graphical methods. J. Am. Stat. Assoc. **79**(387), 531–554 (1984)

Eells, W.C.: The relative merits of circles and bars for representing component parts. J. Am. Stat. Assoc. **21**(154), 119–132 (1926)

Fenton, S.: Pie charts are bad. Personal journal on the web (2009). https://www.stevefenton.co.uk/2009/04/pie-charts-are-bad/. Accessed 10 Jan 2019

Few, S.: Save the pies for dessert. Visual Business Intelligence Newsletter (2007). http://www.perceptualedge.com/articles/08-21-07.pdf. Accessed 10 Jan 2019

Gabrielle, B.: Why Tufte is flat-out wrong about pie charts. Web log post, Speaking PowerPoint - The new language of business (2013)

Heer, J., Bostock, M.: Crowdsourcing graphical perception: using mechanical turk to assess visualization design. In: Proceedings of the SIGCHI Conference on Human Factors in Computing Systems, pp. 203–212. ACM (2010)

Kosara, R.: In defense of pie charts. Web log post. eagereyes (2011). http://eagereyes.org/criticism/in-defense-of-pie-charts. Accessed 10 Jan 2019

Lima, M.: Why humans love pie charts - an historical and evolutionary perspective. Noteworthy - The Journal Blog (2018). https://blog.usejournal.com/why-humans-love-pie-charts-9cd346000bdc

Nussbaumer, C.: Death to pie charts. Web log post. Storytelling with Data (2011). http://www.storytellingwithdata.com/2011/07/death-to-pie-charts.html. Accessed 10 Jan 2019

Peck, E.M.M., Yuksel, B.F., Ottley, A., Jacob, R. J., Chang, R.: Using fNIRS brain sensing to evaluate information visualization interfaces. In: Proceedings of the SIGCHI Conference on Human Factors in Computing Systems, CHI 2013, pp. 473–482. ACM (2013)

R Core Team. R: A Language and Environment for Statistical Computing. R Foundation for Statistical Computing, Vienna, Austria (2019). http://www.R-project.org

Siirtola, H.: The cost of pie charts. In: To appear in 23rd International Conference on Information Visualisation (IV2019), July 2019

Simkin, D., Hastie, R.: An information-processing analysis of graph perception. J. Am. Stat. Assoc. **82**(398), 454–465 (1987)

Skau, D., Kosara, R.: Arcs, angles, or areas: individual data encodings in pie and donut charts. Comput. Graph. Forum **35**, 121–130 (2016)

Spence, I., Lewandowsky, S.: Displaying proportions and percentages. Appl. Cogn. Psychol. **5**, 61–77 (1991)

Tufte, E.R.: The Visual Display of Quantitative Information. Graphics Press, Cheshire (1983)

von Huhn, R.: Further studies in the graphic use of circles and bars: a discussion of the Eell's experiment. J. Am. Stat. Assoc. **22**(157), 31–39 (1927)

Wickham, H.: ggplot2: Elegant Graphics for Data Analysis. Use R!, 1st edn. Springer, New York (2010). https://doi.org/10.1007/978-0-387-98141-3

Wickham, H.: tidyverse: Easily Install and Load 'Tidyverse' Packages. R package version 1.1.1 (2017)

Wickham, H., Grolemund, G.: R for Data Science: Import, Tidy, Transform, Visualize, and Model Data. O'Reilly Media, Sebastopol (2016)

Same Same but Different: Exploring the Effects of the Stroop Color Word Test in Virtual Reality

Romina Poguntke[1(✉)], Markus Wirth[2], and Stefan Gradl[2]

[1] University of Stuttgart, Stuttgart, Germany
romina.poguntke@vis.uni-stuttgart.de
[2] Friedrich-Alexander-Universität Erlangen-Nürnberg (FAU), Erlangen, Germany
{markus.wirth,stefan.gradl}@fau.de

Abstract. Virtual reality (VR) is used for different trainings e.g. for pilots, athletes, and surgeons. Dangerous and difficult situations are often focused in such simulations in VR, targeting to learn how to perform well under stress. However, there has been little work on understanding stress perception in VR compared to the real-world situation. In this paper we present an investigation of how users experience a stressful task in VR compared to in a classic office environment. Specifically, we investigate the subjective stress experience and physiological arousal with 15 participants performing the Stroop color word test either on a regular desktop screen, in VR, or in VR requiring head movements. Our findings suggest that stressful tasks are perceived less stressful when being performed in VR compared to the real environment as long as there is no additional stress factor, such as head movement involved. Our work indicates that it may be valuable to transfer stressful tasks, currently done in traditional office environments into VR.

Keywords: Virtual reality · Stress · Human-computer interaction

1 Introduction and Background

Virtual reality (VR) is becoming increasingly popular for researchers in different domains and for various purposes, e.g. rehabilitation [6,18,25], sports [24], and gaming [5]. Moreover VR has been proven to be an important tool for simulating stressful and cognitively demanding scenarios in e.g. military trainings [3,5], pilot flight trainings [13,14], other dangerous working environments, such as petrol refinery [7]. Aiming to train soldiers, flight pilots, and also firefighters stress elicitation in VR has pointed towards an important research gap. To not interrupt immersion in the VR scenario and elicit stress at the same time, there is a need for effectively stress inducing tasks that can be applied in VR. Aiming to elicit stress in VR, Legkov et al. [12] asked participants to react on approaching objects in a space shooter scenario. Measuring the Galvanic Skin Response

© IFIP International Federation for Information Processing 2019
Published by Springer Nature Switzerland AG 2019
D. Lamas et al. (Eds.): INTERACT 2019, LNCS 11747, pp. 699–708, 2019.
https://doi.org/10.1007/978-3-030-29384-0_42

(GSR) and the subjective stress level, they found that their dual task paradigm increased physiological arousal and affected certain stress dimensions. Jönsson et al. [10] validated if the Trier Social Stress Test (TSST) [11], a standardized and validated task mainly used for laboratory studies, performed in VR also induces stress. They found that the cortisol level in the participants' saliva had increased by 88% and also the heart rate and heart rate variability showed a solid indication of experienced social stress. Based on these results, stress induction in VR has been studied [1,4,17]. However, there has been little work on the role of stress in VR. Particularly the investigation of the effects of stress elicitation in virtual environments compared to classic desktop based scenarios has been neglected so far. VR represents a promising approach to be applied as a training technique for learning to deal with heavy stressors. To address this research gap, we explore the transferability of stressful tasks from office to virtual environments using the Stroop color word test [21], a well established stress elicitation task [26], to observe stress perception in VR.

With this work, we contribute the first investigation of transferring it from its classic desktop screen version into VR. Through the stress assessment based on a three dimensional structure comprising engagement, worry, and distress, and the evaluation of heart rate variability, we provide first insights in the exploration of stressful tasks in VR and prospective effects of transferring these tasks from reality into virtual environments.

2 Implementation

Subsequently, we will explain what the Stroop color word test is and how we implemented it in our three experimental conditions.

2.1 Stroop Color Word Test

Among the classical version of the Stroop color word test [21] and several distinct versions that exist, we took the Stroop color word version for this work presenting both, the congruent and incongruent condition (cf. Fig. 2). This task is commonly used in HCI [26] and intensifies physiological reactions [20], moreover it can be easily implemented in VR which is an advantage when considering

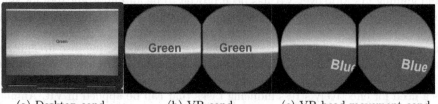

(a) Desktop cond.   (b) VR cond.   (c) VR head movement cond.

Fig. 1. Depicts the three conditions compromising our independent variable.

the transferability of a stress inducing task. While 'congruent' means that words are displayed in the color that they signify, 'incongruent' refers to the incongruence between the color of the word and in its actual meaning. For example, in the congruent condition the word 'red' is being presented in red and in the incongruent conditions it is painted in blue (cf. Fig. 1). Hereby the participant's task is to name the word's color and neglect the color that the word is designating.

2.2 Implementation of the Stroop Test in VR

For our user study setup, we utilized the HTC Vive virtual reality system connected to a PC consisting of a 3.7 GHz Intel Xeon processor, 16 GB RAM and a GeForce GTX 970 graphics card with a display size of 17, 3 in. (Full-HD, 1.920 × 1080) (cf. Fig. 1a). To render the stimuli of the Stroop color word test, we employed the Unity 3D engine[1]. For each condition, two sequences of 120 randomly selected Stroop items were generated at the beginning. Randomization was based on the subject ID, thus an individual sequence was generated for each participant. To get an equal distribution of Stroop items among all participants, two initial static buckets containing all items were created: one for the incongruent and one for the congruent test. The incongruent bucket contained each possible color combination ten times, the congruent bucket each stimulus 30 times. For each participant, the sequence of Stroop items that was presented, was randomly drawn from these buckets until they were empty. For the desktop screen and the VR condition, all stimuli were displayed in the centered field of view. For the VR head movement condition, the Stroop items were displayed at a pseudorandom position in the field of view of the participants in the virtual reality. This means that a random position was selected in either the left/right (50° from the center field of view) or lower/upper (50.5° from the center field of view) hemisphere of the subject with the constraint that no hemisphere could be selected two subsequent times.

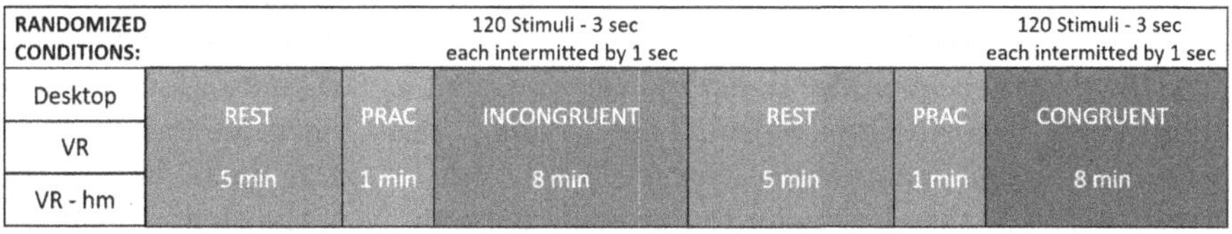

RANDOMIZED CONDITIONS:	120 Stimuli - 3 sec each intermitted by 1 sec					120 Stimuli - 3 sec each intermitted by 1 sec
Desktop	REST	PRAC	INCONGRUENT	REST	PRAC	CONGRUENT
VR						
VR - hm	5 min	1 min	8 min	5 min	1 min	8 min

Fig. 2. Study design showing the sequence of trials including the three conditions (desktop screen, VR, VR requiring head movements). We let the participants perform a practice trial before each of the two trials (incongruent, congruent) started, resulting in four trials in total preceded by a five minutes resting period.

---

[1] https://unity3d.com/.

3   User Study

For our user study we invited 15 participants and randomly split them into three equally sized groups, resulting in an in-between-subject design. Whereas one group experienced the Stroop color test in VR and another group performed head movements in VR, the third group conducted the test on a regular desktop screen positioned on an office desk. We randomized the sequence of three conditions for each participant according to Latin square.

3.1   Measures

As independent variables, we designed three different conditions how the Stroop color word test should be performed: (a) sitting in front of a desktop screen and all stimuli presented in the centered field of view, (b) in VR and the stimuli also presented in the centered field of view, and (c) in VR but the stimuli appeared as described above in the visual field of the participant. The latter condition was introduced based on the observations that the vestibular system being involved in head movements, was found to have an influence on the susceptibility to motion sickness [19]. Thus, we were interested if requiring head movements to accomplish the task would increase stress perception. As dependent variables we assessed the subjectively perceived stress level employing the Short Stress State Questionnaire (SSSQ) [8]; also used by Legkov et al. [12] to observe stress reactions induced in VR. Likewise, we recorded physiological data, i.e. heart rate (HR) and heart rate variability (HRV) to monitor if the physiological arousal corresponding to stress also varies among our conditions as could be shown in related work for VR experiences in general [2,18]. For recording physiological data we used the Nexus Kit 4 by MindMedia[2].

3.2   Procedure and Data Collection

Before we started with the evaluation, participants were explained the study's purpose and procedure. After giving their written consent, we asked each one to place the three gel electrodes connected to a two channel ExG sensor for assessing HR and HRV to themselves; meaning the negative (black) electrode was attached at the right collar bone, the positive (red) electrode on the midaxial line on the lateral aspect of the chest, and the ground electrode near the right leg on the chest. Inspired by previous study designs [22], we specified the sequence of trials as depicted in Fig. 2. Before the initial resting phase of five minutes, baseline measurements started, each participant was asked to fill in the first part ('At the moment') of the Short Stress State Questionnaire [8] for assessing the baseline stress level. Then, there was a one minute practice phase; by this we ensured that everyone understood the task. It was followed by an eight minute incongruent phase. During that time the participants were presented 120 words, either on the desktop screen or in VR, for 3 s intermitted by one second. After another

---

[2] https://www.mindmedia.com/de/produkte/nexus-4/.

five minutes of resting and a one minute practice trial, the congruent phase lasted eight minutes followed, presented in the same manner as the incongruent condition. When the last Stroop color test trial was completed, all participants were asked to complete the second part of the Short Stress State Questionnaire referring to their stress perception 'During the task' (Fig. 3).

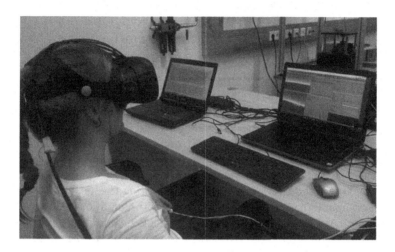

Fig. 3. Participant wearing the HTC Vive VR glasses performing the Stroop test in VR while measuring heart rate and heart rate variability.

3.3 Participants

Our sample consisted of 15 participants ($M = 23.5$, $SD = 2.5$ years), among these were seven females – in each group at least two females. The majority (ten people) were VR novices, while three stated to have some VR experience and two others said they had been using VR "a lot". Recruiting our participants via university mailing lists and personal acquisition, we had eleven students, one PhD student, one teacher and two engineers among our sample. The experimental procedure had been approved by the ethics committee of our institution.

4   Results

For the physiological data analysis, we removed the first and last 30 s of the baseline and the experimental (incongruent, congruent) sessions to avoid primacy effects. Prior to the statistical calculations, we normalized the data according to each participant's baseline values. We focused on the physiological measures HR and HRV using the standard formula provided by the manufacturers processing software[3] for HRV value calculation.

---

[3] https://www.mindmedia.com/en/products/biotrace-software/.

Table 1. Table shows means and standard deviations of the incongruent and congruent trials for heart rate and heart rate variability according to the three different conditions. While high values indicate increased arousal for HR, lower values are associated with high arousal for HRV [23].

	HR		HRV	
	incongr.	con.	incongr.	con.
Desktop	1.00 (0.02)	1.00 (0.06)	1.12 (0.37)	1.26 (0.66)
VR	1.04 (0.23)	1.01 (0.22)	0.99 (0.60)	1.25 (0.45)
VR-hm	1.08 (0.07)	1.04 (0.06)	0.93 (0.36)	1.05 (0.56)

Physiological Measures. During the incongruent trial, participants showed slightly higher HR values in the VR condition and also for the head movement condition, compared to performing the Stroop test in front of a desktop screen (cf. Table 1). For the congruent trial, the results were similar to those for the incongruent one, but overall the values were little lower as can be obtained from Table 1. Regarding the HRV, we observed that during the incongruent condition in VR, participants had lower HRV values in both conditions, namely VR and VR requiring head movements, indicating physiological arousal (cf. Table 1). In front of the desktop screen, the HRV was higher with an average of 1.12. Again, these results are similar to the HRV values recorded during the congruent trial showing that this trial resulted in lower physiological arousal (cf., Table 1).

Performance. As performance measures, we recorded the error rate. Most errors in the incongruent condition were made in VR requiring head movements ($M = 1.4$, $SD = 2.2$) followed by the Stroop at a desktop screen ($M = 1.0$, $SD = 1.0$) and in VR-only the average errors were 0.6 ($SD = 1.3$). In the congruent condition there occurred only one error in VR requiring head movements.

Subjective Measures. For the SSSQ results, we calculated the difference between the pre-test and post-test SSSQ scores ((post-score − pre-score) / pre-score standard deviation) [15] resulting in a so-called change score. Hereby positive scores signify a higher stress rating after the task was accomplished and negative change scores mean that stress was higher before the task. Since the SSSQ has an underlying three factorial structure divided into Disstress, Worry, and Engagement [9] we present the results according to these factors in Fig. 4. The desktop screen condition induced the most distress with an average change score of 12.45 ($SD = 12.90$), while for the Stroop test performed in VR, the participants felt almost not stressed at all ($M = -0.57$, $SD = 1.27$). When head movements in VR were required, the distress increased to an average score of 3.50 ($SD = 9.37$). Referring to the sub-dimension worry, there was no change when the Stroop test was performed in front of a desktop screen ($M = 0.02$, $SD = 7.39$). And for both VR conditions we observed that worry was even decreasing compared to the baseline measurement, namely to an average of -1.81 in VR ($SD = 1.93$) and

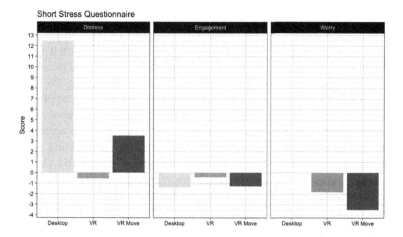

Fig. 4. Results from the SSSQ [8] according to its three dimensions *Engagement, Distress,* and *Worry* showing that the Stroop test in VR does not have been perceived as stressful in VR as in the desktop screen condition.

to -3.48 ($SD = 3.78$) when head movements were required in VR. For engagement there was no difference in the VR condition ($M = -0.42$, $SD = 3.65$) and for the desktop screen condition ($M = -1.40$, $SD = 4.51$) as well as the head movement requiring one ($M = -1.28$, $SD = 2.48$), there were only minor changes signifying that engagement was lower after the Stroop test.

Inferential Statistical Analysis. Since our data was not normally distributed, which is required for parametric tests, we used non-parametric tests. Thus, we performed a Kruskal-Wallis test aiming to reveal differences among our three conditions. No significant results could be found here. We further investigated correlations between the different variables. For this, we used the Spearman rank coefficient which is also robust against outliers in our data. We found a strongly positive correlation between the stress assessing SSSQ overall score and it's two underlying dimensions distress ($r = .862, p = .000$) and worry ($r = .601, p = .018$).

5 Discussion

Our results show that the participants subjectively perceived the task on a desktop screen as the most stressful ($M = 12.45$), whereas the same task in VR has been rated almost not stressful at all with an average of -0.57 signifying that there has been almost no difference between the stress level before and after the task. The participants rated the VR condition requiring head movements more stressful ($M = 3.50$), which suggests that the involvement of motor skills acts as an additional stress factor. Whereas the standard deviation of distress perception in VR had been low with an average of 1.27, it was exceeded by the two other conditions. Particularly in the desktop screen variant, there were two participants for whom there was almost no change between the distress level before and after the Stroop test, while three other participants felt enormously stressed having a change score of 14.14 and respectively 19.80. These differences underline the subjective perception of stress that is challenging [26]. Moreover, our results are supported by prior work [12] where the SSSQ was applied and distress increased with the presentation of a stressful task, while worry decreased. In contrast, during the two most stressful conditions, desktop screen and VR requiring head movements, engagement was low after performing the Stroop test ($M = -1.40$, $M = -1.28$) indicating that stress dominated then. This is further strengthened by the correlational analysis revealing that engagement was the only dimension of the SSSQ that didn't correlate significantly with its total score and thus insufficiently reflected the participant's stress perception. Again, in VR there was almost no difference before and after the task ($M = -0.42$). For worry we found almost no difference when being performed on a desktop screen ($M = 0.02$). In the VR conditions it even decreased after finishing the task ($M = -1.81$, $M = -3.48$) what can be explained with a feeling of relief after having accomplished the test. Regarding the physiological data we recorded, the results show that our participants had lower arousal values in HR ($M = 1.00$) and HRV ($M = 1.12$) during the desktop screen task. While arousal had been mild but slightly higher in the VR condition for HR ($M = 1.04$), and HRV ($M = 0.99$), there was a greater rise in HR ($M = 1.08$) and respectively a decrease in HRV ($M = 0.93$). These findings show that the participants experienced higher physiological arousal in both VR conditions, what is supported by the results for the subjective measures. However, performing motor skills seems to increase only the subjective stress perception but does not affect physiological arousal. Thus, the Stroop color word test seems not suitable for inducing stress in participants when it is transfered into VR. To successfully evoke subjectively perceived stress, there is the requirement of moving the head as an additional factor. This is in line with the findings from research on the reason for why head-mounted displays (HMDs) used for VR are causing visual stress. Mon-Williams et al. [16] stated the that vertical gaze angle is a crucial factor and that therefore the HMD needs to be placed in the correct vertical position for each user individually. Consequently, the presentation of the stimuli in the virtual space shifted on both, the x- and y-axis, could have provoked a level of stress in the user that is perceived only subjectively.

Although we believe, that this piece of work yields important insights in the perception and the transfer of stress in VR, we have to acknowledge that due to our limited number of participants, future work should repeat this experiment involving a greater sample so that the observed tendencies can be verified statistically. Nevertheless, our results show that inducing stress in VR cannot be adopted on a one to one basis for VR and thus could benefit from further investigations, particularly focusing on the design of stressful tasks for VR.

6   Conclusion and Future Work

In this paper, we explored whether a stressful task can be transferred into VR. The results show that participants felt higher distress and lower engagement when the test was performed in the office environment compared to the VR condition. Likewise, the involvement of motor skills in the virtual environment led also to higher distress and lower engagement, what could only be observed in the subjective data. Hence, our findings suggest that the Stroop color word test is not suitable for inducing stress when being performed in VR and when being adopted one to one. To successfully evoke subjectively felt stress, e.g. as part of an VR flight simulation scenario to practice reactions under pressure, an additional requirement is needed, e.g. to perform motor skills. Consequently future work should focus on the exploration and determination of suitable motor skill tasks in VR to elicit stress. Through the initial exploration of the transferability of stressful tasks into VR, we believe to provide a valuable starting point for further investigations in the underlying mechanics, to ultimately design effective training scenarios for VR.

Acknowledgements. This work was partly conducted within the Amplify project funded from the European Research Council (ERC) (grant agreement no. 683008).

References

1. Annerstedt, M., et al.: Inducing physiological stress recovery with sounds of nature in a virtual reality forest - results from a pilot study. Physiol. Behav. **118**, 240–250 (2013)
2. Calvert, S.L., Tan, S.L.: Impact of virtual reality on young adults' physiological arousal and aggressive thoughts: Interaction versus observation. J. Appl. Dev. Psychol. **15**(1), 125–139 (1994)
3. Council, N.R.: Modeling and simulation: linking entertainment and defence (1997)
4. Diemer, J., Mühlberger, A., Pauli, P., Zwanzger, P.: Virtual reality exposure in anxiety disorders: impact on psychophysiological reactivity. World J. Biol. Psychiatry **15**(6), 427–442 (2014)
5. Fong, G.: Adapting cots games for military simulation. In: Proceedings 2004 International Conference Virtual Reality Continuum Applications Industry, VRCAI 2004, pp. 269–272. ACM, New York (2004)
6. Gradl, S., Wirth, M., Zillig, T., Eskofier, B.M.: Visualization of heart activity in virtual reality: a biofeedback application using wearable sensors. In: Proceedings 15th International Conference on Wearable Implantable Body Sensor Networks, pp. 152–155, March 2018
7. Haller, M., Kurka, G., Volkert, J., Wagner, R.: omVR–A safety training system for a virtual refinery. In: Proceedings ISMCR 1999 Topical Workshop Virtual Reality Advanced Human Robot Systems, ISMCR 1999, pp. 291–298 (1999)
8. Helton, W.S.: Validation of a short stress state questionnaire. In: Proceedings Human Factors Ergonomics Society Annual Meeting, vol. 48, no. 11, pp. 1238–1242 (2004)
9. Helton, W.S., Näswall, K.: Short stress state questionnaire. Eur. J. Psychol. Assess. **31**(1), 20–30 (2015)

10. Jönsson, P., Wallergård, M., Österberg, K., Hansen, R.M., et al.: Cardiovascular and cortisol reactivity and habituation to a virtual reality version of the trier social stress test: a pilot study. Psychoneuroendocrino **35**(9), 1397–1403 (2010)
11. Kirschbaum, C., Pirke, K.M., Hellhammer, D.H.: The 'trier social stress test' - a tool for investigating psychobiological stress responses in a laboratory setting. Neuropsychobiology **28**, 76–81 (1993)
12. Legkov, P., Izdebski, K., Kärcher, S., König, P.: Dual task based cognitive stress induction and its influence on path integration. In: Proceedings 23rd Symposium Virtual Reality Software Technology, pp. 41:1–41:5. ACM, New York (2017)
13. Loftin, R.B., Kenney, P.: Training the hubble space telescope flight team (1995)
14. Markov-Vetter, D., Moll, E., Staadt, O.: Evaluation of 3d selection tasks in parabolic flight conditions: pointing task in augmented reality user interfaces. In: Proceedings 11th International Conference Virtual Reality Continuum and its Applications in Industry, VRCAI 2012, pp. 287–294. ACM, New York (2012)
15. Matthews, G., Joyner, L., Gilliland, K., Campbell, S., Falconer, S., Huggins, J.: Validation of a comprehensive stress state questionnaire: towards a state 'big three'. In: Personality Psychology Europe, pp. 335–350. Tilburg University Press (1999)
16. Mon-Williams, M., Plooy, A., et al.: Gaze angle: a possible mechanism of visual stress in virtual reality headsets. Ergonomics **41**(3), 280–285 (1998)
17. Montero-López, E., Santos-Ruiz, A., García-Ríos, M.C., Rodríguez-Blázquez, R., Pérez-García, M., Peralta-Ramírez, M.I.: A virtual reality approach to the trier social stress test: contrasting two distinct protocols. Behav. Res. Methods **48**(1), 223–232 (2016)
18. Moore, K., Wiederhold, B.K., Wiederhold, M.D., Riva, G.: Panic and agoraphobia in a virtual world. CyberPsychology Behav. **5**(3), 197–202 (2002)
19. Paillard, A., et al.: Motion sickness susceptibility in healthy subjects and vestibular patients: effects of gender, age and trait-anxiety. J. Vestib. Res. **23**(4,5), 203–209 (2013)
20. Renaud, P., Blondin, J.P.: The stress of stroop performance: physiological and emotional responses to color-word interference, task pacing, and pacing speed. Int. J. Psychophysiol. **27**(2), 87–97 (1997)
21. Stroop, J.R.: Studies of interference in serial verbal reactions. J. Exp. Psychol. **18**(6), 643–662 (1935)
22. Svetlak, M., Bob, P., Cernik, M., Kukleta, M.: Electrodermal complexity during the stroop colour word test. Auton. Neurosci. Basic Clin. **152**, 101–107 (2010)
23. Tarbell, S.E., Millar, A., Laudenslager, M., Palmer, C., Fortunato, J.E.: Anxiety and physiological responses to the trier social stress test for children in adolescents with cyclic vomiting syndrome. Auton. Neurosci. Basic Clin. **202**, 79–85 (2017)
24. Wirth, M., et al.: Assessment of perceptual-cognitive abilities among athletes in virtual environments: exploring interaction concepts for soccer players. In: Proceedings of the 2018 Designing Interactive Systems Conference, pp. 1013–1023. ACM, New York (2018)
25. Yeh, S.C., et al.: An integrated system: virtual reality, haptics and modern sensing technique (VHS) for post-stroke rehabilitation. In: Proceedings of the ACM Symposium Virtual Reality Software Technology, VRST 2005, pp. 59–62. ACM, New York (2005)
26. Zhai, J., Barreto, A.: Stress recognition using non-invasive technology. In: Proceedings of International Florida Artificial Intelligence Research Society Conference, pp. 395–400 (2006)

Interaction Design for Culture and Development I

"Why Would You Buy from a Stranger?" Understanding Saudi Citizens' Motivations and Challenges in Social Commerce

Aisha Ahmed AlArfaj[1,2(✉)], Ellis Solaiman, and Lindsay Marshall[1]

[1] School of Computing, Newcastle University, Newcastle upon Tyne, UK
[2] College of Computer and Information Sciences,
Princess Nourah bint Abdulrahman University, Riyadh, Saudi Arabia
aiaalarfaj@pnu.edu.sa

Abstract. Consumers in many countries like the Kingdom of Saudi Arabia (KSA) are increasingly turning to social media platforms like Instagram and WhatsApp to buy and sell products and services. Commercial activities within these platforms are increasing in popularity because of important qualities they provide, such as convenience of use, social aspects, and the variety of the types of products available. Using social media in this way has become popular, even though social platforms lack support for conducting e-commerce. In our study, we aim to understand this new trend, to investigate the needs of social media consumers within KSA, and to investigate how social platforms can be better designed to meet those needs. Using data collected through interviews with 26 social media users, we discuss and propose design directions and trust mechanisms for supporting commercial activity within social media platforms with the aim of improving user experience and increasing user acceptance.

Keywords: Social commerce · Social media applications · E-commerce · Peer-to-peer exchange · Trust · Social features · Commercial functions · Consumer needs

1 Introduction

The rise of technology and Internet connectivity has led to new methods of commerce and communication. This is evident through popular world leading e-commerce platforms like Amazon and eBay, as well as popular social media platforms such as Facebook and Instagram [1]. While e-commerce has grown quickly since overcoming early problems such as; trust; information security; and general customer satisfaction [2], social media is also now used by commercial enterprises in what has come to be known as social commerce (s-commerce). However, s-commerce is still at the development stage, and is plagued by problems that need to be investigated and solved.

Western countries have been at the forefront of the development and adoption of internet technologies, and many countries around the world are catching up, particularly in terms of using social media for communication [3], and also for commerce [4]. There is a clear need for new research in none Western countries where important cultural factors can have a strong influence on the way users perceive and make use of

© IFIP International Federation for Information Processing 2019
Published by Springer Nature Switzerland AG 2019
D. Lamas et al. (Eds.): INTERACT 2019, LNCS 11747, pp. 711–732, 2019.
https://doi.org/10.1007/978-3-030-29384-0_43

online technology for commercial activity [11, 12]. The focus of this study, KSA (Kingdom of Saudi Arabia), is among the largest proportional users of social media because of its collectivist culture that places a high value on family and social groups [5]. Moreover, there is massive growth every year in the use of social media platforms in Saudi Arabia, being one of the top countries for annual growth of social media users in 2018 [6]. Conducting the study in Saudi Arabia will help us understand the motivations and needs of a particular social group that has not been widely studied compared to other user populations such as users in the West. For such reasons, this study focuses on Saudi Arabian users, which is a relatively new context for HCI.

From a technological perspective, previous studies that have investigated social media commercial use have mostly examined the use of Facebook [7, 8]. However, currently the most popular social media network used as an s-commerce platform in Arabic countries such as Saudi Arabia, Kuwait, and Egypt is Instagram [9]. Therefore, conducting a study on the use of Instagram will help us understand a different platform that has not been a focus of study before. A few social media platforms have indeed started to add some commercial functionality [9, 10], but much more needs to be done. Also, designers should understand the preferences of users from different cultures. In order to be able to design future social media applications or improve existing ones, particularly for conducting business transactions whilst also providing optimal user satisfaction, it is essential to investigate the experiences and needs of both the providers (sellers), and the consumers who use these applications [13, 14, 34, 40]. In this paper, the focus is placed on the needs of the consumer, while future work will consider the needs of the seller [13].

The aim of this study is to explore user routines and behaviours, and to investigate the factors behind the success of social media-based businesses in KSA. A principal objective of our work is to understand the users and how they make use of current platforms to conduct business. The study focuses on trust in the context of social and cultural aspects to provide design directions for s-commerce platforms, specifically for social features, commercial functions and trust mechanisms.

In summary, our paper makes the following contributions:

- Provides an understanding of the behaviours, routines, and needs of consumers while conducting commerce through social media platforms (Social Commerce) in the context of the Kingdom of Saudi Arabia.
- We investigate factors influencing trust, before, during, and after conducting commerce using social media platforms.
- We discuss and propose design directions and trust mechanisms for social media platforms in order to improve the social commerce platform and to help in minimising the feeling of risk thereby enhancing trust while conducting commerce on such platforms.

2 Background

2.1 Social Commerce (S-commerce)

S-commerce is a new area of research that encompasses many disciplines, including psychology, marketing, computer science, business, and sociology. As a result, s-commerce has a variety of different definitions. In general, it can be defined as a development in which individuals are connected, and can execute commercial transactions by using social networks [17]. It can also be defined as a form of e-commerce in cyberspace that makes use of user-generated content and social media to conduct commercial transactions [18]. The social commerce concept was introduced by Yahoo in 2005 [19]. Since 2008, research on s-commerce has grown [20]. Some social media networks such as Facebook have recently started to introduce commercial functions on their applications [9, 10].

Several studies point to the importance of s-commerce, as they both increase business values and revenues, as well as enhancing the shopping experience of customers [8]. Some of these studies even suggest that in future people will no longer use traditional e-commerce as a way to buy or sell because of the significantly increased use of social media applications in business [8]. The reason behind the growing use of these applications is their increasing social acceptability and their ability to meet people's need more effectively than traditional e-business channels [15]. Recently, several studies have presented literature reviews on s-commerce, and they provide a foundation for future research [8, 20]. In addition, some HCI studies explore the use of social media for commercial activities [7, 21]. They investigate user experiences of s-commerce platforms and provide some design directions mostly for Facebook. Another previous research study examined the acceptance of social commerce in Saudi Arabia and found that there is a positive association between habit, price saving, social support and social commerce constructs on the one hand, and behavioral intentions on the other hand [22]. However, there is still a lack of studies that examine user routines and behavior in using s-commerce platforms [16], especially in KSA.

2.2 Features of E-commerce and Social Commerce

E-commerce comprises three categories of technical features, which are transactional features, relational features, and social features [23]. Transactional features support activities such as searching for a product or placing an order. Relational features involve relationships between consumers and sellers, such as membership or loyalty programmes. Social features are related to the relationship between consumers and their interactions, such as ratings and reviews. These features can be categorised as promoting and attracting others, creating self-identity and a sense of community, generating content, and acting collectively [23]. In the social commerce business model, consumers play the main role [8], and for this reason, social features should be further considered and studied.

A recent study of user preferences found the essential features to implement in s-commerce platforms are "Comment", "Like" and "Send" button [16]. These mostly help in reviewing and ranking the products and provide consumers with the knowledge that impacts their purchase decision and their shopping experience [8, 16]. These studies are helpful in designing s-commerce platforms and understanding the impact of these features on purchase activities. However, to our knowledge, there is a lack of research into the impact of these features on trust.

2.3   Trust

Trust is one of the essential factors in human interaction, especially in the context of online shopping [24]. It can affect the success of e-commerce [25], as it has a significant effect on consumers' buying intentions [26]. In other words, e-commerce would not reach its full potential without trust [27]. In e-commerce, trust has been defined as individuals' beliefs regarding sellers' ability, benevolence, and integrity [24]. From these beliefs, consumers can feel more confident in trusting the other party [24].

In commerce activities, trust is commonly divided into two main categories; hard and soft trust [26]. Hard trust focuses on security and technical aspects, where soft trust concerns the quality of vendors' services and knowledge. This study focuses on soft trust, which is related to users' perceptions of trust [26].

In order to enhance users ability and feelings to perceived trust, three mechanisms have been discussed in previous studies [28]. The first mechanism is process-based, and is based on the history of previous transactions. This type can be affected by customer satisfaction, which builds reputation [28]. Therefore, trust can be affected by the experience of customers during online shopping [24]; new customers can be attracted by the existing consumers [24]. Reputation systems can create trust between peers based on previous experience [2, 29], which also can be presented by reviews [20]. The second mechanism is characteristics-based, related to the person, which can be established by similarities such as sex and nationality [28]. For example, a previous study explored how family and friends' recommendations initiated mobile commerce activities and encouraged trust in the site [26]. The third mechanism is the institutional-based mechanism, related to formal societal structures which are commonly established by a third party [28]. Another study discussed a calculative-based mechanism, related to cost and payment, which in this case are the consumers' rational assessment of the cost and benefits of the other party [24].

A key concern of HCI research is to develop design features to improve the trust of e-commerce platforms [7, 30, 31]. Irina et al. in [32] discussed the importance of design in gathering trust, especially concerning visual, reputational, and contextual factors. There are some features that can establish trust, such as social channels where users can communicate and build their trust network, and profiles [19]. If these channels are used to send recommendations, particularly to friends and family, then trust in a product or service is generally improved [1, 26]. Moreover, when people find that their family or friends (even friends of friends [33]), like a service or product and post it on social networks, this will be perceived by them as a recommendation [34].

Furthermore, social features can build trust through [23]: reviews, recommendations, promotion tags and ratings generated by trustworthy social content (user-generated content) [19]. In addition, the relational features can also build trust by encouraging relationships between the sellers and consumers [23]. Therefore, there is a need to have trust creation features [14]. Trust can also be established by purchase knowledge (vendor's reputation, previous experience with the vendor, reports from trusted third parties), interface properties (familiarity and attitude) and informational content [25]. Another study discussed the effect of images on building trust [32].

2.4   The Context: The Kingdom of Saudi Arabia (KSA)

The Saudi Arabian culture includes two main systems, Islam, and tribalism [35]. Islam is the national religion of KSA. It is a system that is also followed in law, and it is related to life. Tribalism is one of the values that is related to the family and the need to show loyalty towards tribe members [36]. Triandis's considered Saudi Arabia to be a modern but collectivistic society as the society relies on trust and helping family members and friends, depending on superiors and supporting subordinates [5]. Collectivism can be defined as the society relies on trust and helping family members and friends, depending on superiors and supporting subordinates [5]. A collectivistic society means that the individuals cooperate with each others [5]. In some collective culture, individuals rely on other people and discuss the options with them before making a decision [22].

The KSA government has established a 2030 vision and one of the vision's programmes is the "National Transformation Program 2020", in which one of the objectives is maximising local content and digital transformation. In addition, one of the initiatives for this programme is to "Design a program to stimulate e-commerce among individuals and businesses and to provide the technical and legal support necessary to start-ups, small and medium-sized enterprises and logistics companies" [37]. For this reason, more studies in KSA should be conducted to support this transformation and to implement the vision.

Maroof is an initiative from the Ministry of Commerce and Investment in the Kingdom of Saudi Arabia, which provides free business services for development and operation [38]. This is known as a new service that supports e-commerce in the kingdom, and is helpful for all e-commerce dealers, whether sellers or buyers [38]. It enhances trust between the buyer and the seller, as well as providing the opportunity for sellers to be involved in a community where they are reviewed by consumers [38].

3   Research Method

We chose a qualitative method (interview) to investigate and understand user behaviours and routines in using s-commerce in KSA. A semi-structured interview study was conducted with social network users based on Lazar et al., where the authors provide guidelines on how to prepare, conduct and analyse interviews [39]. This was completed over three months, from May to July 2017. Our initial research questions focused on understanding how Saudis use social media for commercial activities, and exploring what trust mechanisms they use for conducting these activities.

3.1 Participants

We recruited 26 participants from KSA by posting a Google form on social media applications such as WhatsApp, Twitter and Instagram in order to reach social media users. The form includes basic questions regarding age, level of education, gender, whether they use social media applications for business, whether they use e-commerce websites, and their contact details. The reasoning behind using the form is that it can assist in gathering a far-ranging sample. We received 67 responses and selected people from different age groups, education levels and buying experiences to establish a variety of participants.

The targeted audience for the interviews was consumers who use social media applications in trading products and services (mostly peer-to-peer); however, it was interesting to ask them whether they have attempted to open a business on a social network to check if they have different perceptions than who did not. The first author conducted all 26 interviews (12 female, 14 male). Ages ranged from 19 to 44; the level of education for 22 participants was undergraduate, and of the remaining participants, three were postgraduate, and 1 had a high school degree. The median monthly income for the participants ranged from approximately $2,200 to $5,500. Our demographics data shows that we have a more general sample.

Each participant used at least two social media applications. The top social media applications, which were used by at least 21 participants, were WhatsApp, Twitter, Instagram and Snapchat. All participants had been using social media applications for at least two years (the range for the sample was from 2 to 10 years). All but one of the participants had used a social media application to conduct commercial transactions, while 22 of the participants had used e-commerce websites. The mobile phone was the most popular device used to buy (19 by smartphone, 3 by tablet, and 4 by laptop).

3.2 Procedure

The first author conducted semi-structured interviews through social media applications such as Line, WhatsApp and Skype, because the participants were Saudi users living in KSA and the location of the interviewer was the United Kingdom. The first author, who is bilingual (Arabic and English), conducted and recorded the interviews with the Saudi participants in Arabic, to allow them to fully express themselves. We then transcribed the interviews, also in Arabic. After conducting 26 interviews, we stopped recruitment because the patterns of the interviewee's experiences were recognised and the last few interviews were confirming them. Examples of the patterns include the similarity in how interviewees find the sellers, such as finding sellers by searching, and through family and friends.

Questions were divided into four main categories (See Appendix A). First, we asked participants general questions about their use of social media applications. Questions included which social media applications they used, when they started to use them, and how long they spent using them each day. The second category of questions examined the commercial use of social media applications. We asked questions exploring which applications they used, how they used these applications, what motivated their use, how trustworthy they considered the applications to be, and how their experience was in general. The third category concerned their use of e-commerce websites. Participants were asked whether they used them, which ones they used, what their experience was, which they preferred, and what device they used for shopping online. The final set of questions collected demographic data. We asked them which city they were currently living in, and what their monthly income was. In the end, participants were offered a $15 gift card to thank them for their time.

3.3 Data Analysis

The interviews were transcribed in Arabic and analysed using thematic analysis. We began by reading all 26 transcripts to identify main themes and develop codes. The first author conducted an initial coding, open coding, so that the first cycle of coding was open to all possible directions, following the techniques described in [40]. We used ATLAS.ti, which is software that assists in the analysis of qualitative data [41], to code our data. The first author coded the transcripts, then, for the second cycle of coding, the codes were grouped under categories and subcategories (e.g. habits before purchasing, trust mechanisms, etc.) and themes by using affinity diagrams, and were translated into English. Axial and selective coding were used to identify the relationships between concepts [42]. The second author analysed two interviews to confirm the codes and categories. Finally, all authors discussed the codes and themes and agreed on them. From coding the first three transcripts, we generated 65 codes; after the fourth and fifth we generated 77 codes. Themes emerged during the iteration. The codes and themes were altered by reading and analysing the coded transcripts.

4 Finding

We first describe the motivations for using social media applications to conduct commercial transactions, followed by a description of three purchasing stages (pre-purchase, purchase, post-purchase), and the factors that affect trust in each stage. Finally, we explain the risks that prevent consumers from buying through social media applications.

4.1 Motivation

When the participants were asked about what motivated them to buy through social networks, the responses pertained to three main categories: (1) Social aspect and Instagram design. (2) Products. (3) Ease, convenience and speed.

Social Aspect and Instagram Design
Commonly, participants described how the availability of social features in Instagram (such as profile, followers, comments and likes), as well as having other social media such as Snapchat, motivates them to buy and trust the sellers on Instagram. First, many (10) participants mentioned that having many e-shops on Instagram, with information on profiles that can be followed, motivates them to buy: *Communicating and following sellers' accounts becomes a passion and addiction-P11.* They indicated that they

follow some sellers' accounts in order to be updated on new and available products. One of the participants mentioned that if he did not have the money to buy a specific product he wanted, then he would follow the account until he could obtain it: *If I find a product that I like but cannot afford its cost, I followed the account until I can buy it in the future-P14.*

Many (15) participants mentioned that they browse through Instagram, which may lead them to view photos of products that someone has tried or are advertised by influencers, or even those posted by sellers' accounts that they followed, which attracts consumers to buy.

Family and friends also influenced most of the participants (23). They receive online and offline recommendations to buy from accounts on Instagram. This supports previous findings regarding the effect of social support on online buying interactions [22]. Furthermore, few (three) participants mentioned that they are motivated to buy to support the sellers as they are from their friends or family members. In the "Finding Sellers and Products" section, we will explain more about family and friends' sharing activities and their effects on trust.

Two participants mentioned that people in Saudi Arabia are active in social media, and this motivates them to use it for everything, not just for the common use of sharing and communicating: *We love to buy by using Instagram and social media applications more than the websites, because we are active in social media, and browsing a website does not suit us, as we do not like them-P2.*

Products

Most of the participants (16) described how product types, availability and uniqueness attracted them to buy from Instagram. They can find unique products, such as new brands, imported goods, customised products or handmade products – for example, t-shirts with Arabic words, or homemade food or sweets. Several participants mentioned that product quality is good, or even considered to be high quality. Some (4) participants indicated that sellers having up-to-date products motivates them to buy from these shops, which means these products are new, and not even available in the physical market: *I follow many sellers on Instagram, as their products are not available in market or e-commerce websites-P16.* Two participants noted that they want to support sellers on Instagram, because they are national people: *I mostly buy from Instagram for two reasons: support national people who run these small businesses and the prices-P13.* In addition, six participants mentioned that product prices are lower than those of market. One of the participants also explained that the ability to compare prices between shops and find the more reasonable prices motivates.

Ease, Convenience and Speed

Almost half of the buyers described the processes of buying a product as easy. Some of the buyers liked being able to communicate with sellers directly. Nine buyers did not want to buy by using a link, they prefer to talk using WhatsApp and order through it: *If I found a website for the sellers' accounts, I may open the links to view and find the products I want, but I will order through WhatsApp as it is easier for me-P2.* They also mentioned that people know how to use Instagram and WhatsApp, it is easy for them to use, and for this reason they use it more than the websites.

Most of the participants agreed that they liked to have products delivered to their home, and that if a seller would not, they may not order. Few (3) participants mentioned that the delivery when they order from Instagram is typically faster than from an e-commerce website: *If I am going to travel and I need a product within a short time, it is easier and faster to order it by Instagram. However, if I do not need it urgently, I am going to order it by Amazon, which may take time-P26.* These results match an earlier study that indicates that members of "sale groups" on Facebook find buying and selling easy and quick [7].

4.2   Pre-purchase

Finding Sellers and Products
Before purchasing a product, consumers need to find the product that they desire, and the seller's account to subsequently place an order. Participants were asked how they find a product/seller account on a social media application. They use three ways to find sellers' accounts, which are family and friends, searching, and advertisements; each way affects consumers' trust differently.

First, it was clear that participants find sellers' accounts mostly from their friends and family, both offline and online. Most of the participants mentioned that they totally trust any accounts that were recommended by their friends or family. The majority of the participants noted that they often receive online recommendations from their friends and family via different methods. This was also the case in a study conducted in North America where it was found that study participants receive recommendations from their friends, which they browse to decide whether to place an order or not [26]. Several (5) of the participants capture the account and send it to a WhatsApp group, which may be composed of close friends, family or even include employees from the same company. Others mentioned their friends under the product's post by writing the friend's account in a comment under the post. They also send direct messages to share the accounts or products that they like, or mentioned each other under the photos in sellers' accounts in Instagram. Additionally, they may take a photo or video and send it by Snapchat. Participants described buying from Instagram as a social habit, because they communicate with their friends and family when deciding whether to buy from a seller's account or not. This indicates that social commerce involves social support that enhances communication with others, which was also found in previous research [8].

Participants described the methods they use for searching to find a product or seller account. First, most of the participants reported that they search using Instagram by two methods: using "hashtags", and using an Instagram search engine, where they can search for people or tags, or they use the account search feature. Six participants reported that it is difficult to search using Instagram (accounts/hashtags), especially due to having unrelated posts using the same hashtags. Participants reported that they had faced difficulties in finding a product when they did not know the sellers' accounts. To overcome this issue, two participants mentioned that they might use Google to search for a product on Instagram as it is the easiest way and better than using hashtags: *I search by using google, and it directs me to what I want, and this is the easiest way and better than using hashtags, where you may get irrelevant results-P3.*

Ten participants find seller accounts from advertisements, mostly through Insta-gram's/Snapchat's accounts belonging to celebrities, influencers, bloggers and spe-cialised accounts (all will be referred as influencers), which mostly provide advice and recommendations in a specific area. Influencers post a photo with a tag or mention a seller account, and this is how people get to about it, or some sellers write a comment about what they sell under an influencer's post. Three participants trust the influencers that they follow and do not need to check anything. However, the rest of the partici-pants reported that they need to check if they should trust these accounts.

Check Seller Practices

Participants described how they gain trust in buying from strangers by checking the sellers' practices, which mostly regard their professional practices, prices, payment, delivery and communication. Commonly, buyers described the importance of sellers' professionalism, which may convince them to trust and buy. They assess profession-alism in different ways, specifically by looking at profiles and the included photos, details, and information. Sixteen of the participants mentioned that they check the posts (photos/videos) in the sellers' profile before ordering. This result implies that the social presence of sellers influences consumer trust, which is consist with previous research [14]. For example, having clear and high-quality posts represents a more professional seller. They reported that they could sense whether the product's quality was good or not from checking the photos. Participants commonly check the included details and information in sellers' profiles to discover more about sellers and products, and whether they should trust them or not. Participants were varied in their views regarding included details and information. Most of them mentioned that having more information about the seller raises the level of trust and makes them feel more comfortable; this infor-mation may include the real name of the seller, their mobile number (it is linked to their national ID), and their personal Twitter account: *I can trust the accounts that include the real name of the sellers and have a mobile number to communicate with them directly-P7.*

Seven participants agreed that it is important to have an official account with, for example, a commercial registration, a logo and a public account. Three participants mentioned that they are willing to trust more if they find a link to the e-shop website included in the seller's profile on Instagram: *Sellers who just have Instagram accounts may close them anytime; however, having a link to a website gives me the feeling of trust-P3.* One of the participants reported that he trusts sellers who deal with physical stores and mentioned the name of stores in their profile.

Most of the participants mentioned that the price and payment methods affect trust and buying decisions. Seven participants felt that they could trust after checking the available prices. They check the price of a product and compare it with other accounts or sites, and, if they find it reasonable, they will trust: *My trust depends on the product that I am going to buy; I will have an average price in mind, if the price is near to my average then I will trust-P14.* Five participants mentioned that they are more willing to trust when buying items that are less risky (not expensive) with regard to money. They would purchase even if they did not feel that they could trust the seller, so if anything went wrong, they would not regret it: *I do not buy expensive products in order not to have regrets if anything goes wrong-P1.*

Eight participants reported that they trust sellers when they can pay cash on delivery. They mentioned that they would look for payment details in sellers' profiles and under the posts, and if they did not find them, they would communicate with the sellers to ask them. However, four participants have trust issues with a seller's account that does not indicate the prices under the products, as they felt sellers would play with prices: *I check whether they include prices for the product or not, if not I would not buy from them. I feel they will change the prices-P15.*

Communicating directly with the sellers and having several contact methods will enhance trust. Nine participants felt more comfortable when they communicated directly with the sellers. They reported that ways of communicating with sellers motivate them and help them to feel more trust. Additionally, they may receive more information and details related to the product, such as more photos, the actual size, and how to use it, which may convince them to buy: *I usually ask the seller to send more photo directly to me before adding the order-P3.*

Some sellers register in Maroof and include it in their profile, which can be considered to be a practice that enhances trust. Eleven participants mentioned that they knew Maroof, but they varied in their use of it: Three of them check it frequently and others only sometimes and they trust the registered sellers: *I just deal with verified e-shops that I found in Maroof-p13.* However, of these eleven, four participants did not use it at all. The reason for that is they did not find it useful, as it does not include many of the sellers' accounts, which was also a concern for some of the participants who do use it: *It is not rich enough; few seller accounts are registered-P25.* Two participants reported that they had heard about it, but did not actually know how to check it. They simply found it written in a seller's profile. The remaining participants, who did not know about the application, mentioned that they were very interested and happy to have such a service – they can trust the sellers who are registered, as they are able to complain if anything goes wrong: *This service will motivate me to buy and trust -P11.* These findings are consistent with previous research that a third party can enhance trust [26].

Some sellers post a screenshot of the positive private comments that have been sent by buyers to gain other buyers' trust. Thirteen participants mentioned that they do not trust an account with such a photo, because they suspect it is a fake used to cover up a seller's negative points. It may have a negative effect, which means instead of increasing trust, it is in some cases a cause for suspicion, and few (2) participants may not buy from accounts using such posts. Two participants reported that other people would believe and trust in such a practice: *to be honest, I do not trust them, but I know a lot of people see the screenshots as a standard with which they can evaluate the account-P2.* A participant mentioned that as a seller in the past, she did it to gain trust, and thinks it is useful. Alternatively, four participants mentioned that they believe this kind of screenshot, and that it may motivate them to trust and buy from the seller's account.

Previous Experiences

Participants also commonly check previous experiences in different ways. They can access these experiences by looking at the number of followers, examining who the followers are (for example, some of their friends or family, or even influencers), number of likes, number of mentions, and checking the comments under each post, which affect trust as well as tags.

One of the participants mentioned that if there were no comments at all, she would not buy from the account. Another participant mentioned that the presence of tags has a strong effect on trust when people post their experiences and tag the seller, because it is more real. For example, personal accounts that include personal experiences of different products and different sellers that they tag. However, five participants mentioned that they did not read the comments because they think they are not helpful. As an example, people taste food differently, one may like this kind, but others may not.

Half of the participants mentioned that having several positive comments and mentions under products motivates them to trust and buy. They read the comments in order to gain an impression of the seller's behaviour and attitude, and to help them to know more about products. For example, these may mention the product's material. One participant mentioned that she would search on Google to read more generally about the products. They described how good experiences affect their trust. Good experiences may include their own, friends, family or previous consumers' experiences: *If anyone tried the product and wrote positive comments, then I trust to buy-P19.* One of the participants mentioned that the most important thing is to look for negative comments, because the positive comments may be fake.

4.3   Purchase

Placing an order depends on what methods sellers provide to communicate and place the order. Mostly they add the WhatsApp number in their profile; two participants mentioned that this method makes them feel more comfortable, as the mobile number is usually linked to their national ID. Five participants reported that orders are placed by sending direct messages within Instagram, which sometimes feels risky; Eight mentioned that calling sellers directly feels safer. One participant mentioned that the order was placed via using a link in their profile.

The payment method is most commonly cash on delivery, as it is safer and can be trusted. However, fifteen participants mentioned that if they have to, they may transfer the money to the seller's account, because it is documented and the bank account should be in KSA. They also mentioned that if they have to transfer the money, they need to know more about the seller and feel that the seller is trustworthy.

Most of the participants reported that they communicate with a representative to deliver their order, with incurs an extra charge. Some sellers may offer a "pick-up" option; however, participants generally prefer products to be delivered to their home, as the pick-up location may be too crowded or may not be nearby. Eight participants mentioned that if accounts are not in Saudi Arabia, of which most will be within the Gulf countries, then deliveries will be made by shipping companies.

4.4   Post-purchase

Two participants mentioned that they check the product and its quality before handing over money. Most of the participants mentioned that they tended not to write comments under products' posts; however, nine of them will write a direct or private message to the seller to thank them, and offer their comments on the products, even telling them about the negative things. Six participants received messages from sellers asking them about their opinion of the products; the participants then provide their feedback. Three participants mentioned that after writing a private message to sellers to thank them, the sellers took a screenshot of the message and posted it under their profile to gain the trust of other customers. Participants who have been asked and took a screenshot of their private message, did not trust this way, and did not like it, but they agreed to do it as they thought it might help the sellers. Two participants told us that they might write a comment under the product post only if the seller was good and polite in communicating with them, but otherwise they would not: *Writing comments is dependent on the sellers, if they were helpful, respectful and kind, then I feel that I have to write to thank them-P1.*

Three participants mentioned that they might write comments, particularly positive comments, under the products, including information about their experience with the product and the seller, or by giving likes to support the sellers: *After buying a product, I may write a comment to help others to know how the product was, and how sellers dealt with me-P26.* One participant described writing negative comments on Instagram as a waste of time, as the sellers can delete them, which the participants had experienced. However, four participants stated that they do not write public comments at all. Their reasons included the matter of privacy, hating to be seen by the public.

4.5   Perceived Risks

Most of the participants described many different risks that they might face when buying through Instagram, mostly regarding sellers' accounts, products and delivery. Ten participants were concerned about dealing with fake accounts and losing their money, in the case of transferring money and nothing being delivered in return.

Half of the participants (13) mentioned that they were concerned about having issues related to the product. These may include receiving a product that is not as the picture/description suggested, receiving a poor quality product, or being sent the wrong size/material: *I ordered a cake from an Instagram account; the picture was great. I received it; it was great and delicious, but it was tiny, which was not clear from the photo. I was embarrassed as I ordered it for a party-P12.* One of the bad experiences was having an issue with a product that was very different from the one in the picture; one participant asked the seller several times to refund, but the seller refused. She then used religion to make the seller afraid, by suggesting that she would pray for God to punish the seller; the seller then agreed to refund: *she gave me the refund after sending to her a lot of prayer to be punished-P9.*

Five participants mentioned they were concerned by the possibility of having issues with delivery. For example, the delivery being late or not arriving on the date or time they were told, especially if payment is made before the product is delivered.

Five participants mentioned refund and exchange as one of the issues that they were concerned about having to face. For example, if payment is made in advance and they have received the product, then it is almost impossible to obtain a refund or an exchange: *I ordered something and asked them to write a message on top of it; they wrote a totally different message. I called them and tried to complain, but nothing happened-P2*. However, nine participants mentioned that they did not feel any risk, especially if they mostly ordered with cash on delivery, as they could check the product before paying the money.

5 Discussion

The aim of this study is to understand the use of social media applications as commercial platforms even though they lack traditional commerce features [7]. Social commerce has different features in other types of commerce. Table 1 shows a comparison between consumer to consumer (C2C) brokered e-commerce, community commerce [7], and social commerce (Instagram and WhatsApp) features discovered in our study (with respect to C2C (consumer to consumer), and B2C (business to consumer). The comparison is conducted with respect to type of sellers, how to find a product, how it is delivered, the payment methods, type of products, and how trust is established. We can see that there are more similarities between community commerce and social commerce. There is some similarity in finding products by monitoring news feeds and having the up-to-date information which they can find by monitoring new posts or news feed. Furthermore, the way trust is established in both community commerce [7] and social commerce, relies more on the social presence and social support. The findings reveal strong agreement with literature on one key theme, which is trust [7, 14, 34]. There are varied trust mechanisms when using social commerce (e.g. Instagram). We can categorise them into four main categories: social aspects (including seller activities), purchase cost and payment method, and Maroof.

5.1 Social Aspect

The main aspect that affects trust is the social aspect. The findings of our study show that family and friends are the main, and sometimes the only, source of consumer trust. People establish trust based on the experience of their family and friends more than anything else [26]. The Saudi culture is a collectivism culture [43], which reveals the importance of the social aspect in designing s-commerce platforms. The preference interface for a collectivist culture should focus on relationships and groups [44]. Previous studies show the effect and role of friends and family on trust [26]. It may be helpful to show the accounts that have been trusted by friends and family. In addition, a study shows that in KSA people trust their family members and even share their authentications [45]. This matches some of our findings, as several participants share their income with their partners or family, by buying for their friends or family, or by giving their visa debit/credit card to their family to use for buying things online.

Furthermore, as Saudi users are active users of social media applications [46], it may be helpful if Instagram had the facility to build a community where buyers could find nearby sellers and sellers could find nearby buyers. This would enable them to communicate and exchange their experiences and even enhance trust. Members of the same community trust each other more [7].

Table 1. Comparison between C2C e-commerce, Community commerce [47] and social commerce features (our study).

	Brokered C2C E-Commerce Example: eBay	Community Commerce Example: Facebook groups	Social commerce Example: Instagram and WhatsApp	Participants perceptions
Sellers	• (C2C)	•Member to member within the same group	• (B2C) • (C2C)	•It is not easy to distinguish between customer or business accounts
Product finding	•Sophisticated search engine and product filters •Product categories	•Monitoring News Feed •Mobile push notifications •Basic search engine •Photo albums for product categories	•Monitoring new posts •Search engines: Google and Instagram (search accounts, search hashtags) •Friends and family •Advertisement	•New posts are reasonable and can catch buyers interest •Searching in general is difficult •Searching by hashtags are likeable but not always related •Friends and family recommendations are helpful •Advertisements sometimes are too much and annoying
Delivery	•Shipped to home	•Drive to pick up on porch	•Drivers hired to deliver from sellers to buyers with extra charge •Shipping company if from a Gulf country •Sometimes pick up	•Delivery costing a large amount of money, but useful, not late. •Reasonable cost; waiting for shipping •Not preferred
Payment	•Escrow payment systems	•Leave payment under the door	•Cash on delivery. •Transfer the money	•Feel safer; do not worry if the delivery is late •Sometime easier but with risk
Marketplace	(Global) •Large pool of products	(Local, Restricted) •Fewer products	(Local, Gulf countries) •Large pool of products and services	•Productive and unique
Trust	•Reputation systems •Escrow payment systems	•Membership in closed group •Regulation of behaviour by admin members & group •Transactions visible to group •Shared group identity •Profiles	•Sellers accounts: profile (content and activities) •Technology (having a website) •Friends and family •Previous experiences •Cash on delivery •Direct communication •Third-party "Maroof" •Cheap product	•Viewing profile can give the first feel of trust; Knowing more, trusting more. •Feel trustworthy •Friends and family create trust •Having previous experiences can establish trust •Feels safer; cannot be fooled •Communicating with the seller give the first feeling of trust •Not enough sellers; trusted as controlled by government

Moreover, one method of benefitting more from the social aspect is to introduce a recommendation system based on use by family and friends, especially in social media applications. This would increase trust, as consumers would know that recommended accounts are ones that their family or friends, or even friends of friends [33], have tried. The findings of our study are consistent with those of Al-Maghrabi, who mentioned that "positive word of mouth" between family and friends may enhance trust in a specific website [47].

In the past, exchanges between users were handled by a third party, whereas now this can be done by social features such as ranking, rating and feedback [48]. Formal reputation or feedback systems can establish trust [23], which does not exist on Instagram. However, some social features can build trust between consumers and sellers [23] and work as rating and feedback systems – for example, mentions, tags, and comments. Our findings show the significant effect of comments on consumers' trust and motivations, which should be added and considered, as reported in [49]. People tend to believe the comments and recommendations made by strangers if there are many responses [26]; as in our case, the participants look at the number of followers, likes and comments. Features such as liking and the number of followers work as a rating system [34]. Therefore, user-generated-content is one of the important factors that may affect trust [19] as well as public relations [50]. Social features can help users to create their own trusted network [19] and to find the sellers [21].

Therefore, s-commerce platforms, in general, need social engagement to enhance trust. Additionally, social engagement is needed when designing for a collectivism culture. People in Saudi Arabia are active users of social media and enjoy sharing with others [46]. For this reason, there is a need to link social media to e-commerce and to integrate commercial functions with social media features. Social media features that are effective for a specific culture, or localised features, can be different depending on the region or culture, as shown in a previous study [51].

Furthermore, from our study, we found that people in Saudi Arabia prefer writing reviews and comments about products in a private and direct message to the seller rather than in public comments. Therefore, it would be helpful to give the seller the ability to publish some of these private messages automatically, after gaining permission from the private message writer instead of capturing the message and post it which may seem fake. Alternatively, after conducting a commercial transaction and having the order delivered, an automatic comment requestor could be sent to the buyer, which could then be published anonymously.

Furthermore, some of our participants trust the influencers who advertise these accounts – a study showed that 15% of consumers trust advertising [49]. When designing s-commerce platforms, adding a feature that shows accounts that are trusted by influencers would be useful.

Trust can also be established from seller activities such as having a professional profile and communicating with consumers directly. Our findings show that consumers trust sellers when they can learn more about them and feel that they are professional. The seller's profile is one of the tools that can enhance trust [7]. Therefore, platforms like Instagram need to be designed to actively encourage sellers to provide more information about themselves, which will help buyers to feel confident about spotting genuine accounts. In addition, sellers should present a professional image by having a commercial registration, which is posted clearly on their account; using clear photos with full details about their products; displaying a logo; and having a clear profile, giving their full details. This result also matches a previous result, which is that high-resolution photos with a wide-angle make participants feel more trust [52]. Therefore, some design features can enhance trust. In an exploratory study on Airbnb, it was reported that people tended to trust accounts on Airbnb because they were professional, attractive and contained high-resolution and wide-angle photos [29]. Another study examined the use of profiles on Etsy, which requires the sellers to create a profile as well as a shop profile [53], which enhances trust [14].

As our participants feel more trust when they find that a seller's account includes an e-commerce website, sellers can enhance trust by creating a website, even if it is just for viewing the products. Website design can affect consumers' trust [54]. This means that consumer trust is enhanced by using technology and being professional. Moreover, it would be useful if Instagram provided a tool for sellers to give them the ability to create their own website on Instagram (maybe as a blog) or by having business accounts that enable consumers to buy directly using Instagram.

5.2 Payment and Purchase Costs

From our study, we found that calculative-based trust is one of the mechanisms that has an impact on the decision to buy and trust in KSA. Some participants trust by rationally assessing the costs and benefits of the other party, which similarly found by [24]. Participants tend to trust and use cash on delivery, which is considered a high Calculative-Based Antecedent [55]. PayPal Insight found that 80% of online purchases in the Middle East use cash on delivery [56]. This also matches a study in China where people tend to use cash on delivery [55] as well as in Turkey [57]. Even though the Saudi culture has a high score in uncertainty avoidance by Hofstede [43], Saudi Arabians take risks sometimes and buy from strangers, especially if the cost is not high or if they can pay with the cash on delivery method. However, it is better to have a payment method that uses the same platform, which in our case is Instagram, as people may then trust it more. Etsy provides customers with the opportunity to make the payment through the website, which enhances trust [58].

5.3 Maroof

The Kingdom of Saudi Arabia is a high power distance culture, and also high in uncertainty avoidance [43]. This is represented by our findings, as people believe in the government and need to have a clear policy and regulation to trust and follow. Therefore, institutional-based trust mechanisms still play a significant role in trust in KSA, especially if provided by the government. Our results show that consumers trust more when the government controls and supports sellers, as it is considered to be a trusted third-party platform. Therefore, in order to enhance trust in these applications, they may be linked to the Maroof service. Accounts belonging to registered sellers could then display a special icon to show registration. Another solution is to have verified account techniques on Instagram. The verifying techniques can help to gain trust, as shown in a previous study on Airbnb – sellers display a verified photo, which has been taken by a photographer sent by Airbnb [52]. Previous studies are consistent with these findings as having a third party to verify the sellers accounts can establish trust [26] We found that there is a potential in Maroof as the participants who did not know about it were encouraged to use it once they had about it from us.

5.4   Limitation of Social Commerce in the Kingdom of Saudi Arabia

The results also show that users face some limitations. Some buyers found difficulties when searching for a product. The difficulties with searching will affect purchase activities because consumers will not be able to find the right product. This can be addressed by adding and enhancing Instagram search engines to suit commercial searches. Another solution is to have a separate application that includes sellers' and buyers' accounts with social features and commercial functions. The current search tools enable users to only search for Users or Hashtags [59]. Some people may find Hashtags attractive, and they were used before as hashtag commerce [60]. However, having many unrelated images frustrates the consumers. Therefore, there should be a mechanism that stops unrelated photos from being displayed.

Delivery is still considered to be an issue; previously, it was one of the factors that slowed down the adoption of e-commerce in KSA [61]. Consumers find that delivery is too expensive. The price of the product may be less than the price for delivery. A suggested solution for this is to have a linked application to Instagram which can calculate the distance between the seller and buyer, and give a delivery cost depending on the distance. In addition, trying to find the nearest representative to the sellers would reduce the cost, similarly to Uber's technique. An article describes how representatives can earn a fortune from delivering products, sometimes around $400 per day [62]. Issues with delivery include the need for consumers to send their home address each time they place an order. A solution for this would be for Instagram to supply a service where consumers can register their home address so that when they order, they do not need to send any details.

One of the challenges of s-commerce in KSA is that people want to feel and touch a product. They also may have issues with product sizes and the materials used in products [63]. A solution for this is to provide the facility to give more details about products, to have a selection of photos taken from different angles, with zooming capabilities, and to show the sizes clearly. Consumers should have almost the same impression as touching and feeling the product. Another solution is to give consumers the ability to view the products from different angles as if it is in front of them, which was found to be effective in another study [29].

6   Conclusions and Future Work

Our study explores how consumers use social media applications to conduct commercial transactions in KSA even though social media platforms lack commercial functionality. The main finding is that social aspects enhance trust and motivate users to buy products and services using these platforms. Therefore, we strongly believe that social media applications, as well as e-commerce websites, should leverage their social features to build additional functionalities that can improve customer experiences while conducting s-commerce. As an example, the methods by which customers review and comment on both products and sellers within social media platforms should be enhanced for commercial purposes. Such methods could include, for example, giving sellers the ability to share publically, private feedback on products when the buyer has given consent to do so. In addition to the findings and recommendations presented in this paper, we have also conducted research to gain a deeper understanding of s-commerce user behaviours and routines from the perspective of the sellers. This work can be found here [13], where we make further recommendations on social commerce functionality with a focus on seller needs. In the future, further studies will be conducted to test the implementation of social commerce functionality discussed in this paper and in [13]. We would like to look more deeply at cultural issues that may influence the design of social commerce platforms in KSA. Moreover, it would be interesting to conduct a comparative study between the perceptions and needs of users in Arabic countries such as Saudi Arabia, and Western countries such as the UK.

7   Appendix A

Section 1- their use of social media applications:

1. Which Social networks do you use most?
2. Since when have you started using social network?
3. How many hours do you spend on social media? Daily/weekly
4. Are your accounts on social media private or public?

   Section 2- the commercial use of social media applications:

5. Do you use social media for online shopping? Why?
6. Which social media application do you prefer more in buying?
7. What motivate you to buy from a shop on social media?
8. How do you use social media for shopping?
9. Can you explain how you find product and buy it by social media?
10. Can you explain your experience in writing and reading comments?
11. What do you like or dislike about this experience?
12. What do you think the risks of buying using social media?
13. How do you trust to buy on social media?

    Section 3- the use of e-commerce websites:

14. Do you shop online by using e-commerce websites and applications? why?
15. Do you prefer buying by websites or by social media and why?

    Section 4- demographic and general information:

16. Gender and age
17. The highest degree of education you have completed
18. Occupation
19. Nationality:
20. What is the device that you use mostly for shopping online?

References

1. Hillman, S., Neustaedter, C., Bowes, J.: The routines and social behaviours of frequent Mcommerce shoppers. In: Proceedings of CHI 2012 Extended Abstracts on Human Factors in Computing Systems, pp. 1841–1846 (2012)
2. Abed, S.S., Dwivedi, Y.K., Williams, M.D.: SMEs' Adoption of E-commerce Using Social Media in a Saudi Arabian Context: a Systematic Literature Review. Int. J. Bus. Inf. Syst. **19**, 159–179 (2015)
3. Alkhowaiter, W.: The power of instagram in building small businesses. In: Dwivedi, Y.K., Mäntymäki, M., Ravishankar, M.N., Janssen, M., Clement, M., Slade, E.L., Rana, N.P., Al-Sharhan, S., Simintiras, A.C. (eds.) I3E 2016. LNCS, vol. 9844, pp. 59–64. Springer, Cham (2016). https://doi.org/10.1007/978-3-319-45234-0_6
4. Makki, E., Chang, L.: Understanding the effects of social media and mobile usage on e-commerce: an exploratory study in Saudi Arabia. Int. Manag. Rev. **11**, 98–110 (2015)
5. Triandis, H.C.: Individualism and collectivism: past, present, and future. In: The Handbook of Culture & Psychology, pp. 52–67 (2001)
6. Chaffey, D.: Global social media research summary (2018). https://www.smartinsights.com/social-media-marketing/
7. Moser, C., Resnick, P., Schoenebeck, S.: Community commerce: facilitating trust in mom-to-mom sale groups on Facebook. In: Conference on Human Factors in Computing Systems (2017)
8. Huang, Z., Benyoucef, M.: From e-commerce to social commerce: a close look at design features. Electron. Commer. Res. Appl. **12**, 246–259 (2013)
9. Gibreel, O., AlOtaibi, D.A., Altmann, J.: Social commerce development in emerging markets. Electron. Commer. Res. Appl. **27**, 152–162 (2018)
10. Facebook Business: New for Facebook Pages: Calls to Action. https://www.facebook.com/business/news/call-to-action-button
11. Wang, C., Zhang, P.: The evolution of social commerce: the people, management, technology, and information dimensions and information dimensions. Commun. Assoc. Inf. Syst. **31**(1), 5 (2012)
12. Gheitasy, A., Abdelnour-Nocera, J., Nardi, B., Rigas, D.: Designing for online collaborative consumption: a study of sociotechnical gaps and social capital. In: Kurosu, M. (ed.) HCI 2014. LNCS, vol. 8512, pp. 683–692. Springer, Cham (2014). https://doi.org/10.1007/978-3-319-07227-2_65
13. AlArfaj, A.A., Solaiman, E.: Investigating commercial capabilities and trust in social media applications for entrepreneurs. In: Proceedings of ACM C&T conference (C&T2019), 11 p. ACM, Vienna (2019)
14. Gheitasy, A., Abdelnour-Nocera, J., Nardi, B.: Socio-technical gaps in online collaborative consumption (OCC): an example of the Etsy community. In: Proceedings of the 33rd Annual International Conference on the Design of Communication - SIGDOC 2015, pp. 1–9 (2015)
15. Lampinen, A., Brown, B.: Market design for HCI : successes and failures of peer-to-peer exchange platforms. In: CHI Conference on Human Factors in Computing Systems, pp. 4331–4343. ACM (2017)
16. Huang, Z., Benyoucef, M.: User preferences of social features on social commerce websites: An empirical study. Technol. Forecast. Soc. Chang. **95**, 57–72 (2015)
17. Stephen, A.T., Toubia, O.: Deriving value from social commerce networks. J. Mark. Res. **47**, 215–228 (2010)
18. Lee, J.Y.: Trust and social commerce. Univ. Pittsburgh Law Rev. **77**, 137–181 (2015)

19. Curty, R.G., Zhang, P.: Social Commerce : Looking Back and Forward. 2007, pp. 1–10 (2011). https://doi.org/10.1002/meet.145.v48
20. Lin, X., Li, Y., Wang, X.: Social commerce research: definition, research themes and the trends. Int. J. Inf. Manage. **37**, 190–201 (2017)
21. Jack, M., Jackson, S.J.: Infrastructure as creative action : online buying, selling, and delivery in Phnom Penh. In: Conference on Human Factors in Computing Systems, pp. 6511–6522 (2017)
22. Sheikh, Z., Islam, T., Rana, S., Hameed, Z., Saeed, U.: Acceptance of social commerce framework in Saudi Arabia (2017). http://dx.doi.org/10.1016/j.tele.2017.08.003
23. Gonçalves Curty, R., Zhang, P.: Website features that gave rise to social commerce: a historical analysis. Electron. Commer. Res. Appl. **12**, 260–279 (2013)
24. Gefen, D., Karahanna, E., Straub, D.W.: Trust and TAM in online shopping: an integrated model. MIS Q. **27**, 51–90 (2003)
25. Egger, F.N.: "Trust me, I'm an online vendor": towards a model of trust for e-commerce system design. In: CHI 2000 Extended Abstracts on Human factors in Computing Systems – ACM, pp. 101–102 (2000)
26. Hillman, S., Neustaedter, C., Bowes, J., Antle, A.: Soft trust and mCommerce shopping behaviours. In: Proceedings of the 14th International Conference on Human-Computer Interaction with Mobile Devices and Services, pp. 113–122 (2012)
27. Jarvenpaa, S., Tractinsky, N., Saarinen, L.: Consumer trust in an internet store: a cross-cultural validation. J. Comput.-Mediated Commun. **5**, 45–71 (2006)
28. Luo, X.: Trust production and privacy concerns on the Internet: a framework based on relationship marketing and social exchange theory. Ind. Mark. Manage. **31**, 111–118 (2002)
29. Finley, K.: Trust in the Sharing Economy: An Exploratory Study. (2012)
30. Lampinen, A., Bellotti, V., Cheshire, C., Gray, M.: CSCW and the sharing economy: the future of platforms as sites of work collaboration and trust. In: Proceedings of the 19th ACM Conference on Computer Supported Cooperative Work and Social Computing Companion - CSCW 2016 Companion, pp. 491–497, 26–February (2016)
31. Riegelsberger, J., Sasse, M., McCarthy, J.: Shiny happy people building trust? Photos on e-commerce websites and consumer trust. In: Proceedings of the SIGCHI Conference on Human Factors in Computing Systems, vol. 5, pp. 121–128 (2003)
32. Kuzheleva-Sagan, I.P., Suchkova, N.A.: Designing trust in the Internet services. AI & Soc. **31**, 381–392 (2016)
33. Swamynathan, G., Wilson, C., Boe, B., Almeroth, K., Zhao, B.Y.: Do social networks improve e-Commerce ? A study on social marketplaces. In: Proceedings of the First Workshop on Online Social Networks, vol. 1, pp. 1–6 (2008)
34. Hillman, S., Neustaedter, C., Pang, C., Oduor, E.: Shared joy is double joy: the social practices of user networks within group shopping sites. In: Conference on Human Factors in Computing Systems, pp. 2417–2426 (2013)
35. Al-shehry, A.M.: Transformation towards e-government in The Kingdom of Saudi Arabia: technological and organisational perspectives. Doctor of Philosophy (PhD), The School of Computing, De Montfort University (2009)
36. Maisel, S.: The new rise of tribalism in Saudi Arabia. Nomadic Peoples **18**, 100–122 (2014). https://doi.org/10.3197/np.2014.180207
37. Al-Saud, M., Bin, S., Bin, A.: 2030 Vision. http://vision2030.gov.sa/en
38. Ministry of Commorce and Investment: About us. https://maroof.sa/Home/About
39. Lazar, J., Feng, J.H.J., Hochheiser, H.: Research methods in human-computer interaction (2017)
40. Saldaña, J.: The Coding Manual for Qualitative Researchers. SAGE Publication, Thousand Oaks (2016)

41. Mads, S., Dam, R.F.: The Encyclopedia of Human-Computer Interaction (2012)
42. Strauss, A.L., Corbin, J.M.: Basics of Qualitative Research : Techniques and Procedures for Developing Grounded Theory (1998)
43. Country Comparison: Saudi Araia - Hofstede Insights. https://www.hofstede-insights.com/country-comparison/saudi-arabia/
44. Marcus, A., Gould, E.W.: Crosscurrents: cultural dimensions and global web user-interface design. Interact. ACM **7**, 32–46 (2000)
45. Flechais, I., Jirotka, M., Alghamdi, D.: In the balance in Saudi Arabia: security, privacy and trust. In: CHI 2013 Extended Abstracts on Human Factors in Computing Systems, pp. 823–828 (2013)
46. Abokhodair, N., Vieweg, S.: Privacy & social media in the context of the Arab Gulf. In: Designing Interactive Systems, pp. 672–683 (2016)
47. Al-maghrabi, T., Dennis, C., Vaux Halliday, S.: Antecedents of continuance intentions towards e-shopping: the case of Saudi Arabia. J. Enterp. Inf. Manag. **24**, 85–111 (2011)
48. Dillahunt, T.R., Malone, A.R.: The promise of the sharing economy among disadvantaged communities. In: Proceedings of the 33rd Annual ACM Conference on Human Factors in Computing Systems - CHI 2015, pp. 2285–2294 (2015)
49. Qualman, E.: Socialnomics: how social media transforms the way we live and do business (2012)
50. Kim, S., Park, H.: Effects of various characteristics of social commerce (s-commerce) on consumers' trust and trust performance. Int. J. Inf. Manage. **33**, 318–332 (2013)
51. Sun, H.: Designing for social commerce experience as cultural consumption. In: Rau, P.L. P. (ed.) IDGD 2011. LNCS, vol. 6775, pp. 402–406. Springer, Heidelberg (2011). https://doi.org/10.1007/978-3-642-21660-2_45
52. Hawlitschek, F., Teubner, T., Adam, M., Borchers, N., Moehlmann, M., Weinhardt, C.: Trust in the sharing economy: an experimental framework. In: Proceedings of the Thirty-Seventh International Conference on Information Systems (ICIS), Dublin, pp. 11–14 (2016)
53. Zifla, E., Wattal, S.: Community engagement in peer-to- peer business: evidence from Etsy.com. In: European Conference on Information Systems (2016)
54. Noor, A.D., Sulaiman, R., Bakar, A.A.: A review of factors that influenced online trust in social commerce. In: International Conference on Information Technology and Multimedia (ICIMU), pp. 118–123 (2014)
55. Chen, N., Rau, P.L.P.: Effects of trust on group buying websites in china. Int. J. Hum.-Comput. Interact. **30**, 615–626 (2014)
56. East, M.: PayPal Insights: e-commerce in the Middle East 2012–2015 (2015)
57. Yoldas, S.: A Research about Buying Behaviours of Online Customers, Comparison of Turkey with UK (2012)
58. Etsy: Etsy: Trust. https://www.etsy.com/uk/trust
59. How do I search on Instagram?. https://help.instagram.com/1482378711987121
60. Leary, D.: Social and hashtag commerce : "order by tweet." In: International Conference on Information Systems (2016)
61. Aljowaidi, M.: A study of e-commerce adoption using the TOE framework in Saudi retailers : firm motivations, implementation and benefits. Doctor of Philosophy (PhD), Business IT and Logistics, RMIT University (2015)
62. AlOnazi, N.: Instagram traders huge profit without licences. http://3alyoum.com/article/95585
63. Alsharif, F.: Investigating the factors affecting on-line shopping adoption in Saudi Arabia. Doctoral dissertation, De Montfort University (2013)

Denouncing Sexual Violence: A Cross-Language and Cross-Cultural Analysis of #MeToo and #BalanceTonPorc

Irene Lopez[1](✉), Robin Quillivic[2], Hayley Evans[3], and Rosa I. Arriaga[3]📵

[1] Universitat Politècnica de Catalunya, Barcelona, Spain
irene.michelle.lopez@est.fib.upc.edu
[2] École centrale de Lille, Lille, France
quillivicrobin@hotmail.fr
[3] Georgia Institute of Technology, Atlanta, GA, USA
hayley.evans@gatech.edu, arriaga@cc.gatech.edu

Abstract. #MeToo, a social media movement that denounced sexual violence against women was lauded as a global phenomenon. In this paper, we present a cross-language and cross-cultural quantitative examination of the English #MeToo and French #BalanceTonPorc. The goal of our study was to examine the global to local adoption and personalization of this social media movement. In part one of our study, we sought to understand linguistic differences by comparing #MeToo tweets in English and #BalanceTonPorc tweets in French. In the second part, we sought to understand cultural differences in the way #MeToo was adopted in the US and India. We found that the movement did not share a unified perspective, instead it was shaped by the culture and social reality of the posters; tweets in French were more aggressive and accusing than those in English, while English tweets from India involved more religion and society than those from the US.

Keywords: Twitter trends · Linguistic analysis · Social movements

1 Introduction

Globally, one in three women is affected by sexual violence in her lifetime [26]. Sexual violence is defined as "any sexual act or an attempt to obtain a sexual act, unwanted sexual comments, or advances, acts to traffic or otherwise directed, against a person's sexuality using coercion, by any person regardless of their relationship to the victim in any setting, including but not limited to home and work" [17]. Survivors of sexual violence have historically remained silent [1], yet in 2017 a global movement denouncing sexual violence unfolded across traditional [4,21,23,38] and social media [32], which is perhaps most recognized in the form of #MeToo.

© IFIP International Federation for Information Processing 2019
Published by Springer Nature Switzerland AG 2019
D. Lamas et al. (Eds.): INTERACT 2019, LNCS 11747, pp. 733–743, 2019.
https://doi.org/10.1007/978-3-030-29384-0_44

Though sexual violence is a gendered-and-cultural phenomenon [17], #MeToo was utilized in various countries to express facts, beliefs, and stories related to sexual violence on social media [2,16]. While #MeToo was used at a global level, various language-specific hashtags were used for the same purpose including but not limited to the Spanish #YoTambien (MeToo), the Italian #QuellaVoltaChe (TheTimeThat), and the French #BalanceTonPorc (DenounceYourPig). While some attention has been paid to the variants of the #MeToo movement [11,25], there has not yet been an empirical study that compares linguistic attributes across the dimensions of language, culture, and place.

Our study analyzes two aspects of the global social media movement denouncing sexual violence. First, we present a cross-language, quantitative examination of the English #MeToo and French #BalanceTonPorc from a data set of 412,582 publicly shared tweets in 2017. Our findings reveal that users of each language participate distinctly, which bears implications for understanding global social media movements that are multilingual. Second, we present an analysis of over a million #MeToo tweets from 2018, written in English, from the US and India. This allows an investigation of cultural differences which affect expression in the same language in a social media movement.

Our research contributes to understanding of global social media movements across language, culture, and place. We examine how this phenomenon takes form for each and characterize user participation across linguistic dimensions, in order to highlight the differences in the movement and how different societies face a global issue.

2   Related Work

Social movements and collective action have been studied extensively within the social computing community [8,13,19,22,35]. Many of these studies have focused on social media movements at the local and national level [9]. However, research has noted that globalization and increased adoption of global communication networks (e.g. Twitter) has shifted the focus of social movements from local or national scale to a global scale [7]. Trans-nationally, members of social networks have advocated for specific causes and goals united through hashtag activism [36] such as Latin America's #NiUnaMenos movement against femicide and gender-based violence. Despite global activism, pluralism of participation exists, and social media movements cannot be detached from underlying influences such as people, events [24], language, culture, and digital media platforms which influence the personalization of collective action [5]. Researchers have also investigated how Twitter reflects the views and perspective of users in India. For example, [18,30] addressed the role that Twitter plays in understanding public health issues, finding similarities and differences between English Twitter users from the US and India. For example, when both groups tweeted about AIDS they focused on disseminating information about prevention and testing, but users from India were less likely to tweet about AIDS or autism and more likely to tweet about tobacco cessation than their US counterparts.

Framing theory, provides yet another way to think about social media movements. It is a concept from mass communication literature, that refers to the process by which media can be manipulated to highlight certain aspects of an issue to orient an individual's thinking and perception around it [14]. Each frame includes a message, audience, participants, platform, context, and high-level moral and conceptual messages. Furthermore, Lakoff [20] states that these "frames" are evoked by language, and therefore the choice and structure of language is critical in frame theory. As mentioned previously, language is an important social lens, and discourse studies can inform socio-historical understanding of meaning as a product of a social group [3]. This makes analyzing tweets on sexual violence among different language communities an important endeavor. One question that should be answered in order to better understand the relationship between the people that speak the language and their cultural values is: *How do people relate the social context to the linguistic system?* In other words, *how do they frame their meaning via semantic exchange?* [14,20]. This question is equally compelling when one considers a shared language in two very different cultures.

To our knowledge, little research has examined this global to local adoption and personalization of social media movements across language and culture in the social computing community. One notable effort in this space was conducted in the examination of the use of English and Arabic tweets during the 2011 Arab Spring [6]. Similarly, our study will adopt a view of the #MeToo movement through the language spheres of English and French. However, rather than focusing on information flow between spheres, we will examine how speakers of each language participated in the #MeToo social media movement concurrently and distinctly. We will investigate unique participation of US #MeToo and French #BalanceTonPorc tweets across language. We will also examine how culture affects the linguistic content of tweets written in English by people from India and the USA.

3   Data

In order to analyze the differences between content in French and English, we gathered a total of 4 datasets. For each language, we gathered tweets related to the global social media phenomena in which users shared content related to sexual violence. As is common, we also compiled control data sets with which we could compare tweets [10]. For the cultural analysis we retrieved 2 data sets, formed by tweets in English which could be attributed to users from the USA or India. In this section, we describe the methods used for acquiring this data.

The first part of our study uses 412,582 publicly shared tweets utilizing the hashtags #MeToo, #MoiAussi, and #BalanceTonPorc shared between October 13, 2017 and November 11, 2017. We collected data using both Twitter API via Tweepy [34] and the Github Library Taspinar[1]. We used each of the hashtags listed and then concatenated our results, dropping duplicates based on the ID associated with the tweets. Tweets collected with the Taspinar Library did not

---

[1] https://github.com/taspinar/twitterscraper (2017).

have information about the user or language, however, we were able to use the tweet ID and Twitter API to complete the data set. We then created columns for hashtags (#), mentions (@), and URLs using a Regex Library. Next we applied a cleaning function which removed all punctuation, numbers, and set all text to lowercase. Finally, we divided the data set by language (English or French) in order to obtain two distinct, language-based data sets.

In order to provide a consistent cross-linguistic analysis, we developed a control data set for both English and French [10]. This comparison allows us to show that differences in tweets is influenced by the social media movement rather than language structure. Queries seeking a "random" set of tweets are not permitted via the Twitter API. Therefore, in order to create our control data set, we collected tweets from the same time period which mentioned common topics. In order to collect tweets on these topics we first collected tweets with the most used French and English words (q = the, it, I, this, a, les, le, j'ai, c'est). We then sourced tweets regarding sports (q = NFL, Liguel), television shows (q = The Voice), and tweets related to commercials (q = contest, concours).

For the second part of our study we used the official Twitter API through the Tweepy library to gather metadata. We retrieved over 2 million tweets which used the hashtag #MeToo and were shared between October 9, 2018 and November 25, 2018; next we used a language detection library to discard those tweets that were not written in English. We then classified the tweets as coming from either "India", "USA" or "Other", discarding the latter. This reduced the number of tweets to 1,511,161; these tweets were divided in two data sets based on country of origin.

The classification of tweets by country was done using the following data when available: (1) the coordinates of the tweet, (2) the coordinates of the bounding box associated with the user who shared the tweet, (3) the location of the user as published in their profile. If the tweet was actually a retweet the information from the original poster was used. If none of this data was available or if the tweet was matched to a country different from the USA or India it was classified as "Other" to be discarded.

4   Methods

To quantify cross language dimensions in our datasets, we define 3 categories of linguistic measures: **(1) affective attributes** marked by words related to emotion as well as the polarity of the emotions expressed, **(2) cognitive attributes** which relate to sensory information, and **(3) linguistic style attributes** related to the use of pronouns and common nouns. To evaluate these measures we use LIWC [27] a well known and validated linguistic analysis tool [15,37]. Previous work in this area identifies this tool and its categories to be valuable in evaluating the linguistic differences on social media for a variety of purposes [9,15,31]. We use two LIWC dictionaries appropriate to the dataset languages. For French, we used Piolat's [29] which corresponds to LIWC 2007. Although an updated version of the official English dictionary exists [28], in order to maintain equivalency between the dictionaries we used the LIWC 2007 as well.

5   Results

Content Discrepancies Between Languages. In our data, we observe that 52% of English tweets contain an external link whereas only 36% of French tweets do in comparison to our control data sets for both languages. These findings make sense if we consider that sharing URLs is in line with the goal of promoting awareness about sexual violence; which is the objective of the #MeToo movement. In the 2018 data sets, the tweets from the USA were also more likely to include URLS which might indicate that it is a tendency which has more to do with the country than the language itself.

Linguistic Differences. We observed many significant statistical differences between the French and English data sets on Table 1 and between the India and USA data sets in Table 2. To identify the significant results we looked at the average differences as well as the differences between the Z-score statistics. (See Tables 1 and 2 for details). We also replaced the p values under 0.0001 with 0.

A Negatively Charged Social Media Movement. #MeToo and #Balance-TonPorc tweets are charged with negative emotions such as anger as one might expect with talk of sexual violence. When compared to our control data set, there is approximately a 50% difference in negative tone of tweet when compared to tweets outside the movement. French tweets have less affect (the emotional charge based on the number of words related to feelings) than English ones and use more aggressive, vulgar language. This difference may be explained by the tone of each social media campaign. #MeToo suggests solidarity whereas #BalanceTonPorc encourages women to "out your pig," as illustrated below:

"#MeToo has been a mix of emotions. I am sharing my story..."

Translation: [Expletive] patriarchy!

In #MeToo tweets from 2018 we observed that tweets from the USA had less affect than tweets from India, meaning that they expressed fewer emotions. This could be due to the fact that the movement in India is just getting started and there are many tweets denouncing abuse.

Cognitive Attributes: Creating Solidarity or Denouncing Perpetrators. The goal of #MeToo was to create a survivor to survivor network whereas #BalanceTonPorc was to identify and denounce perpetrators of sexual violence. Our analyses show that denouncing individuals is much less likely in the English than the French data set, as seen below:

"#MeToo is inclusive because of our shared words and experiences among women- that is the whole point."

Translation: Agh! Indeed, I think we will have a special category for the white males who do not like this hashtag!"

Table 1. 2017 Dataset: LIWC Cross-Language Results, Z statistics calculated with a Wilcoxon Rank Sum test and the size effect with Cohen's indicator

	$\mu\,(FR_C)$	$\mu\,(EN_C)$	Z_C	$\mu\,(FR)$	$\mu\,(EN)$	Z_{2017}	P_{2017}	d_{2017}
Affective attributes								
Affect (emotion)	7.774	7.035	16.88	5.167	6.749	−41.83	0	−0.188
Posemo	6.436	5.126	43.35	2.631	3.303	−16.01	0	−0.103
Negemo	1.301	1.88	−78.92	2.705	3.417	−23.98	0	−0.122
Anger	0.477	0.846	−55.5	1.122	2.302	−49.9	0	−0.261
Swear	0.208	0.396	−28.31	0.303	0.212	7.3	0	0.048
Cognitive attributes								
Hear	0.447	0.649	−38.15	0.794	1.104	−9.89	0	−0.096
See	0.961	0.992	−21.85	0.785	0.501	16.94	0	0.117
Feel	0.43	0.447	−9.18	0.539	0.346	11.4	0	0.097
Linguistic style attributes								
Interpersonal Focus								
I	2.603	4.565	−209.6	2.933	2.799	13.29	0	0.023
We	0.358	0.599	−39.41	0.293	1.14	−32.77	0	−0.192
She/He	3.654	0.811	264.2	4.268	0.768	143.4	0	0.895
They	0.267	0.462	−36.25	0.448	0.485	−5.65	0	−0.017
Social personal concerns								
Family	0.223	0.237	−6.93	0.953	0.265	41.79	0	0.322
Friend	0.289	0.194	9.57	0.257	0.127	9.22	0	0.106
Social	3.718	7.67	−283.4	4.558	11.129	−142.8	0	−0.619
Health	0.506	0.493	0.49	0.602	0.385	13.54	0	0.1
Body	0.536	0.637	−26.46	1.304	0.375	48.53	0	0.371
Relig	0.18	0.274	−16.96	0.209	0.281	−3.45	0.001	−0.032
Sexual	0.276	0.553	−39.7	1.292	1.632	−15.57	0	−0.091

Furthermore, tweets from the French data set were more likely to describe the appearance of the perpetrator along with their own feelings about the encounter.

Translation: That guy...with a very unhealthy and insistent stare.

Tweets from India were also much more likely to denounce an individual than tweets from the US, but they were less likely to give a clear description of an attack.

Linguistic Style Attributes: Use of Pronouns. There are notable differences between the use of pronouns in the social media movements of #MeToo and #BalanceTonPorc. The measure of the English "I" and French "j" or "j" show that French tweets utilize the first person more often. English tweets utilize "we" 90% more than in the French data set.

Table 2. 2018 Dataset: LIWC Cross-Language Results, Z statistics calculated with a Wilcoxon Rank Sum test and the size effect with Cohen's indicator

	μ (USA)	μ (India)	Z_{2018}	P_{2018}	d_{2018}
Affective attributes					
Affect (emotion)	5.402	5.74	−43.39	0	−0.072
Posemo	2.467	2.545	−20.75	0	−0.023
Negemo	2.914	3.152	−41.33	0	−0.067
Anger	1.967	1.874	35.46	0	0.033
Swear	0.103	0.059	11.23	0	0.069
Cognitive attributes					
Hear	0.848	0.874	−4.35	0	−0.015
See	0.603	0.37	62.13	0	0.162
Feel	0.288	0.193	55.68	0	0.105
Linguistic style attributes					
Interpersonal focus					
I	1.814	1.43	45.77	0	0.119
We	0.694	0.457	75.07	0	0.155
She/He	1.531	1.483	7.06	0	0.017
They	0.506	0.542	−13.87	0	−0.024
Social personal concerns					
Family	0.326	0.39	17.52	0	−0.049
Friend	0.102	0.132	−4.68	0	−0.045
Social	9.158	9.221	−3.29	0.001	−0.009
Health	0.236	0.226	−4.16	0	0.01
Body	0.253	0.307	−25.69	0	−0.051
Relig	0.244	0.781	−98.45	0	−0.277
Sexual	1.152	0.987	48.74	0	0.08

"#MeToo is here to stay! We must challenge sexual harassment!"

When comparing India and the USA, personal pronouns are used more often with the exception of the third person plural "they". The latter is used more frequently in tweets from India, where the focus seems to be placed on men as a group and in society in general.

"Men in the social sector are equally oppressive and abusive. They hide behind the cloak of 'wokeness' and understanding consent..."

Use of Words Related to Family Ties

Both French and English tweets use words related to family (e.g. father, uncle). However, these were much more present in the French data set, often denouncing family members who were involved in perpetrating sexual violence. This is not surprising considering approximately 30% of child sex offenders are family members [33]. Rather than naming or tagging these perpetrators, French tweets identified the familial relationship.

Translation: My uncle who abused me, from when I was X to X years old...

Description of Assault
The French tweets more often described details and characteristics of the sexual violence than did English tweets.

Translation: This guy who puts his hand on my bottom...

When compared to the US, tweets from India are much more often related with religion and contain more references to body parts, although the language used is less explicit as reflected in the lower score on the "sexual" category.

6   Discussion

In 2017, #MeToo, a social media movement that denounced sexual violence against women was lauded as a global phenomenon [4, 21, 23, 32, 38]. In this paper, we presented a cross-language and cultural based quantitative examination of the English #MeToo and French #BalanceTonPorc. The goal of our study was to examine the global to local adoption and personalization of this social media movement. We sought to understand linguistic and cultural differences between the US and France and the US and India, respectively.

We found that the global movement did not share a unified perspective. Tweets from the US, France, and India all demonstrated semantics which indicate a unique, local social perspective. It was not the case that there was a global #MeToo that denounced sexual violence but rather that two linguistic and two cultural communities found their own voice. We believe that this likely stems from the initial framing set out in the US [12] which called for solidarity and support; whereas in French [11] the call was to share experiences and identify the perpetrators. It could also be argued that these distinctive frames [14, 20] oriented participant's thinking about how to respond to these first tweets. Thus, as the volume of tweets increased, our evidence shows that these frames were reinforced throughout the data sets for each language.

When comparing English #MeToo and French #BalanceTonPorc tweets we found that the latter were more likely to include words that indicated that there was a narrative rather than simply raising awareness. We found that compared to English, French tweets were more likely to be in the first person, more likely to include body terms and number words. Further, they were more likely to include male family terms. The French tweets were also found to have a more negative emotional valence and vulgar words. All this underscores the fact that French women were more likely to include their personal story about how old they were and what happened to them. This shows that the 2017 datasets were able to prove that the differences between the #MeToo and #BalanceTonPorc tweets were not only due to different languages but to the fact that the French movement focused on denouncing attacks.

When we look at #MeToo from a cultural versus a linguistic lens a different narrative appears. Here we see that shared language does not reflect a shared expression. Tweets from each country posted content which adjusted to the needs and customs of their societies. Indian tweets were more likely to refer to religious themes, shared less explicit content, and had a bigger focus on denouncing society and men as a group.

In conclusion, our analysis is in line with other findings that microblogs such as Twitter can shed light on contemporary events. Despite some limitations, our findings open up new avenues of research in the area of social computing.

References

1. Ahrens, C.E.: Silent and silenced: the disclosure and non-disclosure of sexual assault. Ph.D. thesis, ProQuest Information & Learning (2002)
2. Anderson, M.: How social media users have discussed sexual harassment since #MeToo went viral. Pew Research Center (2018). https://www.pewresearch.org/fact-tank/2018/10/11/how-social-media-users-have-discussed-sexual-harassment-since-metoo-went-viral/
3. Angermuller, J., Maingueneau, D., Wodak, R.: The Discourse Studies Reader: Main Currents in Theory and Analysis. John Benjamins Publishing Company, Amsterdam (2014)
4. Armour, N., Axon, R.: USA gymnastics: sexual assault investigation urges cultural change. USA Today (2017)
5. Bennett, W.L., Segerberg, A.: Digital media and the personalization of collective action: social technology and the organization of protests against the global economic crisis. Inf. Commun. Soc. **14**(6), 770–799 (2011)
6. Bruns, A., Highfield, T., Burgess, J.: The Arab Spring and social media audiences: English and Arabic Twitter users and their networks. Am. Behav. Sci. **57**(7), 871–898 (2013)
7. Castells, M.: The new public sphere: global civil society, communication networks, and global governance. Ann. Am. Acad. Polit. Soc. Sci. **616**(1), 78–93 (2008)
8. Choudhary, A., Hendrix, W., Lee, K., Palsetia, D., Liao, W.K.: Social media evolution of the Egyptian revolution. Commun. ACM **55**(5), 74–80 (2012)
9. De Choudhury, M., Jhaver, S., Sugar, B., Weber, I.: Social media participation in an activist movement for racial equality. In: Tenth International AAAI Conference on Web and Social Media (2016)
10. De Choudhury, M., Sharma, S.S., Logar, T., Eekhout, W., Nielsen, R.C.: Gender and cross-cultural differences in social media disclosures of mental illness. In: Proceedings of the 2017 ACM Conference on Computer Supported Cooperative Work and Social Computing, pp. 353–369. ACM (2017)
11. Donadio, R.: #BalanceTonPorc is France's #MeToo. The Atlantic (2017). https://www.theatlantic.com/international/archive/2017/10/the-weinstein-scandal-seen-from-france/543315/
12. Donadio, R.: A year ago, Alyssa Milano started a conversation about #MeToo. NBC News (2017). https://www.nbcnews.com/news/us-news/year-ago-alyssa-milano-started-conversation-about-metoo-these-women-n920246

13. Eltantawy, N., Wiest, J.B.: The Arab Spring - social media in the Egyptian revolution: reconsidering resource mobilization theory. Int. J. Commun. **5**, 18 (2011)
14. Entman, R.M.: Framing: toward clarification of a fractured paradigm. J. Commun. **43**(4), 51–58 (1993)
15. Farnadi, G., et al.: Computational personality recognition in social media. User Model. User-Adap. Inter. **26**(2–3), 109–142 (2016)
16. Haynes, S., Chen, A.: How #MeToo is taking on a life of its own in Asia. Time Mag. (2018). http://time.com/longform/me-too-asia-china-south-korea/
17. Kalra, G., Bhugra, D.: Sexual violence against women: understanding cross-cultural intersections. Indian J. Psychiatry **55**(3), 244 (2013)
18. Karusala, N., Kumar, N., Arriaga, R.: #autism: Twitter as a lens to explore differences in autism awareness in India and the United States. In: Proceedings of the Tenth International Conference on Information and Communication Technologies and Development, p. 41. ACM (2019)
19. Khatua, A., Cambria, E., Khatua, A.: Sounds of silence breakers: exploring sexual violence on Twitter. In: 2018 IEEE/ACM International Conference on Advances in Social Networks Analysis and Mining (ASONAM), pp. 397–400. IEEE (2018)
20. Lakoff, G.: Simple framing. Rockridge Institute, vol. 14 (2006)
21. The Local: 1.001 Norwegian artists denounce sexual harassment (2017). https://www.thelocal.no/20171123/1000-norwegian-artists-denounce-sexual-harassment
22. Manikonda, L., Beigi, G., Liu, H., Kambhampati, S.: Twitter for sparking a movement, reddit for sharing the moment: #MeToo through the lens of social media. arXiv preprint arXiv:1803.08022 (2018)
23. News, G.: Miss Peru contestants cite gender-based violence stats instead of their bra size (2017). https://globalnews.ca/news/3835335/miss-peru-contestants-cited-gender-based-violence-stats-instead-of-their-bra-size/
24. Olesen, T.: Transnational publics: new spaces of social movement activism and the problem of global long-sightedness. Curr. Sociol. **53**(3), 419–440 (2005)
25. Onwuachi-Willig, A.: What about #UsToo: the invisibility of race in the #MeToo movement. Yale LJF **128**, 105 (2018)
26. Organization, W.H.: Violence against women (2011). https://www.who.int/news-room/fact-sheets/detail/violence-against-women
27. Pennebaker, J.W., Booth, R.J., Francis, M.E.: LIWC 2007: linguistic inquiry and word count. LIWC.net, Austin, Texas (2007)
28. Pennebaker, J.W., Boyd, R.L., Jordan, K., Blackburn, K.: The development and psychometric properties of LIWC2015. Technical report (2015)
29. Piolat, A., Booth, R.J., Chung, C.K., Davids, M., Pennebaker, J.W.: La version française du dictionnaire pour le liwc: modalités de construction et exemples d'utilisation. Psychologie française **56**(3), 145–159 (2011)
30. Quadri, S., Karusala, N., Arriaga, R.I.: #AutismAwareness: a longitudinal study to characterize tweeting patterns for Indian and US users. In: Proceedings of the 9th Indian Conference on Human Computer Interaction, pp. 11–19. ACM (2018)
31. Ramirez-Esparza, N., Chung, C.K., Kacewicz, E., Pennebaker, J.W.: The psychology of word use in depression forums in English and in Spanish: texting two text analytic approaches. In: ICWSM (2008)
32. Respers, L.: #MeToo: social media flooded with personal stories of assault. CNN (2017). https://edition.cnn.com/2017/10/15/entertainment/me-too-twitter-alyssa-milano/index.html
33. Richards, K.: Misperceptions about child sex offenders. Trends and Issues in Crime and Criminal Justice, September 2011

34. Roesslein, J.: Tweepy documentation
35. Schneider, K.T., Carpenter, N.J.: Sharing #MeToo on Twitter: incidents, coping responses, and social reactions. Int. J. Equality Divers. Incl. (2019)
36. Stache, L.C.: Advocacy and political potential at the convergence of hashtag activism and commerce. Feminist Media Stud. **15**(1), 162–164 (2015)
37. Wang, Y., Weber, I., Mitra, P.: Quantified self meets social media: sharing of weight updates on Twitter. In: Proceedings of the 6th International Conference on Digital Health Conference, pp. 93–97. ACM (2016)
38. Zacharek, S., Dockterman, E., Sweetland, H.: Time person of the year 2017: the silence breakers. Time Mag. (2017). http://time.com/time-person-of-the-year-2017-silence-breakers

Dhana Labha: A Financial Management Application to Underbanked Communities in Rural Sri Lanka

Thilina Halloluwa[1(✉)] and Dhaval Vyas[2]

[1] University of Colombo School of Computing, Colombo, Sri Lanka
tch@ucsc.cmb.ac.lk
[2] University of Queensland, Brisbane, Australia
d.vyas@uq.edu.au

Abstract. This paper presents findings from field trial of a mobile application called 'Dhana Labha' in a rural Sri Lankan community. Dhana Labha was designed to be used by the community members to manage their personal finances, oversee their performance in managing multiple microfinance loans and assist in loan collection. We distributed the application among thirty eight microfinance clients and studied their use over a period of six months. Our findings show that the use of Dhana Labha had a positive impact on existing local practices and financial awareness while prompting the participants to develop unexpected new practices around microfinance workflows. Our findings highlight the importance of understanding existing sociocultural practices for designing applications, as they strongly affect and shape the use of technology in a constrained setting.

Keywords: Microfinance · ICTD · Sociocultural practices · Qualitative study

1 Introduction

Financial management is vital in achieving long term as well as short term goals of an individual. Banking institutions play a critical role in this regard by providing various financial services such as savings, loans, and insurance. However, while these services have expanded their reach by introducing several Information and Communication Technology (ICT) based solutions, over 2 billion individuals remain outside the reach of formal banks [11] due to various reasons such as lack of financial infrastructure and credit history [73]. In these situations, microfinance institutions (MFIs) offer a solution by providing loans to these communities without collateral [72]. In the developing world, microfinance has taken a prominent role to support people whom the banks are unwilling to provide loans. These individuals are known as underbanked [27], who have limited access to financial institutions or unbanked [28], who do not have any access to financial institutions.

Microfinance is traditionally a coordinative process, in which micro-loans are released to a group of people instead of an individual. In recent times, the fields of HCI and ICTD have seen a growing number of studies around microfinance related

D. Lamas et al. (Eds.): INTERACT 2019, LNCS 11747, pp. 744–767, 2019.
https://doi.org/10.1007/978-3-030-29384-0_45

activities (e.g. [1, 3, 15, 16, 51, 52, 73, 74]). However, while there is a collective agreement on the potential of ICT to support microfinance activities, most of the technology interventions have focused on enhancing transactional as well as procedural aspects of microfinance [57, 65, 71, 73]. Yet, over the years, studies have shown that various social and cultural practices are at the root of the success of microfinance (e.g. [15, 20, 51]). In this paper, we report on the experiences of deployment of a mobile phone based financial management application that was designed to support the collaborative work associated with microfinance workflows in rural Sri Lanka. The application is meant to be used only by microfinance clients (members, group leaders and centre leaders) and not by the microfinance institutes (MFIs). The design and specific functionalities of the application, Dhana Labha, was informed from ethnographic work (e.g. [20, 38, 61]) conducted in similar contexts. Dhana Labha enables people to manage their finances and oversee microfinance loans. We distributed it to a rural underbanked community in Sri Lanka. We recruited participants via two MFIs operating within that community. The study was carried out over a period of six months with thirty-eight microfinance clients from eight microfinance groups. Instead of evaluating our mobile application, we focused more on using it as a probing tool [24] to understand the changes in experiences brought forward by this intervention.

The main contribution of this paper lies with the empirical findings where we describe how we used Dhana Labha as a technology probe to understand how the people living in a constrained environment with limited exposure to technology use a mobile application to manage their finances and microfinance related activities. By doing so, we elaborate on how the application influenced current local practices. Further, we describe how the application brought forward unexpected changes such as creating physical leaderboards, introducing physical badges while facilitating discussions around finances. These practices enabled building reputations and closing the gaps between social classes. It also had a positive effect on the awareness of the participants' financial situation. we report that these users are firmly accustomed to their existing sociocultural practices, and that attachment led them to use Dhana Labha in a way that the application was internalised and became a part of their current practice. As a result, we advocate that socio-cultural aspects need to be at the centre when designing for microfinance in Sri Lanka. We conclude by presenting design insights for suture researchers focusing on sustained use of technology in a constrained setting aimed at supporting existing sociocultural practices through application design.

2   Related Work

2.1   HCI in Constrained Environments

In recent years, HCI practitioners have shown a larger interest in identifying research opportunities associated with cross-cultural design space which mainly targets HCI design for developing regions. The term "postcolonialism" generally refers to segments of people from lands which were previously colonized [2, 29]. However, within the context of HCI, postcolonialism refers to methods that aim to engage and empower the community. Postcolonial computing is a term coined through this interest which advocates a shift in perspective focusing mainly on power differences, authority, legal issues, participation, intelligibility and cultural aspects [29]. Therefore, many argue that some of the assumptions made by the researchers in the developed world may prove to be invalid in these constrained environments. For example, researchers have found that the UI elements and image representations took for granted in a developed country considered to be strange in developing countries [44].

Researchers have identified that gamification and use of game elements as a potential means of encourage participation specially with younger users [18, 32, 41]. They claim that it is easier for rural children to relate to technological tools if the tools simulate their real life experiences (e.g. traditional games [32] or a popular sport such as cricket [41]). Medhi-Thies et al. [46] highlight the importance of mediators when introducing technology in marginalized communities due to the low literacy rates of participants. Wyche et al. [68] present their observations on the challenges people in the developing world where poverty, lack of electricity, network issues are facing when attempting to use Facebook. Jose et al. [30] identify social influence, curiosity, lifecycle of mobile as well as its content, privacy and security as the main reasons for upgrading to a new mobile phone in their attempt to design an ultra-low cost smartphone for the poor communities in India. Kolko et al. [37], suggest that the focus should be on work ecosystems and aspects such as power consumptions and interface. They discovered a significant difference in the extent of collaboration between high resource and low resource settings. Overall, researchers agree that it is important to develop a holistic understanding of cultural and social aspects when designing for users in these marginalized constrained environments.

2.2 Financial Matters in HCI

Understanding an individual's interactions with money is essential when designing financial applications [34]. Thus, many studies have been carried out to understand how individuals in different cultures and contexts interact with personal finances.

Vines et al. [63] have studied the personal finances of older adults in the UK to understand the strategies used to manage their finances. After a longitudinal study, the researchers advocate that the new technology interventions should explore means of strengthening the traditional methods instead of replacing them. A recent study done in China [69] has looked at the monetary practices of older adults' finances in China. The study reports that participants were relying on traditional methods even though there existed numerous technologically enhanced solutions due to their simple lifestyle. Vines et al. [64] further studied the low-income individuals and reported how they organise their finances by planning, prioritising, hiding, and delaying their transactions. Vyas et al. [66, 67] have studied the Australian families and reported that these families have come up with creative methods and rely on physical tools to live well on less income. This fact has prompted the researchers to question whether pursuing the development of technological tools is a viable option [67]. They also point out that financial matters have the potential to bring families together and reported on family collaborations around financial matters [58].

Financial Matters in ICTD. While there are several attempts to understand the financial management practices of individuals from the developed world (e.g., [30, 52, 54, 55]), there is a lack of similar studies involving marginalised populations in developing countries. Studies have shown that when designing for non-literate users, features such as voice-annotation support, local language support, and graphical cues, need to be implemented [48]. Similarly, Kumar, Martin, and O'Neill [39] have looked into the financial practices of Indians, with the intention of understanding how mobile payment mechanisms could be integrated into current payment workflows. They report that the potential is high in India to adopt these new payment mechanisms if they are literate. Mesfin et al. [49] on features of mobile money applications for rural Ethiopia suggest that designers should focus more on social, cultural and religious practices as well as on embedded social meanings when introducing technology interventions. Halloluwa et al. [19] have explored the values associated with the financial affairs of rural Sri Lankans using participatory design workshops. They report three central themes (supporting family, Independence and spiritual beliefs) which acts as the driving force behind the financial decisions of rural Sri Lankans and suggest that the tools should focus on empowering these communities through technology.

2.3   Microfinance and Poverty

Over the years, various studies have illustrated the effectiveness of microfinance, its potential to improve the financial status of low-income families [12, 22, 42, 43, 45, 70]. Furthermore, studies have found that microfinance has a positive impact on local economy [36], entrepreneurship [10], education [23], community engagement [8], social mobilisation [31] and social empowerment is widely accepted [33]. Microfinance can also reduce gender inequality [33, 74] and tends to empower women particularly in male-dominated cultures [26, 60]. Goodman [16] claim that even though microfinance has a defined set of workflows, people tend to modify them to fit into their existing borrowing practices. In their work with Bolivian underbanked community, Velasco and Marconi [62] report that there is a diversification of microfinance groups. They report that these groups are now transformed into supportive units which even conduct businesses together. Over the years, microfinance has attracted plenty of criticisms mainly due to the way loans are utilised. Several low-income families utilise borrowed money to meet household expenses and daily consumption instead of utilising it to generate income [14]. Several bad habits also contribute to the negative impact of microfinance. For example, Fernando [13] reports that some MFI clients meet loan repayments by borrowing money from individual moneylenders. They would even secure their loans with local traders in exchange for grocery items. Furthermore, the interest rates of MFIs are significantly higher than formal banks mainly due to higher operating costs [55]. As a result of the unproductive use of funds as well as higher interact rates have increased the personal debt of individuals which has led to increases in poverty [5] as well as emotional turmoil [59]. Overall, the influence of microfinance, as well as its impact on poverty reduction, appears to be variable and inconclusive [54].

2.4 Designing for Microfinance

Due to the prominence of microfinance within the financial affairs of the poor, HCI community has recently started showing greater interest in microfinance workflows (e.g., [1, 15, 20, 51]). Notably, studies have been conducted to investigate ways to enhance these workflows. MFIs collect payments by visiting their members weekly or monthly depending on financial company policies. However, due to different schedules, and busy lifestyles some members may forget about the collection dates. Thus, Sambasivan et al. [56] have explored the impact of a mobile-based message broadcasting system which was used to send payment reminders. They describe the impact of such a system on aspects such as trust and individual identities. Similarly, O'Neil et al. [51] have looked into the lives of auto-rickshaw drivers who are continually on the road to make a living. Therefore, they have explored the possibility of using mobile money to collect payments. They report that mobile money applications alone would not be sufficiently successful, and any such technologies should be embedded into the broader loan repayment ecosystem. Complementing this work, Halloluwa et al. [20] have explored the broader loan repayment ecosystems of a rural Sri Lankan community. They report that sociocultural aspects such as trust, credibility, community engagement and familial support are central to the success of microfinance. Adeel et al. [1] have studied another aspect of microfinance that has gone unnoticed. They claim that loan officers are providing many services outside of their work requirement such as introducing new markets and offering financial advice, which plays a significant role in making microfinance work.

MFIs mostly operate in the rural regions of developing countries where infrastructural facilities are limited. Plogmann et al. [53] claim that lack of technological infrastructure as well as the distance (geographical as well as cultural) between MFI clients and technical experts is one of the significant barriers for introducing technological solutions to this community. It is evident that most current technological interventions to the underbanked community have been introduced focusing on the procedural and transactional aspects of microfinance [20]. However, Barton et al. [6] suggest that by expanding that focus onto microfinance clients and not entirely on MFIs, the designers will be able to develop a different perspective towards microfinance which can lead to more efficient, and sustainable solutions to current issues in microfinance.

3 The Setting

3.1 Rural Sri Lankan Society

Sri Lanka is an island nation with a population of 21 million, out of which 77.4% lives in rural regions [40]. The hierarchy of the Sri Lankan society is mainly patriarchal, particularly in rural regions [9]. Since this is socially and culturally entrenched, the involvement of women [21] and children [17] in financial decision making is limited.

3.2 Microfinance Institutions (MFIs), Centres and Groups

The primary financial service of microfinance is to provide micro-loans without collateral. However, to compensate for the lack of collateral, MFIs follow a group-based lending mechanism which ensures repayment [4, 62, 72]. That is, instead of releasing loans to an individual, the MFIs require their clients to be grouped. Several groups collectively form a centre. A leader will be selected for the centre. In addition, each group will have its own group leader. Leaders are responsible for making sure that their members do not miss payments. The MFI will allocate a loan officer (LO) to each centre. LOs make weekly/monthly visits to the centres to provide financial services. The centre leader is responsible for hosting the meetings. In most cases, a centre leader would also act as a group leader [20].

4 The Application

Specific features of the application are inspired by previous work with underbanked communities in Sri Lanka (e.g. [4, 20, 61]).

4.1 Dhana Labha and Personal Finances

Dhana Labha supports the individual members to manage their personal finances by inserting their expenses as well as their income. They can also view their transactions in a news feed filtered according to categories (Fig. 1-a). There is a separate form for them to add their loan related information which gets added to the feed as an expense. They can also view all the information about their loans such as the remaining balance, next instalment and overdue amounts (Fig. 1-b). At the initial setup, the members are prompted to select a language, either Sinhala (a native language) or English.

4.2 Dhana Labha and Common Microfinance Workflows in Sri Lanka

Collecting Payments. The centres are required to conduct regular meetings. The appointed LO will attend these meetings to release loans and collect repayments. However, prior research has shown that there are several activities carried out by the leaders in the background to ensure timely payments from their members [20]. Visiting the members one or two days prior to the meeting date to collect payments or remind about the payments is one such crucial activity. This allows the leaders to be informed about the payments of their members well in advance which in turn helps them to take necessary actions to cover for members who are struggling to make payments [19, 20].

Dhana Labha allows the group leaders to manage their groups (Fig. 1-c, d). Since most leaders manage multiple loans from different MFIs, the application allows them to create multiple groups, multiple loans and add members. Once that is done, the leaders can connect group members with their respective groups and loans. The application generates a weekly/monthly payment chart with colour codes (Fig. 1-e). Leaders can insert their members' payment records to the application when they do home visits. The colour of each week changes depending on the payment. At the end of each week, the application generates a leaderboard for each group based on the loan repayment progress (Fig. 1-f).

Releasing a Loan. The loans are released to group members based on trust. That is, when one member obtains a loan, the others in the group become guarantors. If one member defaults on loan, all the members will be held accountable, and all further loans of the centre will be compromised. In addition, the loans are released in multiple rounds which allows the MFIs to evaluate a member's repayment capability as well as trustworthiness [4, 20]. The leaderboard as well as the scoring system integrated to it is designed to assist members to build up their credentials and showcase their trustworthiness to the MFIs (Fig. 1-f). A member can make a payment in full or as a partial payment. The application awards a single mark for full payment and a proportion of the payment as a mark for a partial payment (i.e. if instalment required is 100 rupees and the member made a 40 rupee payment, 0.4 marks will be awarded). 0 mark is given for a missed payment. Multiple borrowing is another common practice [61] supported by Dhana Labha. Members can create multiple loans and connect their profiles with those loans to manage loans obtained from multiple MFIs.

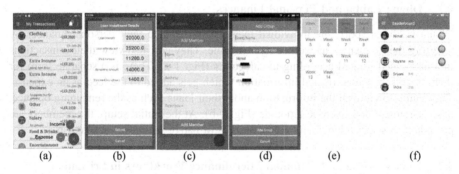

(a)   (b)   (c)   (d)   (e)   (f)

Fig. 1. (a) The transaction feed (b) The loan information sheet (c) group member adding (d) adding members to groups (e) The weekly payment chart with colour codes; full payments are indicated in green, yellow indicates partial payment and red indicate missed payments. (f) The group leaderboard with scores (Color figure online)

5   The Study

5.1   Participants

The participants were recruited in collaboration with two MFIs operating in the Gampaha district, Sri Lanka. We distributed the application to members of eight groups, comprising 38 members. All of them had access to economical smartphones. In addition, five LOs took part in our study. However, their participation was limited to individual interviews. They were not given the access to the application.

5.2 Data Collection and Analysis

A qualitative approach was followed in collecting and analysing data. Two members of the research team conducted weekly, face-to-face, semi-structured interviews with the members at the microfinance centres and interviewed the leaders at their homes. We also conducted interviews with the LOs involved at the end of the study. We used telephone interviews in cases where participants could not meet us in person. Audio recordings of the interviews were made, and whenever required, photographs were taken of the interviewees. While one member of the research team conducted the interview, the other member took notes.

All the interviews were conducted in the Sinhala language. Since one of the authors is from a different geographic location, the interview data was translated and transcribed. The transcriptions were collectively coded, and themes were derived through the thematic analysis method [7]. Audio recordings, photographs as well as transcriptions were shared among the authors and explored individually. Afterwards, a cross analysis was conducted to compare the findings. Further discussions were conducted to resolve conflicting interpretations of data.

6 Findings

6.1 General Use of Dhana Labha

The application allowed the participants (both members and leaders) to manage their personal finances by adding their incomes and expenses to the application. They were also able to oversee multiple microfinance loans. Additionally, the leaders were able to manage their groups through the application. They took the application with them when they visit their group members to collect payments or remind meeting dates and updated payment chart in their presence (Fig. 2-a). The leaderboard was only available to the leaders, and they would show it to the other members when they attend the meetings. Our interviews with the members suggested that our participants were excited about the intervention and found it useful.

Ramesh is a taxi driver who earns irregular incomes throughout the day. Here is how he explained his experience with Dhana Labha.

"Dhana Labha has made it easier for me to keep track of my transactions because my phone is always with me. I really like the charts of the application since it summarises my expenses." – Ramesh

Thilaka, who works as a domestic worker stated that she prefers to write down her income and expenses in a notebook since she did not keep her phone with her while working out of fear of damaging it. At the end of each day, she would transfer her notes to the mobile phone (Fig. 2-b).

"At the moment I get paid daily, but at the end of each month, I have to lend from my employer to cover for my loans. Dhana Labha has shown me that I spend small amounts of money each day for fast food and sweets which accumulates into a larger sum. Therefore, I have decided to ask for a weekly payment instead of a daily one. Hope that will help me save some money – Thilaka

This statement of her showed us how Dhana Labha helped her to reflect on her transactions which led her to make better financial decisions.

Overall, our participants stated that the application is engaging and useful. Yet, we saw that members gradually reduced their use of the application for entering their daily expenses. They would only enter data once in two or three days. They were mostly interested in microfinance portion of the application where they were able to see how other members progress with their loans.

We initially approached forty six members from 10 groups for the study. However, after the first week of use, two groups (eight members) opted out of the study. One group claimed that they do not trust the application and they fear that the MFI may use the application against them in some way.

"We do not want them to introduce something like this. The way it was is better. [...] In the past, we could negotiate with the leader and get a grace period." – Members of a group who opted out

It was clear that some these members thought that the application would take away their chances to negotiate with their leaders on payments. The other group opted out stating their concern over the data usage of the application.

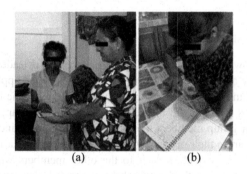

(a)   (b)

Fig. 2. (a) A group leader visiting a house of a member with the application to collect payment (b) A member adding her transactions to the application by referring to her notebook

Family Communication. Our findings also revealed that Dhana Labha had prompted the members to initiate conversations among family members regarding financial matters.

Nimal is a cook who works at a roadside hotel in the city. Additionally, he undertakes occasional catering jobs to various village functions. Both Nimal and his wife Lakmini have been obtaining loans from MFIs for the past five years. However, in addition to MFI loans, Nimal has obtained several other loans from local money lenders without Lakmini's knowledge. After we introduced the application, they have started inserting all their financial transactions, which showed Lakmini that they are in a lot more debt than she initially suspected.

"I never knew that my husband is in this much debt. I used to trouble him to start our own food stall. Now I think it is better to help him pay all these debts and then start working on a food stall" – Lakmini

Gunadasa, who runs a boutique shop with his wife wanted to get their son to join the family business. However, being a traditional Sri Lankan father, whom children always look up to as an authoritative figure, he has found it difficult to initiate such a discussion with his son.

"I always wanted to talk about financial matters with my older son. But I could not find a suitable topic. With Dhana Labha, I have something my son understands better than me. And he helps me enter all my expenses while I talk about financial matters" – Gunadasa

Both of these statements show that the application helped initiate discus around finances within the families. This is significant because typically within the Sri Lankan rural regions, the father is considered to be the breadwinner and financial matters rarely discussed with the children or wife.

Prioritizing Payments and Improving Awareness. Members also reported that the application helped them prioritize their payments. For example, our participants stated that they used to pawn their gold jewelry whenever they struggle to pay the instalments. While this helps them pay for a single loan instalment, they end up having two debts, instead of one. However, most MFIs do not add additional interest to missed payments. The application has helped Kamala to understand just that. The loan instalment details form (Fig. 1-b) of the application has shown her that she is behind her instalments and yet the instalment amount does not change weekly.

"I saw that my week's instalment for this week is 500 rupees and if I pay next week, the instalment is 1000 rupees. That is when I realised; the MFI is not charging an additional interest. But my gold loan charges a 1% interest per day. So I decided to pay the gold loan this week and pay my MFI loan next week." – Kamala

Pasisni has a practice of taking loans from one MFI to repay another MFI's loan. The charts in the application have helped Pasini to realise that she has a lot of debt and with her current income that she will never be able to repay. We also interviewed some members about the colour codes in the weekly payment chart (Fig. 1-c), and they said that they always wanted to have it green and hated to see red.

"Yes we are poor, but we are proud people. We took a loan because we knew we could pay for it. When I saw my record is marked in red, I felt ashamed." – Upendra

Seeing red in their records have made them feel as if they had done something shameful.

6.2   Trustworthiness and Credibility

MFIs employ a variety of tactics to determine the trustworthiness or the credibility of individuals. Conducting loan rounds, marking attendance are some of those tactics [20]. However, in many cases, the LOs rely heavily on group and centre leaders' words to understand the trustworthiness of members. As a result, an individual occupying a higher social standing can obtain a loan easily compared to someone from a lower social standing.

Our findings revealed that it is the people who occupy lower social standings that are more enthusiastic about the use of the application – particularly the visual elements such as leaderboards and charts. Nilupa, a domestic worker, has been using microfinance for several years and has faced difficulties in the past to make payments on time. This has painted a negative picture of her in the eyes of LOs as well as the other members.

"The whole group, as well as the villagers, looked down on me, and it is tough to get a larger loan approved since no one trusted me to pay. Wait and see; I will win the whole thing." –
Nilupa

While Nilupa has not missed any payments recently, her previous negative track record had made it very difficult for her to get a larger loan approved. The application has given her a way to show others who looked down on her that she too is a proud and credible person.

While using the application, she led the leaderboard on several occasions, and she was hopeful that she would be able to get a larger loan approved. Her group members have confirmed that over the past six months, she has not missed a single payment not only with the MFI we worked with but also with other the MFIs Nilupa interacts with. One MFI has even released a loan of 20000 rupees which was previously rejected.

"The change in her is amazing. At one point we were even not sure if we wanted to work with her. She has missed many payments before. Her group leader has specifically asked me not to release a larger loan to Nilupa. Hopefully, she will continue this" – Nilupa's LO

It was clear that leading the leaderboard has given her a taste of social recognition among her peers and this has motivated her and helped to improve her self-confidence.

We also observed the application is having a positive impact on the members' lives outside the microfinance centres. Prema, another member who was considered to be struggling to make repayments, has not just paid all her microfinance instalments but also paid the debts she had to the village boutique shop. When prompted, she clarified that initially, it was only her husband who was earning, and she took loans to support the family. The husband paid the loans. But Prema's desire to show her peers that she too is a trustworthy individual has motivated her to find a job at a local grocery.

"This whole experience has shown me what I can really do. If I could not pay the instalments, it would have been visible to everybody. I told my husband that I do not want to be laughed at anymore. I am happy that I took the initiative." – Prema

While all the excerpts above highlights how Dhana Labha helped to motivate our participants and helped them to reflect on their financial decisions, the MFIs have seen another use for the application. One LO stated that now it is easier for her to reject loan requests as the mobile application clearly show the group members' standings to the group.

"I am planning to come up with a method to determine whether to release a loan or not based on these application scores. If they do not have a good score, I can easily point it out." – An LO

And she believes that by increasing the awareness of members about the application and letting them know that this is a community driven initiative instead of something introduced by the MFIs, she would be able to make transparent decisions on loan rejections.

6.3   Missed Payments and Coercion

Members missing payments is a common issue in microfinance. To discourage this the Los withhold future loans of other members when a member of their group misses a payment. As a result, the group leaders take many precautions to make sure all their members make payments on time. A common practice is for the group leader to compensate for the member who missed a payment. But there are many occasions where they use tactics such as Public shaming [33] or the use of coercion [20] to collect payments. Interestingly, our intervention showed us that this type of technology intervention has a potential to reduce the occurrence such harmful practices.

Kumari is a centre leader who manages more than five groups. Since she is managing such a large number of people, it was difficult for her to compensate when multiple members miss payments. Therefore, she stated that she takes precautionary actions to make sure her members pay on time. Sometimes, this may even be through unethical and in some case unlawful means, such as threatening family members or even publicly humiliating members.

> *"I am not proud of it. But these MFI loans are a huge part of how we support our families. If the MFIs stop visiting, we will lose everything. I am prepared to collect the instalments by any means necessary." – Kumari*

However, Kumari said that over the past six months, she only had to use coercive tactics once. The LOs we worked with, as well as the leaders, claimed that there is an overall drop in missed payments. Even the members who were really struggling to pay would at least make a partial payment to show their commitment to the loans.

While group leaders claimed that they have not had to use coercive tactics, several members stated that the leaders are now using the colour codes of the application to influence payments.

> *"She came to our place and showed me her phone. She said that since I have red in my weekly sheet, I would not be able to take the next loan. She said that she had not shown it the LO yet, but if I did not pay up, she would do it." – Rangika (a member from Kumari's group)*

When a member misses a payment, instead of public shaming, this leader has threatened to show the application to the MFIs and stop them from releasing the next loan.

6.4   Social Negotiations Around the Application

Even though initially, one group opted out from the study stating concerns that application prevents them from negotiating with the leader, we realised that several members have come to an understanding with their leaders to mark the payments even though the payment is not made. They would pay it at a later day of the month, and the leader will cover for them while charging an additional interest. While the leaders may not accept such a negotiation with all the members, they were happy to do so for a trustworthy person.

> *"You see, earlier, when we ask leaders to cover for us, they would always say many things claiming that we have missed the payments regularly. Now the application shows that we have not, which make it easier to ask for a loan from the leader." – Wasana's group members*

These members have figured out that they can use Dhana Labha to negotiate with their leaders as well as LOs in a more meaningful way while justifying their claims.

Dileka is a centre leader who believes that members should take responsibility for their own loans and she should not have to visit them frequently to collect payments.

> *"I know the other leaders are doing many immoral things to collect payments. I simply do not want to stoop to that level. If they do not pay, I will try my best to cover for this loan cycle. But after that, I will not work with them." – Dileka*

However, because of her attitudes towards the role of a group leader, she has struggled to collect payments from group members in the past. As a result, some MFIs have even stopped visiting her centre claiming that she is not taking responsibility for her members. The application has given Dileka an alternative tactic of which she feels comfortable using.

> *"It was common for my members to make a partial payment to me and bring the balance on the meeting date. Now, they see their week slots become yellow when they make partial payments, and almost immediately they agree to pay in full so that it would become green." – Dileka*

She has realised that her members are very conscious of the colour scheme and they always wanted to have it in green. This has made her life as a centre leader easier since she does not have to visit the members to collect payments as frequently.

6.5 New Practices Influenced by the Application

Our interventions revealed that users had built additional practices around the functionalities of the application. Creating a handwritten leaderboard and introducing tangible badges are examples.

Fig. 3. Nadee describing her handwritten leaderboard

Fig. 4. Nilanthi proudly wearing the two badges and showing us her weekly payment chart

Handwritten Leaderboard. Priyanwada is a centre leader who has been interacting with MFIs for the past ten years. She found that her members are now showing an eagerness which was not there before.

"Earlier, they would just visit the centre, make the payments and leave. But now I see many of them talk about their loans and their financial situations with each other. I think the leaderboard and the charts of the application plays a major role in this because it helps to visualise their finances." – Priyanwada

Nadee is a centre leader who runs a children's nursery. Currently, she leads two groups. Nadee has seen that while all of her members seem eager about the application and the charts, only four of her members were actively using the application. The members were more interested in seeing the leaderboard (which was available only in the leader's phone) than to see their own finances. Therefore, Nadee decided to create a physical leaderboard at her centre (Fig. 3). After each meeting, she would update the board in front of all the members.

She especially found that her members are engaging in discussions over the leaderboard where they kept asking how the winner is selected as well as how the score is calculated. Following is an except where she explained this change.

"It is amazing how it all worked out. As you know, most of our members are not educated, and they did not really care to learn about the interest rates. Initially, I tried teaching them but gave up very soon because none of them showed any interest. But now all of a sudden, they want to know the calculations behind the leaderboard." – Nadee

Creating Identity Through Badges. Inspired by the leaderboard and the members' eagerness towards it, one MFI has introduced a badge system to their members. These were plastic badges given to the overall best member of the group (best member badge) and to the members who made the full instalment payments for three consecutive weeks (loan leader badge) (Fig. 4).

"The lives of our clients' are a bit simple. But this has created a sort of competition among them. Something they have not experienced before" – LO

It was clear that the game like experience and the opportunity to compete with each other have given a refreshing change to the monotonous lives of these members which in turn motivated them to manage their finances better.

Nilanthi is a boutique shop owner who has been interacting with multiple MFIs for the past three years. She has been awarded both the badges.

"We have not experienced such a thing in a long time. We had these when we were schooling. I remember our teacher gave us stars when we were small. I think this has a similar effect. I feel proud of myself for being able to have been awarded the two badges." – Nilanthi

The members went on saying;

"Now we do not have to look at leaders' phone all the time. We know who is performing best in our group" – Senani

These practices have allowed them to build an identity for themselves as a credible person within their community and the badges allow them to have a sense of achievement. Evidently these members have accepted it as an opportunity where they can elevate their social status within the community.

The LO confirmed that they are planning to introduce the handwritten leaderboard as well as the badge system to rest of their MFI centres as this seems to motivate the members to become better re-payers.

7 Discussion

The following sections further elaborate our findings by exploring them through a postcolonial lens. We also discuss our opinions on sustained use of technology over a period of six months and share our design insights on the use of technology in a constrained setting.

7.1 Lessons Learned from a Postcolonial Perspective

As mentioned earlier, the term postcolonialism in HCI refers to the methods that aim to engage and empower marginalized communities. This section elaborates on how certain aspects of postcoloniality came into play in different stages of this research.

Participation and Power Differences. We experienced that our participant responses are too polite and respectful. They often hesitated to give any negative feedback regarding the application or their experiences participating in the study. There were many occasions where we had to revisit a participant to obtain further clarifications. They would often address us as 'Sir' or 'Mahaththaya' (Sinhalese to sir). Instead of talking freely, they would always stand up and answer. Some participants were keenly interested in getting to use new technology or interact with devices. As a result, they kept on providing complements instead of sharing their genuine experiences. Therefore, treating these compliments with this context in mind is critical when researching with a similar community. In cases where the researcher is from a developed country, it is advisable to employ a local researcher or a representative who understands the innate practices, beliefs as well as the hierarchies.

Communication. Communicating without ambiguity is another focal point in postcolonial computing research [29]. Even though one author was a local researcher who were familiar with local customs, this was one of the main challenges we encountered. Particularly when discussing the participants' innate financial experiences.

One reason for reluctance could mainly be due to the sensitive nature of the topic; 'Personal Finances', which is considered an impolite subject to discuss with strangers. Another reason for their reluctance could have been the social class difference, as we were perceived as educated urban dwellers who had intruded into their rural community. Later they confided that they feared that we would collect their stories and publicize them, which would reflect negatively on their social lives. Even though we explained that the informed consent collection process and ethics committee guidelines prevented us from disclosing any of their personal information, the participants were not convinced and continued to show their distrust. Approaching the same participant through different members of the community whom they trust was a tactic we used to earn their trust. Sharing our personal experiences and discuss matters beyond personal finances such as their previous work experiences and various stories of the past were some of the frequent topics of discussions. Consequently, we had to spend several days outside the period of study conduct getting to know the participants and visiting their homes to build a strong relationship. While one may view this as a waste of time, this helped us to develop a greater understanding of their everyday lives as well as develop a holistic image of how they operate within the community.

7.2 Sustained Use of Technology by Promoting Actions Beyond the Status Quo

This study showed that there is a potential to motivate the sustained use of technology by promoting actions beyond their current state of affairs. We realized that Dhana Labha have promoted new practices around the application outside of its intended use.

Community and Family Connectedness. Dhana Labha was never intended to be used as a communication tool. For example, it did not have social elements such as messaging or connecting members together since the aim of the application was to support personal finance and microfinance workflows. Nonetheless, we observed that our application contributed towards initiating discussions around finances at various levels.

Typically, a microfinance centre is formed as a focal point of loan collection [4]. The members would obtain loans from multiple MFIs which conduct meetings on the same date [61]. As a result, a member would usually visit a centre to mark their attendance and immediately would leave the centre so that they can attend the next MFI's meeting. However, with the introduction of scores and leaderboard, participants got inspired to know more about how the scores were calculated. We speculate that this is mainly to know how they can outperform the other group members. Once they understood that they lose marks when they miss a payment or make a partial payment, they would then talk to other members to learn how they were able to make payments. This has inadvertently prompted them to discuss their financial affairs with other members as well as LOs. Nadee has understood the value of this and has taken the initiative to create a handwritten leaderboard at her centre. She now realises that her members are engaging more with fellow members as well as the LOs over their financial practices.

As mentioned earlier, the Sri Lankan society is traditionally patriarchal where males are seen as the breadwinners of the family. As a result, most husbands would not usually discuss the financial affairs with their wives. In addition, finances are considered an adult-related affair and the involvement of children is limited. While there are cases where children are expected to earn money by performing light chores in the village, most parents prefer to keep their children away from everyday activities associated with loans and repayments. We believe that this is mainly out of fear of losing their socially and culturally accepted position of "breadwinner" within the family. In this study, Dhana Labha has provided opportunities for the males to initiate discussions with their families. In Gunadasa's case, he was able to get his son involved as he was struggling to enter his transactions to the mobile application. Nimal was able to finally share his actual financial standings with his wife so that she would help him pay the additional loans he took from money lenders.

Social Empowerment and Recognition. While we observed that some of the participants were eager to use Dhana Labha for its intended use (managing finances, collecting loans, etc.), it is the simple value-added features such as the leaderboard and instalment payment chart that captivated their interest. Even though the caste system does not have a prominent presence in the Sri Lankan community, the social status or class play a significant role. For example, a village baker or an astrologer are considered to be occupying a higher social class whereas the domestic workers or labourers are considered from a lower social class. Even the MFIs take into account these social standings when deciding on releasing loans as well as choosing group/centre leaders [20]. As a result, it is challenging for a person from a lower social class to obtain a larger loan, not to mention becoming a leader. The leaderboard has given those individuals occupying lower social classes a form of recognition as well as a means to gain respect from their peers, which has motivated them to continue without missing payments. We realise that these members place a significantly high value on such recognition. Nilupa's and Prema's experiences provide excellent examples of this. In Prema's case, she not only paid off all her debt to other money lenders but also went on and found a job so that she can maintain her successful practices. The group members, as well as the LOs, have confirmed the fact that these members carry themselves more confidently within the centres. It also speaks volumes of the impact Dhana Labha had on empowering them.

Reducing Harmful Practices. Members missing payments or defaulting loans is one of the main issues the MFIs need to be aware of, particularly since MFIs release loans without obtaining any collateral. It is not only damaging to the MFI, it has an adverse effect on the members as well as the community. For example, members who miss several payments tend to take additional loans from individual lenders that ultimately leads to more debt [13, 33]. The remaining group members will also have their future loans rejected which may cause community unrest among the group members. Therefore to mitigate missed payments, the MFIs follow a set of proven practices such as conducting loan rounds and taking attendance [10, 72], which allows them to monitor the loan payment patterns of individuals.

However, we identified that the notion of winning something over the other members had triggered a chain reaction which ultimately reduced the number of missed payments. Another such tactic of MFIs to reduce missed payments is to only accept influential people within the community as centre leaders [20]. The rationale behind this is that a leader who is socially respected and influential would take actions to influence the members to make payments. Sometime, the MFIs may completely discontinue the centre. Hence, the leaders usually make sure that their members pay on time and in cases where they are unable to pay, the leaders themselves will cover their payments. However, they could only cover for a member for a limited number of times. On instances where members would continue to miss payments, some leaders resorted to using violent actions such as verbally and physically threatening the families and forcefully collecting payments. Through our explorations, we observed that our intervention had a positive influence on such harmful practices. Several leaders have mentioned that now there is an intrinsic motivation among the members who previously were notorious for missing payments since they wanted to win over the others. In addition, even in difficult cases, the weekly instalment payment chart was enough to influence members to make full payments. While one can argue this to be a different form of coercive tactic, it is harmless compared to the previously utilised methods such as physical/verbal abuse and public shaming (e.g. [13, 20, 33]).

We believe that the continued use of Dhana Labha was due to the collective outcomes described above which mainly extended the functionalities of Dhana Labha beyond the confines of single use while promoting actions outside the status quo.

7.3 Design Implications for Future Work

Complimenting the prior work on socio-cultural practices and their influence on the microfinance workflows (e.g. [1, 15, 20, 51]), our work demonstrated just how those practices are attuned to the lives of our participants. However, this habituation led us to critically question the focus on existing technology introductions for the microfinance sector, which has mainly aimed at supporting MFIs and its related organisational and transactional practices (e.g. [57, 65, 71]). Instead, we discuss implications where the focus would be to support community engagement and connect these underbanked communities together.

Gamification in a Constrained Setting. The participant's use of Dhana Labha prompted us to wonder that there may be a potential for a social network that incorporates gamified elements. The participants' eagerness towards the leaderboard and physical badges shown a great potential to motivate users make timely payments and improved group participation. And since this is a practices proven to be successful in few other contexts in similar environments, particularly in encouraging participation (e.g. [18, 47]), it would be interesting to study how these communities would react to a full gamified experience with leaderboards, badges through the application, awards, and discussion boards. By expanding the use of application beyond the confines of single usage, we may able to inspire improved social networking. Understanding how such enhanced social experiences through technology impacts on the participants day to day lives could be an interesting research avenue. At the current state, the members can only see their own transactions, and only the leaders could see the loan progress of the other members. Instead, in our next iteration, we plan to share the leaderboard with all our participants so that they could see their standings.

How these plans could be implemented is another interesting question given the various constraints we have to operate in. On the one hand, the use of such an application may have a financial cost for the users because any social communication has to be done through a data network. Though we are aware that mobile data cost is minuscule in Sri Lanka (e.g. [25, 50]), changing the perception of these people towards the use of mobile internet could be challenging. This was evident for us when one group opted out claiming that they fear the application will "eat up" their data allocations. On the other hand, we do not believe our participants are familiar with such social elements and sophisticated features. The economical smartphones they use may not be adequality powerful to handle those features either.

We believe that most of these constraints can be overcome simply by conducting a few training workshops with the participants. For example, we could improve their awareness of data charges and the economical data packages offered by internet service providers. Therefore, if they were made aware of these and taught how to activate these packages, we believe that they could be motivated to use Dhana Labha for social networking.

Visibility Through Situated Displays. Another potential line of work is exploring the use of situated displays. What impact would Dhana Labha have if it could communicate through a situated display at the microfinance centre to a broader audience? This suggestion is inspired by Nadee's handwritten leaderboard and how it prompted the members to compete with each other as well as initiate discussions. All members of the centre could be automatically connected and synchronised to the display when they arrive at the centre. It would be interesting to investigate how to scale this up and understand the impact of such an intervention at a larger scale. There could be multiple centres within a single community because a centre would consist of around 25-30 members. This means that a single MFI may operate in multiple centres within the same community. Therefore, if the MFIs could derive information from these displays, it may also allow them to maintain a decentralised database of their centres and members. Since our findings suggested that our participants were eager to win over their peers and showcase their credibility, initiating a centre-wise competition and examine how that impacts social and community relationships could be of interest.

As a Learning Tool. It would also be interesting to see how Dhana Labha could be used as a learning tool to provide much needed financial literacy to the underbanked. For instance, Nadee stated that most of her members are unaware of interest rates or uninterested in learning about them. As a result, most of them are unaware that they are actually agreeing to pay a significantly larger interest rate to MFIs than what formal banking institutions are charging [55]. Despite many attempts by Nadee to teach her members about these financial aspects, she had failed to do so due to lack of interest from her members. Instances such as Gunadasa's experience of getting his son involved in a discussion on family finances, Dhana Labha helping Thilaka to reflect on her transactions and Kamala prioritizing her payments led us to question whether there is a potential to use the same application to improve the financial literacy of these families. Helping these communities improve their financial literacy and awareness can help them better manage their personal finances which in turn may have a positive impact on their overall financial situation.

8 Conclusion

In this paper, we have presented a six-month-long exploratory study aimed at understanding the effects of introducing a financial management application to the underbanked rural community in Sri Lanka. Through our findings, we reveal that our application impacted on several levels of our participants and their families' lives. Notably, we saw that our participants used it to showcase their credibility and to socially negotiate as well as to foster new practices. We also identified that our intervention had a positive impact on some of the critical aspects of microfinance such as members missing multiple payments which accumulate into a more substantial debt as well as the use of coercion in collecting payments. Moreover, the application helped to improve our participant's awareness of their financial status. Consequently, we realised that even though the functionalities of the application mainly supported microfinance workflows and managed personal finance, the participants' existing socio-cultural practices strongly influenced and shaped the use of technology.

The insights derived from this research highlight that the current practices of participants are habituated to their lives in such a way, that they look for ways to seamlessly merge technologically driven solutions with their practices. These findings led us to question the technology centred visions for designing within the ICTD domain. Realising the importance of understanding the microfinance community and its inherent sociocultural practices, this study provides design insights for future technology designers who aim at introducing technological aids to the underbanked community. We suggest that researchers should explore ways to promote additional actions beyond the current state of affairs through technology since those were the aspects proved to be having a broader impact and promoted sustained use of technology over a longer period which is critical in new technology interventions.

References

1. Adeel, M., Nett, B., Gurbanova, T., Wulf, V., Randall, D.: The challenges of microfinance innovation: understanding 'private services'. In: Bertelsen, O., Ciolfi, L., Grasso, M., Papadopoulos, G. (eds.) ECSCW 2013, pp. 269–286. Springer, London (2013). https://doi.org/10.1007/978-1-4471-5346-7_14
2. Ahmed, S.I., Mim, N.J., Jackson, S.J.: Residual mobilities: infrastructural displacement and post-colonial computing in Bangladesh. In: Proceedings of the 33rd Annual ACM Conference on Human Factors in Computing Systems, pp. 437–446 (2015)
3. Alawattage, C., Graham, C., Wickramasinghe, D.: Microaccountability and biopolitics: microfinance in a Sri Lankan village. Account. Organ. Soc. 72, 1–23 (2018)
4. Atapattu, A.: State of microfinance in Sri Lanka. In: State of Microfinance in SAARC Countries, Colombo (2009)
5. Barman, D., Mathur, H.P., Kalra, V.: Role of microfinance interventions in financial inclusion: a comparative study of microfinance models. Vis.: J. Bus. Perspect. 13(3), 51–59 (2009)
6. Barton, S., del Busto, C., Rodriquez, C., Liu, A.: Client-focused MFI technologies case study (microREPORT #77), Washington (2007)
7. Braun, V., Clarke, V.: Using thematic analysis in psychology. Qual. Res. Psychol. 3, 77–101 (2006)
8. Brook, R.M., Hillyer, K.J., Bhuvaneshwari, G.: Microfinance for community development, poverty alleviation and natural resource management in peri-urban Hubli-Dharwad, India. Environ. Urban. 20(1), 149–163 (2008)
9. Casinader, R.A., Fernando, S., Gamage, K.: Women's issues and men's roles: Sri Lankan village experience. In: Momse, J.H. (ed.) Geography of Gender in the Third World, pp. 309–322. State University of New York Press, Albany (1987)
10. Dean, K., Valdivia, M.: Teaching entrepreneurship: Impact of business training on microfinance clients and institutions. Rev. Econ. Stat. 93(2), 510–527 (2011)
11. Demirguc-Kunt, A., Klapper, L., Singer, D., Van Oudheusden, P.: The global findex database 2014: measuring financial inclusion around the world (2015)

12. Diniz, E.H., Pozzebon, M., Jayo, M.: The role of ICT in improving microcredit: the case of correspondent banking in Brazil. Cahier du GReSI **08**, 03 (2008)

13. Fernando, J.L.: Microfinance: Perils and Prospects. Routledge (2006)

14. Friedmann, J.: Empowerment: the Politics of Alternative Development (1992)

15. Ghosh, I., Chen, J., Ming, J., Abouzied, A.: The persistence of paper: a case study in microfinance from Ghana. In: Proceedings of the Seventh International Conference on Information and Communication Technologies and Development, p. 13 (2015)

16. Goodman, R.: Borrowing money, exchanging relationships: making microfinance fit into local lives in Kumaon, India. World Dev. **93**, 362–373 (2017)

17. Halloluwa, T., Vyas, D., Usoof, H., Bandara, P., Brereton, M., Hewagamage, P.: Designing for financial literacy: co-design with children in rural Sri Lanka. In: Bernhaupt, R., Dalvi, G., Joshi, A., Balkrishan, D.K., O'Neill, J., Winckler, M. (eds.) INTERACT 2017. LNCS, vol. 10513, pp. 313–334. Springer, Cham (2017). https://doi.org/10.1007/978-3-319-67744-6_21

18. Halloluwa, T., Vyas, D., Usoof, H., Hewagamage, K.P.: Gamification for development: a case of collaborative learning in Sri Lankan primary schools. Pers. Ubiquitous Comput. **22** (2), 391–407 (2017)

19. Halloluwa, T., Bandara, P., Usoof, H., Vyas, D.: Value for money: co-designing with underbanked women from rural Sri Lanka. In: Proceedings of the 30th Australian Conference on Computer-Human Interaction, OZCHI 2018, pp. 1–12 (2018)

20. Halloluwa, T., Usoof, H., Vyas, D.: Sociocultural practices that make microfinance work: a case study from Sri Lanka. In: Proceedings of the ACM: Human-Computer Interaction, pp. 1–21 (2018)

21. Herath, H.M.A.: Place of women in Sri Lankan society: measures for their empowerment for development and good governance. Vidyodaya J. Manag. **01**(1), 1–14 (2015)

22. Herath, H.M.W.A., Guneratne, L.H.P., Sanderatne, N.: Impact of microfinance on women's empowerment: a case study on two microfinance institutions in Sri Lanka. Sri Lanka J. Soc. Sci. **38**(1), 51–61 (2015)

23. Holvoet, N.: Impact of microfinance programs on children's education. ESR Rev. **6**(2), 27 (2004)

24. Hutchinson, H., Bederson, B.B., Druin, A., et al.: Technology probes: inspiring design for and with families. In: Proceedings of the SIGCHI Conference on Human Factors in Computing Systems (CHI 2003), vol. 5, pp. 17–24 (2003)

25. Hutchison: Hutchison Telecommunications Sri Lanka—the best 3G Internet provider Pack Comparison (2018). https://www.hutch.lk/pack-compare/. Accessed 19 Dec 2018

26. International Labour Office: Small change, big changes: women and microfinance, Geneva (2008). http://www.ilo.org/wcmsp5/groups/public/@dgreports/@gender/documents/meeting document/wcms_091581.pdf. Accessed 4 June 2018

27. Investopedia: Underbanked. Investopedia (2017). http://www.investopedia.com/terms/u/ underbanked.asp. Accessed 4 Sept 2017

28. Investopedia: Unbanked. Investopedia (2017). http://www.investopedia.com/terms/u/ unbanked.asp. Accessed 4 Sept 2017

29. Irani, L., Vertesi, J., Dourish, P., Philip, K., Grinter, R.E.: Postcolonial computing: a lens on design and development. In: Proceedings of the 2010 CHI Conference on Human Factors in Computing Systems (2010)

30. Ghosh, S., Seshagiri, S., Ponnada, A.: Exploring regional user experience for designing ultra low cost smart phones. In: CHI Extended Abstracts on Human Factors in Computing Systems, pp. 768–776 (2016)

31. Kabeer, N., Sulaiman, M.: Assessing the impact of social mobilization: Nijera Kori and the construction of collective capabilities in rural Bangladesh. J. Hum. Dev. Capab. **16**(1), 47–68 (2015)

32. Kam, M., Mathur, A., Kumar, A., Canny, J.: Designing digital games for rural children: a study of traditional village games in India. In: Proceedings of the SIGCHI Conference on Human Factors in Computing Systems, CHI 2009, pp. 31–40 (2009)
33. Karim, L.: Microfinance and Its Discontents: Women in Debt in Bangladesh. University of Minnesota Press (2011)
34. Kaye, J., Vertesi, J., Ferreira, J., Brown, B., Perry, M.: #CHIMoney: financial interactions, digital cash, capital exchange and mobile money. In: Proceedings of the Extended Abstracts of the 32nd Annual ACM Conference on Human Factors in Computing Systems - CHI EA 2014, pp. 111–114 (2014)
35. Kaye, J.J., McCuistion, M., Gulotta, R., Shamma, D.A.: Money talks: tracking personal finances. In: Proceedings of the 32nd Annual ACM Conference on Human Factors in Computing Systems – CHI 2014, pp. 521–530 (2014)
36. Khandker, S.R.: Microfinance and poverty: evidence using panel data from Bangladesh. World Bank Econ. Rev. 19(2), 263–286 (2005)
37. Kolko, B.E., et al.: Adapting collaborative radiological practice to low-resource environments. In: Proceedings of the ACM 2012 Conference on Computer Supported Cooperative Work, pp. 97–106 (2012)
38. Kongovi, V., Sinha, S.: Microfinance sector in Sri Lanka: opportunities and growth strategies (2014)
39. Kumar, D., Martin, D., O'Neill, J.: The times they are a-changin'. In: Proceedings of the 2011 Annual Conference on Human Factors in Computing Systems – CHI 2011, p. 1413 (2011)
40. Sri Lanka: Computer Literacy Statistics - 2014 Department of Census and Statistics (2014)
41. Larson, M., Rajput, N., Singh, A., Srivastava, S.: I want to be Sachin Tendulkar!: a spoken English Cricket game for rural students. In: Proceedings of the 2013 Conference on Computer Supported Cooperative Work, pp. 1353–1364 (2013)
42. Ledgerwood, V., White, V.: Transforming Microfinance Institutions: Providing Full Financial Services to the Poor. World Bank Publications, Washington, DC (2006)
43. Louis, P., Seret, A., Baesens, B.: Financial efficiency and social impact of microfinance institutions using self-organizing maps. World Dev. 46, 197–210 (2013)
44. Marsden, G.: Designing technology for the developing world. Interactions 13(2), 39–59 (2006)
45. Mohummed Shofi Mazumder and Wencong Lu: What impact does microfinance have on rural livelihood? A comparison of governmental and non-governmental microfinance programs in Bangladesh. World Dev. 68, 336–354 (2015)
46. Medhi-Thies, I., Ferreira, P., Gupta, N., O'Neill, J., Cutrell, E.: KrishiPustak: a social networking system for low- literate farmers. In: Proceedings of the 18th ACM Conference on Computer Supported Cooperative Work & Social Computing, pp. 1670–1681 (2015)
47. Medhi, I., Gautama, S.N., Toyama, K.: A comparison of mobile money-transfer UIs for non-literate and semi-literate users. In: Proceedings of the 27th International Conference on Human Factors in Computing Systems, pp. 1741–1750 (2009)
48. Woldmariam, M.F., Ghinea, G., Atnafu, S., Groenli, T.M.: Monetary practices of traditional rural communities in Ethiopia: implications for new financial technology design. Hum.-Comput. Interact. 0024, 1–45 (2016)
49. Mobitel: Plans and Rates – Prepaid—Mobitel (2018). http://www.mobitel.lk/broadband/plans-and-rates-prepaid. Accessed 19 Dec 2018
50. O'Neill, J., Dhareshwar, A., Muralidhar, S.H.: Working digital money into a cash economy: the collaborative work of loan payment. Comput. Support. Coop. Work. (CSCW) 26, 4–6 (2017)

51. Parikh, T.S., Javid, P., Ghosh, K., Toyama, K.: Mobile phones and paper documents: evaluating a new approach for capturing microfinance data in rural India. In: Proceedings of the 2006 CHI Conference on Human Factors in Computing Systems, pp. 551–560 (2006)

52. Plogmann, S., Adeel, M., Nett, B., Wulf, V.: The role of social capital and cooperation infrastructures within microfinance. In: Lewkowicz, M., Hassanaly, P., Wulf, V., Rohde, M. (eds.) Proceedings of COOP 2010, pp. 223–243. Springer, London (2010). https://doi.org/10.1007/978-1-84996-211-7_13

53. Rooyen, C., Stewart, R., de Wet, T.: The impact of microfinance in sub-saharan Africa: a systematic review of the evidence. World Dev. 40(11), 2249–2262 (2012)

54. Rosenberg, R., Gaul, S., Ford, W., Tomilova, O.: Microcredit interest rates and their determinants: 2004–2011. In: Köhn, D. (ed.) Microfinance 3.0, pp. 69–104. Springer, Heidelberg (2013). https://doi.org/10.1007/978-3-642-41704-7_4

55. Sambasivan, N., Weber, J., Cutrell, E.: Designing a phone broadcasting system for urban sex workers in India. In: Proceedings of the 2011 CHI Conference on Human Factors in Computing Systems, pp. 267–276 (2011)

56. Singh, V., Padhi, P.: Information and communication technology in microfinance sector: case study of three Indian MFIs. IIM Kozhikode Soc. Manag. Rev. 4(2), 106–123 (2015)

57. Snow, S., Vyas, D., Brereton, M.: Sharing, saving, and living well on less: supporting social connectedness to mitigate financial hardship. Int. J. Hum.-Comput. Interact. 33(5), 345–356 (2017)

58. Srinivasan, M.: Getting sucked into a quicksand of debt. dailymirror. fhttp://www.dailymirror.lk/article/Getting-sucked-into-a-quicksand-of-debt-133083.html. Accessed 1 Nov 2017

59. Swain, R.B., Wallentin, F.Y.: Does microfinance empower women? Evidence from self-help groups in India. Int. Rev. Appl. Econ. 23(5), 541–556 (2009)

60. Tilakaratna, G., Hulme, D.: Microfinance and multiple borrowing in Sri Lanka: another microcredit bubble in South Asia? South Asia Econ. J. 16(1), 46–63 (2015)

61. Velasco, C., Marconi, R.: Group dynamics, gender and microfinance in Bolivia. J. Int. Dev. 16(3), 519–528 (2004)

62. Vines, J., Blythe, M., Dunphy, P., Monk, A.: Eighty something: banking for the older old. In: Proceedings of the 25th BCS Conference on Human-Computer Interaction, pp. 64–73 (2011)

63. Vines, J., Dunphy, P., Monk, A.: Pay or delay: the role of technology when managing a low income. In: Proceedings of the SIGCHI Conference on Human Factors in Computing Systems, pp. 501–510 (2014)

64. Vong, J., Song, I.: Mobility technology solutions can reduce interest rates of microfinance loans. In: Vong, J., Song, I. (eds.) Emerging Technologies for Emerging Markets Topics in Intelligent Engineering and Informatics, vol. 11, pp. 11–24. Springer, Singapore (2015). https://doi.org/10.1007/978-981-287-347-7_2

65. Vyas, D., Snow, S., Brereton, M., Dulleck, U., Boyen, X.: Being thrifty on a $100K wage: austerity in family finances. In: Proceedings of the ACM Conference on Computer Supported Cooperative Work, CSCW 2015, pp. 167–170 (2015)

66. Vyas, D., Snow, S., Roe, P., Brereton, M.: Social organization of household finance: understanding artful financial systems in the home. In: Proceedings of the 19th ACM Conference on Computer-Supported Cooperative Work & Social Computing, pp. 1777–1789 (2016)

67. Wyche, S.P., Lampe, C., Rangaswamy, N., Peters, A., Monroy-Hernández, A., Antin, J.: Facebook in the developing world: the myths and realities underlying a socially networked world. In: CSCW Companion 2014: Proceedings of the Companion Publication of the 17th ACM Conference on Computer Supported Cooperative Work & Social Computing, pp. 121–124 (2014)

68. Yang, P.-J., Ding, X.: Today's life style and yesterday's life experiences: a study of financial practices of retirees in China. In: Companion: Proceedings of the 19th ACM Conference on Computer Supported Cooperative Work and Social Computing Companion, CSCW 2016, pp. 441–444 (2016)

69. Sultana, H., Jamal, M.A.: Impact of microfinance on women empowerment through poverty alleviation: an assessment of socio- economic conditions in Chennai City of Tamil Nadu. Asian J. Poverty Stud. 3(2), 175 183 (2017)

70. Yeow, A., Chuen, D.L.K., Tan, R., Chia, M.: Indonesian Microfinance Institutions (MFI) Move to Technology – TBOP's Prodigy Experience. Elsevier Inc. (2018)

71. Yunus, M.: Banker to the Poor: The Story of the Grameen Bank. Aurum Press LTD, London (2003)

72. Zamora, J.: Mobile as a means to electrification in Uganda. In: Proceedings of the First African Conference on Human Computer Interaction – AfriCHI 2016, pp. 187–191 (2016)

73. Zhang, Q., Posso, A.: Microfinance and gender inequality: cross-country evidence. Appl. Econ. Lett. 24(20), 1494–1498 (2017)

74. Zimmerman, J., et al.: Teens, parents, and financial literacy. In: Proceedings of the Designing Interactive Systems Conference, pp. 312–322 (2016)

Fostering Interaction Between Locals and Visitors by Designing a Community-Based Tourism Platform on a Touristic Island

Mara Dionisio[1,2(✉)], Cláudia Silva[2], and Valentina Nisi[2,3]

[1] FCT/NOVA, Campus da Caparica, Lisbon, Portugal
msgdionisio@gmail.com
[2] ITI/LARSYS, Madeira-ITI, Campus da Penteada, Funchal, Portugal
silvaclaudia01@gmail.com, valentina.nisi@gmail.com
[3] Universidade da Madeira, Campus da Penteada, Funchal, Portugal

Abstract. More people are traveling than ever before. This intense and disproportionate growth in tourism may, however, generate negative environmental and social effects, especially on islands. In order to address this issue, this article presents the design and evaluation of Há-Vita, an interactive web platform, whose goal is to foster awareness of local nature and folk knowledge and create connections between locals and visitors. We explored these design goals through different research methods, such as user studies with tourists in hotel lobbies, as well as focus groups consisting of two different groups of local residents and a group of visitors. Theoretically, Há-Vita is grounded in the concept of "community-based tourism ventures," which is concerned with environmental preservation via ecotourism practices and, at the same time, the empowerment of local communities. Furthermore, the design rationale of the platform is also inspired by the authenticity theory, which examines tourists' pursuit of meaningful interactions with locals. Our results indicate that, despite time constraints (for visitors), locals and visitors were willing to interact with each other as they acknowledged authentic benefits in such interaction. Furthermore, our focus groups with locals have shown the potential to stimulate different levels of local empowerment based on the community-based tourism framework in the design iterations of Há-Vita.

Keywords: Community empowerment · Tourism ·
Nature and culture preservation · Design · HCI · Tourism sustainability

1 Introduction

Tourism is now an activity within the reach of millions, and this has enabled the travel and hosting industry to flourish globally. In particular, islands are special places with a natural attraction for tourists, due to their unique environmental and cultural attributes. On many islands, tourism is usually the answer to socio-economic constraints, contributing as the prime source of economic welfare and job creation for the locals who inhabit these isolated regions [1]. Intense and disproportionate tourism growth may, however, generate damaging environmental and social effects. Tourism pressures can

© IFIP International Federation for Information Processing 2019
Published by Springer Nature Switzerland AG 2019
D. Lamas et al. (Eds.): INTERACT 2019, LNCS 11747, pp. 768–787, 2019.
https://doi.org/10.1007/978-3-030-29384-0_46

endanger endemic species as well as generate friction in the local community as visitors may adopt behaviors that go against the island culture or traditional values [2, 3]. This friction may lead locals to dislike tourism and to develop coping mechanisms to avoid contact with visitors [3, 4], generating unexpected consequences in the long run. It is crucial that the growth of the travel and tourism sectors continues with the investment and development taking place in an open and sustainable manner, motivating the empowerment of local communities and protection of cultural habitats [5–7].

As seen in the work of Dourish and Foth et al. [4, 8], issues relating to nature or the environment have been the focus of several studies in HCI research. Those studies have looked at how information and communication technologies (ICTs) may foster environmental sustainability, behavioral change, and social benefit. The potential and effectiveness of HCI interventions in eco-friendly practices require inquiry into the contexts in which those practices arise. In HCI research, environmental and ecological concerns are typically framed as a psychological problem of "bad habits," where the solution is to motivate and inform people to act pro-environmentally [9]. However, environmental and ecological concerns go beyond personal or individual responsibility, as they also have a political dimension that must be considered before eventually becoming part of any effective solution in HCI interventions. The contradictory dual reality of islands, which heavily rely on tourism revenues but also struggle with the damaging effects of it, provides a perfect example of what Dourish calls the HCI discourse that "obscures political and cultural contexts of environmental practice, which on the other hand must be considered as part of an effective solution" [8].

Concerned with the interaction between locals and visitors towards environmental and cultural preservation, this work uses as an example of analysis the Archipelago of Madeira, an established tourist destination and home to the Laurisilva forest (UNESCO World Heritage site since 1999). In 2013, tourism accounted for 24% of GDP and 15% of employment in the region [10].

This context led to the design of Há-Vita, an interactive web platform based on the concept of "community-based tourism ventures" [5] which is defined as initiatives that aim to care for the environment (ecotourism) as well as ensuring the empowerment of local communities. Through the fostering of interactions (online and offline) between visitors and locals, the goal of the platform is to raise awareness of local values, the natural heritage, folk knowledge and traditions. Our main contributions for the Interact community are: (i) the description of the design and rationale of the Há-Vita web platform, (ii) the discussion regarding the benefits of such platforms for locals and tourists, as we conducted studies with both groups, and iii) the discussion of the user feedback regarding the Há-Vita prototypes and preliminary considerations for the future design iterations.

Over the next two sections, we describe the conceptual framework and related work that supported the motivation and design of the platform. Then, in Sect. 4, the design of the platform following a design research approach [11], is reported. In Sect. 5, we delve into the findings of several studies, followed by a discussion of the findings against the empowerment framework and laying out preliminary reflections for future designers of platforms with similar goals to Há-Vita.

2   Conceptual Framework

In order to address the two different target groups in our study, locals and visitors, the design rationale of Há-Vita draws on the combination of two different, but complementary, conceptual approaches to tourism. First, "Community-Based Tourism" (CBT) [5, 12–15], in which locals are the primary beneficiaries of the tourism. Second, the "authentic" experience [16], a tourism trend that aims to provide unique and local experiences to tourists. Next, we will explain how, and why, these concepts serve as the basis of Há-Vita.

2.1   Community-Based Tourism and Four Levels of Empowerment

CBT looks at how local communities can exert control over the activities taking place in their environment based on past studies of how community-based tourism [13, 15], tourism conducted and controlled by locals, may empower local communities by diversifying the local economy, generating entrepreneurial opportunities for residents from different backgrounds, preserving culture, conserving the environment, and providing educational opportunities. Although one may say that CBT is related to the complex and broad literature on community engagement across different disciplines such as Political Science [17] and Urban HCI [18], the literature about CBT is quite developed and has been recognized in the context of tourism development, namely 'sustainable tourism' (ST) [19, 20], but also cultural tourism [19] and ecotourism [5]. For the latter, and aligned with the same concerns of our design rationales, there is a specific branch in the literature called "Community-based tourism ventures" (CBTV). This refers to initiatives that aim to care for the environment (ecotourism) as well as ensuring the empowerment of local communities. This approach to ecotourism is a response to tourism activities that are controlled by outside operators, foreign tourism companies, or contexts in which most of the economic benefits fall naturally (accrue) to the government, rather than returning benefits to local communities [5]. This approach is inspiring to our work since it prioritizes the quality of life of people and the conservation of environmental resources in the local community. Community-based tourism is not, however, exempt from challenges and is often criticized by scholars [12, 19]. This critical outlook of CBT is anchored in the problematic assumptions embedded within the community concept itself, as Noel Salazar emphasizes in his work [19]. Within the literature on CBT [12, 19], and also community engagement [17], different authors criticize the idea of community as being a construct and vague, and that is not taken into account by CBT studies. Blackstock [12], for example, argues that the literature on CBT, as presented since the 1990s, fails in three major regards towards community development: Firstly, it tends to take a functional approach to community involvement (not having the transformative intent of community development and not focusing on community empowerment). Secondly, it tends to treat the host community as a homogeneous bloc. Thirdly, it neglects the (external power-based) structural constraints on local control of the tourism industry. Additionally, Manyara and Jones [13] found several challenges for "development of indigenous small and medium tourism enterprises (SMTEs)." Some of these obstacles are: access to the global marketplace, literacy and numeracy, sector-specific skills, access to capital, resource ownership and lack of government support through appropriate policy and legislative framework [13].

Okazaki [14] concluded that, to mitigate the failures of CBT, the first step in tourism planning should be to examine the current situation with respect to community participation and then to indicate the initiatives that are required to promote it. In addition to Okazaki's attempt to address issues found with CBT, we recall the previous point made by Blackstock [12] that we should focus on community empowerment, and we draw on the principles or signs of empowerment proposed by Regina Scheyvens with regard to CBTV [5]. She explains the signs of local empowerment and disempowerment derived from these four levels:

(1) Economic Empowerment: Cash earned is shared between many households in the community and there are visible signs of improvement; Economic Disempowerment: Only a few individuals/families gain direct financial benefits from ecotourism, most profits go to local elites, outside operators, government agencies, etc.;

(2) Psychological Empowerment: Self-esteem of community members is enhanced because of outside recognition of the uniqueness and value of their culture, natural resources and their traditional knowledge; Psychological Disempowerment: Many people have not shared in the benefits of ecotourism, yet they may face hardships because of reduced access to the resources of a protected area;

(3) Social Empowerment: Social cohesion that may improve individuals and families as individuals and families work together towards the ecotourism activities; Social Disempowerment: The community takes on outside values and loses respect for traditional culture and for elders. Rather than cooperation there is competition for the perceived benefits of ecotourism;

(4) Political Empowerment: Refers to the structure that represents the needs and interests of all community groups and provides a forum through which people can raise questions; Political Disempowerment: The majority of community members feel they have little or no say over whether the ecotourism initiative operates or the way in which it operates;

Drawing on these studies that have used the four levels of empowerment, we anchor the analysis of our data to understanding how local communities in Madeira might be empowered through the control of a digital media platform.

2.2 Authenticity

Authenticity theory is connected with what van Nuenen [21] presents as "the modern discourse of anti-tourism, which consists of a traveler's desire to reach beyond superficial experiences that the tourism industry fosters." Van Nuenen is drawing from Goffman's theories, dating back to 1959 [22], in which Goffman provides an analysis of social interactions framed by the metaphor of "front and back regions" of a theatre. The front is the meeting place of hosts and guests (e.g., reception offices, parlors) and the back is "where members of the home team retire between performances to relax and to prepare" (e.g., kitchens, boiler rooms). Building on Goffman's [22] division into front and back regions, MacCannell [2, 23] says that touristic experience is underlined by the same structural tendencies. Increasingly, tourists' ambitions move towards experiencing the local life, being like locals; there is a desire to experience "back regions" and being "one of them," in this case being one of the locals, or at least having access to the truth, to the intimacy of locals.

What is relevant for us in having this theory as a framework is that part of this authentic experience involves a pursuit of more meaningful interactions with locals [23]. In MacCannell's words: "the touristic way of getting in with the natives is the entry into a quest for authentic experiences, perceptions and insights" [23]. This theory informs us not to design something that serves only as staged authenticity but a platform that enables visitors to engage with local life through developing ties with residents.

3 Related Work

3.1 Interaction Between Locals and Tourists

Past studies have revealed that the interaction between locals and tourists have developed in many forms and through different services (e.g., Couchsurfing, Airbnb, HomeAway [24]) and situations, either online or offline [25]. More recently, this interaction between locals and tourists has been part of a broader discussion of what constitutes an authentic experience [2, 23] for tourists [3, 26] in the context of digital media and tourism (see vayable.com [27], Urban Buddy [28], Spotted by Locals [29]). Echoing our context and design rationale, Moyle et al. [25] explored the cultural interaction between local communities and visitors to islands using social exchange theory to enhance the understanding of the island experience, in Bruny Island in Tasmania, and Magnetic Island in Queensland, Australia. The authors found that locals have a variety of motivations for social interaction with visitors, ranging from solely economic, to a genuine desire to share culture and traditions, and avoid superficial and hostile contact. However, the most common reason for interaction was economic. Nevertheless, those who do not rely on tourism to live "often expressed a genuine desire to interact in order to provide quality and meaningful experiences." It is also insightful to note that these authors point out that locals who have lived longer on the islands conceptualize the interaction with visitors as a "process of storytelling," either during an economic transaction or just socially. For those, pride plays a crucial role in interactions in which the sharing of history, culture, and environment is valued. While the authors found that some locals blame tourists for the deterioration of local infrastructure, they found a number of conditions that may facilitate the interaction between local and visitors, such as "festivals, events, and markets", where "locals could choose to interact with visitors, with a time limit, and without any major perceived threat to locals' lifestyle."

These authors provide several suggestions that may inform our current work. First, the education of the island communities is relevant in order to prepare and adapt for a shifting global landscape in which visitors have more interest in experiencing each destination more holistically. Also, the authors advocate for the inclusion of the visitors' perspective in future studies about interaction between locals and visitors to small islands. To date, we have not found studies similar to ours that survey tourists in regards to the interaction between locals and visitors, nor specifically on islands.

As a result, our study fills a gap in the literature by not only adding the perspective of visitors in such interactions, but also incorporating their impressions in the design of an interactive system.

While Moyle et al. talk about interaction between locals and visitors in general, without making distinctions between online and offline interactions, Chung et al. [24, 30] look at this type of interaction in online communities, and the role of an offline meeting in building online friendships. By using Social Network Analysis, Chung [24] found that locals and tourists build friendships in an online community through offline events. Moreover, they argue that that locals and tourists make their friendships in an online travel community, but online friendships are likely to be formed after a face-to-face meeting, not only by online interactions. On a note relevant to our project, Chung et al. [30] conclude that the fact that online users generally build friendships after face-to-face meeting provides destination marketing organizations with significant practical implications.

By developing the Há-Vita conceptual design further, we aim at not only providing information about nature and culture but also facilitating meaningful interactions with locals. We push forward the trend/concept of designing digital media platforms for interactions between locals as we offer deeper contact with the locals' way of living and raise awareness towards the local values. Furthermore, this work also builds on, and takes forward, the recommendations of the work by Moyle et al. [25] and takes into consideration the feedback of both locals and visitors in the design of the platform.

4 Designing the Há-Vita Platform

For the design of the Há-Vita platform, we followed a research through design approach [11]. We drew inspiration from the relevant literature on community-based tourism, the initial field research conducted when gathering the video content and the authors' inside knowledge as active members of the local community[1]. We also followed the advice of Norman and Stappers: "when political, economic, social and cultural variables interact, it is best to proceed slowly, with incremental steps" [31]. The development of the prototype evolved into two stages. Stage 1 describes the conception and content design of the platform based on the gathered literature, informal interactions with local scientists, local artisans, with details in subsection below (4.1). Stage 2, Subsect. 4.2, describes how based on the video interview topics, the platform allows visitors to engage in activities around the island that allow them deeper contact with the locals and their way of life.

---

[1] All authors were resident on the island at the time of the study and contributed equally to the design of the platform. The first author is native and highly engaged in preserving local values and environmental care, and she was the primary facilitator of the focus groups. The second author has a background in journalism and extensive experience working with communities and conducted most of the interviews, while informally involving the community in the project, and was also one of the facilitators in the focus groups. The third author is the Principal Investigator of the project with extensive experience in community storytelling and interactive media.

4.1   Stage 1: Há-Vita 1.0

Content Creation: We chose to produce video interviews as this format offers the visitors the sense to "get to know" community members and hear from them first hand. Utilizing the journalistic principle of having different points of view in a story, we carefully chose our interviewees based on their expertise and knowledge on local heritage, crafts, and biodiversity. The interviewees represented two different sources: (1) Scientific knowledge holders and (2) Local folk knowledge holders. All interviewees were informed of the general project goal to stimulate and instill in tourists an interest in the natural heritage and folk knowledge of Madeira. To scientists, we asked open-ended questions regarding technical distinctions of terms such as native and endemic plants, or the causes of wildfires or floods on the island. To local residents, we posed general questions about their knowledge and experience with the flora, fauna, and traditional products of Madeira. The content and thematic areas addressed in the platform were directly affected by the interactions with the locals as they generated a snowball effect for content development; locals suggested themes and stories, or put us in contact with other locals that they thought could contribute to the platform. After three months of work, we managed to gather 18 interviews of various length, the content and themes of which was analyzed and yielded seven main categories: Laurisilva, Madeira's Fauna, Traditional Products, Hydrological Balance, Macaronesian Forests, Invasive Species, and Natural Disasters (represented in Fig. 1).

Conceptualization of the Interface: The Há-Vita homepage presents a promotional video introducing the platform's main goal. The top of the page contains a drop-down menu, where clicking on the word *Episodes* leads to the identification of the seven themes, drawn from the interviews and extensive interactions with the locals. The icons in the drop-down menu expand, and by clicking inside the expansion, the visitors are forwarded to the page where the locals express their knowledge regarding the chosen topic (Fig. 1). The interface was deployed in a customized WordPress template.

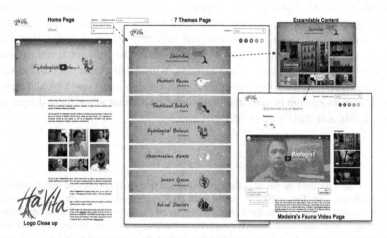

Fig. 1. Há-Vita graphical elements highlighting the connection to Madeira's nature and traditions (e.g., the main logo represents of one of the indigenous trees; Icon 3 from main categories depicts Poncha on of the traditional beverages of Madeira)

Há-Vita 1.0 provided us with a working repository of video content, and interviews with the local community, in a non-linear, modular fashion. At this stage, the communication between the visitors and the locals was still quite restricted, being only granted through comments to the videos. In order to enable a sense of empowerment of locals through the interaction with visitors, we needed to make the platform more interactive.

4.2   Stage 2: Há-Vita 2.0

Past studies have suggested [25] that direct involvement of local communities in touristic activities could benefit both visitors and locals. On the visitors' side it would provide the opportunity for an authentic experience, and for the locals it would provide empowerment. In Fig. 2, the connection between local empowerment, tourists, nature, and the island's cultural values is present. Locals can be contributors not only concerning content for the main themes, but they can also contribute by organizing activities. Those who contribute to the video content appear to the right side of each video. Below the picture, there is a highlight if the local offers an activity. By clicking that section visitors will be able to see which activity is proposed. Visitors can also have an overview of all locals participating in the platform, while locals have access to a backend allowing them to manage their connection with the visitors (Fig. 3).

Fig. 2. Features enabling visitors to connect with locals. *Left*: hovering on the locals' photographs keywords showcases a summary of who the local is. *Right*: Activities showcase a description, date, type contribution, explanation on how to sign up and a contact form in case doubts arise.

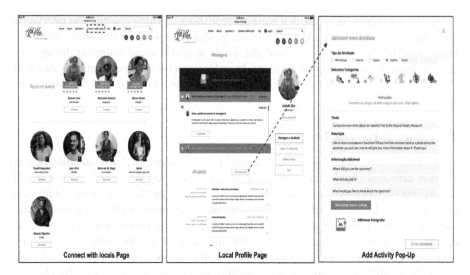

| Connect with locals Page | Local Profile Page | Add Activity Pop-Up |

Fig. 3. Left: Complete list of all the locals participating in the platform with whom visitors and connect, and instructions how they can connect. Types of possible connections: Sending messages or enrolling in activities. *Center:* Locals profile page featuring the contacts from the visitors and activities they are currently organizing; *Right:* Locals form for adding a new activity.

5   Evaluation of Há-Vita Platform

The overall concept and design of Há-Vita were evaluated in several stages. We ran a pilot test with visitors of the Island to gather first insights, followed by a series of focus groups with three distinct user segments: the local residents, the local scientists, and the tourists. In the next section, we describe this process of evaluation and its findings.

5.1   Pilot Study of Há-Vita 1.0

The pilot study aimed at testing the research protocol, as well as evaluating the effectiveness of the content on the users and, finally, the website graphical user interface. A table was set up in a hotel lobby with a computer and tablets (Fig. 4). Researchers invited the guests to interact with the platform. A semi-structured interview was designed to probe into three main areas: (A) Content, (B) Interface (C) Connection with locals. The whole protocol lasted 15/20 min. 12 European guests, age range 14 to 65, participated in the pilot and were rewarded with a locally produced vegetal sponge.

Interviews were recorded and later transcribed into Nvivo software. Main results are summarized in Table 1.

Table 1. Results of the pilot study, grouped by Nvivo nodes and illustrative quotes.

Platform Content: (1) Design and interaction were simple; (2) Participants enjoyed and found the content shared by the locals relevant; (3) Scientific content was valued to confirm knowledge obtained during their explorations; (4) Videos featuring the locals sharing folk content was perceived as being authentic; (5) Há-Vita had enabled them to gather new knowledge about Madeira and its ecosystem; (6) Added motivation to explore the island more; (7) Participants imagined accessing Há-Vita, before and during the travel;

PSU1- "she is really authentic, (...) I could meet her out in the street, and she would just talk to me like this..."

PB1-"I haven't realized it been so many natural disasters! (...) deforestation, so that's what I discovered, and I also feel... sympathy for the people who were caught in the natural disasters..."

PJI1-"I was unaware of all this unique nature, there is more than you realize, different birds, plants, different species"

PSU4- "I think the combination of being out there and then catching up with background is very good..."

Improvements: (1) Include advice on what to do or not do in order to preserve local nature, biodiversity, and traditions; (2) Videos should be tied with locations around the island (e.g., That bird can be found in X location/city); (3) Add a clear message about the website goal; (4) Add a short textual description before the video summarizing the subject;

PSU6- "It is simple to navigate and go around it... (says spontaneously before the question)"

PGH1-"(...) interesting videos, but it doesn't become clear... what you want to tell me..".

PSIT1- "just tell us want we can do ... people don't like to think..."

Visitors and locals' interaction: (1) the videos triggered curiosity about the locals; (2) Some participants felt prompted to interact with the interviewee while locals or others foresee difficulties in the communication and logistics;

PS2-"(...) I would ask the best places to go, about to finding about locals, what they are doing, maybe there are traditional festival going on if there is something very special happening..."

PSU7- "The Poncha lady, I think that is really authentic. I would ask for recipes, how to find the herbs out in the trails"

PA1-"(...)not really, only between a group of friends, but not me, myself"

PSH2- "That is very difficult because they obviously speak a different language (...)"

Implications of the Findings for the Há-Vita Design and Follow-Up Study: While the platform was generally well received, visitors are transient individuals and do not usually have time to divert from their holidays plans. As a result, most of them engaged in the study in a rushed and reluctant way, echoing [25] findings. Therefore, we changed our method to a focus group discussion in order to have participants committed to discussing the platform for a longer period of time and to probe more in-depth opinions.

5.2 Focus Groups Study

The new study was designed to understand how different stakeholders would respond to the concept of the Há-Vita platform, involving local community members who held "popular/folk knowledge" (e.g., popular wisdom about medicinal plants), local "experts" (e.g., local scientists and tourists operators) and visitors of Madeira island (Fig. 4). The sessions were moderated by two facilitators and two assistants who helped in the setting up and documentation of the sessions (always the same across sessions). Sessions were recorded both in audio and on video; observations and non-verbal interactions were noted.

Fig. 4. Images from the conducted evaluation sessions

Design of the Focus-Group Session. The facilitator presented the general purpose of the focus group (FG), introduced the research team, and gathered consent forms. This was followed by an icebreaker activity and then the Há-Vita platform was showcased, projected onto a large screen followed by a discussion designed to elicit comments and feedback on the platform. Throughout the text, we have replaced the participants' names with identity codes (IC) referring to which FG and the id of the participant (e.g., FVC: Focus Visitors Letterfakename) (Table 2).

Table 2. Characterization of the participants and focus group sessions

Sessions/Participants General Characterization	Duration/No Participants
Local Community: Age ranging from mid-thirties to late sixty, residents in Nun's Valley locality; Elderly handcrafters, farmers and stay-at-home women, or retired people, but all were active members of the community center; IC's: FLC; FLL; FLA; FLM; FLJ; FLMR	80 min/6
Experts Community: Participants with different expertise: 1 environmental researcher/geographer (FERQ), 1 Biologist (FECG); 4 participants with background in tourism (one travel agent (FERP), one guest relations manager (FESC), the head of the government touristic projects (FECN) and a tourism Professor from the local university (FELM);	120 min/6
Visitors: 6 females and one male with ages ranging from 24 to 44; All participants had a higher education degree; 2 participants were Portuguese (from mainland Portugal), 1 Romanian, 1 Italian, 1 German, 1 Turkish and 1 Spanish; IC's: FVMM, FVMF, FVIA	60 min/7

5.3   Results

In this section, we present the main results from the focus group (FG). All FG were recorded and audio files transcribed. The resulting data was analyzed by two researchers using a thematic analysis approach supported by Nvivo software. Firstly, researchers used open coding to create high-level categories individually, then reviewed and merged their separate efforts into new common categories. Secondly, the researchers grouped the information into affinity diagrams used to explain the relationships between categories. Thirdly, researchers organized the most frequent concepts and insights found for each focus group, followed by the description of each one with illustrative quotes given by users in the interviews. We will present the results from each focus group separately. The overall findings and discussion are presented in Sect. 6 (Tables 3, 4 and 5).

Table 3. Summary of the local community focus group.

Positive reactions of the community to the multimedia content of Há-Vita platform:
(1) Participants enjoyed watching its content and felt proud of viewing the local community members featured in the video interviews (FLC2); (2) Most enjoyed videos: The Laurisilva Video (featuring a priest-scientist), the Traditional Products explained by locals themselves, and the Exotic Species video; (3) The community members expressed a desire to collaborate in producing further content and suggested several topics they would like to contribute to (FLC1, FLC1)

FLC1: "This is a great initiative... will you continue making more videos?"
FLC2: "We have great things (...)why not showcase them to others..."
FLC1: "More wickerwork, it's a local handcraft and a thing they might like. Here are also women who know how to embroider, by showing the embroidery of Madeira"

Há-Vita a catalyst for interaction between the local community and visitors:
(1) Participants were very open to, and happy with, the idea of having a deeper and more authentic connection with the tourists (FLC4); (2) Participants recognized in the Há-Vita platform an opportunity to share the local culture eventually leading to attracting people to the small village and retaining them (FLC3). Apart from festivals/parties, tourists visit the location just for sightseeing purposes, spending little time in the village itself (5–10 min); (3) Participants were excited about the idea of organizing workshops for tourists and immediately started brainstorming types of workshops (FLA4, FLL1). The workshops would be very valuable, not only for economic reasons but also to keep traditions alive (see FLM2). They mentioned that some of the customs/traditions are being lost since younger generations are not interested in them. However, if there is (business) potential in the workshops, they might change their minds (FLM1). (4) The local community also expressed interest in learning something from the visitors (referring to a cultural exchange)

FLC4: "We want to welcome them all, as long as they're good people"
FLC3: "(...) promoting the products would be a great help. It's very important, It's good for the local business, to expose the parish itself. FLM [complementing]: Because we don't want tourists who arrive here to stay only for 5 min, have a coffee and leave
FLM2: "it's not just about selling [the baskets] there must be teaching and learning"
FLM1: "the workshops could be also a way to attract youngers to learn these crafts... at first could be just for fun but then they might enjoy it"
FLA4: "This godmother of mine would love to make some chestnut soup, to dry and tread the chestnuts.; FLL1 (complementing): More wicker work, it's a local handcraft and a thing they might like. There are also women who know the embroidery of Madeira"

Concerns: (1) Participants were worried that such a platform could not be developed in time within their lifespan that would be something more for their children or grandchildren to take advantage of; (2) Participants expressed that they would not be able to interact with the digital platform to add information, videos, or propose workshops, and they would need help from their children or grandchildren (FLA6)

FLA6: "It's too much work for us, it would have to be my daughter or Mr Manuel's daughter it's difficult for us"

Table 4. Summary of the local experts focus group

Há-Vita general impressions: (1) Local experts enjoyed Há-Vita and considered it a good start to be further expanded. They found the content interesting and dynamic, except for the "Natural Disasters" which was labeled as too sensitive to be disclosed to the visitors in this open way; (2) Participants valued the initiatives that promoted the connection between tourists and locals through organized workshops as it would help support locals' small business initiatives as well as farming and agriculture (FERQ1, FERP2, FERP3). Participants mentioned that these types of "connecting" activities would make visitors care about the location and revisit Madeira (FECG1).; (3) Participants found the idea of a network of "Contacts, Activities, and people" novel and worth pursuing (FERP1)
FERQ1: "(...) it should be either a monetary offer or a fixed price. If we have something to offer, there are costs involved. FECG1: Otherwise people don't show up." (complementing) FERP1:"There is a platform... Be local, where people can sell a product. In September, if I have the grape harvest, and people can sign up for my activity. Tourists do look for these things..."   *FECG1: "These types of connections are what makes visitors feel well, come back and pass on the good word about Madeira*   *FERP2: "Some tourists go to some typical houses, that are not on a known route. They already know there is this man who offers a liquor (...) and most of the times the tourist leaves a monetary gratification and that man already won his day. (...)"*   *FERQ2: "We have a collaboration with some hotels (...) Their guests sign up and participate in the tree planting/reforestation activities. Some become members (of the association)"*
Concerns and future suggestions: (1) Some of the local knowledge holders may present a lack of familiarity with technology and foreign languages and this should be taken into account in future iterations; (2) Several political issues were mentioned, such as more government intervention and support to preserve the local natural heritage (FERP7, FERP6). Há-Vita could work as a place where locals could publicly emphasize threats to the environment in order to draw the attention of the government; (3) Experts worried about the popularity of Madeira as a tourist destination and how that is affecting the resources of the island (in particular the natural trails and Laurisilva forest) (FERP6); (4) Participants suggested that Há-Vita could have the role of an educational tool regarding the local values (FERP8, FECN2); (5) Participants suggested to highlight the features that support direct communication and interaction between locals and visitors. Furthermore, a calendar showcasing activities would facilitate planning and participation before reaching the destination
FERP7: "Everyone wants to "gain" from the tourism but they don't want to protect the "product of madeira" – it's Nature, locals don't participants in the volunteering activities"   *FERP8: "Tourism need to be educated – e.g. not to pick plants, feed birds and not to go on trails who are closed - "they need to learn the household rules"*   *FECN2: "Even though I work for the government... it needs to be educated as well"*   *FERP6: "Similar to other cities, limits must be imposed ... if we don't preserve and limit ... everything will be destroyed (referring to Laurisilva forest, and limits in the trails)"*

Table 5. Summary of the visitors focus group

Appreciation for the authenticity and dynamic content: (1) Participants appreciated how the information was presented in an informative and timely way and how the short and dynamic videos help to keep the focus on the content (FVIA2, FVMF2). In particular, they enjoyed the authenticity of the local people featuring on videos, and the mix between popular and scientific knowledge; in particular, the experts' reasoning as opposed to an emotional perspective (FVIA1); (2) Participants mentioned that the platform can become a powerful database of knowledge and they mentioned, Padre Nóbrega (a community cherished priest and botanist) who passed away soon after releasing the interview with the Há-Vita production team; (3) Participants also shared that they learn new things about Madeira from the video content. Several users highlighted the richness of information and authenticity value of the video about the exotic plants (luffas), the medicinal plants, and the video explaining the origins of Poncha

FVIA: "I also like that idea that you put "normal" people in the videos, that is really cool. It is nice to have experts but also just the locals... it gives a sense of authenticity"
FVMF2: "The graphic elements helped to retain the information of what the people were saying.
FVIA2: "it's like dynamic, this moderation between the videos"
FVMF3: "(...) that database, that recorded knowledge. Because, that priest already died, right? His way of presenting information is really interesting. You see, he really feels passionate about it"

Suggestions to strengthen the Há-Vita platform and stimulate the connection between visitors and locals: (1) The activities proposed by the locals should be laid out clearly so that people know exactly what to do and what to expect (FVGA1). When volunteering activities, clearly state why they are important and what benefits they can have for the local community. Explain what is unique about the workshops/activities promoted through Há-Vita (FVIA5, FVMF3). Echoing the "Experts" group, participants suggested a more efficient way to present the activities, for example in a calendar or a map, so that visitors could plan the activities according to their stay (FVMF4, FVSG1); (2) Expand and add more content and topics; there could be a crowdsourcing component where people could submit their videos about specific topics; (3) Use infographics to summarize the information from specific videos. Finally, they expressed the desire to have more videos inside each of the main categories and express the interest in having fun facts or curiosities that could be added as text or images in the webpage of each main topic; (4) In terms of the design and videos of the website, participants pointed out small improvements, such as the quality of sound in specific videos, keeping the consistency between videos in the flow and pace of the content (e.g. Some videos were more balanced than others in terms of pace and some videos had more infographics than others)

FVIA5: "For community spirit, sometimes don't need the same language, I feel like if you really want to do something you do"; FVMF3 (complementing):" put there, like lady doesn't speak English but it's a fun activity, or you're gonna meet the locals, it's a very interesting experience"
FVGA1: "You could write as a traveler what is the benefit/contribution? Is it the time? Is the place? It takes one hour or tell me that you will bring me to this place where I have never been before"
FVSG1:" (...) little more information about the people who speak and maybe a little bit of summary of the content... in the beginning or after." FVMF4 (complementing):": "(..) if we could see the map of Madeira and activities, and everything that they are talking about. We can know where about"

6 Discussion

The section is divided into three subsections: (1) Enabling Local Empowerment, where we discuss the potential for Há-Vita to empower residents through the four levels of community-based tourism; (2) Authenticity and Visitor Experience discusses to what extent tourists found the content and experience that the platform offers authentic, and (3) Preliminary insights and general lessons learned distilled from our experience that inform the development of similar platforms with the design rationale of raising awareness about local values while fostering connections between locals and visitors.

6.1 Enabling Local Empowerment

Economic Empowerment. In the FGs, locals, especially those from Nun's Valley, expressed a striking enthusiasm and willingness to organize activities for visitors such as workshops, tours, and visits to specific local areas. Although our participants did not stress economic benefits per se, they were open to engaging with visitors through Há-Vita and receiving a financial reward for the activities they could eventually organize. For example, locals were interested in the possibility of charging visitors for events such as wicker basket workshops as well as benefiting from a fair favor exchange. Visitors could, for instance, engage with locals from less urbanized areas in a fair exchange such as helping out in the winemaking and then receive a traditional lunch. A platform like Há-Vita could add value to the community and location by proclaiming new and authentic activities for tourists to engage in (FERP2); It could also lead to an "indirect" economic benefit that would come from the spread of the destination positive image (FECG1).

Psychological Empowerment. During the FG in Nun's Valley, locals showed pride while watching their community represented on Há-Vita, through their comments and facial expressions (FLC2). They voiced that the platform was a powerful means to showcase local traditions to visitors. For this reason, several participants said out loud that they wanted to further contribute with novel content. They also proposed activities in which they could share their culture and crafts (FLC1). This need for more information was later on reinforced in the FG with visitors, in which they recognized how the multimedia part of the platform could become a "powerful database of knowledge" (FVMF3). Based on these results, Há-Vita could function as a self-esteem empowering tool for the community members, because it highlights values of the local culture, natural resources, and traditional knowledge.

Social Empowerment. In our FGs, Há-Vita emerged as a potentially socially empowering tool by improving individuals' and families' cohesion while working together towards the ecotourism goals and activities. Locals in Nun's Valley mentioned how such a platform could be used to trigger youth interest and instill pride in learning old customs and traditions (FLM1). Elderly participants manifested a need for having the assistance from their children or grandchildren to use Há-Vita and communicating in foreign languages (FLA6). On one hand, this lack of digital literacy and foreign languages could be seen as an issue but it could provide the local community with bonding opportunities across generations as they work together, leading to an improvement of digital literacy for those elder locals. The FG with locals (scientific knowledge), revealed a certain level of disempowerment of the locals. From their words, companies are basically the only entities that profit from the tourism, but do not take action to protect the main "product of Madeira," which is nature and culture (FERP7).

Political Empowerment. In the FG with scientific knowledge holders, participants spent a significant time discussing how Há-Vita might support community political empowerment. They discussed how the platform could provide themselves with a forum, in which people could speak out about pressing issues allowing them to address the regional government, to raise questions and suggestions. These participants were very concerned with tourism policies and pointed out the need to raise the regional government's awareness towards nature and traditions (FECN2). These findings led us to further envision Há-Vita as a potential channel of social and political change. This would address the concerns of Di Salvo et al. [9] and Manyara et al. [13] and could generate collective action by influencing policy and regulations regarding tourism and environmental preservation and awareness.

6.2   Authenticity and Visitor Experience

In general, our results suggested that visitors perceived the video content as authentic and engaging. Participants appreciated Há-Vita as a medium that offers insights into the cultural background of the local community and nature through video content. In this way, our findings reinforce our design rationale of providing starting grounds for interactions with locals. Such interaction could even begin before arriving at the destination, as suggested not only by several participants but also by Moyle et al. [25]. Likewise, Há-Vita could allow alternative touristic experiences benefiting those visitors wanting to enter "back regions" of the locale [15] but also promoting alternative routes and situations, eventually taking pressure off some of the most visited places. Indeed, our findings showed that most of the visitors that we engaged with were surprised to learn about the island's difficulties (PB1). Tourism Board's webpages often promote destinations as immaculate places and, as visitors learned about alternative facts, it contrasted with the "paradise" image of the destination they held before the visualization of Há-Vita. At the same time, however, the experience of browsing Há-Vita brought the visitors closer to the authentic reality of the island (PSU1, PSU7, FVIA).

Our findings suggest that Há-Vita shone a light on the island's values (biodiversity, folk knowledge and traditions), not only for visitors but also for the rest of the stakeholders (PJI1). Locals and visitors both manifested an interest in extending and regularly updating the Há-Vita content. This resonates with what Novacek [32] suggested, that by utilizing multimedia content we were able to engage the public not only in the biodiversity of the island but also with its traditions and folk knowledge (FVMF2, FVIA2). Moreover, visitors found the content interesting because it added to their touristic experience and local field trips. While local experts praised the website for its ecological and local values message, we were also encouraged to be more assertive and clear when posting these messages (such as "house rules"), making clear calendars, communication channels, and information more easily available (FVGA1, PSIT1).

Establishing connections between visitors and locals does not come without challenges, something that has been previously approached in the CBT literature [13]. Locals may have unique expertise but may not know how to share it with visitors. As seen previously, this could be related to digital literacy issues or due to language barriers. The latter was also a concern shared by visitors. However, they were open and willing to make efforts to overcome this (FVIA5).

6.3 Summary of Preliminary Insights

Design for Local Values Conservation, Valorization and Authenticity: Local values can be lost over time. Hence, it is crucial to continually capture and preserve ephemeral and intangible heritage. Video interviews with local testimonials revealed themselves to be a great way to promote empathy and connection between visitors and locals; designers should leverage the pleasure of teaching and pride that locals have towards their local values; promote a balance between folk and scientific knowledge, and between reason and emotional content; if possible, complementary media such as infographics, animations, and visual summaries should be used to help viewers retain information.

Design for Digital (il-)Literacy and Inter-generational Exchange: Locals enjoy seeing themselves, their products, and people they know personally, represented on the platform. However, digital literacy may be one of the biggest challenges for future design iterations of Há-Vita and similar platforms. Future design efforts could mitigate this challenge by facilitating inter-generational exchange and interaction, for example, through participatory design workshops. Besides this, the design process of such platforms should support elderly people and younger generations to co-create content and activities together, which could be also promoted in workshops.

Design for Platform Prosperity: At the current stage, Há-Vita only has content produced by the researchers themselves. In order to ensure sustainability of such a project, content creation workshops could be delivered to locals, so they could also contribute with content creation. Another approach is allowing crowdsourced content and subsequent monitoring mechanisms to ensure its quality. Future design efforts should delve into analyzing what would be the best format for the platform, whether a website or a mobile application (or even a mixed approach). Further research should address if locals (especially those with lower digital literacy) would be more comfortable in adding activities and content by using a custom-made application available on their mobile phones. Concerning the visitors' experience, designers should cater for different stages in the visitor experience; prior to the arrival to the location, but also during their stay. The design may leverage, for example, on a supplementary mobile application that supports a visitor's stay on the island by triggering relevant content based on their whereabouts. Furthermore, activities promoted by locals should be laid out clearly so that visitors know exactly what to expect (e.g., language, duration, outcomes, costs). When of volunteering activities, locals should clearly state why they are important and what difference they will make towards the local community.

Design Carefully Around CTB Problematic Issues by Opening Up to Dialogue:
We must acknowledge the risks and drawbacks of fostering community-based tourism and design around such things as: exploitation of visitors/locals; imbalance between the offered experience and the cost; addressing political concerns in its content and ensuring that locals have the means to control the benefits of exchanges with visitors. Designers could consider deploying strategies such as the integration of testimonies and evaluation of the proposed activities and hosts. Future iterations should account for exchanges of information between locals, visitors, and government regarding problematic issues by providing open communication channels like forums of discussion.

7 Future Work

Finding the best strategy to reach out to tourists, who are transient individuals and usually do not have much spontaneous time to spend, remains an open challenge. In the next iterations of Há-Vita, we aim to include a more significant sample and quantitative data, drawing for example on Há-Vita data generated through Google Analytics. Furthermore, it is important to realize that it will be hard to fully achieve our goal of empowering locals and stimulate interactions between locals and visitors, with design or video interviews only. It should be aided, as suggested by Di Salvo et al. [9], by administration collectives at the regional and national level. These local partners, as in the case of the Regional Tourism Board, may be able to facilitate the long-term engagement of both locals and visitors with the platform. Such steps would be fundamental in order to plan and run longitudinal studies for the platform. Finally, it would be crucial to thoroughly study how to achieve some sort of sustainability of the platform itself, and the impact of such a platform, both on the visitors' experience and on the local ecosystem.

8 Conclusion

In this paper, we presented the design and discussion of an Há-Vita, an online platform aimed at fostering awareness towards local nature and folk knowledge, as well as fostering connections between visitors and locals. We presented our design approach, and then discussions derived from our studies, in connection with the presented theoretical framework. This work makes specific contributions by further developing the trend of providing visitors with an authentic experience that not only has the potential to benefit the tourist experience, but also to empower the local community. Furthermore, we are filling a gap in the literature by adding the perspective of both visitors and locals in the interaction between them and laying out the barriers and strategies of undertaking user studies with visitors. Finally, we provided a discussion that may inform the design choices of future platforms with similar goals.

Acknowledgments. We wish to acknowledge our fellow researchers Ana Bettencourt, Dina Dionisio and the support of following funding entities: LARSyS (UID/EEA/50009/2019), MITIExcell (M1420-01-0145-FEDER-000002) and FCT Grant (PD/BD/114142/2015).

References

1. Center for Responsible Travel: The Case for Responsible Travel: Trends & Statistics 2015 (2015)
2. MacCannell, D.: The Tourist: A New Theory of the Leisure Class. University of California Press, London (1976)
3. Tussyadiah, I.P.: Toward a theoretical foundation for experience design in tourism. J. Travel Res. **53**, 543–564 (2014). https://doi.org/10.1177/0047287513513172
4. Foth, M., Satchell, C., Paulos, E., Igoe, T., Ratti, C.: Pervasive Persuasive Technology and Environmental Sustainability, p. 76 (2008)
5. Scheyvens, R.: Ecotourism and the empowerment of local communities. Tour. Manag. **20**, 245–249 (1999). https://doi.org/10.1016/S0261-5177(98)00069-7
6. Baudouin, P.: On Digital Accessibility and ICT (Coverage and Use) for the Outermost Regions, p. 28 (2017)
7. Barros, C.P., Machado, L.P.: The length of stay in tourism. Ann. Tour. Res. **37**, 692–706 (2010)
8. Dourish, P.: HCI and environmental sustainability: the politics of design and the design of politics. In: Proceedings of the 8th ACM Conference on Designing Interactive Systems, pp. 1–10. ACM, New York (2010). https://doi.org/10.1145/1858171.1858173
9. DiSalvo, C., Sengers, P., Brynjarsdóttir, H.: Mapping the landscape of sustainable HCI. In: Proceedings of the SIGCHI Conference on Human Factors in Computing Systems, pp. 1975–1984. ACM, New York (2010). https://doi.org/10.1145/1753326.1753625
10. ACIF, KPMG: Documento Estrategico Turismo Madeira-2015-2020 (2015)
11. Zimmerman, J., Forlizzi, J., Evenson, S.: Research through design as a method for interaction design research in HCI. In: Proceedings of the SIGCHI Conference on Human Factors in Computing Systems, pp. 493–502. ACM (2007)
12. Blackstock, K.: A critical look at community based tourism. Community Dev. J. **40**, 39–49 (2005). https://doi.org/10.1093/cdj/bsi005
13. Manyara, G., Jones, E.: Community-based tourism enterprises development in Kenya: an exploration of their potential as avenues of poverty reduction. J. Sustain. Tour. **15**, 628–644 (2007). https://doi.org/10.2167/jost723.0
14. Okazaki, E.: A community-based tourism model: its conception and use. J. Sustain. Tour. **16**, 511–529 (2008). https://doi.org/10.1080/09669580802159594
15. Sebele, L.S.: Community-based tourism ventures, benefits and challenges: Khama Rhino Sanctuary Trust, Central District, Botswana. Tour. Manag. **31**, 136–146 (2010). https://doi.org/10.1016/j.tourman.2009.01.005
16. Cohen, E.: Authenticity and commoditization in tourism. Ann. Tour. Res. **15**, 371–386 (1988). https://doi.org/10.1016/0160-7383(88)90028-X
17. Head, B.W.: Community engagement: participation on whose terms? Aust. J. Polit. Sci. **42**, 441–454 (2007). https://doi.org/10.1080/10361140701513570
18. Fredericks, J., Amayo Caldwell, G., Tomitsch, M.: Middle-out design: collaborative community engagement in urban HCI. In: Presented at the 2 December (2016). https://doi.org/10.1145/3010915.3010997

19. Salazar, N.B.: Community-based cultural tourism: issues, threats and opportunities. J. Sustain. Tour. **20**, 9–22 (2012). https://doi.org/10.1080/09669582.2011.596279

20. Dangi, T.B., Jamal, T.: An integrated approach to "sustainable community-based tourism". Sustainability **8**, 475 (2016). https://doi.org/10.3390/su8050475

21. van Nuenen, T.: The production of locality on peer-to-peer platforms. Cogent Soc. Sci. **2**, 1215780 (2016). https://doi.org/10.1080/23311886.2016.1215780

22. Goffman, E.: The presentation of Self in Everyday Life. 1959. Gardeb City NY (2002)

23. MacCannell, D.: Staged authenticity: arrangements of social space in tourist settings. Am. J. Sociol. **79**, 589–603 (1973)

24. Chung, J.Y.: Online friendships in a hospitality exchange network: a sharing economy perspective. Int. J. Contemp. Hosp. Manag. **29**, 3177–3190 (2017). https://doi.org/10.1108/IJCHM-08-2016-0475

25. Moyle, B., Weiler, B., Croy, G.: Tourism interaction on islands: the community and visitor social exchange. Int. J. Cult. Tour. Hosp. Res. **4**, 96–107 (2010). https://doi.org/10.1108/17506181011045172

26. Pine, B.J., Gilmore, J.H.: The Experience Economy. Harvard Business Press, Boston (2011)

27. Things to Do in - Well Anywhere| Your Personal Tour Guide| Vayable. https://www.vayable.com/

28. Jaffe, E.: The app that turns tourists into locals. http://www.theatlanticcities.com/technology/2013/08/urban-buddy-turns-tourists-locals/6513/

29. Spotted by locals: city guides by insiders. https://www.spottedbylocals.com/

30. Chung, J.Y., Buhalis, D., Petrick, J.F.: The Use of Social Network Analysis to Examine the Interactions between Locals and Tourists in an Online Community, p. 9 (2010)

31. Norman, D.A., Stappers, P.J.: DesignX: complex sociotechnical systems. She Ji J. Des. Econ. Innov. **1**, 83–106 (2015). https://doi.org/10.1016/j.sheji.2016.01.002

32. Novacek, M.J.: Engaging the public in biodiversity issues. Proc. Natl. Acad. Sci. **105**, 11571–11578 (2008). https://doi.org/10.1073/pnas.0802599105

Ustaad: A Mobile Platform for Teaching Illiterates

Syed Ali Umair Tirmizi, Yashfa Iftikhar, Sarah Ali, Ahmed Ehsan,
Ali Ehsan[✉], and Suleman Shahid

Lahore University of Management Sciences, Lahore, Pakistan
{18030004, 17030013, 17030026, 17030009, 17030008,
suleman.shahid}@lums.edu.pk

Abstract. According to a recent statistical analysis conducted in 2018, more than 40% of the population has no reading or writing skills especially in rural areas of Pakistan. On the contrary, the mobile phone users have grown at a very steep rate even with a stagnant literacy rate. We formed a user-driven approach to research, develop and test a prototype mobile application that could be used to teach illiterates basic reading, writing and counting skills without using traditional schooling techniques. This first of a kind application provided the user the ability to customize their own learning plan. Focusing on native language Urdu, the application teaches them the required skill they need for daily life activities such as writing their own name, scenario-based calculations, identifying commonly used words.

Keywords: User-centered design · Illiteracy · Mobile phones · Human-computer-interaction

1 Introduction

Pakistan is in the throes of an educational crisis, the literacy rate in Pakistan is lowest among the South Asian countries, with a current literacy rate of 55% [2] in the most populated province; Punjab, has witnessed a significant decline in literacy rate from 64% to 59% during the years of 2016–2017 [3]. The definition of literacy in Pakistan was recently redefined as: "The ability to read and understand a simple text in any language from a newspaper or magazine, write a simple letter and perform a basic mathematical calculation (i.e. counting and addition/subtraction)" after the Population and Housing Census 2017 [1]. However, technology is making huge strides in the country with a growing number of mobile phone subscribers each year. Recent statistics by telecommunication authority of the country, PTA revealed that over 150 million mobile subscribers are present in Pakistan who may have access to 4G and 3G technology and currently more than 67 million already on high speed mobile internet [15]. These internet-enabled smartphones provide a special medium for education in native language Urdu among illiterates especially in adults who cannot start or resume schooling due to different social reasons.

Using the definition of literacy described in the Population and Housing Census 2017 [1] in our study, we examined the illiterate adults in rural parts of Lahore.

© IFIP International Federation for Information Processing 2019
Published by Springer Nature Switzerland AG 2019
D. Lamas et al. (Eds.): INTERACT 2019, LNCS 11747, pp. 788–796, 2019.
https://doi.org/10.1007/978-3-030-29384-0_47

Through user-centered design, we develop a prototype application called Ustaad to teach basic reading, writing and counting skills through mobile phone. We tested the application with adults from different backgrounds having little or no formal education and showed that self-learning can be increased through tailor-made application for illiterates. This presents a framework for teaching native language to users belonging to low literacy areas by developing skills useful in day to day life in a short amount of time.

2 Related Work

Recently, work done in ICT4D has provided more useful applications to people who have received little or no formal education. Improvising techniques such as pictures, emoji, voice and sometimes haptic inputs for text have been included in applications as aids for illiterate users. A certain study was done to help illiterate people combat one of the most frequent problems they face which is texting someone [5]. Using techniques such as speech-to-text, pictures and reusing previous messages the study concluded that illiterate people use mobile quite frequently but avoid text-based applications as such SMS applications, chat messengers and when required use some traditional tricks to combat this problem such as asking a relative for help or stickers/emoji. The prototype of the study focused on providing such a solution based on common interaction techniques using interactive and text-free design.

Such strides are also part of medical and emergency services where an emphatic research and development project resulted in the first aid iOS application that teaches illiterates first aid procedures in Mardan area of KPK province in Pakistan [6]. The study focused on the usability of a sketch-based interface vs an image-based interface for teaching first aid activities in low literacy area showing sketch based far more effective in illiterate people. With the introduction of mobile computing and the rapid growth of mobile users, the need to develop an interface that can be used by both illiterates and literates has also taken strides. HCI introduces a new aspect to mobile computing where interfaces are being designed to facilitate more illiterates. The key factor in such research is a combination of Graphics and voice I/Os [7, 8] such as done by IBM India. Although voice-based technology is making great strides in helping less educated interact more with computers and a mobile device such as Web Spoken technology by IBM Research India [9] but it still isn't as effective as visual aids due to complex nature of speech synthesis and speech generation. Technologies such as pattern recognition, deep learning have made visual inputs a lot easier to implement in computer systems making human-computer interaction closer to human interaction. Hand gestures also shown in studies [10] is shown to be an effective tool for recognition and gesture-based inputs. Research conducted in Switzerland among illiterate people ended up recommending icons, colors, and symbols are very important feature of design for mobile phone interfaces for illiterate and semi-literate users [11].

Most of the previous work done focuses on children [12–14]. These applications allowed pre-decided learning plans with a fixed amount of words without any support for customized input. Few works which targeted illiterate adults focused on facilitating rather than actually teaching illiterates in reading writing and calculation [4]. This is the first systematic study on illiterates with focus on Pakistan's native language with customized learning and curriculum planning with the ability to input their own choice of words through voice.

3 User Research

We conducted user research using a blend of contextual inquiry and interviews. Since our candidates are illiterate, other user research methods like surveys and questionnaires cannot be applied. Around 20–25 Semi-structured interviews were conducted in different rural areas of Lahore that collected information regarding education background technology used and what problems they face in day to day tasks due to illiteracy. This would fuel our prototype design.

3.1 Participants

We recruited the participants for our user research from Lahore where around 60% of the population is illiterate. We conducted 23 interviews of people for the user research phase, with age 18 and above, around which 21 were male while around 2 were female.

3.2 Interview Questions

Users were asked 24–26 questions in total and some questions were added or dropped according to a response from the user. First few questions were used to gather data about user such as age, profession, and formal education. The second part focused on a situation where the user were require to read and write words or sentences and the last part of the interview focused on the user's view of technology. Users were asked if they use technology and how much skill they already have with it. Users were asked if that technology required them to touch screen or use tracer pen. Some interactive questions were added to see how much knowledge the user has common signs and symbols.

3.3 Findings

The set of findings can be divided into three parts. The first part of the findings is related to the level of literacy and causes. The second part focuses on technology and if they use it and third focusing on how they cope with a situation involving literacy. The user interviewed often seemed to be disengaged with the idea of learning from start and often showed disapproval of the idea of formal education if given chance now. In our interview, we had a blend of people, some who hadn't studied at all, some who had been to school for some time. 73.9% of our candidates were the ones who had never been to any school. 87.5% of them refused when inquired whether they could read or write a small sentence in any language. Similarly, 47.8% of people knew and could recognize numbers when shown to them. 54.5% of our interviewee's told us that they can perform some small basic calculations of addition and subtraction, however, in reality, 23.5% of our candidates answered the sum of 35 and 25 correctly (For their ease we told them the numbers both in English and Urdu). We showed them some basic symbols of a tick, cross, forward and backward arrows which are generally used in many places. 65.25% of the candidates weren't able to identify any one of the symbols. In order to evaluate the extent to which our candidates are technology literate, we asked them whether they could operate mobile phones, computers. 47.8% of our candidates could use a simple mobile or smart mobile. 21.7% of people couldn't operate any mobile phone. None could operate a computer/laptop.

A question where the user was asked how they do contact finding and adding on their mobile phone received a lot of people saying they use someone for help or use pictures. Some said they use icons or shape of letters and numbers. A common practice among illiterate smartphone user was saving contact name along with a picture. One user said, "I have a smart mobile and for contacts, I have saved, I also have pictures along". Some user also said they use voice recording services on the messaging application. A user said "I don't do messages. I am on WhatsApp and I do voice message. My friends know that since I cannot read, they only reply using voice message".

This developed the base on how to thinking and designing something that could be used to teach these basic tasks to illiterates by technologies they use most. It should have visual and audio cues as well as provide important educational perspective to the user in their daily life with minimal effort required.

4 Design and Development

The design phase incorporated the findings in the user research phase with certain features; the solution was an Android mobile application that only uses large icons and voice for interaction. Audio input kept minimalistic and targeted common words and names. Use of color, icons and common cultural signs also incorporated. Another application called Ustaad Tracker was used for tracking the progress of the user and allowing an expert to set the education plan. We added the shortlisted sub-tasks derived from user research in the application. Those subtasks are reading/writing common words, reading/writing numbers, reading/writing custom words, and performing scenario/story based calculation. The major target of the study was to make the user able to read and write his name and the learning was evaluated automatically using accuracy.

To have a better look at the requirements of users, we designed a low fidelity prototype and tested it on 5 participants. Users found the screen flow simple and easy to navigate but some users pointed out repeating voice instruction if no action has been performed for a while.

Inspired by the lessons from the testing with prototype and interview results, we here describe the final android application called "Ustaad" which provides the facility to learn basic and customized words using the phone. The solution is divided into two mobile based applications that would be running on commonly available mobile OS (android). Main Application would be labeled Ustaad, A standalone application meant to be designed for the user. The objective of this application is to make user practice all three tasks which are reading, writing and counting that will help them transition into literate phase. A companion application called Ustaad tracker would be a complimentary application that can be downloaded by the helper of a user to track the process and set an educational plan for the user to follow. Helper is someone related to the user or someone user often goes to for help regarding literacy tasks. The helper can devise an educational plan for the user, picking section they want the user to attempt before moving to next as shown in Fig. 4. It can be linked to the main Ustaad application through the setting's button.

The Ustaad application (Fig. 1) was based on a prototype developed before. It would again have 3 sections of reading, writing, and calculation. Each section will have certain subsections. For reading section user will have each icon for learning to read number, words, and name. Each subsection will have a testing phase where the user will have to identify the spoken word by selecting options. For the writing section, a special tracer would be developed. The user would be able to see words, numbers, and name in the form of the dotted line as shown in Fig. 2 and would be asked to practice. The performance of user will measure and accuracy will be shown after. For calculation, section user will be shown a scenario teaching number based on previous sections. Here the user will be able to see calculations are to be performed and then he will be tested as shown in Fig. 3.

Fig. 1. Reading number

Fig. 2. Writing name using dotted line

Fig. 3. Scenario based calculation section.

Fig. 4. Ustaad tracker application; user list (left), task for a specific user (right)

5 Evaluation

Our evaluation phase consisted of 13 participants with age ranging from 19 to 60 plus with all belonging from Lahore. The participants recruited had no or little formal education with the same social background as participants from the user research phase. A testing methodology followed to find the difficulty faced by users and flaws highlighted by them. The facial expressions of the users and their activity on the application were recorded. We also conducted pre-test and post-test using questionnaires to measure the time spends on each task by the user, recorded the emotional response of user for each task, measure the accuracy of steps user performs in each task and measure the user's accuracy of tracing words. We recorded the user's facial expressions as well as their activity on mobile application through two different cameras. The user will be asked to sign a consent form and will be informed about the amount of time it will take for completing the test. We briefed them different scenarios and ask them to perform a list of tasks for each scenario by doing so we can evaluate the usability, effectiveness, efficiency and enjoyable of our application. Afterward, a post-test questionnaire will be asked which include question based on the experience of the user from the application and how much learning they achieved.

We measured both quantitative data along with emotional and subjective response of users. The first measurement was the time taken by the user (TTU) to perform certain sections and subsections in minutes. Second important measurement was the user's facial expression during testing. We also calculated how accurately the user was able to perform the given tasks. For this, we divide each task into the fine-grained steps and calculate accuracy by aggregating the correctly performed steps then dividing it by the total number of steps needed to perform that task mathematically shown in Fig. 5.

$$\forall_{T_{i=0}}^{n} \quad Accuracy = \frac{\sum_{k=0}^{m_i} T_{ik}}{\sum_{j=1}^{n_i} T_{ij}}$$

Where:
T_i = Task i
n = Total number of tasks
T_{ij} = Each step j in task i
n_i = Total number of steps in a T_i
T_{ik} = Each correctly performed step k in task i
m_i = Total number of correct steps in a T_i

$$Accuracy = \frac{I}{max(W, T)}$$

Where:
T = Total numbers of pixels in the filled text
W = Total numbers of pixels in canvas that user traced on
I = Intersection of T and W

Fig. 5. Task accuracy formula   **Fig. 6.** Tracing accuracy formula

Moreover, we also measured the accuracy of the Urdu text traced by the user when he/she is provided an outline of the text. This will be calculated and logged by the application. The formula for accuracy is shown in Fig. 6. Accuracy results are shown in Table 1.

Table 1. Tracing accuracy examples

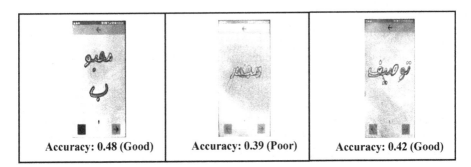

| Accuracy: 0.48 (Good) | Accuracy: 0.39 (Poor) | Accuracy: 0.42 (Good) |

6 Results and Discussion

The result section can be divided into 2 major sections: quantitative data gathered by mobile facility based on measurements and user feedback from the post-test interview.

6.1   Quantitative Results

An average TTU was 30 min for each testing session because we had to explain the concept of application testing to the user beforehand and their unfamiliarity with technology added even more time to the equation. For reading time more than 60% of users on average took a minute or less. Majority of user took more time for names and common words than numbers. In the writing section, around 75% of the people were able to complete this task with average TTU less than 2 min while the remaining 25% failed to perform the task at all. The calculation section was completed by most users in 2 min with average TTU less than a minute.

In emotional responses, the most dominant emotional reactions were Neutral, Confusion, and Joy. Neutral reaction meant that they were able to understand the task pretty well e.g. Learn calculation scenario had 4 neutral reactions. Joy meant that they were able to really enjoy the task at hand; participants really enjoyed writing their own name, reading common words with pictures, and learning calculation with scenarios.

The confusion mostly occurred when the user gets lost in the navigation but some users were confused from the very start till the very end. These totally confused users are those users who seldom use a mobile phone.

In terms of accuracy; the percentage of steps correctly taken by the user to complete a particular task, around 55.6% of the people were able to perform the writing task with 100% accuracy, 11.1% performed it with 75% accuracy, another 11.1% performed it with 50% accuracy and 22.2% were not able to perform the task at all. In reading most of the users were able to identify written numbers correctly but navigation issues were most dominant in reading custom words and common words. More often the user got lost. Around 55.6% of the people were able to perform the calculation task with 100% accuracy, 11.1% performed it with 75% accuracy, another 11.1% performed it with 50% accuracy and 22.2% were not able to perform the task at all.

6.2   User Feedback

When we asked the candidate that from a scale of 1 (worst) to 5 (best), how much did the like our application, 23.1% of them rated 5, 38.5% rated 4, 30.8% of them rated 3, while only 7.7% of them rated 2. When asked about the interface of the application we received an extremely positive response as 84.6% categorized the interface in Good and Very Good category. The most user found that writing own name was the most interesting section of the application. Around 91% of users found the application to be of the daily user while some also said there was room for improvement. When it comes to benefits, we had a very positive response as 92.3% believed that they will be able to write their name after using our app, while a 100% believed that they will be able to read and write basic words, numbers, and perform basic calculations. When asked which task they found the most difficult to understand interestingly enough 23.1% of them said write Your Name task. This might be because it involved tracing of their own name which is naturally difficult to convey and perform. In general, around 70% of user found the application easy to use while 30% found it difficult to navigate.

We clearly observed different candidates found the application more suited to them. A user said "Yes if I get a chance, I will dedicate some time for it. I will give 1 to 2 h daily". People found application as an alternative for formal education which is expensive as well as time-consuming for an adult doing a job to support a family. To the question would they like to learn in future one user replied "Yes, but only if it is limited to a smartphone. If I have to go to a university, then it will be difficult for me because I have kids so I don't have time". His reply explained that for a worker with a family to support, a smartphone application is far suitable as time spent and learning will be according to their affordance.

7 Discussion

The inability to read, write, and calculate not only makes illiterates dependent on others but influences their self-esteem and increase their feeling of distress. Our statistics suggest that a significant amount (87%) of the candidates considered literacy as important and are willing to spend some time given the opportunity to learn. At the same time, these individuals are busy with jobs and families so, as some candidates pointed out, formal institution offering years of formal education won't work for them. Unfortunately, not much attention is being paid towards these individuals although they represent a significant part of society.

The Ustaad application is the first of its kind, as targets illiterate adults and teaches them how to read, write and calculate without following any formal education curriculum. It skips the initial alphabet learning and helps the user learn the required words in a more intuitive manner. This method of learning has proven to be very effective as almost all the interviewed candidates agreed that using Ustaad will successfully teach them basic reading, writing, and calculations skills.

8 Conclusion and Future Work

All of our candidates agreed that the application will help them get better in reading, writing, and calculation. Most of them found the application delightful to use and would use the app if installed on their mobile phones. Some of the candidates did highlight some usability issues including finding the navigation difficult and confusion in mapping intention to action. Our evaluation process proves that after solving these usability issues, our app can make illiterate less dependent on others as they themselves will be able to read, write and calculate through repetition. The study offers a framework for teaching any language using technology to users belonging to countries with low literacy and a similar socio-economic situation like Pakistan.

Although the work offers a detailed insight to literacy problems in Pakistan along with a possible solution, further work is required in the form a longitudinal study to see the effect of the application on illiterates in a longer period of use.

References

1. Govt redefines literacy for count (Tribune). https://tribune.com.pk/story/1341159/govt-redefines-literacy-count/
2. Literacy Rate of Education in Pakistan 2016 (Archivist Online). http://www.archivistonline.pk/literacy-rate-in-pakistan/
3. Literacy Rate in Pakistan Drops by 2% in 2016–17 (Pro Pakistani). https://propakistani.pk/2017/05/26/literacy-rate-pakistan-drops-2-2016-17/
4. Wang, X., Kota, K.K., Reddy, K., Baran, D., Bhatia, N.: Litebox: design for adult literacy (2018). https://doi.org/10.1145/3170427.3180654
5. Friscira, E., Knoche, H., Huang, J.: Getting in touch with text: designing a mobile phone application for illiterate users to harness SMS. In: Proceedings of the 2nd ACM Symposium on Computing for Development, p. 5. ACM (2012)
6. Shah, S.Z.A., Khan, I.A., Maqsood, I., Khan, T.A., Khan, Y.: First-aid application for illiterates and its usability evaluation. In: 2015 13th International Conference on Frontiers of Information Technology (FIT), pp. 125–131. IEEE (2015)
7. Agarwal, S.K., Grover, J., Kumar, A., Puri, M., Singh, M., Remy, C.: Visual conversational interfaces to empower low-literacy users. In: Kotzé, P., Marsden, G., Lindgaard, G., Wesson, J., Winckler, M. (eds.) Human-Computer Interaction – INTERACT 2013. LNCS, vol. 8120, pp. 729–736. Springer, Heidelberg (2013). https://doi.org/10.1007/978-3-642-40498-6_67
8. Remy, C., Agarwal, S.K., Kumar, A., Srivastava, S.: Supporting voice content sharing among underprivileged people in Urban India. In: Kotzé, P., Marsden, G., Lindgaard, G., Wesson, J., Winckler, M. (eds.) Human-Computer Interaction – INTERACT 2013. LNCS, vol. 8120, pp. 489–506. Springer, Heidelberg (2013). https://doi.org/10.1007/978-3-642-40498-6_38
9. Kumar, A., Agarwal, S.K.: Spoken web: using voice as an accessibility tool for disadvantaged people in developing regions. ACM SIGACCESS Access. Comput. **104**, 3–11 (2012)
10. Pavlovic, V.I., Sharma, R., Huang, T.S.: Visual interpretation of hand gestures for human-computer interaction: a review. IEEE Trans. Pattern Anal. Mach. Intell. **7**, 677–695 (1997)
11. Knoche, H., Huang, J.: Text is not the enemy-how illiterates use their mobile phones. In: NUIs for New Worlds: New Interaction Forms and Interfaces for Mobile Applications in Developing Countries-CHI 2012 Workshop (2012)
12. Learn Urdu. A simple and interesting app to learn reading and writing Urdu language 2018. https://play.google.com/store/apps/details?id=com.LearnUrdu.Free. Accessed 02 Sep 2018
13. Kids Urdu Qaida. An application to learn and recognize Urdu language alphabets (2015). https://play.google.com/store/apps/details?id=com.suave.urduqaida. Accessed 04 Sep 2018
14. Kids Urdu Learner: Urdu Qaida, Games and Poems 2018. Urdu learning application for kids. http://www.overleaf.com/. Accessed 01 Nov 2018
15. Telecom Indicators. PTA (2019). https://www.pta.gov.pk/en/telecom-indicators. Accessed 5 Oct 2018

Author Index

Printed in the United States
By Bookmasters